A
FLEETWAY
LIBRARY

BATTLE
PICTURE
LIBRARY

SIX OF
THE BEST

HIT THE DIRT!

The publishers would like to thank the team at IPC Media Ltd and DC
Comics for their help in compiling this book, particularly David Abbott.

Published in 2010 by Prion
An imprint of the Carlton Publishing Group
20 Mortimer Street
London
W1T 3JW

Copyright © IPC Media 2010

Published under licence from DC Comics

A catalogue record for this book is available from the British Library.

ISBN 978 1 85375 759 4

Printed and bound in Singapore

10 9 8 7 6 5 4 3 2 1

A FLEETWAY LIBRARY

BATTLE PICTURE LIBRARY

SIX OF THE BEST

HIT THE DIRT!

SIX OF THE BEST
COMIC-BOOK
ADVENTURES FROM

BATTLE
PICTURE
LIBRARY

GENERAL EDITOR:
STEVE HOLLAND

PRION

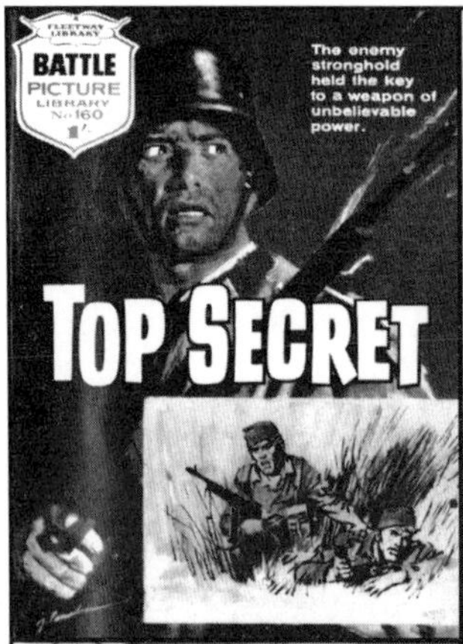
BATTLE
PICTURE
LIBRARY
No.160
1/-
The enemy stronghold held the key to a weapon of unbelievable power.
TOP SECRET

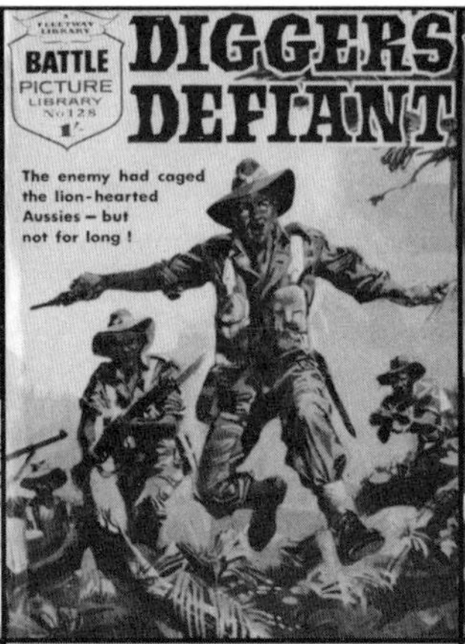
BATTLE
PICTURE
LIBRARY
No.128
1/-
DIGGERS DEFIANT
The enemy had caged the lion-hearted Aussies – but not for long !

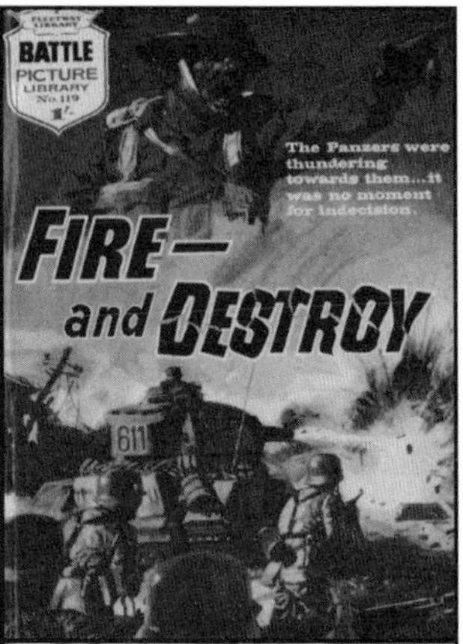
BATTLE
PICTURE
LIBRARY
No.119
1/-
The Panzers were thundering towards them... it was no moment for indecision.
FIRE— and DESTROY
611

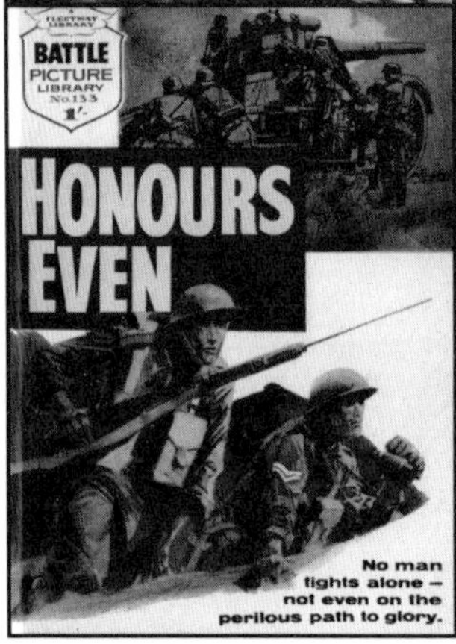
BATTLE
PICTURE
LIBRARY
No.133
1/-
HONOURS EVEN
No man fights alone – not even on the perilous path to glory.

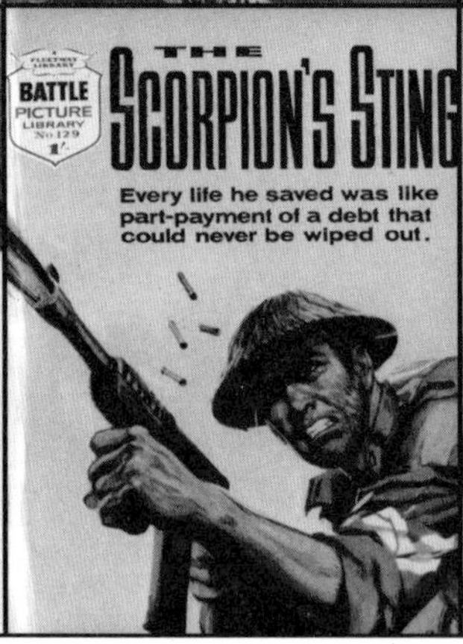
BATTLE
PICTURE
LIBRARY
No.129
1/-
THE SCORPION'S STING
Every life he saved was like part-payment of a debt that could never be wiped out.

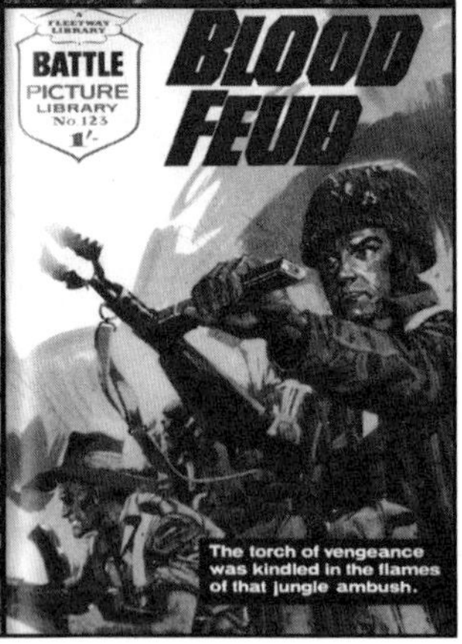
BATTLE
PICTURE
LIBRARY
No.125
1/-
BLOOD FEUD
The torch of vengeance was kindled in the flames of that jungle ambush.

CONTENTS

INTRODUCTION

Blood, toil, tears and sweat. On 13 May 1940, Churchill summed up the coming ordeal in France with these words, quoting a phrase originally spoken by Theodore Roosevelt 43 years earlier when he was appointed Assistant Secretary of the American Navy. Churchill, who had held a similar position as First Lord of the Admiralty, had just been appointed Prime Minister and was making his first speech to the Houses of Parliament.

"We have before us an ordeal of the most grievous kind," said Churchill. One wonders if even he imagined the years of bitter fighting, of struggle and sacrifice that it would take before the Allies could claim victory. "Victory at all costs," was Churchill's aim. "Victory in spite of all terror. Victory, however long and hard the road may be, for without victory there is no survival."

That long, hard road was paved with the kind of adventures celebrated in *Battle Picture Library*, the comic strip pocket book published as a companion to *War Picture Library* and *Air Ace Picture Library*. Whilst War had tried to cover all three services in its early days, Air Ace picked up the gauntlet of telling thrilling tales of aerial conflict and *War at Sea Picture Library* (which was to arrive in 1962) served the Navy in the same capacity. *Battle* concentrated its stories on the war on the ground when it debuted in 1961, although the various titles overlapped in their coverage somewhat, as you will see in some of the following stories.

Within a few months of releasing its first issue, *Battle* was publishing four issues a month; at the end of the decade, this rose to six a month and then eight a month for most of the 1970s before slipping back to six a month for the last few years of its 24-year run. Many of the later issues were reprints, but in the heydays of the 1960s, *Battle* published 375 stories—an astonishing 22,000 pages of artwork.

Those 22,000 pages spanned the world, from the beaches of Italy and landing grounds of France to the fields and streets of Europe and the jungles of Burma. Even where the stories covered the same theatre, the action was never the same. Take two of the tales reprinted here: both "Blood Feud" and "Diggers Defiant" are set in the Far East, but they share little beyond a common background.

None of the stories glamorises war: the writers knew that it was only from the worst of situations that some found the courage to become heroes and even those heroes could be flawed, like glory seeker Johnny Gledhill, risk-taker Corporal Todd, former killer Dan Mevin, or Clem Harvey, court-martialled down to the ranks for a deadly mistake.

What these stories do share is a sense of the blood, toil, tears and sweat that Allied troops suffered for the six years of World War II.

Steve Holland

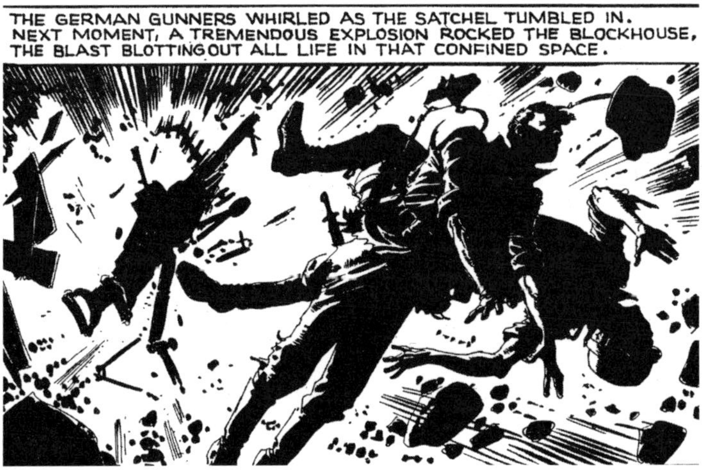
THE GERMAN GUNNERS WHIRLED AS THE SATCHEL TUMBLED IN. NEXT MOMENT, A TREMENDOUS EXPLOSION ROCKED THE BLOCKHOUSE, THE BLAST BLOTTING OUT ALL LIFE IN THAT CONFINED SPACE.

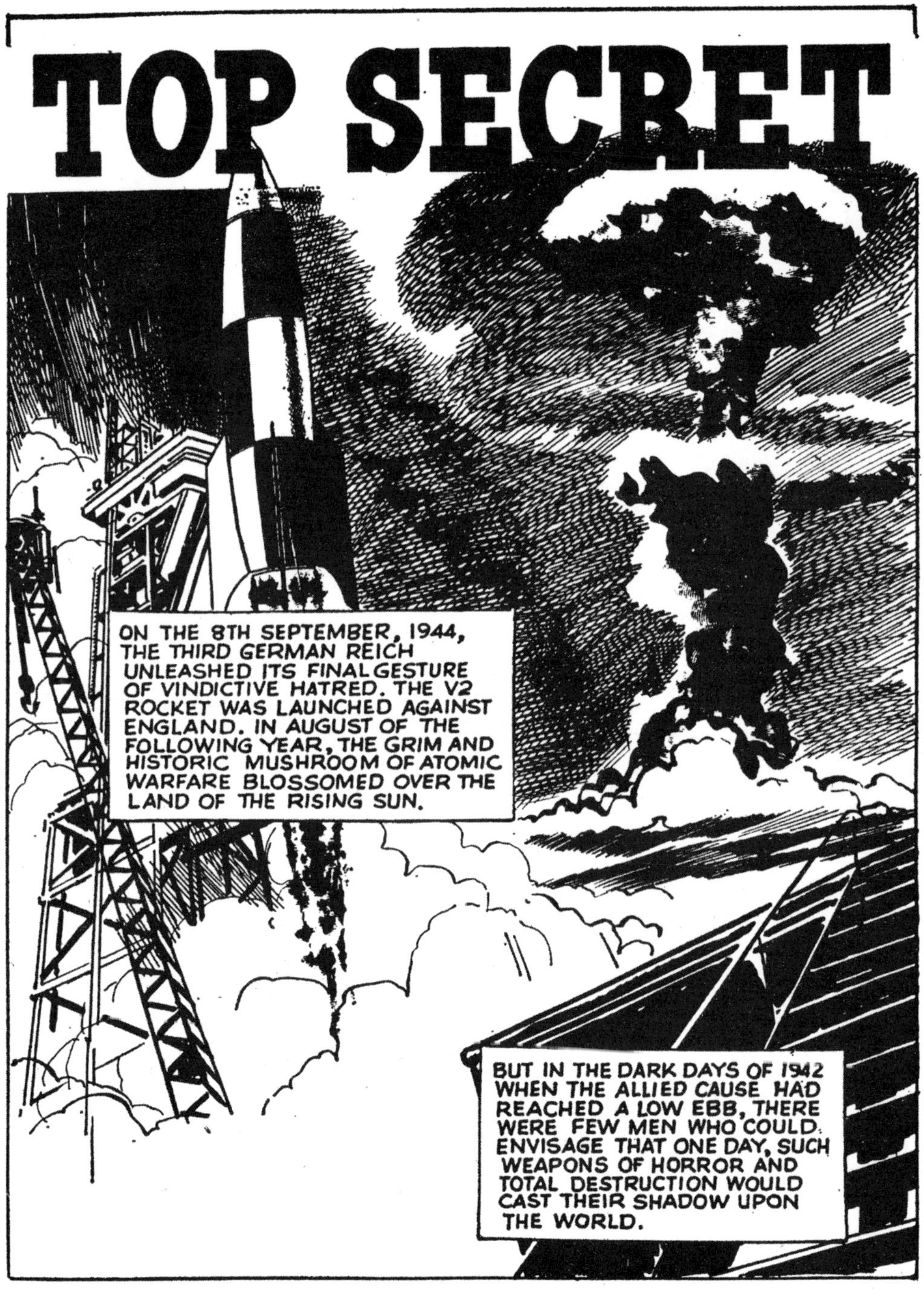
TOP SECRET
ON THE 8TH SEPTEMBER, 1944, THE THIRD GERMAN REICH UNLEASHED ITS FINAL GESTURE OF VINDICTIVE HATRED. THE V2 ROCKET WAS LAUNCHED AGAINST ENGLAND. IN AUGUST OF THE FOLLOWING YEAR, THE GRIM AND HISTORIC MUSHROOM OF ATOMIC WARFARE BLOSSOMED OVER THE LAND OF THE RISING SUN.
BUT IN THE DARK DAYS OF 1942 WHEN THE ALLIED CAUSE HAD REACHED A LOW EBB, THERE WERE FEW MEN WHO COULD ENVISAGE THAT ONE DAY, SUCH WEAPONS OF HORROR AND TOTAL DESTRUCTION WOULD CAST THEIR SHADOW UPON THE WORLD.

Chapter 1. Operation Warlock

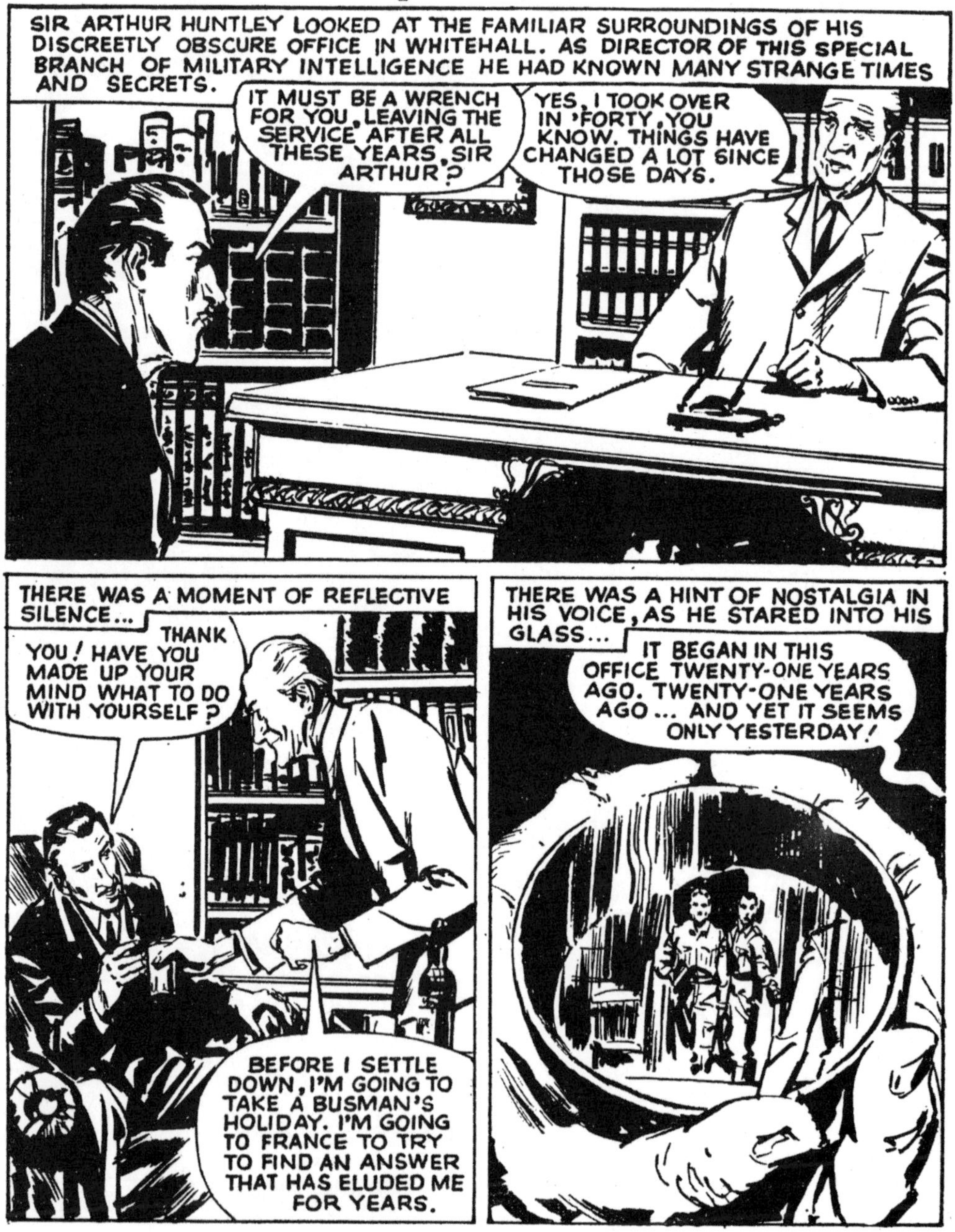
SIR ARTHUR HUNTLEY LOOKED AT THE FAMILIAR SURROUNDINGS OF HIS DISCREETLY OBSCURE OFFICE IN WHITEHALL. AS DIRECTOR OF THIS SPECIAL BRANCH OF MILITARY INTELLIGENCE HE HAD KNOWN MANY STRANGE TIMES AND SECRETS.
IT MUST BE A WRENCH FOR YOU, LEAVING THE SERVICE AFTER ALL THESE YEARS, SIR ARTHUR?
YES, I TOOK OVER IN 'FORTY, YOU KNOW. THINGS HAVE CHANGED A LOT SINCE THOSE DAYS.
THERE WAS A MOMENT OF REFLECTIVE SILENCE...
THANK YOU! HAVE YOU MADE UP YOUR MIND WHAT TO DO WITH YOURSELF?
BEFORE I SETTLE DOWN, I'M GOING TO TAKE A BUSMAN'S HOLIDAY. I'M GOING TO FRANCE TO TRY TO FIND AN ANSWER THAT HAS ELUDED ME FOR YEARS.
THERE WAS A HINT OF NOSTALGIA IN HIS VOICE, AS HE STARED INTO HIS GLASS...
IT BEGAN IN THIS OFFICE TWENTY-ONE YEARS AGO. TWENTY-ONE YEARS AGO... AND YET IT SEEMS ONLY YESTERDAY!

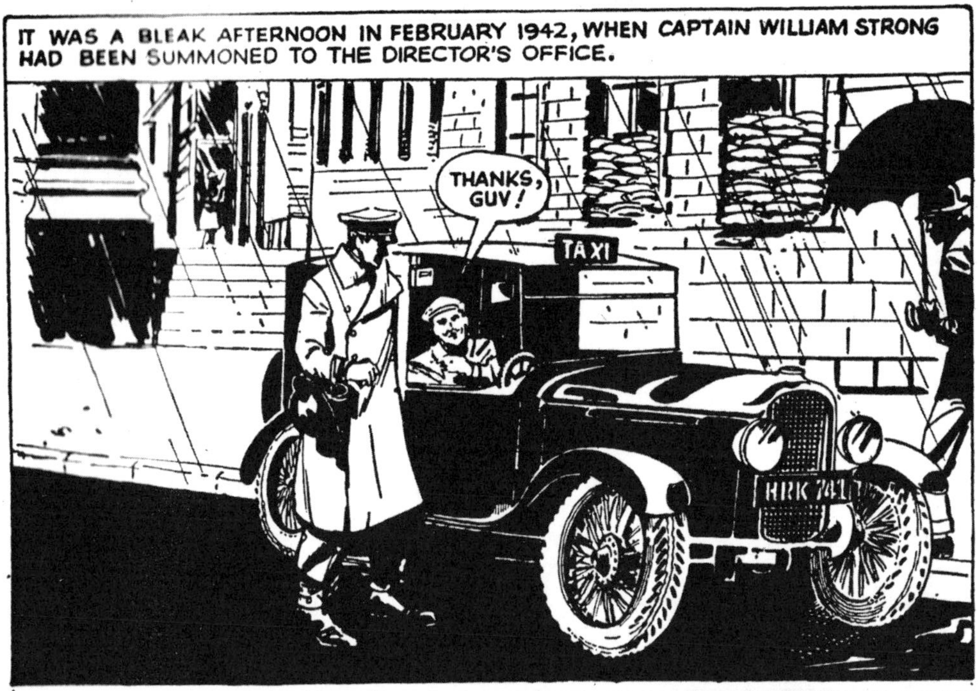
IT WAS A BLEAK AFTERNOON IN FEBRUARY 1942, WHEN CAPTAIN WILLIAM STRONG HAD BEEN SUMMONED TO THE DIRECTOR'S OFFICE.
THANKS, GUV!
TAXI

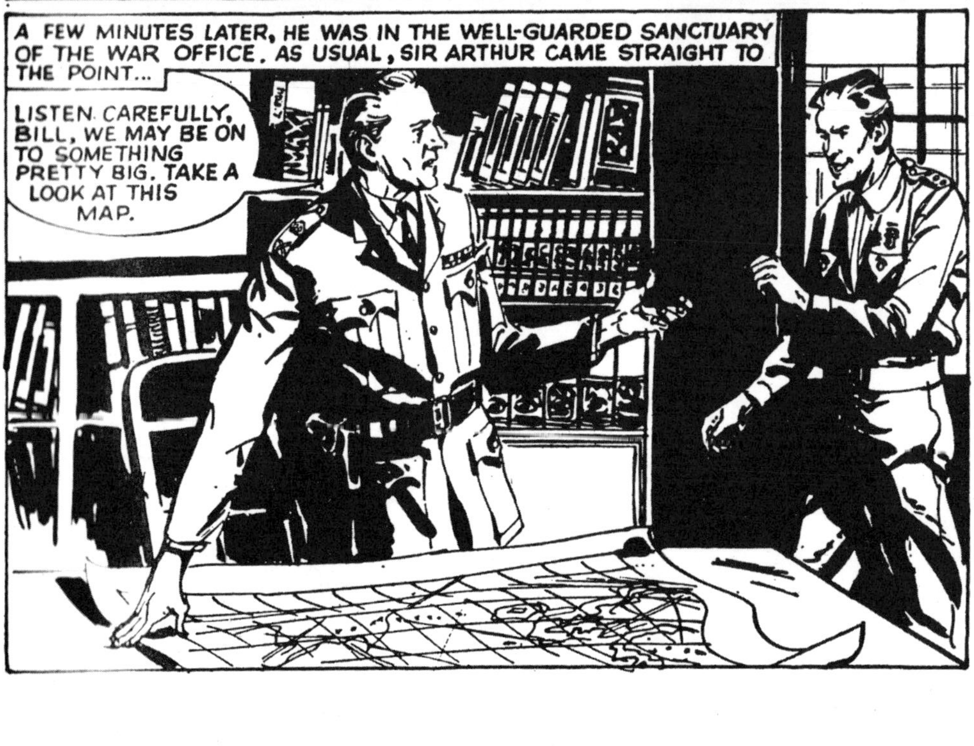
A FEW MINUTES LATER, HE WAS IN THE WELL-GUARDED SANCTUARY OF THE WAR OFFICE. AS USUAL, SIR ARTHUR CAME STRAIGHT TO THE POINT...
LISTEN CAREFULLY, BILL, WE MAY BE ON TO SOMETHING PRETTY BIG. TAKE A LOOK AT THIS MAP.

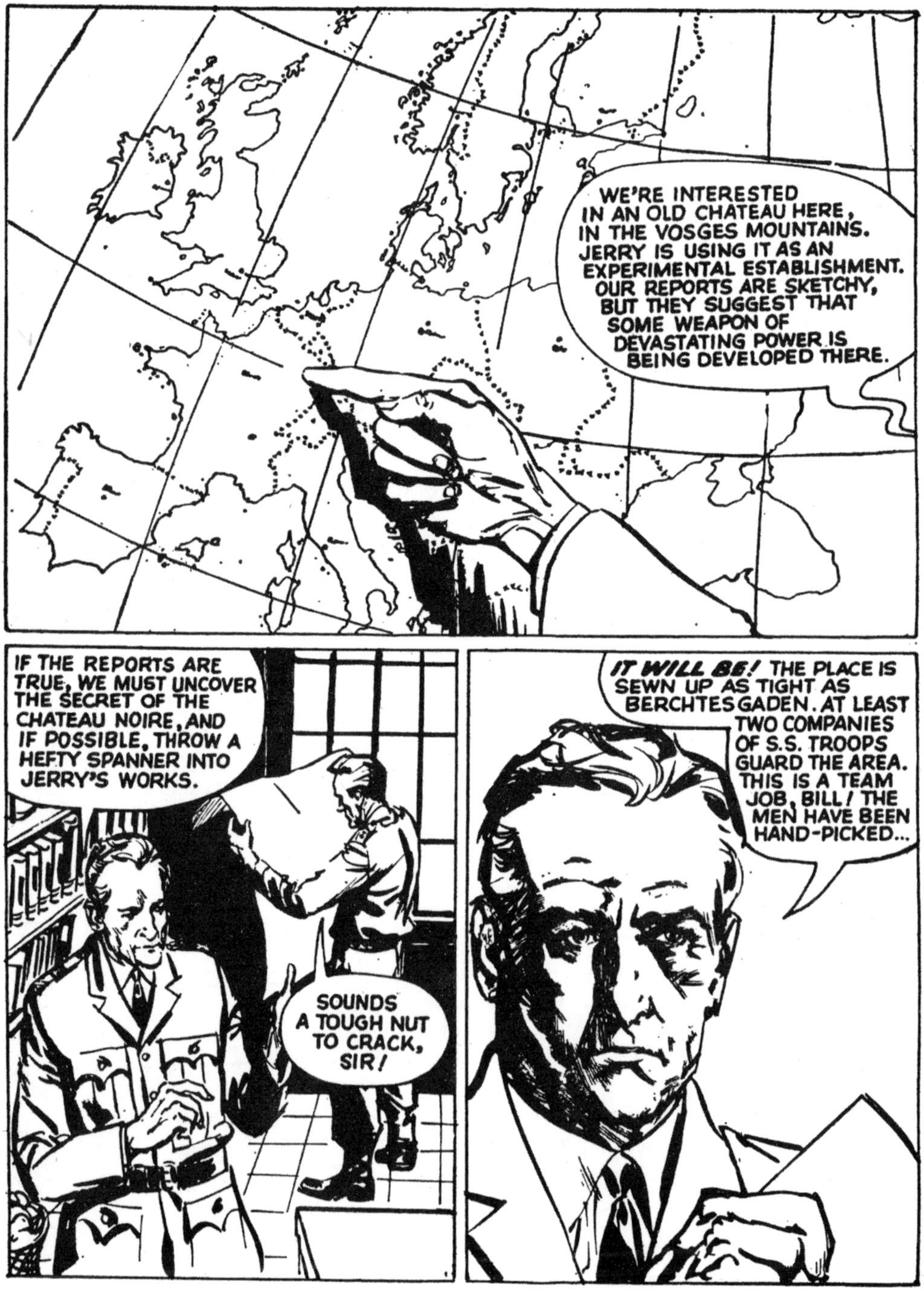
WE'RE INTERESTED IN AN OLD CHATEAU HERE, IN THE VOSGES MOUNTAINS. JERRY IS USING IT AS AN EXPERIMENTAL ESTABLISHMENT. OUR REPORTS ARE SKETCHY, BUT THEY SUGGEST THAT SOME WEAPON OF DEVASTATING POWER IS BEING DEVELOPED THERE.
IF THE REPORTS ARE TRUE, WE MUST UNCOVER THE SECRET OF THE CHATEAU NOIRE, AND IF POSSIBLE, THROW A HEFTY SPANNER INTO JERRY'S WORKS.
SOUNDS A TOUGH NUT TO CRACK, SIR!
IT WILL BE! THE PLACE IS SEWN UP AS TIGHT AS BERCHTESGADEN. AT LEAST TWO COMPANIES OF S.S. TROOPS GUARD THE AREA. THIS IS A TEAM JOB, BILL! THE MEN HAVE BEEN HAND-PICKED...

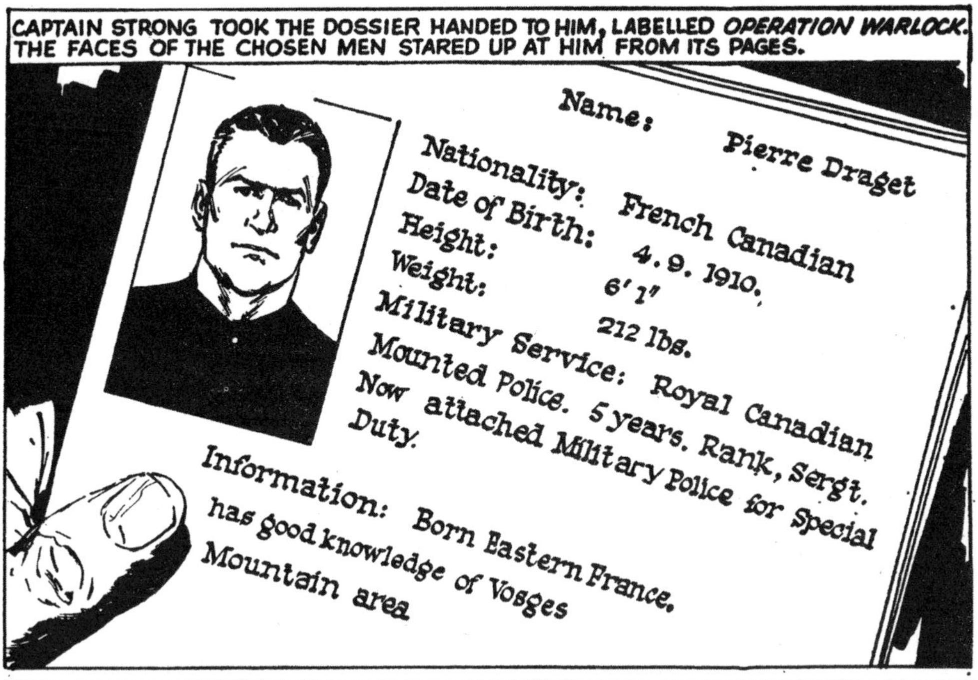
CAPTAIN STRONG TOOK THE DOSSIER HANDED TO HIM, LABELLED *OPERATION WARLOCK*. THE FACES OF THE CHOSEN MEN STARED UP AT HIM FROM ITS PAGES.
Name: Pierre Draget
Nationality: French Canadian
Date of Birth: 4.9. 1910.
Height: 6'1"
Weight: 212 lbs.
Military Service: Royal Canadian Mounted Police. 5 years. Rank, Sergt. Now attached Military Police for Special Duty.
Information: Born Eastern France, has good knowledge of Vosges Mountain area

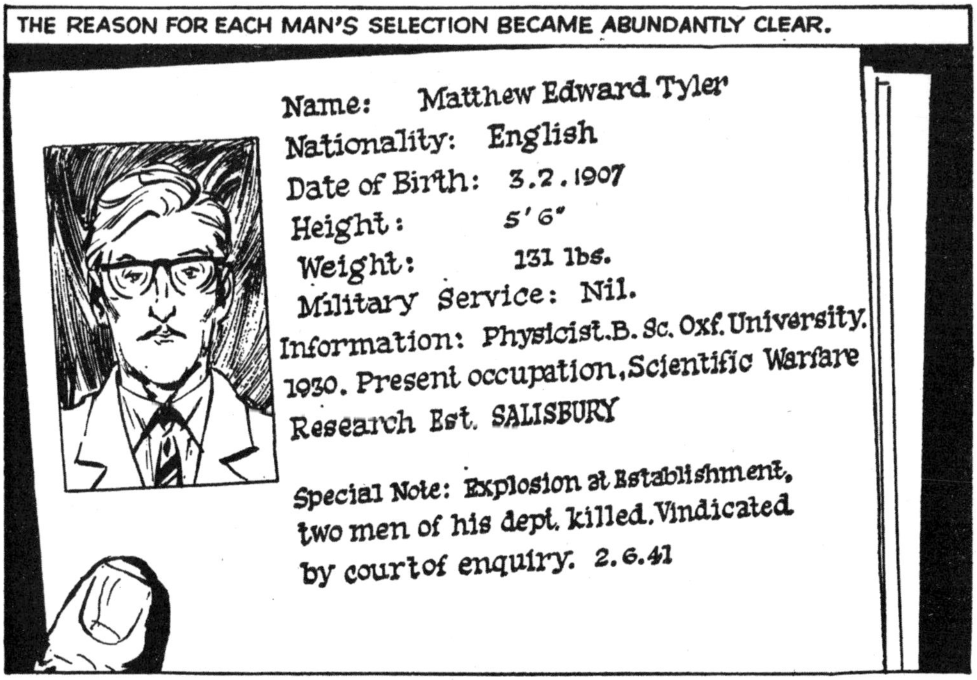
THE REASON FOR EACH MAN'S SELECTION BECAME ABUNDANTLY CLEAR.
Name: Matthew Edward Tyler
Nationality: English
Date of Birth: 3.2.1907
Height: 5'6"
Weight: 131 lbs.
Military Service: Nil.
Information: Physicist. B. Sc. Oxf. University. 1930. Present occupation, Scientific Warfare Research Est. SALISBURY
Special Note: Explosion at Establishment, two men of his dept. killed. Vindicated by court of enquiry. 2.6.41

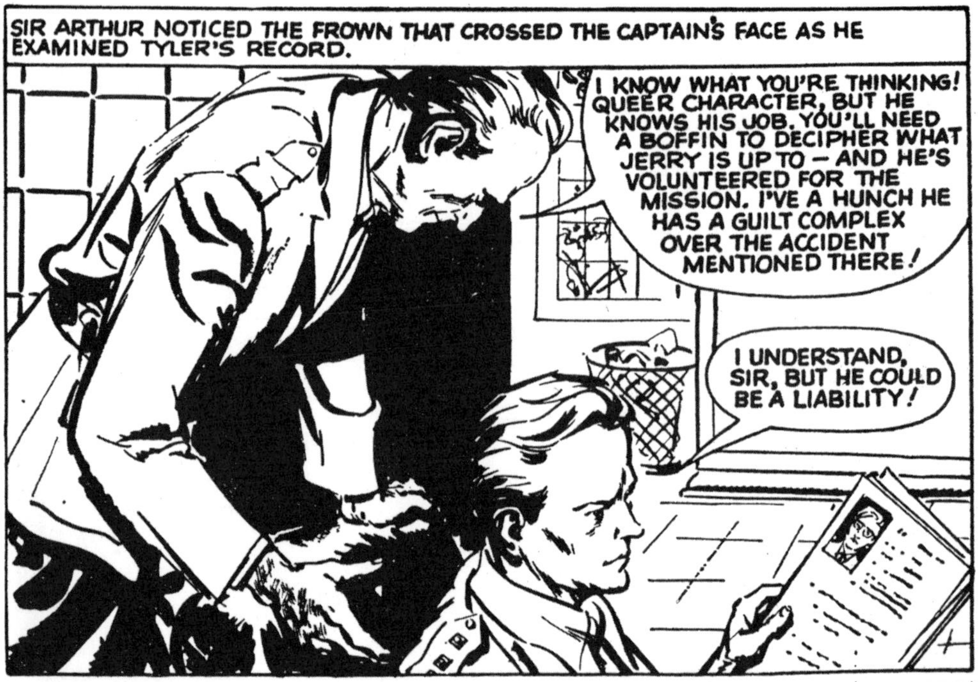
SIR ARTHUR NOTICED THE FROWN THAT CROSSED THE CAPTAIN'S FACE AS HE EXAMINED TYLER'S RECORD.
I KNOW WHAT YOU'RE THINKING! QUEER CHARACTER, BUT HE KNOWS HIS JOB. YOU'LL NEED A BOFFIN TO DECIPHER WHAT JERRY IS UP TO – AND HE'S VOLUNTEERED FOR THE MISSION. I'VE A HUNCH HE HAS A GUILT COMPLEX OVER THE ACCIDENT MENTIONED THERE!
I UNDERSTAND, SIR, BUT HE COULD BE A LIABILITY!

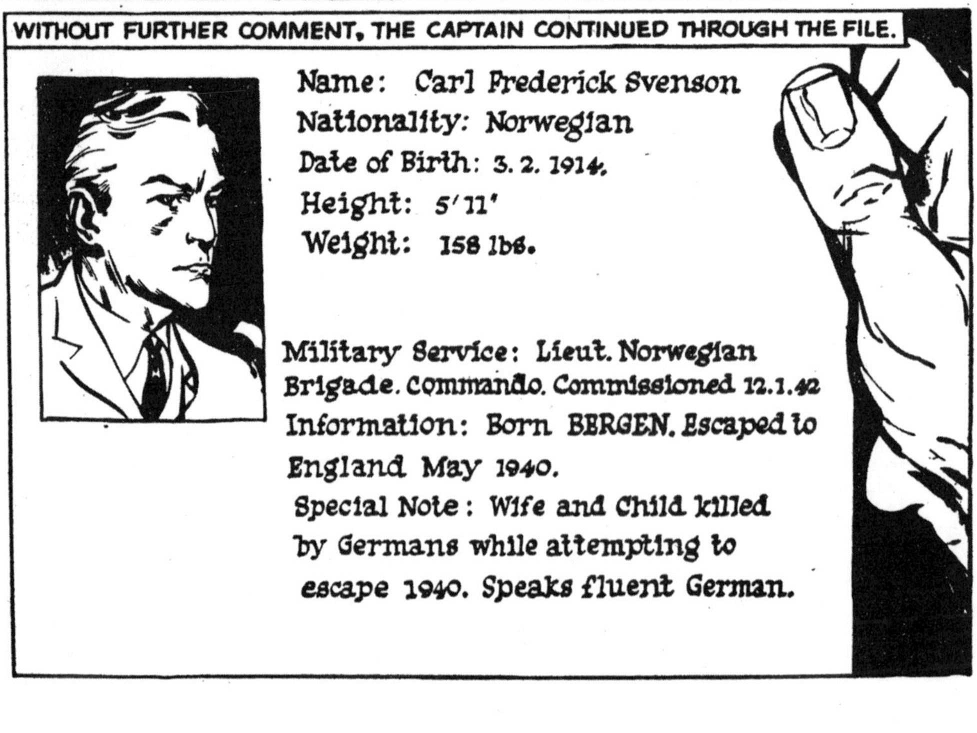
WITHOUT FURTHER COMMENT, THE CAPTAIN CONTINUED THROUGH THE FILE.
Name: Carl Frederick Svenson
Nationality: Norwegian
Date of Birth: 3. 2. 1914.
Height: 5'11'
Weight: 158 lbs.
Military Service: Lieut. Norwegian Brigade. Commando. Commissioned 12.1.42
Information: Born BERGEN. Escaped to England May 1940.
Special Note: Wife and Child killed by Germans while attempting to escape 1940. Speaks fluent German.

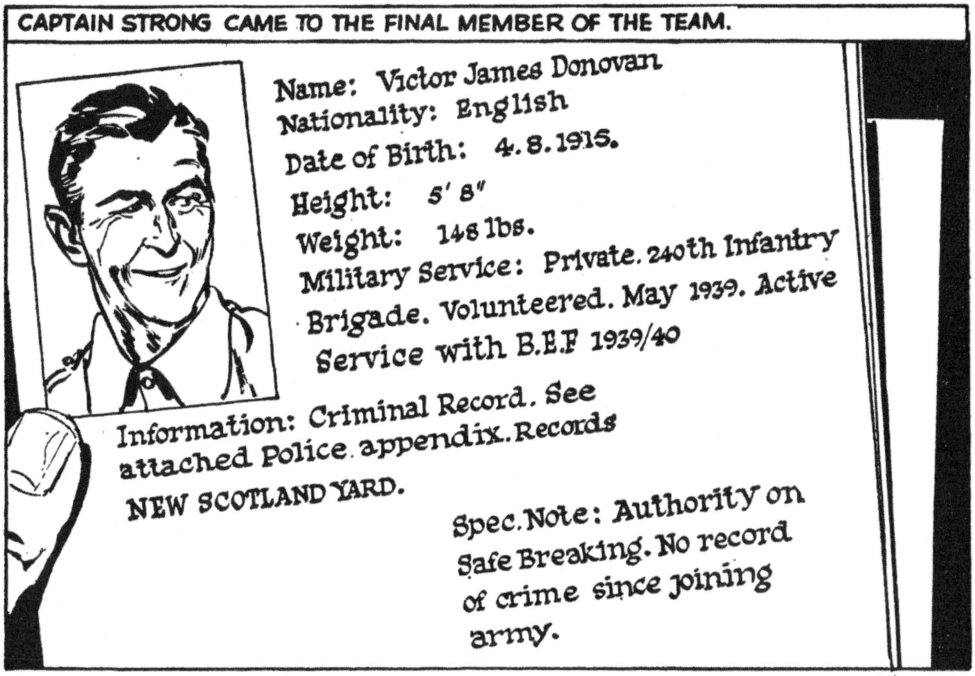
CAPTAIN STRONG CAME TO THE FINAL MEMBER OF THE TEAM.
Name: Victor James Donovan
Nationality: English
Date of Birth: 4. 8. 1915.
Height: 5' 8"
Weight: 148 lbs.
Military Service: Private. 240th Infantry Brigade. Volunteered. May 1939. Active Service with B.E.F 1939/40
Information: Criminal Record. See attached Police appendix. Records NEW SCOTLAND YARD.
Spec. Note: Authority on Safe Breaking. No record of crime since joining army.

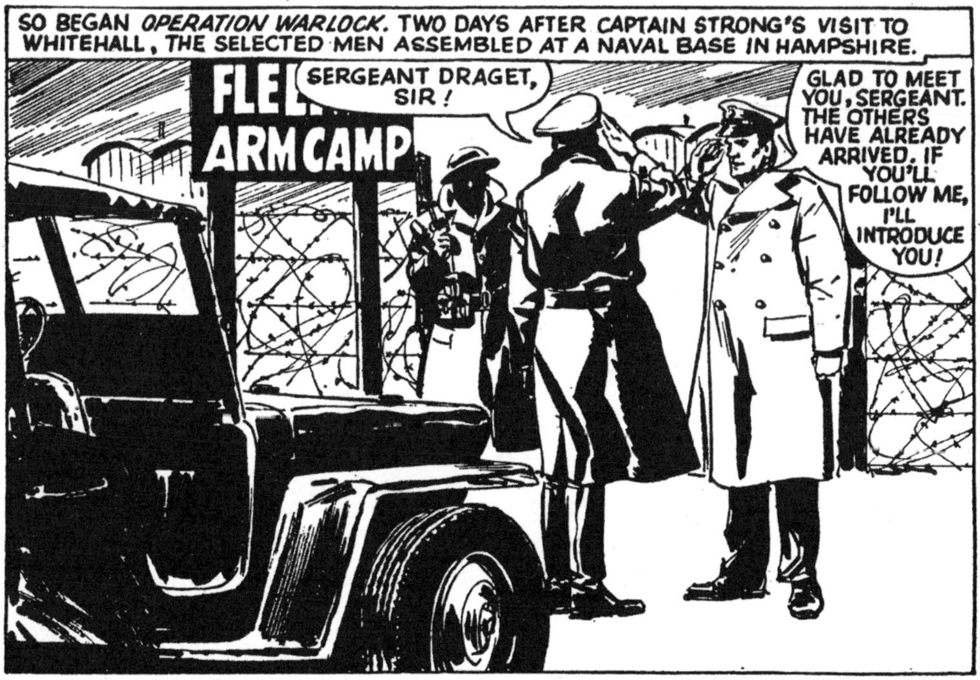
SO BEGAN *OPERATION WARLOCK*. TWO DAYS AFTER CAPTAIN STRONG'S VISIT TO WHITEHALL, THE SELECTED MEN ASSEMBLED AT A NAVAL BASE IN HAMPSHIRE.
FLE
ARM CAMP
SERGEANT DRAGET, SIR!
GLAD TO MEET YOU, SERGEANT. THE OTHERS HAVE ALREADY ARRIVED. IF YOU'LL FOLLOW ME, I'LL INTRODUCE YOU!

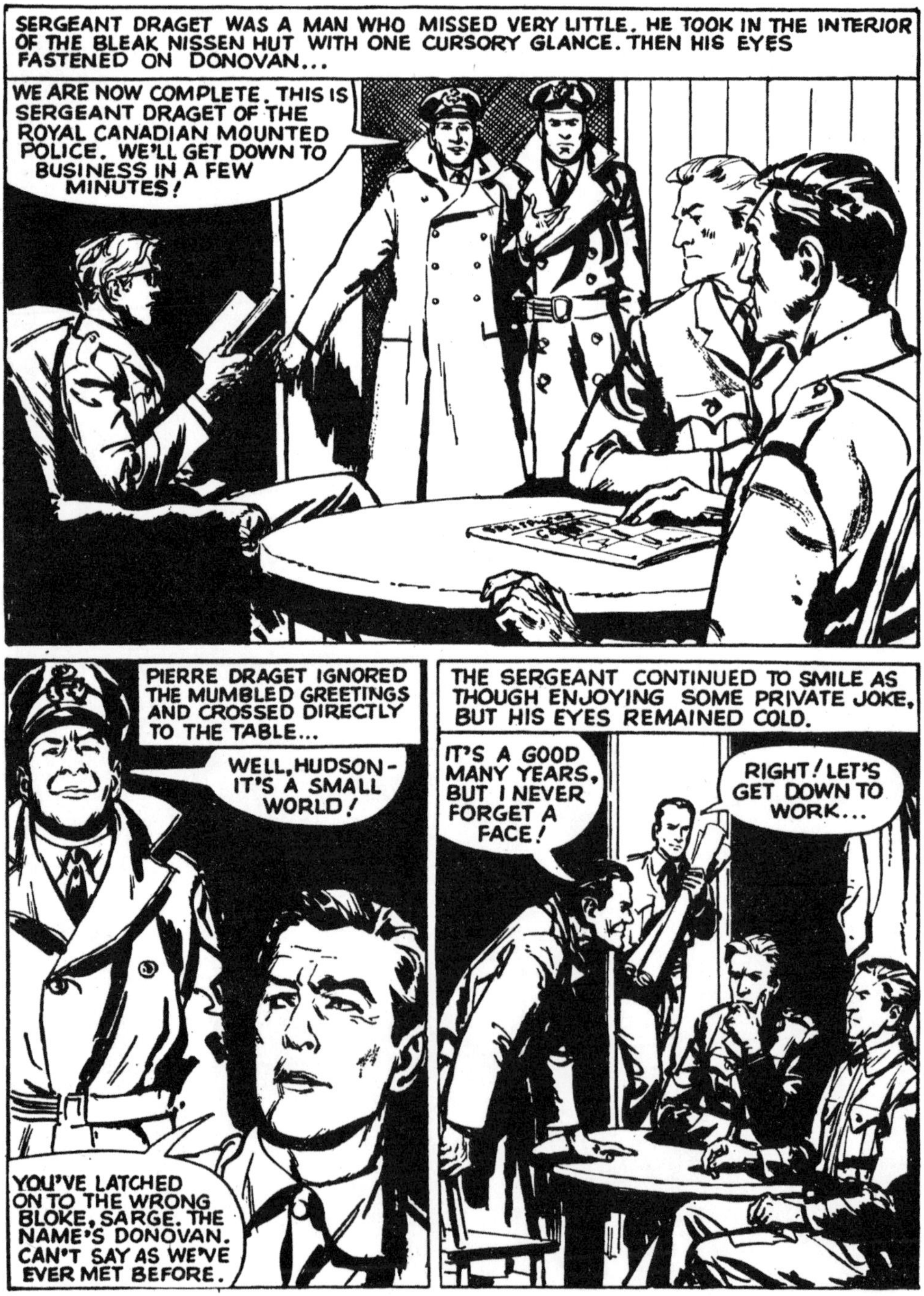
SERGEANT DRAGET WAS A MAN WHO MISSED VERY LITTLE. HE TOOK IN THE INTERIOR OF THE BLEAK NISSEN HUT WITH ONE CURSORY GLANCE. THEN HIS EYES FASTENED ON DONOVAN...
WE ARE NOW COMPLETE. THIS IS SERGEANT DRAGET OF THE ROYAL CANADIAN MOUNTED POLICE. WE'LL GET DOWN TO BUSINESS IN A FEW MINUTES!
PIERRE DRAGET IGNORED THE MUMBLED GREETINGS AND CROSSED DIRECTLY TO THE TABLE...
WELL, HUDSON - IT'S A SMALL WORLD!
YOU'VE LATCHED ON TO THE WRONG BLOKE, SARGE. THE NAME'S DONOVAN. CAN'T SAY AS WE'VE EVER MET BEFORE.
THE SERGEANT CONTINUED TO SMILE AS THOUGH ENJOYING SOME PRIVATE JOKE, BUT HIS EYES REMAINED COLD.
IT'S A GOOD MANY YEARS, BUT I NEVER FORGET A FACE!
RIGHT! LET'S GET DOWN TO WORK...

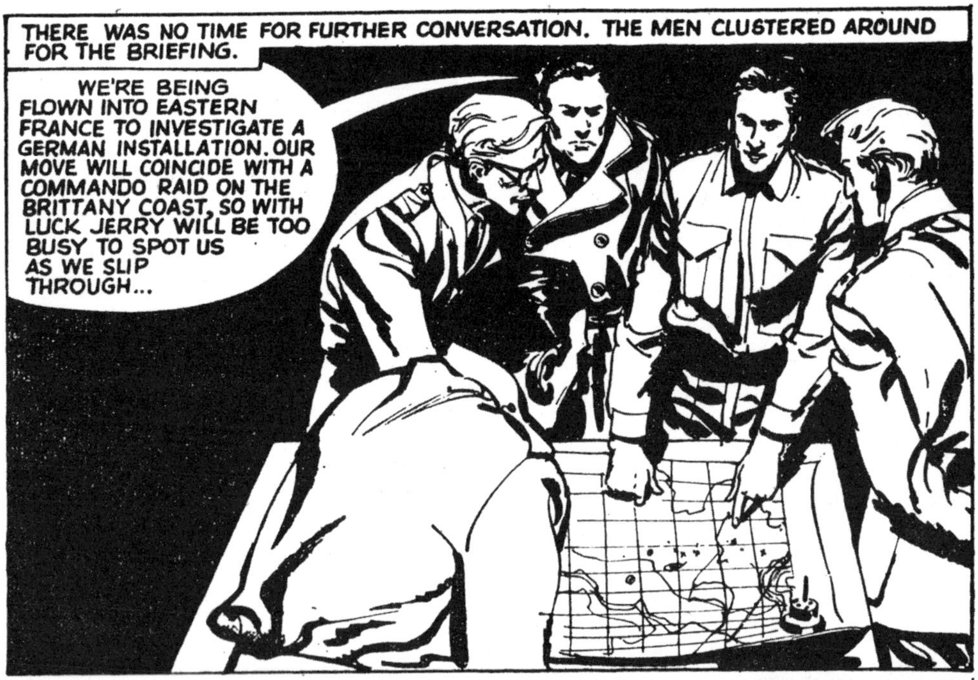
THERE WAS NO TIME FOR FURTHER CONVERSATION. THE MEN CLUSTERED AROUND FOR THE BRIEFING.
WE'RE BEING FLOWN INTO EASTERN FRANCE TO INVESTIGATE A GERMAN INSTALLATION. OUR MOVE WILL COINCIDE WITH A COMMANDO RAID ON THE BRITTANY COAST, SO WITH LUCK JERRY WILL BE TOO BUSY TO SPOT US AS WE SLIP THROUGH...

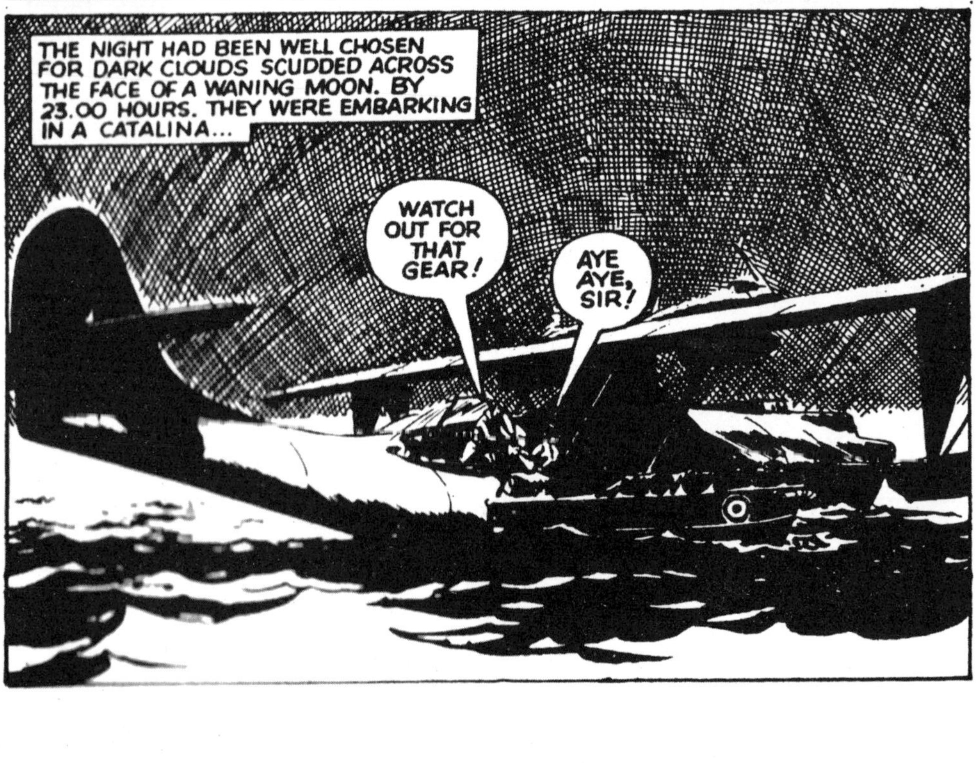
THE NIGHT HAD BEEN WELL CHOSEN FOR DARK CLOUDS SCUDDED ACROSS THE FACE OF A WANING MOON. BY 23.00 HOURS. THEY WERE EMBARKING IN A CATALINA...
WATCH OUT FOR THAT GEAR!
AYE AYE, SIR!

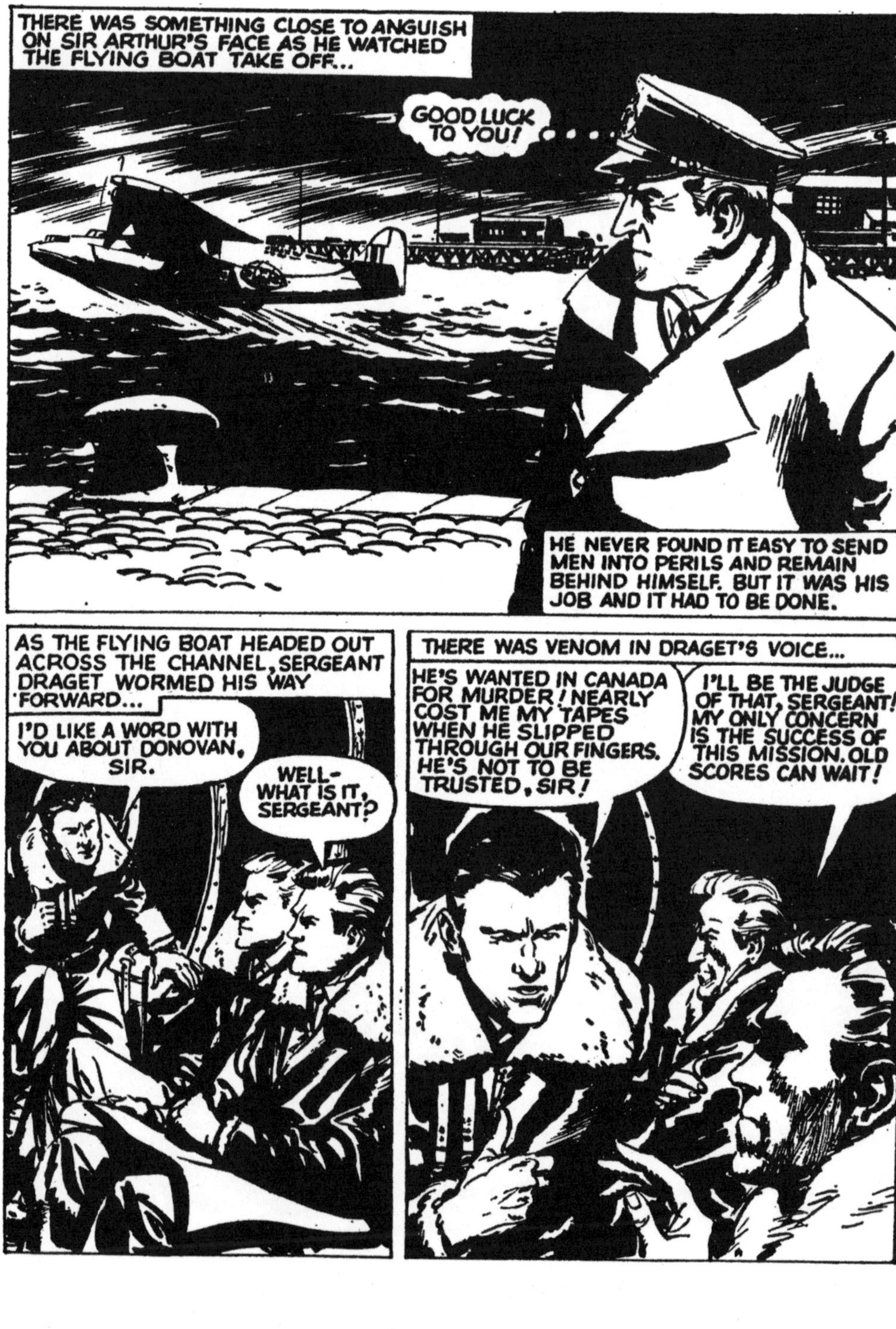
THERE WAS SOMETHING CLOSE TO ANGUISH ON SIR ARTHUR'S FACE AS HE WATCHED THE FLYING BOAT TAKE OFF...
GOOD LUCK TO YOU!
HE NEVER FOUND IT EASY TO SEND MEN INTO PERILS AND REMAIN BEHIND HIMSELF. BUT IT WAS HIS JOB AND IT HAD TO BE DONE.
AS THE FLYING BOAT HEADED OUT ACROSS THE CHANNEL, SERGEANT DRAGET WORMED HIS WAY FORWARD...
I'D LIKE A WORD WITH YOU ABOUT DONOVAN, SIR.
WELL- WHAT IS IT, SERGEANT?
THERE WAS VENOM IN DRAGET'S VOICE...
HE'S WANTED IN CANADA FOR MURDER! NEARLY COST ME MY TAPES WHEN HE SLIPPED THROUGH OUR FINGERS. HE'S NOT TO BE TRUSTED, SIR!
I'LL BE THE JUDGE OF THAT, SERGEANT! MY ONLY CONCERN IS THE SUCCESS OF THIS MISSION. OLD SCORES CAN WAIT!

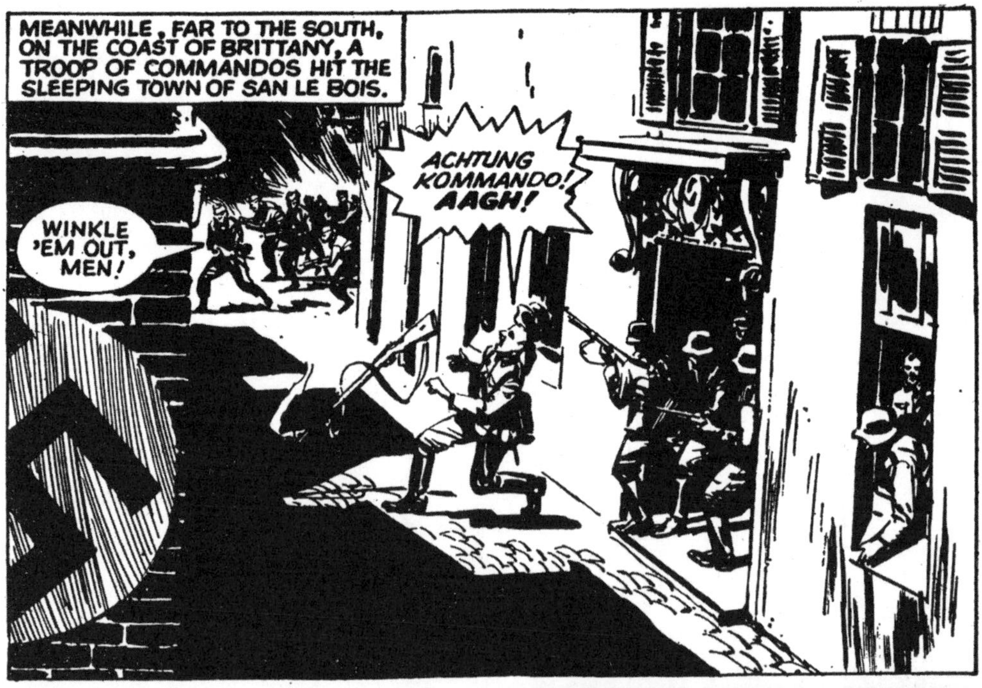
MEANWHILE, FAR TO THE SOUTH, ON THE COAST OF BRITTANY, A TROOP OF COMMANDOS HIT THE SLEEPING TOWN OF SAN LE BOIS.
WINKLE 'EM OUT, MEN!
ACHTUNG KOMMANDO! AAGH!

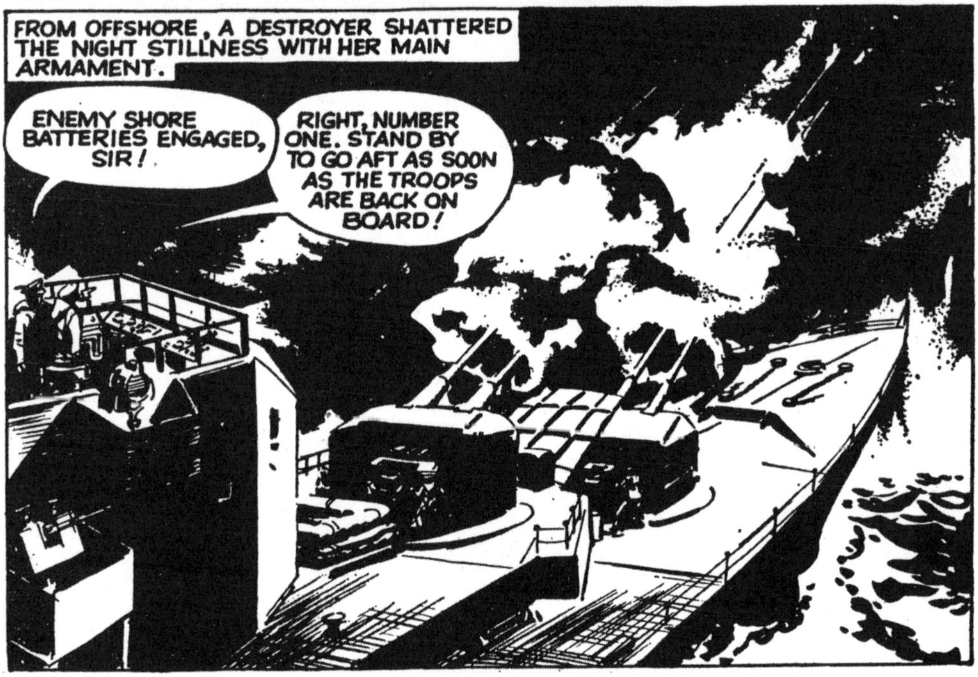
FROM OFFSHORE, A DESTROYER SHATTERED THE NIGHT STILLNESS WITH HER MAIN ARMAMENT.
ENEMY SHORE BATTERIES ENGAGED, SIR!
RIGHT, NUMBER ONE. STAND BY TO GO AFT AS SOON AS THE TROOPS ARE BACK ON BOARD!

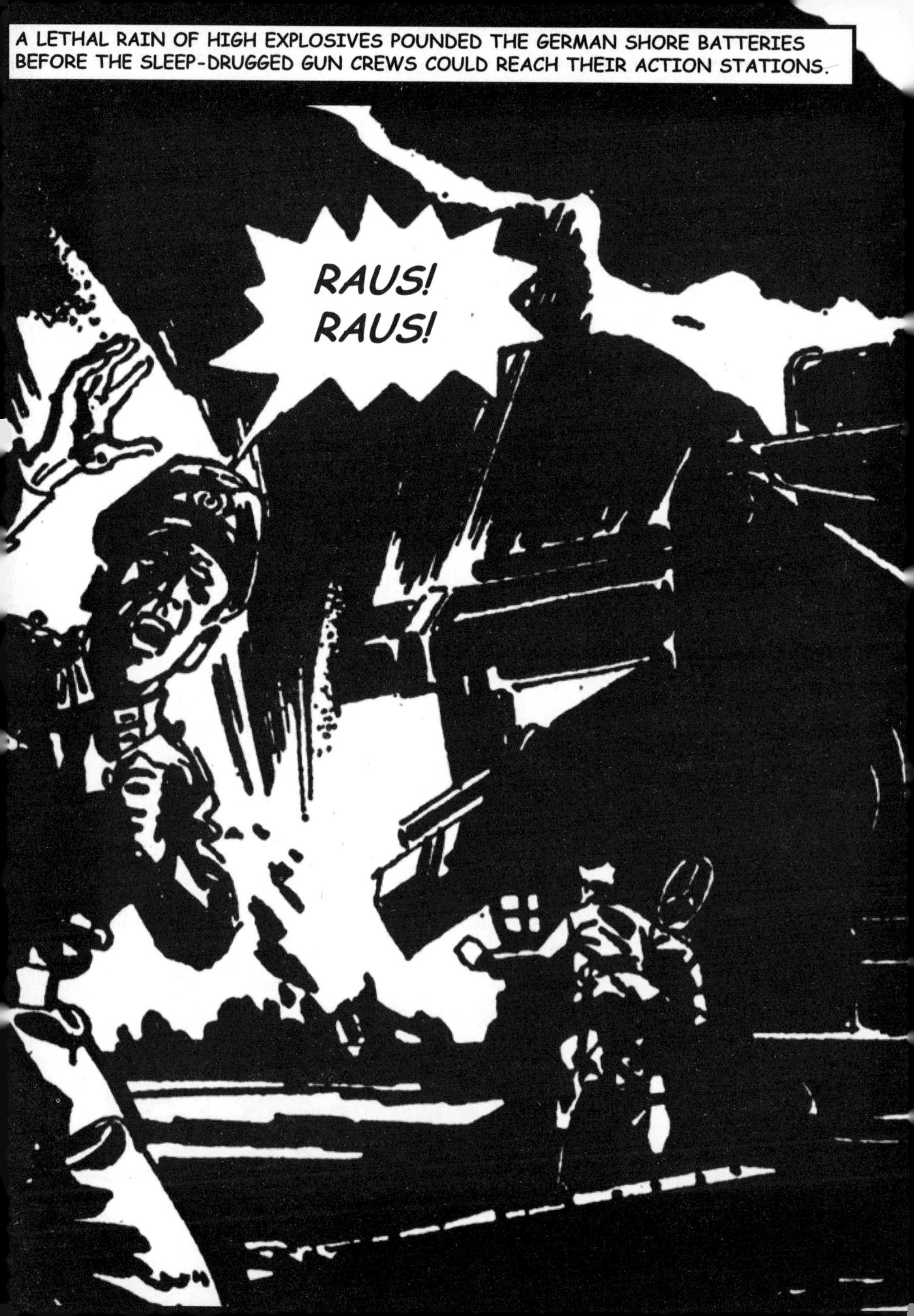
A LETHAL RAIN OF HIGH EXPLOSIVES POUNDED THE GERMAN SHORE BATTERIES BEFORE THE SLEEP-DRUGGED GUN CREWS COULD REACH THEIR ACTION STATIONS.
RAUS! RAUS!

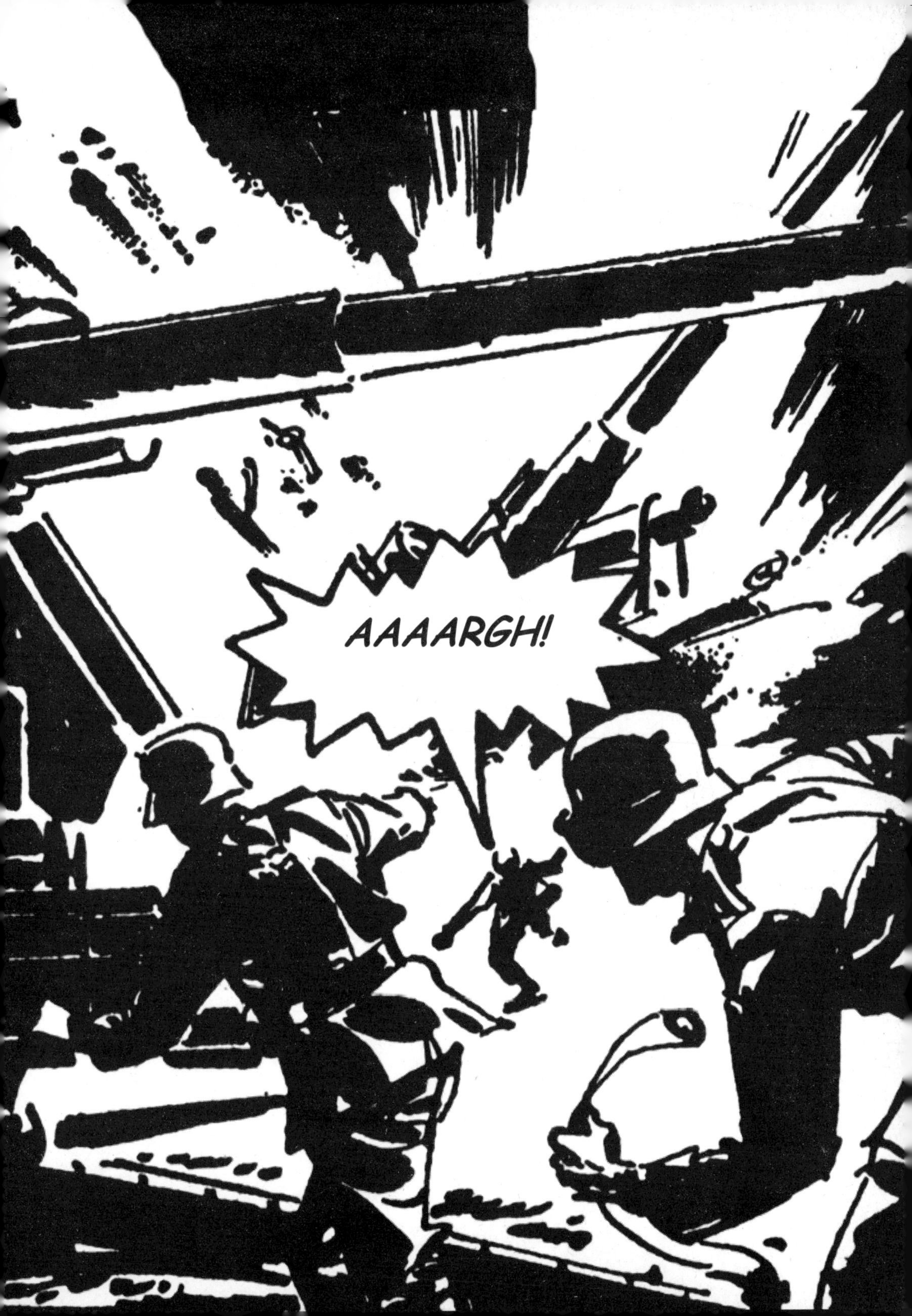
AAAARGH!

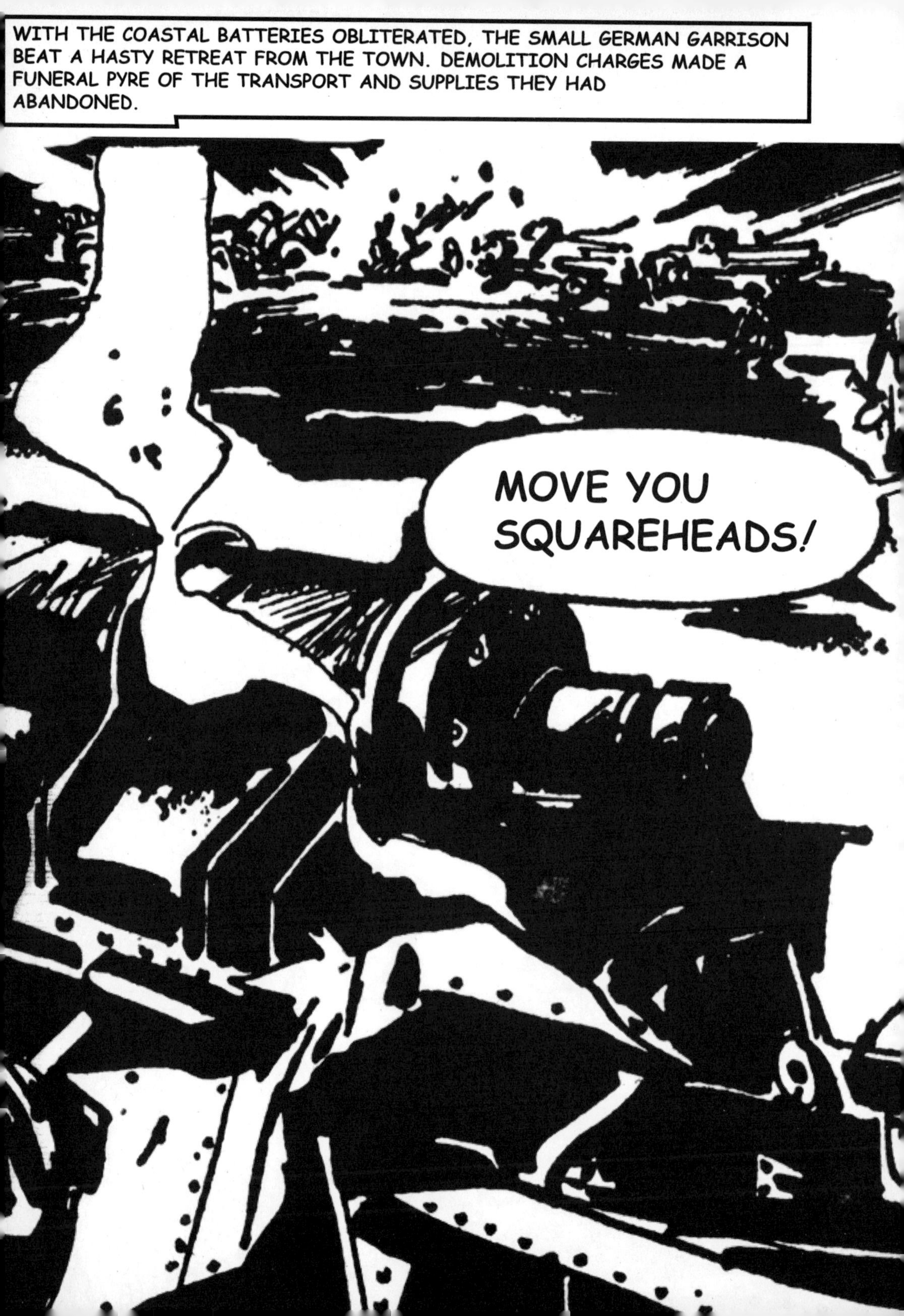
WITH THE COASTAL BATTERIES OBLITERATED, THE SMALL GERMAN GARRISON BEAT A HASTY RETREAT FROM THE TOWN. DEMOLITION CHARGES MADE A FUNERAL PYRE OF THE TRANSPORT AND SUPPLIES THEY HAD ABANDONED.
MOVE YOU SQUAREHEADS!

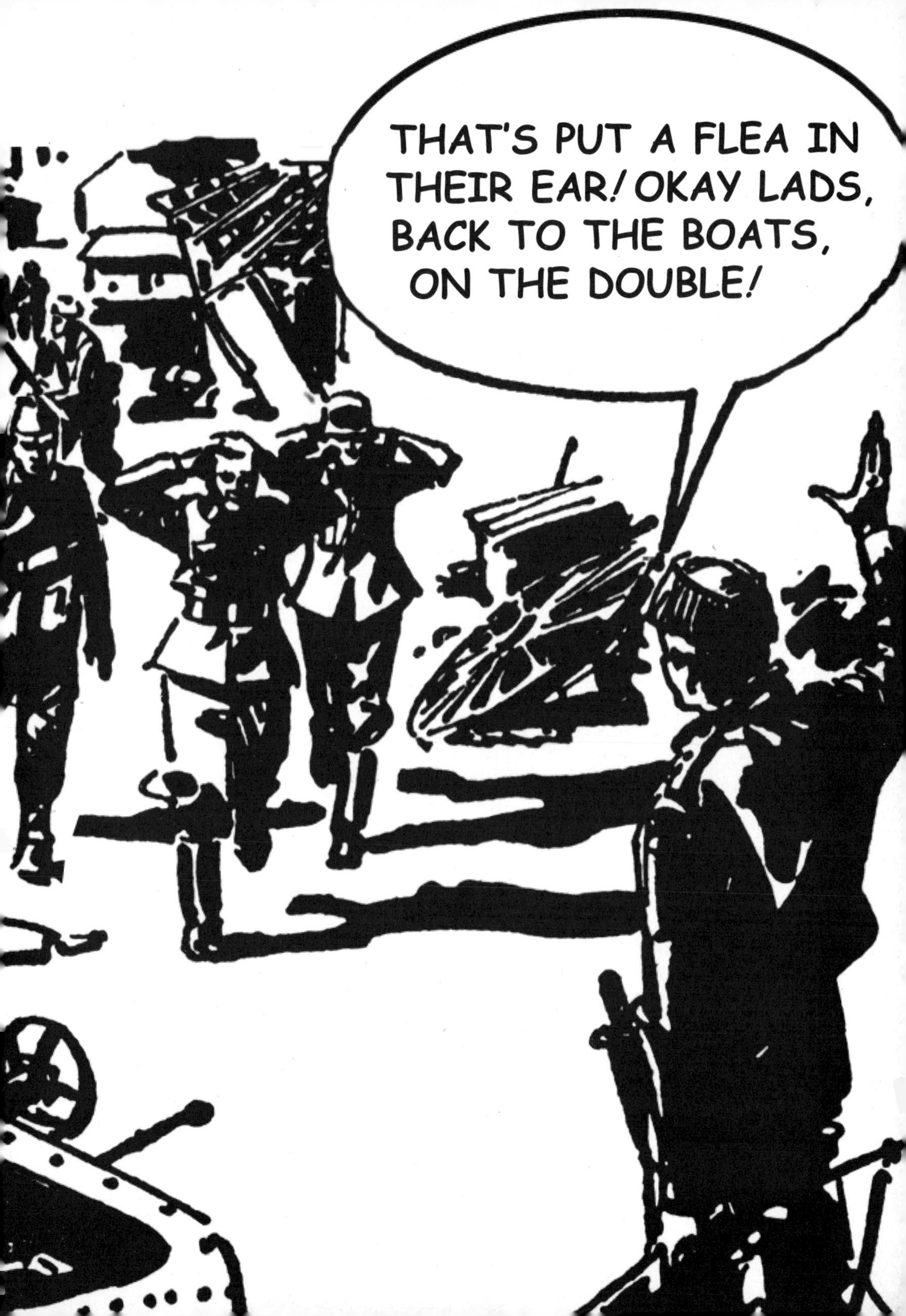
THAT'S PUT A FLEA IN THEIR EAR! OKAY LADS, BACK TO THE BOATS, ON THE DOUBLE!

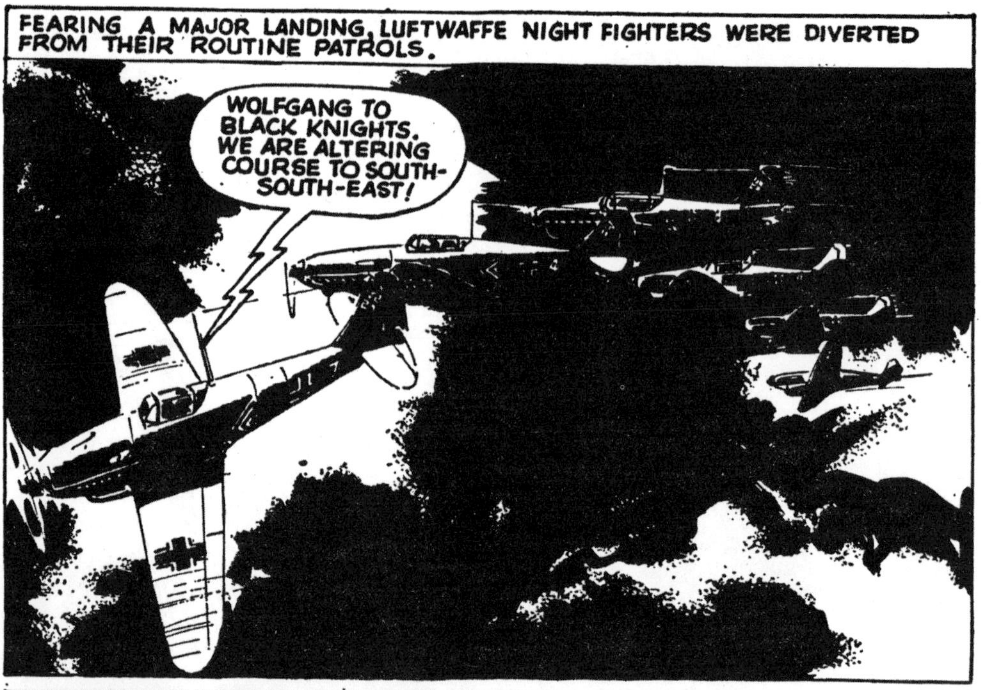
FEARING A MAJOR LANDING, LUFTWAFFE NIGHT FIGHTERS WERE DIVERTED FROM THEIR ROUTINE PATROLS.
WOLFGANG TO BLACK KNIGHTS. WE ARE ALTERING COURSE TO SOUTH-SOUTH-EAST!

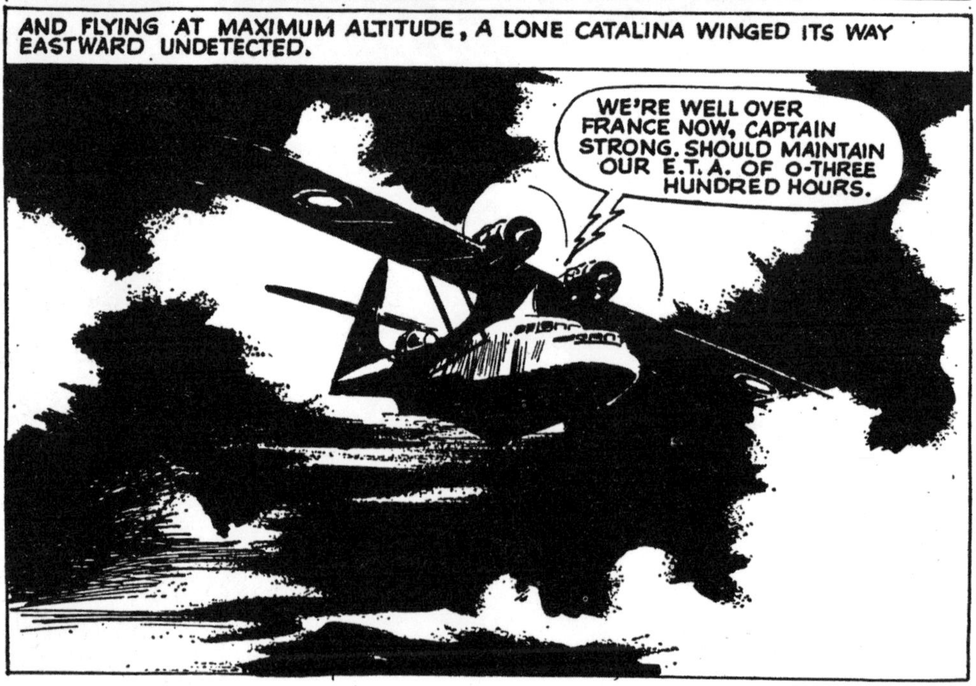
AND FLYING AT MAXIMUM ALTITUDE, A LONE CATALINA WINGED ITS WAY EASTWARD UNDETECTED.
WE'RE WELL OVER FRANCE NOW, CAPTAIN STRONG. SHOULD MAINTAIN OUR E.T.A. OF O-THREE HUNDRED HOURS.

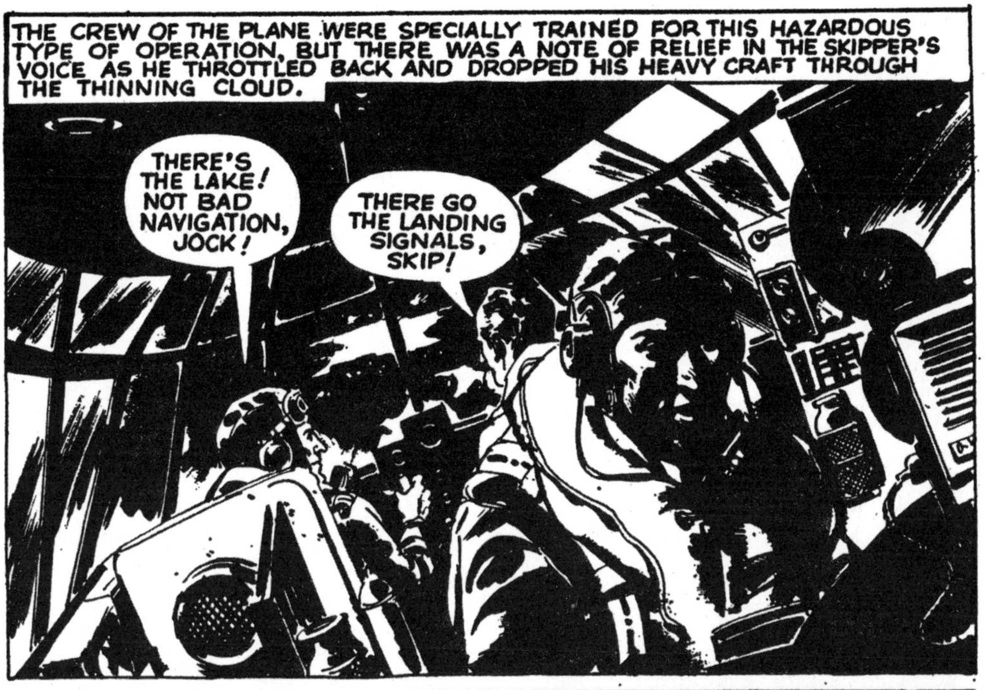
THE CREW OF THE PLANE WERE SPECIALLY TRAINED FOR THIS HAZARDOUS TYPE OF OPERATION, BUT THERE WAS A NOTE OF RELIEF IN THE SKIPPER'S VOICE AS HE THROTTLED BACK AND DROPPED HIS HEAVY CRAFT THROUGH THE THINNING CLOUD.
THERE'S THE LAKE! NOT BAD NAVIGATION, JOCK!
THERE GO THE LANDING SIGNALS, SKIP!

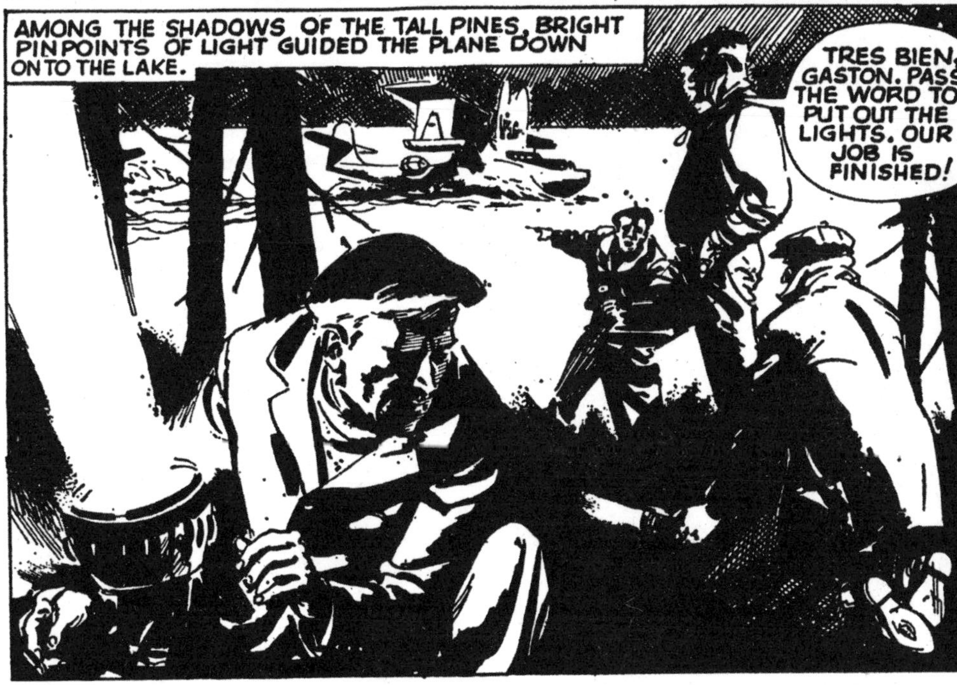
AMONG THE SHADOWS OF THE TALL PINES, BRIGHT PINPOINTS OF LIGHT GUIDED THE PLANE DOWN ONTO THE LAKE.
TRES BIEN, GASTON. PASS THE WORD TO PUT OUT THE LIGHTS. OUR JOB IS FINISHED!

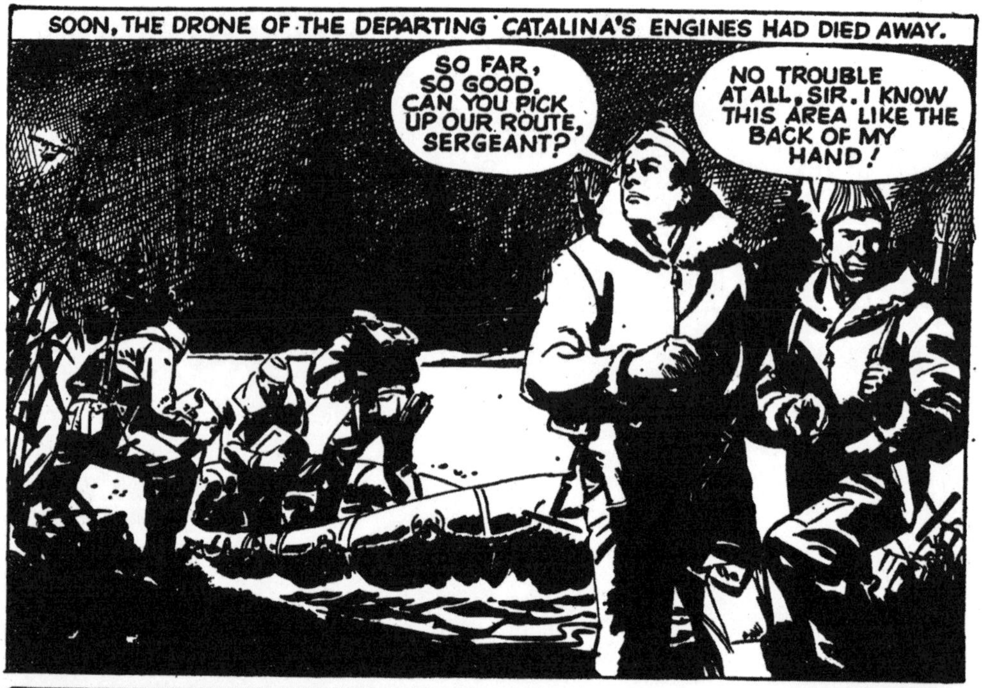
SOON, THE DRONE OF THE DEPARTING CATALINA'S ENGINES HAD DIED AWAY.
SO FAR, SO GOOD. CAN YOU PICK UP OUR ROUTE, SERGEANT?
NO TROUBLE AT ALL, SIR. I KNOW THIS AREA LIKE THE BACK OF MY HAND!

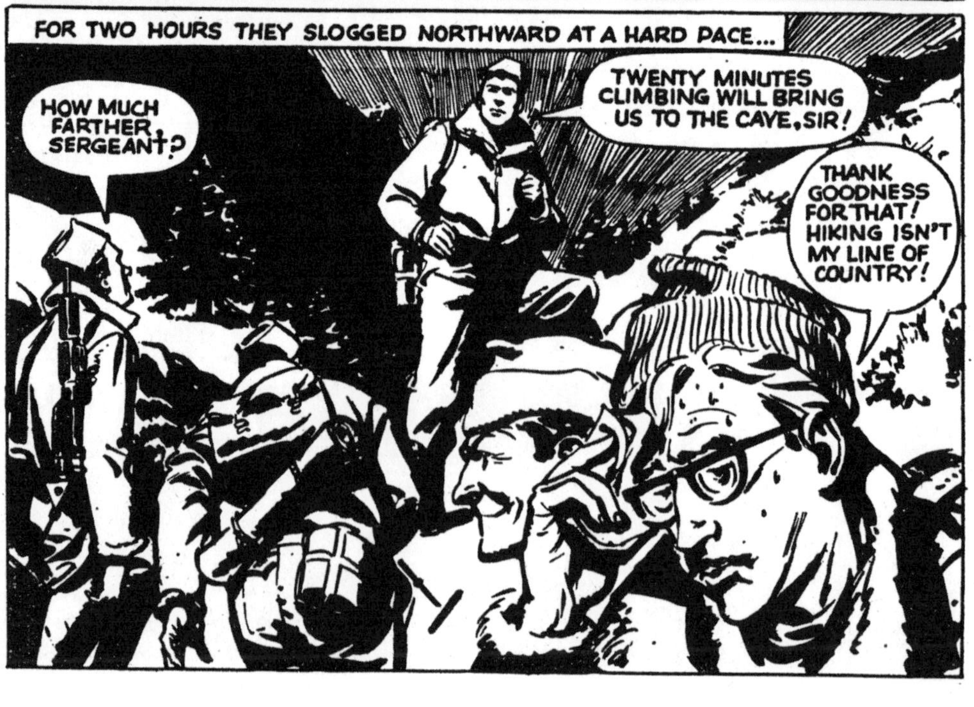
FOR TWO HOURS THEY SLOGGED NORTHWARD AT A HARD PACE...
HOW MUCH FARTHER, SERGEANT?
TWENTY MINUTES CLIMBING WILL BRING US TO THE CAVE, SIR!
THANK GOODNESS FOR THAT! HIKING ISN'T MY LINE OF COUNTRY!

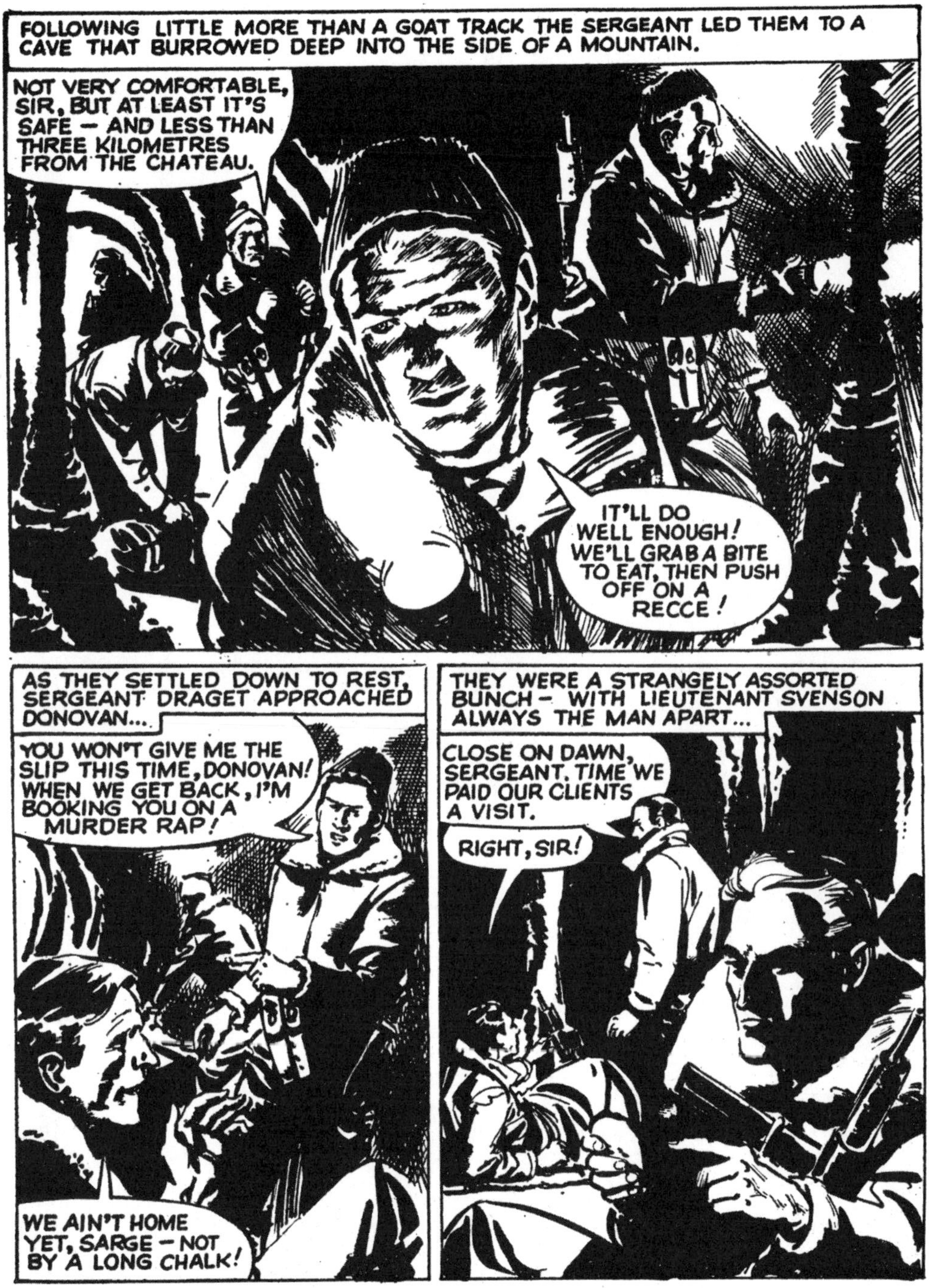
FOLLOWING LITTLE MORE THAN A GOAT TRACK THE SERGEANT LED THEM TO A CAVE THAT BURROWED DEEP INTO THE SIDE OF A MOUNTAIN.
NOT VERY COMFORTABLE, SIR, BUT AT LEAST IT'S SAFE — AND LESS THAN THREE KILOMETRES FROM THE CHATEAU.
IT'LL DO WELL ENOUGH! WE'LL GRAB A BITE TO EAT, THEN PUSH OFF ON A RECCE!
AS THEY SETTLED DOWN TO REST, SERGEANT DRAGET APPROACHED DONOVAN...
YOU WON'T GIVE ME THE SLIP THIS TIME, DONOVAN! WHEN WE GET BACK, I'M BOOKING YOU ON A MURDER RAP!
WE AIN'T HOME YET, SARGE — NOT BY A LONG CHALK!
THEY WERE A STRANGELY ASSORTED BUNCH — WITH LIEUTENANT SVENSON ALWAYS THE MAN APART...
CLOSE ON DAWN, SERGEANT. TIME WE PAID OUR CLIENTS A VISIT.
RIGHT, SIR!

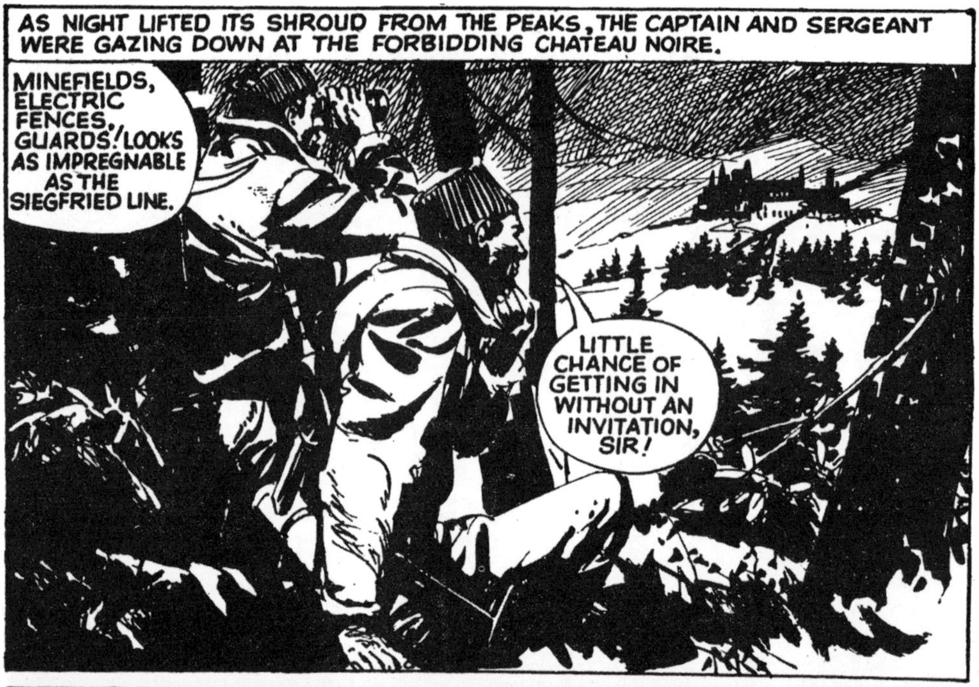
AS NIGHT LIFTED ITS SHROUD FROM THE PEAKS, THE CAPTAIN AND SERGEANT WERE GAZING DOWN AT THE FORBIDDING CHATEAU NOIRE.
MINEFIELDS, ELECTRIC FENCES, GUARDS! LOOKS AS IMPREGNABLE AS THE SIEGFRIED LINE.
LITTLE CHANCE OF GETTING IN WITHOUT AN INVITATION, SIR!

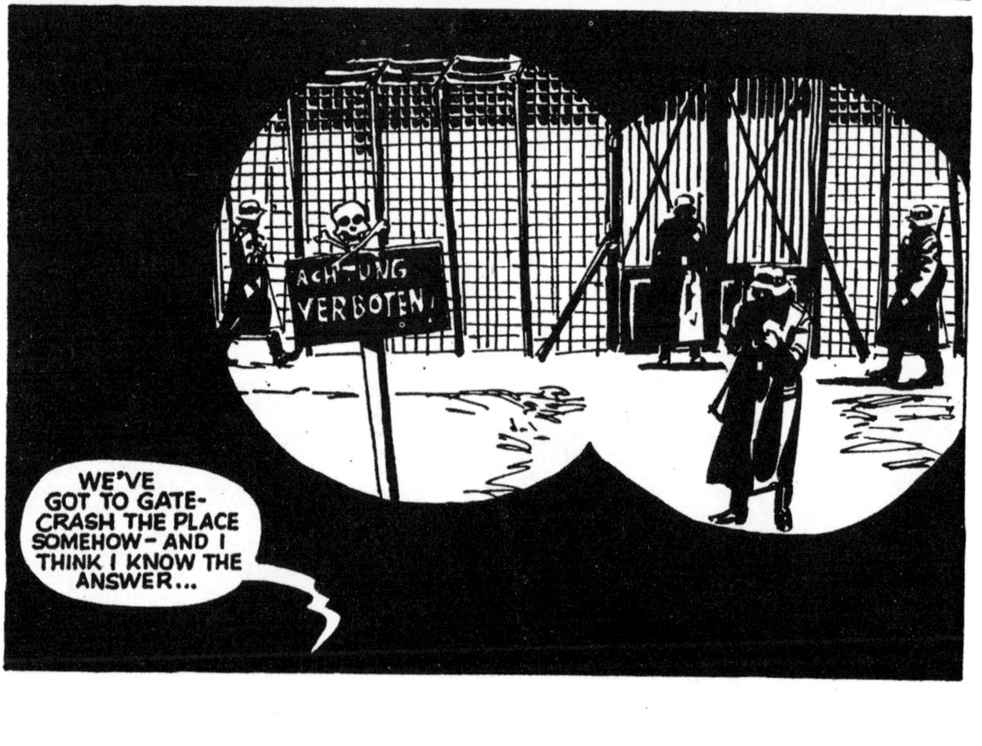
ACHTUNG VERBOTEN!
WE'VE GOT TO GATE-CRASH THE PLACE SOMEHOW - AND I THINK I KNOW THE ANSWER...

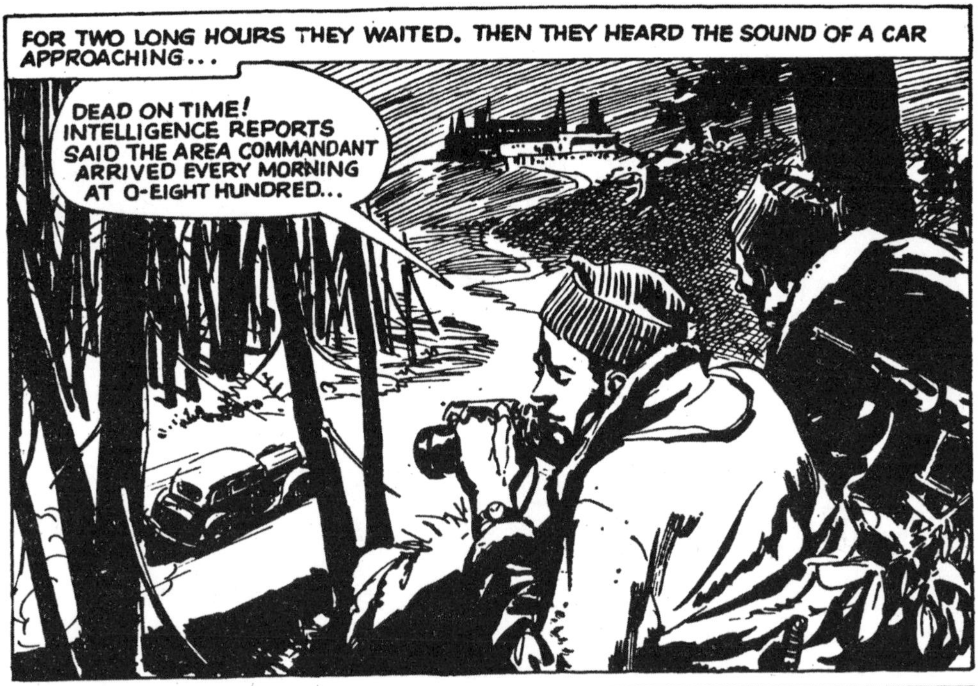
FOR TWO LONG HOURS THEY WAITED. THEN THEY HEARD THE SOUND OF A CAR APPROACHING...
DEAD ON TIME! INTELLIGENCE REPORTS SAID THE AREA COMMANDANT ARRIVED EVERY MORNING AT O-EIGHT HUNDRED...

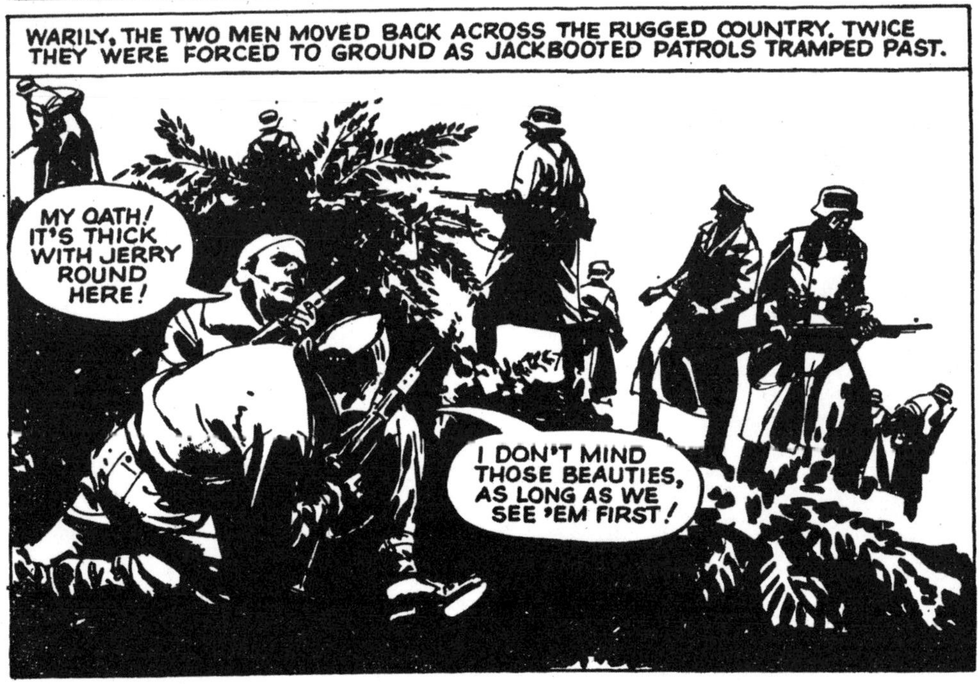
WARILY, THE TWO MEN MOVED BACK ACROSS THE RUGGED COUNTRY. TWICE THEY WERE FORCED TO GROUND AS JACKBOOTED PATROLS TRAMPED PAST.
MY OATH! IT'S THICK WITH JERRY ROUND HERE!
I DON'T MIND THOSE BEAUTIES, AS LONG AS WE SEE 'EM FIRST!

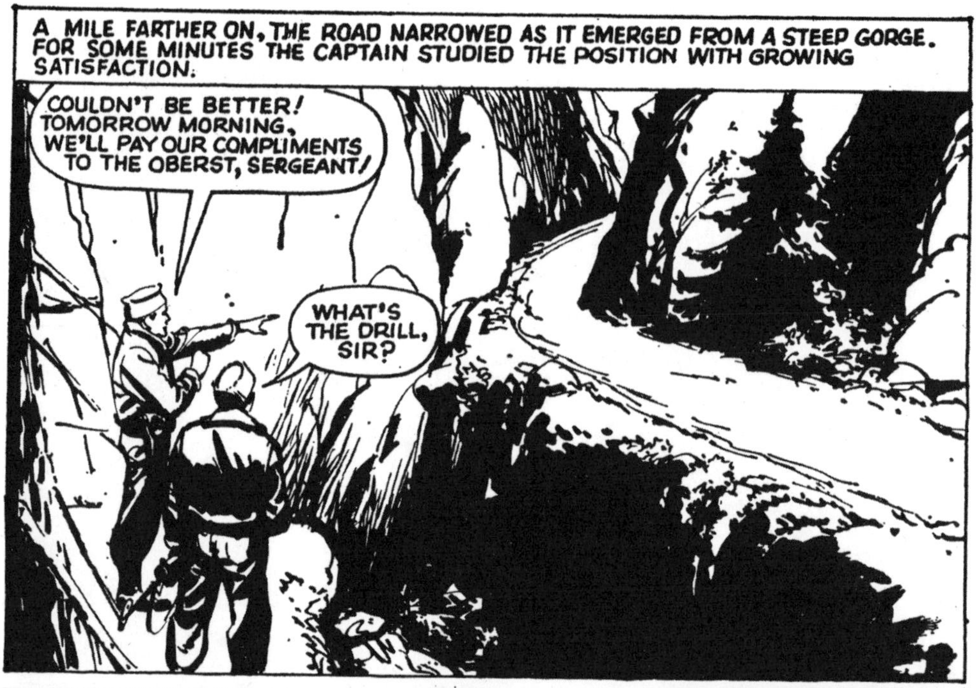
A MILE FARTHER ON, THE ROAD NARROWED AS IT EMERGED FROM A STEEP GORGE. FOR SOME MINUTES THE CAPTAIN STUDIED THE POSITION WITH GROWING SATISFACTION.
COULDN'T BE BETTER! TOMORROW MORNING, WE'LL PAY OUR COMPLIMENTS TO THE OBERST, SERGEANT!
WHAT'S THE DRILL, SIR?

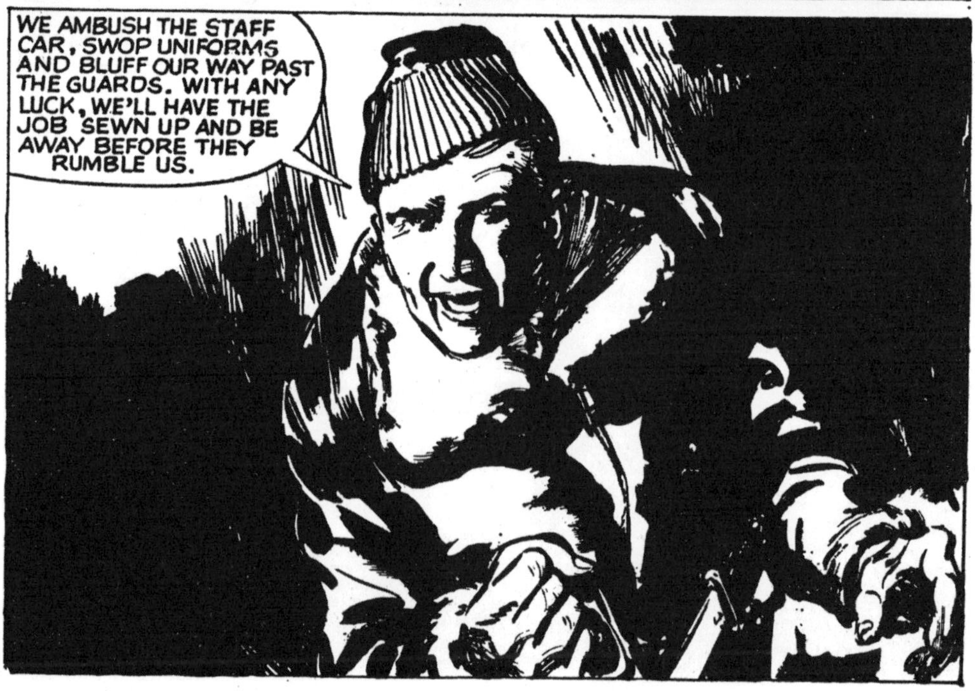
WE AMBUSH THE STAFF CAR, SWOP UNIFORMS AND BLUFF OUR WAY PAST THE GUARDS. WITH ANY LUCK, WE'LL HAVE THE JOB SEWN UP AND BE AWAY BEFORE THEY RUMBLE US.

Chapter 2. Phantoms of the Night

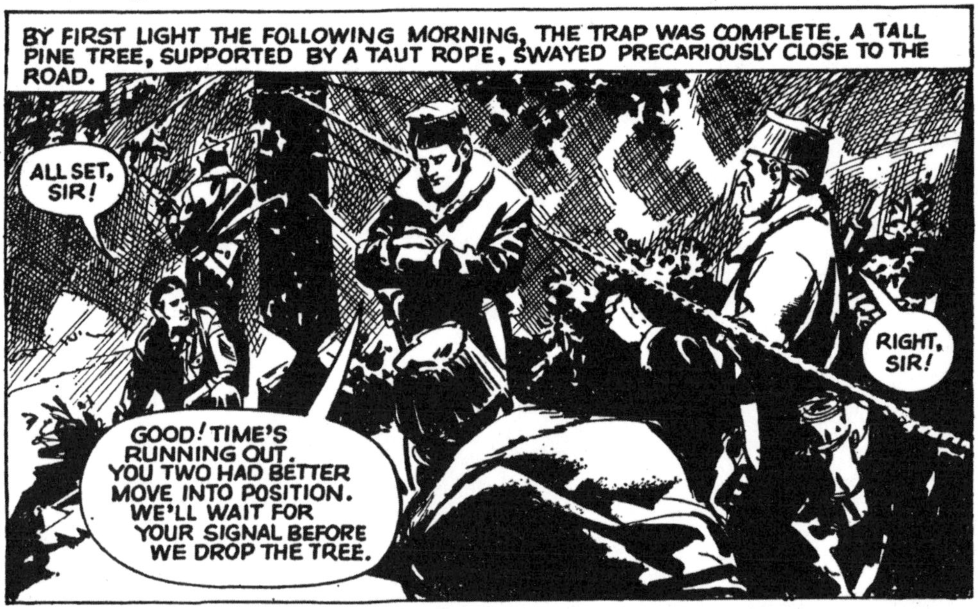
BY FIRST LIGHT THE FOLLOWING MORNING, THE TRAP WAS COMPLETE. A TALL PINE TREE, SUPPORTED BY A TAUT ROPE, SWAYED PRECARIOUSLY CLOSE TO THE ROAD.
ALL SET, SIR!
RIGHT, SIR!
GOOD! TIME'S RUNNING OUT. YOU TWO HAD BETTER MOVE INTO POSITION. WE'LL WAIT FOR YOUR SIGNAL BEFORE WE DROP THE TREE.

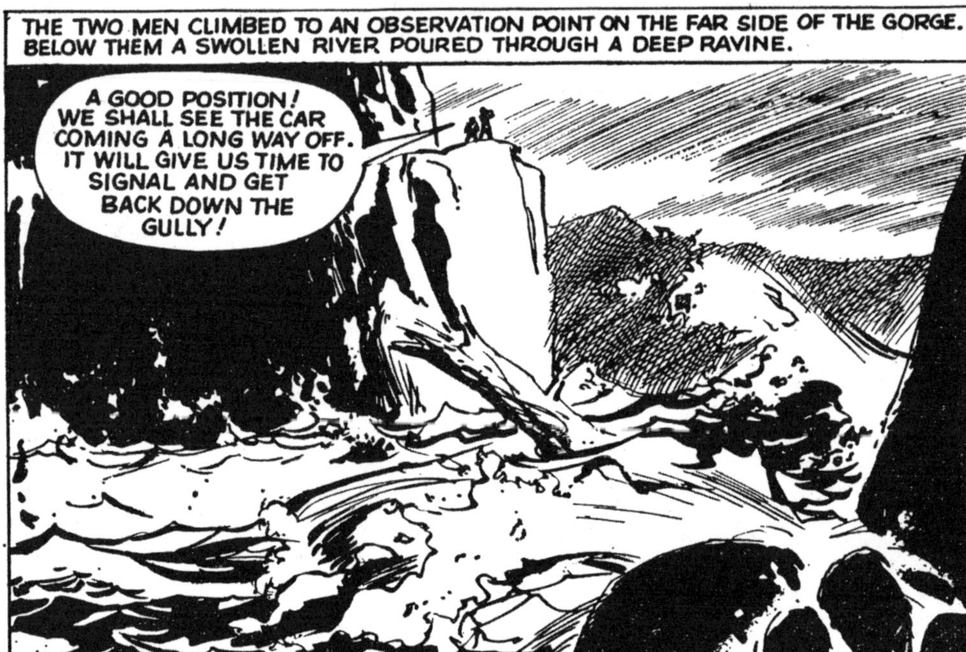
THE TWO MEN CLIMBED TO AN OBSERVATION POINT ON THE FAR SIDE OF THE GORGE. BELOW THEM A SWOLLEN RIVER POURED THROUGH A DEEP RAVINE.
A GOOD POSITION! WE SHALL SEE THE CAR COMING A LONG WAY OFF. IT WILL GIVE US TIME TO SIGNAL AND GET BACK DOWN THE GULLY!

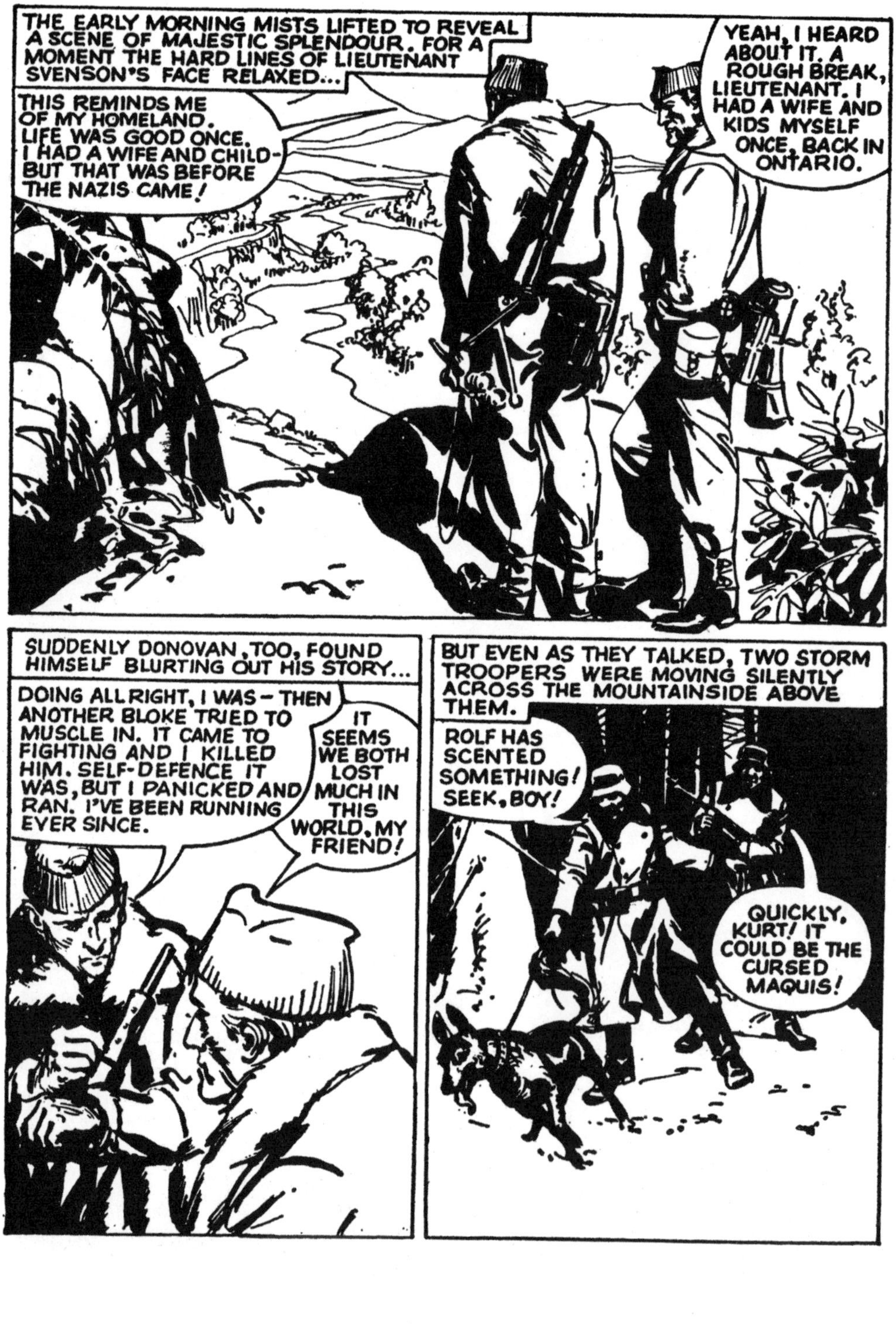
THE EARLY MORNING MISTS LIFTED TO REVEAL A SCENE OF MAJESTIC SPLENDOUR. FOR A MOMENT THE HARD LINES OF LIEUTENANT SVENSON'S FACE RELAXED...
THIS REMINDS ME OF MY HOMELAND. LIFE WAS GOOD ONCE. I HAD A WIFE AND CHILD- BUT THAT WAS BEFORE THE NAZIS CAME!
YEAH, I HEARD ABOUT IT. A ROUGH BREAK, LIEUTENANT. I HAD A WIFE AND KIDS MYSELF ONCE, BACK IN ONTARIO.
SUDDENLY DONOVAN, TOO, FOUND HIMSELF BLURTING OUT HIS STORY...
DOING ALL RIGHT, I WAS - THEN ANOTHER BLOKE TRIED TO MUSCLE IN. IT CAME TO FIGHTING AND I KILLED HIM. SELF-DEFENCE IT WAS, BUT I PANICKED AND RAN. I'VE BEEN RUNNING EVER SINCE.
IT SEEMS WE BOTH LOST MUCH IN THIS WORLD, MY FRIEND!
BUT EVEN AS THEY TALKED, TWO STORM TROOPERS WERE MOVING SILENTLY ACROSS THE MOUNTAINSIDE ABOVE THEM.
ROLF HAS SCENTED SOMETHING! SEEK, BOY!
QUICKLY, KURT! IT COULD BE THE CURSED MAQUIS!

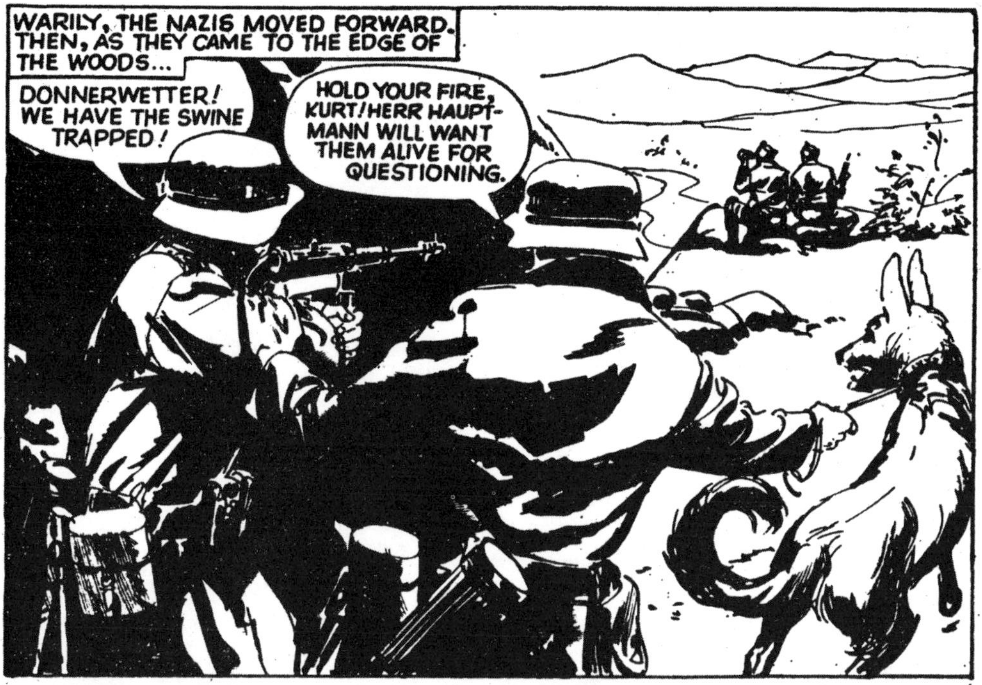
WARILY, THE NAZIS MOVED FORWARD. THEN, AS THEY CAME TO THE EDGE OF THE WOODS...
DONNERWETTER! WE HAVE THE SWINE TRAPPED!
HOLD YOUR FIRE, KURT! HERR HAUPTMANN WILL WANT THEM ALIVE FOR QUESTIONING.

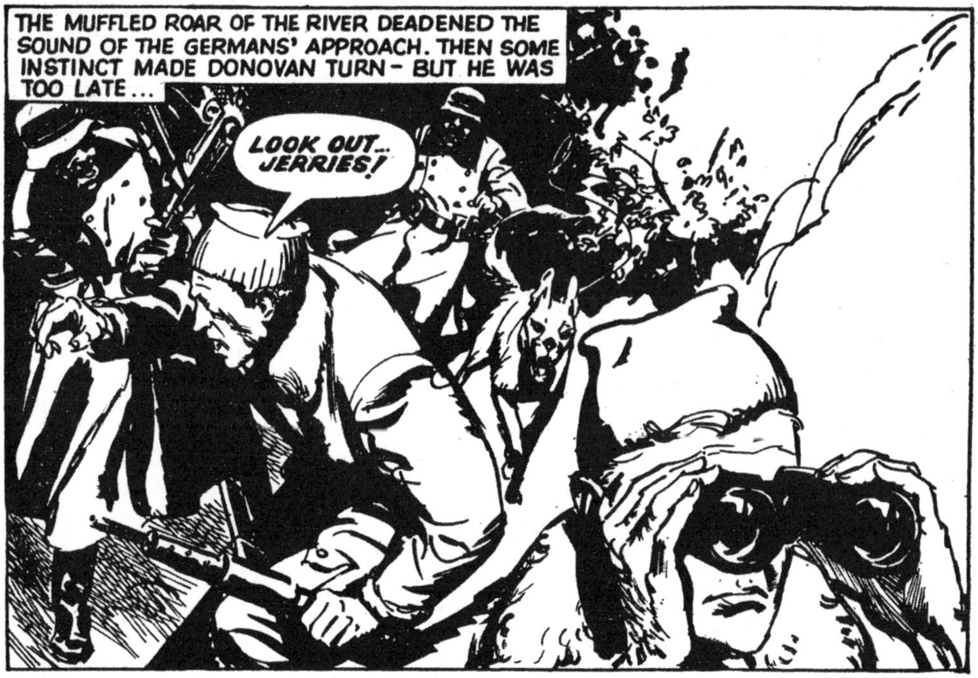
THE MUFFLED ROAR OF THE RIVER DEADENED THE SOUND OF THE GERMANS' APPROACH. THEN SOME INSTINCT MADE DONOVAN TURN – BUT HE WAS TOO LATE...
LOOK OUT... JERRIES!

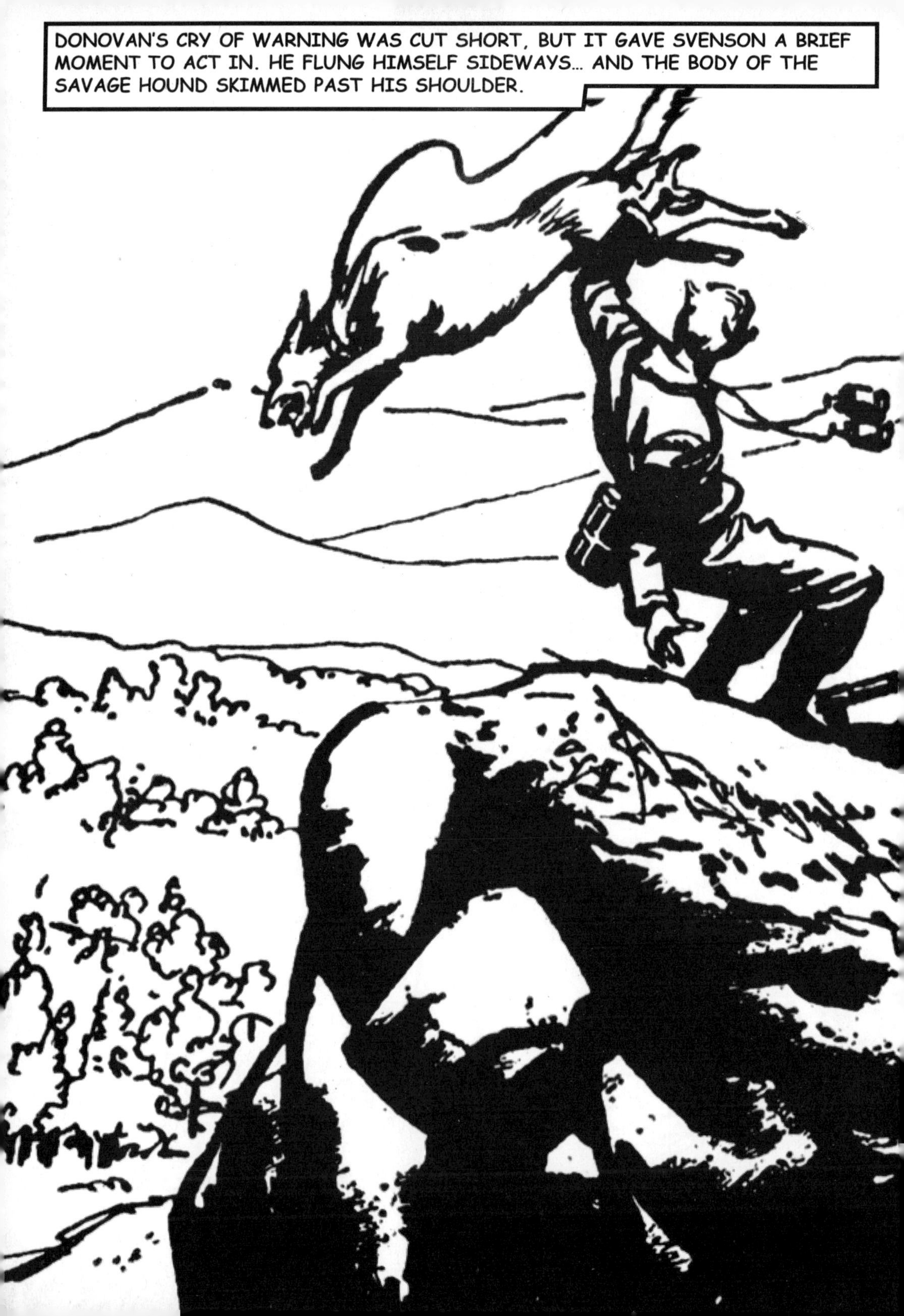
DONOVAN'S CRY OF WARNING WAS CUT SHORT, BUT IT GAVE SVENSON A BRIEF MOMENT TO ACT IN. HE FLUNG HIMSELF SIDEWAYS… AND THE BODY OF THE SAVAGE HOUND SKIMMED PAST HIS SHOULDER.

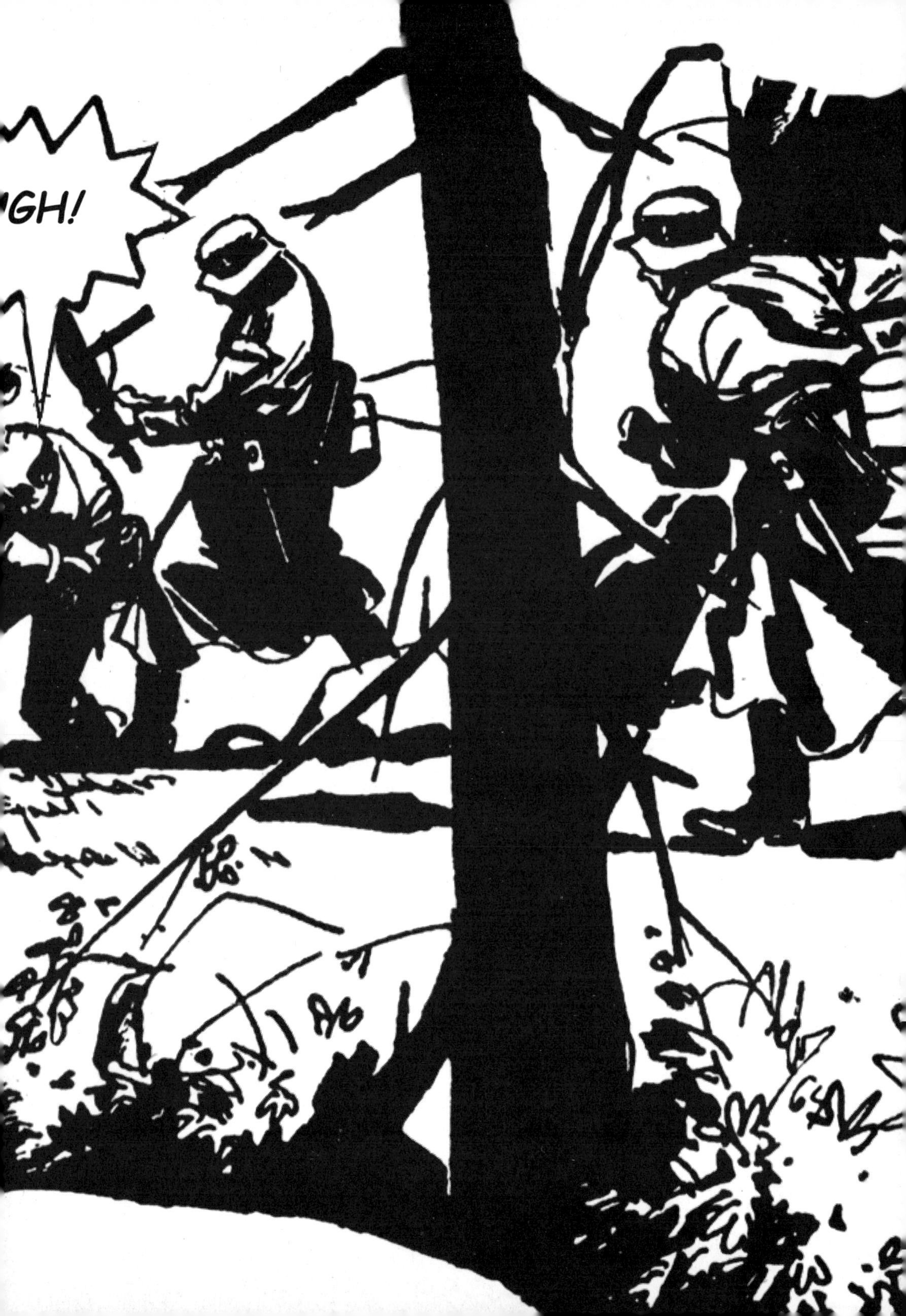
GH!

WITH THE SPEED OF A STRIKING COBRA THE NORWEGIAN LUNGED AT THE NEAREST NAZI AND, WITH A DESPAIRING WAIL , THE MAN PITCHED OUTWARD INTO SPACE.

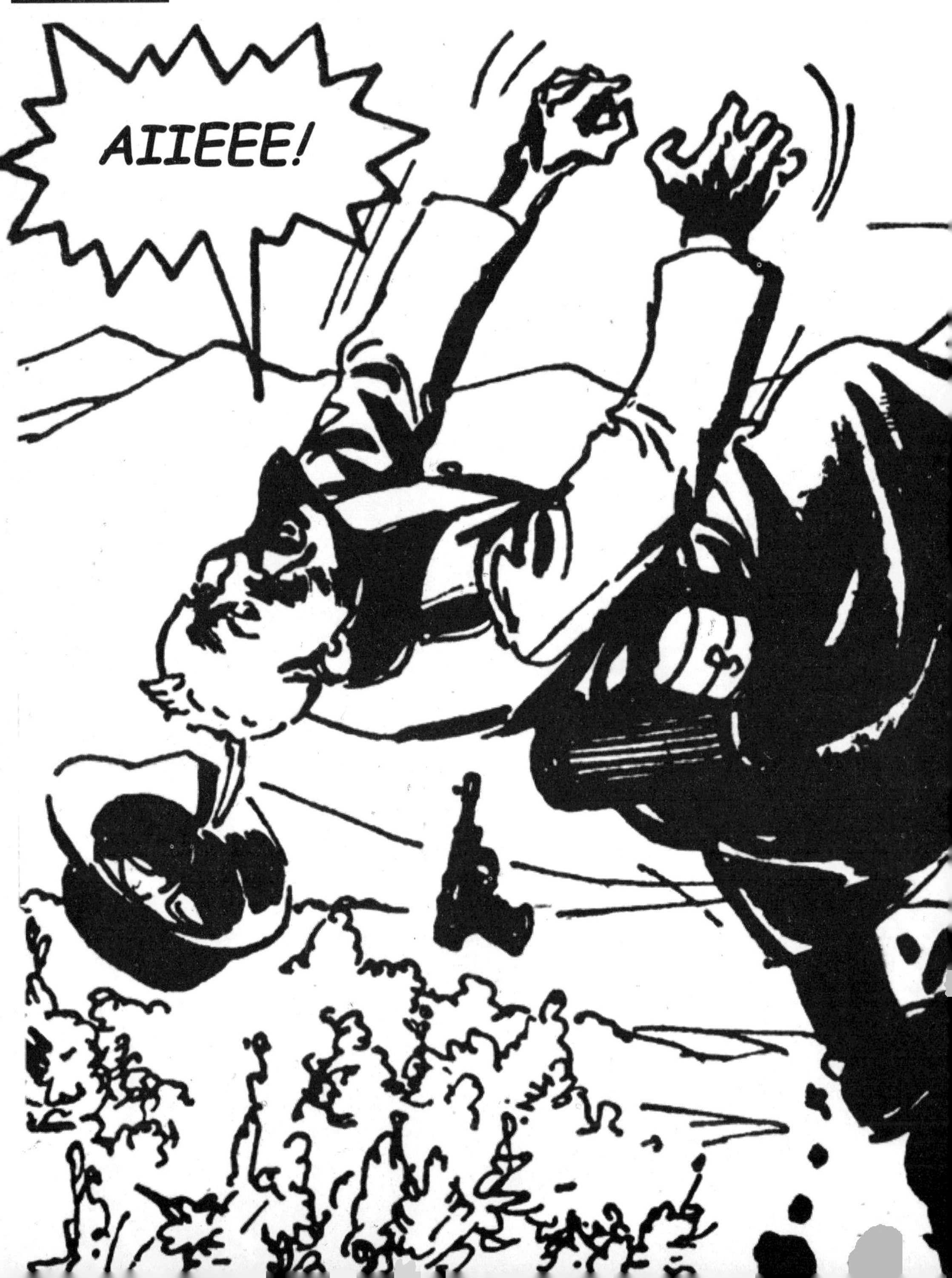
AIIEEE!

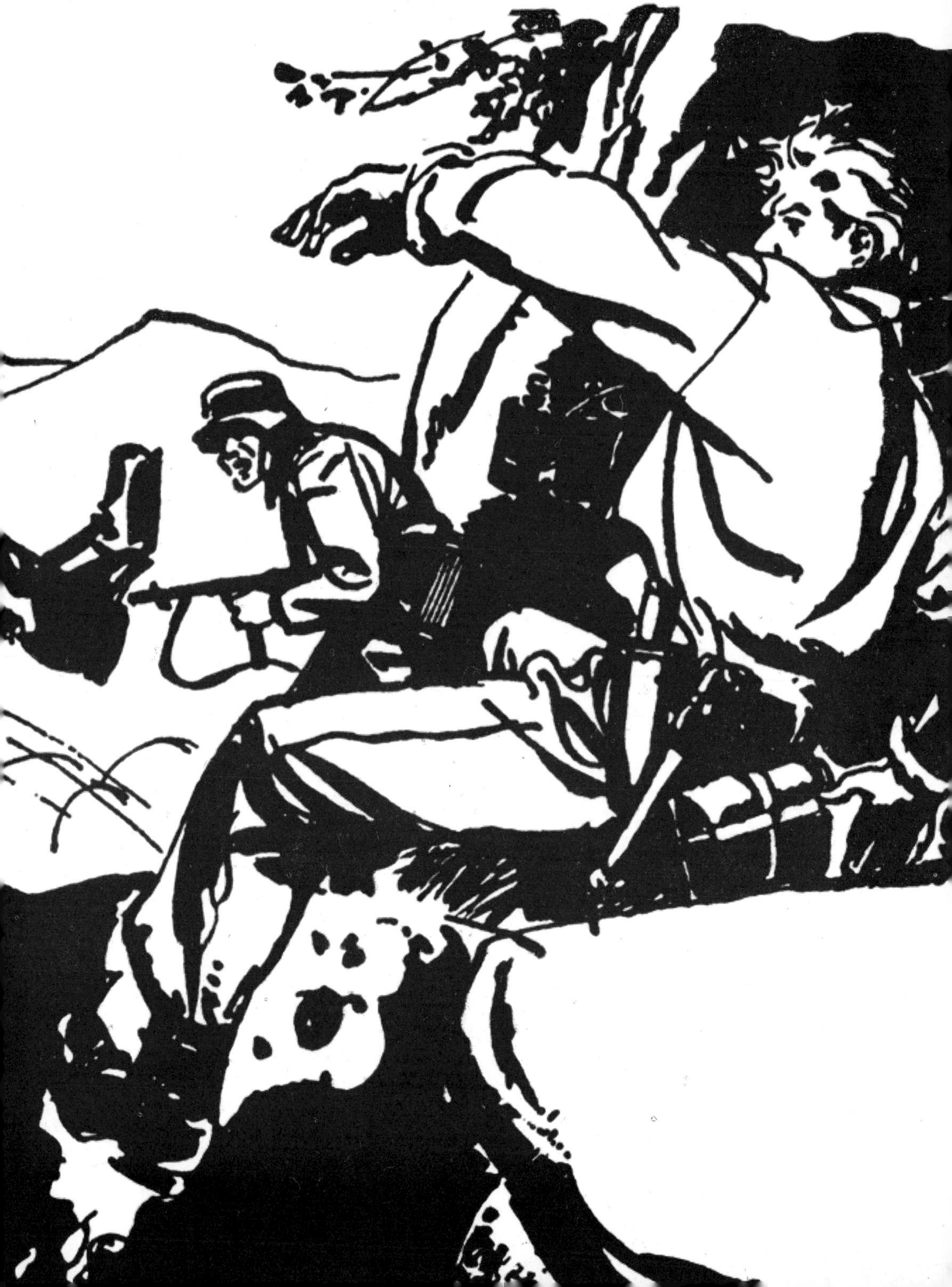

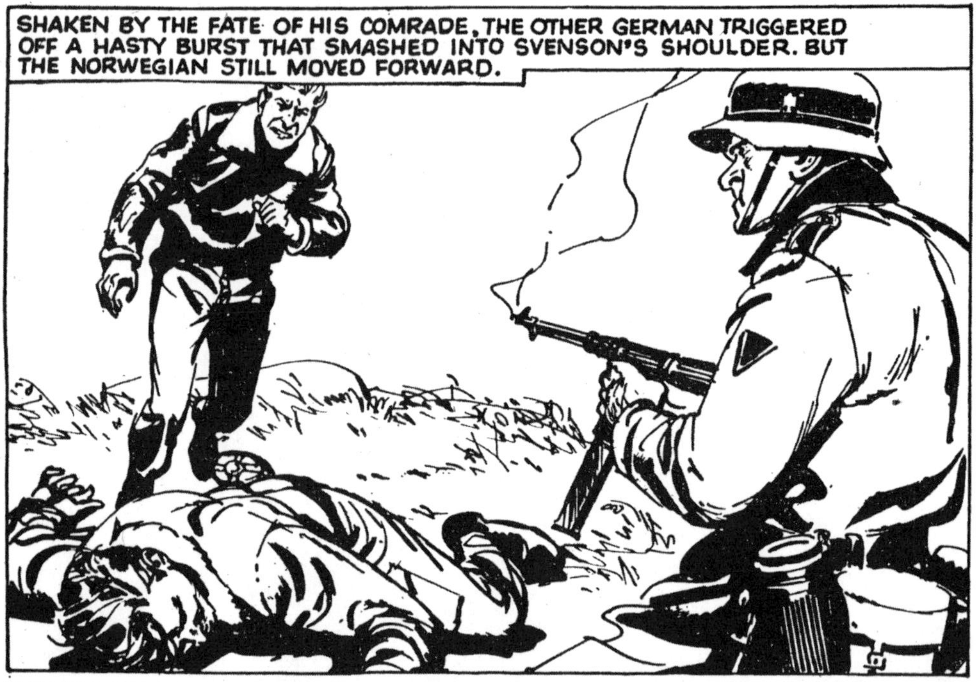
SHAKEN BY THE FATE OF HIS COMRADE, THE OTHER GERMAN TRIGGERED OFF A HASTY BURST THAT SMASHED INTO SVENSON'S SHOULDER. BUT THE NORWEGIAN STILL MOVED FORWARD.

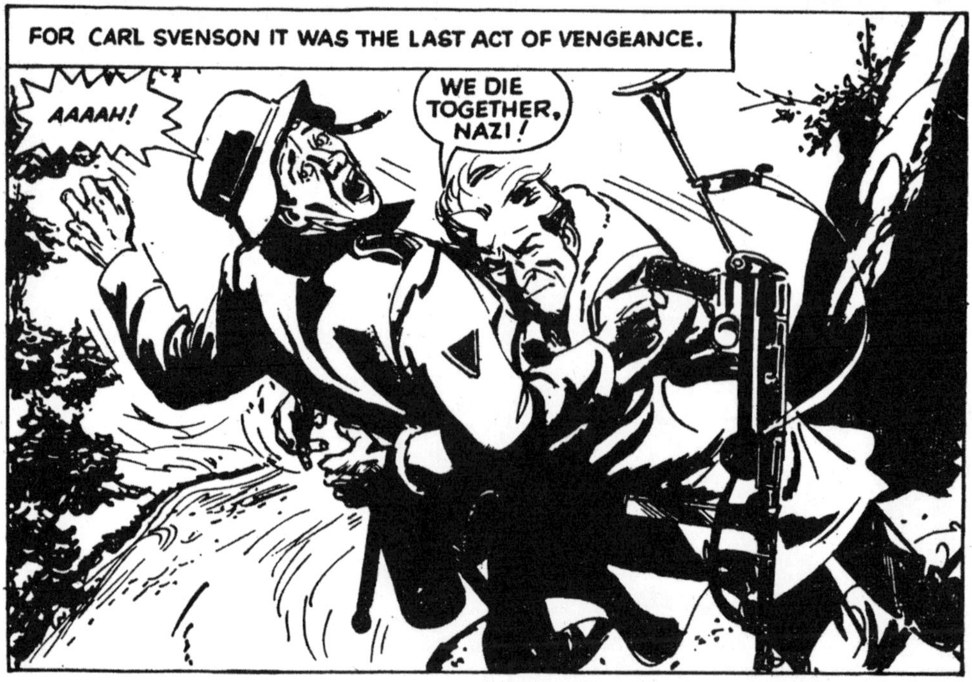
FOR CARL SVENSON IT WAS THE LAST ACT OF VENGEANCE.
AAAAH!
WE DIE TOGETHER, NAZI!

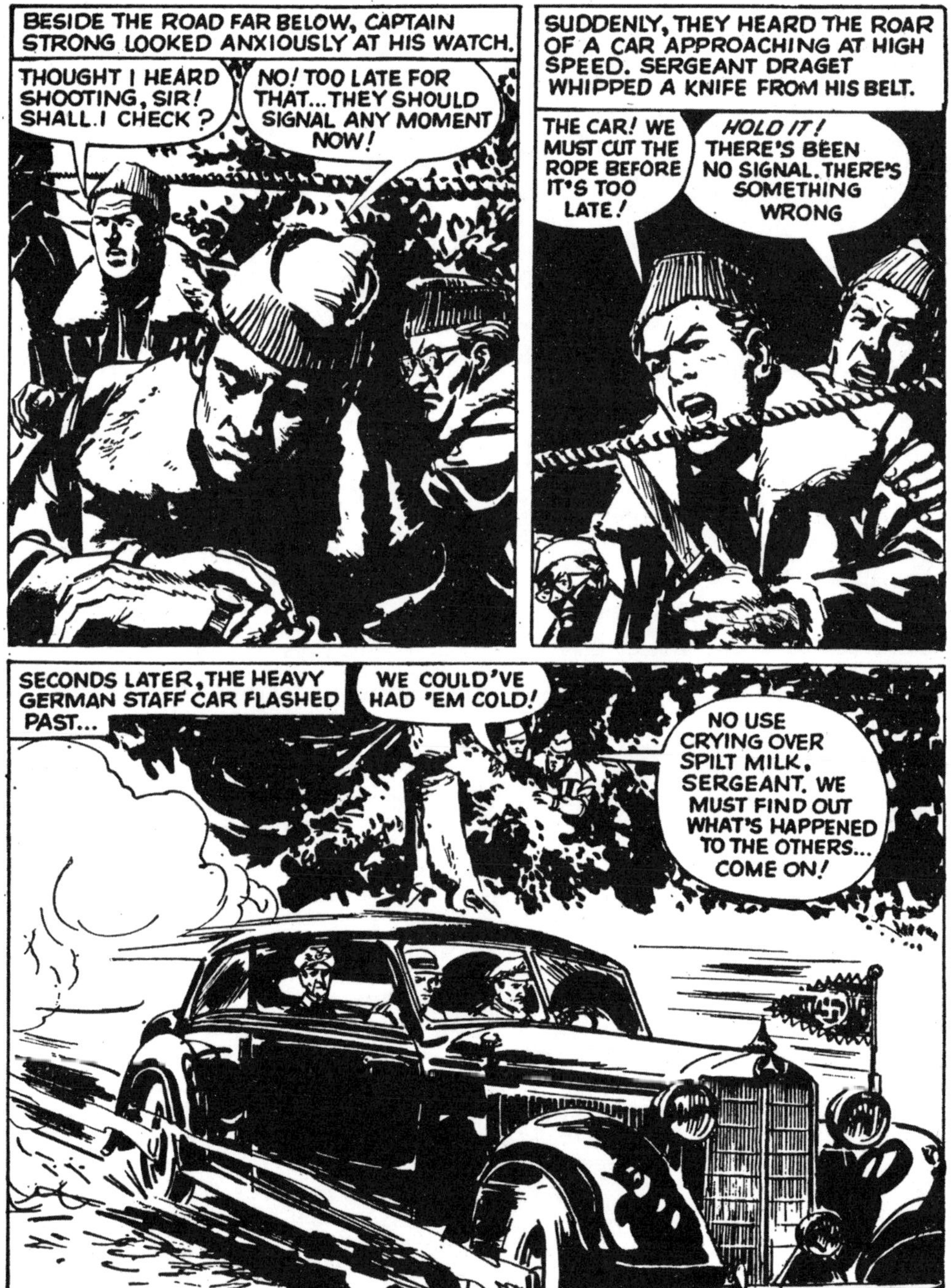
BESIDE THE ROAD FAR BELOW, CAPTAIN STRONG LOOKED ANXIOUSLY AT HIS WATCH.
THOUGHT I HEARD SHOOTING, SIR! SHALL I CHECK?
NO! TOO LATE FOR THAT... THEY SHOULD SIGNAL ANY MOMENT NOW!
SUDDENLY, THEY HEARD THE ROAR OF A CAR APPROACHING AT HIGH SPEED. SERGEANT DRAGET WHIPPED A KNIFE FROM HIS BELT.
THE CAR! WE MUST CUT THE ROPE BEFORE IT'S TOO LATE!
HOLD IT! THERE'S BEEN NO SIGNAL. THERE'S SOMETHING WRONG
SECONDS LATER, THE HEAVY GERMAN STAFF CAR FLASHED PAST...
WE COULD'VE HAD 'EM COLD!
NO USE CRYING OVER SPILT MILK, SERGEANT. WE MUST FIND OUT WHAT'S HAPPENED TO THE OTHERS... COME ON!

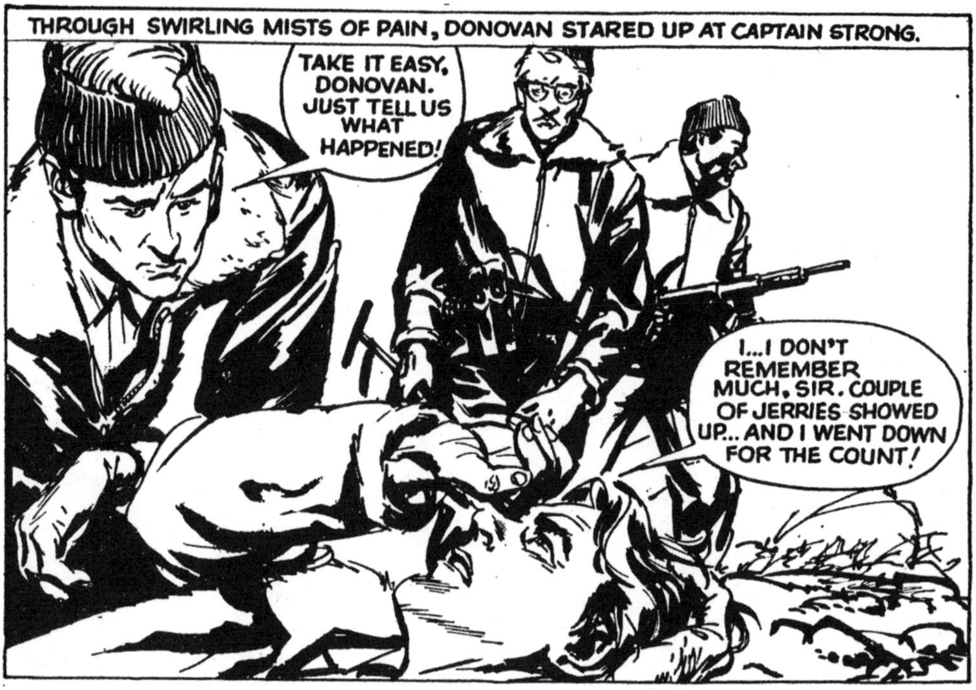
THROUGH SWIRLING MISTS OF PAIN, DONOVAN STARED UP AT CAPTAIN STRONG.
TAKE IT EASY, DONOVAN. JUST TELL US WHAT HAPPENED!
I...I DON'T REMEMBER MUCH, SIR. COUPLE OF JERRIES SHOWED UP... AND I WENT DOWN FOR THE COUNT!

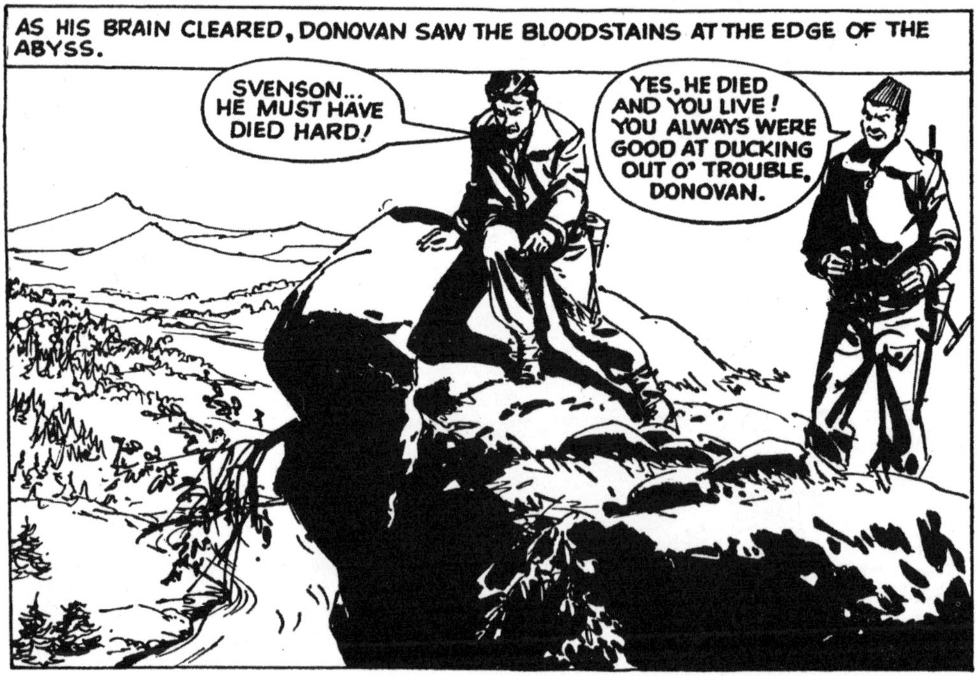
AS HIS BRAIN CLEARED, DONOVAN SAW THE BLOODSTAINS AT THE EDGE OF THE ABYSS.
SVENSON... HE MUST HAVE DIED HARD!
YES, HE DIED AND YOU LIVE! YOU ALWAYS WERE GOOD AT DUCKING OUT O' TROUBLE, DONOVAN.

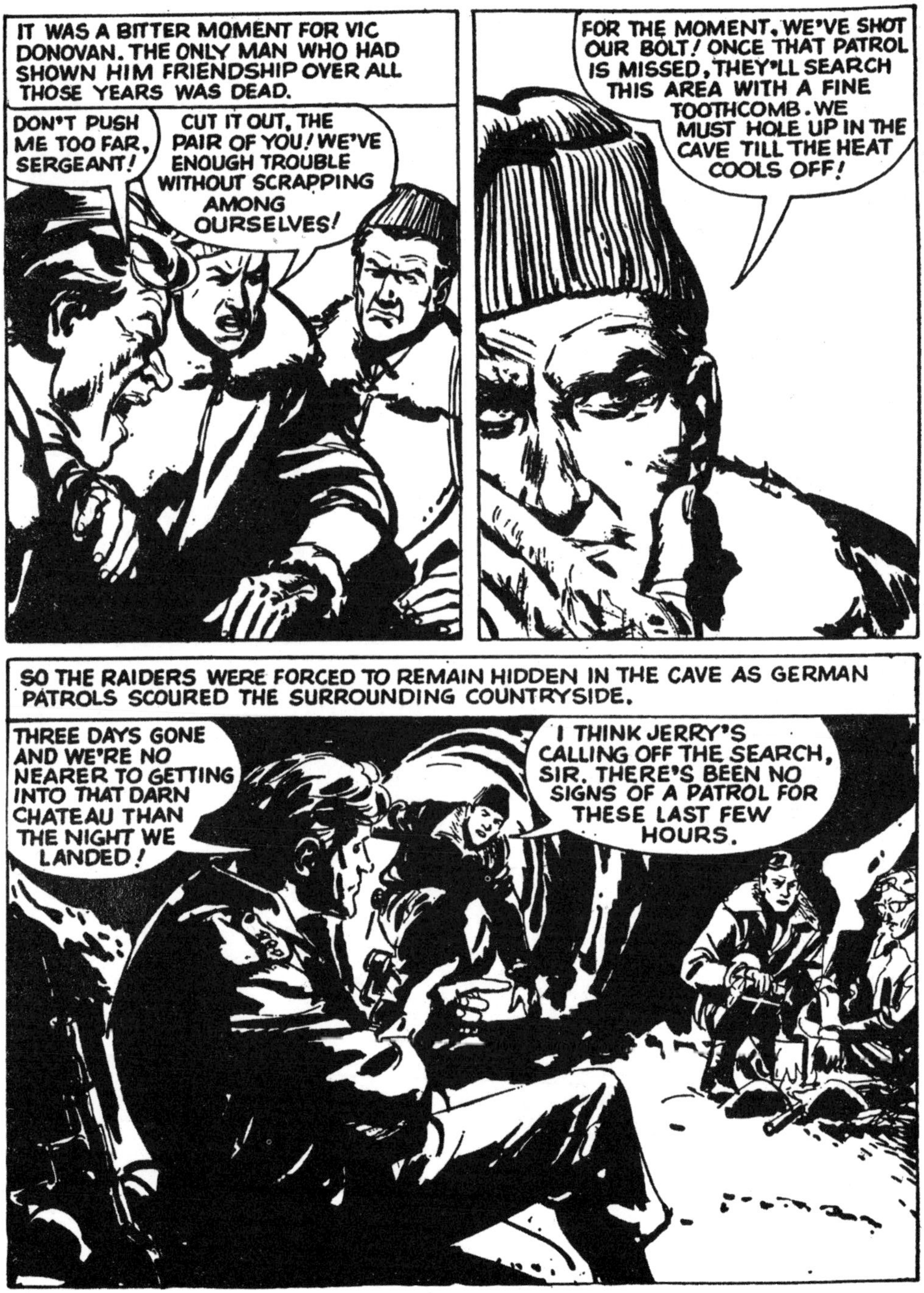
IT WAS A BITTER MOMENT FOR VIC DONOVAN. THE ONLY MAN WHO HAD SHOWN HIM FRIENDSHIP OVER ALL THOSE YEARS WAS DEAD.
DON'T PUSH ME TOO FAR, SERGEANT!
CUT IT OUT, THE PAIR OF YOU! WE'VE ENOUGH TROUBLE WITHOUT SCRAPPING AMONG OURSELVES!
FOR THE MOMENT, WE'VE SHOT OUR BOLT! ONCE THAT PATROL IS MISSED, THEY'LL SEARCH THIS AREA WITH A FINE TOOTHCOMB. WE MUST HOLE UP IN THE CAVE TILL THE HEAT COOLS OFF!
SO THE RAIDERS WERE FORCED TO REMAIN HIDDEN IN THE CAVE AS GERMAN PATROLS SCOURED THE SURROUNDING COUNTRYSIDE.
THREE DAYS GONE AND WE'RE NO NEARER TO GETTING INTO THAT DARN CHATEAU THAN THE NIGHT WE LANDED!
I THINK JERRY'S CALLING OFF THE SEARCH, SIR. THERE'S BEEN NO SIGNS OF A PATROL FOR THESE LAST FEW HOURS.

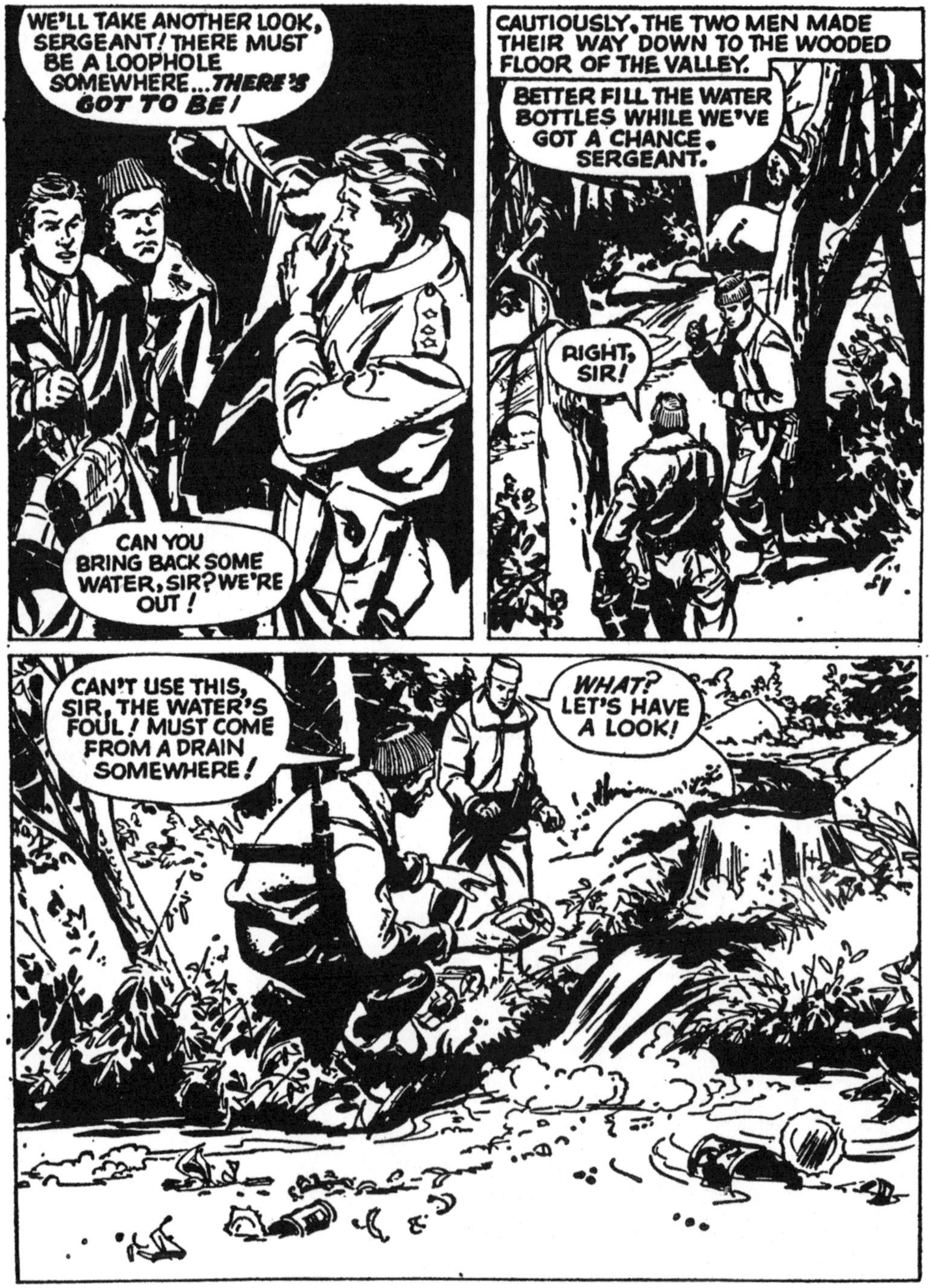
WE'LL TAKE ANOTHER LOOK, SERGEANT! THERE MUST BE A LOOPHOLE SOMEWHERE... THERE'S GOT TO BE!
CAN YOU BRING BACK SOME WATER, SIR? WE'RE OUT!
CAUTIOUSLY, THE TWO MEN MADE THEIR WAY DOWN TO THE WOODED FLOOR OF THE VALLEY.
BETTER FILL THE WATER BOTTLES WHILE WE'VE GOT A CHANCE, SERGEANT.
RIGHT, SIR!
CAN'T USE THIS, SIR, THE WATER'S FOUL! MUST COME FROM A DRAIN SOMEWHERE!
WHAT? LET'S HAVE A LOOK!

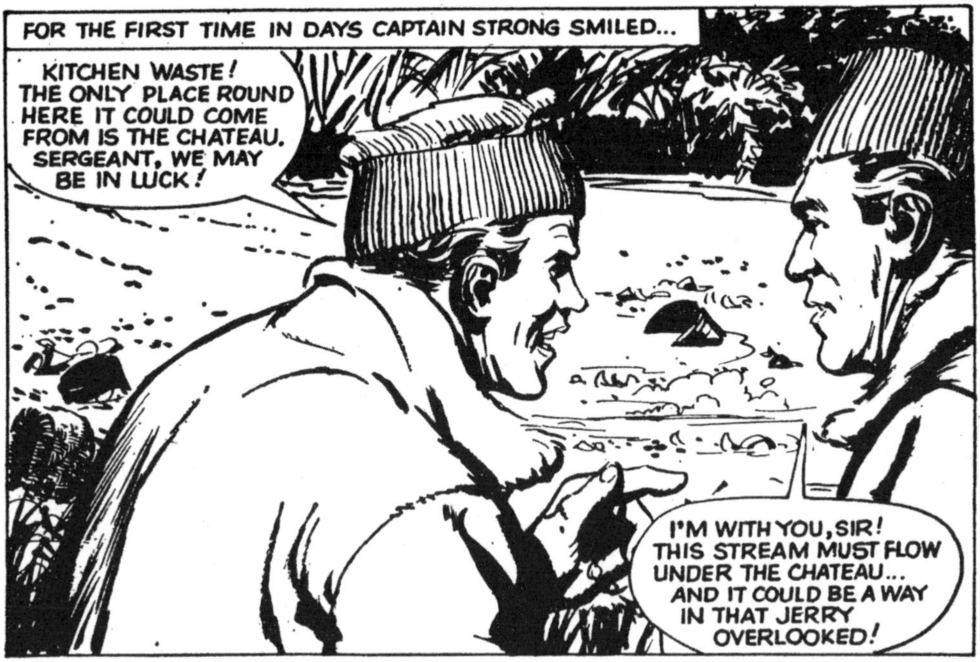
FOR THE FIRST TIME IN DAYS CAPTAIN STRONG SMILED...
KITCHEN WASTE! THE ONLY PLACE ROUND HERE IT COULD COME FROM IS THE CHATEAU. SERGEANT, WE MAY BE IN LUCK!
I'M WITH YOU, SIR! THIS STREAM MUST FLOW UNDER THE CHATEAU... AND IT COULD BE A WAY IN THAT JERRY OVERLOOKED!

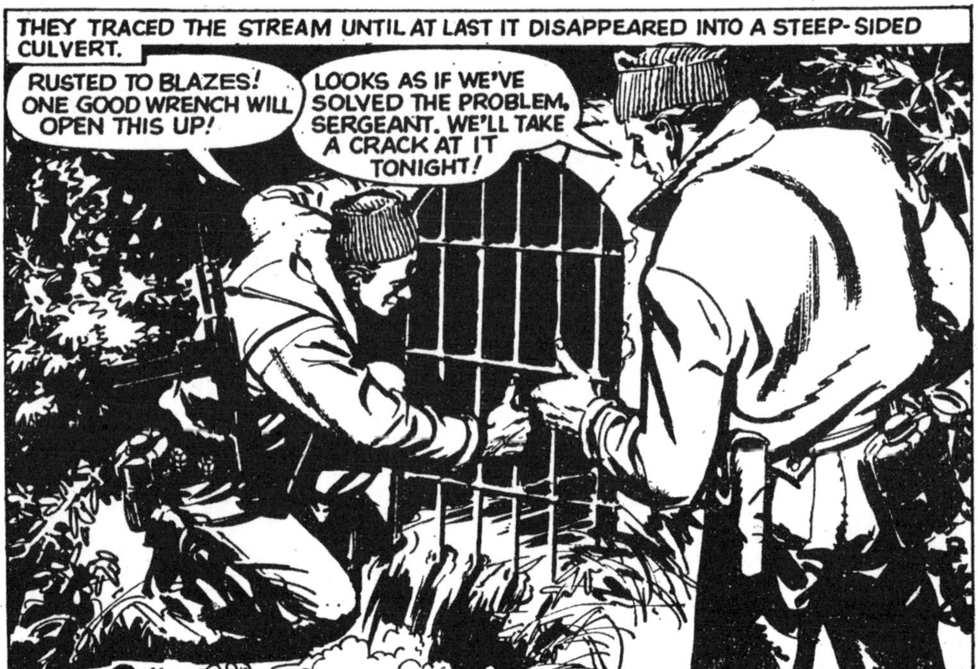
THEY TRACED THE STREAM UNTIL AT LAST IT DISAPPEARED INTO A STEEP-SIDED CULVERT.
RUSTED TO BLAZES! ONE GOOD WRENCH WILL OPEN THIS UP!
LOOKS AS IF WE'VE SOLVED THE PROBLEM, SERGEANT. WE'LL TAKE A CRACK AT IT TONIGHT!

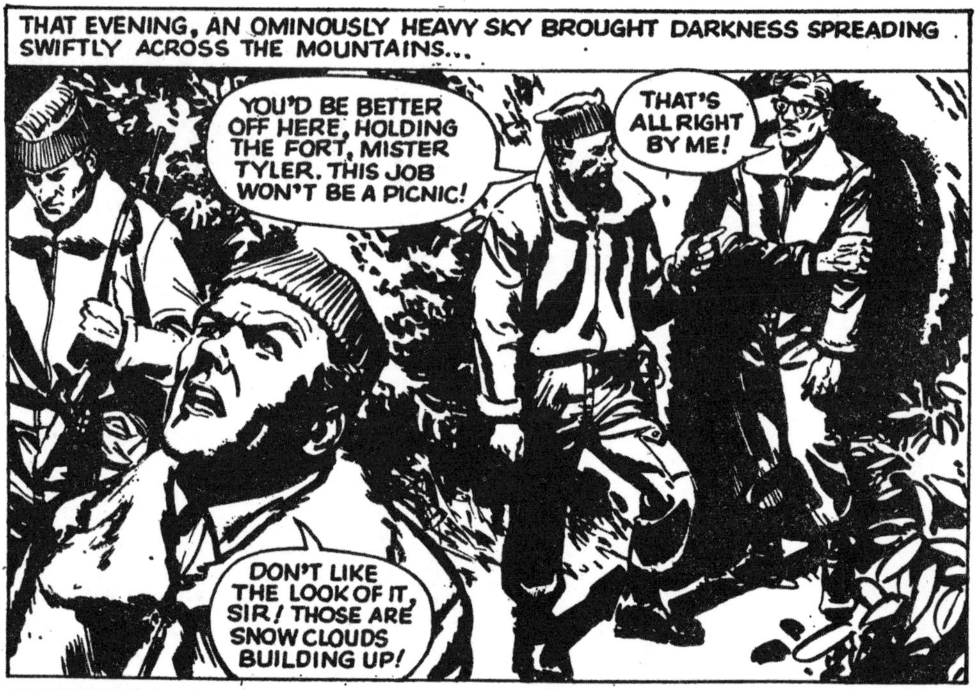
THAT EVENING, AN OMINOUSLY HEAVY SKY BROUGHT DARKNESS SPREADING SWIFTLY ACROSS THE MOUNTAINS...
YOU'D BE BETTER OFF HERE, HOLDING THE FORT, MISTER TYLER. THIS JOB WON'T BE A PICNIC!
THAT'S ALL RIGHT BY ME!
DON'T LIKE THE LOOK OF IT, SIR! THOSE ARE SNOW CLOUDS BUILDING UP!

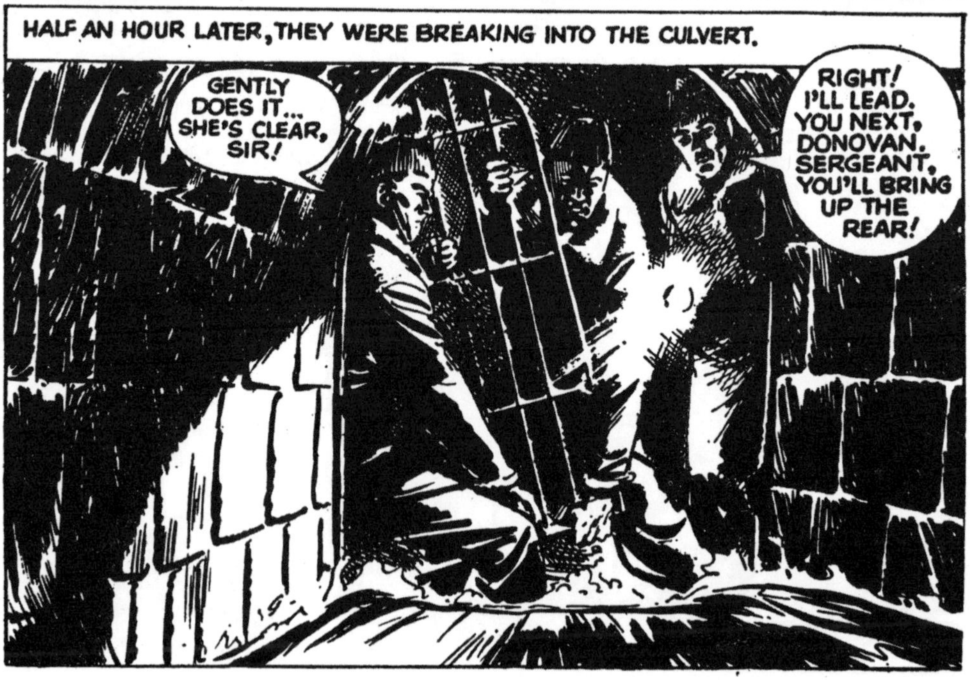
HALF AN HOUR LATER, THEY WERE BREAKING INTO THE CULVERT.
GENTLY DOES IT... SHE'S CLEAR, SIR!
RIGHT! I'LL LEAD. YOU NEXT, DONOVAN. SERGEANT, YOU'LL BRING UP THE REAR!

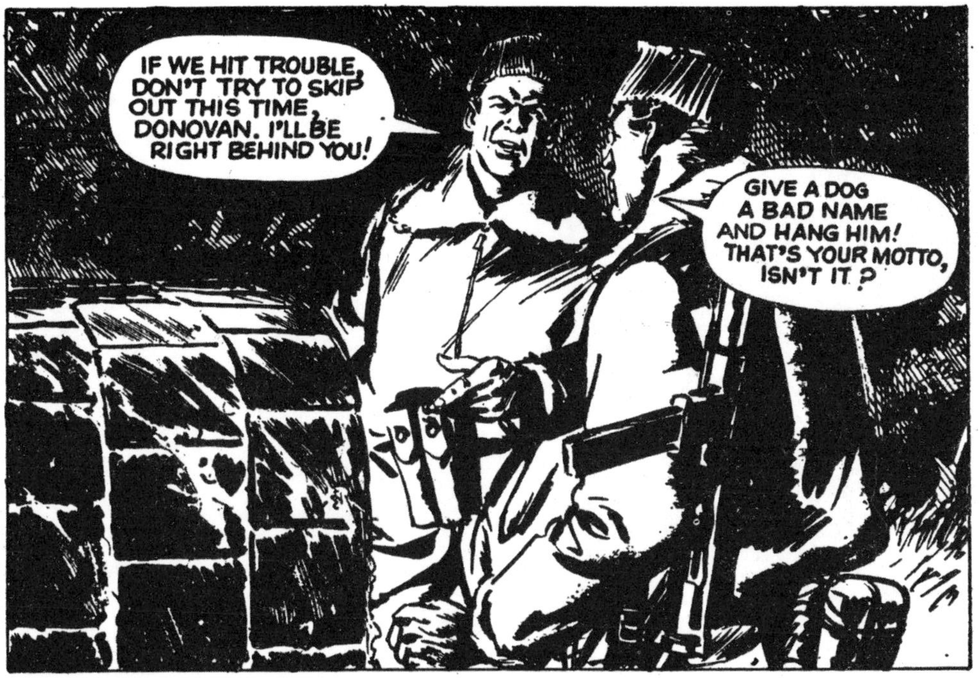
IF WE HIT TROUBLE, DON'T TRY TO SKIP OUT THIS TIME, DONOVAN. I'LL BE RIGHT BEHIND YOU!
GIVE A DOG A BAD NAME AND HANG HIM! THAT'S YOUR MOTTO, ISN'T IT?

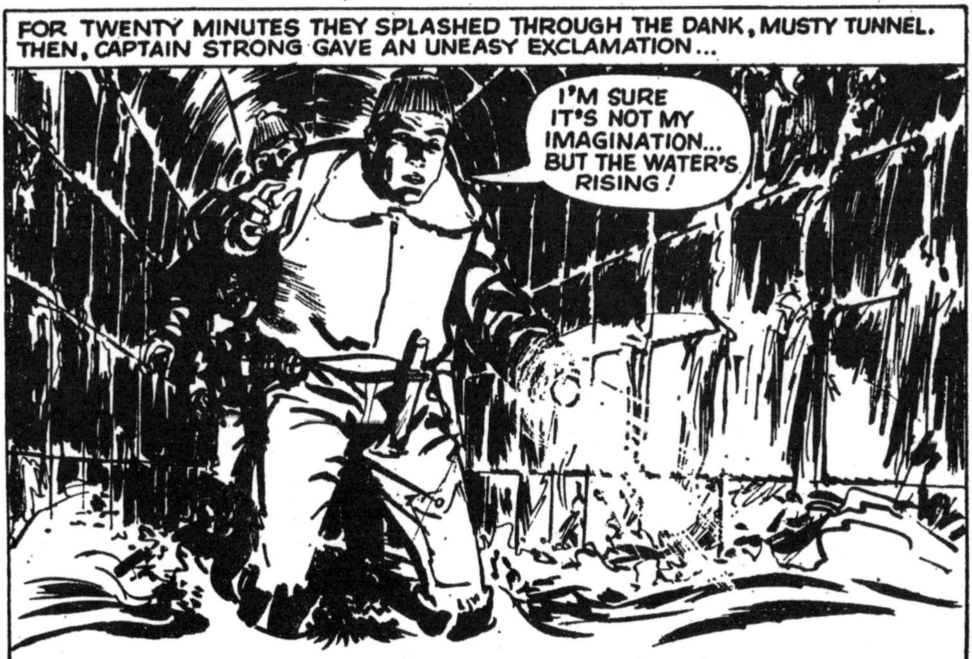
FOR TWENTY MINUTES THEY SPLASHED THROUGH THE DANK, MUSTY TUNNEL. THEN, CAPTAIN STRONG GAVE AN UNEASY EXCLAMATION...
I'M SURE IT'S NOT MY IMAGINATION... BUT THE WATER'S RISING!

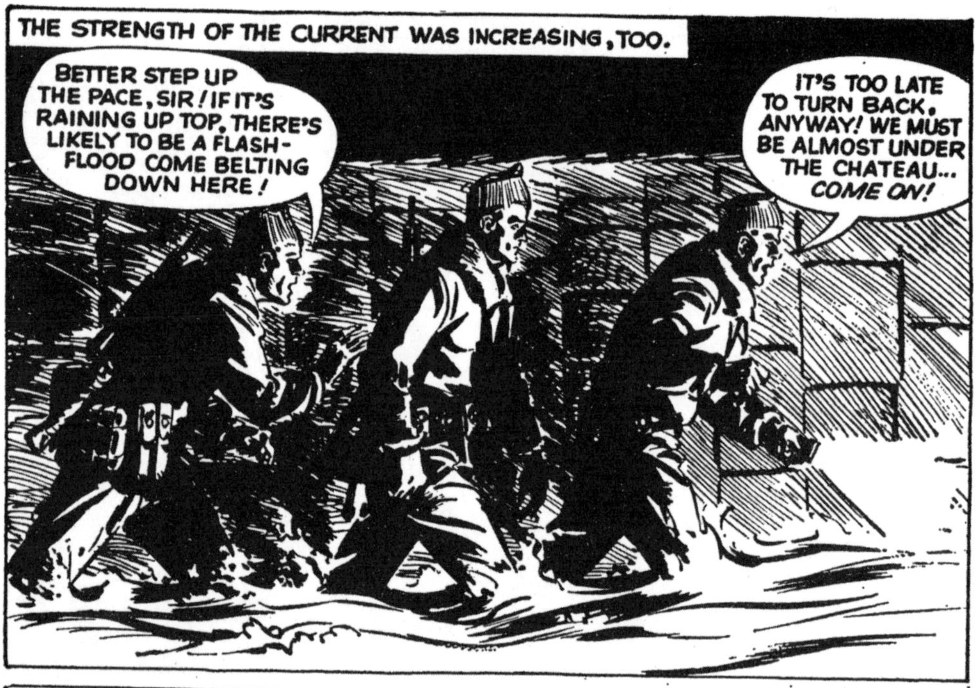
THE STRENGTH OF THE CURRENT WAS INCREASING, TOO.
BETTER STEP UP THE PACE, SIR! IF IT'S RAINING UP TOP, THERE'S LIKELY TO BE A FLASH-FLOOD COME BELTING DOWN HERE!
IT'S TOO LATE TO TURN BACK, ANYWAY! WE MUST BE ALMOST UNDER THE CHATEAU... COME ON!

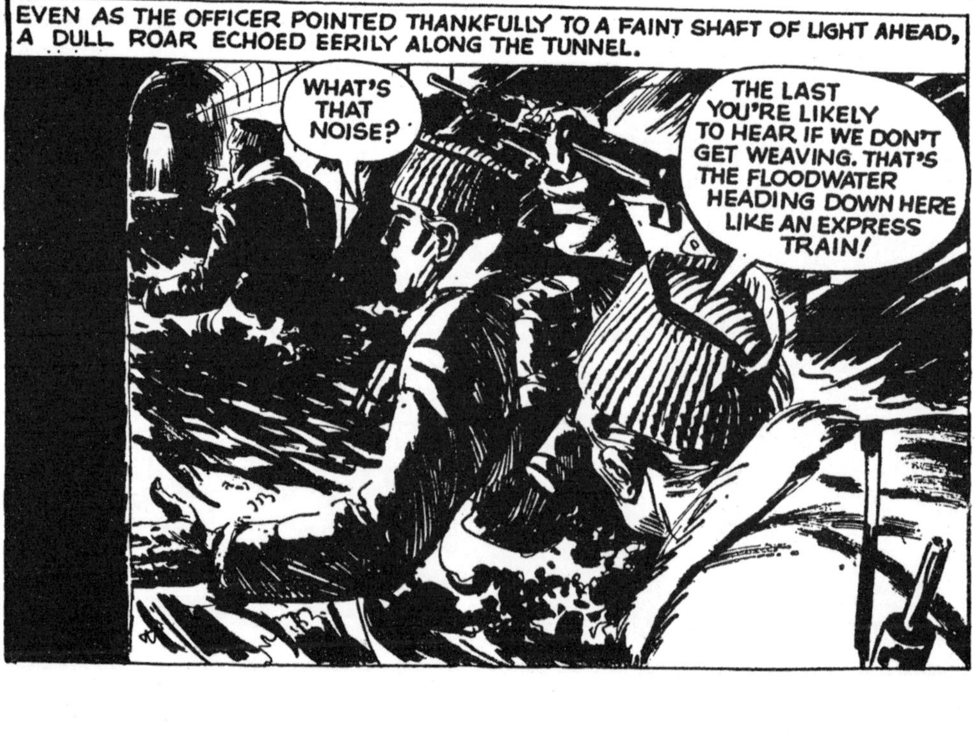
EVEN AS THE OFFICER POINTED THANKFULLY TO A FAINT SHAFT OF LIGHT AHEAD, A DULL ROAR ECHOED EERILY ALONG THE TUNNEL.
WHAT'S THAT NOISE?
THE LAST YOU'RE LIKELY TO HEAR IF WE DON'T GET WEAVING. THAT'S THE FLOODWATER HEADING DOWN HERE LIKE AN EXPRESS TRAIN!

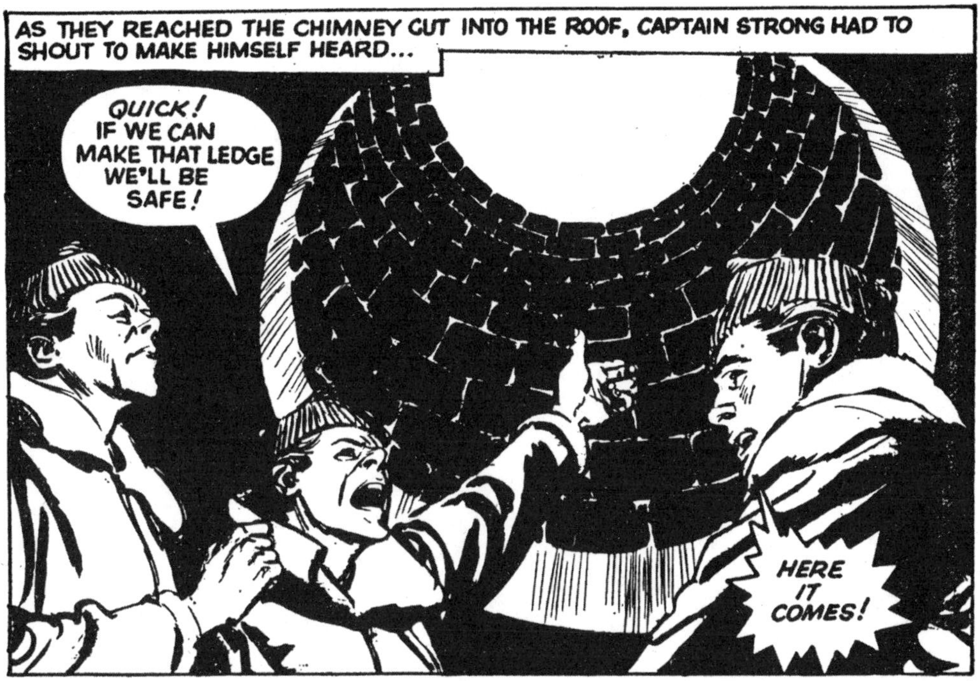
AS THEY REACHED THE CHIMNEY CUT INTO THE ROOF, CAPTAIN STRONG HAD TO SHOUT TO MAKE HIMSELF HEARD...
QUICK! IF WE CAN MAKE THAT LEDGE WE'LL BE SAFE!
HERE IT COMES!

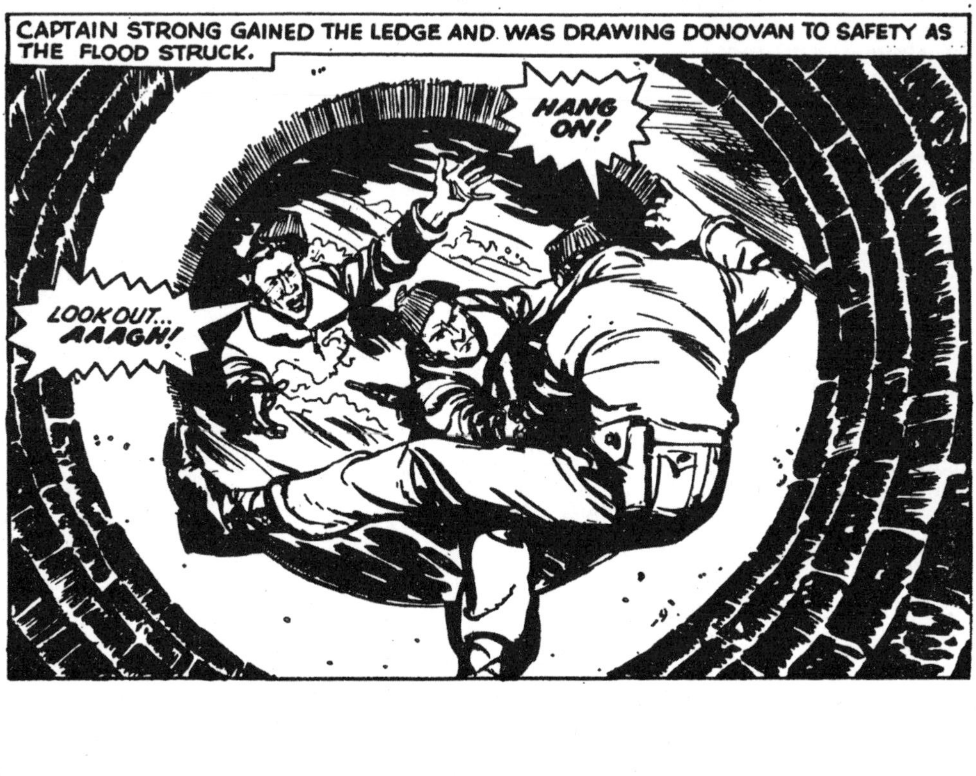
CAPTAIN STRONG GAINED THE LEDGE AND WAS DRAWING DONOVAN TO SAFETY AS THE FLOOD STRUCK.
HANG ON!
LOOK OUT... AAAGH!

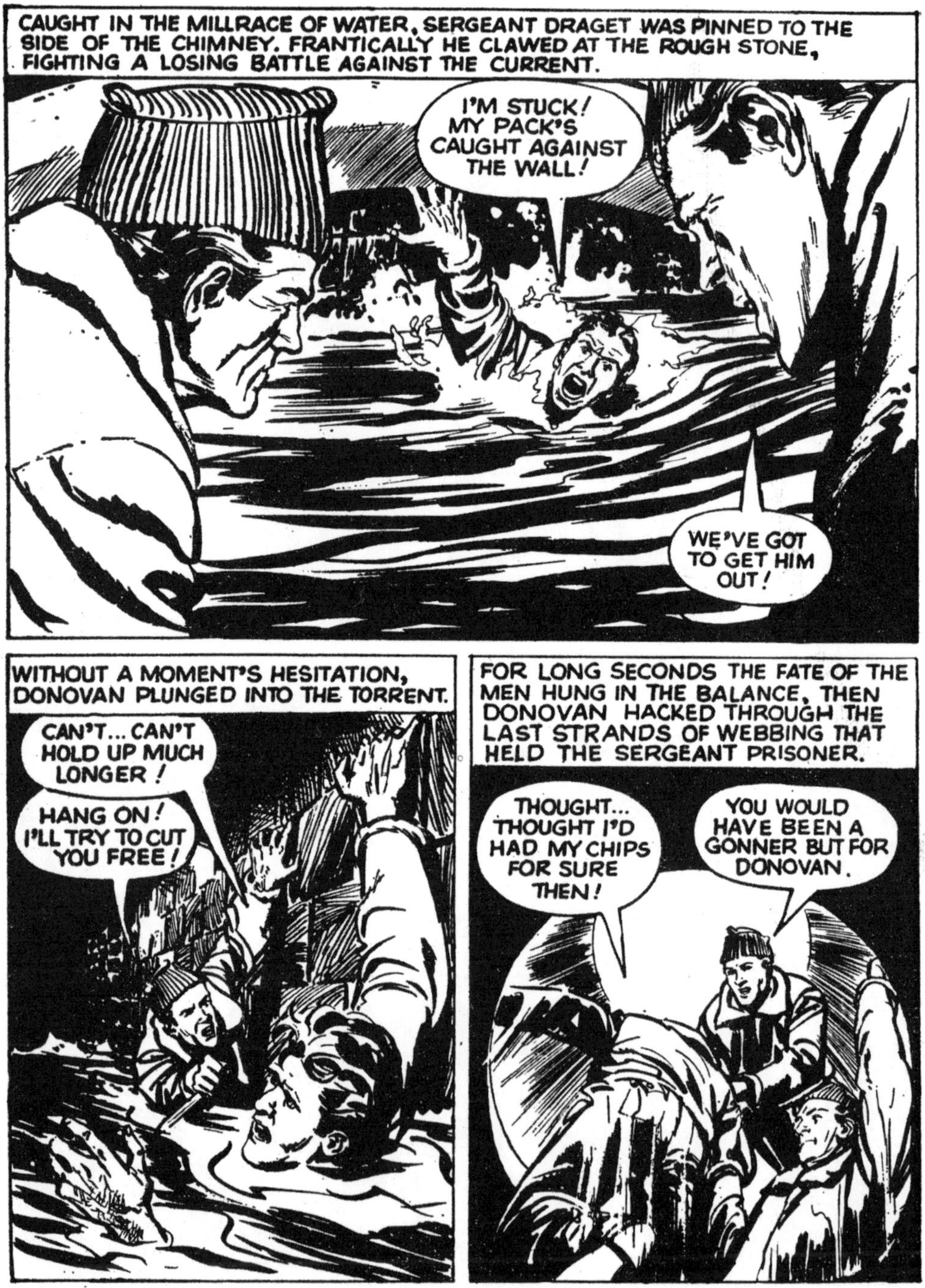
CAUGHT IN THE MILLRACE OF WATER, SERGEANT DRAGET WAS PINNED TO THE SIDE OF THE CHIMNEY. FRANTICALLY HE CLAWED AT THE ROUGH STONE, FIGHTING A LOSING BATTLE AGAINST THE CURRENT.
I'M STUCK! MY PACK'S CAUGHT AGAINST THE WALL!
WE'VE GOT TO GET HIM OUT!
WITHOUT A MOMENT'S HESITATION, DONOVAN PLUNGED INTO THE TORRENT.
CAN'T... CAN'T HOLD UP MUCH LONGER!
HANG ON! I'LL TRY TO CUT YOU FREE!
FOR LONG SECONDS THE FATE OF THE MEN HUNG IN THE BALANCE, THEN DONOVAN HACKED THROUGH THE LAST STRANDS OF WEBBING THAT HELD THE SERGEANT PRISONER.
THOUGHT... THOUGHT I'D HAD MY CHIPS FOR SURE THEN!
YOU WOULD HAVE BEEN A GONNER BUT FOR DONOVAN.

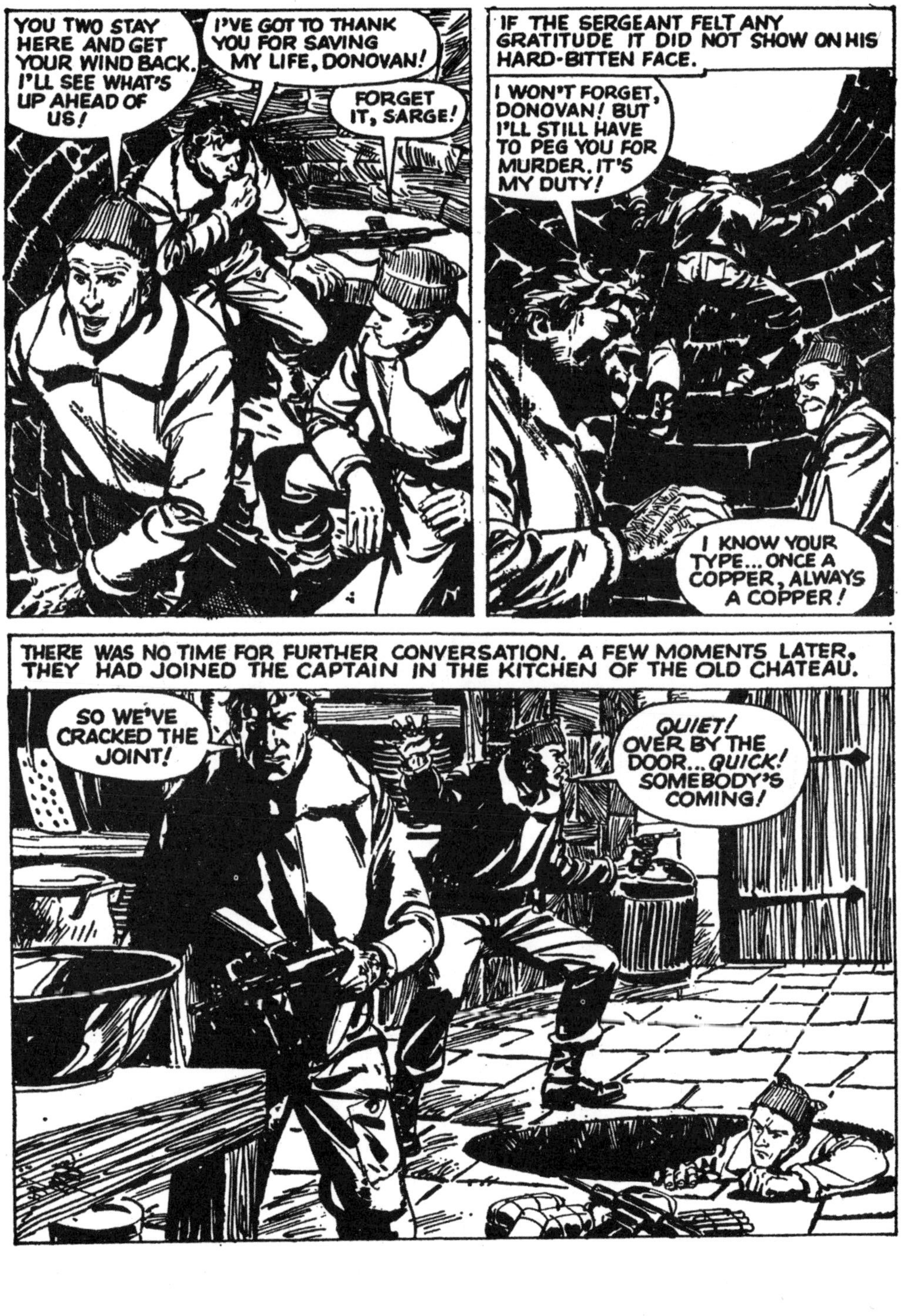
YOU TWO STAY HERE AND GET YOUR WIND BACK. I'LL SEE WHAT'S UP AHEAD OF US!
I'VE GOT TO THANK YOU FOR SAVING MY LIFE, DONOVAN!
FORGET IT, SARGE!
IF THE SERGEANT FELT ANY GRATITUDE IT DID NOT SHOW ON HIS HARD-BITTEN FACE.
I WON'T FORGET, DONOVAN! BUT I'LL STILL HAVE TO PEG YOU FOR MURDER. IT'S MY DUTY!
I KNOW YOUR TYPE... ONCE A COPPER, ALWAYS A COPPER!
THERE WAS NO TIME FOR FURTHER CONVERSATION. A FEW MOMENTS LATER, THEY HAD JOINED THE CAPTAIN IN THE KITCHEN OF THE OLD CHATEAU.
SO WE'VE CRACKED THE JOINT!
QUIET! OVER BY THE DOOR... QUICK! SOMEBODY'S COMING!

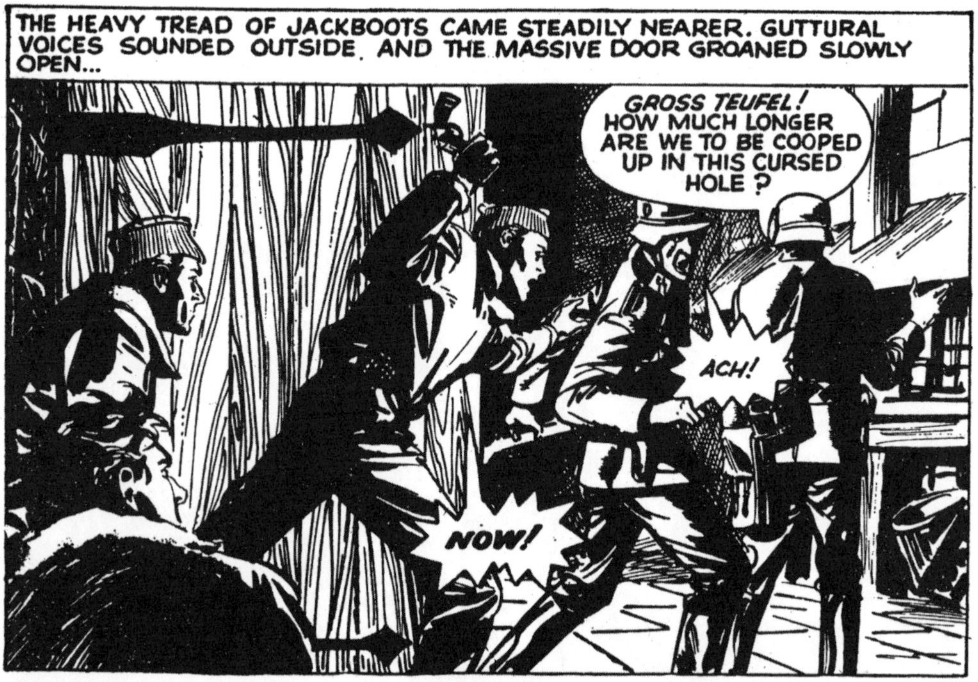
THE HEAVY TREAD OF JACKBOOTS CAME STEADILY NEARER. GUTTURAL VOICES SOUNDED OUTSIDE. AND THE MASSIVE DOOR GROANED SLOWLY OPEN...
GROSS TEUFEL! HOW MUCH LONGER ARE WE TO BE COOPED UP IN THIS CURSED HOLE ?
ACH!
NOW!

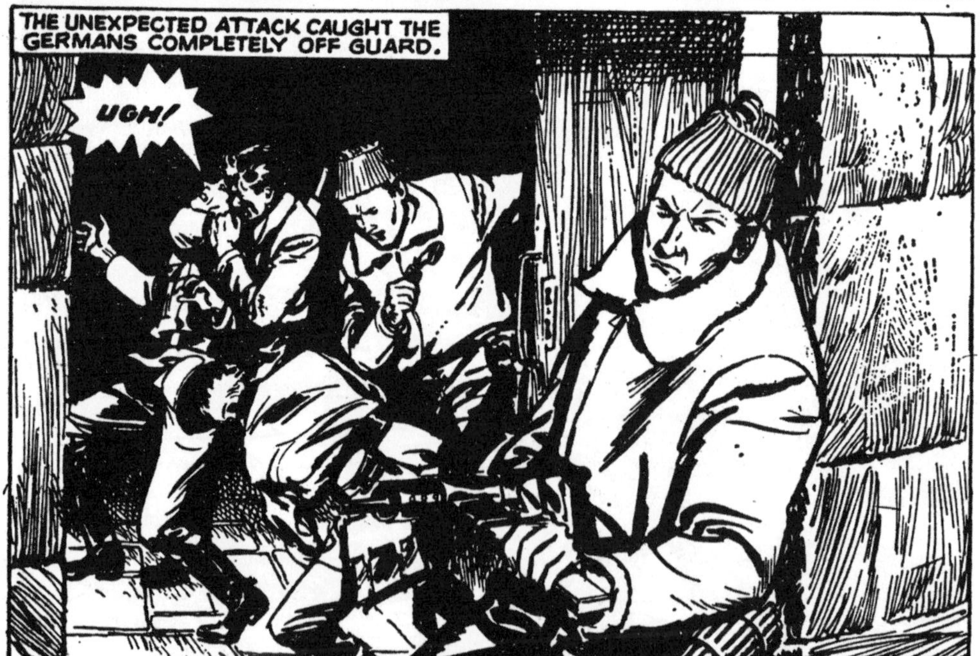
THE UNEXPECTED ATTACK CAUGHT THE GERMANS COMPLETELY OFF GUARD.
UGH!

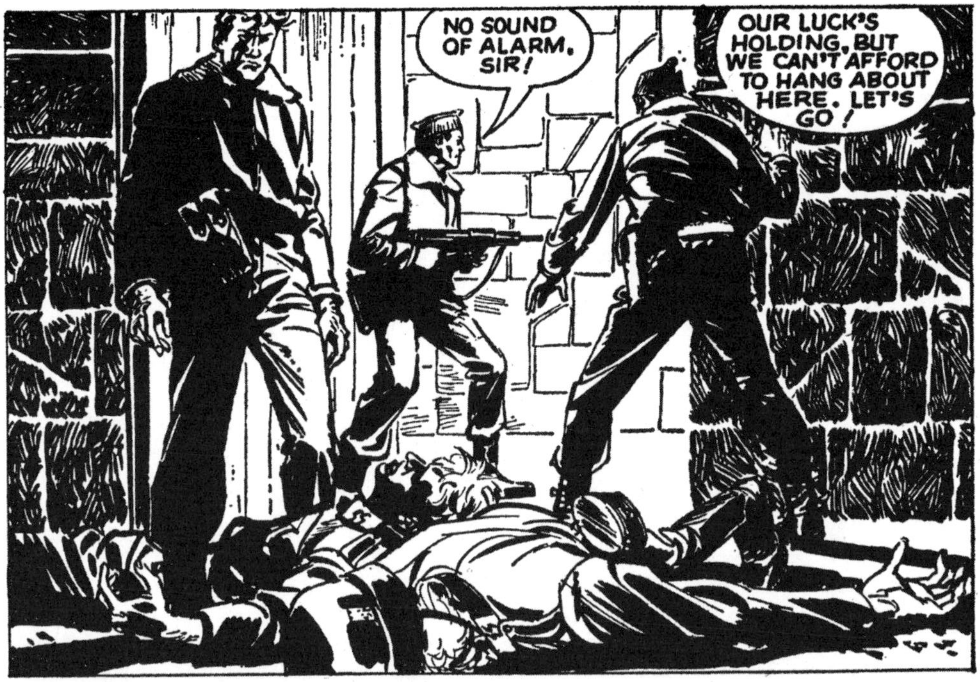
NO SOUND OF ALARM, SIR!
OUR LUCK'S HOLDING, BUT WE CAN'T AFFORD TO HANG ABOUT HERE. LET'S GO!

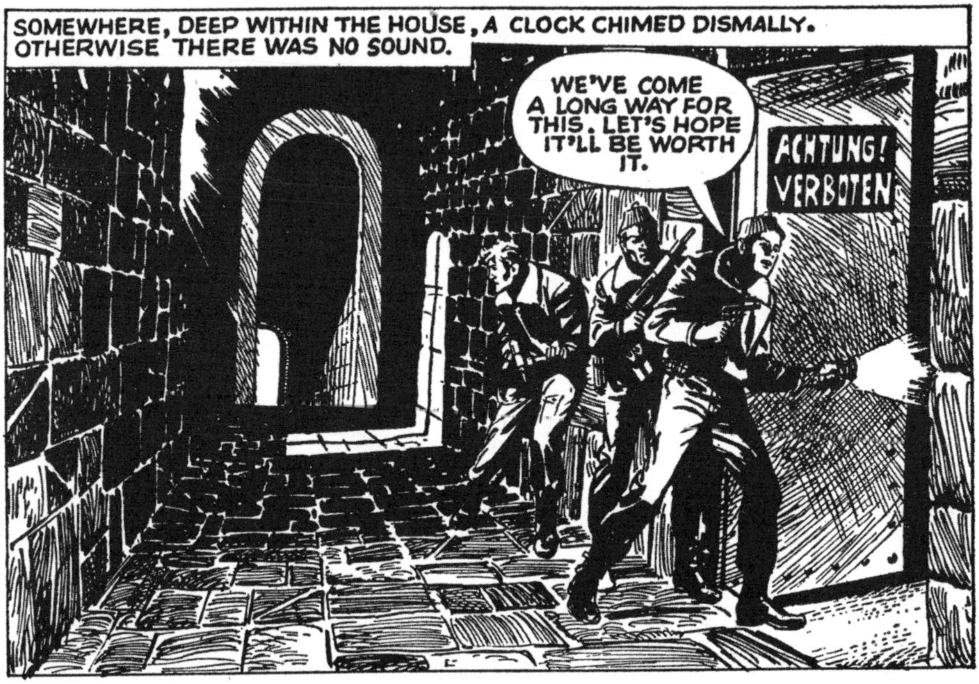
SOMEWHERE, DEEP WITHIN THE HOUSE, A CLOCK CHIMED DISMALLY. OTHERWISE THERE WAS NO SOUND.
WE'VE COME A LONG WAY FOR THIS. LET'S HOPE IT'LL BE WORTH IT.
ACHTUNG! VERBOTEN

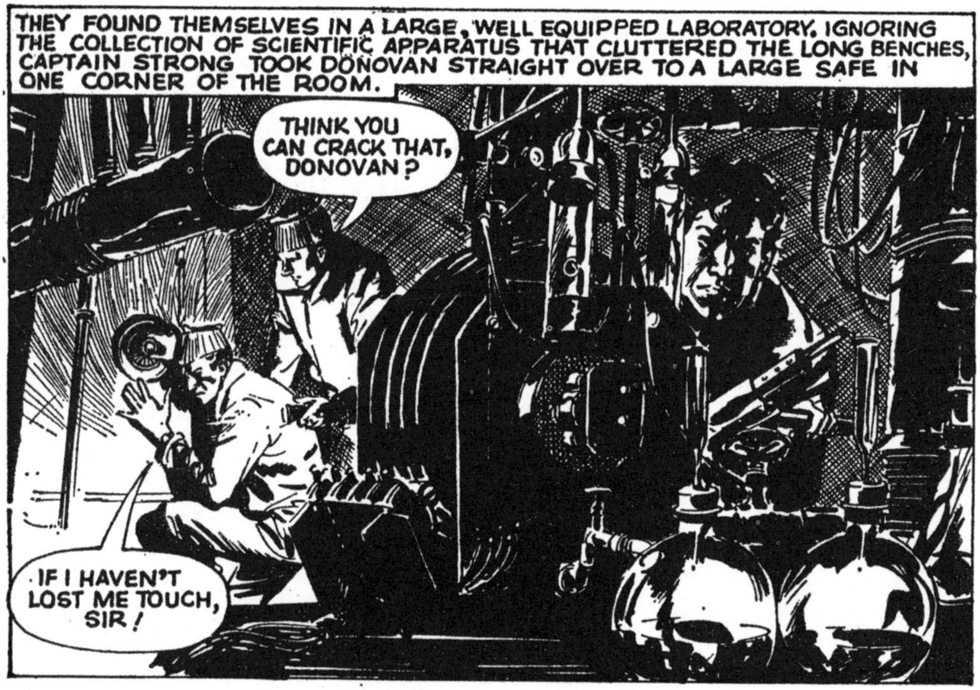
THEY FOUND THEMSELVES IN A LARGE, WELL EQUIPPED LABORATORY. IGNORING THE COLLECTION OF SCIENTIFIC APPARATUS THAT CLUTTERED THE LONG BENCHES, CAPTAIN STRONG TOOK DONOVAN STRAIGHT OVER TO A LARGE SAFE IN ONE CORNER OF THE ROOM.
THINK YOU CAN CRACK THAT, DONOVAN?
IF I HAVEN'T LOST ME TOUCH, SIR!

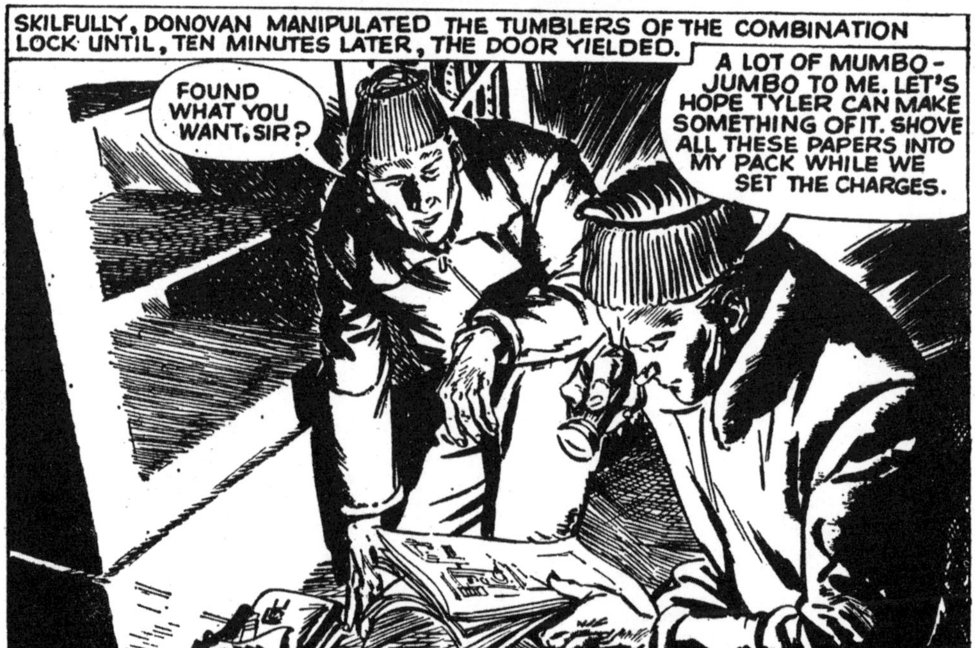
SKILFULLY, DONOVAN MANIPULATED THE TUMBLERS OF THE COMBINATION LOCK UNTIL, TEN MINUTES LATER, THE DOOR YIELDED.
FOUND WHAT YOU WANT, SIR?
A LOT OF MUMBO-JUMBO TO ME. LET'S HOPE TYLER CAN MAKE SOMETHING OF IT. SHOVE ALL THESE PAPERS INTO MY PACK WHILE WE SET THE CHARGES.

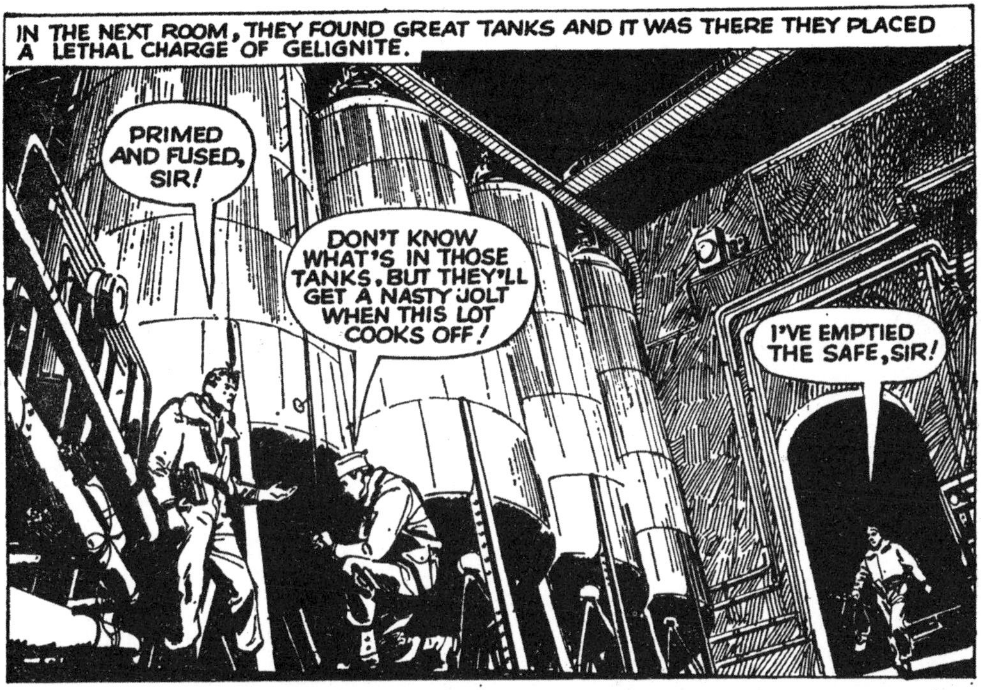
IN THE NEXT ROOM, THEY FOUND GREAT TANKS AND IT WAS THERE THEY PLACED A LETHAL CHARGE OF GELIGNITE.
PRIMED AND FUSED, SIR!
DON'T KNOW WHAT'S IN THOSE TANKS, BUT THEY'LL GET A NASTY JOLT WHEN THIS LOT COOKS OFF!
I'VE EMPTIED THE SAFE, SIR!

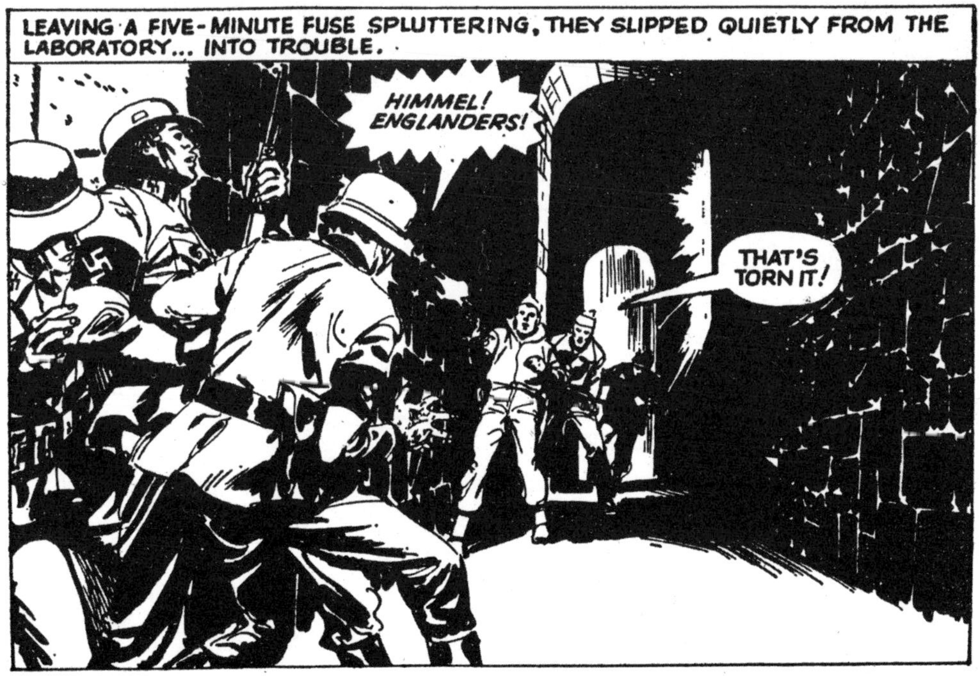
LEAVING A FIVE-MINUTE FUSE SPLUTTERING, THEY SLIPPED QUIETLY FROM THE LABORATORY... INTO TROUBLE.
HIMMEL! ENGLANDERS!
THAT'S TORN IT!

Chapter 3. *Avalanche!*

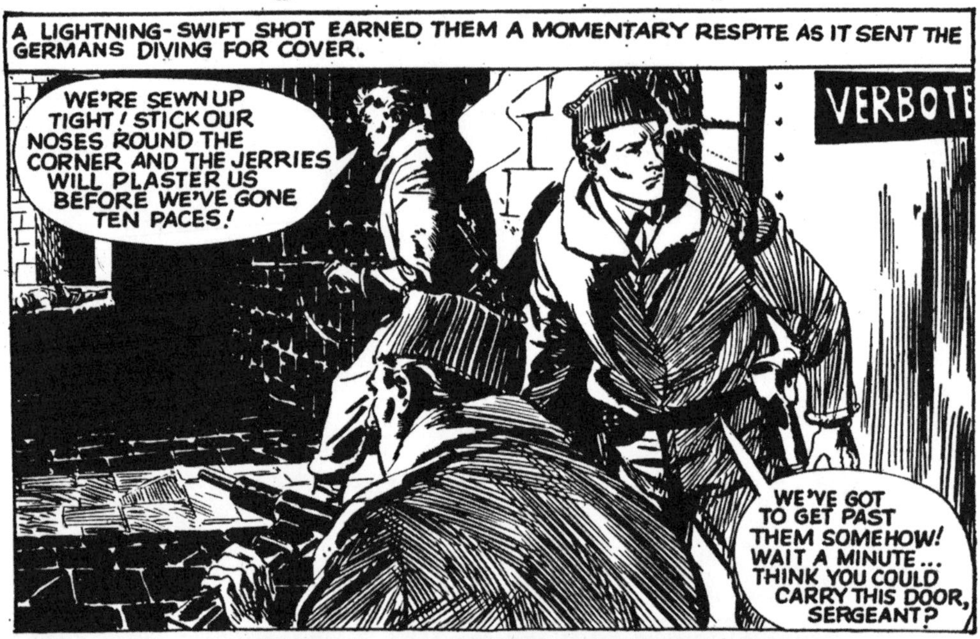
A LIGHTNING-SWIFT SHOT EARNED THEM A MOMENTARY RESPITE AS IT SENT THE GERMANS DIVING FOR COVER.
WE'RE SEWN UP TIGHT! STICK OUR NOSES ROUND THE CORNER AND THE JERRIES WILL PLASTER US BEFORE WE'VE GONE TEN PACES!
VERBOTE
WE'VE GOT TO GET PAST THEM SOMEHOW! WAIT A MINUTE... THINK YOU COULD CARRY THIS DOOR, SERGEANT?

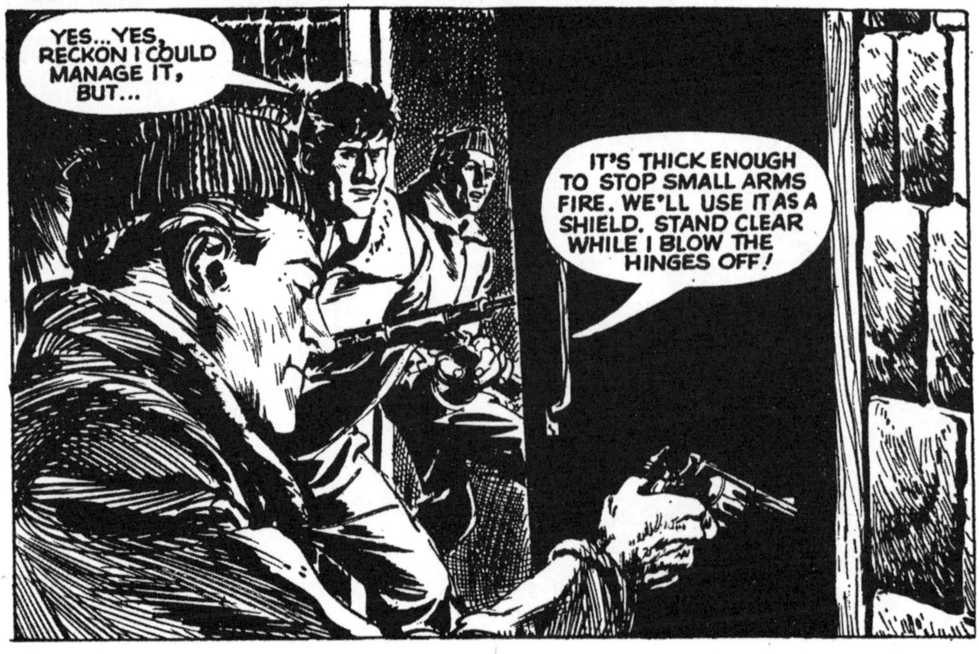
YES...YES, RECKON I COULD MANAGE IT, BUT...
IT'S THICK ENOUGH TO STOP SMALL ARMS FIRE. WE'LL USE IT AS A SHIELD. STAND CLEAR WHILE I BLOW THE HINGES OFF!

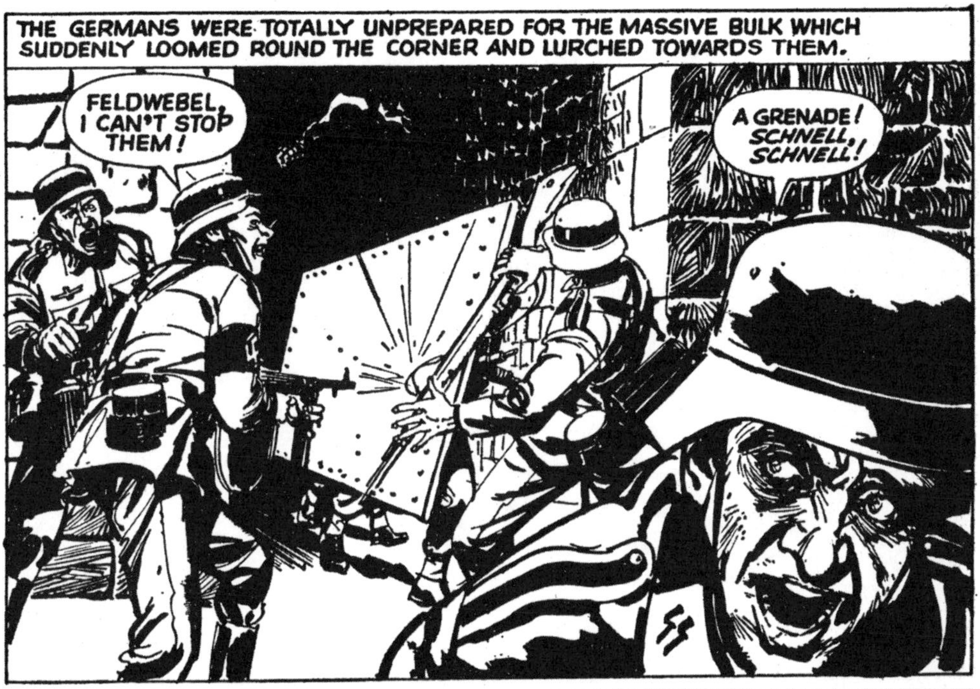
THE GERMANS WERE TOTALLY UNPREPARED FOR THE MASSIVE BULK WHICH SUDDENLY LOOMED ROUND THE CORNER AND LURCHED TOWARDS THEM.
FELDWEBEL, I CAN'T STOP THEM!
A GRENADE! SCHNELL, SCHNELL!

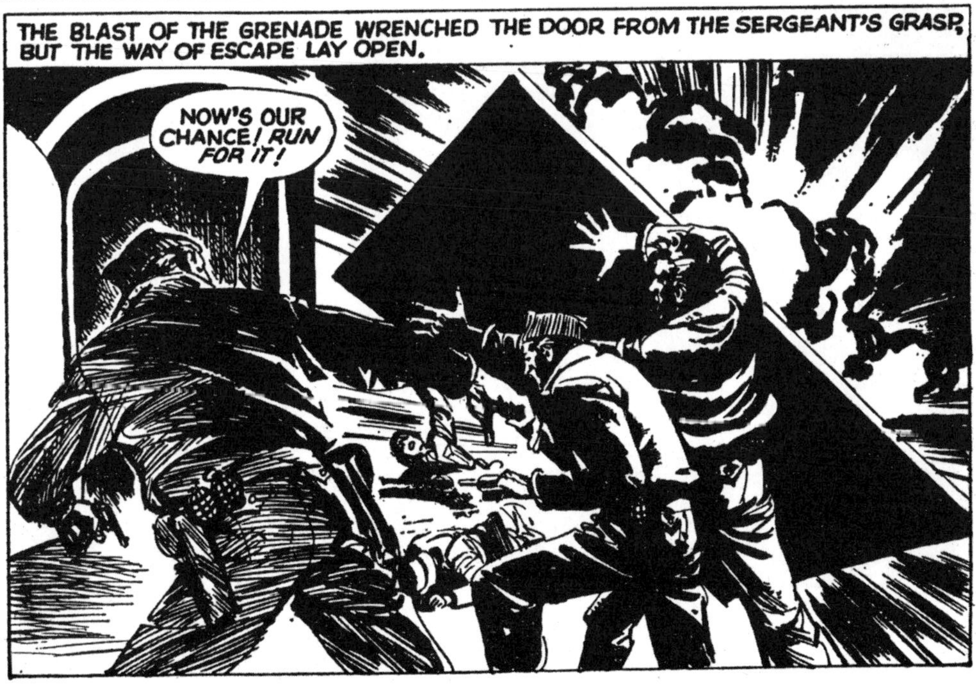
THE BLAST OF THE GRENADE WRENCHED THE DOOR FROM THE SERGEANT'S GRASP, BUT THE WAY OF ESCAPE LAY OPEN.
NOW'S OUR CHANCE! RUN FOR IT!

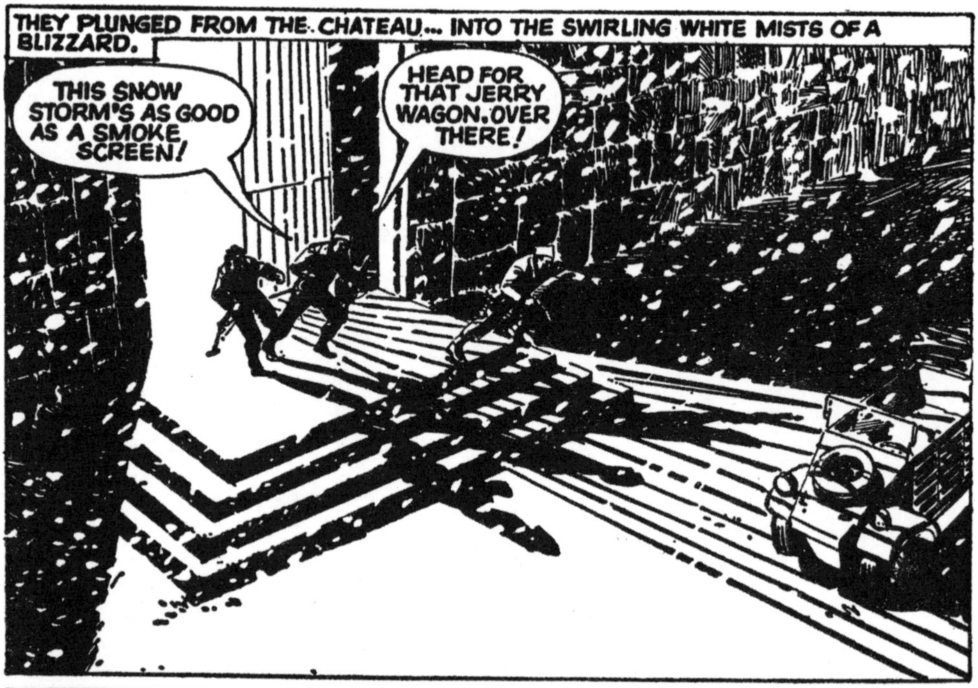
THEY PLUNGED FROM THE CHATEAU... INTO THE SWIRLING WHITE MISTS OF A BLIZZARD.
THIS SNOW STORM'S AS GOOD AS A SMOKE SCREEN!
HEAD FOR THAT JERRY WAGON, OVER THERE!

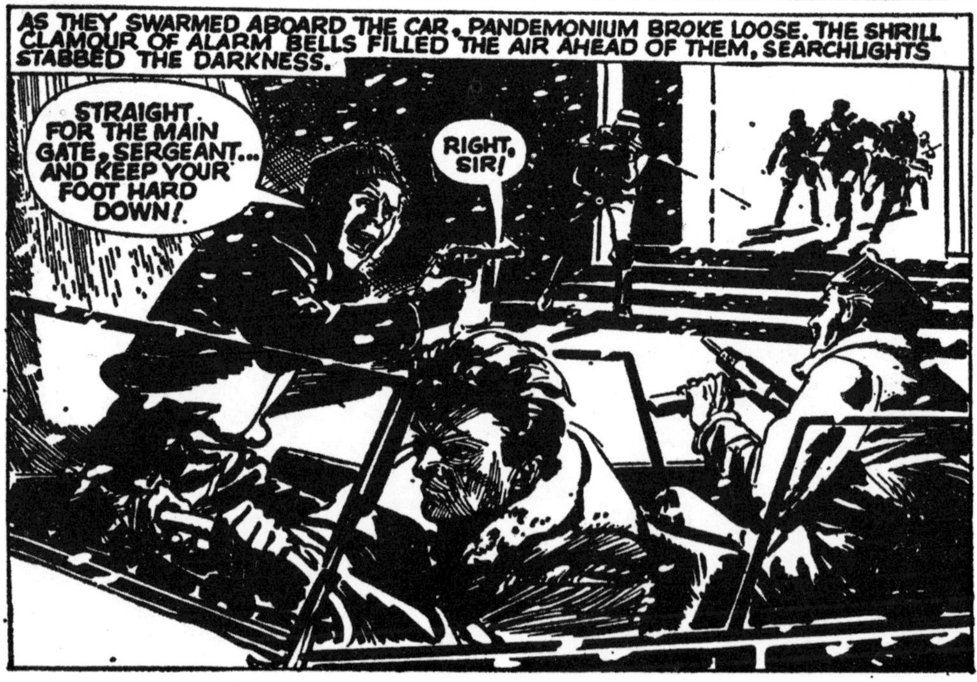
AS THEY SWARMED ABOARD THE CAR, PANDEMONIUM BROKE LOOSE. THE SHRILL CLAMOUR OF ALARM BELLS FILLED THE AIR AHEAD OF THEM, SEARCHLIGHTS STABBED THE DARKNESS.
STRAIGHT FOR THE MAIN GATE, SERGEANT... AND KEEP YOUR FOOT HARD DOWN!
RIGHT, SIR!

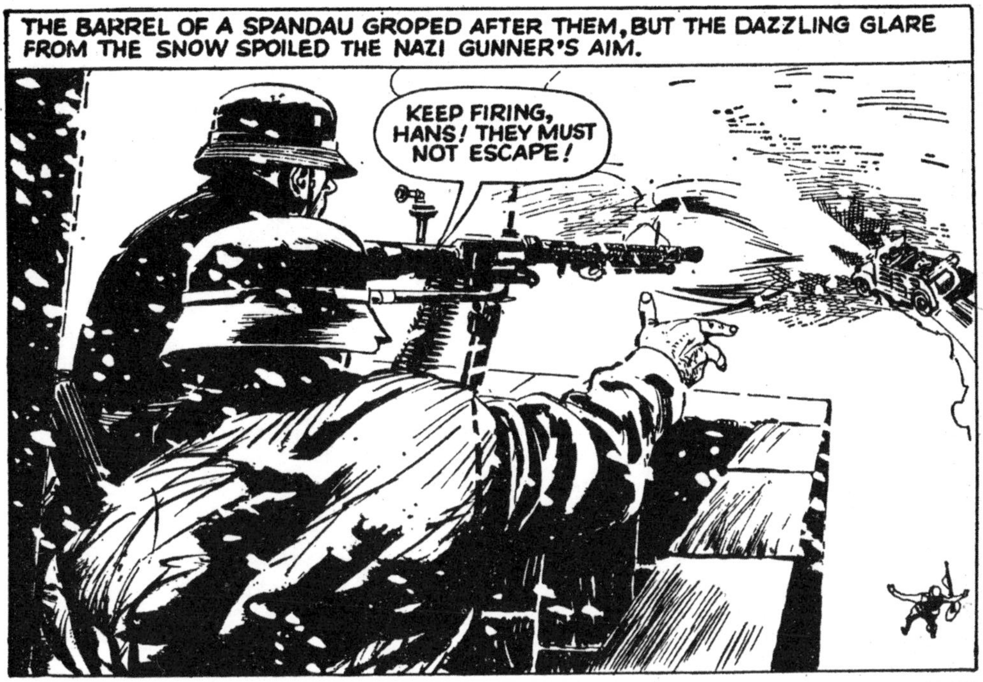
THE BARREL OF A SPANDAU GROPED AFTER THEM, BUT THE DAZZLING GLARE FROM THE SNOW SPOILED THE NAZI GUNNER'S AIM.
KEEP FIRING, HANS! THEY MUST NOT ESCAPE!

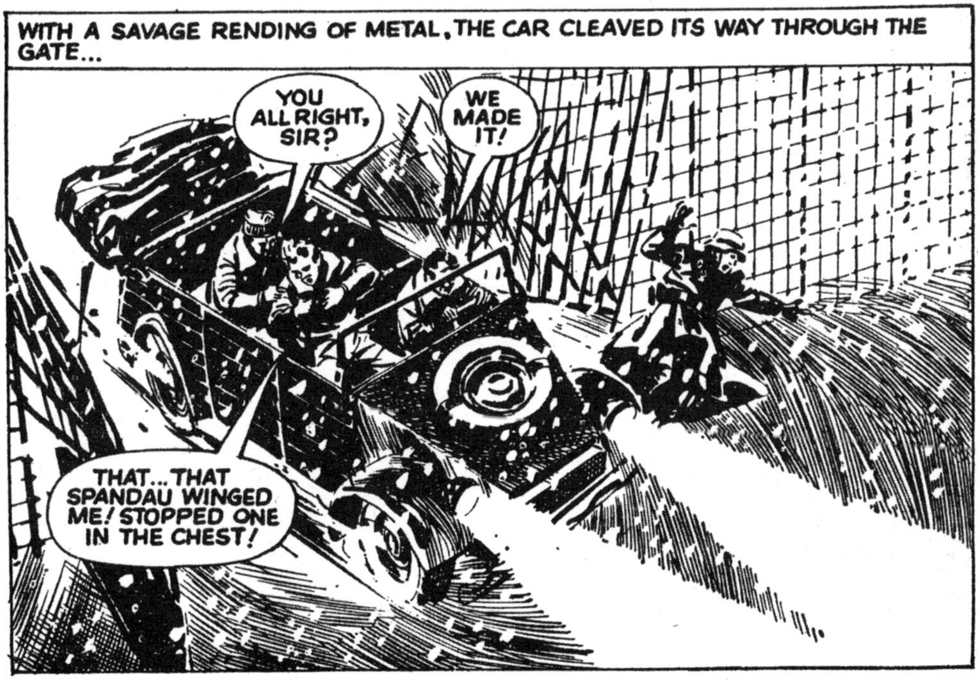
WITH A SAVAGE RENDING OF METAL, THE CAR CLEAVED ITS WAY THROUGH THE GATE...
YOU ALL RIGHT, SIR?
WE MADE IT!
THAT... THAT SPANDAU WINGED ME! STOPPED ONE IN THE CHEST!

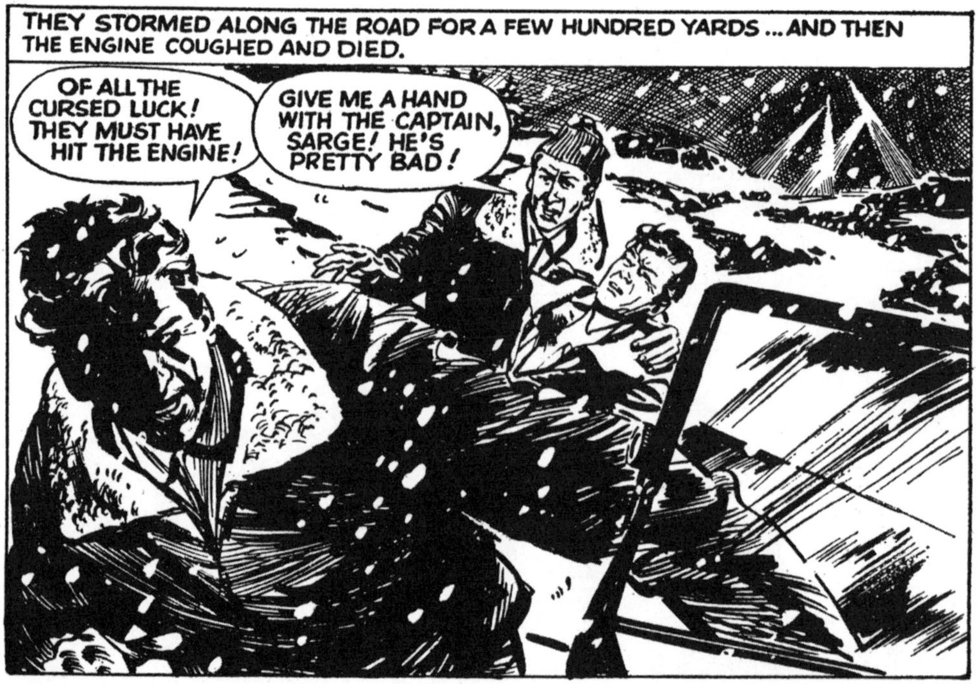
THEY STORMED ALONG THE ROAD FOR A FEW HUNDRED YARDS ... AND THEN THE ENGINE COUGHED AND DIED.
OF ALL THE CURSED LUCK! THEY MUST HAVE HIT THE ENGINE!
GIVE ME A HAND WITH THE CAPTAIN, SARGE! HE'S PRETTY BAD!

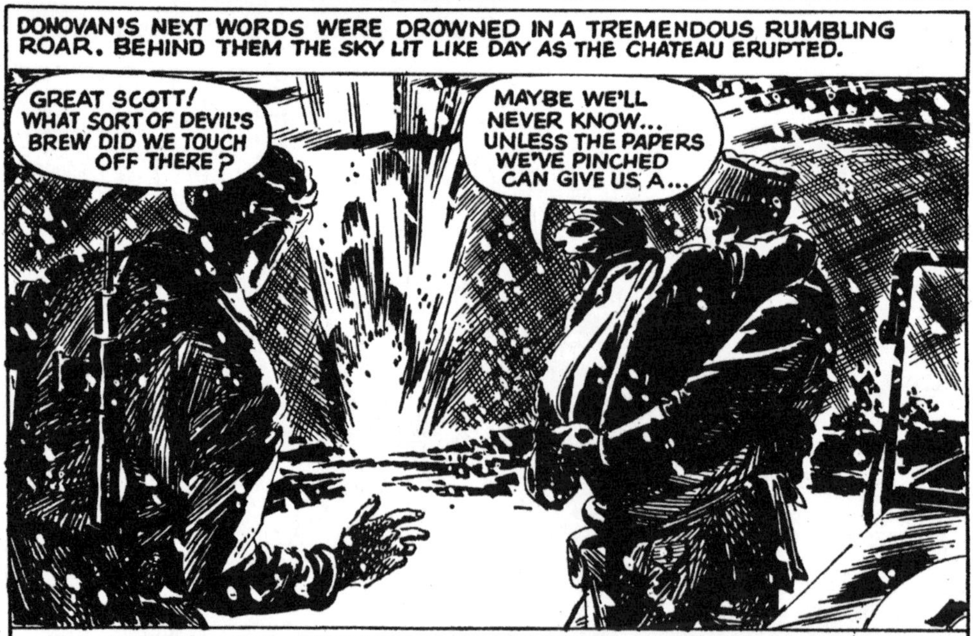
DONOVAN'S NEXT WORDS WERE DROWNED IN A TREMENDOUS RUMBLING ROAR. BEHIND THEM THE SKY LIT LIKE DAY AS THE CHATEAU ERUPTED.
GREAT SCOTT! WHAT SORT OF DEVIL'S BREW DID WE TOUCH OFF THERE?
MAYBE WE'LL NEVER KNOW... UNLESS THE PAPERS WE'VE PINCHED CAN GIVE US A...
THE CAPTAIN'S VOICE TRAILED OFF AS HE FAINTED IN DONOVAN'S ARMS...

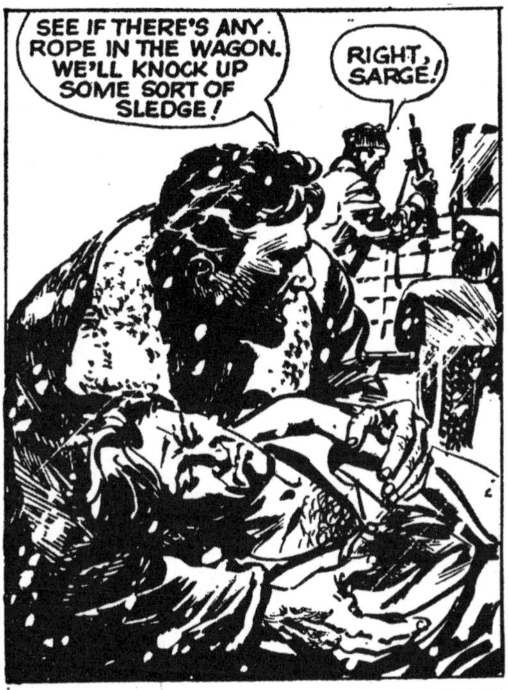
SEE IF THERE'S ANY ROPE IN THE WAGON. WE'LL KNOCK UP SOME SORT OF SLEDGE!
RIGHT, SARGE!

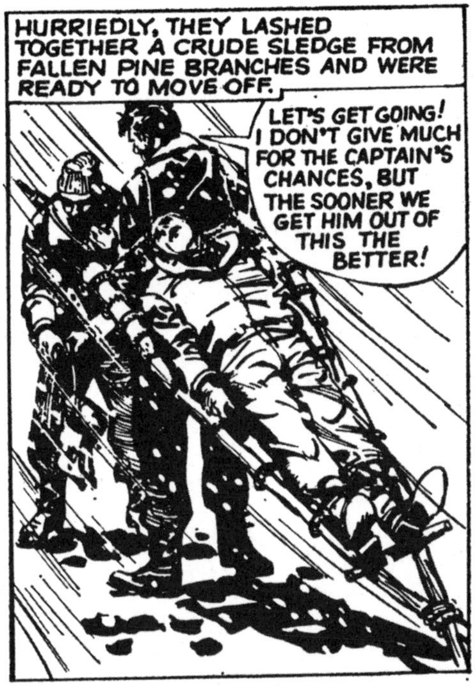
HURRIEDLY, THEY LASHED TOGETHER A CRUDE SLEDGE FROM FALLEN PINE BRANCHES AND WERE READY TO MOVE OFF.
LET'S GET GOING! I DON'T GIVE MUCH FOR THE CAPTAIN'S CHANCES, BUT THE SOONER WE GET HIM OUT OF THIS THE BETTER!

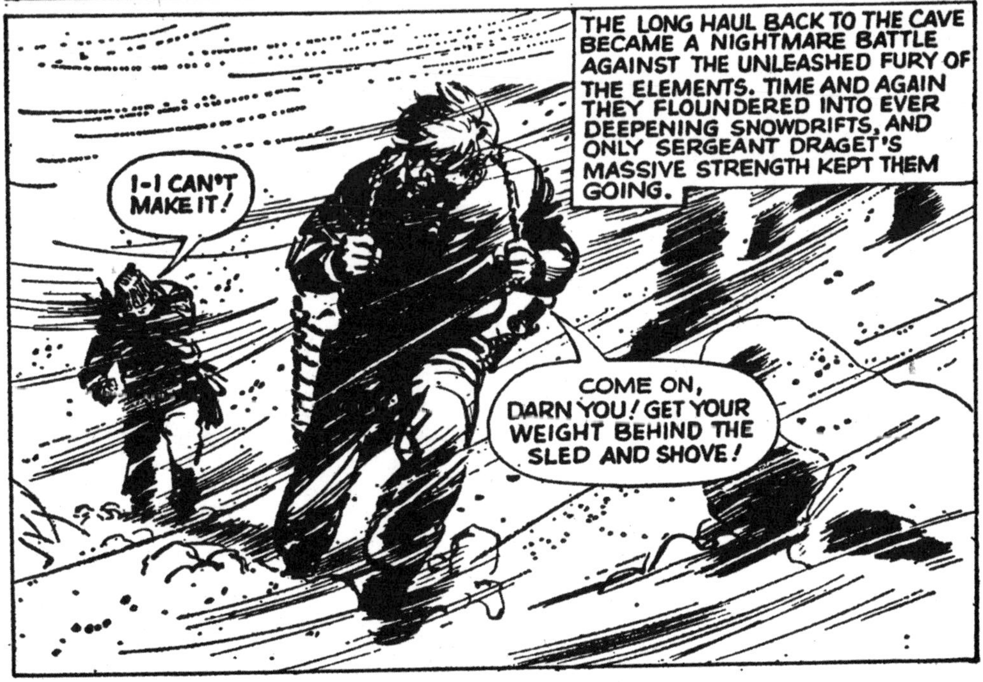
THE LONG HAUL BACK TO THE CAVE BECAME A NIGHTMARE BATTLE AGAINST THE UNLEASHED FURY OF THE ELEMENTS. TIME AND AGAIN THEY FLOUNDERED INTO EVER DEEPENING SNOWDRIFTS, AND ONLY SERGEANT DRAGET'S MASSIVE STRENGTH KEPT THEM GOING.
I-I CAN'T MAKE IT!
COME ON, DARN YOU! GET YOUR WEIGHT BEHIND THE SLED AND SHOVE!

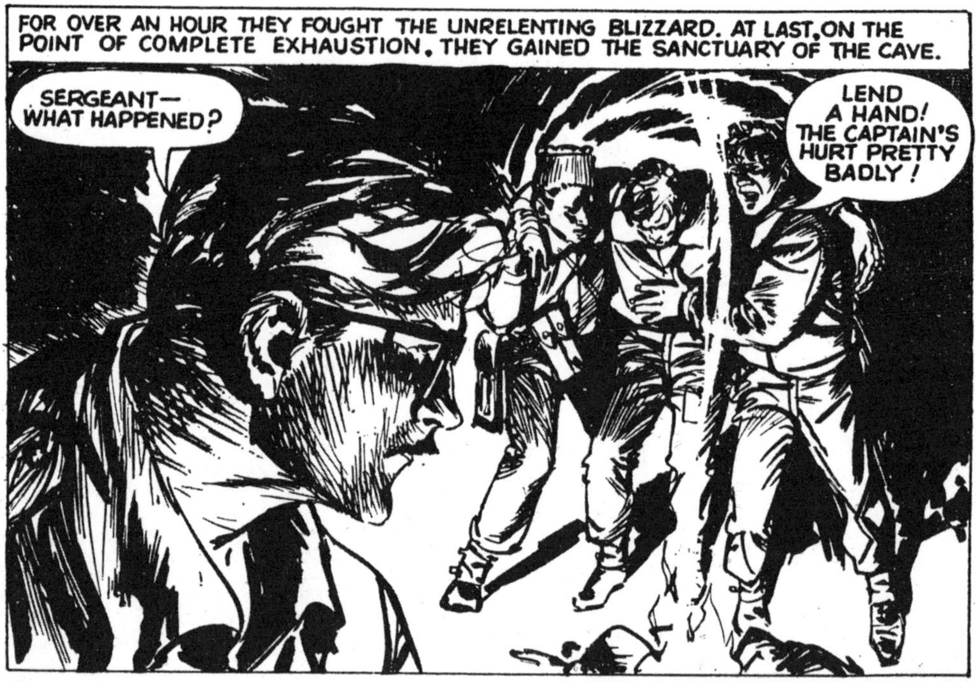
FOR OVER AN HOUR THEY FOUGHT THE UNRELENTING BLIZZARD. AT LAST, ON THE POINT OF COMPLETE EXHAUSTION, THEY GAINED THE SANCTUARY OF THE CAVE.
SERGEANT— WHAT HAPPENED?
LEND A HAND! THE CAPTAIN'S HURT PRETTY BADLY!

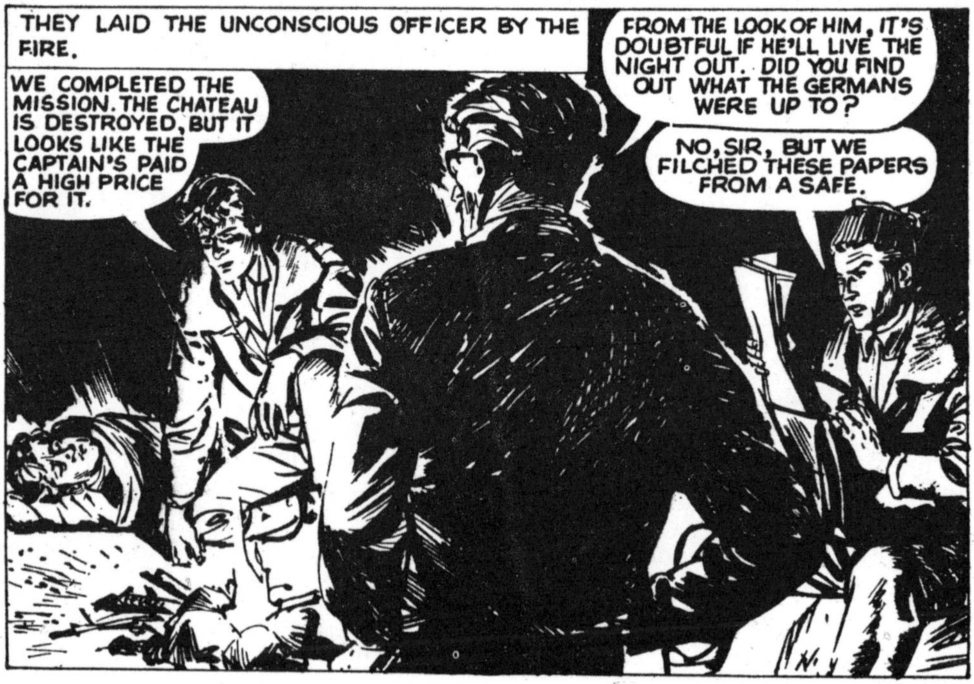
THEY LAID THE UNCONSCIOUS OFFICER BY THE FIRE.
FROM THE LOOK OF HIM, IT'S DOUBTFUL IF HE'LL LIVE THE NIGHT OUT. DID YOU FIND OUT WHAT THE GERMANS WERE UP TO?
WE COMPLETED THE MISSION. THE CHATEAU IS DESTROYED, BUT IT LOOKS LIKE THE CAPTAIN'S PAID A HIGH PRICE FOR IT.
NO, SIR, BUT WE FILCHED THESE PAPERS FROM A SAFE.

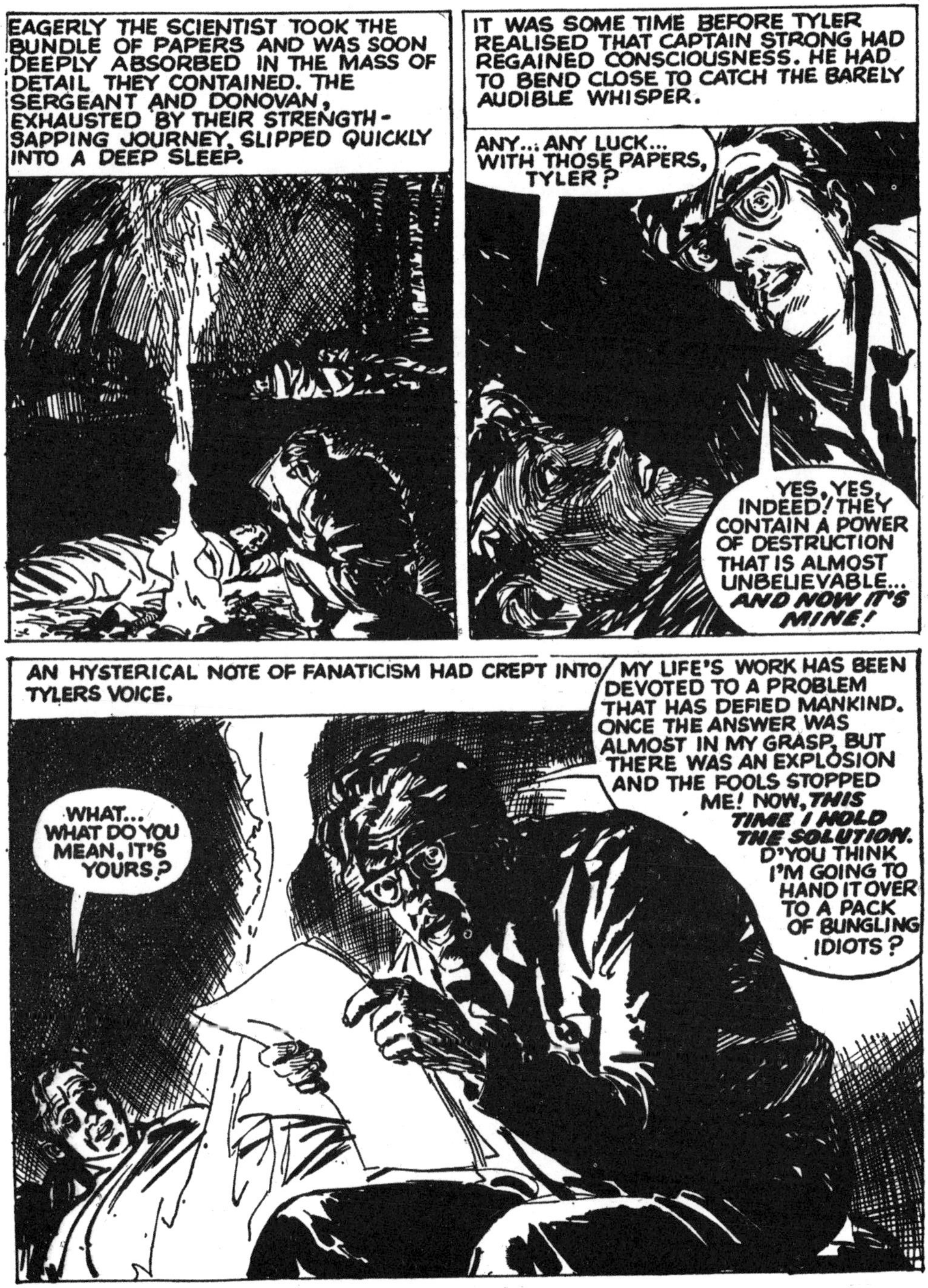
EAGERLY THE SCIENTIST TOOK THE BUNDLE OF PAPERS AND WAS SOON DEEPLY ABSORBED IN THE MASS OF DETAIL THEY CONTAINED. THE SERGEANT AND DONOVAN, EXHAUSTED BY THEIR STRENGTH-SAPPING JOURNEY, SLIPPED QUICKLY INTO A DEEP SLEEP.
IT WAS SOME TIME BEFORE TYLER REALISED THAT CAPTAIN STRONG HAD REGAINED CONSCIOUSNESS. HE HAD TO BEND CLOSE TO CATCH THE BARELY AUDIBLE WHISPER.
ANY... ANY LUCK... WITH THOSE PAPERS, TYLER?
YES, YES, INDEED! THEY CONTAIN A POWER OF DESTRUCTION THAT IS ALMOST UNBELIEVABLE... AND NOW IT'S MINE!
AN HYSTERICAL NOTE OF FANATICISM HAD CREPT INTO TYLERS VOICE.
MY LIFE'S WORK HAS BEEN DEVOTED TO A PROBLEM THAT HAS DEFIED MANKIND. ONCE THE ANSWER WAS ALMOST IN MY GRASP, BUT THERE WAS AN EXPLOSION AND THE FOOLS STOPPED ME! NOW, THIS TIME I HOLD THE SOLUTION. D'YOU THINK I'M GOING TO HAND IT OVER TO A PACK OF BUNGLING IDIOTS?
WHAT... WHAT DO YOU MEAN, IT'S YOURS?

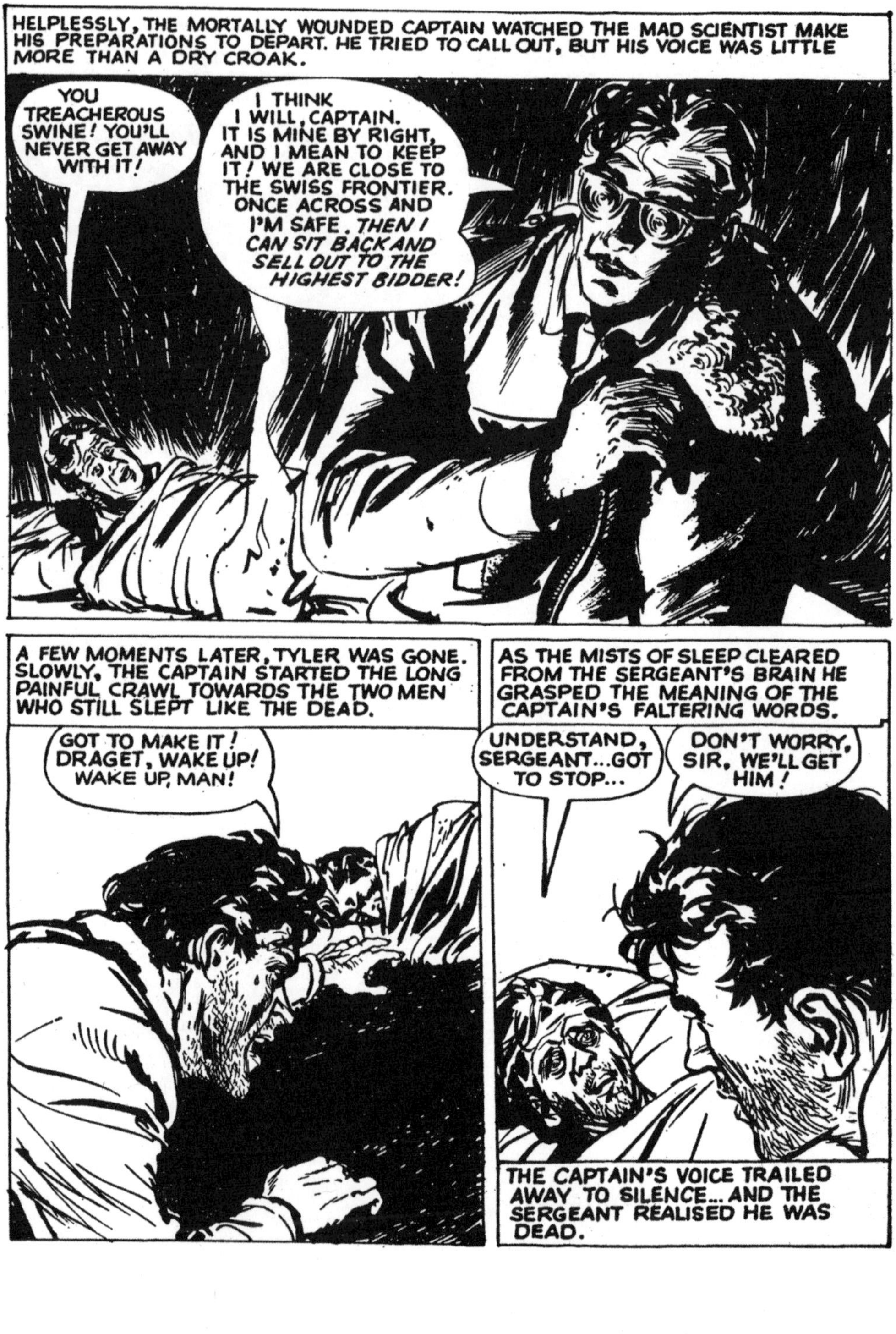
HELPLESSLY, THE MORTALLY WOUNDED CAPTAIN WATCHED THE MAD SCIENTIST MAKE HIS PREPARATIONS TO DEPART. HE TRIED TO CALL OUT, BUT HIS VOICE WAS LITTLE MORE THAN A DRY CROAK.
YOU TREACHEROUS SWINE! YOU'LL NEVER GET AWAY WITH IT!
I THINK I WILL, CAPTAIN. IT IS MINE BY RIGHT, AND I MEAN TO KEEP IT! WE ARE CLOSE TO THE SWISS FRONTIER. ONCE ACROSS AND I'M SAFE. THEN I CAN SIT BACK AND SELL OUT TO THE HIGHEST BIDDER!
A FEW MOMENTS LATER, TYLER WAS GONE. SLOWLY, THE CAPTAIN STARTED THE LONG PAINFUL CRAWL TOWARDS THE TWO MEN WHO STILL SLEPT LIKE THE DEAD.
GOT TO MAKE IT! DRAGET, WAKE UP! WAKE UP, MAN!
AS THE MISTS OF SLEEP CLEARED FROM THE SERGEANT'S BRAIN HE GRASPED THE MEANING OF THE CAPTAIN'S FALTERING WORDS.
UNDERSTAND, SERGEANT...GOT TO STOP...
DON'T WORRY, SIR, WE'LL GET HIM!
THE CAPTAIN'S VOICE TRAILED AWAY TO SILENCE... AND THE SERGEANT REALISED HE WAS DEAD.

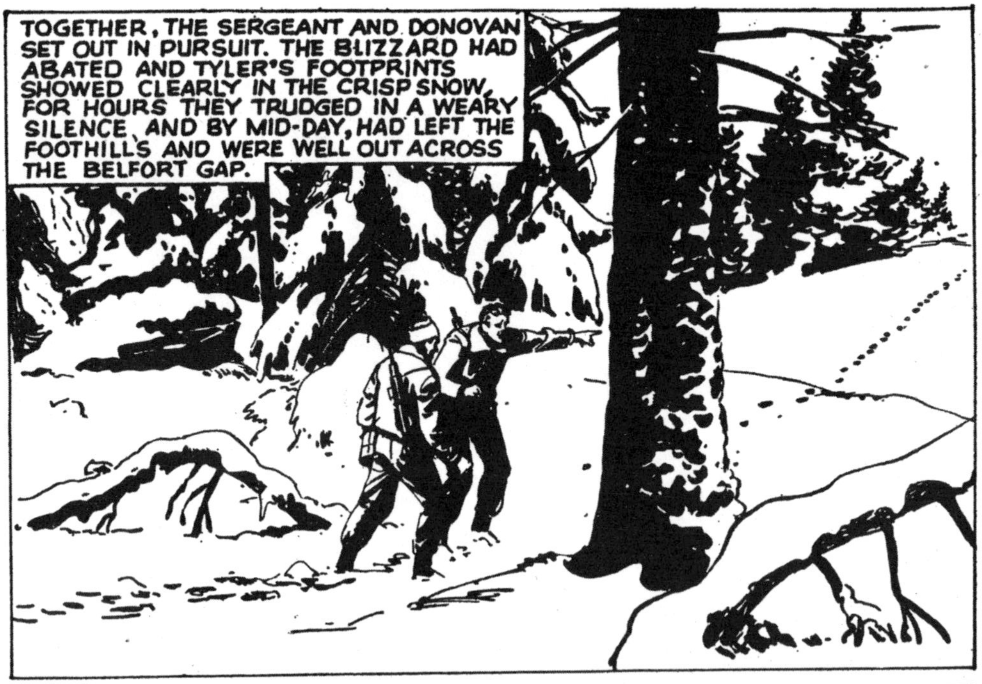
TOGETHER, THE SERGEANT AND DONOVAN SET OUT IN PURSUIT. THE BLIZZARD HAD ABATED AND TYLER'S FOOTPRINTS SHOWED CLEARLY IN THE CRISP SNOW. FOR HOURS THEY TRUDGED IN A WEARY SILENCE AND BY MID-DAY, HAD LEFT THE FOOTHILLS AND WERE WELL OUT ACROSS THE BELFORT GAP.

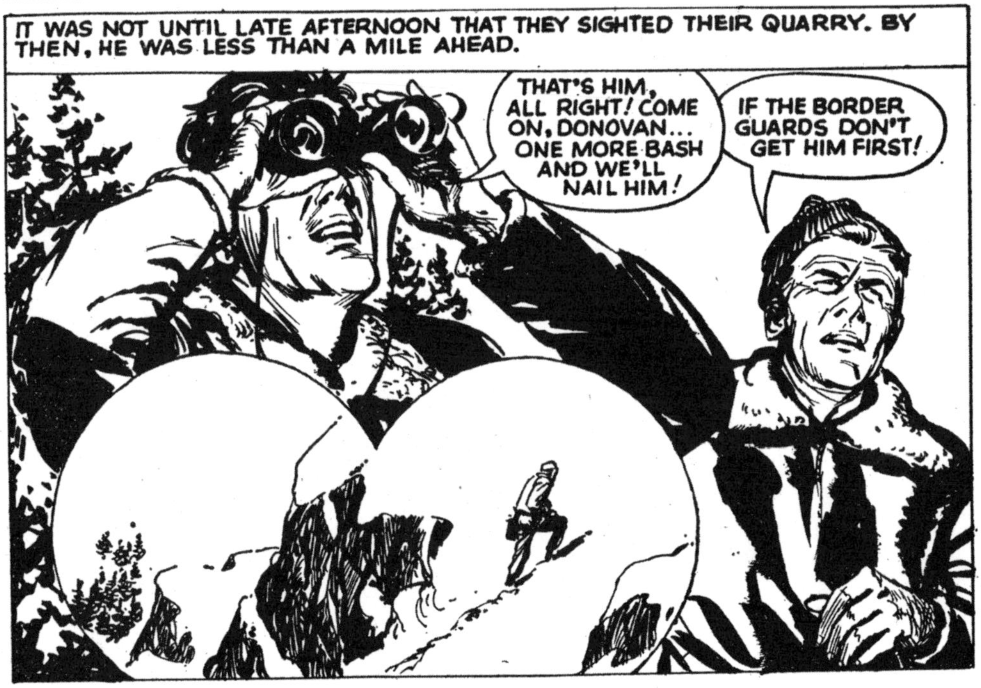
IT WAS NOT UNTIL LATE AFTERNOON THAT THEY SIGHTED THEIR QUARRY. BY THEN, HE WAS LESS THAN A MILE AHEAD.
THAT'S HIM, ALL RIGHT! COME ON, DONOVAN... ONE MORE BASH AND WE'LL NAIL HIM!
IF THE BORDER GUARDS DON'T GET HIM FIRST!

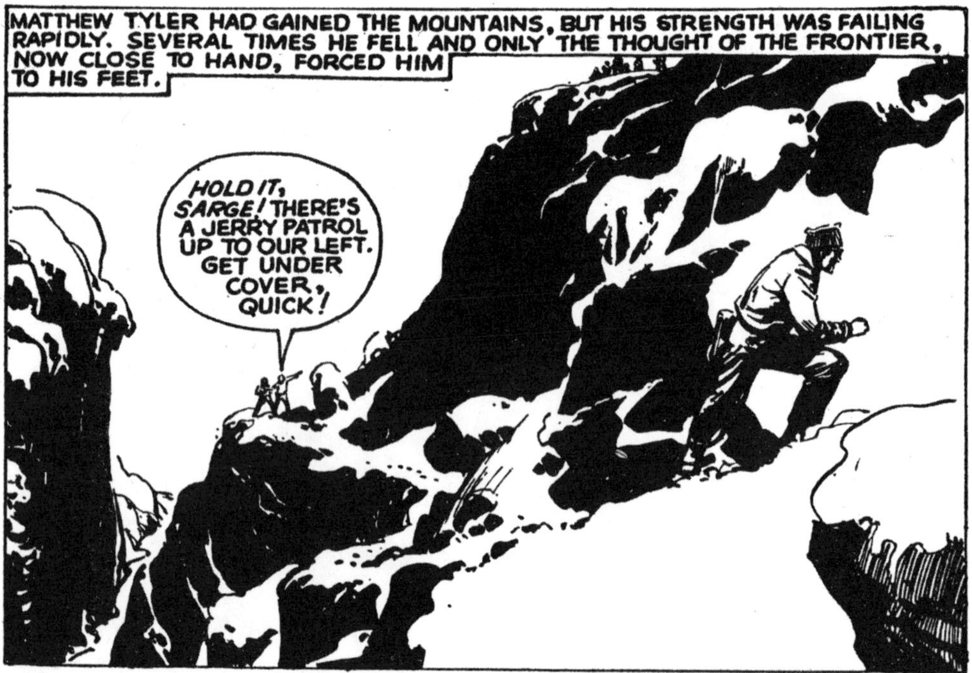
MATTHEW TYLER HAD GAINED THE MOUNTAINS, BUT HIS STRENGTH WAS FAILING RAPIDLY. SEVERAL TIMES HE FELL AND ONLY THE THOUGHT OF THE FRONTIER, NOW CLOSE TO HAND, FORCED HIM TO HIS FEET.
HOLD IT, SARGE! THERE'S A JERRY PATROL UP TO OUR LEFT. GET UNDER COVER, QUICK!

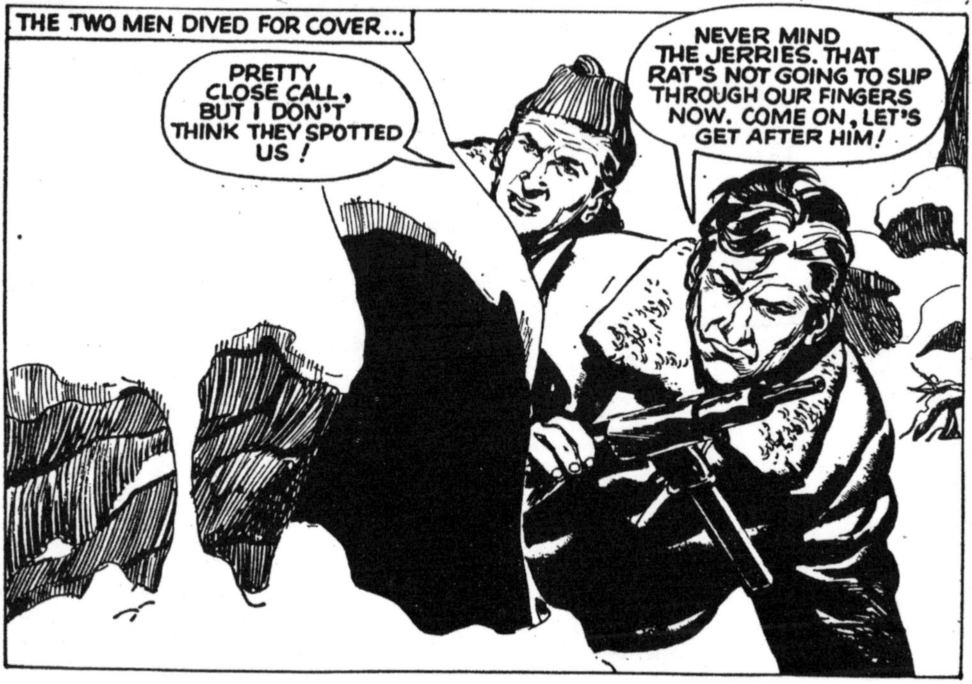
THE TWO MEN DIVED FOR COVER...
PRETTY CLOSE CALL, BUT I DON'T THINK THEY SPOTTED US!
NEVER MIND THE JERRIES. THAT RAT'S NOT GOING TO SLIP THROUGH OUR FINGERS NOW. COME ON, LET'S GET AFTER HIM!

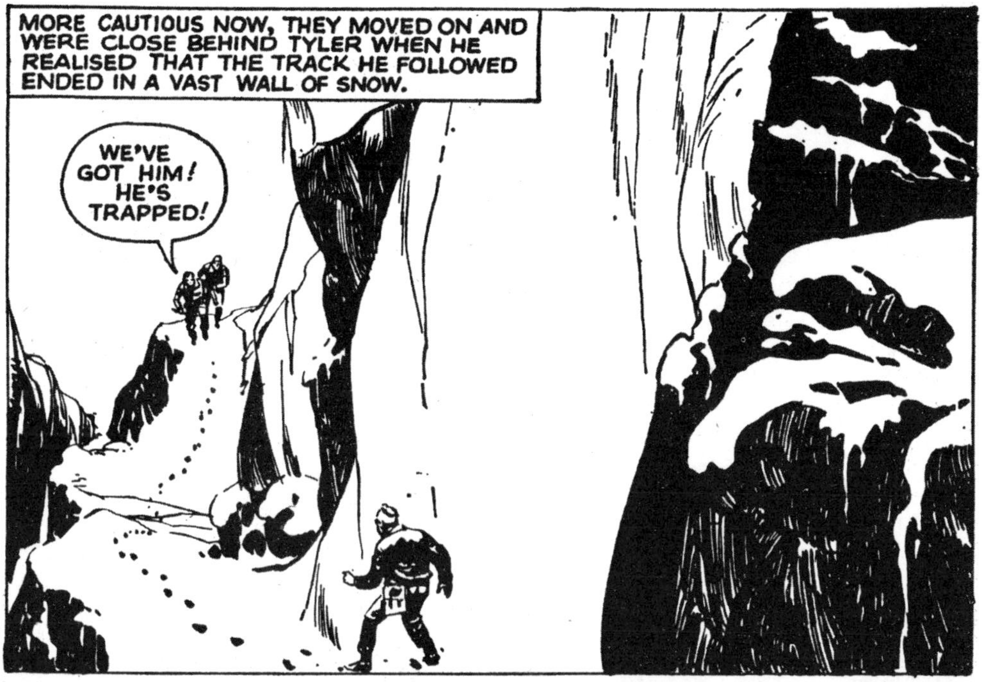
MORE CAUTIOUS NOW, THEY MOVED ON AND WERE CLOSE BEHIND TYLER WHEN HE REALISED THAT THE TRACK HE FOLLOWED ENDED IN A VAST WALL OF SNOW.
WE'VE GOT HIM! HE'S TRAPPED!

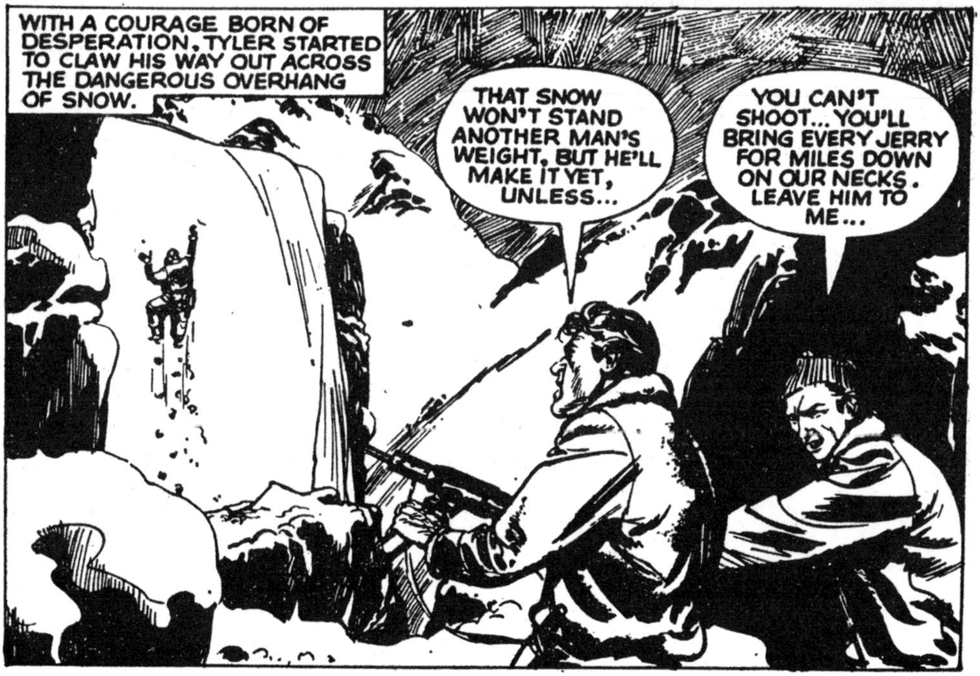
WITH A COURAGE BORN OF DESPERATION, TYLER STARTED TO CLAW HIS WAY OUT ACROSS THE DANGEROUS OVERHANG OF SNOW.
THAT SNOW WON'T STAND ANOTHER MAN'S WEIGHT, BUT HE'LL MAKE IT YET, UNLESS...
YOU CAN'T SHOOT... YOU'LL BRING EVERY JERRY FOR MILES DOWN ON OUR NECKS. LEAVE HIM TO ME...

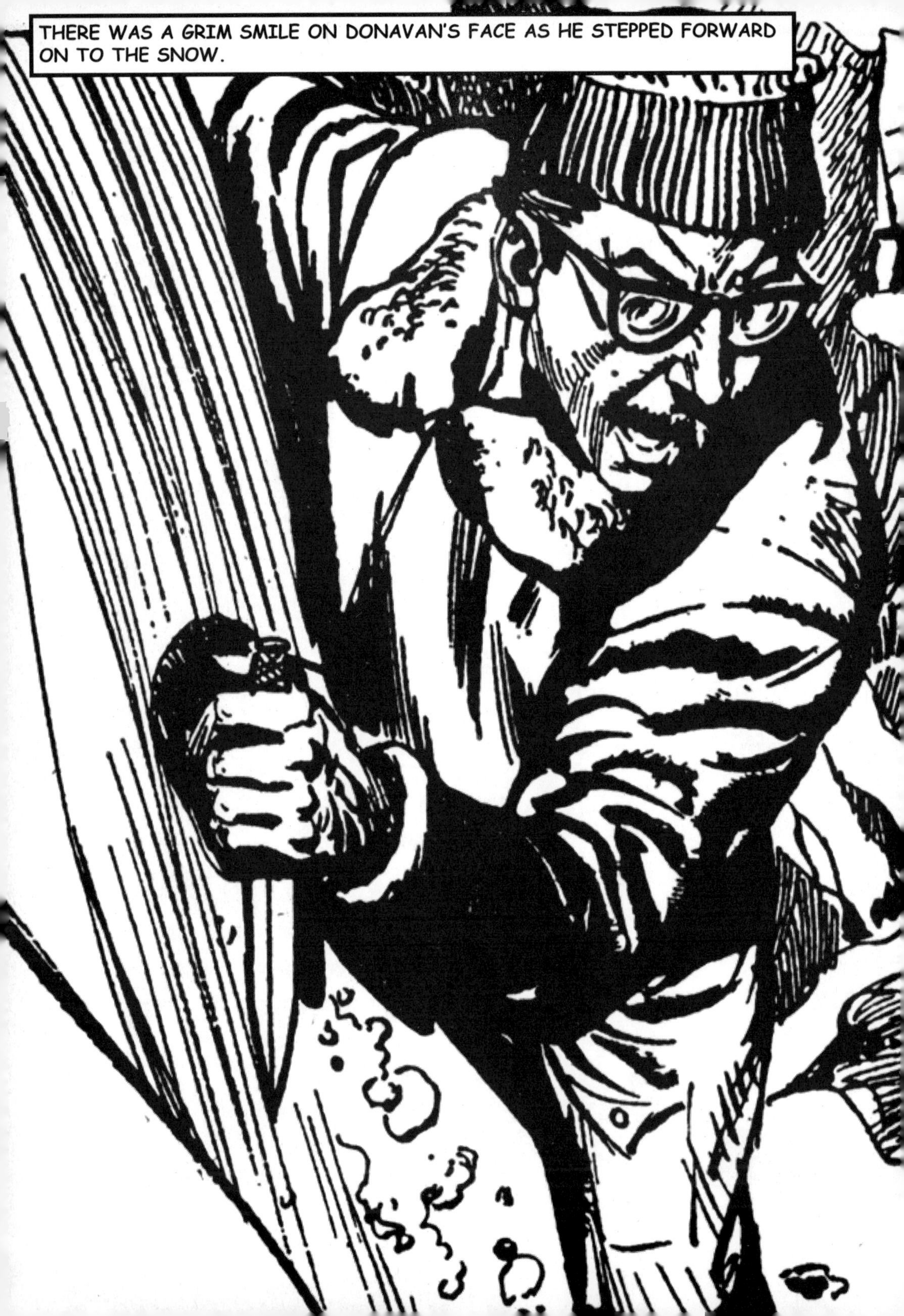
THERE WAS A GRIM SMILE ON DONAVAN'S FACE AS HE STEPPED FORWARD ON TO THE SNOW.

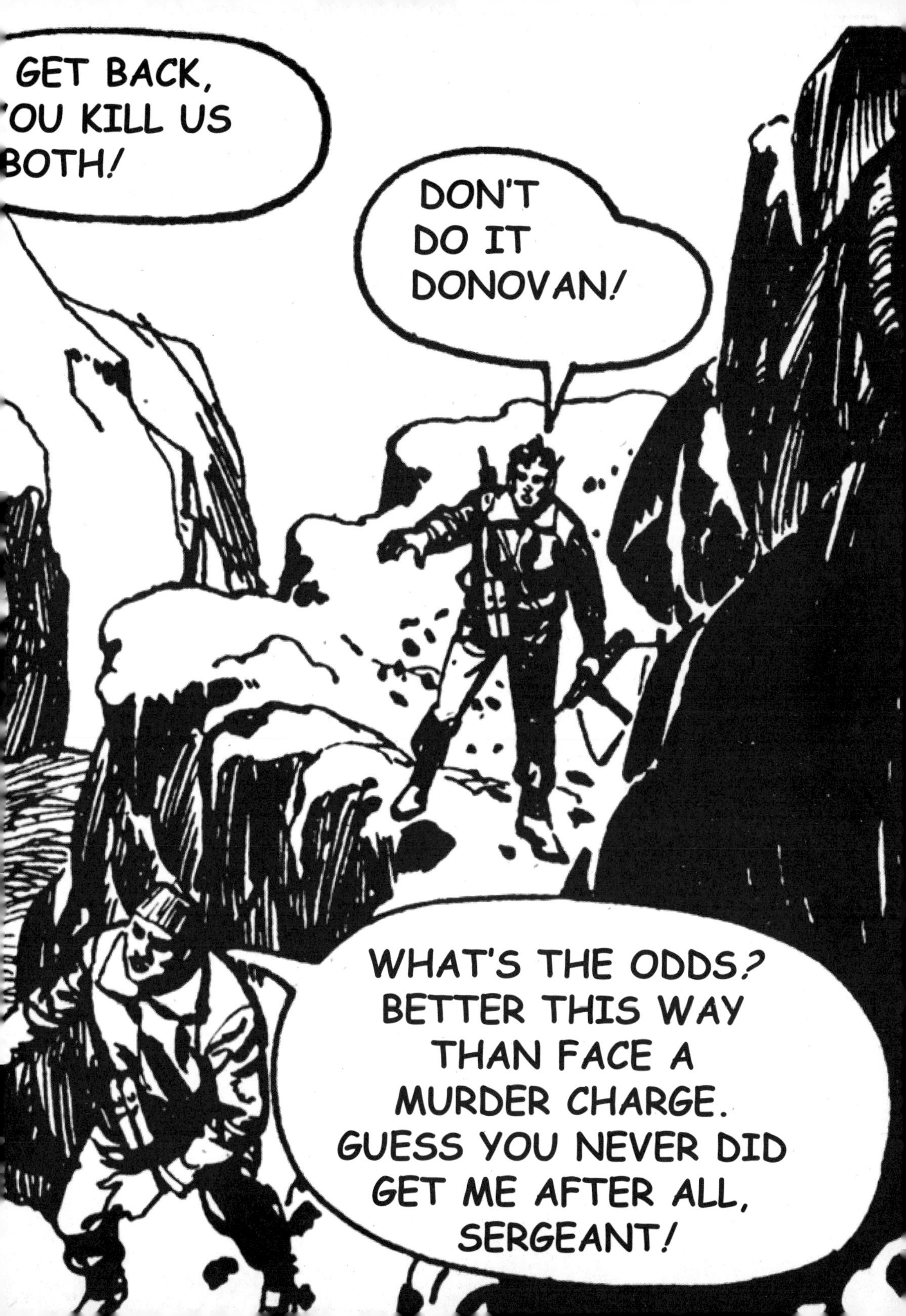
GET BACK, 'OU KILL US BOTH!
DON'T DO IT DONOVAN!
WHAT'S THE ODDS? BETTER THIS WAY THAN FACE A MURDER CHARGE. GUESS YOU NEVER DID GET ME AFTER ALL, SERGEANT!

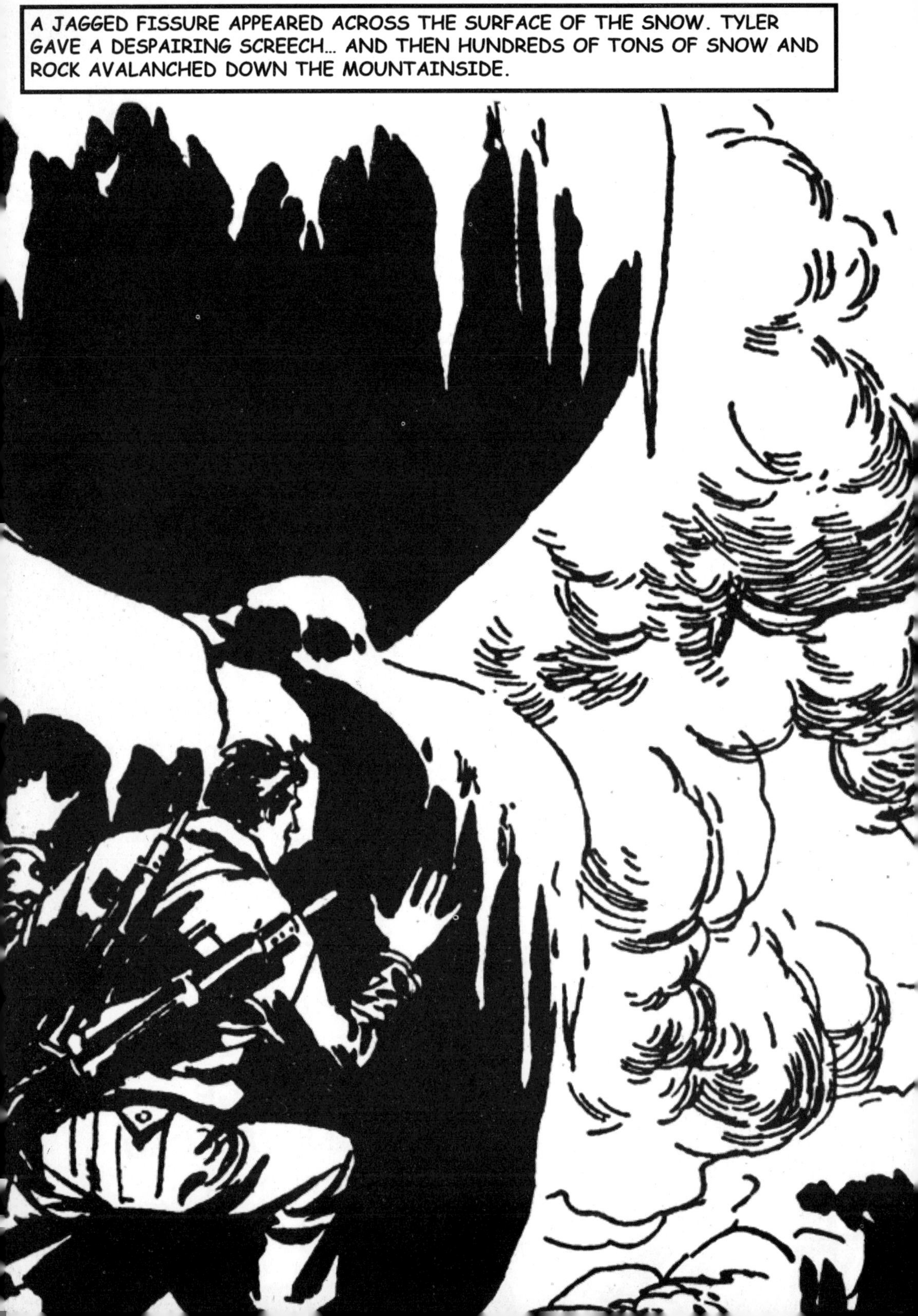
A JAGGED FISSURE APPEARED ACROSS THE SURFACE OF THE SNOW. TYLER GAVE A DESPAIRING SCREECH... AND THEN HUNDREDS OF TONS OF SNOW AND ROCK AVALANCHED DOWN THE MOUNTAINSIDE.

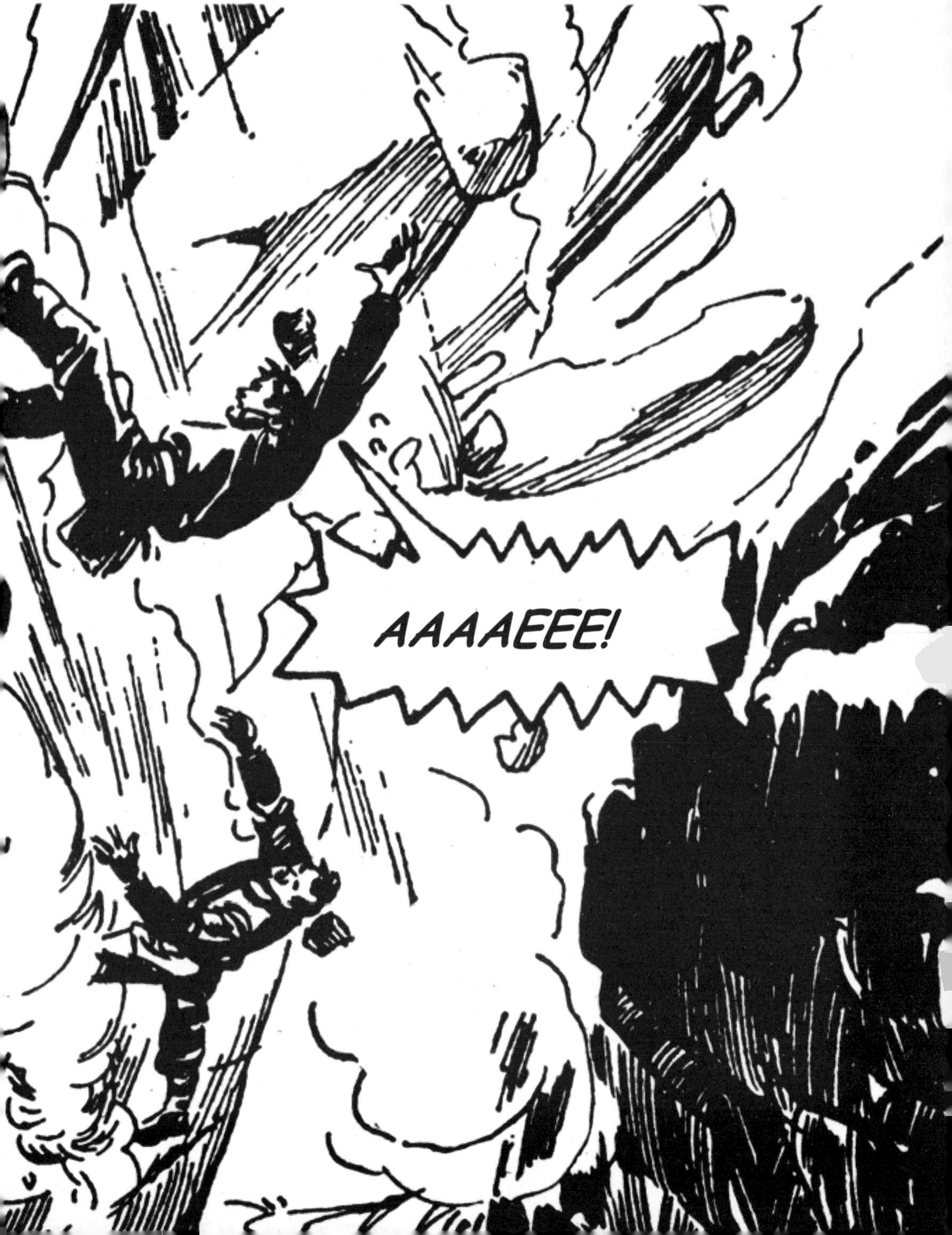
AAAAEEE!

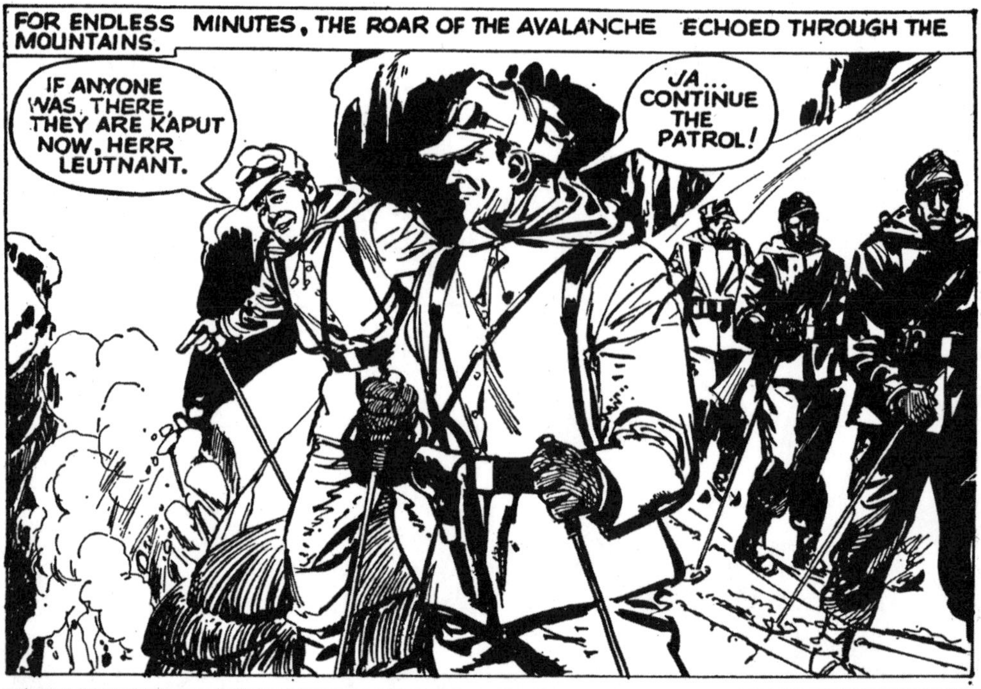
FOR ENDLESS MINUTES, THE ROAR OF THE AVALANCHE ECHOED THROUGH THE MOUNTAINS.
IF ANYONE WAS THERE, THEY ARE KAPUT NOW, HERR LEUTNANT.
JA... CONTINUE THE PATROL!

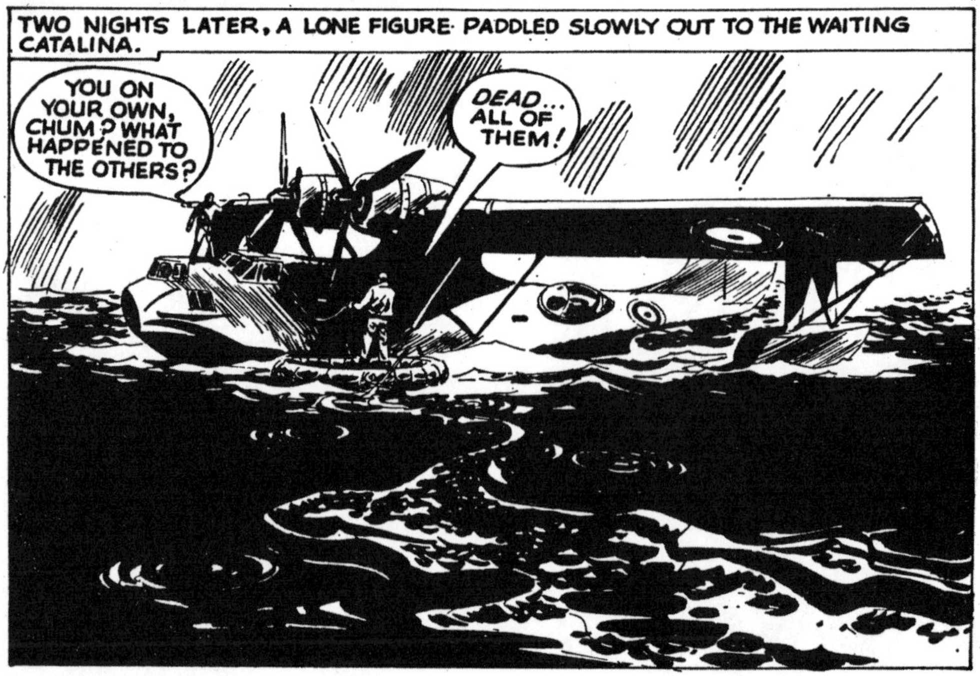
TWO NIGHTS LATER, A LONE FIGURE PADDLED SLOWLY OUT TO THE WAITING CATALINA.
YOU ON YOUR OWN, CHUM? WHAT HAPPENED TO THE OTHERS?
DEAD... ALL OF THEM!

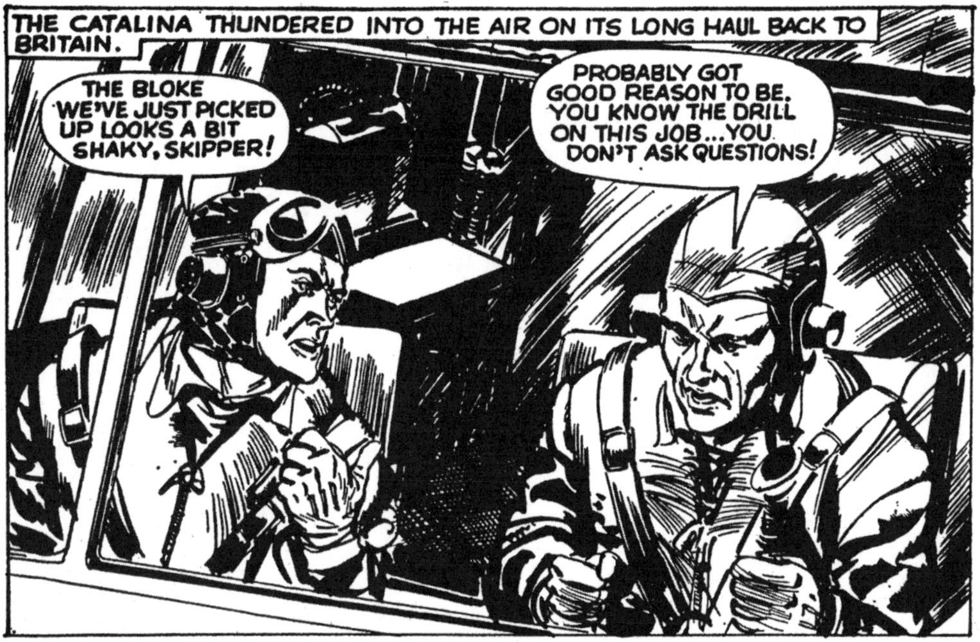
THE CATALINA THUNDERED INTO THE AIR ON ITS LONG HAUL BACK TO BRITAIN.
THE BLOKE WE'VE JUST PICKED UP LOOKS A BIT SHAKY, SKIPPER!
PROBABLY GOT GOOD REASON TO BE. YOU KNOW THE DRILL ON THIS JOB... YOU DON'T ASK QUESTIONS!

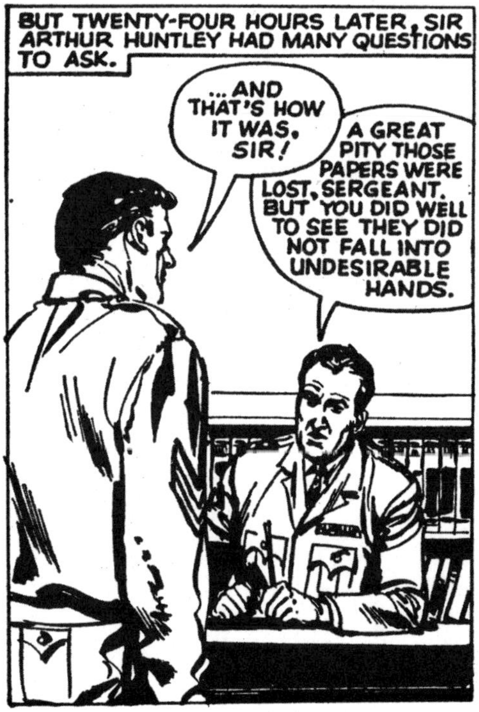
BUT TWENTY-FOUR HOURS LATER, SIR ARTHUR HUNTLEY HAD MANY QUESTIONS TO ASK.
...AND THAT'S HOW IT WAS, SIR!
A GREAT PITY THOSE PAPERS WERE LOST, SERGEANT. BUT YOU DID WELL TO SEE THEY DID NOT FALL INTO UNDESIRABLE HANDS.

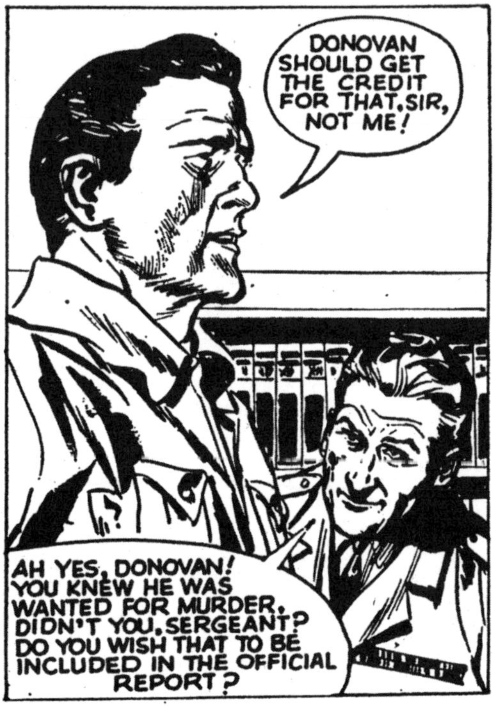
DONOVAN SHOULD GET THE CREDIT FOR THAT, SIR, NOT ME!
AH YES, DONOVAN! YOU KNEW HE WAS WANTED FOR MURDER, DIDN'T YOU, SERGEANT? DO YOU WISH THAT TO BE INCLUDED IN THE OFFICIAL REPORT?

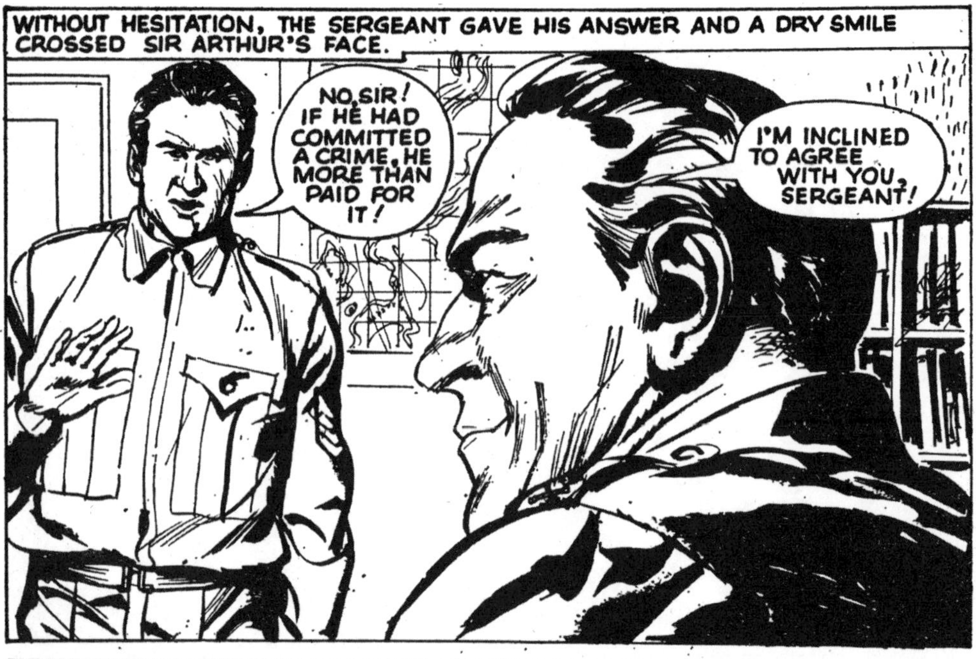
WITHOUT HESITATION, THE SERGEANT GAVE HIS ANSWER AND A DRY SMILE CROSSED SIR ARTHUR'S FACE.
NO, SIR! IF HE HAD COMMITTED A CRIME, HE MORE THAN PAID FOR IT!
I'M INCLINED TO AGREE WITH YOU, SERGEANT!

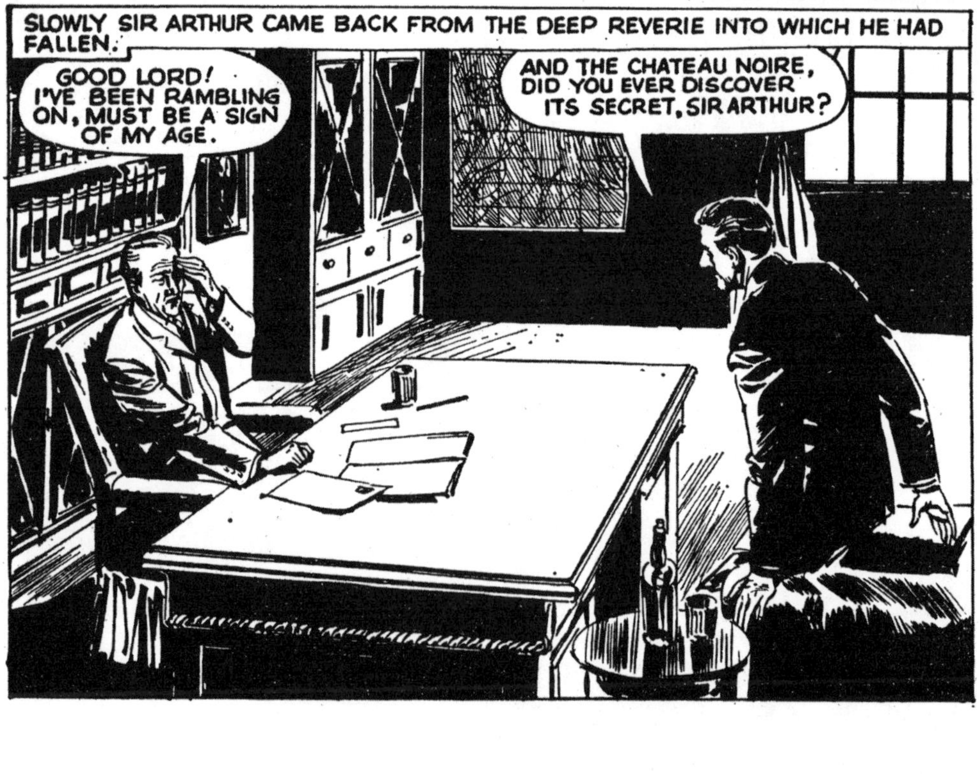
SLOWLY SIR ARTHUR CAME BACK FROM THE DEEP REVERIE INTO WHICH HE HAD FALLEN.
GOOD LORD! I'VE BEEN RAMBLING ON, MUST BE A SIGN OF MY AGE.
AND THE CHATEAU NOIRE, DID YOU EVER DISCOVER ITS SECRET, SIR ARTHUR?

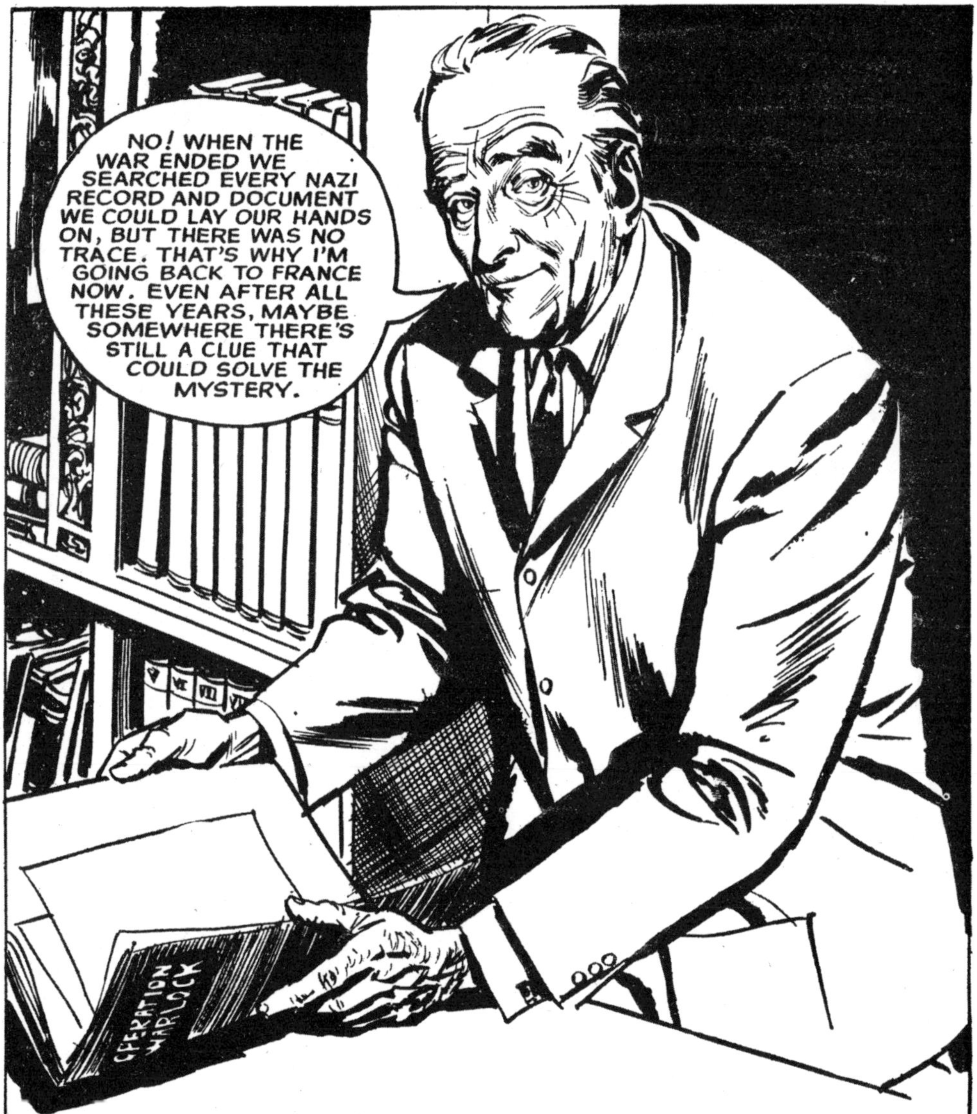
NO! WHEN THE WAR ENDED WE SEARCHED EVERY NAZI RECORD AND DOCUMENT WE COULD LAY OUR HANDS ON, BUT THERE WAS NO TRACE. THAT'S WHY I'M GOING BACK TO FRANCE NOW. EVEN AFTER ALL THESE YEARS, MAYBE SOMEWHERE THERE'S STILL A CLUE THAT COULD SOLVE THE MYSTERY.
OPERATION WARLOCK
BUT IT IS DOUBTFUL IF SIR ARTHUR HUNTLEY WILL EVER BE ABLE TO CLOSE HIS FILE. THE MOUNTAINS GUARD THEIR SECRETS WELL.

DIGGERS DEFIANT

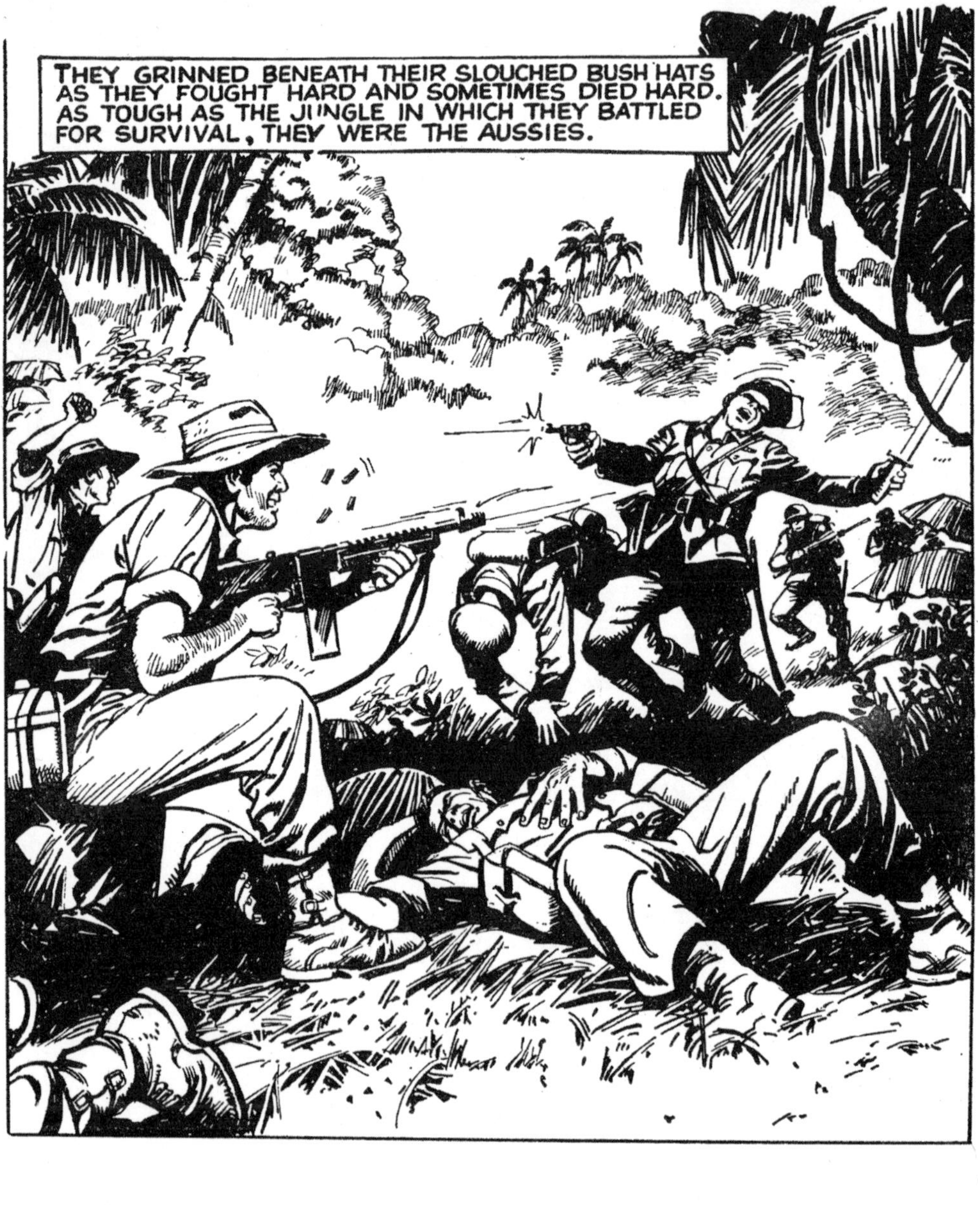
THEY GRINNED BENEATH THEIR SLOUCHED BUSH HATS AS THEY FOUGHT HARD AND SOMETIMES DIED HARD. AS TOUGH AS THE JUNGLE IN WHICH THEY BATTLED FOR SURVIVAL, THEY WERE THE AUSSIES.

Chapter 1. Fight for Freedom

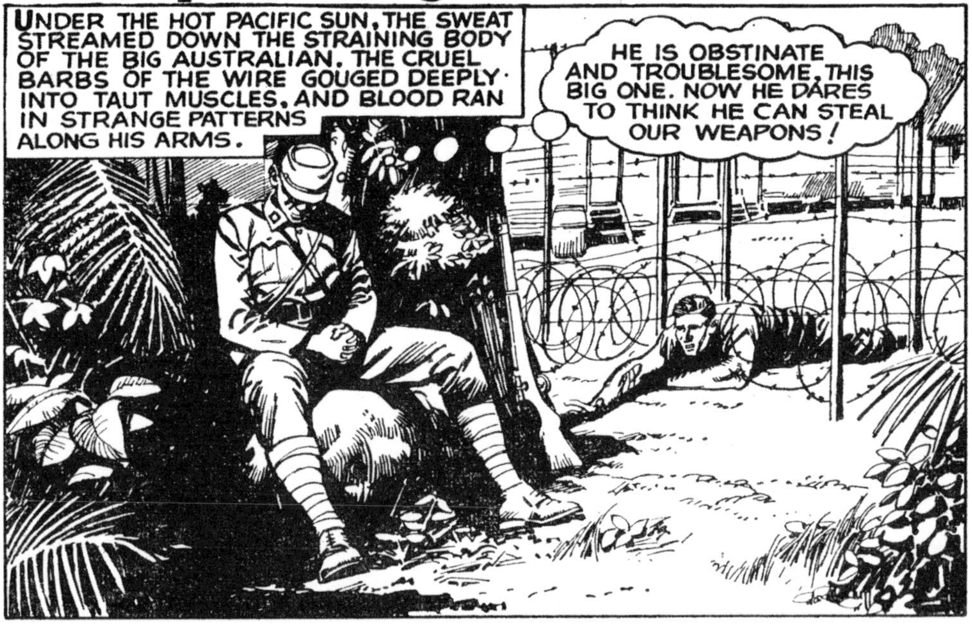
UNDER THE HOT PACIFIC SUN, THE SWEAT STREAMED DOWN THE STRAINING BODY OF THE BIG AUSTRALIAN. THE CRUEL BARBS OF THE WIRE GOUGED DEEPLY INTO TAUT MUSCLES, AND BLOOD RAN IN STRANGE PATTERNS ALONG HIS ARMS.
HE IS OBSTINATE AND TROUBLESOME, THIS BIG ONE. NOW HE DARES TO THINK HE CAN STEAL OUR WEAPONS!

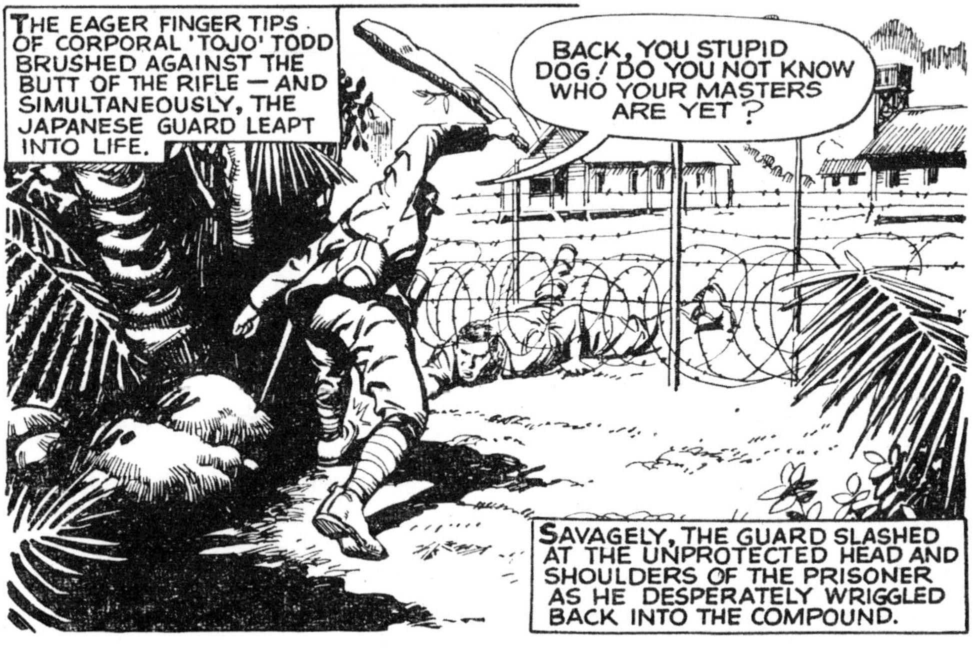
THE EAGER FINGER TIPS OF CORPORAL 'TOJO' TODD BRUSHED AGAINST THE BUTT OF THE RIFLE — AND SIMULTANEOUSLY, THE JAPANESE GUARD LEAPT INTO LIFE.
BACK, YOU STUPID DOG! DO YOU NOT KNOW WHO YOUR MASTERS ARE YET?
SAVAGELY, THE GUARD SLASHED AT THE UNPROTECTED HEAD AND SHOULDERS OF THE PRISONER AS HE DESPERATELY WRIGGLED BACK INTO THE COMPOUND.

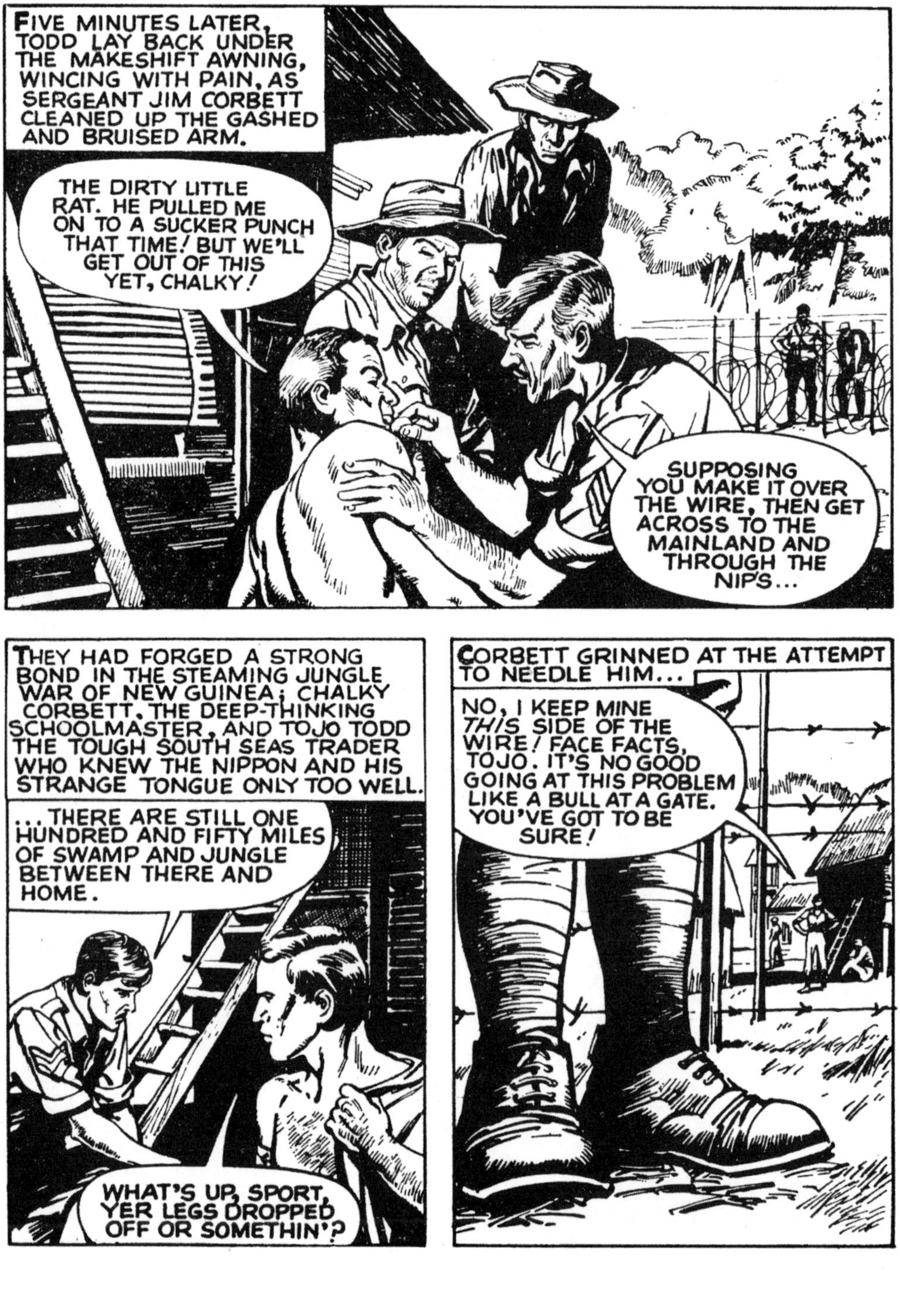
FIVE MINUTES LATER, TODD LAY BACK UNDER THE MAKESHIFT AWNING, WINCING WITH PAIN, AS SERGEANT JIM CORBETT CLEANED UP THE GASHED AND BRUISED ARM.
THE DIRTY LITTLE RAT. HE PULLED ME ON TO A SUCKER PUNCH THAT TIME! BUT WE'LL GET OUT OF THIS YET, CHALKY!
SUPPOSING YOU MAKE IT OVER THE WIRE, THEN GET ACROSS TO THE MAINLAND AND THROUGH THE NIP'S...
THEY HAD FORGED A STRONG BOND IN THE STEAMING JUNGLE WAR OF NEW GUINEA; CHALKY CORBETT, THE DEEP-THINKING SCHOOLMASTER, AND TOJO TODD THE TOUGH SOUTH SEAS TRADER WHO KNEW THE NIPPON AND HIS STRANGE TONGUE ONLY TOO WELL.
...THERE ARE STILL ONE HUNDRED AND FIFTY MILES OF SWAMP AND JUNGLE BETWEEN THERE AND HOME.
WHAT'S UP, SPORT, YER LEGS DROPPED OFF OR SOMETHIN'?
CORBETT GRINNED AT THE ATTEMPT TO NEEDLE HIM...
NO, I KEEP MINE *THIS* SIDE OF THE WIRE! FACE FACTS, TOJO. IT'S NO GOOD GOING AT THIS PROBLEM LIKE A BULL AT A GATE. YOU'VE GOT TO BE SURE!

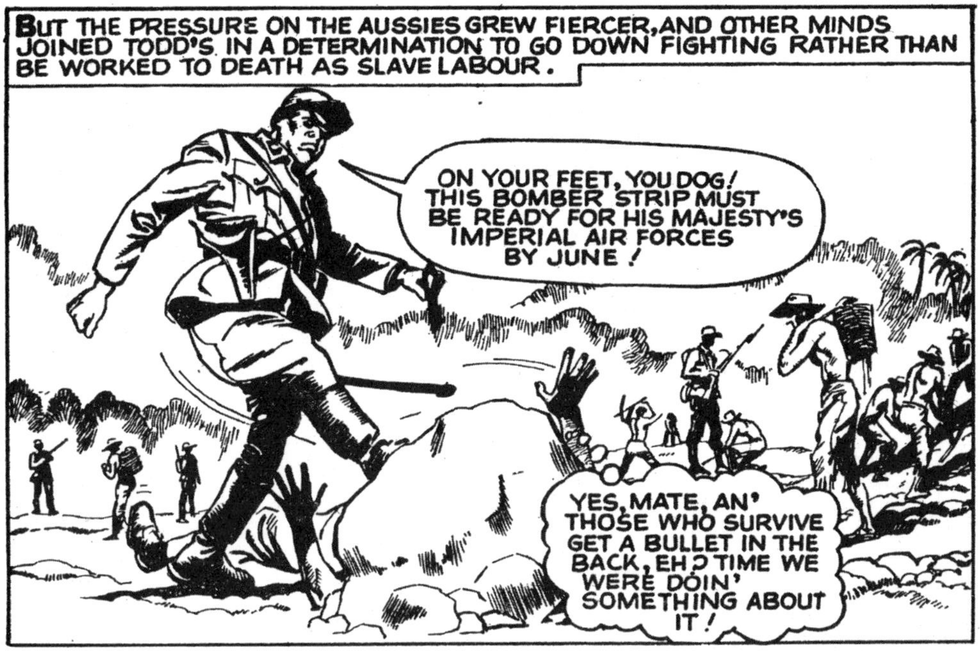
BUT THE PRESSURE ON THE AUSSIES GREW FIERCER, AND OTHER MINDS JOINED TODD'S IN A DETERMINATION TO GO DOWN FIGHTING RATHER THAN BE WORKED TO DEATH AS SLAVE LABOUR.
ON YOUR FEET, YOU DOG! THIS BOMBER STRIP MUST BE READY FOR HIS MAJESTY'S IMPERIAL AIR FORCES BY JUNE!
YES, MATE, AN' THOSE WHO SURVIVE GET A BULLET IN THE BACK, EH? TIME WE WERE DOIN' SOMETHING ABOUT IT!

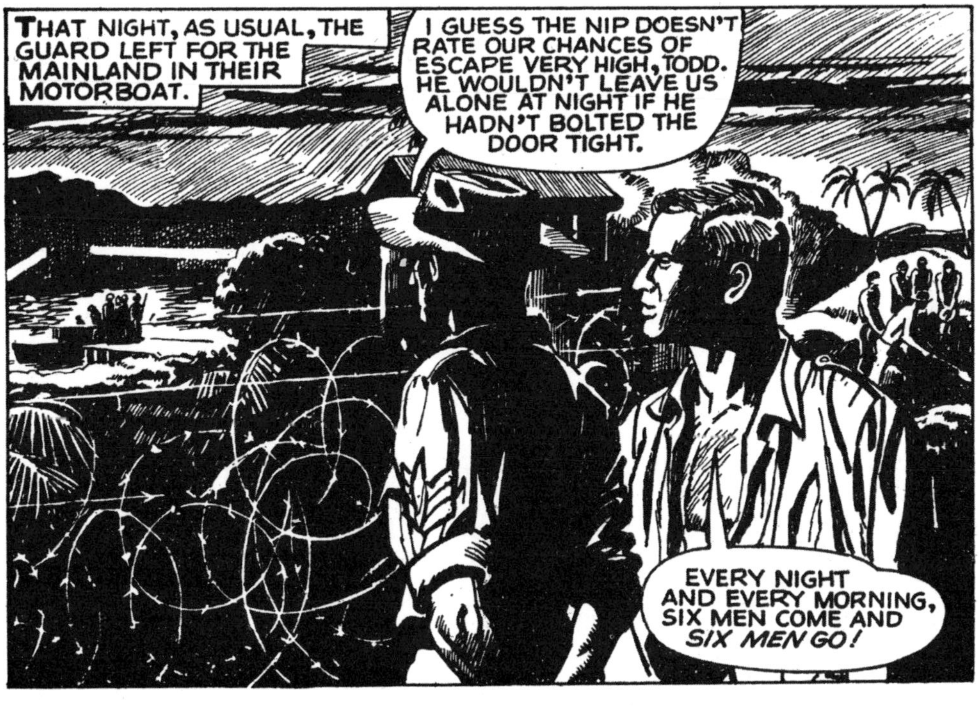
THAT NIGHT, AS USUAL, THE GUARD LEFT FOR THE MAINLAND IN THEIR MOTORBOAT.
I GUESS THE NIP DOESN'T RATE OUR CHANCES OF ESCAPE VERY HIGH, TODD. HE WOULDN'T LEAVE US ALONE AT NIGHT IF HE HADN'T BOLTED THE DOOR TIGHT.
EVERY NIGHT AND EVERY MORNING, SIX MEN COME AND *SIX MEN GO!*

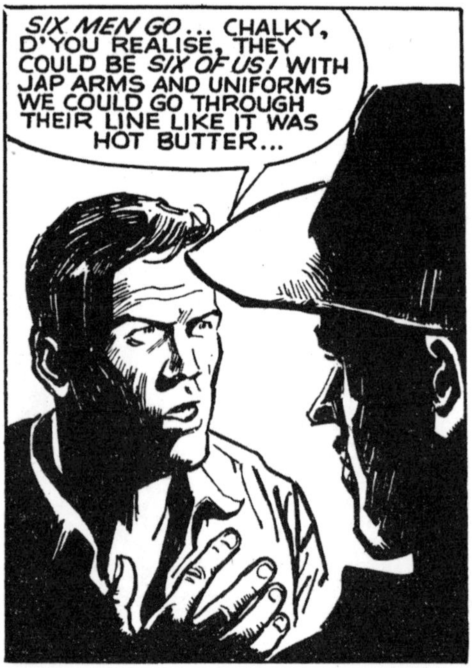
SIX MEN GO... CHALKY, D'YOU REALISE, THEY COULD BE SIX OF US! WITH JAP ARMS AND UNIFORMS WE COULD GO THROUGH THEIR LINE LIKE IT WAS HOT BUTTER...

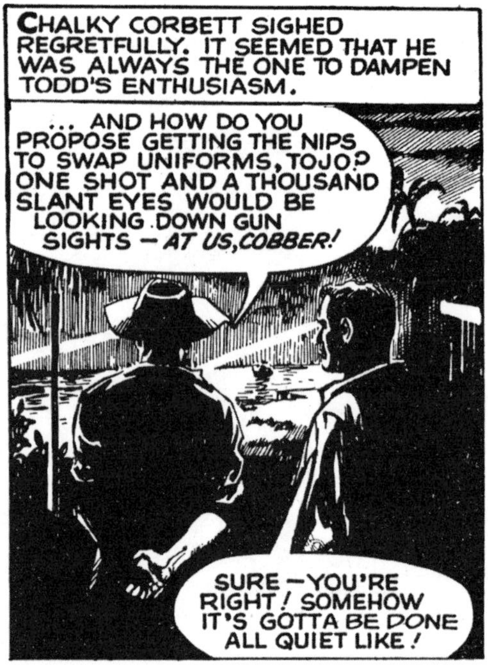
CHALKY CORBETT SIGHED REGRETFULLY. IT SEEMED THAT HE WAS ALWAYS THE ONE TO DAMPEN TODD'S ENTHUSIASM.
... AND HOW DO YOU PROPOSE GETTING THE NIPS TO SWAP UNIFORMS, TOJO? ONE SHOT AND A THOUSAND SLANT EYES WOULD BE LOOKING DOWN GUN SIGHTS — AT US, COBBER!
SURE — YOU'RE RIGHT! SOMEHOW IT'S GOTTA BE DONE ALL QUIET LIKE!

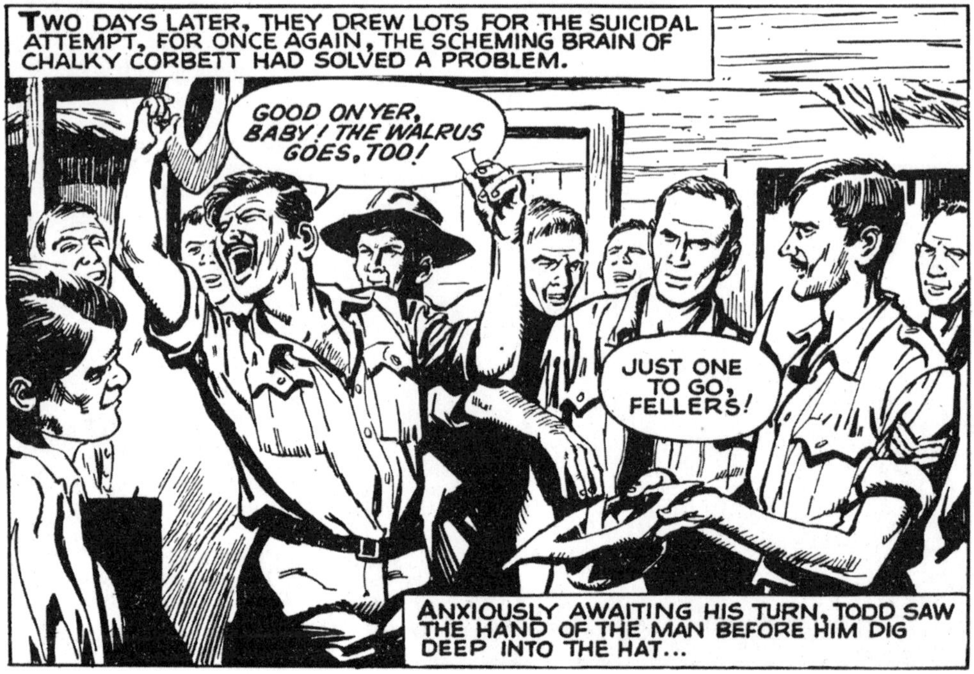
TWO DAYS LATER, THEY DREW LOTS FOR THE SUICIDAL ATTEMPT, FOR ONCE AGAIN, THE SCHEMING BRAIN OF CHALKY CORBETT HAD SOLVED A PROBLEM.
GOOD ONYER, BABY! THE WALRUS GOES, TOO!
JUST ONE TO GO, FELLERS!
ANXIOUSLY AWAITING HIS TURN, TODD SAW THE HAND OF THE MAN BEFORE HIM DIG DEEP INTO THE HAT...

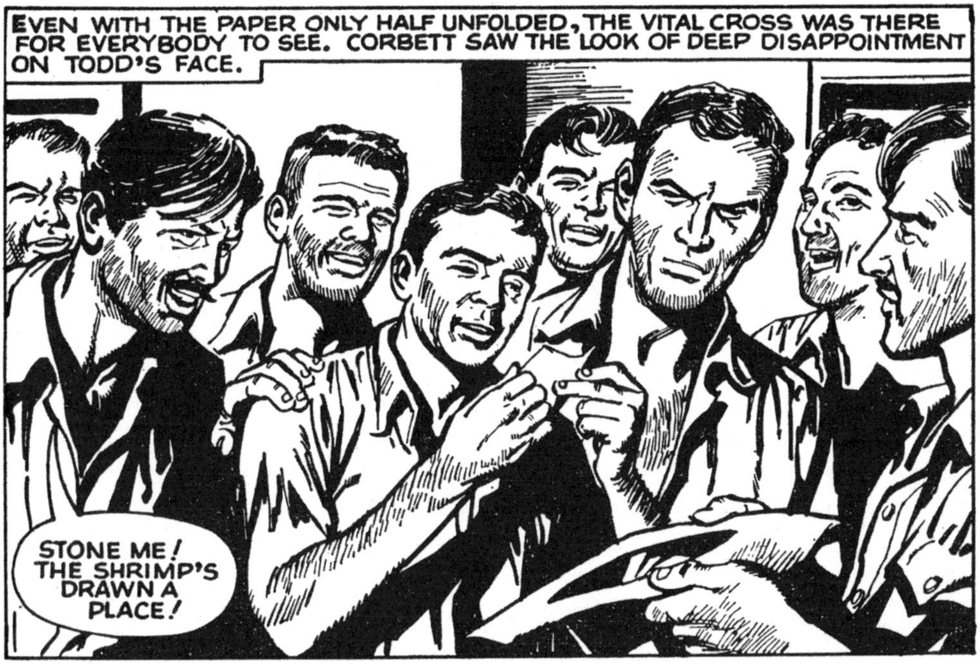
EVEN WITH THE PAPER ONLY HALF UNFOLDED, THE VITAL CROSS WAS THERE FOR EVERYBODY TO SEE. CORBETT SAW THE LOOK OF DEEP DISAPPOINTMENT ON TODD'S FACE.
STONE ME! THE SHRIMP'S DRAWN A PLACE!

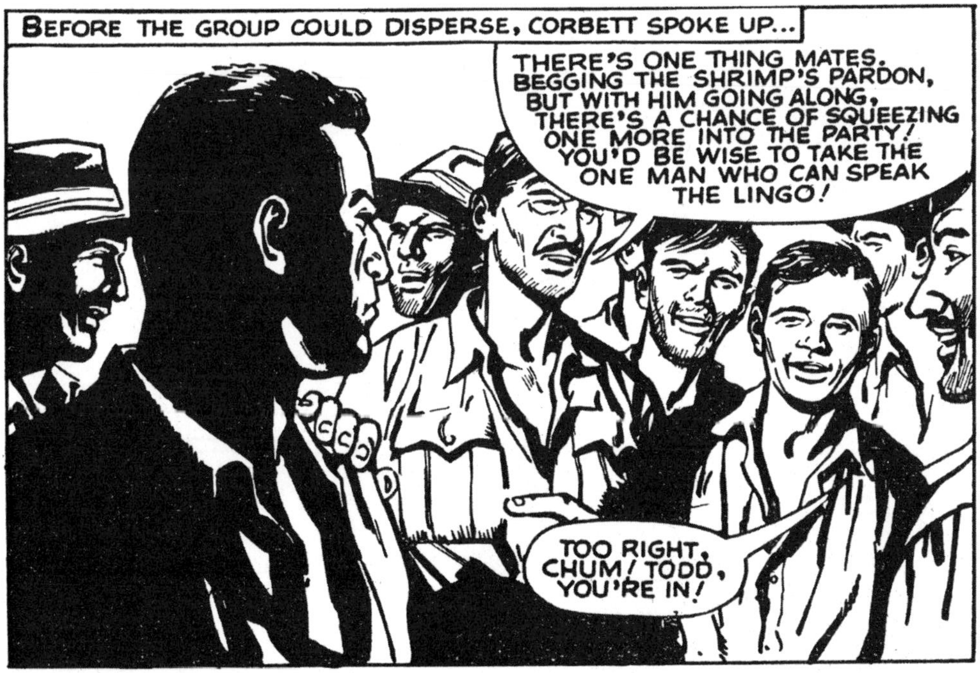
BEFORE THE GROUP COULD DISPERSE, CORBETT SPOKE UP...
THERE'S ONE THING MATES. BEGGING THE SHRIMP'S PARDON, BUT WITH HIM GOING ALONG, THERE'S A CHANCE OF SQUEEZING ONE MORE INTO THE PARTY! YOU'D BE WISE TO TAKE THE ONE MAN WHO CAN SPEAK THE LINGO!
TOO RIGHT, CHUM! TODD, YOU'RE IN!

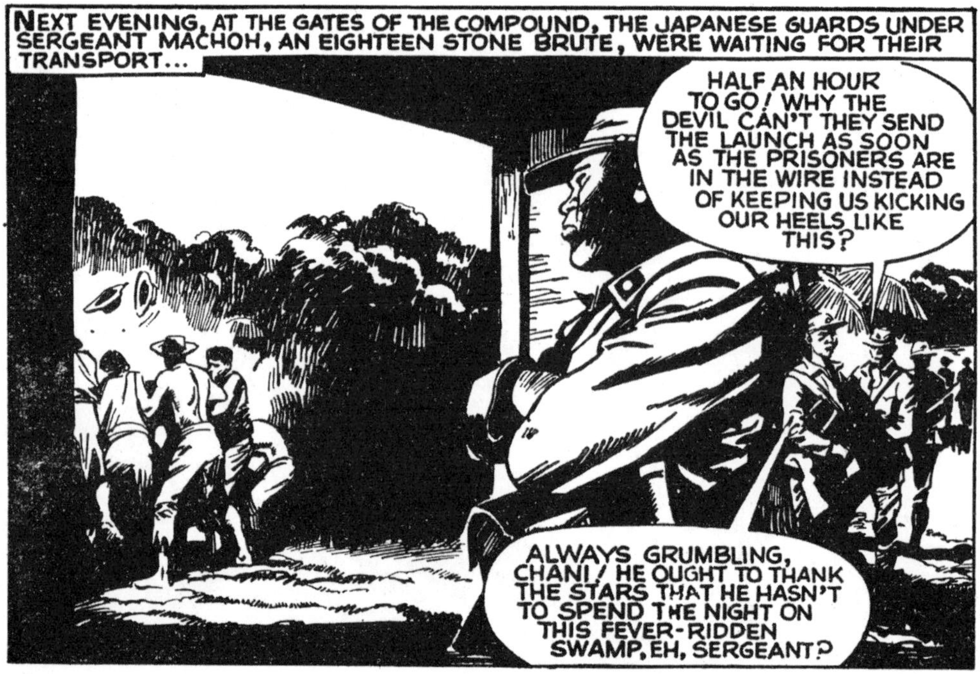
NEXT EVENING, AT THE GATES OF THE COMPOUND, THE JAPANESE GUARDS UNDER SERGEANT MACHOH, AN EIGHTEEN STONE BRUTE, WERE WAITING FOR THEIR TRANSPORT...
HALF AN HOUR TO GO! WHY THE DEVIL CAN'T THEY SEND THE LAUNCH AS SOON AS THE PRISONERS ARE IN THE WIRE INSTEAD OF KEEPING US KICKING OUR HEELS LIKE THIS?
ALWAYS GRUMBLING, CHANI! HE OUGHT TO THANK THE STARS THAT HE HASN'T TO SPEND THE NIGHT ON THIS FEVER-RIDDEN SWAMP, EH, SERGEANT?

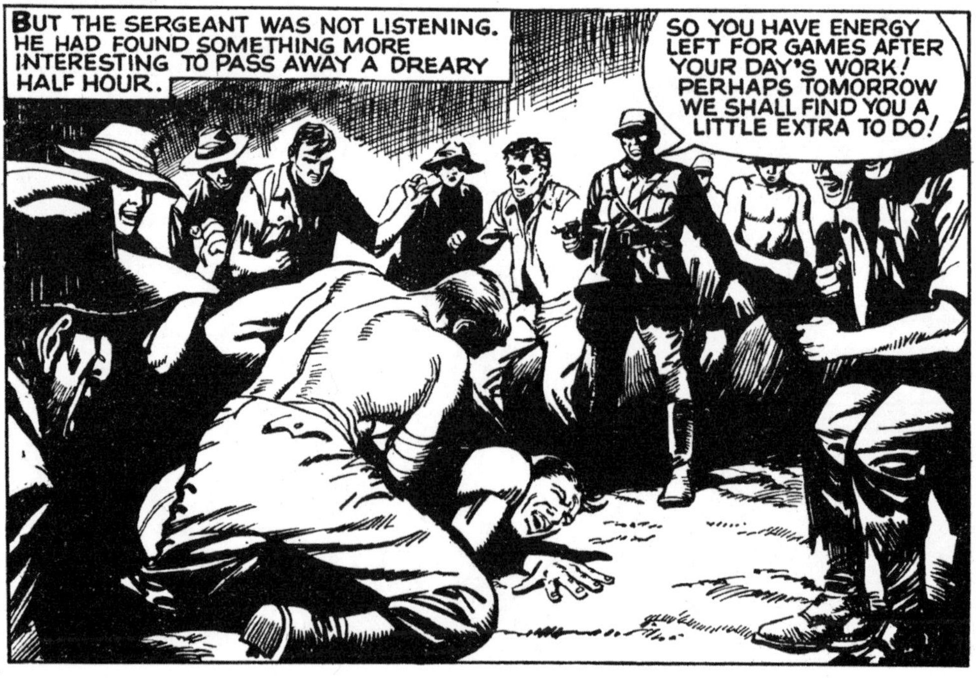
BUT THE SERGEANT WAS NOT LISTENING. HE HAD FOUND SOMETHING MORE INTERESTING TO PASS AWAY A DREARY HALF HOUR.
SO YOU HAVE ENERGY LEFT FOR GAMES AFTER YOUR DAY'S WORK! PERHAPS TOMORROW WE SHALL FIND YOU A LITTLE EXTRA TO DO!

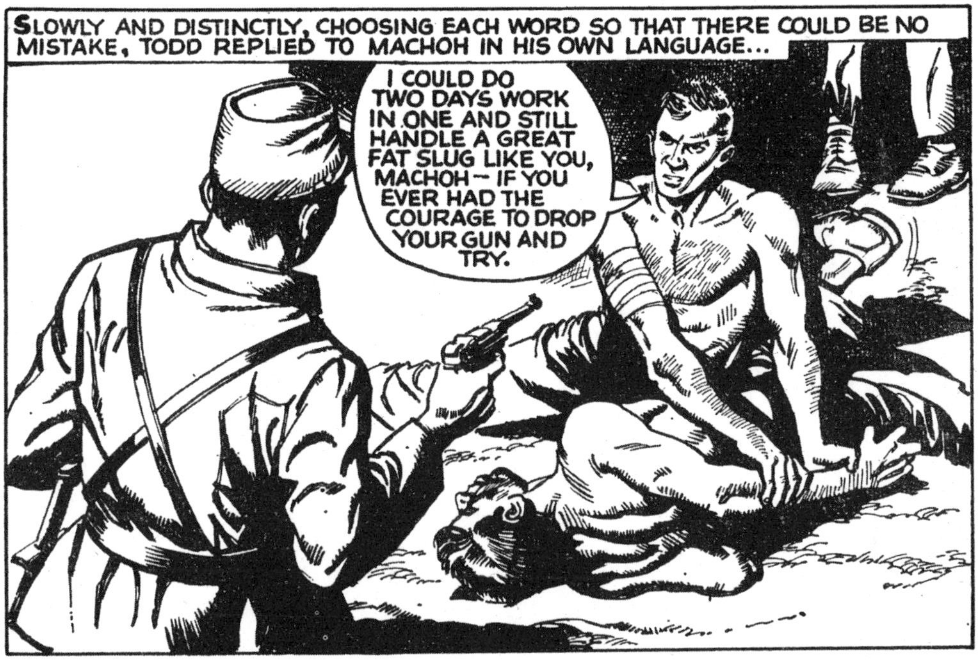
SLOWLY AND DISTINCTLY, CHOOSING EACH WORD SO THAT THERE COULD BE NO MISTAKE, TODD REPLIED TO MACHOH IN HIS OWN LANGUAGE...
I COULD DO TWO DAYS WORK IN ONE AND STILL HANDLE A GREAT FAT SLUG LIKE YOU, MACHOH — IF YOU EVER HAD THE COURAGE TO DROP YOUR GUN AND TRY.

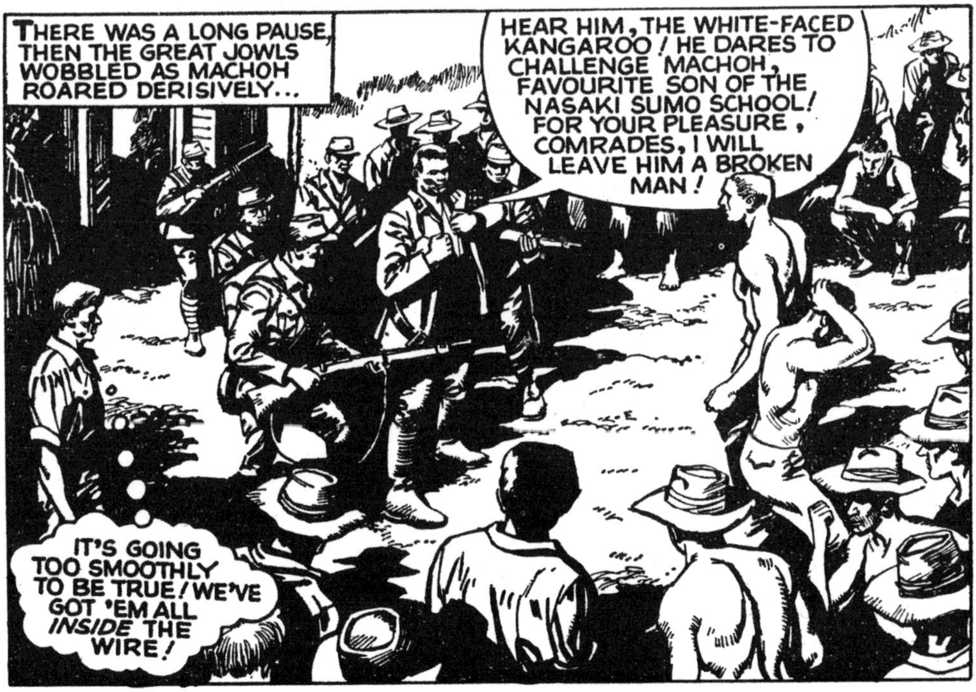
THERE WAS A LONG PAUSE, THEN THE GREAT JOWLS WOBBLED AS MACHOH ROARED DERISIVELY...
HEAR HIM, THE WHITE-FACED KANGAROO! HE DARES TO CHALLENGE MACHOH, FAVOURITE SON OF THE NASAKI SUMO SCHOOL! FOR YOUR PLEASURE, COMRADES, I WILL LEAVE HIM A BROKEN MAN!
IT'S GOING TOO SMOOTHLY TO BE TRUE! WE'VE GOT 'EM ALL *INSIDE* THE WIRE!

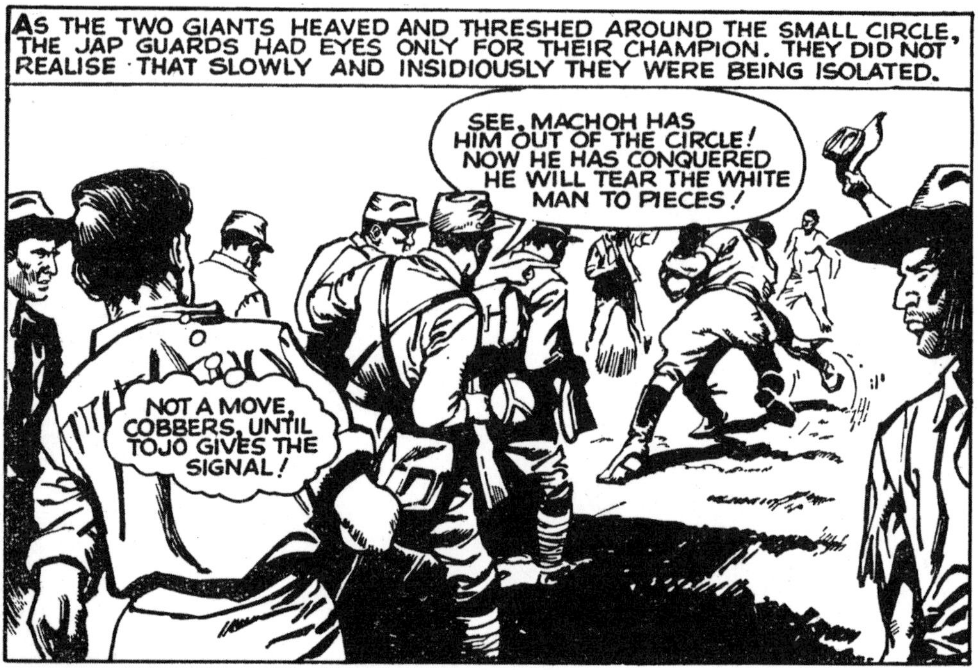
AS THE TWO GIANTS HEAVED AND THRESHED AROUND THE SMALL CIRCLE, THE JAP GUARDS HAD EYES ONLY FOR THEIR CHAMPION. THEY DID NOT REALISE THAT SLOWLY AND INSIDIOUSLY THEY WERE BEING ISOLATED.
SEE, MACHOH HAS HIM OUT OF THE CIRCLE! NOW HE HAS CONQUERED HE WILL TEAR THE WHITE MAN TO PIECES!
NOT A MOVE, COBBERS, UNTIL TOJO GIVES THE SIGNAL!

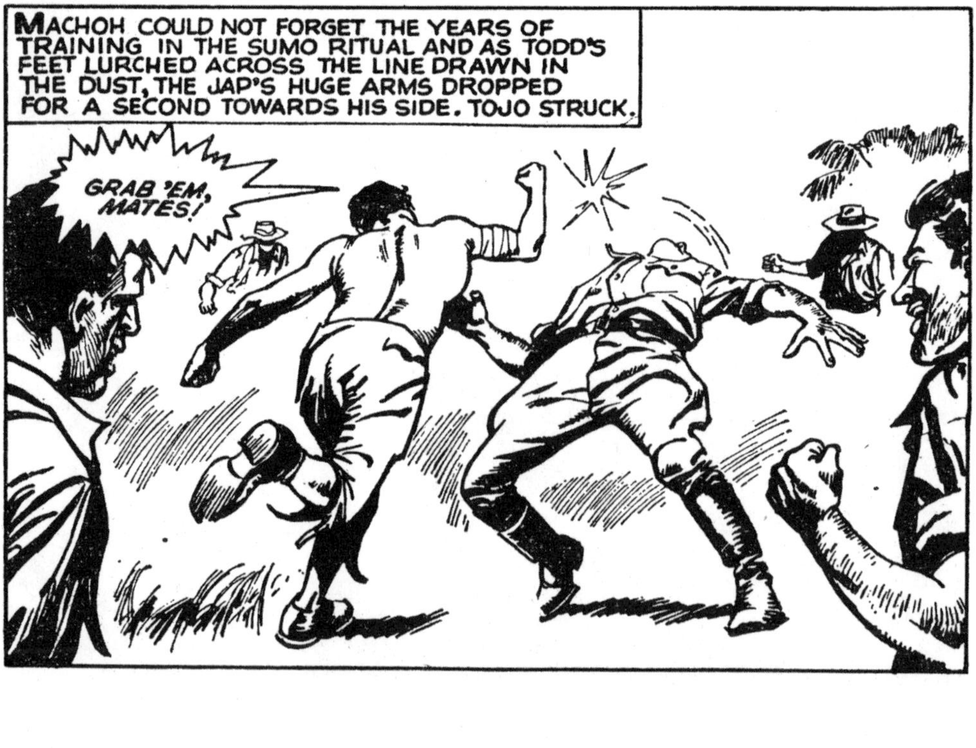
MACHOH COULD NOT FORGET THE YEARS OF TRAINING IN THE SUMO RITUAL AND AS TODD'S FEET LURCHED ACROSS THE LINE DRAWN IN THE DUST, THE JAP'S HUGE ARMS DROPPED FOR A SECOND TOWARDS HIS SIDE. TOJO STRUCK.
GRAB 'EM, MATES!

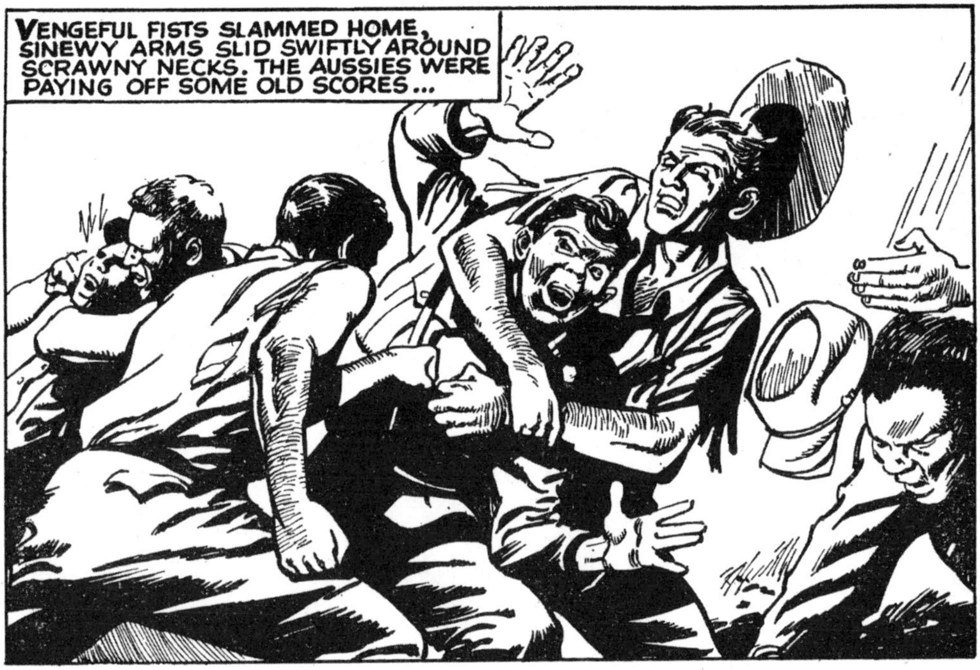
VENGEFUL FISTS SLAMMED HOME, SINEWY ARMS SLID SWIFTLY AROUND SCRAWNY NECKS. THE AUSSIES WERE PAYING OFF SOME OLD SCORES...

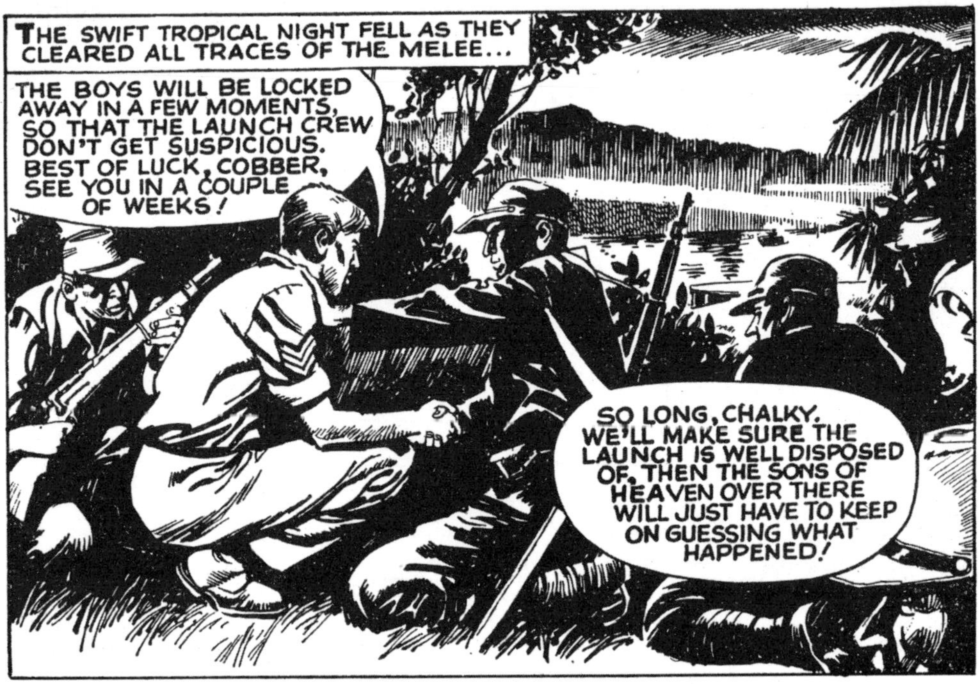
THE SWIFT TROPICAL NIGHT FELL AS THEY CLEARED ALL TRACES OF THE MELEE...
THE BOYS WILL BE LOCKED AWAY IN A FEW MOMENTS, SO THAT THE LAUNCH CREW DON'T GET SUSPICIOUS. BEST OF LUCK, COBBER, SEE YOU IN A COUPLE OF WEEKS!
SO LONG, CHALKY. WE'LL MAKE SURE THE LAUNCH IS WELL DISPOSED OF, THEN THE SONS OF HEAVEN OVER THERE WILL JUST HAVE TO KEEP ON GUESSING WHAT HAPPENED!

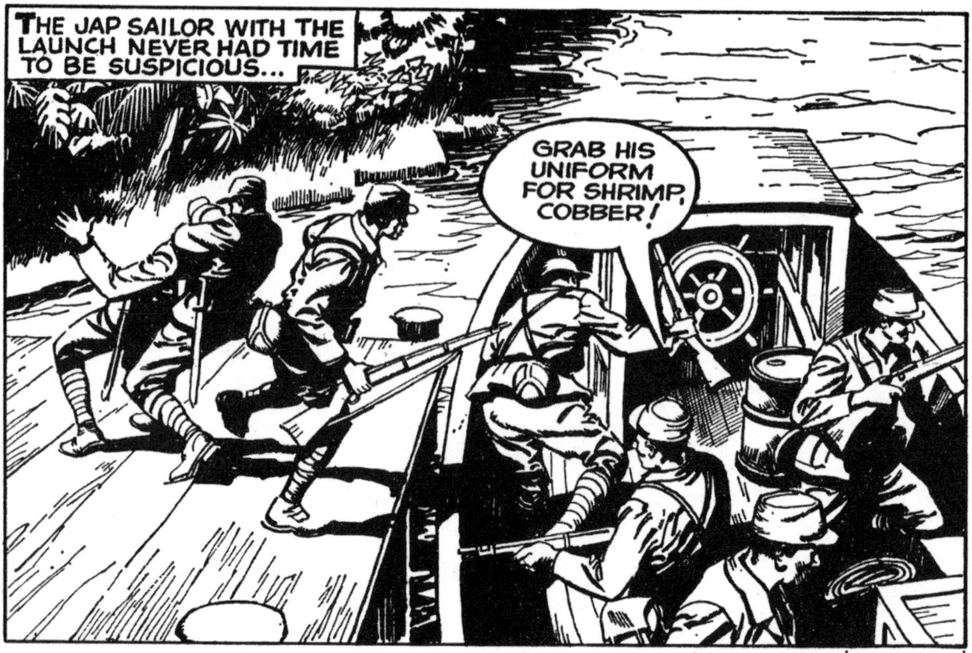
THE JAP SAILOR WITH THE LAUNCH NEVER HAD TIME TO BE SUSPICIOUS...
GRAB HIS UNIFORM FOR SHRIMP, COBBER!

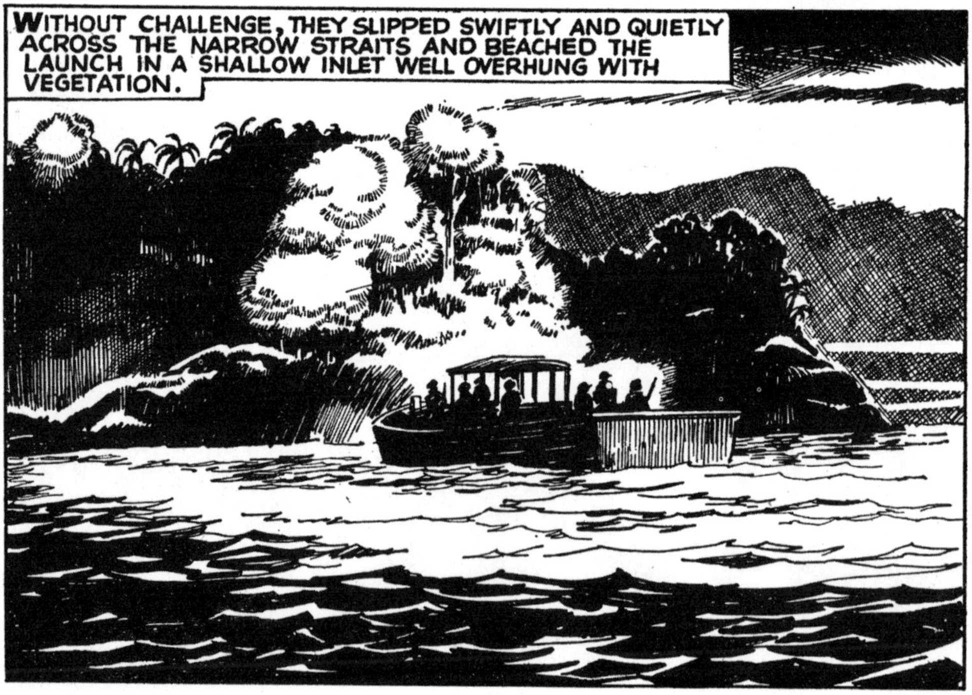
WITHOUT CHALLENGE, THEY SLIPPED SWIFTLY AND QUIETLY ACROSS THE NARROW STRAITS AND BEACHED THE LAUNCH IN A SHALLOW INLET WELL OVERHUNG WITH VEGETATION.

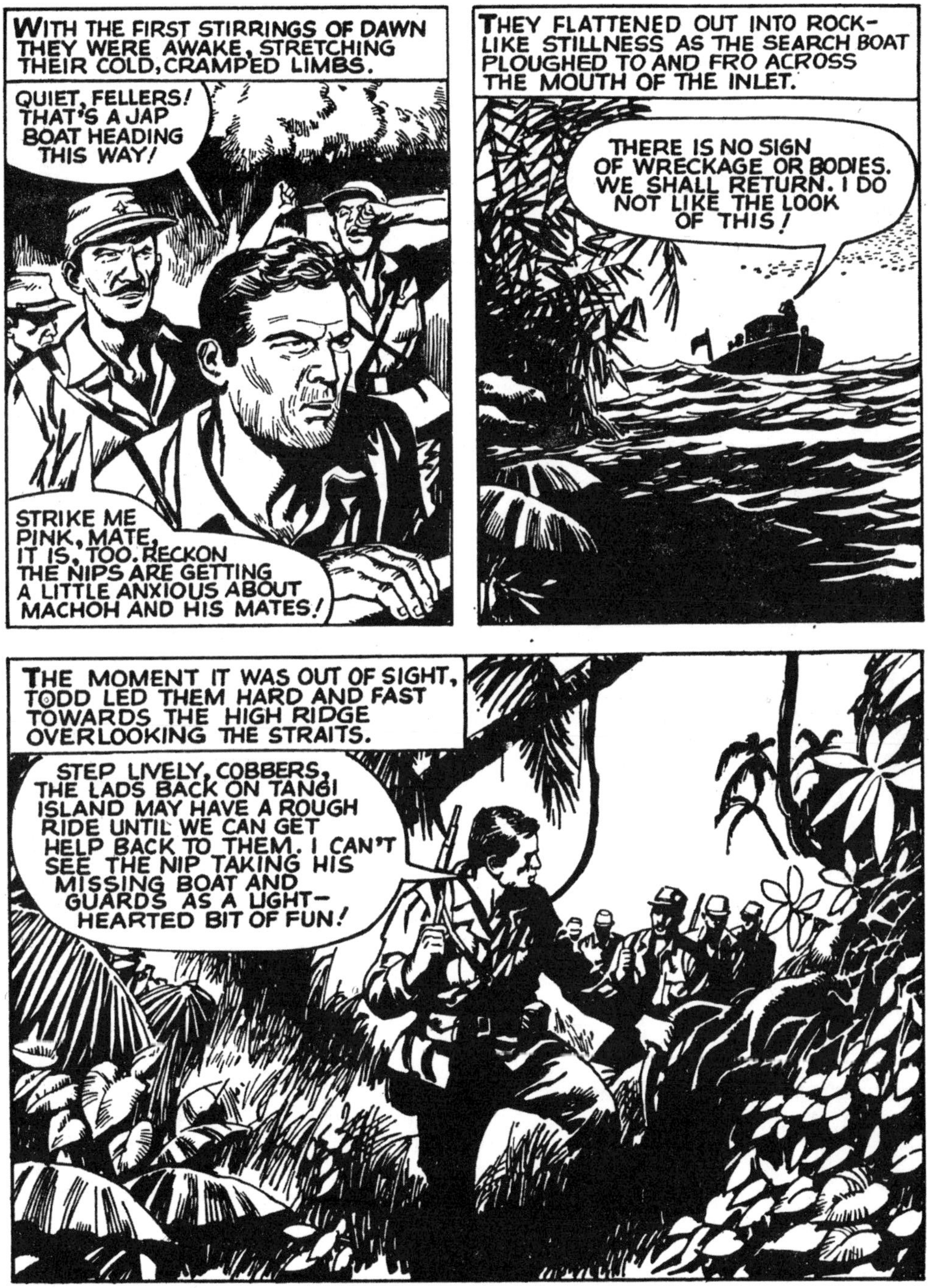
WITH THE FIRST STIRRINGS OF DAWN THEY WERE AWAKE, STRETCHING THEIR COLD, CRAMPED LIMBS.
QUIET, FELLERS! THAT'S A JAP BOAT HEADING THIS WAY!
STRIKE ME PINK, MATE, IT IS, TOO. RECKON THE NIPS ARE GETTING A LITTLE ANXIOUS ABOUT MACHOH AND HIS MATES!
THEY FLATTENED OUT INTO ROCK-LIKE STILLNESS AS THE SEARCH BOAT PLOUGHED TO AND FRO ACROSS THE MOUTH OF THE INLET.
THERE IS NO SIGN OF WRECKAGE OR BODIES. WE SHALL RETURN. I DO NOT LIKE THE LOOK OF THIS!
THE MOMENT IT WAS OUT OF SIGHT, TODD LED THEM HARD AND FAST TOWARDS THE HIGH RIDGE OVERLOOKING THE STRAITS.
STEP LIVELY, COBBERS, THE LADS BACK ON TANGI ISLAND MAY HAVE A ROUGH RIDE UNTIL WE CAN GET HELP BACK TO THEM. I CAN'T SEE THE NIP TAKING HIS MISSING BOAT AND GUARDS AS A LIGHT-HEARTED BIT OF FUN!

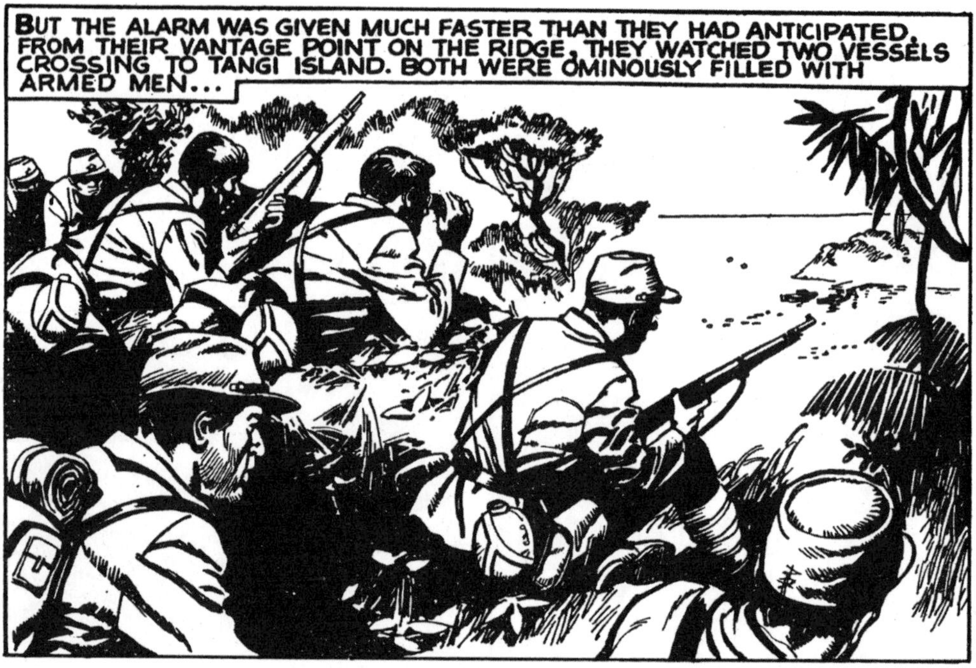
BUT THE ALARM WAS GIVEN MUCH FASTER THAN THEY HAD ANTICIPATED. FROM THEIR VANTAGE POINT ON THE RIDGE, THEY WATCHED TWO VESSELS CROSSING TO TANGI ISLAND. BOTH WERE OMINOUSLY FILLED WITH ARMED MEN...

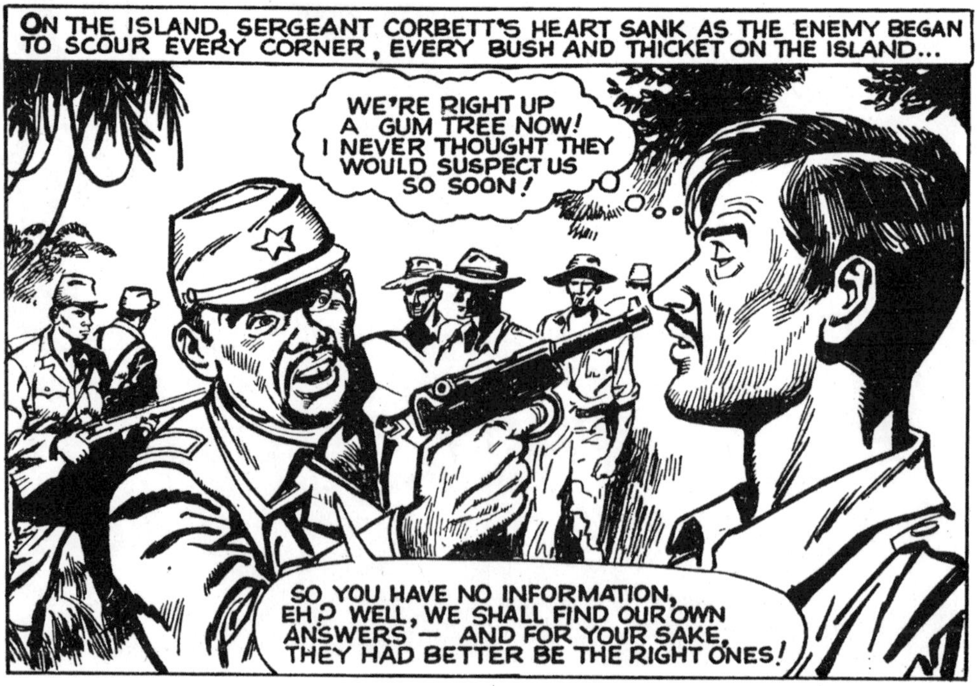
ON THE ISLAND, SERGEANT CORBETT'S HEART SANK AS THE ENEMY BEGAN TO SCOUR EVERY CORNER, EVERY BUSH AND THICKET ON THE ISLAND...
WE'RE RIGHT UP A GUM TREE NOW! I NEVER THOUGHT THEY WOULD SUSPECT US SO SOON!
SO YOU HAVE NO INFORMATION, EH? WELL, WE SHALL FIND OUR OWN ANSWERS — AND FOR YOUR SAKE, THEY HAD BETTER BE THE RIGHT ONES!

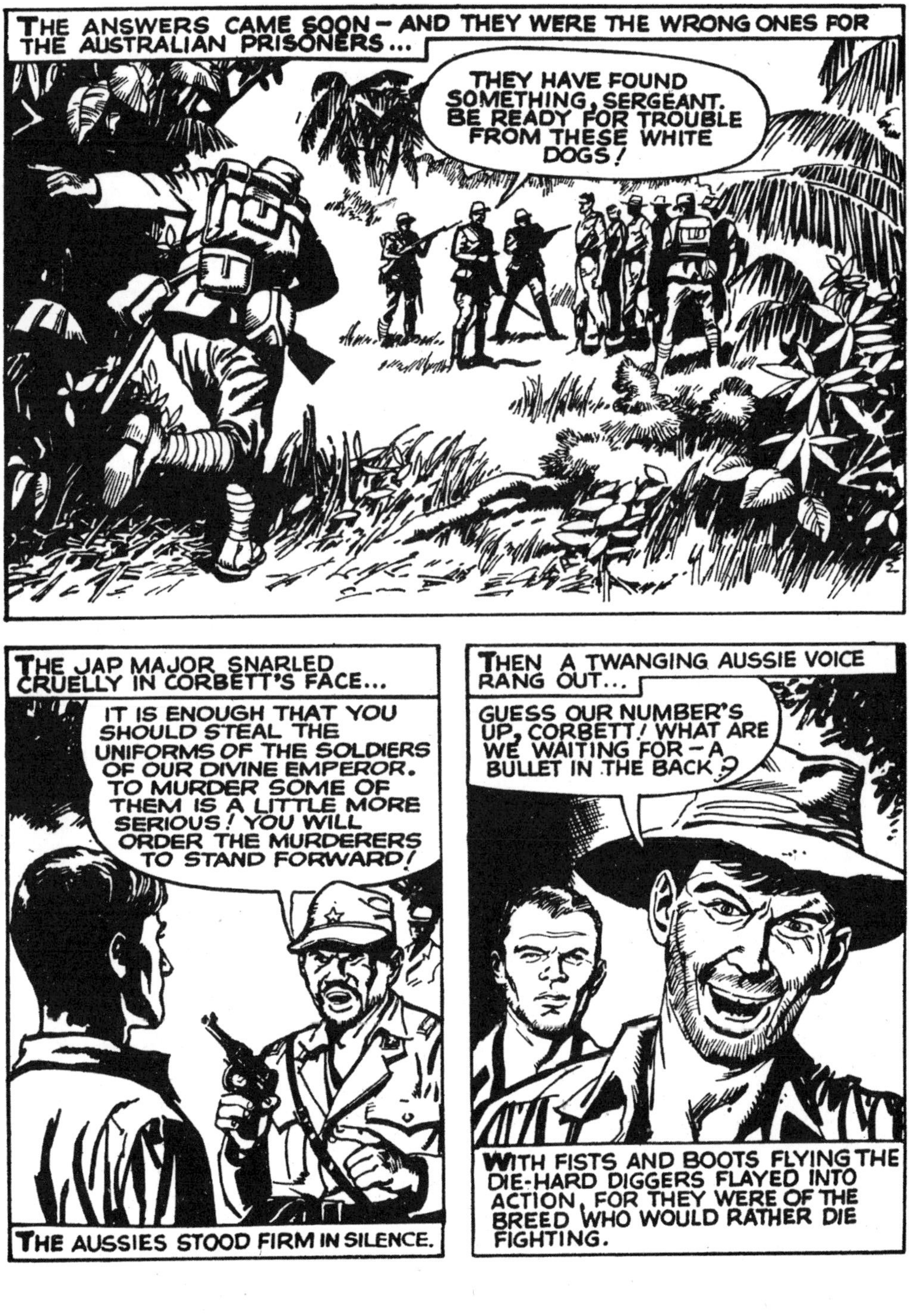
THE ANSWERS CAME SOON — AND THEY WERE THE WRONG ONES FOR THE AUSTRALIAN PRISONERS...
THEY HAVE FOUND SOMETHING, SERGEANT. BE READY FOR TROUBLE FROM THESE WHITE DOGS!
THE JAP MAJOR SNARLED CRUELLY IN CORBETT'S FACE...
IT IS ENOUGH THAT YOU SHOULD STEAL THE UNIFORMS OF THE SOLDIERS OF OUR DIVINE EMPEROR. TO MURDER SOME OF THEM IS A LITTLE MORE SERIOUS! YOU WILL ORDER THE MURDERERS TO STAND FORWARD!
THE AUSSIES STOOD FIRM IN SILENCE.
THEN A TWANGING AUSSIE VOICE RANG OUT...
GUESS OUR NUMBER'S UP, CORBETT! WHAT ARE WE WAITING FOR — A BULLET IN THE BACK?
WITH FISTS AND BOOTS FLYING THE DIE-HARD DIGGERS FLAYED INTO ACTION, FOR THEY WERE OF THE BREED WHO WOULD RATHER DIE FIGHTING.

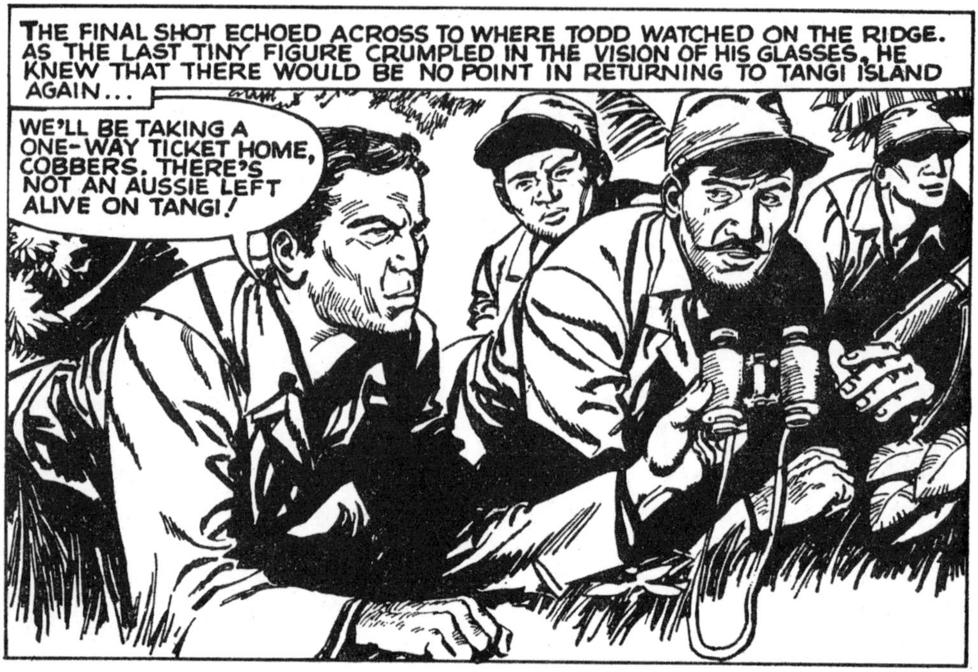
THE FINAL SHOT ECHOED ACROSS TO WHERE TODD WATCHED ON THE RIDGE. AS THE LAST TINY FIGURE CRUMPLED IN THE VISION OF HIS GLASSES, HE KNEW THAT THERE WOULD BE NO POINT IN RETURNING TO TANGI ISLAND AGAIN...
WE'LL BE TAKING A ONE-WAY TICKET HOME, COBBERS. THERE'S NOT AN AUSSIE LEFT ALIVE ON TANGI!

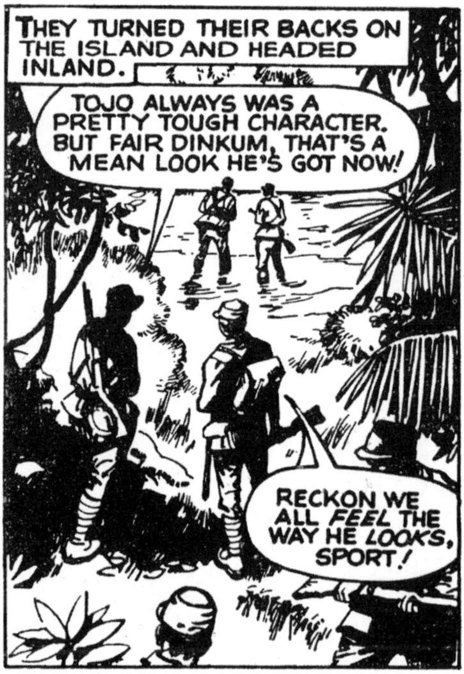
THEY TURNED THEIR BACKS ON THE ISLAND AND HEADED INLAND.
TOJO ALWAYS WAS A PRETTY TOUGH CHARACTER. BUT FAIR DINKUM, THAT'S A MEAN LOOK HE'S GOT NOW!
RECKON WE ALL FEEL THE WAY HE LOOKS, SPORT!

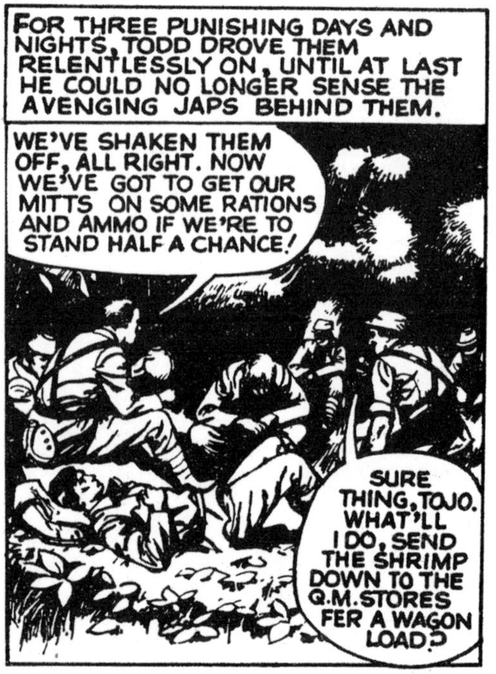
FOR THREE PUNISHING DAYS AND NIGHTS, TODD DROVE THEM RELENTLESSLY ON, UNTIL AT LAST HE COULD NO LONGER SENSE THE AVENGING JAPS BEHIND THEM.
WE'VE SHAKEN THEM OFF, ALL RIGHT. NOW WE'VE GOT TO GET OUR MITTS ON SOME RATIONS AND AMMO IF WE'RE TO STAND HALF A CHANCE!
SURE THING, TOJO. WHAT'LL I DO, SEND THE SHRIMP DOWN TO THE Q.M. STORES FER A WAGON LOAD?

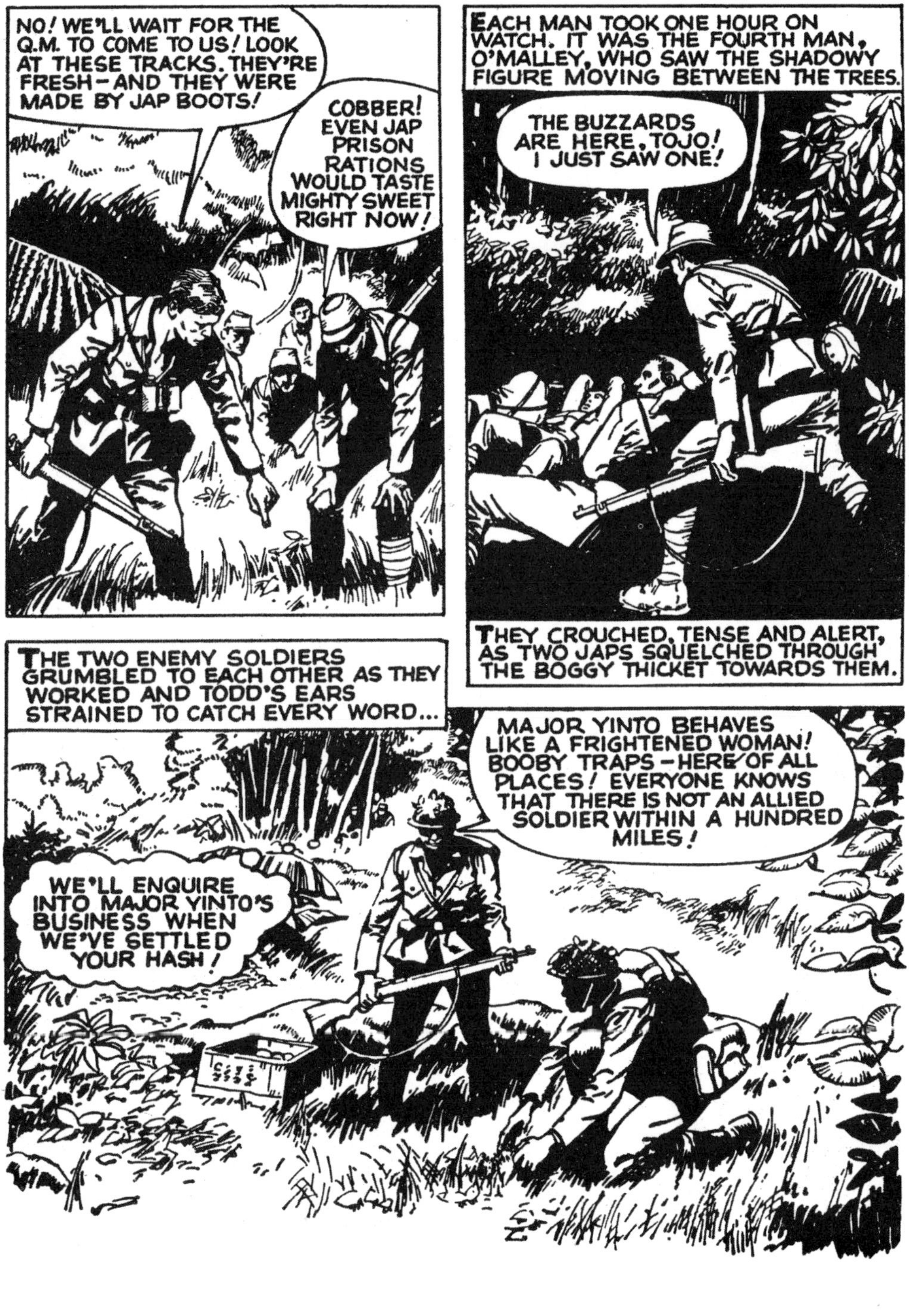
NO! WE'LL WAIT FOR THE Q.M. TO COME TO US! LOOK AT THESE TRACKS. THEY'RE FRESH—AND THEY WERE MADE BY JAP BOOTS!
COBBER! EVEN JAP PRISON RATIONS WOULD TASTE MIGHTY SWEET RIGHT NOW!
EACH MAN TOOK ONE HOUR ON WATCH. IT WAS THE FOURTH MAN, O'MALLEY, WHO SAW THE SHADOWY FIGURE MOVING BETWEEN THE TREES.
THE BUZZARDS ARE HERE, TOJO! I JUST SAW ONE!
THEY CROUCHED, TENSE AND ALERT, AS TWO JAPS SQUELCHED THROUGH THE BOGGY THICKET TOWARDS THEM.
THE TWO ENEMY SOLDIERS GRUMBLED TO EACH OTHER AS THEY WORKED AND TODD'S EARS STRAINED TO CATCH EVERY WORD...
MAJOR YINTO BEHAVES LIKE A FRIGHTENED WOMAN! BOOBY TRAPS—HERE OF ALL PLACES! EVERYONE KNOWS THAT THERE IS NOT AN ALLIED SOLDIER WITHIN A HUNDRED MILES!
WE'LL ENQUIRE INTO MAJOR YINTO'S BUSINESS WHEN WE'VE SETTLED YOUR HASH!

AN HOUR LATER, THE AUSSIES CROUCHED AT THE EDGE OF THE JAP CAMP, POISED READY FOR THE SIGNAL FROM TODD.

NOW, LISTEN! WALRUS AN' ME PAY A SOCIAL CALL ON THE MAJOR. THE SHRIMP AND O'MALLEY FORAGE FOR GRUB AND AMMO. THE REST KEEP WATCH FOR THE BOOBY SQUADS RETURNING!

OKAY, TOJO!

MAJOR YINTO'S EYES STARED UNBELIEVINGLY AT THE MUZZLE OF THE JAP RIFLE WHEN TODD AND WALRUS BURST IN UPON HIM.

NOW, MY LITTLE ORIENTAL CHUM! WHAT'S YOUR BUSINESS AROUND HERE? YOU'RE NOT DOING ALL THAT BUSH CLEARANCE FOR EXERCISE!

YOU INSOLENT DOG!

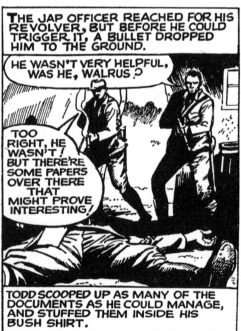

THE JAP OFFICER REACHED FOR HIS REVOLVER, BUT BEFORE HE COULD TRIGGER IT, A BULLET DROPPED HIM TO THE GROUND.

HE WASN'T VERY HELPFUL, WAS HE, WALRUS?

TOO RIGHT, HE WASN'T! BUT THERE'RE SOME PAPERS OVER THERE THAT MIGHT PROVE INTERESTING!

TODD SCOOPED UP AS MANY OF THE DOCUMENTS AS HE COULD MANAGE, AND STUFFED THEM INSIDE HIS BUSH SHIRT.

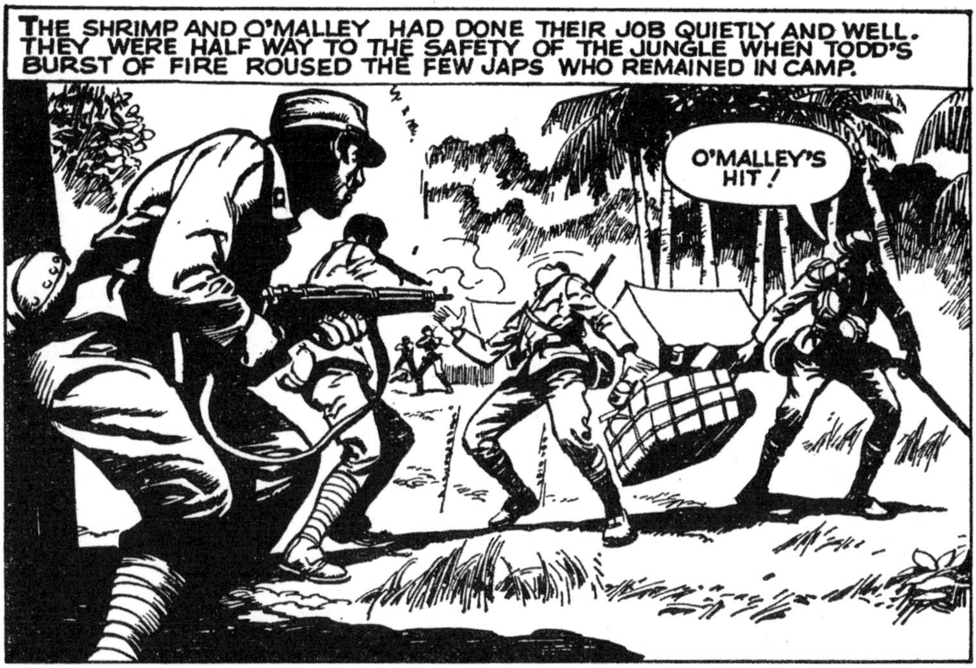
THE SHRIMP AND O'MALLEY HAD DONE THEIR JOB QUIETLY AND WELL. THEY WERE HALF WAY TO THE SAFETY OF THE JUNGLE WHEN TODD'S BURST OF FIRE ROUSED THE FEW JAPS WHO REMAINED IN CAMP.
O'MALLEY'S HIT!

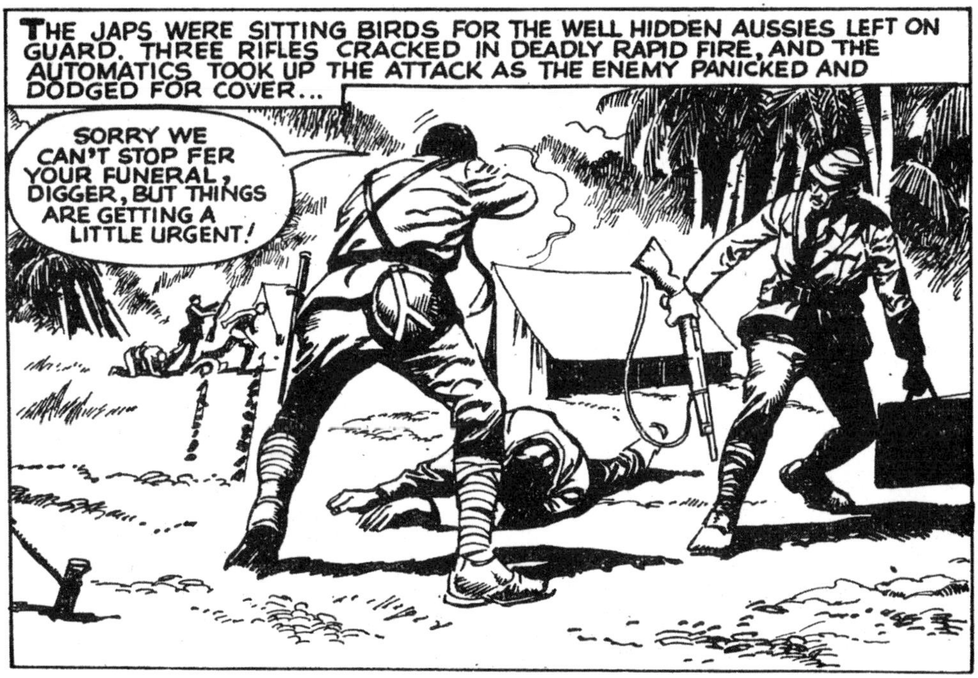
THE JAPS WERE SITTING BIRDS FOR THE WELL HIDDEN AUSSIES LEFT ON GUARD. THREE RIFLES CRACKED IN DEADLY RAPID FIRE, AND THE AUTOMATICS TOOK UP THE ATTACK AS THE ENEMY PANICKED AND DODGED FOR COVER...
SORRY WE CAN'T STOP FER YOUR FUNERAL, DIGGER, BUT THINGS ARE GETTING A LITTLE URGENT!

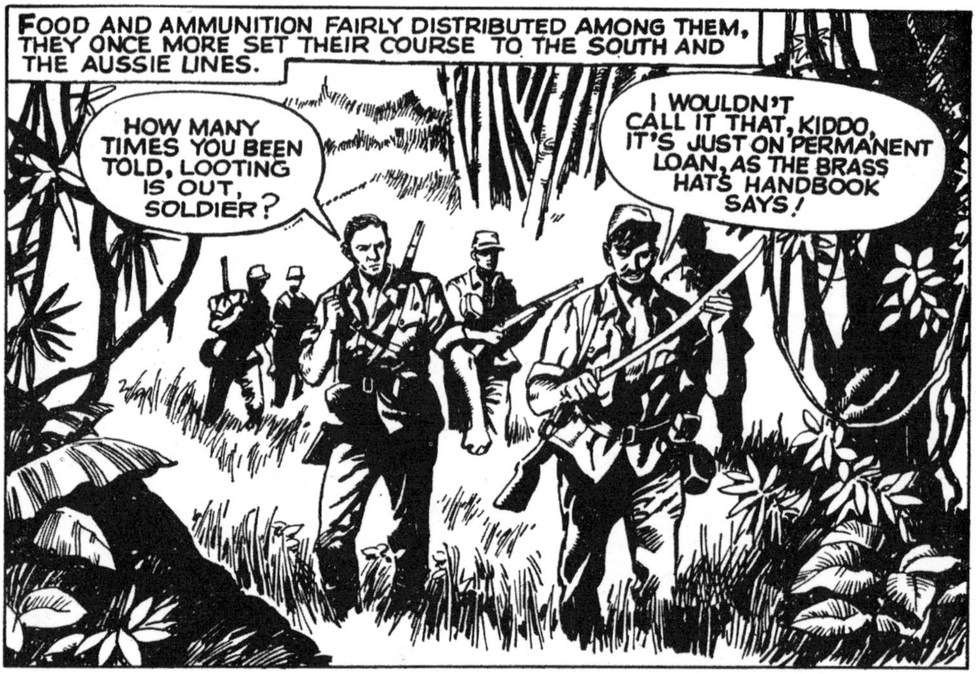
FOOD AND AMMUNITION FAIRLY DISTRIBUTED AMONG THEM, THEY ONCE MORE SET THEIR COURSE TO THE SOUTH AND THE AUSSIE LINES.
HOW MANY TIMES YOU BEEN TOLD, LOOTING IS OUT, SOLDIER?
I WOULDN'T CALL IT THAT, KIDDO, IT'S JUST ON PERMANENT LOAN, AS THE BRASS HATS HANDBOOK SAYS!

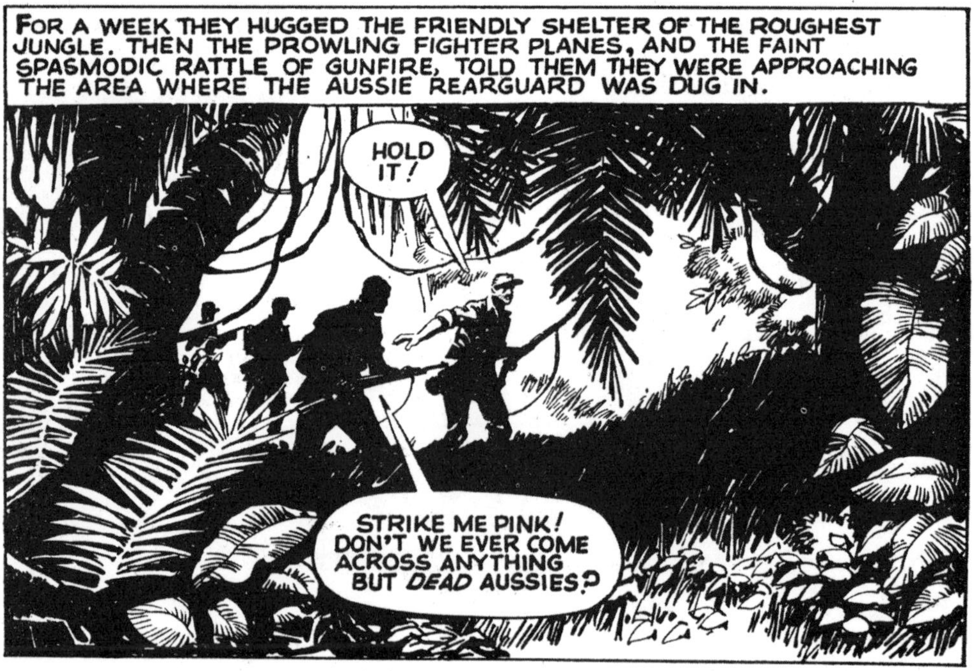
FOR A WEEK THEY HUGGED THE FRIENDLY SHELTER OF THE ROUGHEST JUNGLE. THEN THE PROWLING FIGHTER PLANES, AND THE FAINT SPASMODIC RATTLE OF GUNFIRE, TOLD THEM THEY WERE APPROACHING THE AREA WHERE THE AUSSIE REARGUARD WAS DUG IN.
HOLD IT!
STRIKE ME PINK! DON'T WE EVER COME ACROSS ANYTHING BUT *DEAD* AUSSIES?

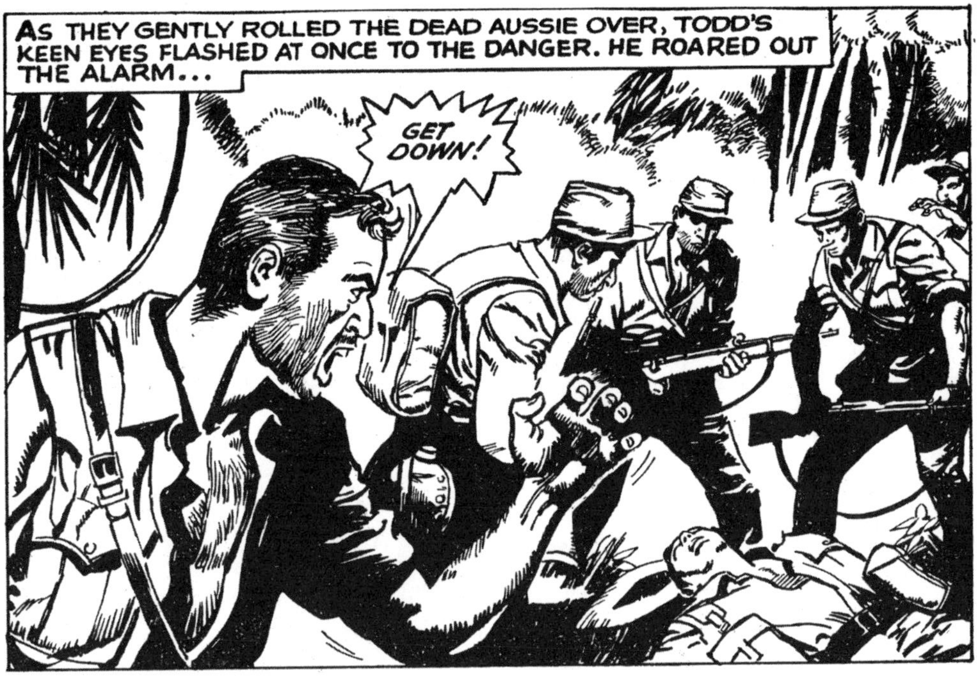
AS THEY GENTLY ROLLED THE DEAD AUSSIE OVER, TODD'S KEEN EYES FLASHED AT ONCE TO THE DANGER. HE ROARED OUT THE ALARM...
GET DOWN!

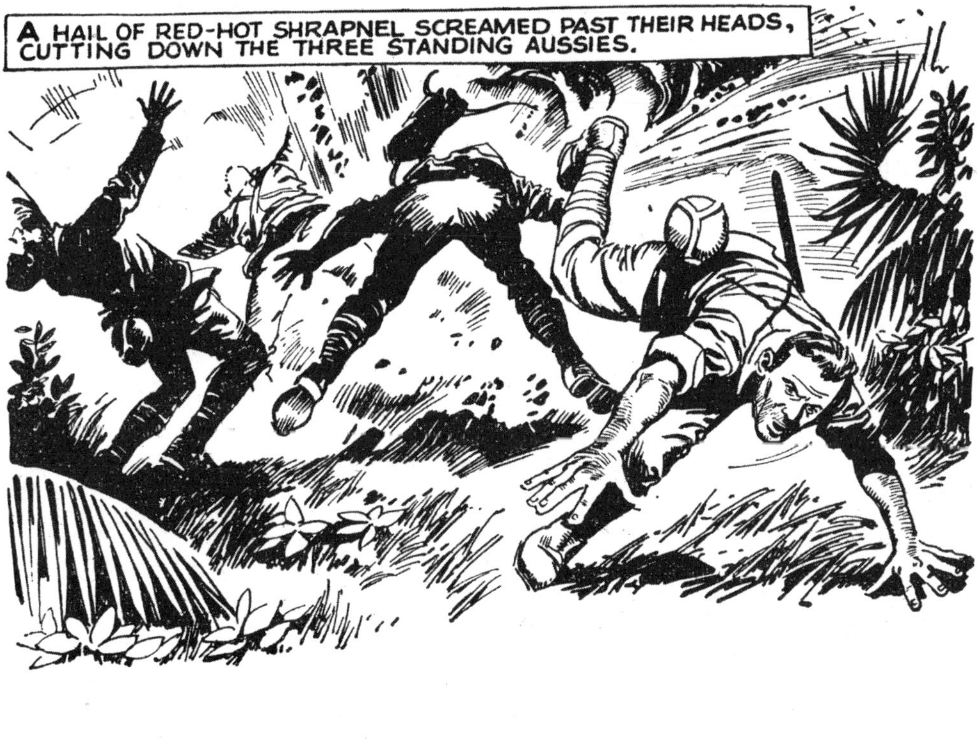
A HAIL OF RED-HOT SHRAPNEL SCREAMED PAST THEIR HEADS, CUTTING DOWN THE THREE STANDING AUSSIES.

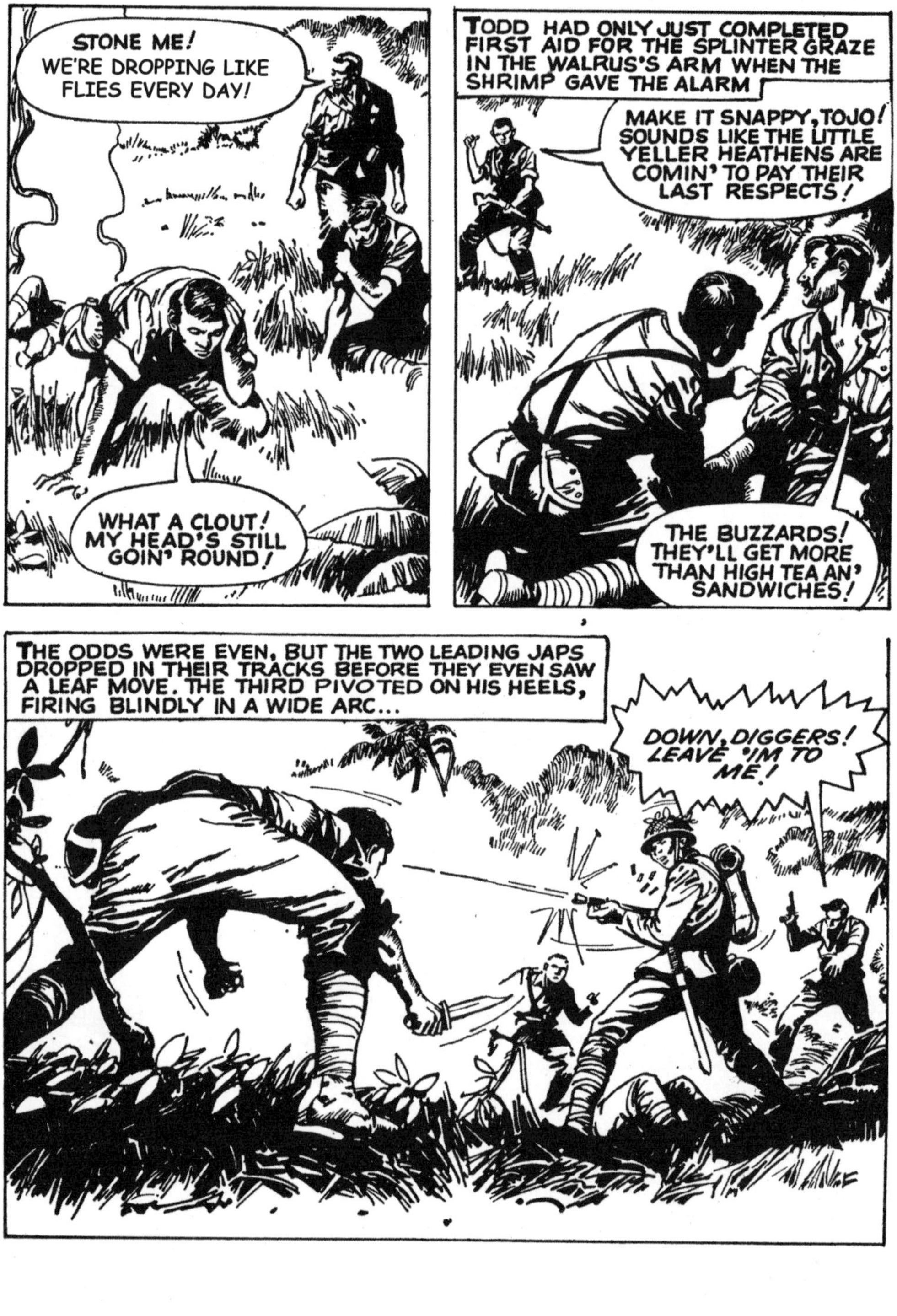
STONE ME! WE'RE DROPPING LIKE FLIES EVERY DAY!
WHAT A CLOUT! MY HEAD'S STILL GOIN' ROUND!
TODD HAD ONLY JUST COMPLETED FIRST AID FOR THE SPLINTER GRAZE IN THE WALRUS'S ARM WHEN THE SHRIMP GAVE THE ALARM
MAKE IT SNAPPY, TOJO! SOUNDS LIKE THE LITTLE YELLER HEATHENS ARE COMIN' TO PAY THEIR LAST RESPECTS!
THE BUZZARDS! THEY'LL GET MORE THAN HIGH TEA AN' SANDWICHES!
THE ODDS WERE EVEN, BUT THE TWO LEADING JAPS DROPPED IN THEIR TRACKS BEFORE THEY EVEN SAW A LEAF MOVE. THE THIRD PIVOTED ON HIS HEELS, FIRING BLINDLY IN A WIDE ARC...
DOWN, DIGGERS! LEAVE 'IM TO ME!

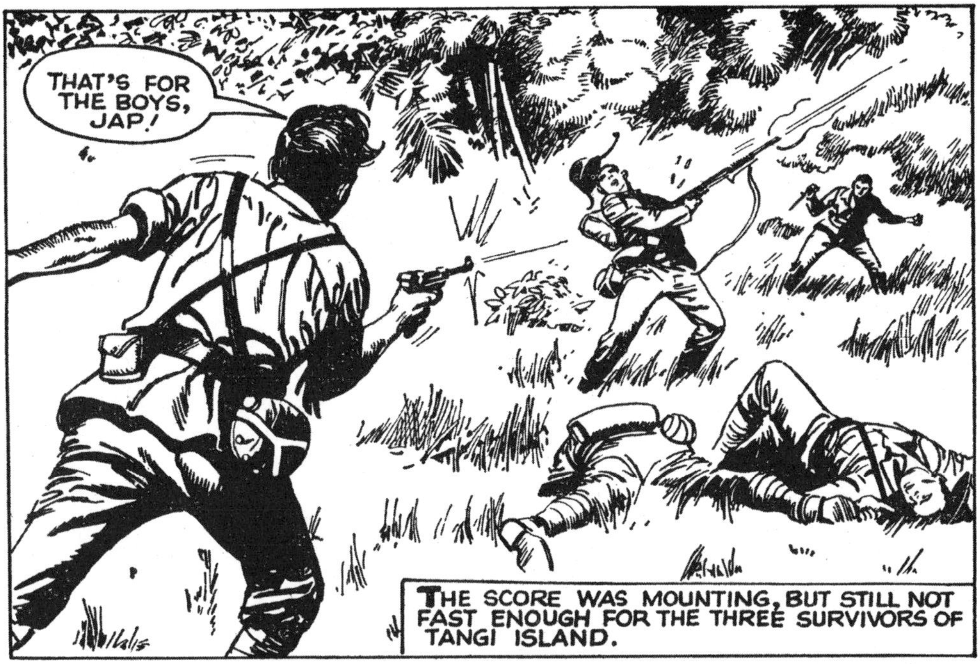
THAT'S FOR THE BOYS, JAP!
THE SCORE WAS MOUNTING, BUT STILL NOT FAST ENOUGH FOR THE THREE SURVIVORS OF TANGI ISLAND.

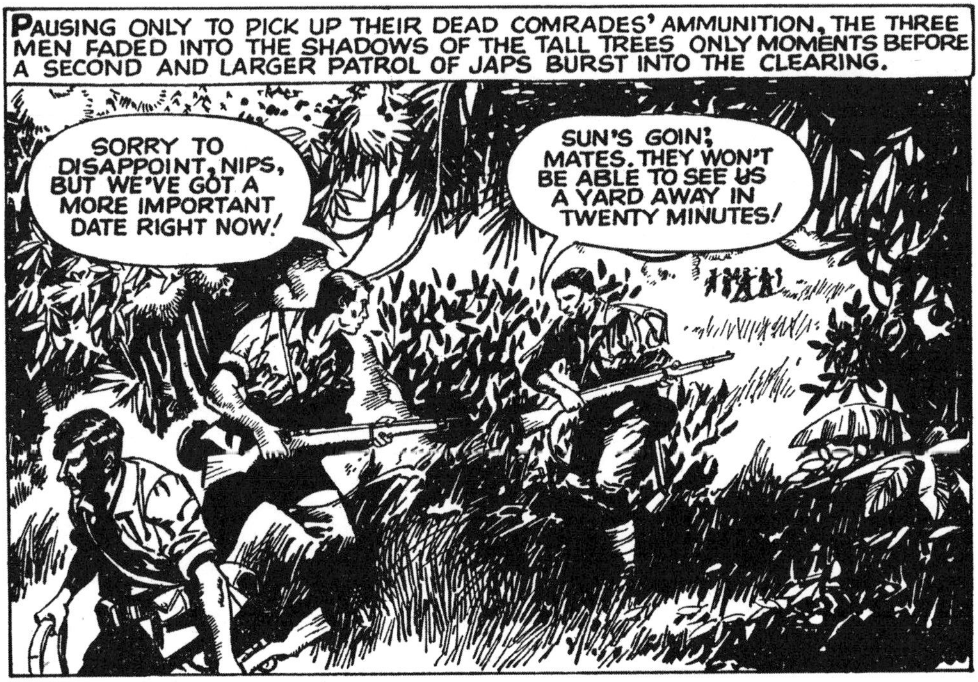
PAUSING ONLY TO PICK UP THEIR DEAD COMRADES' AMMUNITION, THE THREE MEN FADED INTO THE SHADOWS OF THE TALL TREES ONLY MOMENTS BEFORE A SECOND AND LARGER PATROL OF JAPS BURST INTO THE CLEARING.
SORRY TO DISAPPOINT, NIPS, BUT WE'VE GOT A MORE IMPORTANT DATE RIGHT NOW!
SUN'S GOIN', MATES. THEY WON'T BE ABLE TO SEE US A YARD AWAY IN TWENTY MINUTES!

Chapter 2. Men Without Mercy

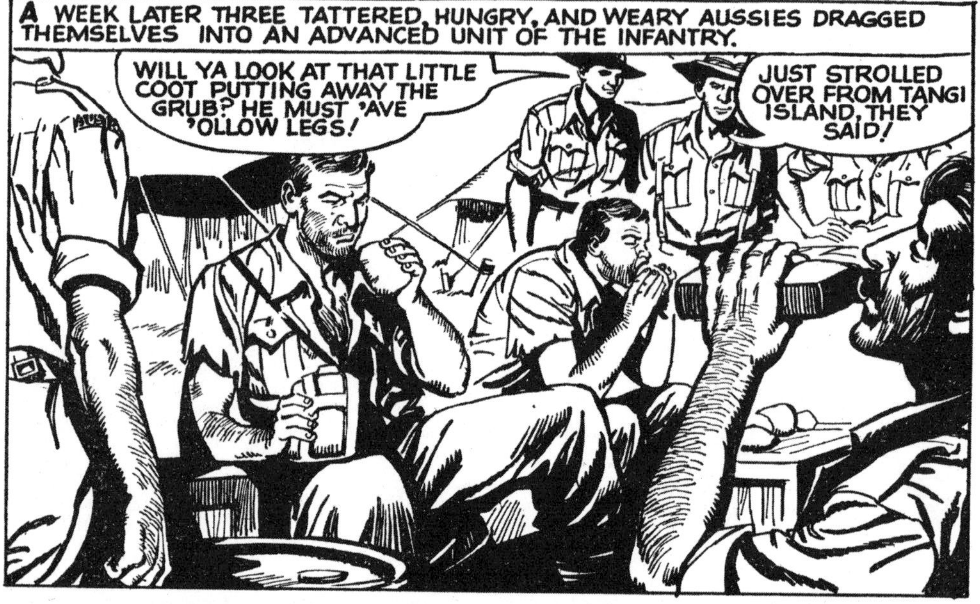
A WEEK LATER THREE TATTERED, HUNGRY, AND WEARY AUSSIES DRAGGED THEMSELVES INTO AN ADVANCED UNIT OF THE INFANTRY.
WILL YA LOOK AT THAT LITTLE COOT PUTTING AWAY THE GRUB? HE MUST 'AVE 'OLLOW LEGS!
JUST STROLLED OVER FROM TANGI ISLAND, THEY SAID!

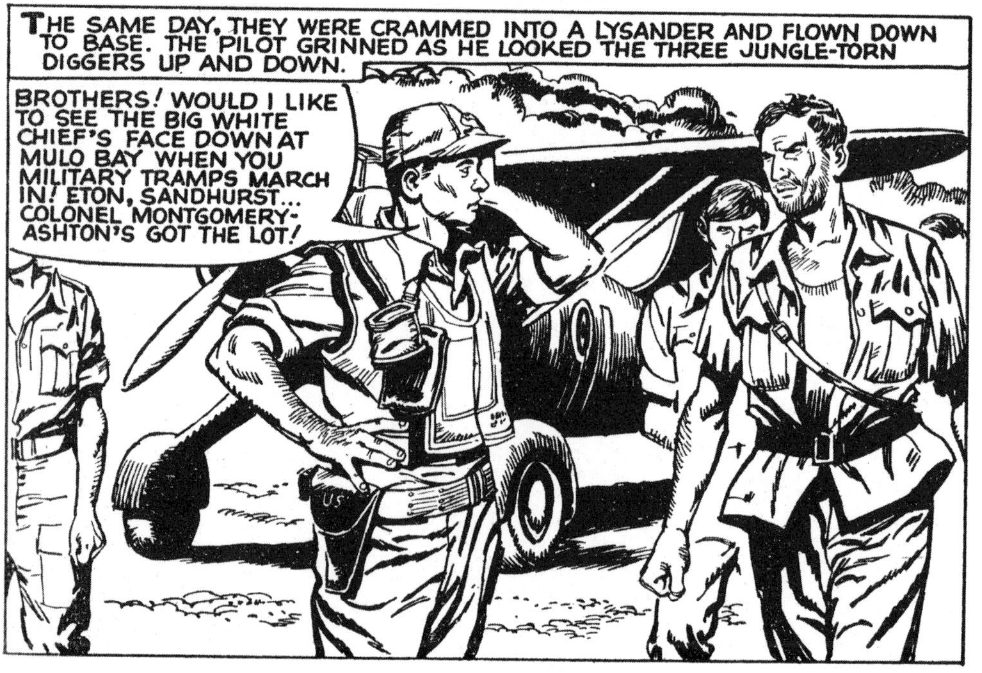
THE SAME DAY, THEY WERE CRAMMED INTO A LYSANDER AND FLOWN DOWN TO BASE. THE PILOT GRINNED AS HE LOOKED THE THREE JUNGLE-TORN DIGGERS UP AND DOWN.
BROTHERS! WOULD I LIKE TO SEE THE BIG WHITE CHIEF'S FACE DOWN AT MULO BAY WHEN YOU MILITARY TRAMPS MARCH IN! ETON, SANDHURST... COLONEL MONTGOMERY-ASHTON'S GOT THE LOT!
US

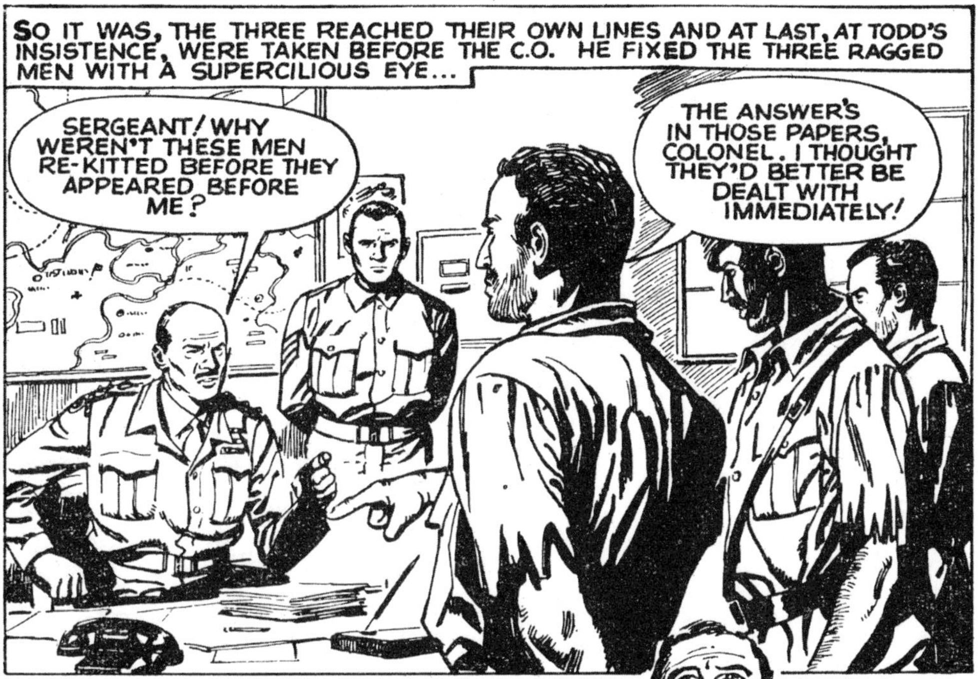
SO IT WAS, THE THREE REACHED THEIR OWN LINES AND AT LAST, AT TODD'S INSISTENCE, WERE TAKEN BEFORE THE C.O. HE FIXED THE THREE RAGGED MEN WITH A SUPERCILIOUS EYE...
SERGEANT! WHY WEREN'T THESE MEN RE-KITTED BEFORE THEY APPEARED BEFORE ME?
THE ANSWER'S IN THOSE PAPERS, COLONEL. I THOUGHT THEY'D BETTER BE DEALT WITH IMMEDIATELY!

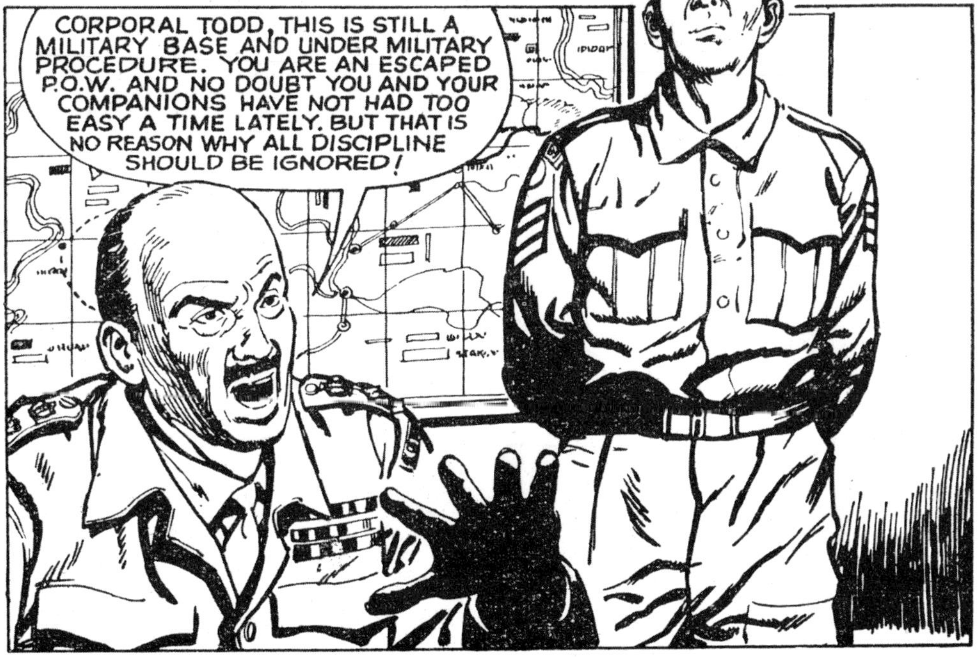
CORPORAL TODD, THIS IS STILL A MILITARY BASE AND UNDER MILITARY PROCEDURE. YOU ARE AN ESCAPED P.O.W. AND NO DOUBT YOU AND YOUR COMPANIONS HAVE NOT HAD TOO EASY A TIME LATELY. BUT THAT IS NO REASON WHY ALL DISCIPLINE SHOULD BE IGNORED!

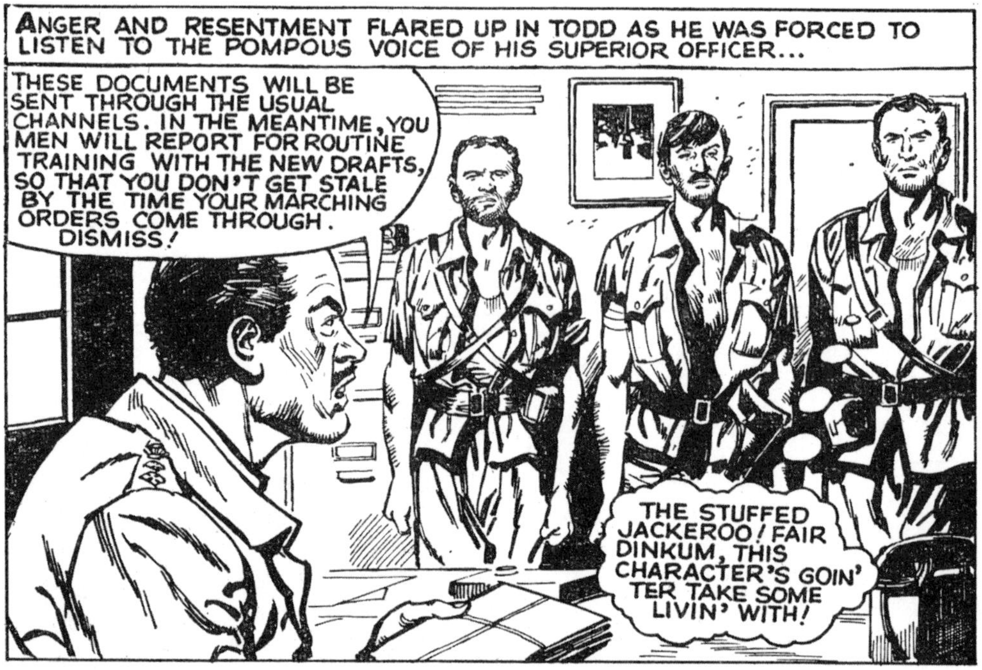
ANGER AND RESENTMENT FLARED UP IN TODD AS HE WAS FORCED TO LISTEN TO THE POMPOUS VOICE OF HIS SUPERIOR OFFICER...
THESE DOCUMENTS WILL BE SENT THROUGH THE USUAL CHANNELS. IN THE MEANTIME, YOU MEN WILL REPORT FOR ROUTINE TRAINING WITH THE NEW DRAFTS, SO THAT YOU DON'T GET STALE BY THE TIME YOUR MARCHING ORDERS COME THROUGH. DISMISS!
THE STUFFED JACKEROO! FAIR DINKUM, THIS CHARACTER'S GOIN' TER TAKE SOME LIVIN' WITH!

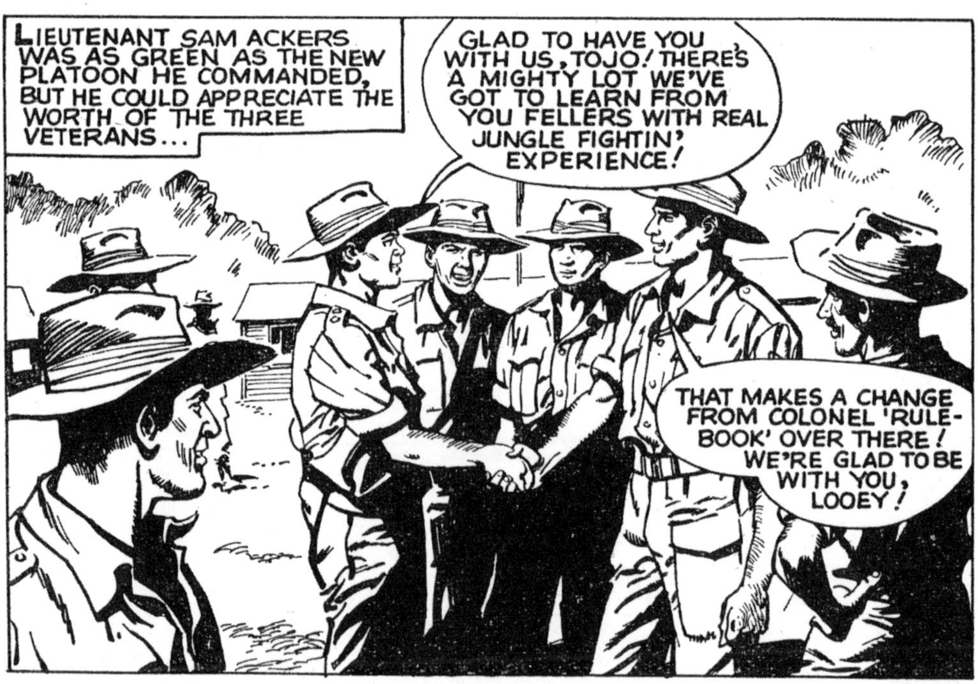
LIEUTENANT SAM ACKERS WAS AS GREEN AS THE NEW PLATOON HE COMMANDED, BUT HE COULD APPRECIATE THE WORTH OF THE THREE VETERANS...
GLAD TO HAVE YOU WITH US, TOJO! THERE'S A MIGHTY LOT WE'VE GOT TO LEARN FROM YOU FELLERS WITH REAL JUNGLE FIGHTIN' EXPERIENCE!
THAT MAKES A CHANGE FROM COLONEL 'RULE-BOOK' OVER THERE! WE'RE GLAD TO BE WITH YOU, LOOEY!

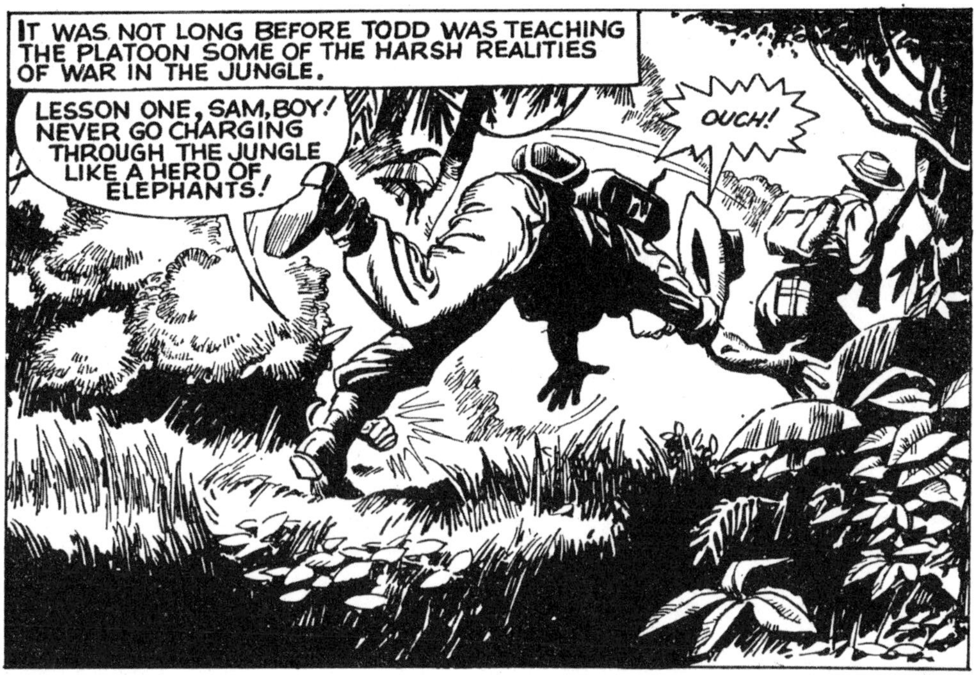
IT WAS NOT LONG BEFORE TODD WAS TEACHING THE PLATOON SOME OF THE HARSH REALITIES OF WAR IN THE JUNGLE.
LESSON ONE, SAM, BOY! NEVER GO CHARGING THROUGH THE JUNGLE LIKE A HERD OF ELEPHANTS!
OUCH!

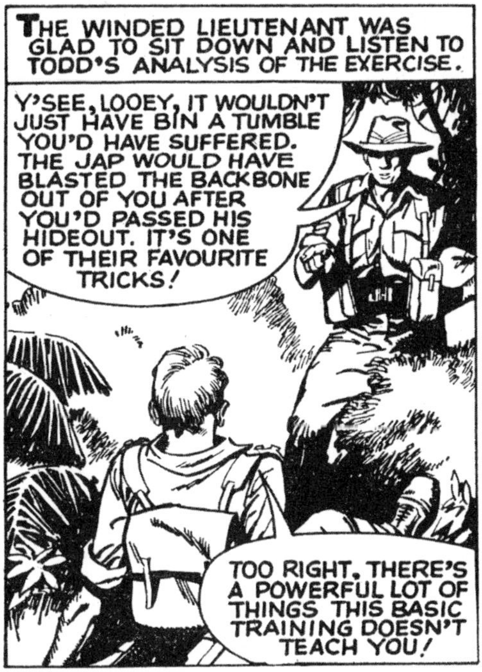
THE WINDED LIEUTENANT WAS GLAD TO SIT DOWN AND LISTEN TO TODD'S ANALYSIS OF THE EXERCISE.
Y'SEE, LOOEY, IT WOULDN'T JUST HAVE BIN A TUMBLE YOU'D HAVE SUFFERED. THE JAP WOULD HAVE BLASTED THE BACKBONE OUT OF YOU AFTER YOU'D PASSED HIS HIDEOUT. IT'S ONE OF THEIR FAVOURITE TRICKS!
TOO RIGHT. THERE'S A POWERFUL LOT OF THINGS THIS BASIC TRAINING DOESN'T TEACH YOU!

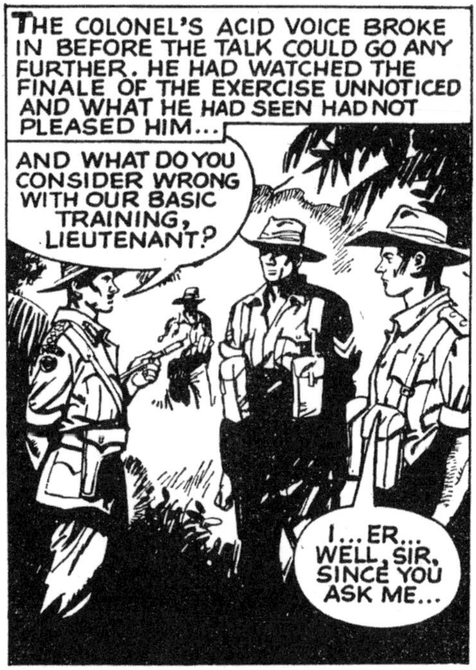
THE COLONEL'S ACID VOICE BROKE IN BEFORE THE TALK COULD GO ANY FURTHER. HE HAD WATCHED THE FINALE OF THE EXERCISE UNNOTICED AND WHAT HE HAD SEEN HAD NOT PLEASED HIM...
AND WHAT DO YOU CONSIDER WRONG WITH OUR BASIC TRAINING, LIEUTENANT?
I... ER... WELL, SIR, SINCE YOU ASK ME...

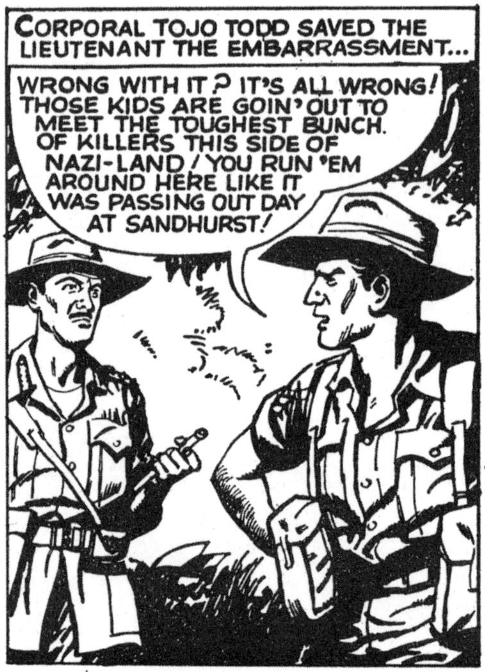
CORPORAL TOJO TODD SAVED THE LIEUTENANT THE EMBARRASSMENT...
WRONG WITH IT? IT'S ALL WRONG! THOSE KIDS ARE GOIN' OUT TO MEET THE TOUGHEST BUNCH OF KILLERS THIS SIDE OF NAZI-LAND! YOU RUN 'EM AROUND HERE LIKE IT WAS PASSING OUT DAY AT SANDHURST!

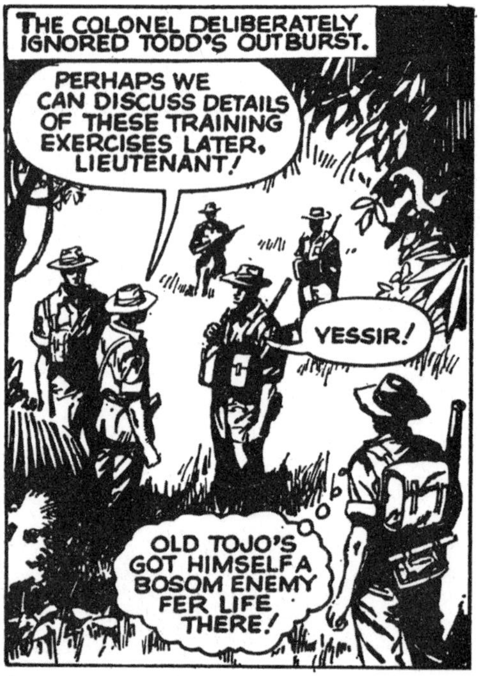
THE COLONEL DELIBERATELY IGNORED TODD'S OUTBURST.
PERHAPS WE CAN DISCUSS DETAILS OF THESE TRAINING EXERCISES LATER, LIEUTENANT!
YESSIR!
OLD TOJO'S GOT HIMSELF A BOSOM ENEMY FER LIFE THERE!

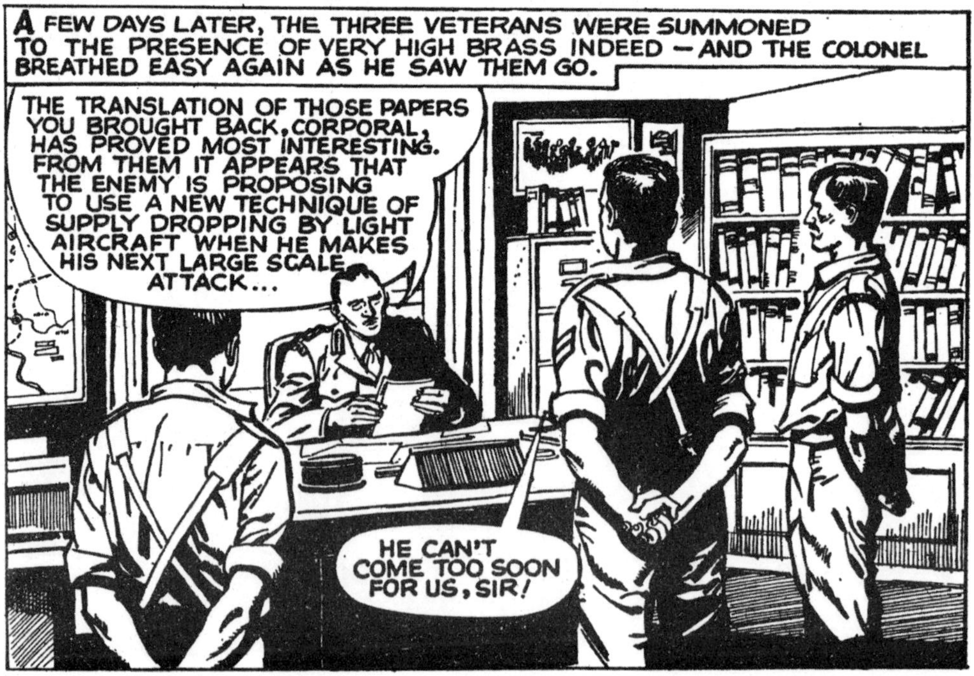
A FEW DAYS LATER, THE THREE VETERANS WERE SUMMONED TO THE PRESENCE OF VERY HIGH BRASS INDEED — AND THE COLONEL BREATHED EASY AGAIN AS HE SAW THEM GO.
THE TRANSLATION OF THOSE PAPERS YOU BROUGHT BACK, CORPORAL, HAS PROVED MOST INTERESTING. FROM THEM IT APPEARS THAT THE ENEMY IS PROPOSING TO USE A NEW TECHNIQUE OF SUPPLY DROPPING BY LIGHT AIRCRAFT WHEN HE MAKES HIS NEXT LARGE SCALE ATTACK...
HE CAN'T COME TOO SOON FOR US, SIR!

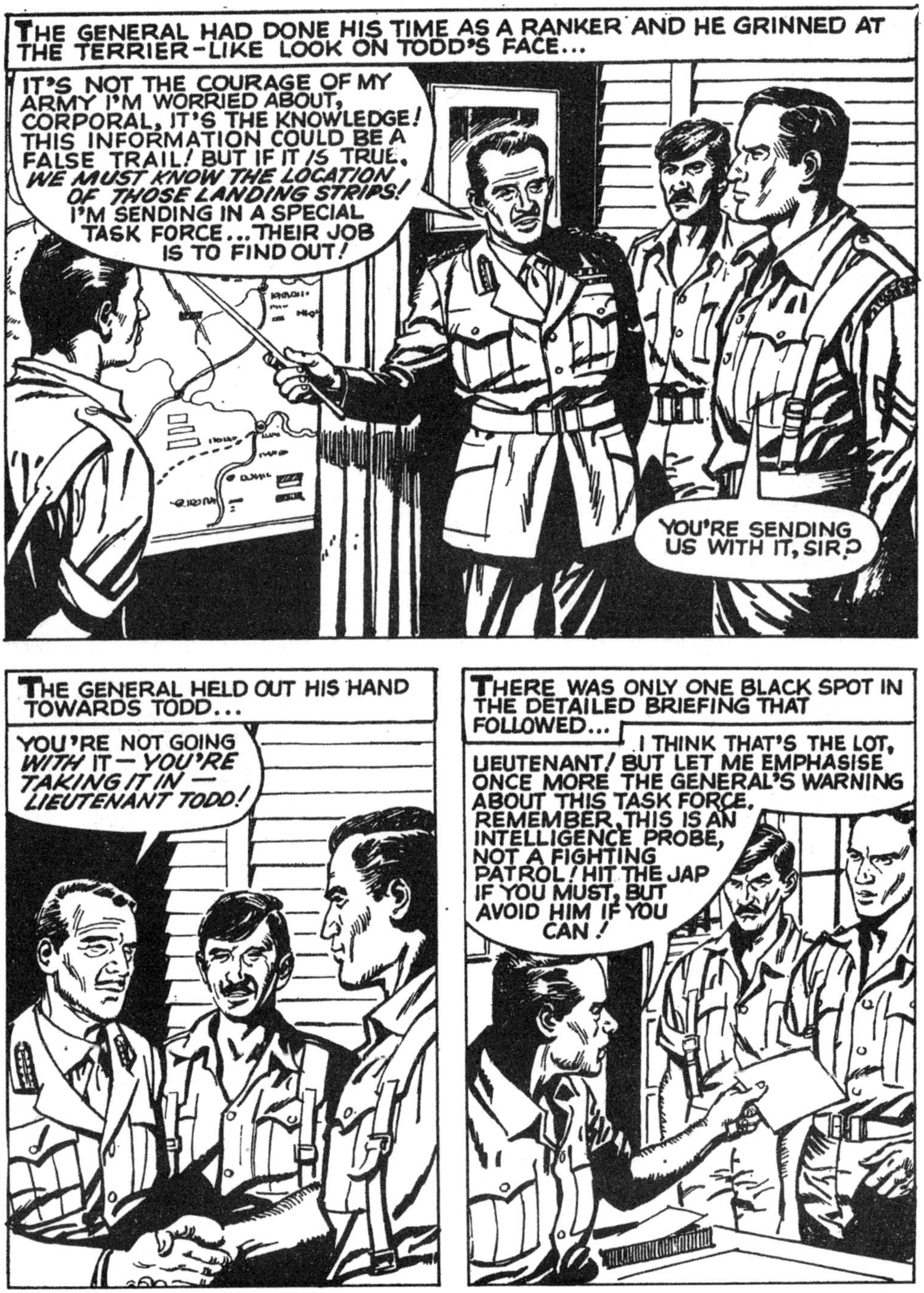
THE GENERAL HAD DONE HIS TIME AS A RANKER AND HE GRINNED AT THE TERRIER-LIKE LOOK ON TODD'S FACE...
IT'S NOT THE COURAGE OF MY ARMY I'M WORRIED ABOUT, CORPORAL, IT'S THE KNOWLEDGE! THIS INFORMATION COULD BE A FALSE TRAIL! BUT IF IT IS TRUE, WE MUST KNOW THE LOCATION OF THOSE LANDING STRIPS! I'M SENDING IN A SPECIAL TASK FORCE... THEIR JOB IS TO FIND OUT!
YOU'RE SENDING US WITH IT, SIR?
THE GENERAL HELD OUT HIS HAND TOWARDS TODD...
YOU'RE NOT GOING WITH IT — YOU'RE TAKING IT IN — LIEUTENANT TODD!
THERE WAS ONLY ONE BLACK SPOT IN THE DETAILED BRIEFING THAT FOLLOWED...
I THINK THAT'S THE LOT, LIEUTENANT! BUT LET ME EMPHASISE ONCE MORE THE GENERAL'S WARNING ABOUT THIS TASK FORCE. REMEMBER, THIS IS AN INTELLIGENCE PROBE, NOT A FIGHTING PATROL! HIT THE JAP IF YOU MUST, BUT AVOID HIM IF YOU CAN!

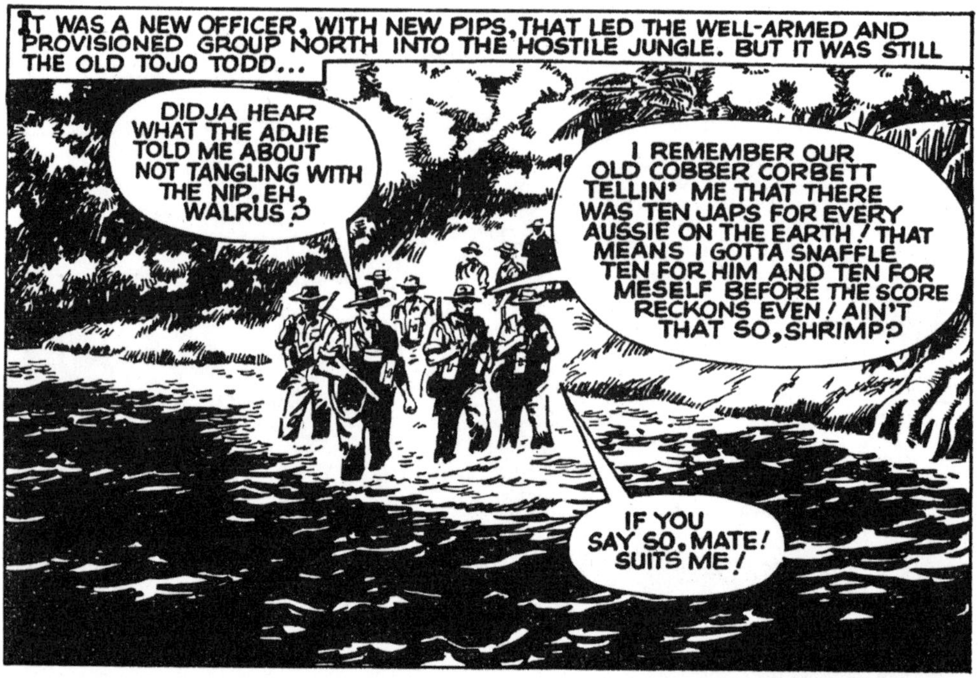
IT WAS A NEW OFFICER, WITH NEW PIPS, THAT LED THE WELL-ARMED AND PROVISIONED GROUP NORTH INTO THE HOSTILE JUNGLE. BUT IT WAS STILL THE OLD TOJO TODD...
DIDJA HEAR WHAT THE ADJIE TOLD ME ABOUT NOT TANGLING WITH THE NIP, EH, WALRUS?
I REMEMBER OUR OLD COBBER CORBETT TELLIN' ME THAT THERE WAS TEN JAPS FOR EVERY AUSSIE ON THE EARTH! THAT MEANS I GOTTA SNAFFLE TEN FOR HIM AND TEN FOR MESELF BEFORE THE SCORE RECKONS EVEN! AIN'T THAT SO, SHRIMP?
IF YOU SAY SO, MATE! SUITS ME!

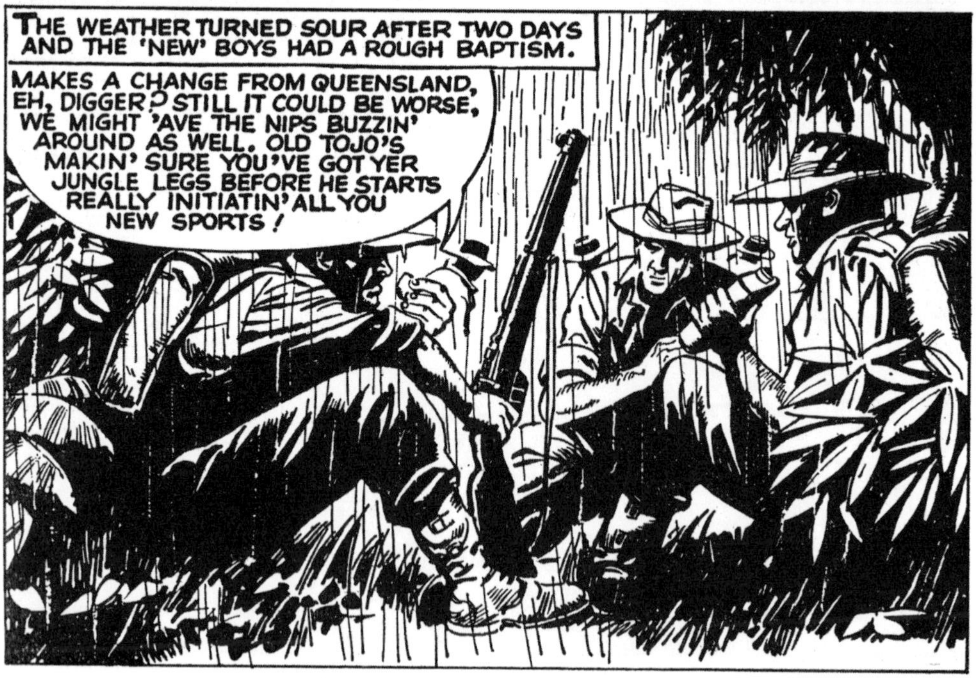
THE WEATHER TURNED SOUR AFTER TWO DAYS AND THE 'NEW' BOYS HAD A ROUGH BAPTISM.
MAKES A CHANGE FROM QUEENSLAND, EH, DIGGER? STILL IT COULD BE WORSE, WE MIGHT 'AVE THE NIPS BUZZIN' AROUND AS WELL. OLD TOJO'S MAKIN' SURE YOU'VE GOT YER JUNGLE LEGS BEFORE HE STARTS REALLY INITIATIN' ALL YOU NEW SPORTS!

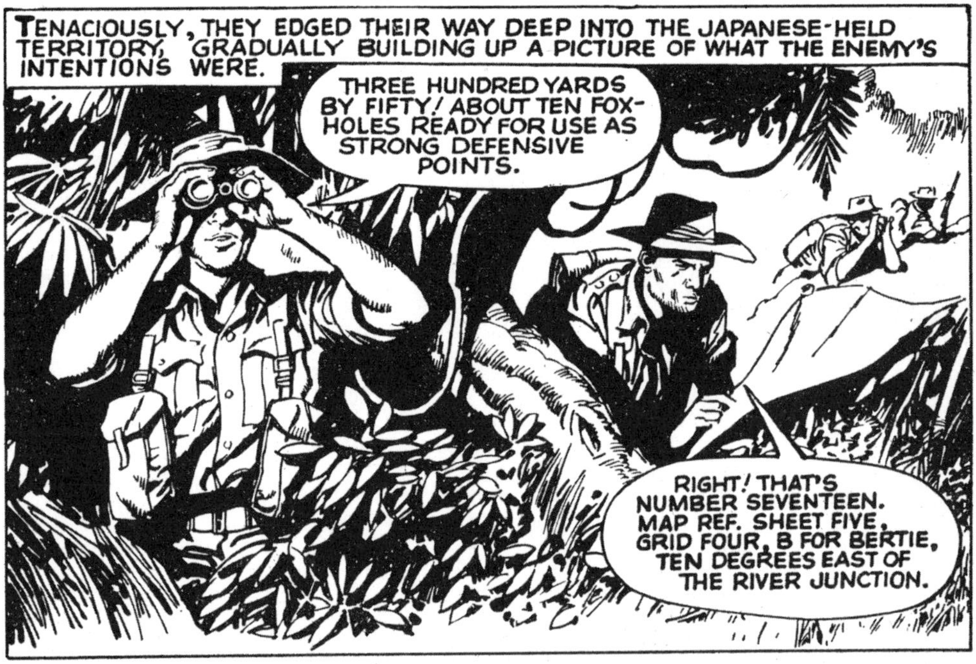
TENACIOUSLY, THEY EDGED THEIR WAY DEEP INTO THE JAPANESE-HELD TERRITORY, GRADUALLY BUILDING UP A PICTURE OF WHAT THE ENEMY'S INTENTIONS WERE.
THREE HUNDRED YARDS BY FIFTY! ABOUT TEN FOX-HOLES READY FOR USE AS STRONG DEFENSIVE POINTS.
RIGHT! THAT'S NUMBER SEVENTEEN. MAP REF. SHEET FIVE, GRID FOUR, B FOR BERTIE, TEN DEGREES EAST OF THE RIVER JUNCTION.

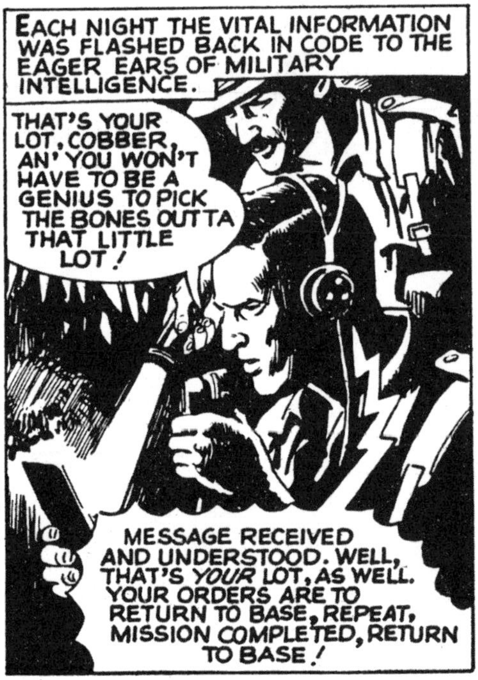
EACH NIGHT THE VITAL INFORMATION WAS FLASHED BACK IN CODE TO THE EAGER EARS OF MILITARY INTELLIGENCE.
THAT'S YOUR LOT, COBBER, AN' YOU WON'T HAVE TO BE A GENIUS TO PICK THE BONES OUTTA THAT LITTLE LOT!
MESSAGE RECEIVED AND UNDERSTOOD. WELL, THAT'S *YOUR* LOT, AS WELL. YOUR ORDERS ARE TO RETURN TO BASE, REPEAT, MISSION *COMPLETED*, RETURN TO BASE!

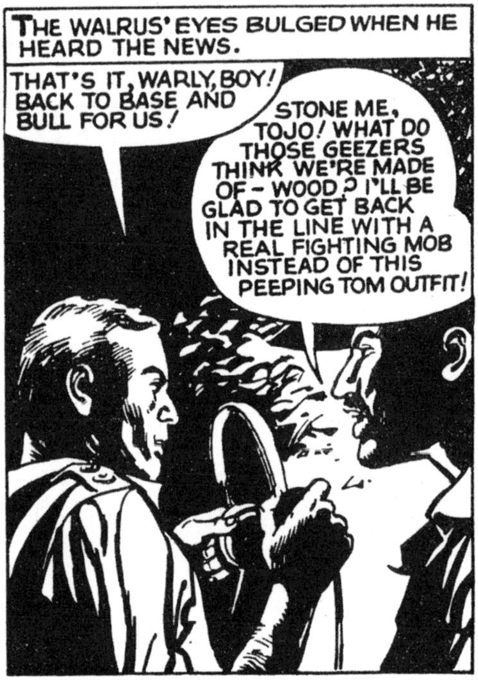
THE WALRUS' EYES BULGED WHEN HE HEARD THE NEWS.
THAT'S IT, WARLY, BOY! BACK TO BASE AND BULL FOR US!
STONE ME, TOJO! WHAT DO THOSE GEEZERS THINK WE'RE MADE OF - WOOD? I'LL BE GLAD TO GET BACK IN THE LINE WITH A REAL FIGHTING MOB INSTEAD OF THIS PEEPING TOM OUTFIT!

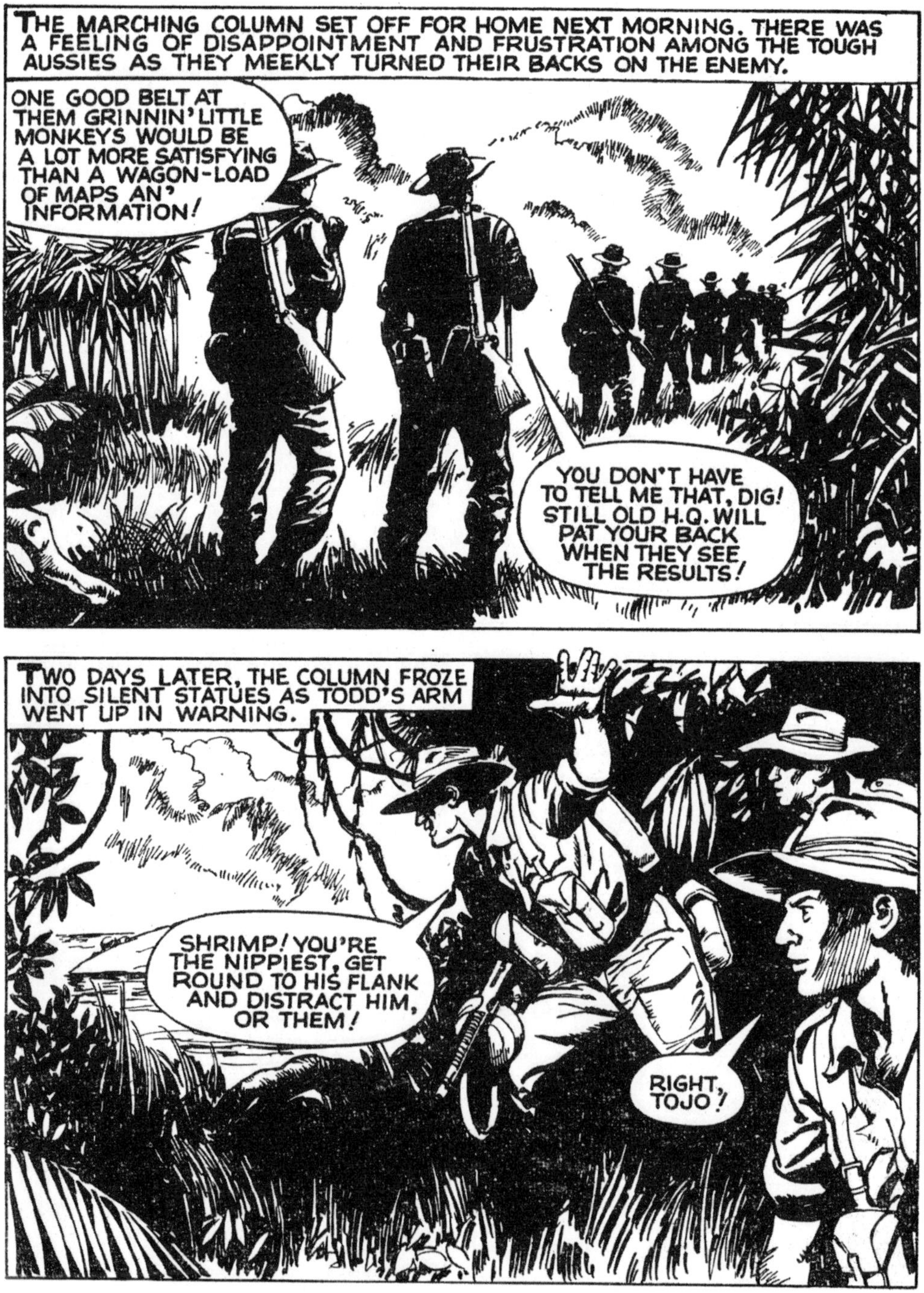
THE MARCHING COLUMN SET OFF FOR HOME NEXT MORNING. THERE WAS A FEELING OF DISAPPOINTMENT AND FRUSTRATION AMONG THE TOUGH AUSSIES AS THEY MEEKLY TURNED THEIR BACKS ON THE ENEMY.
ONE GOOD BELT AT THEM GRINNIN' LITTLE MONKEYS WOULD BE A LOT MORE SATISFYING THAN A WAGON-LOAD OF MAPS AN' INFORMATION!
YOU DON'T HAVE TO TELL ME THAT, DIG! STILL OLD H.Q. WILL PAT YOUR BACK WHEN THEY SEE THE RESULTS!
TWO DAYS LATER, THE COLUMN FROZE INTO SILENT STATUES AS TODD'S ARM WENT UP IN WARNING.
SHRIMP! YOU'RE THE NIPPIEST, GET ROUND TO HIS FLANK AND DISTRACT HIM, OR THEM!
RIGHT, TOJO!

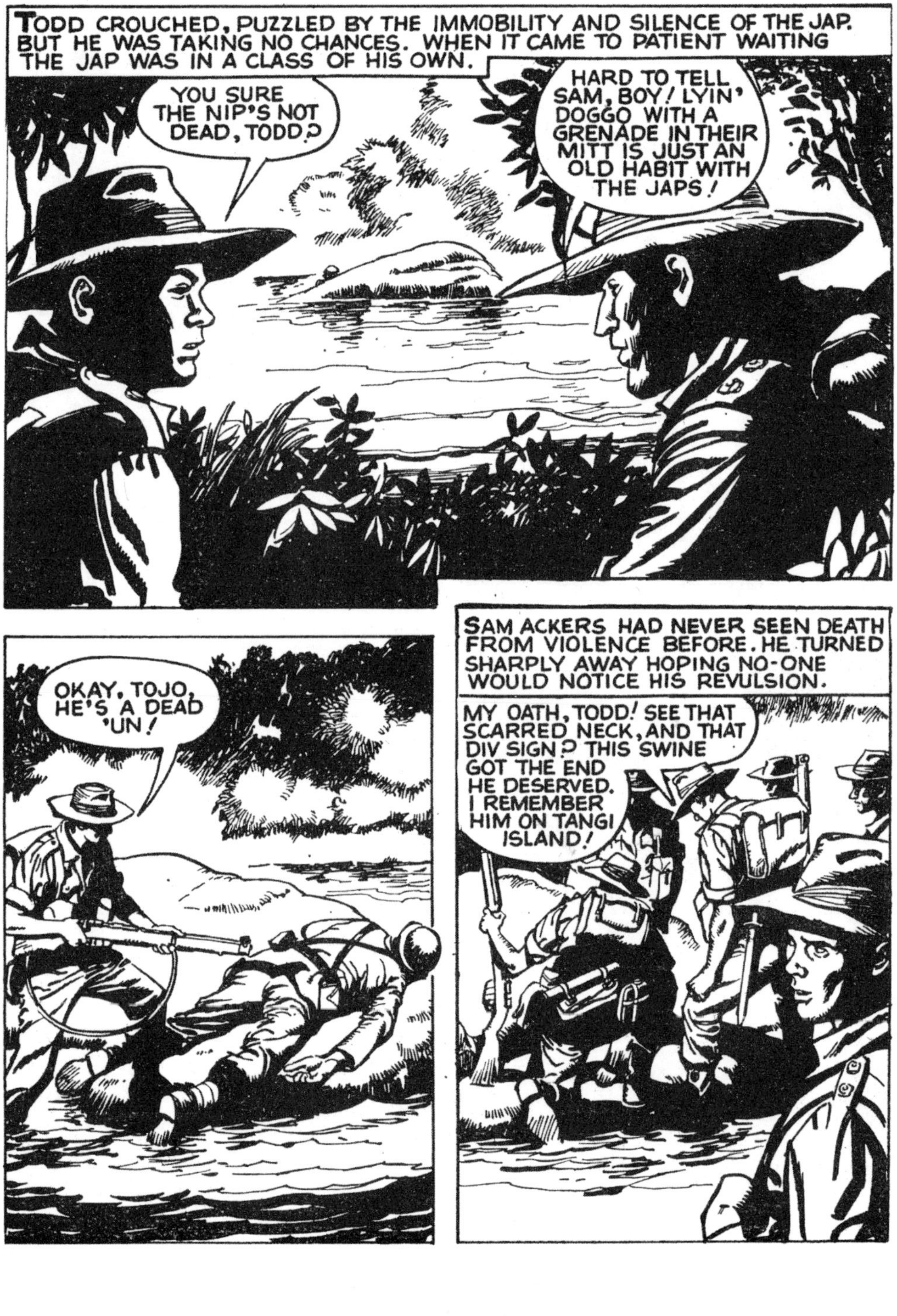
TODD CROUCHED, PUZZLED BY THE IMMOBILITY AND SILENCE OF THE JAP. BUT HE WAS TAKING NO CHANCES. WHEN IT CAME TO PATIENT WAITING THE JAP WAS IN A CLASS OF HIS OWN.
YOU SURE THE NIP'S NOT DEAD, TODD?
HARD TO TELL SAM, BOY! LYIN' DOGGO WITH A GRENADE IN THEIR MITT IS JUST AN OLD HABIT WITH THE JAPS!
OKAY, TOJO, HE'S A DEAD 'UN!
SAM ACKERS HAD NEVER SEEN DEATH FROM VIOLENCE BEFORE. HE TURNED SHARPLY AWAY HOPING NO-ONE WOULD NOTICE HIS REVULSION.
MY OATH, TODD! SEE THAT SCARRED NECK, AND THAT DIV SIGN? THIS SWINE GOT THE END HE DESERVED. I REMEMBER HIM ON TANGI ISLAND!

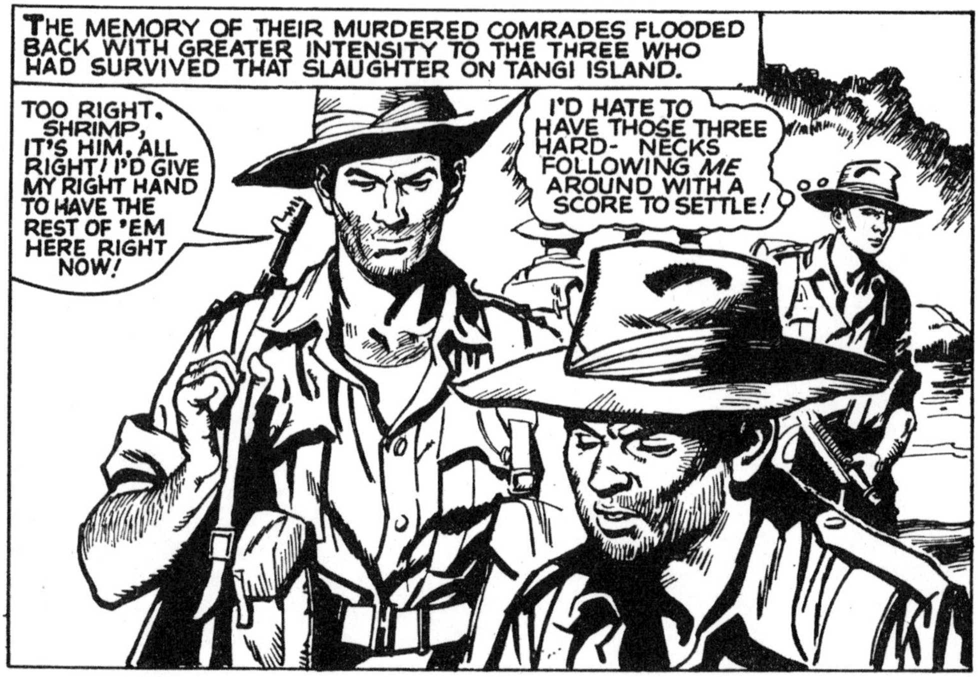
THE MEMORY OF THEIR MURDERED COMRADES FLOODED BACK WITH GREATER INTENSITY TO THE THREE WHO HAD SURVIVED THAT SLAUGHTER ON TANGI ISLAND.
TOO RIGHT, SHRIMP, IT'S HIM, ALL RIGHT! I'D GIVE MY RIGHT HAND TO HAVE THE REST OF 'EM HERE RIGHT NOW!
I'D HATE TO HAVE THOSE THREE HARD- NECKS FOLLOWING *ME* AROUND WITH A SCORE TO SETTLE!

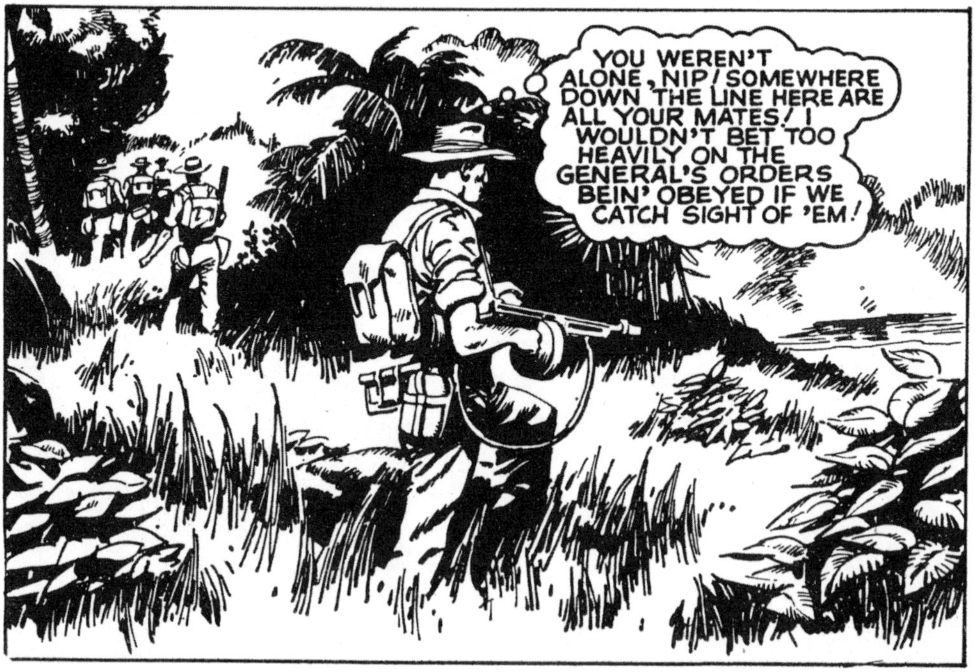
YOU WEREN'T ALONE, NIP! SOMEWHERE DOWN THE LINE HERE ARE ALL YOUR MATES! I WOULDN'T BET TOO HEAVILY ON THE GENERAL'S ORDERS BEIN' OBEYED IF WE CATCH SIGHT OF 'EM!

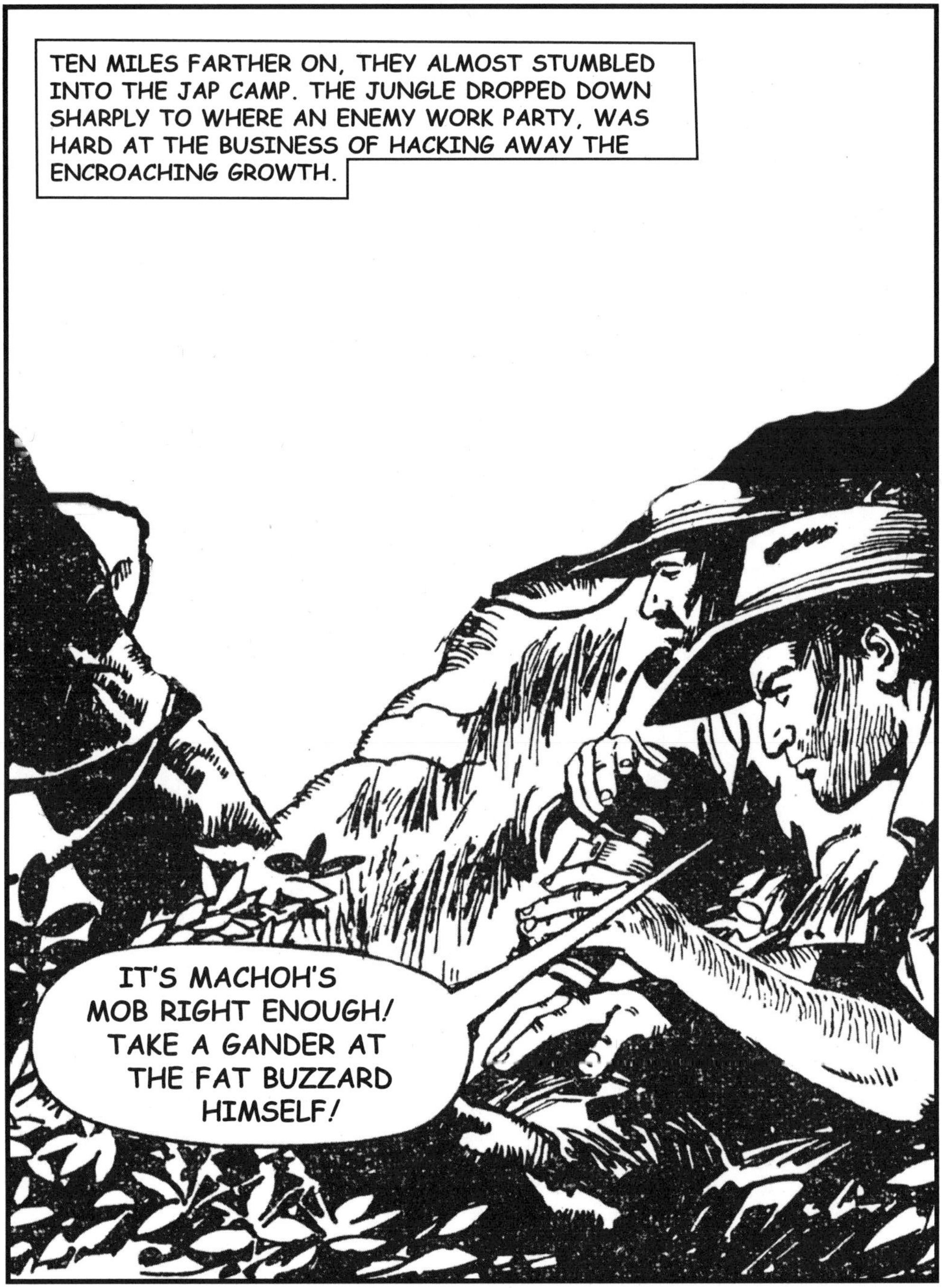
TEN MILES FARTHER ON, THEY ALMOST STUMBLED INTO THE JAP CAMP. THE JUNGLE DROPPED DOWN SHARPLY TO WHERE AN ENEMY WORK PARTY, WAS HARD AT THE BUSINESS OF HACKING AWAY THE ENCROACHING GROWTH.
IT'S MACHOH'S MOB RIGHT ENOUGH! TAKE A GANDER AT THE FAT BUZZARD HIMSELF!

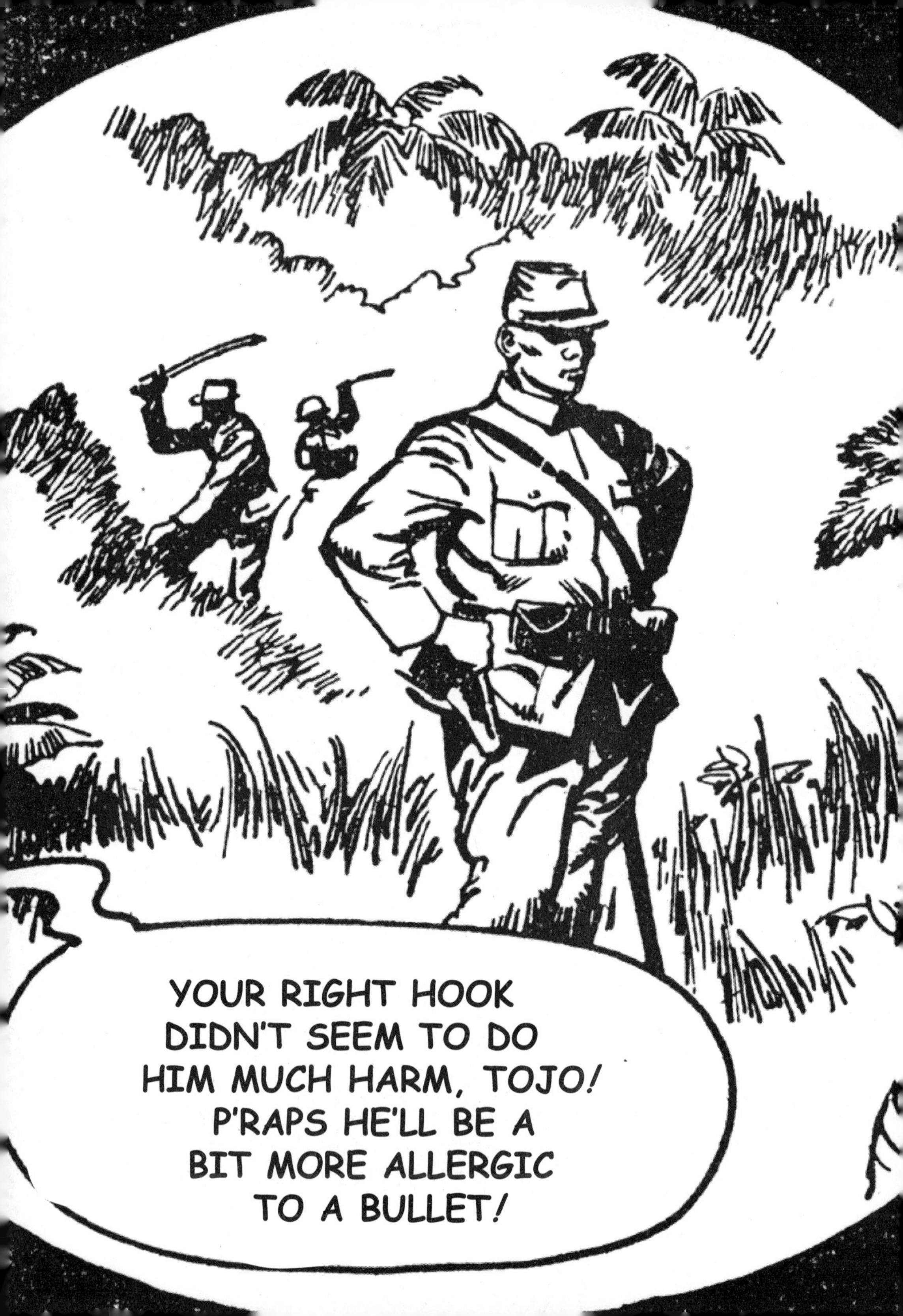
YOUR RIGHT HOOK DIDN'T SEEM TO DO HIM MUCH HARM, TOJO! P'RAPS HE'LL BE A BIT MORE ALLERGIC TO A BULLET!

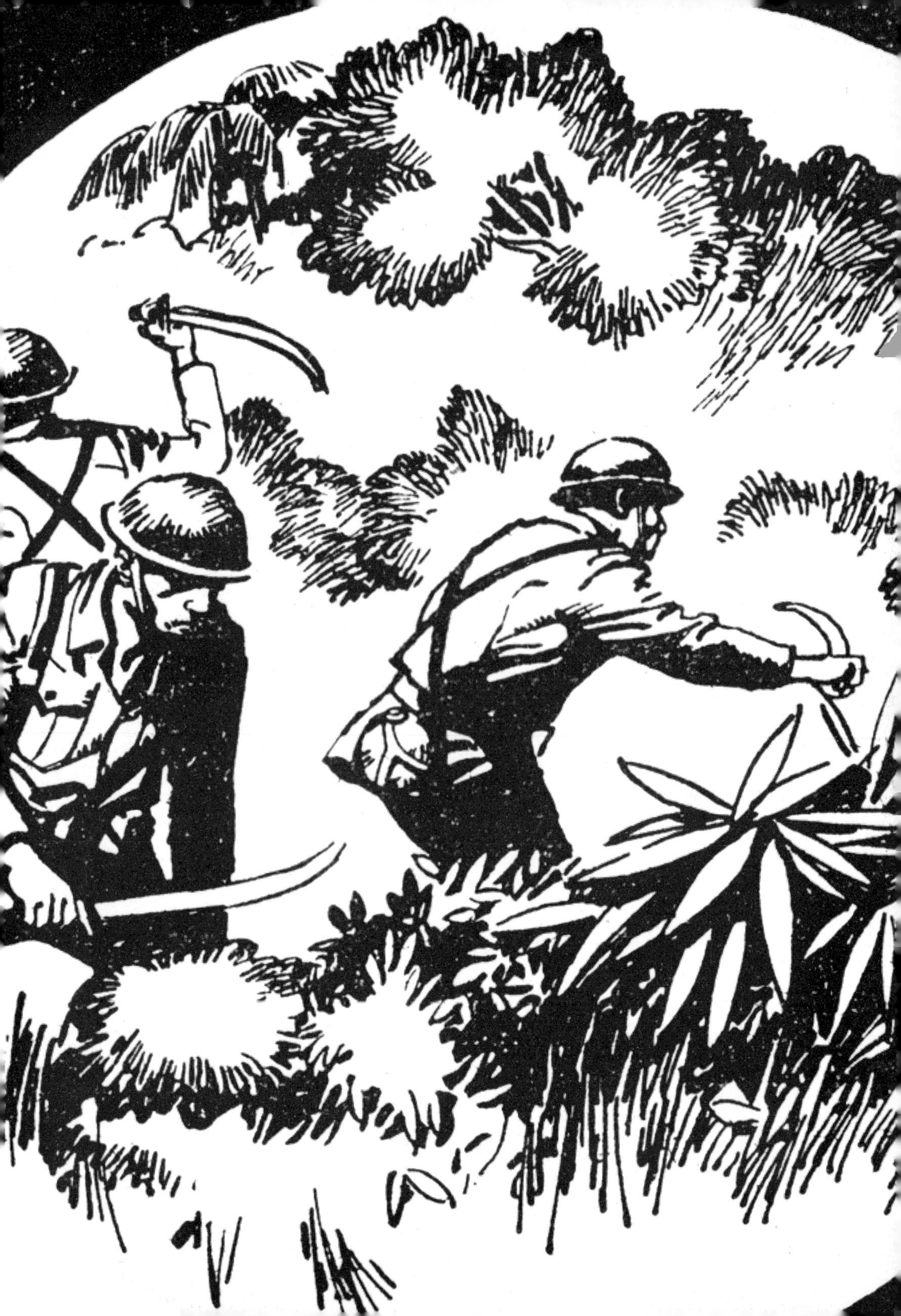

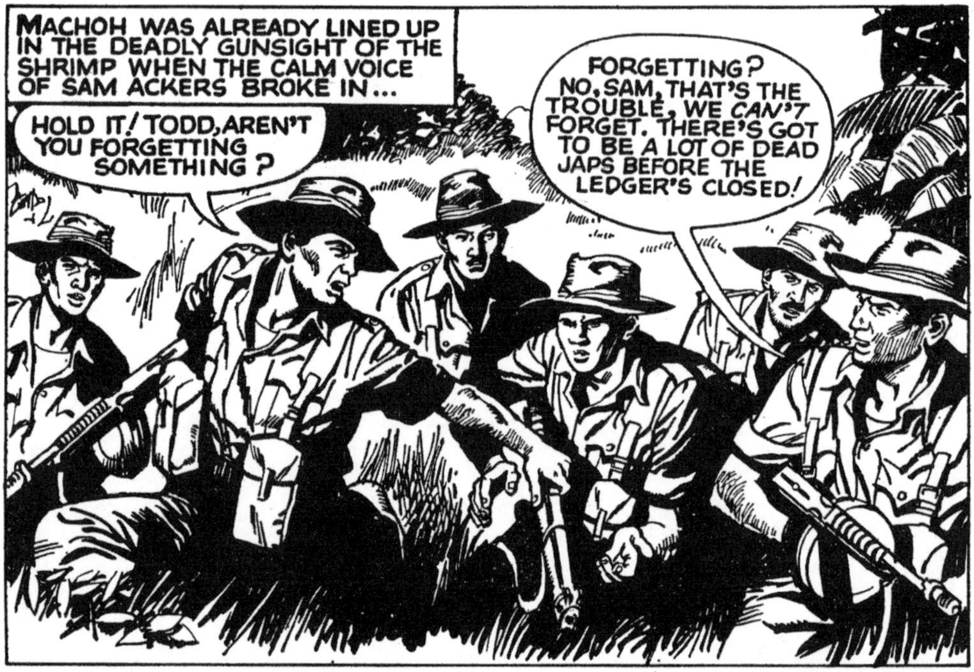
MACHOH WAS ALREADY LINED UP IN THE DEADLY GUNSIGHT OF THE SHRIMP WHEN THE CALM VOICE OF SAM ACKERS BROKE IN...
HOLD IT! TODD, AREN'T YOU FORGETTING SOMETHING?
FORGETTING? NO, SAM, THAT'S THE TROUBLE, WE *CAN'T* FORGET. THERE'S GOT TO BE A LOT OF DEAD JAPS BEFORE THE LEDGER'S CLOSED!

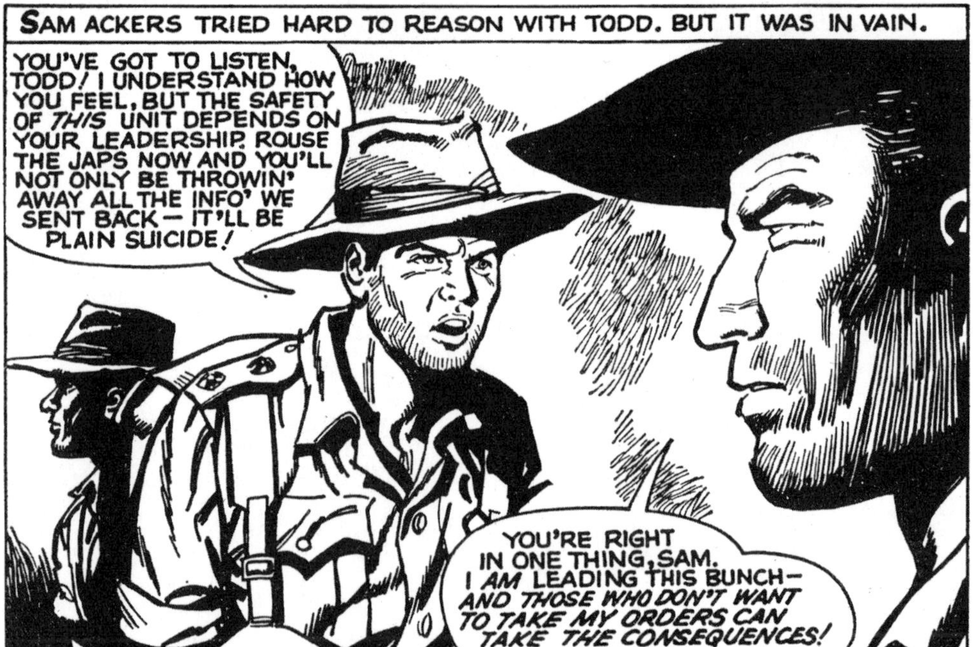
SAM ACKERS TRIED HARD TO REASON WITH TODD. BUT IT WAS IN VAIN.
YOU'VE GOT TO LISTEN, TODD! I UNDERSTAND HOW YOU FEEL, BUT THE SAFETY OF *THIS* UNIT DEPENDS ON YOUR LEADERSHIP. ROUSE THE JAPS NOW AND YOU'LL NOT ONLY BE THROWIN' AWAY ALL THE INFO' WE SENT BACK — IT'LL BE PLAIN SUICIDE!
YOU'RE RIGHT IN ONE THING, SAM. I *AM* LEADING THIS BUNCH — AND *THOSE WHO DON'T WANT TO TAKE MY ORDERS CAN TAKE THE CONSEQUENCES!*

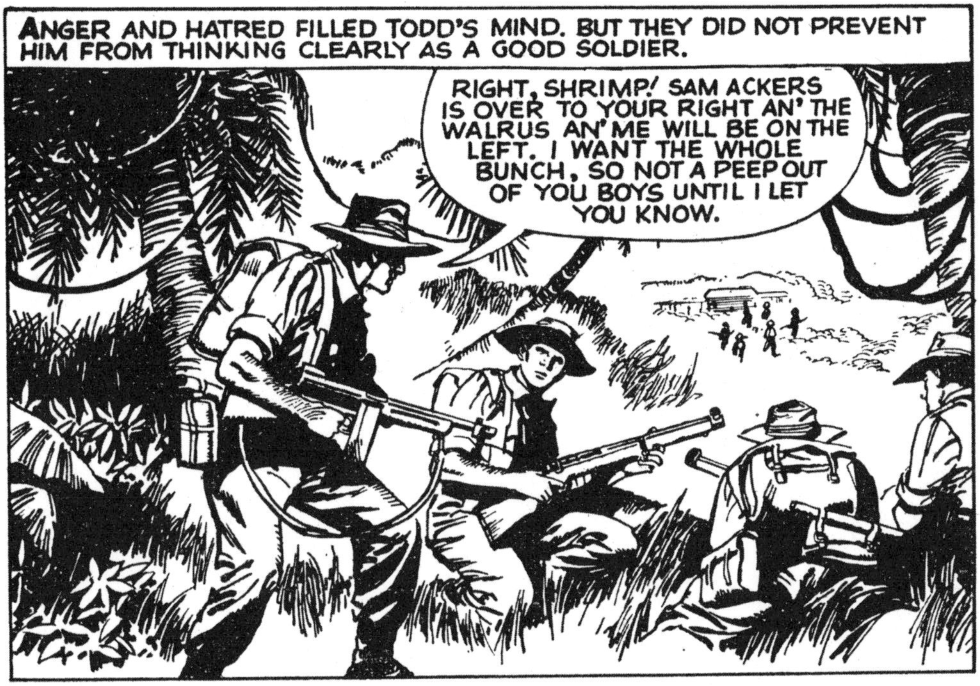
ANGER AND HATRED FILLED TODD'S MIND. BUT THEY DID NOT PREVENT HIM FROM THINKING CLEARLY AS A GOOD SOLDIER.
RIGHT, SHRIMP! SAM ACKERS IS OVER TO YOUR RIGHT AN' THE WALRUS AN' ME WILL BE ON THE LEFT. I WANT THE WHOLE BUNCH, SO NOT A PEEP OUT OF YOU BOYS UNTIL I LET YOU KNOW.

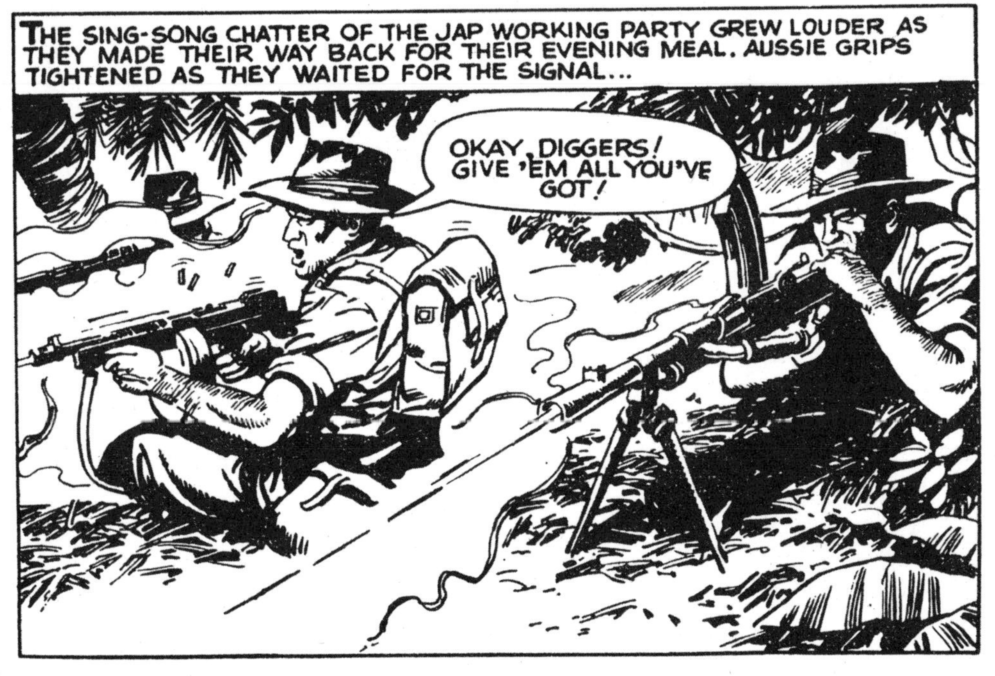
THE SING-SONG CHATTER OF THE JAP WORKING PARTY GREW LOUDER AS THEY MADE THEIR WAY BACK FOR THEIR EVENING MEAL. AUSSIE GRIPS TIGHTENED AS THEY WAITED FOR THE SIGNAL...
OKAY, DIGGERS! GIVE 'EM ALL YOU'VE GOT!

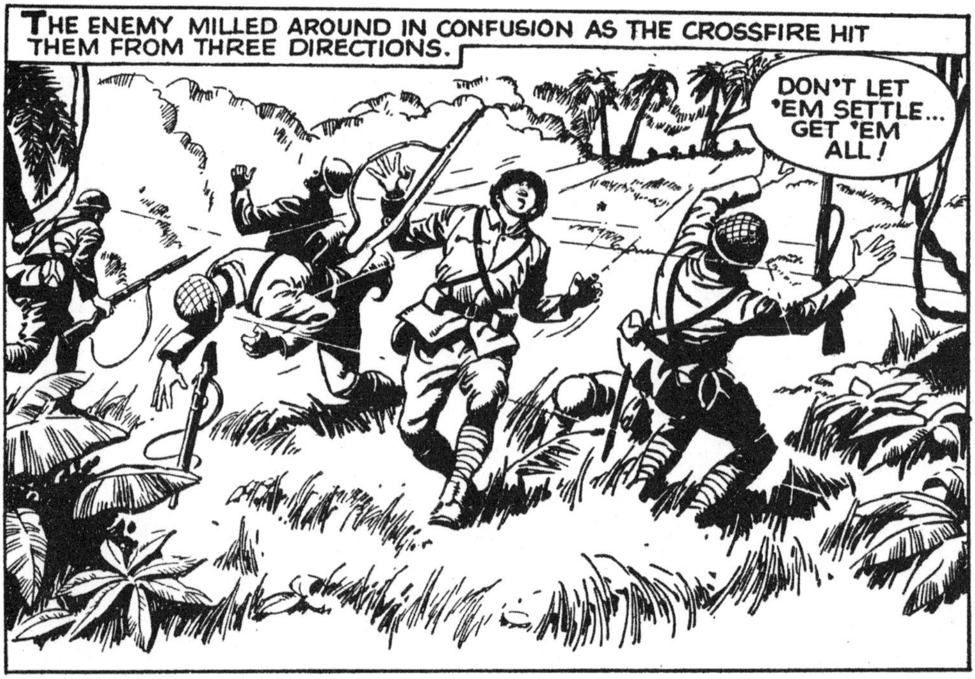
THE ENEMY MILLED AROUND IN CONFUSION AS THE CROSSFIRE HIT THEM FROM THREE DIRECTIONS.
DON'T LET 'EM SETTLE... GET 'EM ALL!

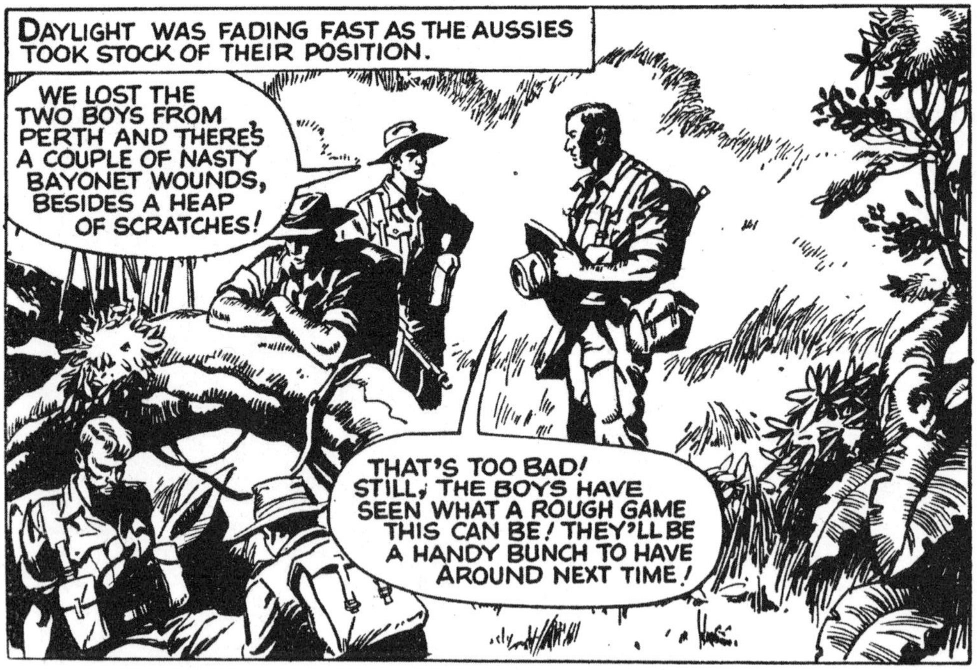
DAYLIGHT WAS FADING FAST AS THE AUSSIES TOOK STOCK OF THEIR POSITION.
WE LOST THE TWO BOYS FROM PERTH AND THERE'S A COUPLE OF NASTY BAYONET WOUNDS, BESIDES A HEAP OF SCRATCHES!
THAT'S TOO BAD! STILL, THE BOYS HAVE SEEN WHAT A ROUGH GAME THIS CAN BE! THEY'LL BE A HANDY BUNCH TO HAVE AROUND NEXT TIME!

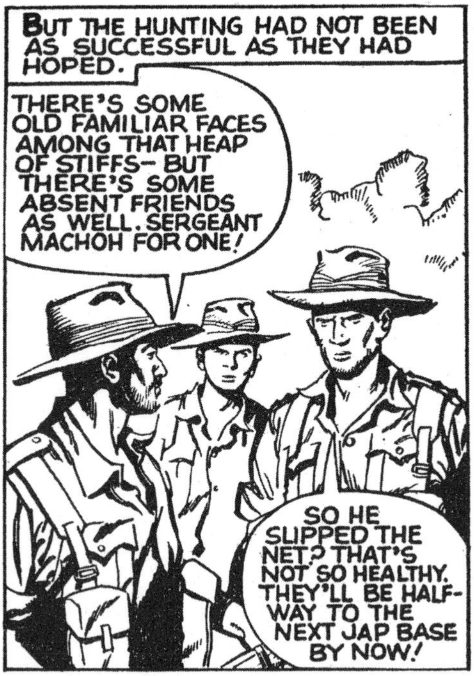
BUT THE HUNTING HAD NOT BEEN AS SUCCESSFUL AS THEY HAD HOPED.
THERE'S SOME OLD FAMILIAR FACES AMONG THAT HEAP OF STIFFS– BUT THERE'S SOME ABSENT FRIENDS AS WELL. SERGEANT MACHOH FOR ONE!
SO HE SLIPPED THE NET? THAT'S NOT SO HEALTHY. THEY'LL BE HALF-WAY TO THE NEXT JAP BASE BY NOW!

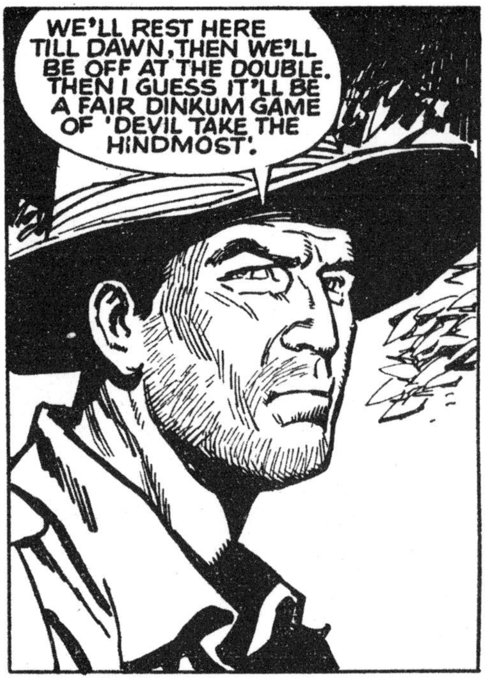
WE'LL REST HERE TILL DAWN, THEN WE'LL BE OFF AT THE DOUBLE. THEN I GUESS IT'LL BE A FAIR DINKUM GAME OF 'DEVIL TAKE THE HINDMOST'.

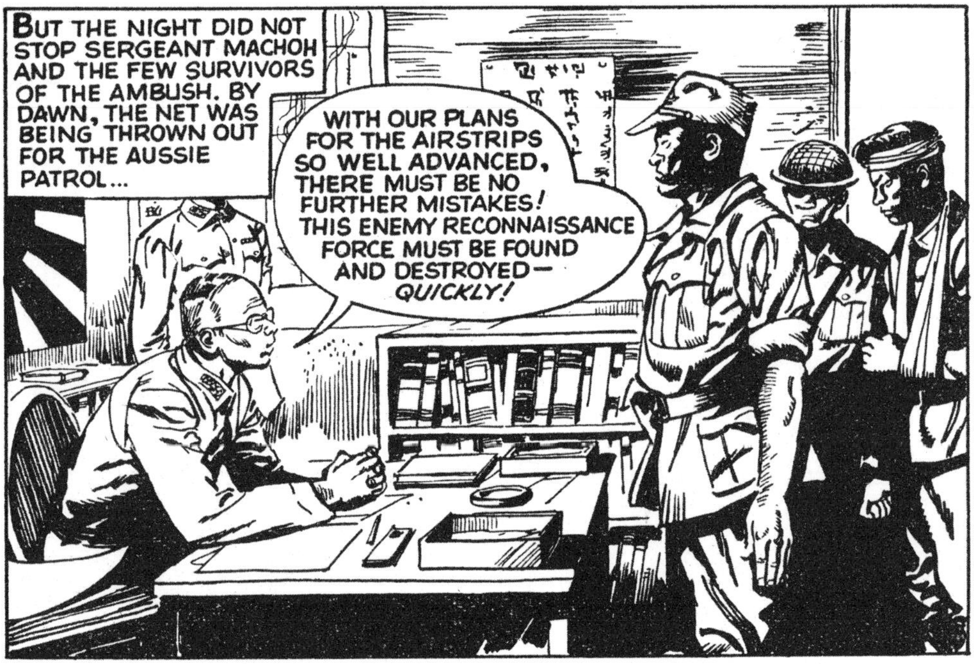
BUT THE NIGHT DID NOT STOP SERGEANT MACHOH AND THE FEW SURVIVORS OF THE AMBUSH. BY DAWN, THE NET WAS BEING THROWN OUT FOR THE AUSSIE PATROL...
WITH OUR PLANS FOR THE AIRSTRIPS SO WELL ADVANCED, THERE MUST BE NO FURTHER MISTAKES! THIS ENEMY RECONNAISSANCE FORCE MUST BE FOUND AND DESTROYED– QUICKLY!

Chapter 3. The Savage Reckoning

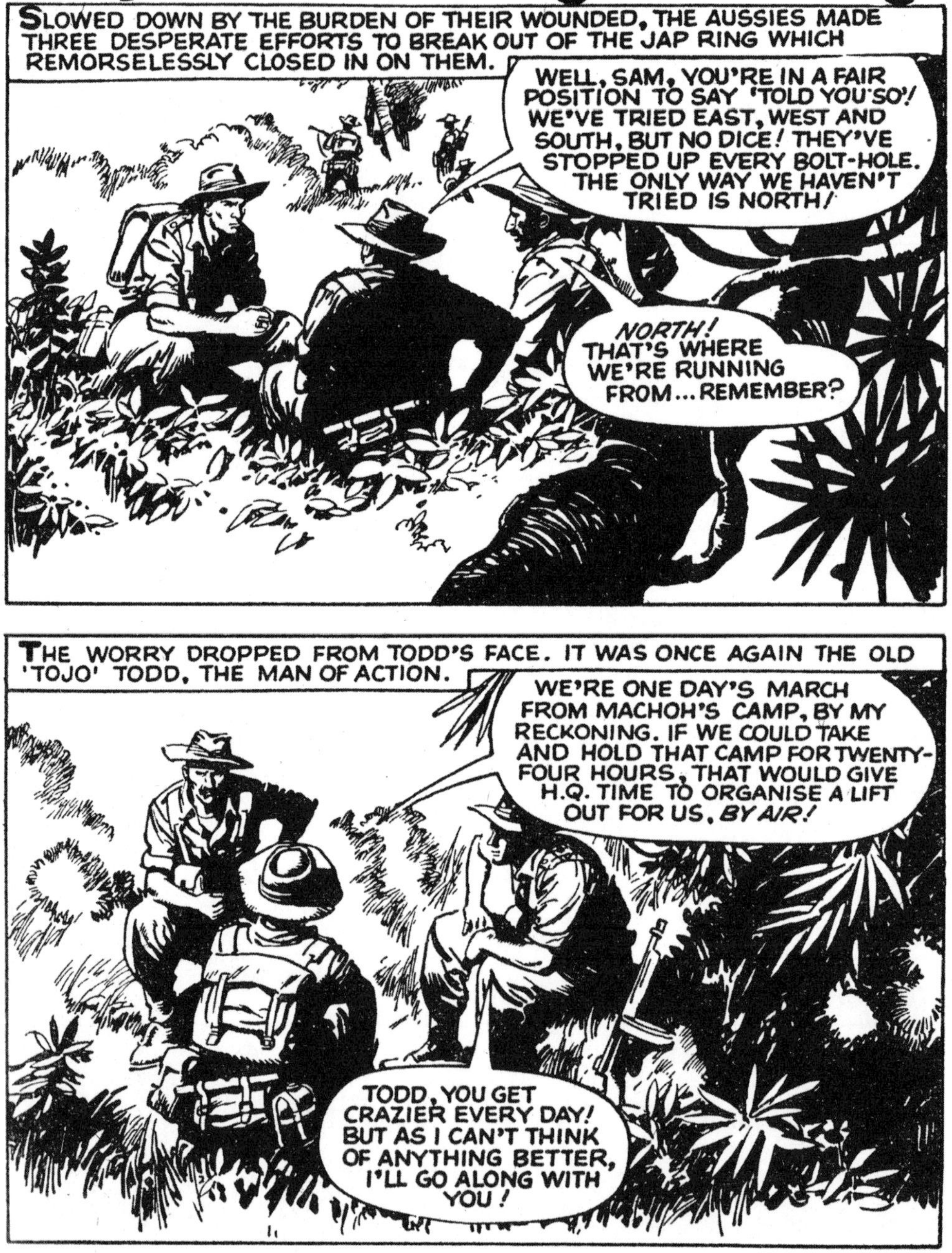
SLOWED DOWN BY THE BURDEN OF THEIR WOUNDED, THE AUSSIES MADE THREE DESPERATE EFFORTS TO BREAK OUT OF THE JAP RING WHICH REMORSELESSLY CLOSED IN ON THEM.
WELL, SAM, YOU'RE IN A FAIR POSITION TO SAY 'TOLD YOU SO'! WE'VE TRIED EAST, WEST AND SOUTH, BUT NO DICE! THEY'VE STOPPED UP EVERY BOLT-HOLE. THE ONLY WAY WE HAVEN'T TRIED IS NORTH!
NORTH! THAT'S WHERE WE'RE RUNNING FROM... REMEMBER?
THE WORRY DROPPED FROM TODD'S FACE. IT WAS ONCE AGAIN THE OLD 'TOJO' TODD, THE MAN OF ACTION.
WE'RE ONE DAY'S MARCH FROM MACHOH'S CAMP, BY MY RECKONING. IF WE COULD TAKE AND HOLD THAT CAMP FOR TWENTY-FOUR HOURS, THAT WOULD GIVE H.Q. TIME TO ORGANISE A LIFT OUT FOR US, BY AIR!
TODD, YOU GET CRAZIER EVERY DAY! BUT AS I CAN'T THINK OF ANYTHING BETTER, I'LL GO ALONG WITH YOU!

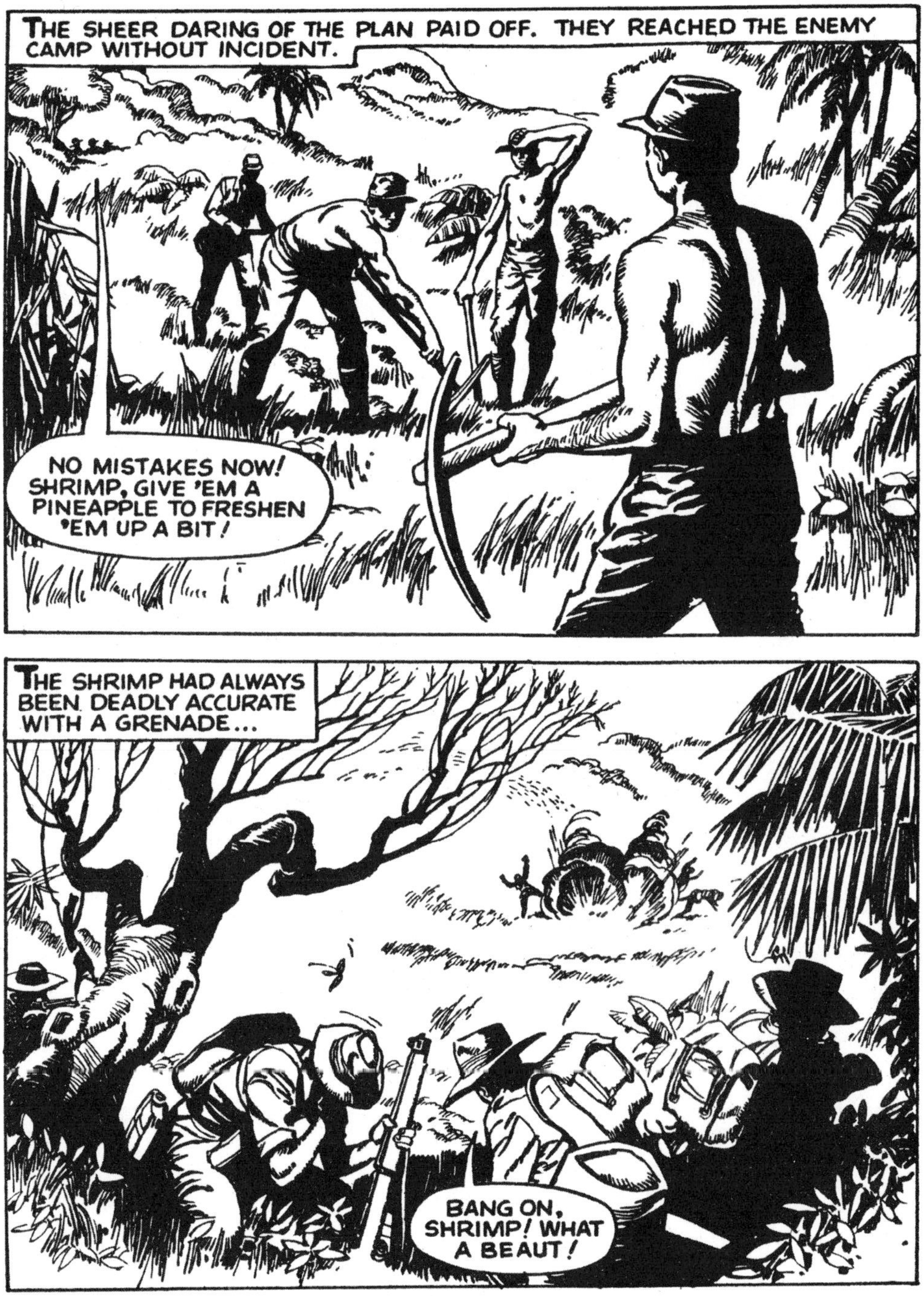
THE SHEER DARING OF THE PLAN PAID OFF. THEY REACHED THE ENEMY CAMP WITHOUT INCIDENT.
NO MISTAKES NOW! SHRIMP, GIVE 'EM A PINEAPPLE TO FRESHEN 'EM UP A BIT!
THE SHRIMP HAD ALWAYS BEEN DEADLY ACCURATE WITH A GRENADE...
BANG ON, SHRIMP! WHAT A BEAUT!

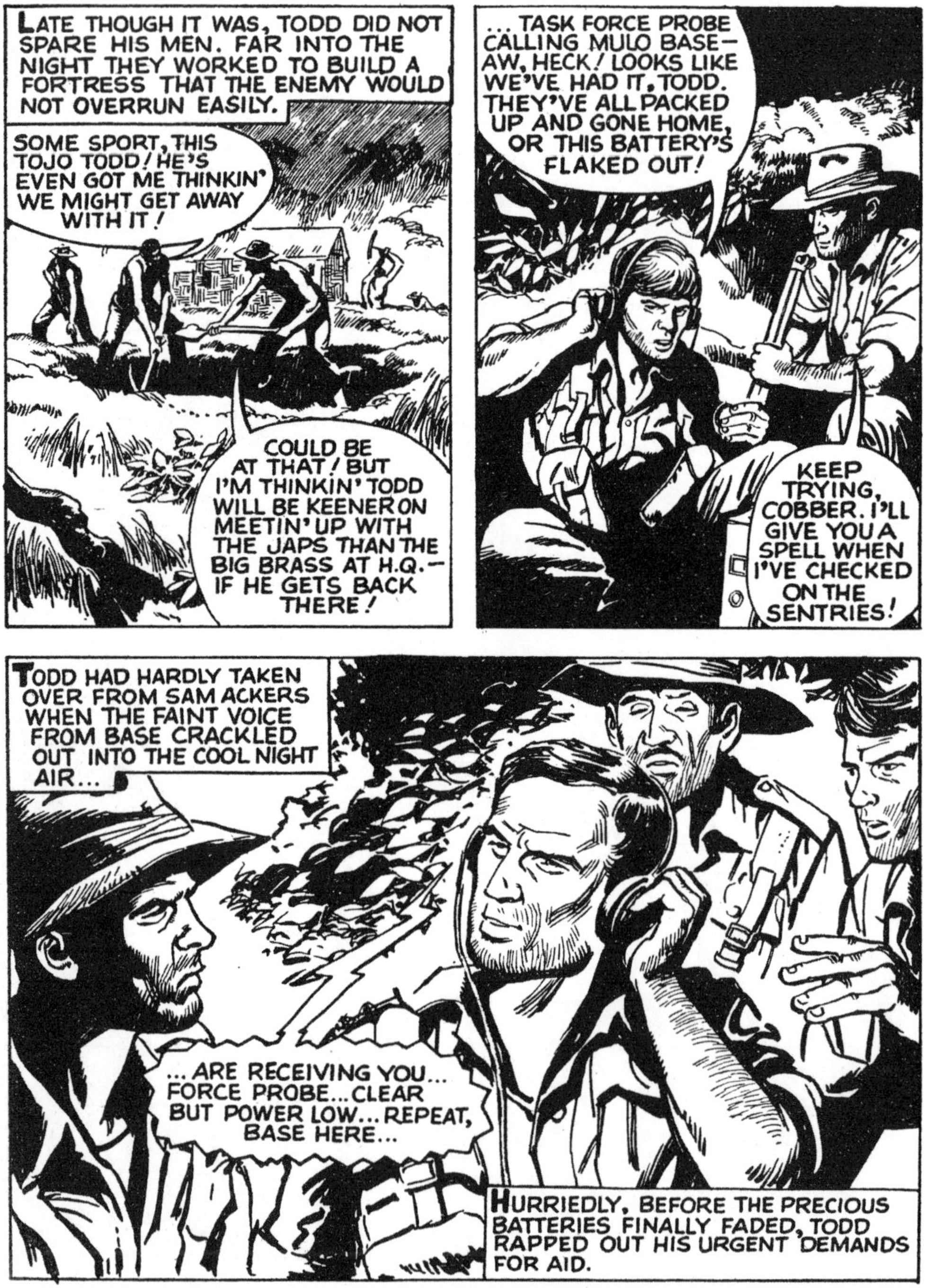
LATE THOUGH IT WAS, TODD DID NOT SPARE HIS MEN. FAR INTO THE NIGHT THEY WORKED TO BUILD A FORTRESS THAT THE ENEMY WOULD NOT OVERRUN EASILY.
SOME SPORT, THIS TOJO TODD! HE'S EVEN GOT ME THINKIN' WE MIGHT GET AWAY WITH IT!
COULD BE AT THAT! BUT I'M THINKIN' TODD WILL BE KEENER ON MEETIN' UP WITH THE JAPS THAN THE BIG BRASS AT H.Q.— IF HE GETS BACK THERE!
... TASK FORCE PROBE CALLING MULO BASE— AW, HECK! LOOKS LIKE WE'VE HAD IT, TODD. THEY'VE ALL PACKED UP AND GONE HOME, OR THIS BATTERY'S FLAKED OUT!
KEEP TRYING, COBBER. I'LL GIVE YOU A SPELL WHEN I'VE CHECKED ON THE SENTRIES!
TODD HAD HARDLY TAKEN OVER FROM SAM ACKERS WHEN THE FAINT VOICE FROM BASE CRACKLED OUT INTO THE COOL NIGHT AIR...
... ARE RECEIVING YOU... FORCE PROBE... CLEAR BUT POWER LOW... REPEAT, BASE HERE...
HURRIEDLY, BEFORE THE PRECIOUS BATTERIES FINALLY FADED, TODD RAPPED OUT HIS URGENT DEMANDS FOR AID.

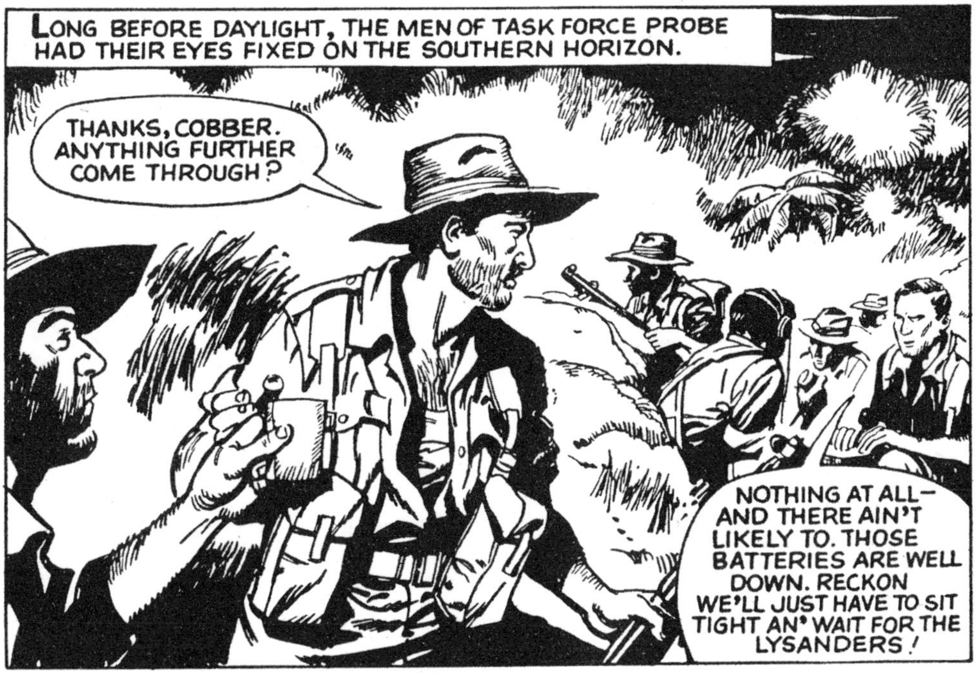
LONG BEFORE DAYLIGHT, THE MEN OF TASK FORCE PROBE HAD THEIR EYES FIXED ON THE SOUTHERN HORIZON.
THANKS, COBBER. ANYTHING FURTHER COME THROUGH?
NOTHING AT ALL— AND THERE AIN'T LIKELY TO. THOSE BATTERIES ARE WELL DOWN. RECKON WE'LL JUST HAVE TO SIT TIGHT AN' WAIT FOR THE LYSANDERS!

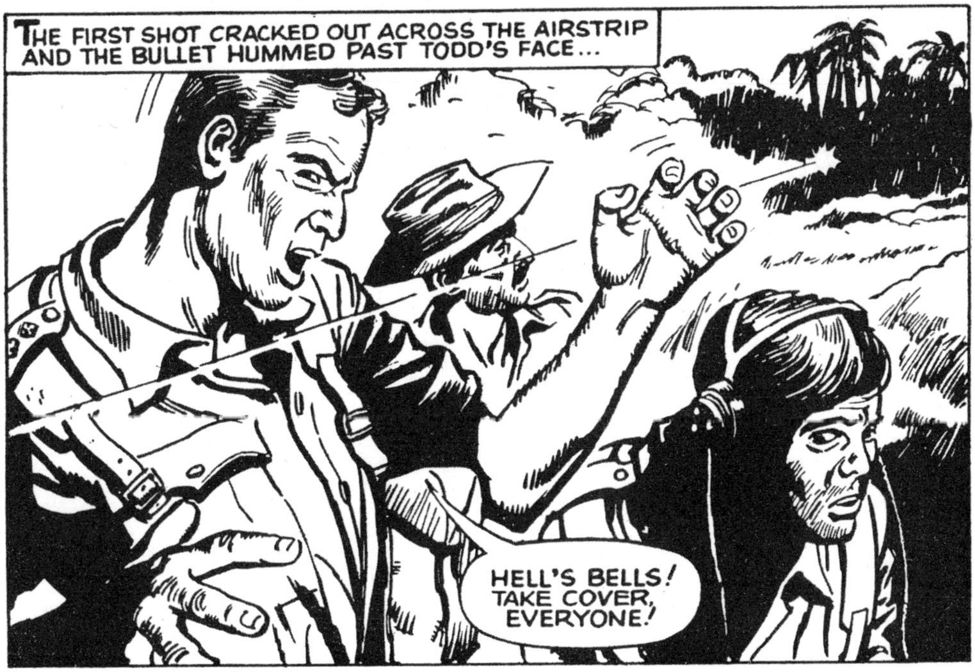
THE FIRST SHOT CRACKED OUT ACROSS THE AIRSTRIP AND THE BULLET HUMMED PAST TODD'S FACE...
HELL'S BELLS! TAKE COVER, EVERYONE!

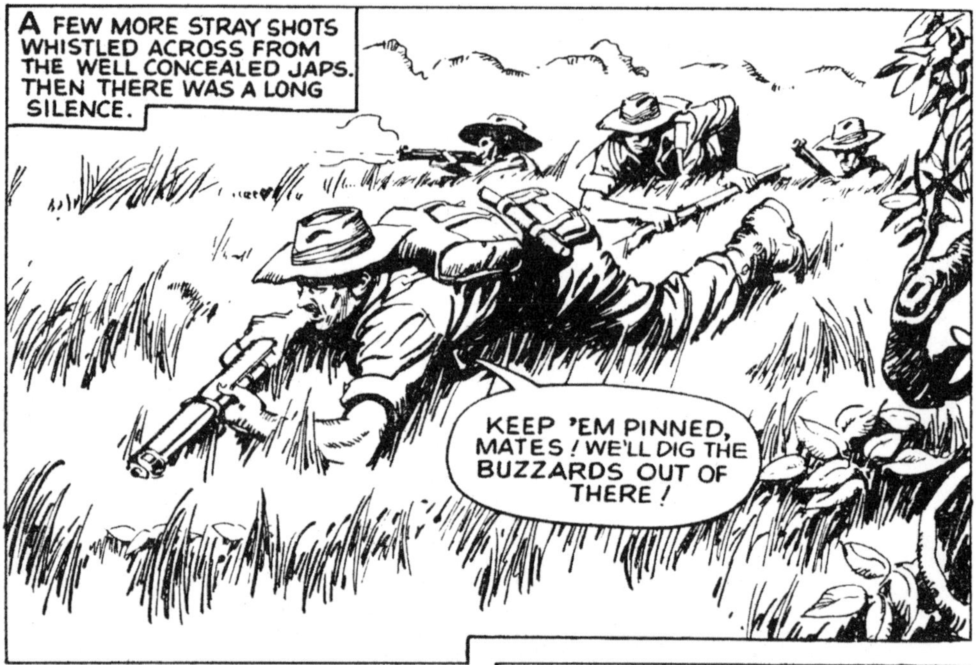
A FEW MORE STRAY SHOTS WHISTLED ACROSS FROM THE WELL CONCEALED JAPS. THEN THERE WAS A LONG SILENCE.
KEEP 'EM PINNED, MATES! WE'LL DIG THE BUZZARDS OUT OF THERE!

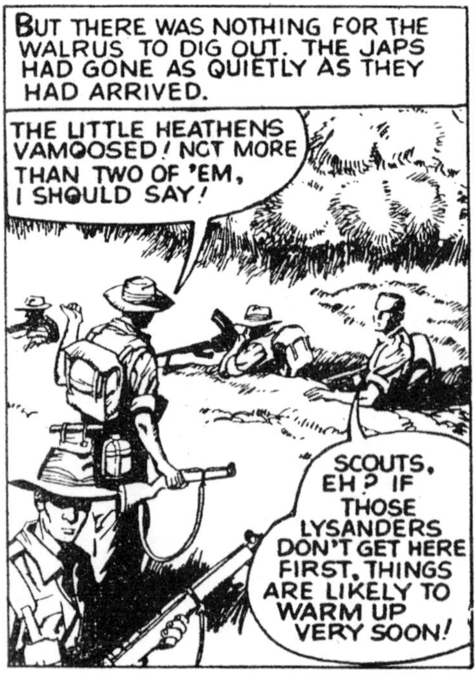
BUT THERE WAS NOTHING FOR THE WALRUS TO DIG OUT. THE JAPS HAD GONE AS QUIETLY AS THEY HAD ARRIVED.
THE LITTLE HEATHENS VAMOOSED! NOT MORE THAN TWO OF 'EM, I SHOULD SAY!
SCOUTS, EH? IF THOSE LYSANDERS DON'T GET HERE FIRST, THINGS ARE LIKELY TO WARM UP VERY SOON!

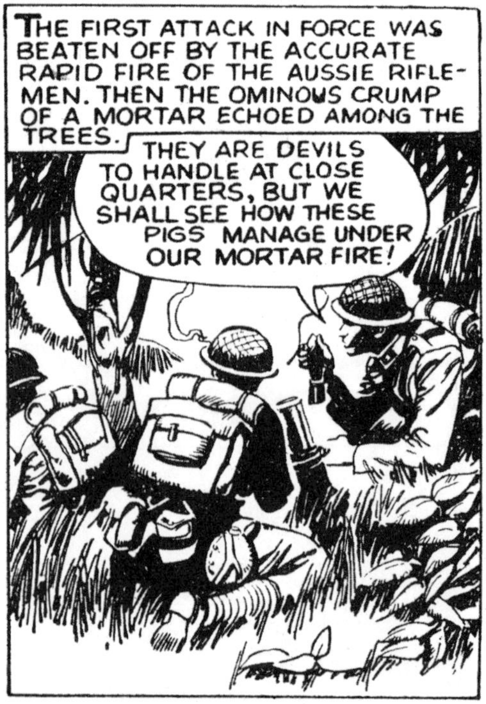
THE FIRST ATTACK IN FORCE WAS BEATEN OFF BY THE ACCURATE RAPID FIRE OF THE AUSSIE RIFLE-MEN. THEN THE OMINOUS CRUMP OF A MORTAR ECHOED AMONG THE TREES.
THEY ARE DEVILS TO HANDLE AT CLOSE QUARTERS, BUT WE SHALL SEE HOW THESE PIGS MANAGE UNDER OUR MORTAR FIRE!

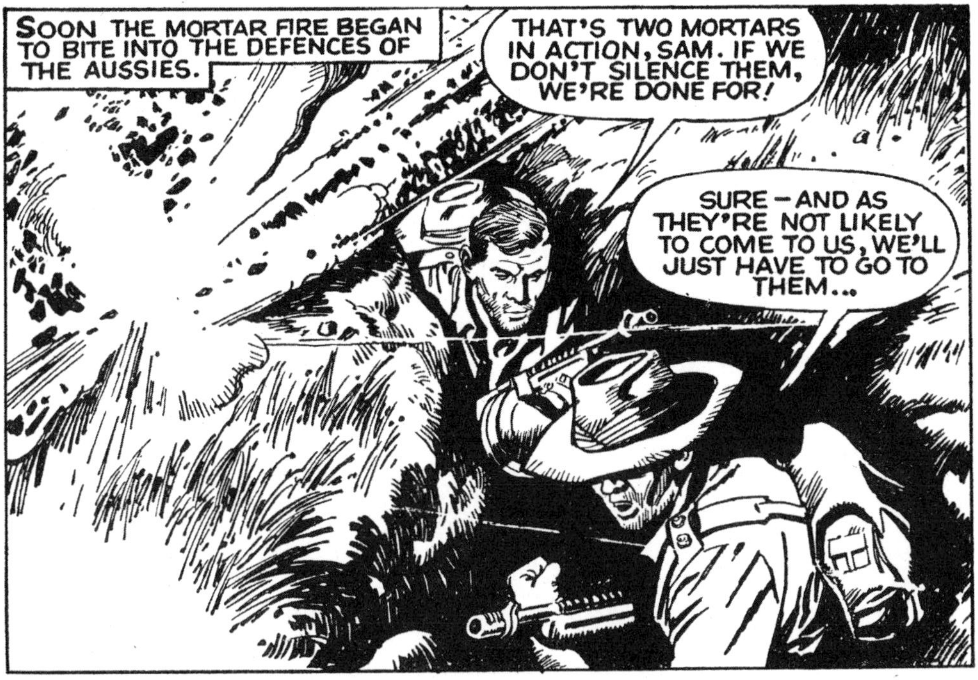
SOON THE MORTAR FIRE BEGAN TO BITE INTO THE DEFENCES OF THE AUSSIES.
THAT'S TWO MORTARS IN ACTION, SAM. IF WE DON'T SILENCE THEM, WE'RE DONE FOR!
SURE – AND AS THEY'RE NOT LIKELY TO COME TO US, WE'LL JUST HAVE TO GO TO THEM...

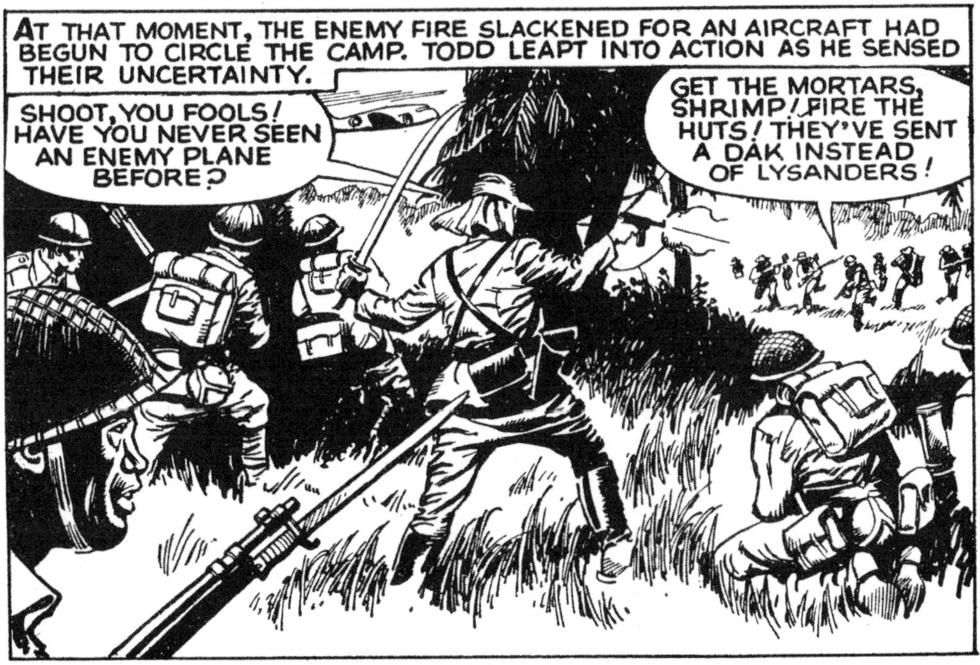
AT THAT MOMENT, THE ENEMY FIRE SLACKENED FOR AN AIRCRAFT HAD BEGUN TO CIRCLE THE CAMP. TODD LEAPT INTO ACTION AS HE SENSED THEIR UNCERTAINTY.
SHOOT, YOU FOOLS! HAVE YOU NEVER SEEN AN ENEMY PLANE BEFORE?
GET THE MORTARS, SHRIMP! FIRE THE HUTS! THEY'VE SENT A DAK INSTEAD OF LYSANDERS!

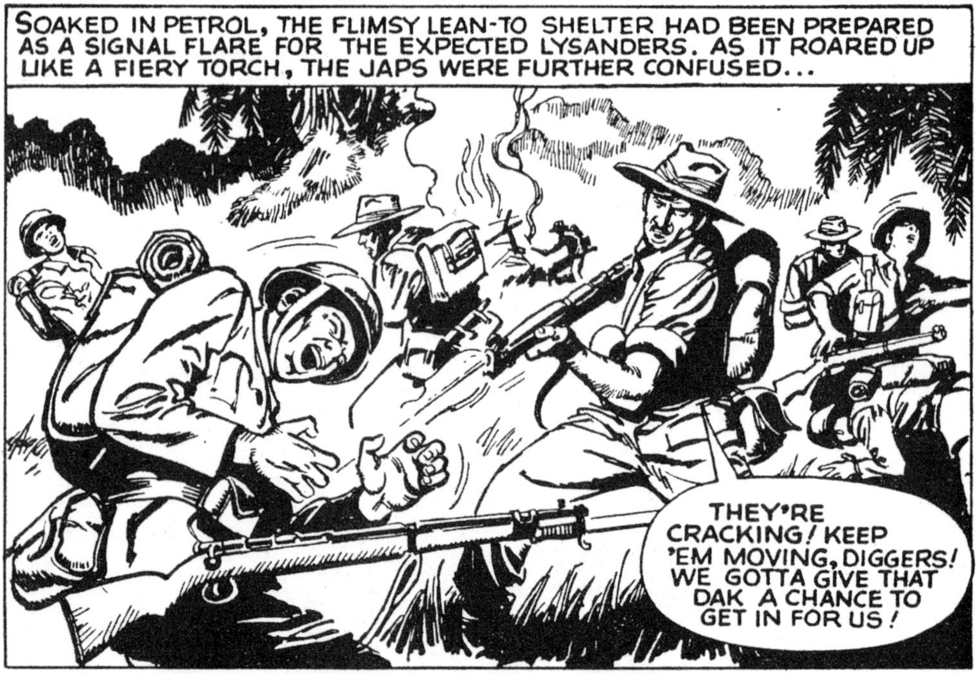
SOAKED IN PETROL, THE FLIMSY LEAN-TO SHELTER HAD BEEN PREPARED AS A SIGNAL FLARE FOR THE EXPECTED LYSANDERS. AS IT ROARED UP LIKE A FIERY TORCH, THE JAPS WERE FURTHER CONFUSED...
THEY'RE CRACKING! KEEP 'EM MOVING, DIGGERS! WE GOTTA GIVE THAT DAK A CHANCE TO GET IN FOR US!

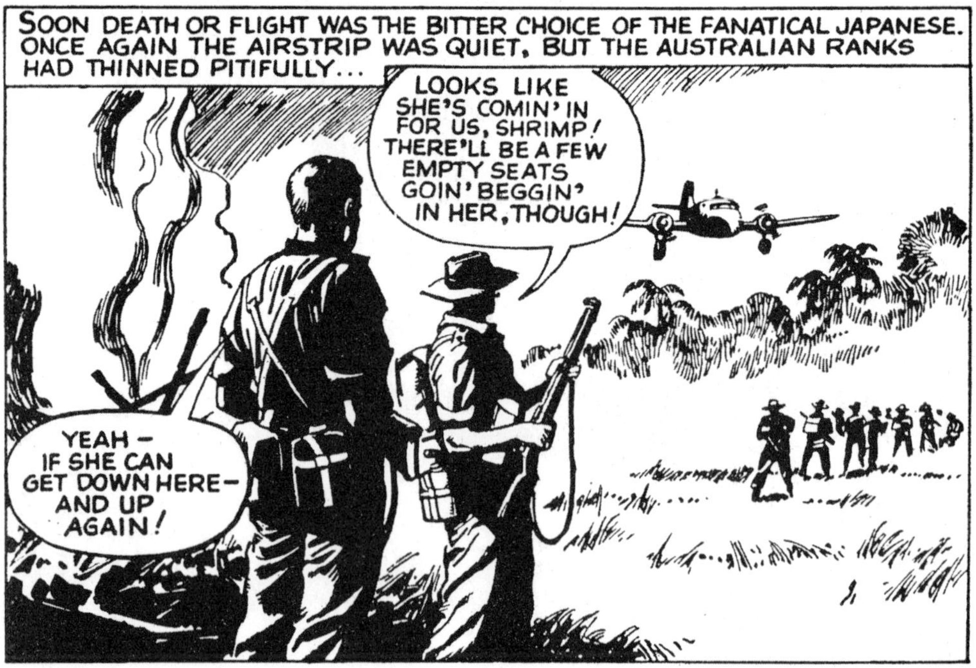
SOON DEATH OR FLIGHT WAS THE BITTER CHOICE OF THE FANATICAL JAPANESE. ONCE AGAIN THE AIRSTRIP WAS QUIET, BUT THE AUSTRALIAN RANKS HAD THINNED PITIFULLY...
LOOKS LIKE SHE'S COMIN' IN FOR US, SHRIMP! THERE'LL BE A FEW EMPTY SEATS GOIN' BEGGIN' IN HER, THOUGH!
YEAH - IF SHE CAN GET DOWN HERE - AND UP AGAIN!

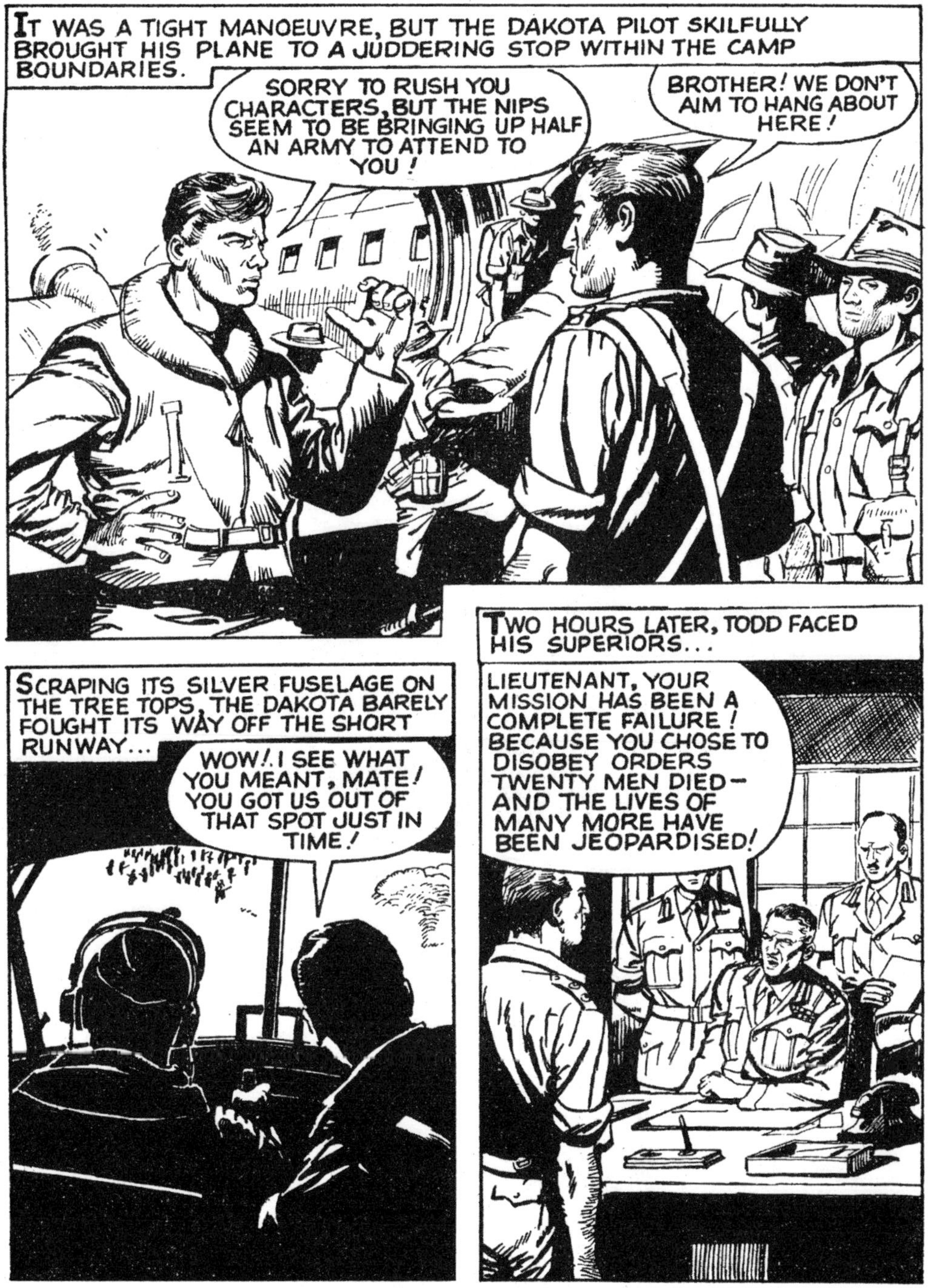
IT WAS A TIGHT MANOEUVRE, BUT THE DAKOTA PILOT SKILFULLY BROUGHT HIS PLANE TO A JUDDERING STOP WITHIN THE CAMP BOUNDARIES.
SORRY TO RUSH YOU CHARACTERS, BUT THE NIPS SEEM TO BE BRINGING UP HALF AN ARMY TO ATTEND TO YOU!
BROTHER! WE DON'T AIM TO HANG ABOUT HERE!
SCRAPING ITS SILVER FUSELAGE ON THE TREE TOPS, THE DAKOTA BARELY FOUGHT ITS WAY OFF THE SHORT RUNWAY...
WOW!. I SEE WHAT YOU MEANT, MATE! YOU GOT US OUT OF THAT SPOT JUST IN TIME!
TWO HOURS LATER, TODD FACED HIS SUPERIORS...
LIEUTENANT, YOUR MISSION HAS BEEN A COMPLETE FAILURE! BECAUSE YOU CHOSE TO DISOBEY ORDERS TWENTY MEN DIED— AND THE LIVES OF MANY MORE HAVE BEEN JEOPARDISED!

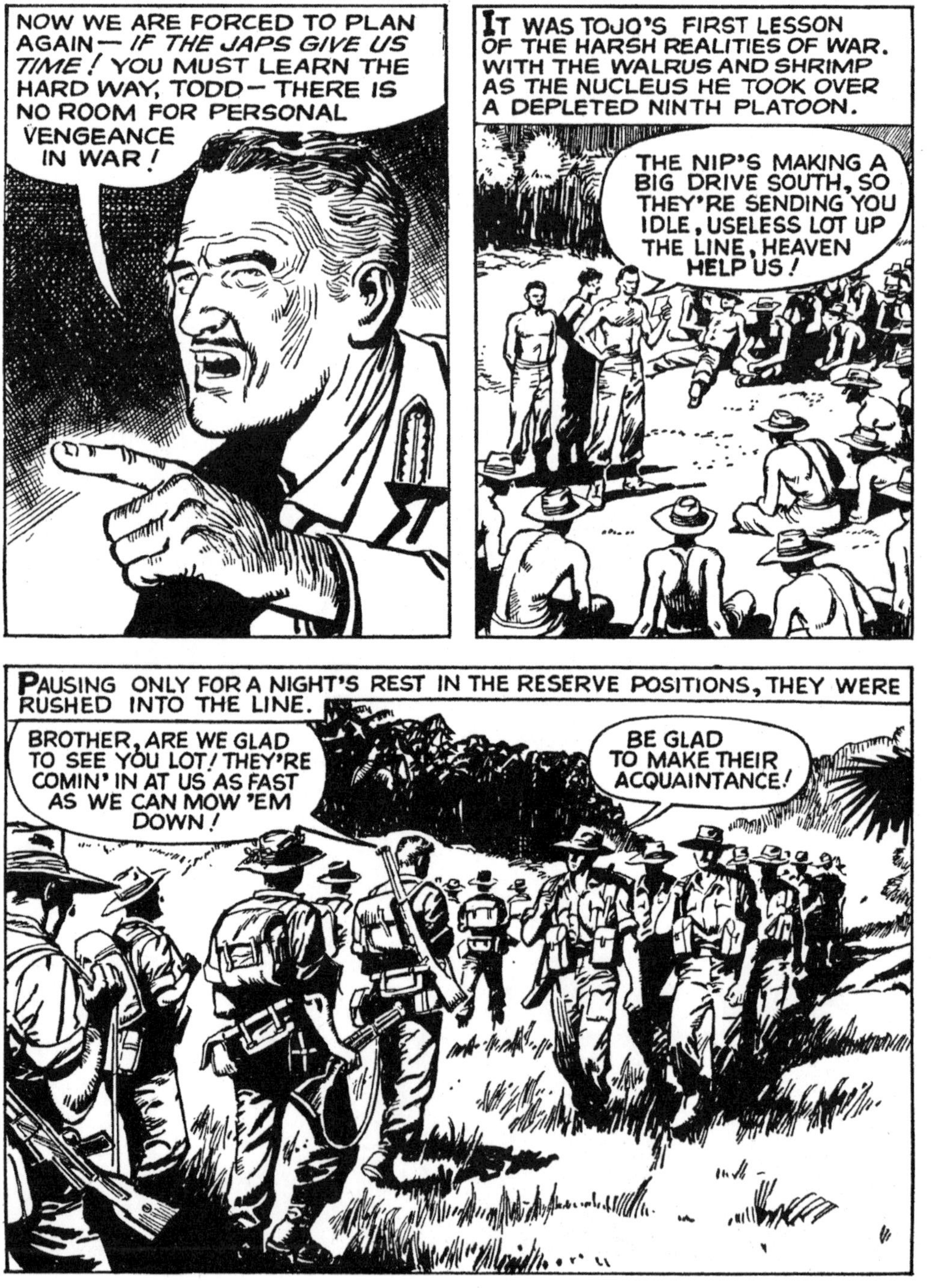
NOW WE ARE FORCED TO PLAN AGAIN— *IF THE JAPS GIVE US TIME!* YOU MUST LEARN THE HARD WAY, TODD— THERE IS NO ROOM FOR PERSONAL VENGEANCE IN WAR!
IT WAS TOJO'S FIRST LESSON OF THE HARSH REALITIES OF WAR. WITH THE WALRUS AND SHRIMP AS THE NUCLEUS HE TOOK OVER A DEPLETED NINTH PLATOON.
THE NIP'S MAKING A BIG DRIVE SOUTH, SO THEY'RE SENDING YOU IDLE, USELESS LOT UP THE LINE, HEAVEN HELP US!
PAUSING ONLY FOR A NIGHT'S REST IN THE RESERVE POSITIONS, THEY WERE RUSHED INTO THE LINE.
BROTHER, ARE WE GLAD TO SEE YOU LOT! THEY'RE COMIN' IN AT US AS FAST AS WE CAN MOW 'EM DOWN!
BE GLAD TO MAKE THEIR ACQUAINTANCE!

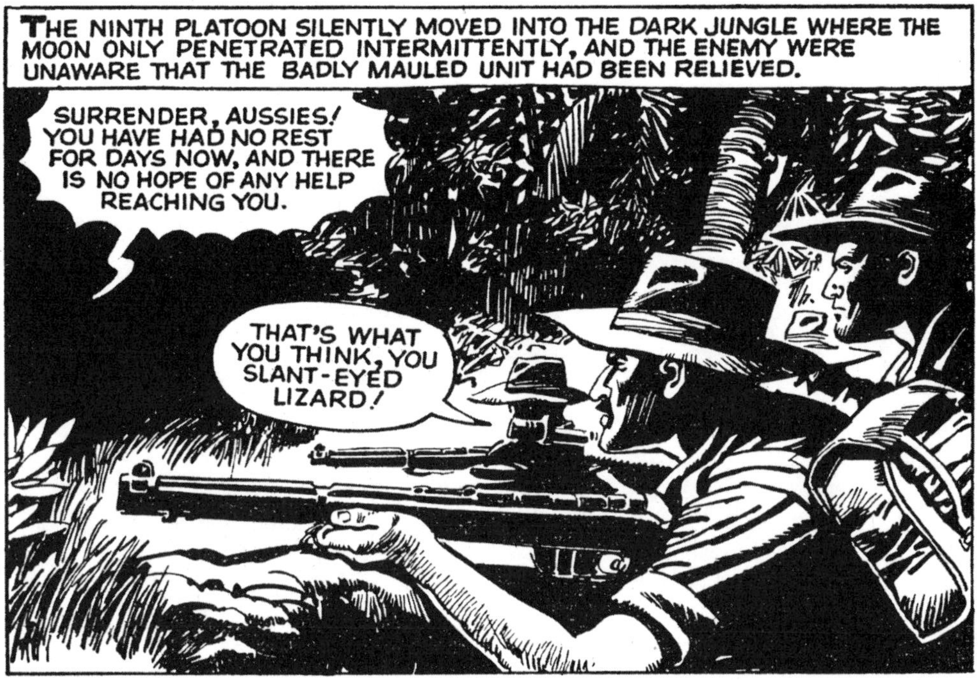
THE NINTH PLATOON SILENTLY MOVED INTO THE DARK JUNGLE WHERE THE MOON ONLY PENETRATED INTERMITTENTLY, AND THE ENEMY WERE UNAWARE THAT THE BADLY MAULED UNIT HAD BEEN RELIEVED.
SURRENDER, AUSSIES! YOU HAVE HAD NO REST FOR DAYS NOW, AND THERE IS NO HOPE OF ANY HELP REACHING YOU.
THAT'S WHAT YOU THINK, YOU SLANT-EYED LIZARD!

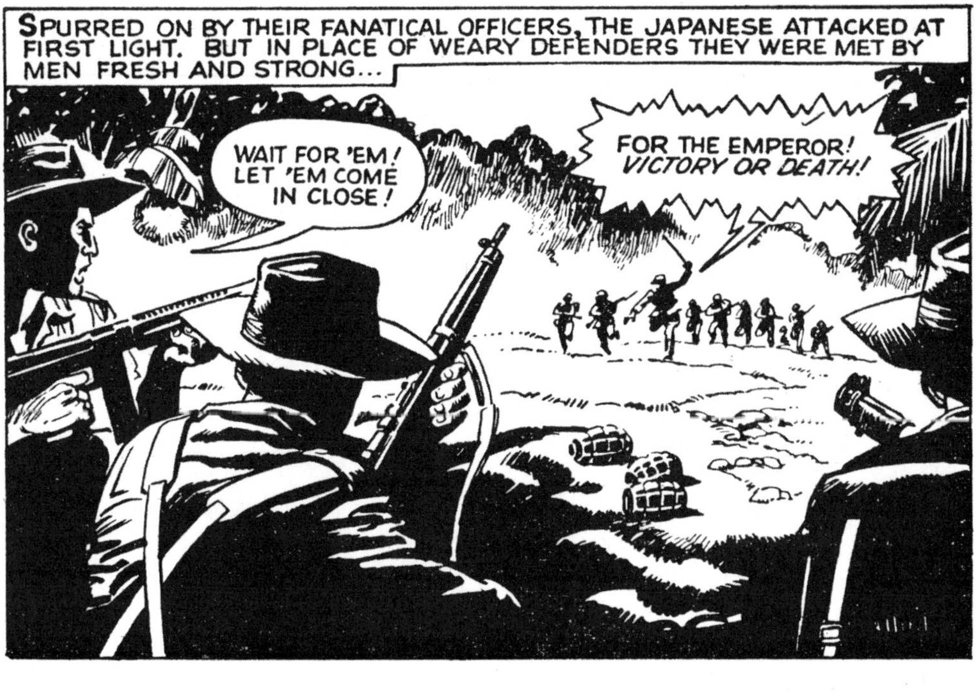
SPURRED ON BY THEIR FANATICAL OFFICERS, THE JAPANESE ATTACKED AT FIRST LIGHT. BUT IN PLACE OF WEARY DEFENDERS THEY WERE MET BY MEN FRESH AND STRONG...
WAIT FOR 'EM! LET 'EM COME IN CLOSE!
FOR THE EMPEROR! *VICTORY OR DEATH!*

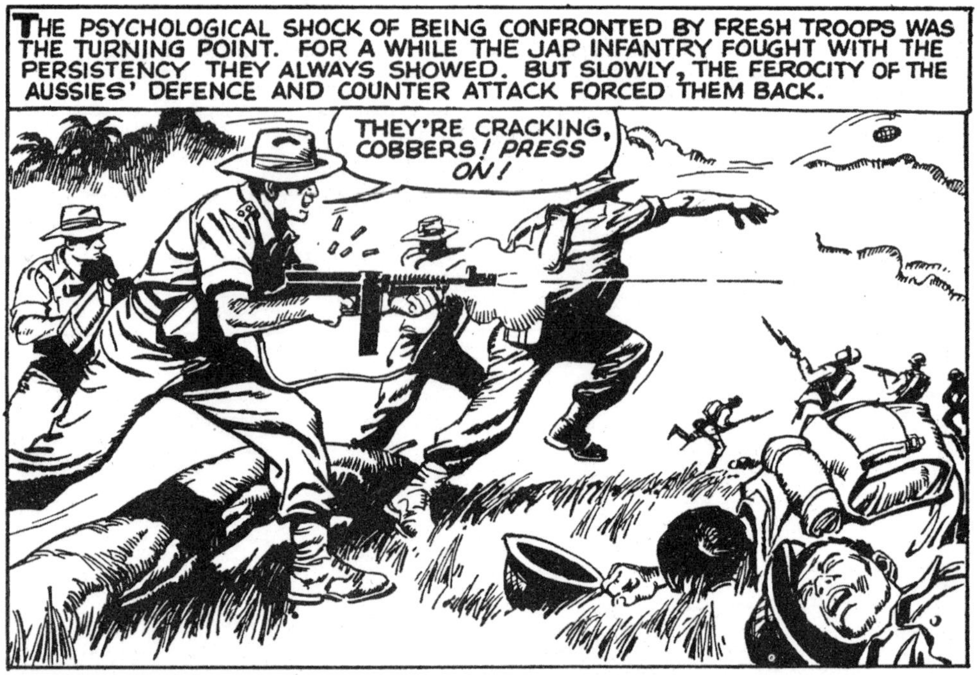
THE PSYCHOLOGICAL SHOCK OF BEING CONFRONTED BY FRESH TROOPS WAS THE TURNING POINT. FOR A WHILE THE JAP INFANTRY FOUGHT WITH THE PERSISTENCY THEY ALWAYS SHOWED. BUT SLOWLY, THE FEROCITY OF THE AUSSIES' DEFENCE AND COUNTER ATTACK FORCED THEM BACK.
THEY'RE CRACKING, COBBERS! PRESS ON!

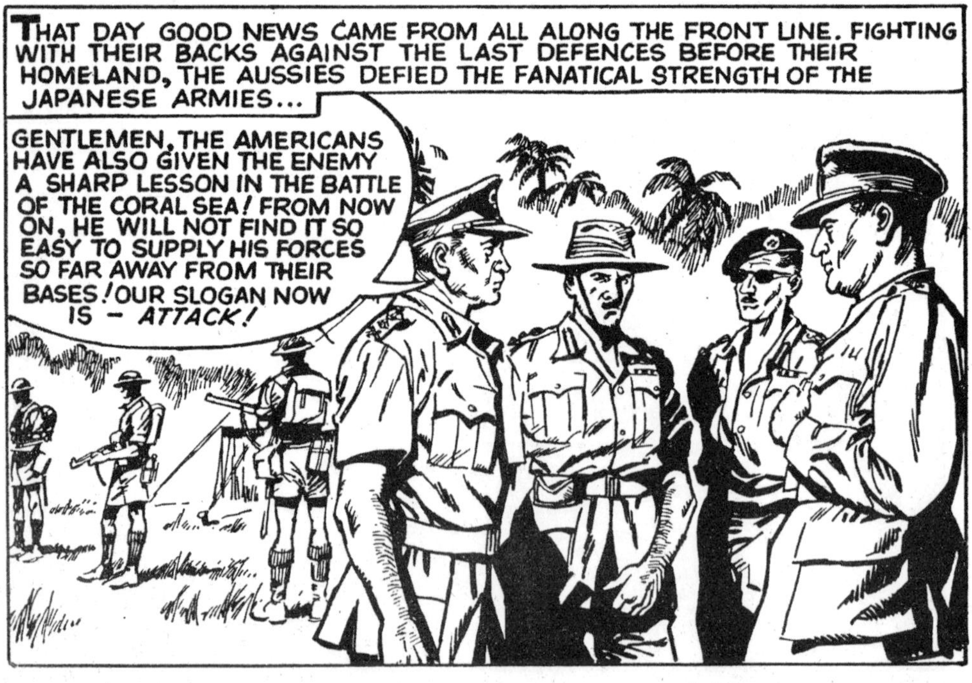
THAT DAY GOOD NEWS CAME FROM ALL ALONG THE FRONT LINE. FIGHTING WITH THEIR BACKS AGAINST THE LAST DEFENCES BEFORE THEIR HOMELAND, THE AUSSIES DEFIED THE FANATICAL STRENGTH OF THE JAPANESE ARMIES...
GENTLEMEN, THE AMERICANS HAVE ALSO GIVEN THE ENEMY A SHARP LESSON IN THE BATTLE OF THE CORAL SEA! FROM NOW ON, HE WILL NOT FIND IT SO EASY TO SUPPLY HIS FORCES SO FAR AWAY FROM THEIR BASES! OUR SLOGAN NOW IS - ATTACK!

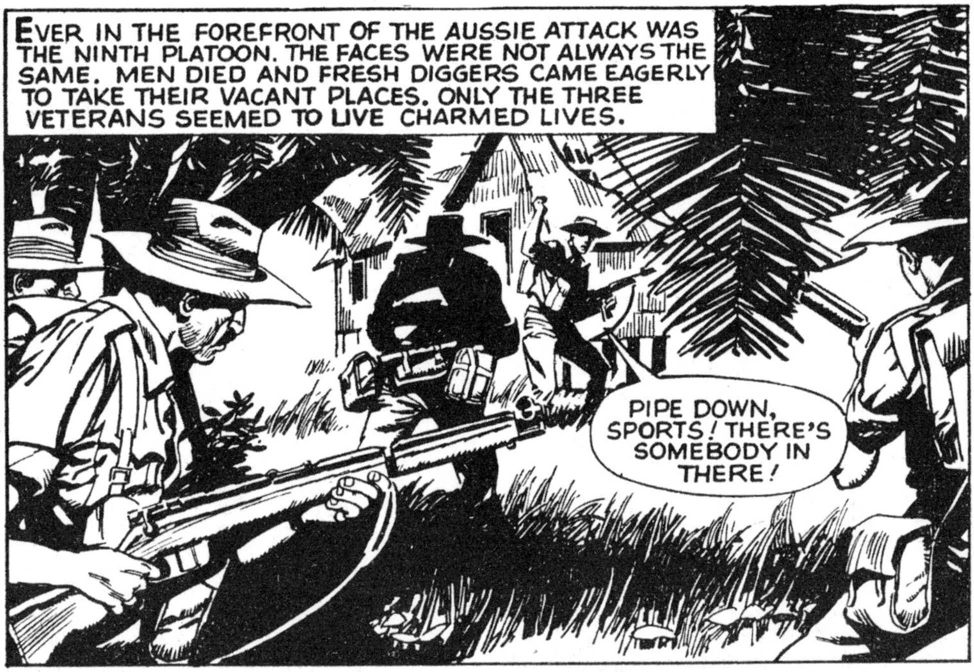
EVER IN THE FOREFRONT OF THE AUSSIE ATTACK WAS THE NINTH PLATOON. THE FACES WERE NOT ALWAYS THE SAME. MEN DIED AND FRESH DIGGERS CAME EAGERLY TO TAKE THEIR VACANT PLACES. ONLY THE THREE VETERANS SEEMED TO LIVE CHARMED LIVES.
PIPE DOWN, SPORTS! THERE'S SOMEBODY IN THERE!

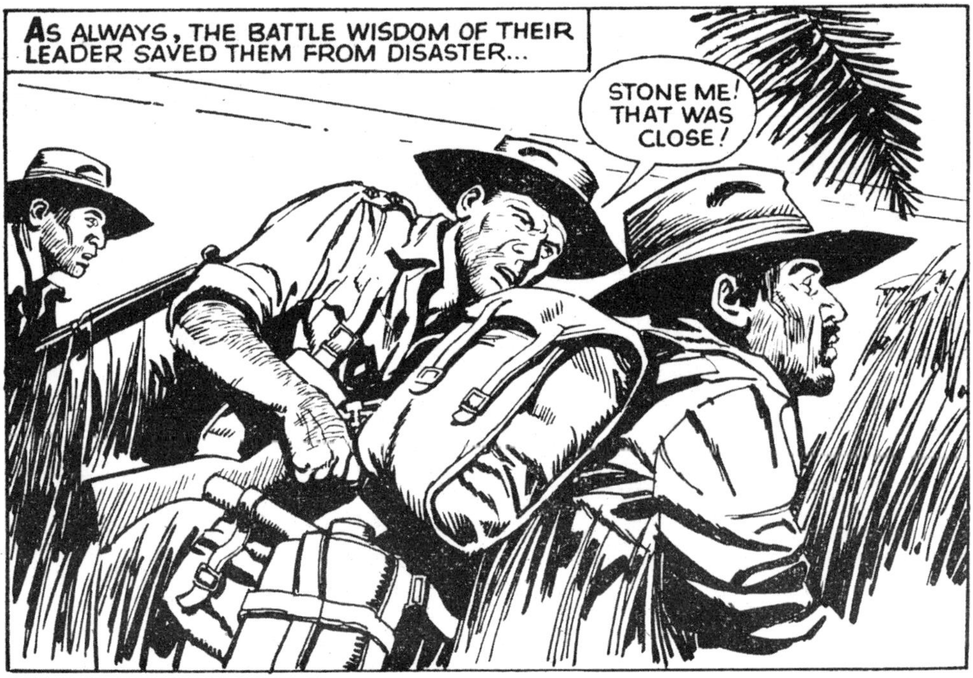
AS ALWAYS, THE BATTLE WISDOM OF THEIR LEADER SAVED THEM FROM DISASTER...
STONE ME! THAT WAS CLOSE!

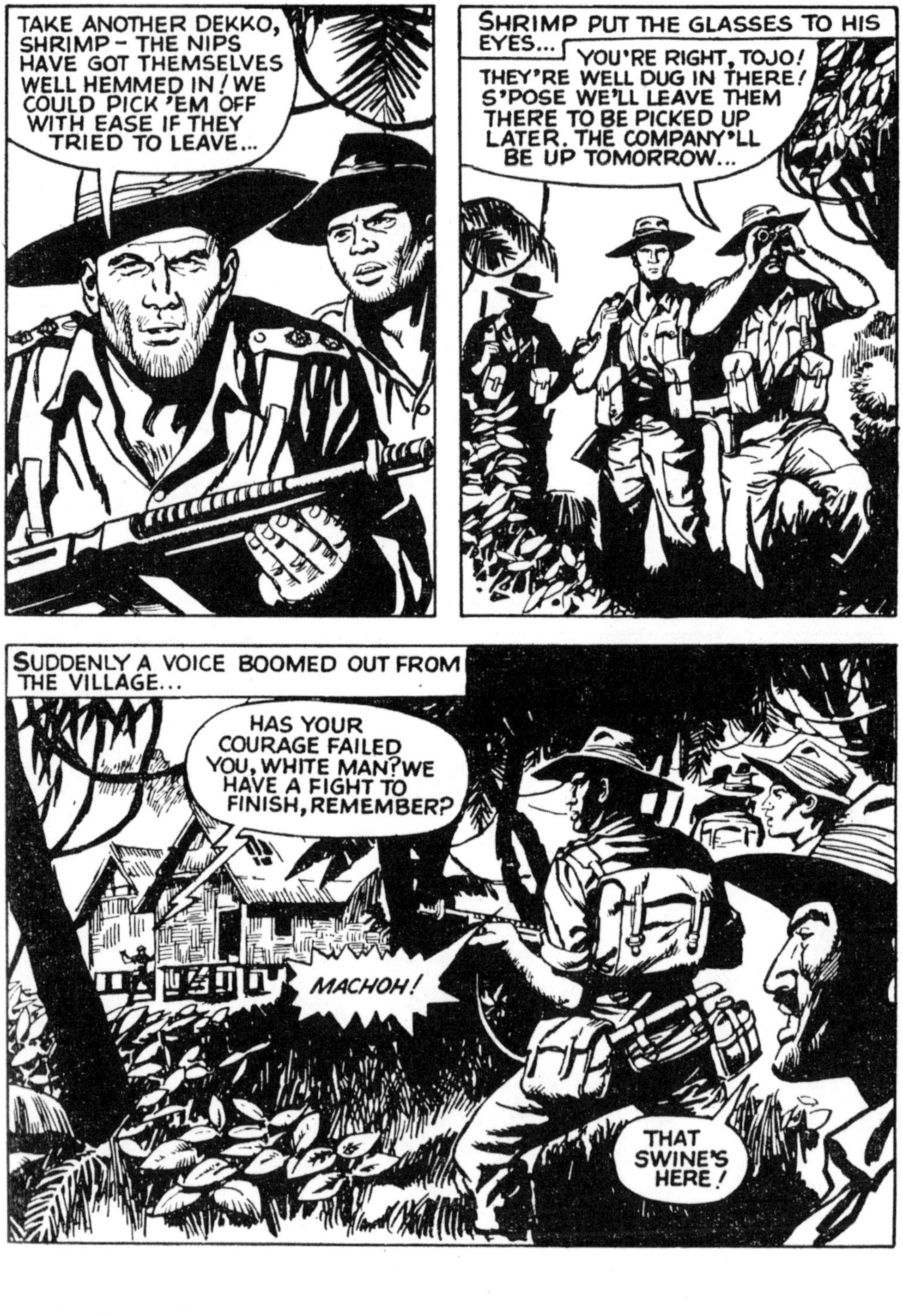
TAKE ANOTHER DEKKO, SHRIMP – THE NIPS HAVE GOT THEMSELVES WELL HEMMED IN! WE COULD PICK 'EM OFF WITH EASE IF THEY TRIED TO LEAVE...
SHRIMP PUT THE GLASSES TO HIS EYES...
YOU'RE RIGHT, TOJO! THEY'RE WELL DUG IN THERE! S'POSE WE'LL LEAVE THEM THERE TO BE PICKED UP LATER. THE COMPANY'LL BE UP TOMORROW...
SUDDENLY A VOICE BOOMED OUT FROM THE VILLAGE...
HAS YOUR COURAGE FAILED YOU, WHITE MAN? WE HAVE A FIGHT TO FINISH, REMEMBER?
MACHOH!
THAT SWINE'S HERE!

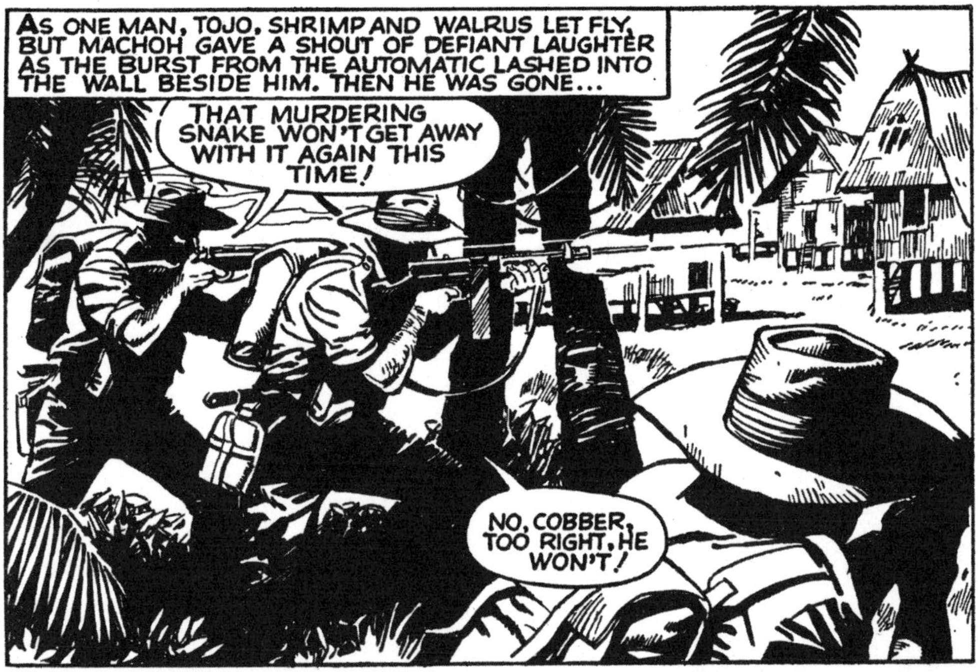
AS ONE MAN, TOJO, SHRIMP AND WALRUS LET FLY, BUT MACHOH GAVE A SHOUT OF DEFIANT LAUGHTER AS THE BURST FROM THE AUTOMATIC LASHED INTO THE WALL BESIDE HIM. THEN HE WAS GONE...
THAT MURDERING SNAKE WON'T GET AWAY WITH IT AGAIN THIS TIME!
NO, COBBER, TOO RIGHT, HE WON'T!

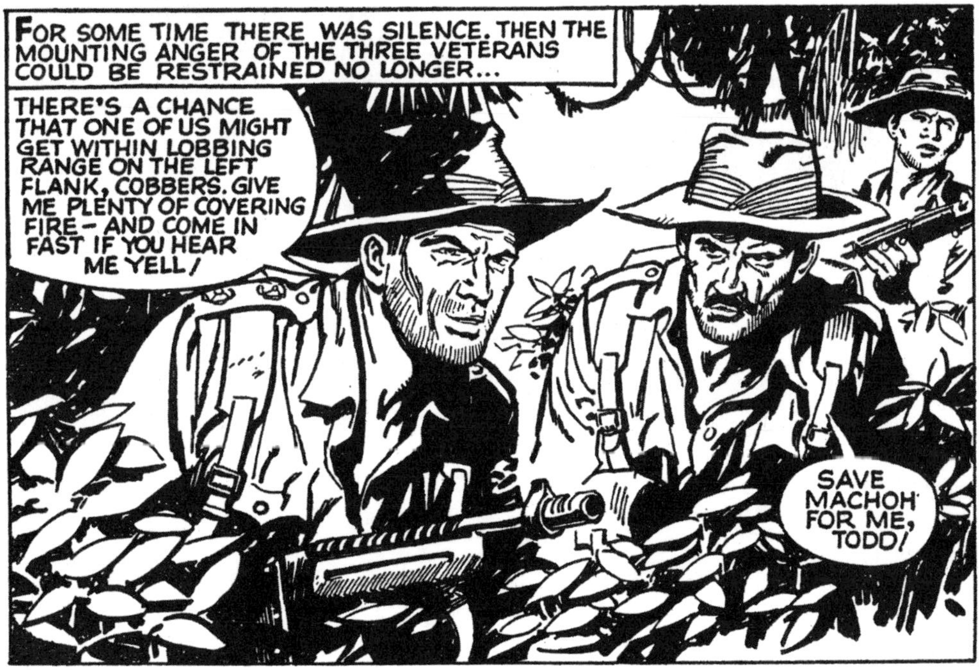
FOR SOME TIME THERE WAS SILENCE. THEN THE MOUNTING ANGER OF THE THREE VETERANS COULD BE RESTRAINED NO LONGER...
THERE'S A CHANCE THAT ONE OF US MIGHT GET WITHIN LOBBING RANGE ON THE LEFT FLANK, COBBERS. GIVE ME PLENTY OF COVERING FIRE — AND COME IN FAST IF YOU HEAR ME YELL!
SAVE MACHOH FOR ME, TODD!

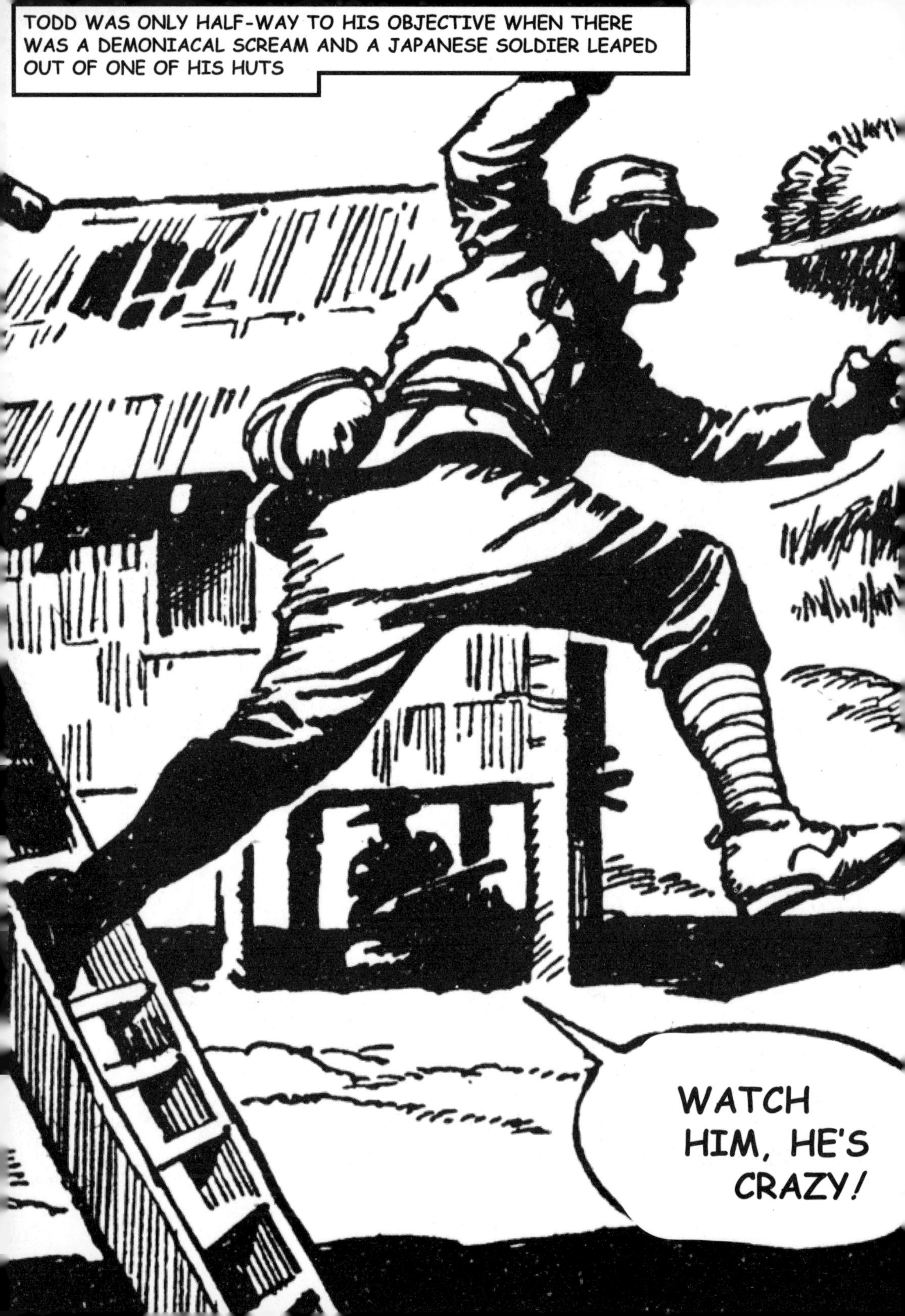
TODD WAS ONLY HALF-WAY TO HIS OBJECTIVE WHEN THERE WAS A DEMONIACAL SCREAM AND A JAPANESE SOLDIER LEAPED OUT OF ONE OF HIS HUTS
WATCH HIM, HE'S CRAZY!

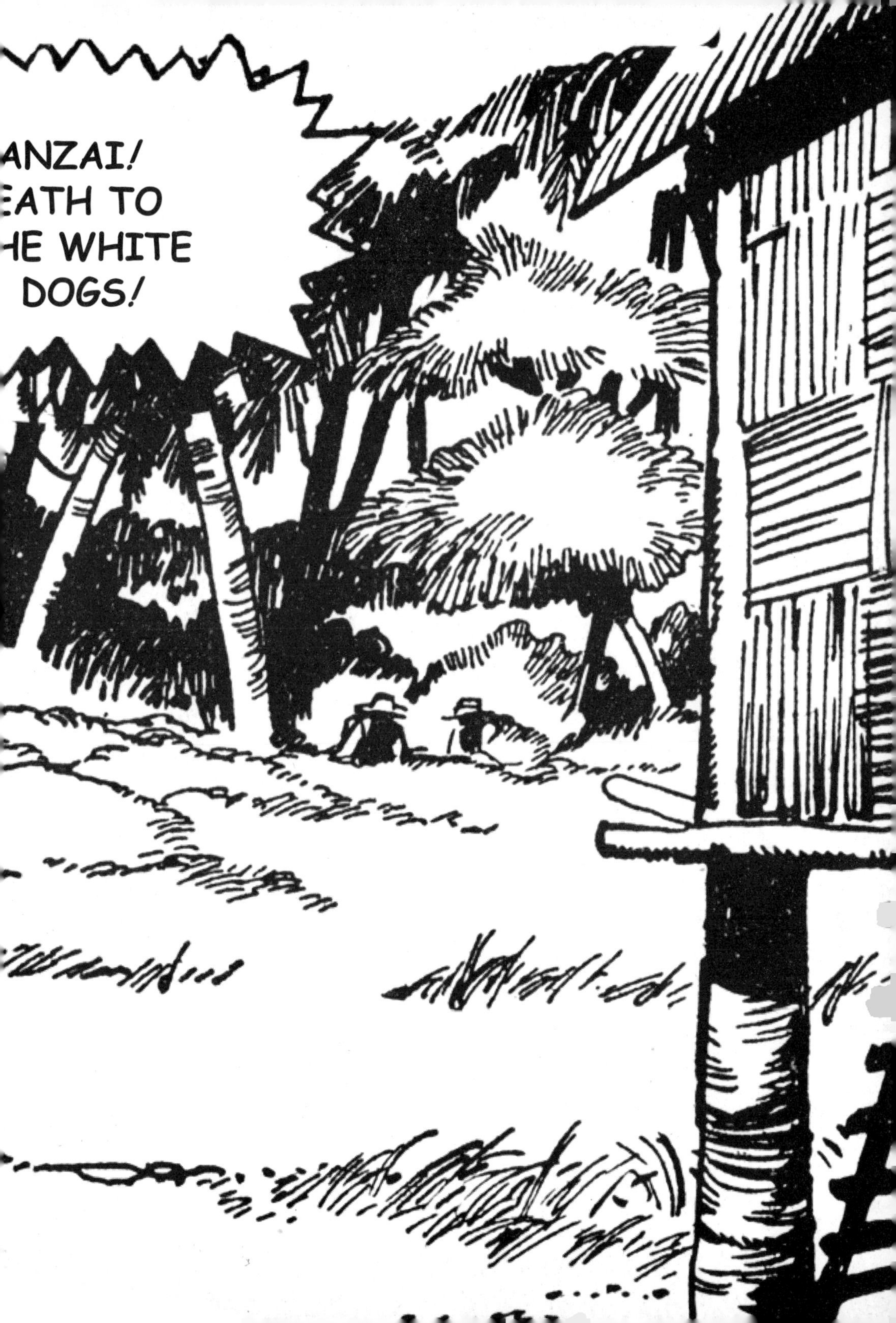
ANZAI! EATH TO HE WHITE DOGS!

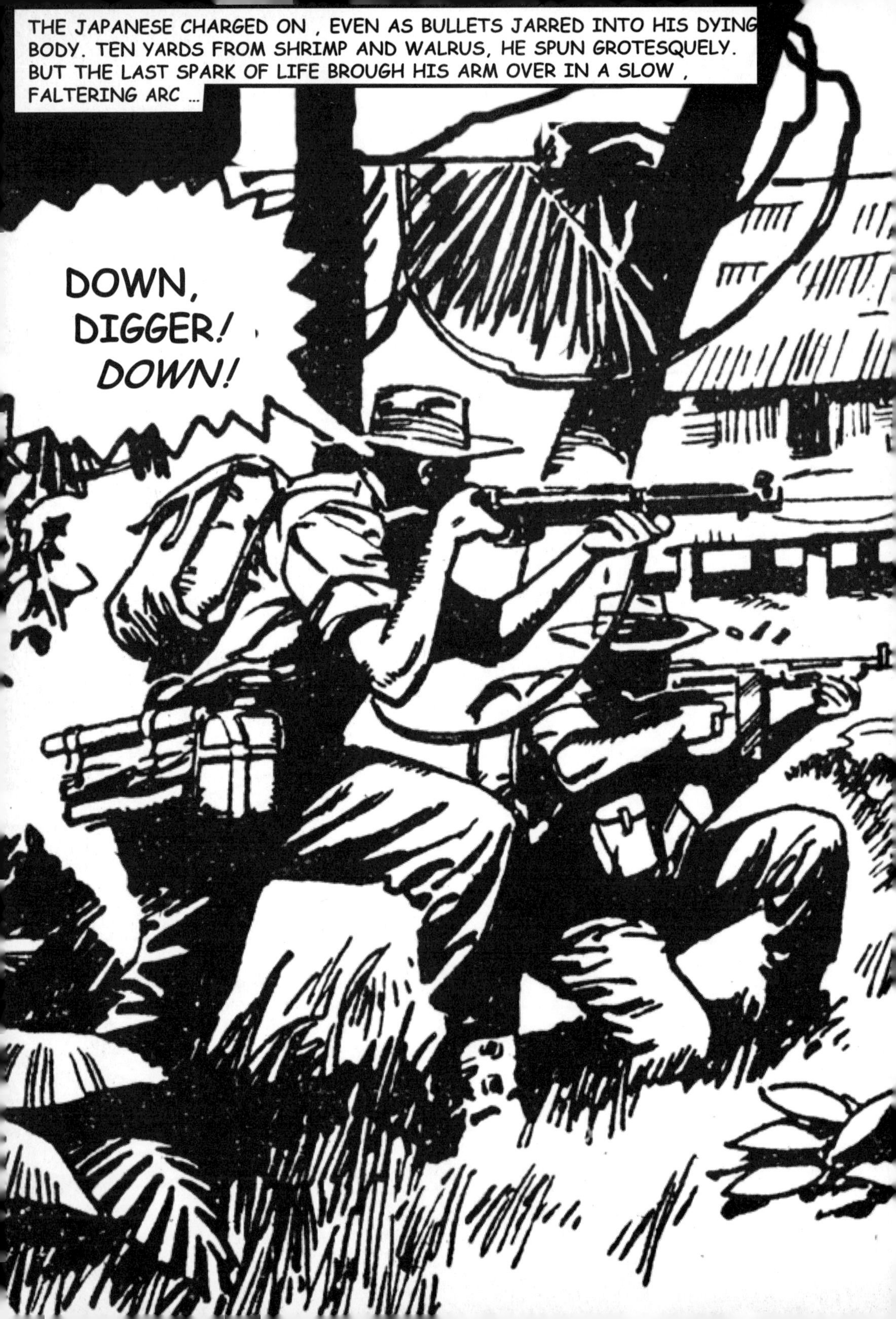
THE JAPANESE CHARGED ON , EVEN AS BULLETS JARRED INTO HIS DYING BODY. TEN YARDS FROM SHRIMP AND WALRUS, HE SPUN GROTESQUELY. BUT THE LAST SPARK OF LIFE BROUGH HIS ARM OVER IN A SLOW , FALTERING ARC ...
DOWN, DIGGER! DOWN!

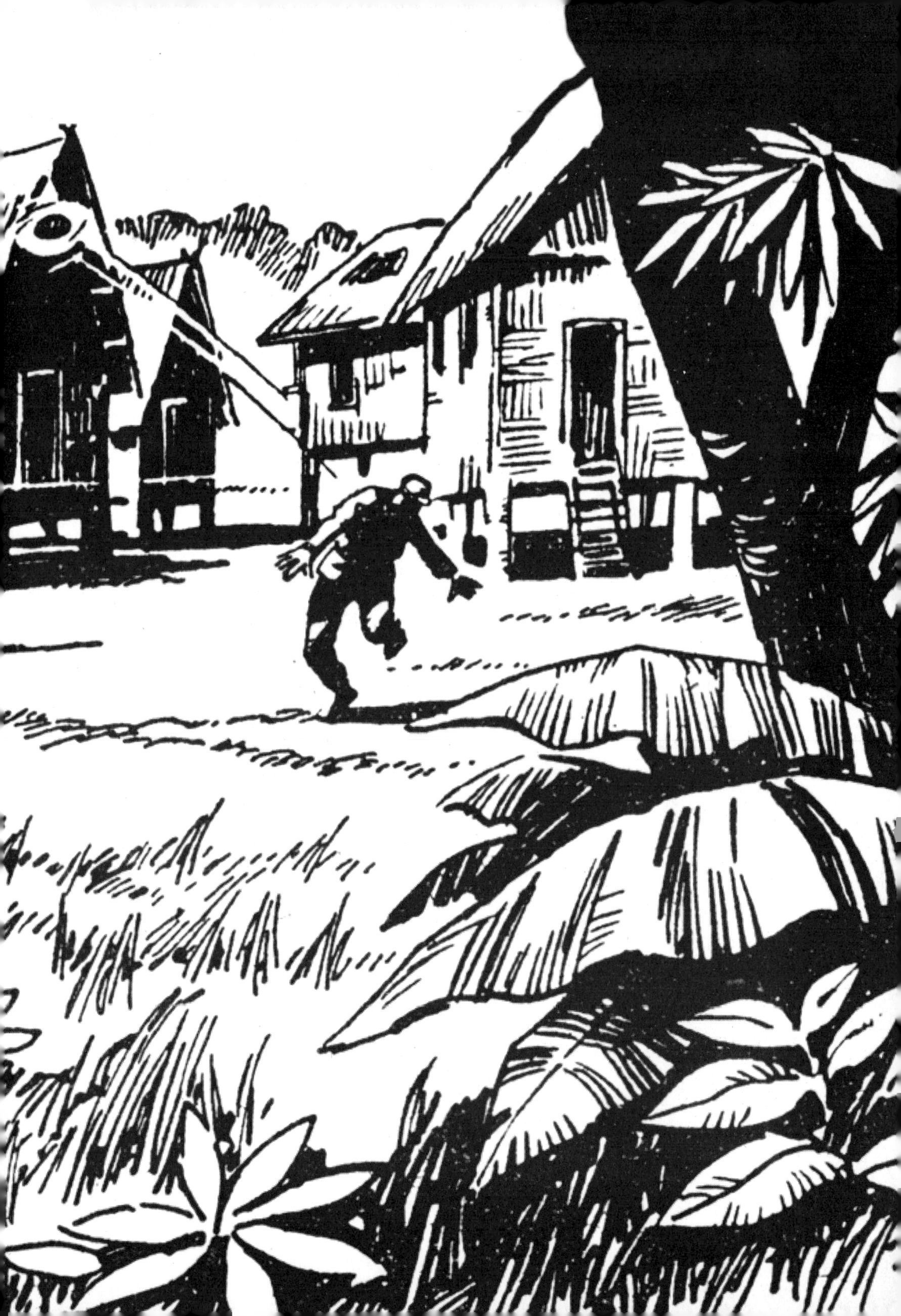

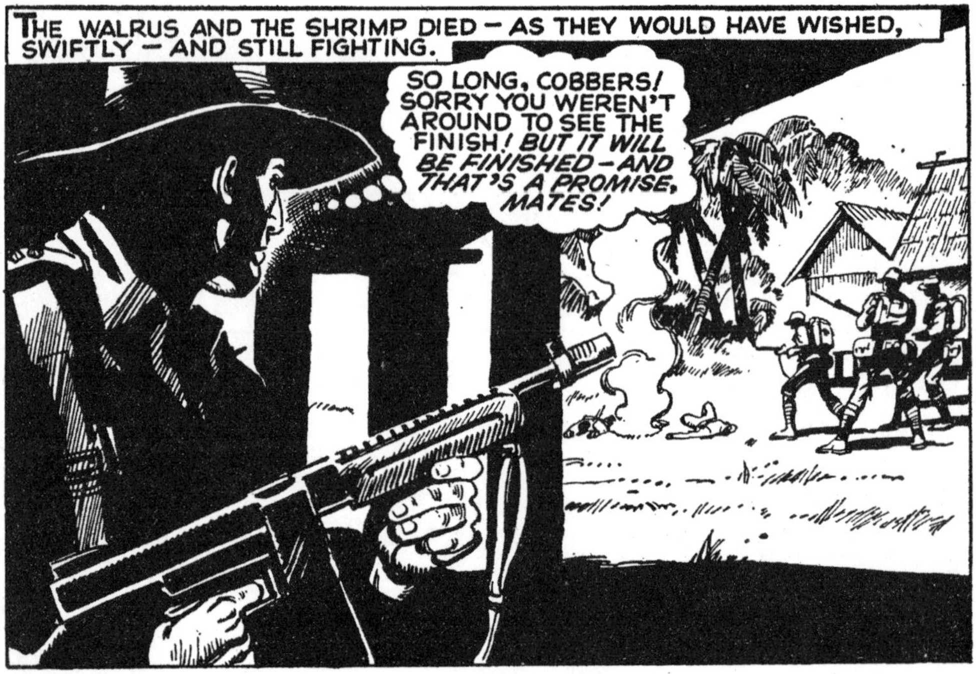
THE WALRUS AND THE SHRIMP DIED — AS THEY WOULD HAVE WISHED, SWIFTLY — AND STILL FIGHTING.
SO LONG, COBBERS! SORRY YOU WEREN'T AROUND TO SEE THE FINISH! BUT IT WILL BE FINISHED — AND THAT'S A PROMISE, MATES!

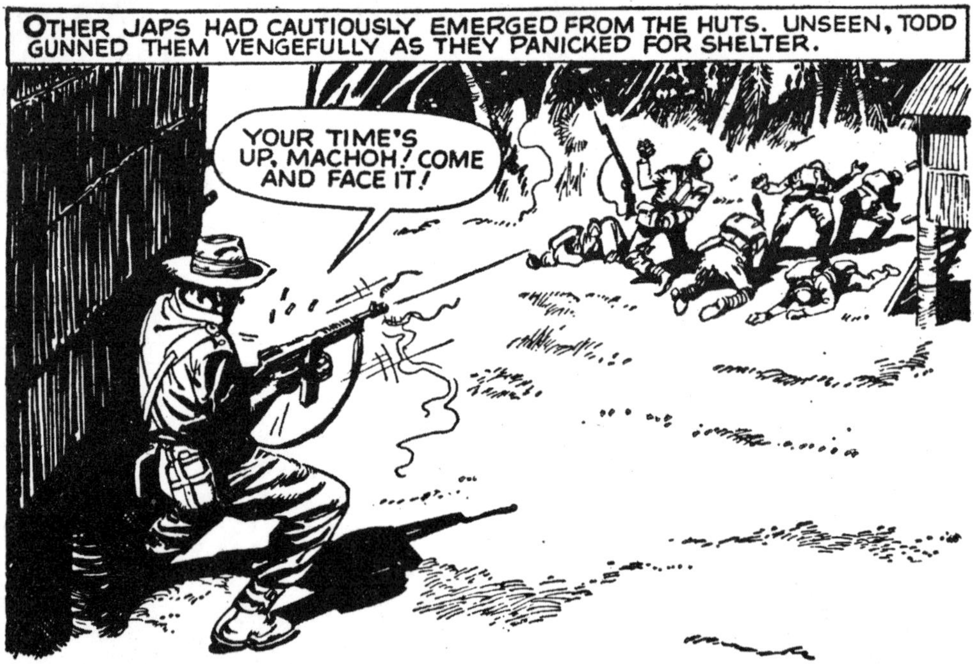
OTHER JAPS HAD CAUTIOUSLY EMERGED FROM THE HUTS. UNSEEN, TODD GUNNED THEM VENGEFULLY AS THEY PANICKED FOR SHELTER.
YOUR TIME'S UP, MACHOH! COME AND FACE IT!

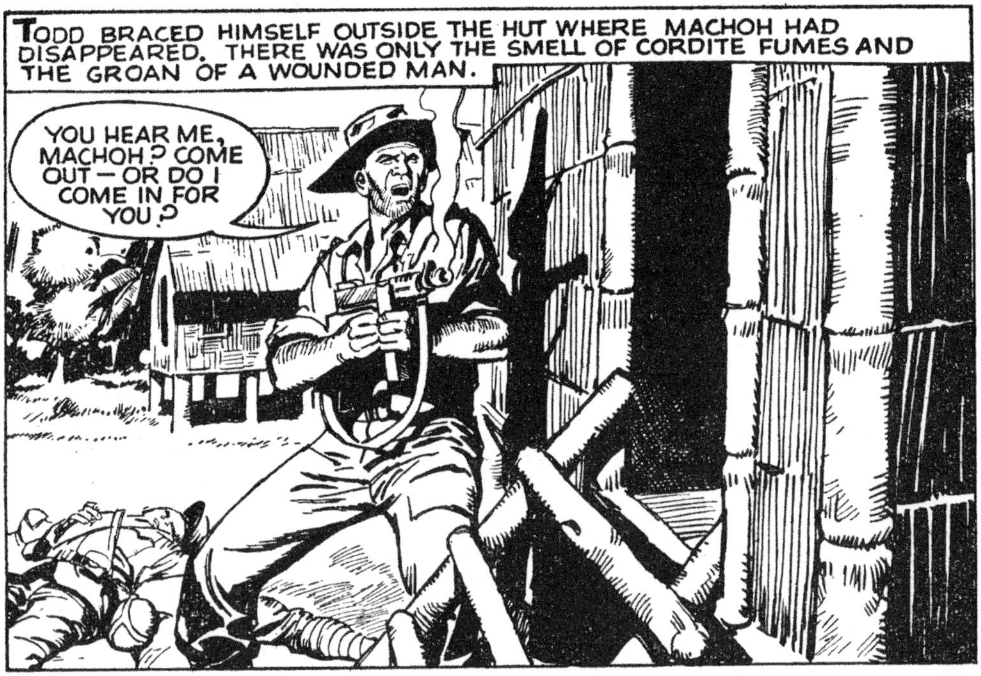
TODD BRACED HIMSELF OUTSIDE THE HUT WHERE MACHOH HAD DISAPPEARED. THERE WAS ONLY THE SMELL OF CORDITE FUMES AND THE GROAN OF A WOUNDED MAN.
YOU HEAR ME, MACHOH? COME OUT — OR DO I COME IN FOR YOU?

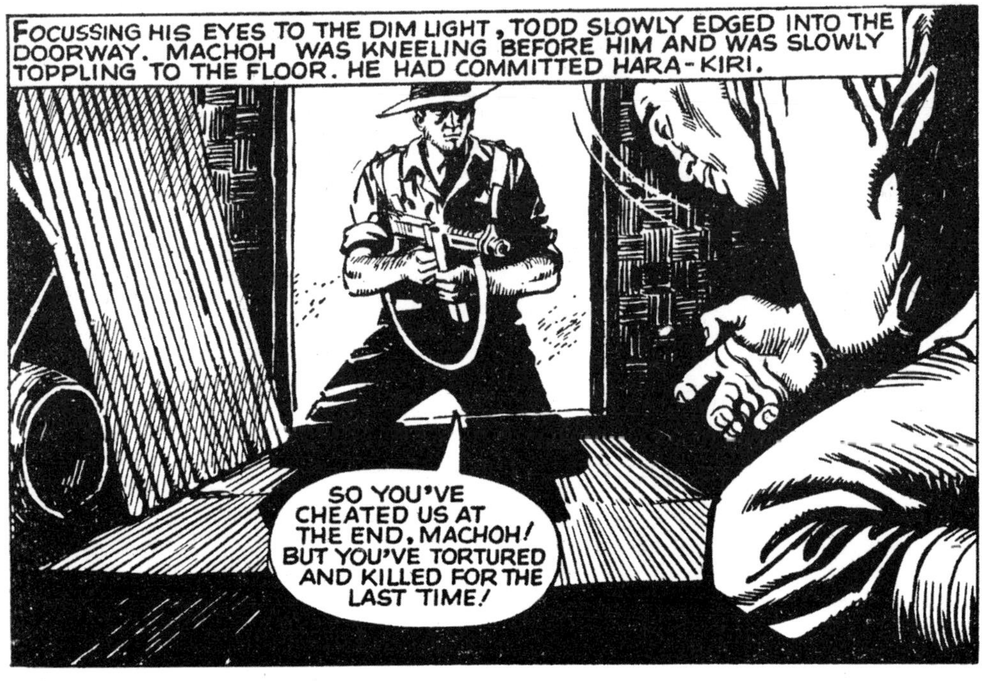
FOCUSSING HIS EYES TO THE DIM LIGHT, TODD SLOWLY EDGED INTO THE DOORWAY. MACHOH WAS KNEELING BEFORE HIM AND WAS SLOWLY TOPPLING TO THE FLOOR. HE HAD COMMITTED HARA-KIRI.
SO YOU'VE CHEATED US AT THE END, MACHOH! BUT YOU'VE TORTURED AND KILLED FOR THE LAST TIME!

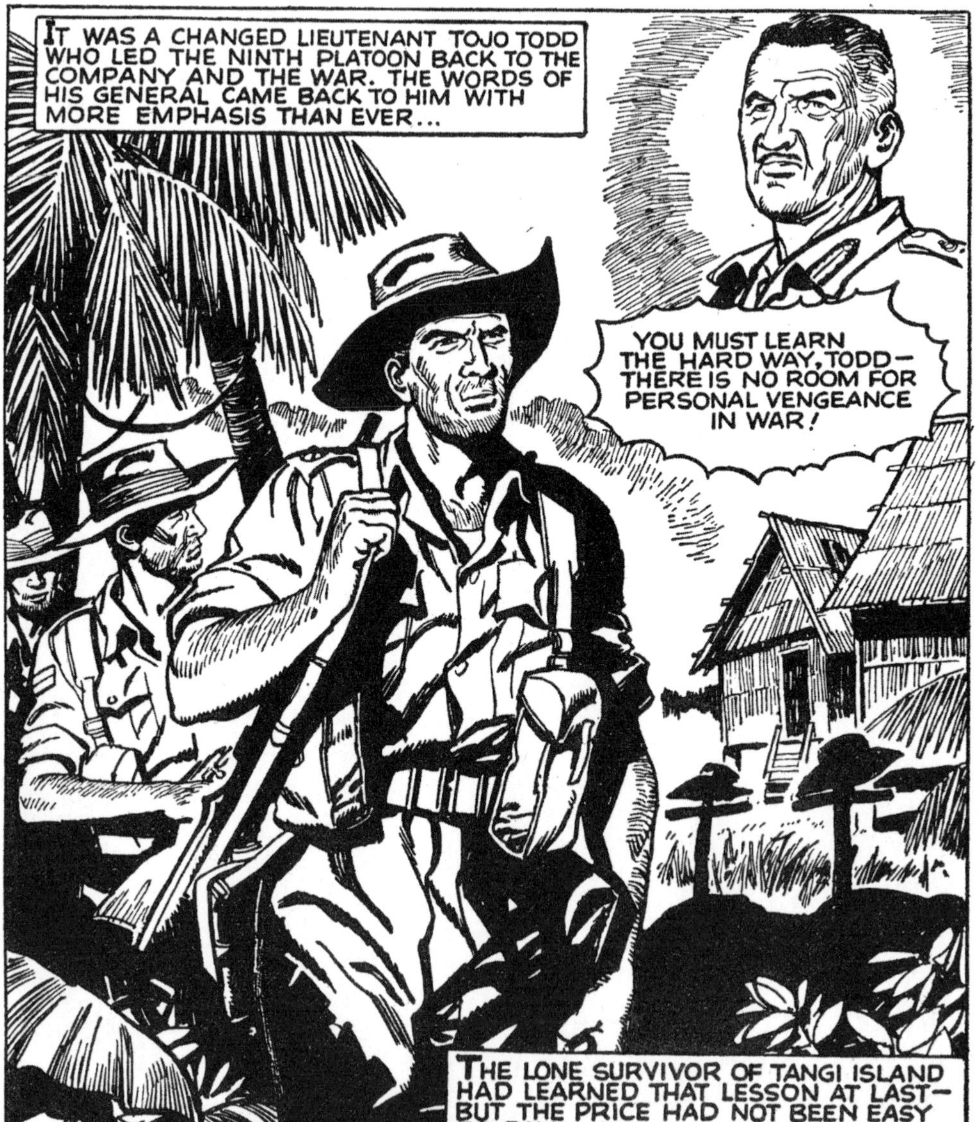
IT WAS A CHANGED LIEUTENANT TOJO TODD WHO LED THE NINTH PLATOON BACK TO THE COMPANY AND THE WAR. THE WORDS OF HIS GENERAL CAME BACK TO HIM WITH MORE EMPHASIS THAN EVER...
YOU MUST LEARN THE HARD WAY, TODD— THERE IS NO ROOM FOR PERSONAL VENGEANCE IN WAR!
THE LONE SURVIVOR OF TANGI ISLAND HAD LEARNED THAT LESSON AT LAST— BUT THE PRICE HAD NOT BEEN EASY TO PAY.

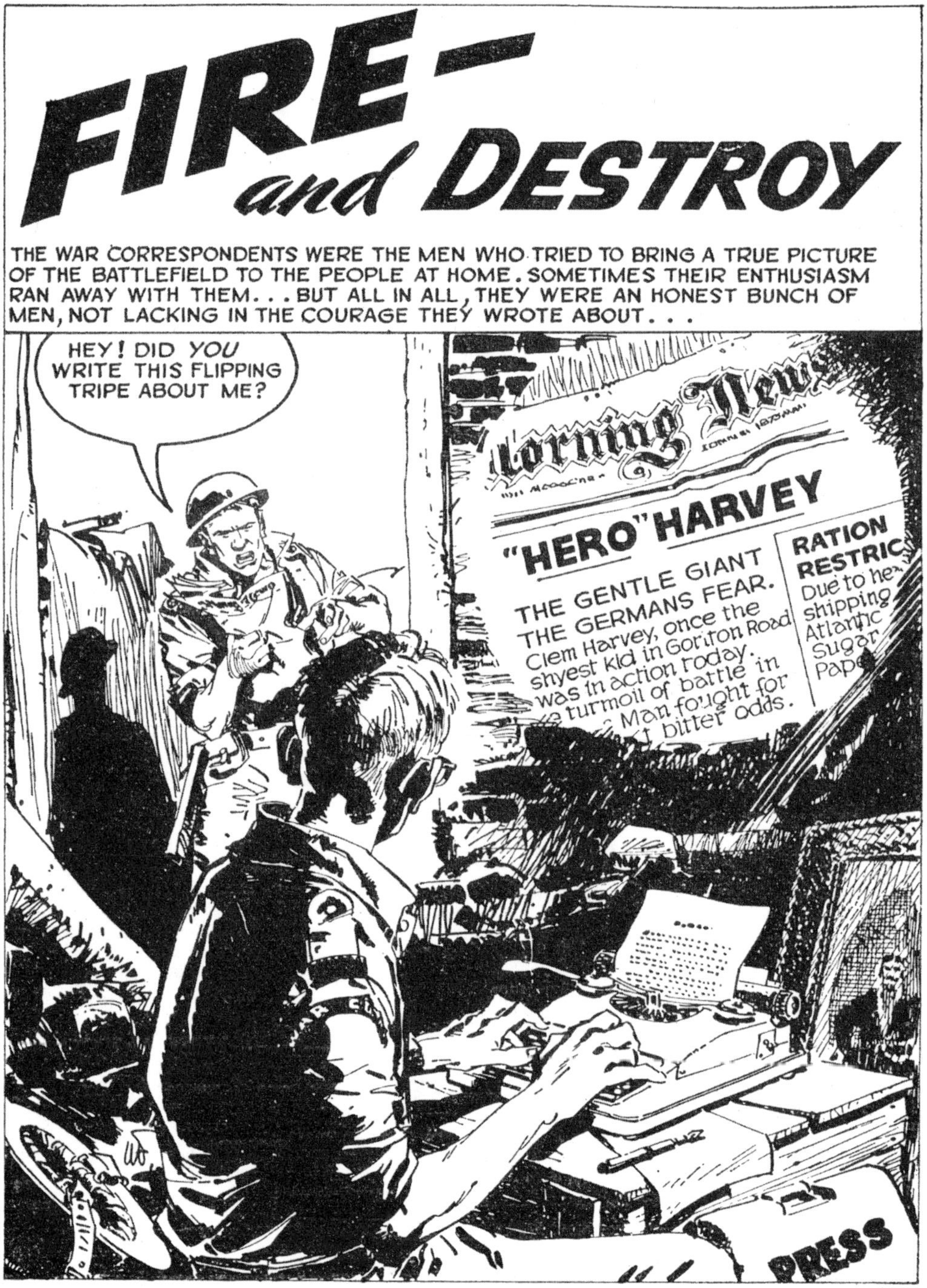
FIRE-and DESTROY
THE WAR CORRESPONDENTS WERE THE MEN WHO TRIED TO BRING A TRUE PICTURE OF THE BATTLEFIELD TO THE PEOPLE AT HOME. SOMETIMES THEIR ENTHUSIASM RAN AWAY WITH THEM. . . BUT ALL IN ALL, THEY WERE AN HONEST BUNCH OF MEN, NOT LACKING IN THE COURAGE THEY WROTE ABOUT. . .
HEY! DID *YOU* WRITE THIS FLIPPING TRIPE ABOUT ME?
"HERO" HARVEY
THE GENTLE GIANT THE GERMANS FEAR.
Clem Harvey, once the shyest kid in Gorton Road was in action today. turmoil of battle in bitter odds.
RATION RESTRIC
Due to he shipping Atlantic Sugar Pape
PRESS

Chapter 1. Death is News

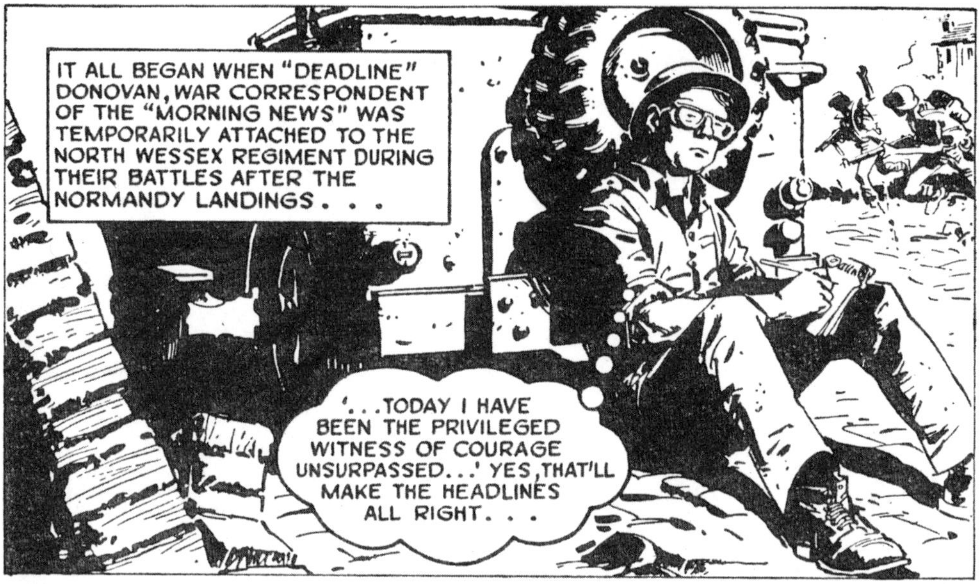
IT ALL BEGAN WHEN "DEADLINE" DONOVAN, WAR CORRESPONDENT OF THE "MORNING NEWS" WAS TEMPORARILY ATTACHED TO THE NORTH WESSEX REGIMENT DURING THEIR BATTLES AFTER THE NORMANDY LANDINGS . . .
'. . .TODAY I HAVE BEEN THE PRIVILEGED WITNESS OF COURAGE UNSURPASSED. . .' YES, THAT'LL MAKE THE HEADLINES ALL RIGHT. . .

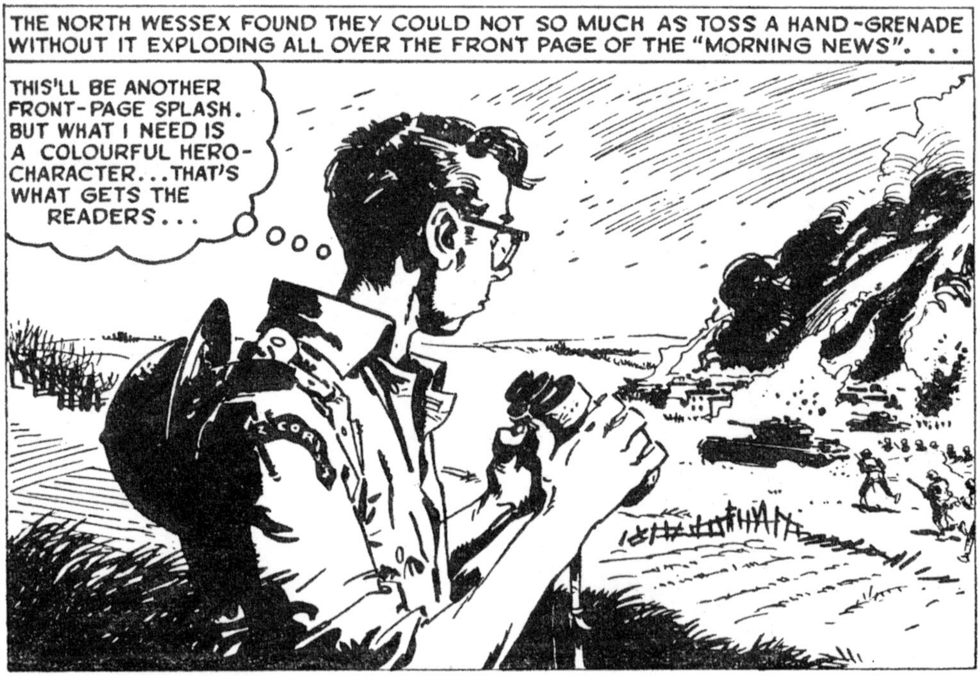
THE NORTH WESSEX FOUND THEY COULD NOT SO MUCH AS TOSS A HAND-GRENADE WITHOUT IT EXPLODING ALL OVER THE FRONT PAGE OF THE "MORNING NEWS". . .
THIS'LL BE ANOTHER FRONT-PAGE SPLASH. BUT WHAT I NEED IS A COLOURFUL HERO-CHARACTER...THAT'S WHAT GETS THE READERS...

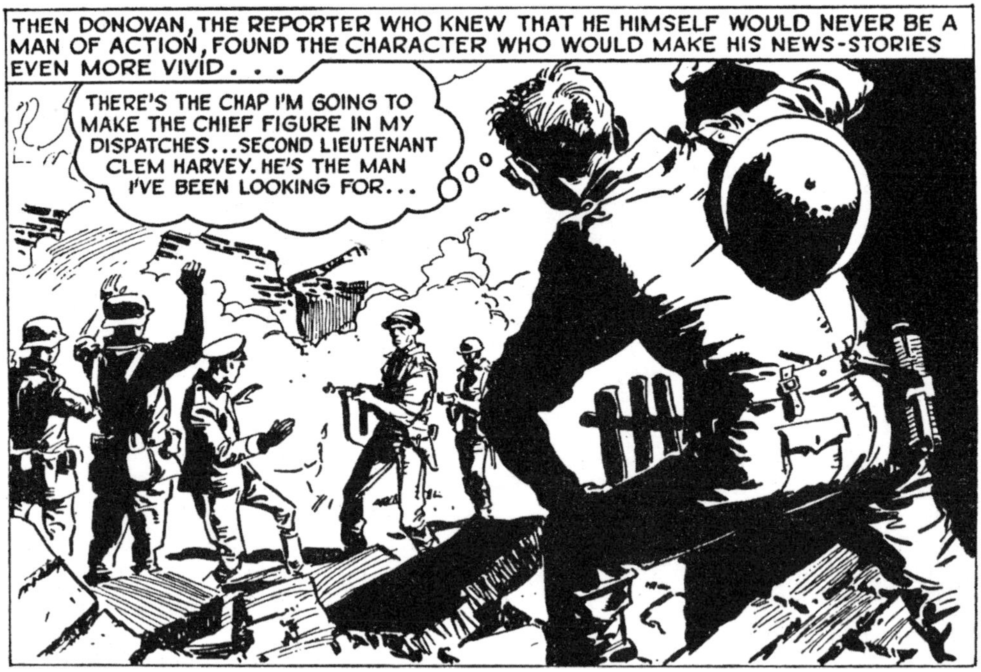
THEN DONOVAN, THE REPORTER WHO KNEW THAT HE HIMSELF WOULD NEVER BE A MAN OF ACTION, FOUND THE CHARACTER WHO WOULD MAKE HIS NEWS-STORIES EVEN MORE VIVID . . .
THERE'S THE CHAP I'M GOING TO MAKE THE CHIEF FIGURE IN MY DISPATCHES...SECOND LIEUTENANT CLEM HARVEY. HE'S THE MAN I'VE BEEN LOOKING FOR...

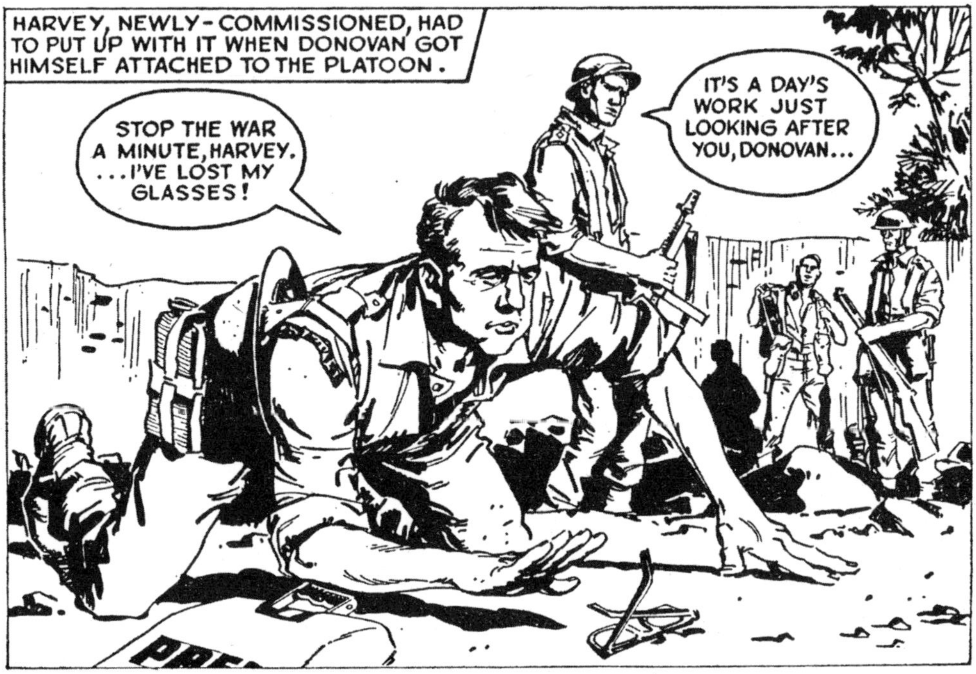
HARVEY, NEWLY-COMMISSIONED, HAD TO PUT UP WITH IT WHEN DONOVAN GOT HIMSELF ATTACHED TO THE PLATOON.
STOP THE WAR A MINUTE, HARVEY. ...I'VE LOST MY GLASSES!
IT'S A DAY'S WORK JUST LOOKING AFTER YOU, DONOVAN...

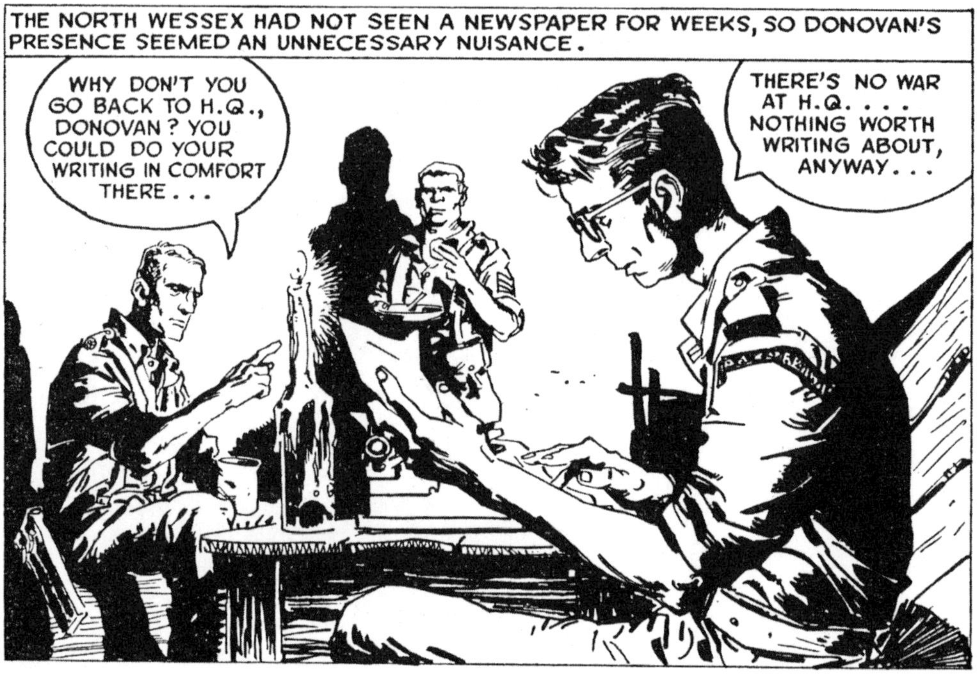
THE NORTH WESSEX HAD NOT SEEN A NEWSPAPER FOR WEEKS, SO DONOVAN'S PRESENCE SEEMED AN UNNECESSARY NUISANCE.
WHY DON'T YOU GO BACK TO H.Q., DONOVAN? YOU COULD DO YOUR WRITING IN COMFORT THERE...
THERE'S NO WAR AT H.Q. . . . NOTHING WORTH WRITING ABOUT, ANYWAY...

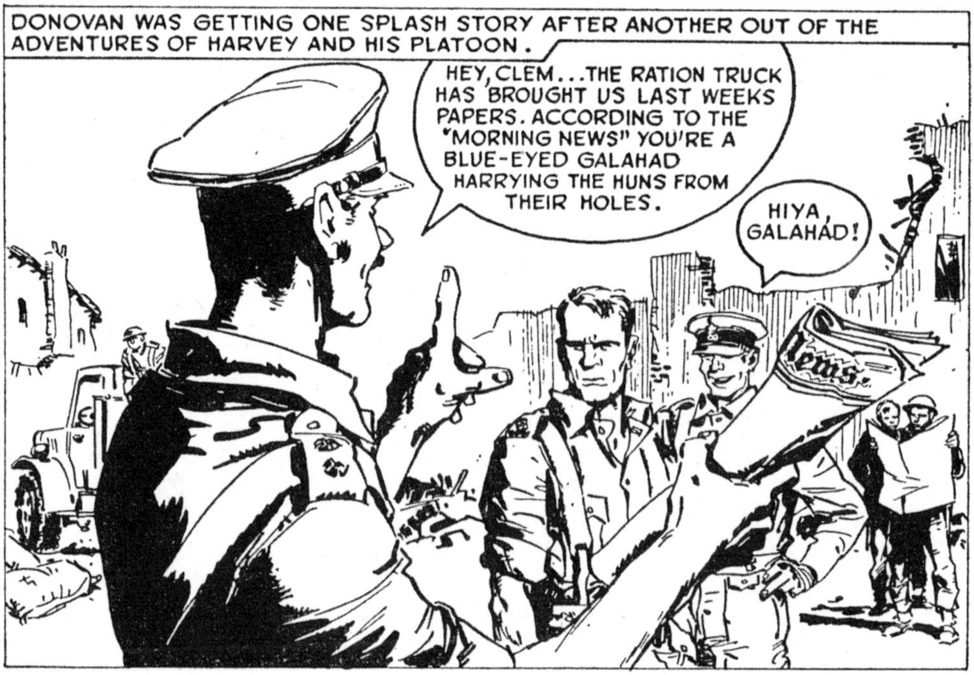
DONOVAN WAS GETTING ONE SPLASH STORY AFTER ANOTHER OUT OF THE ADVENTURES OF HARVEY AND HIS PLATOON.
HEY, CLEM...THE RATION TRUCK HAS BROUGHT US LAST WEEKS PAPERS. ACCORDING TO THE "MORNING NEWS" YOU'RE A BLUE-EYED GALAHAD HARRYING THE HUNS FROM THEIR HOLES.
HIYA, GALAHAD!

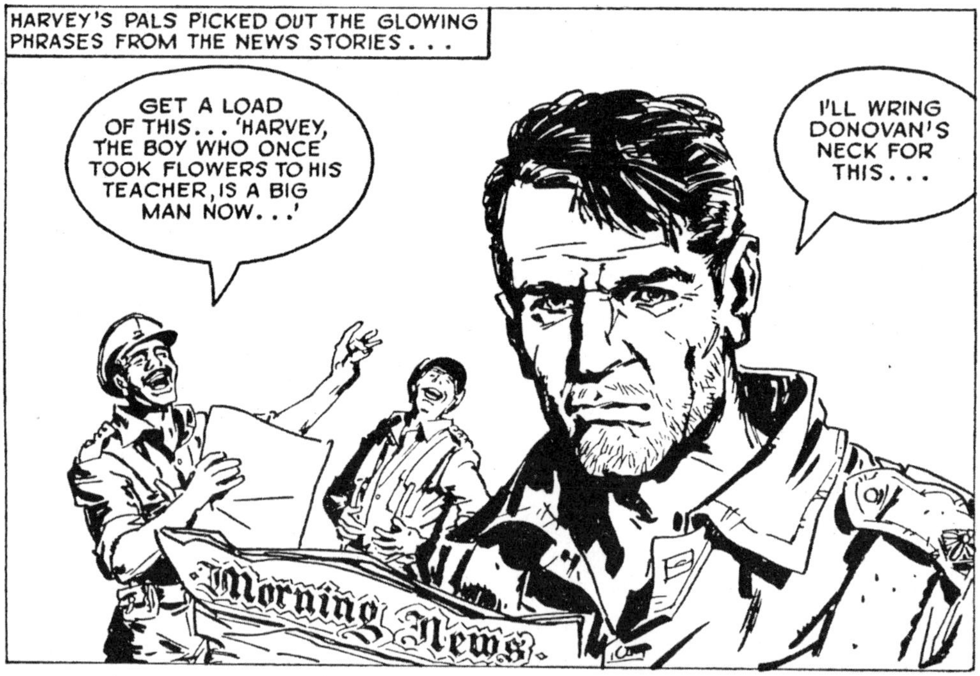
HARVEY'S PALS PICKED OUT THE GLOWING PHRASES FROM THE NEWS STORIES . . .
GET A LOAD OF THIS . . . 'HARVEY, THE BOY WHO ONCE TOOK FLOWERS TO HIS TEACHER, IS A BIG MAN NOW . . .'
I'LL WRING DONOVAN'S NECK FOR THIS . . .
Morning News

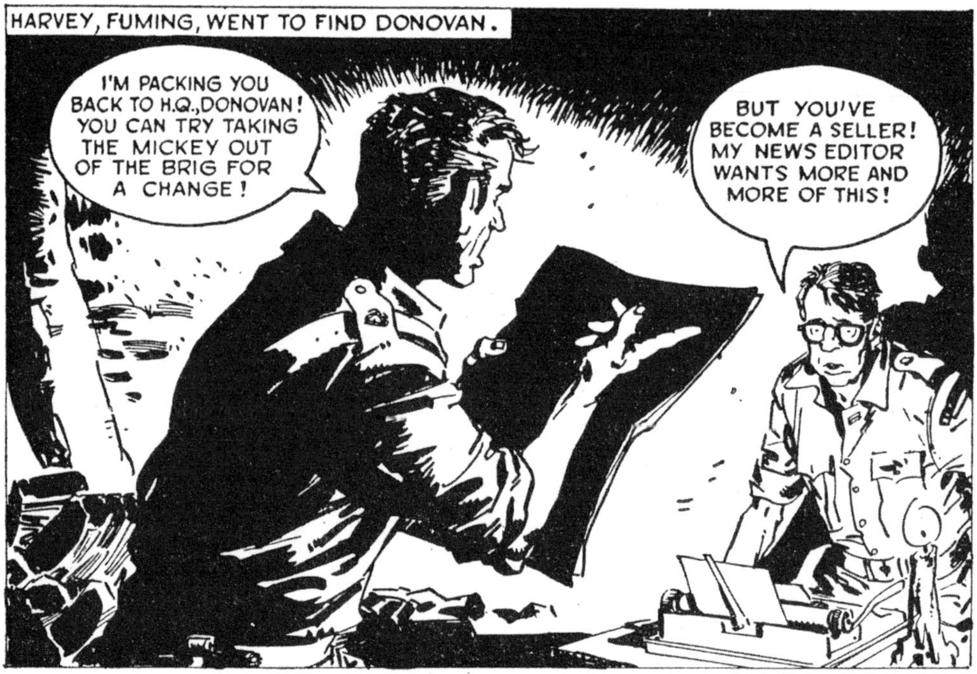
HARVEY, FUMING, WENT TO FIND DONOVAN.
I'M PACKING YOU BACK TO H.Q., DONOVAN! YOU CAN TRY TAKING THE MICKEY OUT OF THE BRIG FOR A CHANGE!
BUT YOU'VE BECOME A SELLER! MY NEWS EDITOR WANTS MORE AND MORE OF THIS!

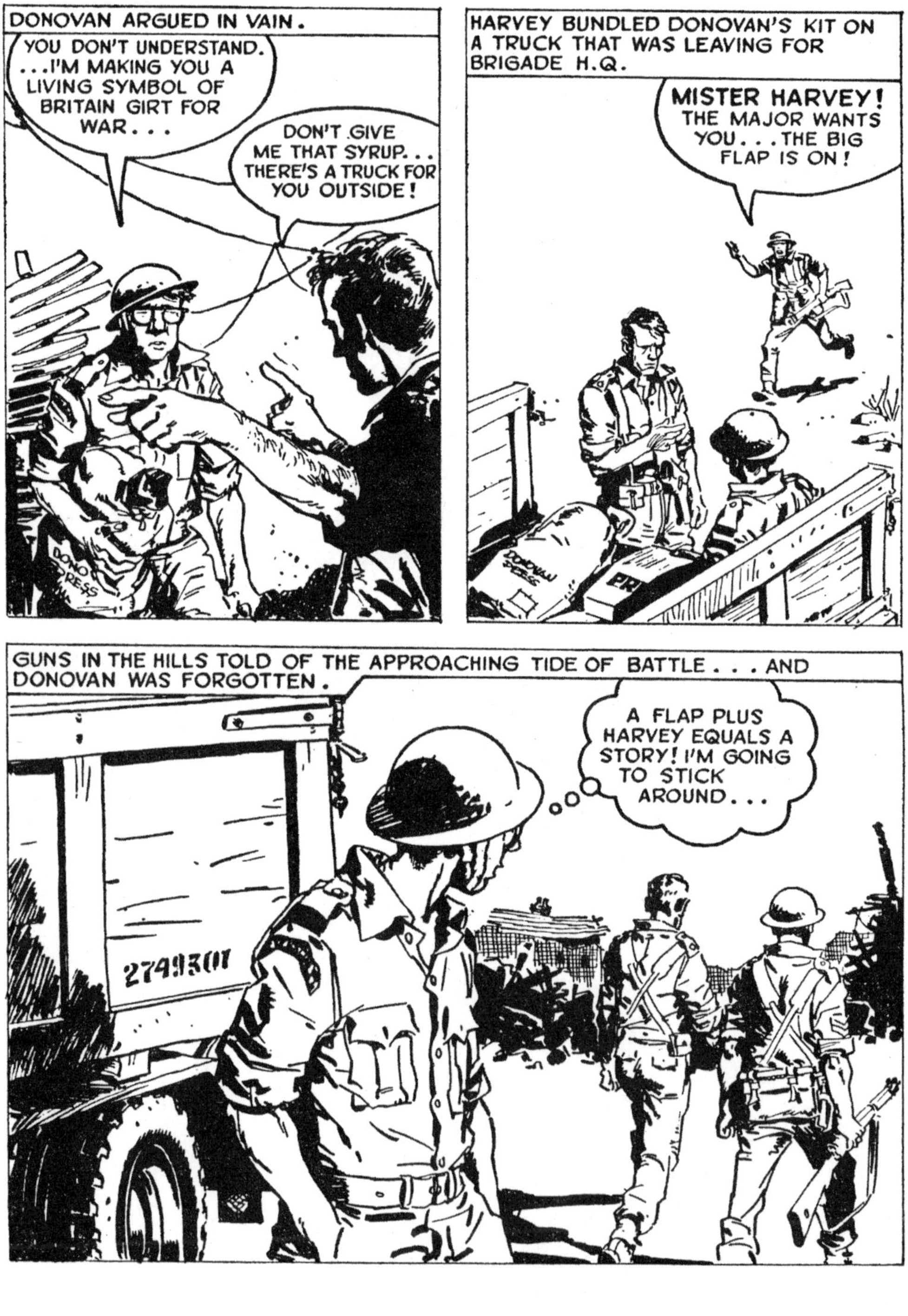
DONOVAN ARGUED IN VAIN.
YOU DON'T UNDERSTAND. ...I'M MAKING YOU A LIVING SYMBOL OF BRITAIN GIRT FOR WAR...
DON'T GIVE ME THAT SYRUP... THERE'S A TRUCK FOR YOU OUTSIDE!
HARVEY BUNDLED DONOVAN'S KIT ON A TRUCK THAT WAS LEAVING FOR BRIGADE H.Q.
MISTER HARVEY! THE MAJOR WANTS YOU...THE BIG FLAP IS ON!
GUNS IN THE HILLS TOLD OF THE APPROACHING TIDE OF BATTLE...AND DONOVAN WAS FORGOTTEN.
A FLAP PLUS HARVEY EQUALS A STORY! I'M GOING TO STICK AROUND...
2749301

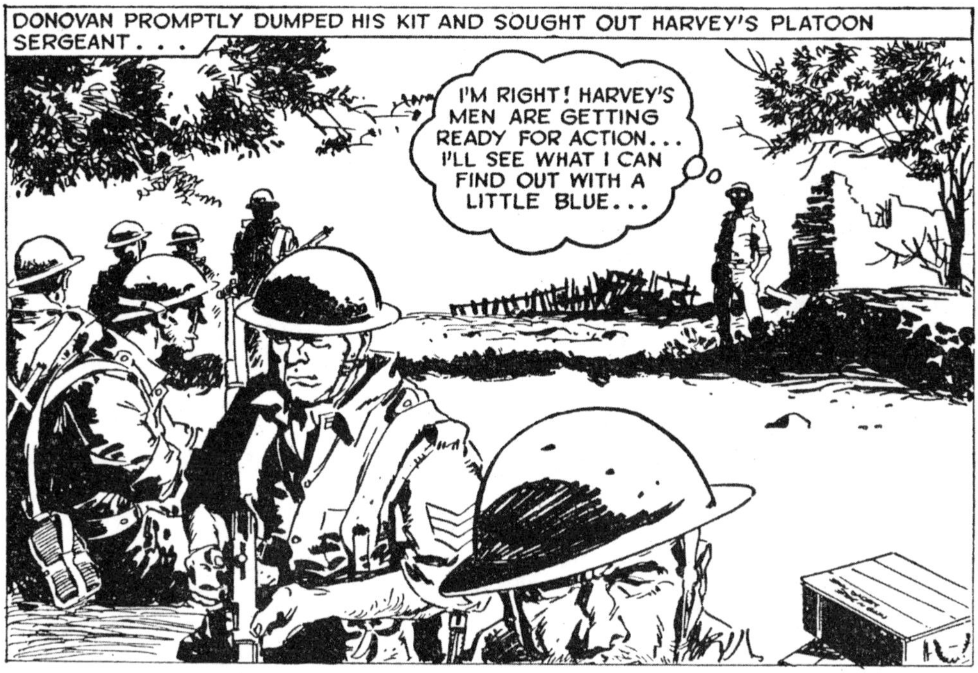
DONOVAN PROMPTLY DUMPED HIS KIT AND SOUGHT OUT HARVEY'S PLATOON SERGEANT . . .
I'M RIGHT! HARVEY'S MEN ARE GETTING READY FOR ACTION... I'LL SEE WHAT I CAN FIND OUT WITH A LITTLE BLUE...

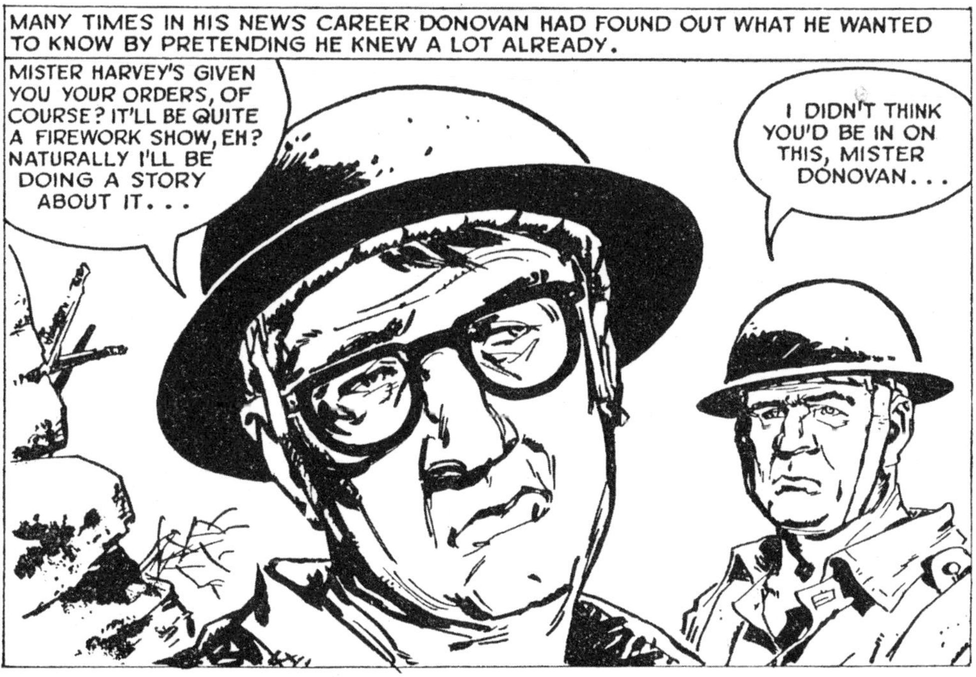
MANY TIMES IN HIS NEWS CAREER DONOVAN HAD FOUND OUT WHAT HE WANTED TO KNOW BY PRETENDING HE KNEW A LOT ALREADY.
MISTER HARVEY'S GIVEN YOU YOUR ORDERS, OF COURSE? IT'LL BE QUITE A FIREWORK SHOW, EH? NATURALLY I'LL BE DOING A STORY ABOUT IT...
I DIDN'T THINK YOU'D BE IN ON THIS, MISTER DONOVAN...

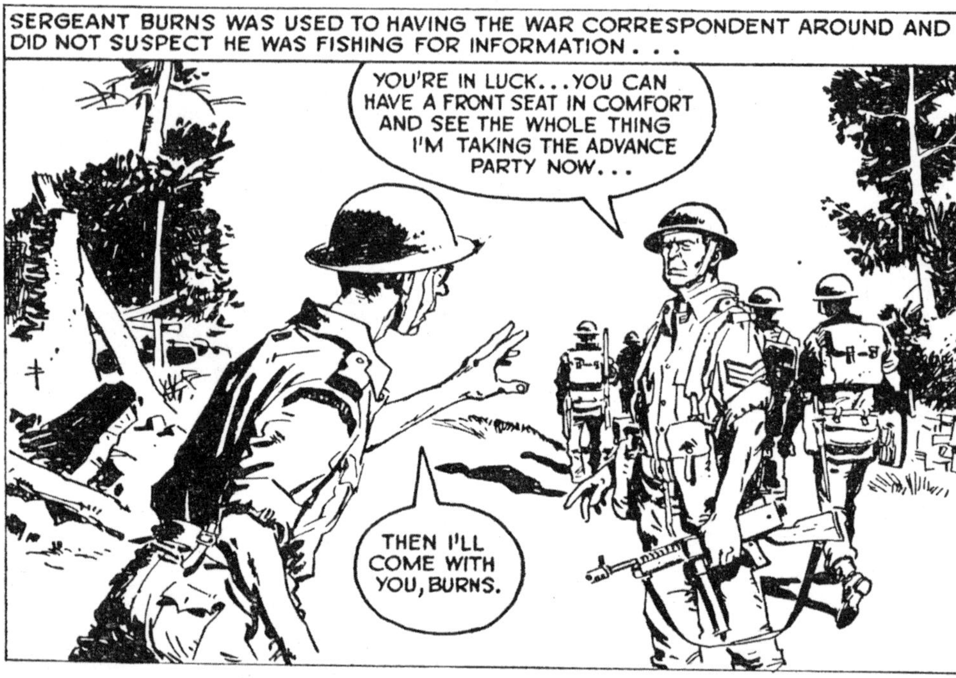
SERGEANT BURNS WAS USED TO HAVING THE WAR CORRESPONDENT AROUND AND DID NOT SUSPECT HE WAS FISHING FOR INFORMATION . . .
YOU'RE IN LUCK...YOU CAN HAVE A FRONT SEAT IN COMFORT AND SEE THE WHOLE THING I'M TAKING THE ADVANCE PARTY NOW...
THEN I'LL COME WITH YOU, BURNS.

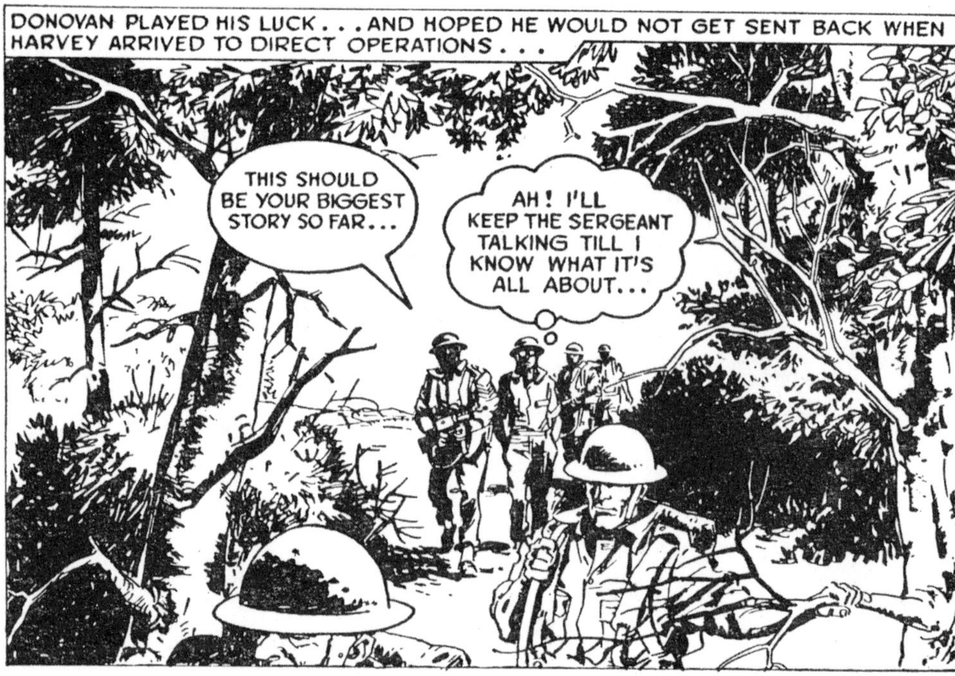
DONOVAN PLAYED HIS LUCK . . . AND HOPED HE WOULD NOT GET SENT BACK WHEN HARVEY ARRIVED TO DIRECT OPERATIONS . . .
THIS SHOULD BE YOUR BIGGEST STORY SO FAR...
AH! I'LL KEEP THE SERGEANT TALKING TILL I KNOW WHAT IT'S ALL ABOUT...

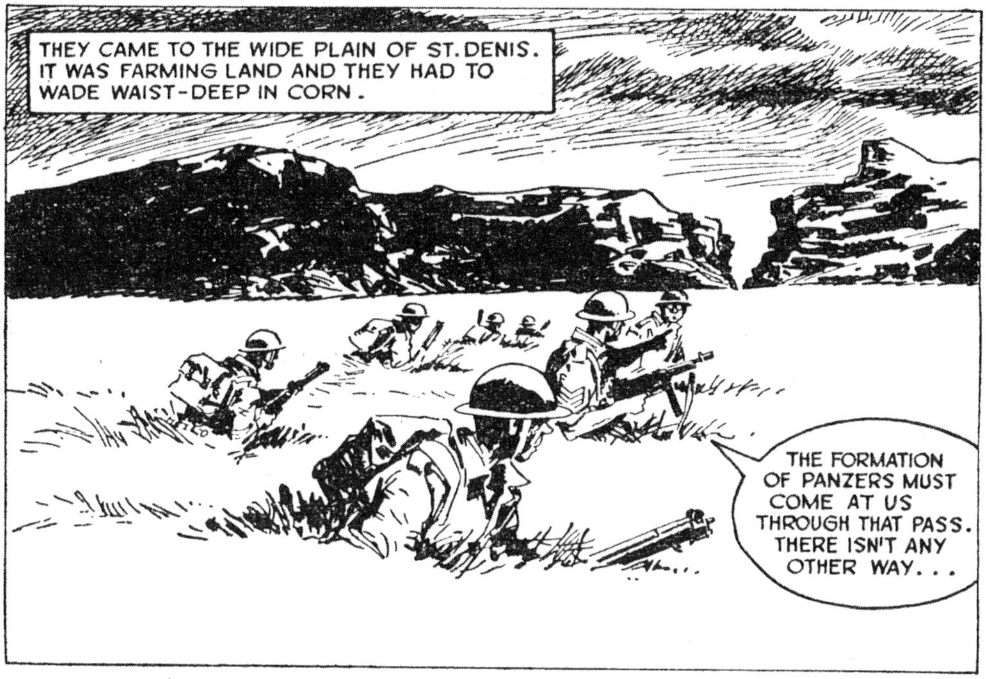
THEY CAME TO THE WIDE PLAIN OF ST. DENIS. IT WAS FARMING LAND AND THEY HAD TO WADE WAIST-DEEP IN CORN.
THE FORMATION OF PANZERS MUST COME AT US THROUGH THAT PASS. THERE ISN'T ANY OTHER WAY...

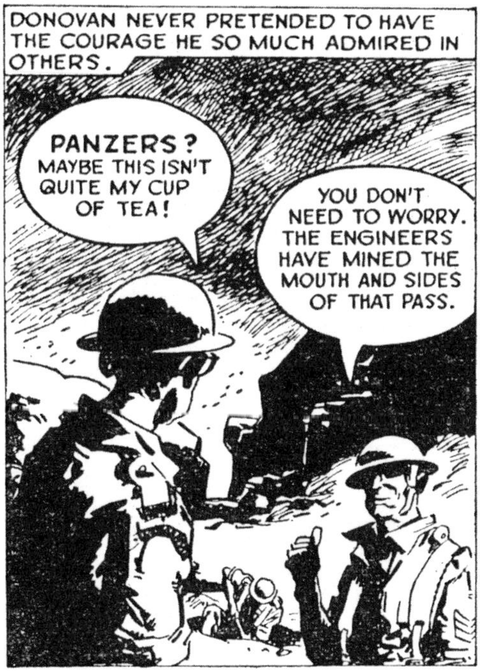
DONOVAN NEVER PRETENDED TO HAVE THE COURAGE HE SO MUCH ADMIRED IN OTHERS.
PANZERS? MAYBE THIS ISN'T QUITE MY CUP OF TEA!
YOU DON'T NEED TO WORRY. THE ENGINEERS HAVE MINED THE MOUTH AND SIDES OF THAT PASS.

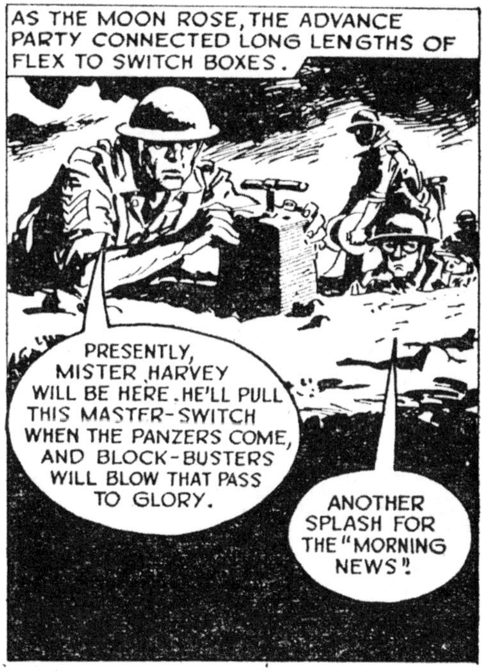
AS THE MOON ROSE, THE ADVANCE PARTY CONNECTED LONG LENGTHS OF FLEX TO SWITCH BOXES.
PRESENTLY, MISTER HARVEY WILL BE HERE. HE'LL PULL THIS MASTER-SWITCH WHEN THE PANZERS COME, AND BLOCK-BUSTERS WILL BLOW THAT PASS TO GLORY.
ANOTHER SPLASH FOR THE "MORNING NEWS".

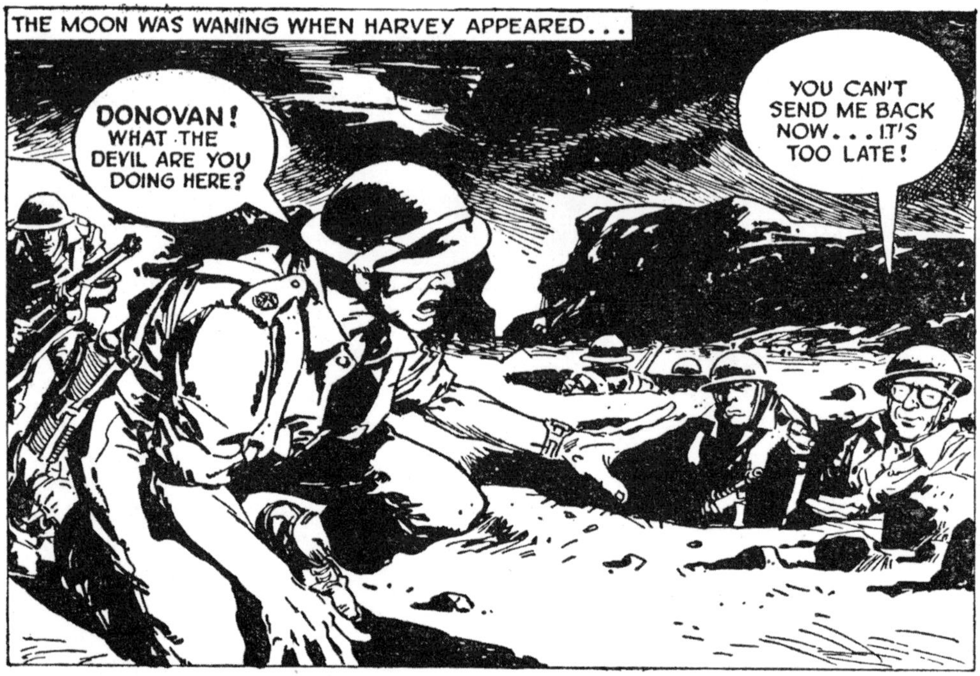
THE MOON WAS WANING WHEN HARVEY APPEARED...
DONOVAN! WHAT THE DEVIL ARE YOU DOING HERE?
YOU CAN'T SEND ME BACK NOW...IT'S TOO LATE!

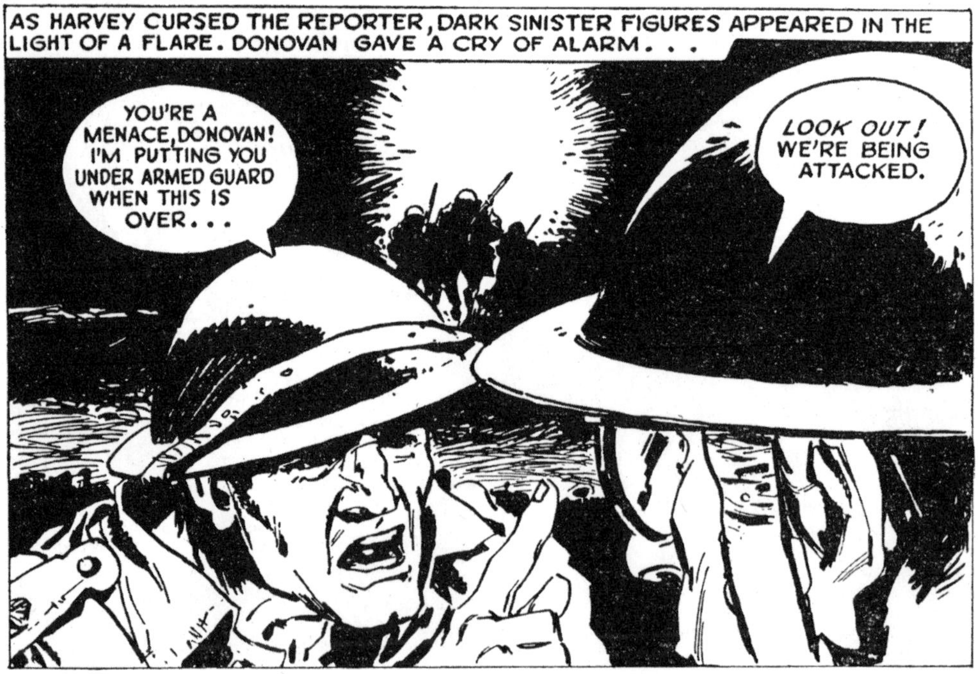
AS HARVEY CURSED THE REPORTER, DARK SINISTER FIGURES APPEARED IN THE LIGHT OF A FLARE. DONOVAN GAVE A CRY OF ALARM...
YOU'RE A MENACE, DONOVAN! I'M PUTTING YOU UNDER ARMED GUARD WHEN THIS IS OVER...
LOOK OUT! WE'RE BEING ATTACKED.

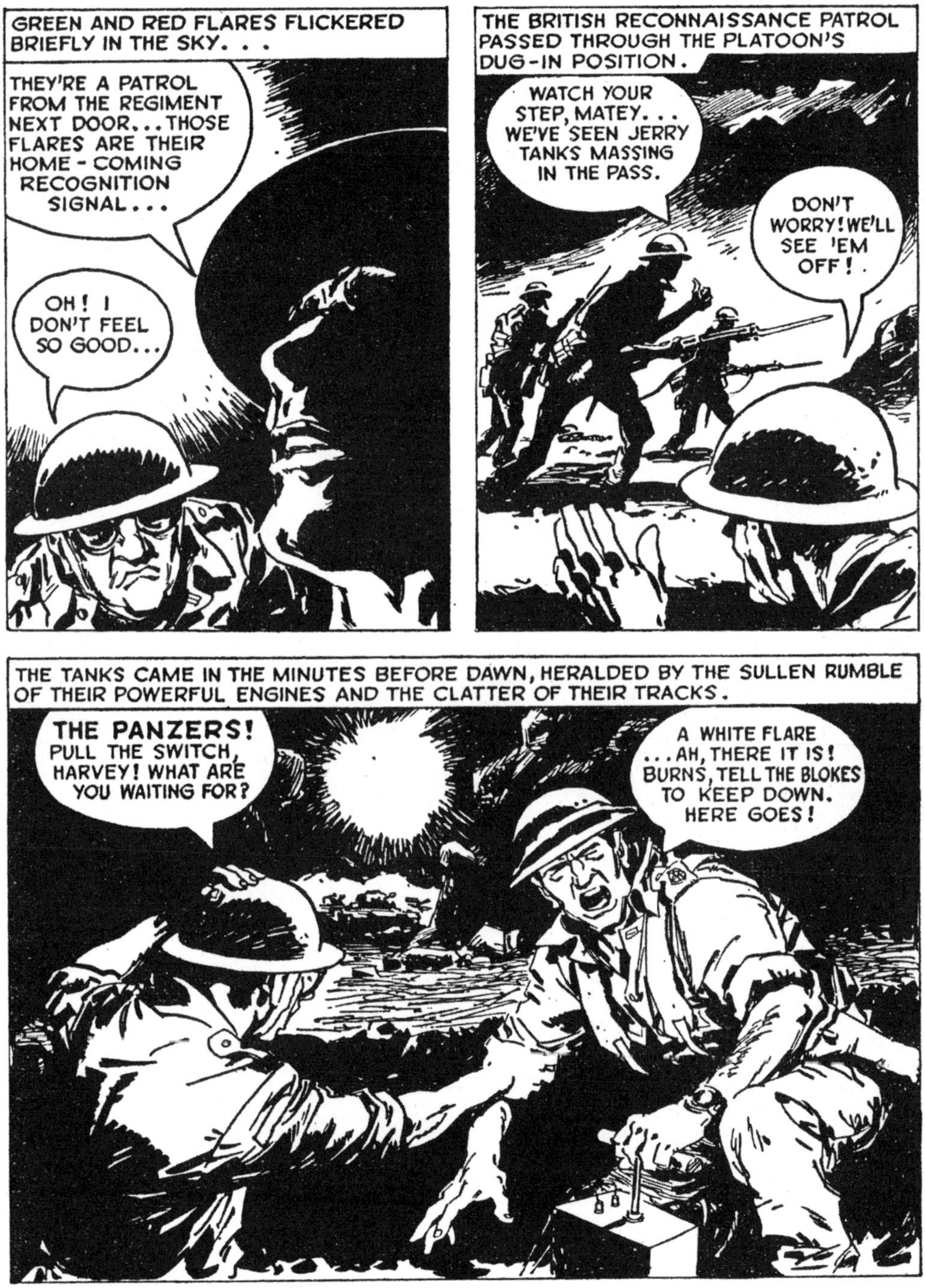
GREEN AND RED FLARES FLICKERED BRIEFLY IN THE SKY. . .
THEY'RE A PATROL FROM THE REGIMENT NEXT DOOR...THOSE FLARES ARE THEIR HOME-COMING RECOGNITION SIGNAL...
OH! I DON'T FEEL SO GOOD...
THE BRITISH RECONNAISSANCE PATROL PASSED THROUGH THE PLATOON'S DUG-IN POSITION.
WATCH YOUR STEP, MATEY... WE'VE SEEN JERRY TANKS MASSING IN THE PASS.
DON'T WORRY! WE'LL SEE 'EM OFF!
THE TANKS CAME IN THE MINUTES BEFORE DAWN, HERALDED BY THE SULLEN RUMBLE OF THEIR POWERFUL ENGINES AND THE CLATTER OF THEIR TRACKS.
THE PANZERS! PULL THE SWITCH, HARVEY! WHAT ARE YOU WAITING FOR?
A WHITE FLARE ...AH, THERE IT IS! BURNS, TELL THE BLOKES TO KEEP DOWN. HERE GOES!

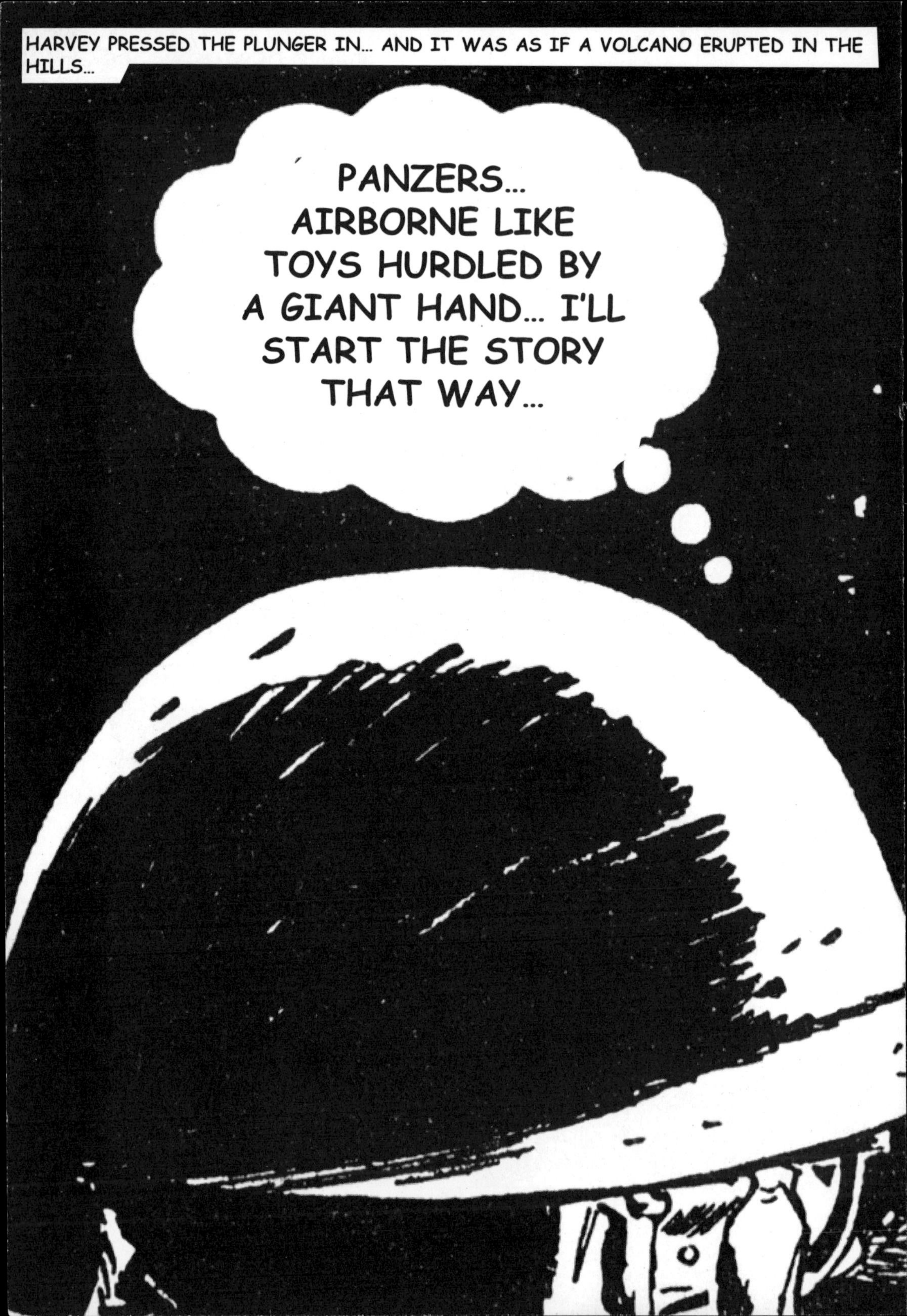
HARVEY PRESSED THE PLUNGER IN... AND IT WAS AS IF A VOLCANO ERUPTED IN THE HILLS...
PANZERS... AIRBORNE LIKE TOYS HURDLED BY A GIANT HAND... I'LL START THE STORY THAT WAY...

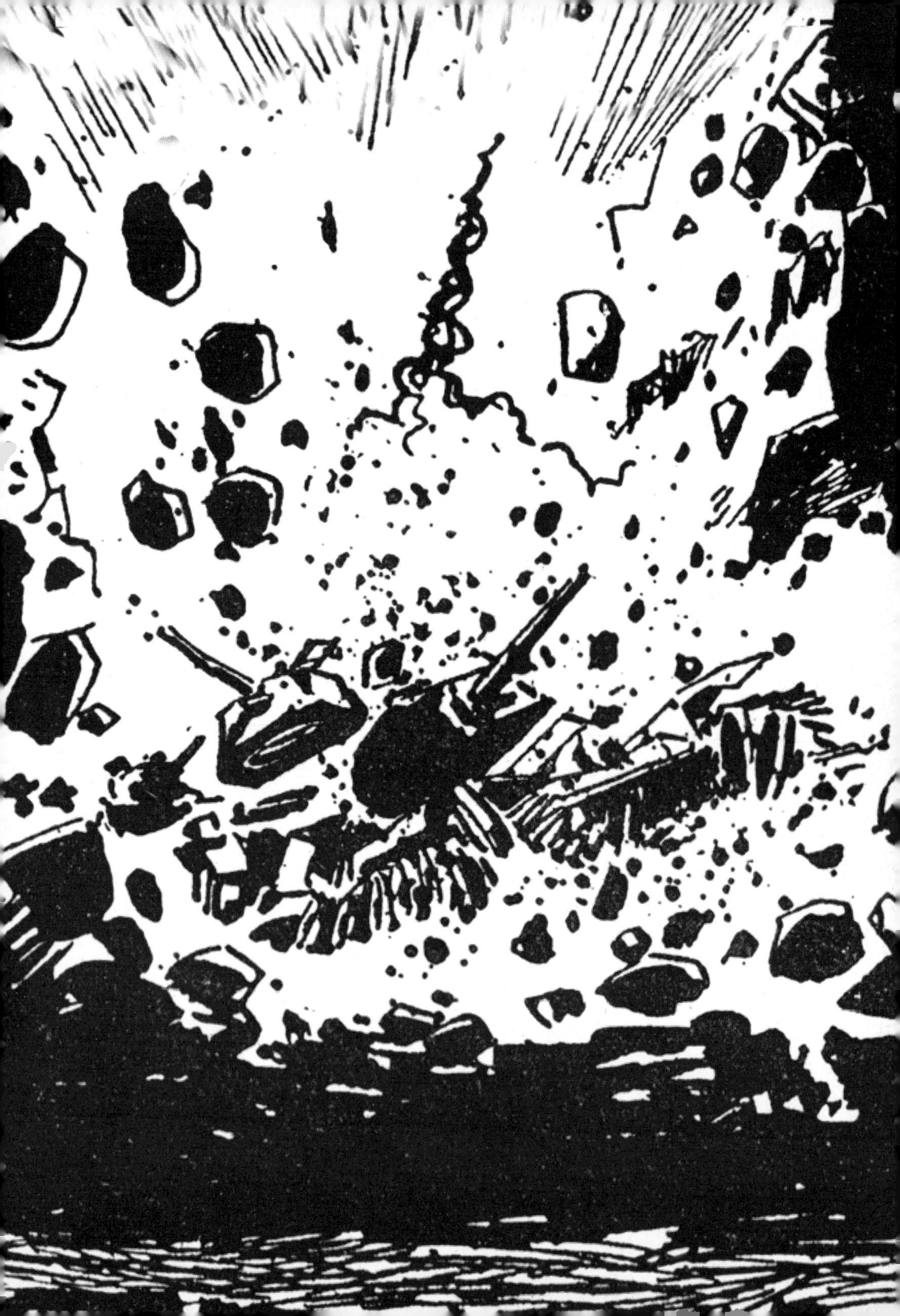

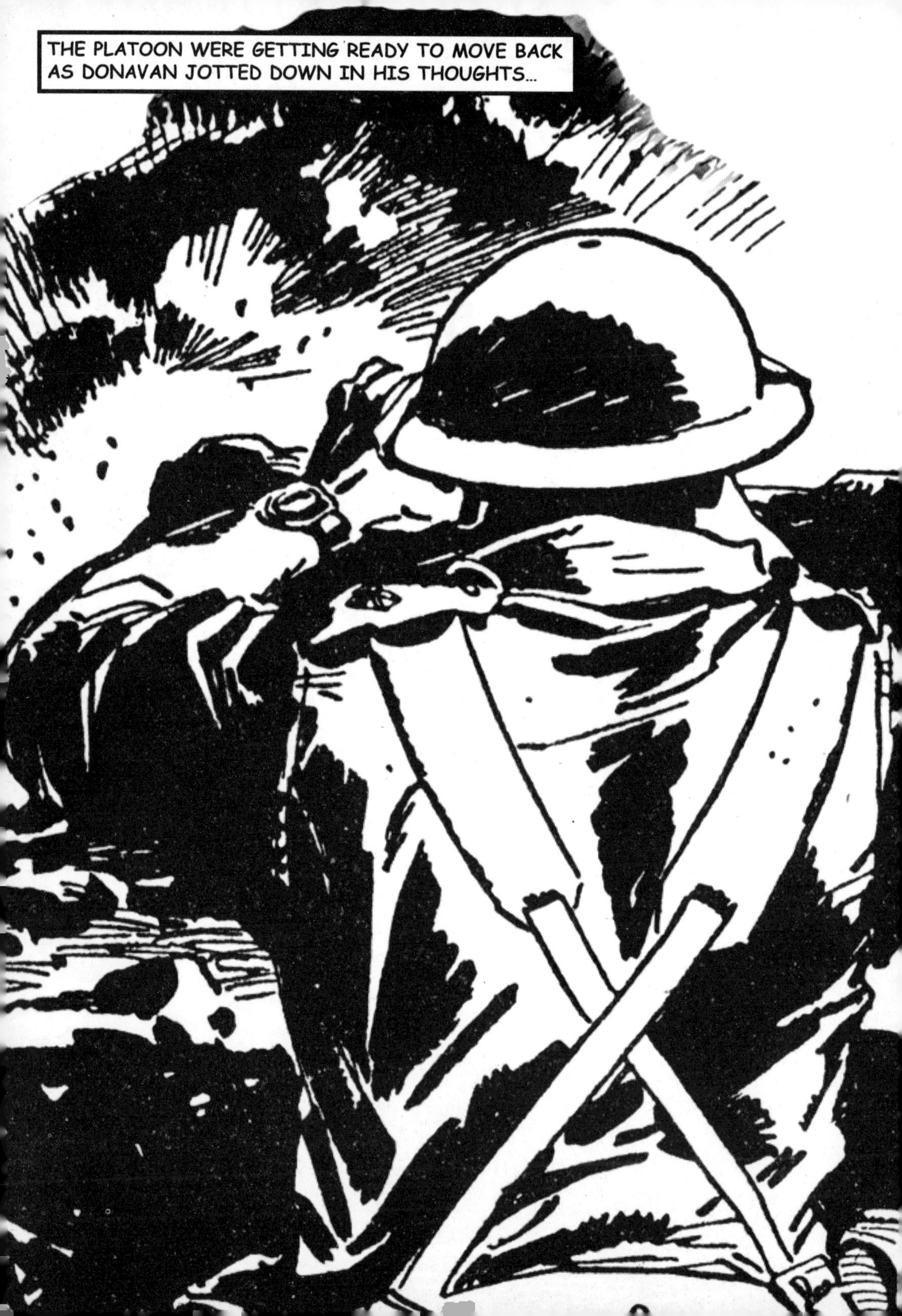
THE PLATOON WERE GETTING READY TO MOVE BACK AS DONAVAN JOTTED DOWN IN HIS THOUGHTS...

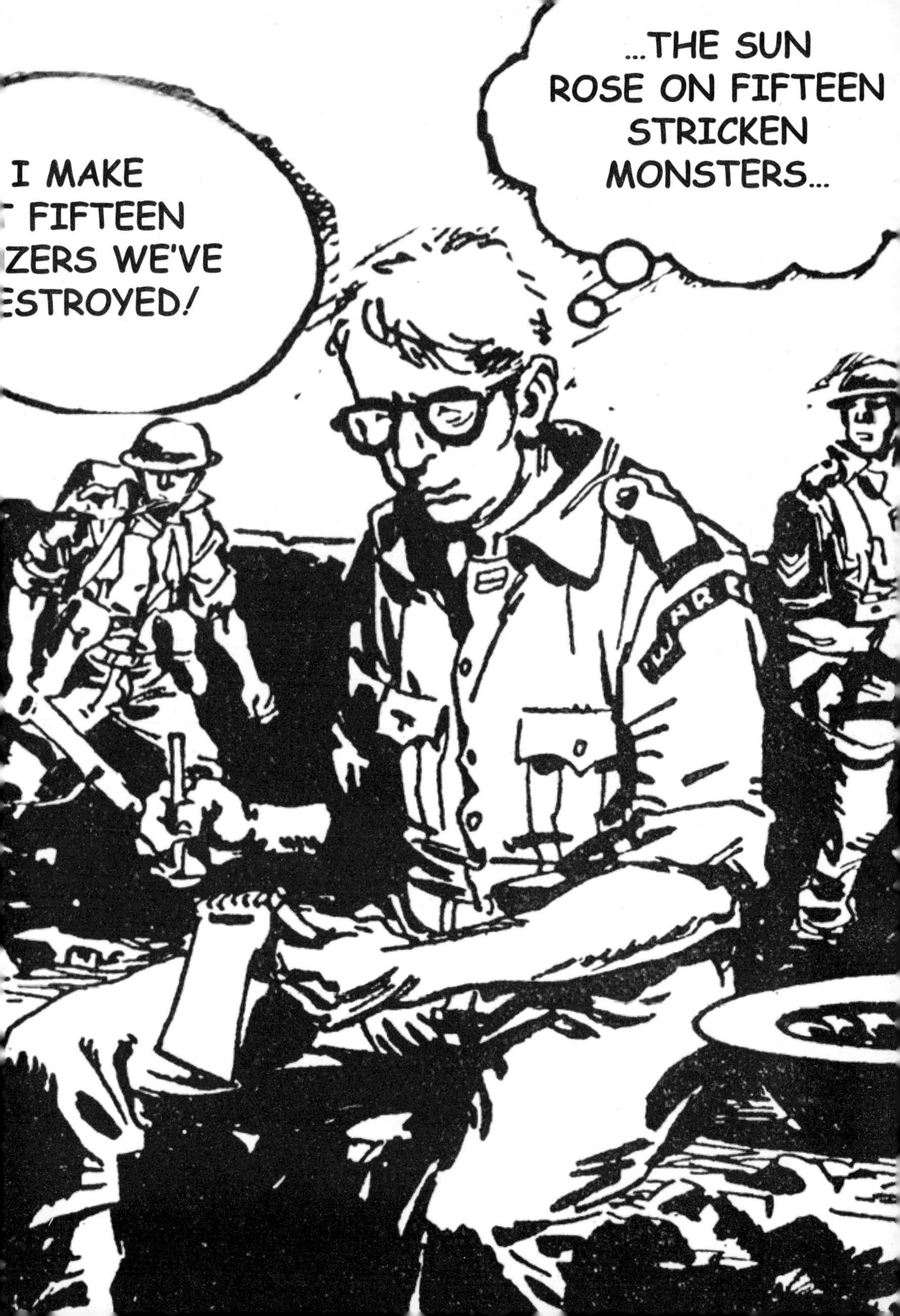
...THE SUN ROSE ON FIFTEEN STRICKEN MONSTERS...
I MAKE
FIFTEEN
ZERS WE'VE
STROYED!

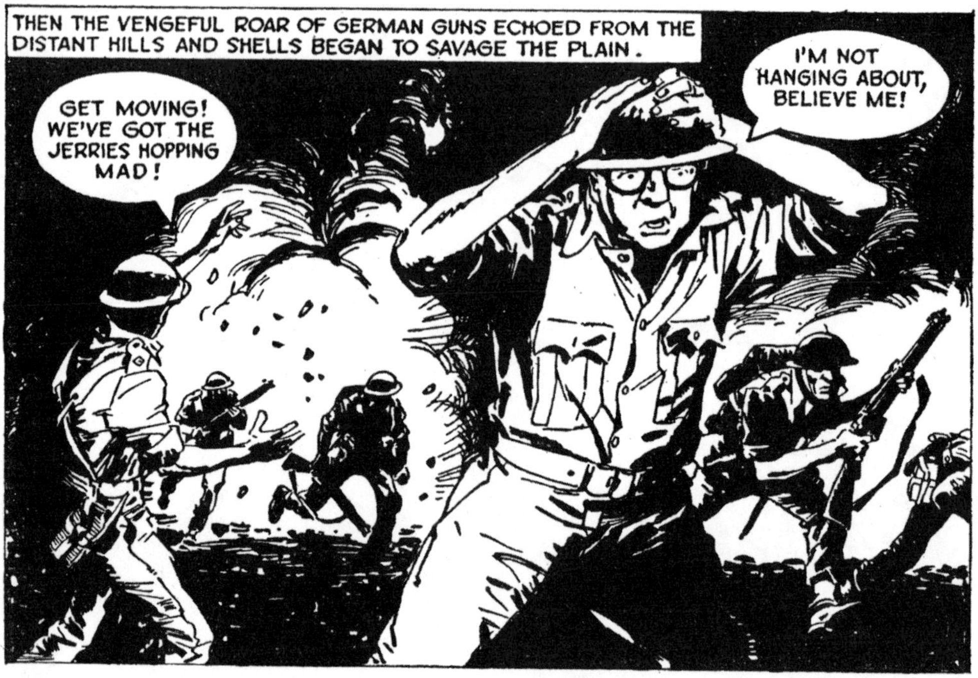
THEN THE VENGEFUL ROAR OF GERMAN GUNS ECHOED FROM THE DISTANT HILLS AND SHELLS BEGAN TO SAVAGE THE PLAIN.
GET MOVING! WE'VE GOT THE JERRIES HOPPING MAD!
I'M NOT HANGING ABOUT, BELIEVE ME!

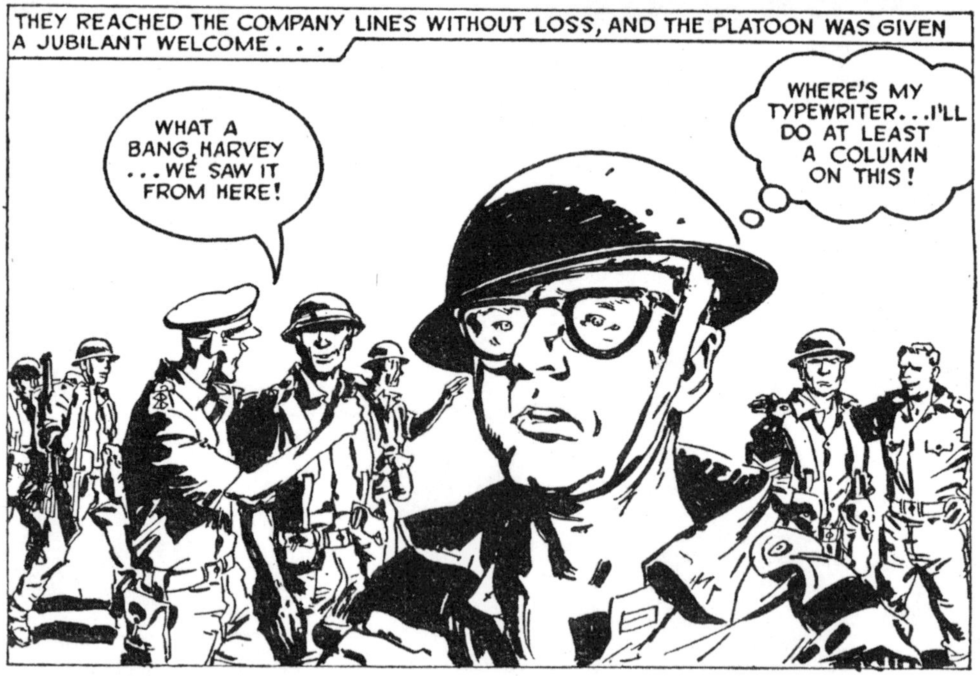
THEY REACHED THE COMPANY LINES WITHOUT LOSS, AND THE PLATOON WAS GIVEN A JUBILANT WELCOME . . .
WHAT A BANG, HARVEY ...WE SAW IT FROM HERE!
WHERE'S MY TYPEWRITER...I'LL DO AT LEAST A COLUMN ON THIS!

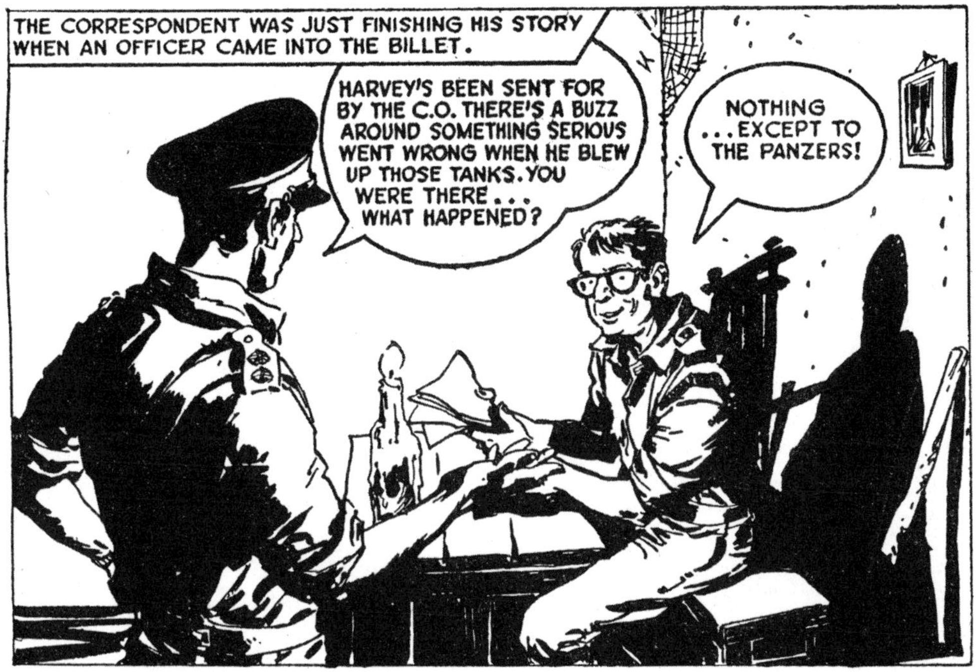
THE CORRESPONDENT WAS JUST FINISHING HIS STORY WHEN AN OFFICER CAME INTO THE BILLET.
HARVEY'S BEEN SENT FOR BY THE C.O. THERE'S A BUZZ AROUND SOMETHING SERIOUS WENT WRONG WHEN HE BLEW UP THOSE TANKS. YOU WERE THERE . . . WHAT HAPPENED?
NOTHING . . . EXCEPT TO THE PANZERS!

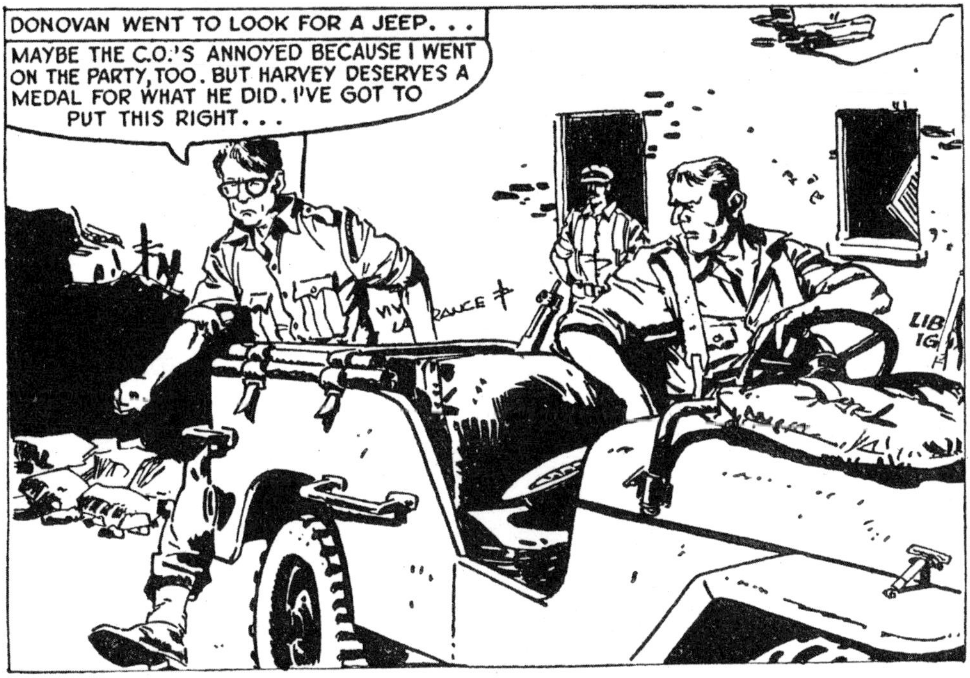
DONOVAN WENT TO LOOK FOR A JEEP. . .
MAYBE THE C.O.'S ANNOYED BECAUSE I WENT ON THE PARTY, TOO. BUT HARVEY DESERVES A MEDAL FOR WHAT HE DID. I'VE GOT TO PUT THIS RIGHT. . .

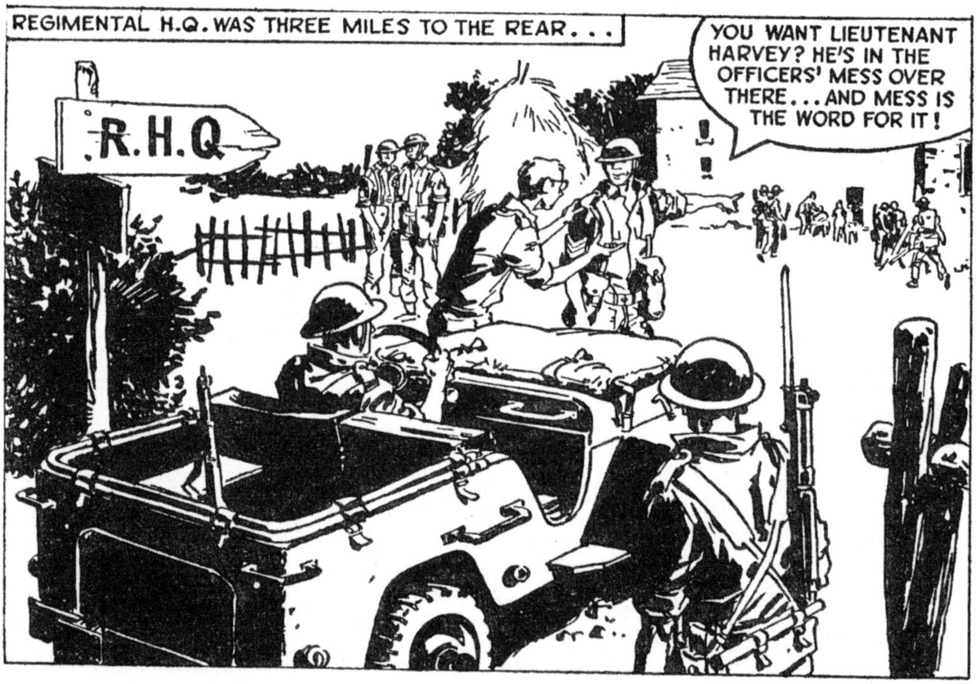
REGIMENTAL H.Q. WAS THREE MILES TO THE REAR . . .
R.H.Q
YOU WANT LIEUTENANT HARVEY? HE'S IN THE OFFICERS' MESS OVER THERE . . . AND MESS IS THE WORD FOR IT!

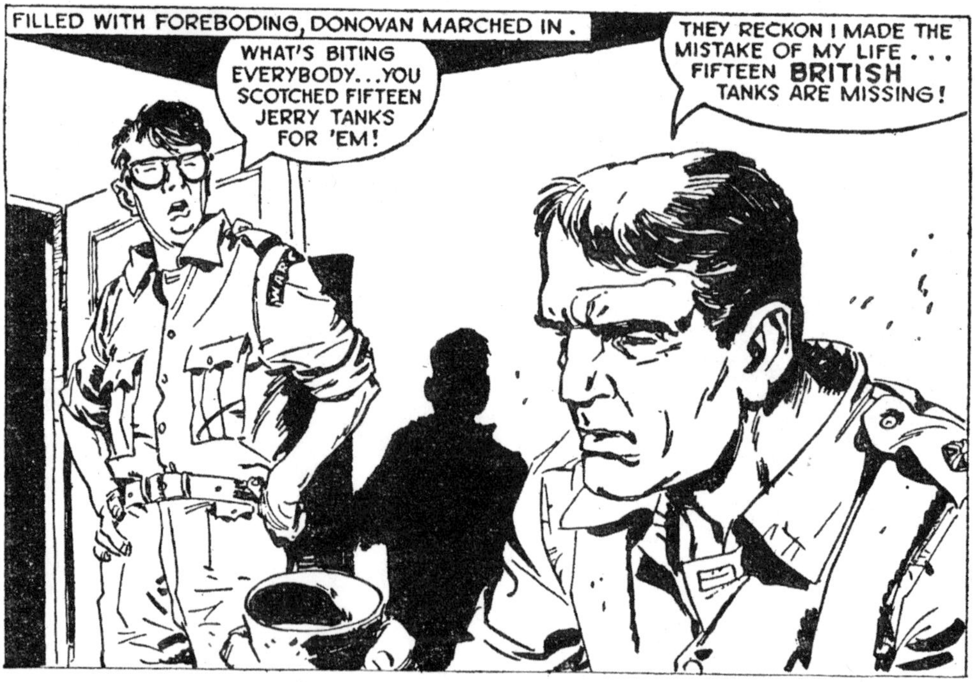
FILLED WITH FOREBODING, DONOVAN MARCHED IN.
WHAT'S BITING EVERYBODY . . . YOU SCOTCHED FIFTEEN JERRY TANKS FOR 'EM!
THEY RECKON I MADE THE MISTAKE OF MY LIFE . . . FIFTEEN BRITISH TANKS ARE MISSING!

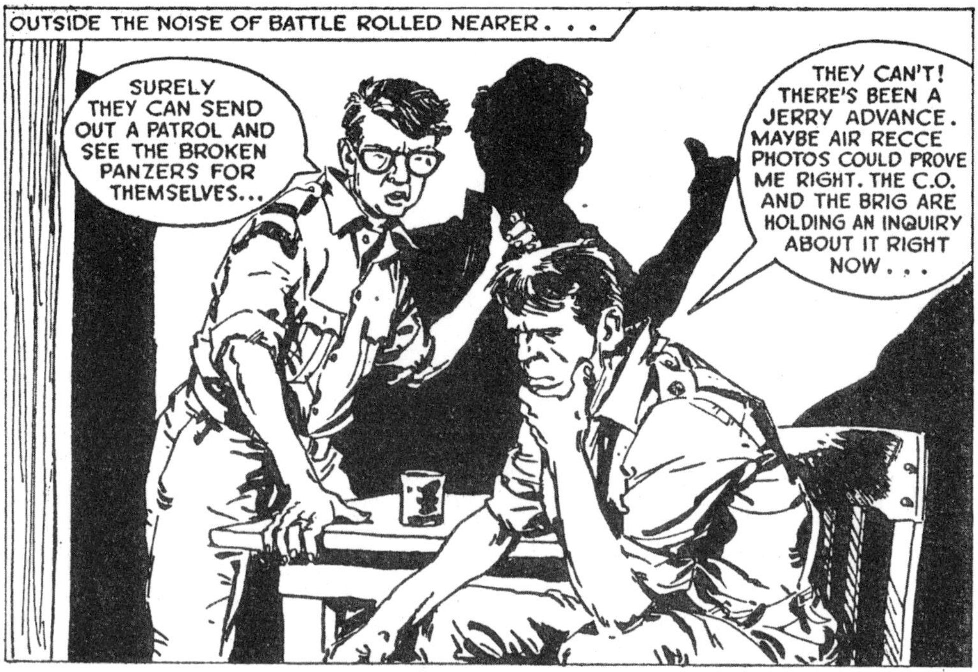
OUTSIDE THE NOISE OF BATTLE ROLLED NEARER . . .
SURELY THEY CAN SEND OUT A PATROL AND SEE THE BROKEN PANZERS FOR THEMSELVES...
THEY CAN'T! THERE'S BEEN A JERRY ADVANCE. MAYBE AIR RECCE PHOTOS COULD PROVE ME RIGHT. THE C.O. AND THE BRIG ARE HOLDING AN INQUIRY ABOUT IT RIGHT NOW . . .

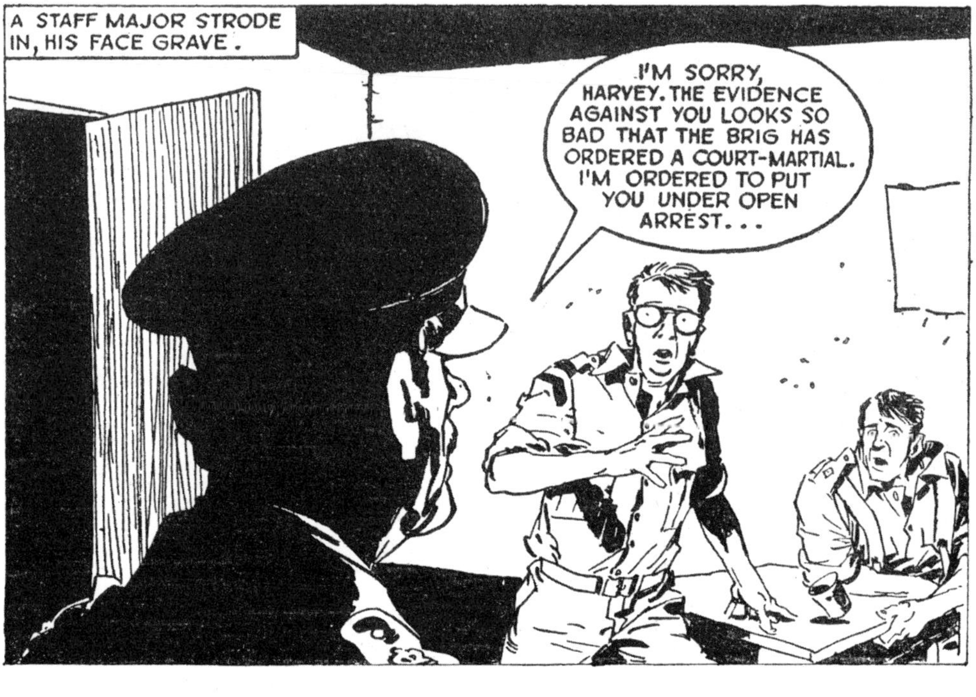
A STAFF MAJOR STRODE IN, HIS FACE GRAVE.
I'M SORRY, HARVEY. THE EVIDENCE AGAINST YOU LOOKS SO BAD THAT THE BRIG HAS ORDERED A COURT-MARTIAL. I'M ORDERED TO PUT YOU UNDER OPEN ARREST . . .

Chapter 2. Tank Buster

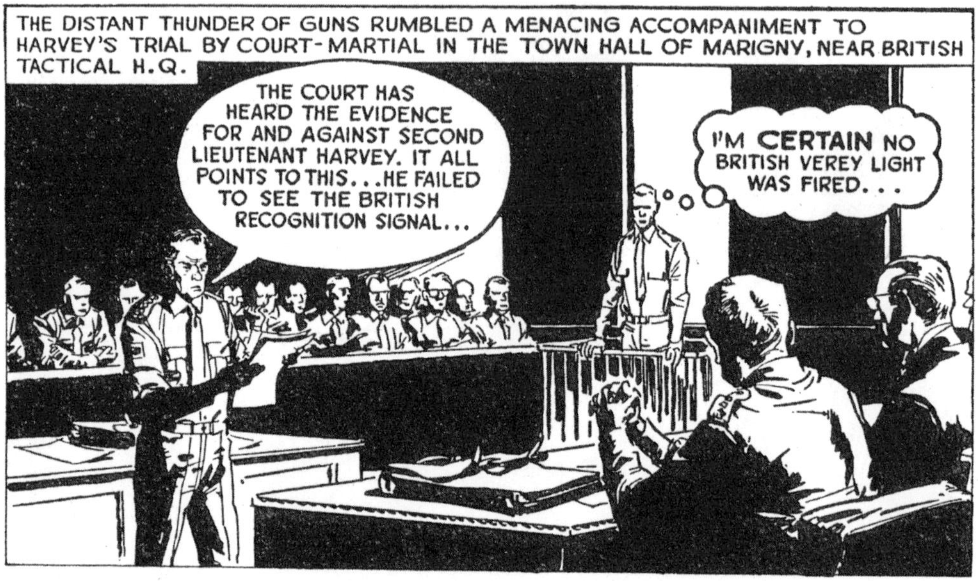
THE DISTANT THUNDER OF GUNS RUMBLED A MENACING ACCOMPANIMENT TO HARVEY'S TRIAL BY COURT-MARTIAL IN THE TOWN HALL OF MARIGNY, NEAR BRITISH TACTICAL H.Q.
THE COURT HAS HEARD THE EVIDENCE FOR AND AGAINST SECOND LIEUTENANT HARVEY. IT ALL POINTS TO THIS...HE FAILED TO SEE THE BRITISH RECOGNITION SIGNAL...
I'M CERTAIN NO BRITISH VEREY LIGHT WAS FIRED...

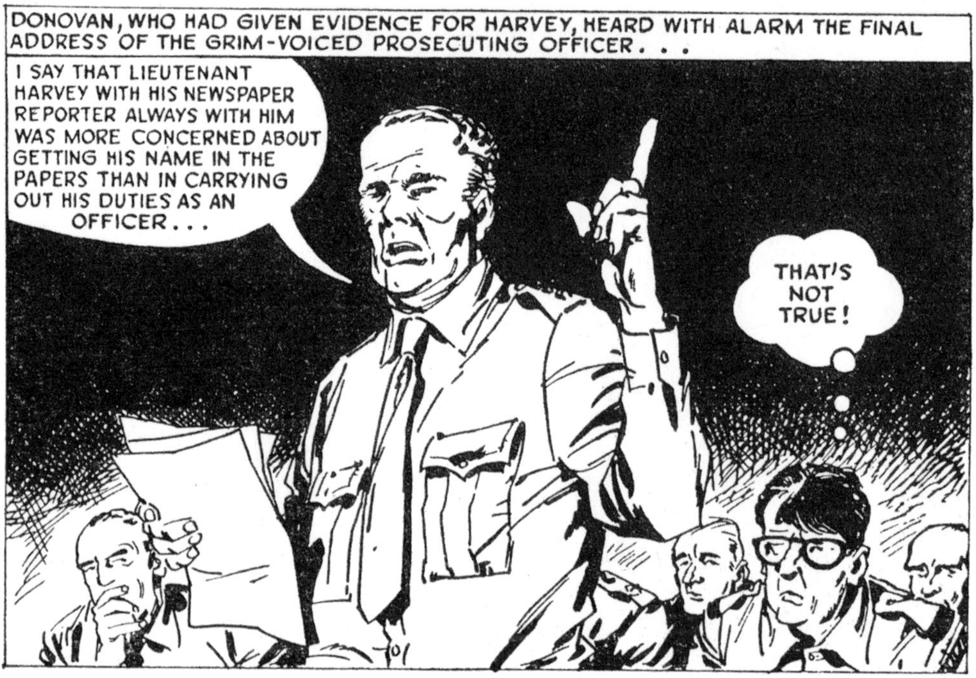
DONOVAN, WHO HAD GIVEN EVIDENCE FOR HARVEY, HEARD WITH ALARM THE FINAL ADDRESS OF THE GRIM-VOICED PROSECUTING OFFICER...
I SAY THAT LIEUTENANT HARVEY WITH HIS NEWSPAPER REPORTER ALWAYS WITH HIM WAS MORE CONCERNED ABOUT GETTING HIS NAME IN THE PAPERS THAN IN CARRYING OUT HIS DUTIES AS AN OFFICER...
THAT'S NOT TRUE!

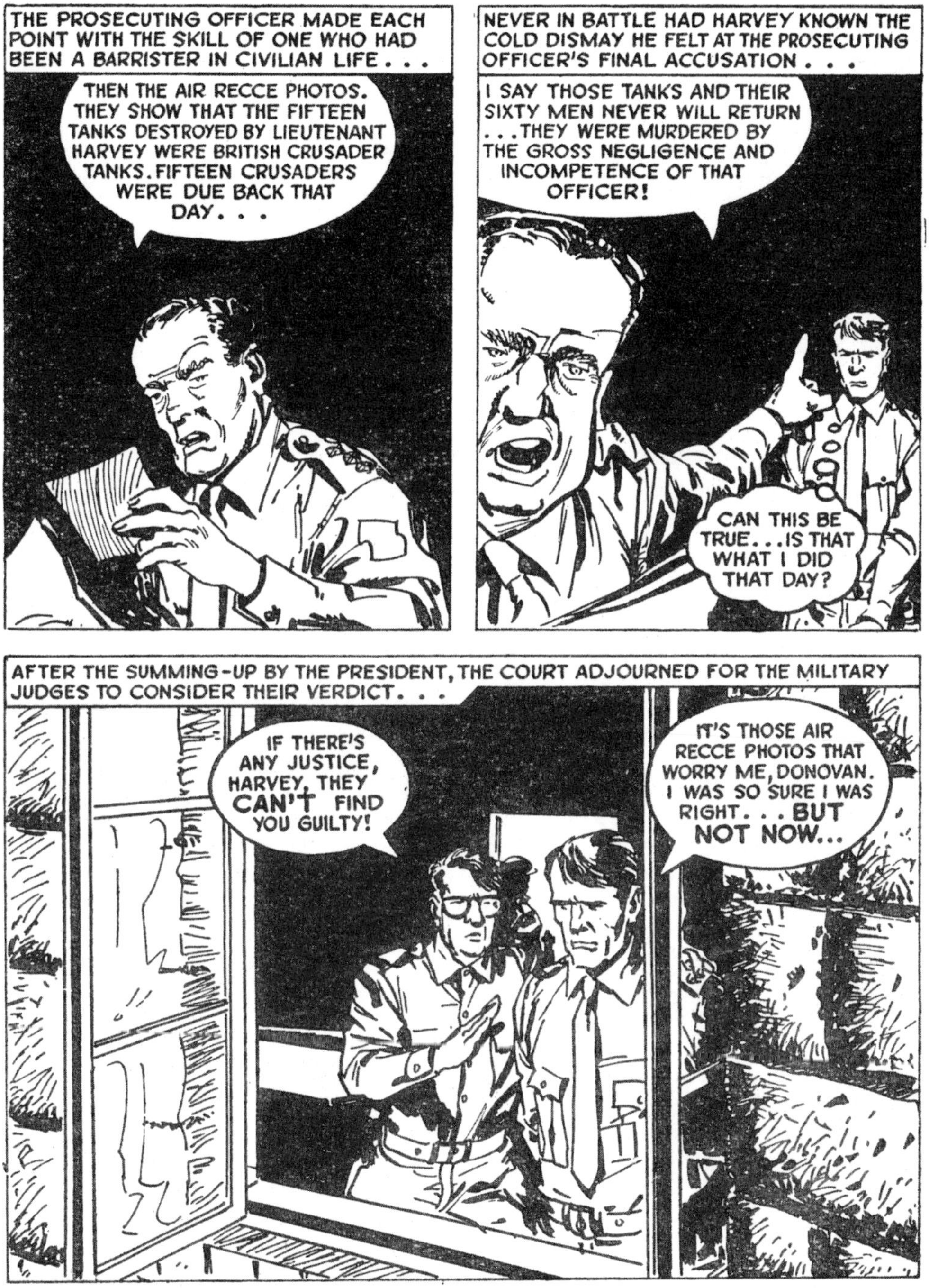
THE PROSECUTING OFFICER MADE EACH POINT WITH THE SKILL OF ONE WHO HAD BEEN A BARRISTER IN CIVILIAN LIFE . . .
THEN THE AIR RECCE PHOTOS. THEY SHOW THAT THE FIFTEEN TANKS DESTROYED BY LIEUTENANT HARVEY WERE BRITISH CRUSADER TANKS. FIFTEEN CRUSADERS WERE DUE BACK THAT DAY . . .
NEVER IN BATTLE HAD HARVEY KNOWN THE COLD DISMAY HE FELT AT THE PROSECUTING OFFICER'S FINAL ACCUSATION . . .
I SAY THOSE TANKS AND THEIR SIXTY MEN NEVER WILL RETURN . . . THEY WERE MURDERED BY THE GROSS NEGLIGENCE AND INCOMPETENCE OF THAT OFFICER!
CAN THIS BE TRUE. . . IS THAT WHAT I DID THAT DAY?
AFTER THE SUMMING-UP BY THE PRESIDENT, THE COURT ADJOURNED FOR THE MILITARY JUDGES TO CONSIDER THEIR VERDICT. . .
IF THERE'S ANY JUSTICE, HARVEY, THEY CAN'T FIND YOU GUILTY!
IT'S THOSE AIR RECCE PHOTOS THAT WORRY ME, DONOVAN. I WAS SO SURE I WAS RIGHT. . . BUT NOT NOW...

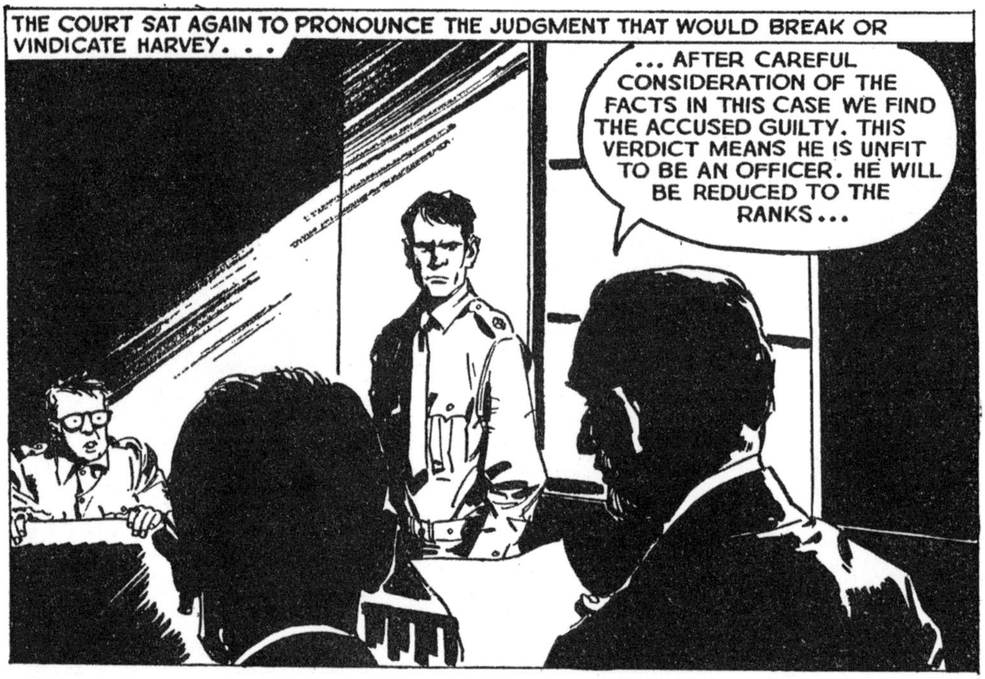
THE COURT SAT AGAIN TO PRONOUNCE THE JUDGMENT THAT WOULD BREAK OR VINDICATE HARVEY. . .
... AFTER CAREFUL CONSIDERATION OF THE FACTS IN THIS CASE WE FIND THE ACCUSED GUILTY. THIS VERDICT MEANS HE IS UNFIT TO BE AN OFFICER. HE WILL BE REDUCED TO THE RANKS...

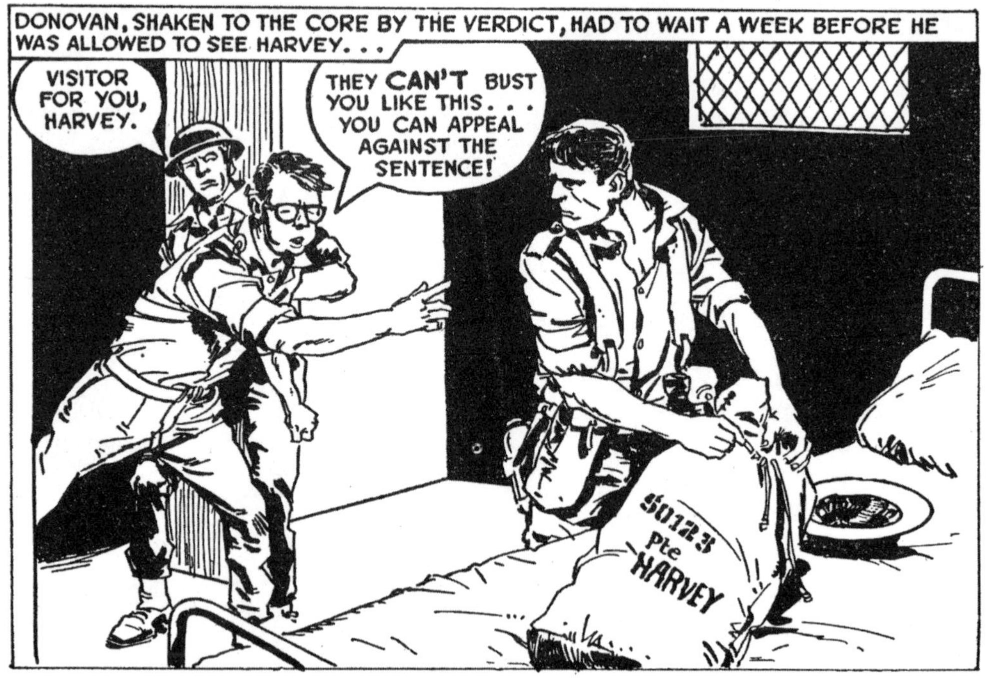
DONOVAN, SHAKEN TO THE CORE BY THE VERDICT, HAD TO WAIT A WEEK BEFORE HE WAS ALLOWED TO SEE HARVEY. . .
VISITOR FOR YOU, HARVEY.
THEY CAN'T BUST YOU LIKE THIS. . . YOU CAN APPEAL AGAINST THE SENTENCE!
50123 Pte HARVEY

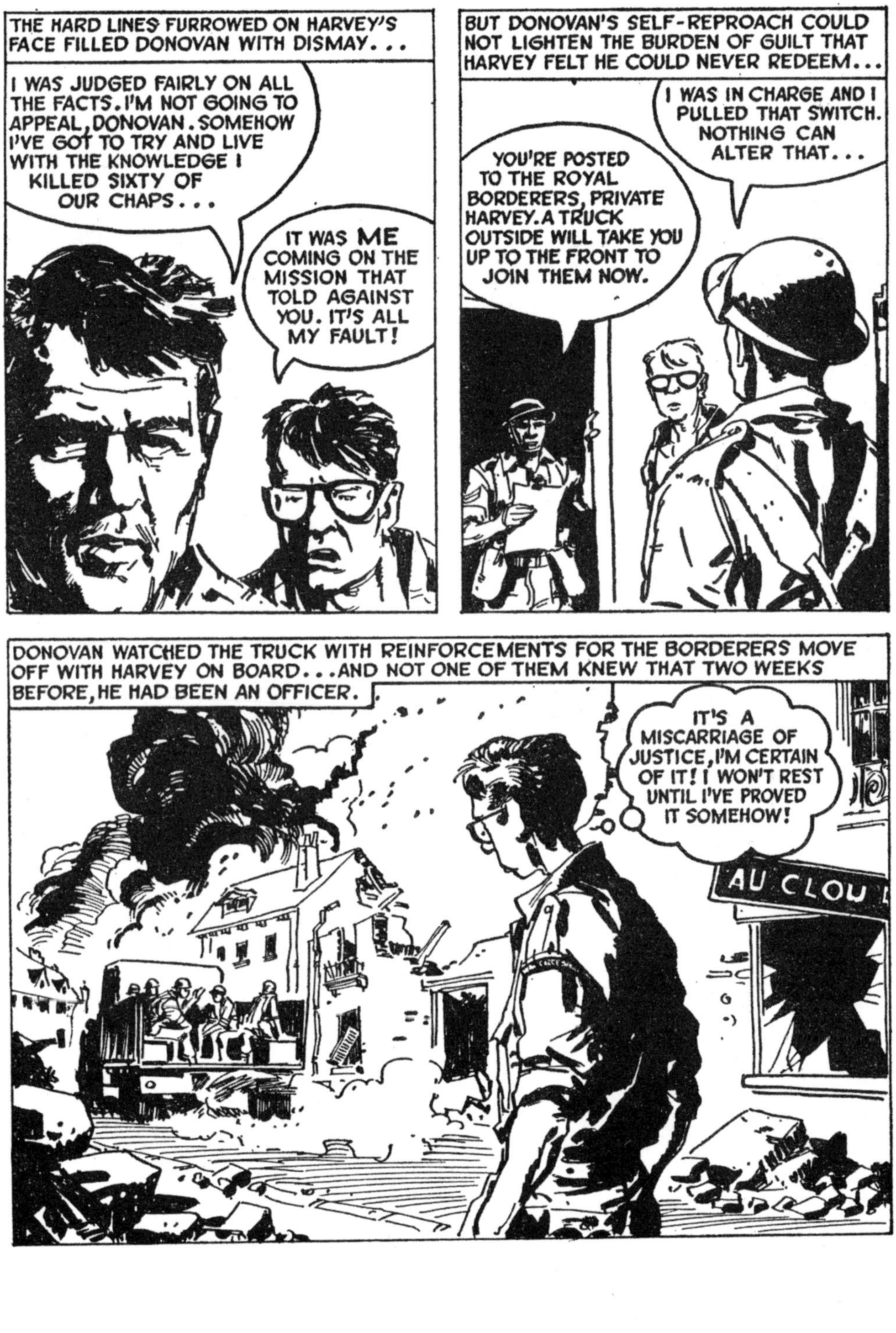
THE HARD LINES FURROWED ON HARVEY'S FACE FILLED DONOVAN WITH DISMAY...
I WAS JUDGED FAIRLY ON ALL THE FACTS. I'M NOT GOING TO APPEAL, DONOVAN. SOMEHOW I'VE GOT TO TRY AND LIVE WITH THE KNOWLEDGE I KILLED SIXTY OF OUR CHAPS...
IT WAS ME COMING ON THE MISSION THAT TOLD AGAINST YOU. IT'S ALL MY FAULT!
BUT DONOVAN'S SELF-REPROACH COULD NOT LIGHTEN THE BURDEN OF GUILT THAT HARVEY FELT HE COULD NEVER REDEEM...
YOU'RE POSTED TO THE ROYAL BORDERERS, PRIVATE HARVEY. A TRUCK OUTSIDE WILL TAKE YOU UP TO THE FRONT TO JOIN THEM NOW.
I WAS IN CHARGE AND I PULLED THAT SWITCH. NOTHING CAN ALTER THAT...
DONOVAN WATCHED THE TRUCK WITH REINFORCEMENTS FOR THE BORDERERS MOVE OFF WITH HARVEY ON BOARD...AND NOT ONE OF THEM KNEW THAT TWO WEEKS BEFORE, HE HAD BEEN AN OFFICER.
IT'S A MISCARRIAGE OF JUSTICE, I'M CERTAIN OF IT! I WON'T REST UNTIL I'VE PROVED IT SOMEHOW!
AU CLOU

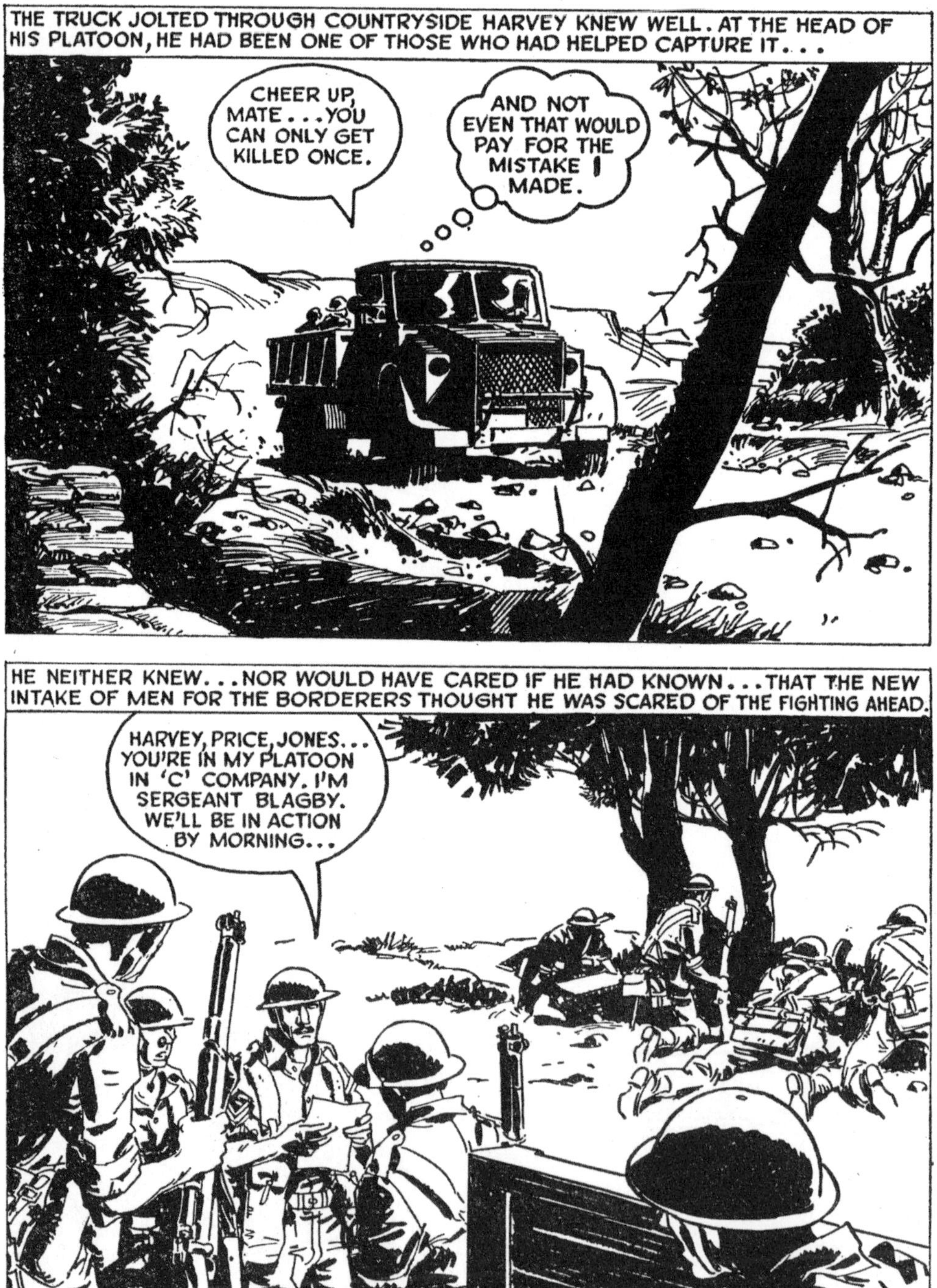
THE TRUCK JOLTED THROUGH COUNTRYSIDE HARVEY KNEW WELL. AT THE HEAD OF HIS PLATOON, HE HAD BEEN ONE OF THOSE WHO HAD HELPED CAPTURE IT...
CHEER UP, MATE...YOU CAN ONLY GET KILLED ONCE.
AND NOT EVEN THAT WOULD PAY FOR THE MISTAKE I MADE.
HE NEITHER KNEW...NOR WOULD HAVE CARED IF HE HAD KNOWN...THAT THE NEW INTAKE OF MEN FOR THE BORDERERS THOUGHT HE WAS SCARED OF THE FIGHTING AHEAD.
HARVEY, PRICE, JONES... YOU'RE IN MY PLATOON IN 'C' COMPANY. I'M SERGEANT BLAGBY. WE'LL BE IN ACTION BY MORNING...

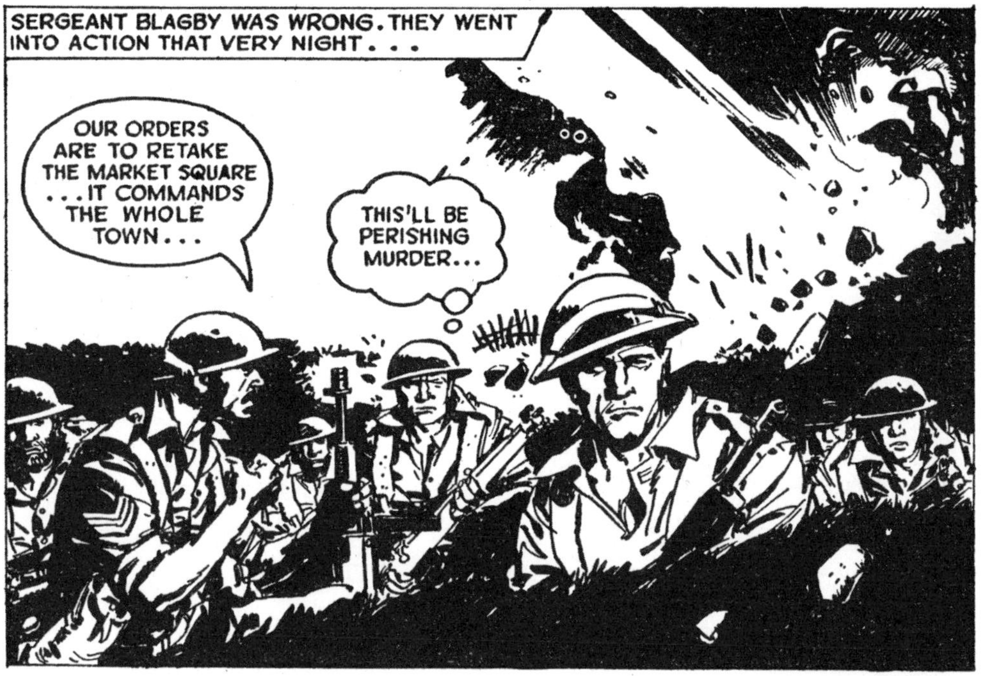
SERGEANT BLAGBY WAS WRONG. THEY WENT INTO ACTION THAT VERY NIGHT . . .
OUR ORDERS ARE TO RETAKE THE MARKET SQUARE . . . IT COMMANDS THE WHOLE TOWN . . .
THIS'LL BE PERISHING MURDER . . .

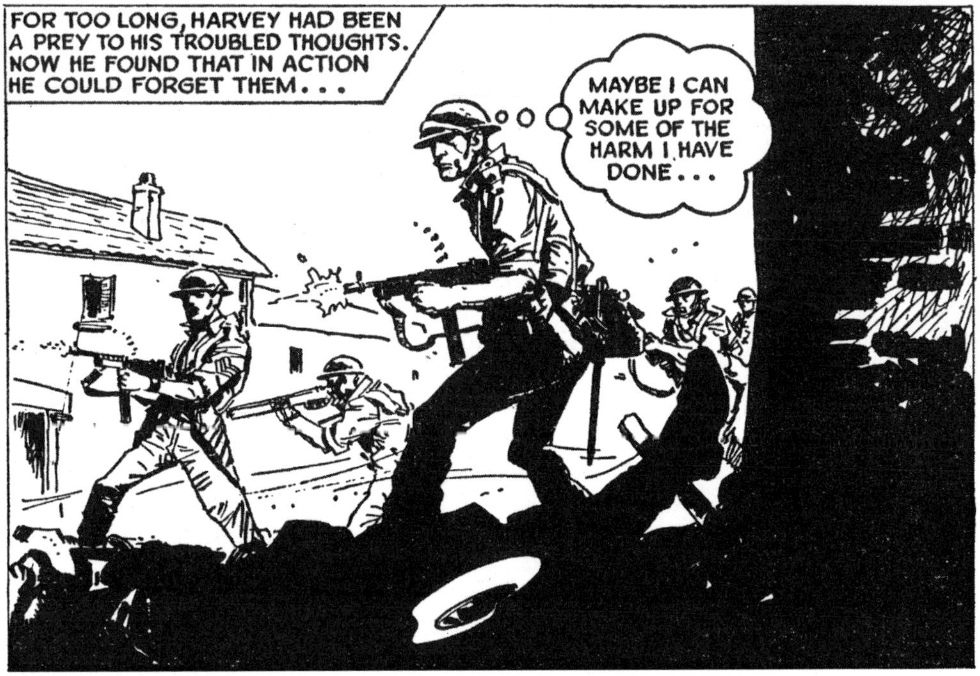
FOR TOO LONG, HARVEY HAD BEEN A PREY TO HIS TROUBLED THOUGHTS. NOW HE FOUND THAT IN ACTION HE COULD FORGET THEM . . .
MAYBE I CAN MAKE UP FOR SOME OF THE HARM I HAVE DONE . . .

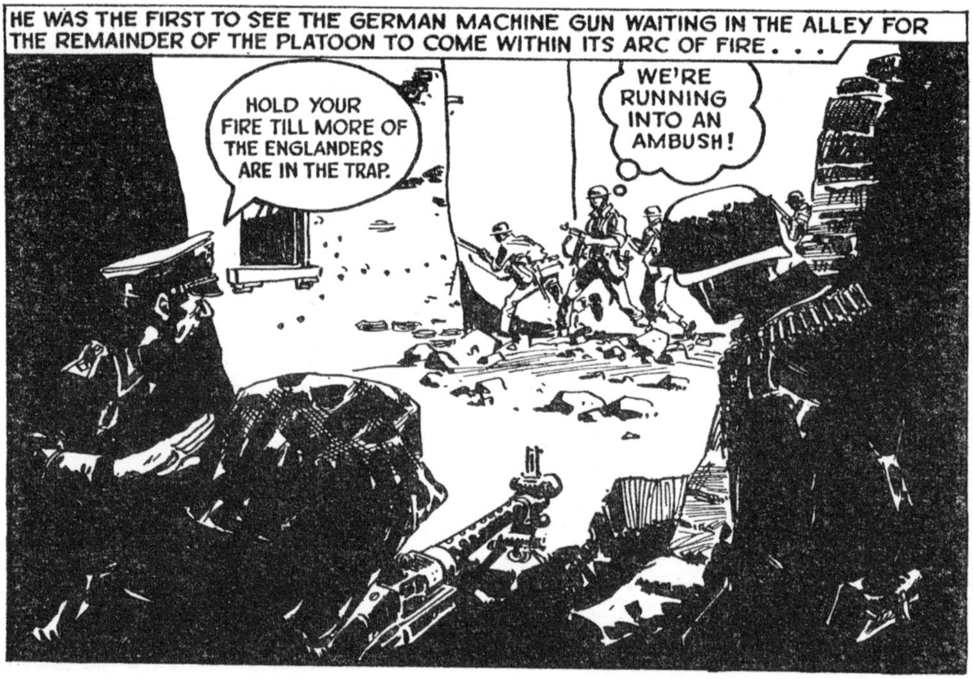
HE WAS THE FIRST TO SEE THE GERMAN MACHINE GUN WAITING IN THE ALLEY FOR THE REMAINDER OF THE PLATOON TO COME WITHIN ITS ARC OF FIRE . . .
HOLD YOUR FIRE TILL MORE OF THE ENGLANDERS ARE IN THE TRAP.
WE'RE RUNNING INTO AN AMBUSH!

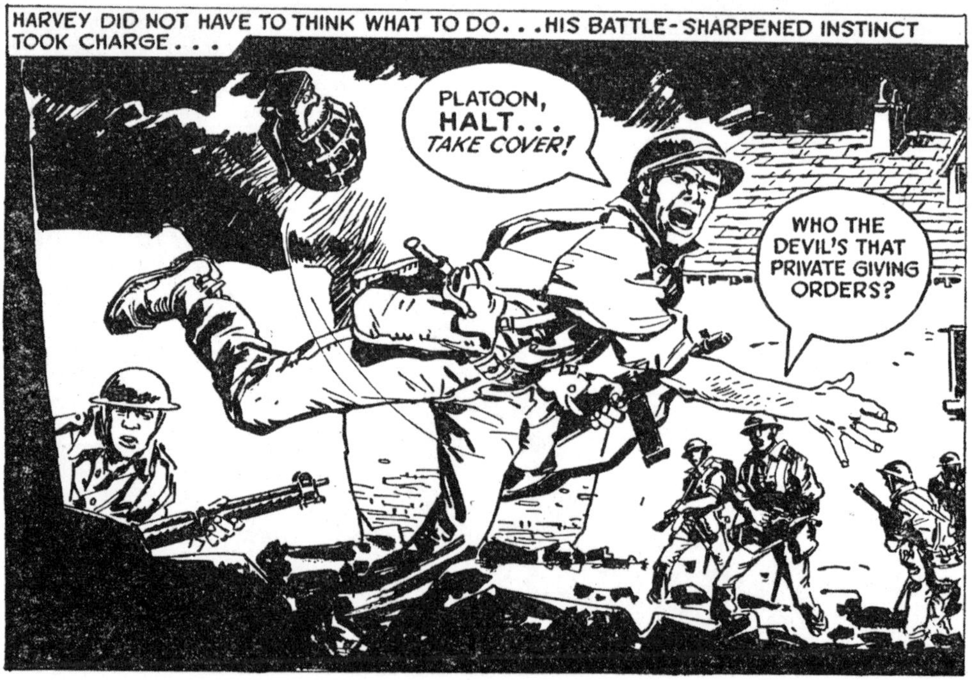
HARVEY DID NOT HAVE TO THINK WHAT TO DO. . .HIS BATTLE-SHARPENED INSTINCT TOOK CHARGE . . .
PLATOON, HALT... TAKE COVER!
WHO THE DEVIL'S THAT PRIVATE GIVING ORDERS?

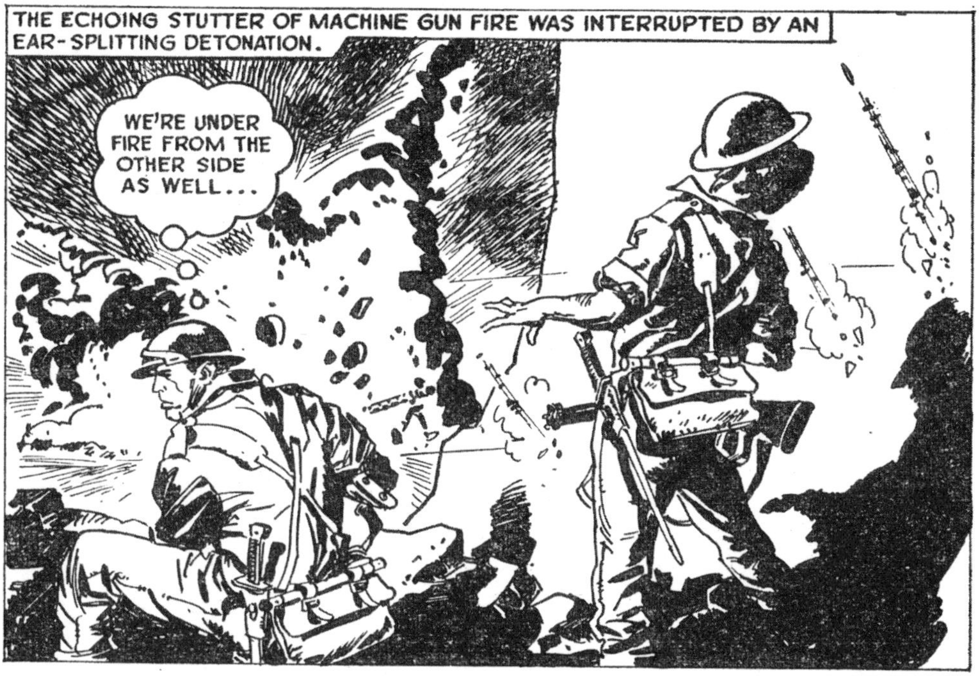
THE ECHOING STUTTER OF MACHINE GUN FIRE WAS INTERRUPTED BY AN EAR-SPLITTING DETONATION.
WE'RE UNDER FIRE FROM THE OTHER SIDE AS WELL...

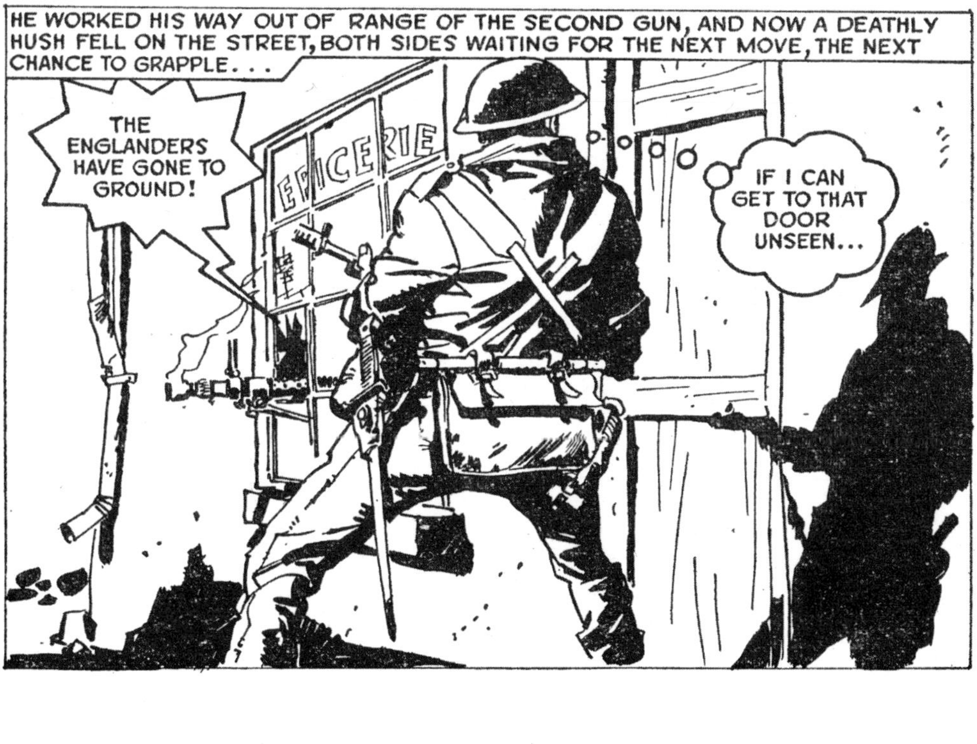
HE WORKED HIS WAY OUT OF RANGE OF THE SECOND GUN, AND NOW A DEATHLY HUSH FELL ON THE STREET, BOTH SIDES WAITING FOR THE NEXT MOVE, THE NEXT CHANCE TO GRAPPLE...
THE ENGLANDERS HAVE GONE TO GROUND!
IF I CAN GET TO THAT DOOR UNSEEN...
EPICERIE

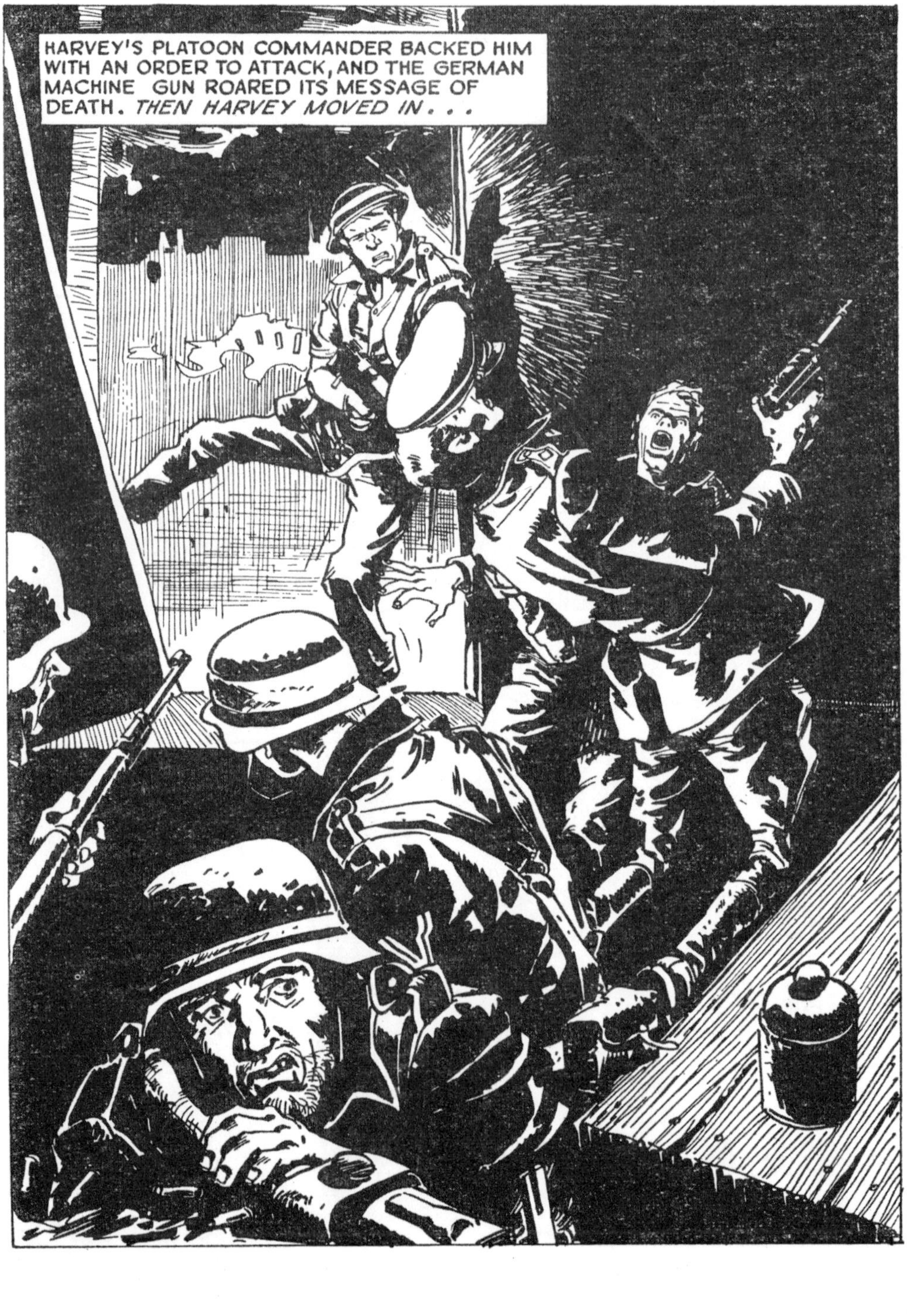
HARVEY'S PLATOON COMMANDER BACKED HIM WITH AN ORDER TO ATTACK, AND THE GERMAN MACHINE GUN ROARED ITS MESSAGE OF DEATH. *THEN HARVEY MOVED IN . . .*

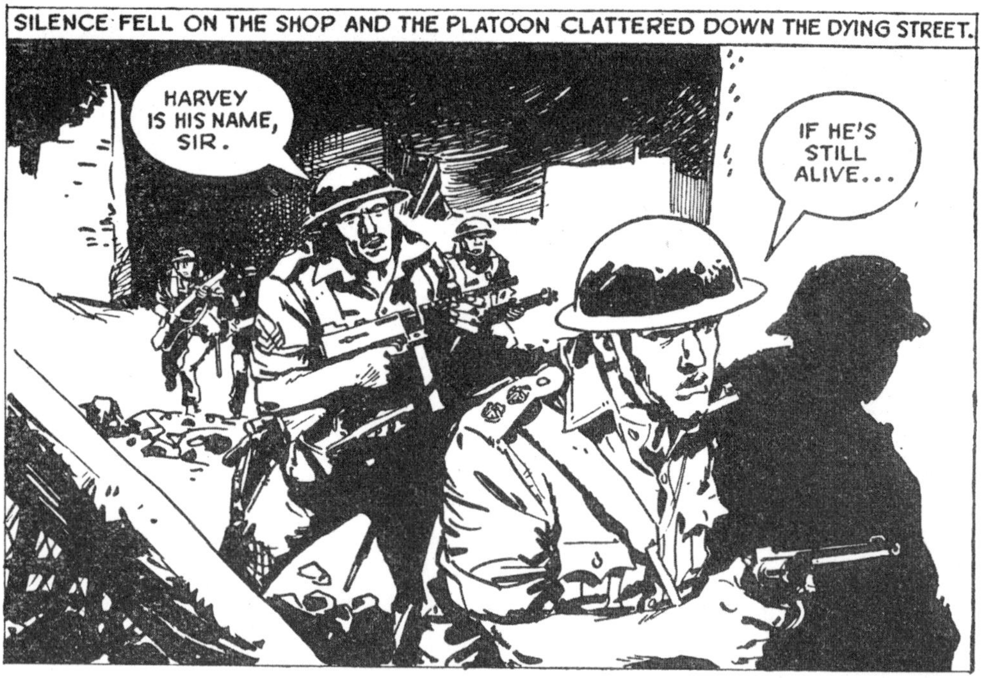
SILENCE FELL ON THE SHOP AND THE PLATOON CLATTERED DOWN THE DYING STREET.
HARVEY IS HIS NAME, SIR.
IF HE'S STILL ALIVE...

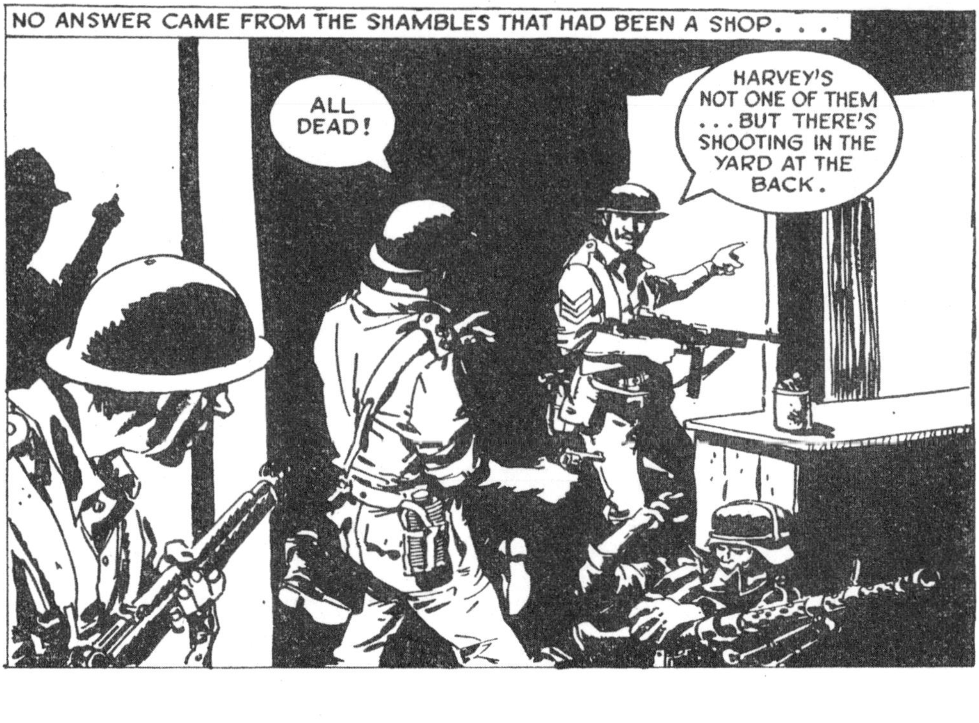
NO ANSWER CAME FROM THE SHAMBLES THAT HAD BEEN A SHOP. . .
ALL DEAD!
HARVEY'S NOT ONE OF THEM ...BUT THERE'S SHOOTING IN THE YARD AT THE BACK.

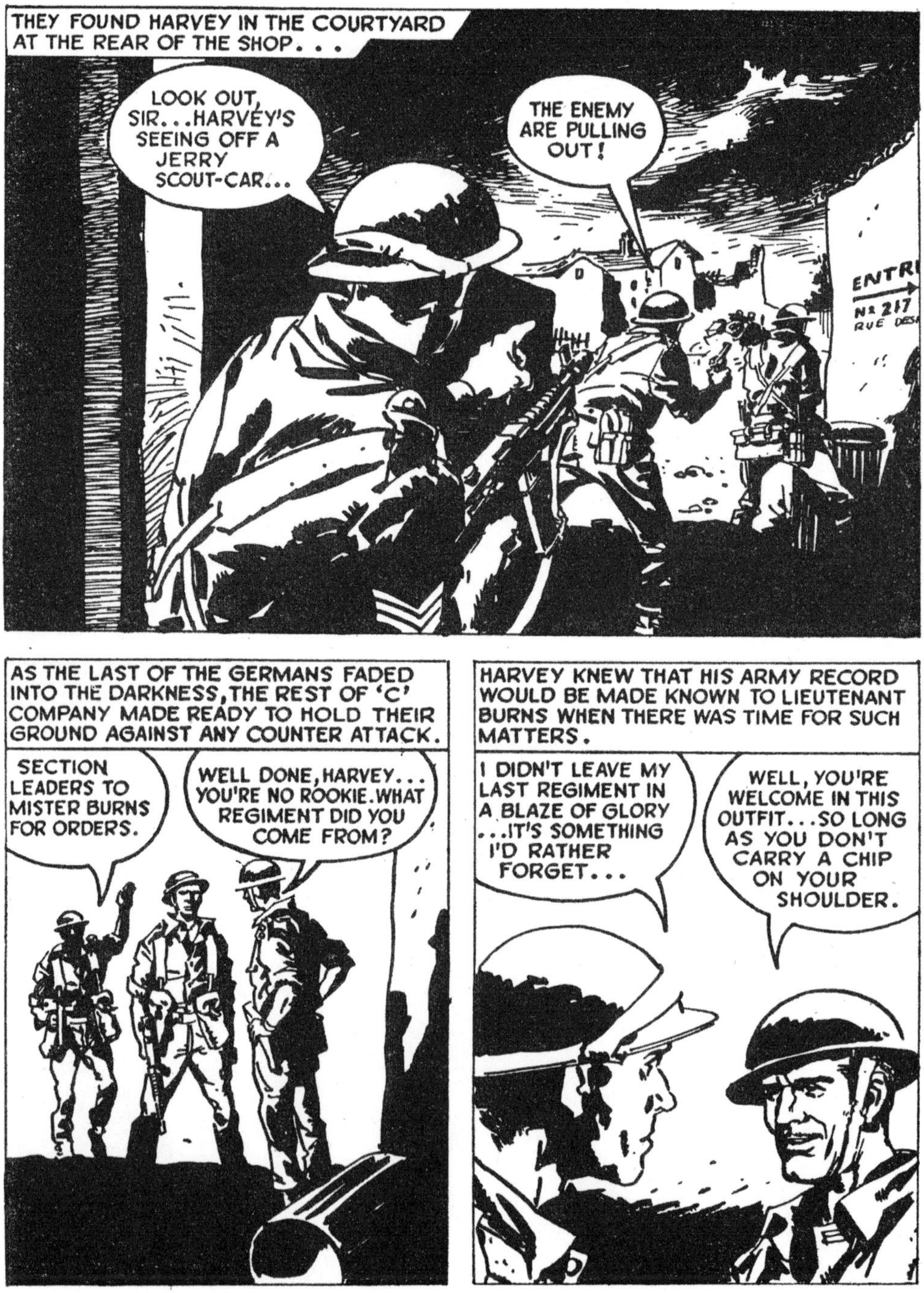
THEY FOUND HARVEY IN THE COURTYARD AT THE REAR OF THE SHOP . . .
LOOK OUT, SIR. . .HARVEY'S SEEING OFF A JERRY SCOUT-CAR...
THE ENEMY ARE PULLING OUT!
AS THE LAST OF THE GERMANS FADED INTO THE DARKNESS, THE REST OF 'C' COMPANY MADE READY TO HOLD THEIR GROUND AGAINST ANY COUNTER ATTACK.
SECTION LEADERS TO MISTER BURNS FOR ORDERS.
WELL DONE, HARVEY... YOU'RE NO ROOKIE. WHAT REGIMENT DID YOU COME FROM?
HARVEY KNEW THAT HIS ARMY RECORD WOULD BE MADE KNOWN TO LIEUTENANT BURNS WHEN THERE WAS TIME FOR SUCH MATTERS.
I DIDN'T LEAVE MY LAST REGIMENT IN A BLAZE OF GLORY . . .IT'S SOMETHING I'D RATHER FORGET...
WELL, YOU'RE WELCOME IN THIS OUTFIT. . . SO LONG AS YOU DON'T CARRY A CHIP ON YOUR SHOULDER.

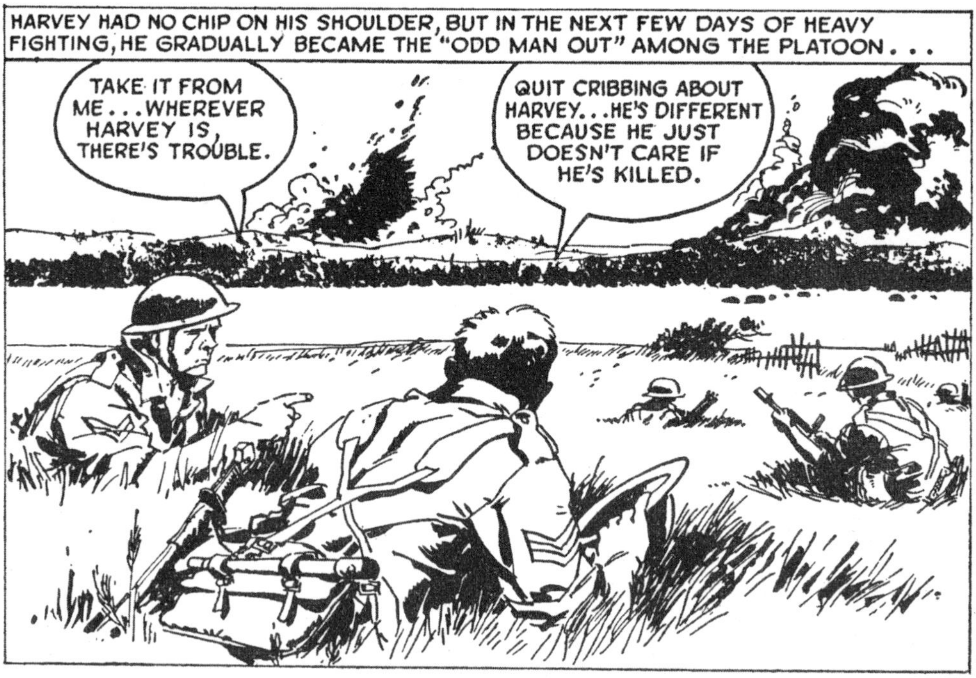
HARVEY HAD NO CHIP ON HIS SHOULDER, BUT IN THE NEXT FEW DAYS OF HEAVY FIGHTING, HE GRADUALLY BECAME THE "ODD MAN OUT" AMONG THE PLATOON . . .
TAKE IT FROM ME . . . WHEREVER HARVEY IS, THERE'S TROUBLE.
QUIT CRIBBING ABOUT HARVEY. . . HE'S DIFFERENT BECAUSE HE JUST DOESN'T CARE IF HE'S KILLED.

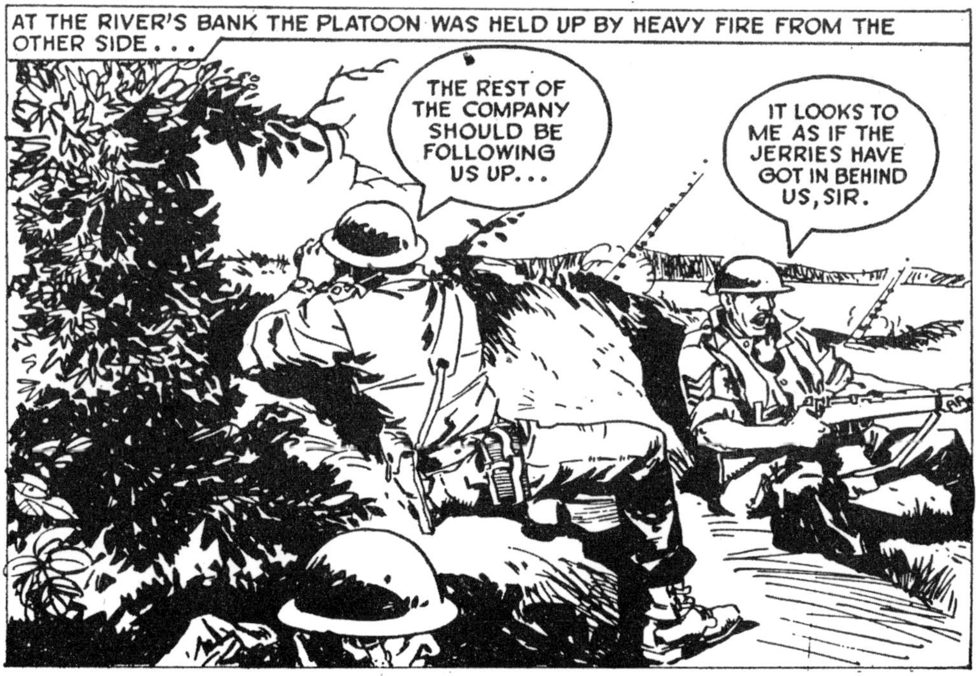
AT THE RIVER'S BANK THE PLATOON WAS HELD UP BY HEAVY FIRE FROM THE OTHER SIDE . . .
THE REST OF THE COMPANY SHOULD BE FOLLOWING US UP . . .
IT LOOKS TO ME AS IF THE JERRIES HAVE GOT IN BEHIND US, SIR.

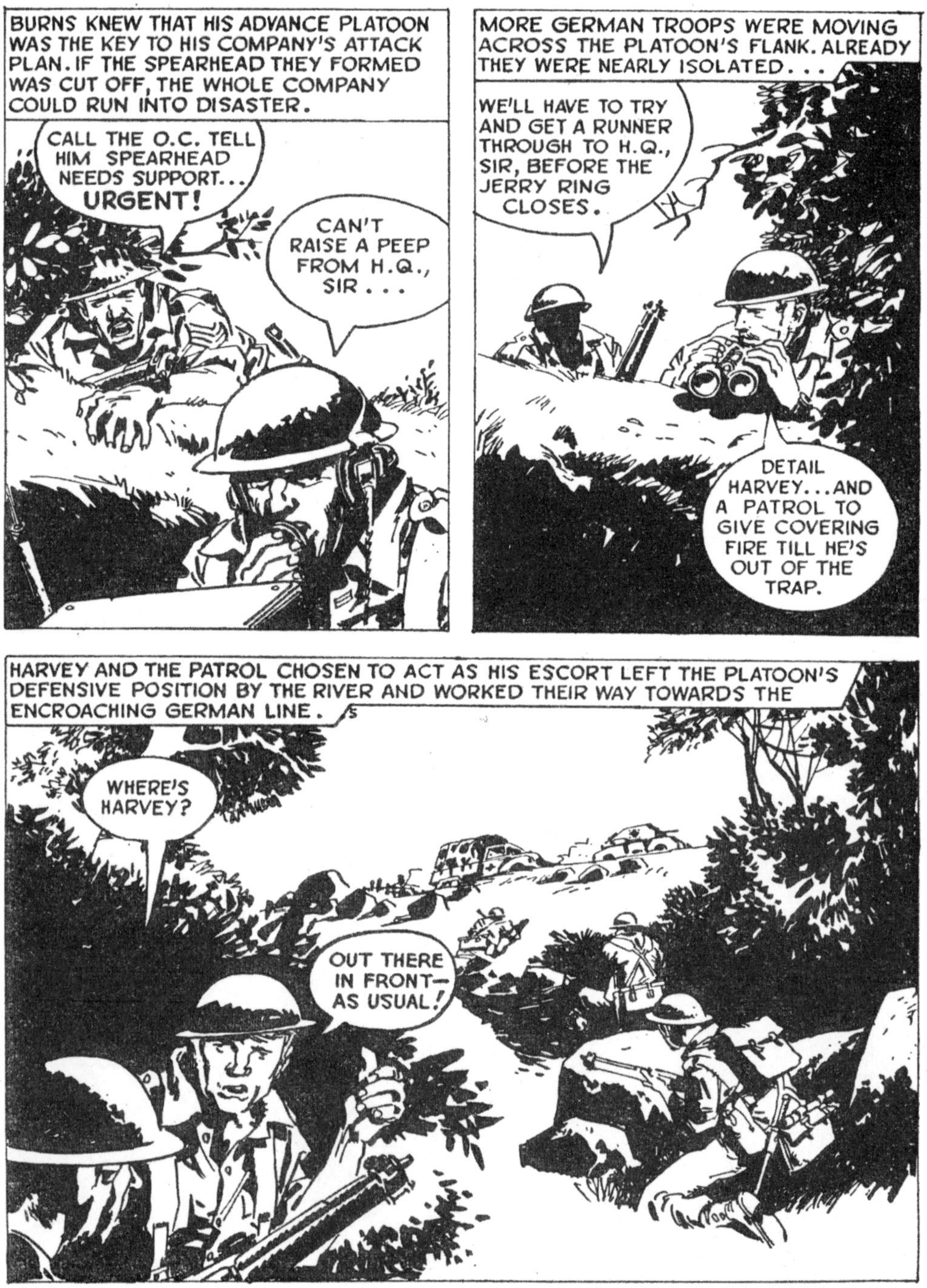
BURNS KNEW THAT HIS ADVANCE PLATOON WAS THE KEY TO HIS COMPANY'S ATTACK PLAN. IF THE SPEARHEAD THEY FORMED WAS CUT OFF, THE WHOLE COMPANY COULD RUN INTO DISASTER.
CALL THE O.C. TELL HIM SPEARHEAD NEEDS SUPPORT... URGENT!
CAN'T RAISE A PEEP FROM H.Q., SIR . . .
MORE GERMAN TROOPS WERE MOVING ACROSS THE PLATOON'S FLANK. ALREADY THEY WERE NEARLY ISOLATED . . .
WE'LL HAVE TO TRY AND GET A RUNNER THROUGH TO H.Q., SIR, BEFORE THE JERRY RING CLOSES.
DETAIL HARVEY...AND A PATROL TO GIVE COVERING FIRE TILL HE'S OUT OF THE TRAP.
HARVEY AND THE PATROL CHOSEN TO ACT AS HIS ESCORT LEFT THE PLATOON'S DEFENSIVE POSITION BY THE RIVER AND WORKED THEIR WAY TOWARDS THE ENCROACHING GERMAN LINE.
WHERE'S HARVEY?
OUT THERE IN FRONT— AS USUAL!

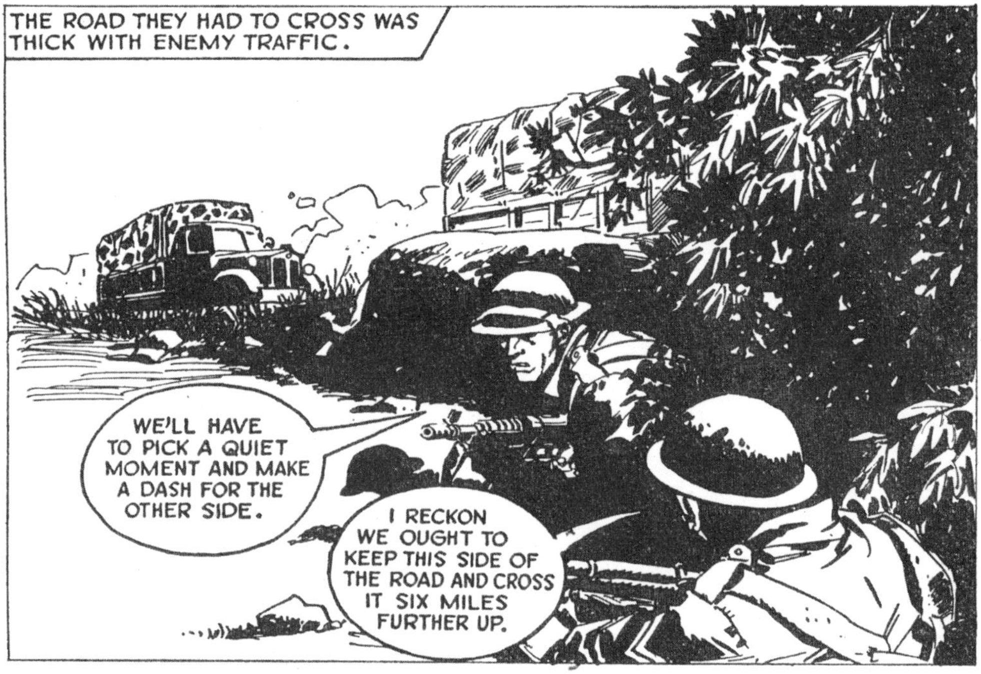
THE ROAD THEY HAD TO CROSS WAS THICK WITH ENEMY TRAFFIC.
WE'LL HAVE TO PICK A QUIET MOMENT AND MAKE A DASH FOR THE OTHER SIDE.
I RECKON WE OUGHT TO KEEP THIS SIDE OF THE ROAD AND CROSS IT SIX MILES FURTHER UP.

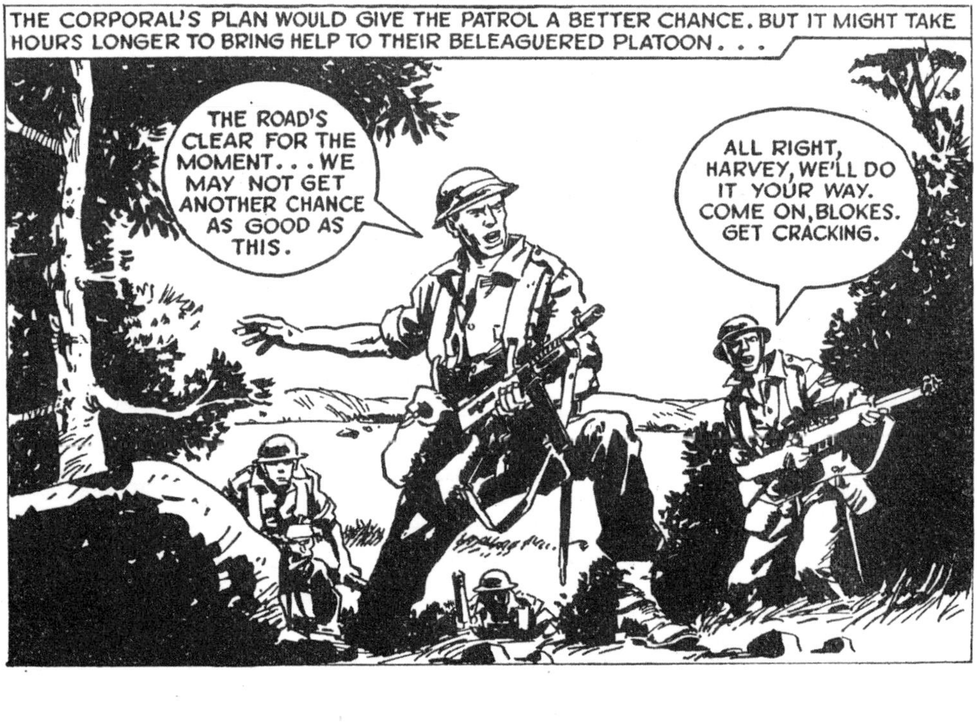
THE CORPORAL'S PLAN WOULD GIVE THE PATROL A BETTER CHANCE. BUT IT MIGHT TAKE HOURS LONGER TO BRING HELP TO THEIR BELEAGUERED PLATOON . . .
THE ROAD'S CLEAR FOR THE MOMENT. . . WE MAY NOT GET ANOTHER CHANCE AS GOOD AS THIS.
ALL RIGHT, HARVEY, WE'LL DO IT YOUR WAY. COME ON, BLOKES. GET CRACKING.

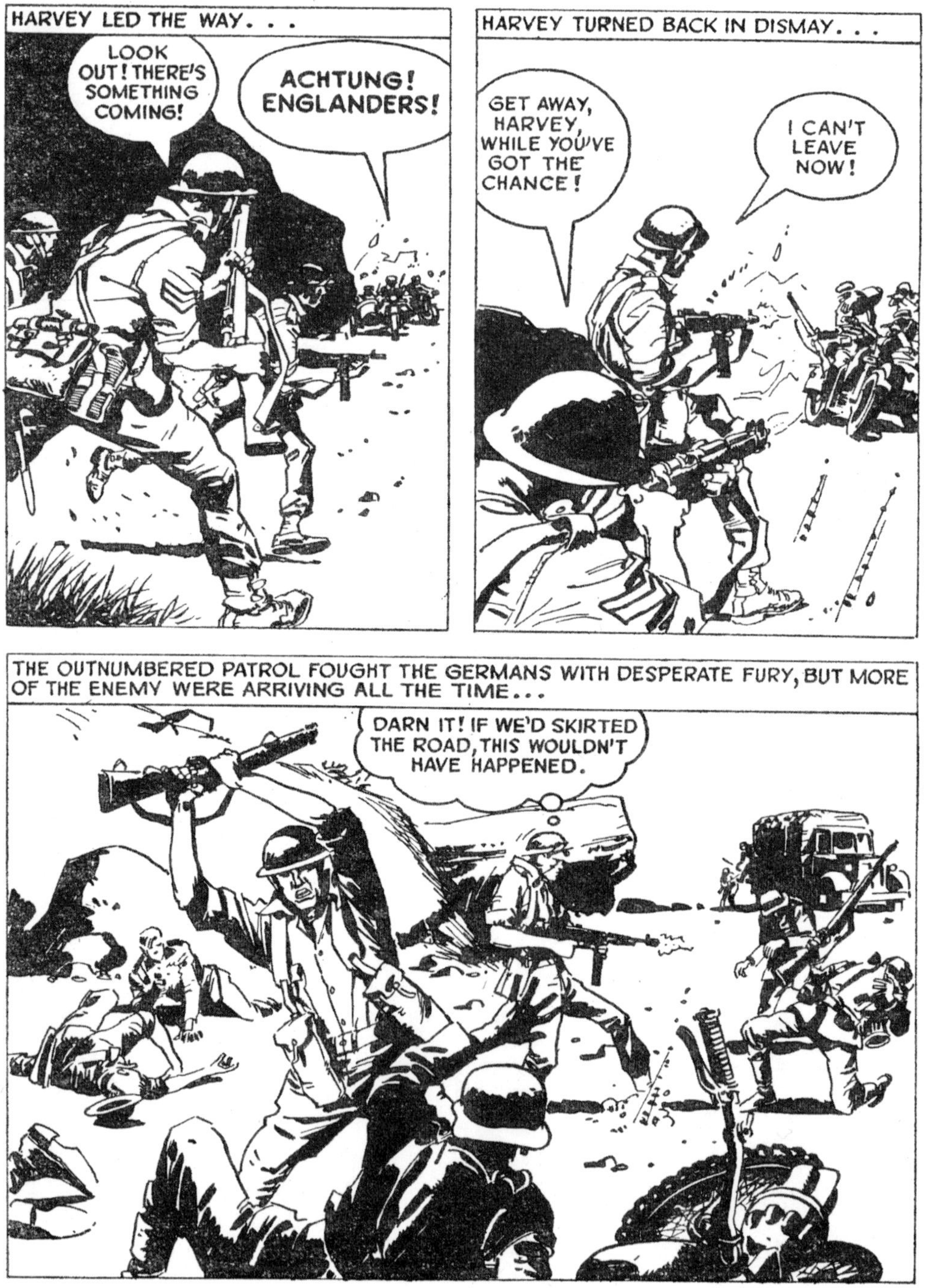
HARVEY LED THE WAY. . .
LOOK OUT! THERE'S SOMETHING COMING!
ACHTUNG! ENGLANDERS!
HARVEY TURNED BACK IN DISMAY. . .
GET AWAY, HARVEY, WHILE YOU'VE GOT THE CHANCE!
I CAN'T LEAVE NOW!
THE OUTNUMBERED PATROL FOUGHT THE GERMANS WITH DESPERATE FURY, BUT MORE OF THE ENEMY WERE ARRIVING ALL THE TIME...
DARN IT! IF WE'D SKIRTED THE ROAD, THIS WOULDN'T HAVE HAPPENED.

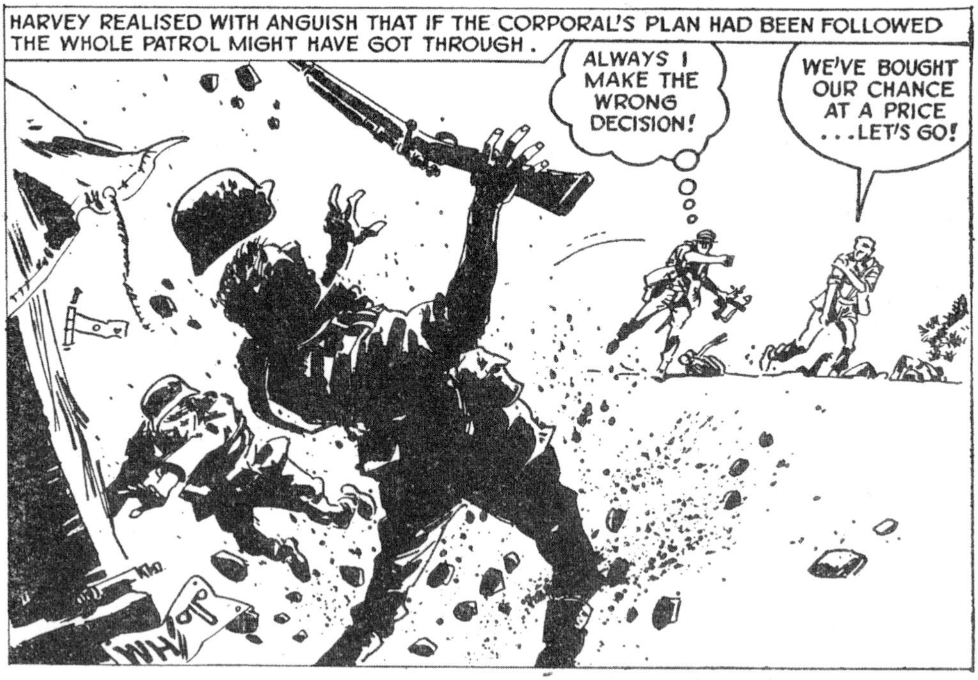
HARVEY REALISED WITH ANGUISH THAT IF THE CORPORAL'S PLAN HAD BEEN FOLLOWED THE WHOLE PATROL MIGHT HAVE GOT THROUGH.
ALWAYS I MAKE THE WRONG DECISION!
WE'VE BOUGHT OUR CHANCE AT A PRICE ...LET'S GO!

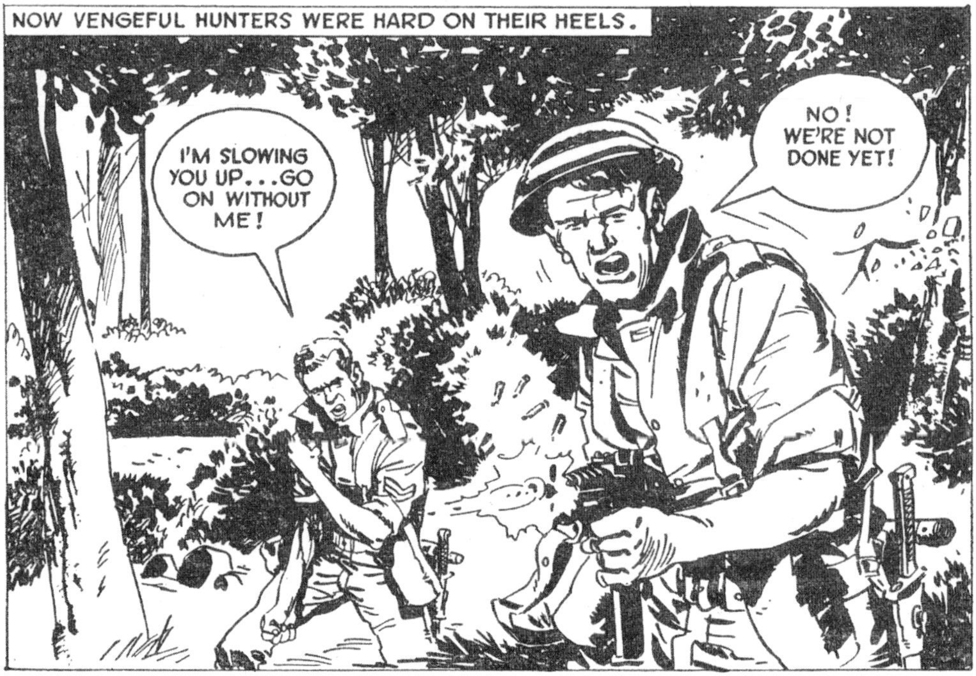
NOW VENGEFUL HUNTERS WERE HARD ON THEIR HEELS.
I'M SLOWING YOU UP...GO ON WITHOUT ME!
NO! WE'RE NOT DONE YET!

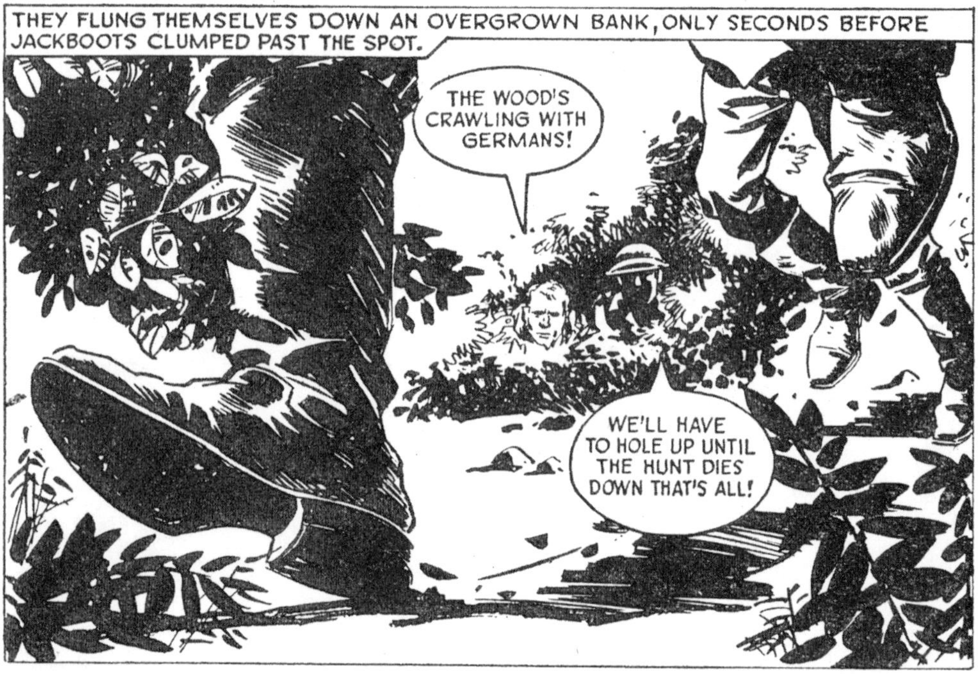
THEY FLUNG THEMSELVES DOWN AN OVERGROWN BANK, ONLY SECONDS BEFORE JACKBOOTS CLUMPED PAST THE SPOT.
THE WOOD'S CRAWLING WITH GERMANS!
WE'LL HAVE TO HOLE UP UNTIL THE HUNT DIES DOWN THAT'S ALL!

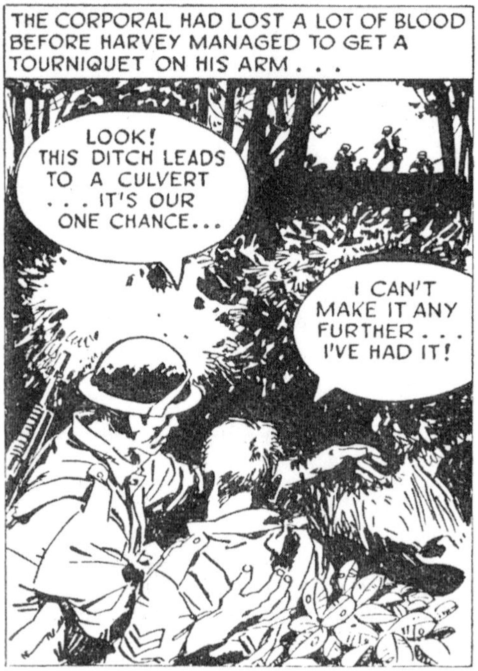
THE CORPORAL HAD LOST A LOT OF BLOOD BEFORE HARVEY MANAGED TO GET A TOURNIQUET ON HIS ARM . . .
LOOK! THIS DITCH LEADS TO A CULVERT . . . IT'S OUR ONE CHANCE...
I CAN'T MAKE IT ANY FURTHER . . . I'VE HAD IT!

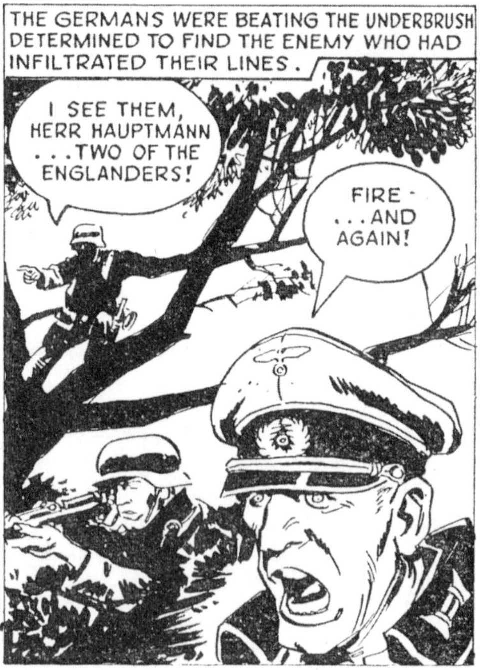
THE GERMANS WERE BEATING THE UNDERBRUSH DETERMINED TO FIND THE ENEMY WHO HAD INFILTRATED THEIR LINES.
I SEE THEM, HERR HAUPTMANN . . . TWO OF THE ENGLANDERS!
FIRE - . . . AND AGAIN!

Chapter 3. The Fatal Order

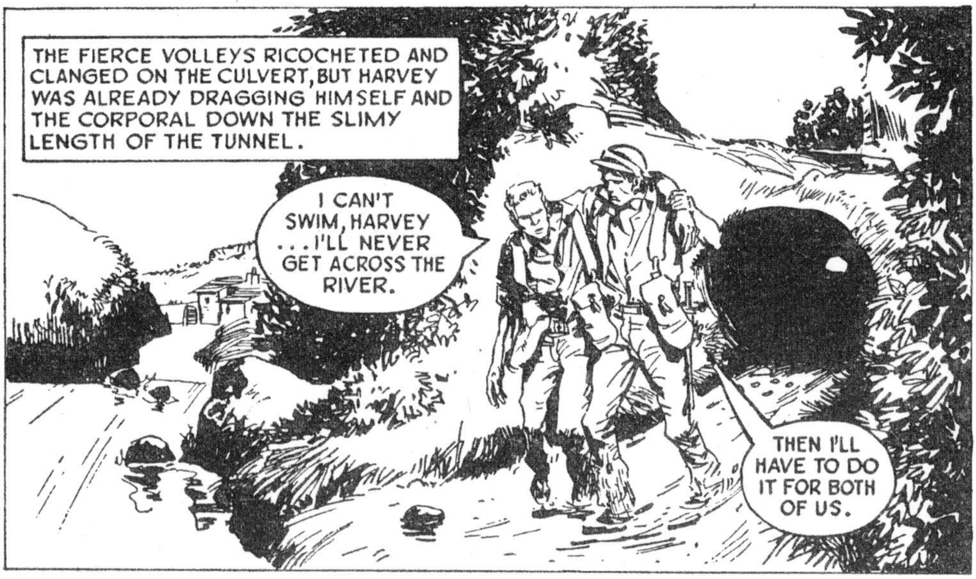
THE FIERCE VOLLEYS RICOCHETED AND CLANGED ON THE CULVERT, BUT HARVEY WAS ALREADY DRAGGING HIMSELF AND THE CORPORAL DOWN THE SLIMY LENGTH OF THE TUNNEL.
I CAN'T SWIM, HARVEY . . . I'LL NEVER GET ACROSS THE RIVER.
THEN I'LL HAVE TO DO IT FOR BOTH OF US.

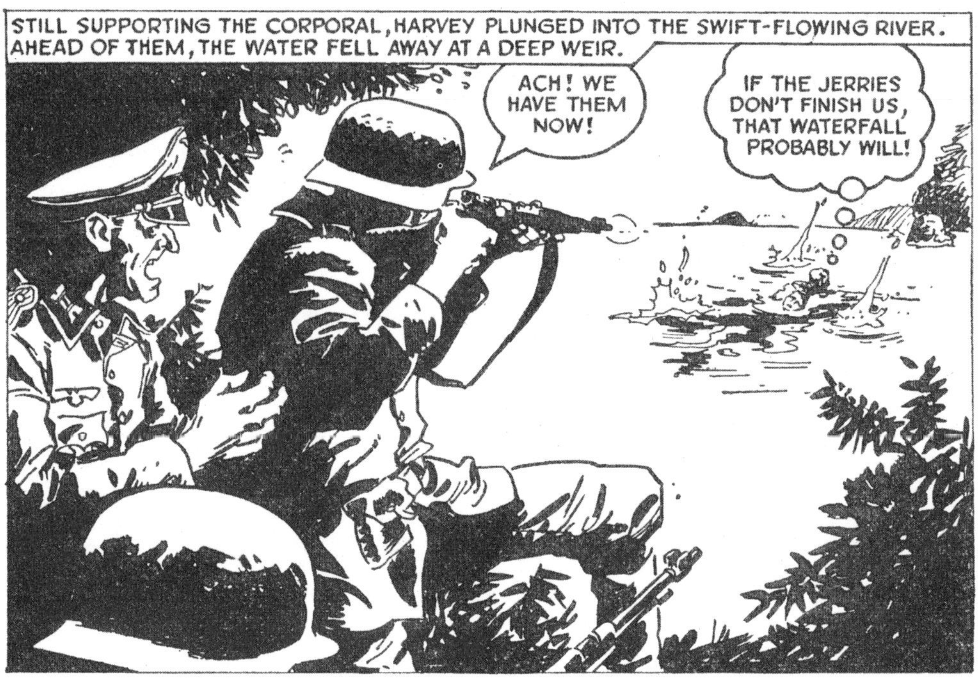
STILL SUPPORTING THE CORPORAL, HARVEY PLUNGED INTO THE SWIFT-FLOWING RIVER. AHEAD OF THEM, THE WATER FELL AWAY AT A DEEP WEIR.
ACH! WE HAVE THEM NOW!
IF THE JERRIES DON'T FINISH US, THAT WATERFALL PROBABLY WILL!

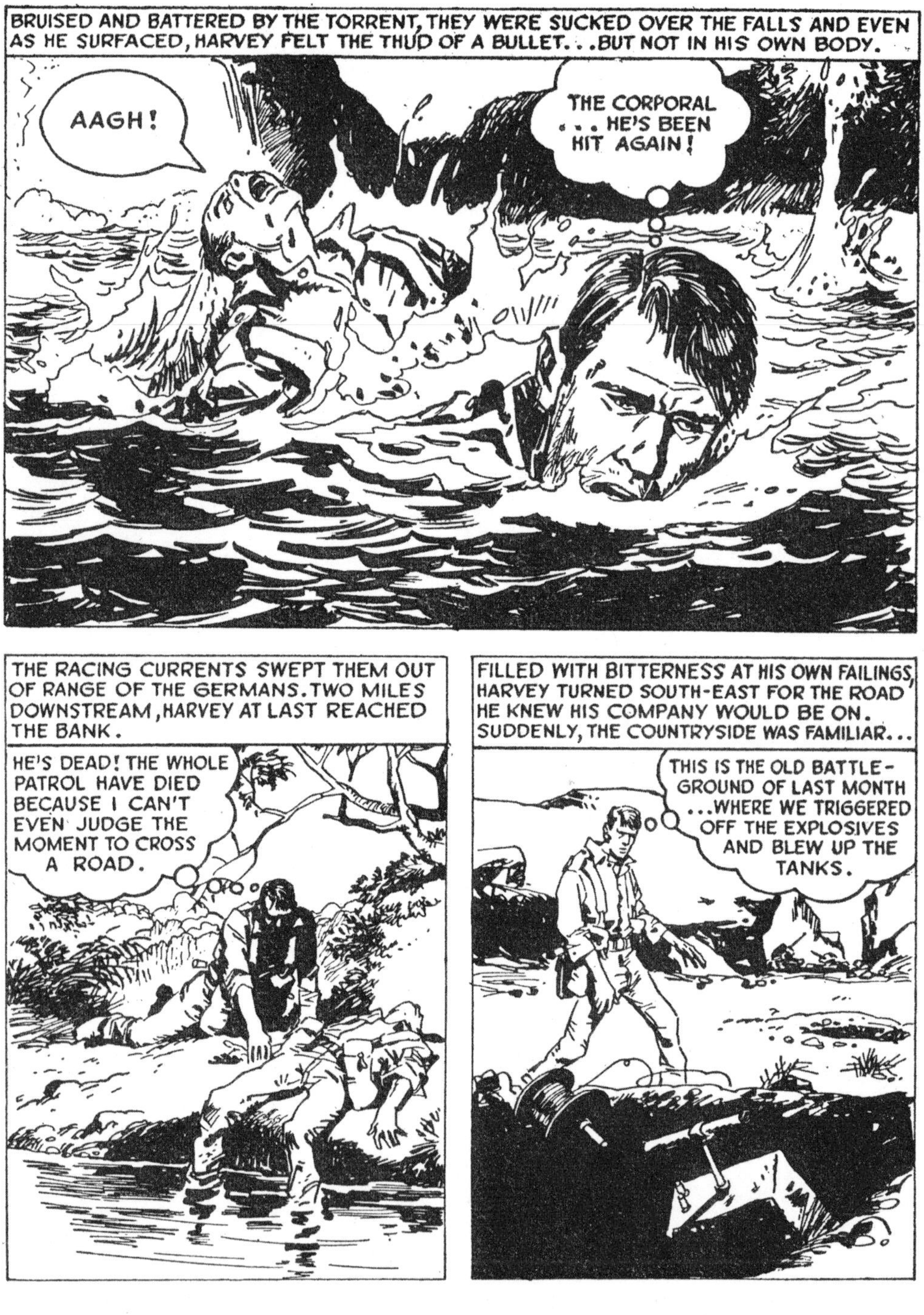
BRUISED AND BATTERED BY THE TORRENT, THEY WERE SUCKED OVER THE FALLS AND EVEN AS HE SURFACED, HARVEY FELT THE THUD OF A BULLET. . .BUT NOT IN HIS OWN BODY.
AAGH!
THE CORPORAL . . . HE'S BEEN HIT AGAIN!
THE RACING CURRENTS SWEPT THEM OUT OF RANGE OF THE GERMANS. TWO MILES DOWNSTREAM, HARVEY AT LAST REACHED THE BANK.
HE'S DEAD! THE WHOLE PATROL HAVE DIED BECAUSE I CAN'T EVEN JUDGE THE MOMENT TO CROSS A ROAD.
FILLED WITH BITTERNESS AT HIS OWN FAILINGS, HARVEY TURNED SOUTH-EAST FOR THE ROAD HE KNEW HIS COMPANY WOULD BE ON. SUDDENLY, THE COUNTRYSIDE WAS FAMILIAR...
THIS IS THE OLD BATTLE-GROUND OF LAST MONTH ...WHERE WE TRIGGERED OFF THE EXPLOSIVES AND BLEW UP THE TANKS.

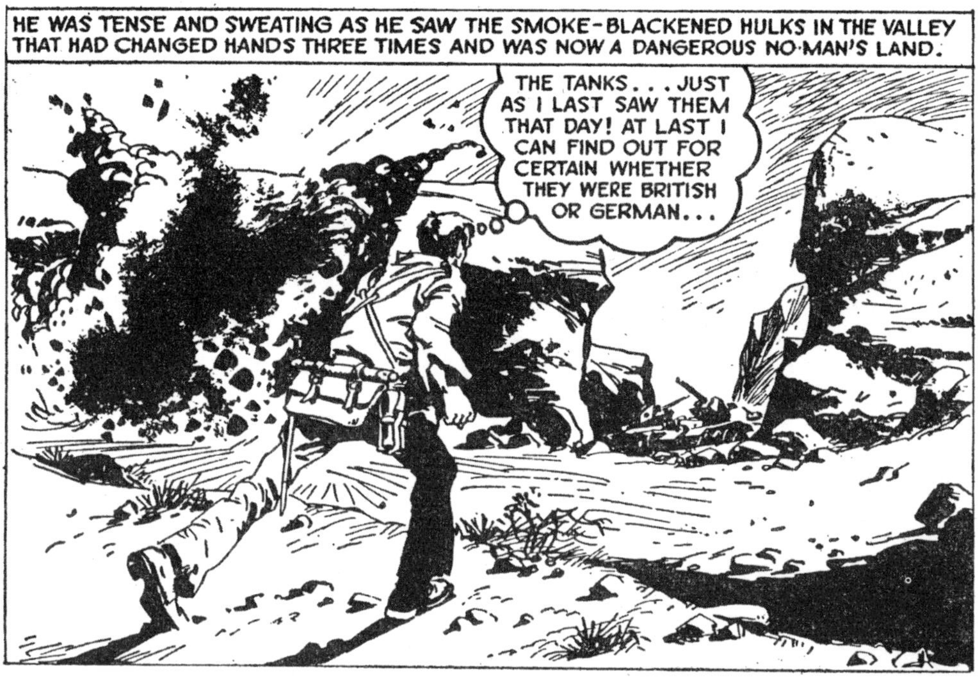
HE WAS TENSE AND SWEATING AS HE SAW THE SMOKE-BLACKENED HULKS IN THE VALLEY THAT HAD CHANGED HANDS THREE TIMES AND WAS NOW A DANGEROUS NO-MAN'S LAND.
THE TANKS . . . JUST AS I LAST SAW THEM THAT DAY! AT LAST I CAN FIND OUT FOR CERTAIN WHETHER THEY WERE BRITISH OR GERMAN . . .

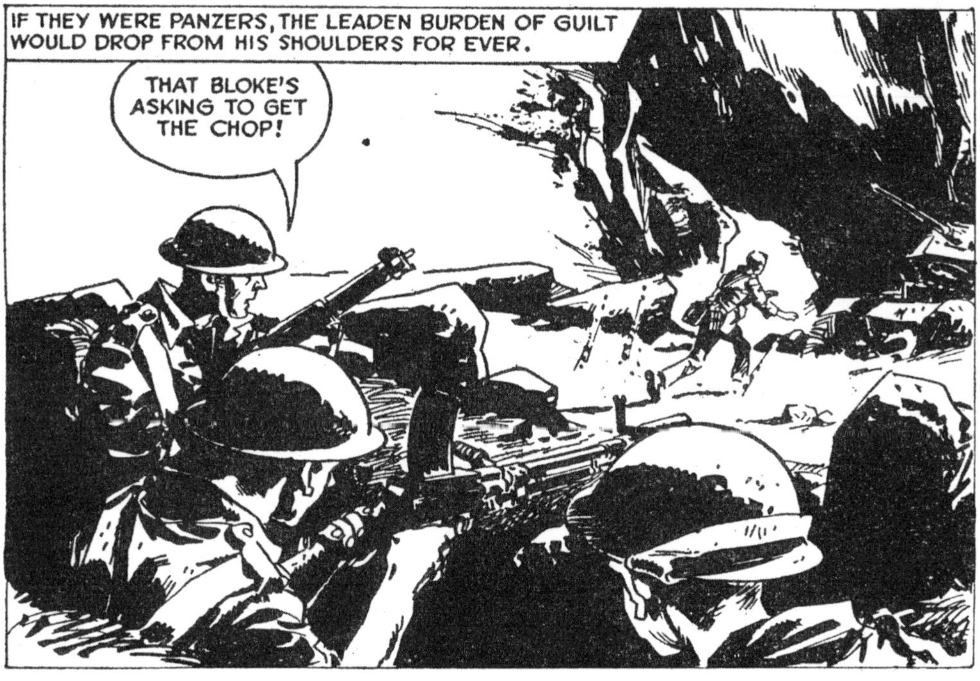
IF THEY WERE PANZERS, THE LEADEN BURDEN OF GUILT WOULD DROP FROM HIS SHOULDERS FOR EVER.
THAT BLOKE'S ASKING TO GET THE CHOP!

THE FIRST TWO TANKS HE CAME TO WERE UNRECOGNISABLE HULKS. THE THIRD AND THE OTHERS HE KNEW AT ONCE...

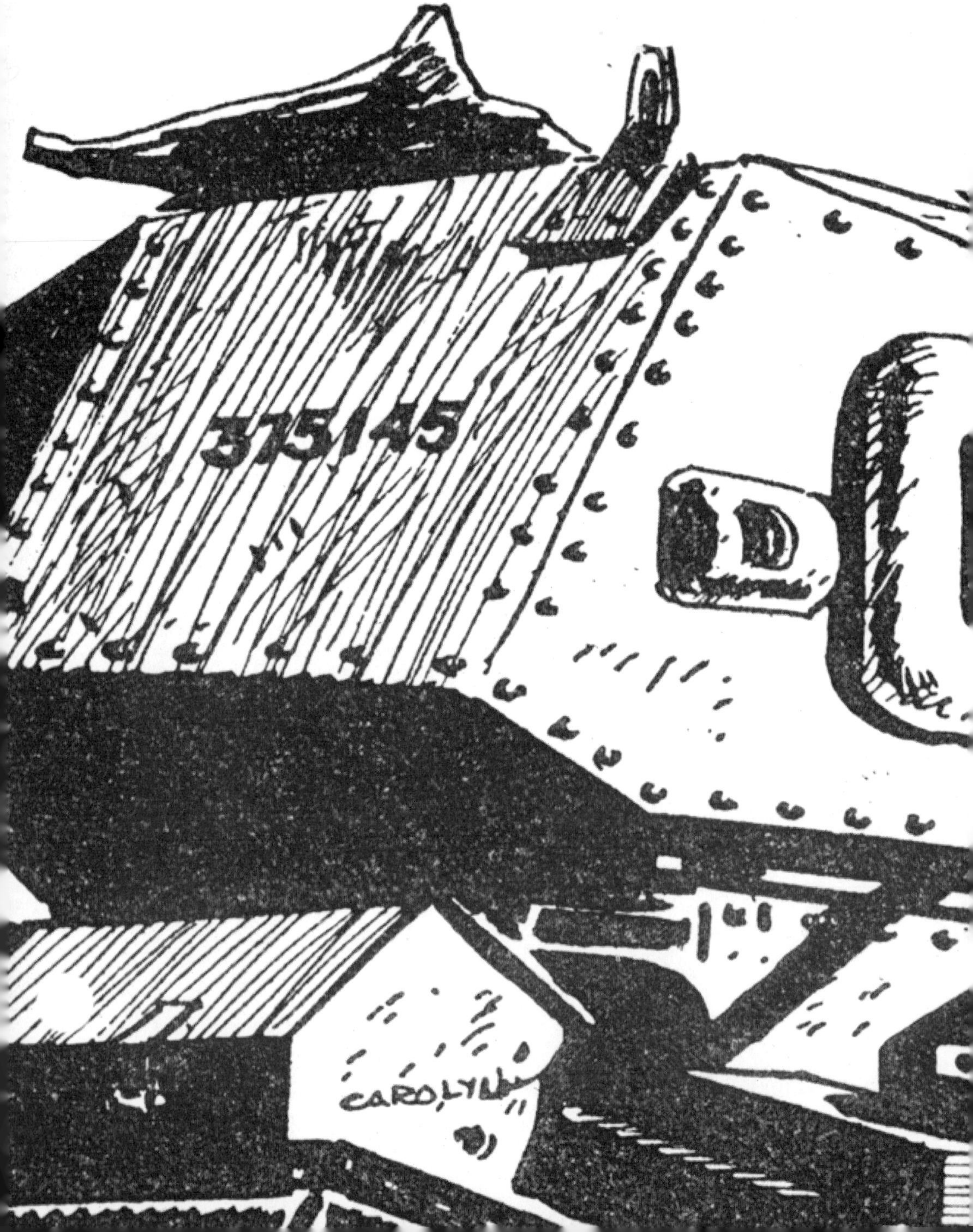

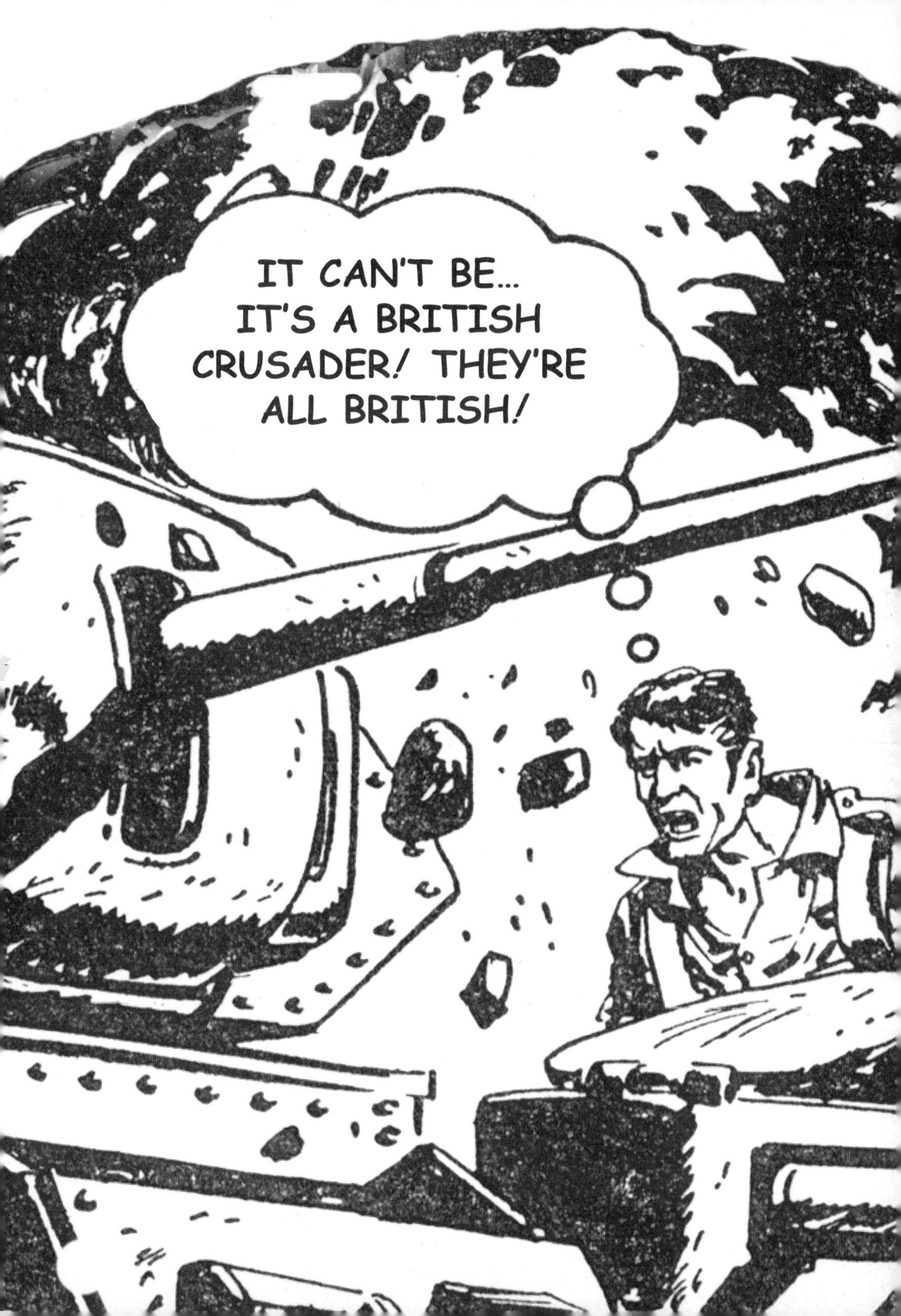
IT CAN'T BE... IT'S A BRITISH CRUSADER! THEY'RE ALL BRITISH!

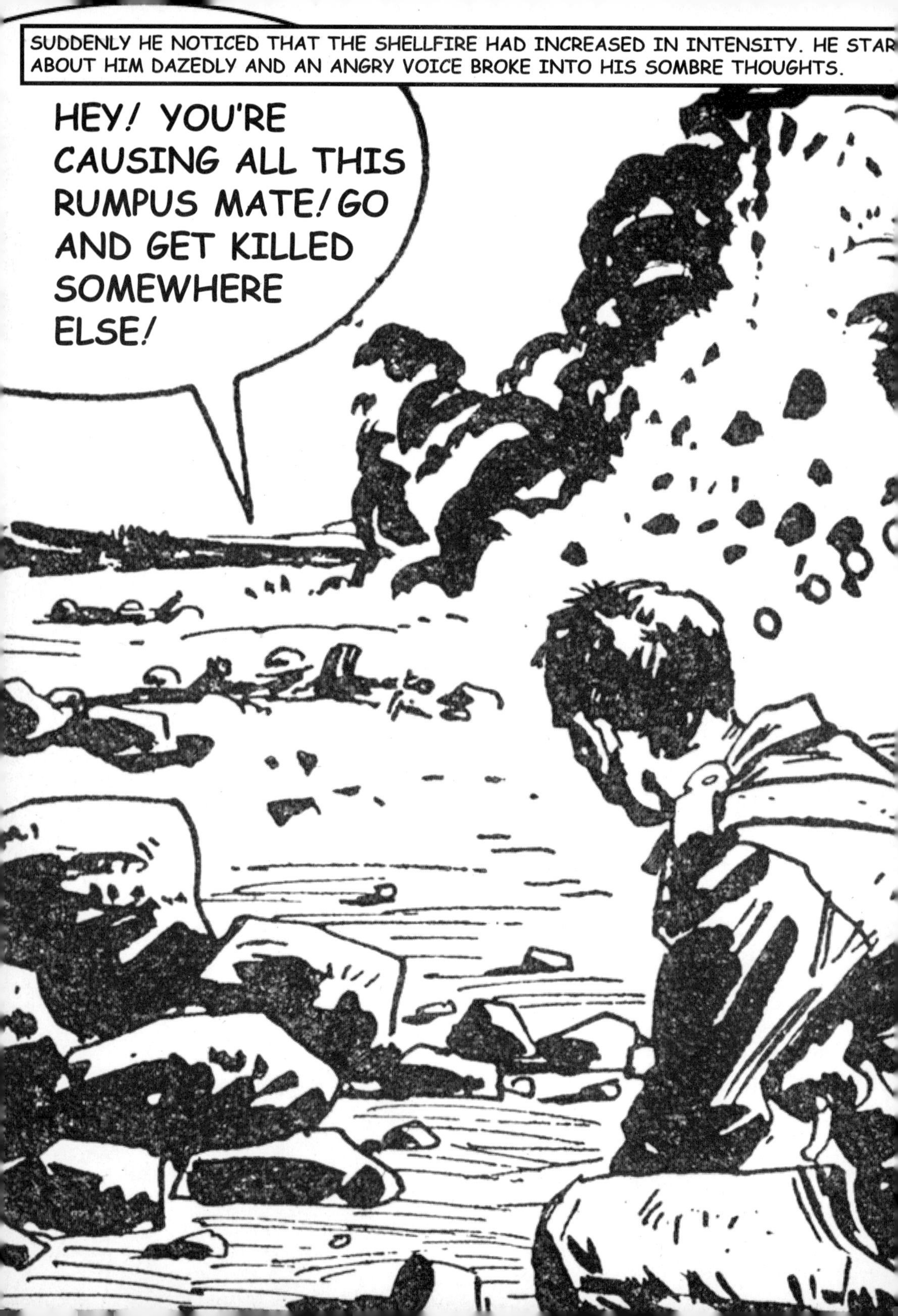
SUDDENLY HE NOTICED THAT THE SHELLFIRE HAD INCREASED IN INTENSITY. HE STAR
ABOUT HIM DAZEDLY AND AN ANGRY VOICE BROKE INTO HIS SOMBRE THOUGHTS.
HEY! YOU'RE CAUSING ALL THIS RUMPUS MATE! GO AND GET KILLED SOMEWHERE ELSE!

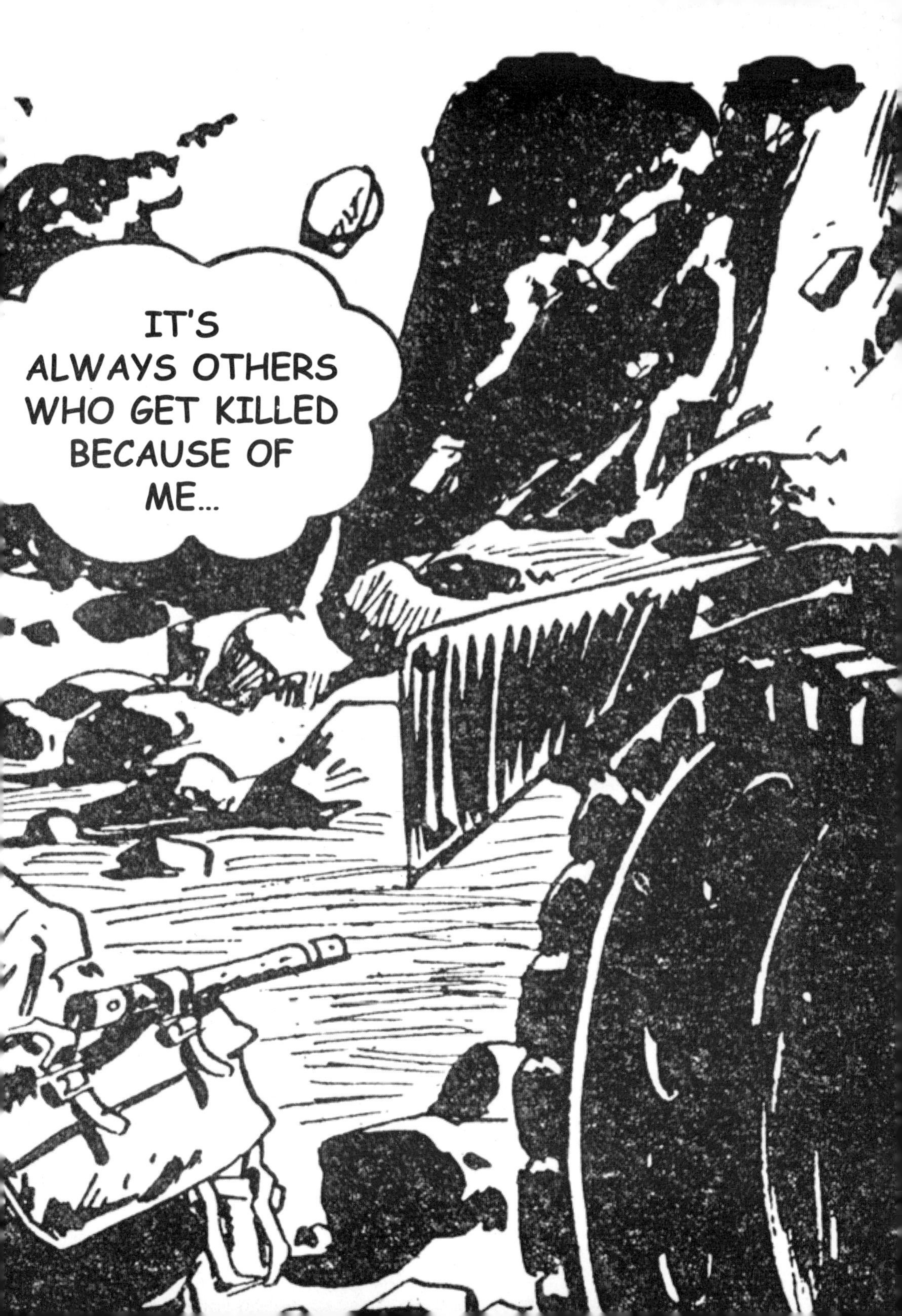
IT'S ALWAYS OTHERS WHO GET KILLED BECAUSE OF ME...

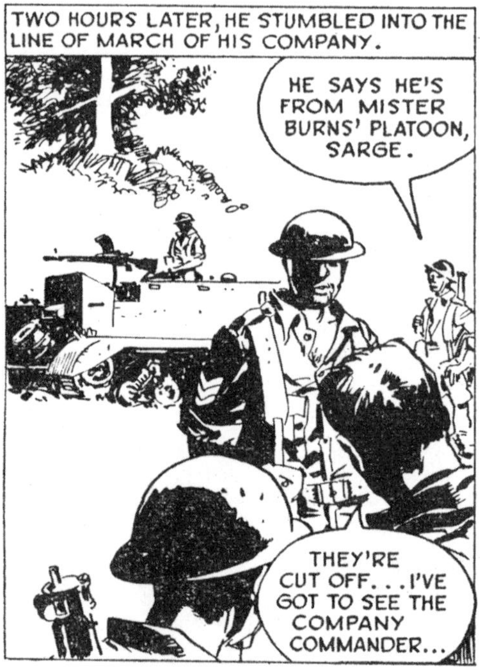
TWO HOURS LATER, HE STUMBLED INTO THE LINE OF MARCH OF HIS COMPANY.
HE SAYS HE'S FROM MISTER BURNS' PLATOON, SARGE.
THEY'RE CUT OFF. . . I'VE GOT TO SEE THE COMPANY COMMANDER...

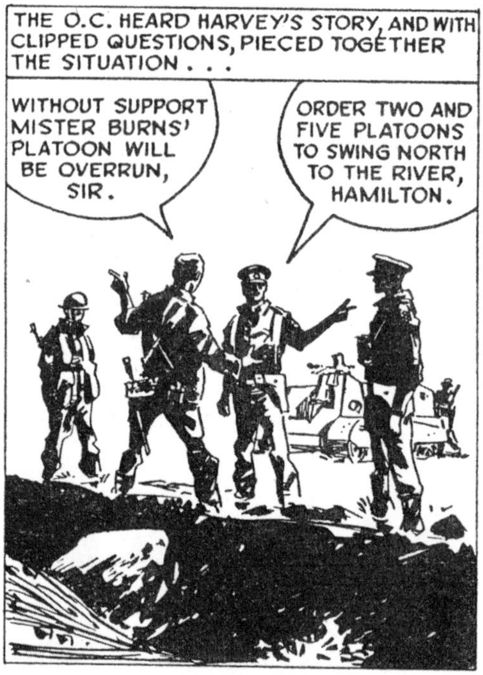
THE O.C. HEARD HARVEY'S STORY, AND WITH CLIPPED QUESTIONS, PIECED TOGETHER THE SITUATION . . .
WITHOUT SUPPORT MISTER BURNS' PLATOON WILL BE OVERRUN, SIR.
ORDER TWO AND FIVE PLATOONS TO SWING NORTH TO THE RIVER, HAMILTON.

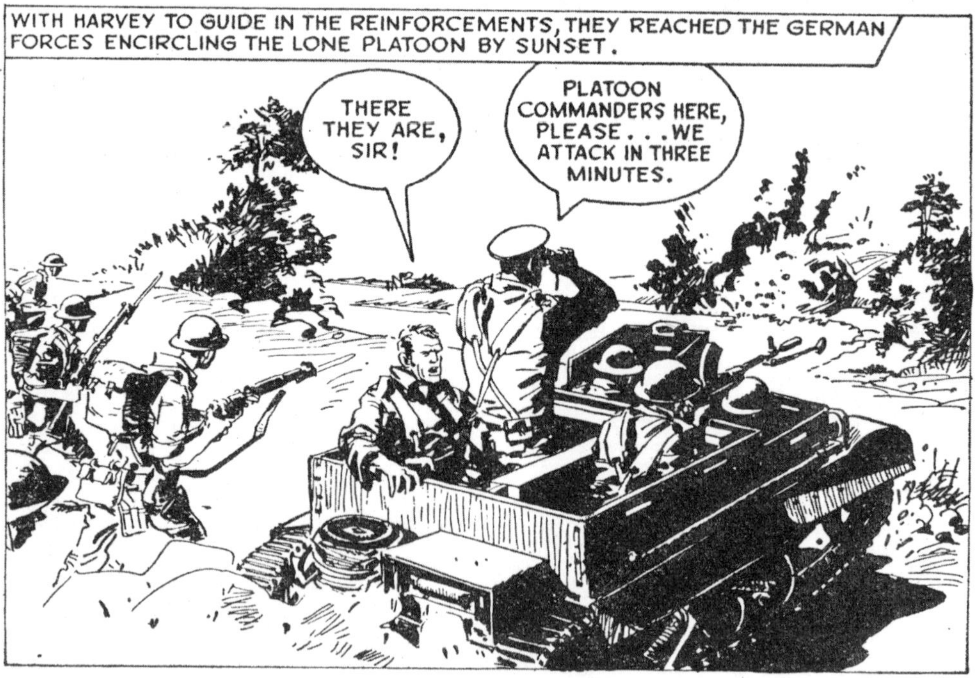
WITH HARVEY TO GUIDE IN THE REINFORCEMENTS, THEY REACHED THE GERMAN FORCES ENCIRCLING THE LONE PLATOON BY SUNSET.
THERE THEY ARE, SIR!
PLATOON COMMANDERS HERE, PLEASE . . . WE ATTACK IN THREE MINUTES.

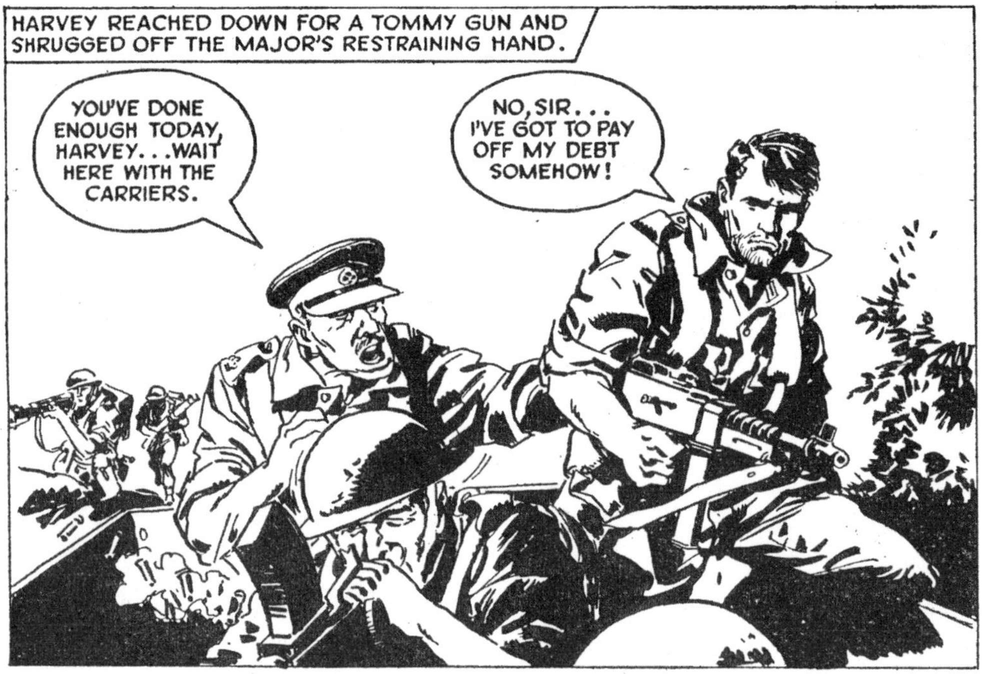
HARVEY REACHED DOWN FOR A TOMMY GUN AND SHRUGGED OFF THE MAJOR'S RESTRAINING HAND.
YOU'VE DONE ENOUGH TODAY, HARVEY...WAIT HERE WITH THE CARRIERS.
NO, SIR... I'VE GOT TO PAY OFF MY DEBT SOMEHOW!

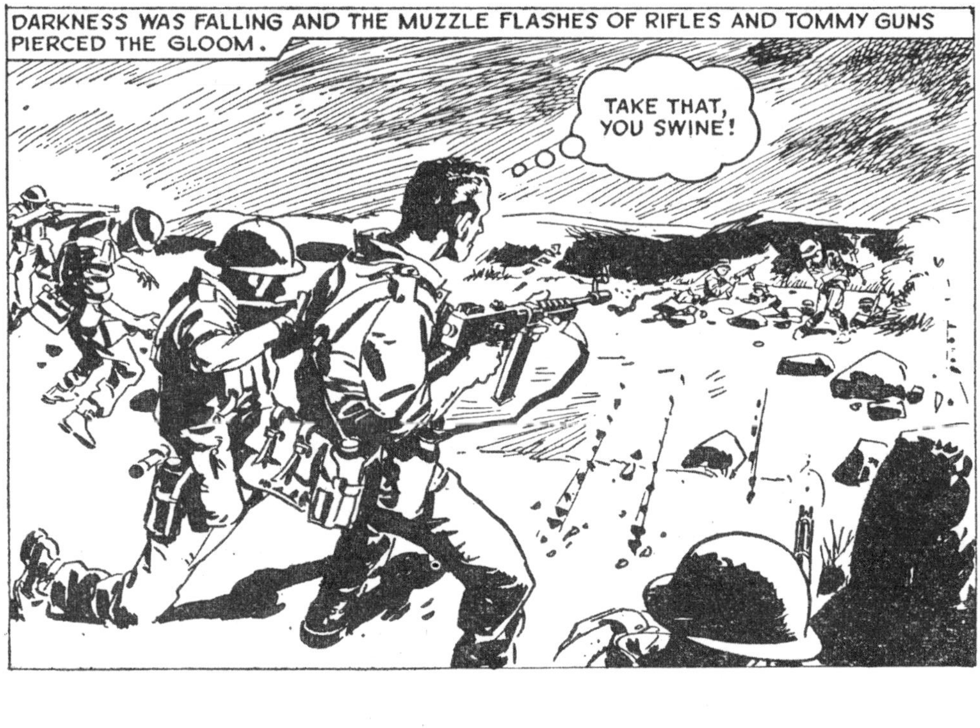
DARKNESS WAS FALLING AND THE MUZZLE FLASHES OF RIFLES AND TOMMY GUNS PIERCED THE GLOOM.
TAKE THAT, YOU SWINE!

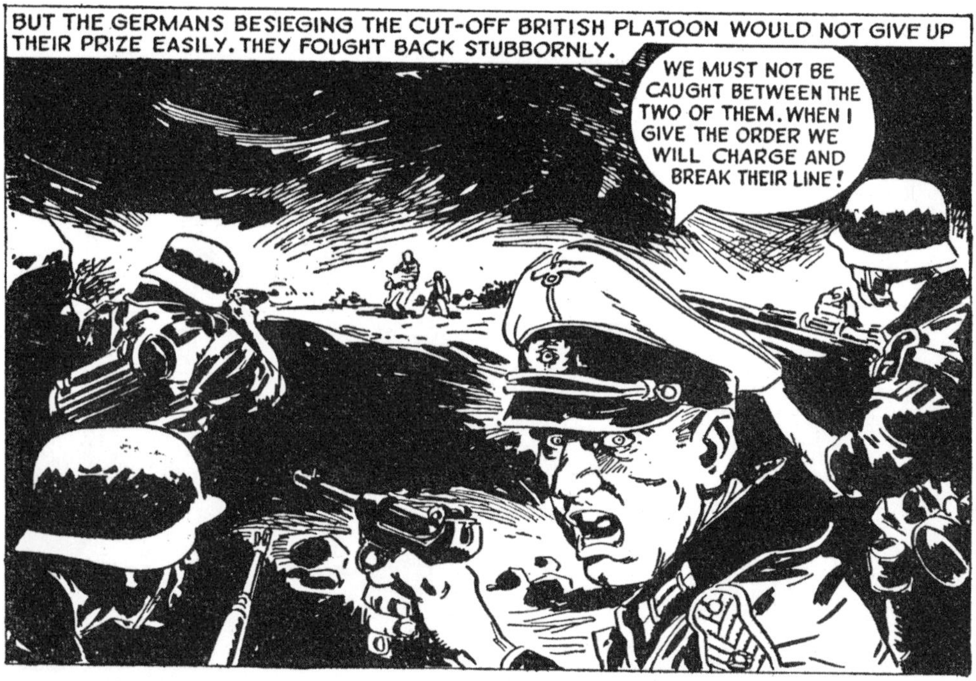
BUT THE GERMANS BESIEGING THE CUT-OFF BRITISH PLATOON WOULD NOT GIVE UP THEIR PRIZE EASILY. THEY FOUGHT BACK STUBBORNLY.
WE MUST NOT BE CAUGHT BETWEEN THE TWO OF THEM. WHEN I GIVE THE ORDER WE WILL CHARGE AND BREAK THEIR LINE!

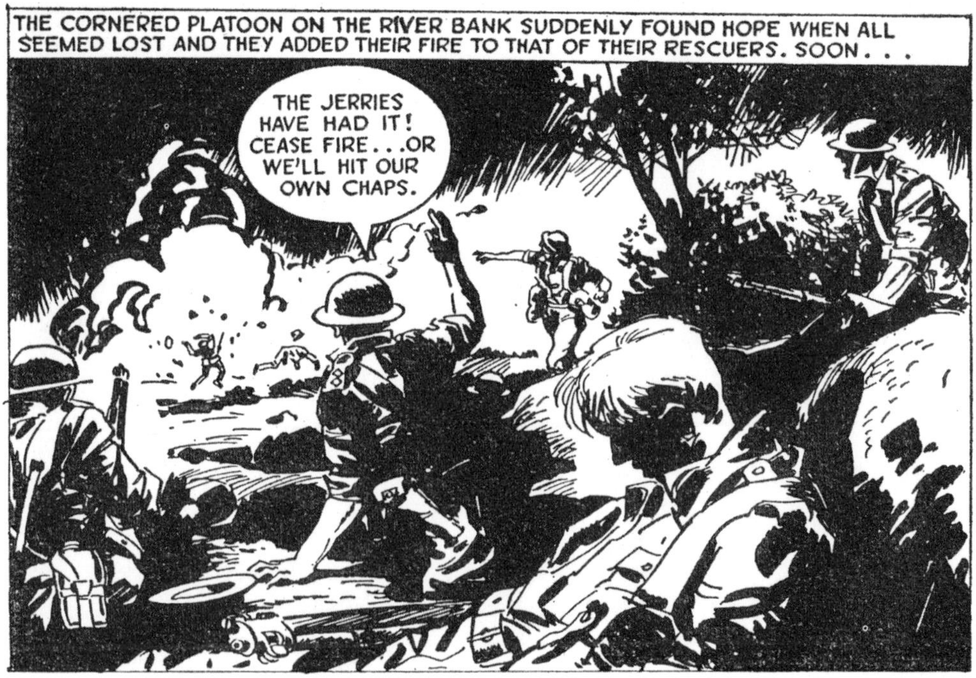
THE CORNERED PLATOON ON THE RIVER BANK SUDDENLY FOUND HOPE WHEN ALL SEEMED LOST AND THEY ADDED THEIR FIRE TO THAT OF THEIR RESCUERS. SOON . . .
THE JERRIES HAVE HAD IT! CEASE FIRE...OR WE'LL HIT OUR OWN CHAPS.

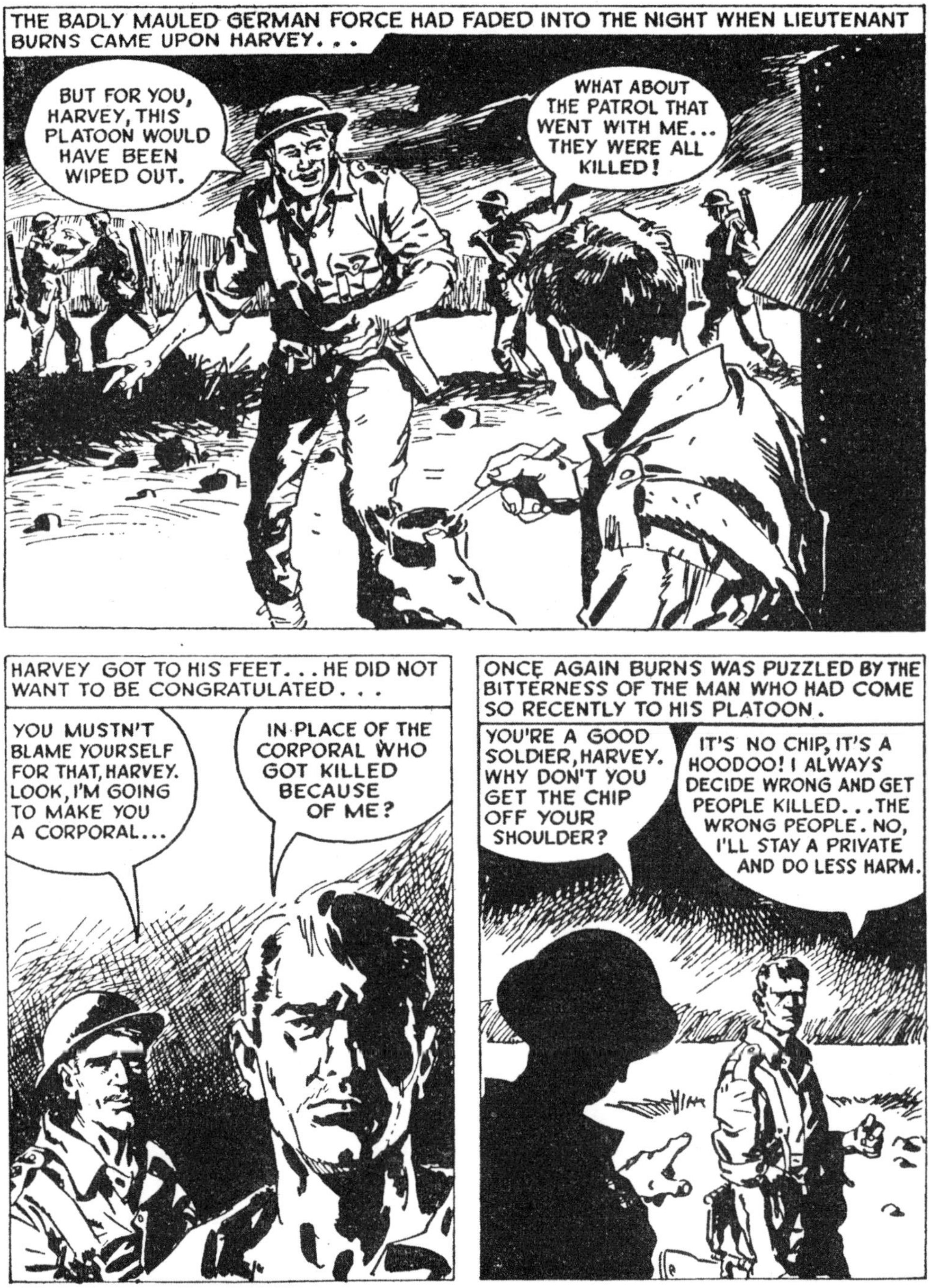
THE BADLY MAULED GERMAN FORCE HAD FADED INTO THE NIGHT WHEN LIEUTENANT BURNS CAME UPON HARVEY. . .
BUT FOR YOU, HARVEY, THIS PLATOON WOULD HAVE BEEN WIPED OUT.
WHAT ABOUT THE PATROL THAT WENT WITH ME... THEY WERE ALL KILLED!
HARVEY GOT TO HIS FEET. . . HE DID NOT WANT TO BE CONGRATULATED. . .
YOU MUSTN'T BLAME YOURSELF FOR THAT, HARVEY. LOOK, I'M GOING TO MAKE YOU A CORPORAL...
IN PLACE OF THE CORPORAL WHO GOT KILLED BECAUSE OF ME?
ONCE AGAIN BURNS WAS PUZZLED BY THE BITTERNESS OF THE MAN WHO HAD COME SO RECENTLY TO HIS PLATOON.
YOU'RE A GOOD SOLDIER, HARVEY. WHY DON'T YOU GET THE CHIP OFF YOUR SHOULDER?
IT'S NO CHIP, IT'S A HOODOO! I ALWAYS DECIDE WRONG AND GET PEOPLE KILLED. . .THE WRONG PEOPLE. NO, I'LL STAY A PRIVATE AND DO LESS HARM.

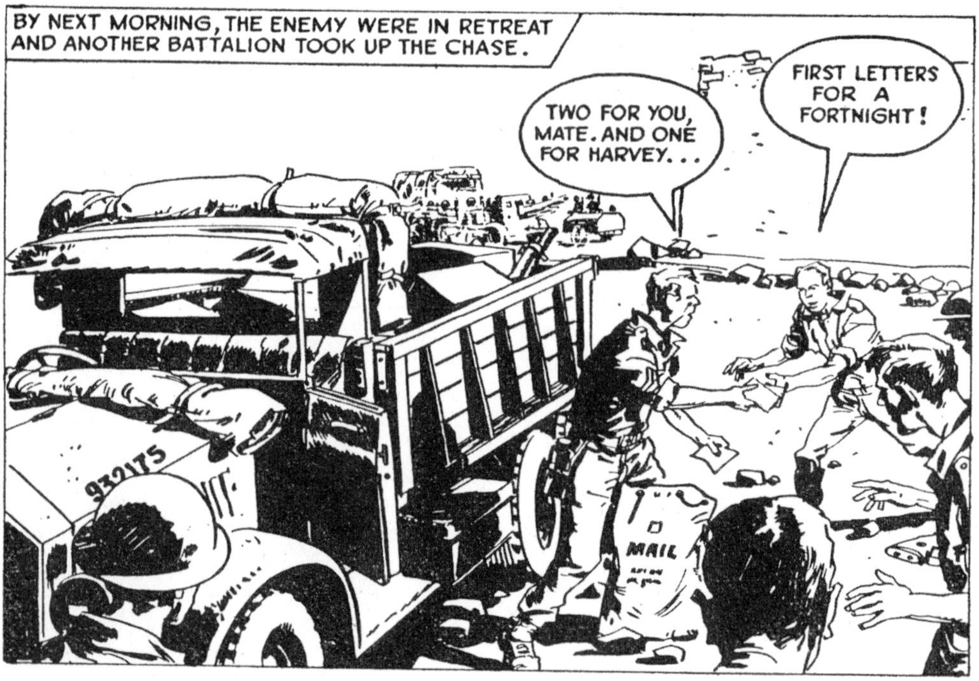
BY NEXT MORNING, THE ENEMY WERE IN RETREAT AND ANOTHER BATTALION TOOK UP THE CHASE.
TWO FOR YOU, MATE. AND ONE FOR HARVEY...
FIRST LETTERS FOR A FORTNIGHT!
MAIL

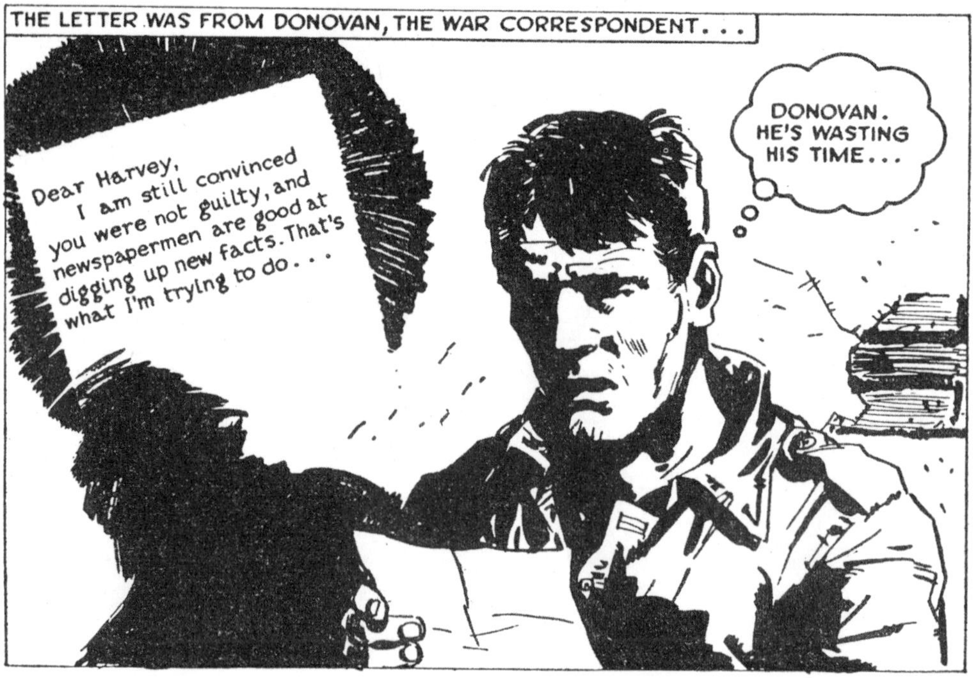
THE LETTER WAS FROM DONOVAN, THE WAR CORRESPONDENT...
Dear Harvey,
I am still convinced you were not guilty, and newspapermen are good at digging up new facts. That's what I'm trying to do...
DONOVAN. HE'S WASTING HIS TIME...

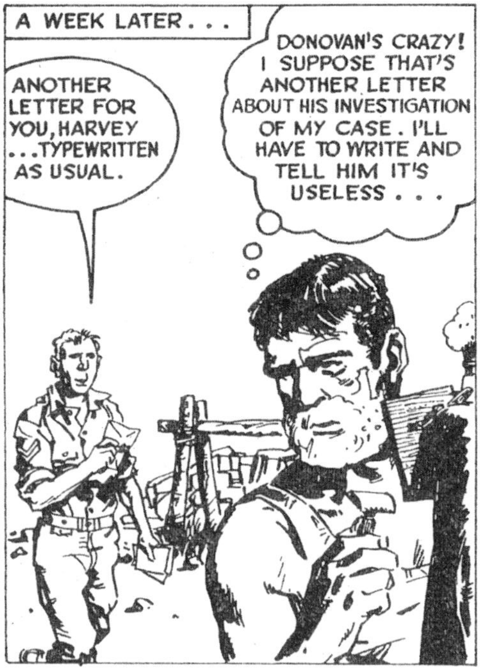
A WEEK LATER . . .
ANOTHER LETTER FOR YOU, HARVEY . . . TYPEWRITTEN AS USUAL.
DONOVAN'S CRAZY! I SUPPOSE THAT'S ANOTHER LETTER ABOUT HIS INVESTIGATION OF MY CASE. I'LL HAVE TO WRITE AND TELL HIM IT'S USELESS . . .

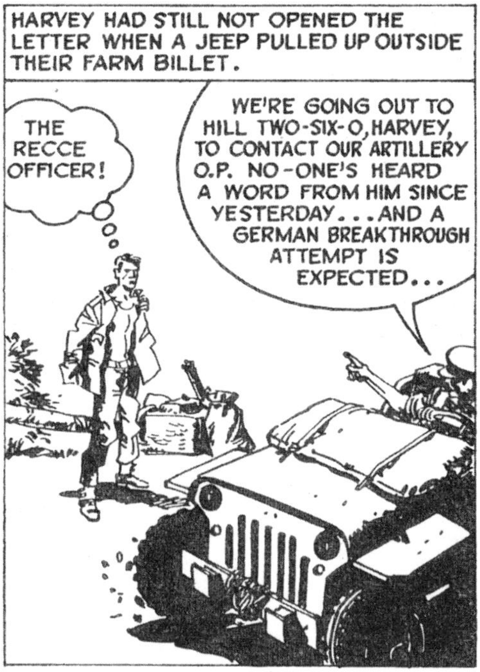
HARVEY HAD STILL NOT OPENED THE LETTER WHEN A JEEP PULLED UP OUTSIDE THEIR FARM BILLET.
THE RECCE OFFICER!
WE'RE GOING OUT TO HILL TWO-SIX-O, HARVEY, TO CONTACT OUR ARTILLERY O.P. NO-ONE'S HEARD A WORD FROM HIM SINCE YESTERDAY . . . AND A GERMAN BREAKTHROUGH ATTEMPT IS EXPECTED . . .

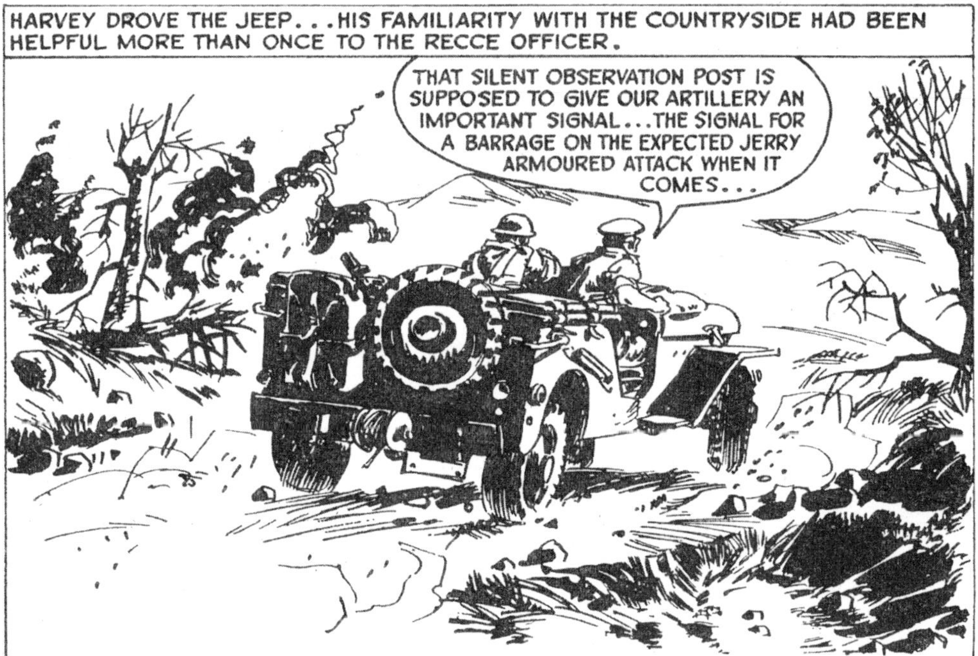
HARVEY DROVE THE JEEP . . . HIS FAMILIARITY WITH THE COUNTRYSIDE HAD BEEN HELPFUL MORE THAN ONCE TO THE RECCE OFFICER.
THAT SILENT OBSERVATION POST IS SUPPOSED TO GIVE OUR ARTILLERY AN IMPORTANT SIGNAL . . . THE SIGNAL FOR A BARRAGE ON THE EXPECTED JERRY ARMOURED ATTACK WHEN IT COMES . . .

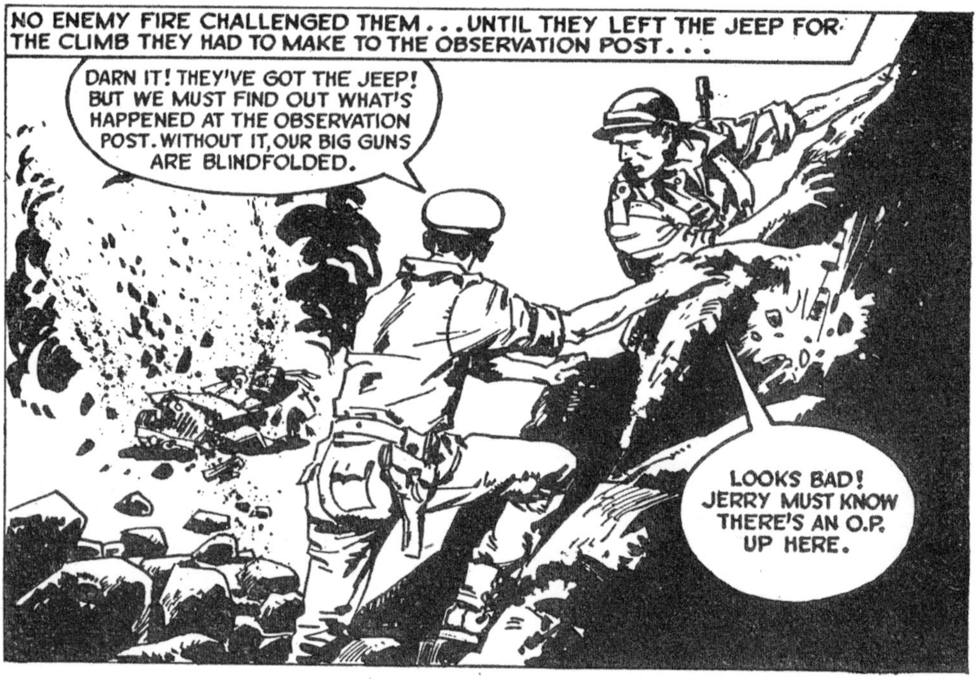
NO ENEMY FIRE CHALLENGED THEM . . . UNTIL THEY LEFT THE JEEP FOR THE CLIMB THEY HAD TO MAKE TO THE OBSERVATION POST . . .
DARN IT! THEY'VE GOT THE JEEP! BUT WE MUST FIND OUT WHAT'S HAPPENED AT THE OBSERVATION POST. WITHOUT IT, OUR BIG GUNS ARE BLINDFOLDED.
LOOKS BAD! JERRY MUST KNOW THERE'S AN O.P. UP HERE.

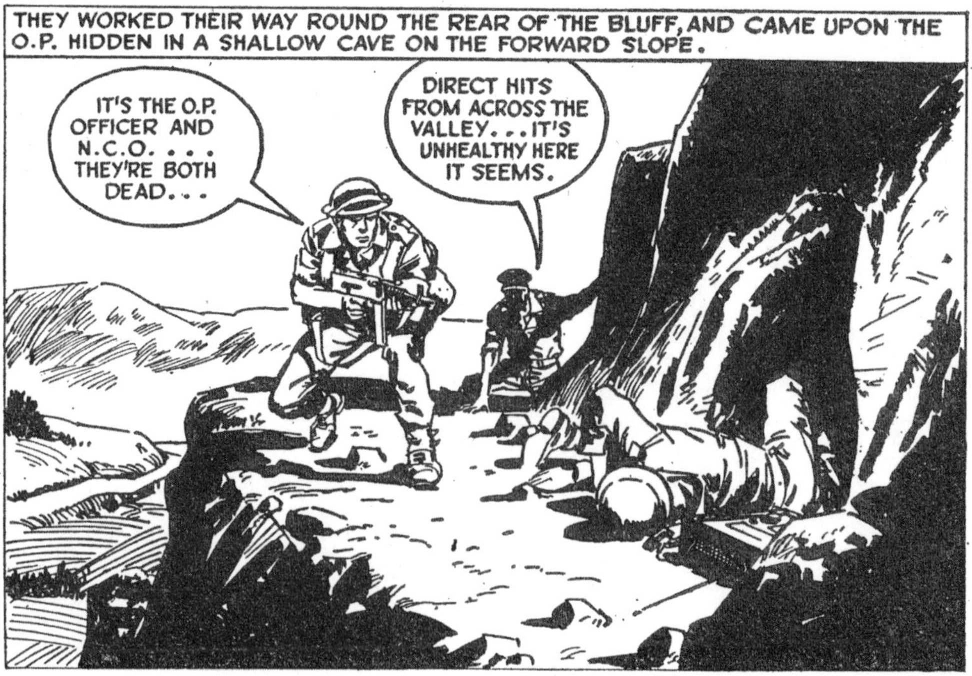
THEY WORKED THEIR WAY ROUND THE REAR OF THE BLUFF, AND CAME UPON THE O.P. HIDDEN IN A SHALLOW CAVE ON THE FORWARD SLOPE.
IT'S THE O.P. OFFICER AND N.C.O. . . . THEY'RE BOTH DEAD . . .
DIRECT HITS FROM ACROSS THE VALLEY . . . IT'S UNHEALTHY HERE IT SEEMS.

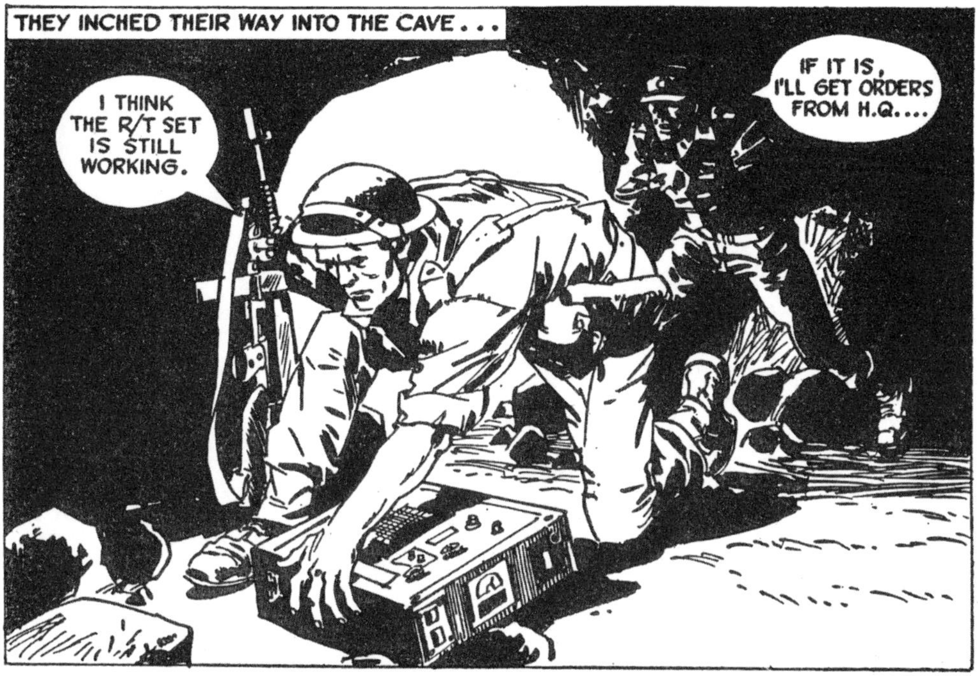
THEY INCHED THEIR WAY INTO THE CAVE . . .
I THINK THE R/T SET IS STILL WORKING.
IF IT IS, I'LL GET ORDERS FROM H.Q. . . .

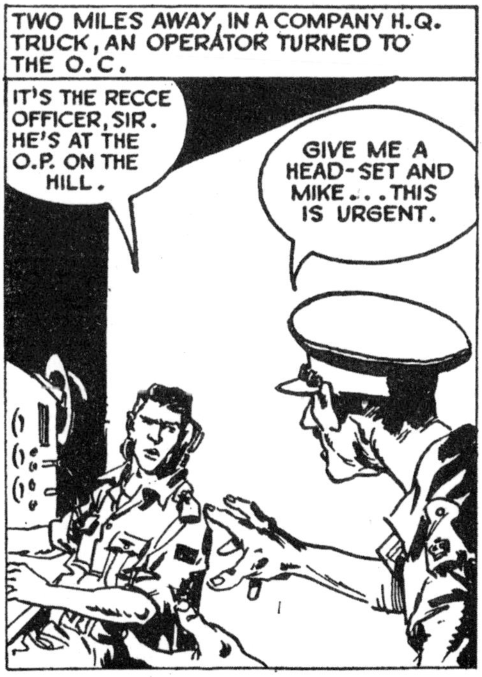
TWO MILES AWAY, IN A COMPANY H.Q. TRUCK, AN OPERATOR TURNED TO THE O.C.
IT'S THE RECCE OFFICER, SIR. HE'S AT THE O.P. ON THE HILL.
GIVE ME A HEAD-SET AND MIKE . . . THIS IS URGENT.

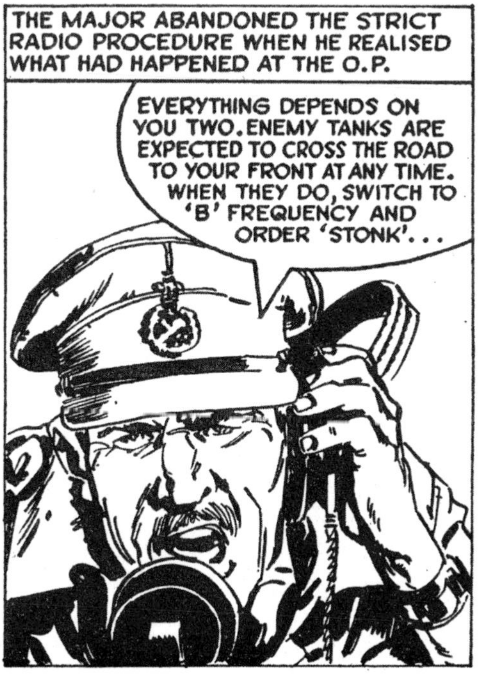
THE MAJOR ABANDONED THE STRICT RADIO PROCEDURE WHEN HE REALISED WHAT HAD HAPPENED AT THE O.P.
EVERYTHING DEPENDS ON YOU TWO. ENEMY TANKS ARE EXPECTED TO CROSS THE ROAD TO YOUR FRONT AT ANY TIME. WHEN THEY DO, SWITCH TO 'B' FREQUENCY AND ORDER 'STONK'. . .

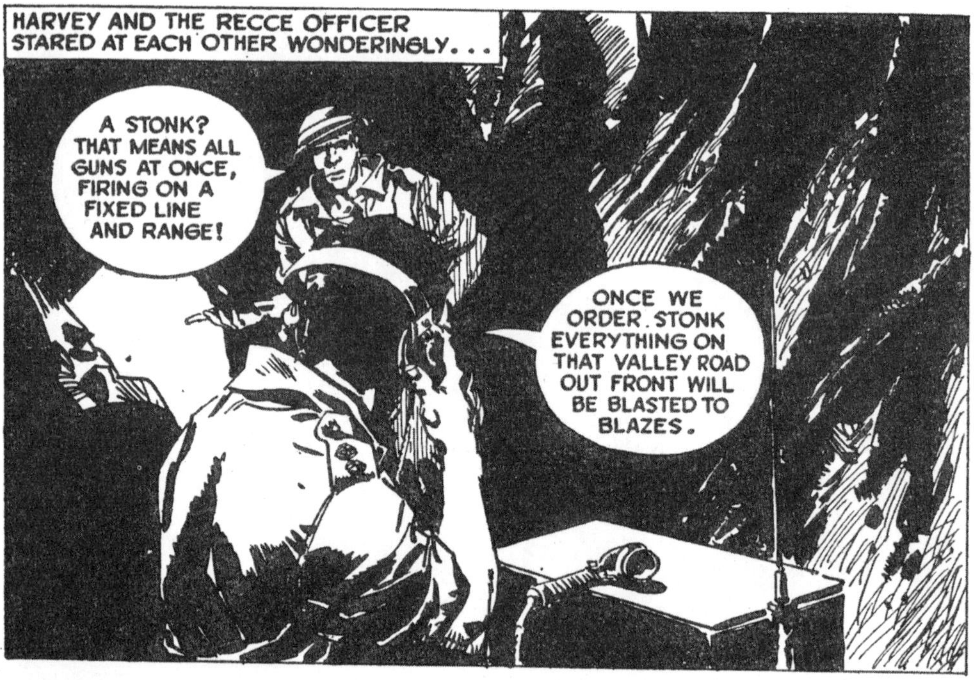
HARVEY AND THE RECCE OFFICER STARED AT EACH OTHER WONDERINGLY. . .
A STONK? THAT MEANS ALL GUNS AT ONCE, FIRING ON A FIXED LINE AND RANGE!
ONCE WE ORDER STONK EVERYTHING ON THAT VALLEY ROAD OUT FRONT WILL BE BLASTED TO BLAZES.

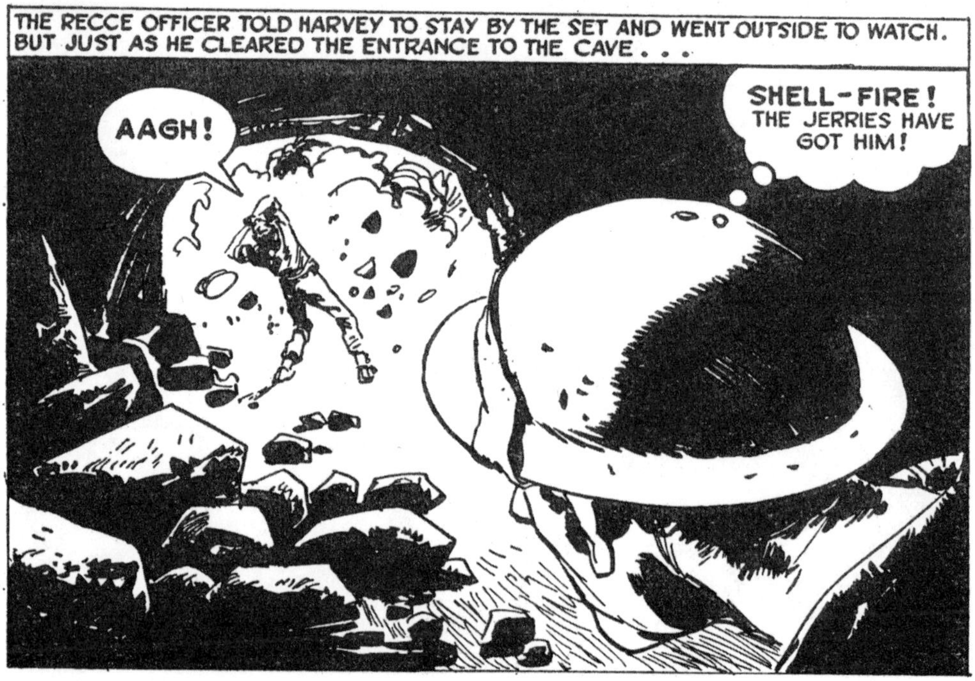
THE RECCE OFFICER TOLD HARVEY TO STAY BY THE SET AND WENT OUTSIDE TO WATCH. BUT JUST AS HE CLEARED THE ENTRANCE TO THE CAVE . . .
AAGH!
SHELL-FIRE! THE JERRIES HAVE GOT HIM!

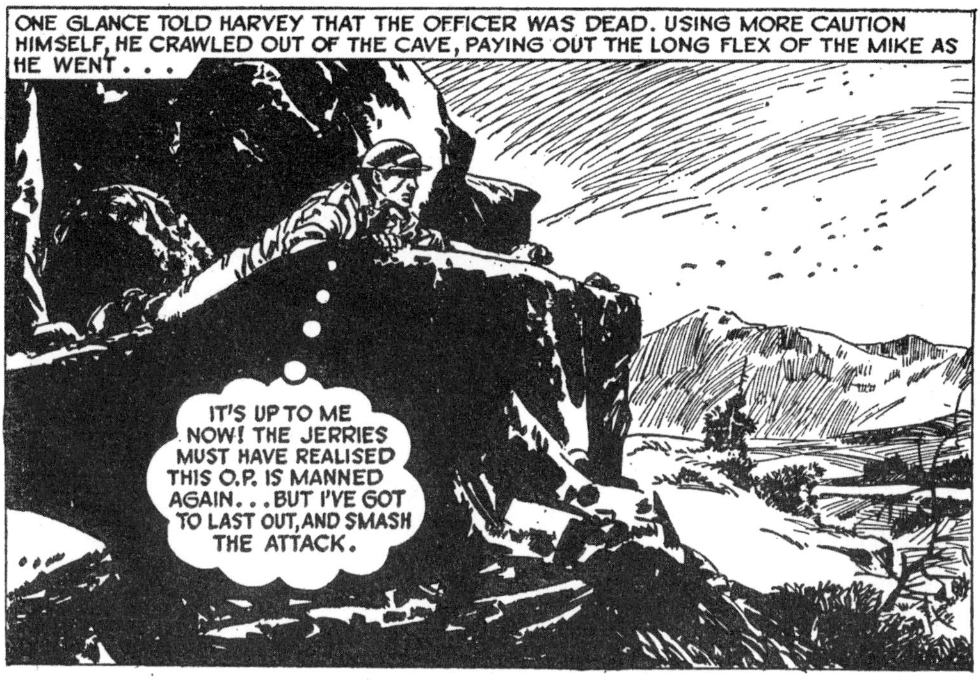
ONE GLANCE TOLD HARVEY THAT THE OFFICER WAS DEAD. USING MORE CAUTION HIMSELF, HE CRAWLED OUT OF THE CAVE, PAYING OUT THE LONG FLEX OF THE MIKE AS HE WENT . . .
IT'S UP TO ME NOW! THE JERRIES MUST HAVE REALISED THIS O.P. IS MANNED AGAIN. . . BUT I'VE GOT TO LAST OUT, AND SMASH THE ATTACK.

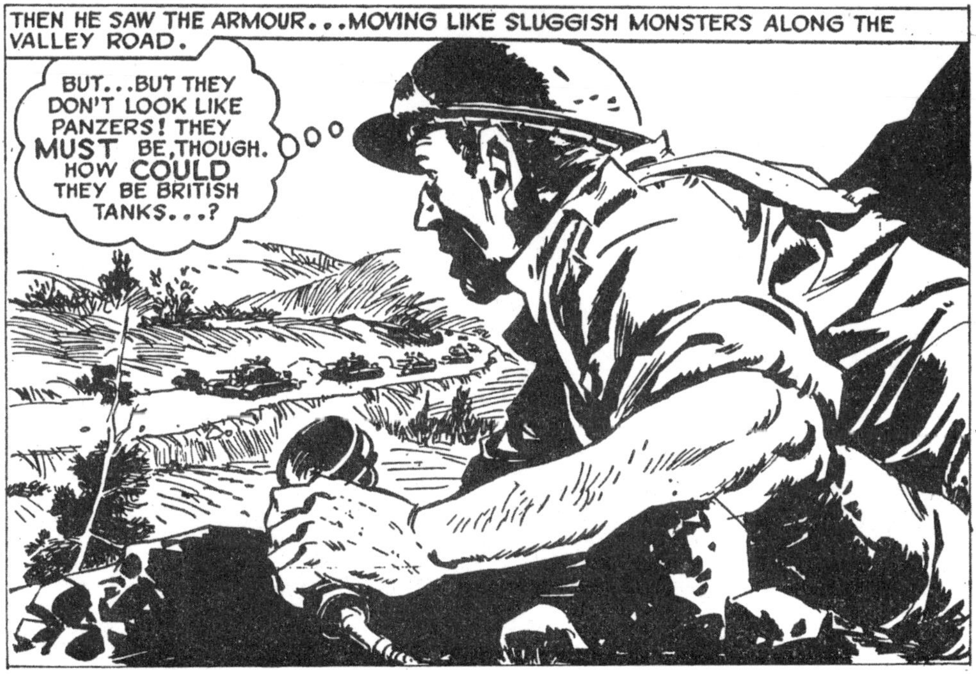
THEN HE SAW THE ARMOUR. . . MOVING LIKE SLUGGISH MONSTERS ALONG THE VALLEY ROAD.
BUT. . . BUT THEY DON'T LOOK LIKE PANZERS! THEY MUST BE, THOUGH. HOW COULD THEY BE BRITISH TANKS. . . ?

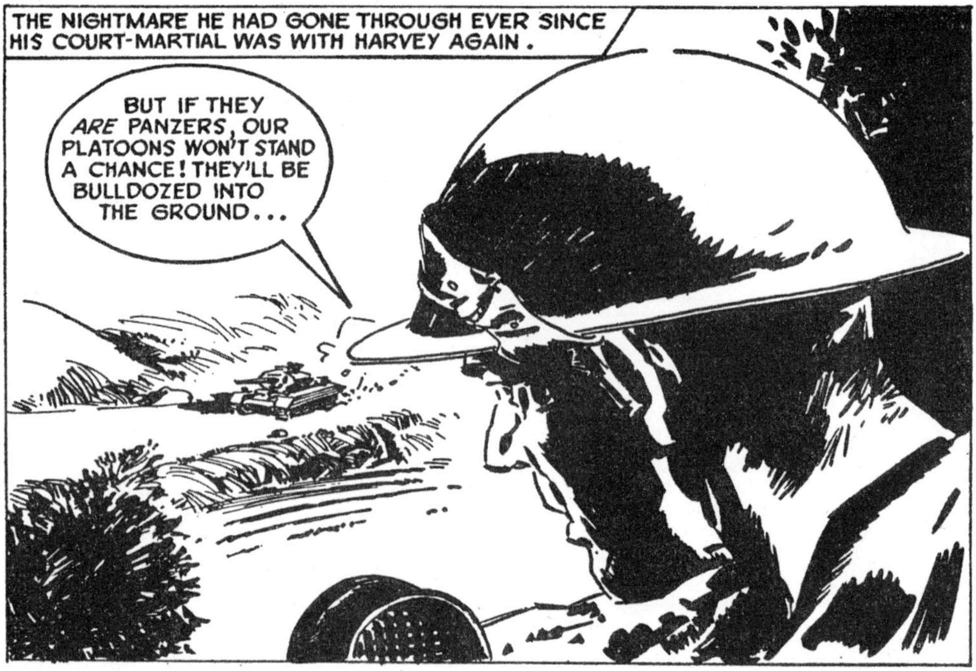
THE NIGHTMARE HE HAD GONE THROUGH EVER SINCE HIS COURT-MARTIAL WAS WITH HARVEY AGAIN.
BUT IF THEY *ARE* PANZERS, OUR PLATOONS WON'T STAND A CHANCE! THEY'LL BE BULLDOZED INTO THE GROUND...

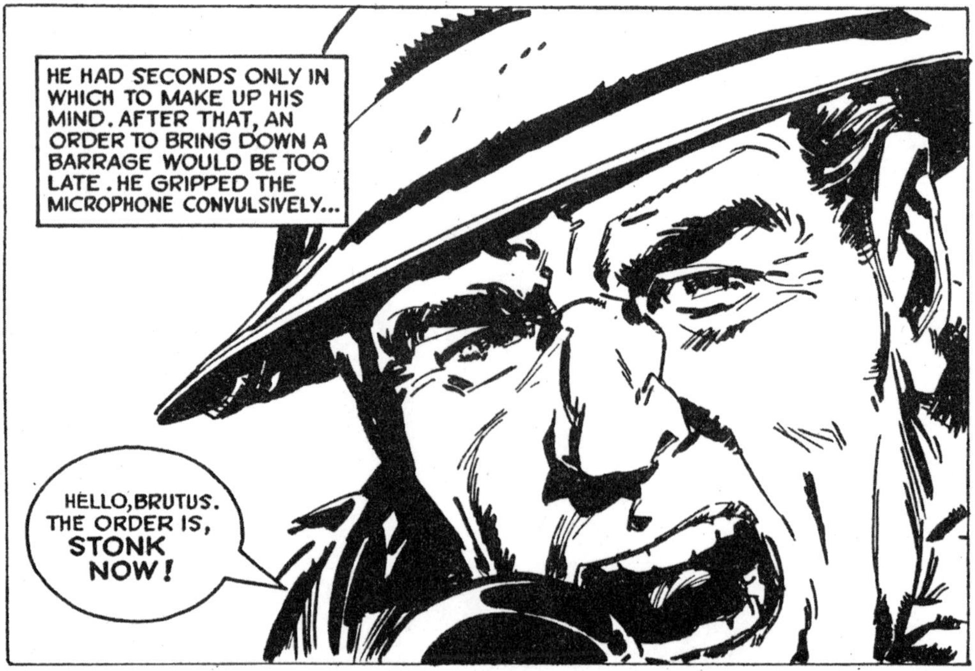
HE HAD SECONDS ONLY IN WHICH TO MAKE UP HIS MIND. AFTER THAT, AN ORDER TO BRING DOWN A BARRAGE WOULD BE TOO LATE. HE GRIPPED THE MICROPHONE CONVULSIVELY...
HELLO, BRUTUS. THE ORDER IS, **STONK NOW!**

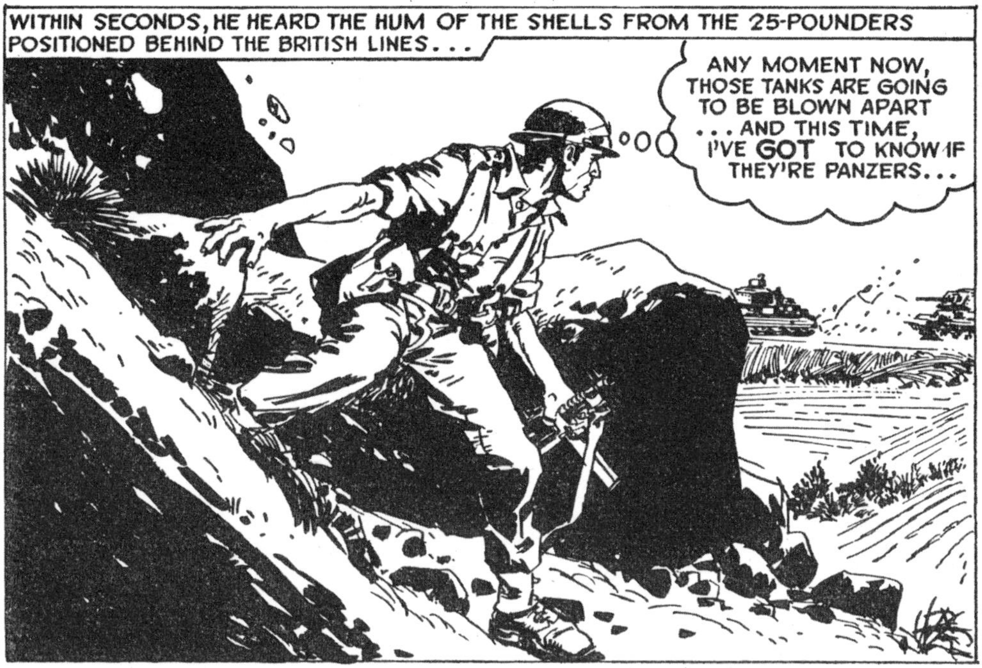
WITHIN SECONDS, HE HEARD THE HUM OF THE SHELLS FROM THE 25-POUNDERS POSITIONED BEHIND THE BRITISH LINES . . .
ANY MOMENT NOW, THOSE TANKS ARE GOING TO BE BLOWN APART . . . AND THIS TIME, I'VE GOT TO KNOW IF THEY'RE PANZERS . . .

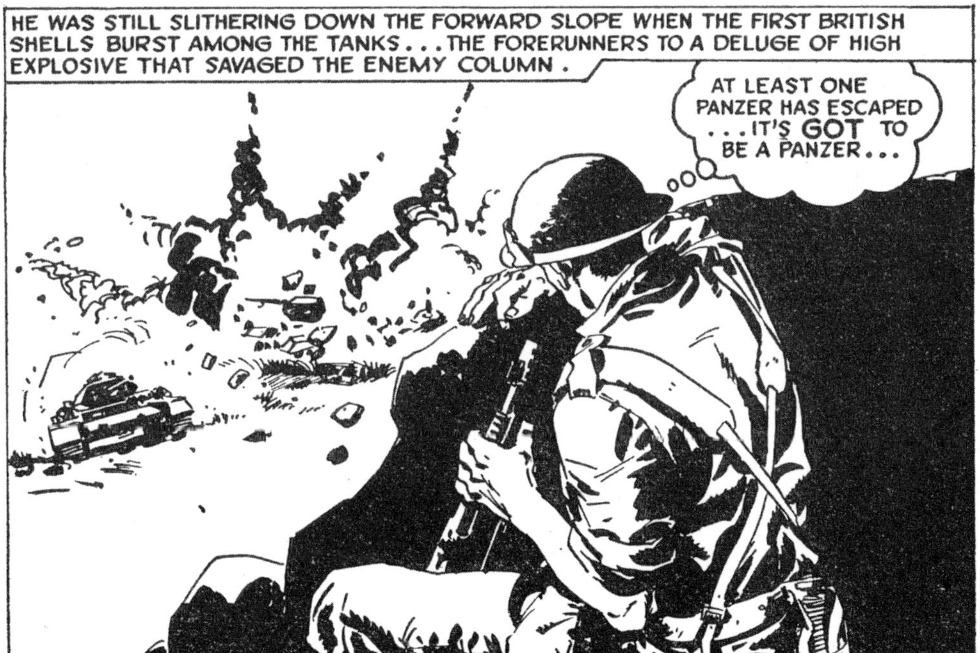
HE WAS STILL SLITHERING DOWN THE FORWARD SLOPE WHEN THE FIRST BRITISH SHELLS BURST AMONG THE TANKS . . . THE FORERUNNERS TO A DELUGE OF HIGH EXPLOSIVE THAT SAVAGED THE ENEMY COLUMN .
AT LEAST ONE PANZER HAS ESCAPED . . . IT'S GOT TO BE A PANZER . . .

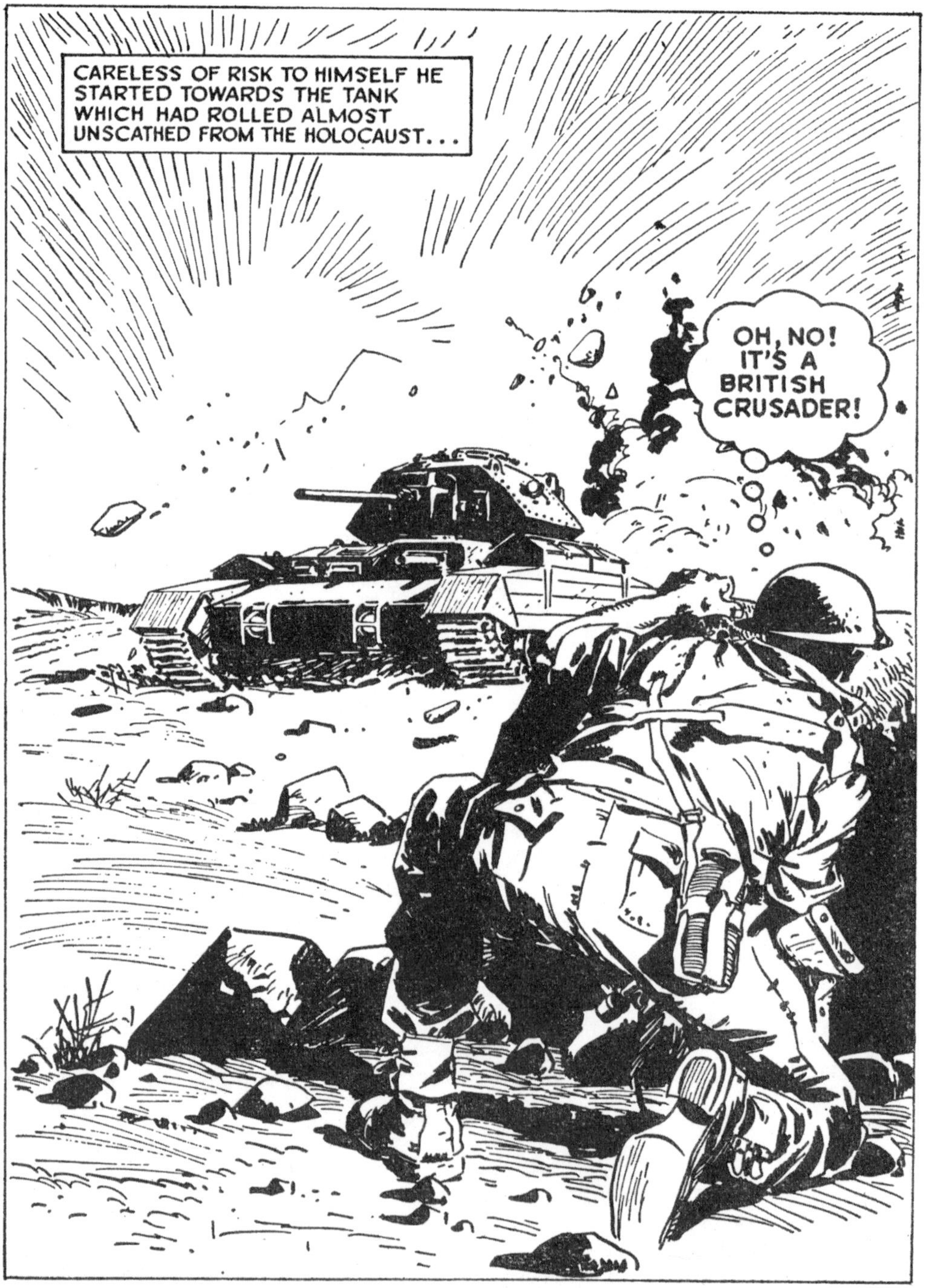
CARELESS OF RISK TO HIMSELF HE STARTED TOWARDS THE TANK WHICH HAD ROLLED ALMOST UNSCATHED FROM THE HOLOCAUST...
OH, NO! IT'S A BRITISH CRUSADER!

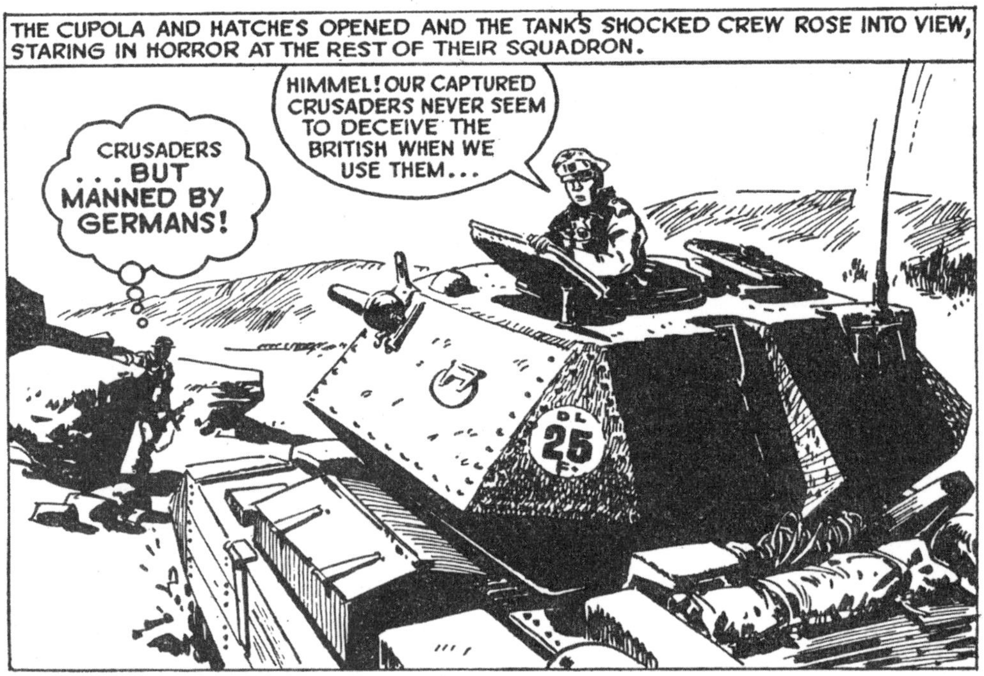
THE CUPOLA AND HATCHES OPENED AND THE TANK'S SHOCKED CREW ROSE INTO VIEW, STARING IN HORROR AT THE REST OF THEIR SQUADRON.
CRUSADERS . . . BUT MANNED BY GERMANS!
HIMMEL! OUR CAPTURED CRUSADERS NEVER SEEM TO DECEIVE THE BRITISH WHEN WE USE THEM...
DL
25

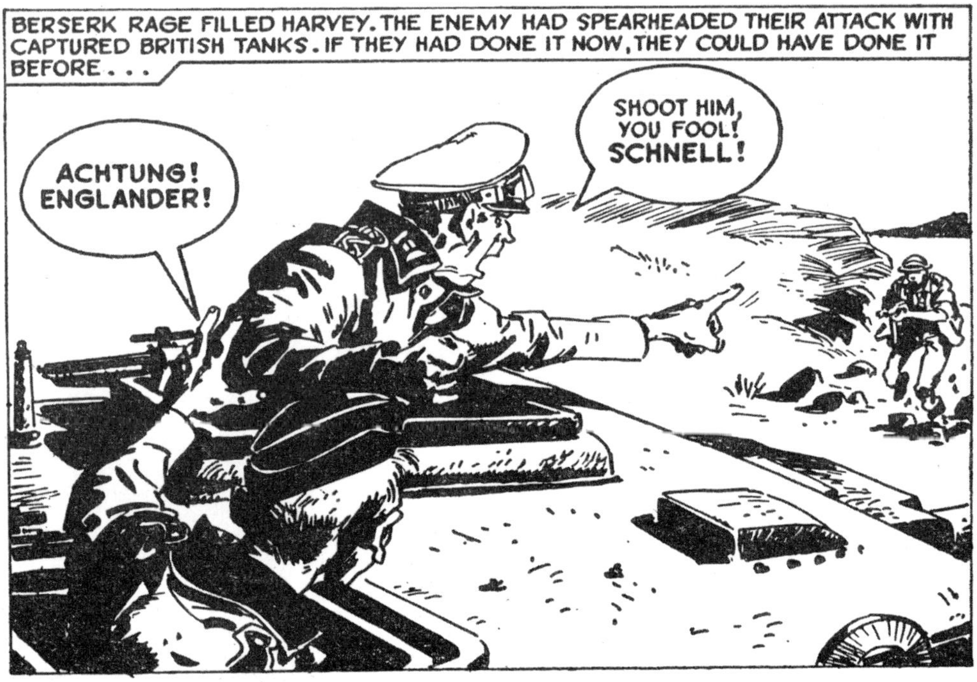
BERSERK RAGE FILLED HARVEY. THE ENEMY HAD SPEARHEADED THEIR ATTACK WITH CAPTURED BRITISH TANKS. IF THEY HAD DONE IT NOW, THEY COULD HAVE DONE IT BEFORE . . .
ACHTUNG! ENGLANDER!
SHOOT HIM, YOU FOOL! SCHNELL!

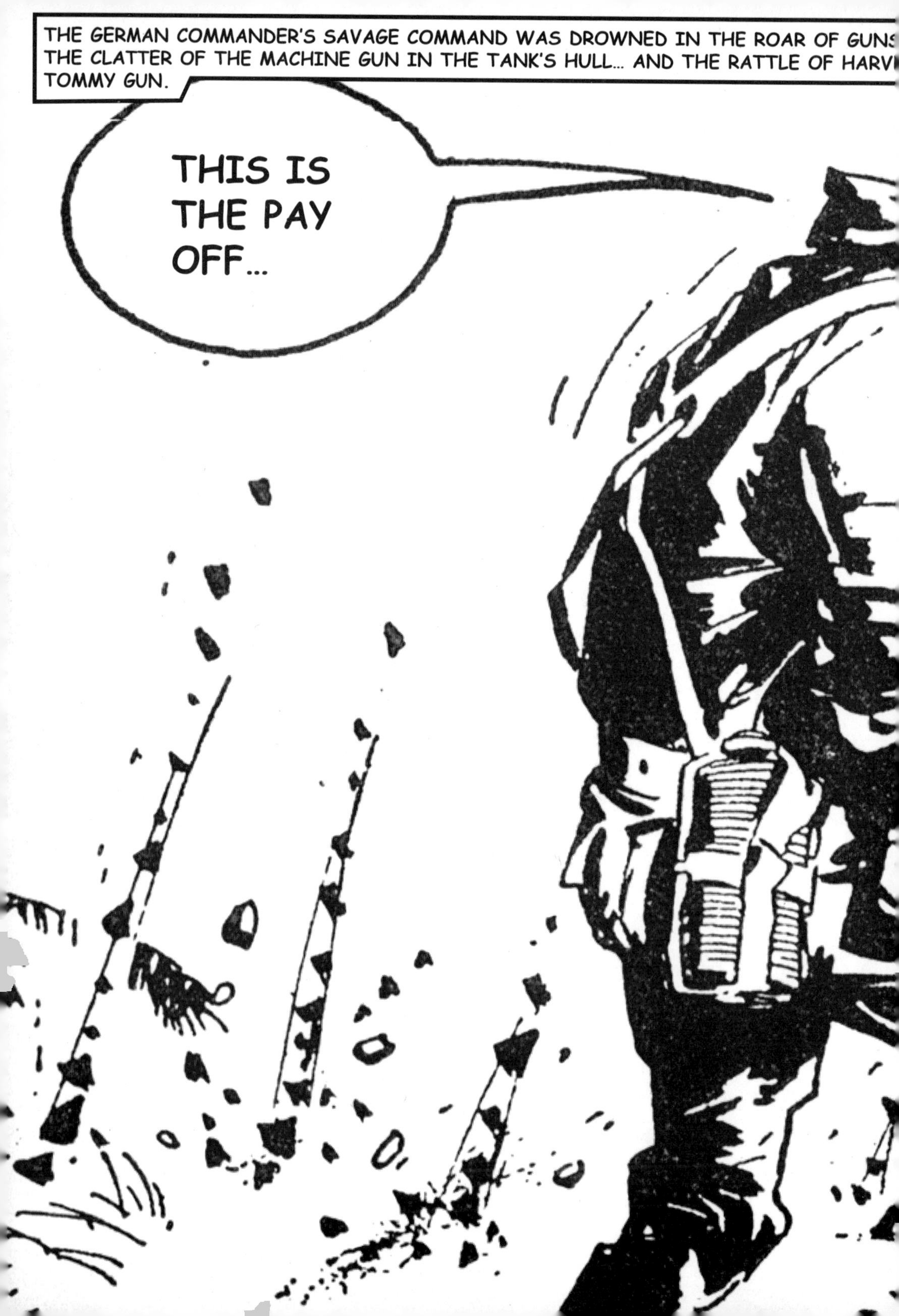
THE GERMAN COMMANDER'S SAVAGE COMMAND WAS DROWNED IN THE ROAR OF GUNS THE CLATTER OF THE MACHINE GUN IN THE TANK'S HULL... AND THE RATTLE OF HARV TOMMY GUN.
THIS IS THE PAY OFF...

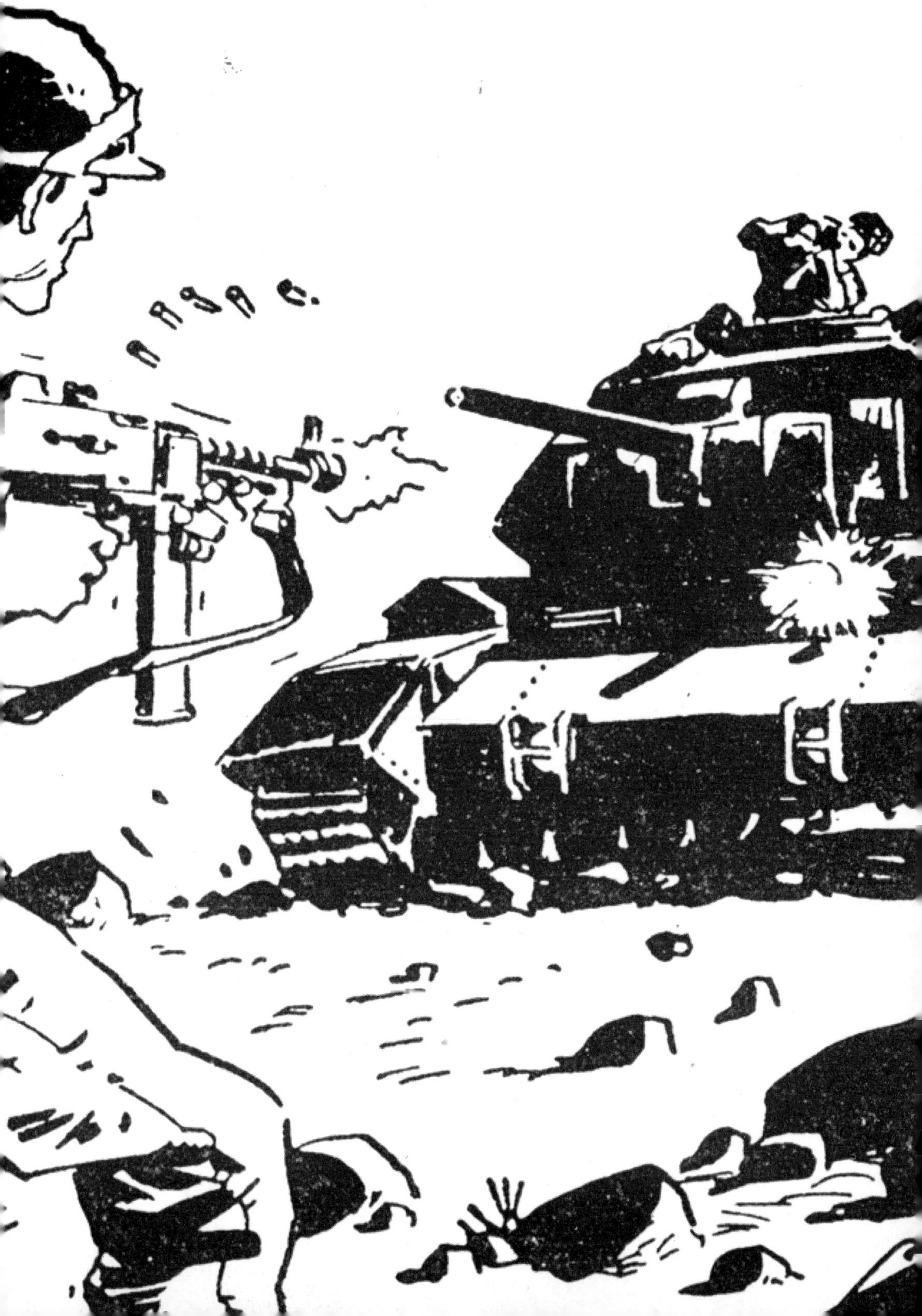

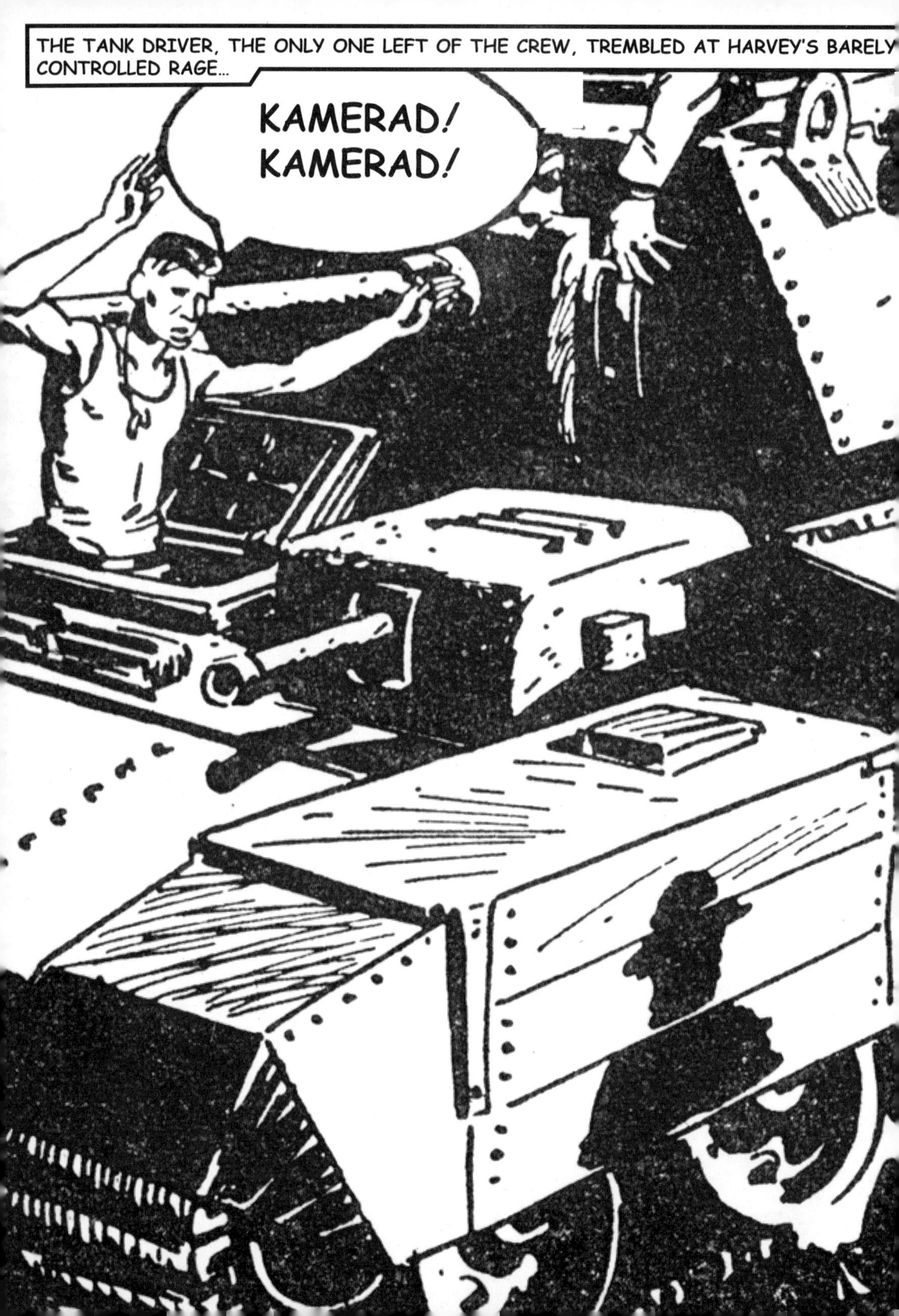
THE TANK DRIVER, THE ONLY ONE LEFT OF THE CREW, TREMBLED AT HARVEY'S BARELY CONTROLLED RAGE...
KAMERAD! KAMERAD!

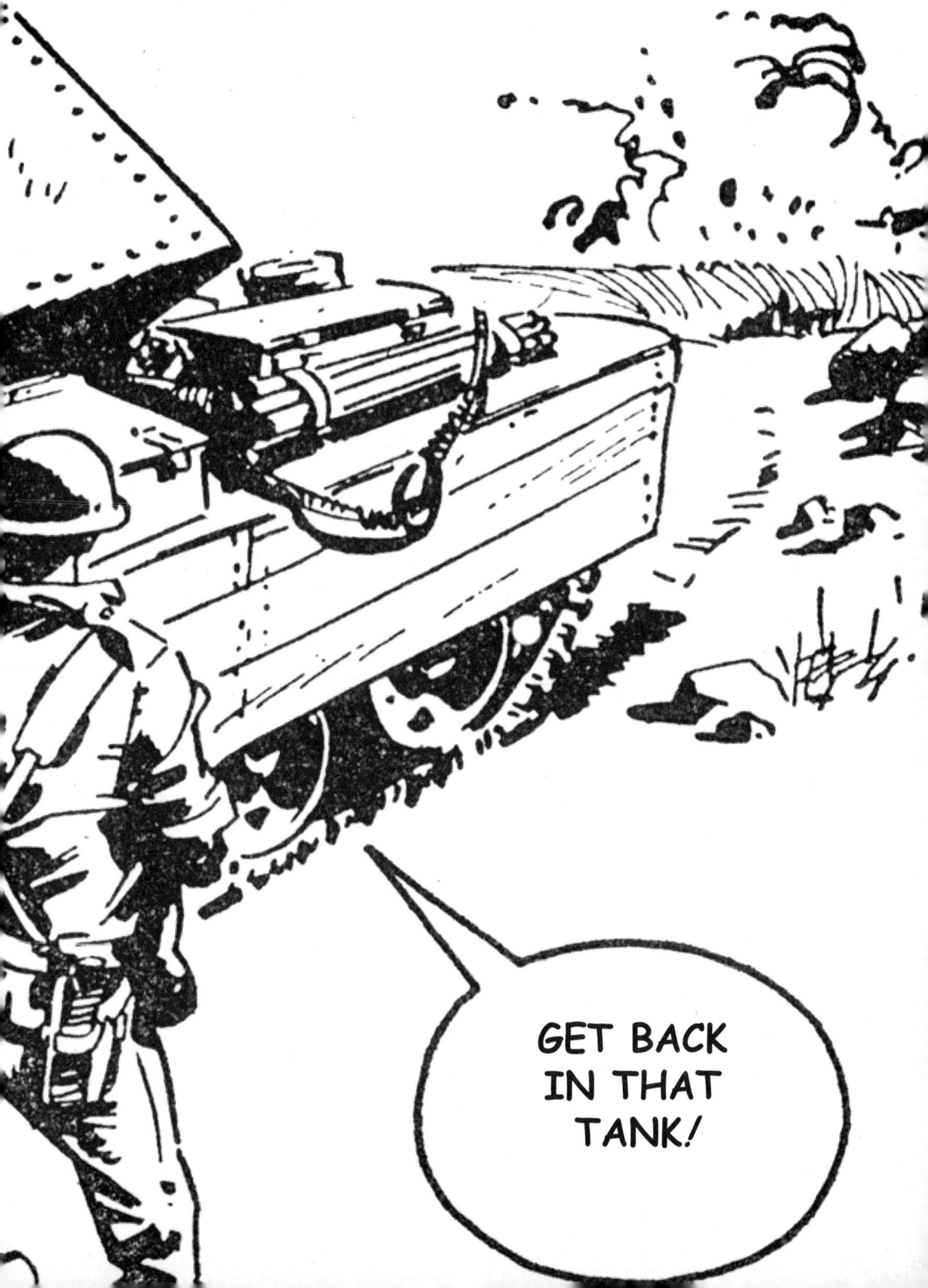
GET BACK IN THAT TANK!

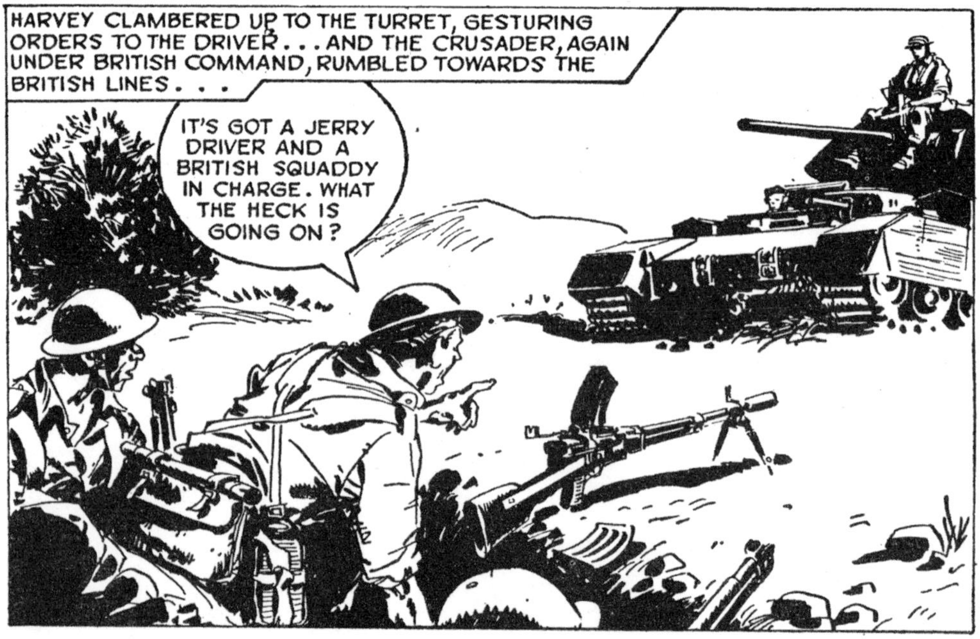
HARVEY CLAMBERED UP TO THE TURRET, GESTURING ORDERS TO THE DRIVER . . . AND THE CRUSADER, AGAIN UNDER BRITISH COMMAND, RUMBLED TOWARDS THE BRITISH LINES . . .
IT'S GOT A JERRY DRIVER AND A BRITISH SQUADDY IN CHARGE. WHAT THE HECK IS GOING ON?

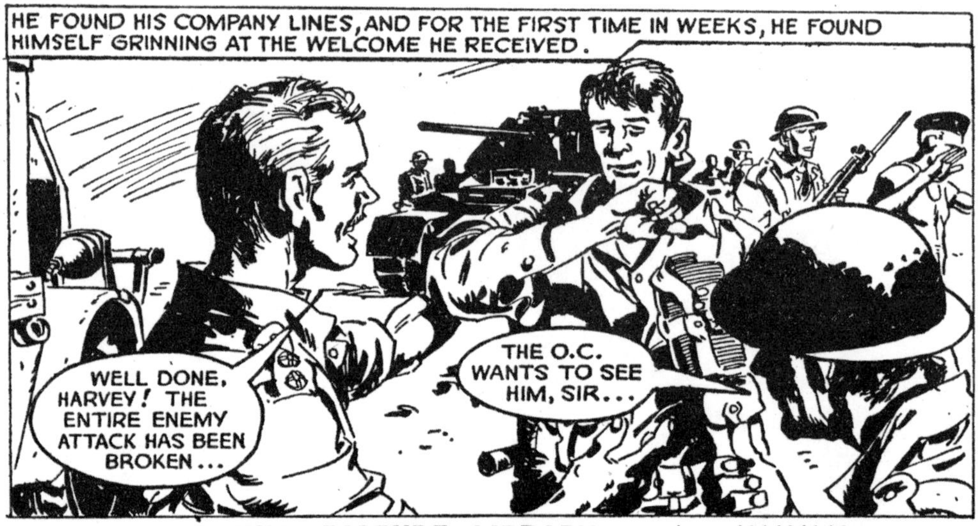
HE FOUND HIS COMPANY LINES, AND FOR THE FIRST TIME IN WEEKS, HE FOUND HIMSELF GRINNING AT THE WELCOME HE RECEIVED.
WELL DONE, HARVEY! THE ENTIRE ENEMY ATTACK HAS BEEN BROKEN...
THE O.C. WANTS TO SEE HIM, SIR...

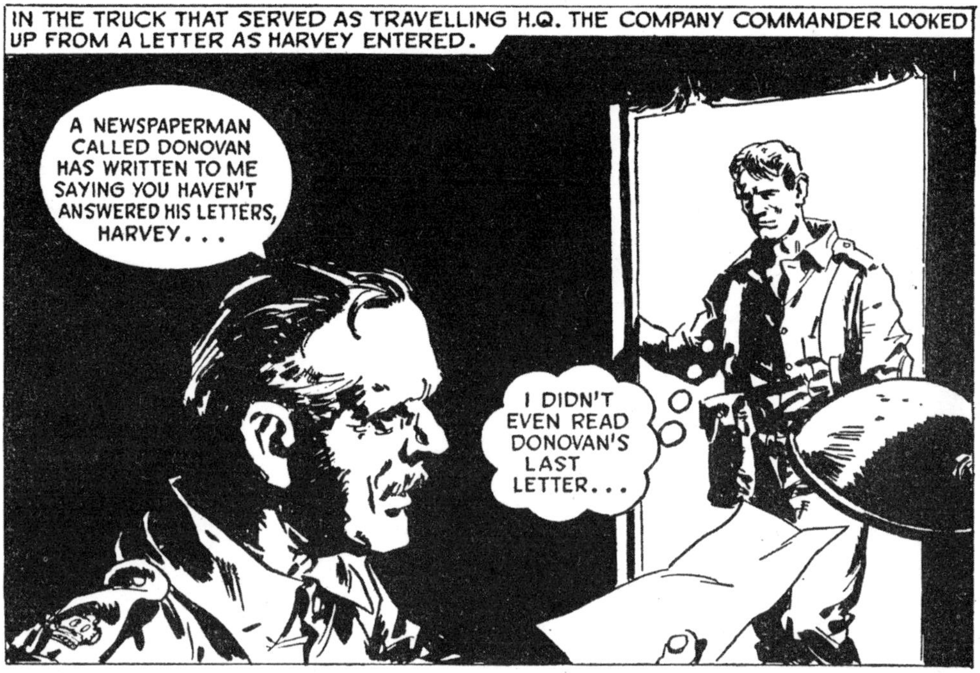
IN THE TRUCK THAT SERVED AS TRAVELLING H.Q. THE COMPANY COMMANDER LOOKED UP FROM A LETTER AS HARVEY ENTERED.
A NEWSPAPERMAN CALLED DONOVAN HAS WRITTEN TO ME SAYING YOU HAVEN'T ANSWERED HIS LETTERS, HARVEY . . .
I DIDN'T EVEN READ DONOVAN'S LAST LETTER . . .

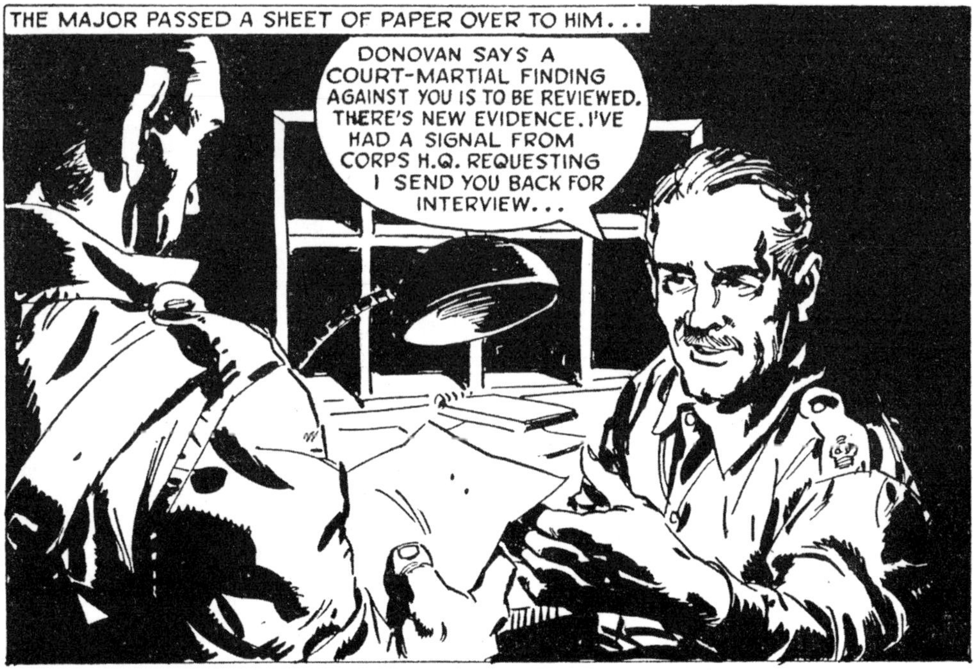
THE MAJOR PASSED A SHEET OF PAPER OVER TO HIM . . .
DONOVAN SAYS A COURT-MARTIAL FINDING AGAINST YOU IS TO BE REVIEWED. THERE'S NEW EVIDENCE. I'VE HAD A SIGNAL FROM CORPS H.Q. REQUESTING I SEND YOU BACK FOR INTERVIEW . . .

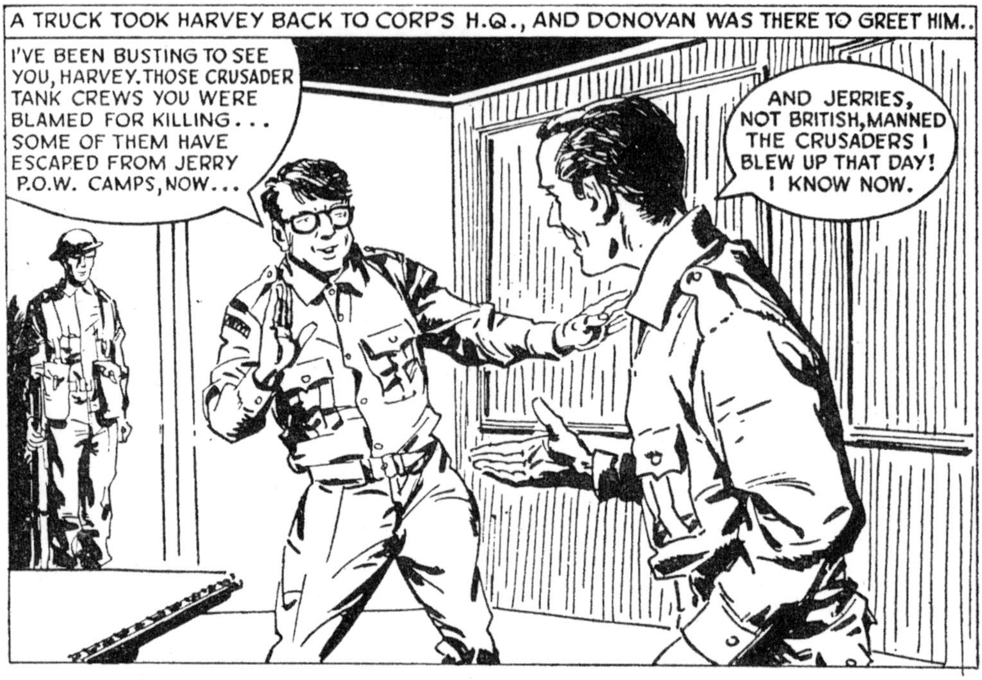
A TRUCK TOOK HARVEY BACK TO CORPS H.Q., AND DONOVAN WAS THERE TO GREET HIM..
I'VE BEEN BUSTING TO SEE YOU, HARVEY. THOSE CRUSADER TANK CREWS YOU WERE BLAMED FOR KILLING... SOME OF THEM HAVE ESCAPED FROM JERRY P.O.W. CAMPS, NOW...
AND JERRIES, NOT BRITISH, MANNED THE CRUSADERS I BLEW UP THAT DAY! I KNOW NOW.

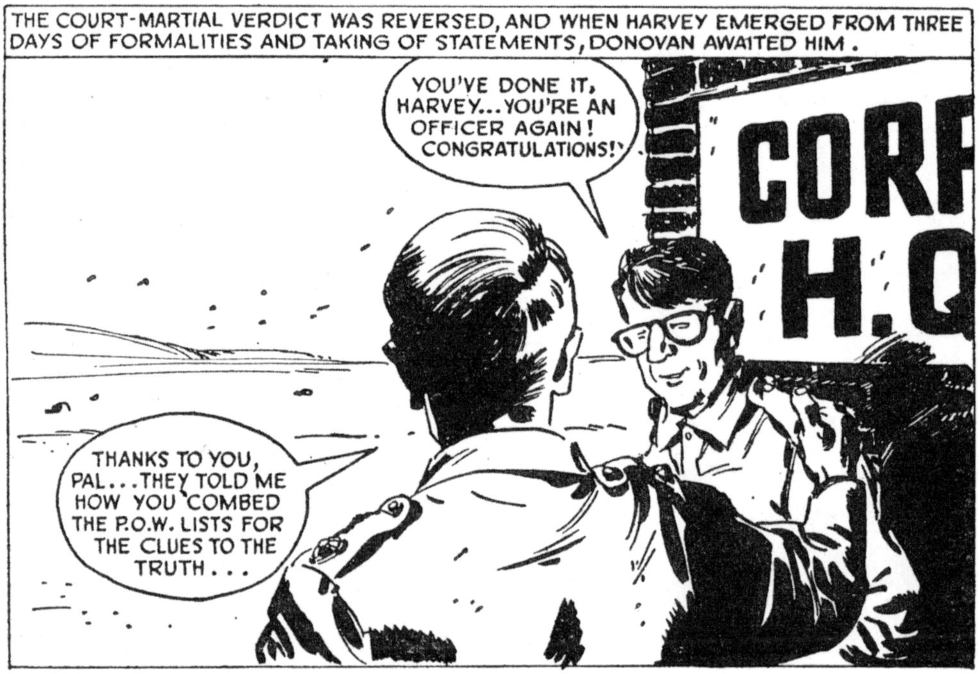
THE COURT-MARTIAL VERDICT WAS REVERSED, AND WHEN HARVEY EMERGED FROM THREE DAYS OF FORMALITIES AND TAKING OF STATEMENTS, DONOVAN AWAITED HIM.
YOU'VE DONE IT, HARVEY...YOU'RE AN OFFICER AGAIN! CONGRATULATIONS!
THANKS TO YOU, PAL...THEY TOLD ME HOW YOU COMBED THE P.O.W. LISTS FOR THE CLUES TO THE TRUTH...

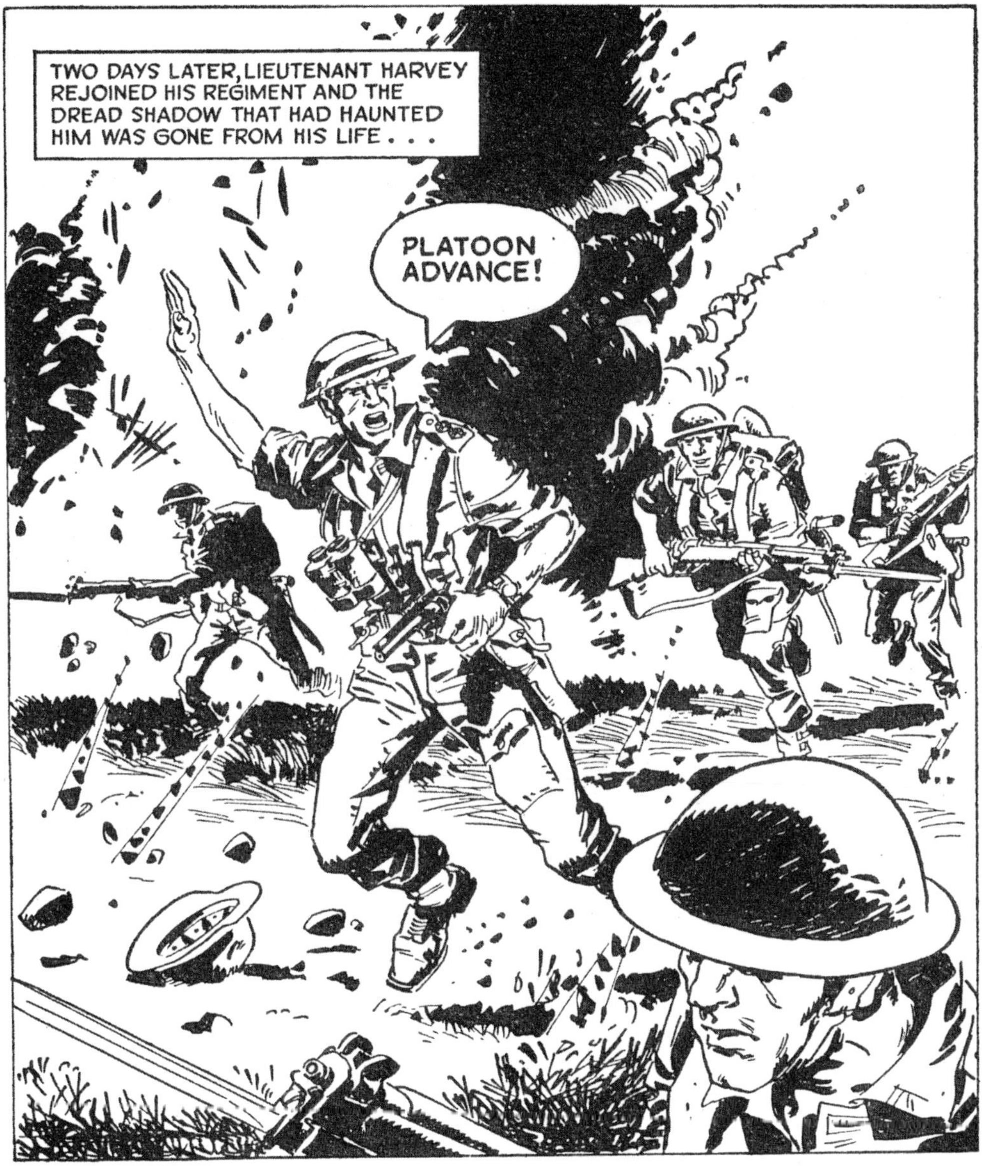
TWO DAYS LATER, LIEUTENANT HARVEY REJOINED HIS REGIMENT AND THE DREAD SHADOW THAT HAD HAUNTED HIM WAS GONE FROM HIS LIFE . . .
PLATOON ADVANCE!

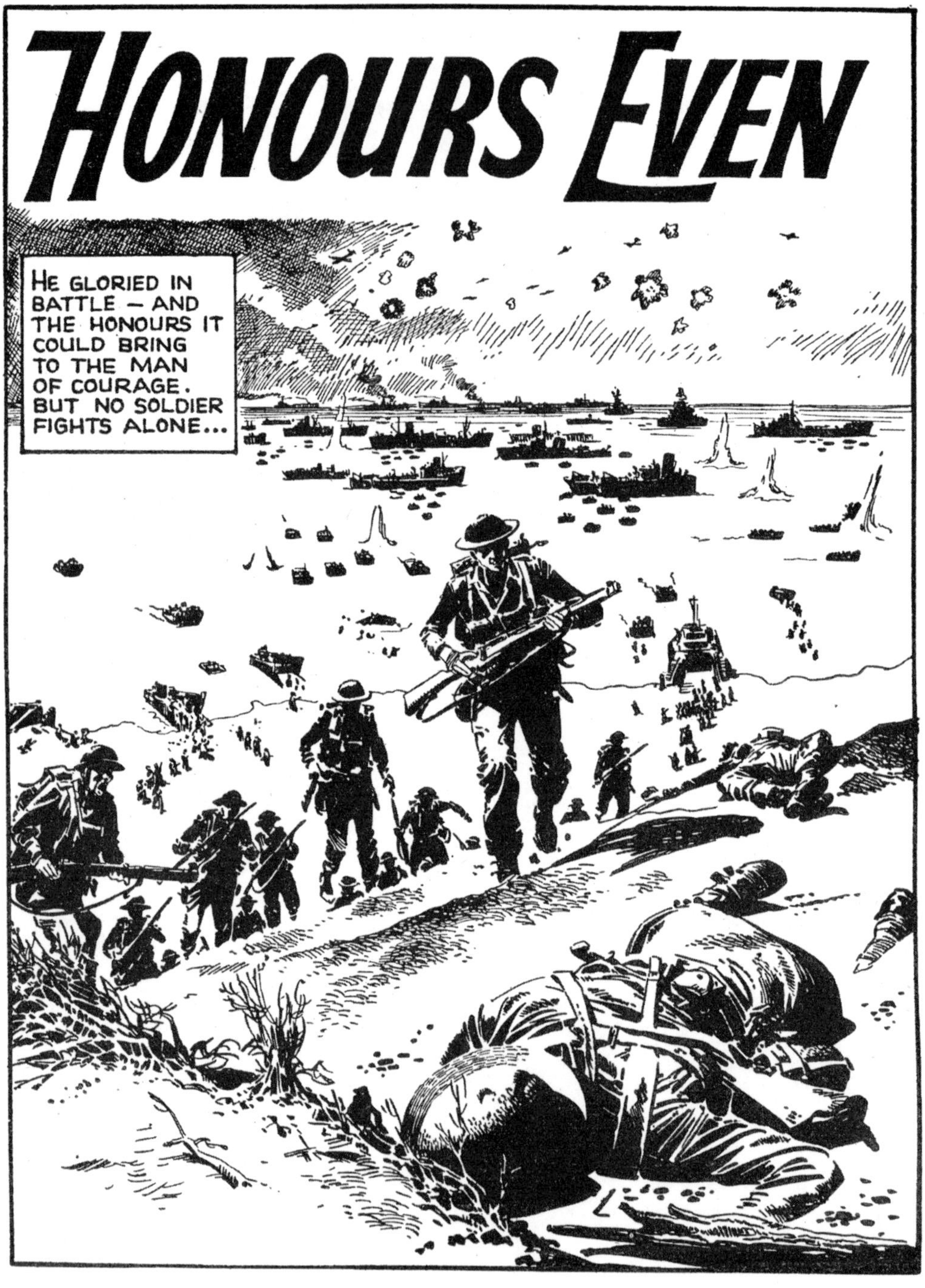
HONOURS EVEN
HE GLORIED IN BATTLE — AND THE HONOURS IT COULD BRING TO THE MAN OF COURAGE. BUT NO SOLDIER FIGHTS ALONE...

Chapter 1. Glory Boy

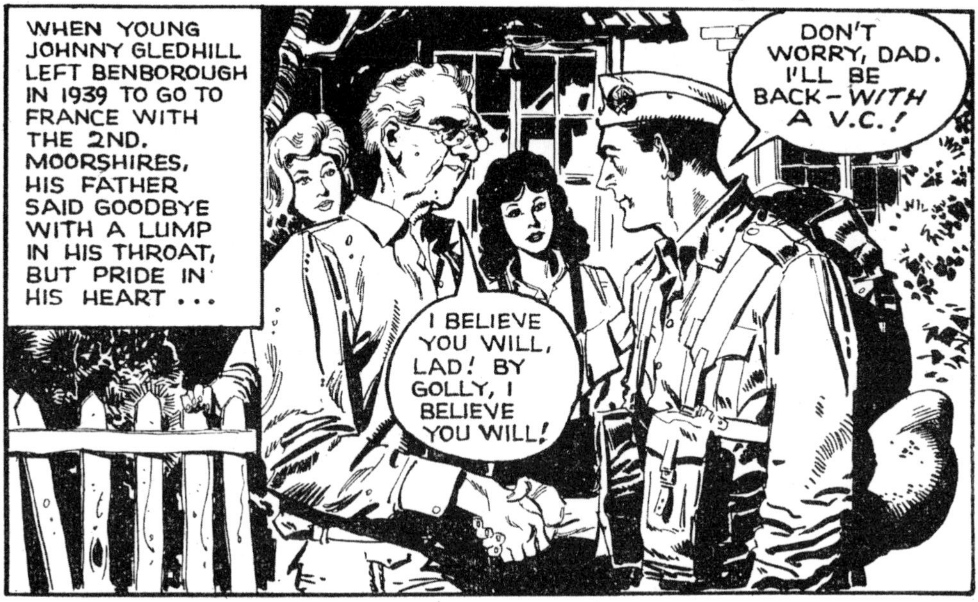
WHEN YOUNG JOHNNY GLEDHILL LEFT BENBOROUGH IN 1939 TO GO TO FRANCE WITH THE 2ND. MOORSHIRES, HIS FATHER SAID GOODBYE WITH A LUMP IN HIS THROAT, BUT PRIDE IN HIS HEART ...
DON'T WORRY, DAD. I'LL BE BACK - WITH A V.C.!
I BELIEVE YOU WILL, LAD! BY GOLLY, I BELIEVE YOU WILL!

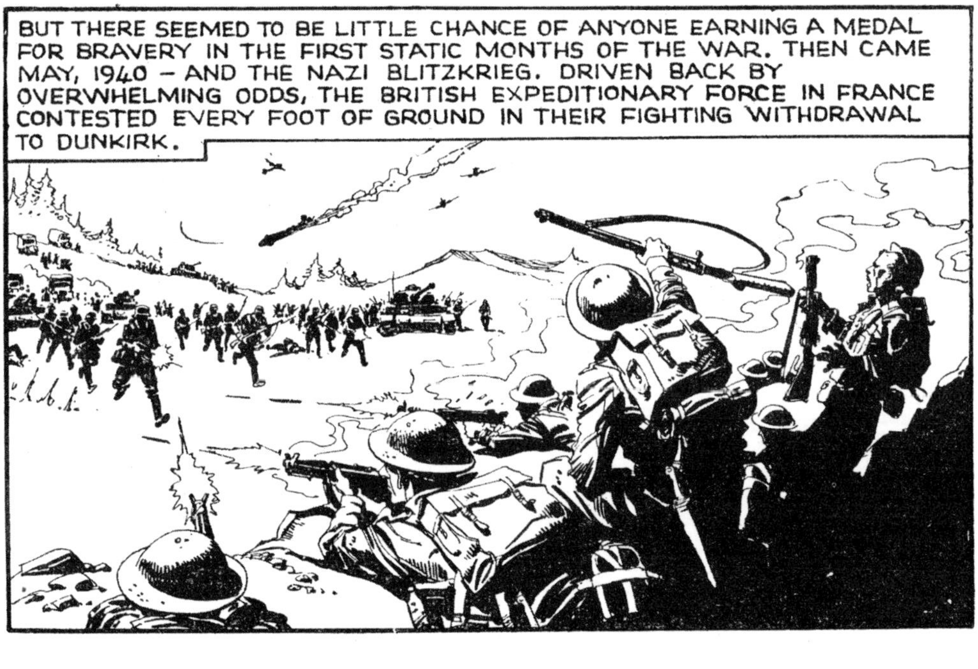
BUT THERE SEEMED TO BE LITTLE CHANCE OF ANYONE EARNING A MEDAL FOR BRAVERY IN THE FIRST STATIC MONTHS OF THE WAR. THEN CAME MAY, 1940 - AND THE NAZI BLITZKRIEG. DRIVEN BACK BY OVERWHELMING ODDS, THE BRITISH EXPEDITIONARY FORCE IN FRANCE CONTESTED EVERY FOOT OF GROUND IN THEIR FIGHTING WITHDRAWAL TO DUNKIRK.

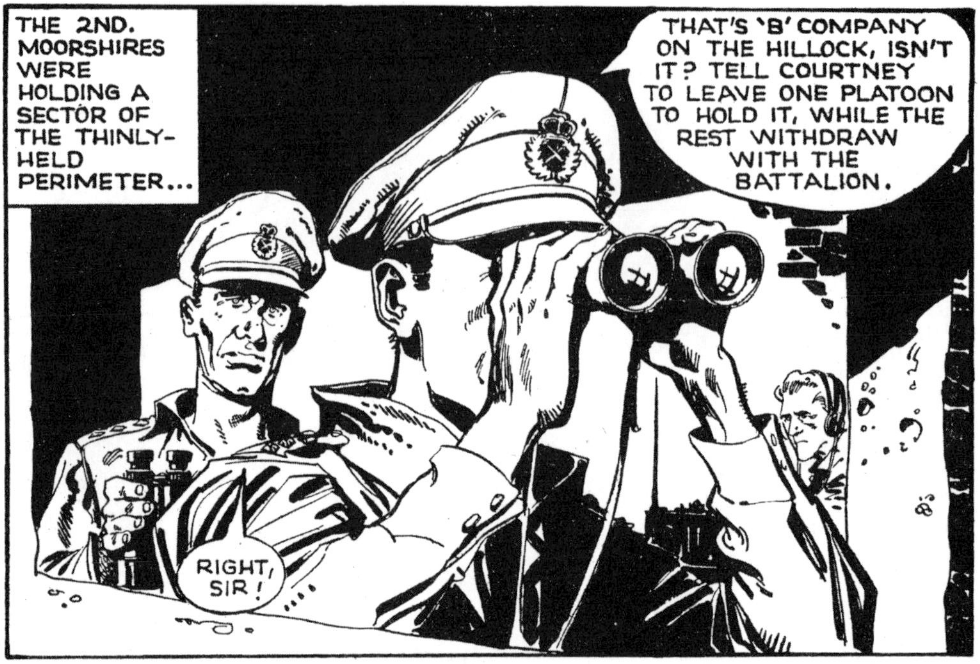
THE 2ND. MOORSHIRES WERE HOLDING A SECTOR OF THE THINLY-HELD PERIMETER...
THAT'S 'B' COMPANY ON THE HILLOCK, ISN'T IT? TELL COURTNEY TO LEAVE ONE PLATOON TO HOLD IT, WHILE THE REST WITHDRAW WITH THE BATTALION.
RIGHT, SIR!

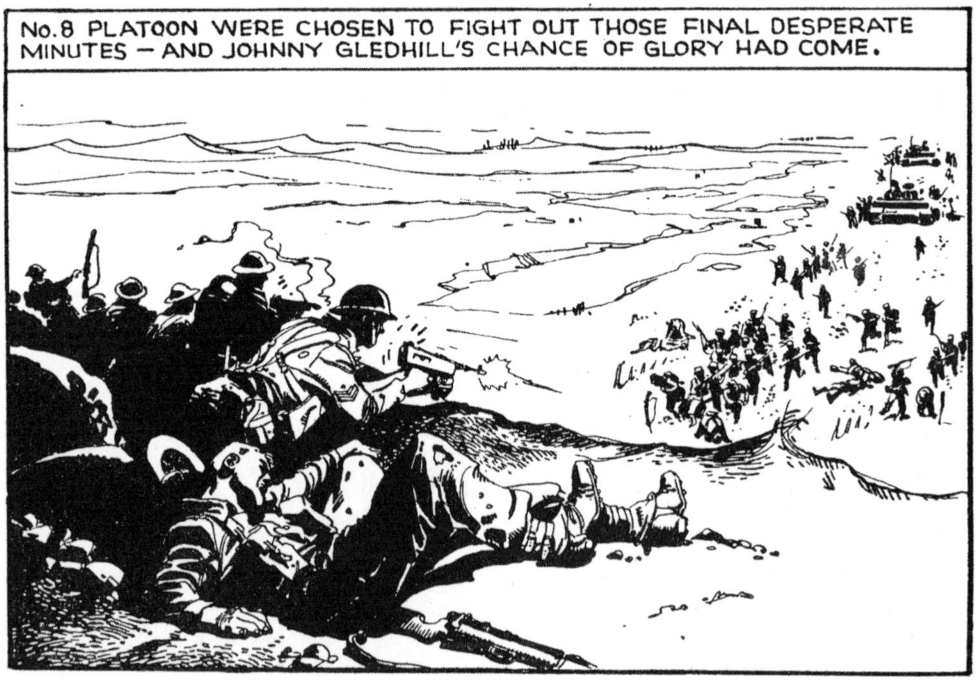
No.8 PLATOON WERE CHOSEN TO FIGHT OUT THOSE FINAL DESPERATE MINUTES – AND JOHNNY GLEDHILL'S CHANCE OF GLORY HAD COME.

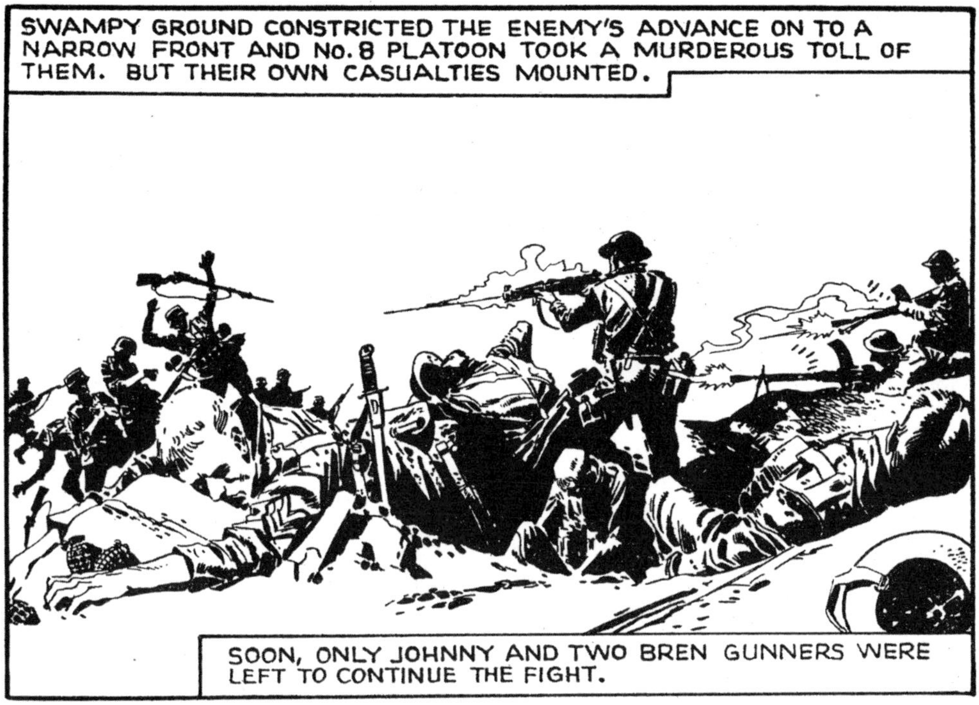
SWAMPY GROUND CONSTRICTED THE ENEMY'S ADVANCE ON TO A NARROW FRONT AND No. 8 PLATOON TOOK A MURDEROUS TOLL OF THEM. BUT THEIR OWN CASUALTIES MOUNTED.
SOON, ONLY JOHNNY AND TWO BREN GUNNERS WERE LEFT TO CONTINUE THE FIGHT.

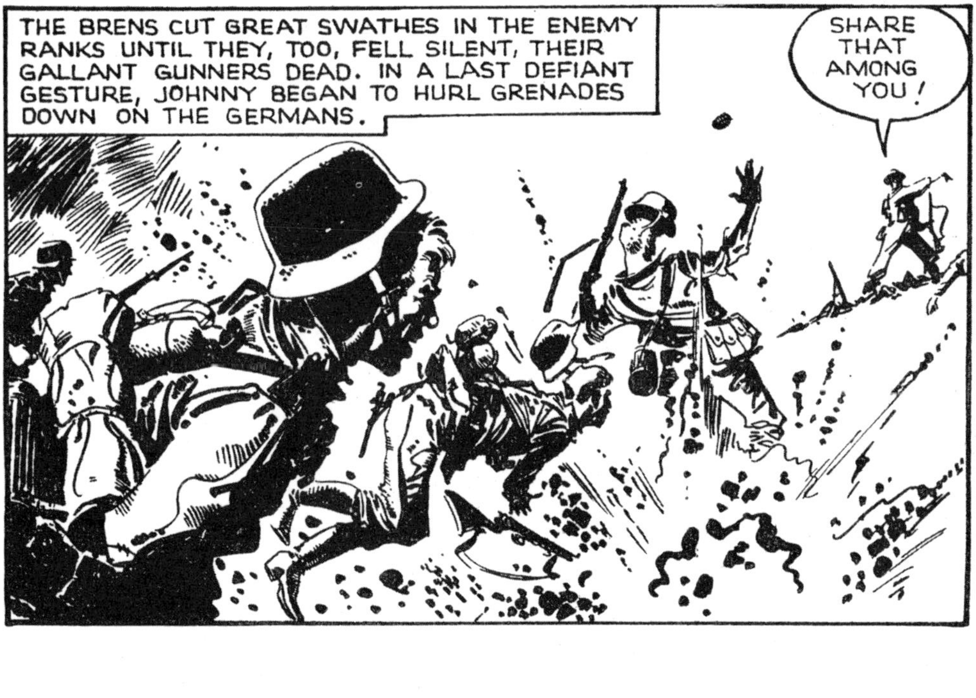
THE BRENS CUT GREAT SWATHES IN THE ENEMY RANKS UNTIL THEY, TOO, FELL SILENT, THEIR GALLANT GUNNERS DEAD. IN A LAST DEFIANT GESTURE, JOHNNY BEGAN TO HURL GRENADES DOWN ON THE GERMANS.
SHARE THAT AMONG YOU!

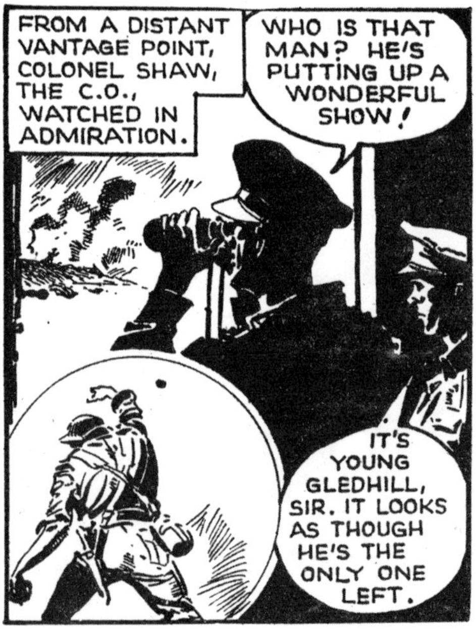
FROM A DISTANT VANTAGE POINT, COLONEL SHAW, THE C.O., WATCHED IN ADMIRATION.
WHO IS THAT MAN? HE'S PUTTING UP A WONDERFUL SHOW!
IT'S YOUNG GLEDHILL, SIR. IT LOOKS AS THOUGH HE'S THE ONLY ONE LEFT.

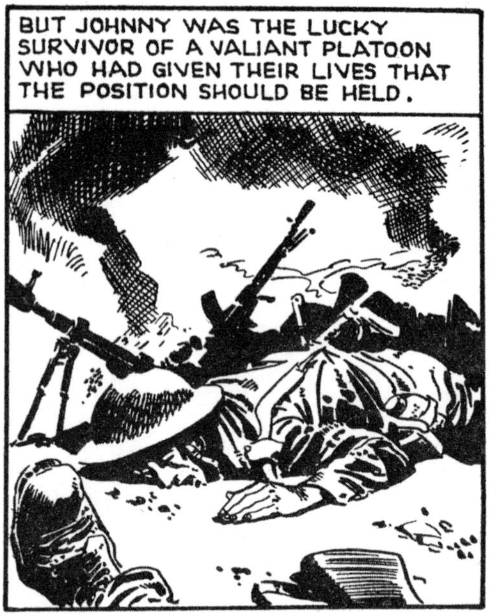
BUT JOHNNY WAS THE LUCKY SURVIVOR OF A VALIANT PLATOON WHO HAD GIVEN THEIR LIVES THAT THE POSITION SHOULD BE HELD.

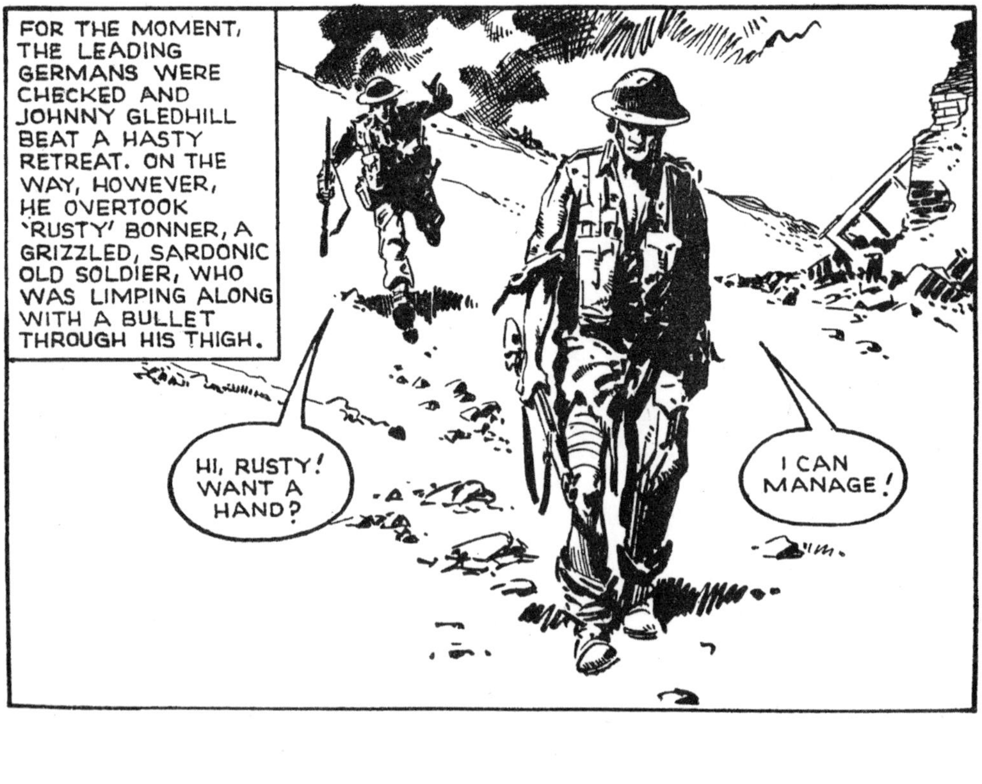
FOR THE MOMENT, THE LEADING GERMANS WERE CHECKED AND JOHNNY GLEDHILL BEAT A HASTY RETREAT. ON THE WAY, HOWEVER, HE OVERTOOK 'RUSTY' BONNER, A GRIZZLED, SARDONIC OLD SOLDIER, WHO WAS LIMPING ALONG WITH A BULLET THROUGH HIS THIGH.
HI, RUSTY! WANT A HAND?
I CAN MANAGE!

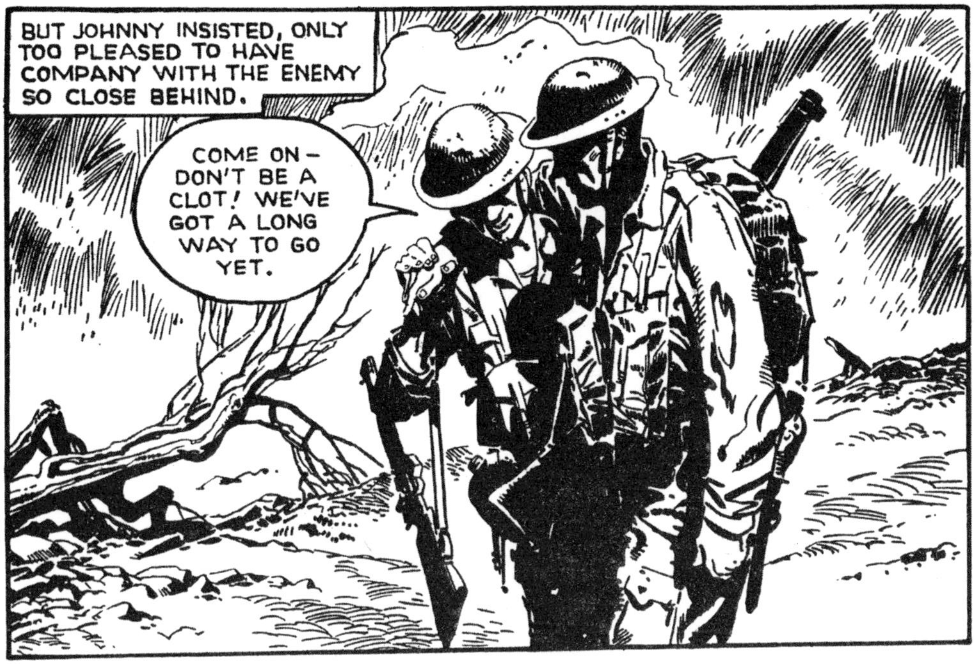
BUT JOHNNY INSISTED, ONLY TOO PLEASED TO HAVE COMPANY WITH THE ENEMY SO CLOSE BEHIND.
COME ON – DON'T BE A CLOT! WE'VE GOT A LONG WAY TO GO YET.

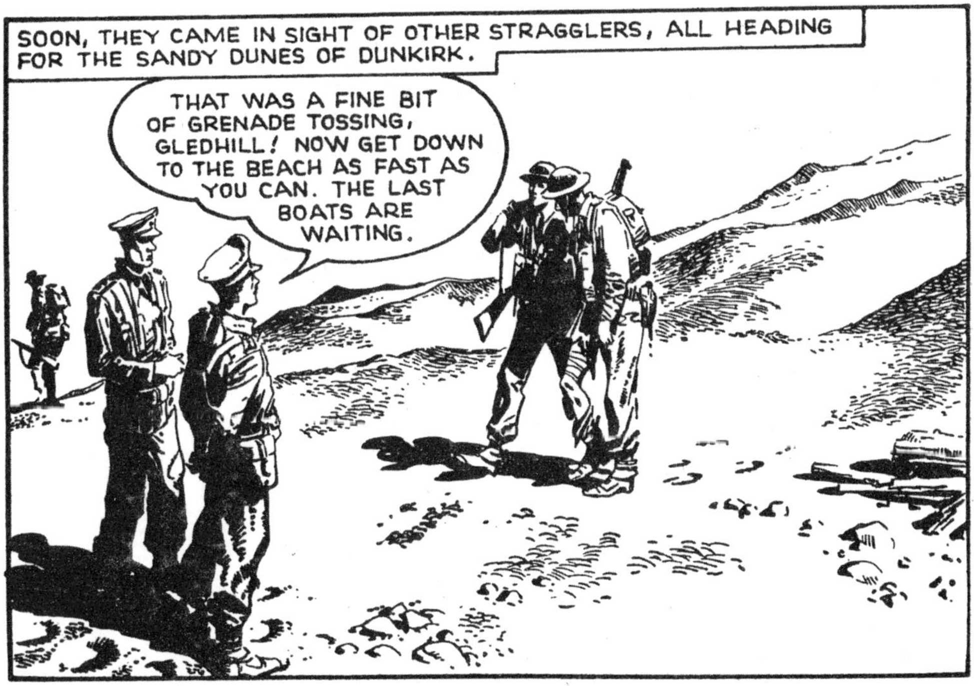
SOON, THEY CAME IN SIGHT OF OTHER STRAGGLERS, ALL HEADING FOR THE SANDY DUNES OF DUNKIRK.
THAT WAS A FINE BIT OF GRENADE TOSSING, GLEDHILL! NOW GET DOWN TO THE BEACH AS FAST AS YOU CAN. THE LAST BOATS ARE WAITING.

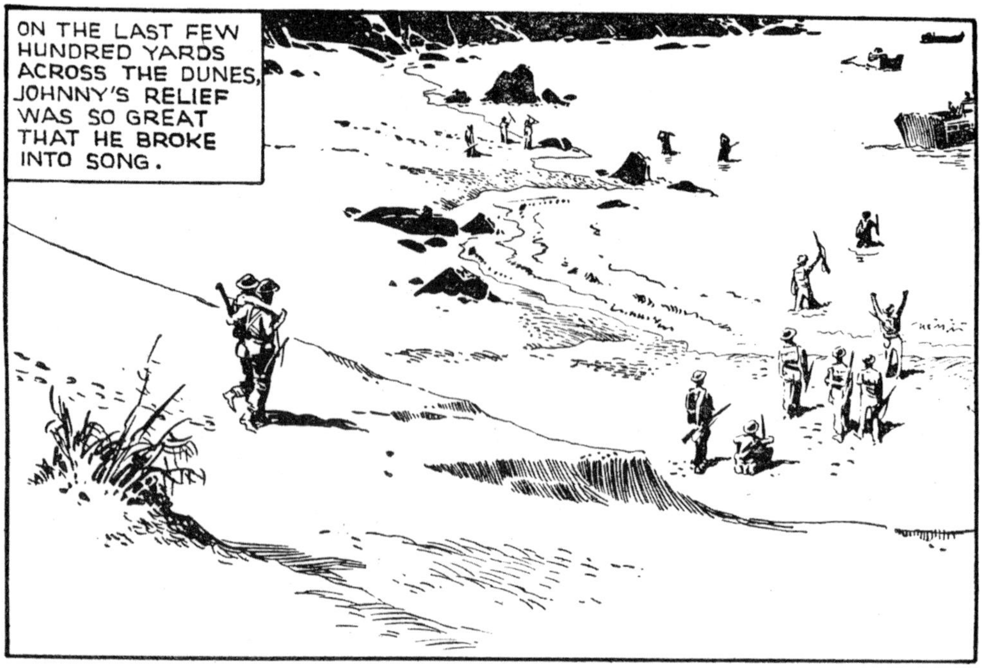
ON THE LAST FEW HUNDRED YARDS ACROSS THE DUNES, JOHNNY'S RELIEF WAS SO GREAT THAT HE BROKE INTO SONG.

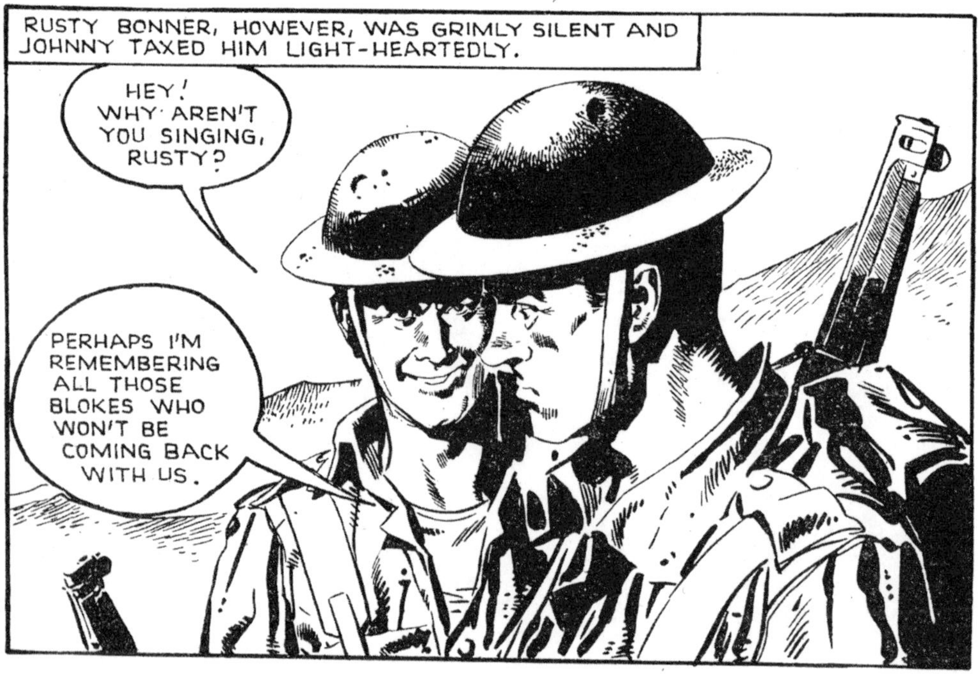
RUSTY BONNER, HOWEVER, WAS GRIMLY SILENT AND JOHNNY TAXED HIM LIGHT-HEARTEDLY.
HEY! WHY AREN'T YOU SINGING, RUSTY?
PERHAPS I'M REMEMBERING ALL THOSE BLOKES WHO WON'T BE COMING BACK WITH US.

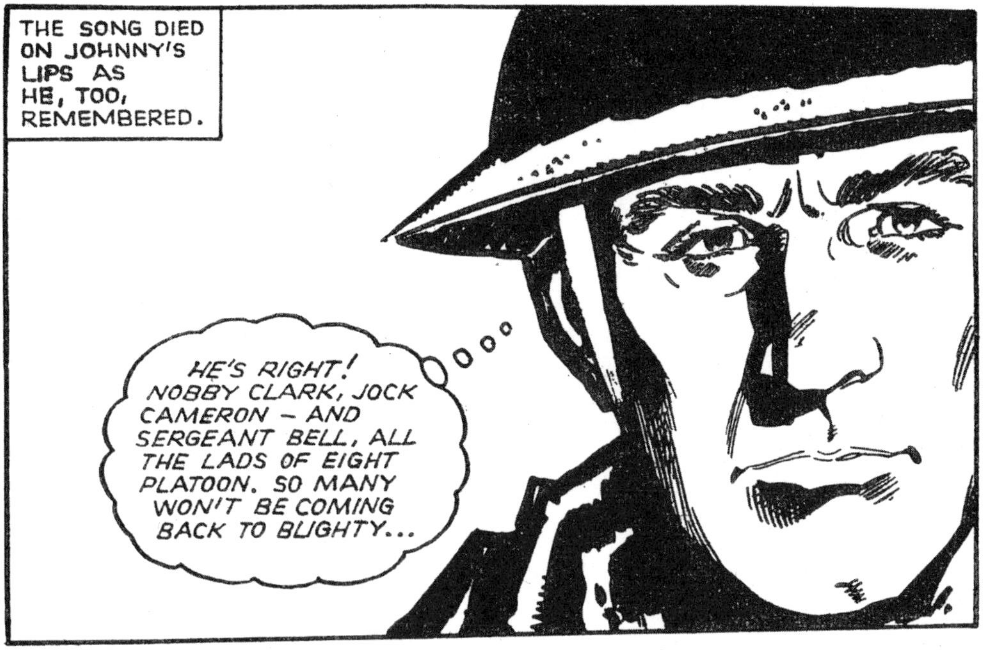
THE SONG DIED ON JOHNNY'S LIPS AS HE, TOO, REMEMBERED.
HE'S RIGHT! NOBBY CLARK, JOCK CAMERON – AND SERGEANT BELL, ALL THE LADS OF EIGHT PLATOON. SO MANY WON'T BE COMING BACK TO BLIGHTY...

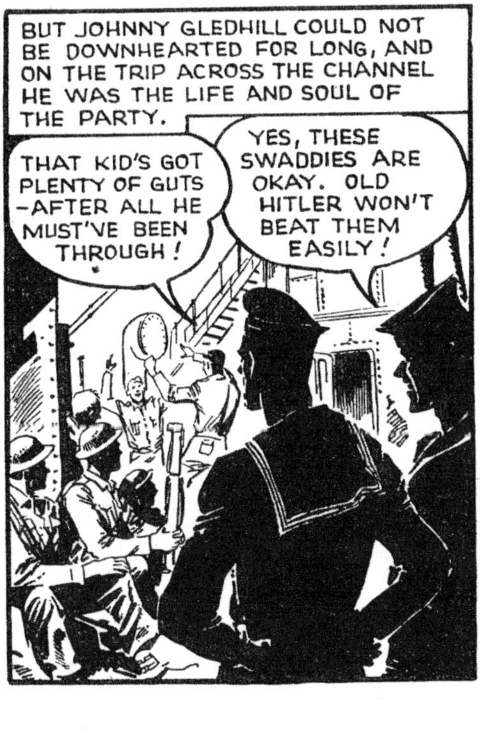
BUT JOHNNY GLEDHILL COULD NOT BE DOWNHEARTED FOR LONG, AND ON THE TRIP ACROSS THE CHANNEL HE WAS THE LIFE AND SOUL OF THE PARTY.
THAT KID'S GOT PLENTY OF GUTS -AFTER ALL HE MUST'VE BEEN THROUGH!
YES, THESE SWADDIES ARE OKAY. OLD HITLER WON'T BEAT THEM EASILY!

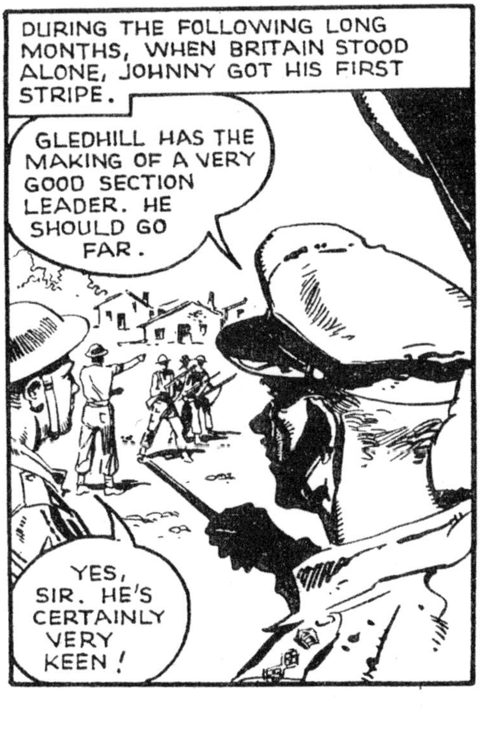
DURING THE FOLLOWING LONG MONTHS, WHEN BRITAIN STOOD ALONE, JOHNNY GOT HIS FIRST STRIPE.
GLEDHILL HAS THE MAKING OF A VERY GOOD SECTION LEADER. HE SHOULD GO FAR.
YES, SIR. HE'S CERTAINLY VERY KEEN!

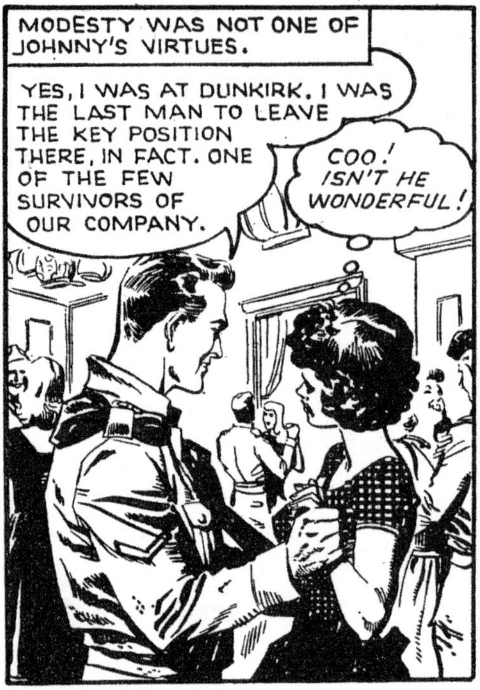
MODESTY WAS NOT ONE OF JOHNNY'S VIRTUES.
YES, I WAS AT DUNKIRK. I WAS THE LAST MAN TO LEAVE THE KEY POSITION THERE, IN FACT. ONE OF THE FEW SURVIVORS OF OUR COMPANY.
COO! ISN'T HE WONDERFUL!

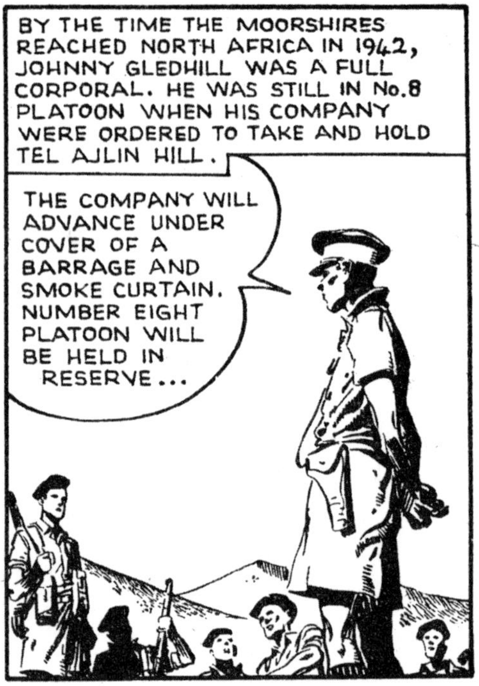
BY THE TIME THE MOORSHIRES REACHED NORTH AFRICA IN 1942, JOHNNY GLEDHILL WAS A FULL CORPORAL. HE WAS STILL IN No.8 PLATOON WHEN HIS COMPANY WERE ORDERED TO TAKE AND HOLD TEL AJLIN HILL.
THE COMPANY WILL ADVANCE UNDER COVER OF A BARRAGE AND SMOKE CURTAIN. NUMBER EIGHT PLATOON WILL BE HELD IN RESERVE...

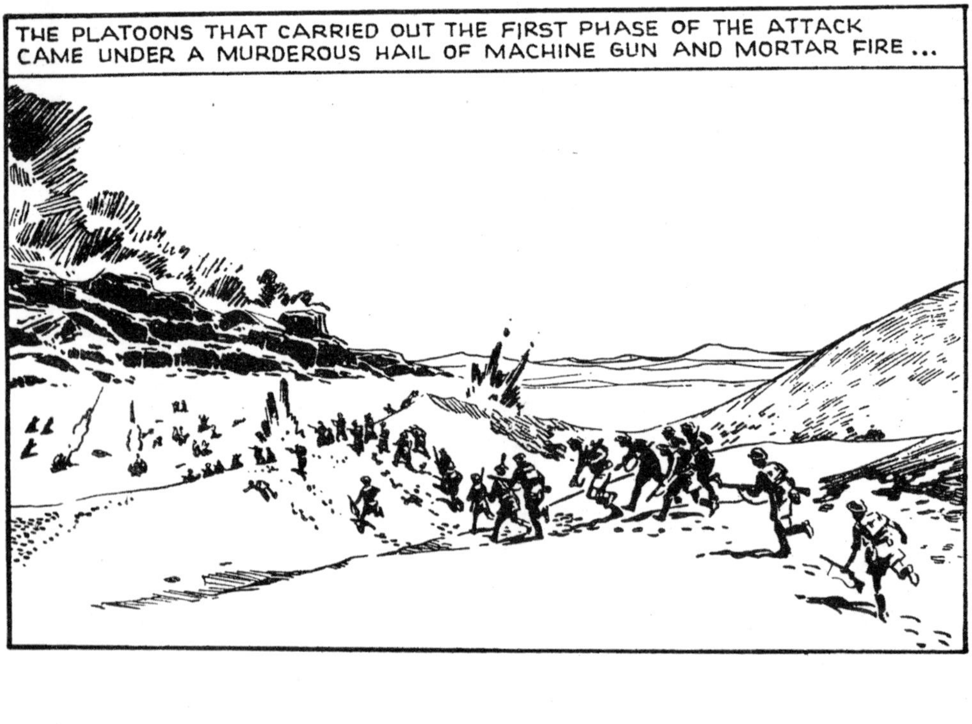
THE PLATOONS THAT CARRIED OUT THE FIRST PHASE OF THE ATTACK CAME UNDER A MURDEROUS HAIL OF MACHINE GUN AND MORTAR FIRE...

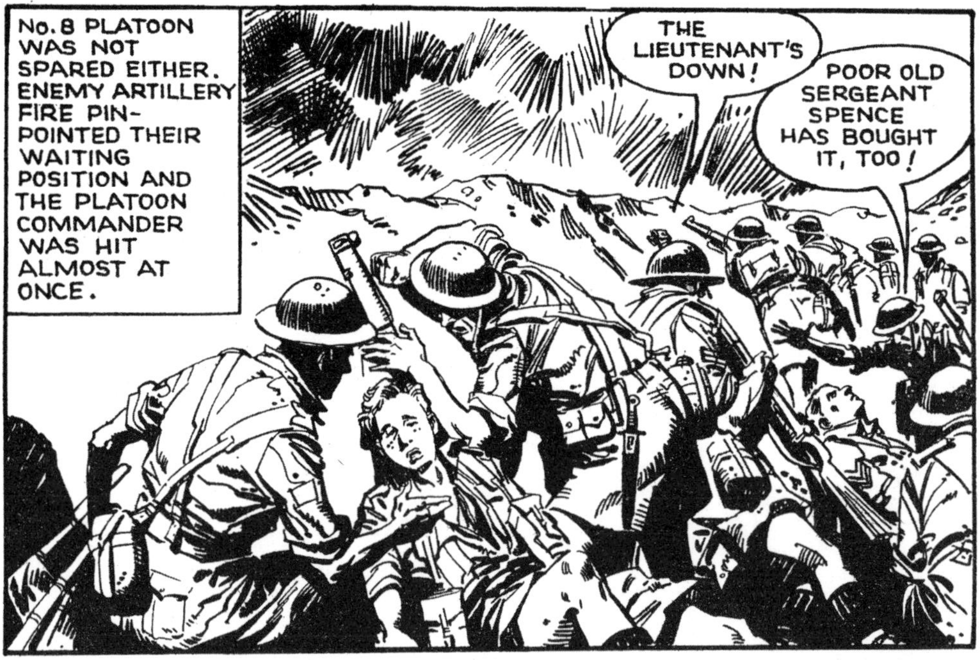
No. 8 PLATOON WAS NOT SPARED EITHER. ENEMY ARTILLERY FIRE PIN-POINTED THEIR WAITING POSITION AND THE PLATOON COMMANDER WAS HIT ALMOST AT ONCE.
THE LIEUTENANT'S DOWN!
POOR OLD SERGEANT SPENCE HAS BOUGHT IT, TOO!

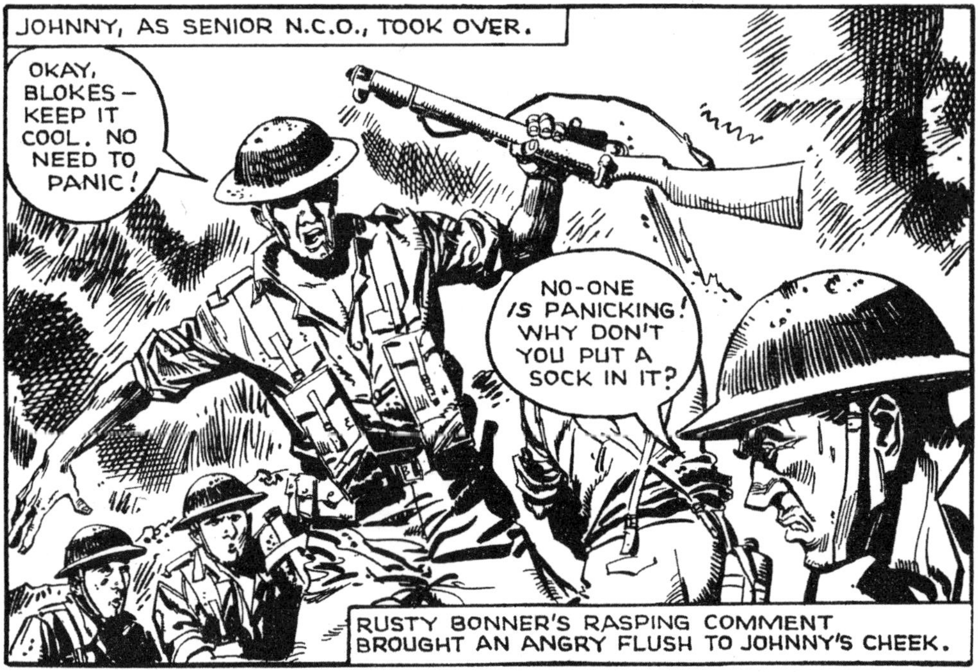
JOHNNY, AS SENIOR N.C.O., TOOK OVER.
OKAY, BLOKES – KEEP IT COOL. NO NEED TO PANIC!
NO-ONE *IS* PANICKING! WHY DON'T YOU PUT A SOCK IN IT?
RUSTY BONNER'S RASPING COMMENT BROUGHT AN ANGRY FLUSH TO JOHNNY'S CHEEK.

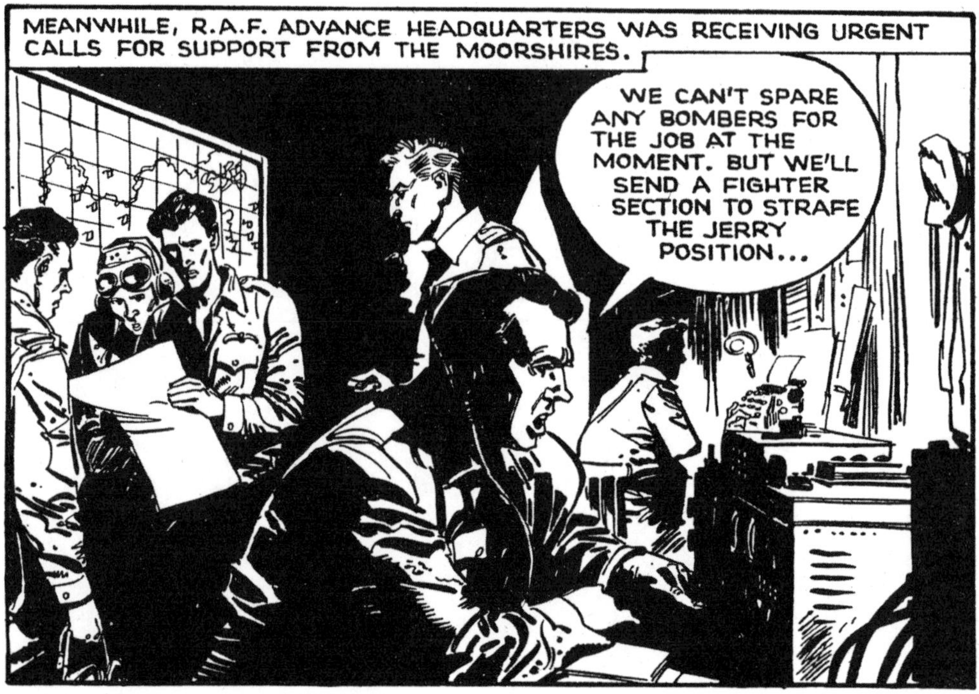
MEANWHILE, R.A.F. ADVANCE HEADQUARTERS WAS RECEIVING URGENT CALLS FOR SUPPORT FROM THE MOORSHIRES.
WE CAN'T SPARE ANY BOMBERS FOR THE JOB AT THE MOMENT. BUT WE'LL SEND A FIGHTER SECTION TO STRAFE THE JERRY POSITION...

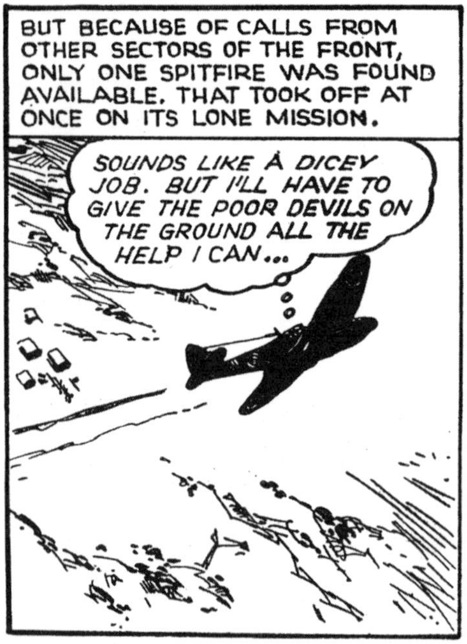
BUT BECAUSE OF CALLS FROM OTHER SECTORS OF THE FRONT, ONLY ONE SPITFIRE WAS FOUND AVAILABLE. THAT TOOK OFF AT ONCE ON ITS LONE MISSION.
SOUNDS LIKE A DICEY JOB. BUT I'LL HAVE TO GIVE THE POOR DEVILS ON THE GROUND ALL THE HELP I CAN...

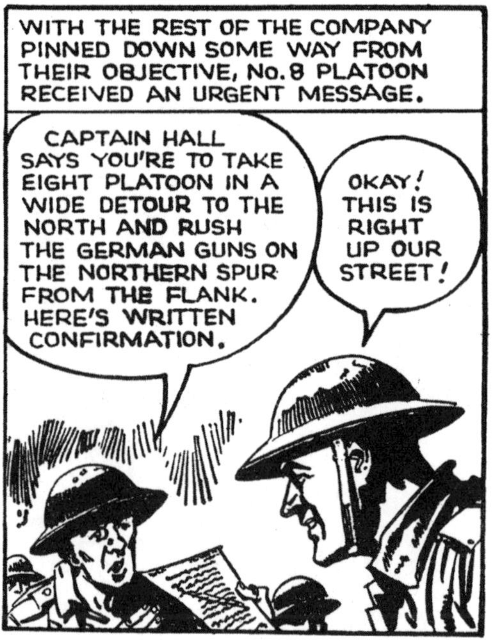
WITH THE REST OF THE COMPANY PINNED DOWN SOME WAY FROM THEIR OBJECTIVE, No. 8 PLATOON RECEIVED AN URGENT MESSAGE.
CAPTAIN HALL SAYS YOU'RE TO TAKE EIGHT PLATOON IN A WIDE DETOUR TO THE NORTH AND RUSH THE GERMAN GUNS ON THE NORTHERN SPUR FROM THE FLANK. HERE'S WRITTEN CONFIRMATION.
OKAY! THIS IS RIGHT UP OUR STREET!

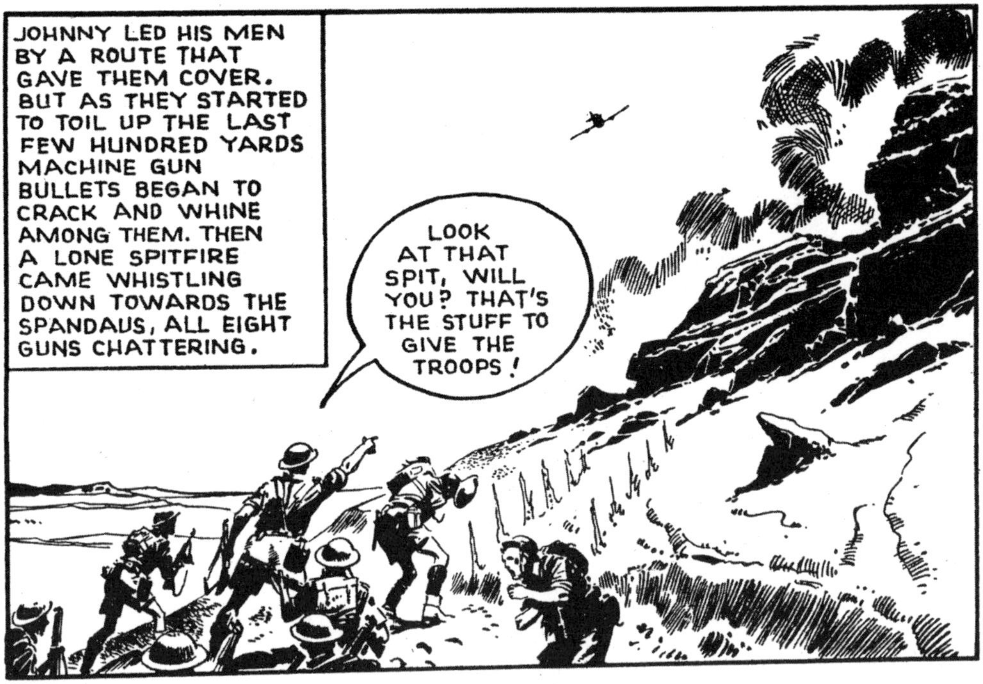
JOHNNY LED HIS MEN BY A ROUTE THAT GAVE THEM COVER. BUT AS THEY STARTED TO TOIL UP THE LAST FEW HUNDRED YARDS MACHINE GUN BULLETS BEGAN TO CRACK AND WHINE AMONG THEM. THEN A LONE SPITFIRE CAME WHISTLING DOWN TOWARDS THE SPANDAUS, ALL EIGHT GUNS CHATTERING.
LOOK AT THAT SPIT, WILL YOU? THAT'S THE STUFF TO GIVE THE TROOPS!

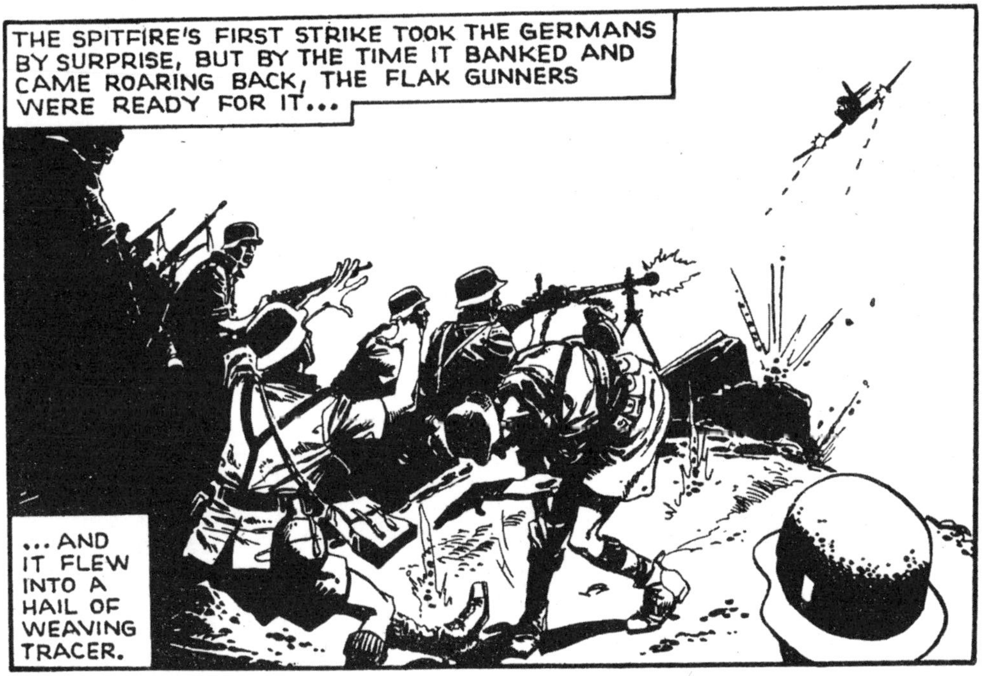
THE SPITFIRE'S FIRST STRIKE TOOK THE GERMANS BY SURPRISE, BUT BY THE TIME IT BANKED AND CAME ROARING BACK, THE FLAK GUNNERS WERE READY FOR IT...
... AND IT FLEW INTO A HAIL OF WEAVING TRACER.

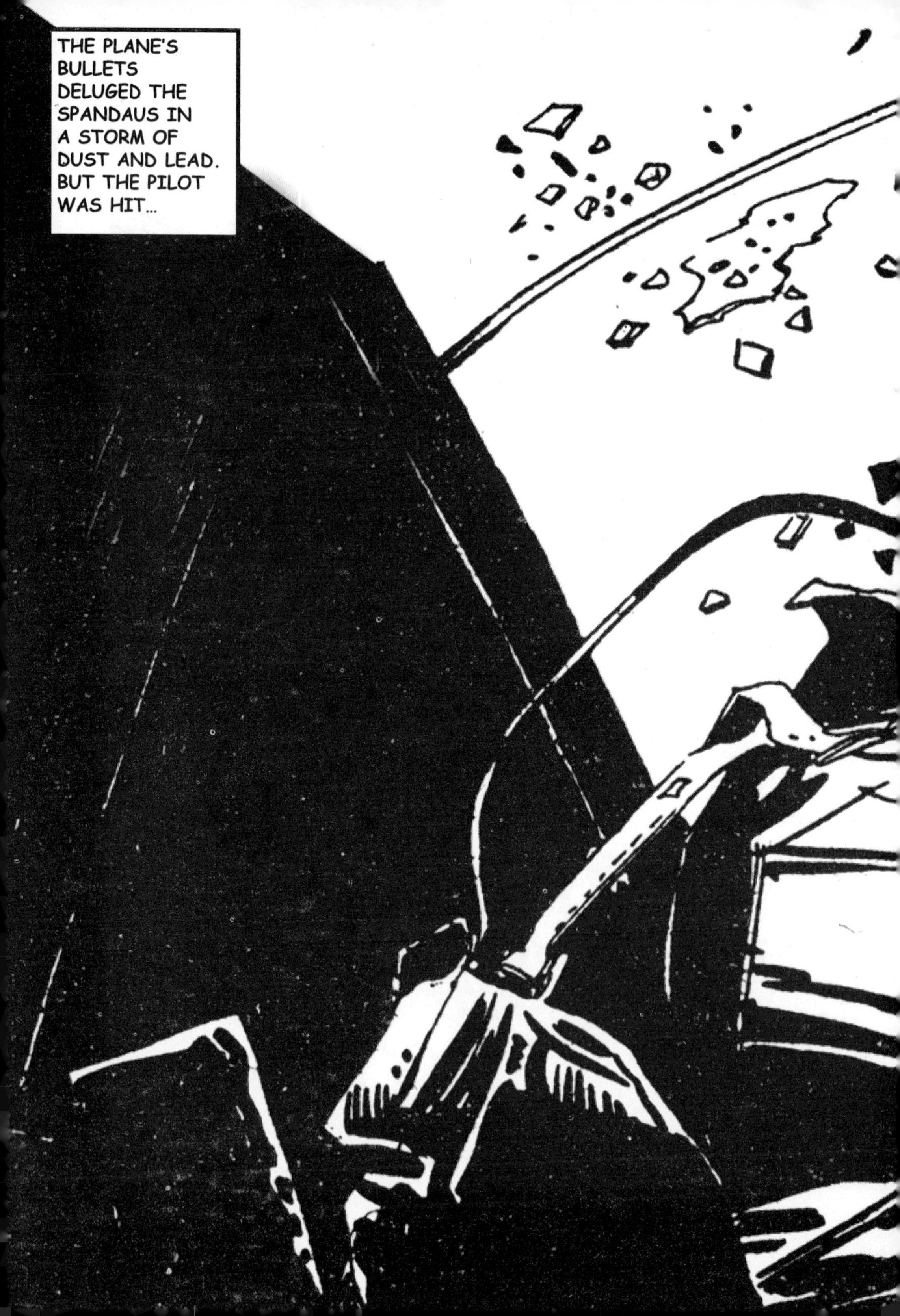
THE PLANE'S BULLETS DELUGED THE SPANDAUS IN A STORM OF DUST AND LEAD. BUT THE PILOT WAS HIT...

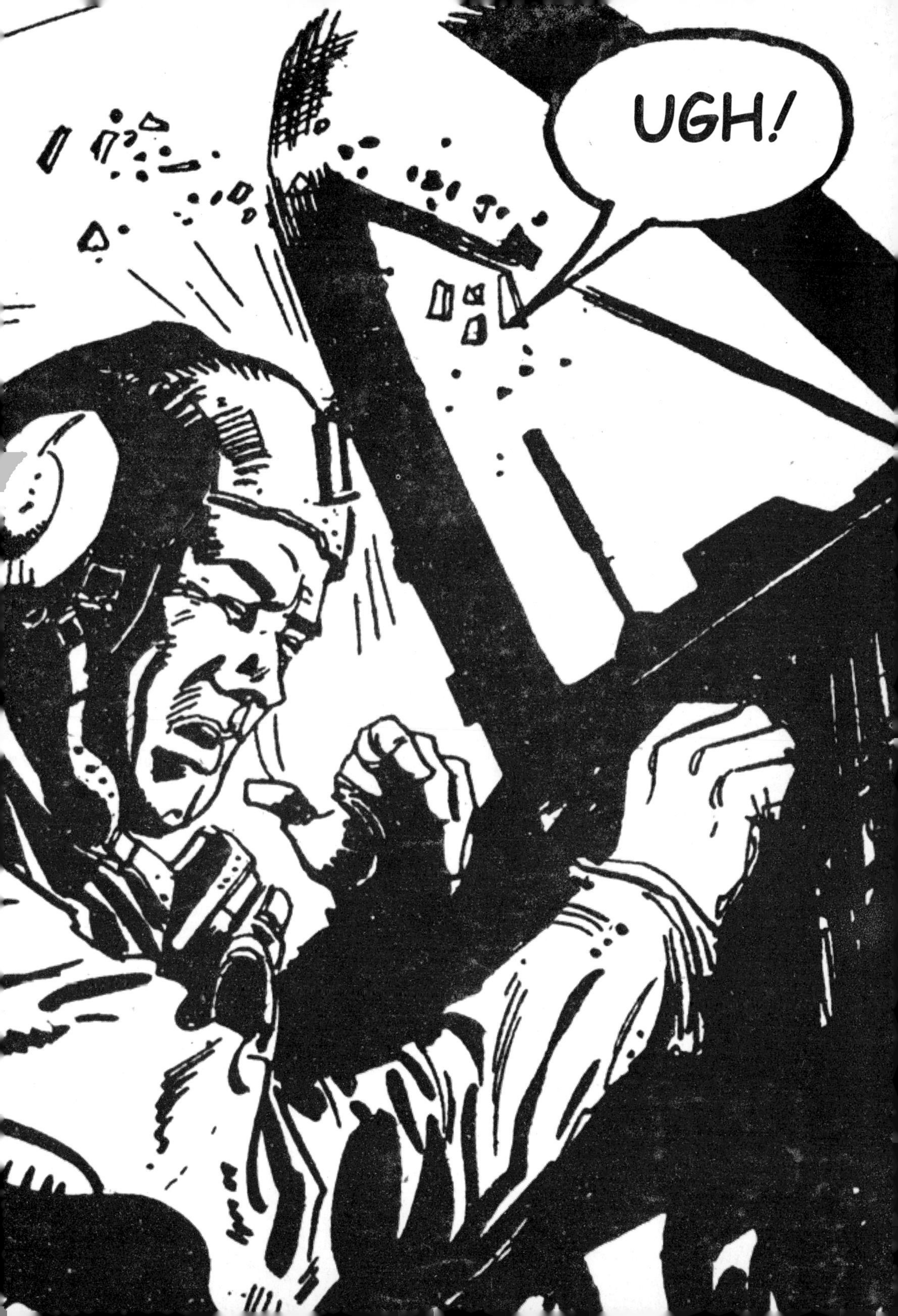
UGH!

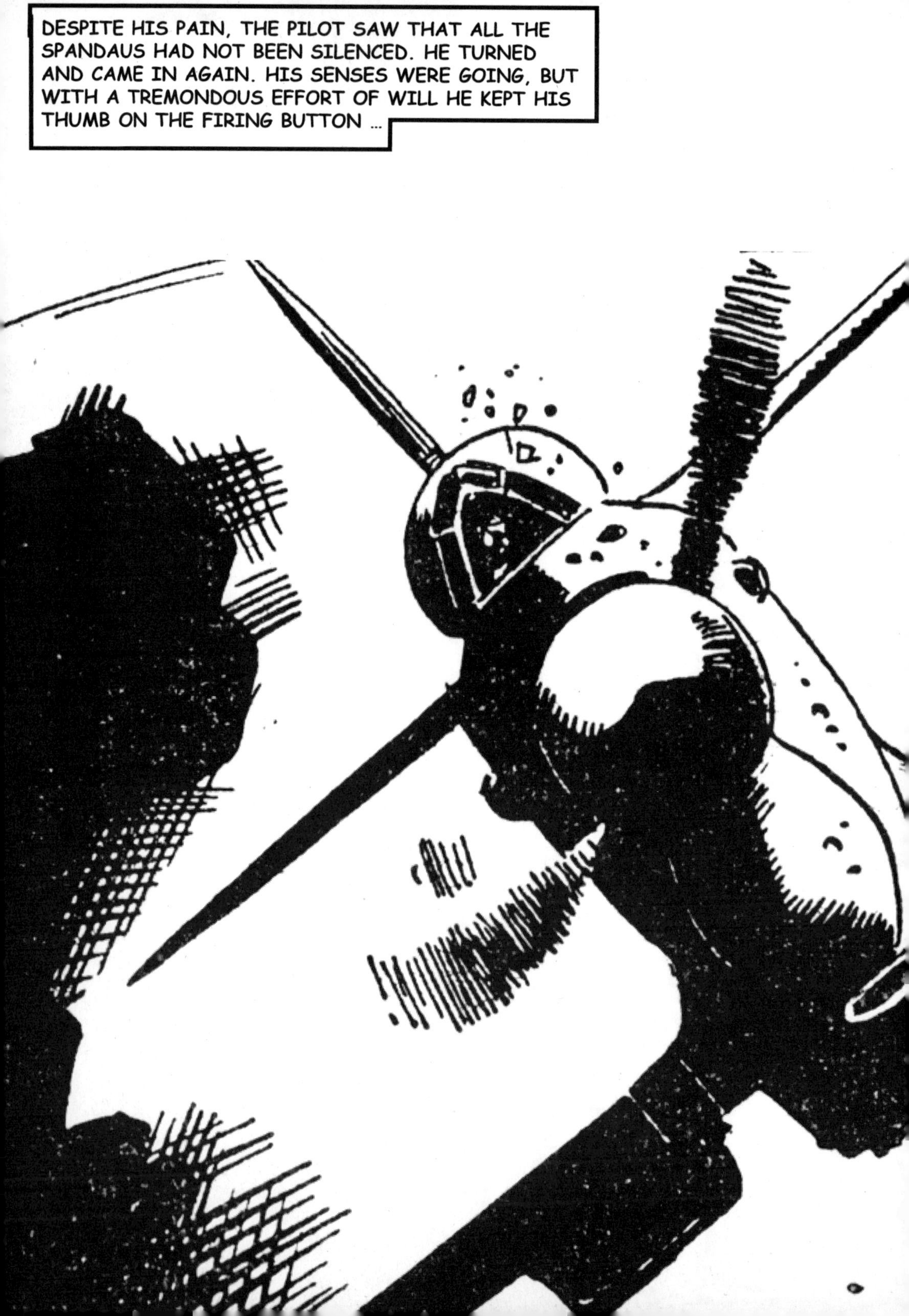
DESPITE HIS PAIN, THE PILOT SAW THAT ALL THE SPANDAUS HAD NOT BEEN SILENCED. HE TURNED AND CAME IN AGAIN. HIS SENSES WERE GOING, BUT WITH A TREMONDOUS EFFORT OF WILL HE KEPT HIS THUMB ON THE FIRING BUTTON ...

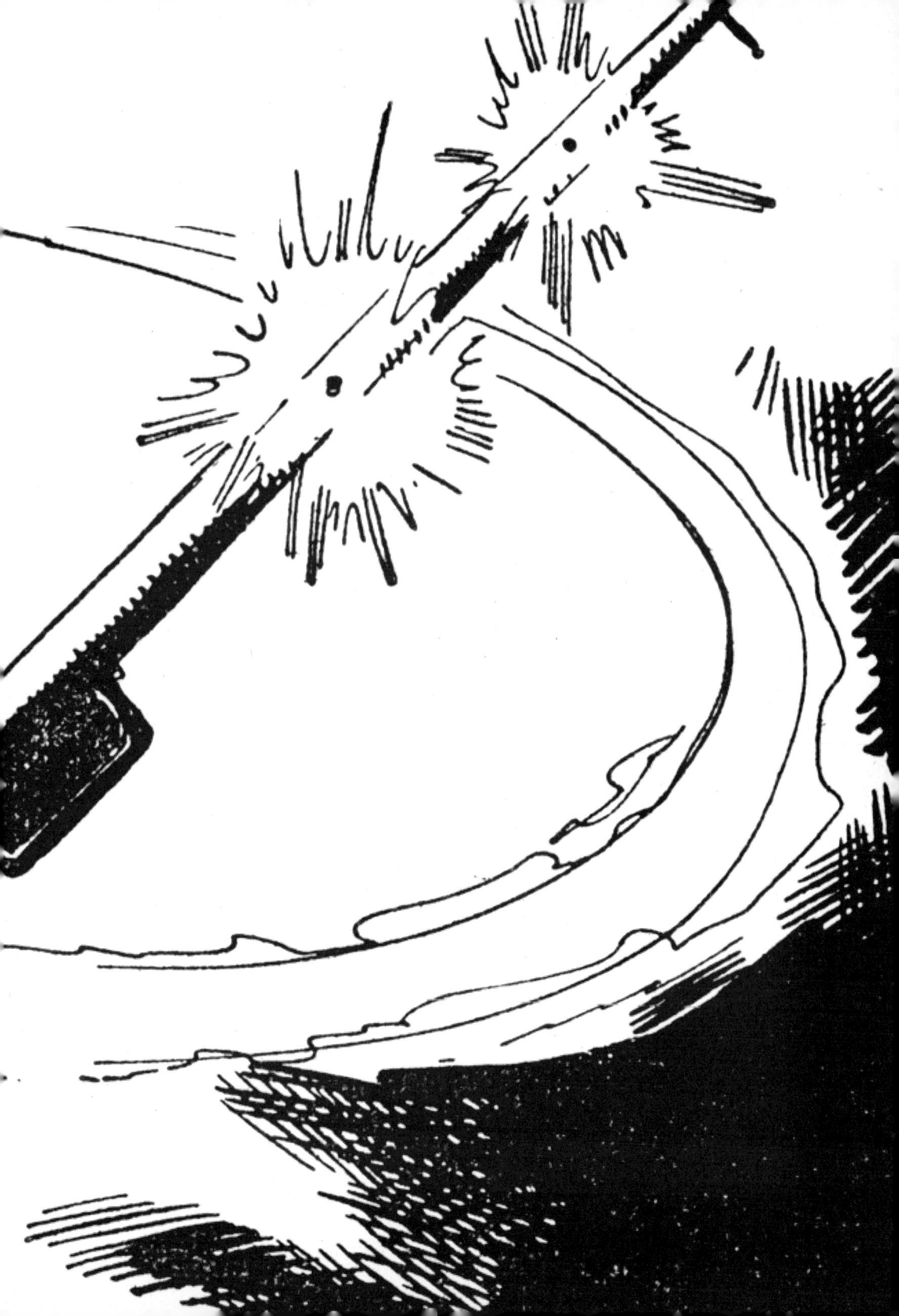

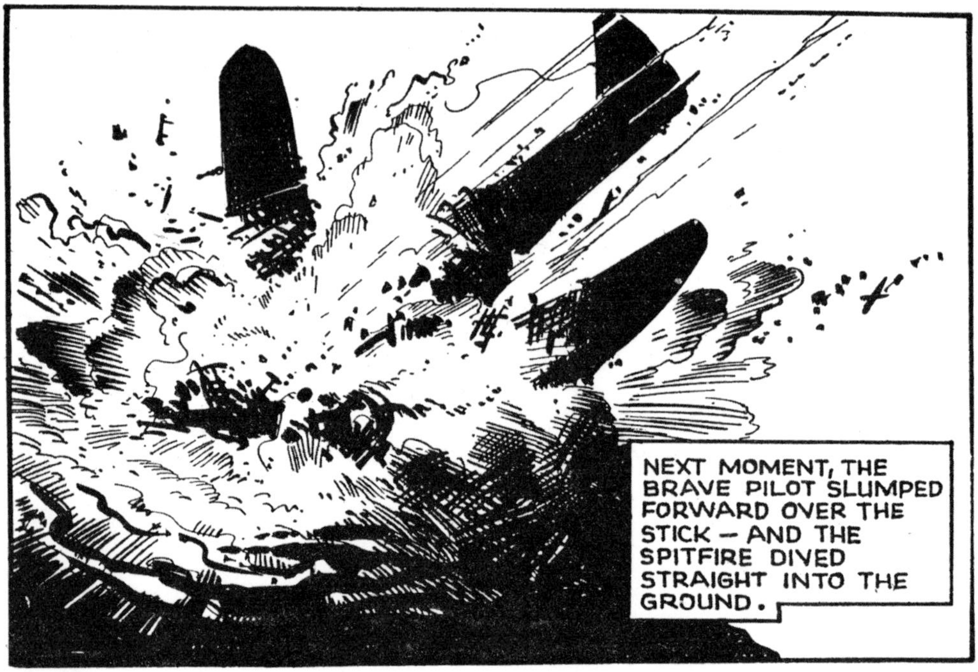
NEXT MOMENT, THE BRAVE PILOT SLUMPED FORWARD OVER THE STICK – AND THE SPITFIRE DIVED STRAIGHT INTO THE GROUND.

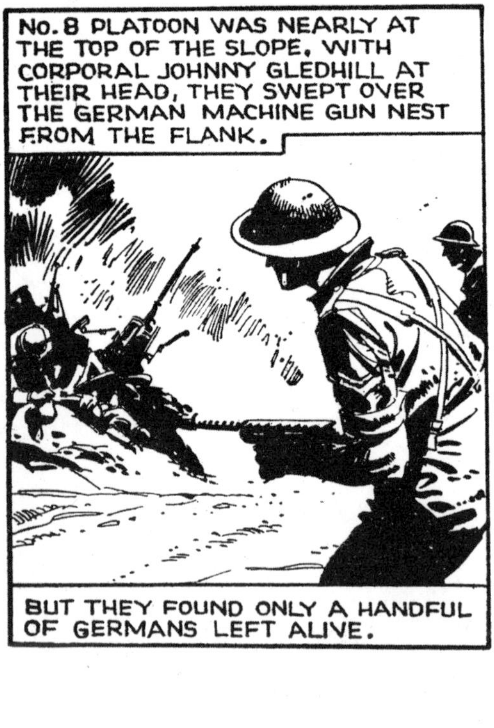
No. 8 PLATOON WAS NEARLY AT THE TOP OF THE SLOPE. WITH CORPORAL JOHNNY GLEDHILL AT THEIR HEAD, THEY SWEPT OVER THE GERMAN MACHINE GUN NEST FROM THE FLANK.
BUT THEY FOUND ONLY A HANDFUL OF GERMANS LEFT ALIVE.

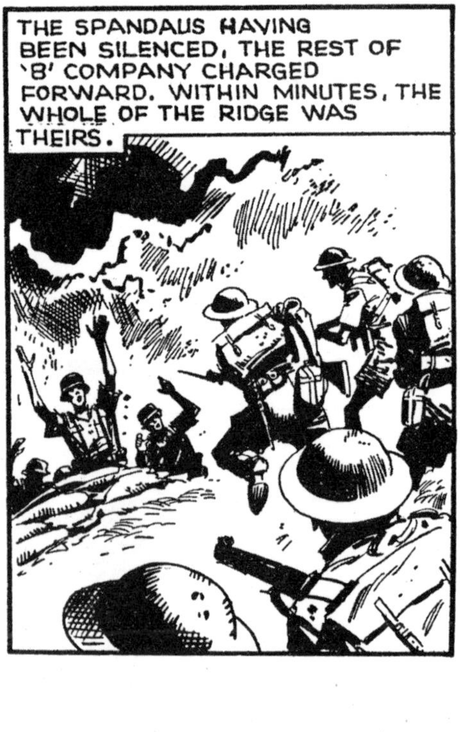
THE SPANDAUS HAVING BEEN SILENCED, THE REST OF 'B' COMPANY CHARGED FORWARD. WITHIN MINUTES, THE WHOLE OF THE RIDGE WAS THEIRS.

Chapter 2. Easy Street

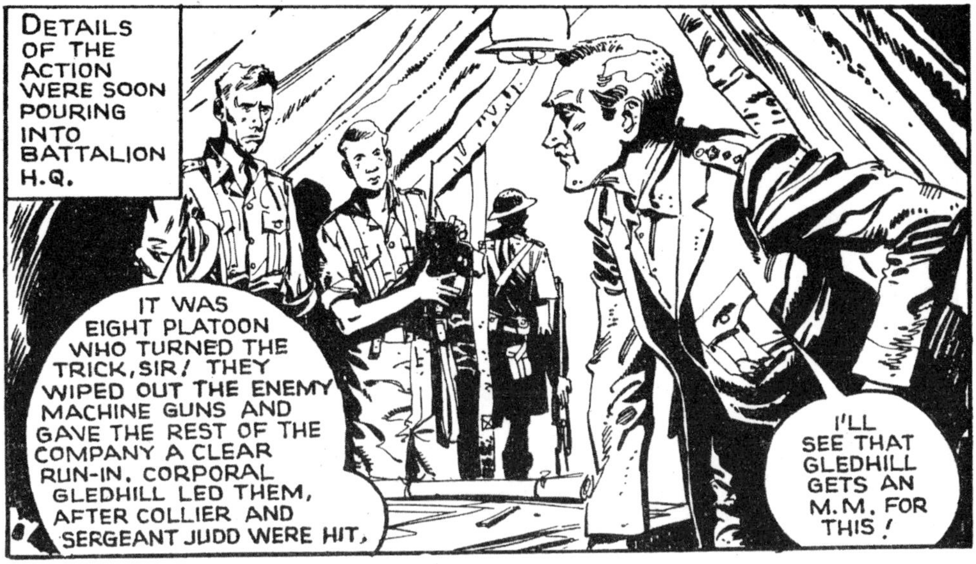
DETAILS OF THE ACTION WERE SOON POURING INTO BATTALION H.Q.
IT WAS EIGHT PLATOON WHO TURNED THE TRICK, SIR! THEY WIPED OUT THE ENEMY MACHINE GUNS AND GAVE THE REST OF THE COMPANY A CLEAR RUN-IN. CORPORAL GLEDHILL LED THEM, AFTER COLLIER AND SERGEANT JUDD WERE HIT.
I'LL SEE THAT GLEDHILL GETS AN M.M. FOR THIS!

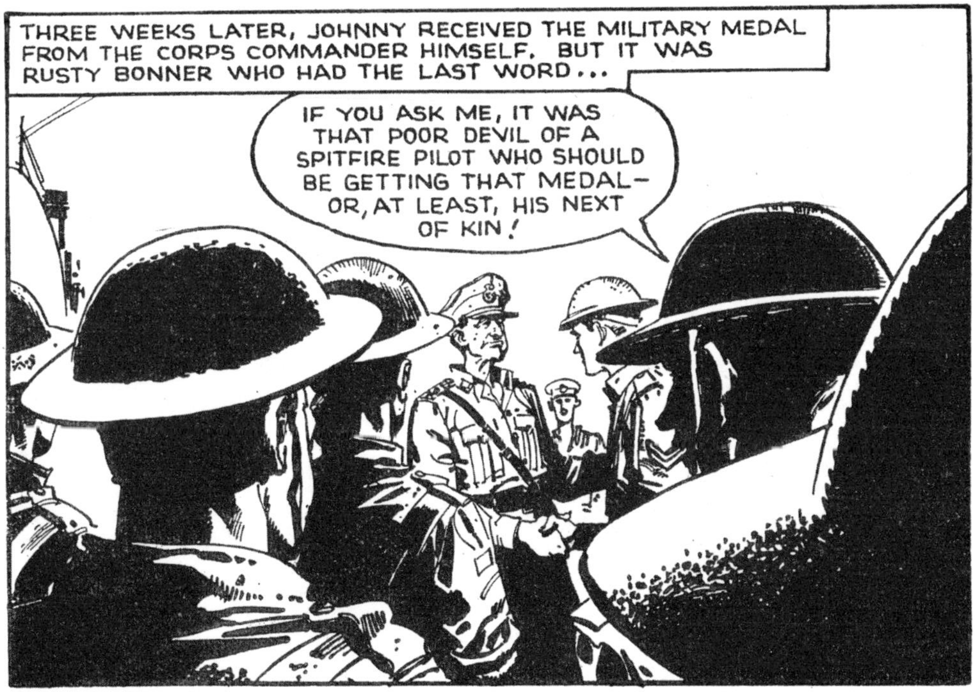
THREE WEEKS LATER, JOHNNY RECEIVED THE MILITARY MEDAL FROM THE CORPS COMMANDER HIMSELF. BUT IT WAS RUSTY BONNER WHO HAD THE LAST WORD...
IF YOU ASK ME, IT WAS THAT POOR DEVIL OF A SPITFIRE PILOT WHO SHOULD BE GETTING THAT MEDAL— OR, AT LEAST, HIS NEXT OF KIN!

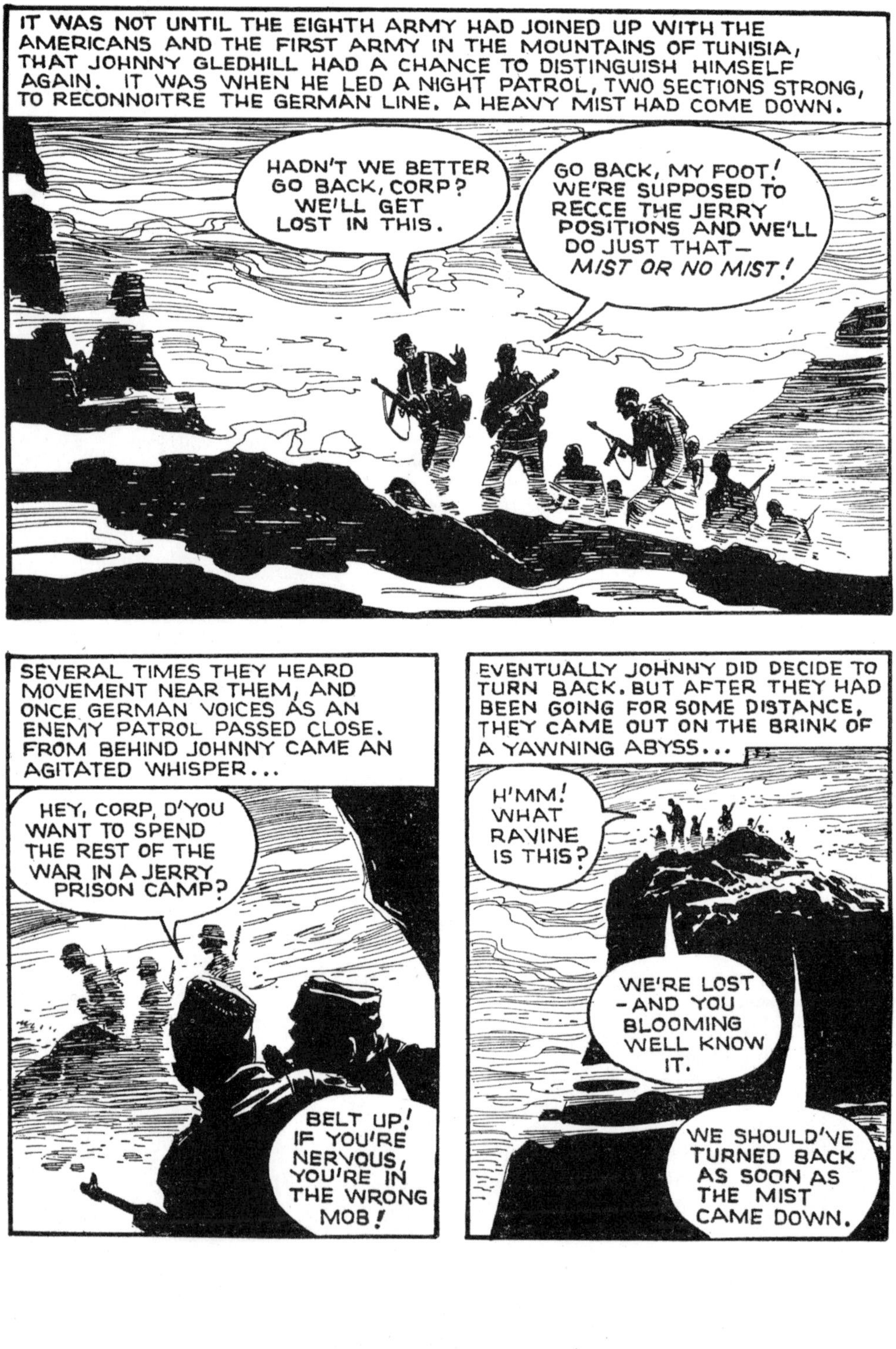
IT WAS NOT UNTIL THE EIGHTH ARMY HAD JOINED UP WITH THE AMERICANS AND THE FIRST ARMY IN THE MOUNTAINS OF TUNISIA, THAT JOHNNY GLEDHILL HAD A CHANCE TO DISTINGUISH HIMSELF AGAIN. IT WAS WHEN HE LED A NIGHT PATROL, TWO SECTIONS STRONG, TO RECONNOITRE THE GERMAN LINE. A HEAVY MIST HAD COME DOWN.
HADN'T WE BETTER GO BACK, CORP? WE'LL GET LOST IN THIS.
GO BACK, MY FOOT! WE'RE SUPPOSED TO RECCE THE JERRY POSITIONS AND WE'LL DO JUST THAT— *MIST OR NO MIST!*
SEVERAL TIMES THEY HEARD MOVEMENT NEAR THEM, AND ONCE GERMAN VOICES AS AN ENEMY PATROL PASSED CLOSE. FROM BEHIND JOHNNY CAME AN AGITATED WHISPER...
HEY, CORP, D'YOU WANT TO SPEND THE REST OF THE WAR IN A JERRY PRISON CAMP?
BELT UP! IF YOU'RE NERVOUS, YOU'RE IN THE WRONG MOB!
EVENTUALLY JOHNNY DID DECIDE TO TURN BACK. BUT AFTER THEY HAD BEEN GOING FOR SOME DISTANCE, THEY CAME OUT ON THE BRINK OF A YAWNING ABYSS...
H'MM! WHAT RAVINE IS THIS?
WE'RE LOST -AND YOU BLOOMING WELL KNOW IT.
WE SHOULD'VE TURNED BACK AS SOON AS THE MIST CAME DOWN.

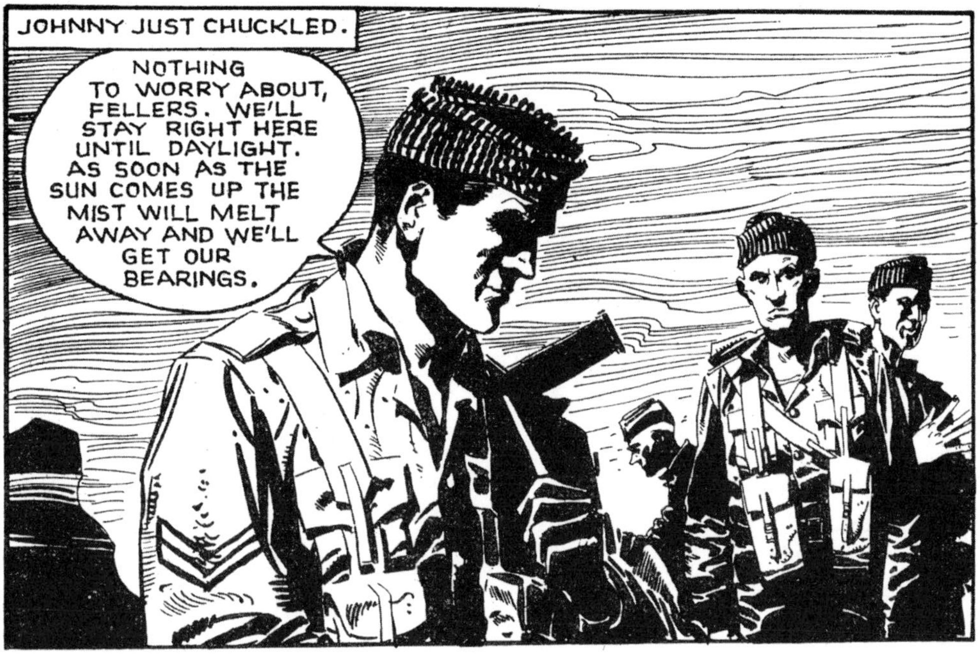
JOHNNY JUST CHUCKLED.
NOTHING TO WORRY ABOUT, FELLERS. WE'LL STAY RIGHT HERE UNTIL DAYLIGHT. AS SOON AS THE SUN COMES UP THE MIST WILL MELT AWAY AND WE'LL GET OUR BEARINGS.

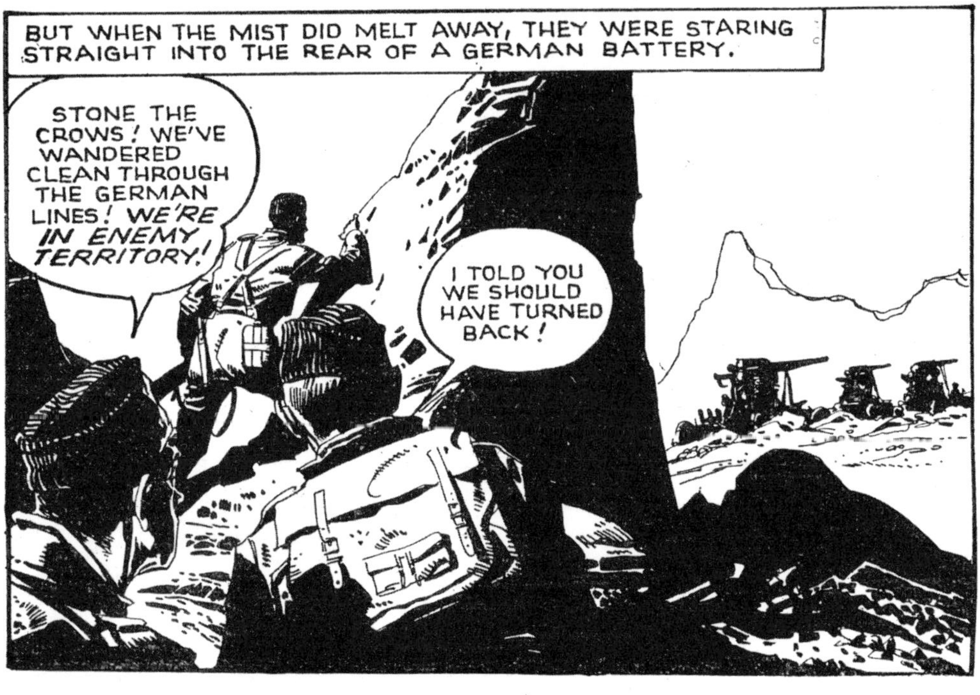
BUT WHEN THE MIST DID MELT AWAY, THEY WERE STARING STRAIGHT INTO THE REAR OF A GERMAN BATTERY.
STONE THE CROWS! WE'VE WANDERED CLEAN THROUGH THE GERMAN LINES! WE'RE IN ENEMY TERRITORY!
I TOLD YOU WE SHOULD HAVE TURNED BACK!

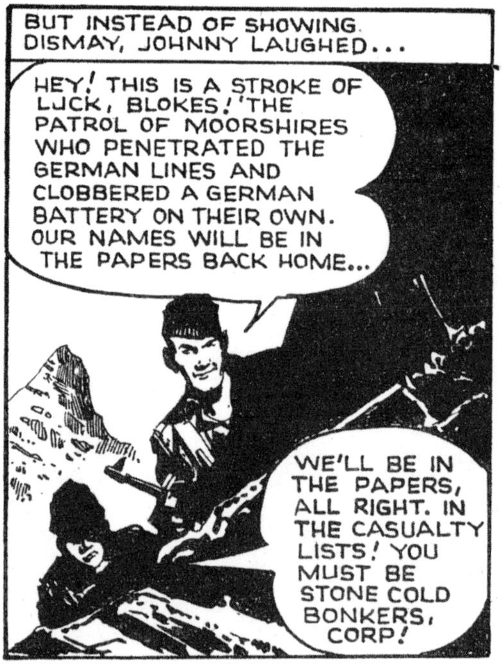
BUT INSTEAD OF SHOWING DISMAY, JOHNNY LAUGHED...
HEY! THIS IS A STROKE OF LUCK, BLOKES! 'THE PATROL OF MOORSHIRES WHO PENETRATED THE GERMAN LINES AND CLOBBERED A GERMAN BATTERY ON THEIR OWN. OUR NAMES WILL BE IN THE PAPERS BACK HOME...
WE'LL BE IN THE PAPERS, ALL RIGHT. IN THE CASUALTY LISTS! YOU MUST BE STONE COLD BONKERS, CORP!

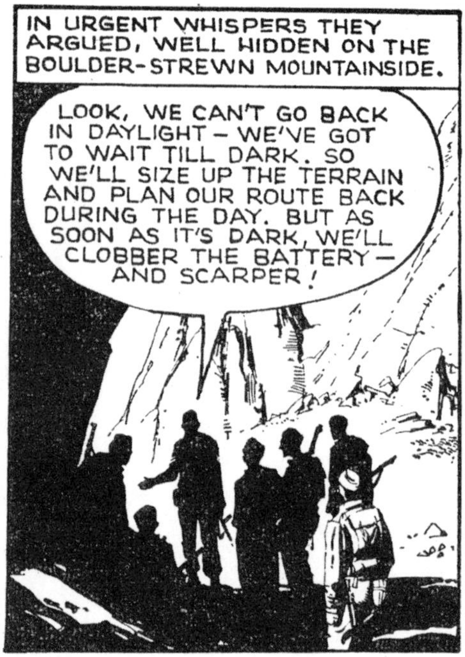
IN URGENT WHISPERS THEY ARGUED, WELL HIDDEN ON THE BOULDER-STREWN MOUNTAINSIDE.
LOOK, WE CAN'T GO BACK IN DAYLIGHT – WE'VE GOT TO WAIT TILL DARK. SO WE'LL SIZE UP THE TERRAIN AND PLAN OUR ROUTE BACK DURING THE DAY. BUT AS SOON AS IT'S DARK, WE'LL CLOBBER THE BATTERY – AND SCARPER!

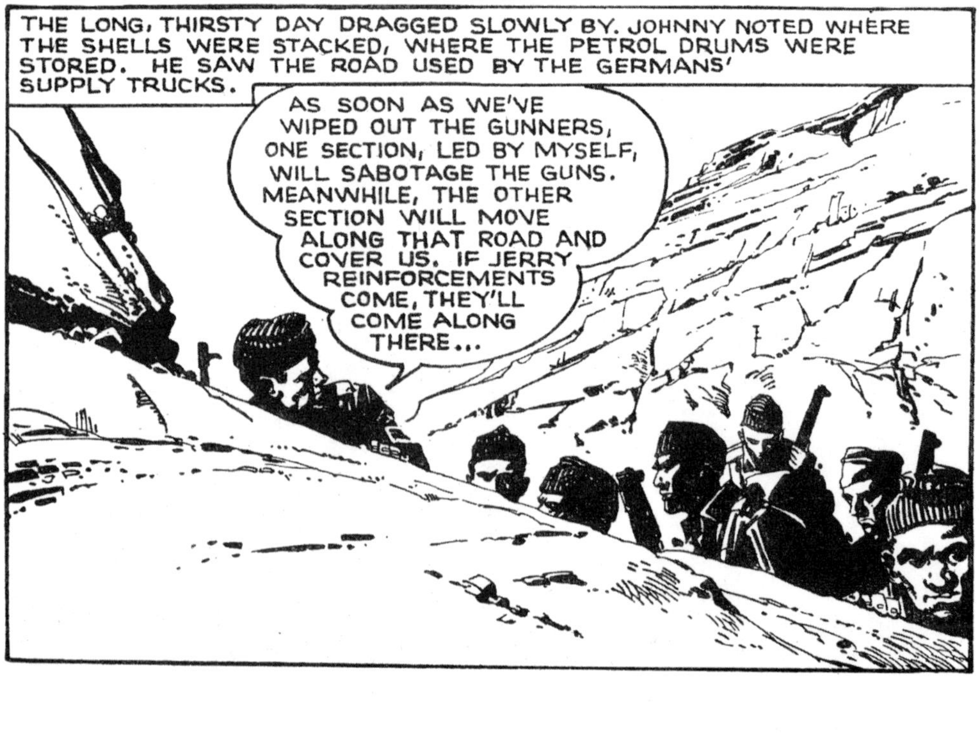
THE LONG, THIRSTY DAY DRAGGED SLOWLY BY. JOHNNY NOTED WHERE THE SHELLS WERE STACKED, WHERE THE PETROL DRUMS WERE STORED. HE SAW THE ROAD USED BY THE GERMANS' SUPPLY TRUCKS.
AS SOON AS WE'VE WIPED OUT THE GUNNERS, ONE SECTION, LED BY MYSELF, WILL SABOTAGE THE GUNS. MEANWHILE, THE OTHER SECTION WILL MOVE ALONG THAT ROAD AND COVER US. IF JERRY REINFORCEMENTS COME, THEY'LL COME ALONG THERE...

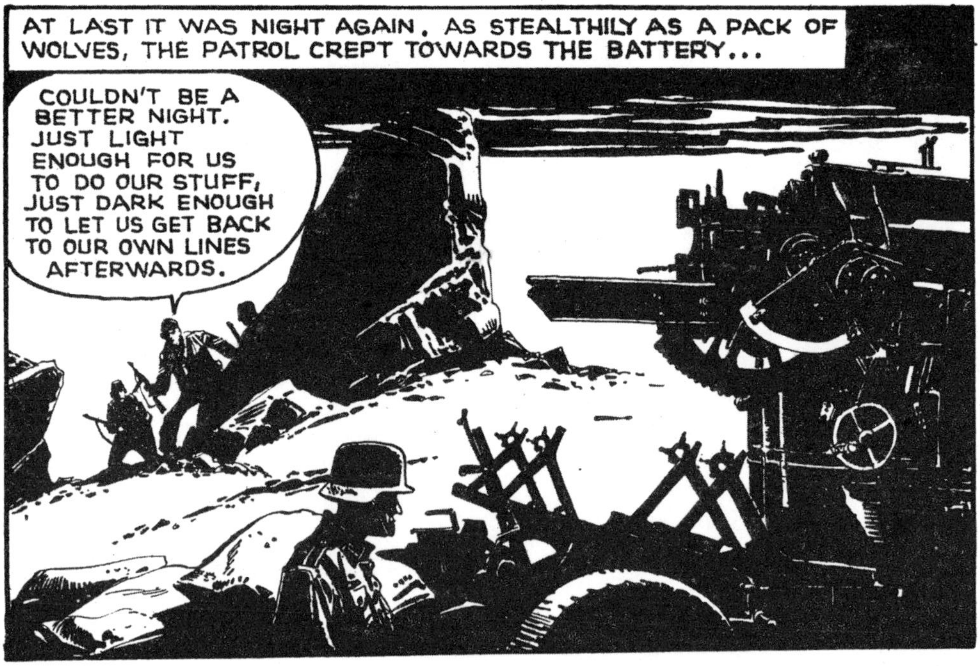
AT LAST IT WAS NIGHT AGAIN. AS STEALTHILY AS A PACK OF WOLVES, THE PATROL CREPT TOWARDS THE BATTERY...
COULDN'T BE A BETTER NIGHT. JUST LIGHT ENOUGH FOR US TO DO OUR STUFF, JUST DARK ENOUGH TO LET US GET BACK TO OUR OWN LINES AFTERWARDS.

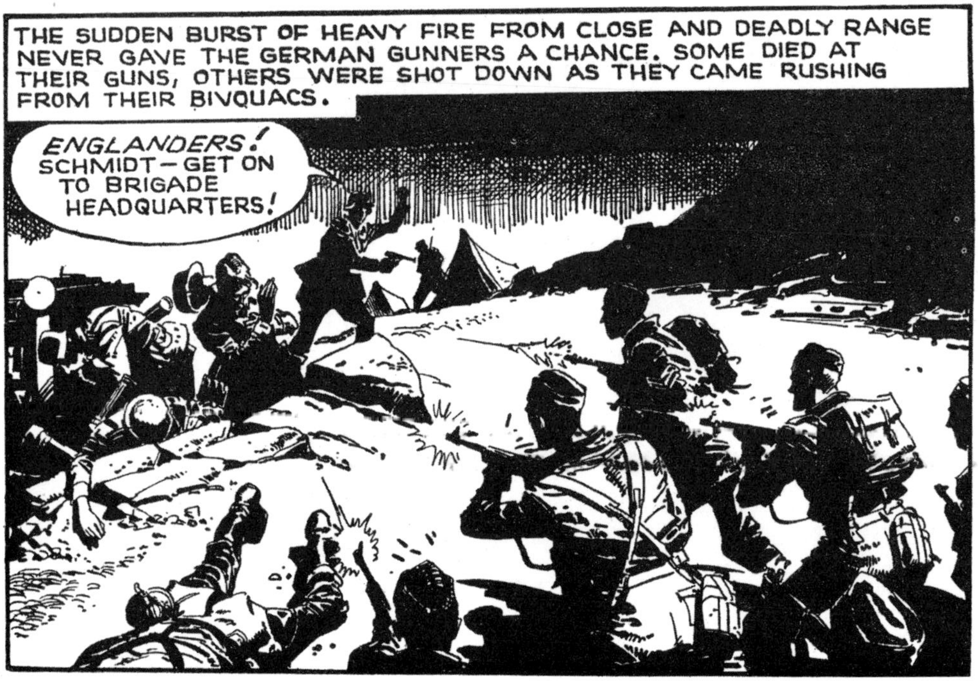
THE SUDDEN BURST OF HEAVY FIRE FROM CLOSE AND DEADLY RANGE NEVER GAVE THE GERMAN GUNNERS A CHANCE. SOME DIED AT THEIR GUNS, OTHERS WERE SHOT DOWN AS THEY CAME RUSHING FROM THEIR BIVOUACS.
ENGLANDERS! SCHMIDT—GET ON TO BRIGADE HEADQUARTERS!

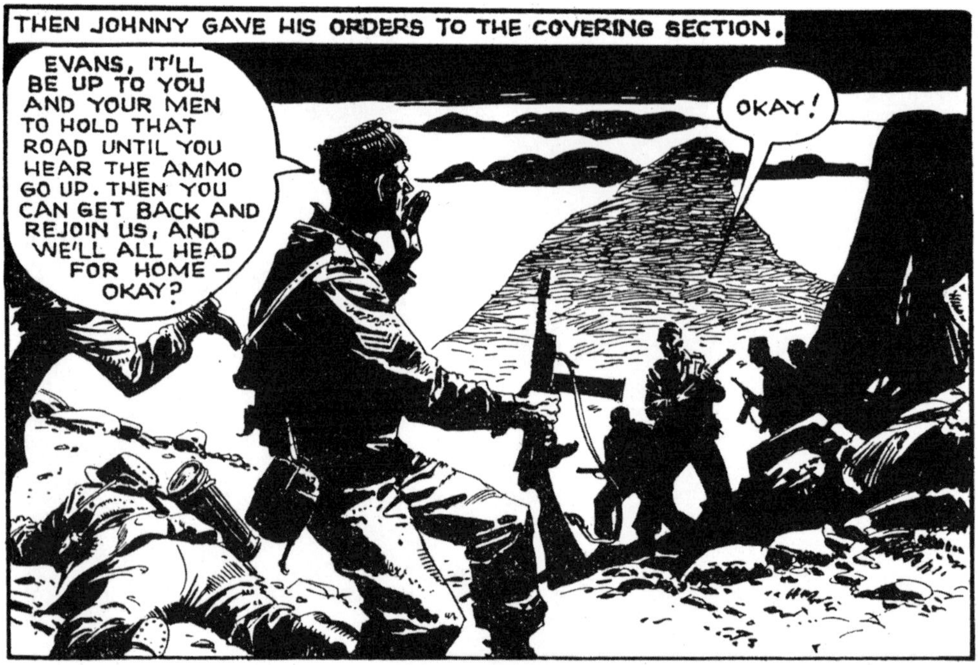
THEN JOHNNY GAVE HIS ORDERS TO THE COVERING SECTION.
EVANS, IT'LL BE UP TO YOU AND YOUR MEN TO HOLD THAT ROAD UNTIL YOU HEAR THE AMMO GO UP. THEN YOU CAN GET BACK AND REJOIN US, AND WE'LL ALL HEAD FOR HOME – OKAY?
OKAY!

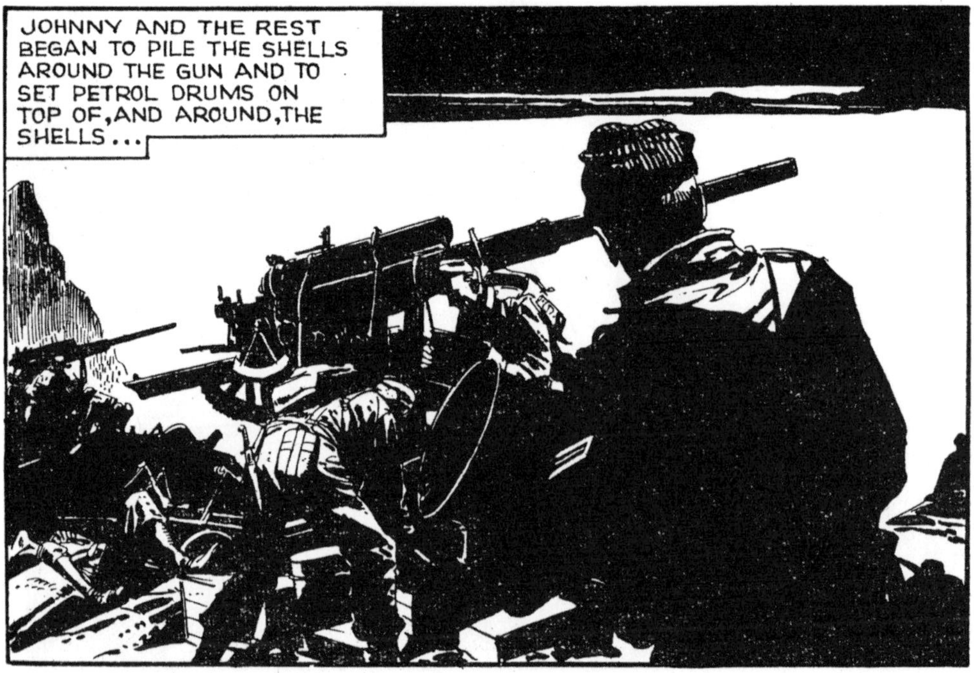
JOHNNY AND THE REST BEGAN TO PILE THE SHELLS AROUND THE GUN AND TO SET PETROL DRUMS ON TOP OF, AND AROUND, THE SHELLS...

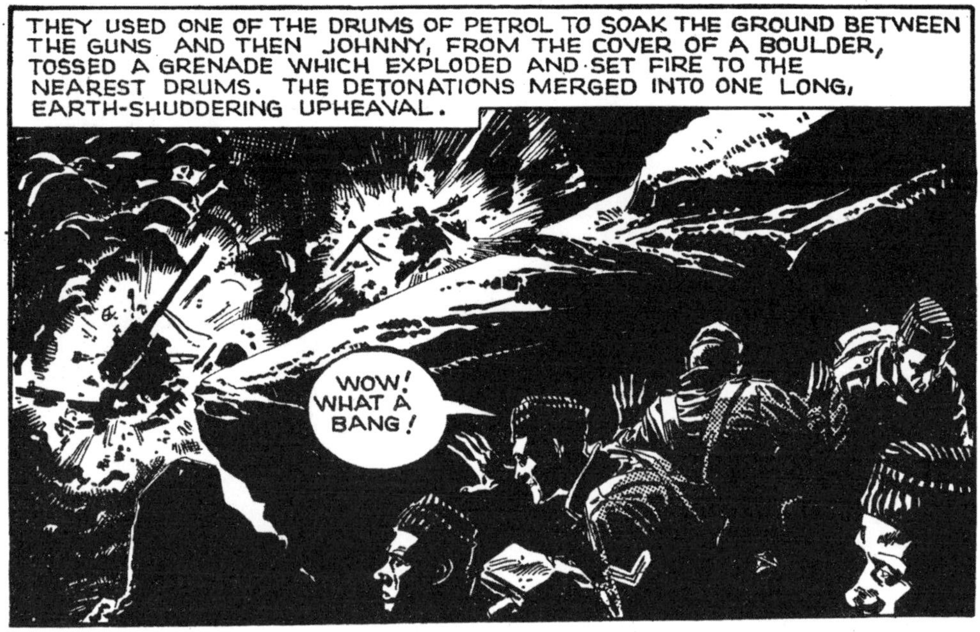
THEY USED ONE OF THE DRUMS OF PETROL TO SOAK THE GROUND BETWEEN THE GUNS AND THEN JOHNNY, FROM THE COVER OF A BOULDER, TOSSED A GRENADE WHICH EXPLODED AND SET FIRE TO THE NEAREST DRUMS. THE DETONATIONS MERGED INTO ONE LONG, EARTH-SHUDDERING UPHEAVAL.
WOW! WHAT A BANG!

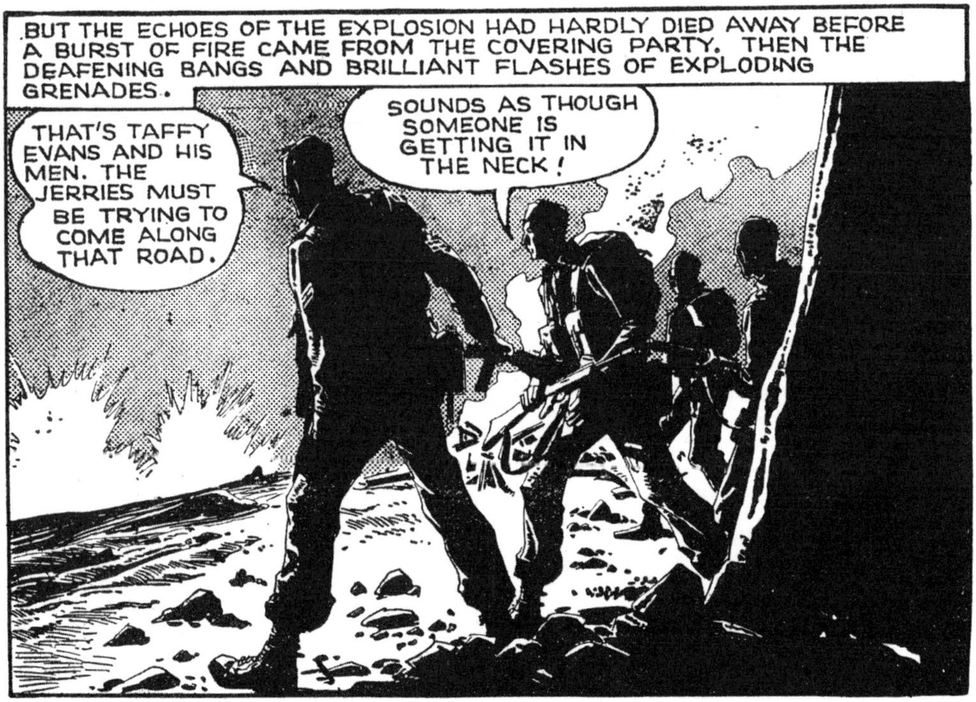
BUT THE ECHOES OF THE EXPLOSION HAD HARDLY DIED AWAY BEFORE A BURST OF FIRE CAME FROM THE COVERING PARTY. THEN THE DEAFENING BANGS AND BRILLIANT FLASHES OF EXPLODING GRENADES.
THAT'S TAFFY EVANS AND HIS MEN. THE JERRIES MUST BE TRYING TO COME ALONG THAT ROAD.
SOUNDS AS THOUGH SOMEONE IS GETTING IT IN THE NECK!

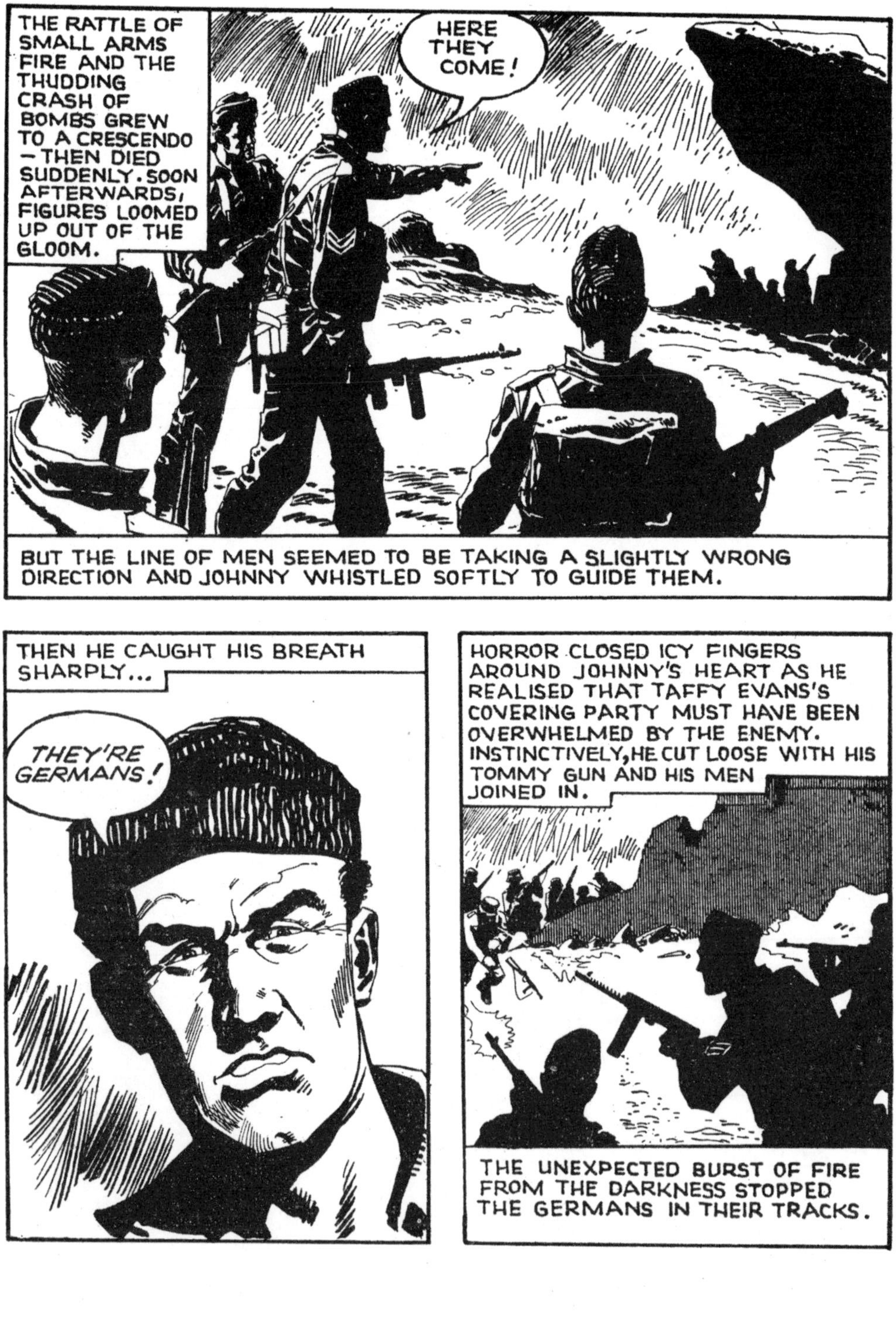
THE RATTLE OF SMALL ARMS FIRE AND THE THUDDING CRASH OF BOMBS GREW TO A CRESCENDO —THEN DIED SUDDENLY. SOON AFTERWARDS, FIGURES LOOMED UP OUT OF THE GLOOM.
HERE THEY COME!
BUT THE LINE OF MEN SEEMED TO BE TAKING A SLIGHTLY WRONG DIRECTION AND JOHNNY WHISTLED SOFTLY TO GUIDE THEM.
THEN HE CAUGHT HIS BREATH SHARPLY...
THEY'RE GERMANS!
HORROR CLOSED ICY FINGERS AROUND JOHNNY'S HEART AS HE REALISED THAT TAFFY EVANS'S COVERING PARTY MUST HAVE BEEN OVERWHELMED BY THE ENEMY. INSTINCTIVELY, HE CUT LOOSE WITH HIS TOMMY GUN AND HIS MEN JOINED IN.
THE UNEXPECTED BURST OF FIRE FROM THE DARKNESS STOPPED THE GERMANS IN THEIR TRACKS.

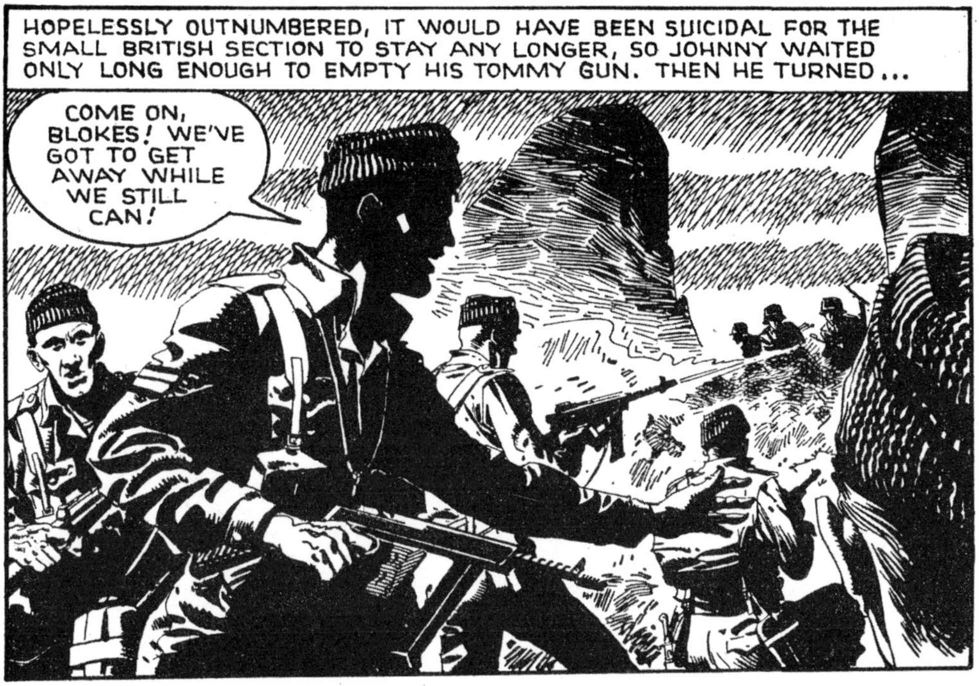
HOPELESSLY OUTNUMBERED, IT WOULD HAVE BEEN SUICIDAL FOR THE SMALL BRITISH SECTION TO STAY ANY LONGER, SO JOHNNY WAITED ONLY LONG ENOUGH TO EMPTY HIS TOMMY GUN. THEN HE TURNED...
COME ON, BLOKES! WE'VE GOT TO GET AWAY WHILE WE STILL CAN!

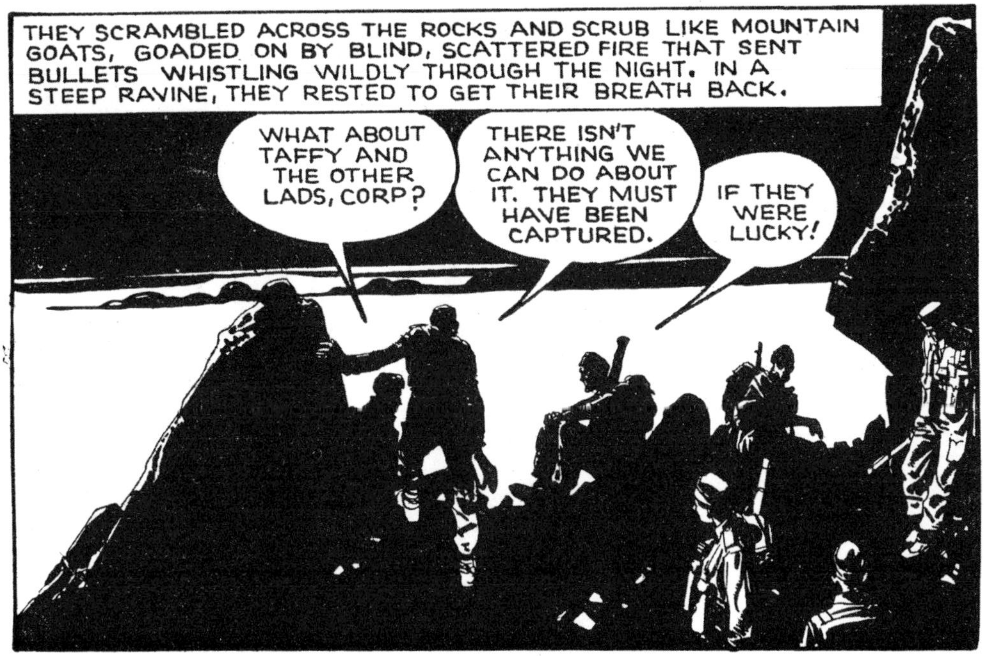
THEY SCRAMBLED ACROSS THE ROCKS AND SCRUB LIKE MOUNTAIN GOATS, GOADED ON BY BLIND, SCATTERED FIRE THAT SENT BULLETS WHISTLING WILDLY THROUGH THE NIGHT. IN A STEEP RAVINE, THEY RESTED TO GET THEIR BREATH BACK.
WHAT ABOUT TAFFY AND THE OTHER LADS, CORP?
THERE ISN'T ANYTHING WE CAN DO ABOUT IT. THEY MUST HAVE BEEN CAPTURED.
IF THEY WERE LUCKY!

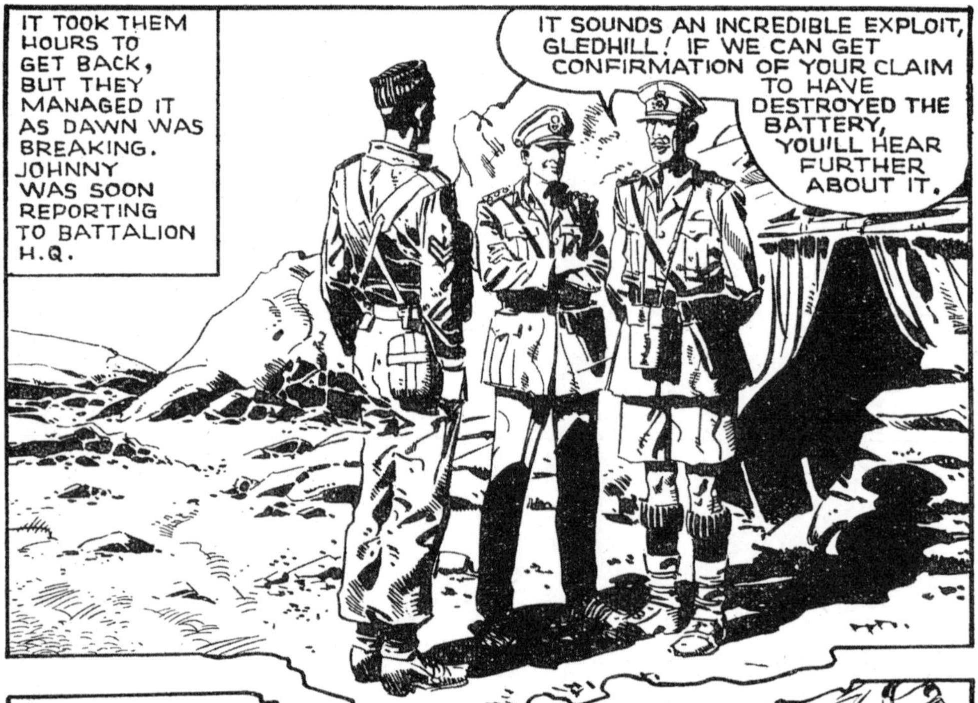
IT TOOK THEM HOURS TO GET BACK, BUT THEY MANAGED IT AS DAWN WAS BREAKING. JOHNNY WAS SOON REPORTING TO BATTALION H.Q.
IT SOUNDS AN INCREDIBLE EXPLOIT, GLEDHILL! IF WE CAN GET CONFIRMATION OF YOUR CLAIM TO HAVE DESTROYED THE BATTERY, YOU'LL HEAR FURTHER ABOUT IT.

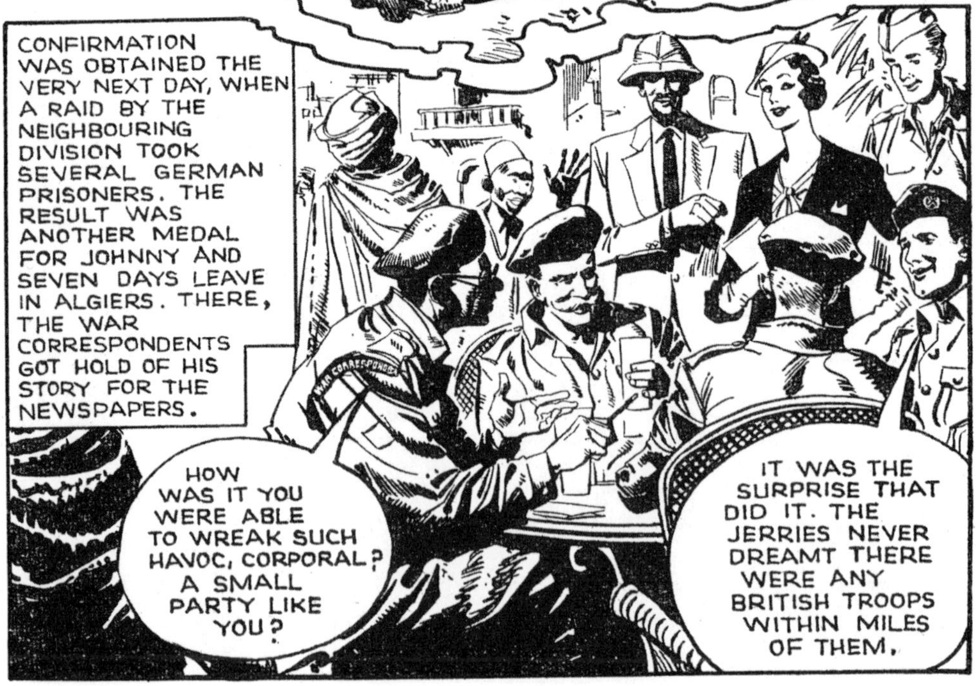
CONFIRMATION WAS OBTAINED THE VERY NEXT DAY, WHEN A RAID BY THE NEIGHBOURING DIVISION TOOK SEVERAL GERMAN PRISONERS. THE RESULT WAS ANOTHER MEDAL FOR JOHNNY AND SEVEN DAYS LEAVE IN ALGIERS. THERE, THE WAR CORRESPONDENTS GOT HOLD OF HIS STORY FOR THE NEWSPAPERS.
HOW WAS IT YOU WERE ABLE TO WREAK SUCH HAVOC, CORPORAL? A SMALL PARTY LIKE YOU?
IT WAS THE SURPRISE THAT DID IT. THE JERRIES NEVER DREAMT THERE WERE ANY BRITISH TROOPS WITHIN MILES OF THEM.

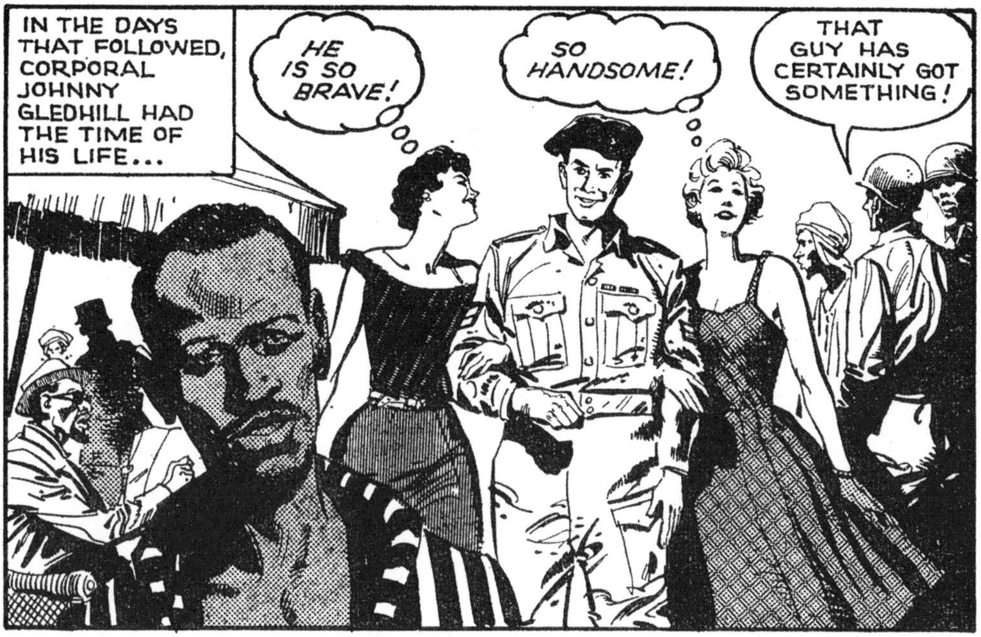
IN THE DAYS THAT FOLLOWED, CORPORAL JOHNNY GLEDHILL HAD THE TIME OF HIS LIFE...
HE IS SO BRAVE!
SO HANDSOME!
THAT GUY HAS CERTAINLY GOT SOMETHING!

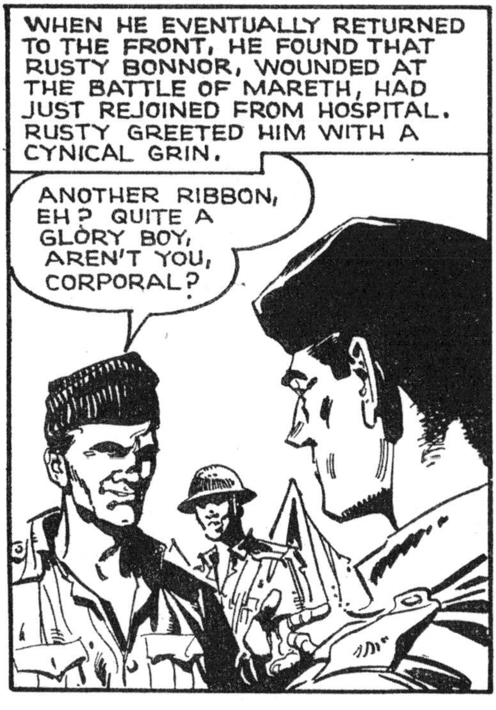
WHEN HE EVENTUALLY RETURNED TO THE FRONT, HE FOUND THAT RUSTY BONNOR, WOUNDED AT THE BATTLE OF MARETH, HAD JUST REJOINED FROM HOSPITAL. RUSTY GREETED HIM WITH A CYNICAL GRIN.
ANOTHER RIBBON, EH? QUITE A GLORY BOY, AREN'T YOU, CORPORAL?

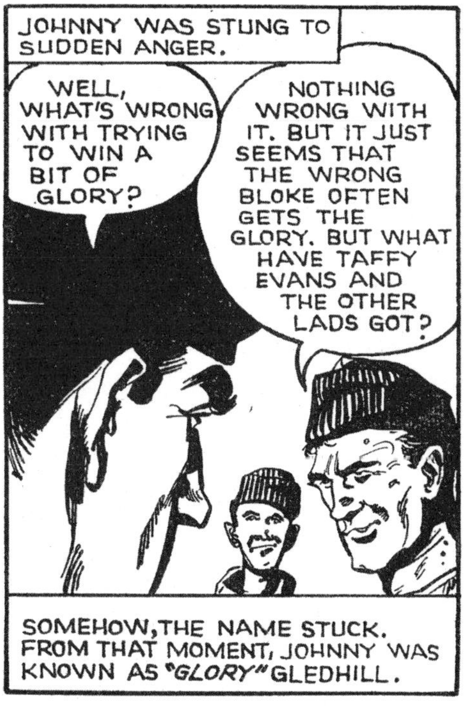
JOHNNY WAS STUNG TO SUDDEN ANGER.
WELL, WHAT'S WRONG WITH TRYING TO WIN A BIT OF GLORY?
NOTHING WRONG WITH IT. BUT IT JUST SEEMS THAT THE WRONG BLOKE OFTEN GETS THE GLORY. BUT WHAT HAVE TAFFY EVANS AND THE OTHER LADS GOT?
SOMEHOW, THE NAME STUCK. FROM THAT MOMENT, JOHNNY WAS KNOWN AS "GLORY" GLEDHILL.

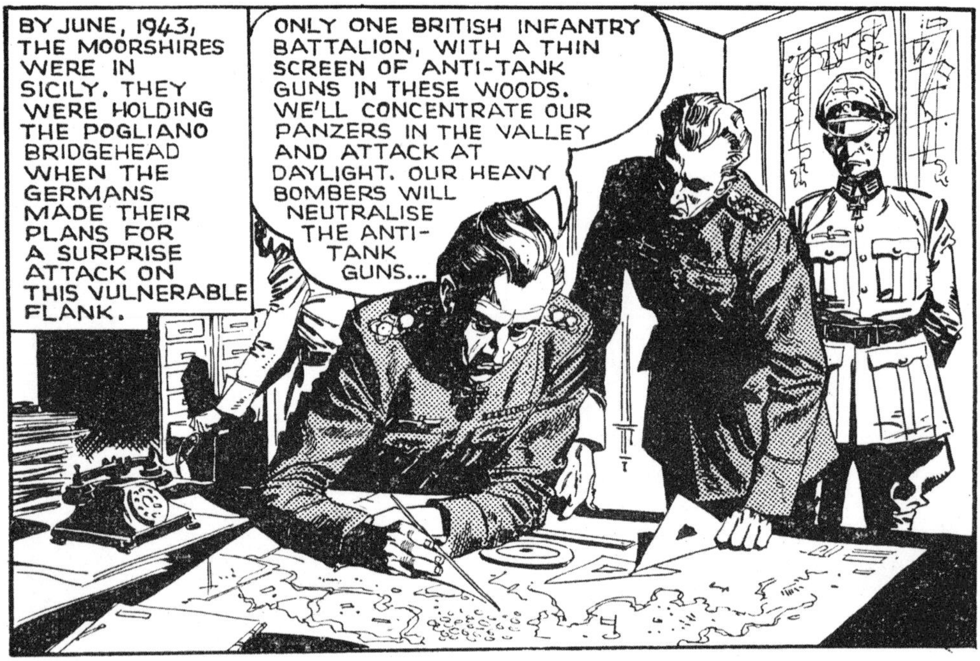
BY JUNE, 1943, THE MOORSHIRES WERE IN SICILY. THEY WERE HOLDING THE POGLIANO BRIDGEHEAD WHEN THE GERMANS MADE THEIR PLANS FOR A SURPRISE ATTACK ON THIS VULNERABLE FLANK.
ONLY ONE BRITISH INFANTRY BATTALION, WITH A THIN SCREEN OF ANTI-TANK GUNS IN THESE WOODS. WE'LL CONCENTRATE OUR PANZERS IN THE VALLEY AND ATTACK AT DAYLIGHT. OUR HEAVY BOMBERS WILL NEUTRALISE THE ANTI-TANK GUNS...

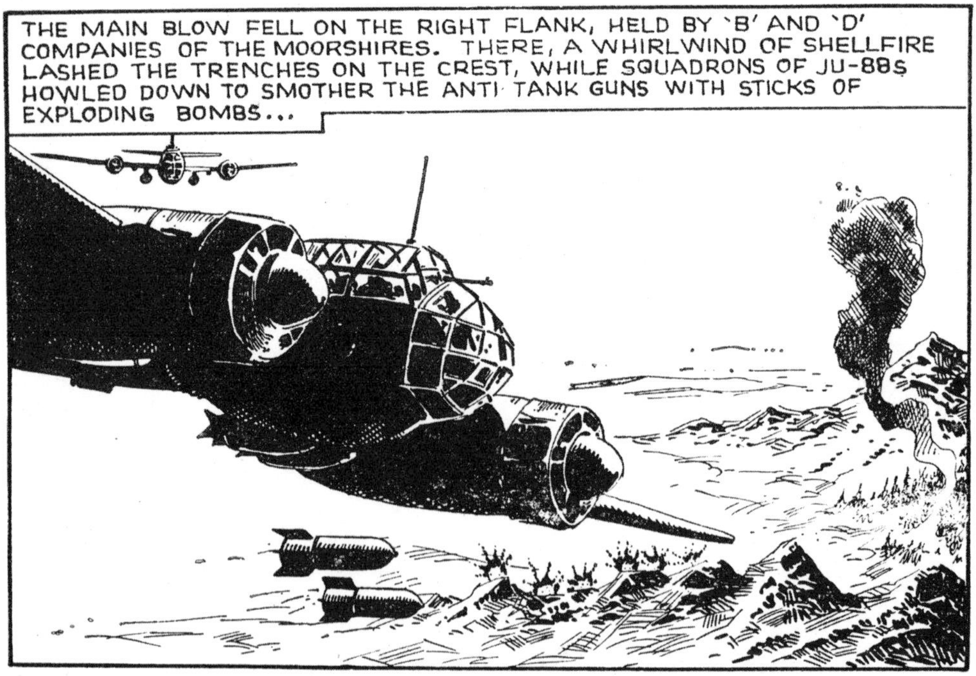
THE MAIN BLOW FELL ON THE RIGHT FLANK, HELD BY 'B' AND 'D' COMPANIES OF THE MOORSHIRES. THERE, A WHIRLWIND OF SHELLFIRE LASHED THE TRENCHES ON THE CREST, WHILE SQUADRONS OF JU-88S HOWLED DOWN TO SMOTHER THE ANTI-TANK GUNS WITH STICKS OF EXPLODING BOMBS...

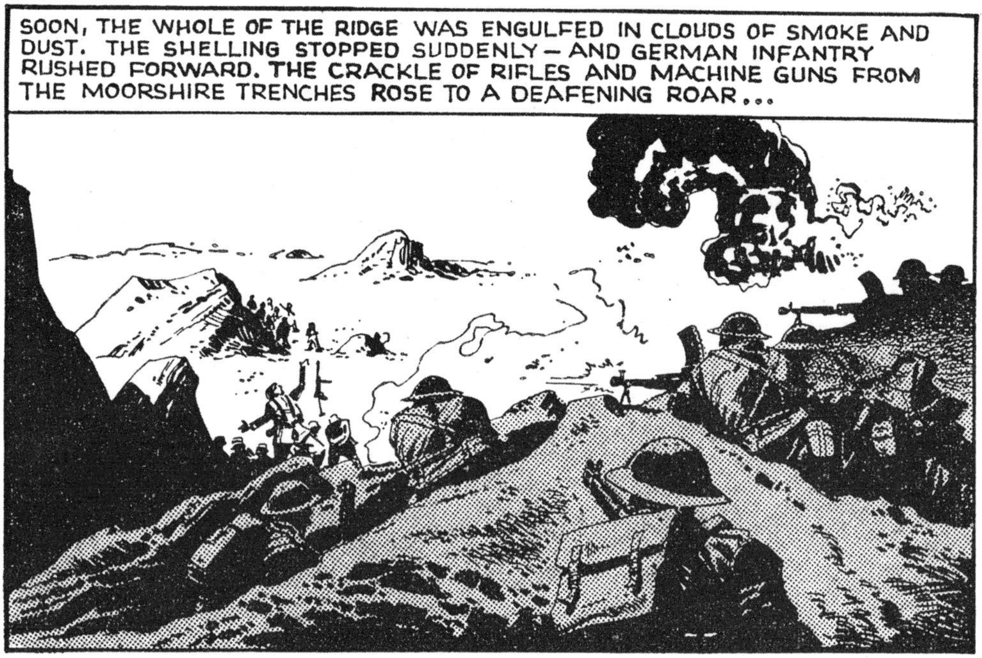
SOON, THE WHOLE OF THE RIDGE WAS ENGULFED IN CLOUDS OF SMOKE AND DUST. THE SHELLING STOPPED SUDDENLY—AND GERMAN INFANTRY RUSHED FORWARD. THE CRACKLE OF RIFLES AND MACHINE GUNS FROM THE MOORSHIRE TRENCHES ROSE TO A DEAFENING ROAR...

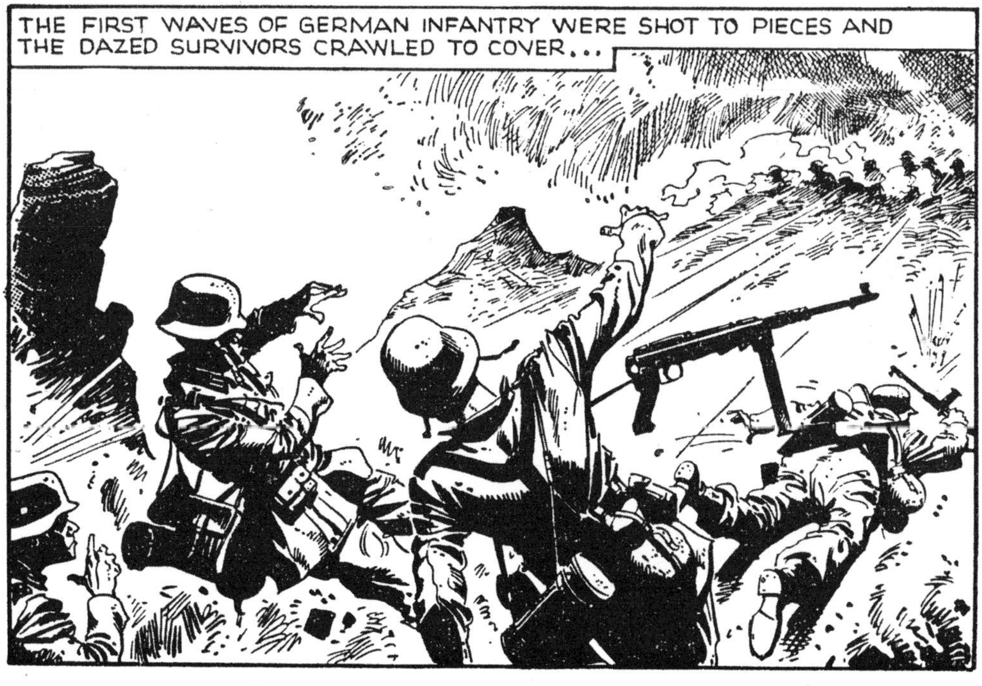
THE FIRST WAVES OF GERMAN INFANTRY WERE SHOT TO PIECES AND THE DAZED SURVIVORS CRAWLED TO COVER...

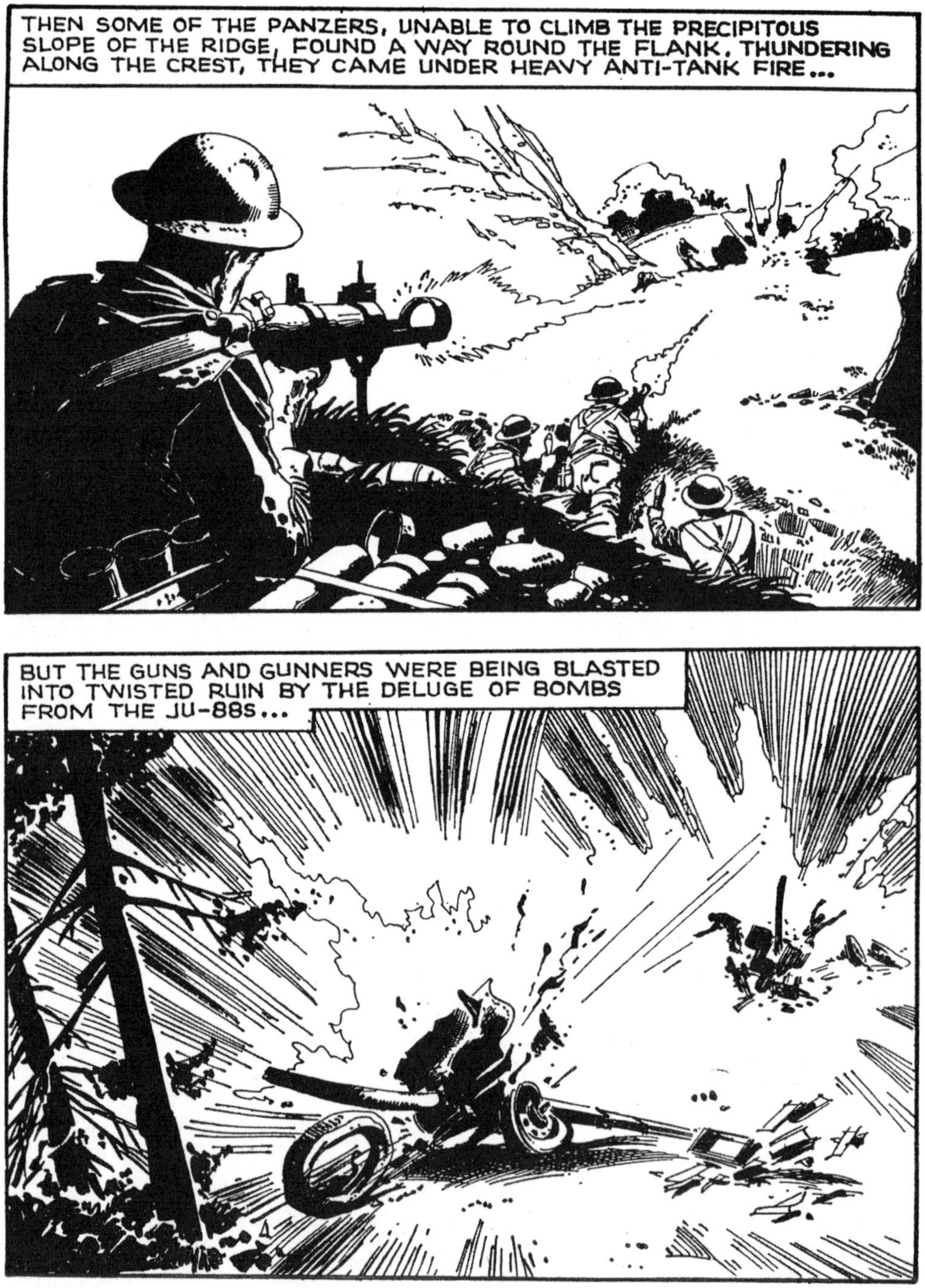
THEN SOME OF THE PANZERS, UNABLE TO CLIMB THE PRECIPITOUS SLOPE OF THE RIDGE, FOUND A WAY ROUND THE FLANK. THUNDERING ALONG THE CREST, THEY CAME UNDER HEAVY ANTI-TANK FIRE...
BUT THE GUNS AND GUNNERS WERE BEING BLASTED INTO TWISTED RUIN BY THE DELUGE OF BOMBS FROM THE JU-88S...

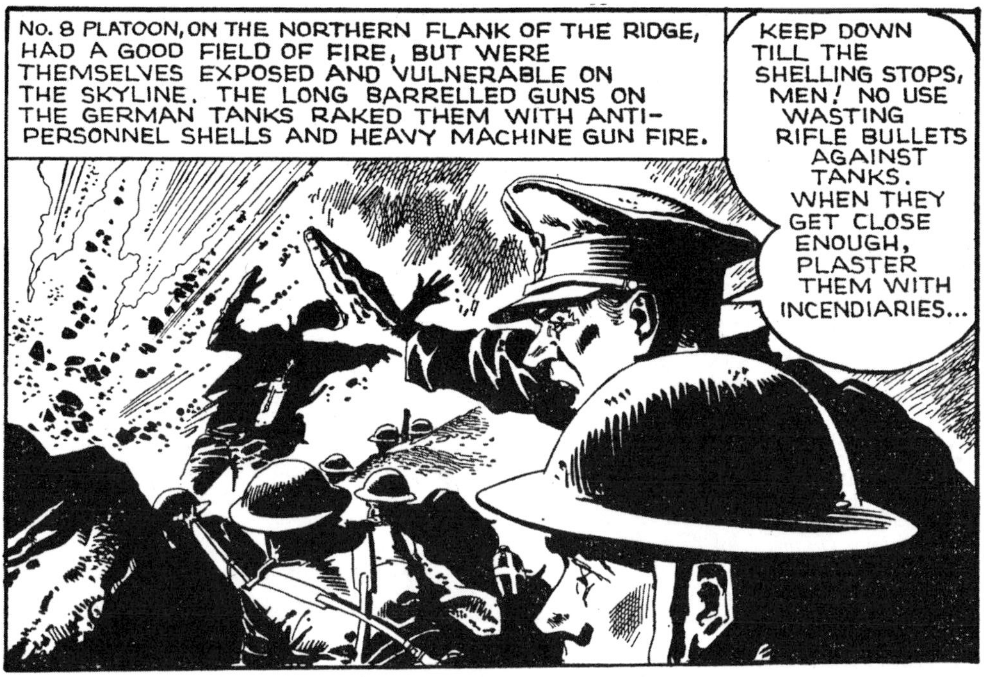
No. 8 PLATOON, ON THE NORTHERN FLANK OF THE RIDGE, HAD A GOOD FIELD OF FIRE, BUT WERE THEMSELVES EXPOSED AND VULNERABLE ON THE SKYLINE. THE LONG BARRELLED GUNS ON THE GERMAN TANKS RAKED THEM WITH ANTI-PERSONNEL SHELLS AND HEAVY MACHINE GUN FIRE.
KEEP DOWN TILL THE SHELLING STOPS, MEN! NO USE WASTING RIFLE BULLETS AGAINST TANKS. WHEN THEY GET CLOSE ENOUGH, PLASTER THEM WITH INCENDIARIES...

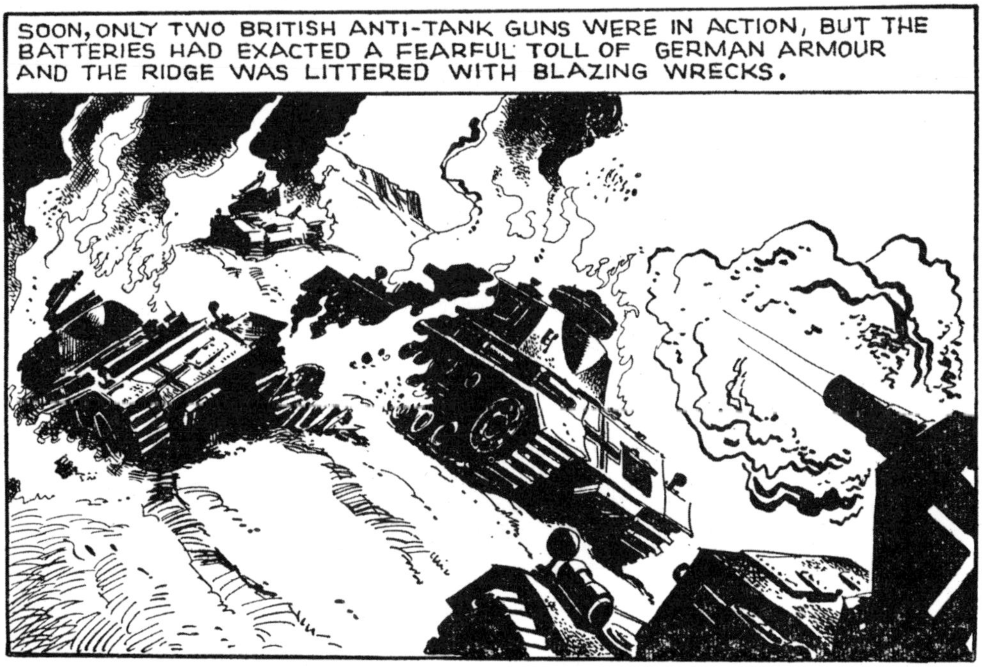
SOON, ONLY TWO BRITISH ANTI-TANK GUNS WERE IN ACTION, BUT THE BATTERIES HAD EXACTED A FEARFUL TOLL OF GERMAN ARMOUR AND THE RIDGE WAS LITTERED WITH BLAZING WRECKS.

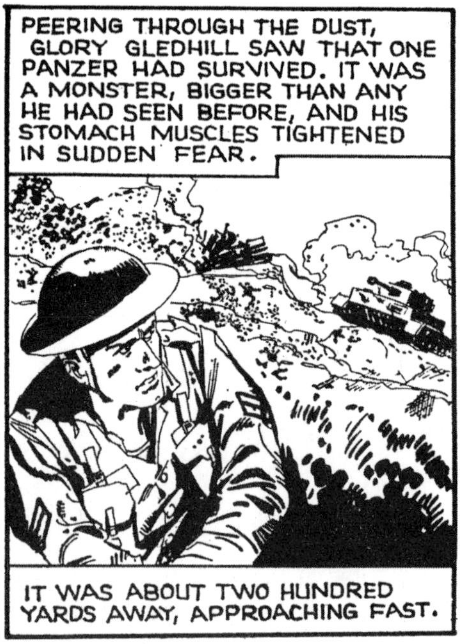
PEERING THROUGH THE DUST, GLORY GLEDHILL SAW THAT ONE PANZER HAD SURVIVED. IT WAS A MONSTER, BIGGER THAN ANY HE HAD SEEN BEFORE, AND HIS STOMACH MUSCLES TIGHTENED IN SUDDEN FEAR.
IT WAS ABOUT TWO HUNDRED YARDS AWAY, APPROACHING FAST.

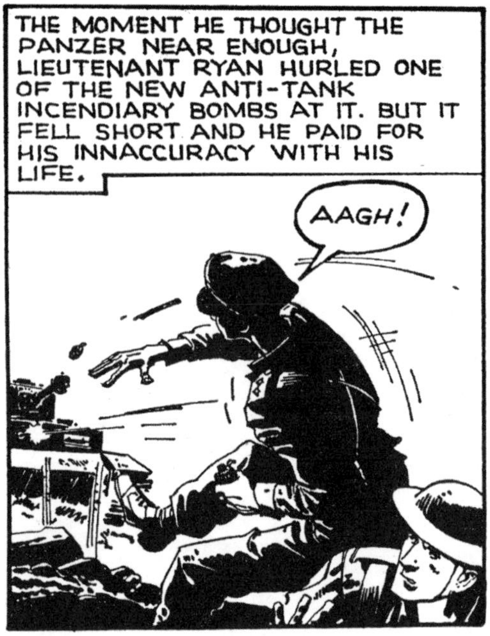
THE MOMENT HE THOUGHT THE PANZER NEAR ENOUGH, LIEUTENANT RYAN HURLED ONE OF THE NEW ANTI-TANK INCENDIARY BOMBS AT IT. BUT IT FELL SHORT AND HE PAID FOR HIS INNACCURACY WITH HIS LIFE.
AAGH!

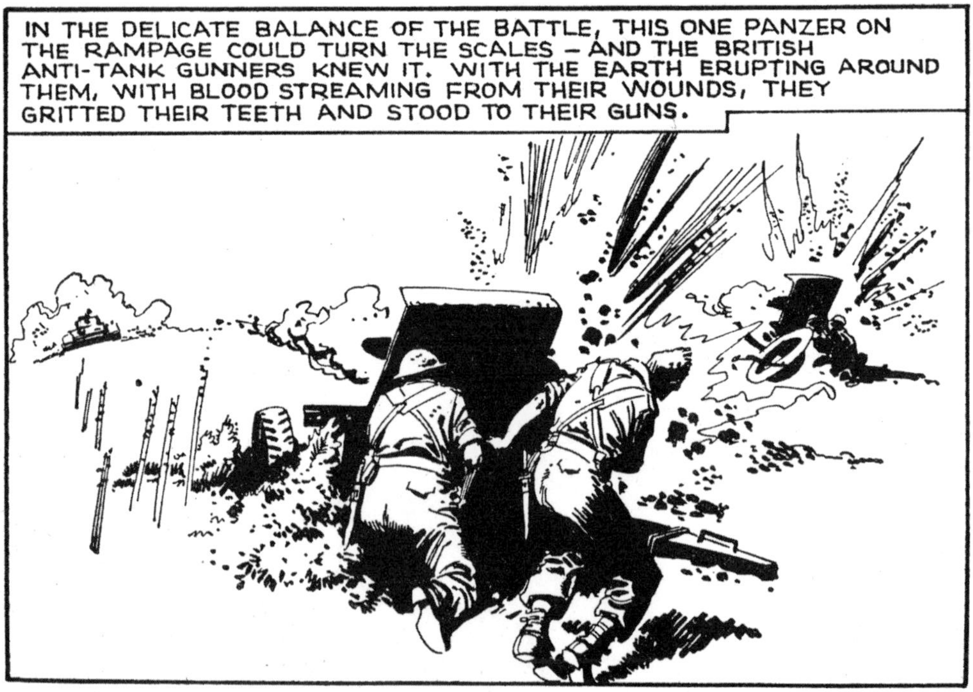
IN THE DELICATE BALANCE OF THE BATTLE, THIS ONE PANZER ON THE RAMPAGE COULD TURN THE SCALES – AND THE BRITISH ANTI-TANK GUNNERS KNEW IT. WITH THE EARTH ERUPTING AROUND THEM, WITH BLOOD STREAMING FROM THEIR WOUNDS, THEY GRITTED THEIR TEETH AND STOOD TO THEIR GUNS.

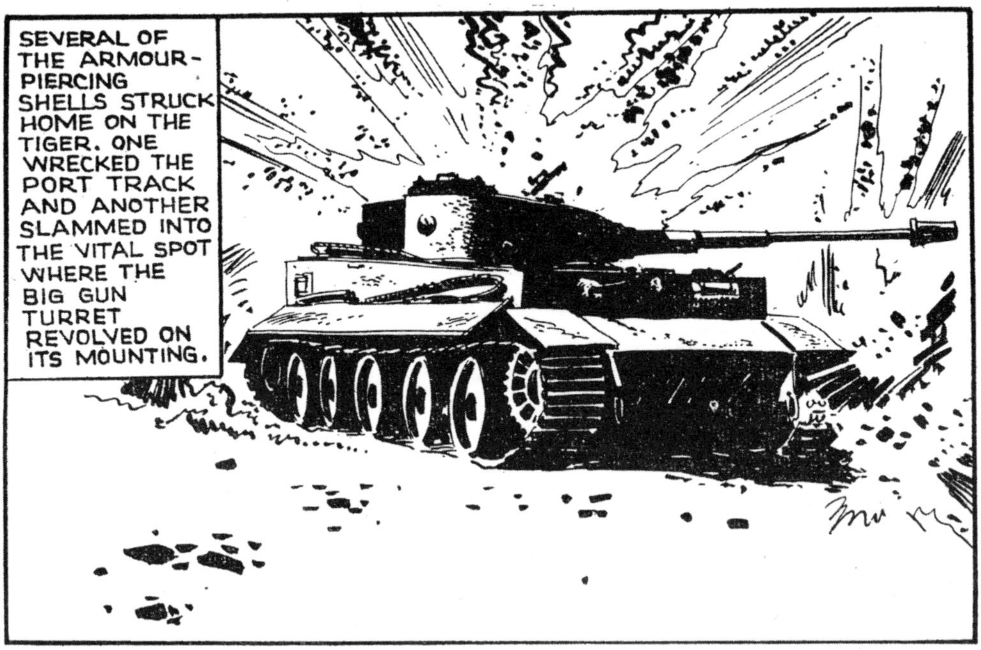
SEVERAL OF THE ARMOUR-PIERCING SHELLS STRUCK HOME ON THE TIGER. ONE WRECKED THE PORT TRACK AND ANOTHER SLAMMED INTO THE VITAL SPOT WHERE THE BIG GUN TURRET REVOLVED ON ITS MOUNTING.

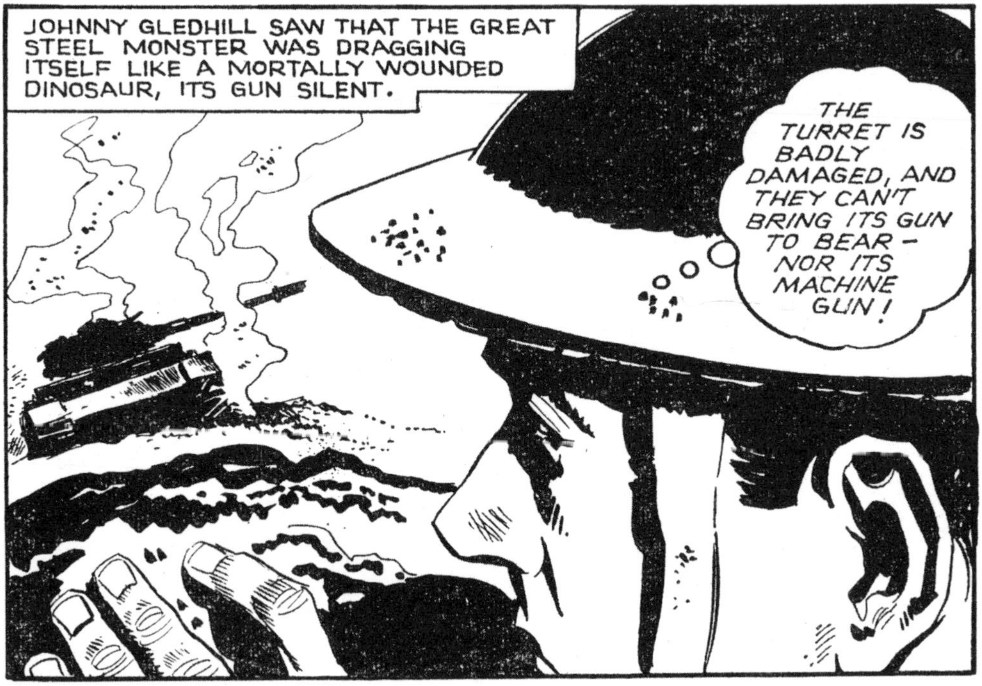
JOHNNY GLEDHILL SAW THAT THE GREAT STEEL MONSTER WAS DRAGGING ITSELF LIKE A MORTALLY WOUNDED DINOSAUR, ITS GUN SILENT.
THE TURRET IS BADLY DAMAGED, AND THEY CAN'T BRING ITS GUN TO BEAR – NOR ITS MACHINE GUN!

HE GRABBED TWO OF THE ANTI-TANK INCENDIARIES FROM BESIDE THE DEAD LIEUTENANT AND SCRAMBLED FROM THE TRENCH. THEN, LIKE DAVID ADVANCING ON GOLIATH, HE RAN FORWARD.

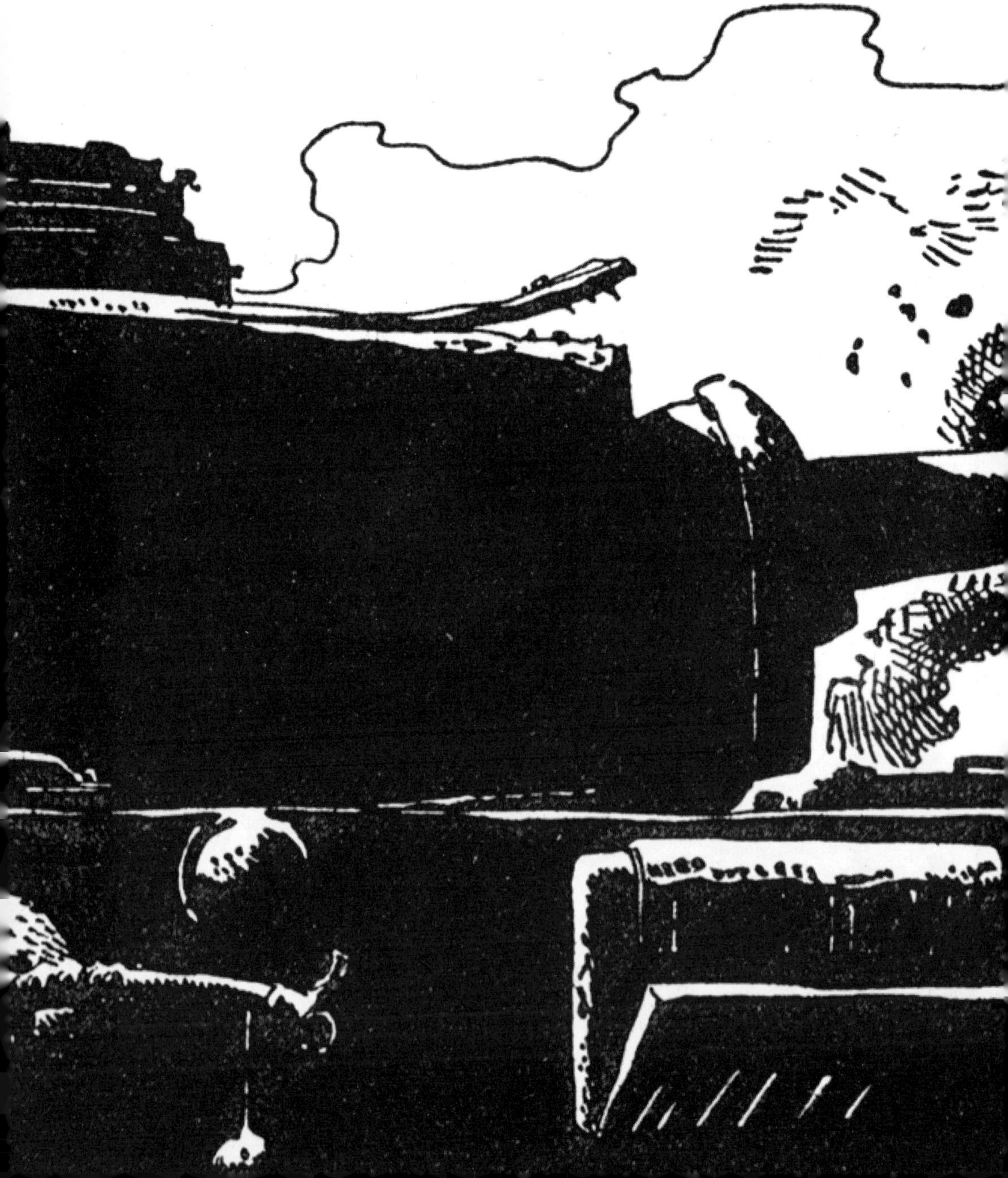

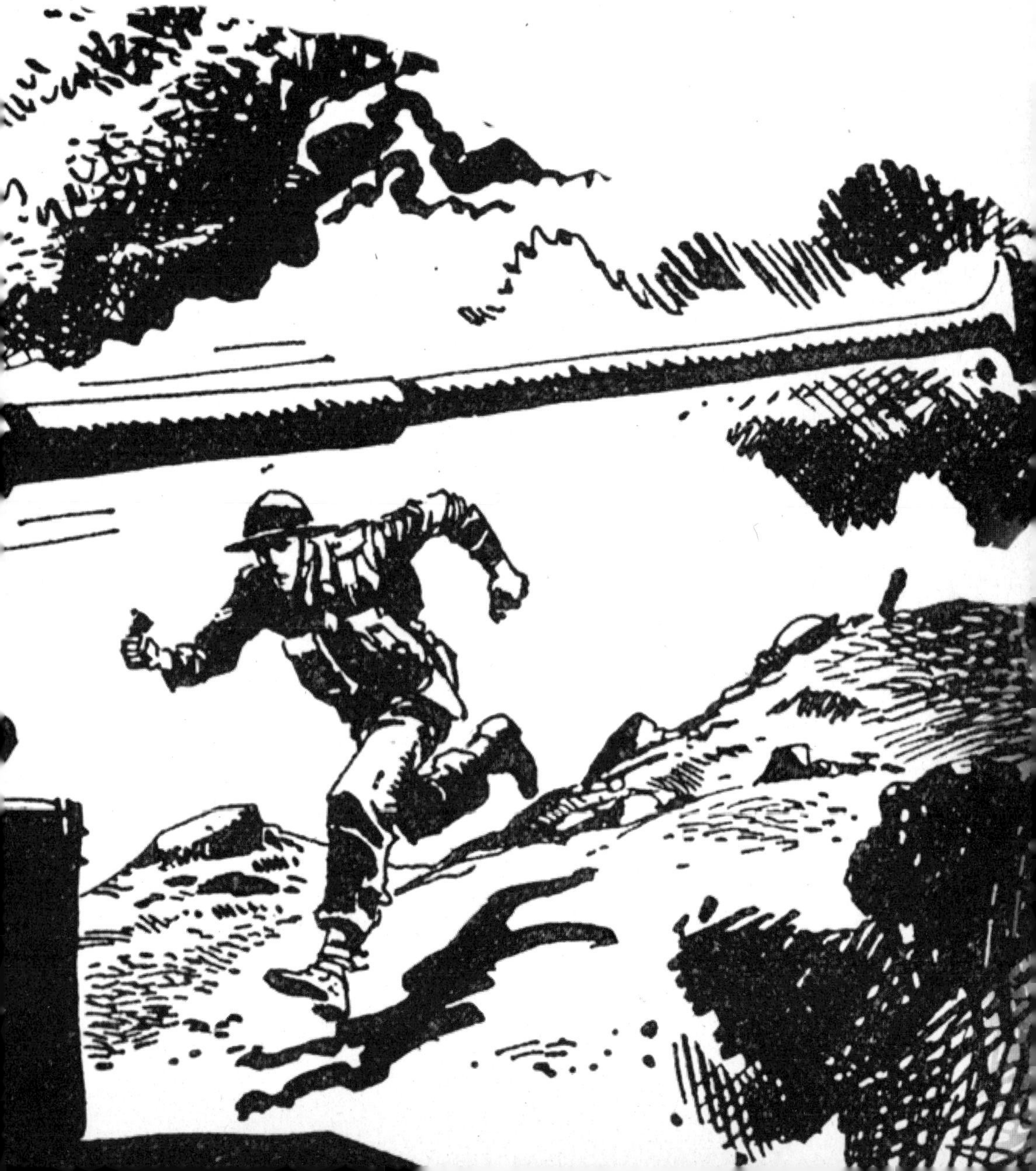

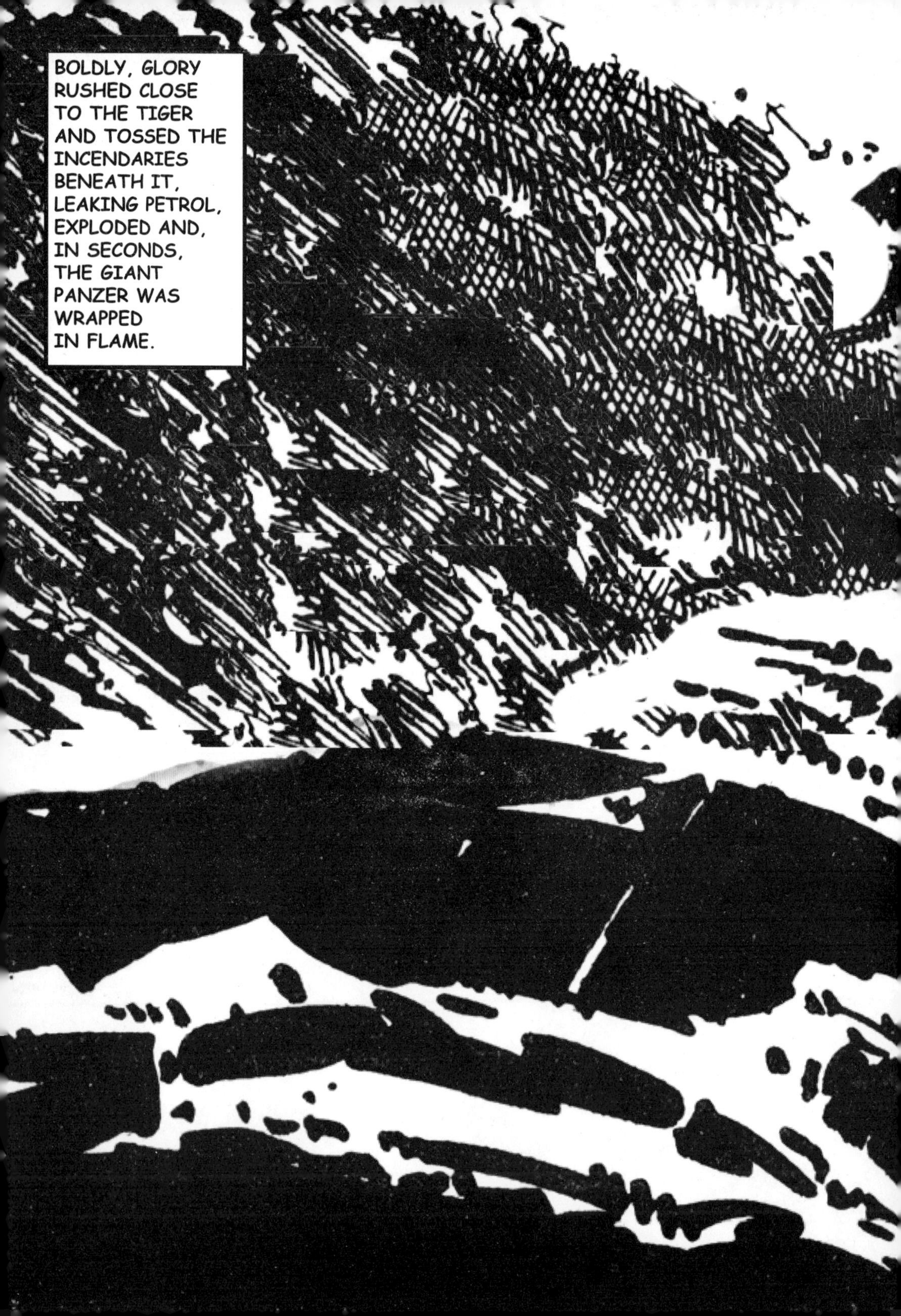
BOLDLY, GLORY RUSHED CLOSE TO THE TIGER AND TOSSED THE INCENDARIES BENEATH IT, LEAKING PETROL, EXPLODED AND, IN SECONDS, THE GIANT PANZER WAS WRAPPED IN FLAME.

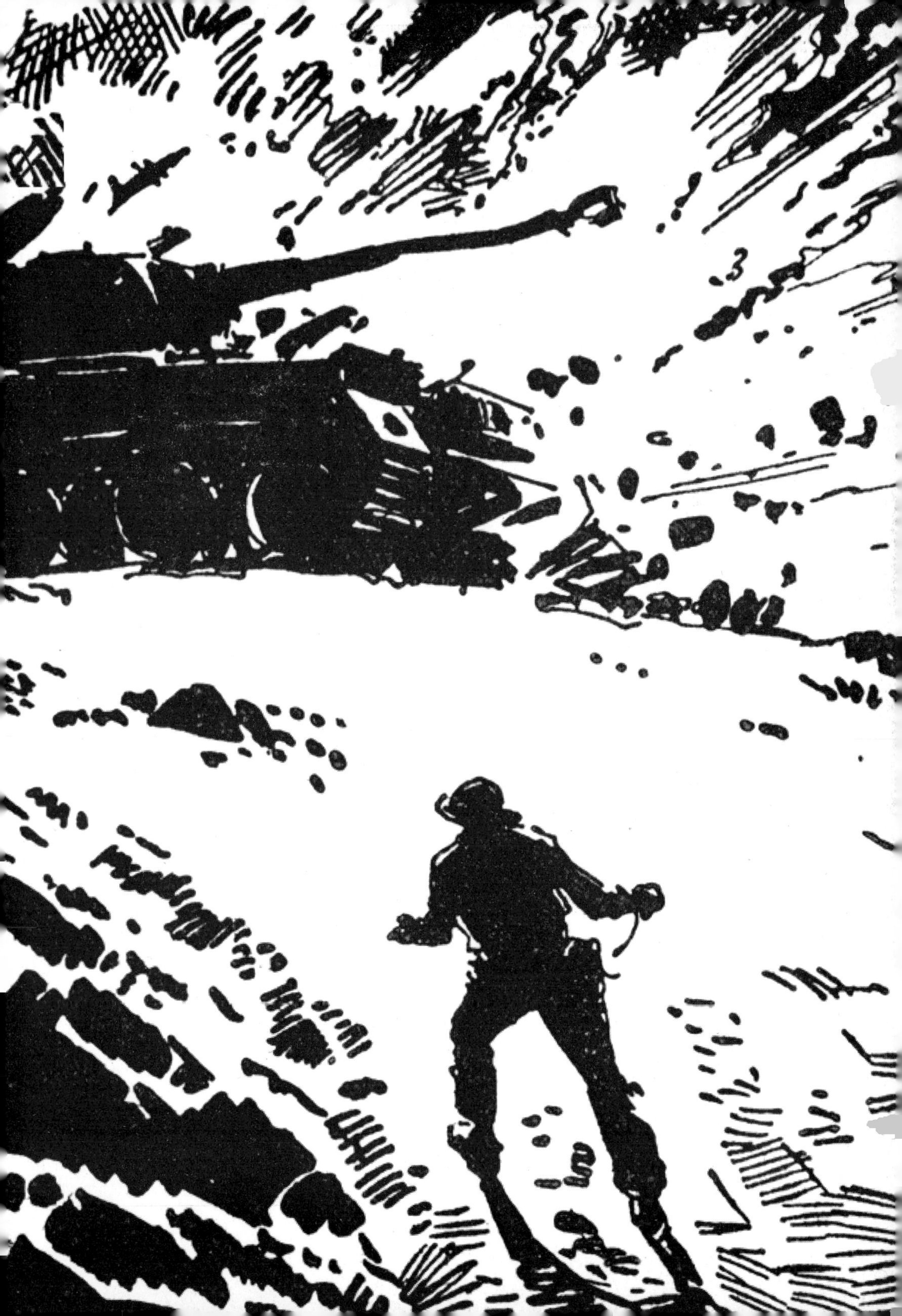

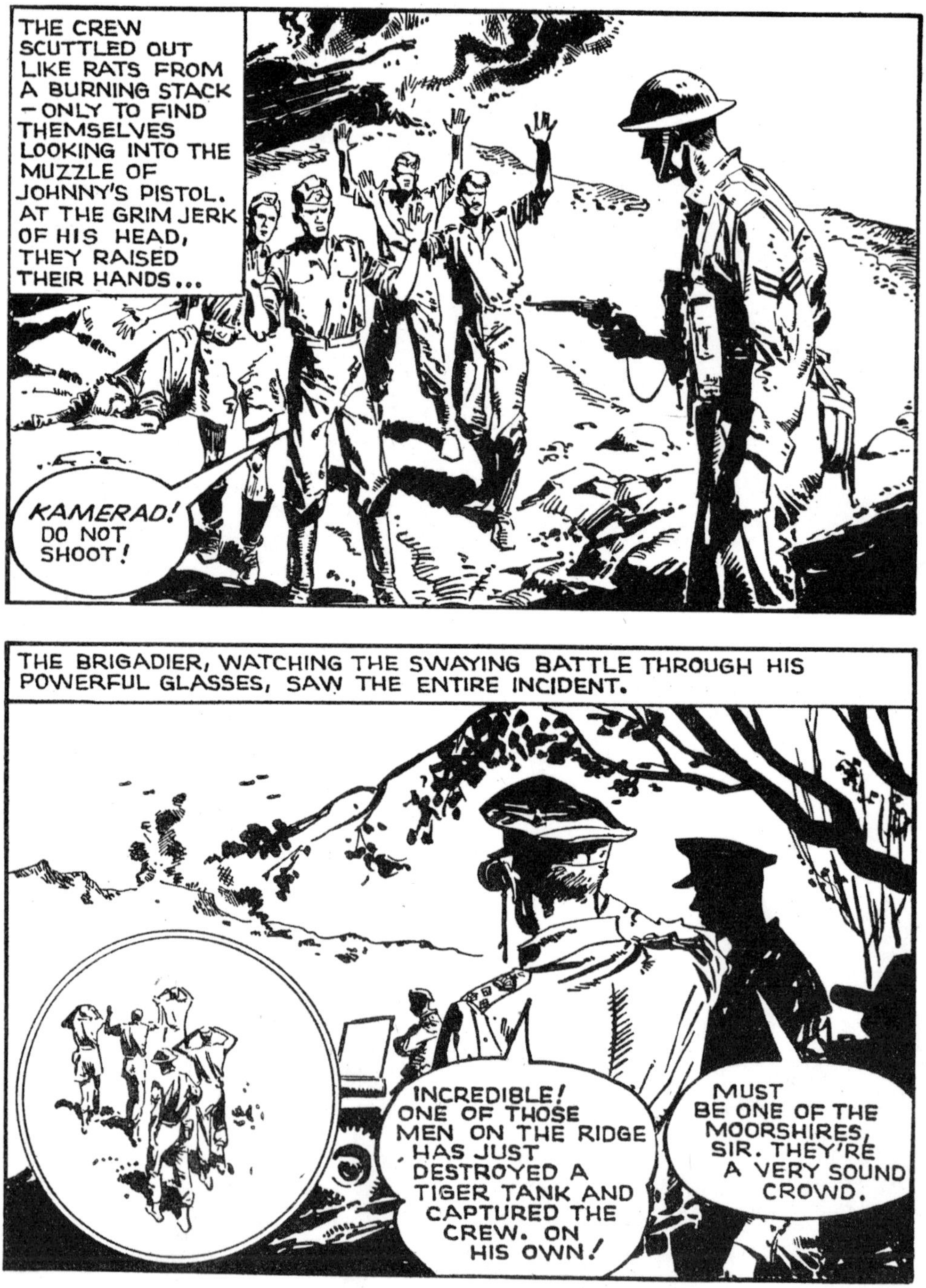
THE CREW SCUTTLED OUT LIKE RATS FROM A BURNING STACK —ONLY TO FIND THEMSELVES LOOKING INTO THE MUZZLE OF JOHNNY'S PISTOL. AT THE GRIM JERK OF HIS HEAD, THEY RAISED THEIR HANDS...
KAMERAD! DO NOT SHOOT!
THE BRIGADIER, WATCHING THE SWAYING BATTLE THROUGH HIS POWERFUL GLASSES, SAW THE ENTIRE INCIDENT.
INCREDIBLE! ONE OF THOSE MEN ON THE RIDGE HAS JUST DESTROYED A TIGER TANK AND CAPTURED THE CREW. ON HIS OWN!
MUST BE ONE OF THE MOORSHIRES, SIR. THEY'RE A VERY SOUND CROWD.

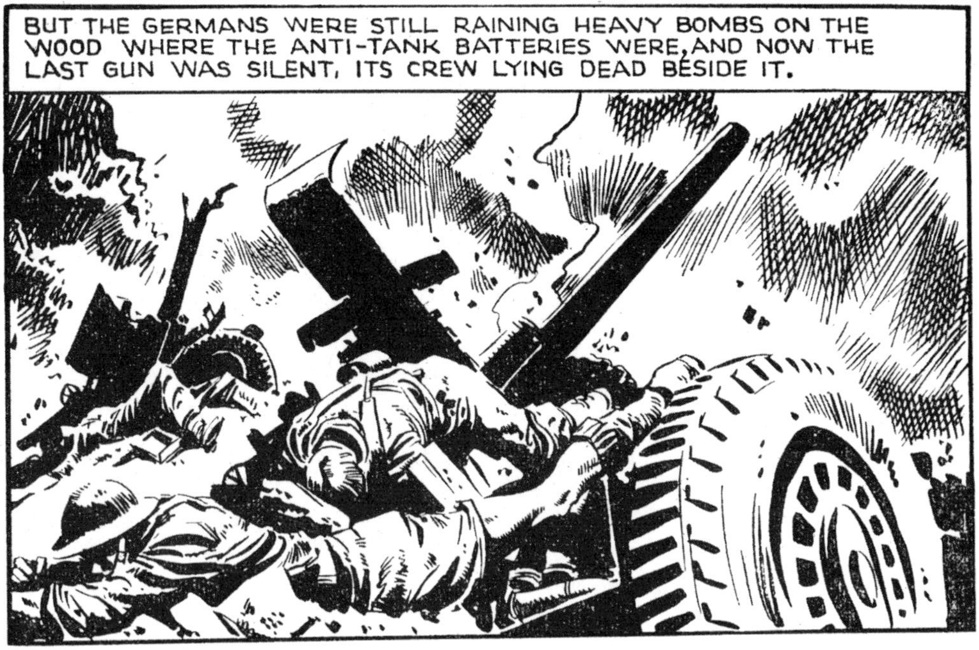
BUT THE GERMANS WERE STILL RAINING HEAVY BOMBS ON THE WOOD WHERE THE ANTI-TANK BATTERIES WERE, AND NOW THE LAST GUN WAS SILENT, ITS CREW LYING DEAD BESIDE IT.

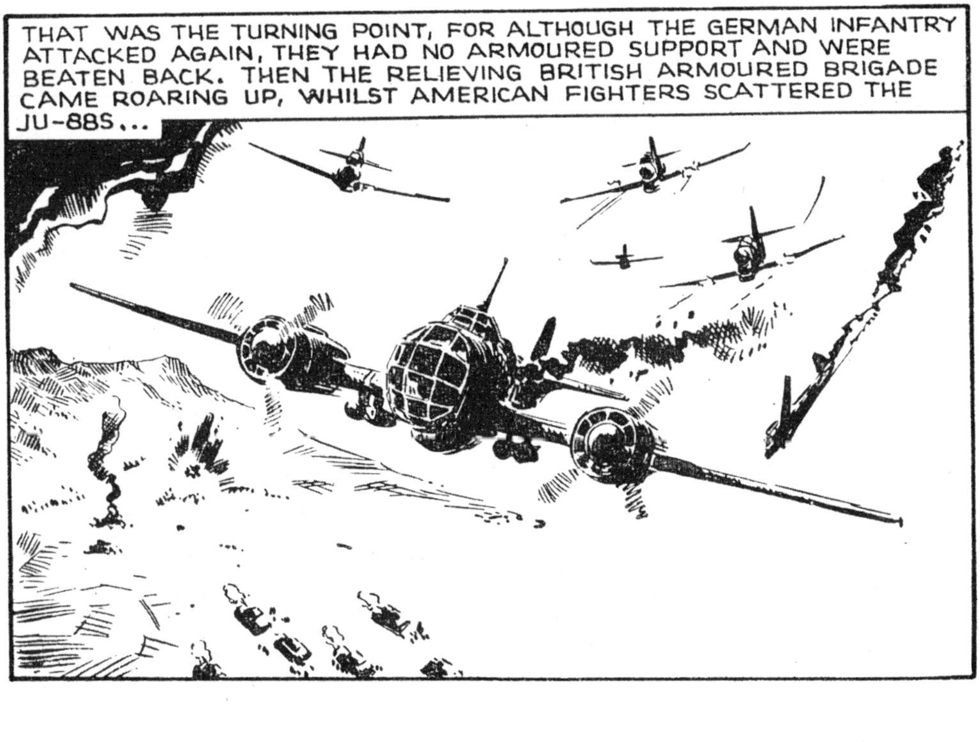
THAT WAS THE TURNING POINT, FOR ALTHOUGH THE GERMAN INFANTRY ATTACKED AGAIN, THEY HAD NO ARMOURED SUPPORT AND WERE BEATEN BACK. THEN THE RELIEVING BRITISH ARMOURED BRIGADE CAME ROARING UP, WHILST AMERICAN FIGHTERS SCATTERED THE JU-88S...

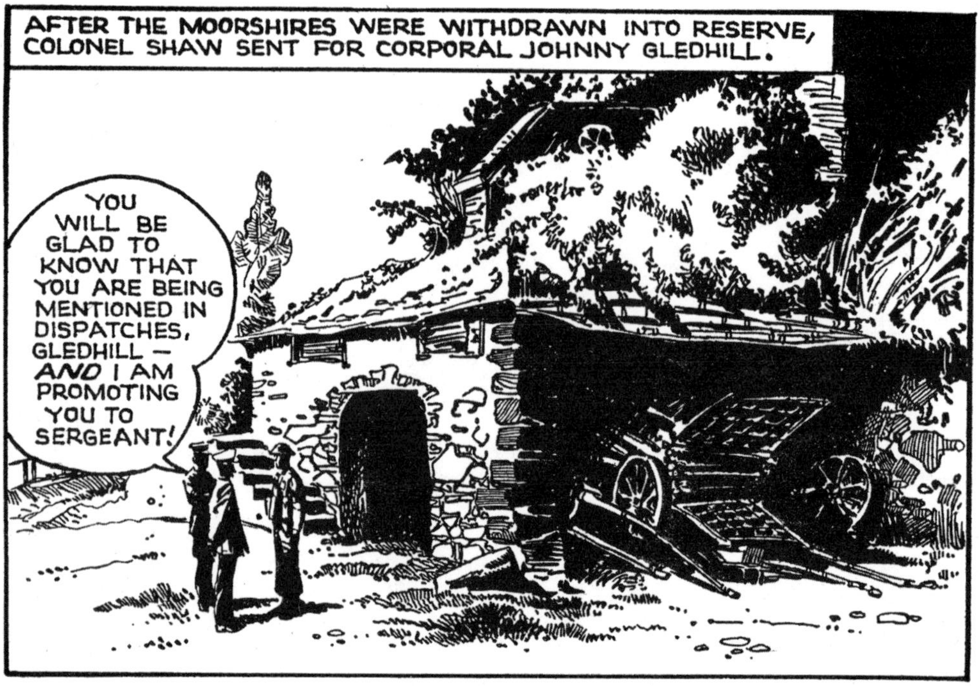
AFTER THE MOORSHIRES WERE WITHDRAWN INTO RESERVE, COLONEL SHAW SENT FOR CORPORAL JOHNNY GLEDHILL.
YOU WILL BE GLAD TO KNOW THAT YOU ARE BEING MENTIONED IN DISPATCHES, GLEDHILL — AND I AM PROMOTING YOU TO SERGEANT!

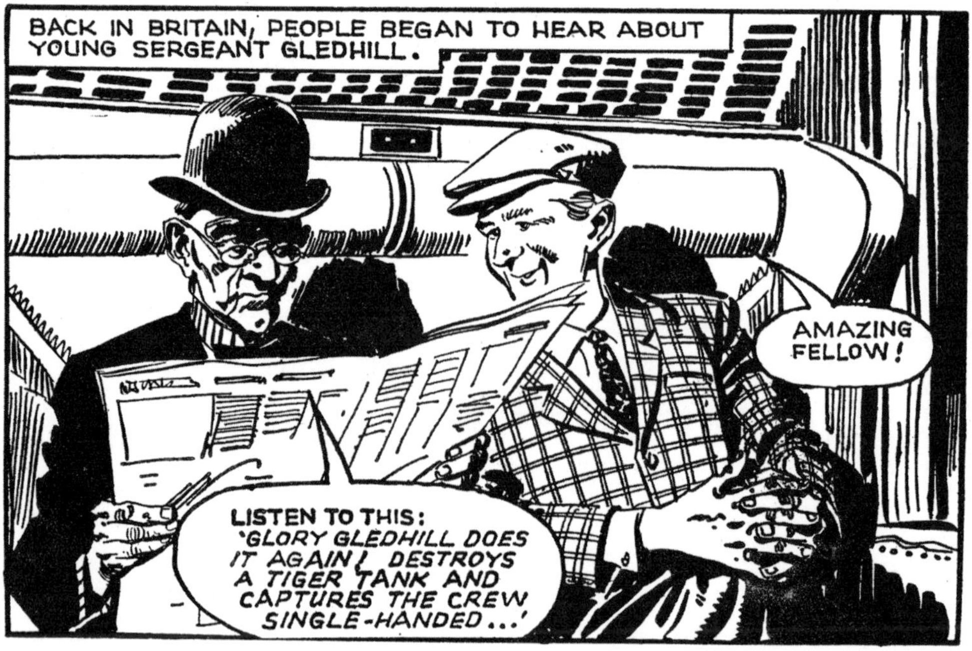
BACK IN BRITAIN, PEOPLE BEGAN TO HEAR ABOUT YOUNG SERGEANT GLEDHILL.
LISTEN TO THIS: 'GLORY GLEDHILL DOES IT AGAIN! DESTROYS A TIGER TANK AND CAPTURES THE CREW SINGLE-HANDED...'
AMAZING FELLOW!

Chapter 3. *To the Last Man*

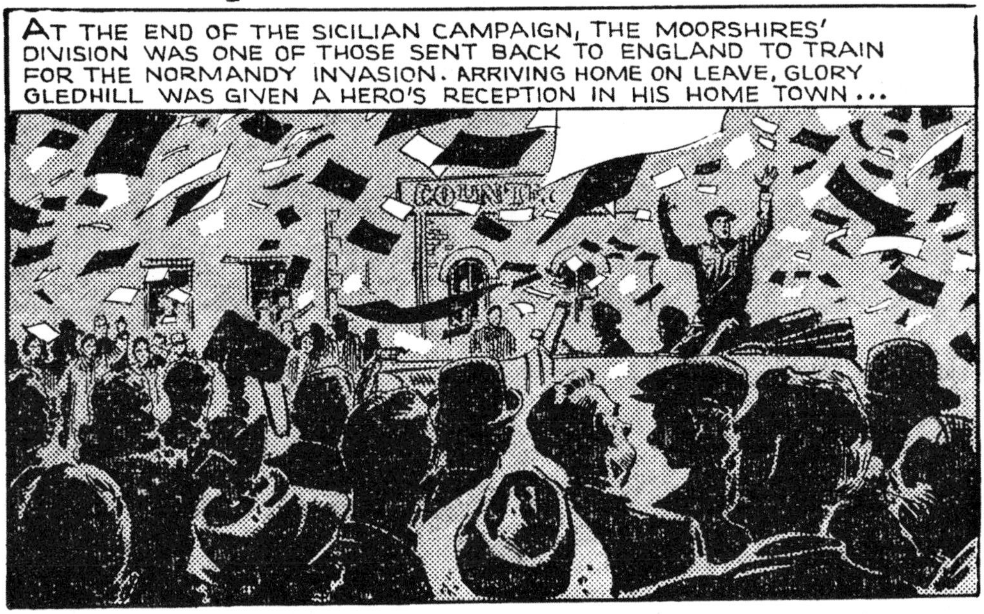
AT THE END OF THE SICILIAN CAMPAIGN, THE MOORSHIRES' DIVISION WAS ONE OF THOSE SENT BACK TO ENGLAND TO TRAIN FOR THE NORMANDY INVASION. ARRIVING HOME ON LEAVE, GLORY GLEDHILL WAS GIVEN A HERO'S RECEPTION IN HIS HOME TOWN...

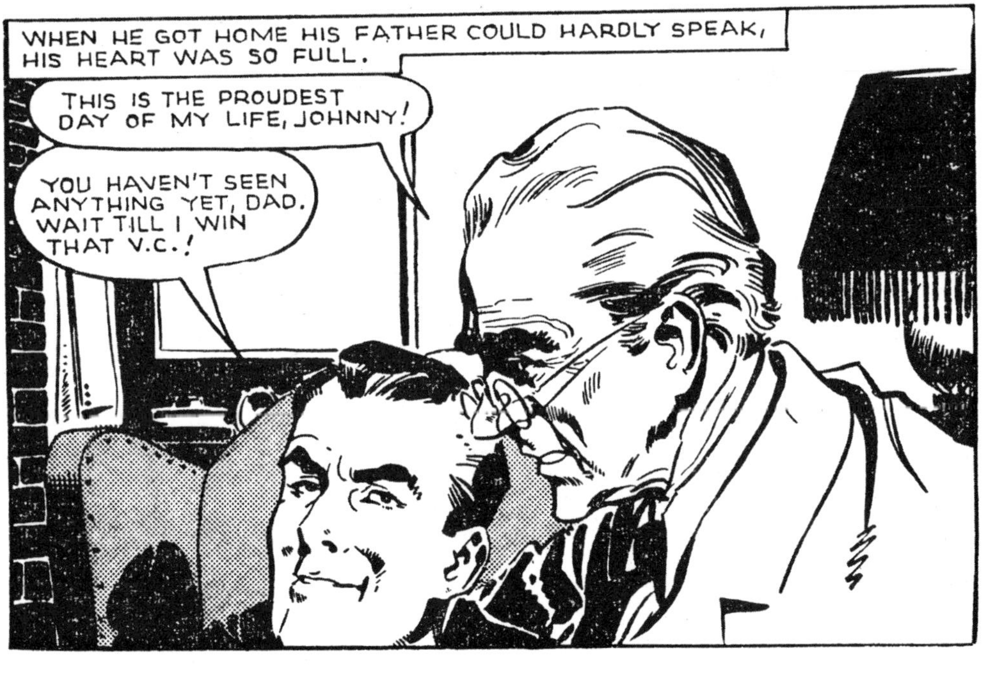
WHEN HE GOT HOME HIS FATHER COULD HARDLY SPEAK, HIS HEART WAS SO FULL.
THIS IS THE PROUDEST DAY OF MY LIFE, JOHNNY!
YOU HAVEN'T SEEN ANYTHING YET, DAD. WAIT TILL I WIN THAT V.C.!

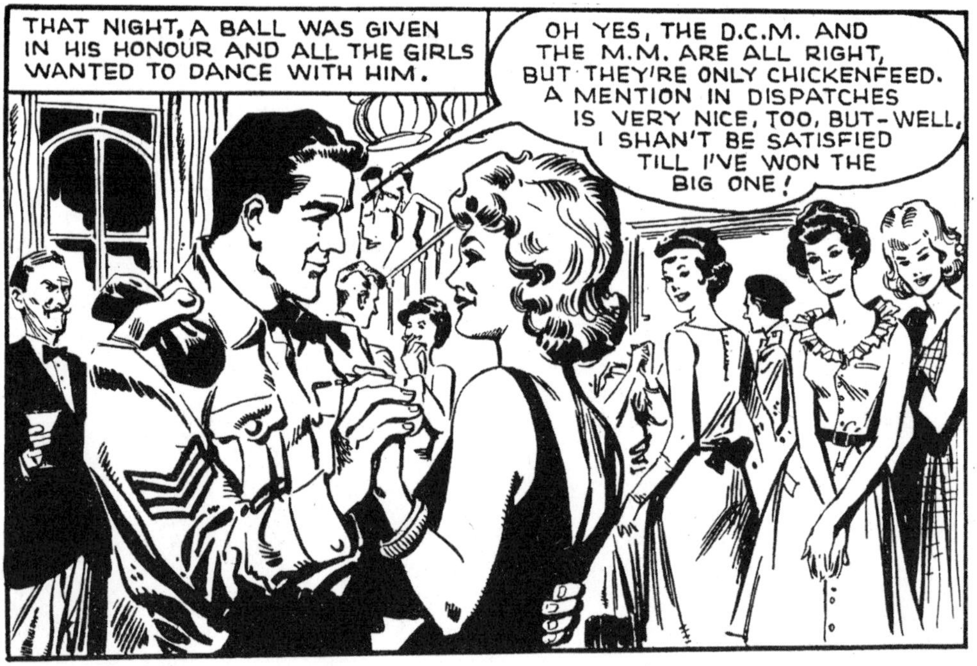
THAT NIGHT, A BALL WAS GIVEN IN HIS HONOUR AND ALL THE GIRLS WANTED TO DANCE WITH HIM.
OH YES, THE D.C.M. AND THE M.M. ARE ALL RIGHT, BUT THEY'RE ONLY CHICKENFEED. A MENTION IN DISPATCHES IS VERY NICE, TOO, BUT-WELL, I SHAN'T BE SATISFIED TILL I'VE WON THE BIG ONE!

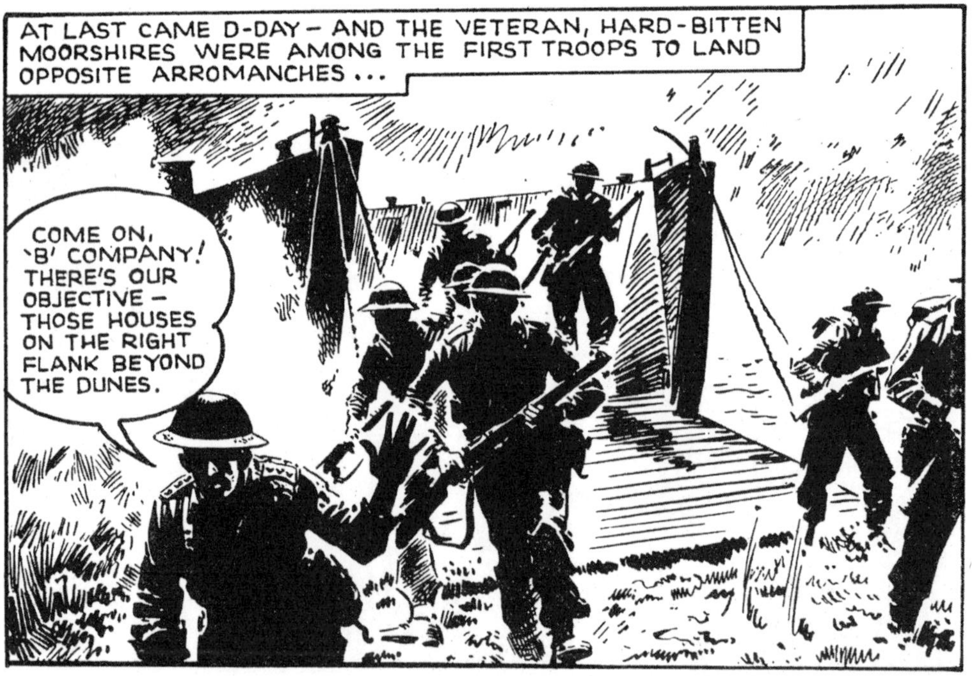
AT LAST CAME D-DAY – AND THE VETERAN, HARD-BITTEN MOORSHIRES WERE AMONG THE FIRST TROOPS TO LAND OPPOSITE ARROMANCHES ...
COME ON, 'B' COMPANY! THERE'S OUR OBJECTIVE – THOSE HOUSES ON THE RIGHT FLANK BEYOND THE DUNES.

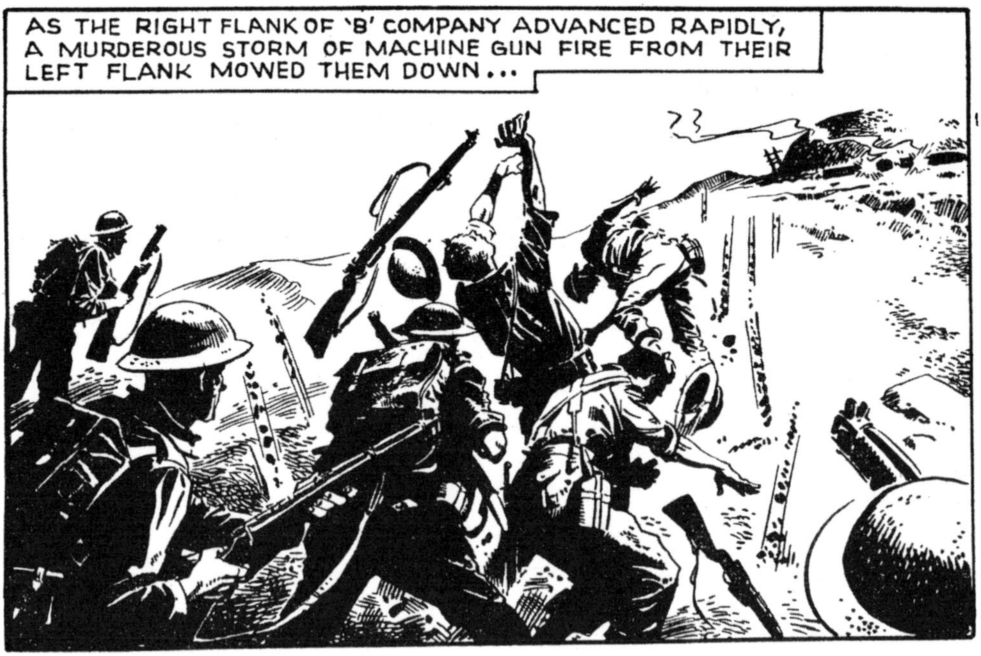
AS THE RIGHT FLANK OF 'B' COMPANY ADVANCED RAPIDLY, A MURDEROUS STORM OF MACHINE GUN FIRE FROM THEIR LEFT FLANK MOWED THEM DOWN...

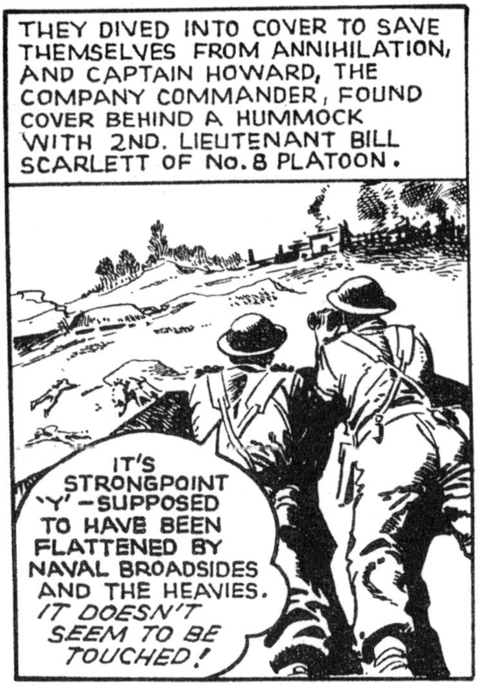
THEY DIVED INTO COVER TO SAVE THEMSELVES FROM ANNIHILATION, AND CAPTAIN HOWARD, THE COMPANY COMMANDER, FOUND COVER BEHIND A HUMMOCK WITH 2ND. LIEUTENANT BILL SCARLETT OF No. 8 PLATOON.
IT'S STRONGPOINT 'Y' – SUPPOSED TO HAVE BEEN FLATTENED BY NAVAL BROADSIDES AND THE HEAVIES. IT DOESN'T SEEM TO BE TOUCHED!

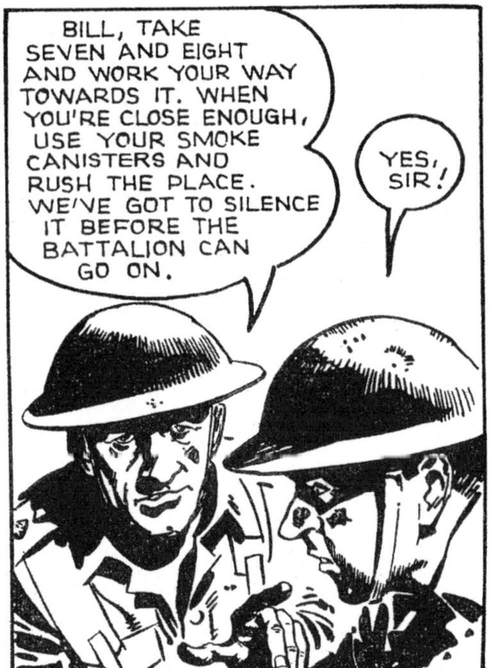
BILL, TAKE SEVEN AND EIGHT AND WORK YOUR WAY TOWARDS IT. WHEN YOU'RE CLOSE ENOUGH, USE YOUR SMOKE CANISTERS AND RUSH THE PLACE. WE'VE GOT TO SILENCE IT BEFORE THE BATTALION CAN GO ON.
YES, SIR!

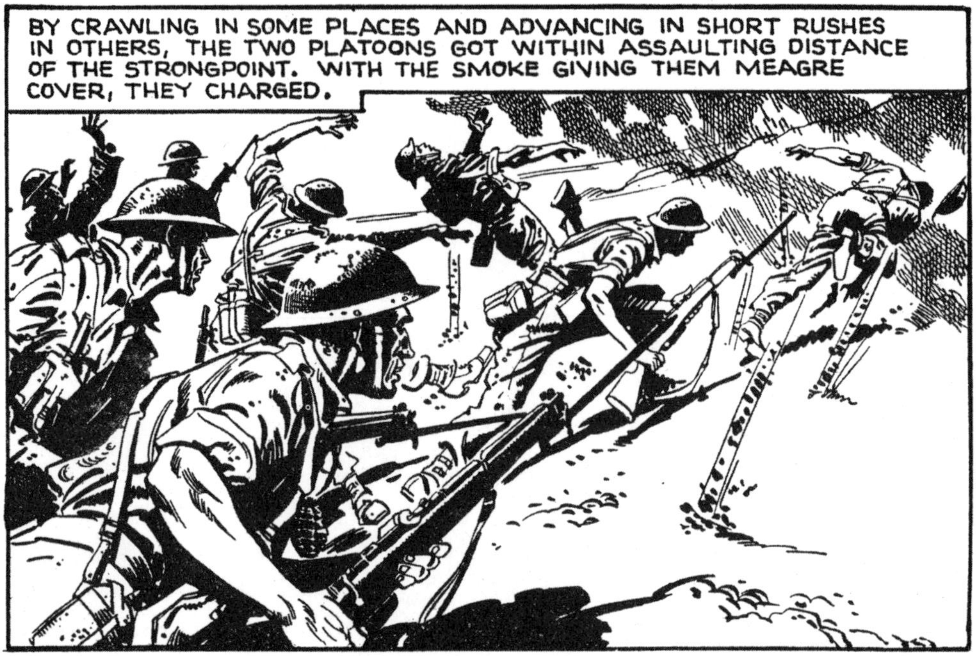
BY CRAWLING IN SOME PLACES AND ADVANCING IN SHORT RUSHES IN OTHERS, THE TWO PLATOONS GOT WITHIN ASSAULTING DISTANCE OF THE STRONGPOINT. WITH THE SMOKE GIVING THEM MEAGRE COVER, THEY CHARGED.

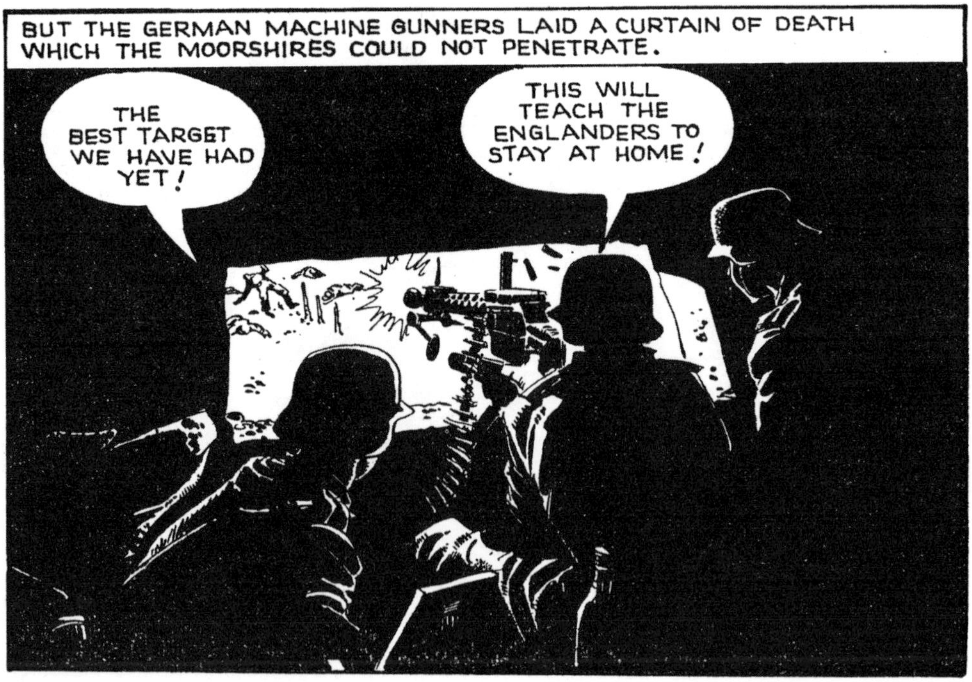
BUT THE GERMAN MACHINE GUNNERS LAID A CURTAIN OF DEATH WHICH THE MOORSHIRES COULD NOT PENETRATE.
THE BEST TARGET WE HAVE HAD YET!
THIS WILL TEACH THE ENGLANDERS TO STAY AT HOME!

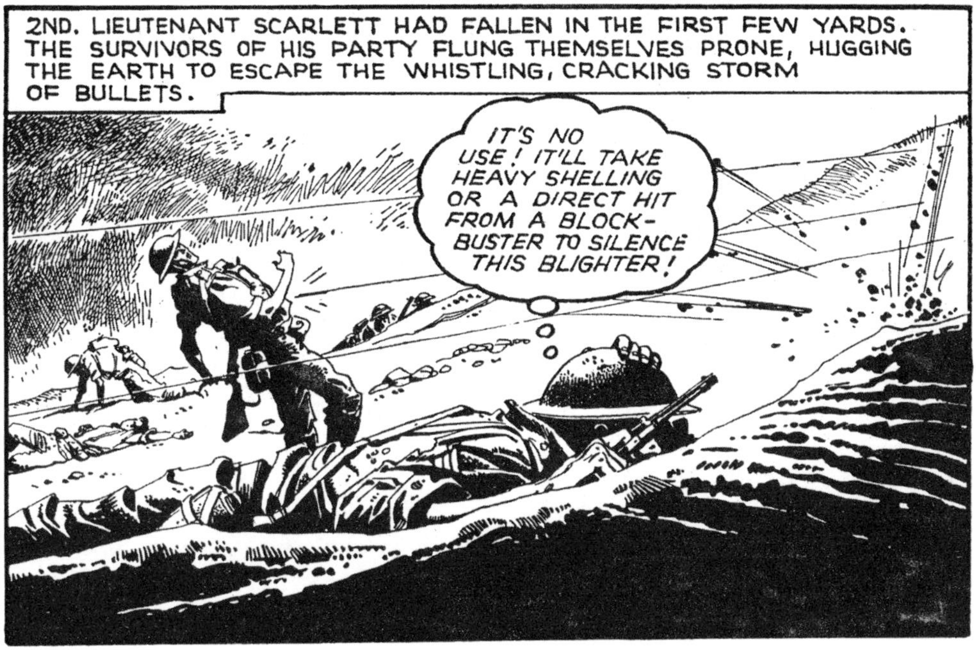
2ND. LIEUTENANT SCARLETT HAD FALLEN IN THE FIRST FEW YARDS. THE SURVIVORS OF HIS PARTY FLUNG THEMSELVES PRONE, HUGGING THE EARTH TO ESCAPE THE WHISTLING, CRACKING STORM OF BULLETS.
IT'S NO USE! IT'LL TAKE HEAVY SHELLING OR A DIRECT HIT FROM A BLOCK-BUSTER TO SILENCE THIS BLIGHTER!

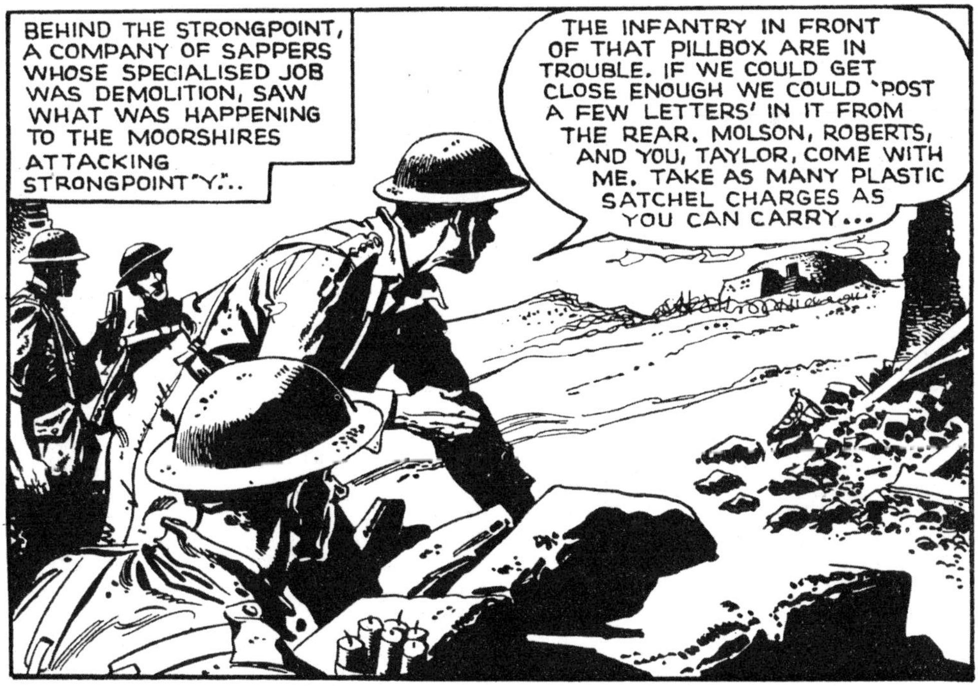
BEHIND THE STRONGPOINT, A COMPANY OF SAPPERS WHOSE SPECIALISED JOB WAS DEMOLITION, SAW WHAT WAS HAPPENING TO THE MOORSHIRES ATTACKING STRONGPOINT "Y"..
THE INFANTRY IN FRONT OF THAT PILLBOX ARE IN TROUBLE. IF WE COULD GET CLOSE ENOUGH WE COULD 'POST A FEW LETTERS' IN IT FROM THE REAR. MOLSON, ROBERTS, AND YOU, TAYLOR, COME WITH ME. TAKE AS MANY PLASTIC SATCHEL CHARGES AS YOU CAN CARRY...

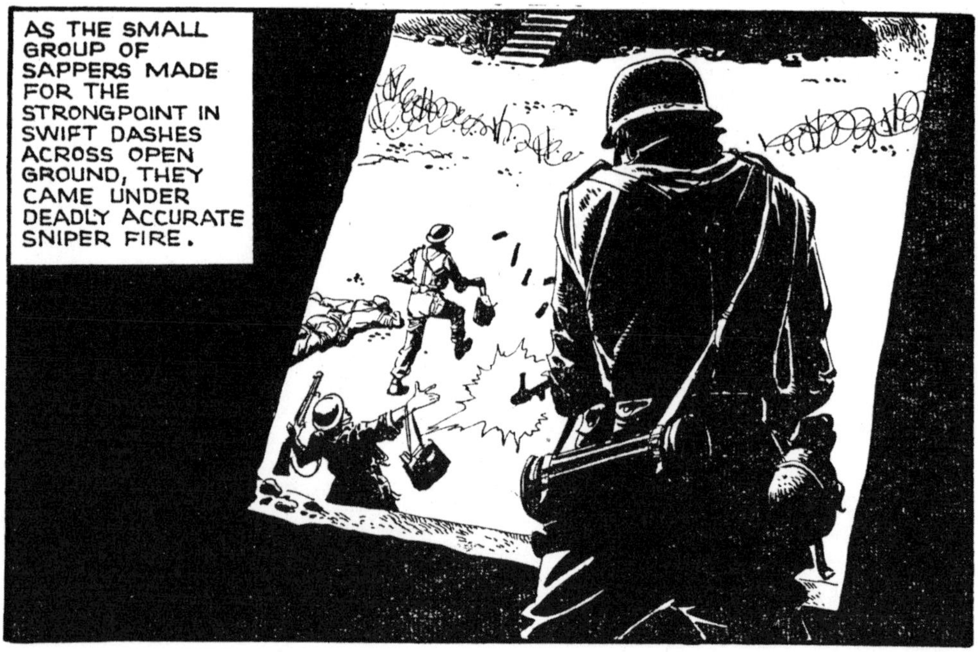
AS THE SMALL GROUP OF SAPPERS MADE FOR THE STRONGPOINT IN SWIFT DASHES ACROSS OPEN GROUND, THEY CAME UNDER DEADLY ACCURATE SNIPER FIRE.

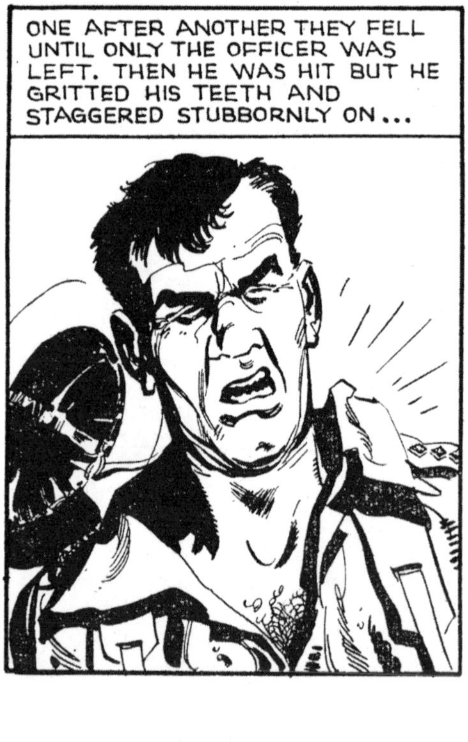
ONE AFTER ANOTHER THEY FELL UNTIL ONLY THE OFFICER WAS LEFT. THEN HE WAS HIT BUT HE GRITTED HIS TEETH AND STAGGERED STUBBORNLY ON...

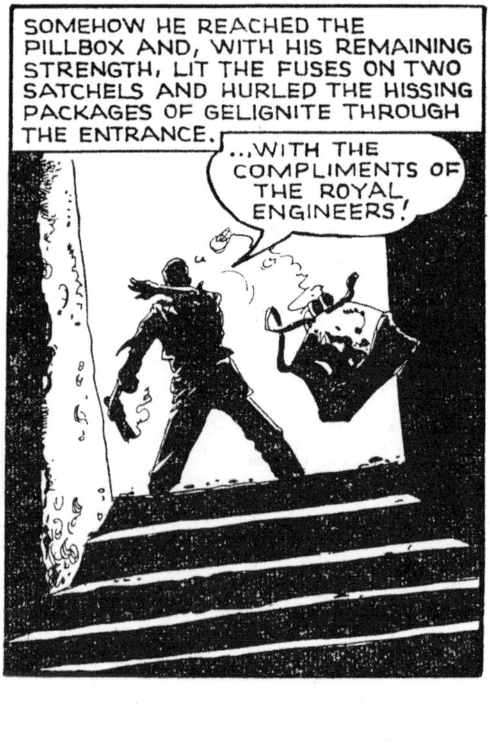
SOMEHOW HE REACHED THE PILLBOX AND, WITH HIS REMAINING STRENGTH, LIT THE FUSES ON TWO SATCHELS AND HURLED THE HISSING PACKAGES OF GELIGNITE THROUGH THE ENTRANCE.
...WITH THE COMPLIMENTS OF THE ROYAL ENGINEERS!

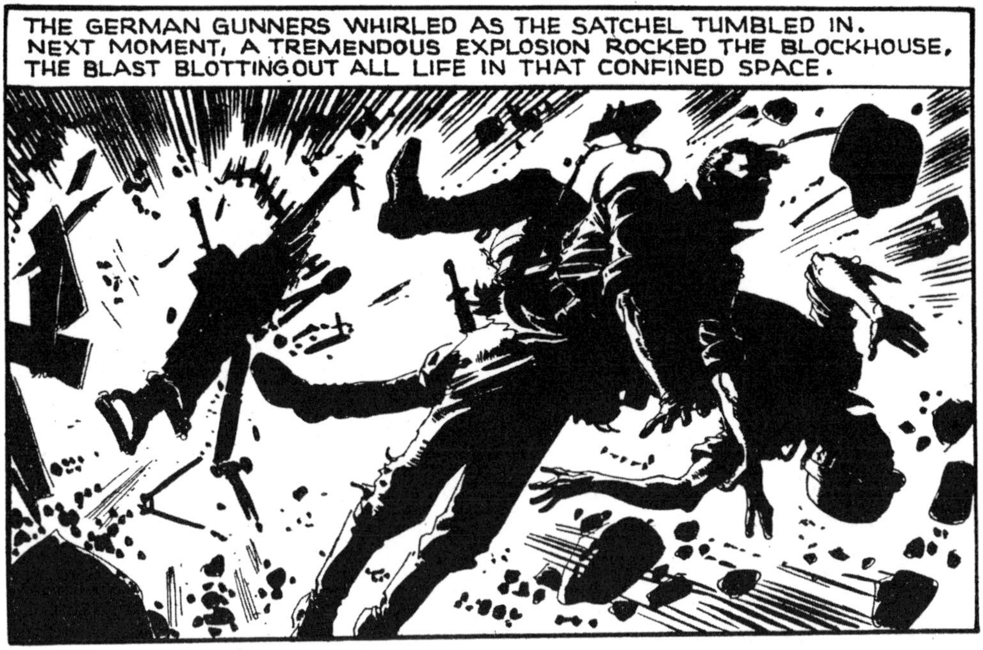
THE GERMAN GUNNERS WHIRLED AS THE SATCHEL TUMBLED IN. NEXT MOMENT, A TREMENDOUS EXPLOSION ROCKED THE BLOCKHOUSE, THE BLAST BLOTTINGOUT ALL LIFE IN THAT CONFINED SPACE.

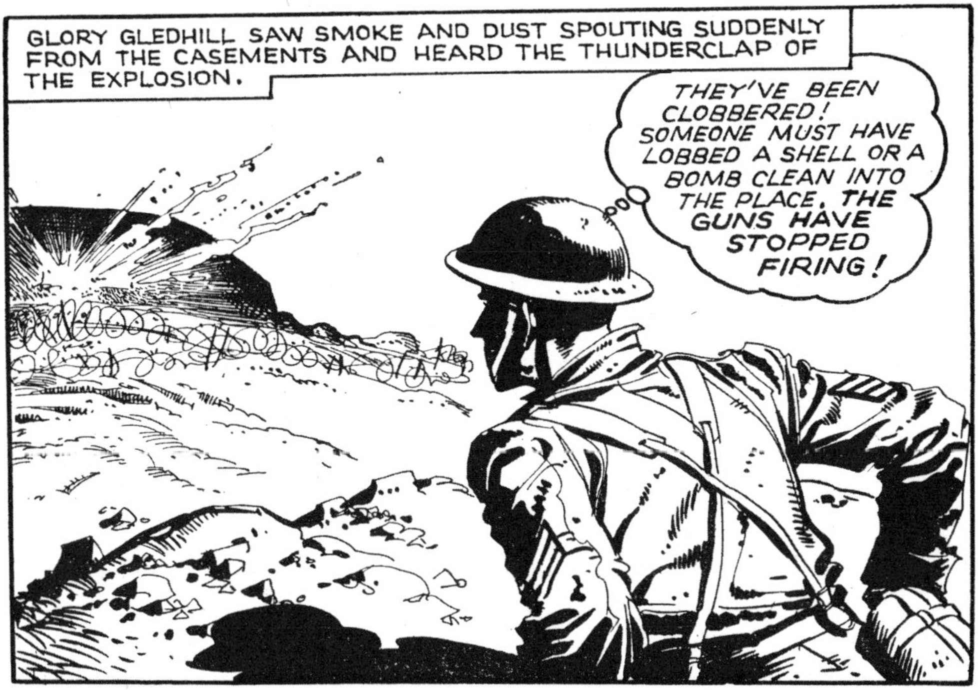
GLORY GLEDHILL SAW SMOKE AND DUST SPOUTING SUDDENLY FROM THE CASEMENTS AND HEARD THE THUNDERCLAP OF THE EXPLOSION.
THEY'VE BEEN CLOBBERED! SOMEONE MUST HAVE LOBBED A SHELL OR A BOMB CLEAN INTO THE PLACE. THE GUNS HAVE STOPPED FIRING!

THE YOUNG SERGEANT HAD AN UNCANNY GIFT FOR SENSING THE RIGHT MOMENT TO TAKE RISKS. HE WAS ON HIS FEET AND RACING TOWARDS THE STRONGPOINT ALMOST BEFORE THE ECHOES OF THE EXPLOSION HAD DIED AWAY...

THERE GOES GLORY AGAIN! MUST BE TRYING TO COMMIT SUICIDE.

THAT'S WHERE YOU'RE WRONG! HE'S GOT IT ALL FIGURED OUT — DOWN TO THE LAST MEDAL!

EVERY MOMENT, GLORY EXPECTED TO FEEL THE NUMBING SHOCK OF A BULLET, BUT HE REACHED THE CONCRETE WALL MIRACULOUSLY UNHARMED.

IN QUICK SUCCESSION, HE SLIPPED TWO HAND GRENADES THROUGH THE NEAREST CASEMENT...

STILL NO SHOTS CAME FROM THE MACHINE GUNS AND THEN THE GRENADES EXPLODED. GLORY DIVED FOR THE PILLBOX ENTRANCE – AND PULLED UP SHORT WHEN HE SAW THE BODY OF A SAPPER CAPTAIN LYING IN FRONT OF IT.

GOOD GRIEF! SO THAT'S WHY THE SPANDAUS STOPPED FIRING! IT WAS THIS POOR BLOKE WHO DID ALL THE DAMAGE!

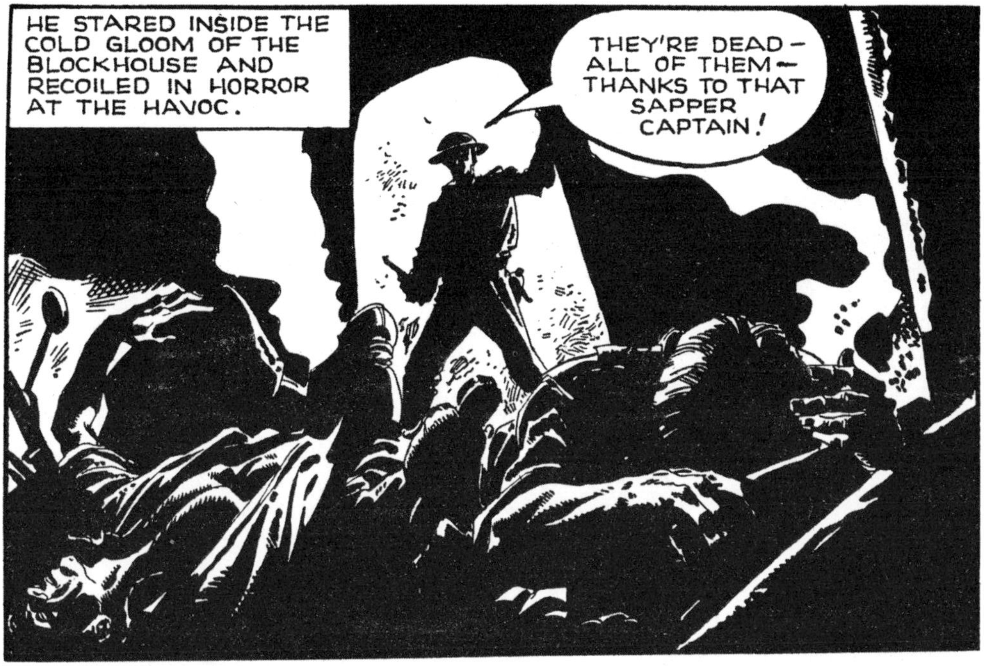
HE STARED INSIDE THE COLD GLOOM OF THE BLOCKHOUSE AND RECOILED IN HORROR AT THE HAVOC.
THEY'RE DEAD - ALL OF THEM - THANKS TO THAT SAPPER CAPTAIN!

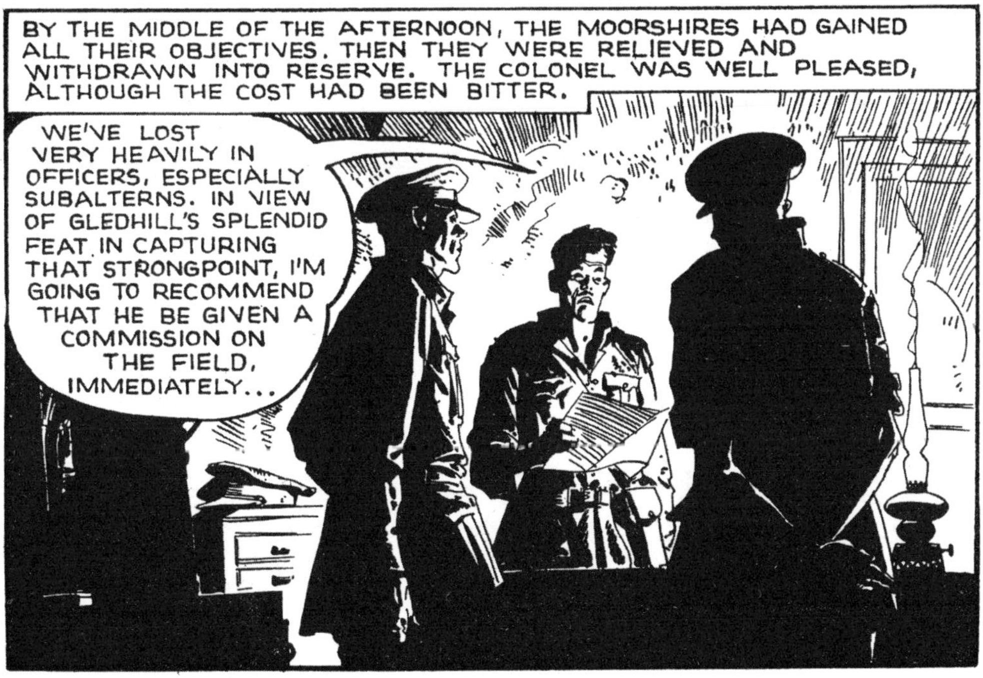
BY THE MIDDLE OF THE AFTERNOON, THE MOORSHIRES HAD GAINED ALL THEIR OBJECTIVES. THEN THEY WERE RELIEVED AND WITHDRAWN INTO RESERVE. THE COLONEL WAS WELL PLEASED, ALTHOUGH THE COST HAD BEEN BITTER.
WE'VE LOST VERY HEAVILY IN OFFICERS, ESPECIALLY SUBALTERNS. IN VIEW OF GLEDHILL'S SPLENDID FEAT IN CAPTURING THAT STRONGPOINT, I'M GOING TO RECOMMEND THAT HE BE GIVEN A COMMISSION ON THE FIELD, IMMEDIATELY...

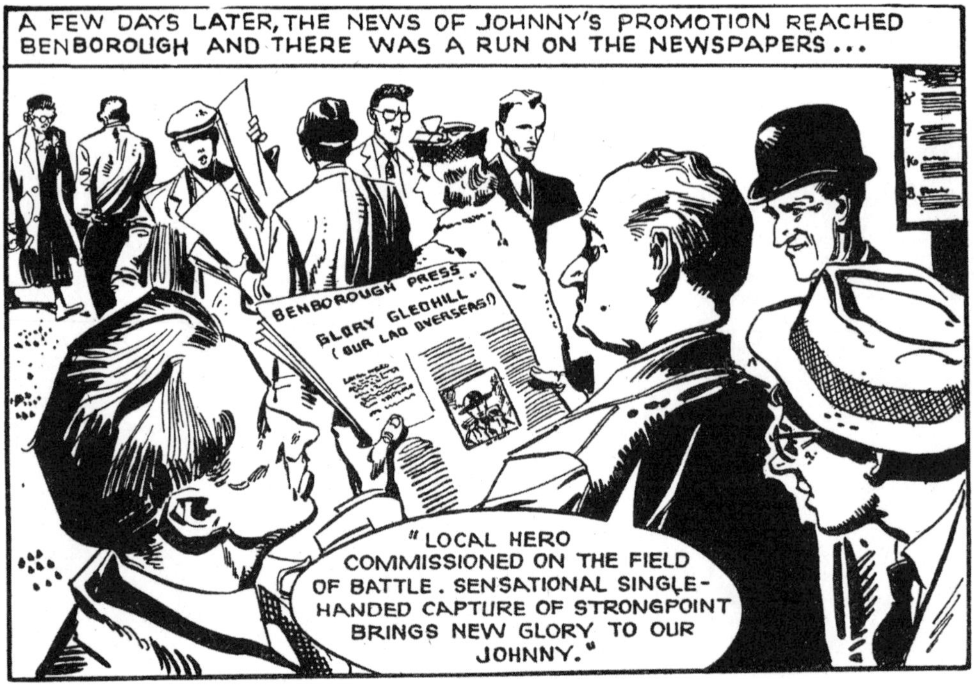
A FEW DAYS LATER, THE NEWS OF JOHNNY'S PROMOTION REACHED BENBOROUGH AND THERE WAS A RUN ON THE NEWSPAPERS...
BENBOROUGH PRESS
GLORY GLEDHILL
(OUR LAD OVERSEAS!)
"LOCAL HERO COMMISSIONED ON THE FIELD OF BATTLE. SENSATIONAL SINGLE-HANDED CAPTURE OF STRONGPOINT BRINGS NEW GLORY TO OUR JOHNNY."

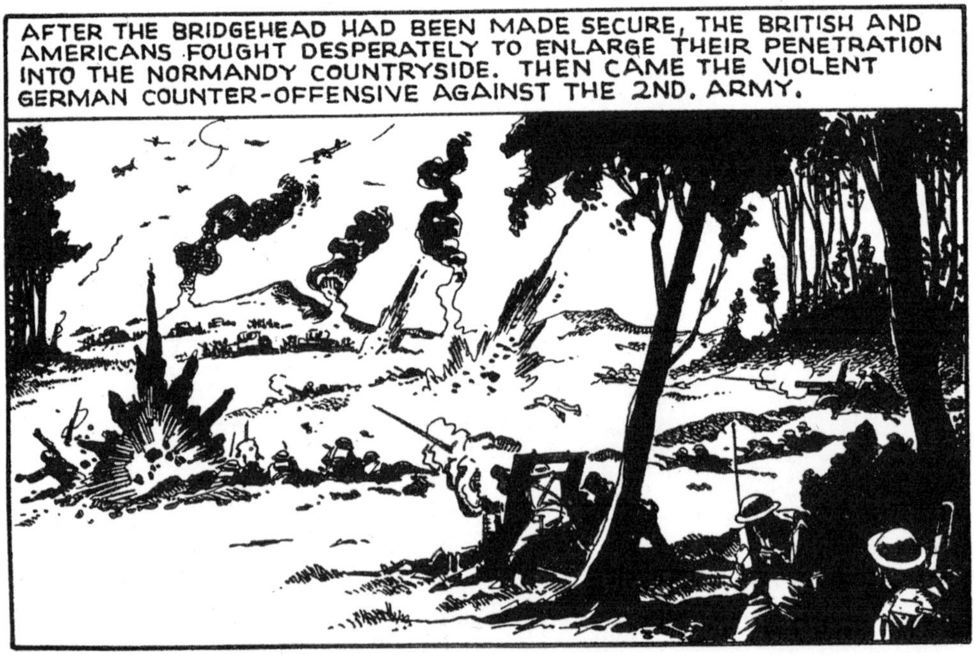
AFTER THE BRIDGEHEAD HAD BEEN MADE SECURE, THE BRITISH AND AMERICANS FOUGHT DESPERATELY TO ENLARGE THEIR PENETRATION INTO THE NORMANDY COUNTRYSIDE. THEN CAME THE VIOLENT GERMAN COUNTER-OFFENSIVE AGAINST THE 2ND. ARMY.

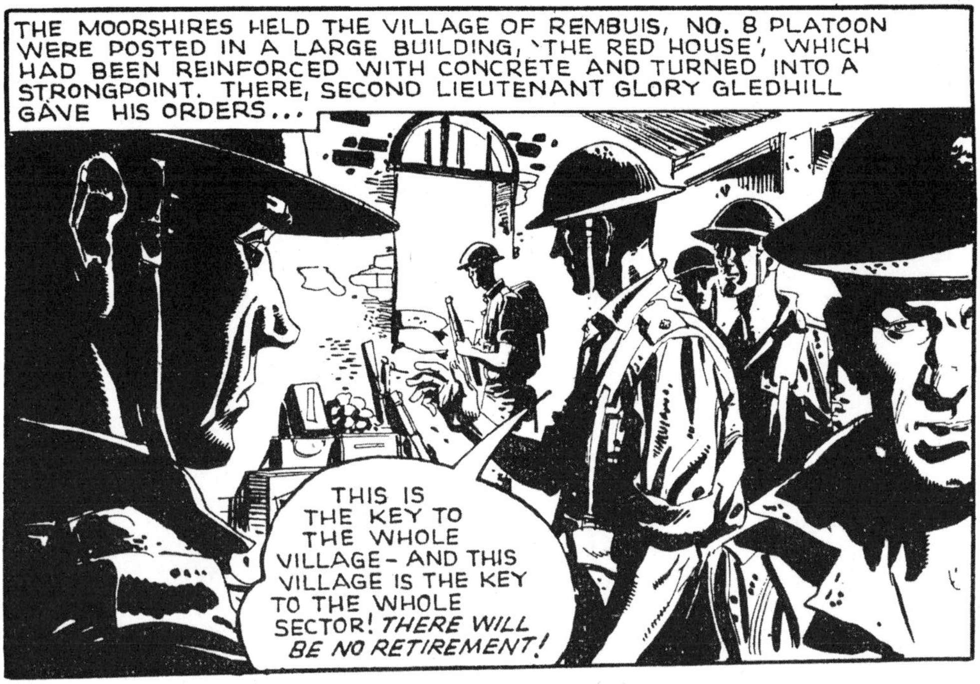
THE MOORSHIRES HELD THE VILLAGE OF REMBUIS, NO. 8 PLATOON WERE POSTED IN A LARGE BUILDING, 'THE RED HOUSE', WHICH HAD BEEN REINFORCED WITH CONCRETE AND TURNED INTO A STRONGPOINT. THERE, SECOND LIEUTENANT GLORY GLEDHILL GAVE HIS ORDERS...
THIS IS THE KEY TO THE WHOLE VILLAGE- AND THIS VILLAGE IS THE KEY TO THE WHOLE SECTOR! *THERE WILL BE NO RETIREMENT!*

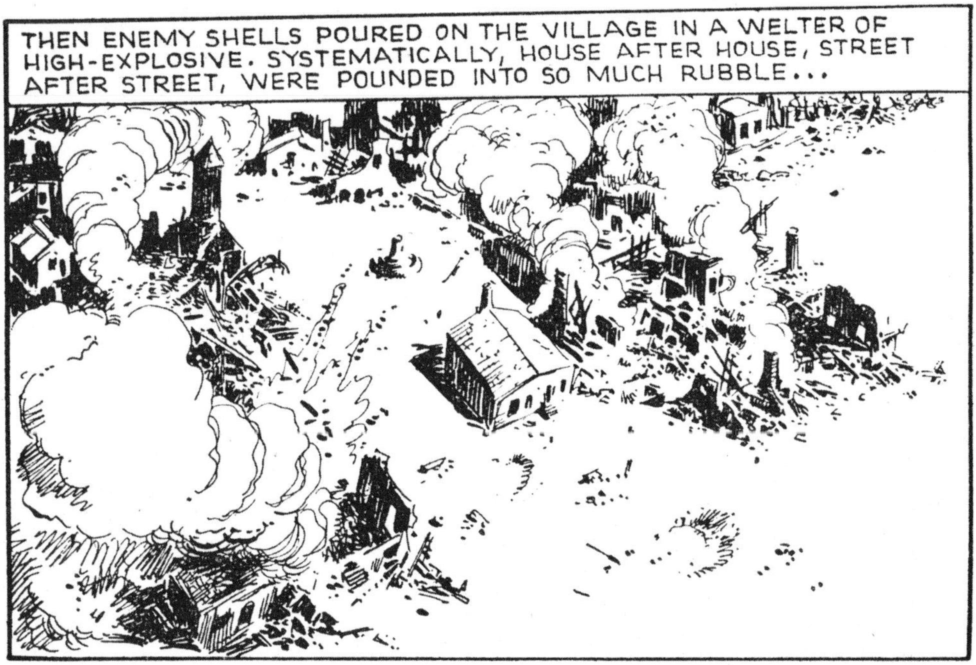
THEN ENEMY SHELLS POURED ON THE VILLAGE IN A WELTER OF HIGH-EXPLOSIVE. SYSTEMATICALLY, HOUSE AFTER HOUSE, STREET AFTER STREET, WERE POUNDED INTO SO MUCH RUBBLE...

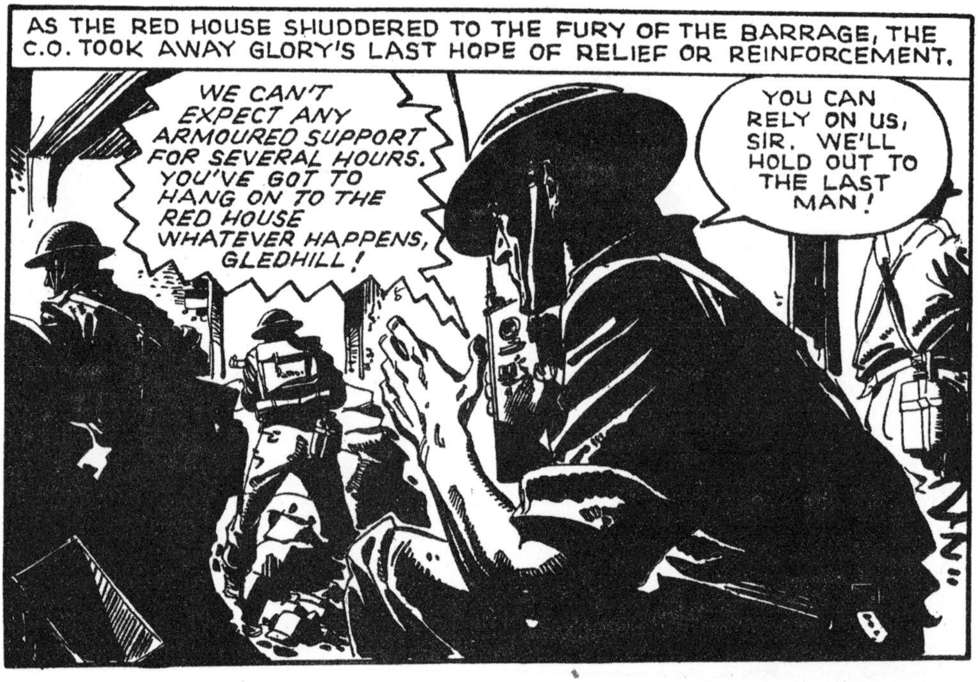
AS THE RED HOUSE SHUDDERED TO THE FURY OF THE BARRAGE, THE C.O. TOOK AWAY GLORY'S LAST HOPE OF RELIEF OR REINFORCEMENT.
WE CAN'T EXPECT ANY ARMOURED SUPPORT FOR SEVERAL HOURS. YOU'VE GOT TO HANG ON TO THE RED HOUSE WHATEVER HAPPENS, GLEDHILL!
YOU CAN RELY ON US, SIR. WE'LL HOLD OUT TO THE LAST MAN!

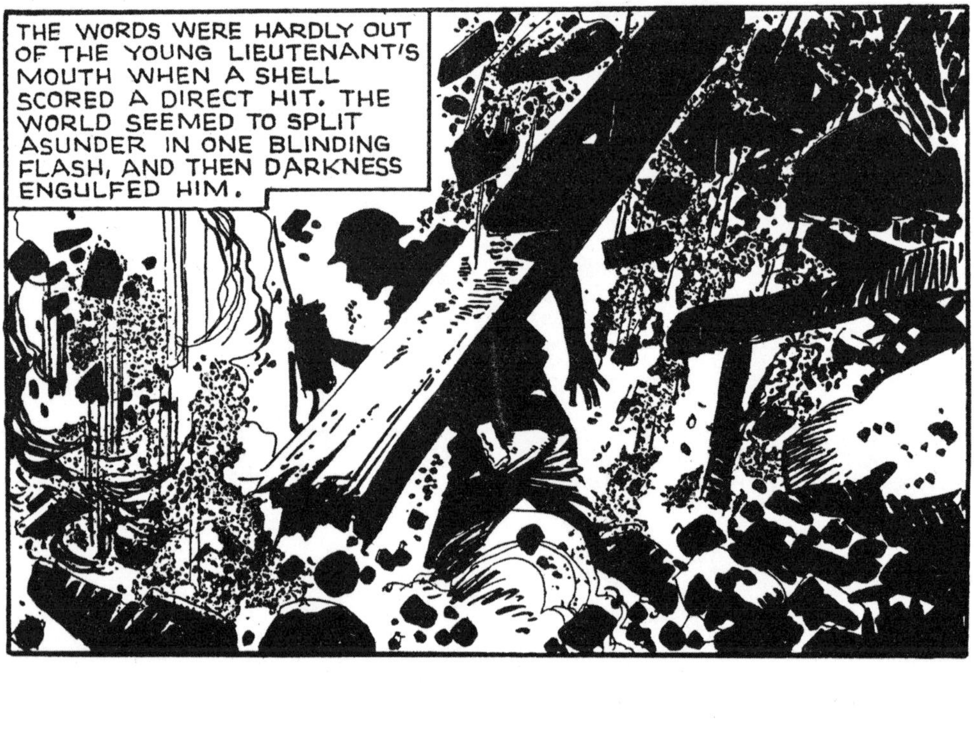
THE WORDS WERE HARDLY OUT OF THE YOUNG LIEUTENANT'S MOUTH WHEN A SHELL SCORED A DIRECT HIT. THE WORLD SEEMED TO SPLIT ASUNDER IN ONE BLINDING FLASH, AND THEN DARKNESS ENGULFED HIM.

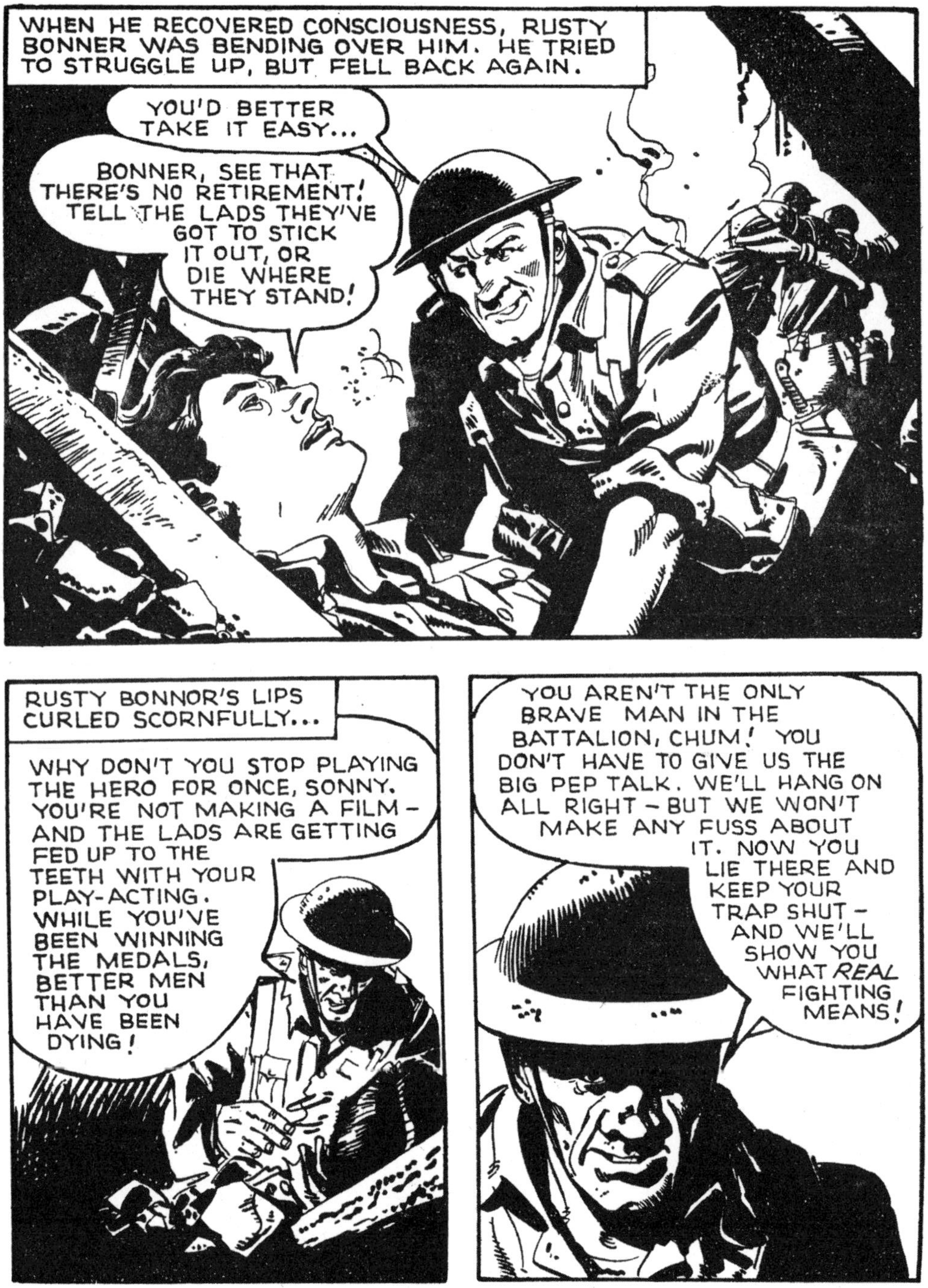
WHEN HE RECOVERED CONSCIOUSNESS, RUSTY BONNER WAS BENDING OVER HIM. HE TRIED TO STRUGGLE UP, BUT FELL BACK AGAIN.
YOU'D BETTER TAKE IT EASY...
BONNER, SEE THAT THERE'S NO RETIREMENT! TELL THE LADS THEY'VE GOT TO STICK IT OUT, OR DIE WHERE THEY STAND!
RUSTY BONNOR'S LIPS CURLED SCORNFULLY...
WHY DON'T YOU STOP PLAYING THE HERO FOR ONCE, SONNY. YOU'RE NOT MAKING A FILM – AND THE LADS ARE GETTING FED UP TO THE TEETH WITH YOUR PLAY-ACTING. WHILE YOU'VE BEEN WINNING THE MEDALS, BETTER MEN THAN YOU HAVE BEEN DYING!
YOU AREN'T THE ONLY BRAVE MAN IN THE BATTALION, CHUM! YOU DON'T HAVE TO GIVE US THE BIG PEP TALK. WE'LL HANG ON ALL RIGHT – BUT WE WON'T MAKE ANY FUSS ABOUT IT. NOW YOU LIE THERE AND KEEP YOUR TRAP SHUT – AND WE'LL SHOW YOU WHAT REAL FIGHTING MEANS!

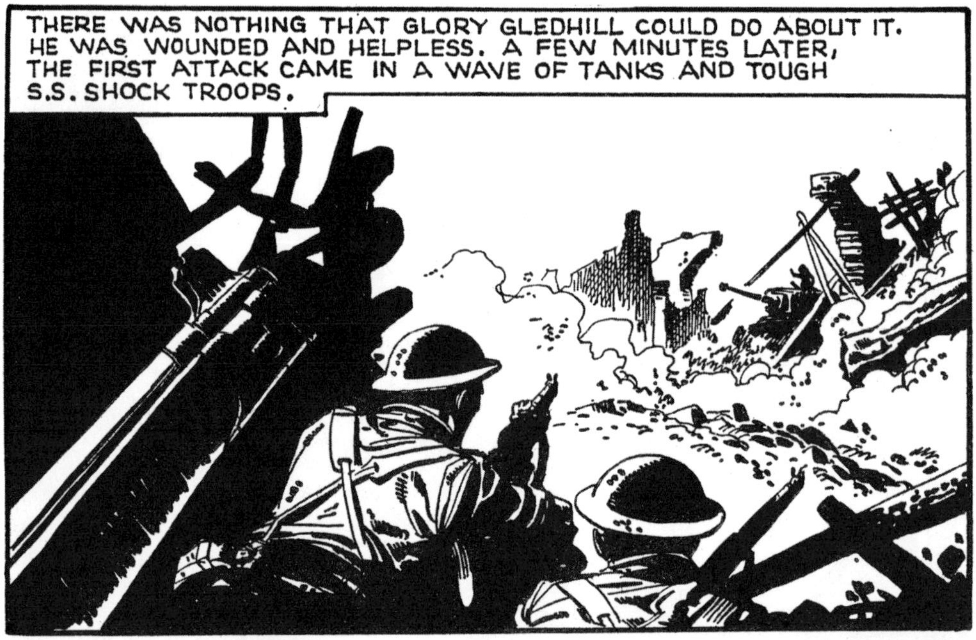
THERE WAS NOTHING THAT GLORY GLEDHILL COULD DO ABOUT IT. HE WAS WOUNDED AND HELPLESS. A FEW MINUTES LATER, THE FIRST ATTACK CAME IN A WAVE OF TANKS AND TOUGH S.S. SHOCK TROOPS.

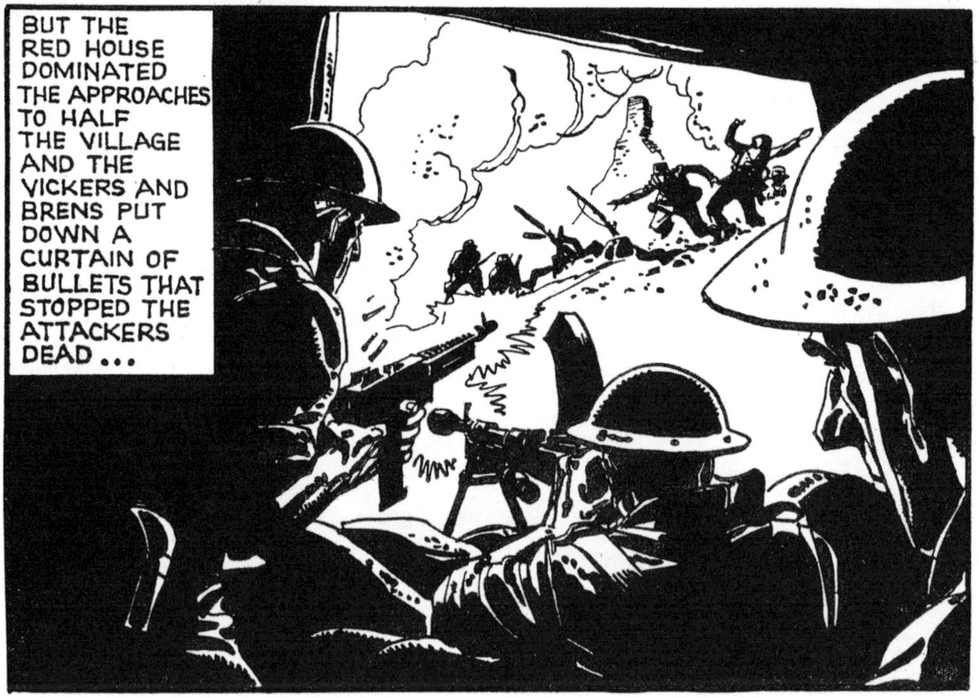
BUT THE RED HOUSE DOMINATED THE APPROACHES TO HALF THE VILLAGE AND THE VICKERS AND BRENS PUT DOWN A CURTAIN OF BULLETS THAT STOPPED THE ATTACKERS DEAD ...

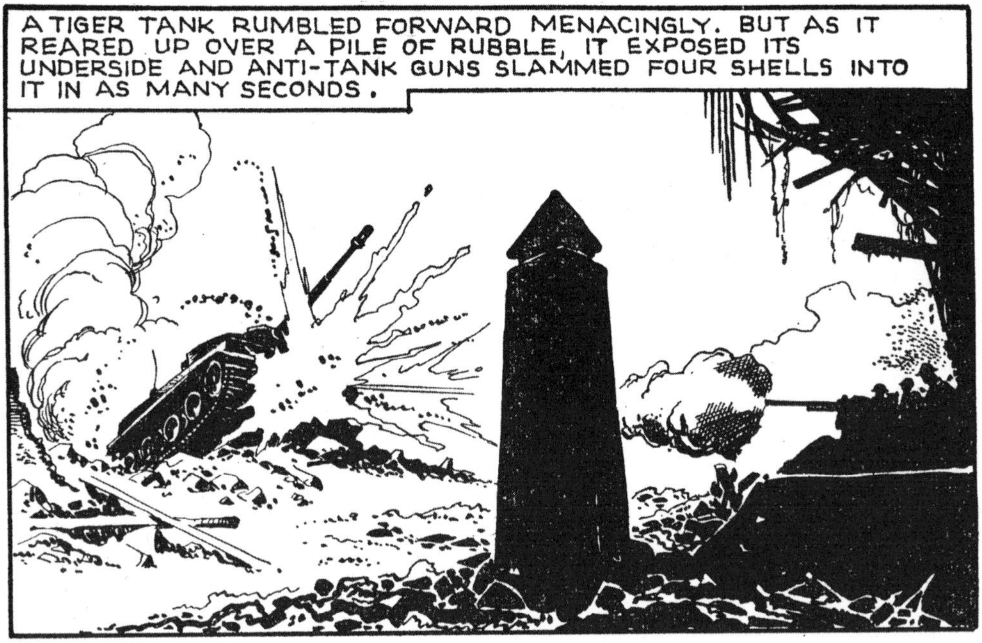
A TIGER TANK RUMBLED FORWARD MENACINGLY. BUT AS IT REARED UP OVER A PILE OF RUBBLE, IT EXPOSED ITS UNDERSIDE AND ANTI-TANK GUNS SLAMMED FOUR SHELLS INTO IT IN AS MANY SECONDS.

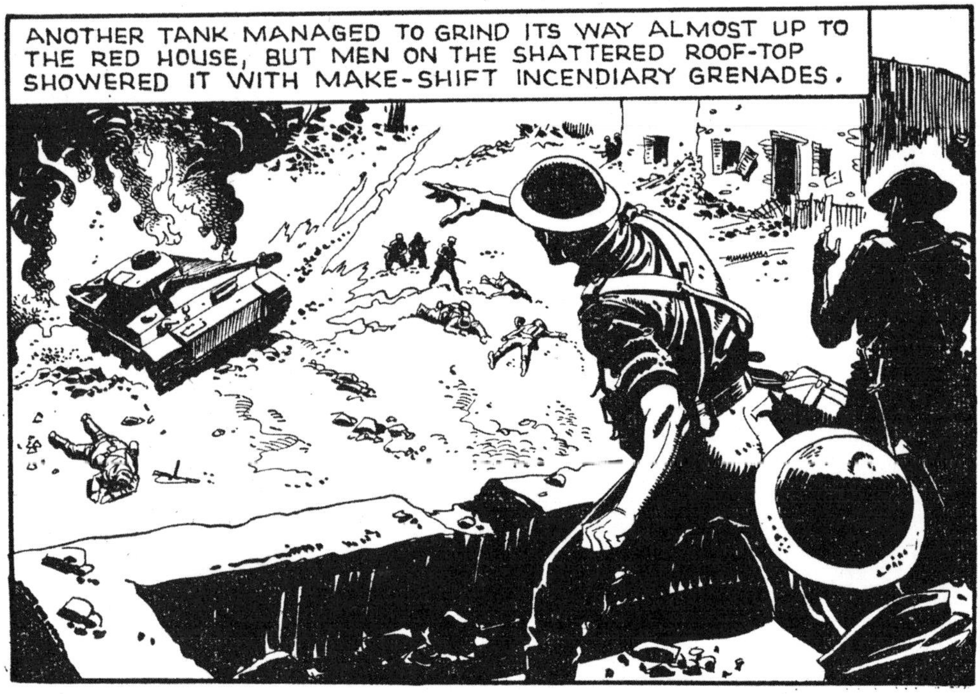
ANOTHER TANK MANAGED TO GRIND ITS WAY ALMOST UP TO THE RED HOUSE, BUT MEN ON THE SHATTERED ROOF-TOP SHOWERED IT WITH MAKE-SHIFT INCENDIARY GRENADES.

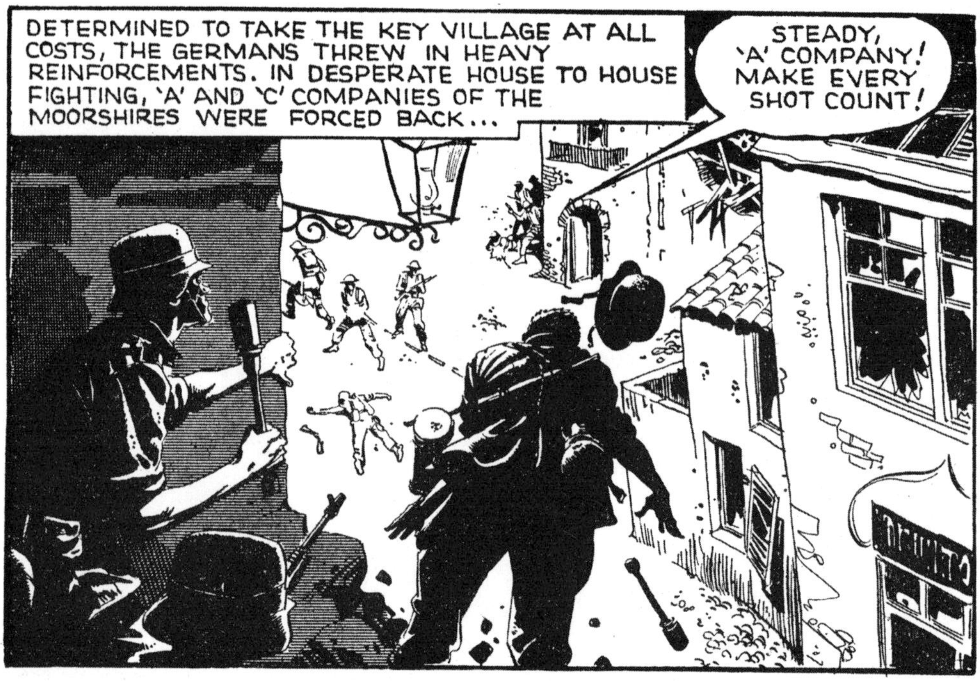
DETERMINED TO TAKE THE KEY VILLAGE AT ALL COSTS, THE GERMANS THREW IN HEAVY REINFORCEMENTS. IN DESPERATE HOUSE TO HOUSE FIGHTING, 'A' AND 'C' COMPANIES OF THE MOORSHIRES WERE FORCED BACK...
STEADY, 'A' COMPANY! MAKE EVERY SHOT COUNT!

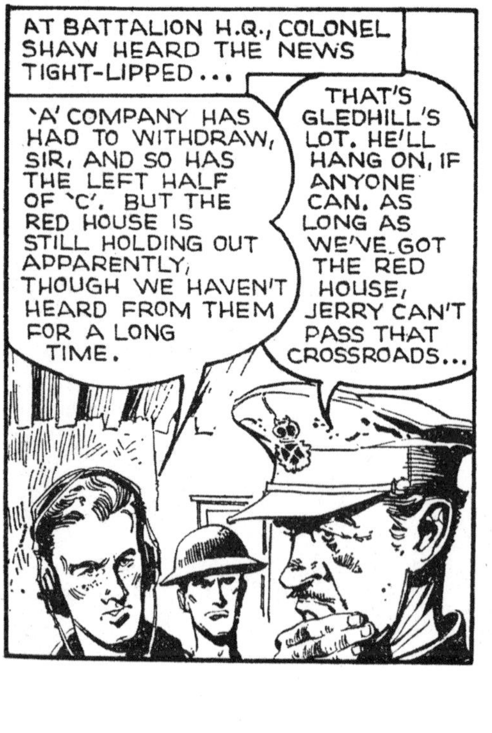
AT BATTALION H.Q., COLONEL SHAW HEARD THE NEWS TIGHT-LIPPED...
'A' COMPANY HAS HAD TO WITHDRAW, SIR, AND SO HAS THE LEFT HALF OF 'C'. BUT THE RED HOUSE IS STILL HOLDING OUT APPARENTLY, THOUGH WE HAVEN'T HEARD FROM THEM FOR A LONG TIME.
THAT'S GLEDHILL'S LOT. HE'LL HANG ON, IF ANYONE CAN. AS LONG AS WE'VE GOT THE RED HOUSE, JERRY CAN'T PASS THAT CROSSROADS...

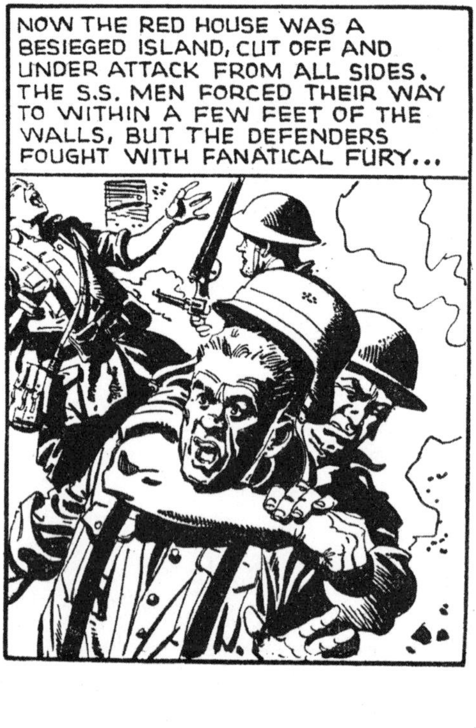
NOW THE RED HOUSE WAS A BESIEGED ISLAND, CUT OFF AND UNDER ATTACK FROM ALL SIDES. THE S.S. MEN FORCED THEIR WAY TO WITHIN A FEW FEET OF THE WALLS, BUT THE DEFENDERS FOUGHT WITH FANATICAL FURY...

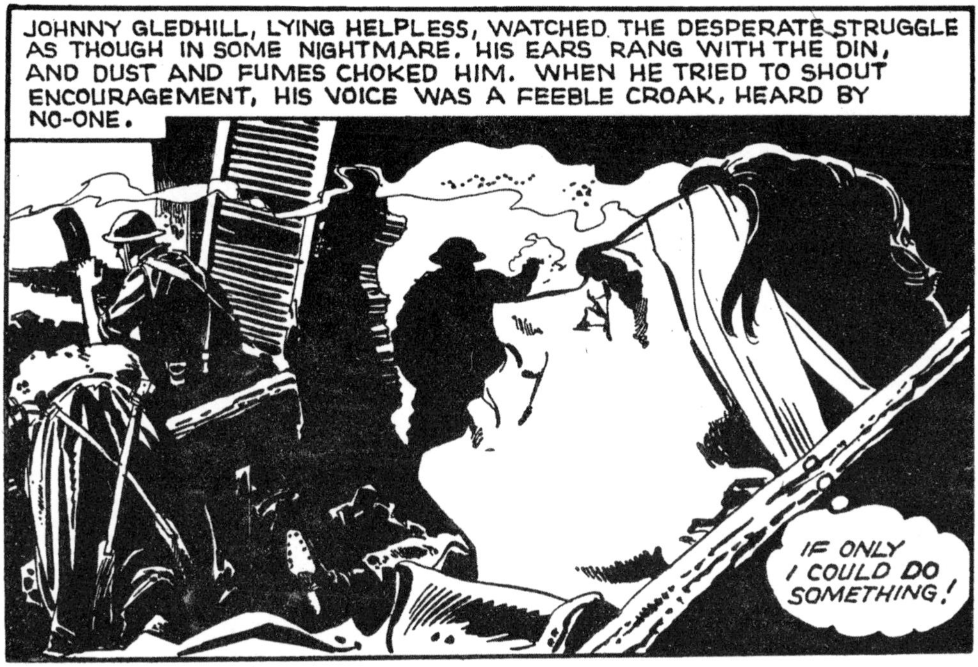
JOHNNY GLEDHILL, LYING HELPLESS, WATCHED THE DESPERATE STRUGGLE AS THOUGH IN SOME NIGHTMARE. HIS EARS RANG WITH THE DIN, AND DUST AND FUMES CHOKED HIM. WHEN HE TRIED TO SHOUT ENCOURAGEMENT, HIS VOICE WAS A FEEBLE CROAK, HEARD BY NO-ONE.
IF ONLY I COULD DO SOMETHING!

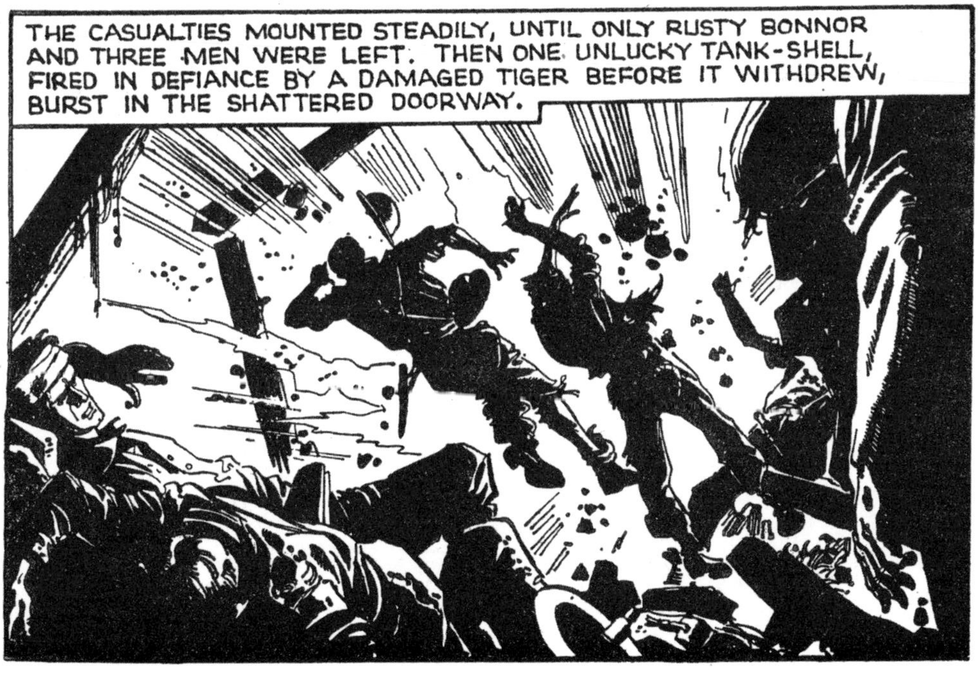
THE CASUALTIES MOUNTED STEADILY, UNTIL ONLY RUSTY BONNOR AND THREE MEN WERE LEFT. THEN ONE UNLUCKY TANK-SHELL, FIRED IN DEFIANCE BY A DAMAGED TIGER BEFORE IT WITHDREW, BURST IN THE SHATTERED DOORWAY.

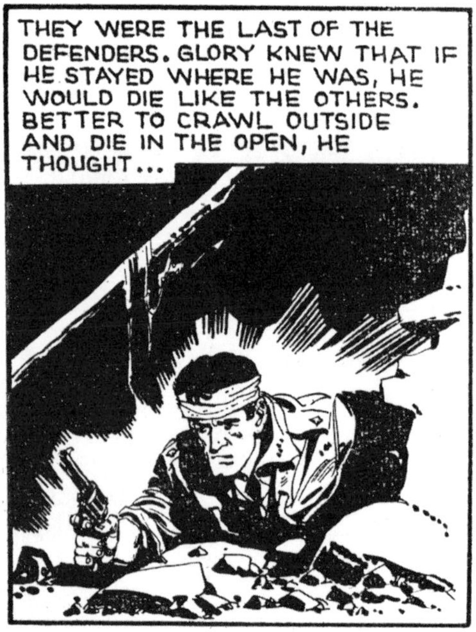
THEY WERE THE LAST OF THE DEFENDERS. GLORY KNEW THAT IF HE STAYED WHERE HE WAS, HE WOULD DIE LIKE THE OTHERS. BETTER TO CRAWL OUTSIDE AND DIE IN THE OPEN, HE THOUGHT...

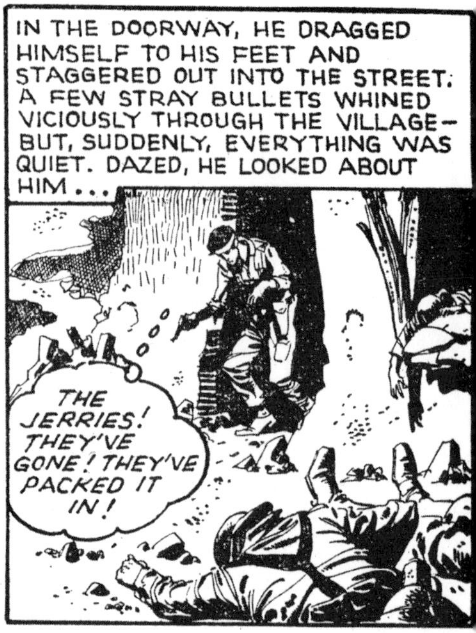
IN THE DOORWAY, HE DRAGGED HIMSELF TO HIS FEET AND STAGGERED OUT INTO THE STREET. A FEW STRAY BULLETS WHINED VICIOUSLY THROUGH THE VILLAGE– BUT, SUDDENLY, EVERYTHING WAS QUIET. DAZED, HE LOOKED ABOUT HIM...
THE JERRIES! THEY'VE GONE! THEY'VE PACKED IT IN!

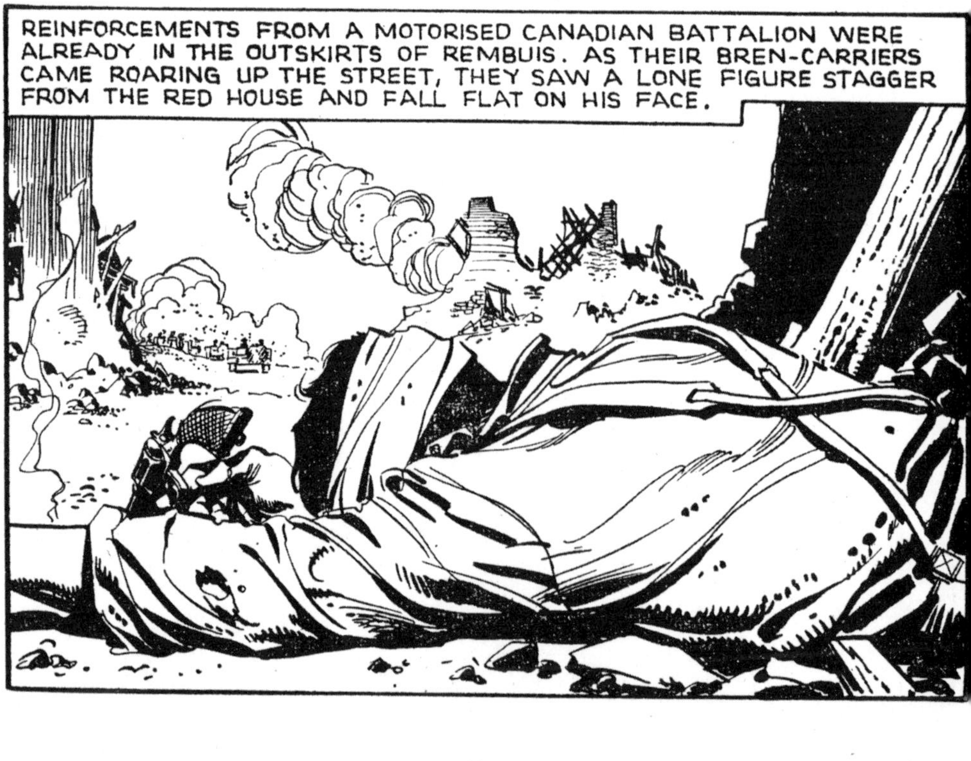
REINFORCEMENTS FROM A MOTORISED CANADIAN BATTALION WERE ALREADY IN THE OUTSKIRTS OF REMBUIS. AS THEIR BREN-CARRIERS CAME ROARING UP THE STREET, THEY SAW A LONE FIGURE STAGGER FROM THE RED HOUSE AND FALL FLAT ON HIS FACE.

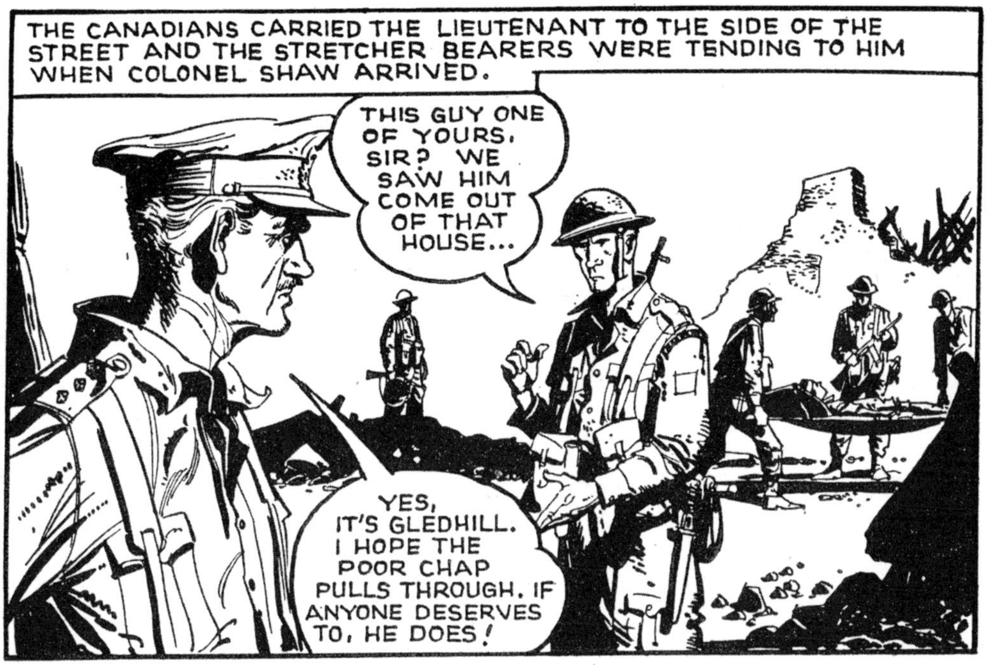
THE CANADIANS CARRIED THE LIEUTENANT TO THE SIDE OF THE STREET AND THE STRETCHER BEARERS WERE TENDING TO HIM WHEN COLONEL SHAW ARRIVED.
THIS GUY ONE OF YOURS, SIR? WE SAW HIM COME OUT OF THAT HOUSE...
YES, IT'S GLEDHILL. I HOPE THE POOR CHAP PULLS THROUGH. IF ANYONE DESERVES TO, HE DOES!

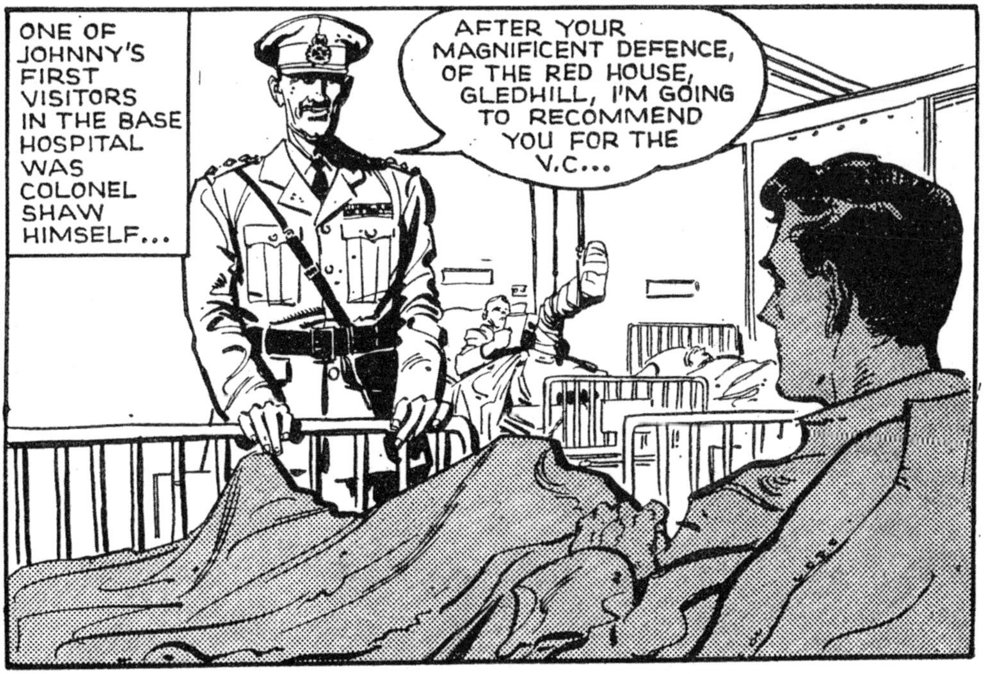
ONE OF JOHNNY'S FIRST VISITORS IN THE BASE HOSPITAL WAS COLONEL SHAW HIMSELF...
AFTER YOUR MAGNIFICENT DEFENCE, OF THE RED HOUSE, GLEDHILL, I'M GOING TO RECOMMEND YOU FOR THE V.C...

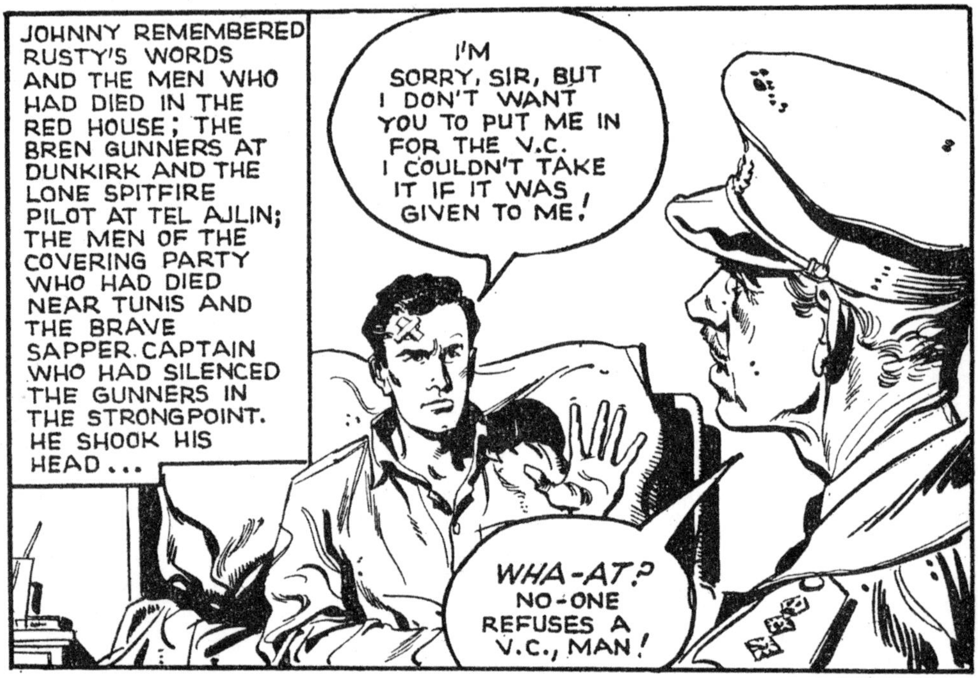
JOHNNY REMEMBERED RUSTY'S WORDS AND THE MEN WHO HAD DIED IN THE RED HOUSE; THE BREN GUNNERS AT DUNKIRK AND THE LONE SPITFIRE PILOT AT TEL AJLIN; THE MEN OF THE COVERING PARTY WHO HAD DIED NEAR TUNIS AND THE BRAVE SAPPER CAPTAIN WHO HAD SILENCED THE GUNNERS IN THE STRONGPOINT. HE SHOOK HIS HEAD . . .
I'M SORRY, SIR, BUT I DON'T WANT YOU TO PUT ME IN FOR THE V.C. I COULDN'T TAKE IT IF IT WAS GIVEN TO ME!
WHA-AT? NO-ONE REFUSES A V.C., MAN!

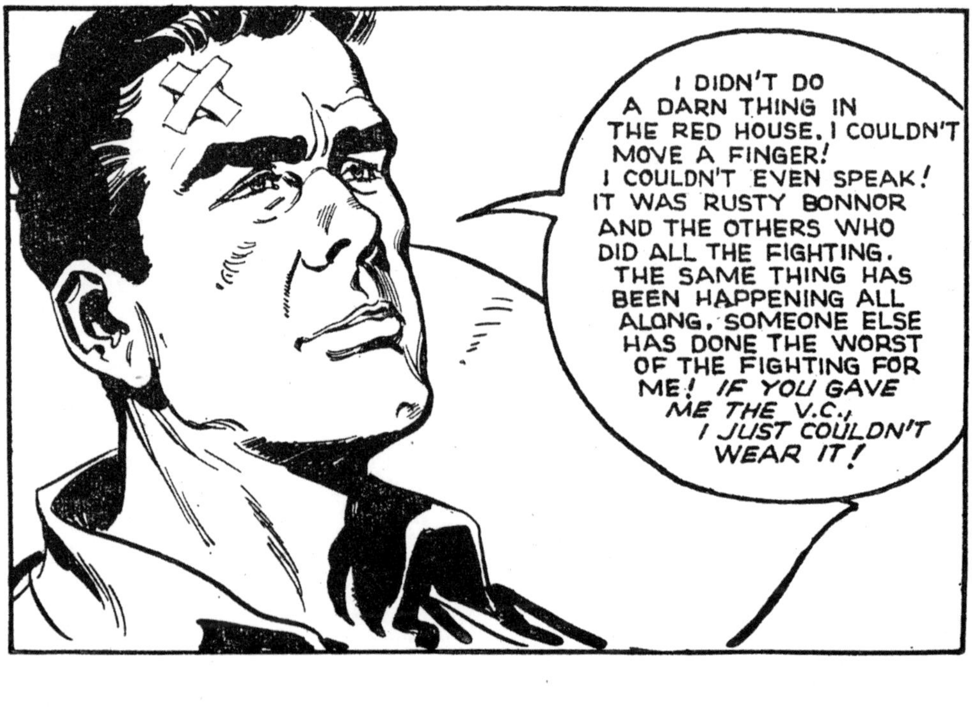
I DIDN'T DO A DARN THING IN THE RED HOUSE. I COULDN'T MOVE A FINGER! I COULDN'T EVEN SPEAK! IT WAS RUSTY BONNOR AND THE OTHERS WHO DID ALL THE FIGHTING. THE SAME THING HAS BEEN HAPPENING ALL ALONG. SOMEONE ELSE HAS DONE THE WORST OF THE FIGHTING FOR ME! IF YOU GAVE ME THE V.C., I JUST COULDN'T WEAR IT!

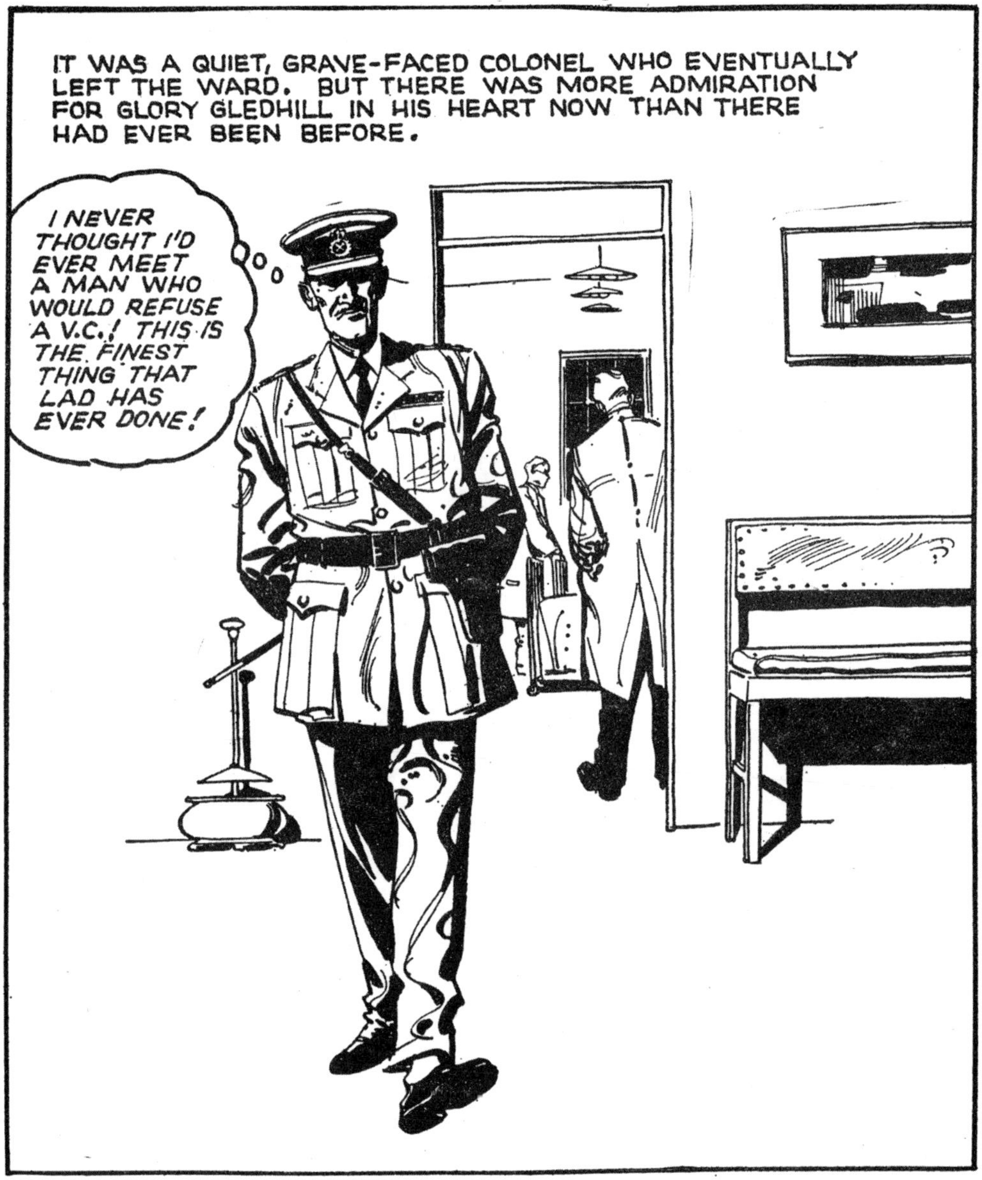
IT WAS A QUIET, GRAVE-FACED COLONEL WHO EVENTUALLY LEFT THE WARD. BUT THERE WAS MORE ADMIRATION FOR GLORY GLEDHILL IN HIS HEART NOW THAN THERE HAD EVER BEEN BEFORE.
I NEVER THOUGHT I'D EVER MEET A MAN WHO WOULD REFUSE A V.C.! THIS IS THE FINEST THING THAT LAD HAS EVER DONE!

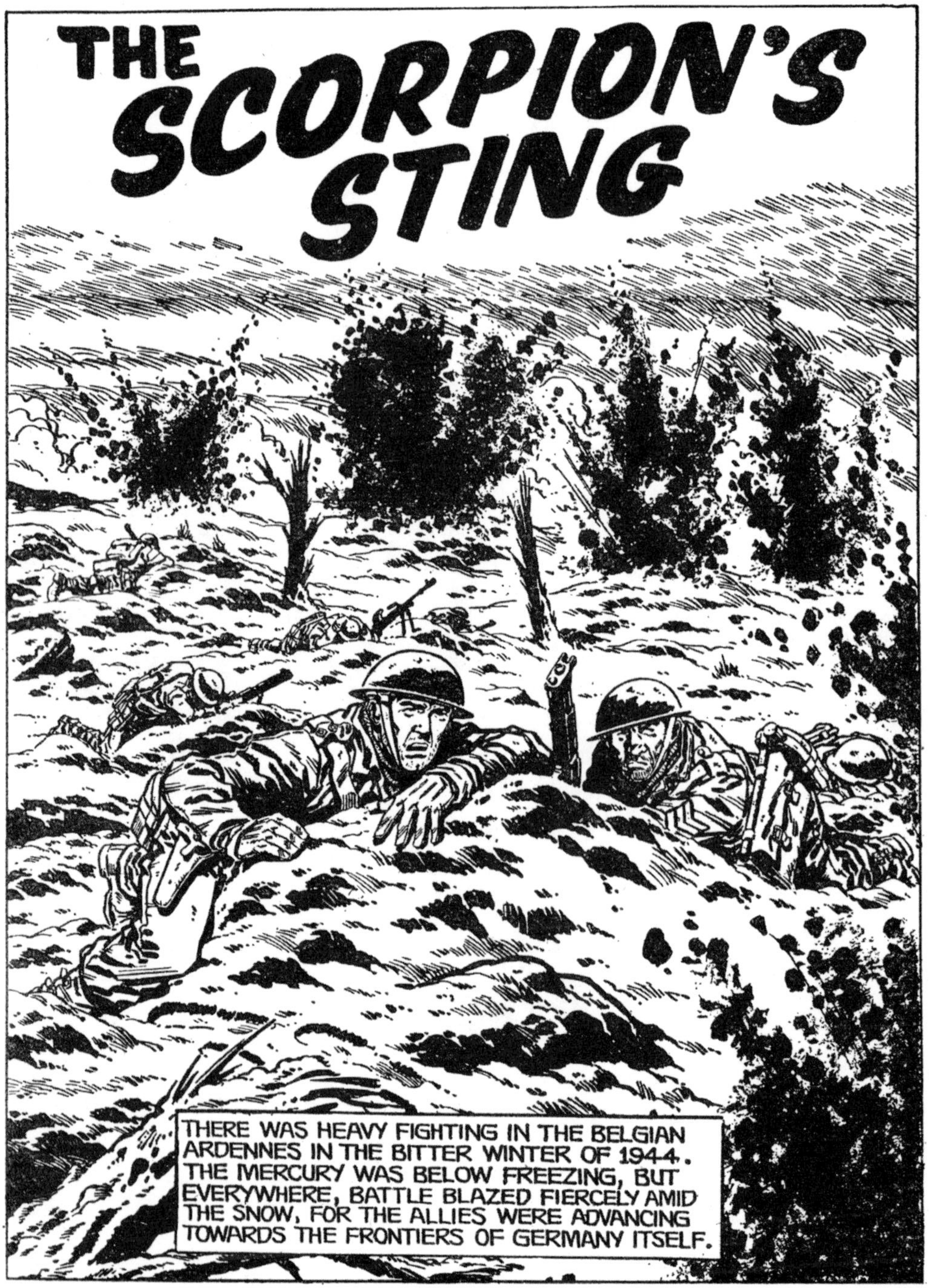
THE SCORPION'S STING
THERE WAS HEAVY FIGHTING IN THE BELGIAN ARDENNES IN THE BITTER WINTER OF 1944. THE MERCURY WAS BELOW FREEZING, BUT EVERYWHERE, BATTLE BLAZED FIERCELY AMID THE SNOW, FOR THE ALLIES WERE ADVANCING TOWARDS THE FRONTIERS OF GERMANY ITSELF.

Chapter 1. Mark of the Brotherhood

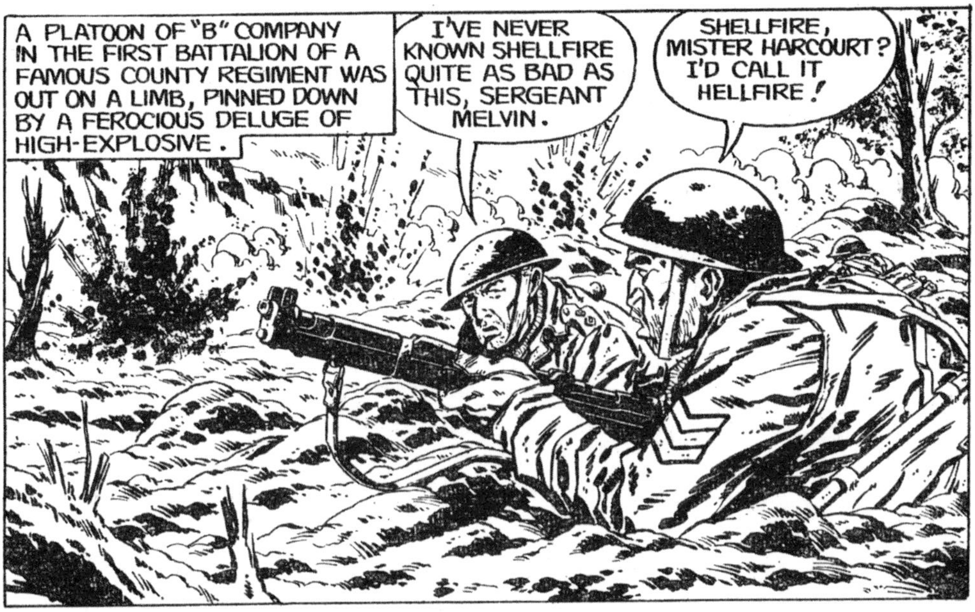
A PLATOON OF "B" COMPANY IN THE FIRST BATTALION OF A FAMOUS COUNTY REGIMENT WAS OUT ON A LIMB, PINNED DOWN BY A FEROCIOUS DELUGE OF HIGH-EXPLOSIVE.
I'VE NEVER KNOWN SHELLFIRE QUITE AS BAD AS THIS, SERGEANT MELVIN.
SHELLFIRE, MISTER HARCOURT? I'D CALL IT HELLFIRE!

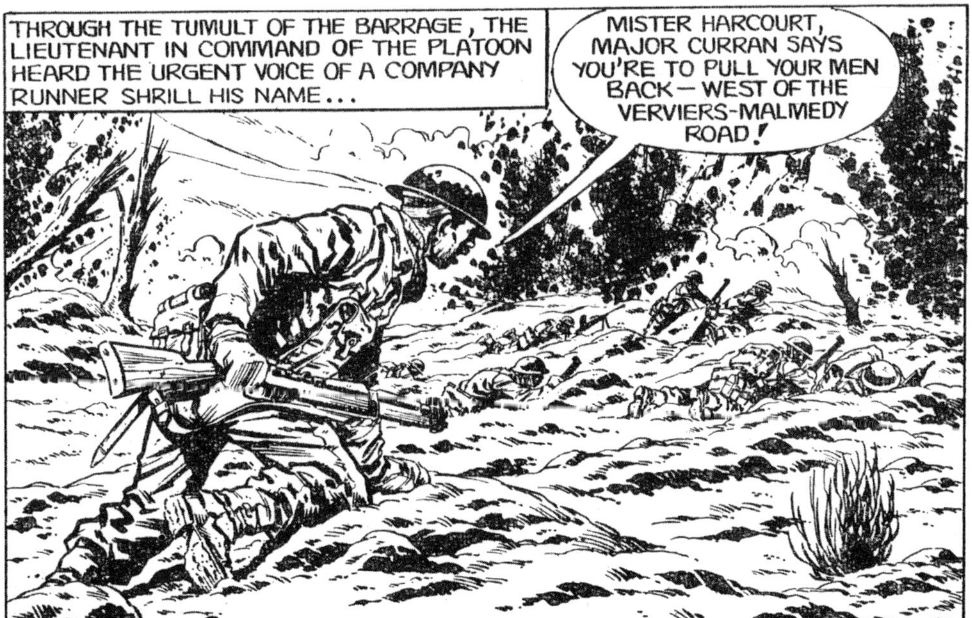
THROUGH THE TUMULT OF THE BARRAGE, THE LIEUTENANT IN COMMAND OF THE PLATOON HEARD THE URGENT VOICE OF A COMPANY RUNNER SHRILL HIS NAME...
MISTER HARCOURT, MAJOR CURRAN SAYS YOU'RE TO PULL YOUR MEN BACK — WEST OF THE VERVIERS-MALMEDY ROAD!

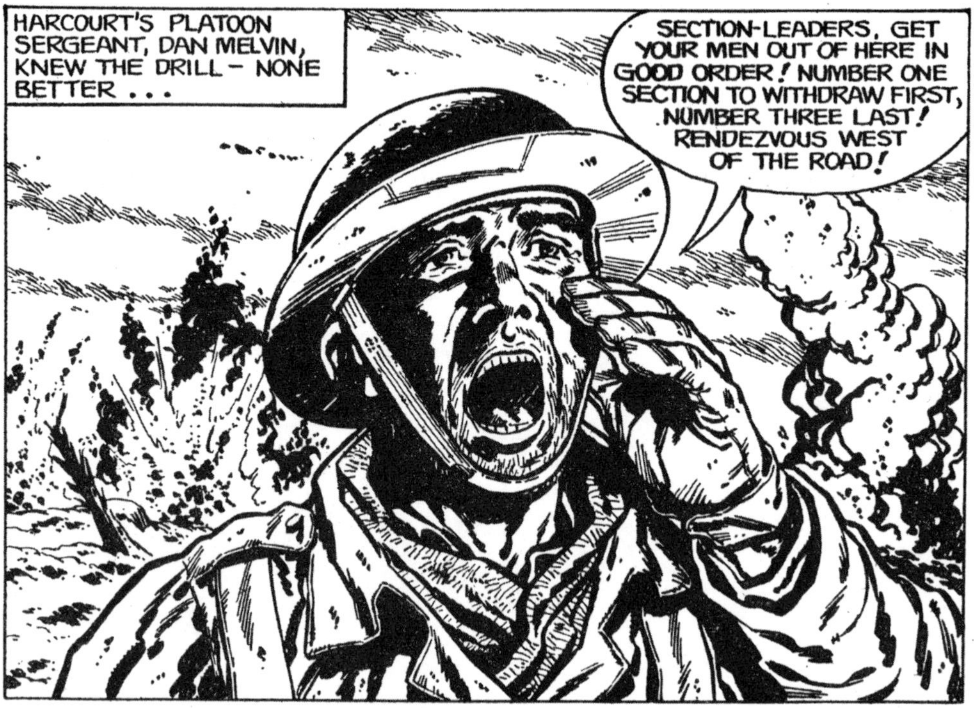
HARCOURT'S PLATOON SERGEANT, DAN MELVIN, KNEW THE DRILL – NONE BETTER . . .
SECTION-LEADERS, GET YOUR MEN OUT OF HERE IN GOOD ORDER! NUMBER ONE SECTION TO WITHDRAW FIRST, NUMBER THREE LAST! RENDEZVOUS WEST OF THE ROAD!

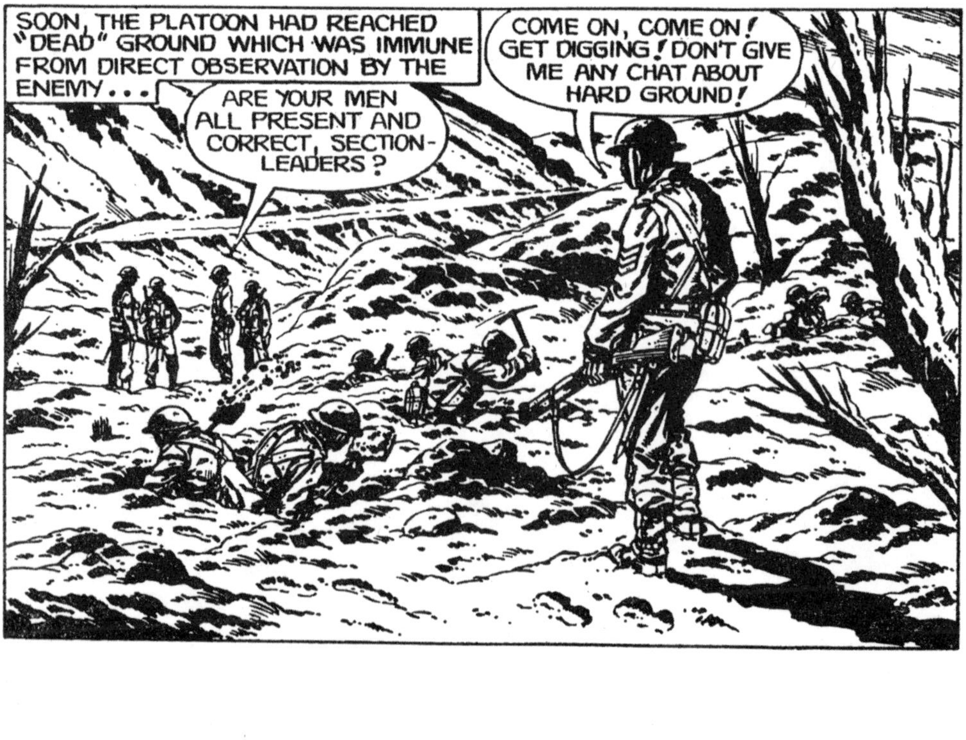
SOON, THE PLATOON HAD REACHED "DEAD" GROUND WHICH WAS IMMUNE FROM DIRECT OBSERVATION BY THE ENEMY . . .
ARE YOUR MEN ALL PRESENT AND CORRECT, SECTION-LEADERS?
COME ON, COME ON! GET DIGGING! DON'T GIVE ME ANY CHAT ABOUT HARD GROUND!

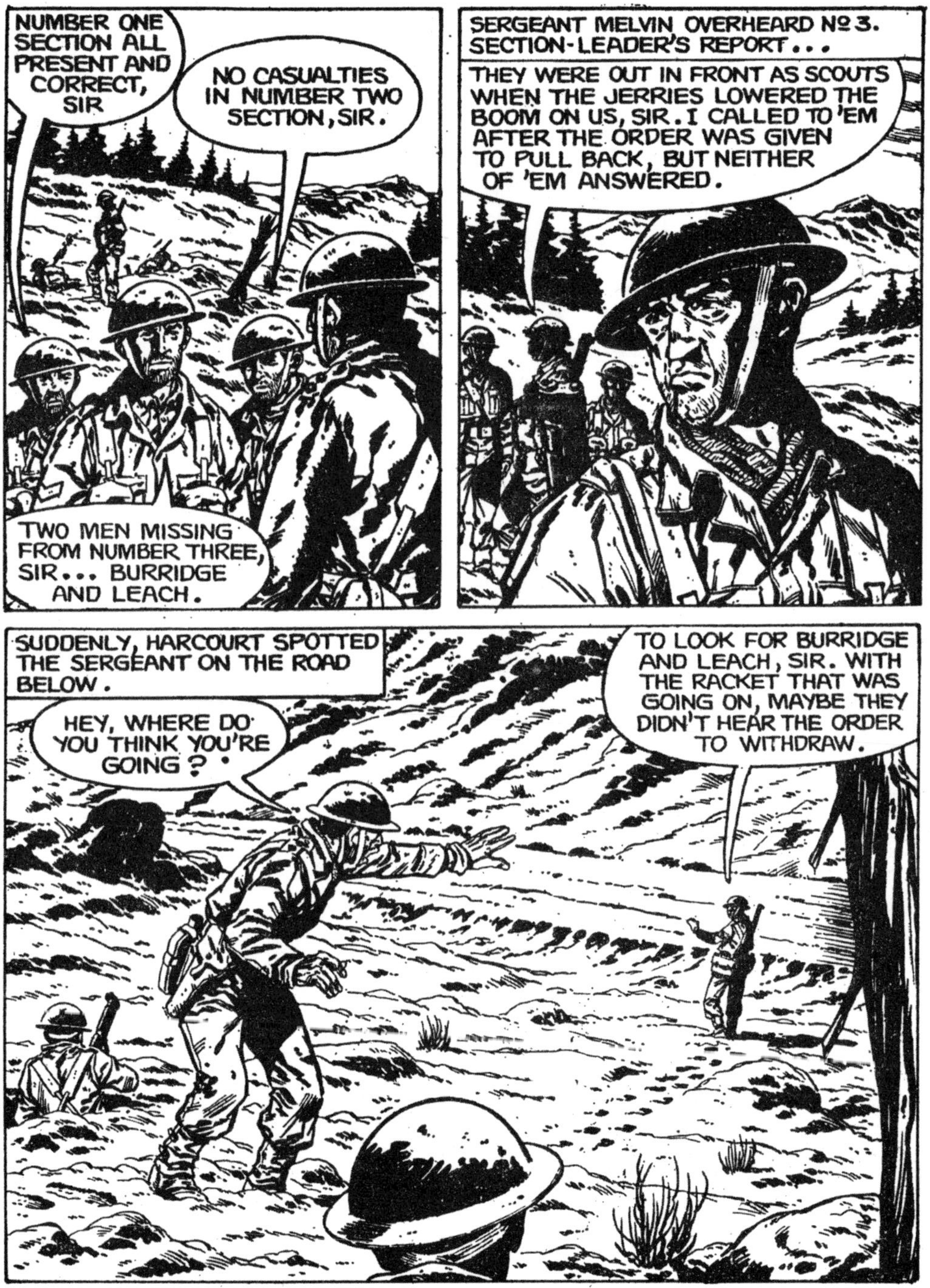
NUMBER ONE SECTION ALL PRESENT AND CORRECT, SIR
NO CASUALTIES IN NUMBER TWO SECTION, SIR.
TWO MEN MISSING FROM NUMBER THREE, SIR... BURRIDGE AND LEACH.
SERGEANT MELVIN OVERHEARD Nº 3. SECTION-LEADER'S REPORT...
THEY WERE OUT IN FRONT AS SCOUTS WHEN THE JERRIES LOWERED THE BOOM ON US, SIR. I CALLED TO 'EM AFTER THE ORDER WAS GIVEN TO PULL BACK, BUT NEITHER OF 'EM ANSWERED.
SUDDENLY, HARCOURT SPOTTED THE SERGEANT ON THE ROAD BELOW.
HEY, WHERE DO YOU THINK YOU'RE GOING?
TO LOOK FOR BURRIDGE AND LEACH, SIR. WITH THE RACKET THAT WAS GOING ON, MAYBE THEY DIDN'T HEAR THE ORDER TO WITHDRAW.

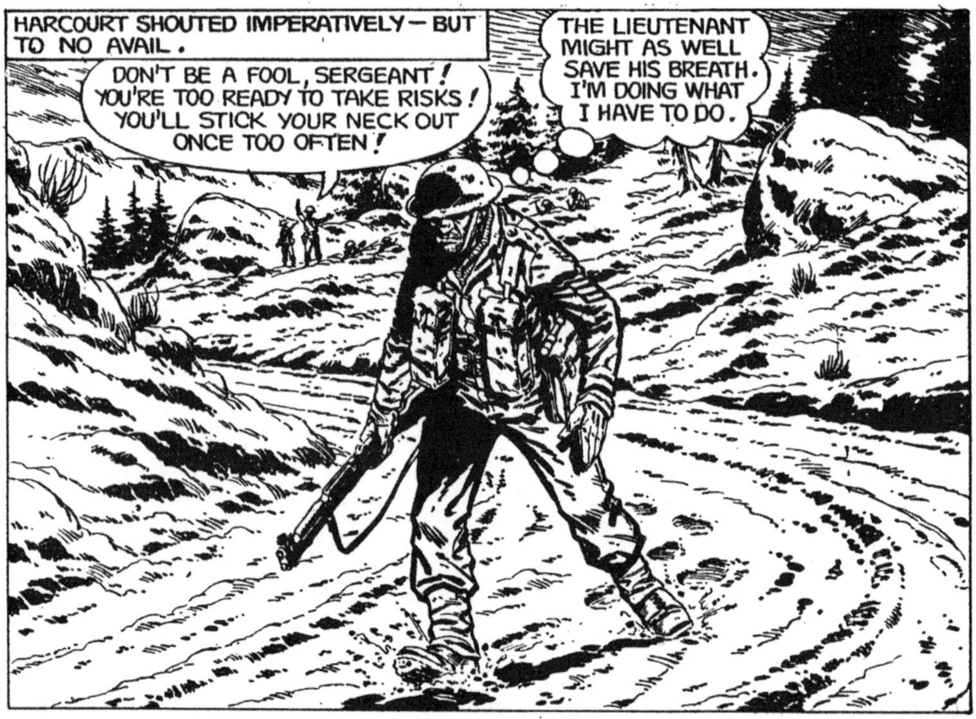
HARCOURT SHOUTED IMPERATIVELY — BUT TO NO AVAIL.
DON'T BE A FOOL, SERGEANT! YOU'RE TOO READY TO TAKE RISKS! YOU'LL STICK YOUR NECK OUT ONCE TOO OFTEN!
THE LIEUTENANT MIGHT AS WELL SAVE HIS BREATH. I'M DOING WHAT I HAVE TO DO.

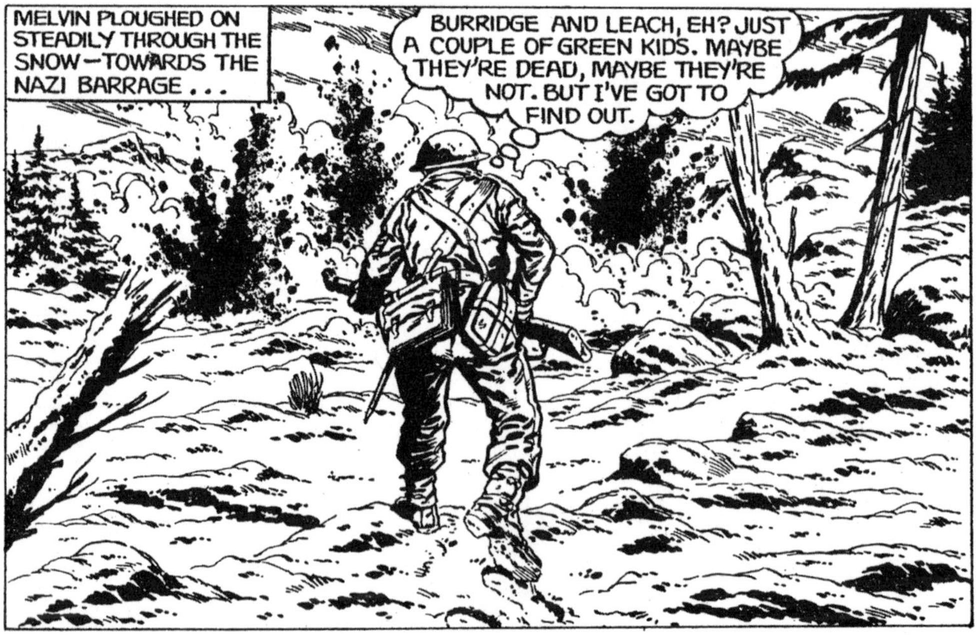
MELVIN PLOUGHED ON STEADILY THROUGH THE SNOW — TOWARDS THE NAZI BARRAGE...
BURRIDGE AND LEACH, EH? JUST A COUPLE OF GREEN KIDS. MAYBE THEY'RE DEAD, MAYBE THEY'RE NOT. BUT I'VE GOT TO FIND OUT.

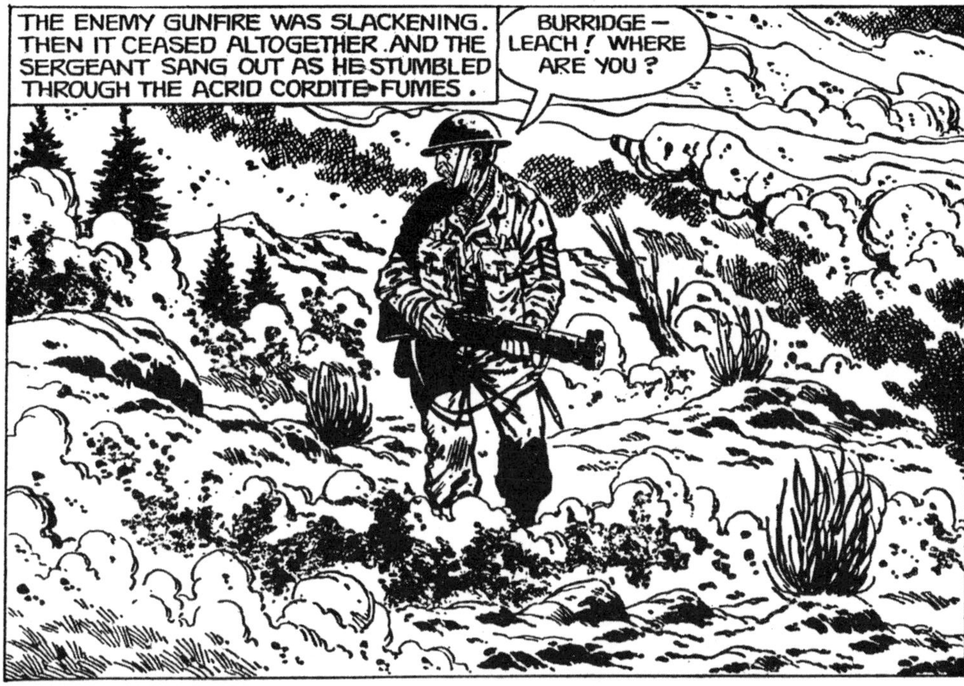
THE ENEMY GUNFIRE WAS SLACKENING. THEN IT CEASED ALTOGETHER. AND THE SERGEANT SANG OUT AS HE STUMBLED THROUGH THE ACRID CORDITE-FUMES.
BURRIDGE — LEACH! WHERE ARE YOU?

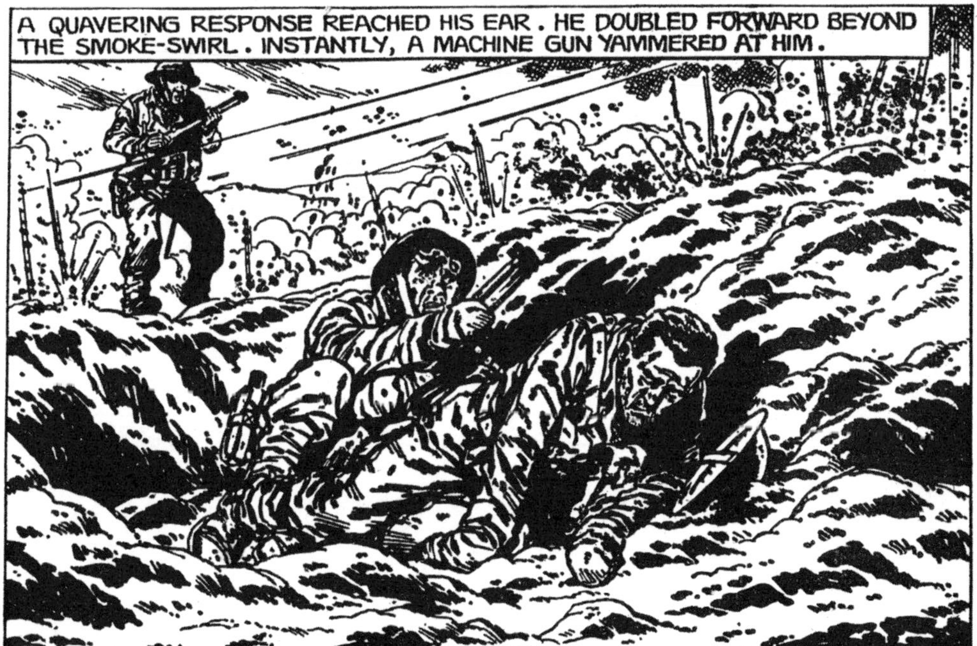
A QUAVERING RESPONSE REACHED HIS EAR. HE DOUBLED FORWARD BEYOND THE SMOKE-SWIRL. INSTANTLY, A MACHINE GUN YAMMERED AT HIM.

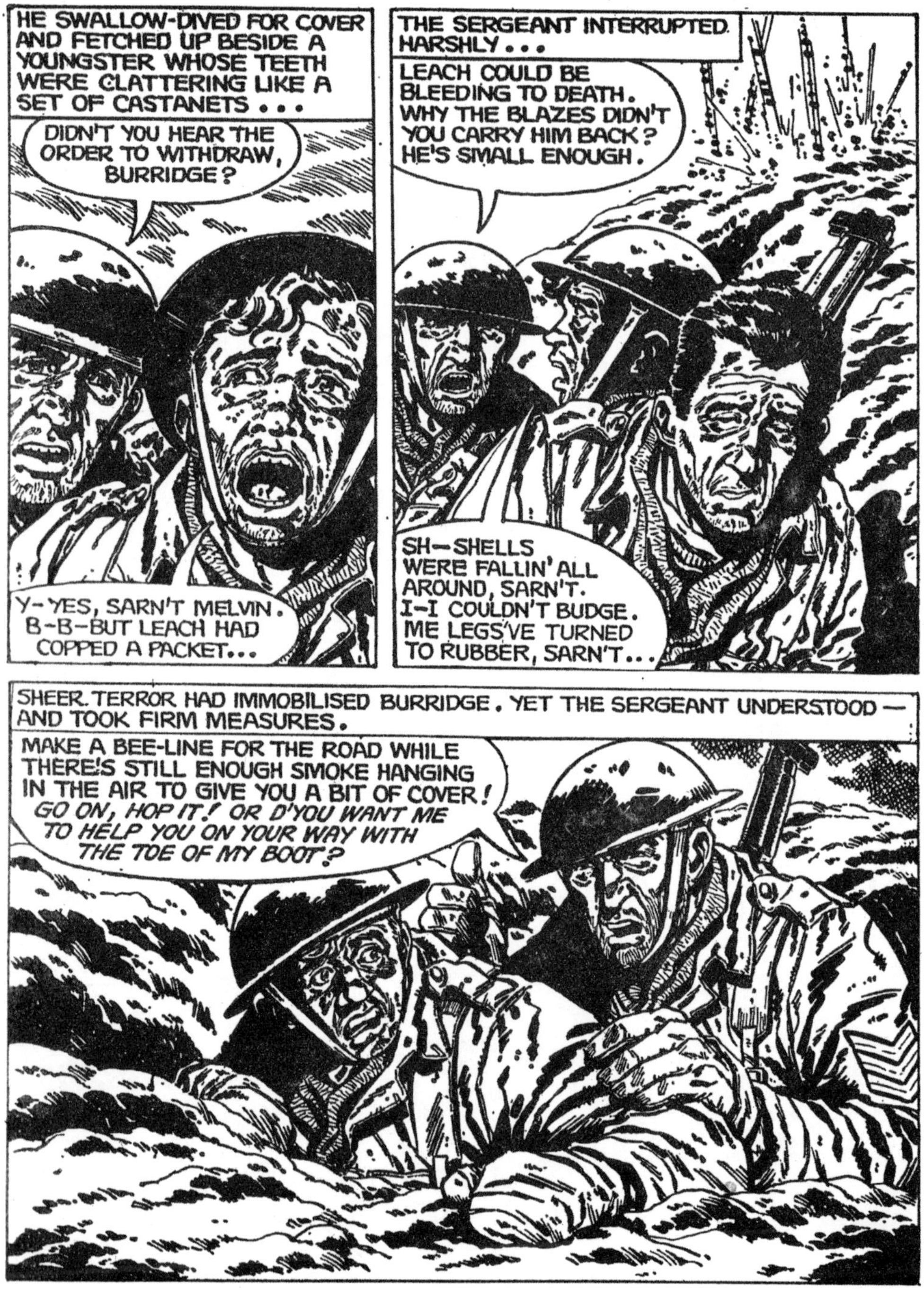
HE SWALLOW-DIVED FOR COVER AND FETCHED UP BESIDE A YOUNGSTER WHOSE TEETH WERE CLATTERING LIKE A SET OF CASTANETS . . .
DIDN'T YOU HEAR THE ORDER TO WITHDRAW, BURRIDGE?
Y-YES, SARN'T MELVIN. B-B-BUT LEACH HAD COPPED A PACKET...
THE SERGEANT INTERRUPTED HARSHLY . . .
LEACH COULD BE BLEEDING TO DEATH. WHY THE BLAZES DIDN'T YOU CARRY HIM BACK? HE'S SMALL ENOUGH.
SH—SHELLS WERE FALLIN' ALL AROUND, SARN'T. I-I COULDN'T BUDGE. ME LEGS'VE TURNED TO RUBBER, SARN'T...
SHEER TERROR HAD IMMOBILISED BURRIDGE. YET THE SERGEANT UNDERSTOOD — AND TOOK FIRM MEASURES.
MAKE A BEE-LINE FOR THE ROAD WHILE THERE'S STILL ENOUGH SMOKE HANGING IN THE AIR TO GIVE YOU A BIT OF COVER! GO ON, HOP IT! OR D'YOU WANT ME TO HELP YOU ON YOUR WAY WITH THE TOE OF MY BOOT?

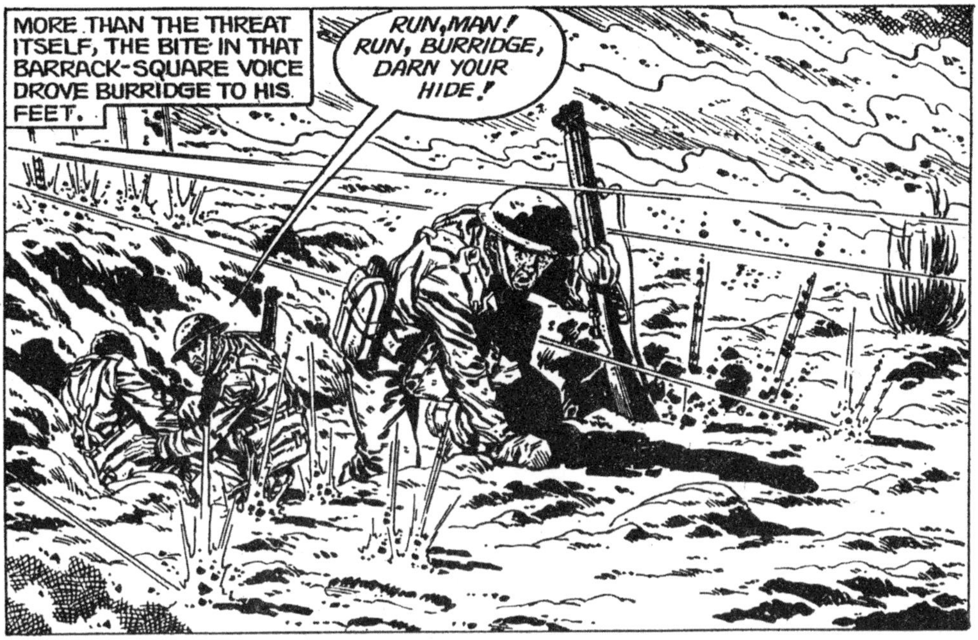
MORE THAN THE THREAT ITSELF, THE BITE IN THAT BARRACK-SQUARE VOICE DROVE BURRIDGE TO HIS FEET.
RUN, MAN! RUN, BURRIDGE, DARN YOUR HIDE!

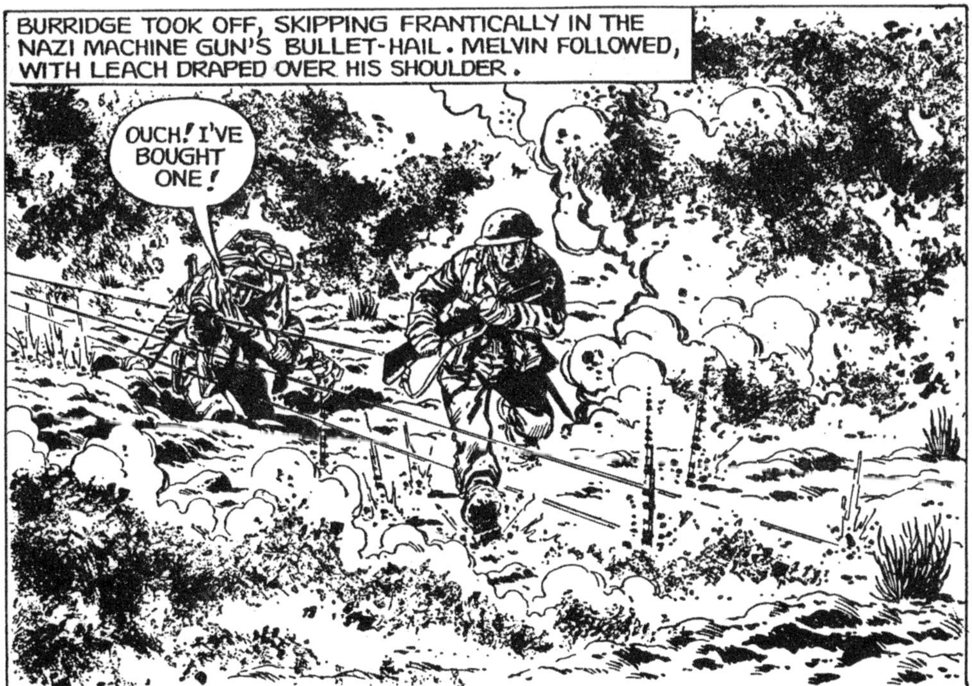
BURRIDGE TOOK OFF, SKIPPING FRANTICALLY IN THE NAZI MACHINE GUN'S BULLET-HAIL. MELVIN FOLLOWED, WITH LEACH DRAPED OVER HIS SHOULDER.
OUCH! I'VE BOUGHT ONE!

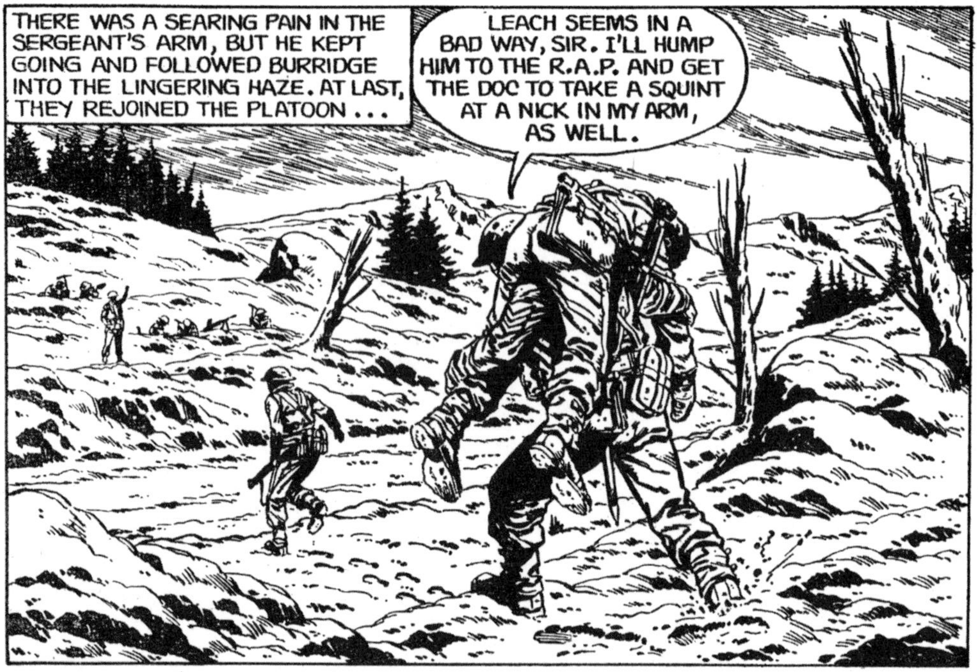
THERE WAS A SEARING PAIN IN THE SERGEANT'S ARM, BUT HE KEPT GOING AND FOLLOWED BURRIDGE INTO THE LINGERING HAZE. AT LAST, THEY REJOINED THE PLATOON . . .
LEACH SEEMS IN A BAD WAY, SIR. I'LL HUMP HIM TO THE R.A.P. AND GET THE DOC TO TAKE A SQUINT AT A NICK IN MY ARM, AS WELL.

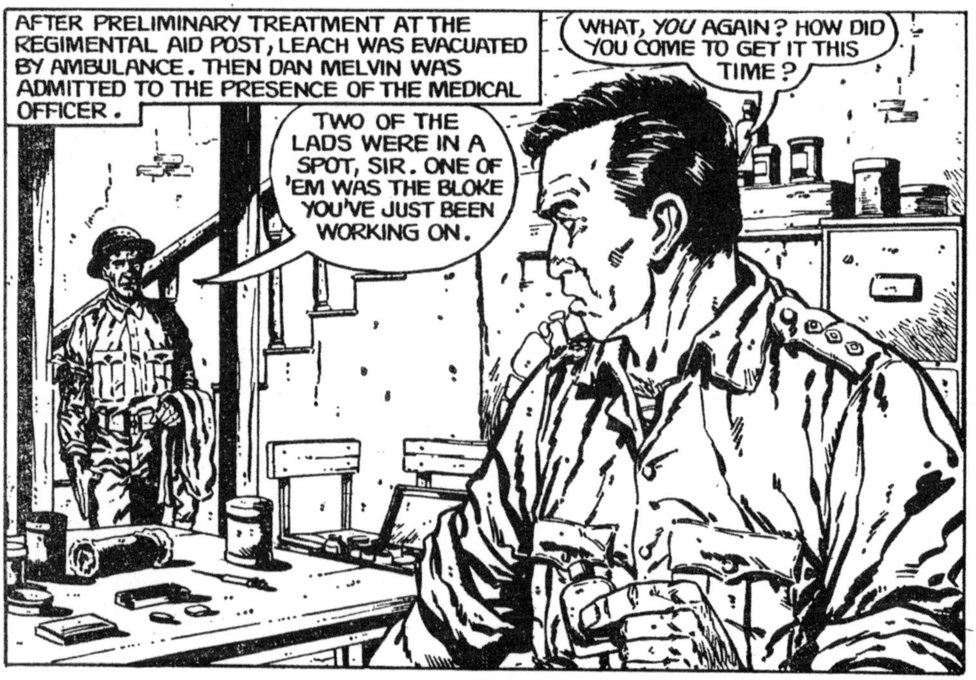
AFTER PRELIMINARY TREATMENT AT THE REGIMENTAL AID POST, LEACH WAS EVACUATED BY AMBULANCE. THEN DAN MELVIN WAS ADMITTED TO THE PRESENCE OF THE MEDICAL OFFICER.
WHAT, *YOU* AGAIN? HOW DID YOU COME TO GET IT THIS TIME?
TWO OF THE LADS WERE IN A SPOT, SIR. ONE OF 'EM WAS THE BLOKE YOU'VE JUST BEEN WORKING ON.

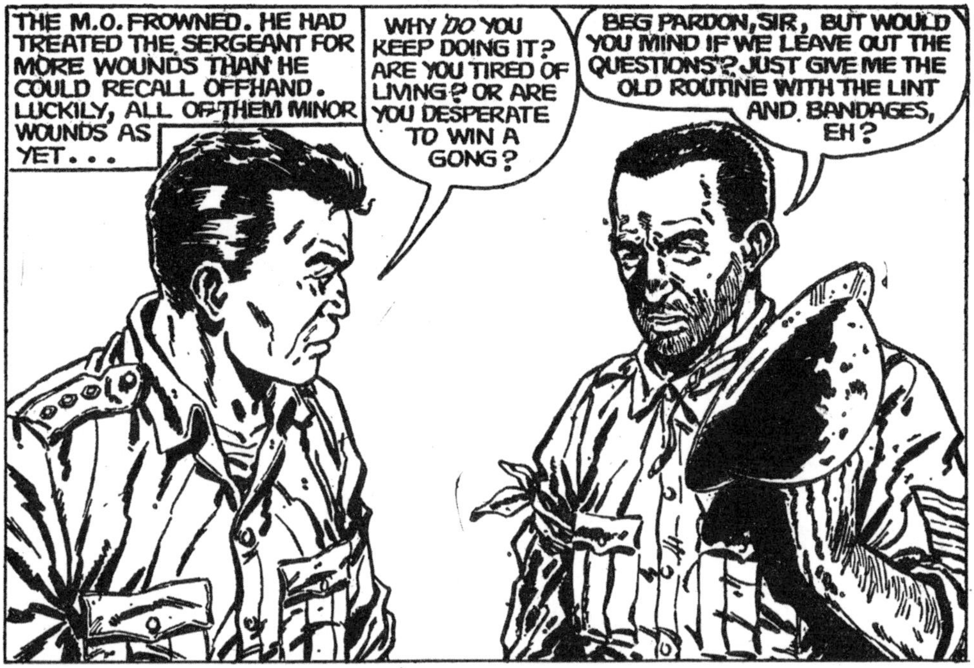
THE M.O. FROWNED. HE HAD TREATED THE SERGEANT FOR MORE WOUNDS THAN HE COULD RECALL OFFHAND. LUCKILY, ALL OF THEM MINOR WOUNDS AS YET...
WHY DO YOU KEEP DOING IT? ARE YOU TIRED OF LIVING? OR ARE YOU DESPERATE TO WIN A GONG?
BEG PARDON, SIR, BUT WOULD YOU MIND IF WE LEAVE OUT THE QUESTIONS? JUST GIVE ME THE OLD ROUTINE WITH THE LINT AND BANDAGES, EH?

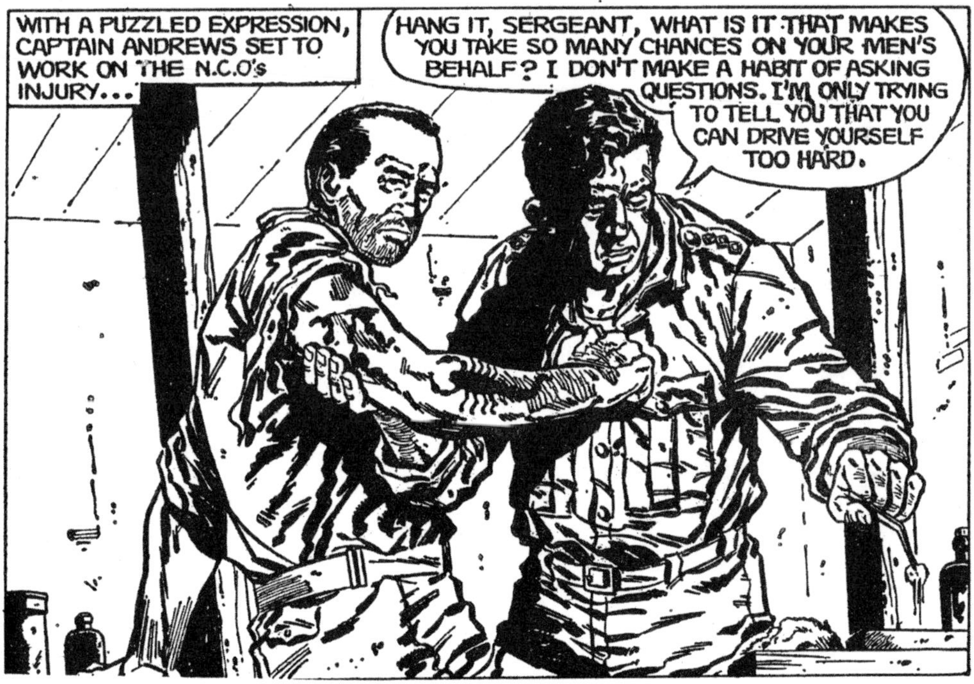
WITH A PUZZLED EXPRESSION, CAPTAIN ANDREWS SET TO WORK ON THE N.C.O's INJURY...
HANG IT, SERGEANT, WHAT IS IT THAT MAKES YOU TAKE SO MANY CHANCES ON YOUR MEN'S BEHALF? I DON'T MAKE A HABIT OF ASKING QUESTIONS. I'M ONLY TRYING TO TELL YOU THAT YOU CAN DRIVE YOURSELF TOO HARD.

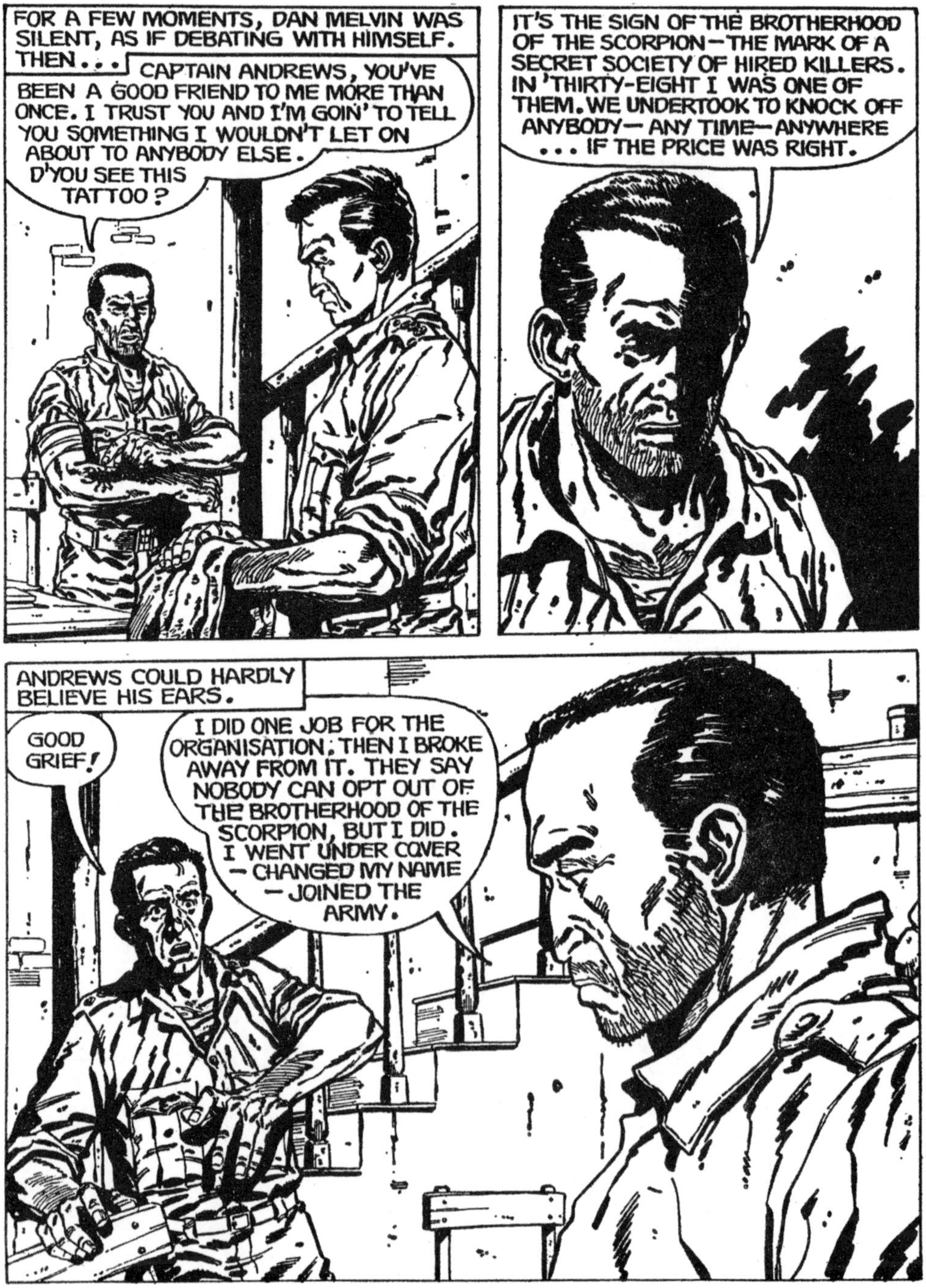
FOR A FEW MOMENTS, DAN MELVIN WAS SILENT, AS IF DEBATING WITH HIMSELF. THEN...
CAPTAIN ANDREWS, YOU'VE BEEN A GOOD FRIEND TO ME MORE THAN ONCE. I TRUST YOU AND I'M GOIN' TO TELL YOU SOMETHING I WOULDN'T LET ON ABOUT TO ANYBODY ELSE.
D'YOU SEE THIS TATTOO?
IT'S THE SIGN OF THE BROTHERHOOD OF THE SCORPION—THE MARK OF A SECRET SOCIETY OF HIRED KILLERS. IN 'THIRTY-EIGHT I WAS ONE OF THEM. WE UNDERTOOK TO KNOCK OFF ANYBODY—ANY TIME—ANYWHERE ... IF THE PRICE WAS RIGHT.
ANDREWS COULD HARDLY BELIEVE HIS EARS.
GOOD GRIEF!
I DID ONE JOB FOR THE ORGANISATION, THEN I BROKE AWAY FROM IT. THEY SAY NOBODY CAN OPT OUT OF THE BROTHERHOOD OF THE SCORPION, BUT I DID. I WENT UNDER COVER —CHANGED MY NAME —JOINED THE ARMY.

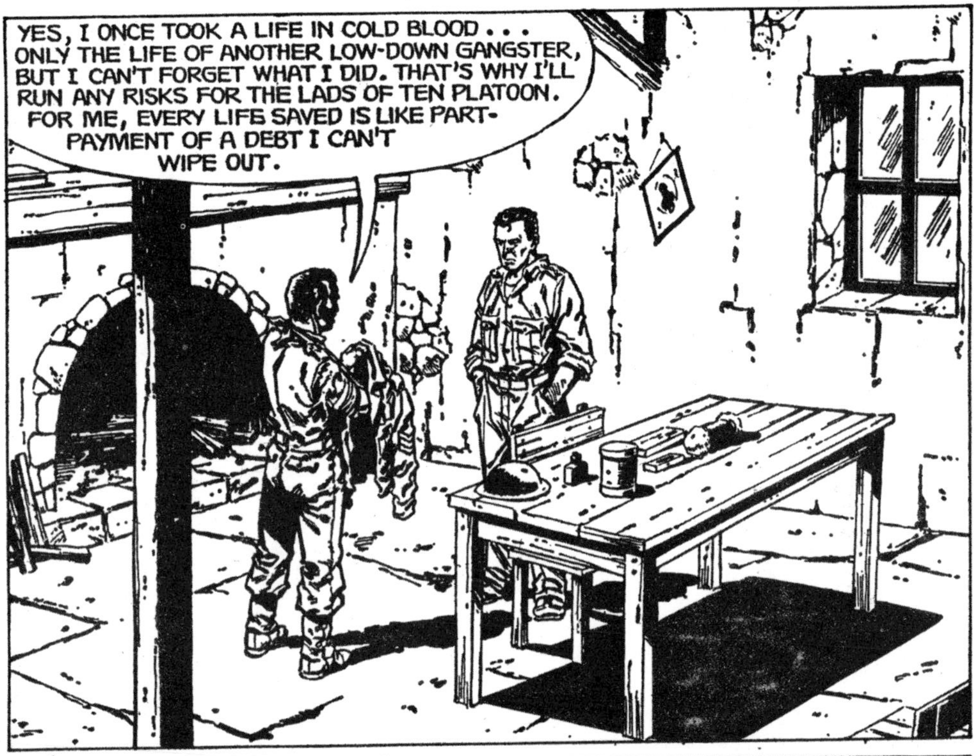
YES, I ONCE TOOK A LIFE IN COLD BLOOD . . . ONLY THE LIFE OF ANOTHER LOW-DOWN GANGSTER, BUT I CAN'T FORGET WHAT I DID. THAT'S WHY I'LL RUN ANY RISKS FOR THE LADS OF TEN PLATOON. FOR ME, EVERY LIFE SAVED IS LIKE PART-PAYMENT OF A DEBT I CAN'T WIPE OUT.

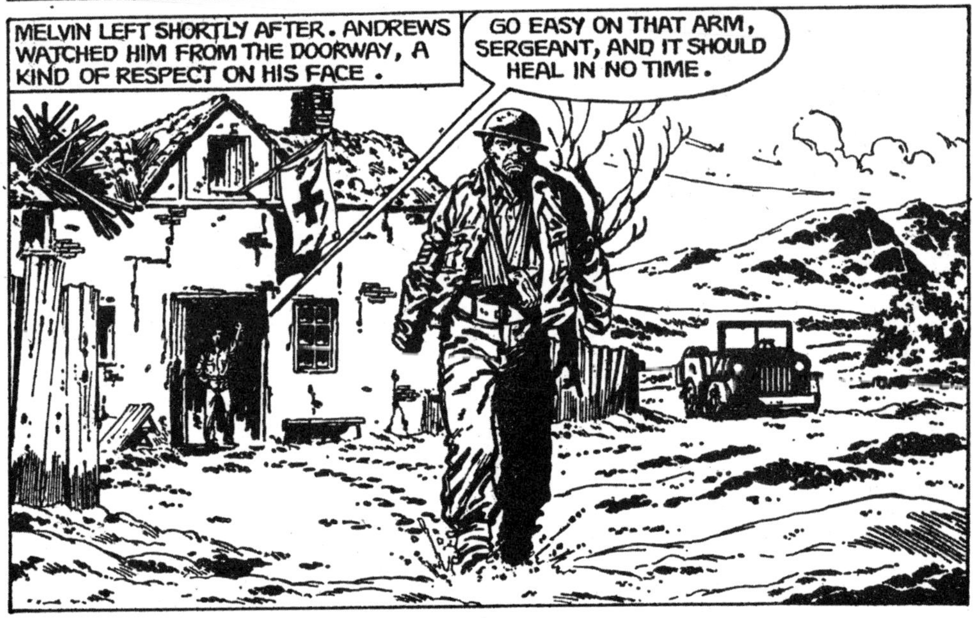
MELVIN LEFT SHORTLY AFTER. ANDREWS WATCHED HIM FROM THE DOORWAY, A KIND OF RESPECT ON HIS FACE.
GO EASY ON THAT ARM, SERGEANT, AND IT SHOULD HEAL IN NO TIME.

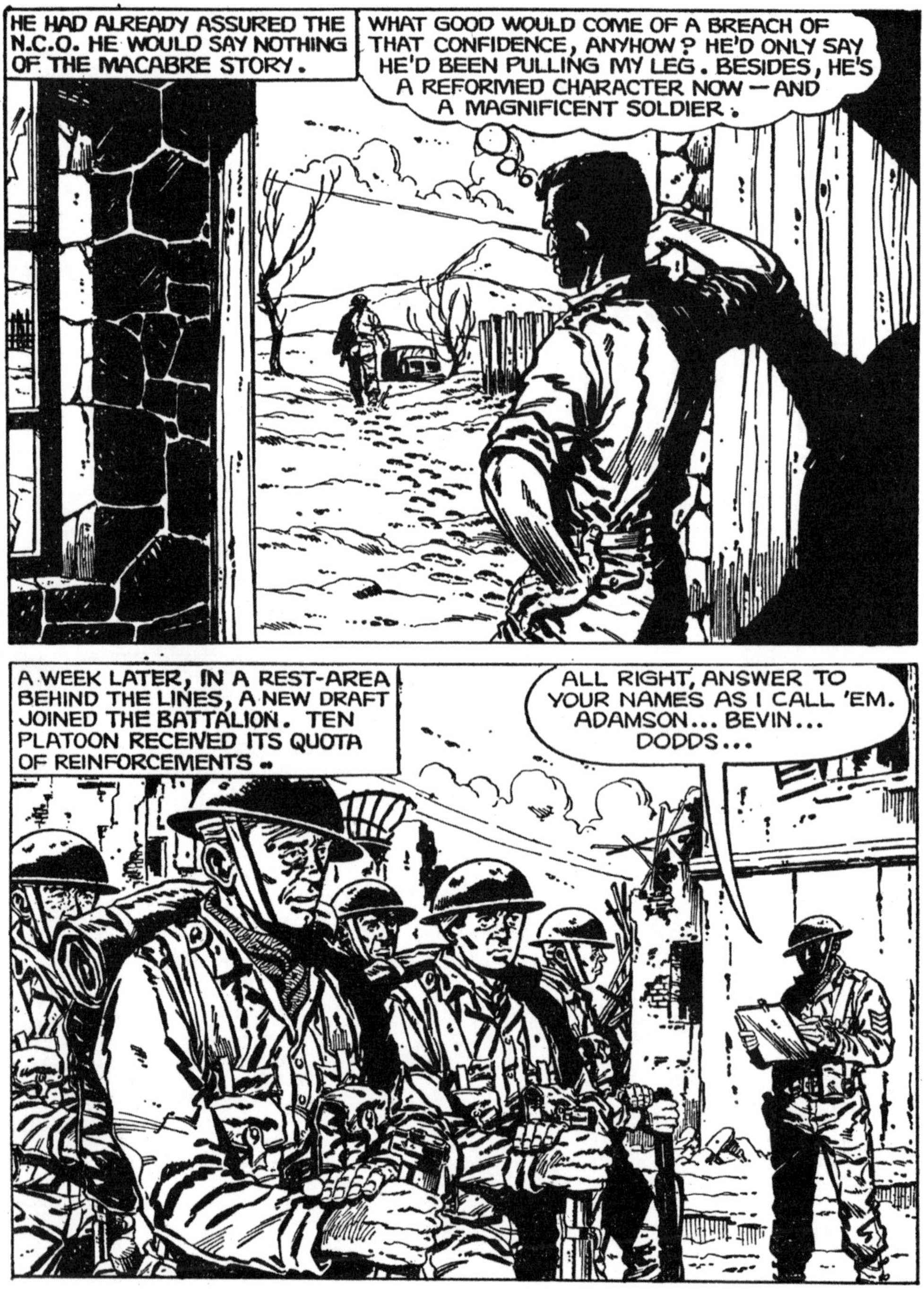
HE HAD ALREADY ASSURED THE N.C.O. HE WOULD SAY NOTHING OF THE MACABRE STORY.
WHAT GOOD WOULD COME OF A BREACH OF THAT CONFIDENCE, ANYHOW? HE'D ONLY SAY HE'D BEEN PULLING MY LEG. BESIDES, HE'S A REFORMED CHARACTER NOW — AND A MAGNIFICENT SOLDIER.
A WEEK LATER, IN A REST-AREA BEHIND THE LINES, A NEW DRAFT JOINED THE BATTALION. TEN PLATOON RECEIVED ITS QUOTA OF REINFORCEMENTS..
ALL RIGHT, ANSWER TO YOUR NAMES AS I CALL 'EM. ADAMSON... BEVIN... DODDS...

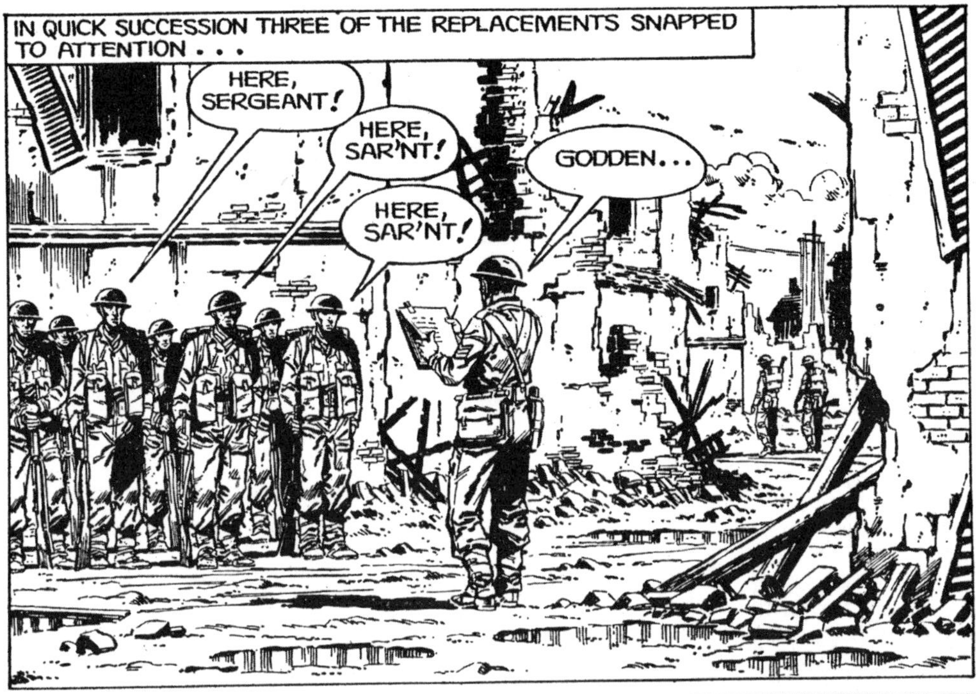
IN QUICK SUCCESSION THREE OF THE REPLACEMENTS SNAPPED TO ATTENTION . . .
HERE, SERGEANT!
HERE, SAR'NT!
HERE, SAR'NT!
GODDEN...

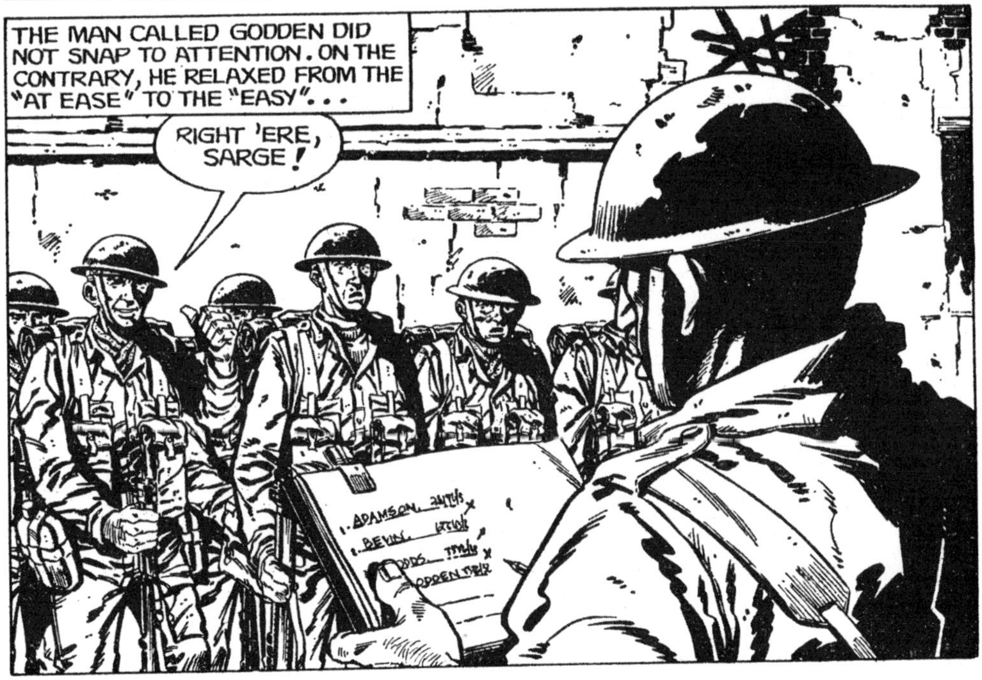
THE MAN CALLED GODDEN DID NOT SNAP TO ATTENTION. ON THE CONTRARY, HE RELAXED FROM THE "AT EASE" TO THE "EASY". . .
RIGHT 'ERE, SARGE!

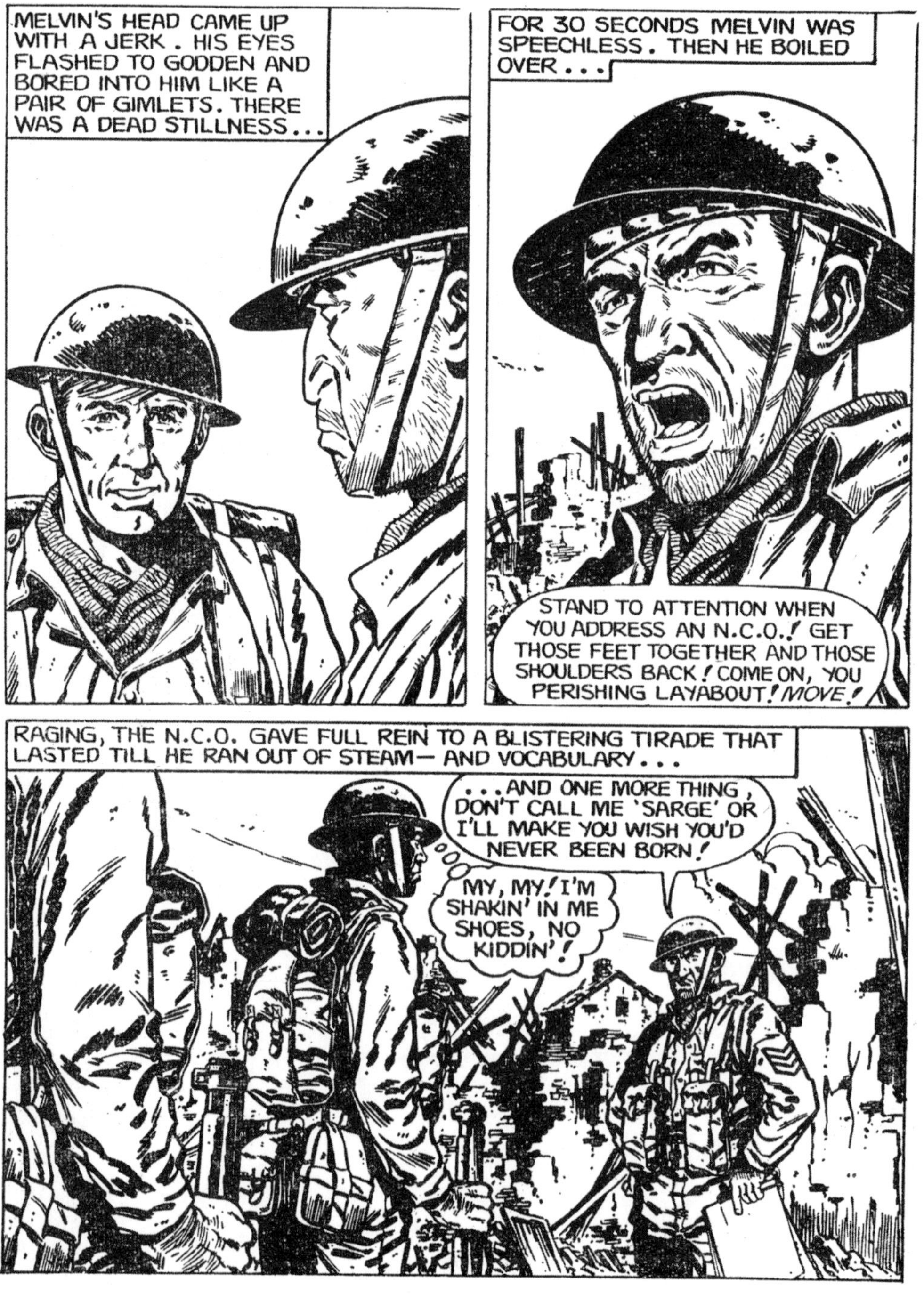
MELVIN'S HEAD CAME UP WITH A JERK. HIS EYES FLASHED TO GODDEN AND BORED INTO HIM LIKE A PAIR OF GIMLETS. THERE WAS A DEAD STILLNESS...
FOR 30 SECONDS MELVIN WAS SPEECHLESS. THEN HE BOILED OVER...
STAND TO ATTENTION WHEN YOU ADDRESS AN N.C.O.! GET THOSE FEET TOGETHER AND THOSE SHOULDERS BACK! COME ON, YOU PERISHING LAYABOUT! MOVE!
RAGING, THE N.C.O. GAVE FULL REIN TO A BLISTERING TIRADE THAT LASTED TILL HE RAN OUT OF STEAM— AND VOCABULARY...
...AND ONE MORE THING, DON'T CALL ME 'SARGE' OR I'LL MAKE YOU WISH YOU'D NEVER BEEN BORN!
MY, MY! I'M SHAKIN' IN ME SHOES, NO KIDDIN'!

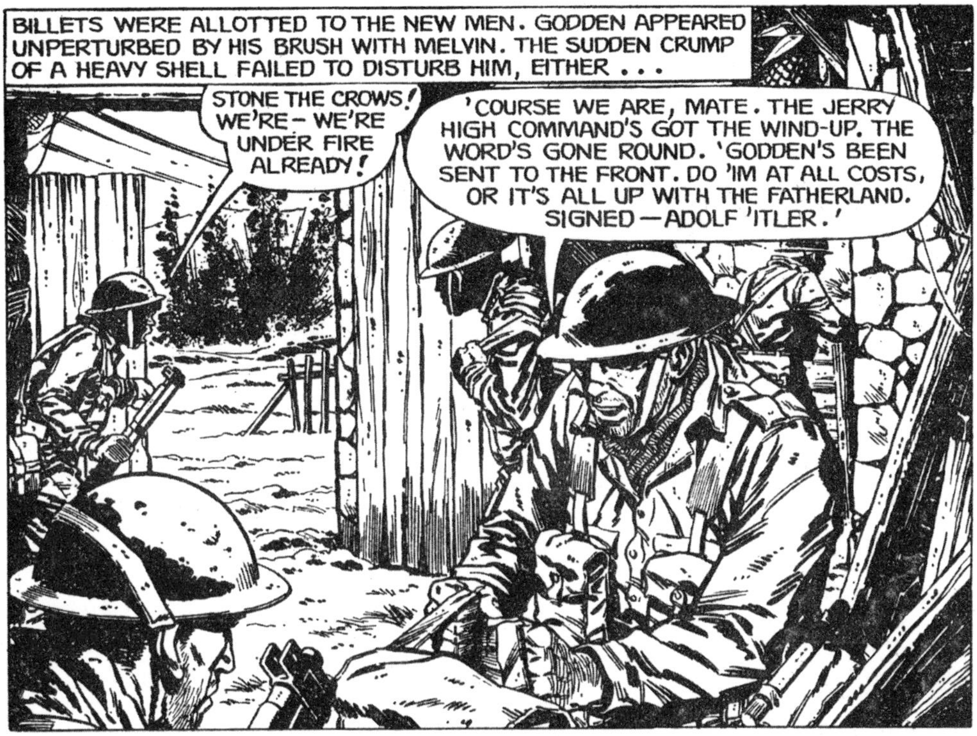
BILLETS WERE ALLOTTED TO THE NEW MEN. GODDEN APPEARED UNPERTURBED BY HIS BRUSH WITH MELVIN. THE SUDDEN CRUMP OF A HEAVY SHELL FAILED TO DISTURB HIM, EITHER . . .
STONE THE CROWS! WE'RE – WE'RE UNDER FIRE ALREADY!
'COURSE WE ARE, MATE. THE JERRY HIGH COMMAND'S GOT THE WIND-UP. THE WORD'S GONE ROUND. 'GODDEN'S BEEN SENT TO THE FRONT. DO 'IM AT ALL COSTS, OR IT'S ALL UP WITH THE FATHERLAND. SIGNED – ADOLF 'ITLER.'

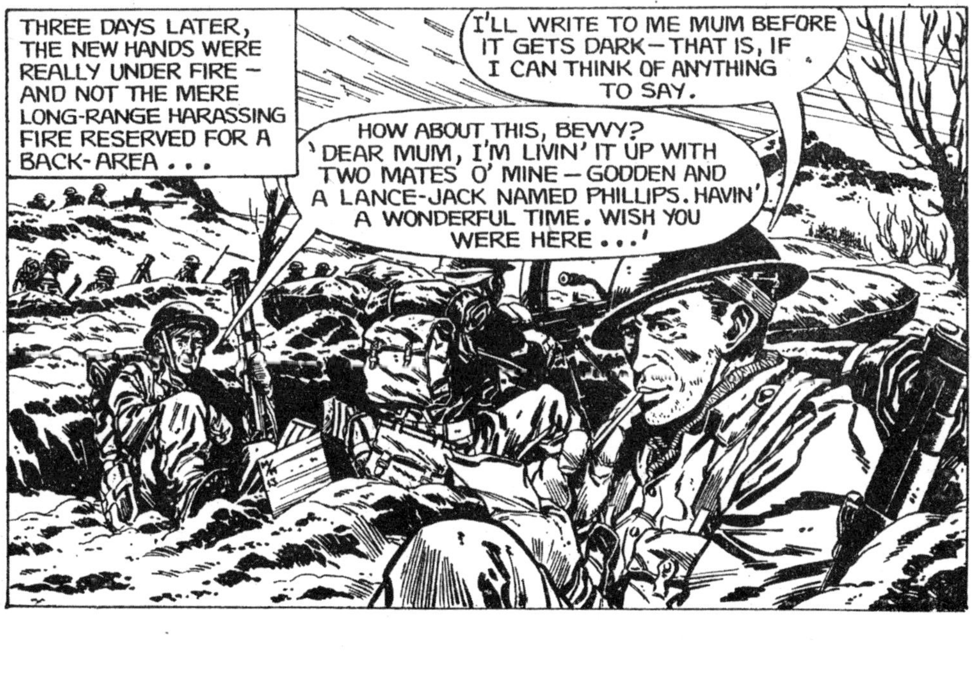
THREE DAYS LATER, THE NEW HANDS WERE REALLY UNDER FIRE – AND NOT THE MERE LONG-RANGE HARASSING FIRE RESERVED FOR A BACK-AREA . . .
I'LL WRITE TO ME MUM BEFORE IT GETS DARK – THAT IS, IF I CAN THINK OF ANYTHING TO SAY.
HOW ABOUT THIS, BEVVY? 'DEAR MUM, I'M LIVIN' IT UP WITH TWO MATES O' MINE – GODDEN AND A LANCE-JACK NAMED PHILLIPS. HAVIN' A WONDERFUL TIME. WISH YOU WERE HERE . . .'

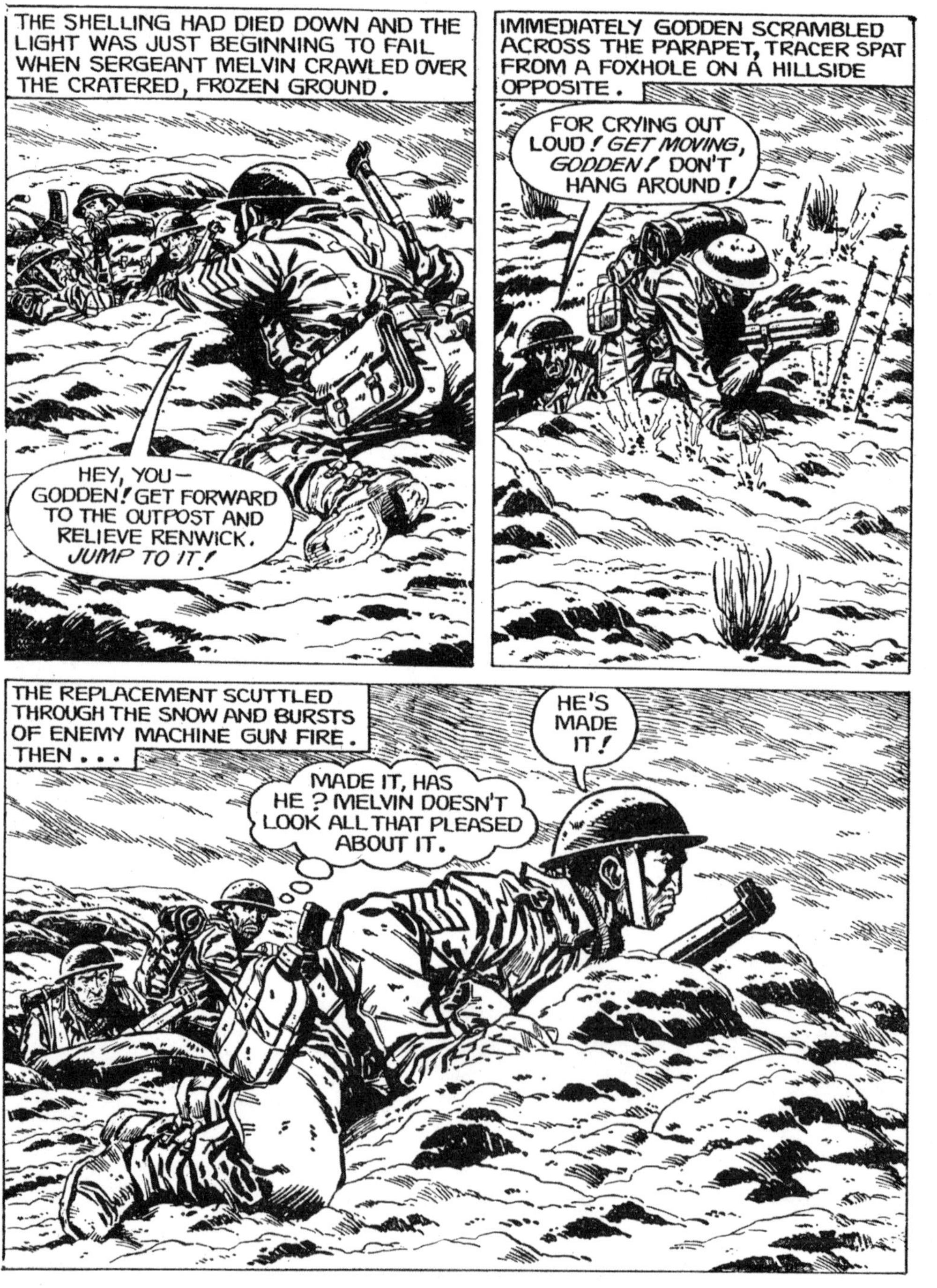
THE SHELLING HAD DIED DOWN AND THE LIGHT WAS JUST BEGINNING TO FAIL WHEN SERGEANT MELVIN CRAWLED OVER THE CRATERED, FROZEN GROUND.
HEY, YOU— GODDEN! GET FORWARD TO THE OUTPOST AND RELIEVE RENWICK. JUMP TO IT!
IMMEDIATELY GODDEN SCRAMBLED ACROSS THE PARAPET, TRACER SPAT FROM A FOXHOLE ON A HILLSIDE OPPOSITE.
FOR CRYING OUT LOUD! GET MOVING, GODDEN! DON'T HANG AROUND!
THE REPLACEMENT SCUTTLED THROUGH THE SNOW AND BURSTS OF ENEMY MACHINE GUN FIRE. THEN . . .
HE'S MADE IT!
MADE IT, HAS HE? MELVIN DOESN'T LOOK ALL THAT PLEASED ABOUT IT.

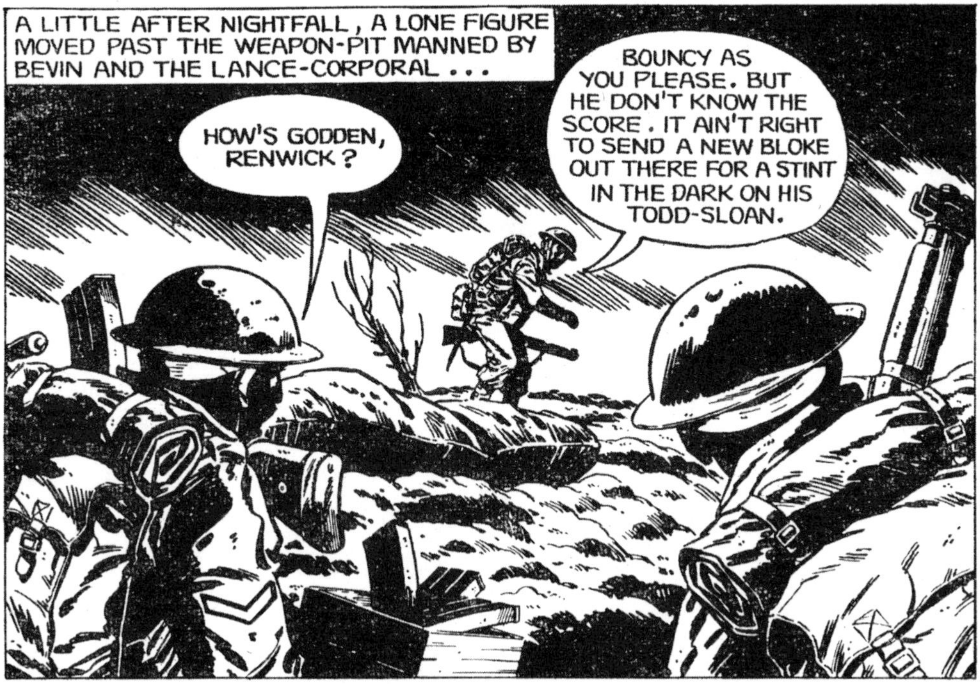
A LITTLE AFTER NIGHTFALL, A LONE FIGURE MOVED PAST THE WEAPON-PIT MANNED BY BEVIN AND THE LANCE-CORPORAL...
HOW'S GODDEN, RENWICK?
BOUNCY AS YOU PLEASE. BUT HE DON'T KNOW THE SCORE. IT AIN'T RIGHT TO SEND A NEW BLOKE OUT THERE FOR A STINT IN THE DARK ON HIS TODD-SLOAN.

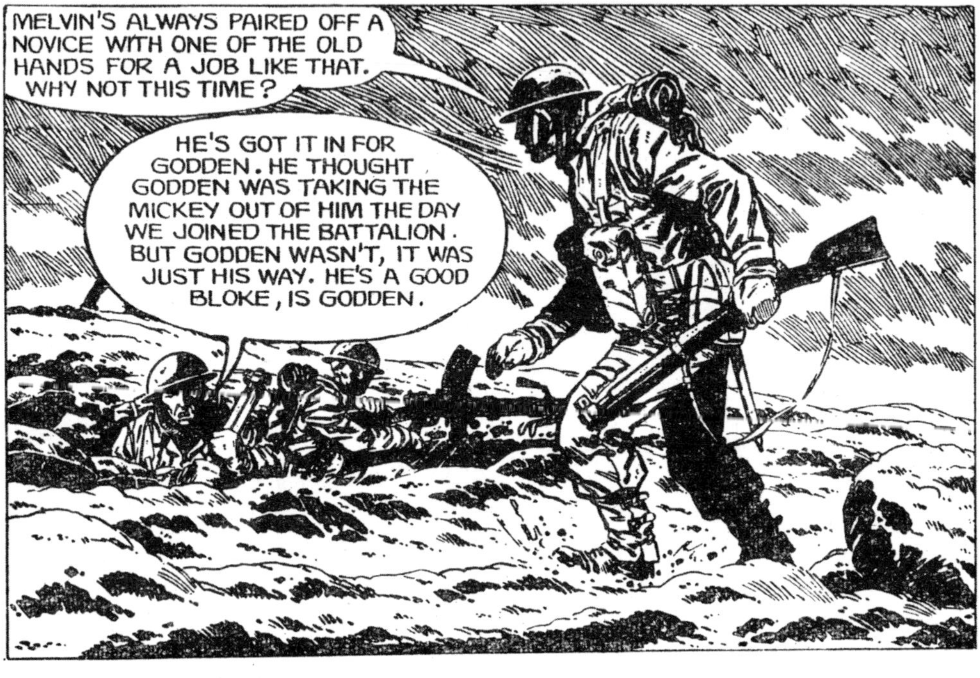
MELVIN'S ALWAYS PAIRED OFF A NOVICE WITH ONE OF THE OLD HANDS FOR A JOB LIKE THAT. WHY NOT THIS TIME?
HE'S GOT IT IN FOR GODDEN. HE THOUGHT GODDEN WAS TAKING THE MICKEY OUT OF HIM THE DAY WE JOINED THE BATTALION. BUT GODDEN WASN'T, IT WAS JUST HIS WAY. HE'S A GOOD BLOKE, IS GODDEN.

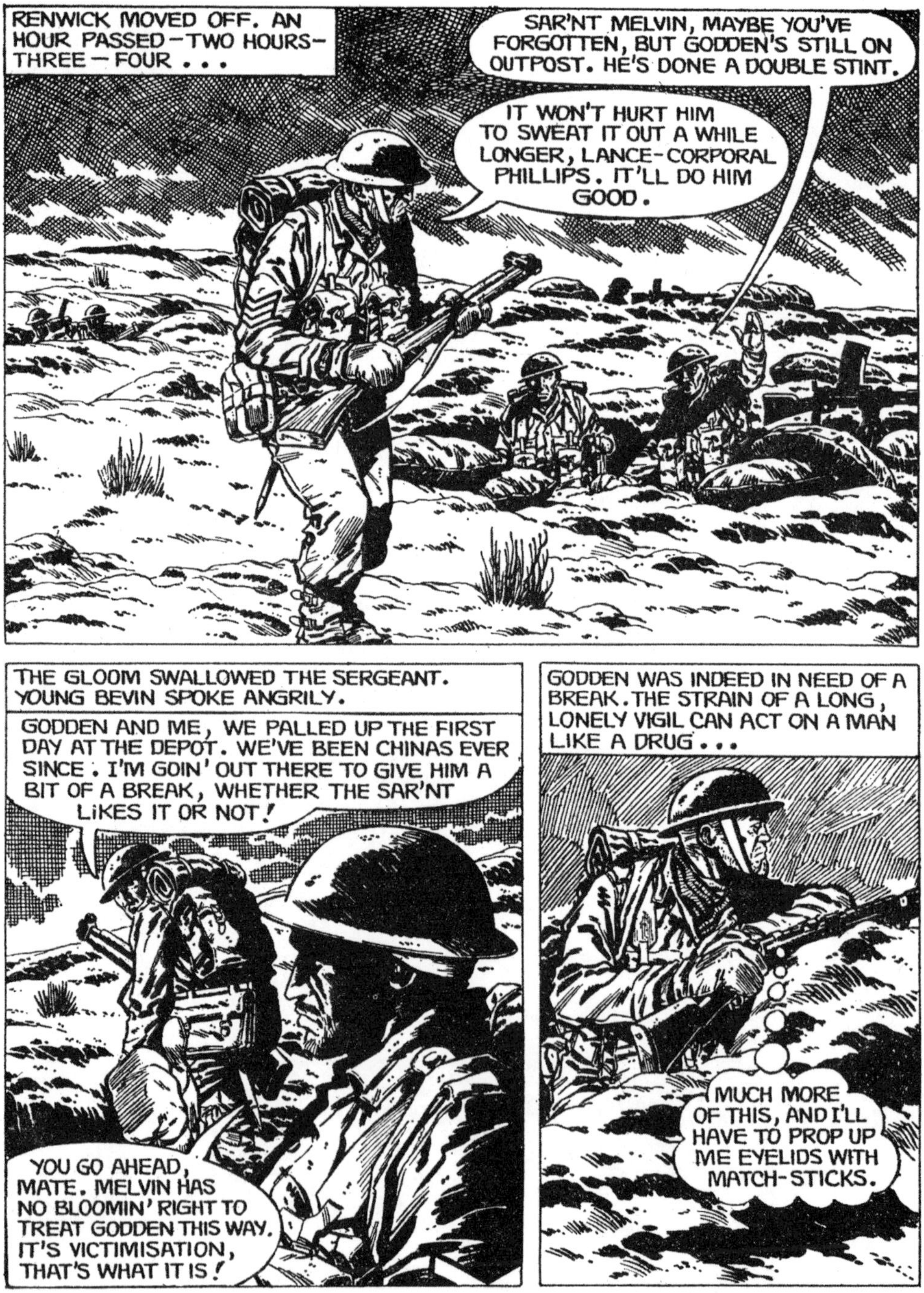
RENWICK MOVED OFF. AN HOUR PASSED – TWO HOURS – THREE – FOUR . . .
SAR'NT MELVIN, MAYBE YOU'VE FORGOTTEN, BUT GODDEN'S STILL ON OUTPOST. HE'S DONE A DOUBLE STINT.
IT WON'T HURT HIM TO SWEAT IT OUT A WHILE LONGER, LANCE-CORPORAL PHILLIPS. IT'LL DO HIM GOOD.
THE GLOOM SWALLOWED THE SERGEANT. YOUNG BEVIN SPOKE ANGRILY.
GODDEN AND ME, WE PALLED UP THE FIRST DAY AT THE DEPOT. WE'VE BEEN CHINAS EVER SINCE. I'M GOIN' OUT THERE TO GIVE HIM A BIT OF A BREAK, WHETHER THE SAR'NT LIKES IT OR NOT!
YOU GO AHEAD, MATE. MELVIN HAS NO BLOOMIN' RIGHT TO TREAT GODDEN THIS WAY. IT'S VICTIMISATION, THAT'S WHAT IT IS!
GODDEN WAS INDEED IN NEED OF A BREAK. THE STRAIN OF A LONG, LONELY VIGIL CAN ACT ON A MAN LIKE A DRUG . . .
MUCH MORE OF THIS, AND I'LL HAVE TO PROP UP ME EYELIDS WITH MATCH-STICKS.

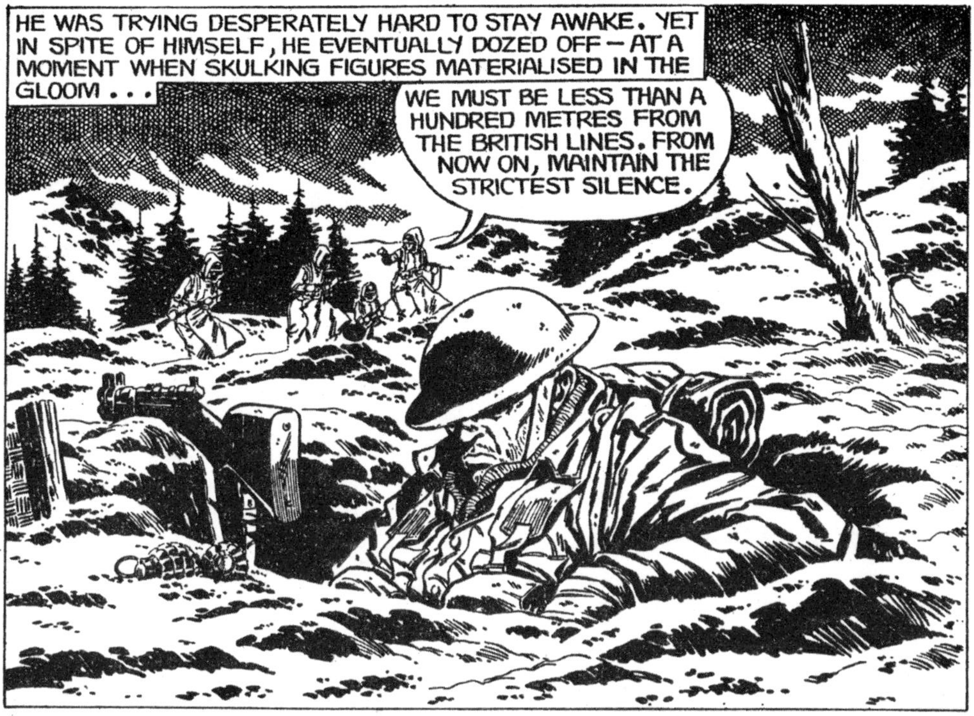
HE WAS TRYING DESPERATELY HARD TO STAY AWAKE. YET IN SPITE OF HIMSELF, HE EVENTUALLY DOZED OFF – AT A MOMENT WHEN SKULKING FIGURES MATERIALISED IN THE GLOOM . . .
WE MUST BE LESS THAN A HUNDRED METRES FROM THE BRITISH LINES. FROM NOW ON, MAINTAIN THE STRICTEST SILENCE.

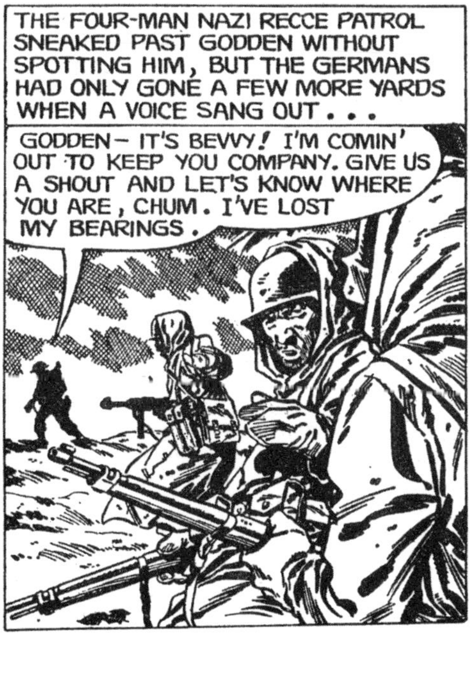
THE FOUR-MAN NAZI RECCE PATROL SNEAKED PAST GODDEN WITHOUT SPOTTING HIM, BUT THE GERMANS HAD ONLY GONE A FEW MORE YARDS WHEN A VOICE SANG OUT . . .
GODDEN– IT'S BEVVY! I'M COMIN' OUT TO KEEP YOU COMPANY. GIVE US A SHOUT AND LET'S KNOW WHERE YOU ARE, CHUM. I'VE LOST MY BEARINGS.

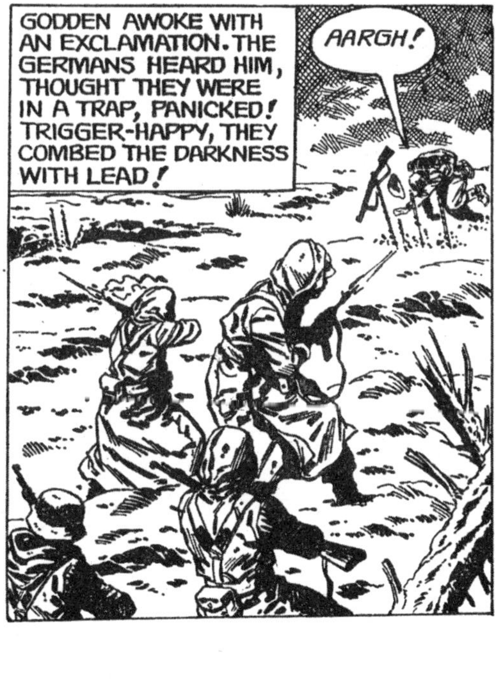
GODDEN AWOKE WITH AN EXCLAMATION. THE GERMANS HEARD HIM, THOUGHT THEY WERE IN A TRAP, PANICKED! TRIGGER-HAPPY, THEY COMBED THE DARKNESS WITH LEAD!
AARGH!

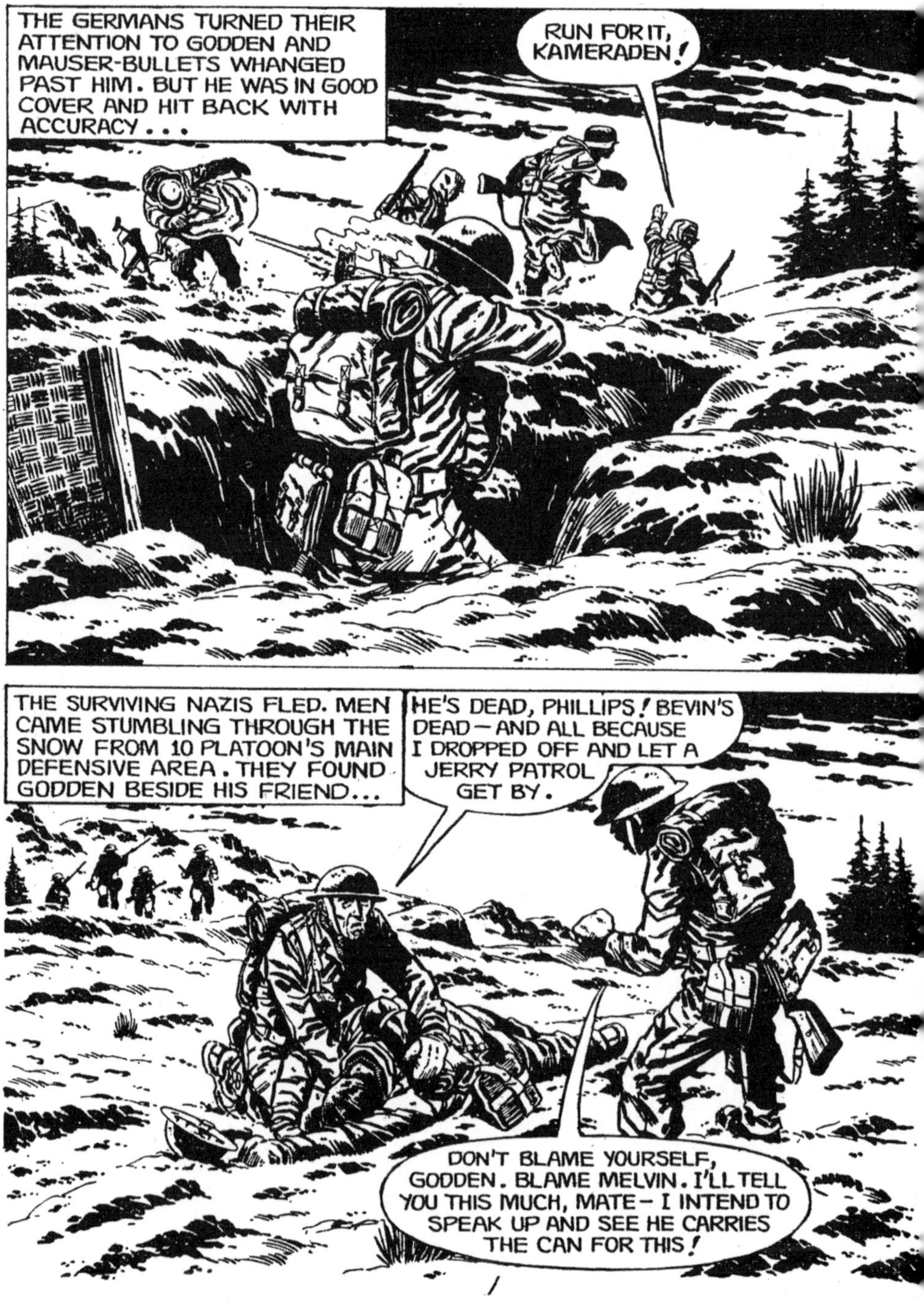
THE GERMANS TURNED THEIR ATTENTION TO GODDEN AND MAUSER-BULLETS WHANGED PAST HIM. BUT HE WAS IN GOOD COVER AND HIT BACK WITH ACCURACY . . .
RUN FOR IT, KAMERADEN!
THE SURVIVING NAZIS FLED. MEN CAME STUMBLING THROUGH THE SNOW FROM 10 PLATOON'S MAIN DEFENSIVE AREA. THEY FOUND GODDEN BESIDE HIS FRIEND...
HE'S DEAD, PHILLIPS! BEVIN'S DEAD — AND ALL BECAUSE I DROPPED OFF AND LET A JERRY PATROL GET BY.
DON'T BLAME YOURSELF, GODDEN. BLAME MELVIN. I'LL TELL YOU THIS MUCH, MATE — I INTEND TO SPEAK UP AND SEE HE CARRIES THE CAN FOR THIS!

Chapter 2. Mission to Albourg

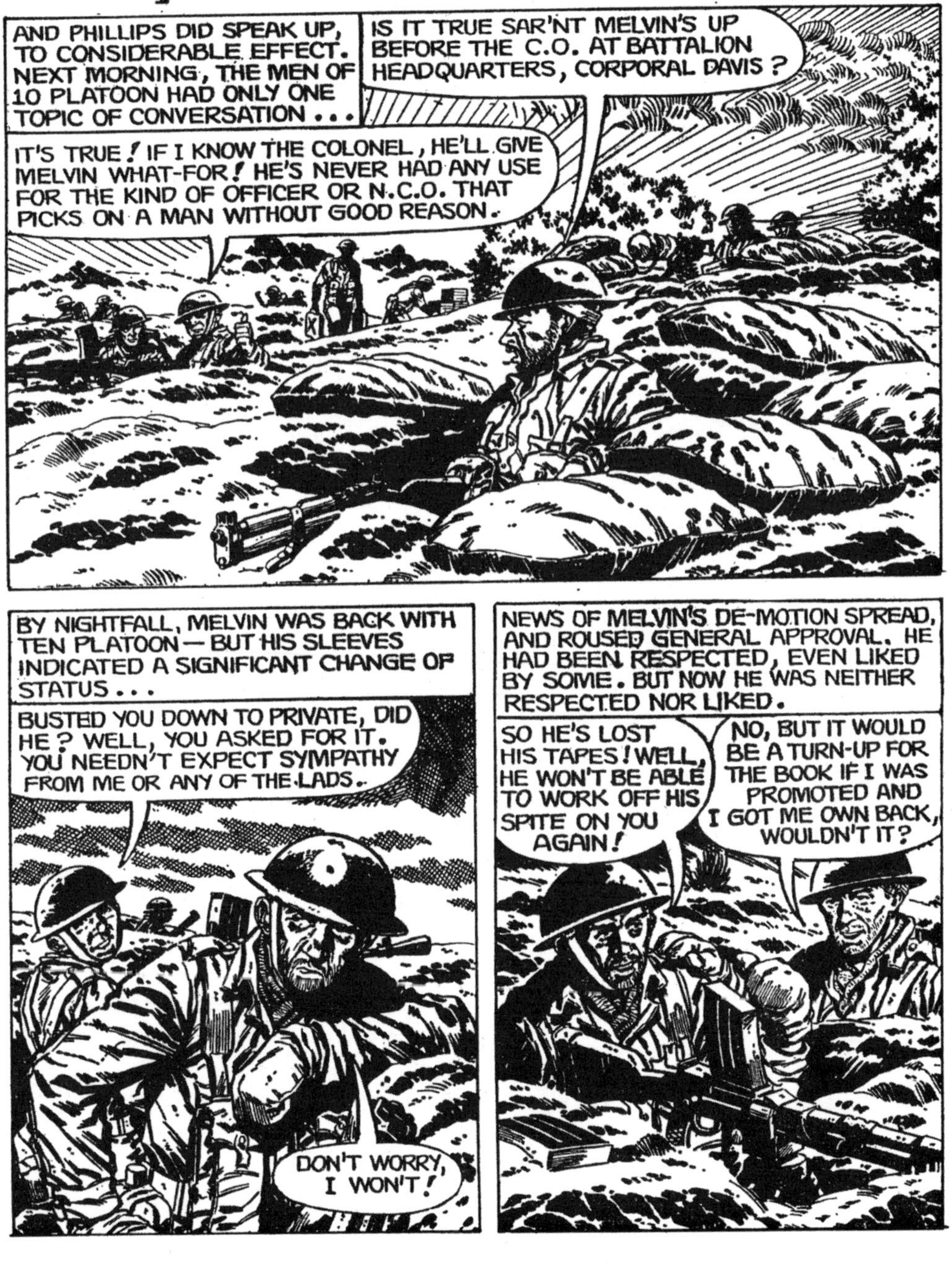
AND PHILLIPS DID SPEAK UP, TO CONSIDERABLE EFFECT. NEXT MORNING, THE MEN OF 10 PLATOON HAD ONLY ONE TOPIC OF CONVERSATION . . .
IS IT TRUE SAR'NT MELVIN'S UP BEFORE THE C.O. AT BATTALION HEADQUARTERS, CORPORAL DAVIS ?
IT'S TRUE ! IF I KNOW THE COLONEL, HE'LL GIVE MELVIN WHAT-FOR ! HE'S NEVER HAD ANY USE FOR THE KIND OF OFFICER OR N.C.O. THAT PICKS ON A MAN WITHOUT GOOD REASON.
BY NIGHTFALL, MELVIN WAS BACK WITH TEN PLATOON — BUT HIS SLEEVES INDICATED A SIGNIFICANT CHANGE OF STATUS . . .
BUSTED YOU DOWN TO PRIVATE, DID HE ? WELL, YOU ASKED FOR IT. YOU NEEDN'T EXPECT SYMPATHY FROM ME OR ANY OF THE LADS.
DON'T WORRY, I WON'T !
NEWS OF MELVIN'S DE-MOTION SPREAD, AND ROUSED GENERAL APPROVAL. HE HAD BEEN RESPECTED, EVEN LIKED BY SOME. BUT NOW HE WAS NEITHER RESPECTED NOR LIKED.
SO HE'S LOST HIS TAPES ! WELL, HE WON'T BE ABLE TO WORK OFF HIS SPITE ON YOU AGAIN !
NO, BUT IT WOULD BE A TURN-UP FOR THE BOOK IF I WAS PROMOTED AND I GOT ME OWN BACK, WOULDN'T IT ?

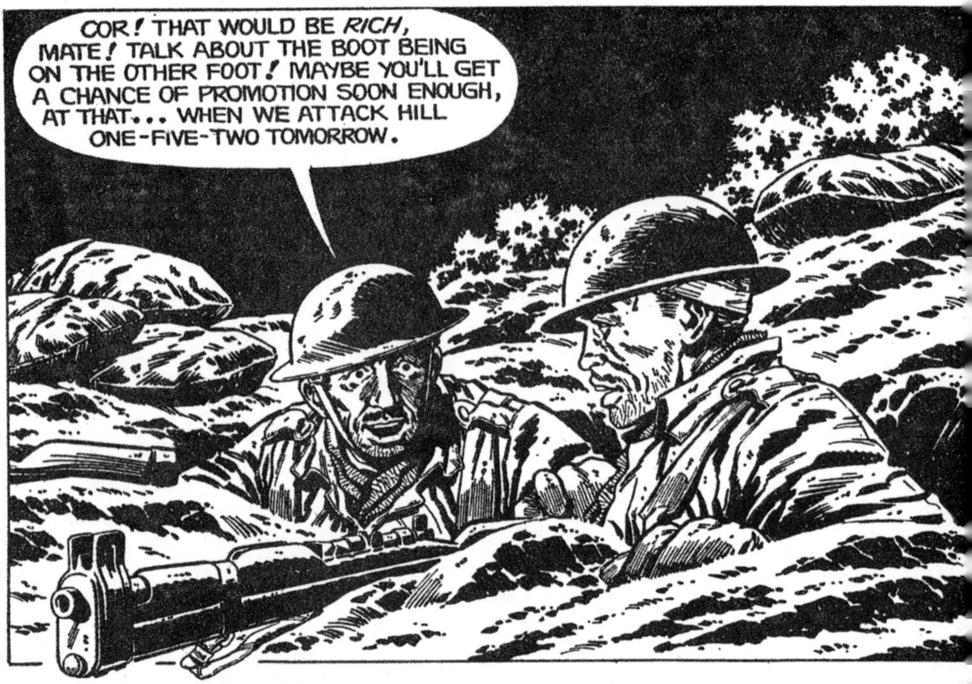
COR! THAT WOULD BE RICH, MATE! TALK ABOUT THE BOOT BEING ON THE OTHER FOOT! MAYBE YOU'LL GET A CHANCE OF PROMOTION SOON ENOUGH, AT THAT... WHEN WE ATTACK HILL ONE-FIVE-TWO TOMORROW.

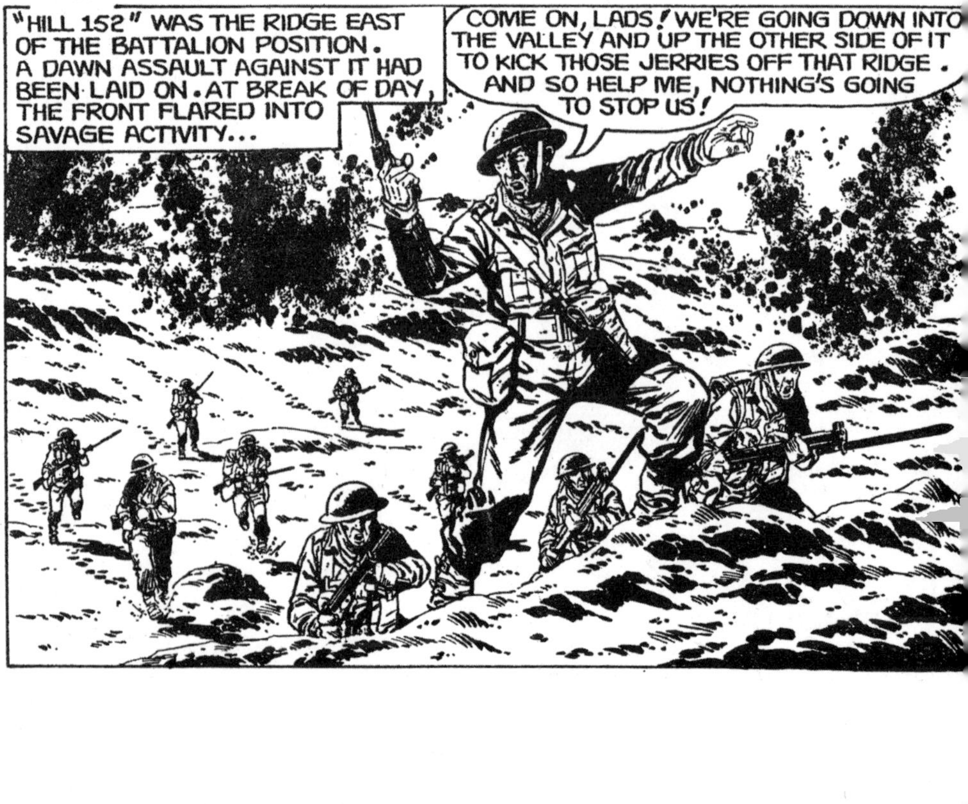
"HILL 152" WAS THE RIDGE EAST OF THE BATTALION POSITION. A DAWN ASSAULT AGAINST IT HAD BEEN LAID ON. AT BREAK OF DAY, THE FRONT FLARED INTO SAVAGE ACTIVITY...
COME ON, LADS! WE'RE GOING DOWN INTO THE VALLEY AND UP THE OTHER SIDE OF IT TO KICK THOSE JERRIES OFF THAT RIDGE. AND SO HELP ME, NOTHING'S GOING TO STOP US!

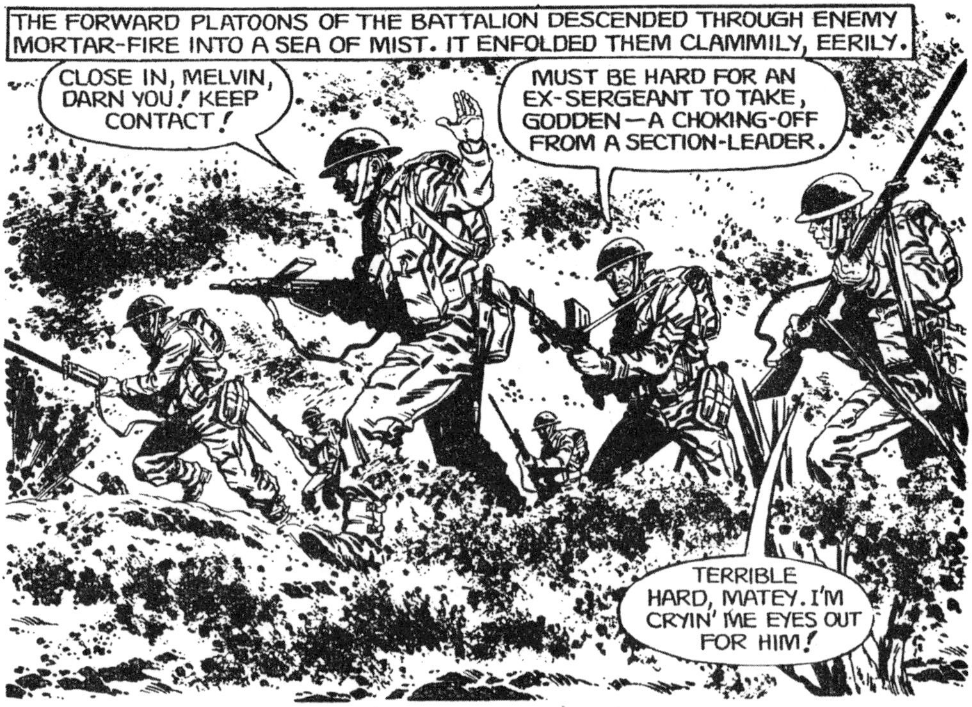
THE FORWARD PLATOONS OF THE BATTALION DESCENDED THROUGH ENEMY MORTAR-FIRE INTO A SEA OF MIST. IT ENFOLDED THEM CLAMMILY, EERILY.
CLOSE IN, MELVIN, DARN YOU! KEEP CONTACT!
MUST BE HARD FOR AN EX-SERGEANT TO TAKE, GODDEN—A CHOKING-OFF FROM A SECTION-LEADER.
TERRIBLE HARD, MATEY. I'M CRYIN' ME EYES OUT FOR HIM!

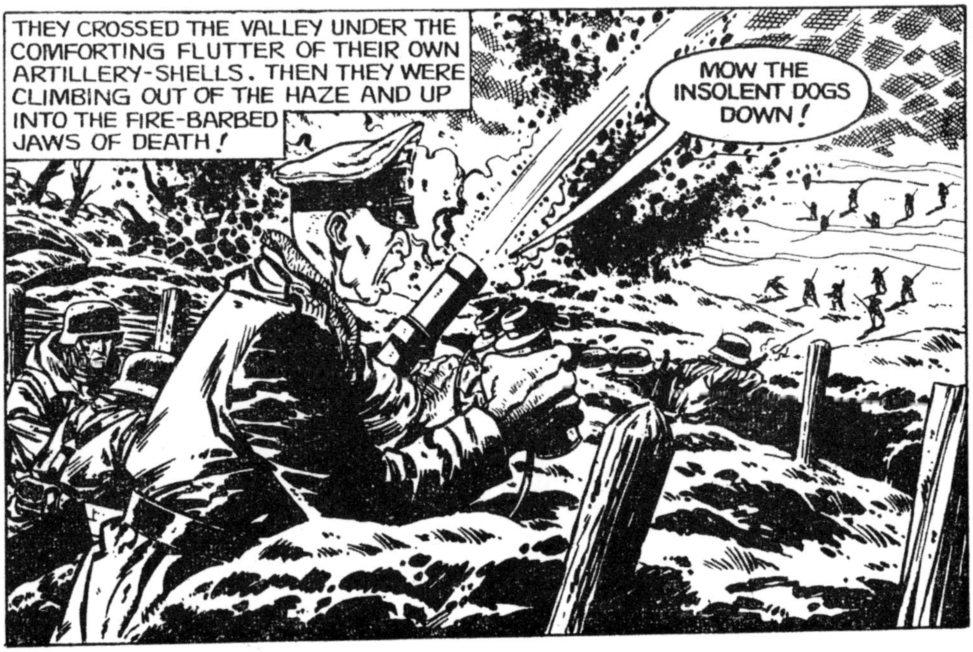
THEY CROSSED THE VALLEY UNDER THE COMFORTING FLUTTER OF THEIR OWN ARTILLERY-SHELLS. THEN THEY WERE CLIMBING OUT OF THE HAZE AND UP INTO THE FIRE-BARBED JAWS OF DEATH!
MOW THE INSOLENT DOGS DOWN!

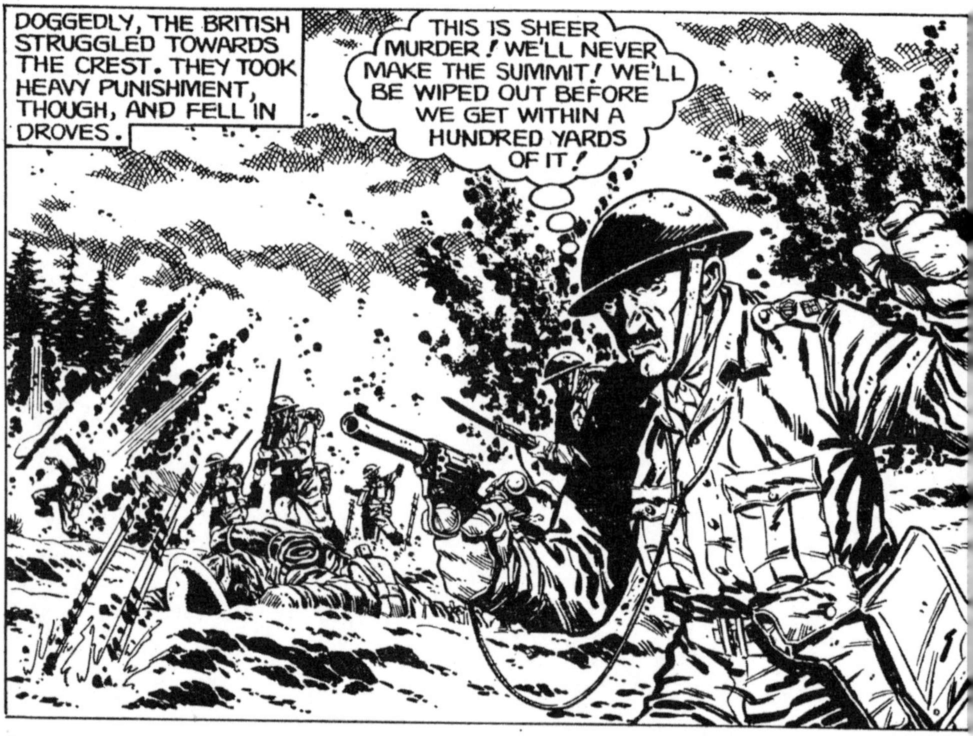
DOGGEDLY, THE BRITISH STRUGGLED TOWARDS THE CREST. THEY TOOK HEAVY PUNISHMENT, THOUGH, AND FELL IN DROVES.
THIS IS SHEER MURDER! WE'LL NEVER MAKE THE SUMMIT! WE'LL BE WIPED OUT BEFORE WE GET WITHIN A HUNDRED YARDS OF IT!

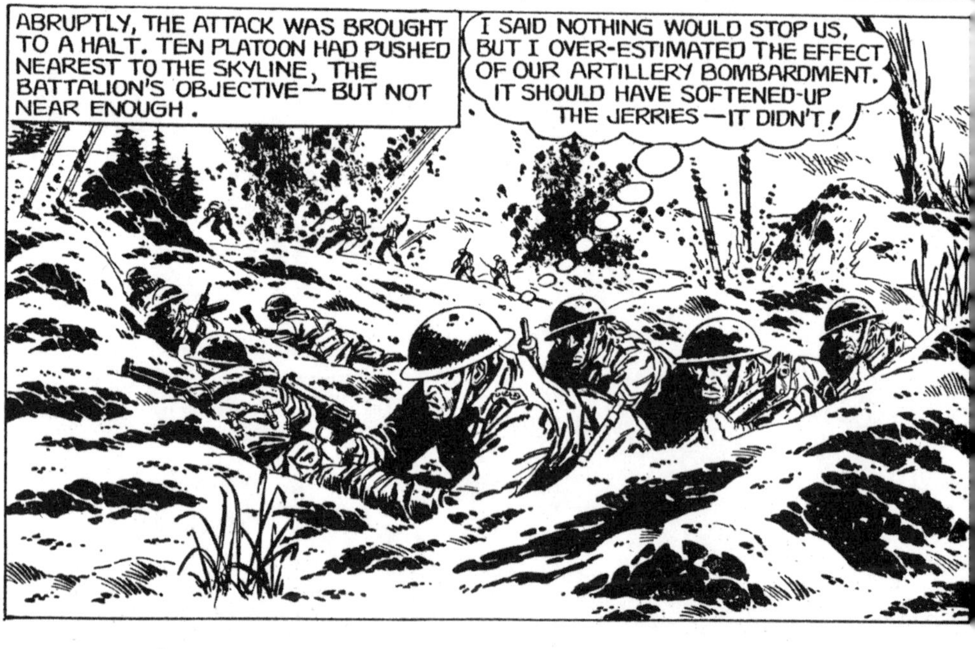
ABRUPTLY, THE ATTACK WAS BROUGHT TO A HALT. TEN PLATOON HAD PUSHED NEAREST TO THE SKYLINE, THE BATTALION'S OBJECTIVE— BUT NOT NEAR ENOUGH.
I SAID NOTHING WOULD STOP US, BUT I OVER-ESTIMATED THE EFFECT OF OUR ARTILLERY BOMBARDMENT. IT SHOULD HAVE SOFTENED-UP THE JERRIES—IT DIDN'T!

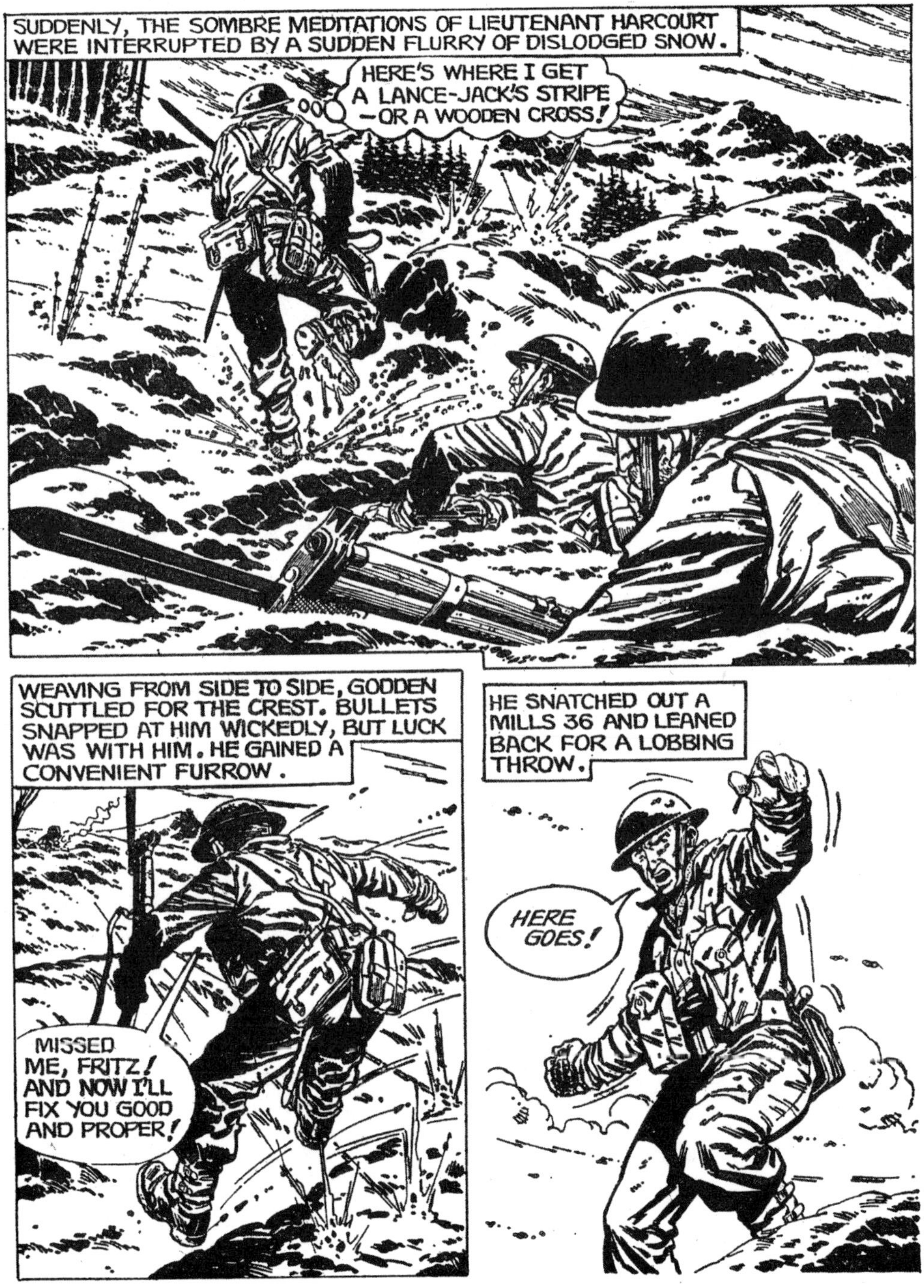
SUDDENLY, THE SOMBRE MEDITATIONS OF LIEUTENANT HARCOURT WERE INTERRUPTED BY A SUDDEN FLURRY OF DISLODGED SNOW.
HERE'S WHERE I GET A LANCE-JACK'S STRIPE —OR A WOODEN CROSS!
WEAVING FROM SIDE TO SIDE, GODDEN SCUTTLED FOR THE CREST. BULLETS SNAPPED AT HIM WICKEDLY, BUT LUCK WAS WITH HIM. HE GAINED A CONVENIENT FURROW.
MISSED ME, FRITZ! AND NOW I'LL FIX YOU GOOD AND PROPER!
HE SNATCHED OUT A MILLS 36 AND LEANED BACK FOR A LOBBING THROW.
HERE GOES!

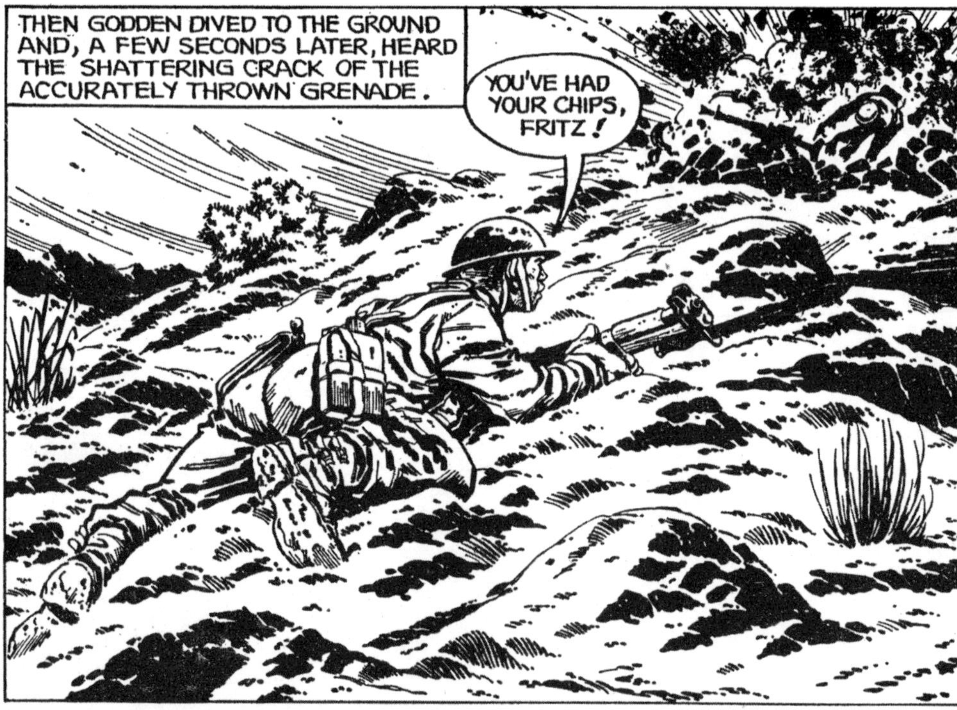
THEN GODDEN DIVED TO THE GROUND AND, A FEW SECONDS LATER, HEARD THE SHATTERING CRACK OF THE ACCURATELY THROWN GRENADE.
YOU'VE HAD YOUR CHIPS, FRITZ!

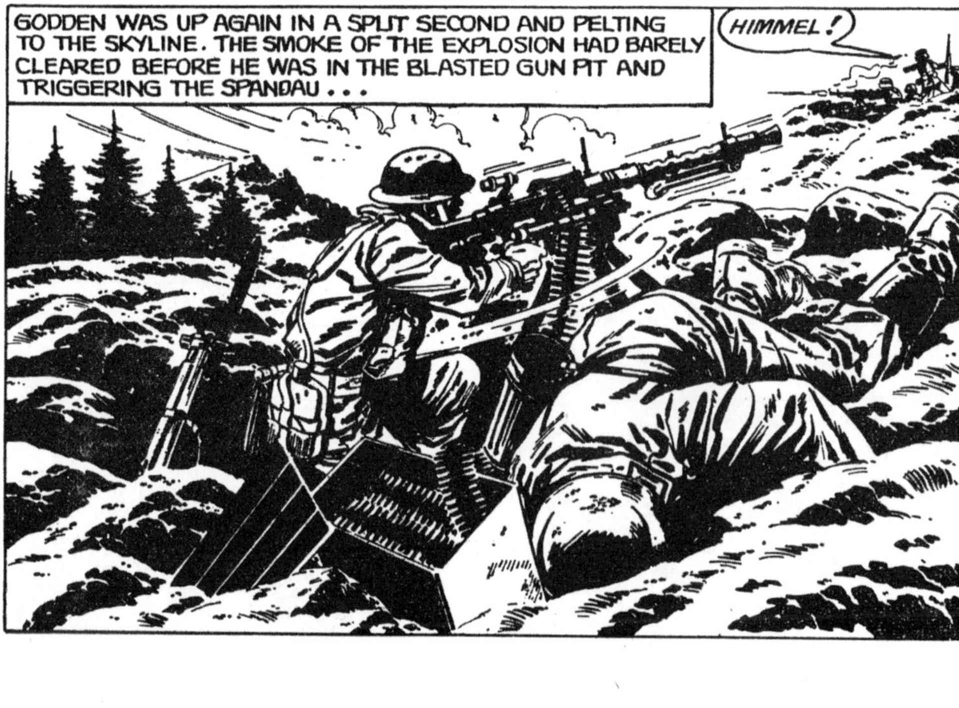
GODDEN WAS UP AGAIN IN A SPLIT SECOND AND PELTING TO THE SKYLINE. THE SMOKE OF THE EXPLOSION HAD BARELY CLEARED BEFORE HE WAS IN THE BLASTED GUN PIT AND TRIGGERING THE SPANDAU . . .
HIMMEL!

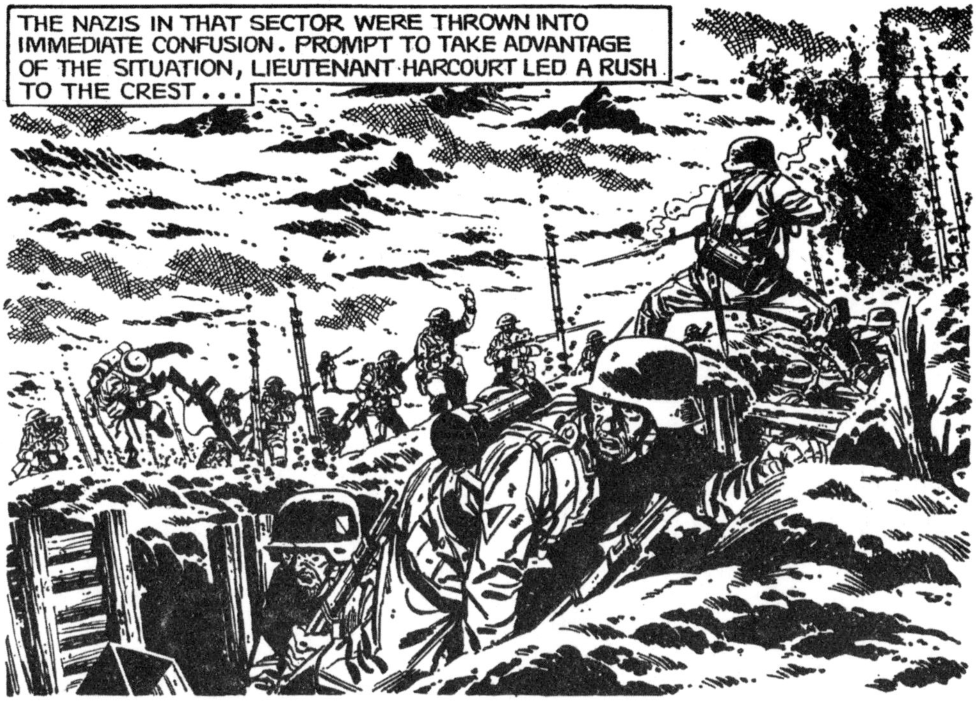
THE NAZIS IN THAT SECTOR WERE THROWN INTO IMMEDIATE CONFUSION. PROMPT TO TAKE ADVANTAGE OF THE SITUATION, LIEUTENANT HARCOURT LED A RUSH TO THE CREST...

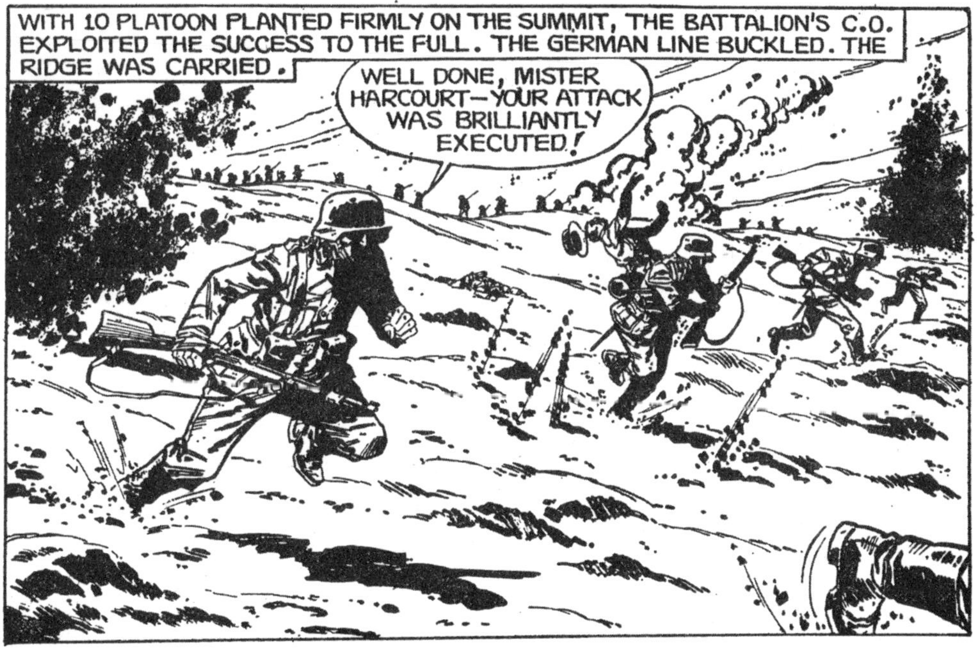
WITH 10 PLATOON PLANTED FIRMLY ON THE SUMMIT, THE BATTALION'S C.O. EXPLOITED THE SUCCESS TO THE FULL. THE GERMAN LINE BUCKLED. THE RIDGE WAS CARRIED.
WELL DONE, MISTER HARCOURT—YOUR ATTACK WAS BRILLIANTLY EXECUTED!

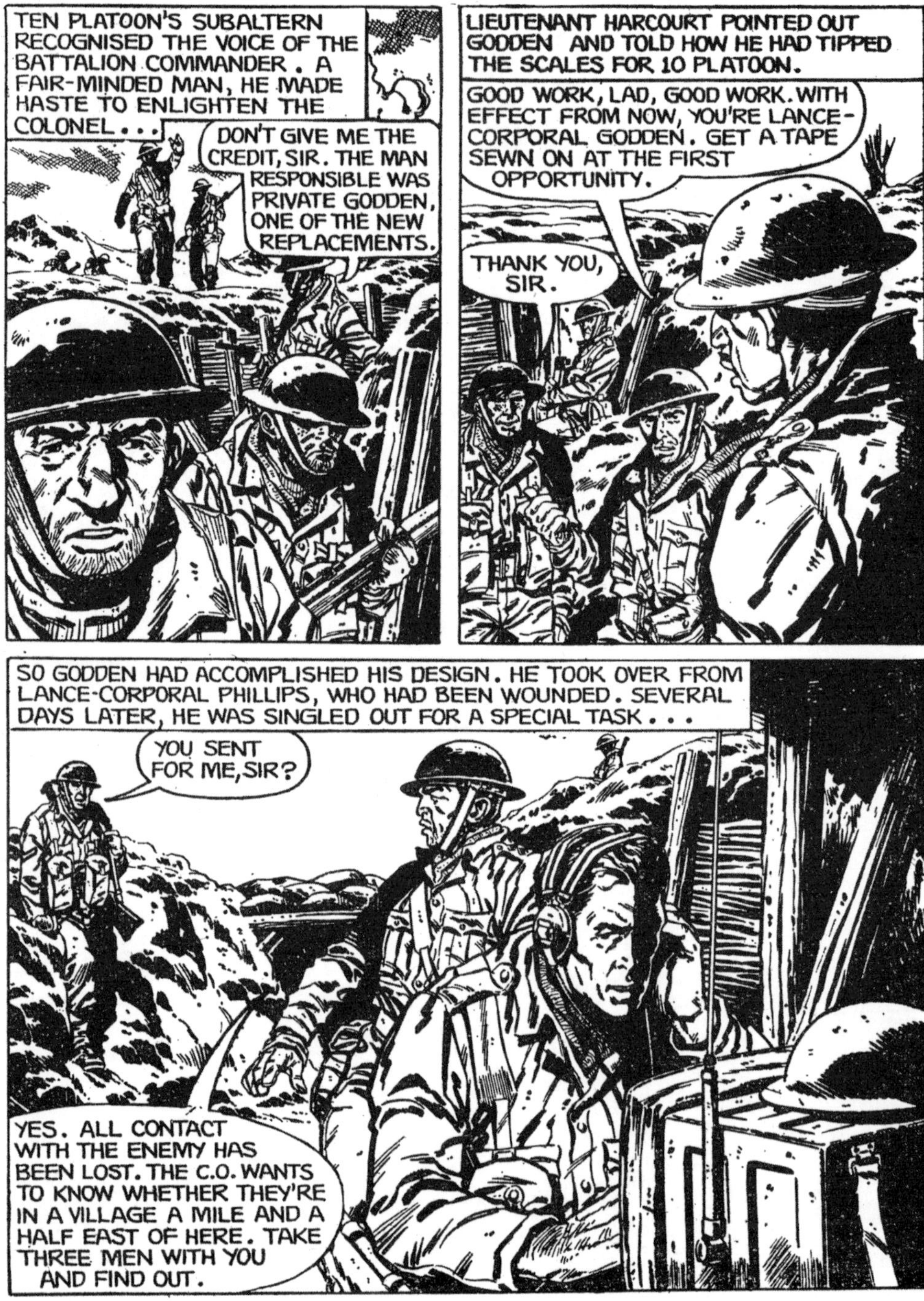
TEN PLATOON'S SUBALTERN RECOGNISED THE VOICE OF THE BATTALION COMMANDER . A FAIR-MINDED MAN, HE MADE HASTE TO ENLIGHTEN THE COLONEL . . .
DON'T GIVE ME THE CREDIT, SIR. THE MAN RESPONSIBLE WAS PRIVATE GODDEN, ONE OF THE NEW REPLACEMENTS.
LIEUTENANT HARCOURT POINTED OUT GODDEN AND TOLD HOW HE HAD TIPPED THE SCALES FOR 10 PLATOON.
GOOD WORK, LAD, GOOD WORK. WITH EFFECT FROM NOW, YOU'RE LANCE-CORPORAL GODDEN. GET A TAPE SEWN ON AT THE FIRST OPPORTUNITY.
THANK YOU, SIR.
SO GODDEN HAD ACCOMPLISHED HIS DESIGN. HE TOOK OVER FROM LANCE-CORPORAL PHILLIPS, WHO HAD BEEN WOUNDED. SEVERAL DAYS LATER, HE WAS SINGLED OUT FOR A SPECIAL TASK . . .
YOU SENT FOR ME, SIR?
YES. ALL CONTACT WITH THE ENEMY HAS BEEN LOST. THE C.O. WANTS TO KNOW WHETHER THEY'RE IN A VILLAGE A MILE AND A HALF EAST OF HERE. TAKE THREE MEN WITH YOU AND FIND OUT.

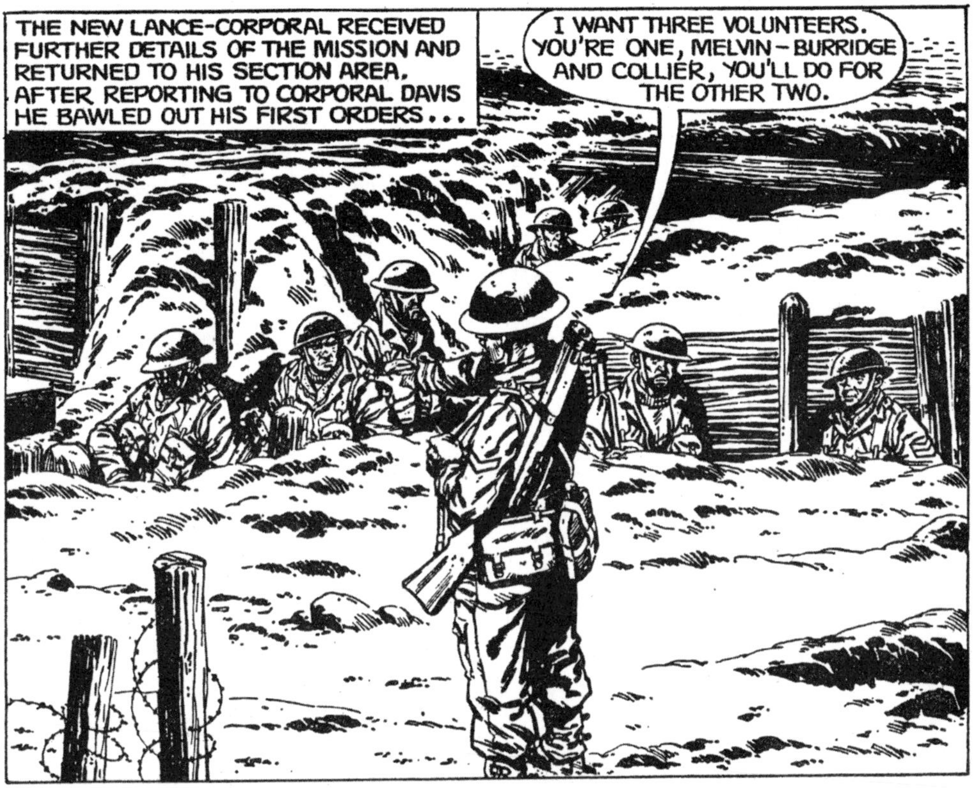
THE NEW LANCE-CORPORAL RECEIVED FURTHER DETAILS OF THE MISSION AND RETURNED TO HIS SECTION AREA. AFTER REPORTING TO CORPORAL DAVIS HE BAWLED OUT HIS FIRST ORDERS...
I WANT THREE VOLUNTEERS. YOU'RE ONE, MELVIN - BURRIDGE AND COLLIER, YOU'LL DO FOR THE OTHER TWO.

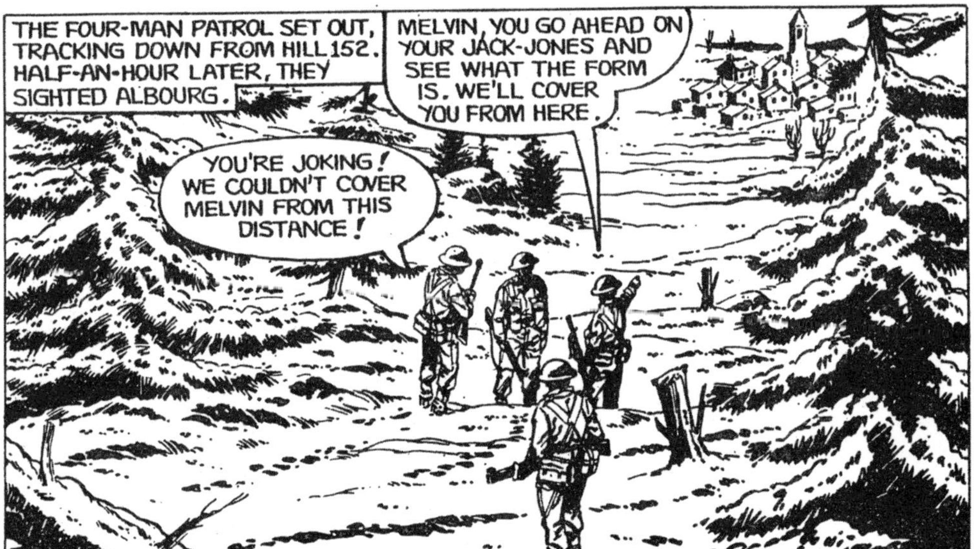
THE FOUR-MAN PATROL SET OUT, TRACKING DOWN FROM HILL 152. HALF-AN-HOUR LATER, THEY SIGHTED ALBOURG.
MELVIN, YOU GO AHEAD ON YOUR JACK-JONES AND SEE WHAT THE FORM IS. WE'LL COVER YOU FROM HERE.
YOU'RE JOKING! WE COULDN'T COVER MELVIN FROM THIS DISTANCE!

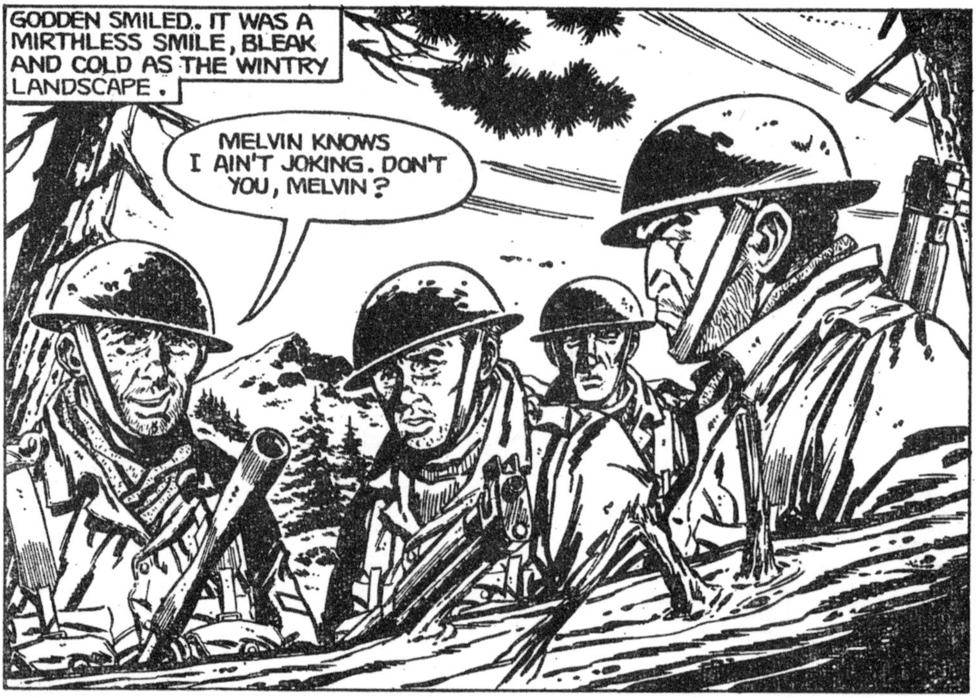
GODDEN SMILED. IT WAS A MIRTHLESS SMILE, BLEAK AND COLD AS THE WINTRY LANDSCAPE.
MELVIN KNOWS I AIN'T JOKING. DON'T YOU, MELVIN?

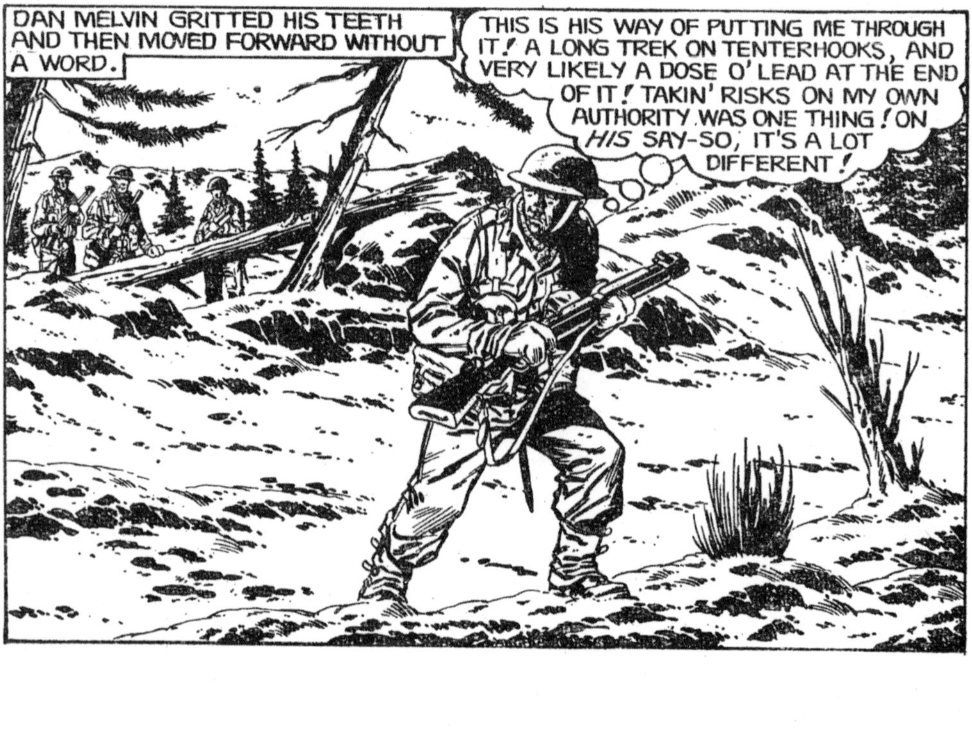
DAN MELVIN GRITTED HIS TEETH AND THEN MOVED FORWARD WITHOUT A WORD.
THIS IS HIS WAY OF PUTTING ME THROUGH IT! A LONG TREK ON TENTERHOOKS, AND VERY LIKELY A DOSE O' LEAD AT THE END OF IT! TAKIN' RISKS ON MY OWN AUTHORITY WAS ONE THING! ON HIS SAY-SO, IT'S A LOT DIFFERENT!

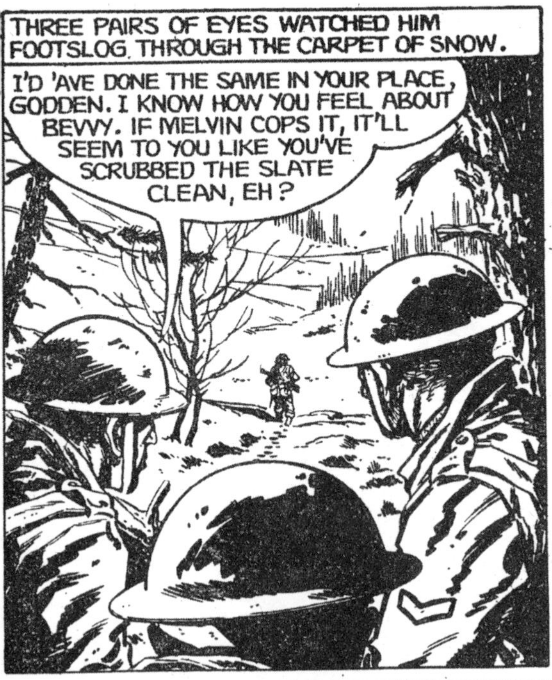
THREE PAIRS OF EYES WATCHED HIM FOOTSLOG THROUGH THE CARPET OF SNOW.
I'D 'AVE DONE THE SAME IN YOUR PLACE, GODDEN. I KNOW HOW YOU FEEL ABOUT BEVVY. IF MELVIN COPS IT, IT'LL SEEM TO YOU LIKE YOU'VE SCRUBBED THE SLATE CLEAN, EH?

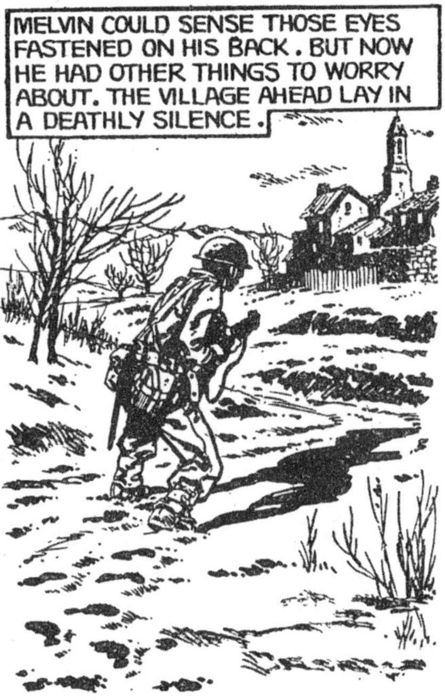
MELVIN COULD SENSE THOSE EYES FASTENED ON HIS BACK. BUT NOW HE HAD OTHER THINGS TO WORRY ABOUT. THE VILLAGE AHEAD LAY IN A DEATHLY SILENCE.

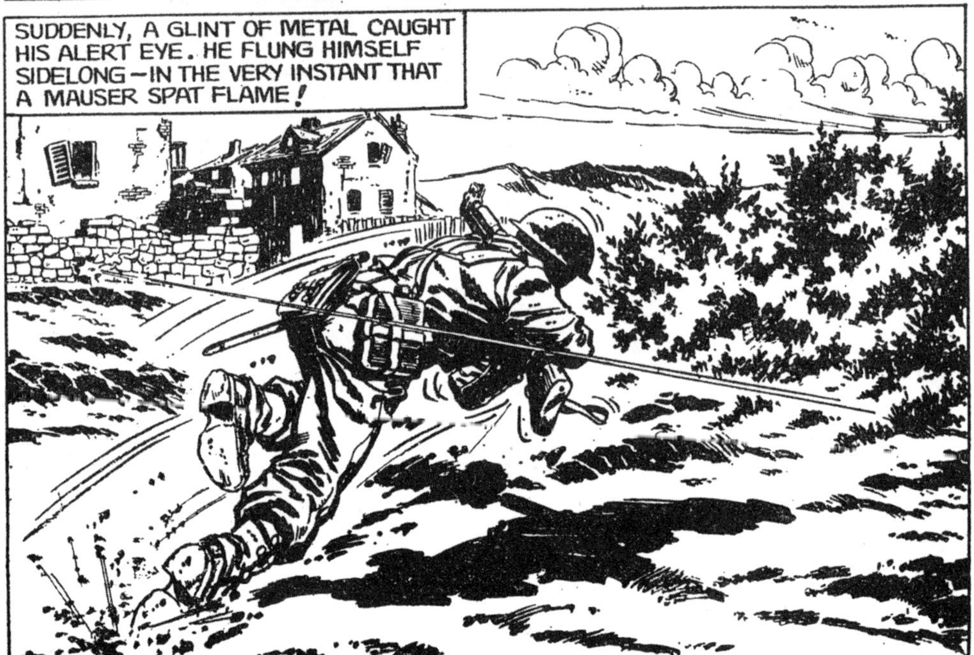
SUDDENLY, A GLINT OF METAL CAUGHT HIS ALERT EYE. HE FLUNG HIMSELF SIDELONG—IN THE VERY INSTANT THAT A MAUSER SPAT FLAME!

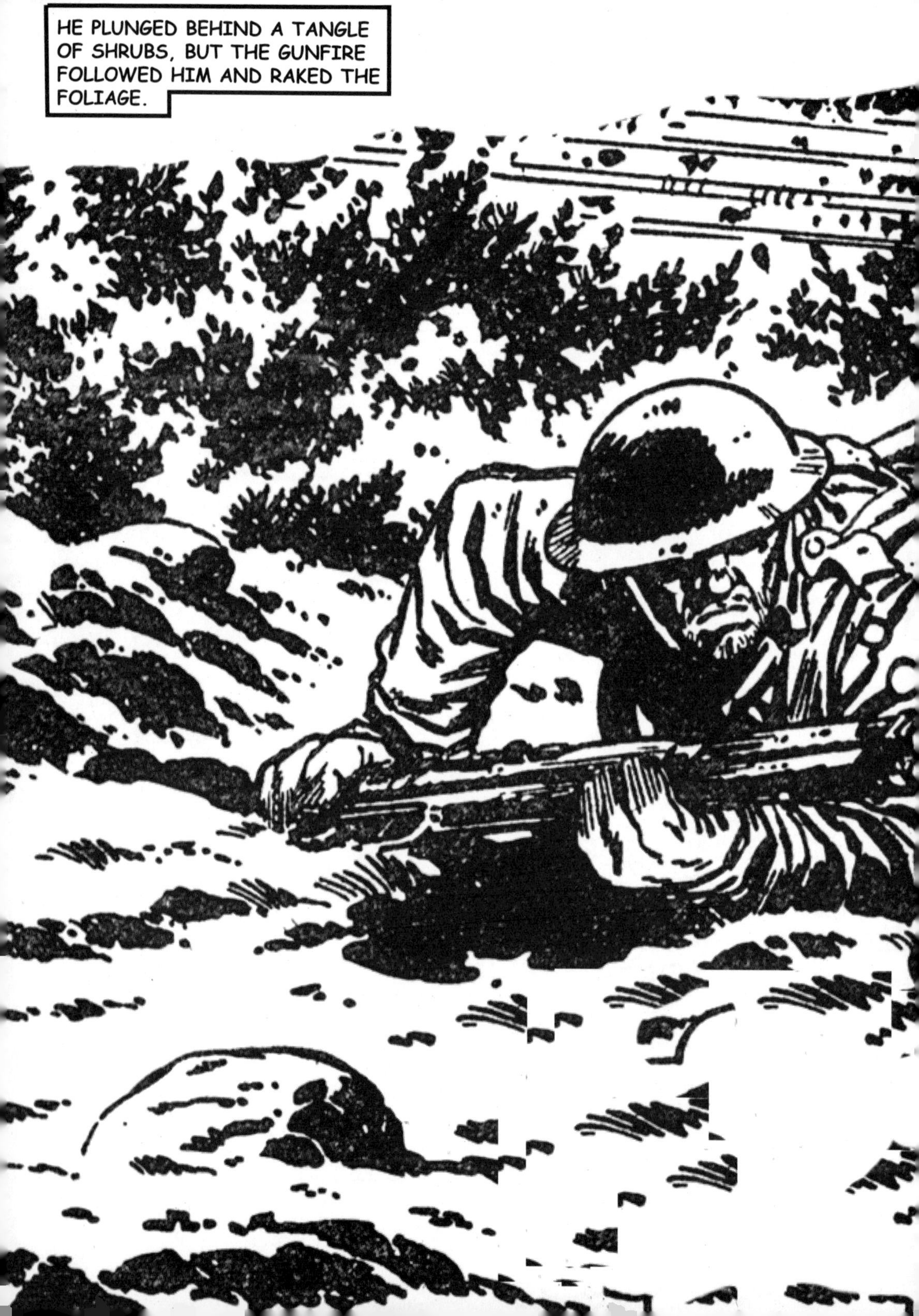
HE PLUNGED BEHIND A TANGLE OF SHRUBS, BUT THE GUNFIRE FOLLOWED HIM AND RAKED THE FOLIAGE.

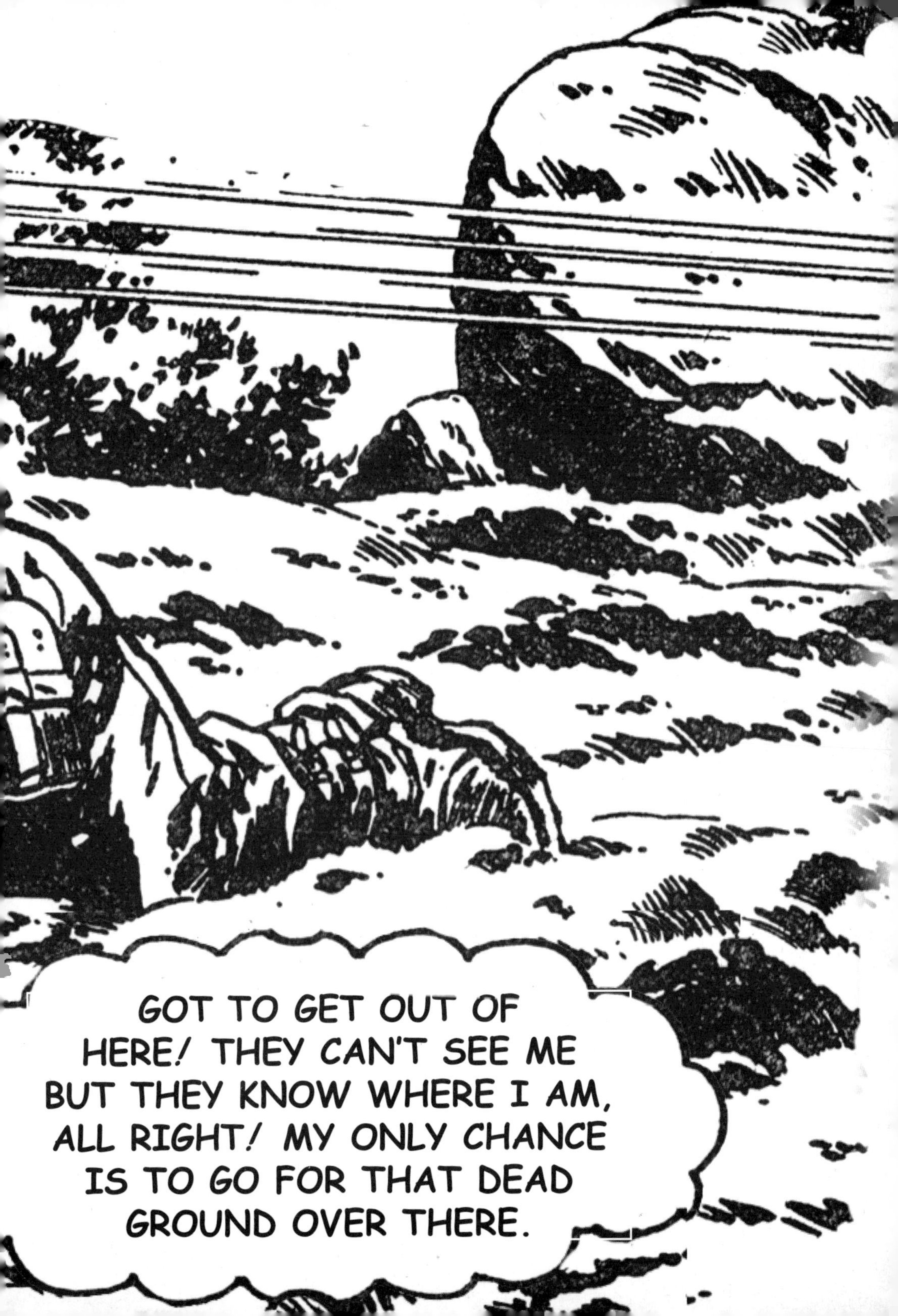
GOT TO GET OUT OF HERE! THEY CAN'T SEE ME BUT THEY KNOW WHERE I AM, ALL RIGHT! MY ONLY CHANCE IS TO GO FOR THAT DEAD GROUND OVER THERE.

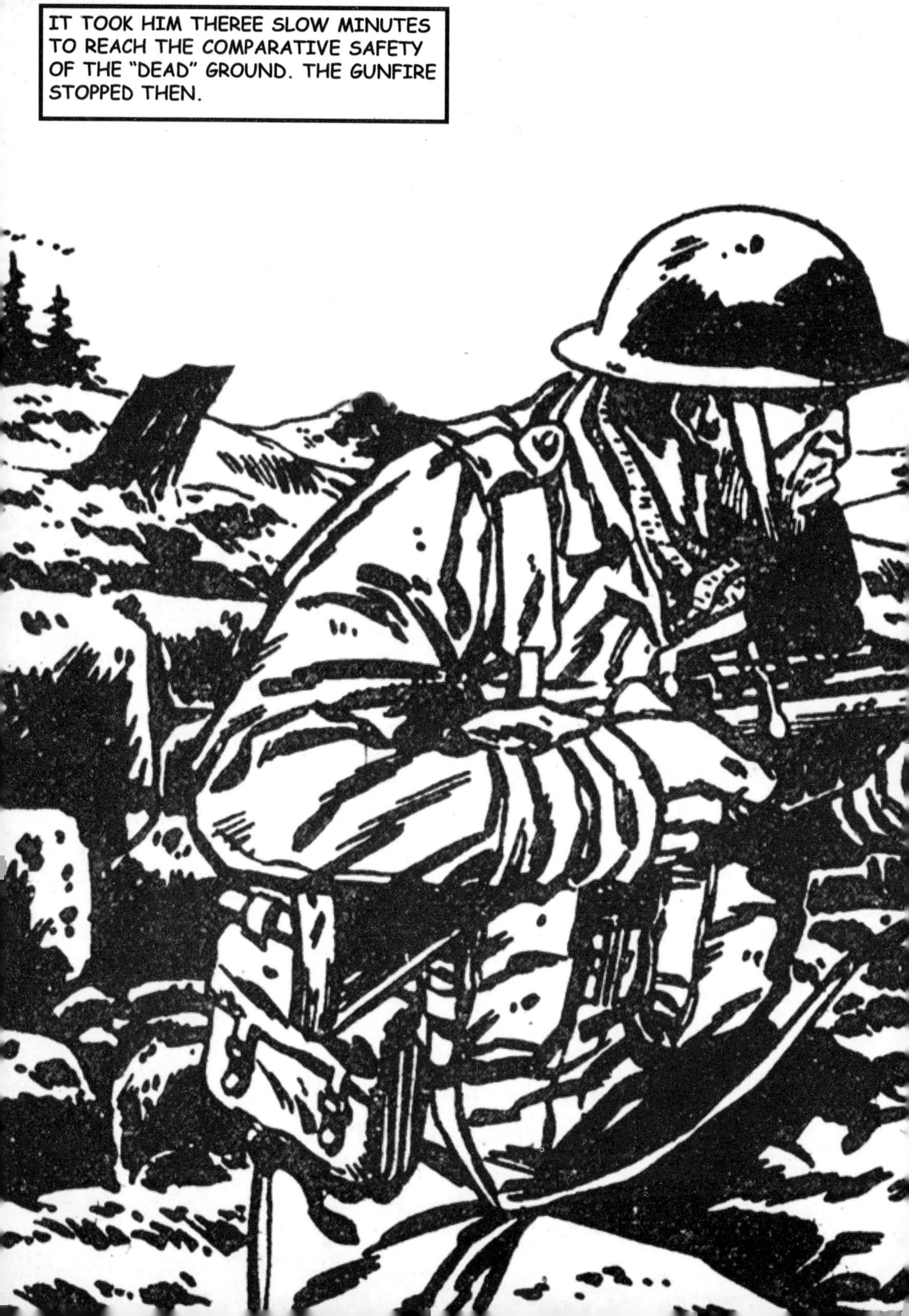
IT TOOK HIM THEREE SLOW MINUTES TO REACH THE COMPARATIVE SAFETY OF THE "DEAD" GROUND. THE GUNFIRE STOPPED THEN.

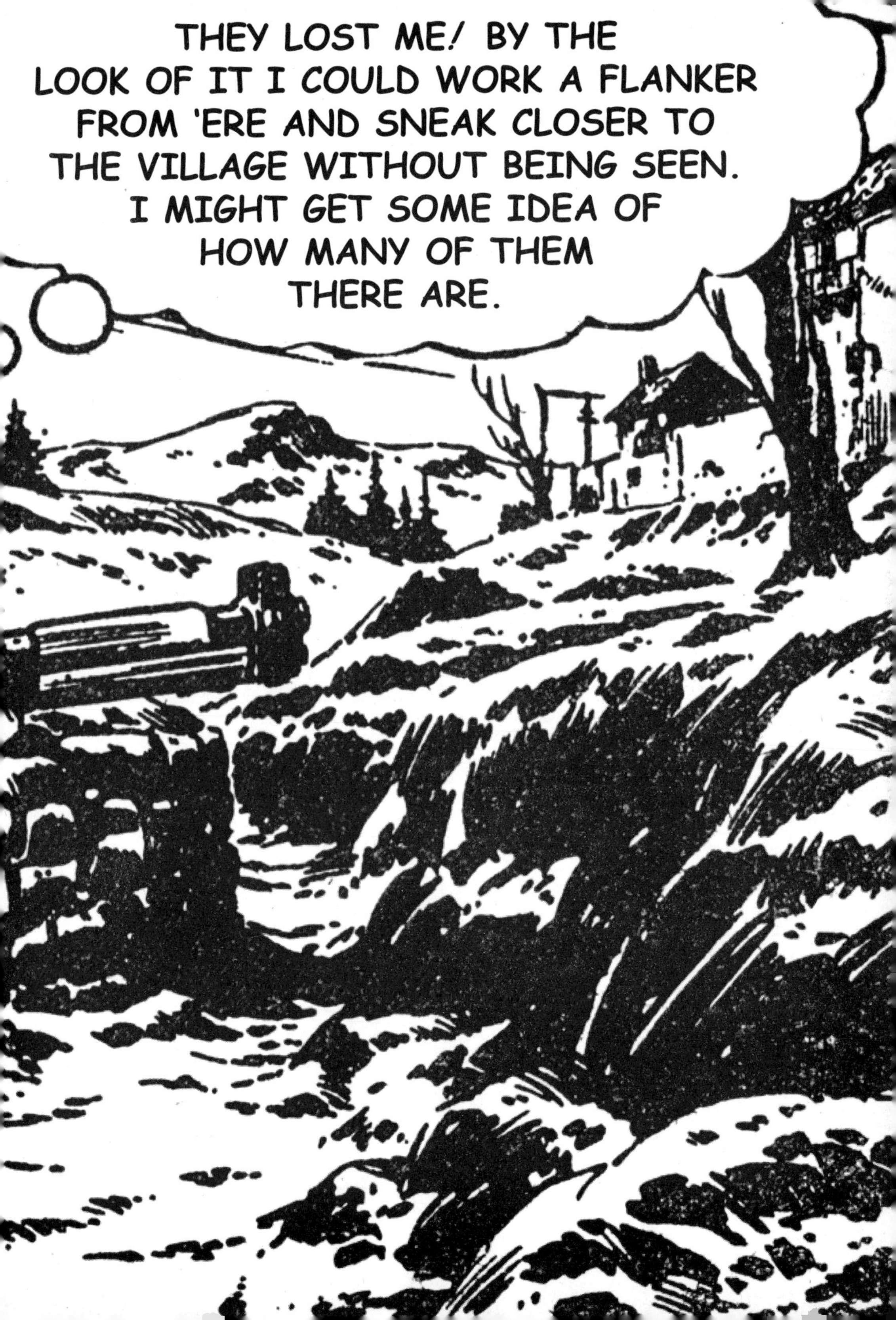
THEY LOST ME! BY THE LOOK OF IT I COULD WORK A FLANKER FROM 'ERE AND SNEAK CLOSER TO THE VILLAGE WITHOUT BEING SEEN. I MIGHT GET SOME IDEA OF HOW MANY OF THEM THERE ARE.

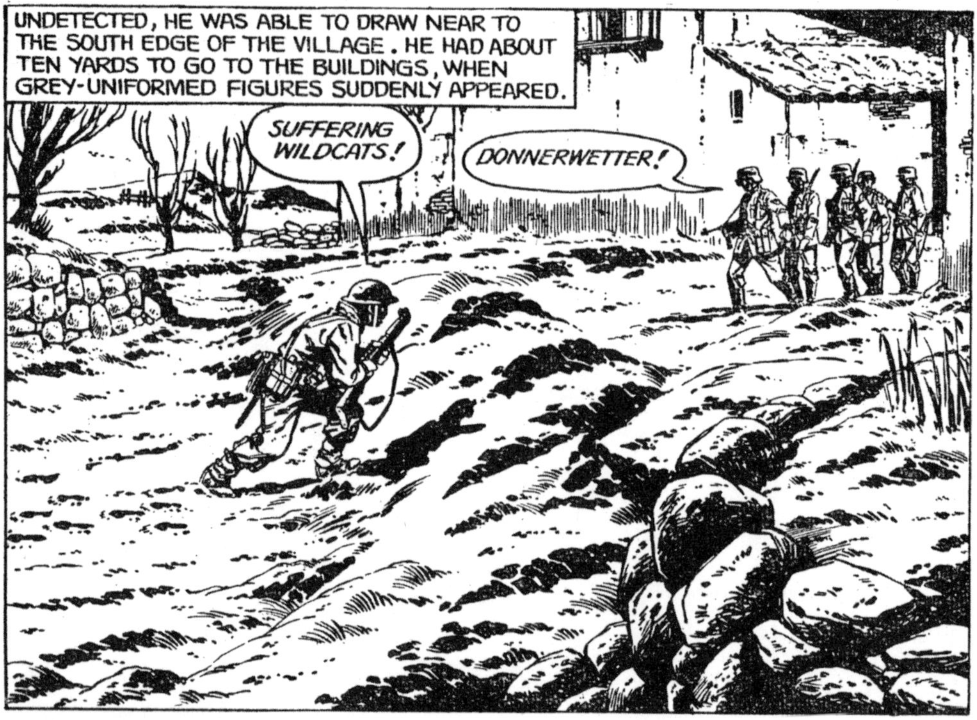
UNDETECTED, HE WAS ABLE TO DRAW NEAR TO THE SOUTH EDGE OF THE VILLAGE. HE HAD ABOUT TEN YARDS TO GO TO THE BUILDINGS, WHEN GREY-UNIFORMED FIGURES SUDDENLY APPEARED.
SUFFERING WILDCATS!
DONNERWETTER!

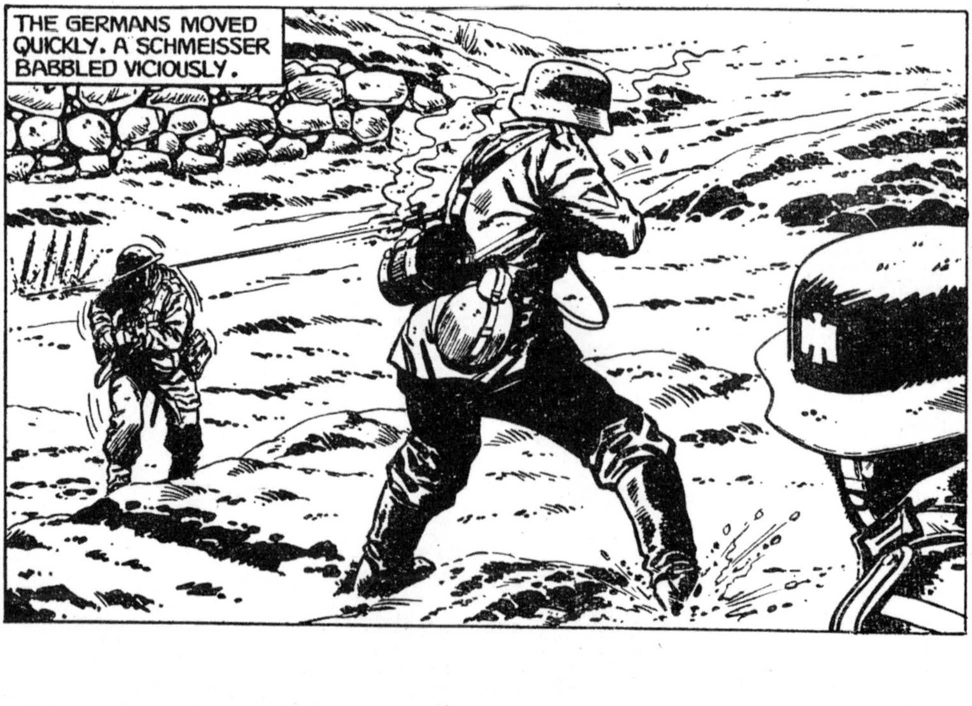
THE GERMANS MOVED QUICKLY. A SCHMEISSER BABBLED VICIOUSLY.

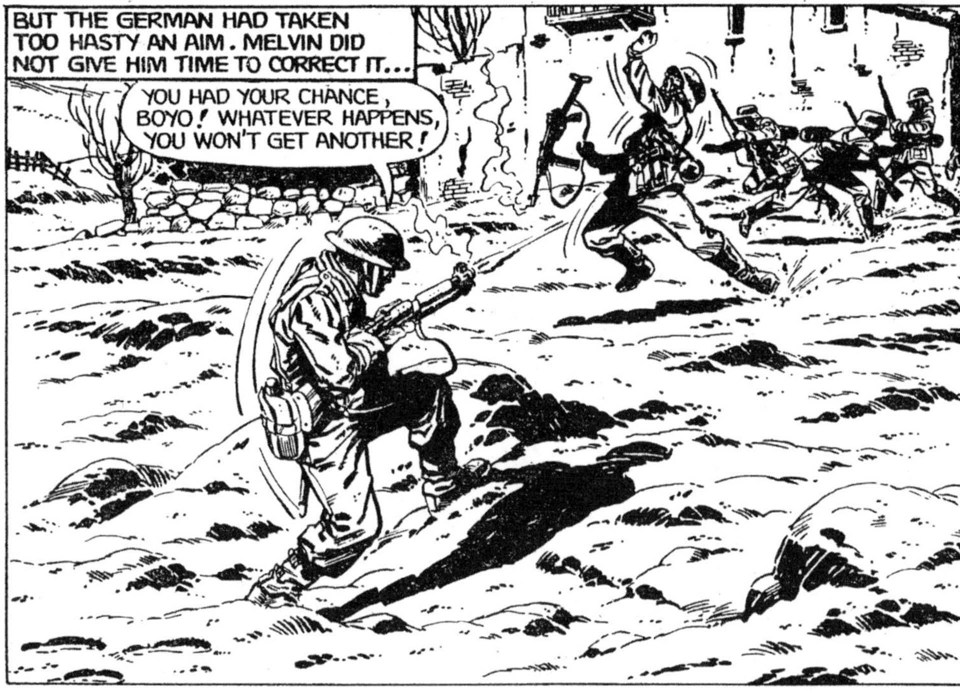
BUT THE GERMAN HAD TAKEN TOO HASTY AN AIM. MELVIN DID NOT GIVE HIM TIME TO CORRECT IT...
YOU HAD YOUR CHANCE, BOYO! WHATEVER HAPPENS, YOU WON'T GET ANOTHER!

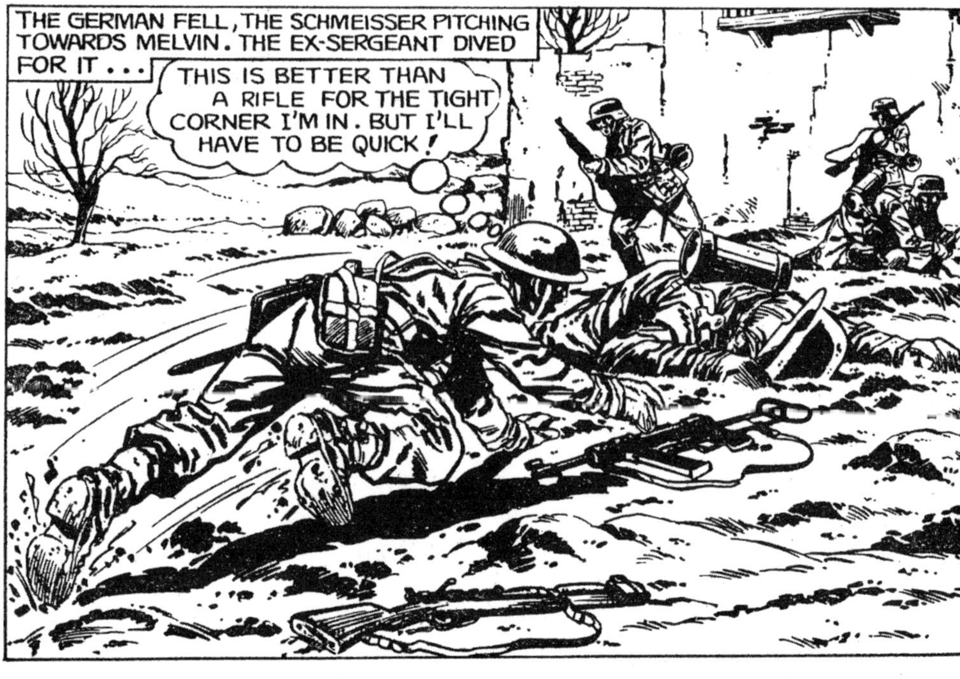
THE GERMAN FELL, THE SCHMEISSER PITCHING TOWARDS MELVIN. THE EX-SERGEANT DIVED FOR IT . . .
THIS IS BETTER THAN A RIFLE FOR THE TIGHT CORNER I'M IN. BUT I'LL HAVE TO BE QUICK!

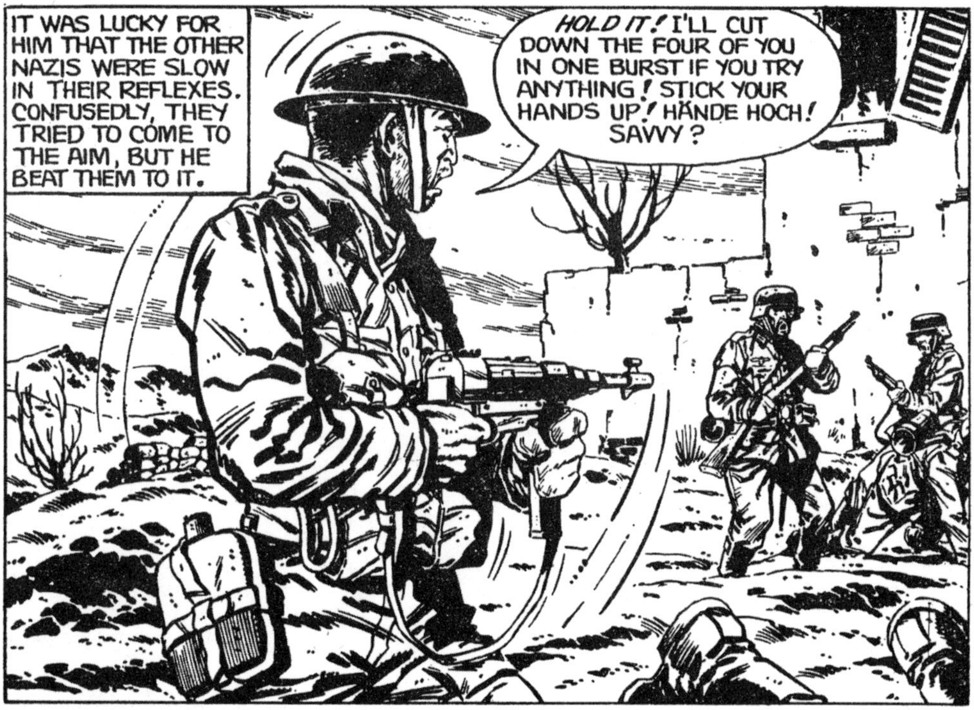
IT WAS LUCKY FOR HIM THAT THE OTHER NAZIS WERE SLOW IN THEIR REFLEXES. CONFUSEDLY, THEY TRIED TO COME TO THE AIM, BUT HE BEAT THEM TO IT.
HOLD IT! I'LL CUT DOWN THE FOUR OF YOU IN ONE BURST IF YOU TRY ANYTHING! STICK YOUR HANDS UP! HÄNDE HOCH! SAVVY?

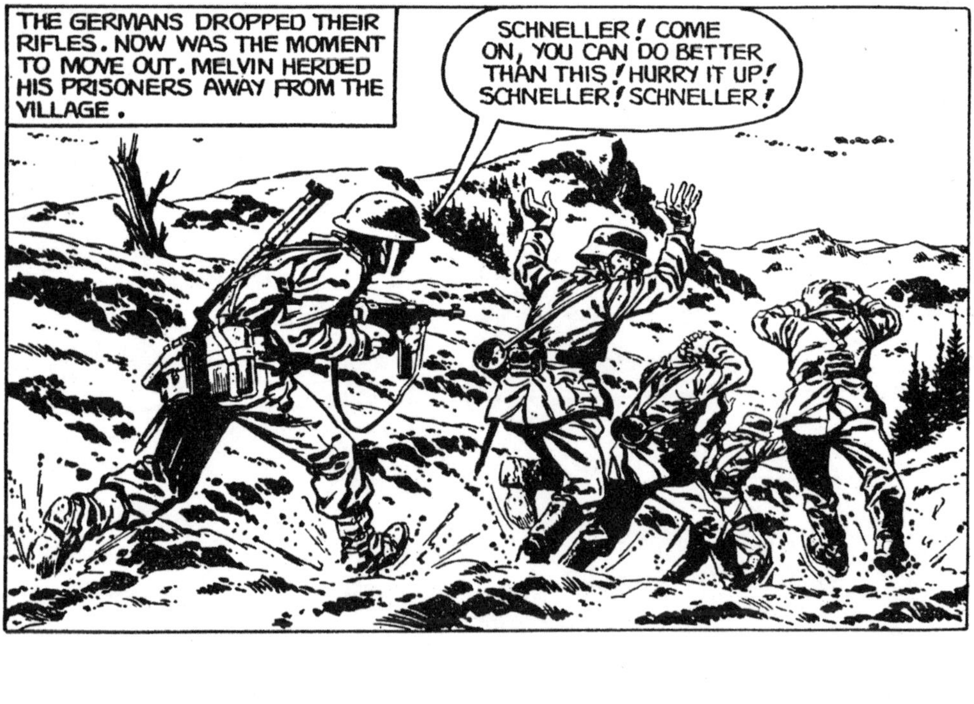
THE GERMANS DROPPED THEIR RIFLES. NOW WAS THE MOMENT TO MOVE OUT. MELVIN HERDED HIS PRISONERS AWAY FROM THE VILLAGE.
SCHNELLER! COME ON, YOU CAN DO BETTER THAN THIS! HURRY IT UP! SCHNELLER! SCHNELLER!

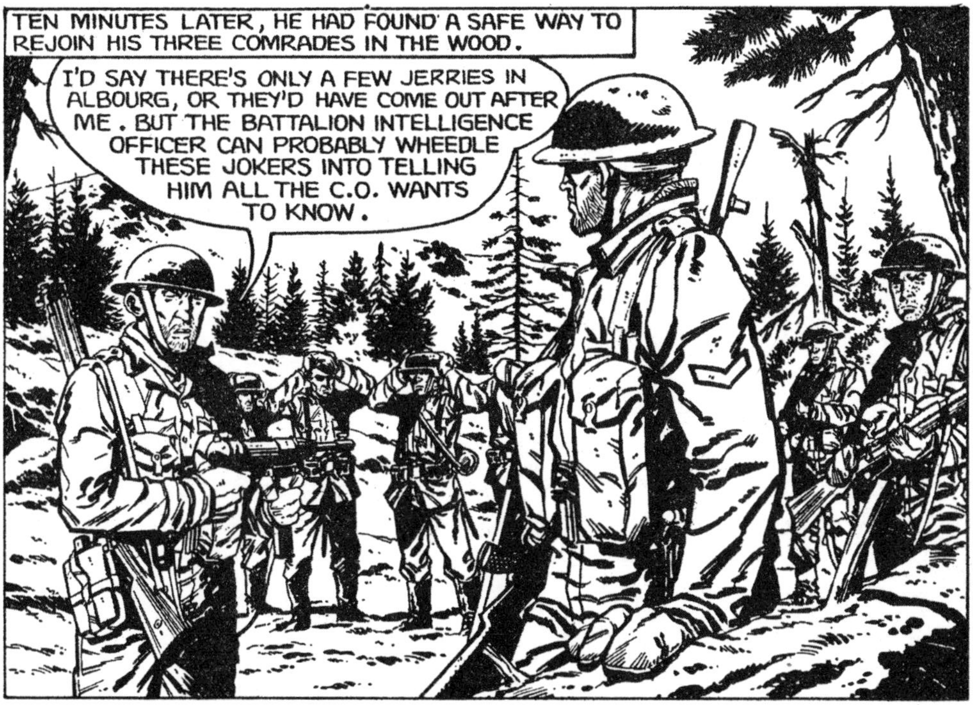
TEN MINUTES LATER, HE HAD FOUND A SAFE WAY TO REJOIN HIS THREE COMRADES IN THE WOOD.
I'D SAY THERE'S ONLY A FEW JERRIES IN ALBOURG, OR THEY'D HAVE COME OUT AFTER ME. BUT THE BATTALION INTELLIGENCE OFFICER CAN PROBABLY WHEEDLE THESE JOKERS INTO TELLING HIM ALL THE C.O. WANTS TO KNOW.

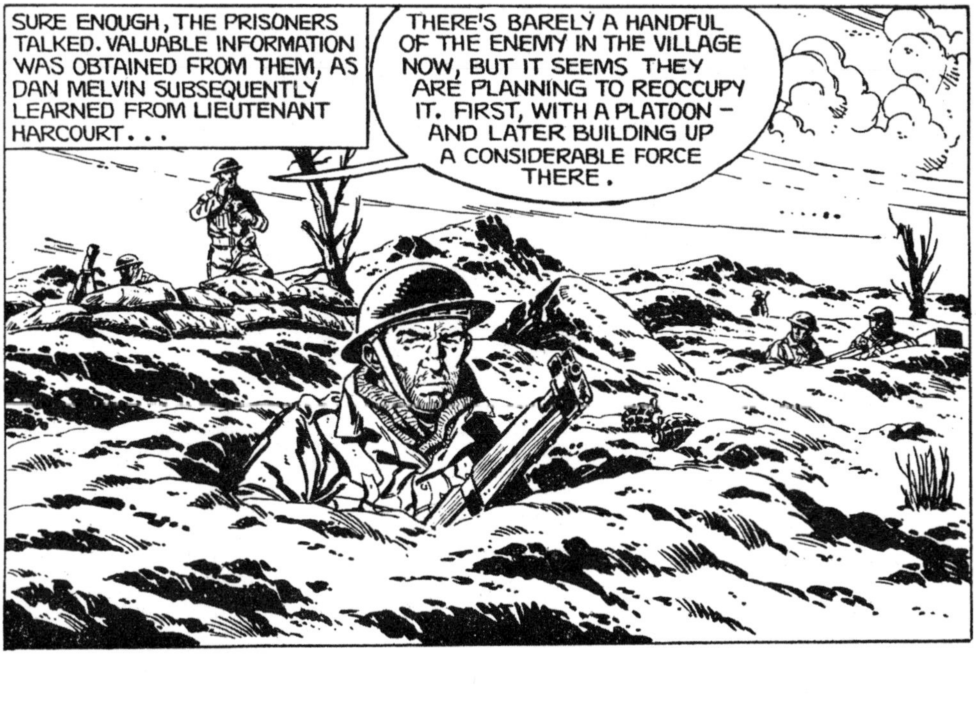
SURE ENOUGH, THE PRISONERS TALKED. VALUABLE INFORMATION WAS OBTAINED FROM THEM, AS DAN MELVIN SUBSEQUENTLY LEARNED FROM LIEUTENANT HARCOURT...
THERE'S BARELY A HANDFUL OF THE ENEMY IN THE VILLAGE NOW, BUT IT SEEMS THEY ARE PLANNING TO REOCCUPY IT. FIRST, WITH A PLATOON – AND LATER BUILDING UP A CONSIDERABLE FORCE THERE.

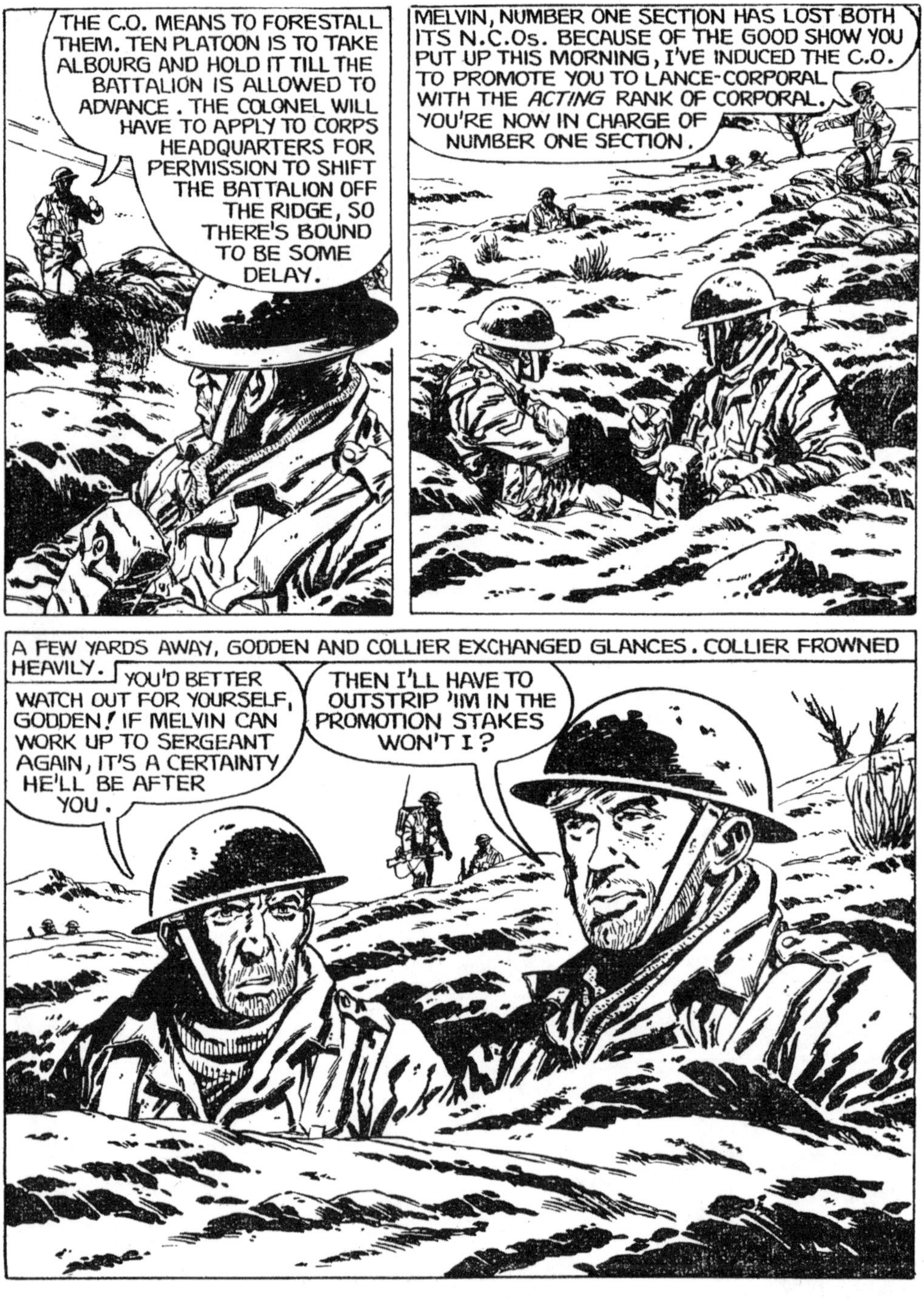
THE C.O. MEANS TO FORESTALL THEM. TEN PLATOON IS TO TAKE ALBOURG AND HOLD IT TILL THE BATTALION IS ALLOWED TO ADVANCE. THE COLONEL WILL HAVE TO APPLY TO CORPS HEADQUARTERS FOR PERMISSION TO SHIFT THE BATTALION OFF THE RIDGE, SO THERE'S BOUND TO BE SOME DELAY.
MELVIN, NUMBER ONE SECTION HAS LOST BOTH ITS N.C.Os. BECAUSE OF THE GOOD SHOW YOU PUT UP THIS MORNING, I'VE INDUCED THE C.O. TO PROMOTE YOU TO LANCE-CORPORAL WITH THE *ACTING* RANK OF CORPORAL. YOU'RE NOW IN CHARGE OF NUMBER ONE SECTION.
A FEW YARDS AWAY, GODDEN AND COLLIER EXCHANGED GLANCES. COLLIER FROWNED HEAVILY.
YOU'D BETTER WATCH OUT FOR YOURSELF, GODDEN! IF MELVIN CAN WORK UP TO SERGEANT AGAIN, IT'S A CERTAINTY HE'LL BE AFTER YOU.
THEN I'LL HAVE TO OUTSTRIP 'IM IN THE PROMOTION STAKES WON'T I?

Chapter 3. To the Death...

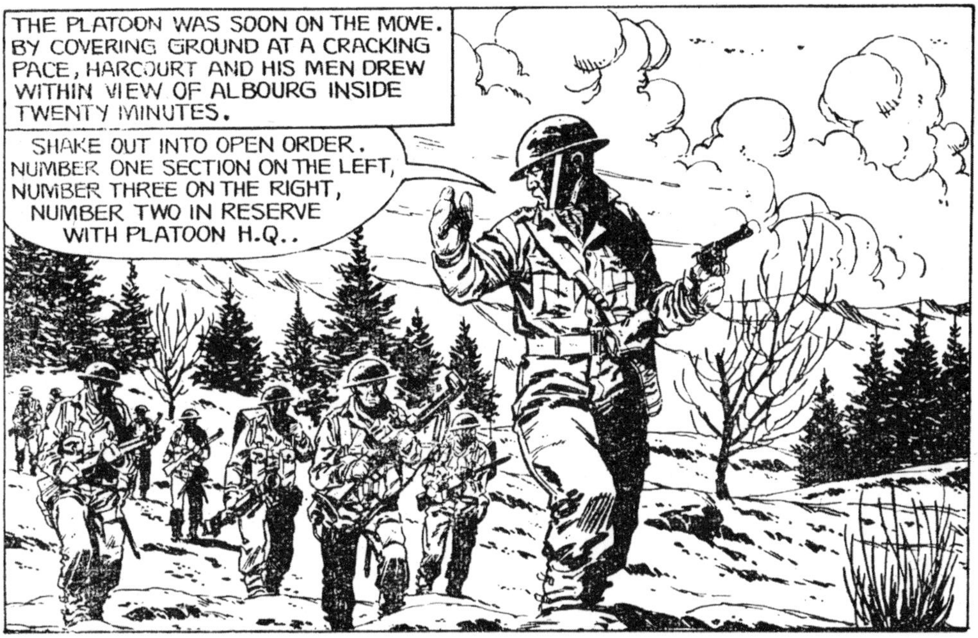
THE PLATOON WAS SOON ON THE MOVE. BY COVERING GROUND AT A CRACKING PACE, HARCOURT AND HIS MEN DREW WITHIN VIEW OF ALBOURG INSIDE TWENTY MINUTES.
SHAKE OUT INTO OPEN ORDER. NUMBER ONE SECTION ON THE LEFT, NUMBER THREE ON THE RIGHT, NUMBER TWO IN RESERVE WITH PLATOON H.Q..

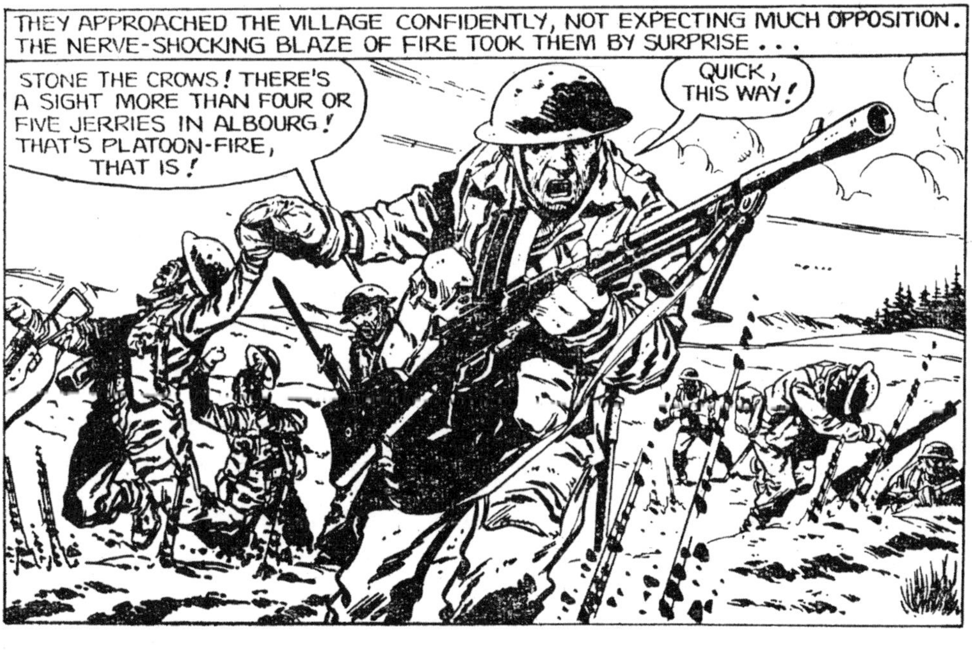
THEY APPROACHED THE VILLAGE CONFIDENTLY, NOT EXPECTING MUCH OPPOSITION. THE NERVE-SHOCKING BLAZE OF FIRE TOOK THEM BY SURPRISE . . .
STONE THE CROWS! THERE'S A SIGHT MORE THAN FOUR OR FIVE JERRIES IN ALBOURG! THAT'S PLATOON-FIRE, THAT IS!
QUICK, THIS WAY!

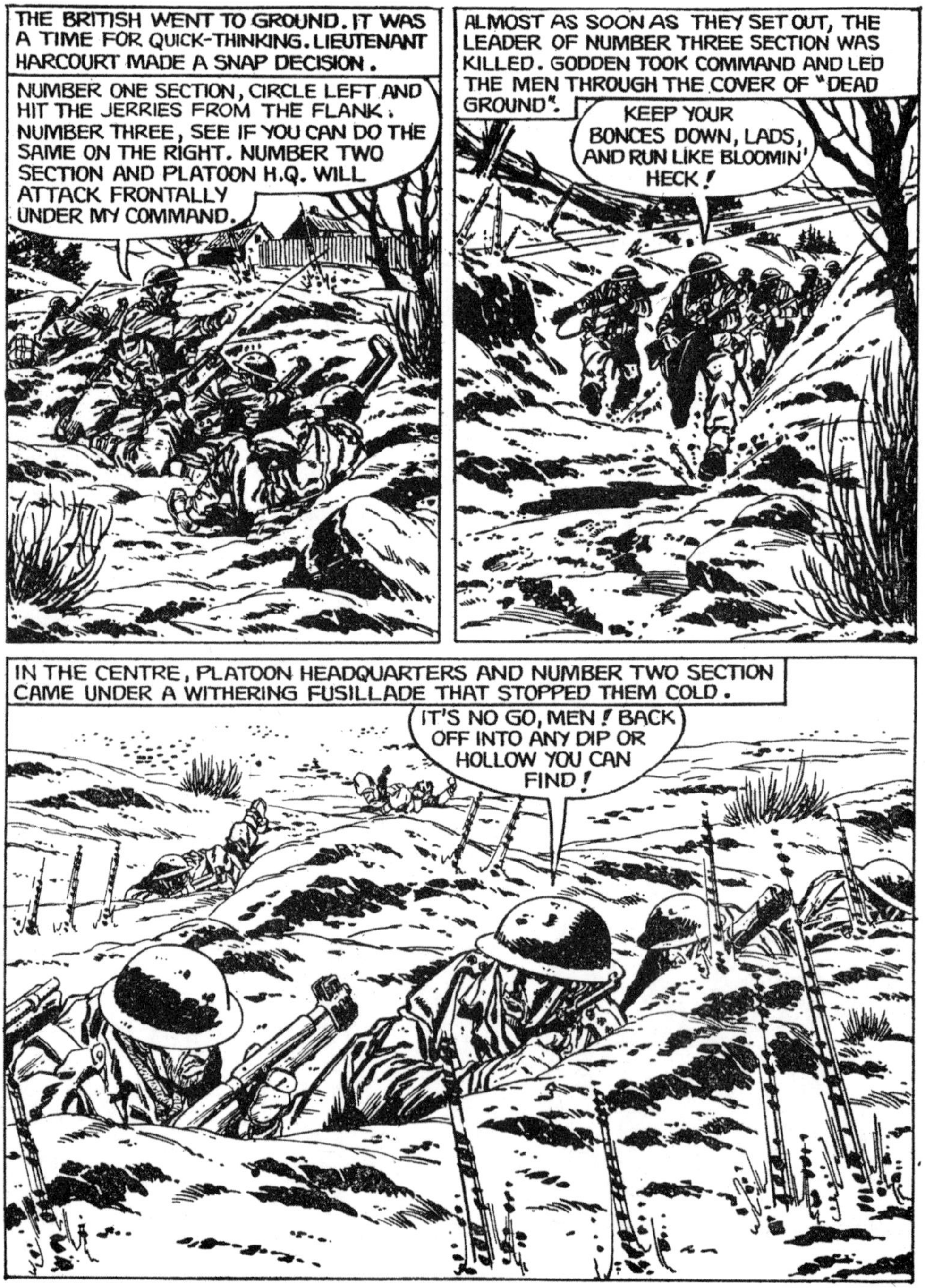
THE BRITISH WENT TO GROUND. IT WAS A TIME FOR QUICK-THINKING. LIEUTENANT HARCOURT MADE A SNAP DECISION.
NUMBER ONE SECTION, CIRCLE LEFT AND HIT THE JERRIES FROM THE FLANK. NUMBER THREE, SEE IF YOU CAN DO THE SAME ON THE RIGHT. NUMBER TWO SECTION AND PLATOON H.Q. WILL ATTACK FRONTALLY UNDER MY COMMAND.
ALMOST AS SOON AS THEY SET OUT, THE LEADER OF NUMBER THREE SECTION WAS KILLED. GODDEN TOOK COMMAND AND LED THE MEN THROUGH THE COVER OF "DEAD GROUND".
KEEP YOUR BONCES DOWN, LADS, AND RUN LIKE BLOOMIN' HECK!
IN THE CENTRE, PLATOON HEADQUARTERS AND NUMBER TWO SECTION CAME UNDER A WITHERING FUSILLADE THAT STOPPED THEM COLD.
IT'S NO GO, MEN! BACK OFF INTO ANY DIP OR HOLLOW YOU CAN FIND!

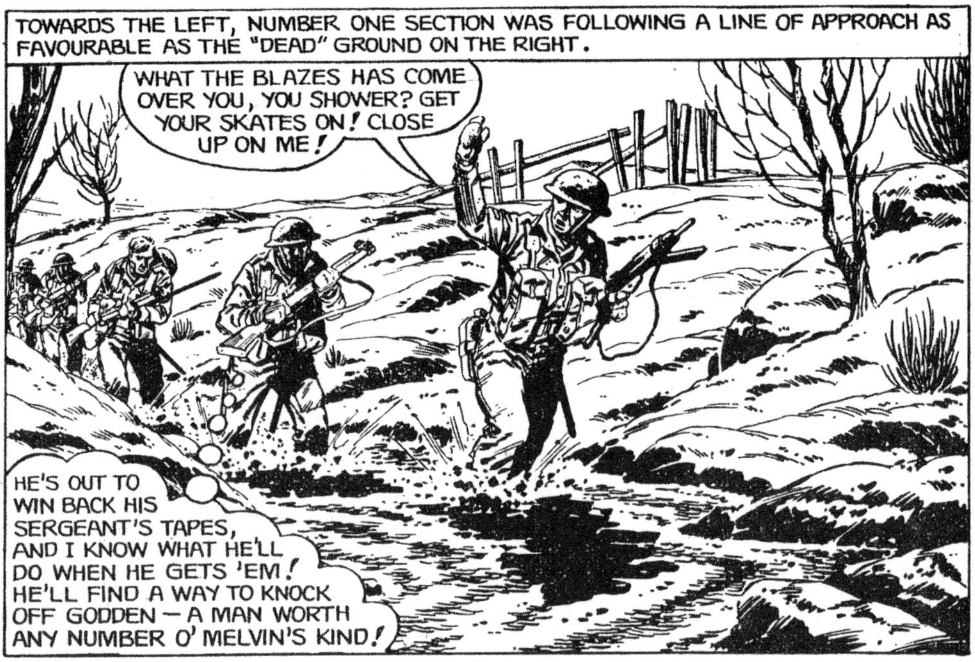
TOWARDS THE LEFT, NUMBER ONE SECTION WAS FOLLOWING A LINE OF APPROACH AS FAVOURABLE AS THE "DEAD" GROUND ON THE RIGHT.
WHAT THE BLAZES HAS COME OVER YOU, YOU SHOWER? GET YOUR SKATES ON! CLOSE UP ON ME!
HE'S OUT TO WIN BACK HIS SERGEANT'S TAPES, AND I KNOW WHAT HE'LL DO WHEN HE GETS 'EM! HE'LL FIND A WAY TO KNOCK OFF GODDEN — A MAN WORTH ANY NUMBER O' MELVIN'S KIND!

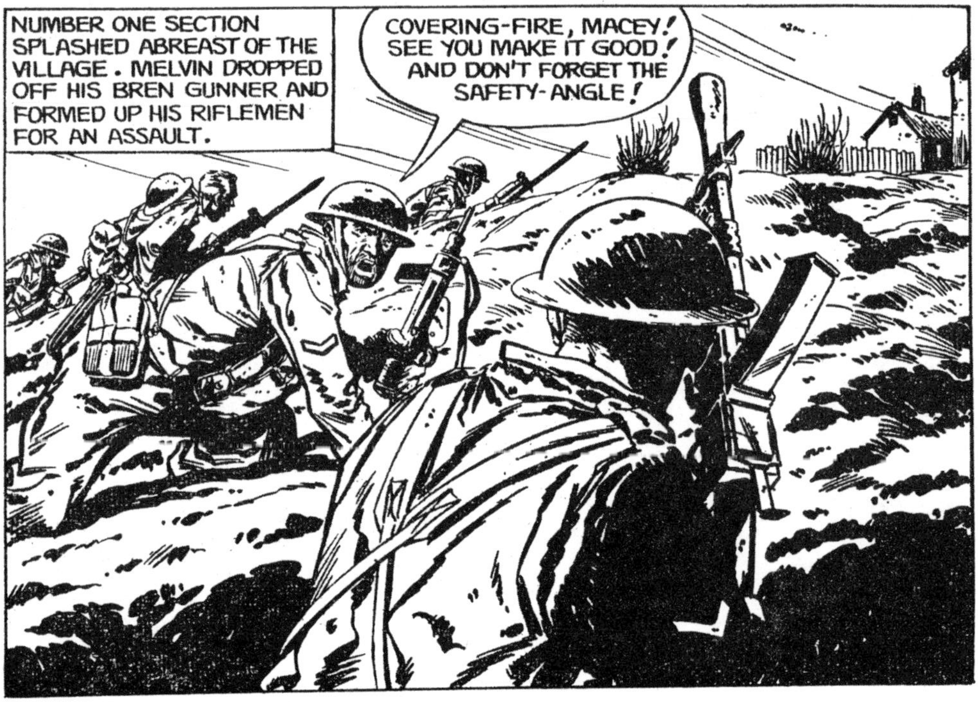
NUMBER ONE SECTION SPLASHED ABREAST OF THE VILLAGE. MELVIN DROPPED OFF HIS BREN GUNNER AND FORMED UP HIS RIFLEMEN FOR AN ASSAULT.
COVERING-FIRE, MACEY! SEE YOU MAKE IT GOOD! AND DON'T FORGET THE SAFETY-ANGLE!

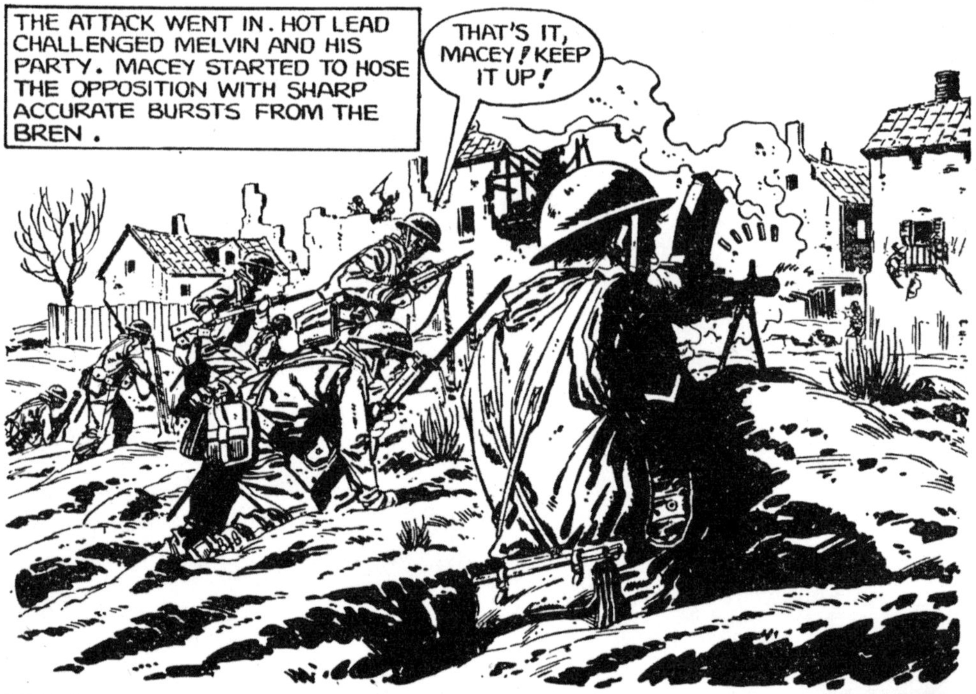
THE ATTACK WENT IN. HOT LEAD CHALLENGED MELVIN AND HIS PARTY. MACEY STARTED TO HOSE THE OPPOSITION WITH SHARP ACCURATE BURSTS FROM THE BREN.
THAT'S IT, MACEY! KEEP IT UP!

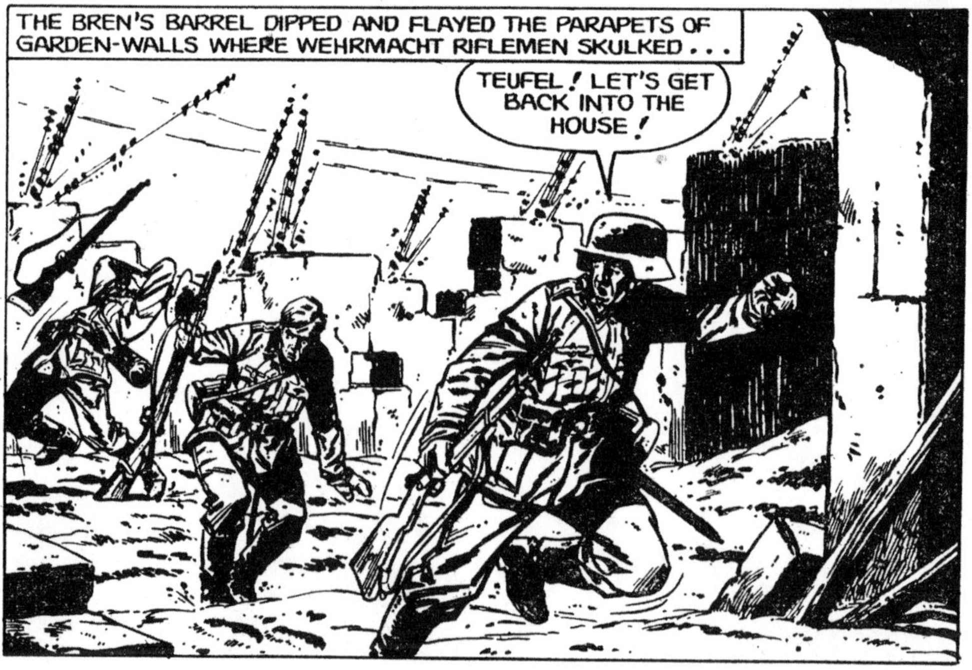
THE BREN'S BARREL DIPPED AND FLAYED THE PARAPETS OF GARDEN-WALLS WHERE WEHRMACHT RIFLEMEN SKULKED...
TEUFEL! LET'S GET BACK INTO THE HOUSE!

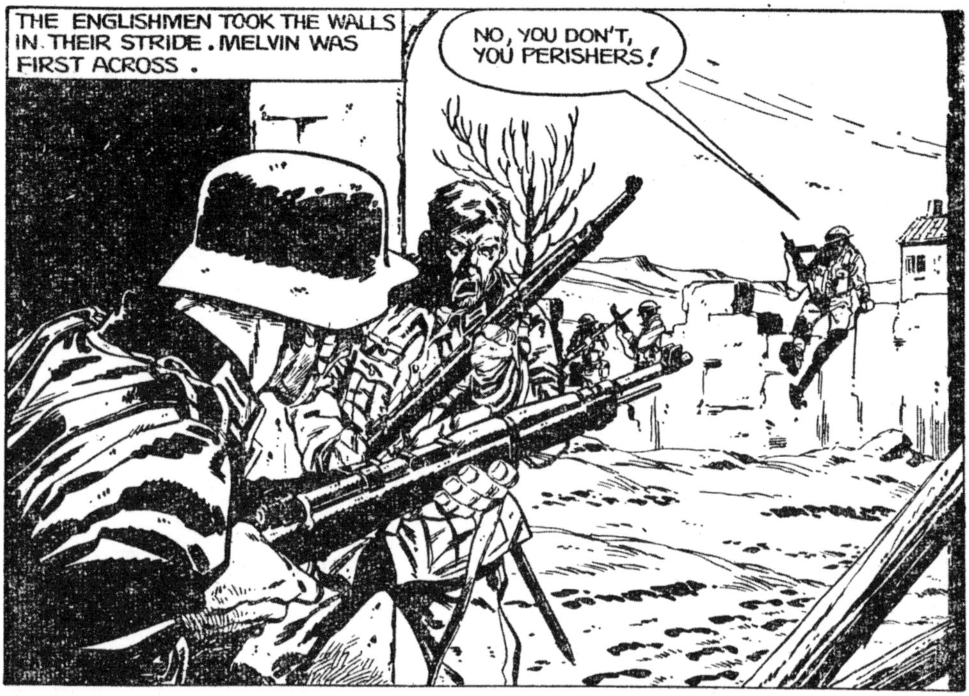
THE ENGLISHMEN TOOK THE WALLS IN THEIR STRIDE. MELVIN WAS FIRST ACROSS.
NO, YOU DON'T, YOU PERISHERS!

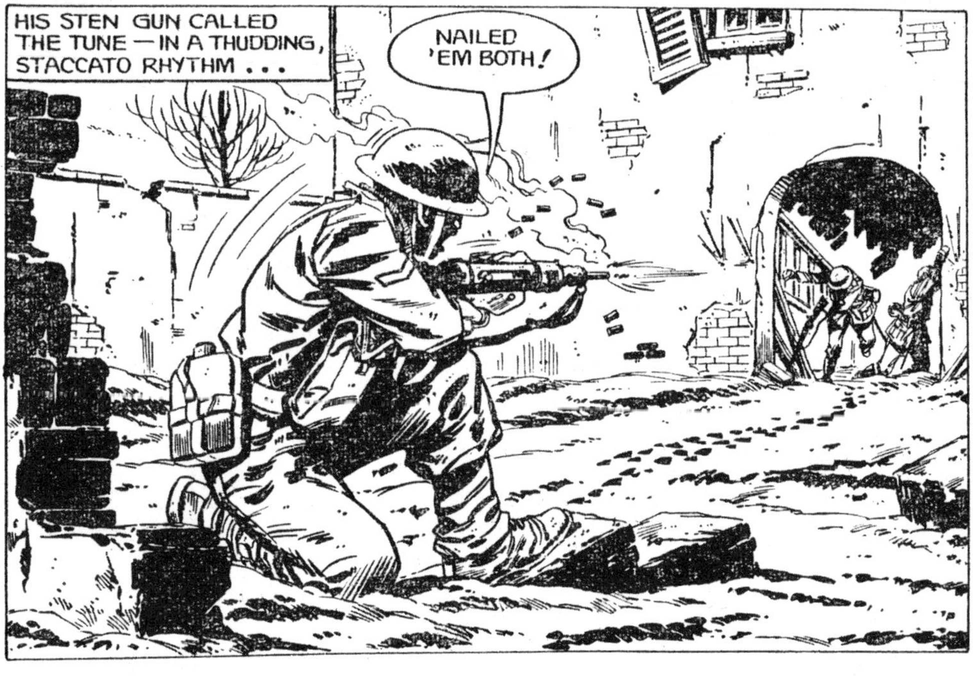
HIS STEN GUN CALLED THE TUNE — IN A THUDDING, STACCATO RHYTHM ...
NAILED 'EM BOTH!

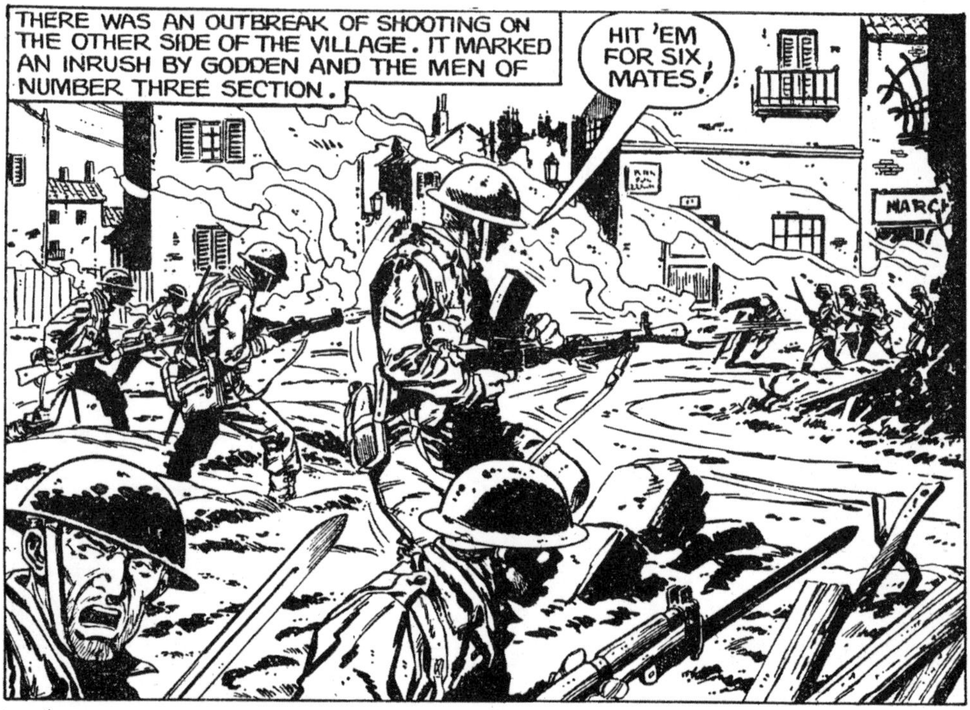
THERE WAS AN OUTBREAK OF SHOOTING ON THE OTHER SIDE OF THE VILLAGE. IT MARKED AN INRUSH BY GODDEN AND THE MEN OF NUMBER THREE SECTION.
HIT 'EM FOR SIX, MATES!
MARC

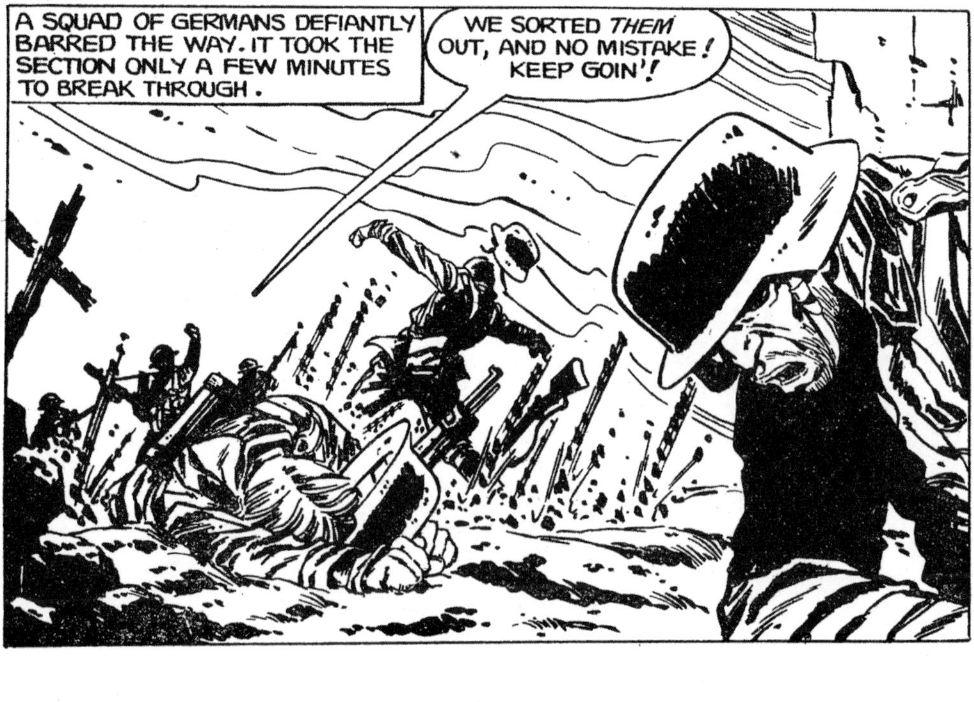
A SQUAD OF GERMANS DEFIANTLY BARRED THE WAY. IT TOOK THE SECTION ONLY A FEW MINUTES TO BREAK THROUGH.
WE SORTED *THEM* OUT, AND NO MISTAKE! KEEP GOIN'!

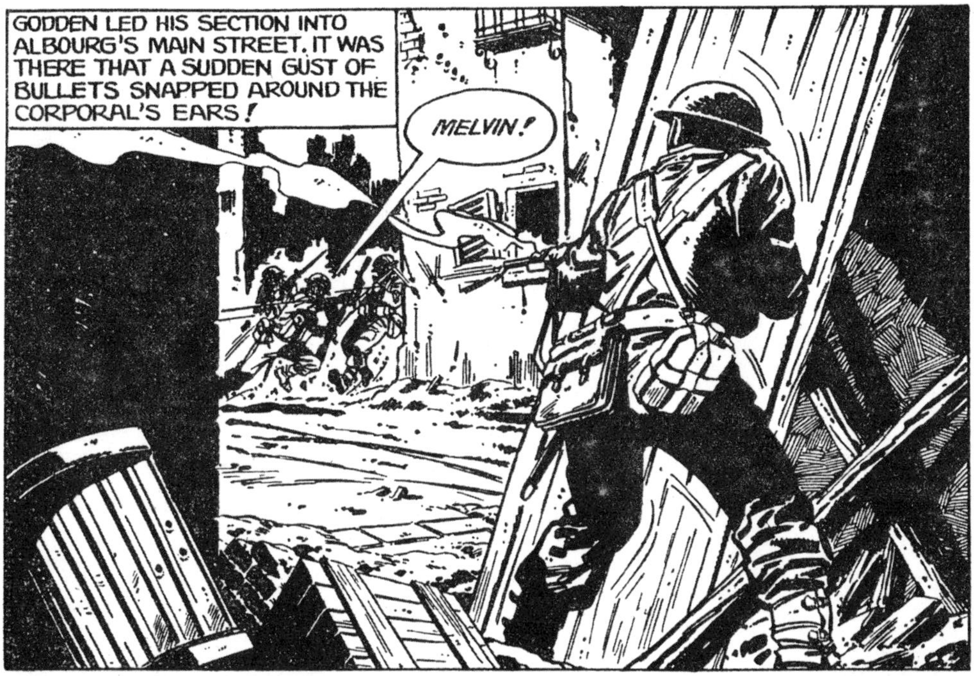
GODDEN LED HIS SECTION INTO ALBOURG'S MAIN STREET. IT WAS THERE THAT A SUDDEN GUST OF BULLETS SNAPPED AROUND THE CORPORAL'S EARS!
MELVIN!

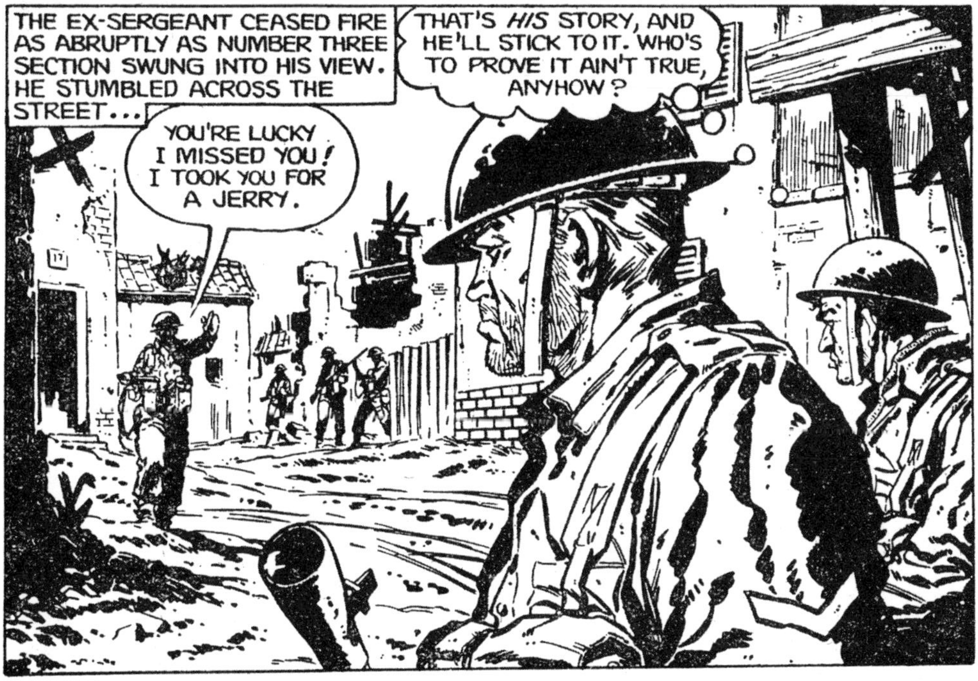
THE EX-SERGEANT CEASED FIRE AS ABRUPTLY AS NUMBER THREE SECTION SWUNG INTO HIS VIEW. HE STUMBLED ACROSS THE STREET...
THAT'S HIS STORY, AND HE'LL STICK TO IT. WHO'S TO PROVE IT AIN'T TRUE, ANYHOW?
YOU'RE LUCKY I MISSED YOU! I TOOK YOU FOR A JERRY.

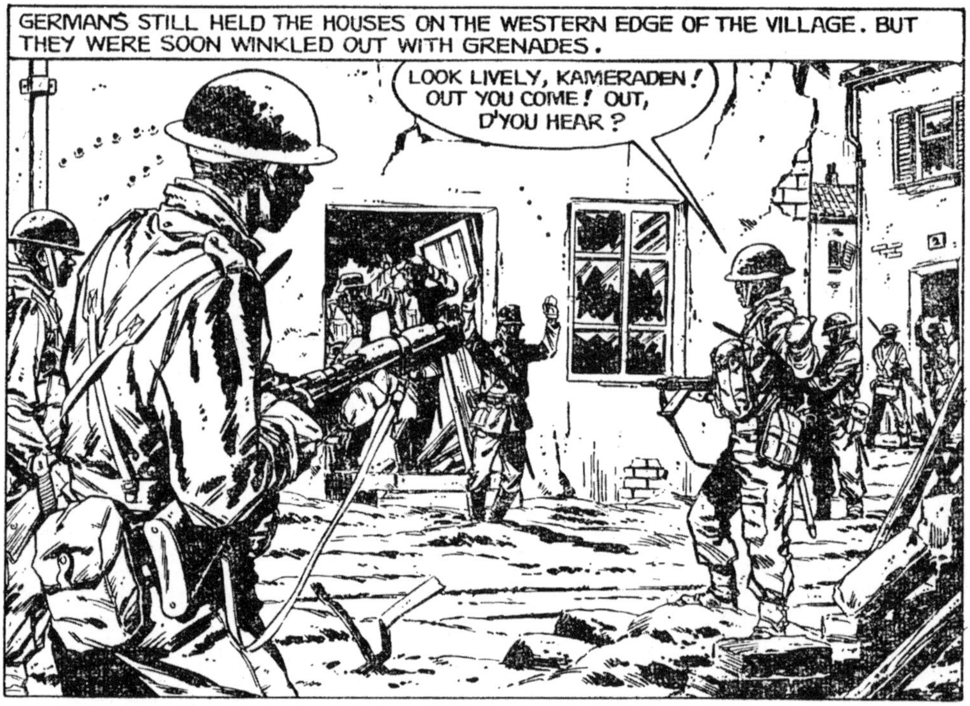
GERMANS STILL HELD THE HOUSES ON THE WESTERN EDGE OF THE VILLAGE. BUT THEY WERE SOON WINKLED OUT WITH GRENADES.
LOOK LIVELY, KAMERADEN! OUT YOU COME! OUT, D'YOU HEAR?

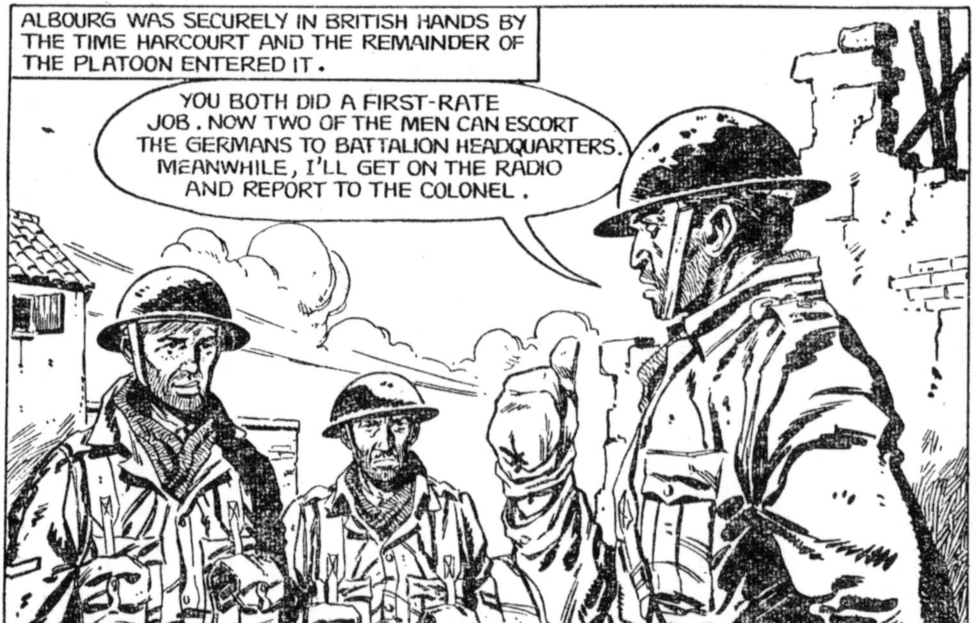
ALBOURG WAS SECURELY IN BRITISH HANDS BY THE TIME HARCOURT AND THE REMAINDER OF THE PLATOON ENTERED IT.
YOU BOTH DID A FIRST-RATE JOB. NOW TWO OF THE MEN CAN ESCORT THE GERMANS TO BATTALION HEADQUARTERS. MEANWHILE, I'LL GET ON THE RADIO AND REPORT TO THE COLONEL.

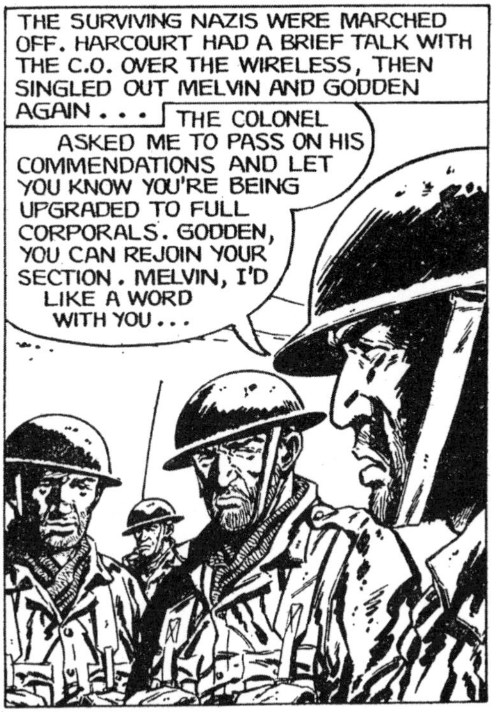
THE SURVIVING NAZIS WERE MARCHED OFF. HARCOURT HAD A BRIEF TALK WITH THE C.O. OVER THE WIRELESS, THEN SINGLED OUT MELVIN AND GODDEN AGAIN . . .
THE COLONEL ASKED ME TO PASS ON HIS COMMENDATIONS AND LET YOU KNOW YOU'RE BEING UPGRADED TO FULL CORPORALS. GODDEN, YOU CAN REJOIN YOUR SECTION. MELVIN, I'D LIKE A WORD WITH YOU . . .

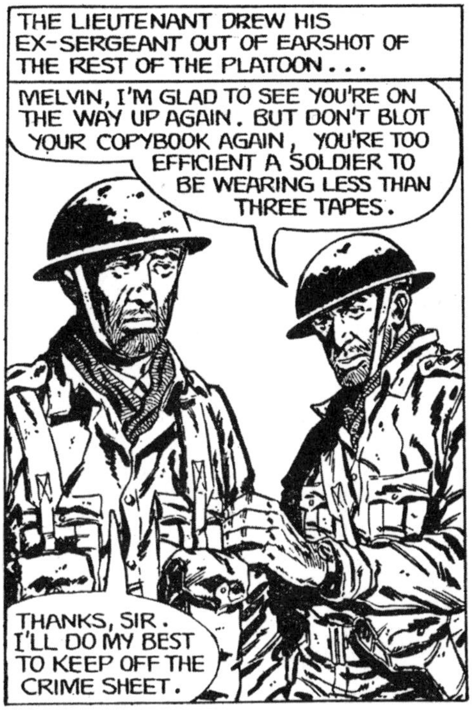
THE LIEUTENANT DREW HIS EX-SERGEANT OUT OF EARSHOT OF THE REST OF THE PLATOON . . .
MELVIN, I'M GLAD TO SEE YOU'RE ON THE WAY UP AGAIN. BUT DON'T BLOT YOUR COPYBOOK AGAIN, YOU'RE TOO EFFICIENT A SOLDIER TO BE WEARING LESS THAN THREE TAPES.
THANKS, SIR. I'LL DO MY BEST TO KEEP OFF THE CRIME SHEET.

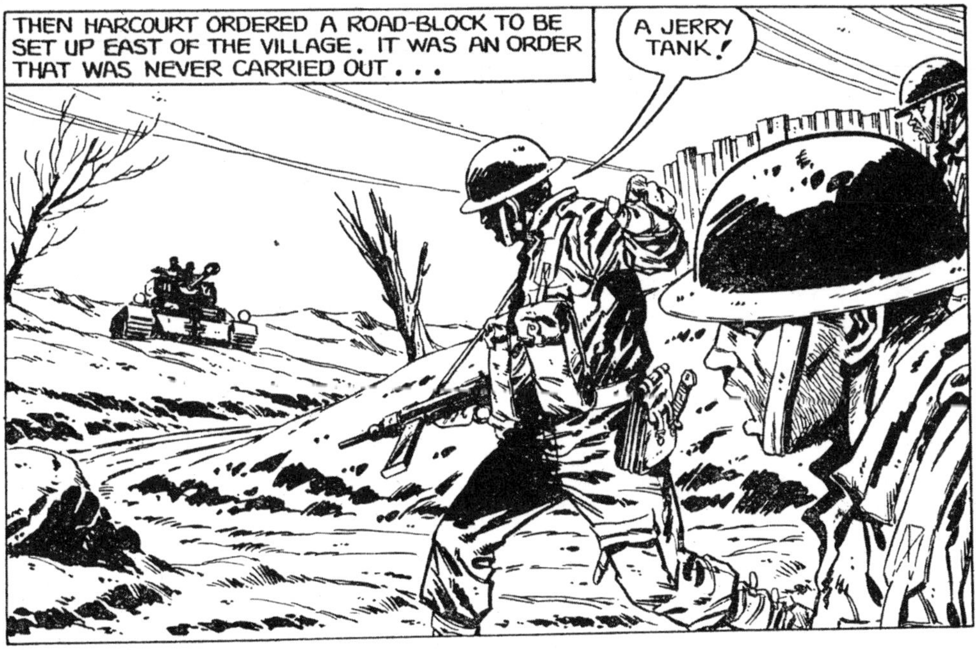
THEN HARCOURT ORDERED A ROAD-BLOCK TO BE SET UP EAST OF THE VILLAGE. IT WAS AN ORDER THAT WAS NEVER CARRIED OUT . . .
A JERRY TANK!

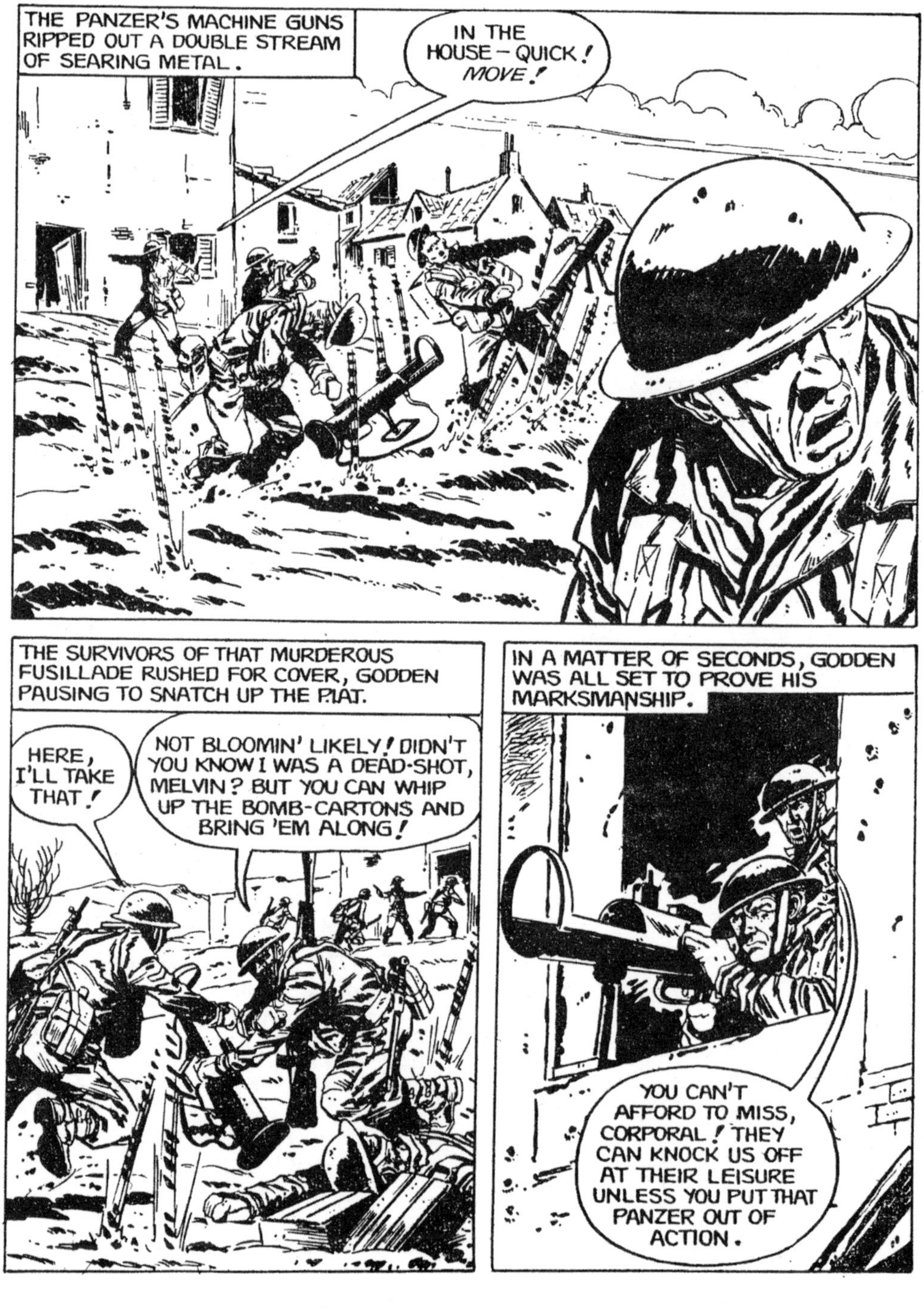
THE PANZER'S MACHINE GUNS RIPPED OUT A DOUBLE STREAM OF SEARING METAL.
IN THE HOUSE – QUICK! *MOVE!*
THE SURVIVORS OF THAT MURDEROUS FUSILLADE RUSHED FOR COVER, GODDEN PAUSING TO SNATCH UP THE P.I.A.T.
HERE, I'LL TAKE THAT!
NOT BLOOMIN' LIKELY! DIDN'T YOU KNOW I WAS A DEAD-SHOT, MELVIN? BUT YOU CAN WHIP UP THE BOMB-CARTONS AND BRING 'EM ALONG!
IN A MATTER OF SECONDS, GODDEN WAS ALL SET TO PROVE HIS MARKSMANSHIP.
YOU CAN'T AFFORD TO MISS, CORPORAL! THEY CAN KNOCK US OFF AT THEIR LEISURE UNLESS YOU PUT THAT PANZER OUT OF ACTION.

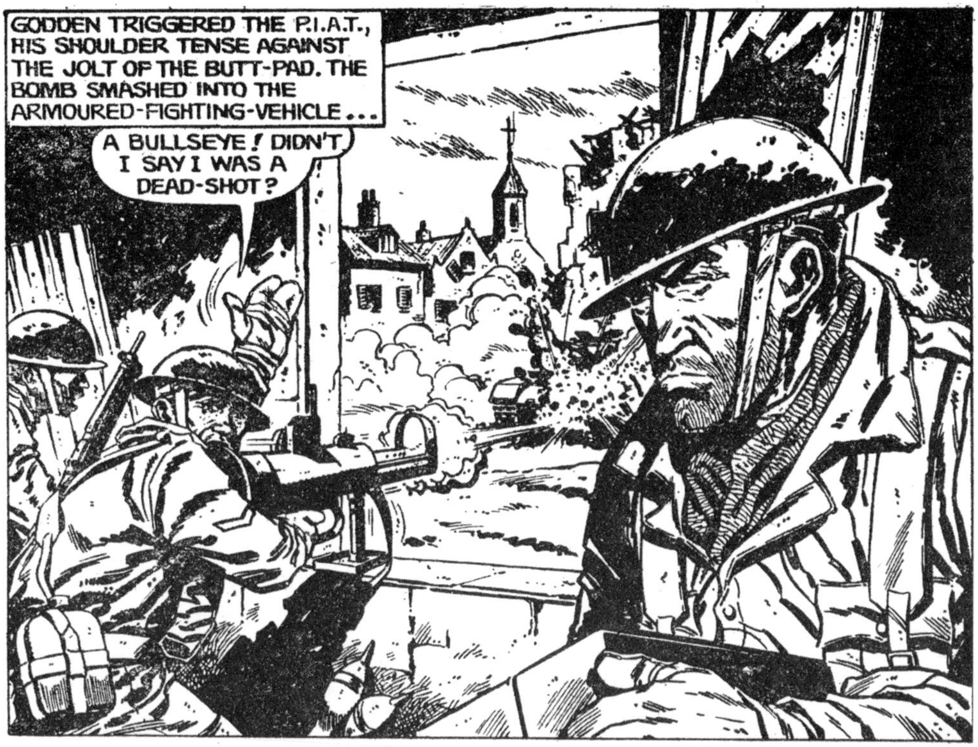
GODDEN TRIGGERED THE P.I.A.T., HIS SHOULDER TENSE AGAINST THE JOLT OF THE BUTT-PAD. THE BOMB SMASHED INTO THE ARMOURED-FIGHTING-VEHICLE...
A BULLSEYE! DIDN'T I SAY I WAS A DEAD-SHOT?

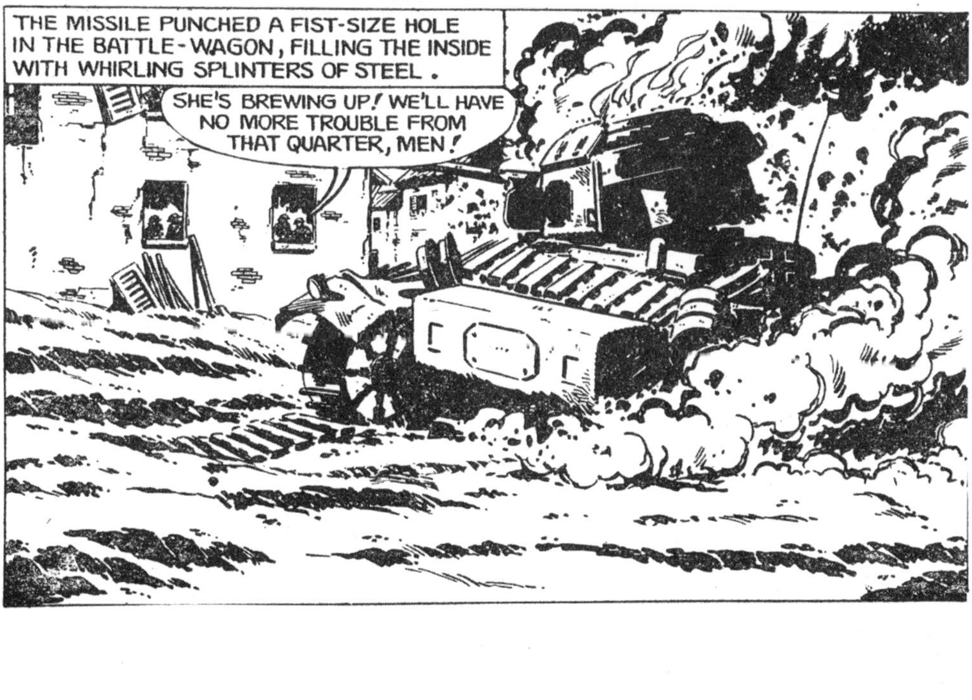
THE MISSILE PUNCHED A FIST-SIZE HOLE IN THE BATTLE-WAGON, FILLING THE INSIDE WITH WHIRLING SPLINTERS OF STEEL.
SHE'S BREWING UP! WE'LL HAVE NO MORE TROUBLE FROM THAT QUARTER, MEN!

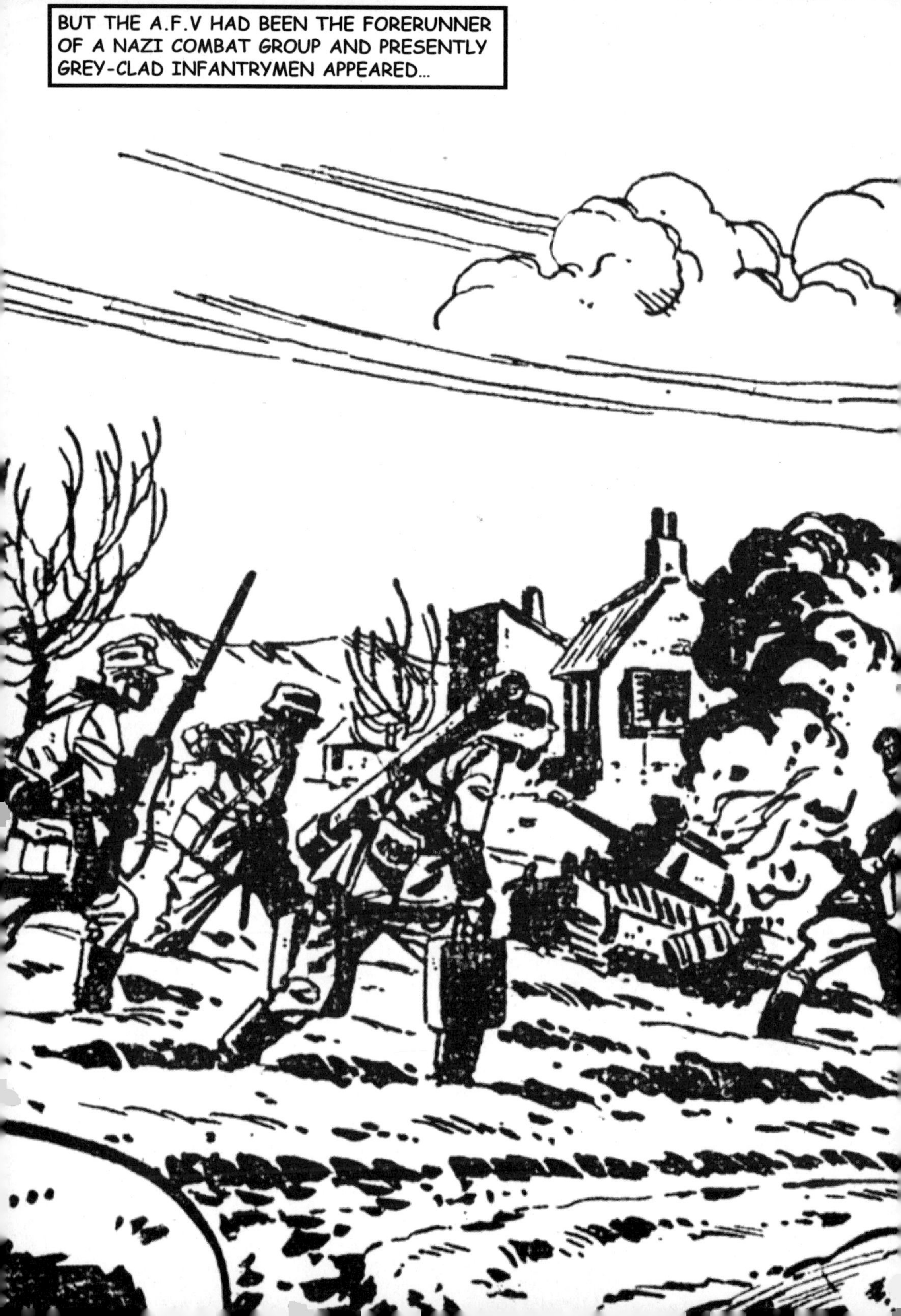
BUT THE A.F.V HAD BEEN THE FORERUNNER OF A NAZI COMBAT GROUP AND PRESENTLY GREY-CLAD INFANTRYMEN APPEARED...

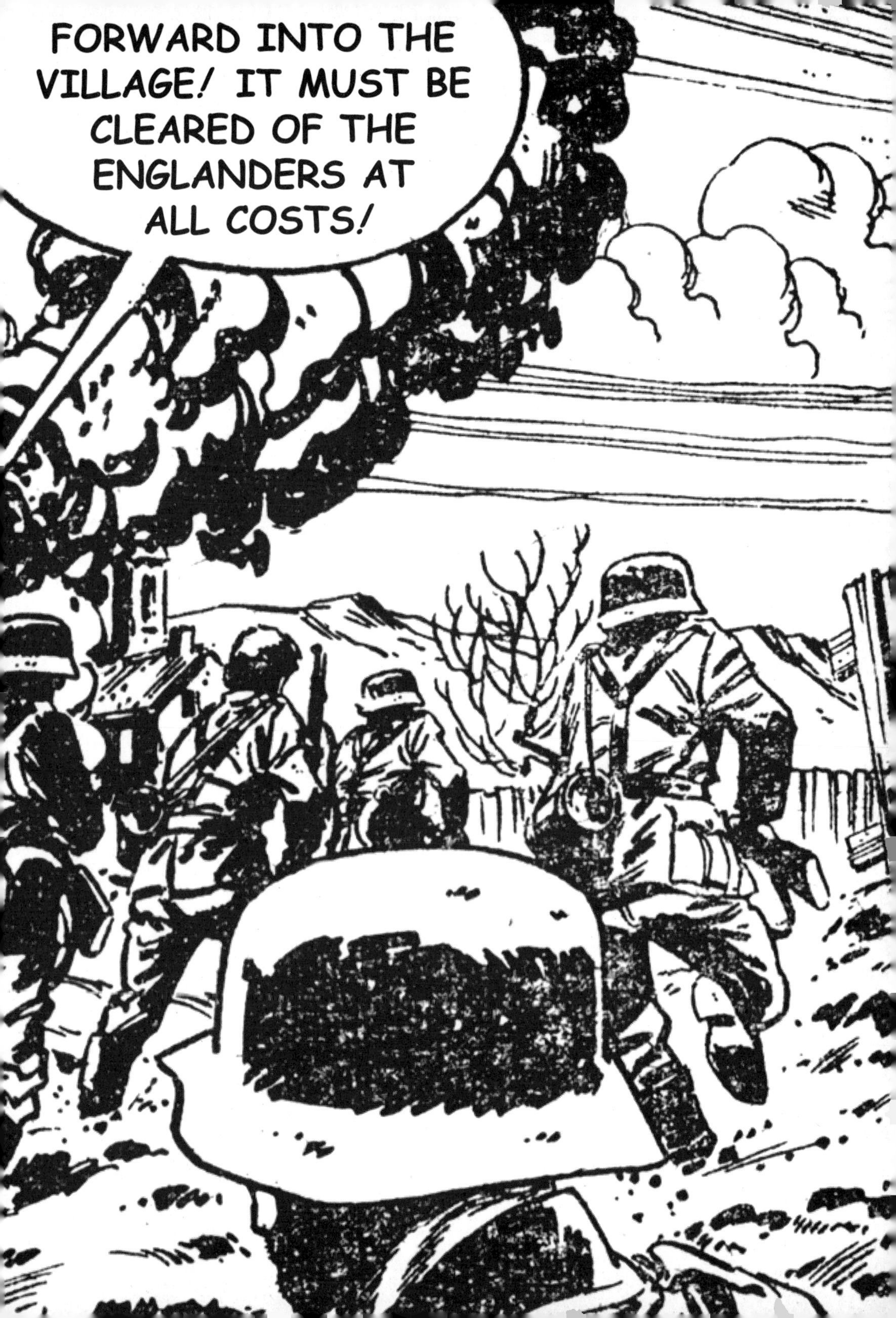
FORWARD INTO THE VILLAGE! IT MUST BE CLEARED OF THE ENGLANDERS AT ALL COSTS!

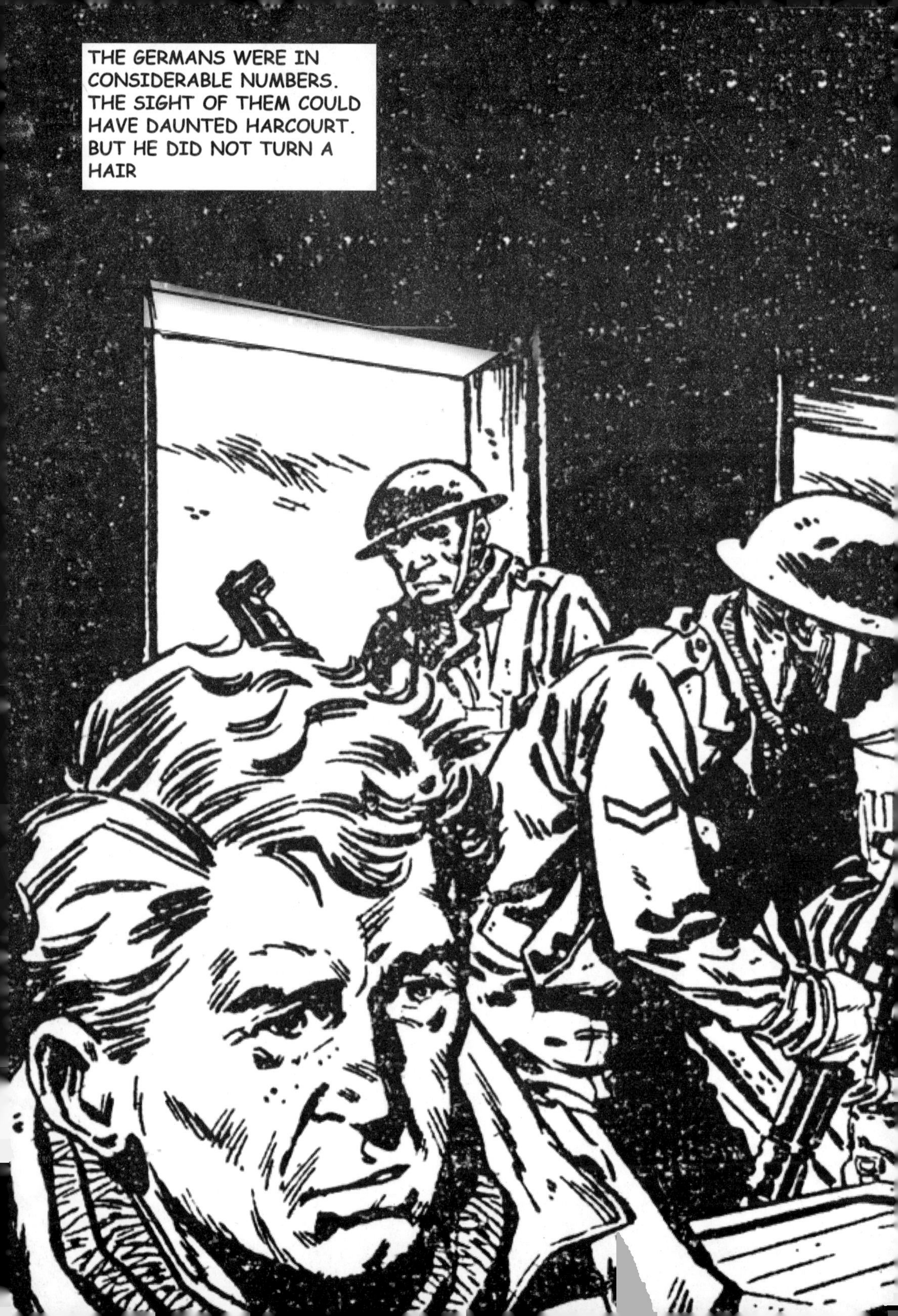
THE GERMANS WERE IN CONSIDERABLE NUMBERS. THE SIGHT OF THEM COULD HAVE DAUNTED HARCOURT. BUT HE DID NOT TURN A HAIR

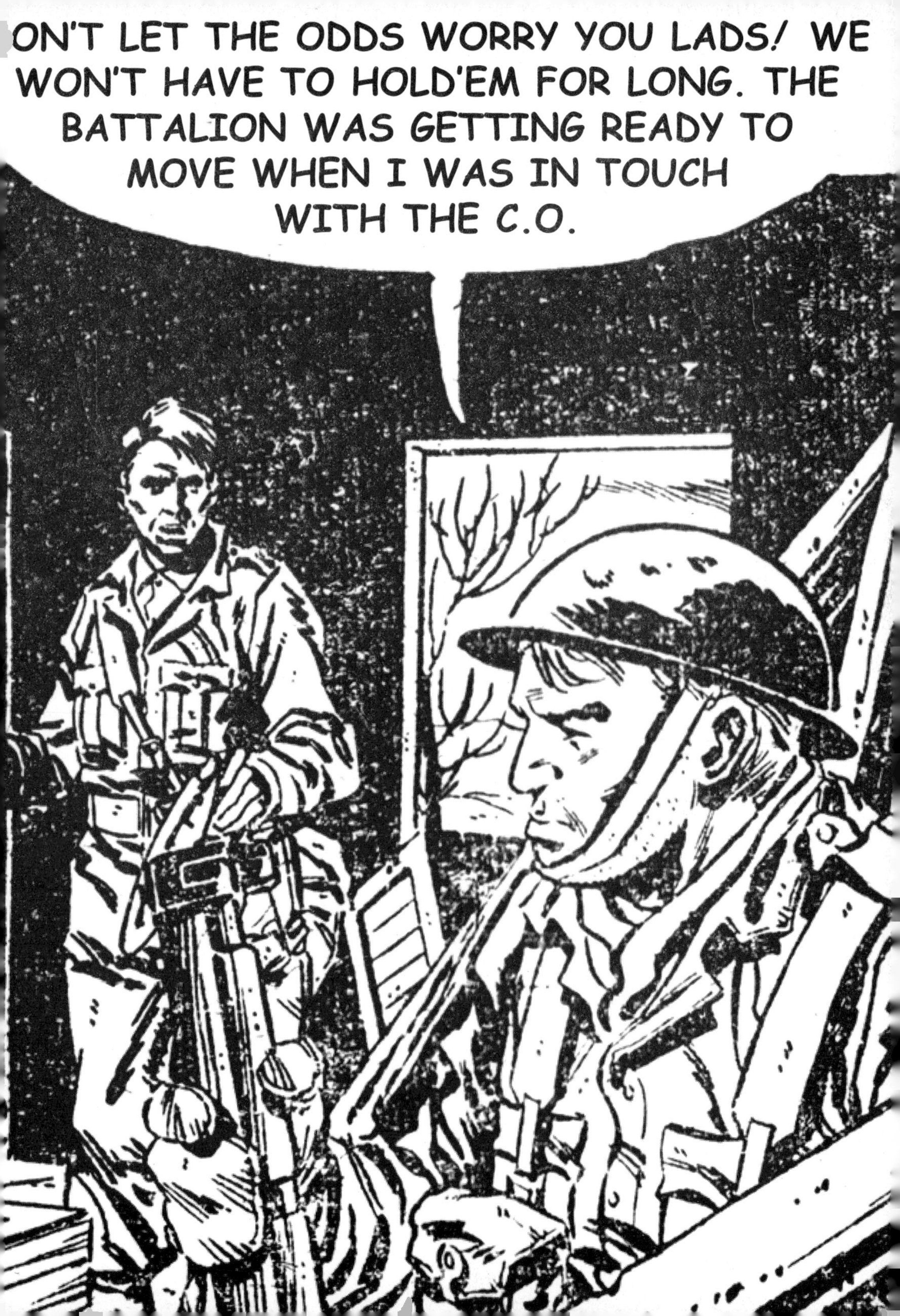
ON'T LET THE ODDS WORRY YOU LADS! WE WON'T HAVE TO HOLD'EM FOR LONG. THE BATTALION WAS GETTING READY TO MOVE WHEN I WAS IN TOUCH WITH THE C.O.

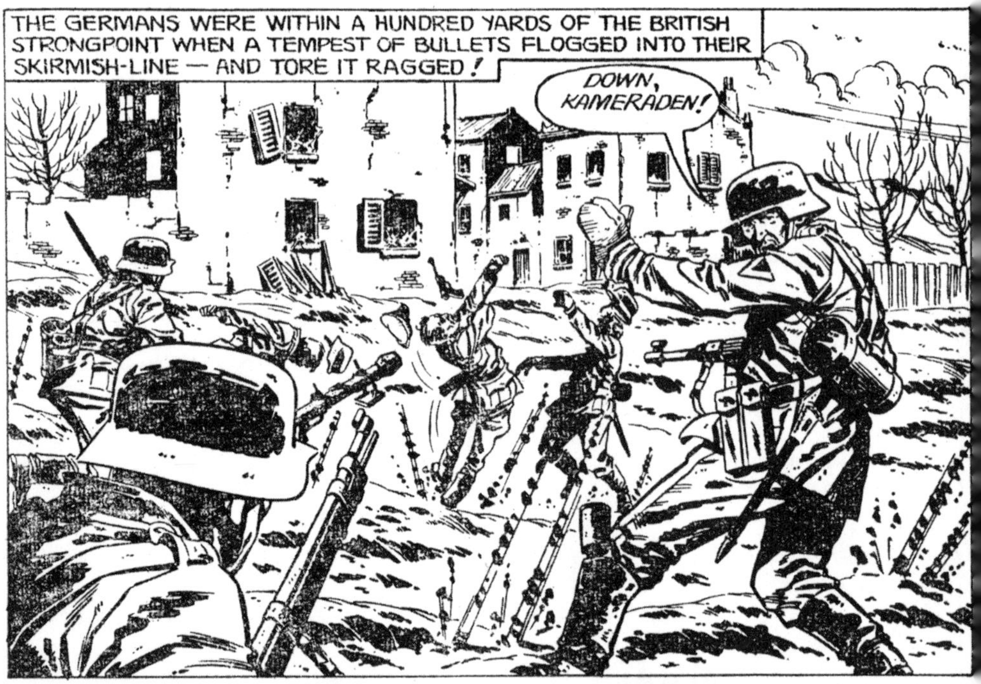
THE GERMANS WERE WITHIN A HUNDRED YARDS OF THE BRITISH STRONGPOINT WHEN A TEMPEST OF BULLETS FLOGGED INTO THEIR SKIRMISH-LINE — AND TORE IT RAGGED!
DOWN, KAMERADEN!

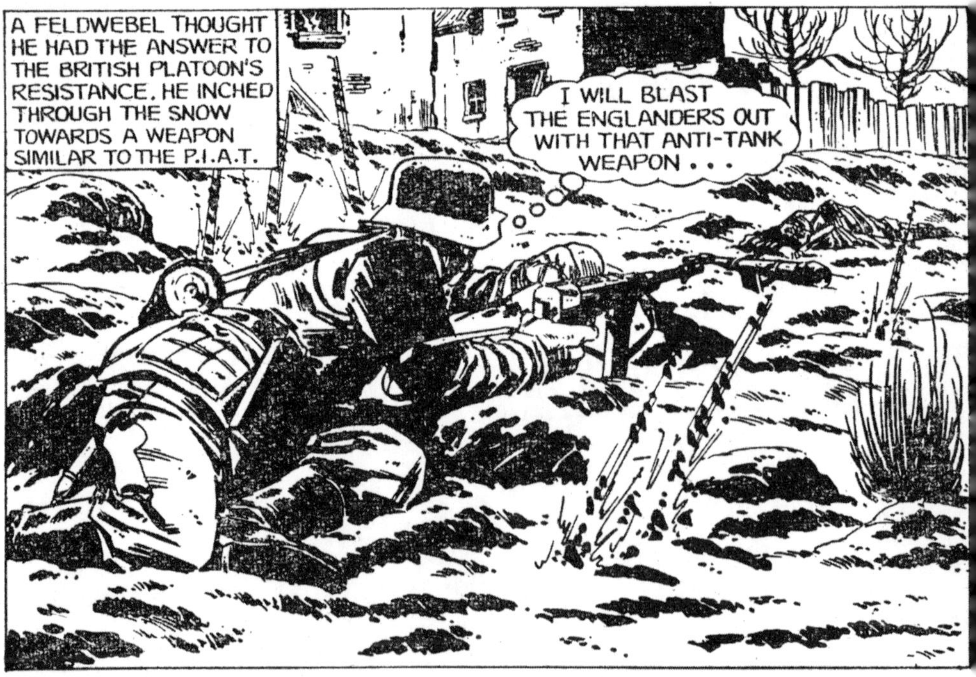
A FELDWEBEL THOUGHT HE HAD THE ANSWER TO THE BRITISH PLATOON'S RESISTANCE. HE INCHED THROUGH THE SNOW TOWARDS A WEAPON SIMILAR TO THE P.I.A.T.
I WILL BLAST THE ENGLANDERS OUT WITH THAT ANTI-TANK WEAPON . . .

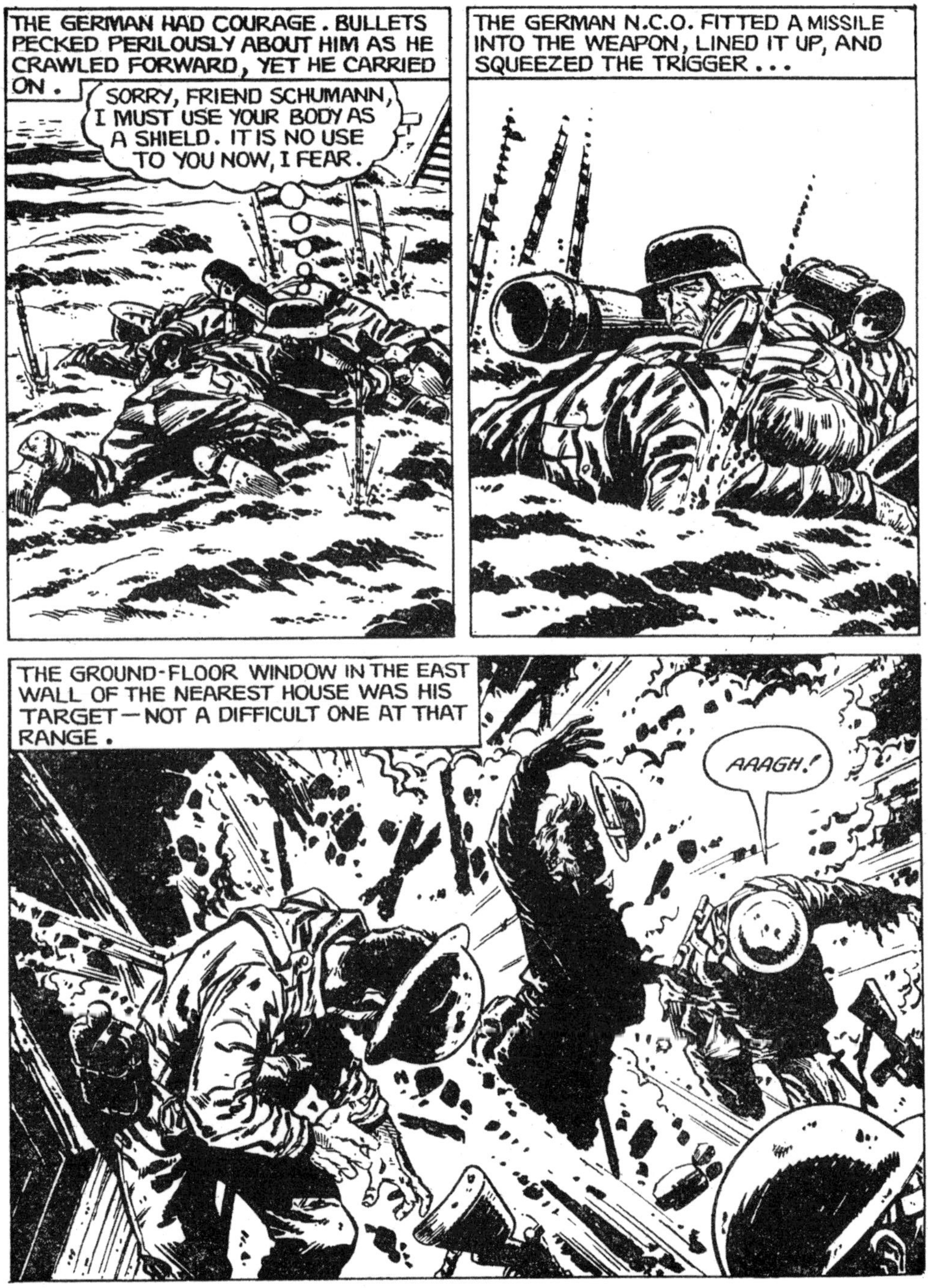
THE GERMAN HAD COURAGE. BULLETS PECKED PERILOUSLY ABOUT HIM AS HE CRAWLED FORWARD, YET HE CARRIED ON.
SORRY, FRIEND SCHUMANN, I MUST USE YOUR BODY AS A SHIELD. IT IS NO USE TO YOU NOW, I FEAR.
THE GERMAN N.C.O. FITTED A MISSILE INTO THE WEAPON, LINED IT UP, AND SQUEEZED THE TRIGGER...
THE GROUND-FLOOR WINDOW IN THE EAST WALL OF THE NEAREST HOUSE WAS HIS TARGET—NOT A DIFFICULT ONE AT THAT RANGE.
AAAGH!

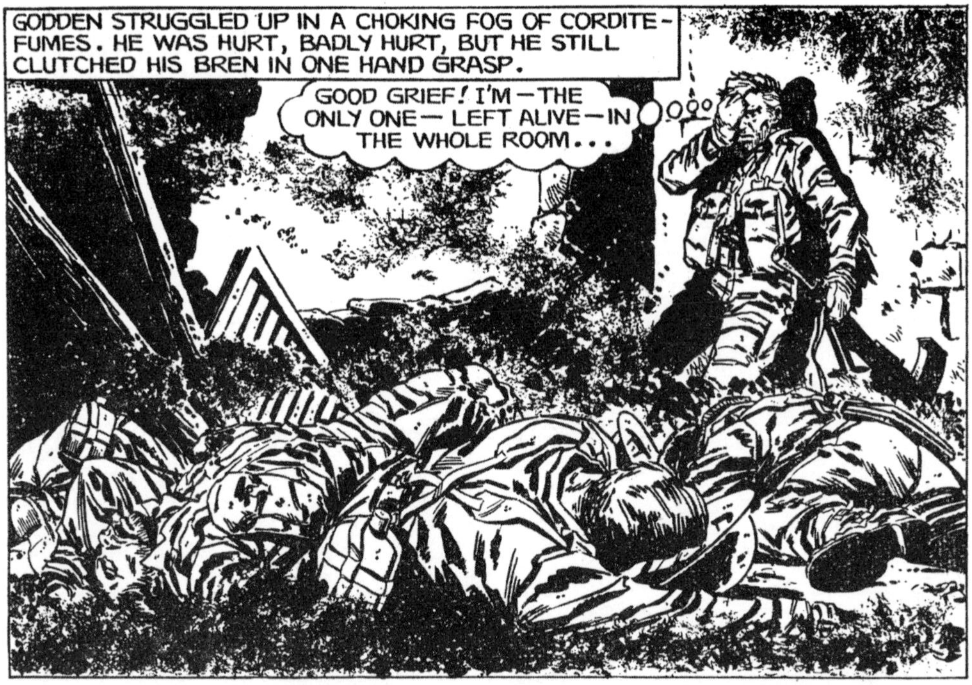
GODDEN STRUGGLED UP IN A CHOKING FOG OF CORDITE-FUMES. HE WAS HURT, BADLY HURT, BUT HE STILL CLUTCHED HIS BREN IN ONE HAND GRASP.
GOOD GRIEF! I'M — THE ONLY ONE — LEFT ALIVE — IN THE WHOLE ROOM...

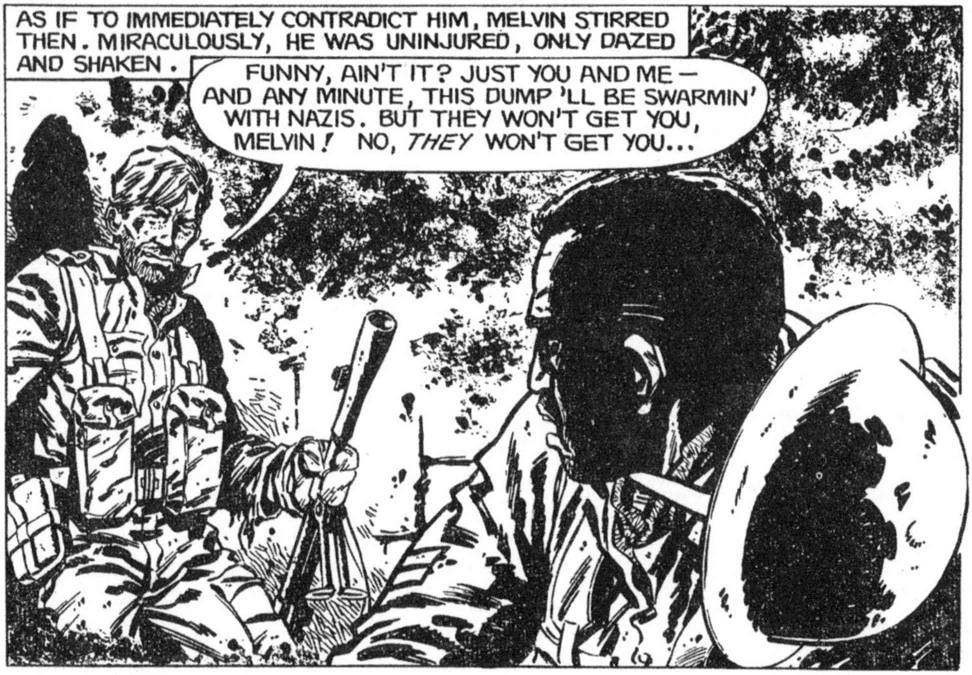
AS IF TO IMMEDIATELY CONTRADICT HIM, MELVIN STIRRED THEN. MIRACULOUSLY, HE WAS UNINJURED, ONLY DAZED AND SHAKEN.
FUNNY, AIN'T IT? JUST YOU AND ME — AND ANY MINUTE, THIS DUMP 'LL BE SWARMIN' WITH NAZIS. BUT THEY WON'T GET YOU, MELVIN! NO, *THEY* WON'T GET YOU...

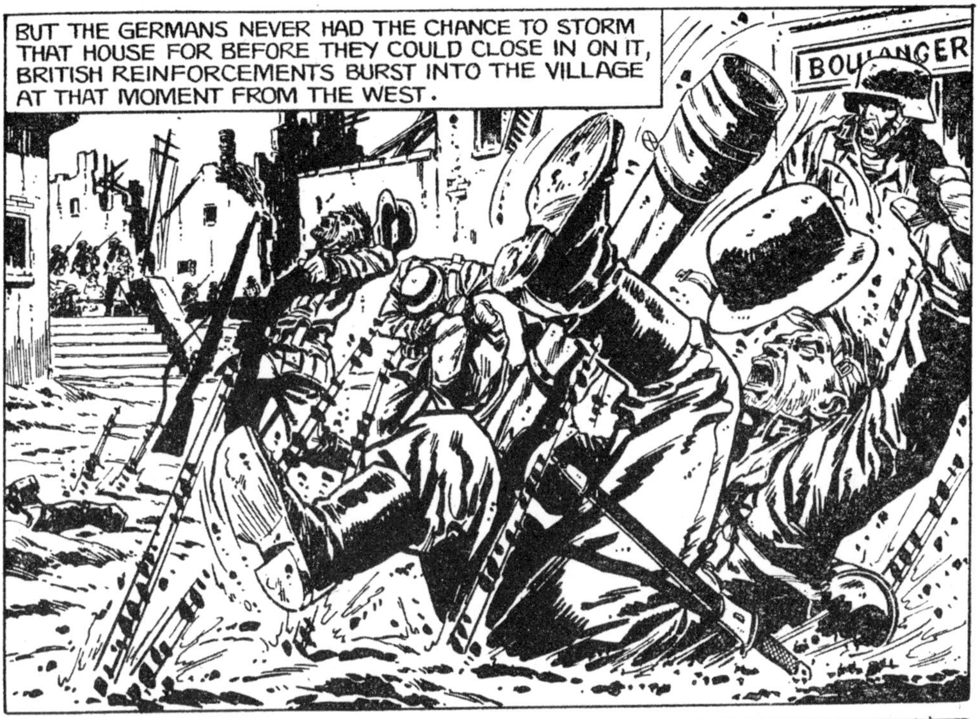
BUT THE GERMANS NEVER HAD THE CHANCE TO STORM THAT HOUSE FOR BEFORE THEY COULD CLOSE IN ON IT, BRITISH REINFORCEMENTS BURST INTO THE VILLAGE AT THAT MOMENT FROM THE WEST.
BOULANGER

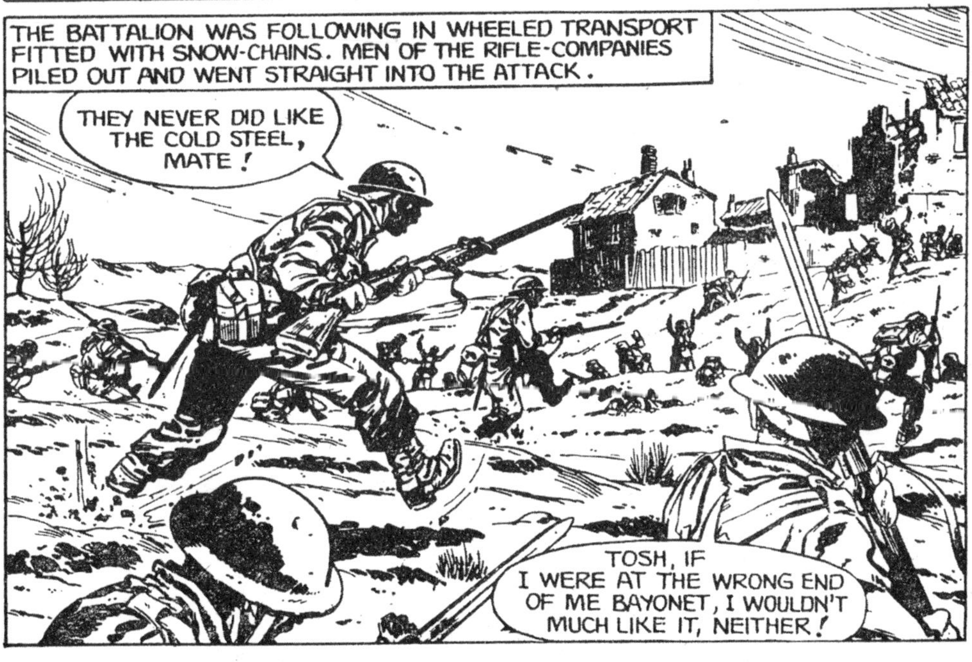
THE BATTALION WAS FOLLOWING IN WHEELED TRANSPORT FITTED WITH SNOW-CHAINS. MEN OF THE RIFLE-COMPANIES PILED OUT AND WENT STRAIGHT INTO THE ATTACK.
THEY NEVER DID LIKE THE COLD STEEL, MATE!
TOSH, IF I WERE AT THE WRONG END OF ME BAYONET, I WOULDN'T MUCH LIKE IT, NEITHER!

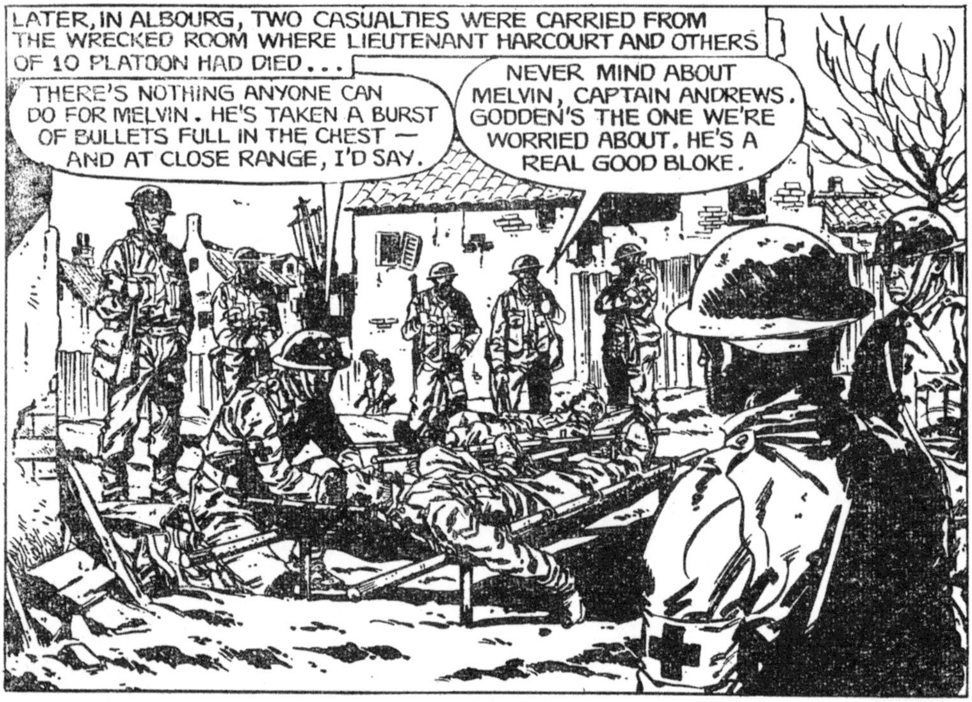
LATER, IN ALBOURG, TWO CASUALTIES WERE CARRIED FROM THE WRECKED ROOM WHERE LIEUTENANT HARCOURT AND OTHERS OF 10 PLATOON HAD DIED...
THERE'S NOTHING ANYONE CAN DO FOR MELVIN. HE'S TAKEN A BURST OF BULLETS FULL IN THE CHEST — AND AT CLOSE RANGE, I'D SAY.
NEVER MIND ABOUT MELVIN, CAPTAIN ANDREWS. GODDEN'S THE ONE WE'RE WORRIED ABOUT. HE'S A REAL GOOD BLOKE.

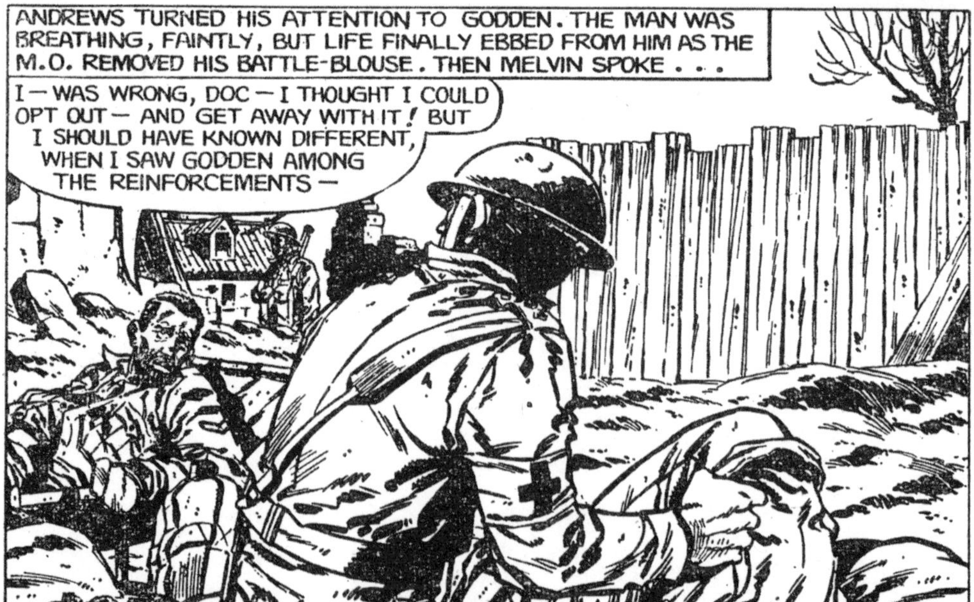
ANDREWS TURNED HIS ATTENTION TO GODDEN. THE MAN WAS BREATHING, FAINTLY, BUT LIFE FINALLY EBBED FROM HIM AS THE M.O. REMOVED HIS BATTLE-BLOUSE. THEN MELVIN SPOKE...
I — WAS WRONG, DOC — I THOUGHT I COULD OPT OUT — AND GET AWAY WITH IT! BUT I SHOULD HAVE KNOWN DIFFERENT, WHEN I SAW GODDEN AMONG THE REINFORCEMENTS —

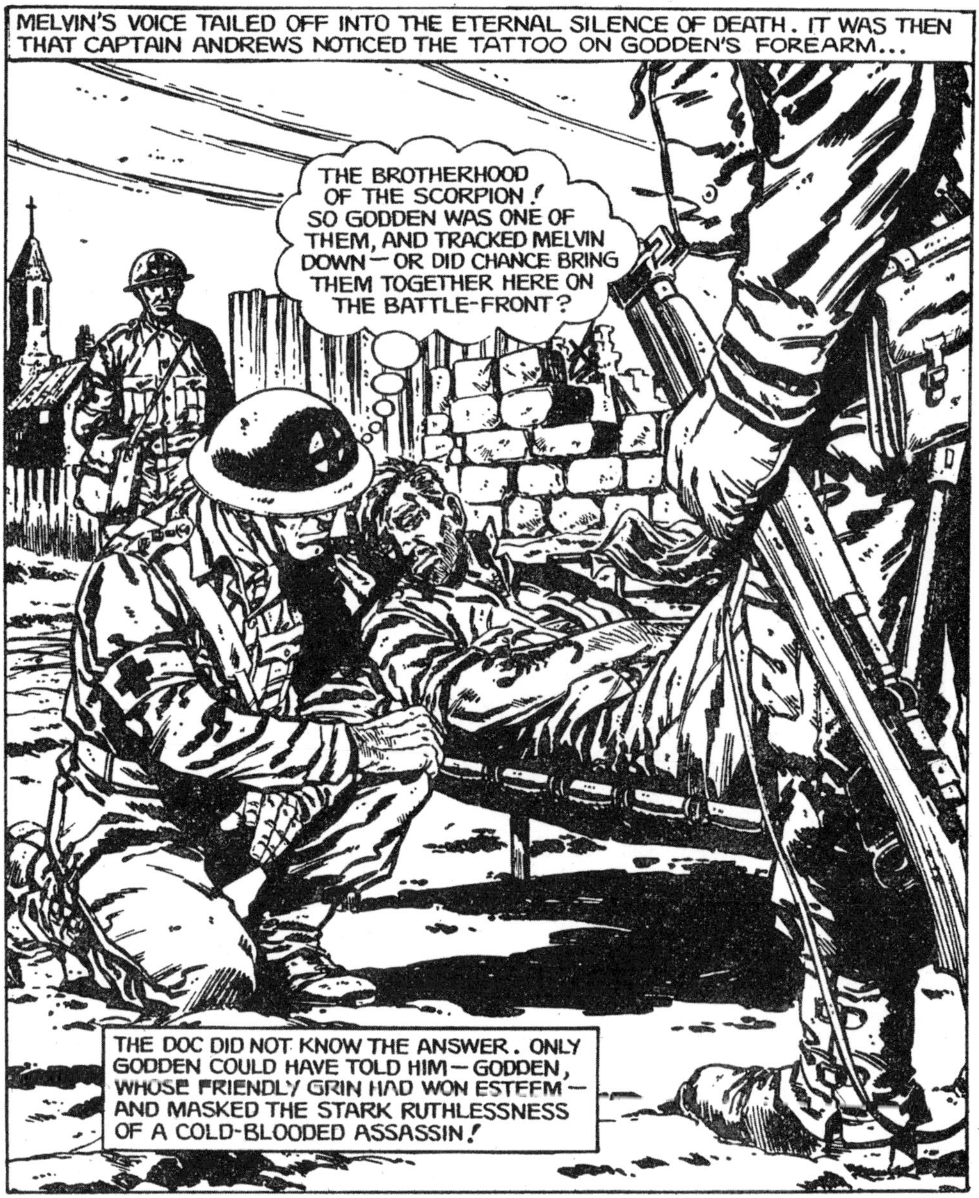
MELVIN'S VOICE TAILED OFF INTO THE ETERNAL SILENCE OF DEATH. IT WAS THEN THAT CAPTAIN ANDREWS NOTICED THE TATTOO ON GODDEN'S FOREARM...
THE BROTHERHOOD OF THE SCORPION! SO GODDEN WAS ONE OF THEM, AND TRACKED MELVIN DOWN — OR DID CHANCE BRING THEM TOGETHER HERE ON THE BATTLE-FRONT?
THE DOC DID NOT KNOW THE ANSWER. ONLY GODDEN COULD HAVE TOLD HIM — GODDEN, WHOSE FRIENDLY GRIN HAD WON ESTEEM — AND MASKED THE STARK RUTHLESSNESS OF A COLD-BLOODED ASSASSIN!

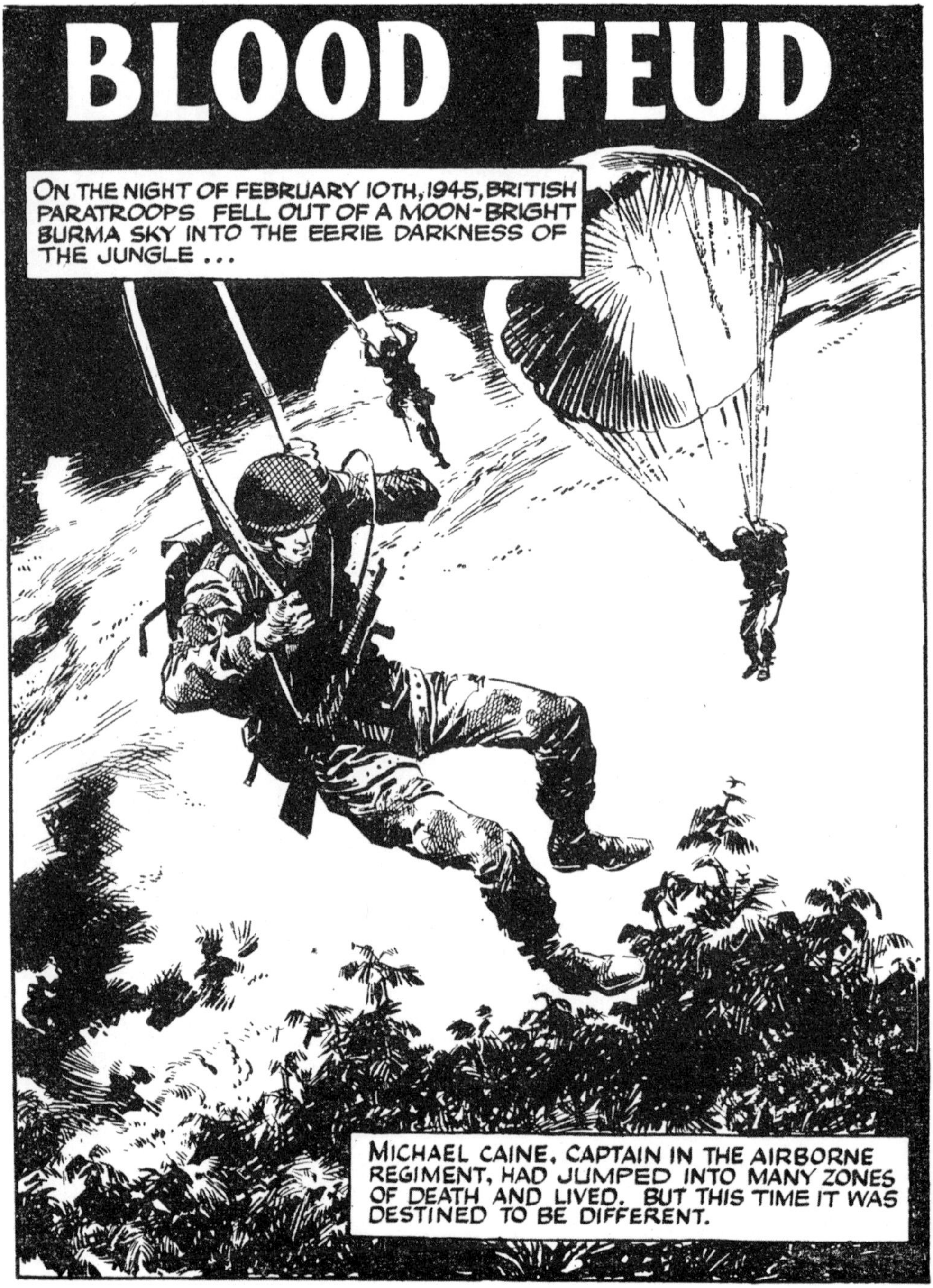
BLOOD FEUD
ON THE NIGHT OF FEBRUARY 10TH, 1945, BRITISH PARATROOPS FELL OUT OF A MOON-BRIGHT BURMA SKY INTO THE EERIE DARKNESS OF THE JUNGLE ...
MICHAEL CAINE, CAPTAIN IN THE AIRBORNE REGIMENT, HAD JUMPED INTO MANY ZONES OF DEATH AND LIVED. BUT THIS TIME IT WAS DESTINED TO BE DIFFERENT.

Chapter 1. River of Fire

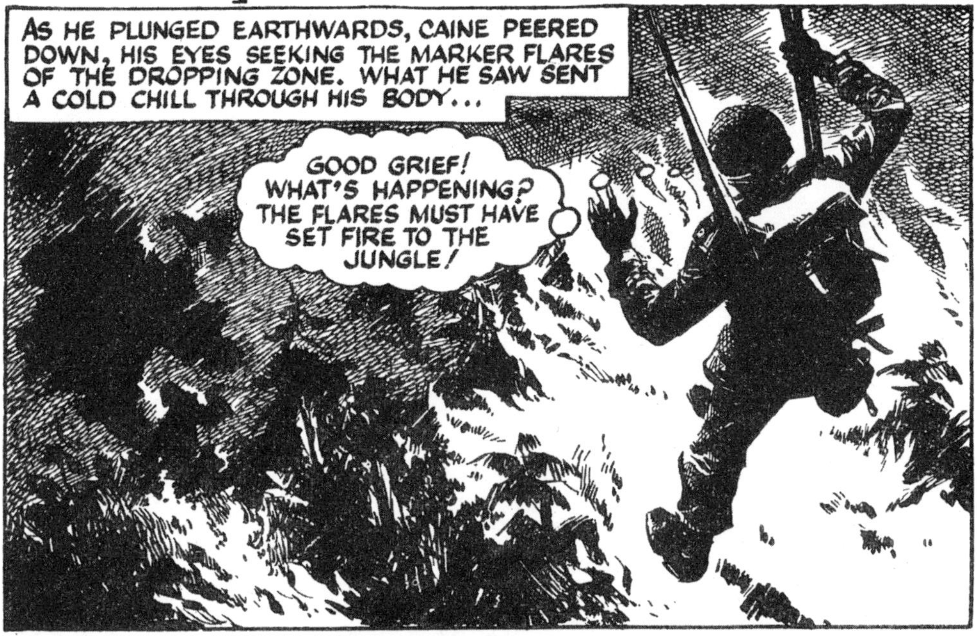
AS HE PLUNGED EARTHWARDS, CAINE PEERED DOWN, HIS EYES SEEKING THE MARKER FLARES OF THE DROPPING ZONE. WHAT HE SAW SENT A COLD CHILL THROUGH HIS BODY...
GOOD GRIEF! WHAT'S HAPPENING? THE FLARES MUST HAVE SET FIRE TO THE JUNGLE!

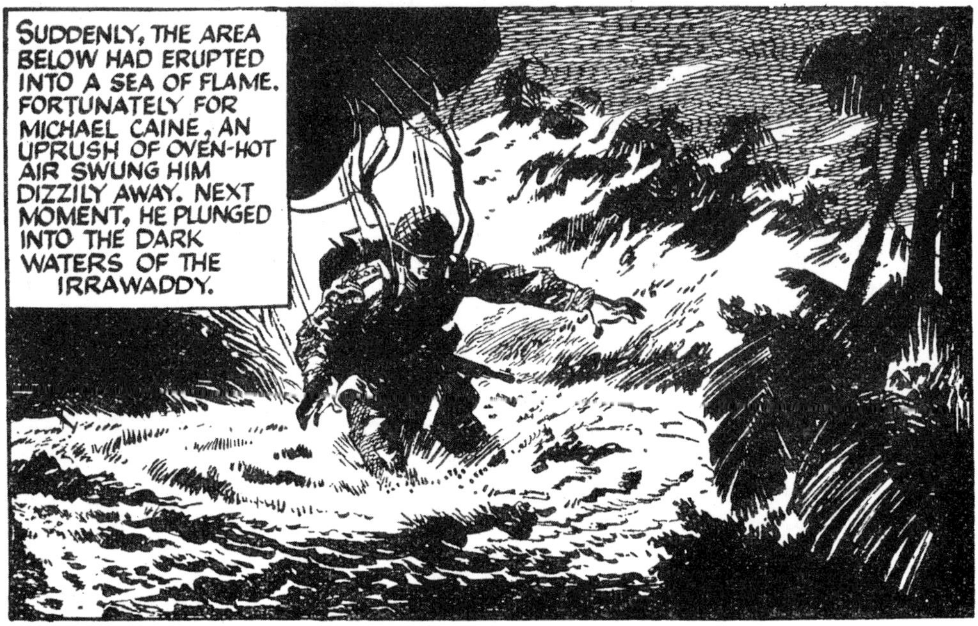
SUDDENLY, THE AREA BELOW HAD ERUPTED INTO A SEA OF FLAME. FORTUNATELY FOR MICHAEL CAINE, AN UPRUSH OF OVEN-HOT AIR SWUNG HIM DIZZILY AWAY. NEXT MOMENT, HE PLUNGED INTO THE DARK WATERS OF THE IRRAWADDY.

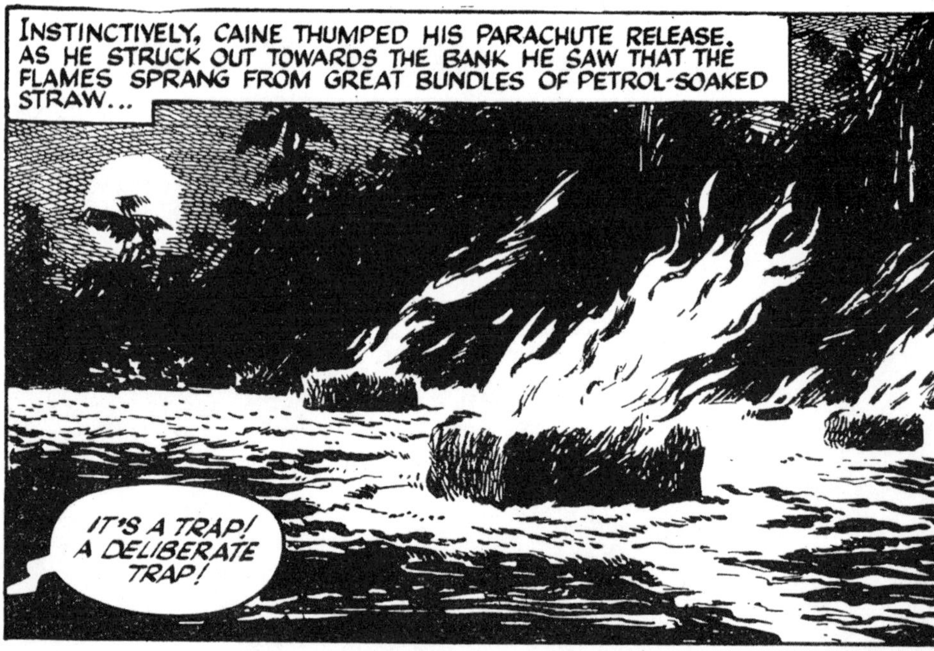
INSTINCTIVELY, CAINE THUMPED HIS PARACHUTE RELEASE. AS HE STRUCK OUT TOWARDS THE BANK HE SAW THAT THE FLAMES SPRANG FROM GREAT BUNDLES OF PETROL-SOAKED STRAW...
IT'S A TRAP! A DELIBERATE TRAP!

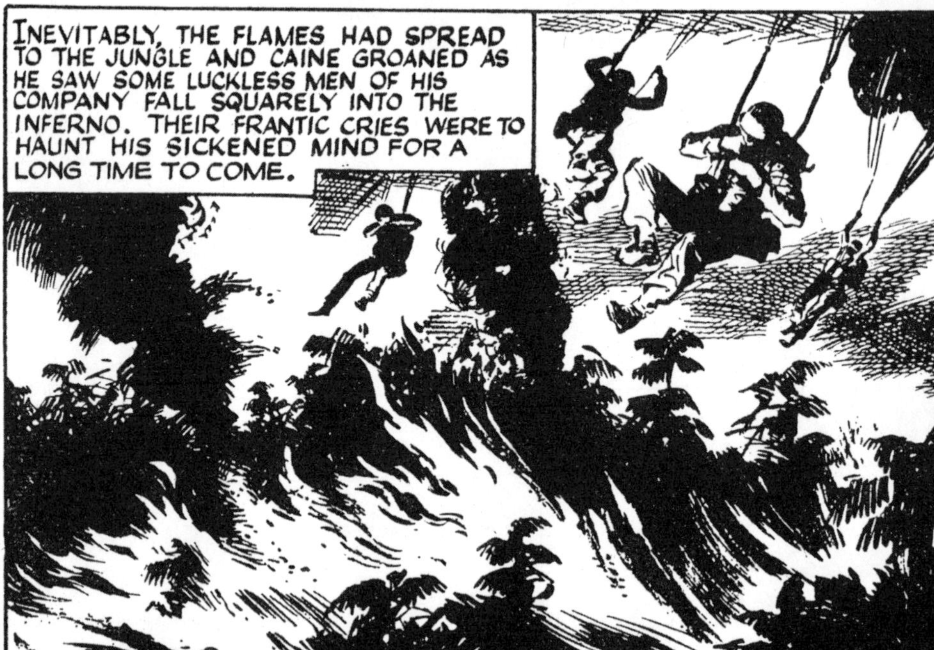
INEVITABLY, THE FLAMES HAD SPREAD TO THE JUNGLE AND CAINE GROANED AS HE SAW SOME LUCKLESS MEN OF HIS COMPANY FALL SQUARELY INTO THE INFERNO. THEIR FRANTIC CRIES WERE TO HAUNT HIS SICKENED MIND FOR A LONG TIME TO COME.

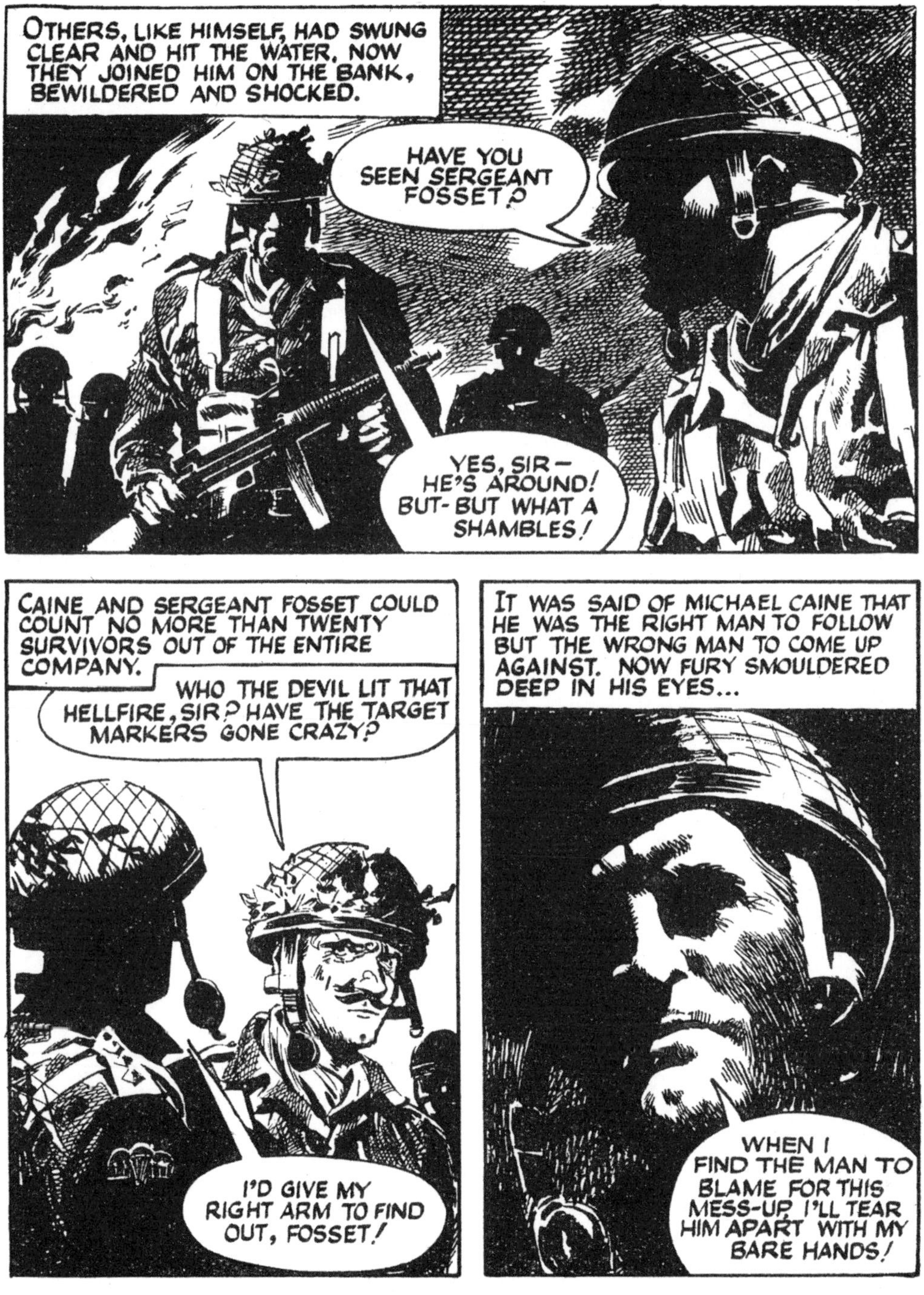
OTHERS, LIKE HIMSELF, HAD SWUNG CLEAR AND HIT THE WATER, NOW THEY JOINED HIM ON THE BANK, BEWILDERED AND SHOCKED.
HAVE YOU SEEN SERGEANT FOSSET?
YES, SIR— HE'S AROUND! BUT-BUT WHAT A SHAMBLES!
CAINE AND SERGEANT FOSSET COULD COUNT NO MORE THAN TWENTY SURVIVORS OUT OF THE ENTIRE COMPANY.
WHO THE DEVIL LIT THAT HELLFIRE, SIR? HAVE THE TARGET MARKERS GONE CRAZY?
I'D GIVE MY RIGHT ARM TO FIND OUT, FOSSET!
IT WAS SAID OF MICHAEL CAINE THAT HE WAS THE RIGHT MAN TO FOLLOW BUT THE WRONG MAN TO COME UP AGAINST. NOW FURY SMOULDERED DEEP IN HIS EYES...
WHEN I FIND THE MAN TO BLAME FOR THIS MESS-UP, I'LL TEAR HIM APART WITH MY BARE HANDS!

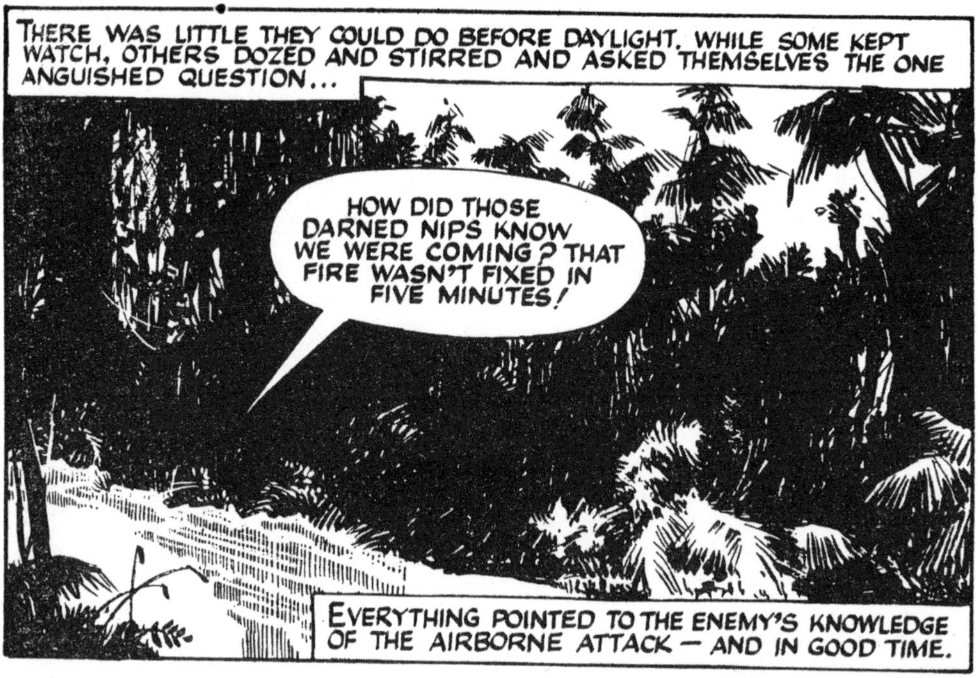
THERE WAS LITTLE THEY COULD DO BEFORE DAYLIGHT. WHILE SOME KEPT WATCH, OTHERS DOZED AND STIRRED AND ASKED THEMSELVES THE ONE ANGUISHED QUESTION...
HOW DID THOSE DARNED NIPS KNOW WE WERE COMING? THAT FIRE WASN'T FIXED IN FIVE MINUTES!
EVERYTHING POINTED TO THE ENEMY'S KNOWLEDGE OF THE AIRBORNE ATTACK — AND IN GOOD TIME.

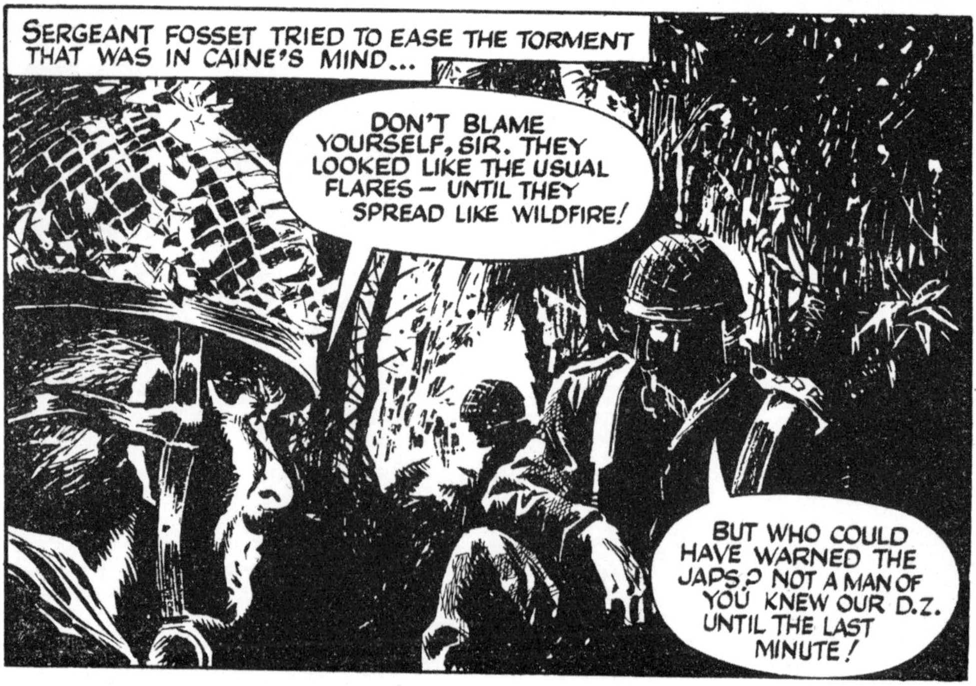
SERGEANT FOSSET TRIED TO EASE THE TORMENT THAT WAS IN CAINE'S MIND...
DON'T BLAME YOURSELF, SIR. THEY LOOKED LIKE THE USUAL FLARES — UNTIL THEY SPREAD LIKE WILDFIRE!
BUT WHO COULD HAVE WARNED THE JAPS? NOT A MAN OF YOU KNEW OUR D.Z. UNTIL THE LAST MINUTE!

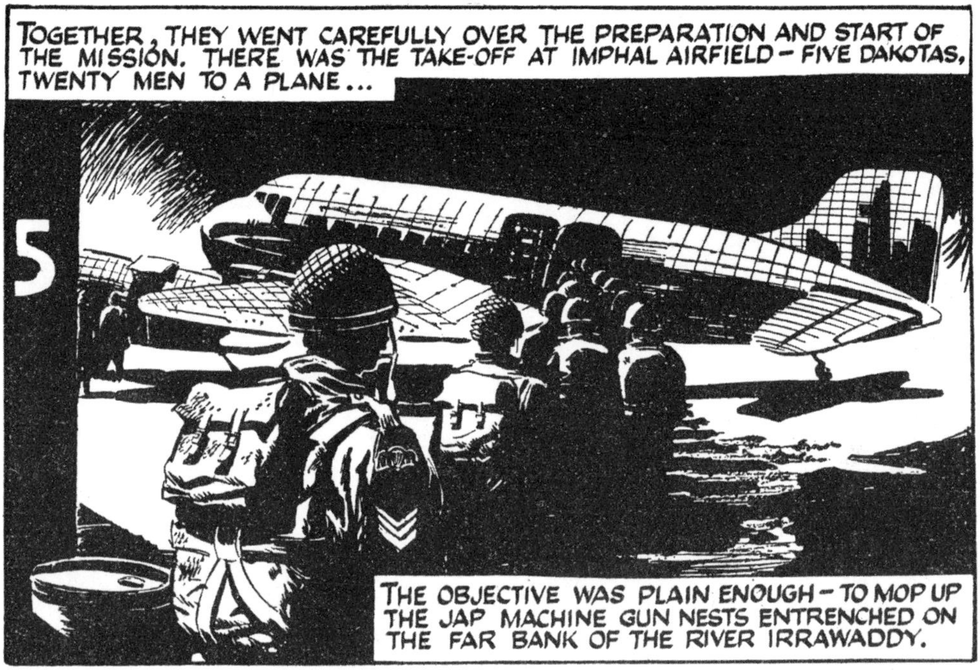
TOGETHER, THEY WENT CAREFULLY OVER THE PREPARATION AND START OF THE MISSION. THERE WAS THE TAKE-OFF AT IMPHAL AIRFIELD - FIVE DAKOTAS, TWENTY MEN TO A PLANE...
5
THE OBJECTIVE WAS PLAIN ENOUGH - TO MOP UP THE JAP MACHINE GUN NESTS ENTRENCHED ON THE FAR BANK OF THE RIVER IRRAWADDY.

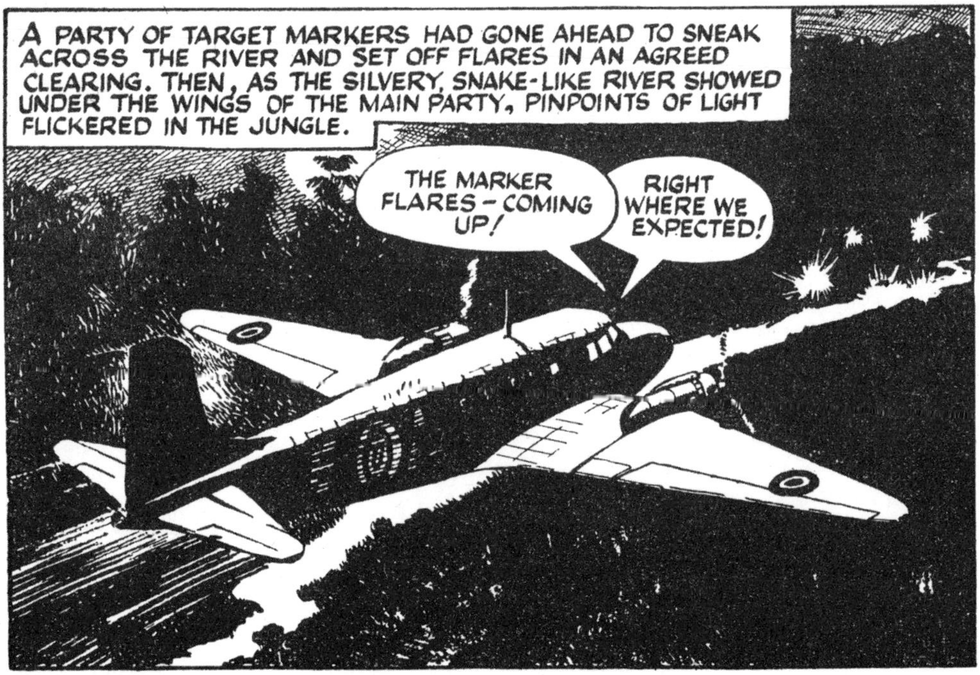
A PARTY OF TARGET MARKERS HAD GONE AHEAD TO SNEAK ACROSS THE RIVER AND SET OFF FLARES IN AN AGREED CLEARING. THEN, AS THE SILVERY, SNAKE-LIKE RIVER SHOWED UNDER THE WINGS OF THE MAIN PARTY, PINPOINTS OF LIGHT FLICKERED IN THE JUNGLE.
THE MARKER FLARES - COMING UP!
RIGHT WHERE WE EXPECTED!

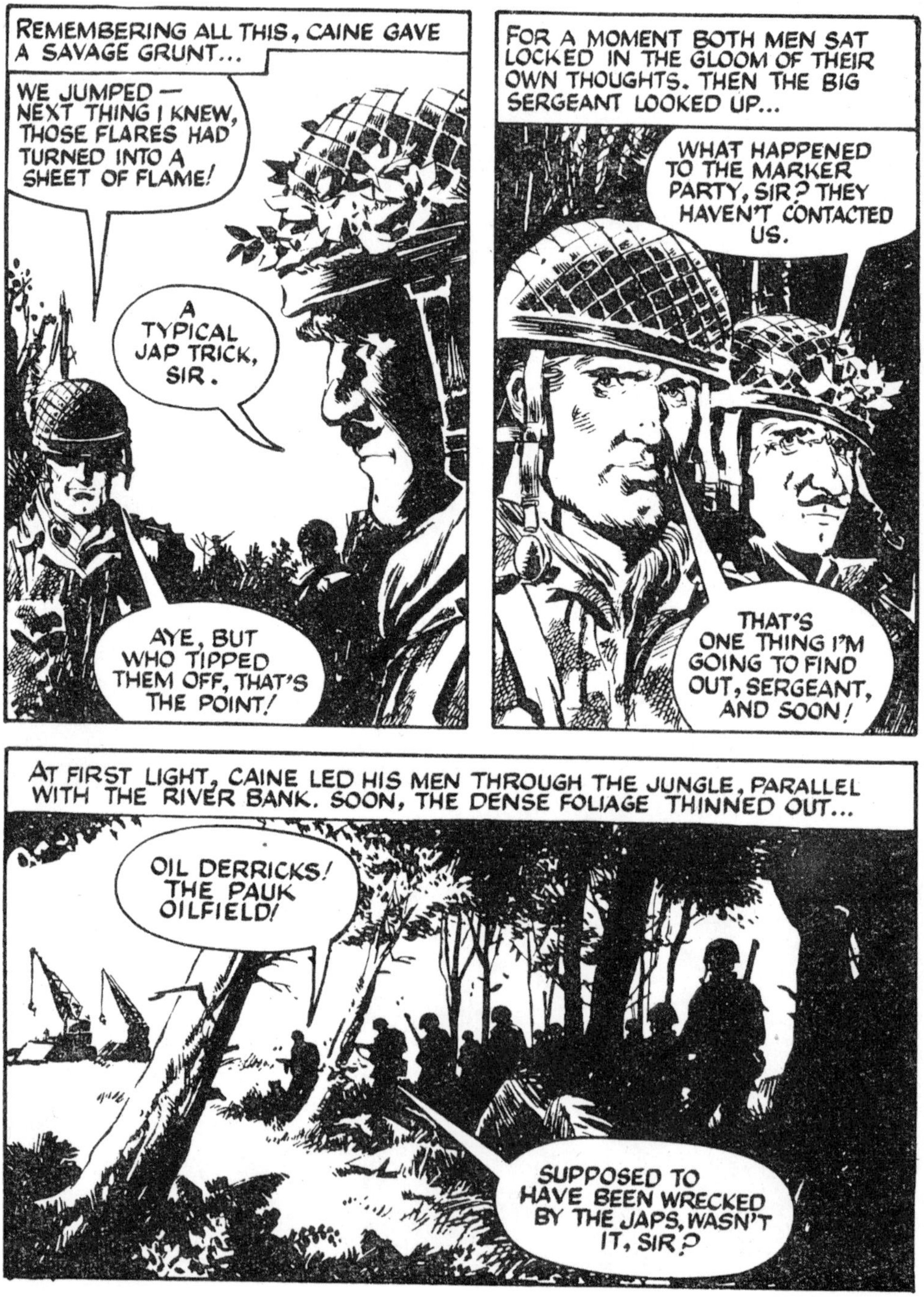
REMEMBERING ALL THIS, CAINE GAVE A SAVAGE GRUNT...
WE JUMPED — NEXT THING I KNEW, THOSE FLARES HAD TURNED INTO A SHEET OF FLAME!
A TYPICAL JAP TRICK, SIR.
AYE, BUT WHO TIPPED THEM OFF, THAT'S THE POINT!
FOR A MOMENT BOTH MEN SAT LOCKED IN THE GLOOM OF THEIR OWN THOUGHTS. THEN THE BIG SERGEANT LOOKED UP...
WHAT HAPPENED TO THE MARKER PARTY, SIR? THEY HAVEN'T CONTACTED US.
THAT'S ONE THING I'M GOING TO FIND OUT, SERGEANT, AND SOON!
AT FIRST LIGHT, CAINE LED HIS MEN THROUGH THE JUNGLE, PARALLEL WITH THE RIVER BANK. SOON, THE DENSE FOLIAGE THINNED OUT...
OIL DERRICKS! THE PAUK OILFIELD!
SUPPOSED TO HAVE BEEN WRECKED BY THE JAPS, WASN'T IT, SIR?

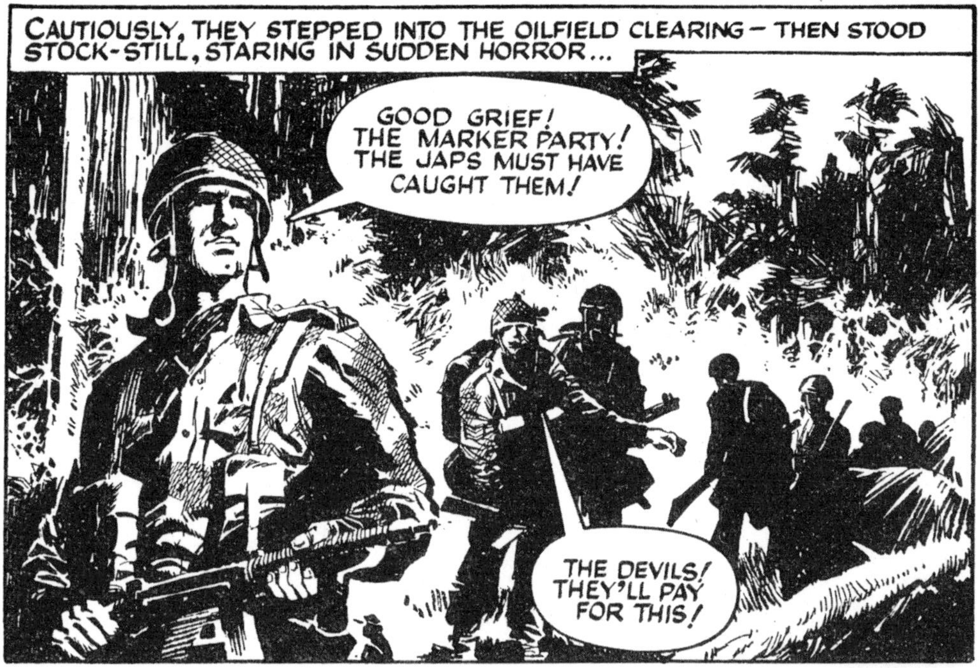
CAUTIOUSLY, THEY STEPPED INTO THE OILFIELD CLEARING – THEN STOOD STOCK-STILL, STARING IN SUDDEN HORROR...
GOOD GRIEF! THE MARKER PARTY! THE JAPS MUST HAVE CAUGHT THEM!
THE DEVILS! THEY'LL PAY FOR THIS!

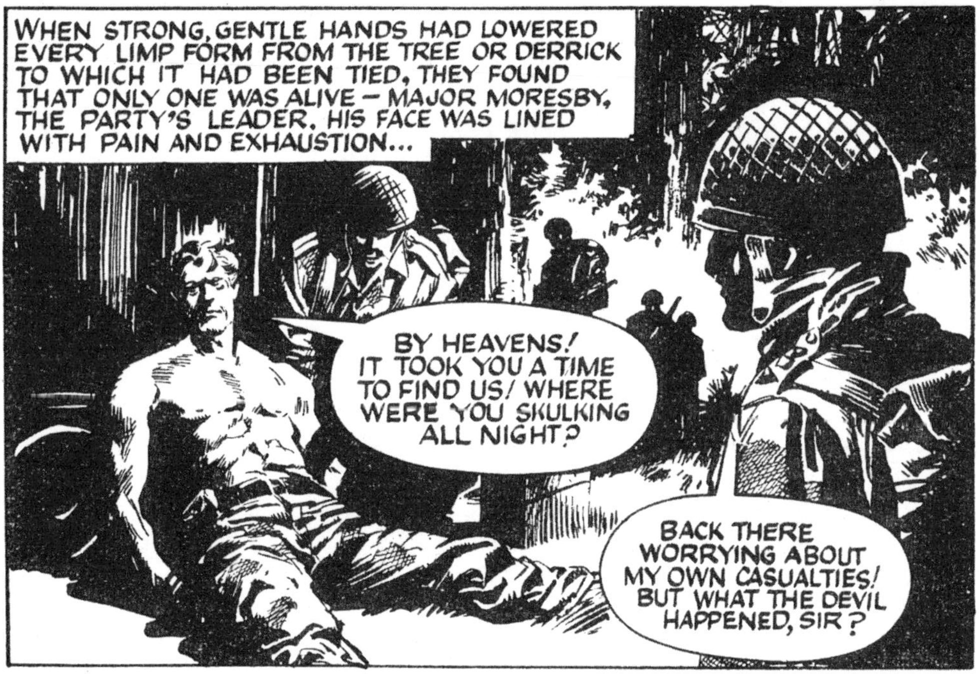
WHEN STRONG, GENTLE HANDS HAD LOWERED EVERY LIMP FORM FROM THE TREE OR DERRICK TO WHICH IT HAD BEEN TIED, THEY FOUND THAT ONLY ONE WAS ALIVE – MAJOR MORESBY, THE PARTY'S LEADER. HIS FACE WAS LINED WITH PAIN AND EXHAUSTION...
BY HEAVENS! IT TOOK YOU A TIME TO FIND US! WHERE WERE YOU SKULKING ALL NIGHT?
BACK THERE WORRYING ABOUT MY OWN CASUALTIES! BUT WHAT THE DEVIL HAPPENED, SIR?

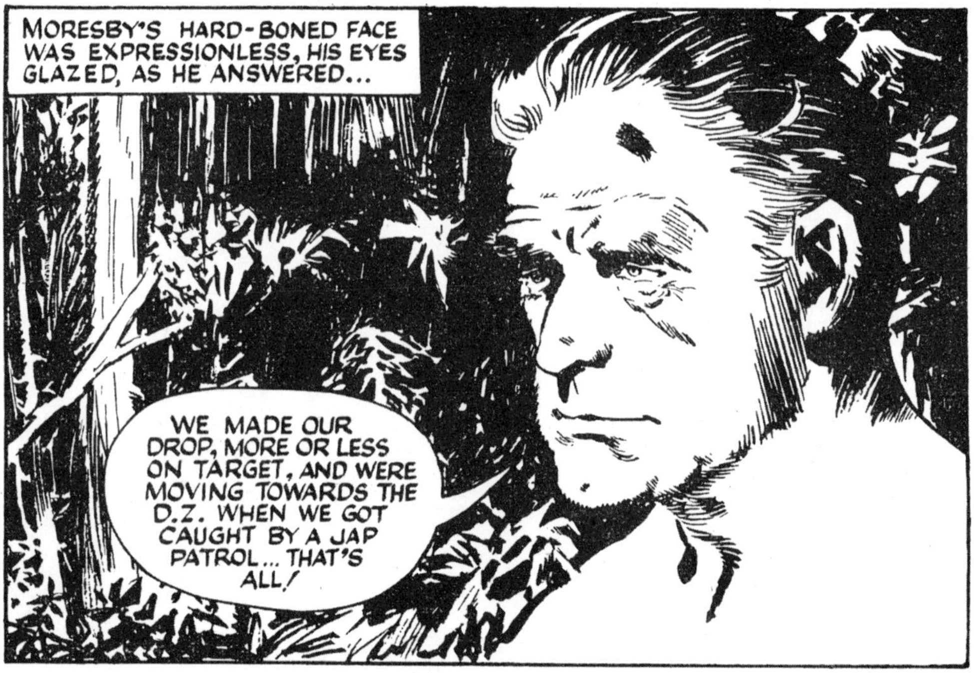
MORESBY'S HARD-BONED FACE WAS EXPRESSIONLESS, HIS EYES GLAZED, AS HE ANSWERED...
WE MADE OUR DROP, MORE OR LESS ON TARGET, AND WERE MOVING TOWARDS THE D.Z. WHEN WE GOT CAUGHT BY A JAP PATROL... THAT'S ALL!

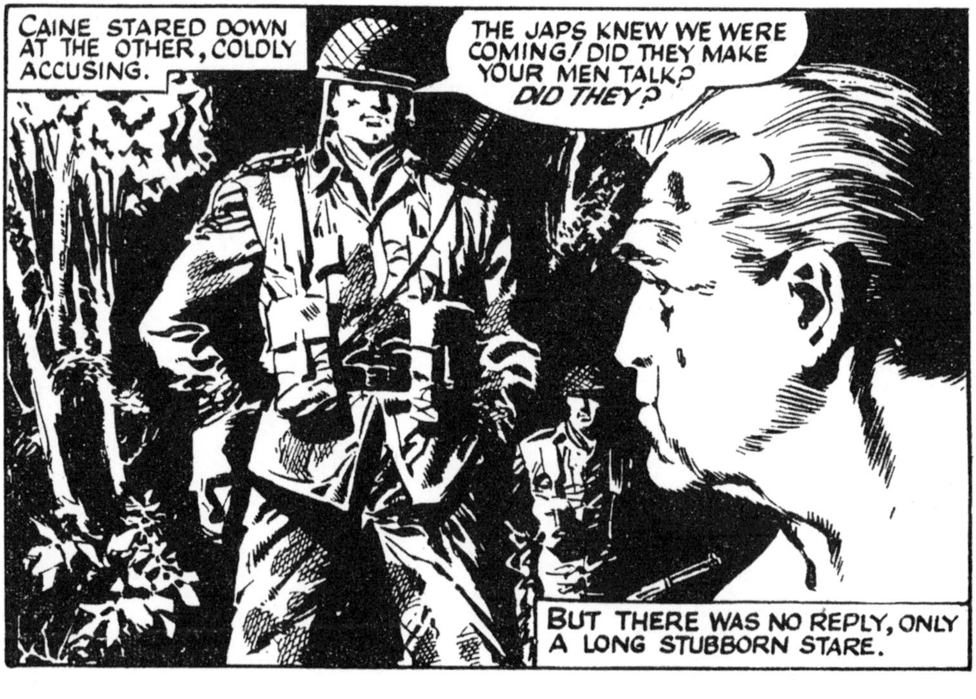
CAINE STARED DOWN AT THE OTHER, COLDLY ACCUSING.
THE JAPS KNEW WE WERE COMING! DID THEY MAKE YOUR MEN TALK? *DID THEY?*
BUT THERE WAS NO REPLY, ONLY A LONG STUBBORN STARE.

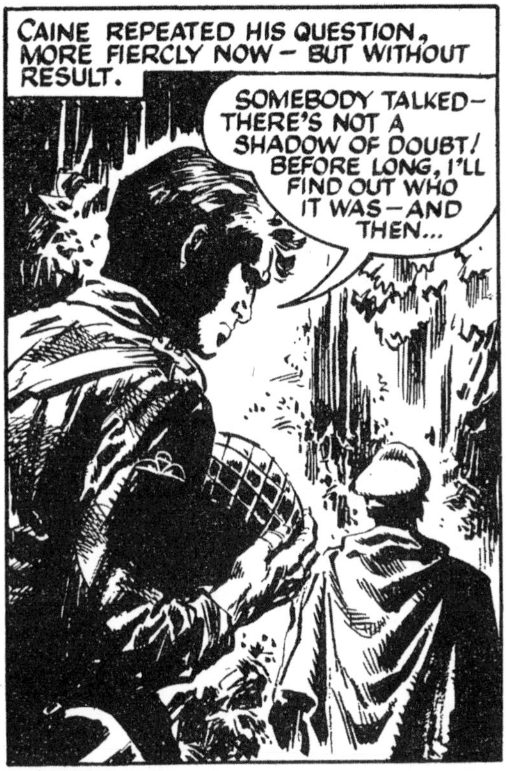
CAINE REPEATED HIS QUESTION, MORE FIERCLY NOW – BUT WITHOUT RESULT.
SOMEBODY TALKED– THERE'S NOT A SHADOW OF DOUBT! BEFORE LONG, I'LL FIND OUT WHO IT WAS–AND THEN...

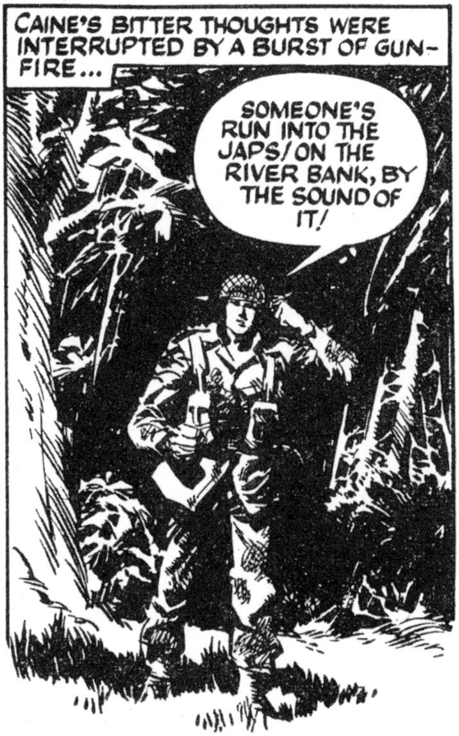
CAINE'S BITTER THOUGHTS WERE INTERRUPTED BY A BURST OF GUN-FIRE...
SOMEONE'S RUN INTO THE JAPS! ON THE RIVER BANK, BY THE SOUND OF IT!

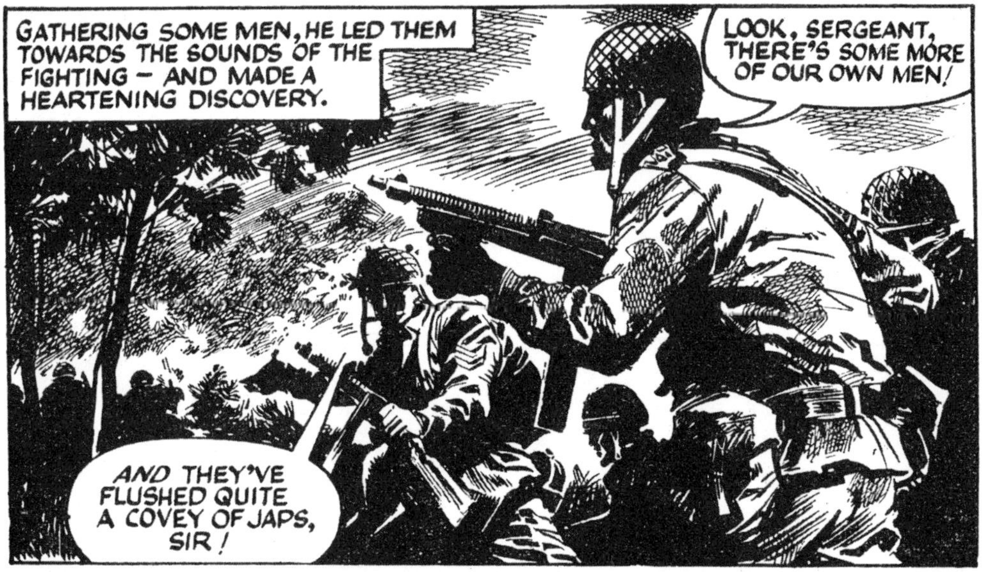
GATHERING SOME MEN, HE LED THEM TOWARDS THE SOUNDS OF THE FIGHTING – AND MADE A HEARTENING DISCOVERY.
LOOK, SERGEANT, THERE'S SOME MORE OF OUR OWN MEN!
AND THEY'VE FLUSHED QUITE A COVEY OF JAPS, SIR!

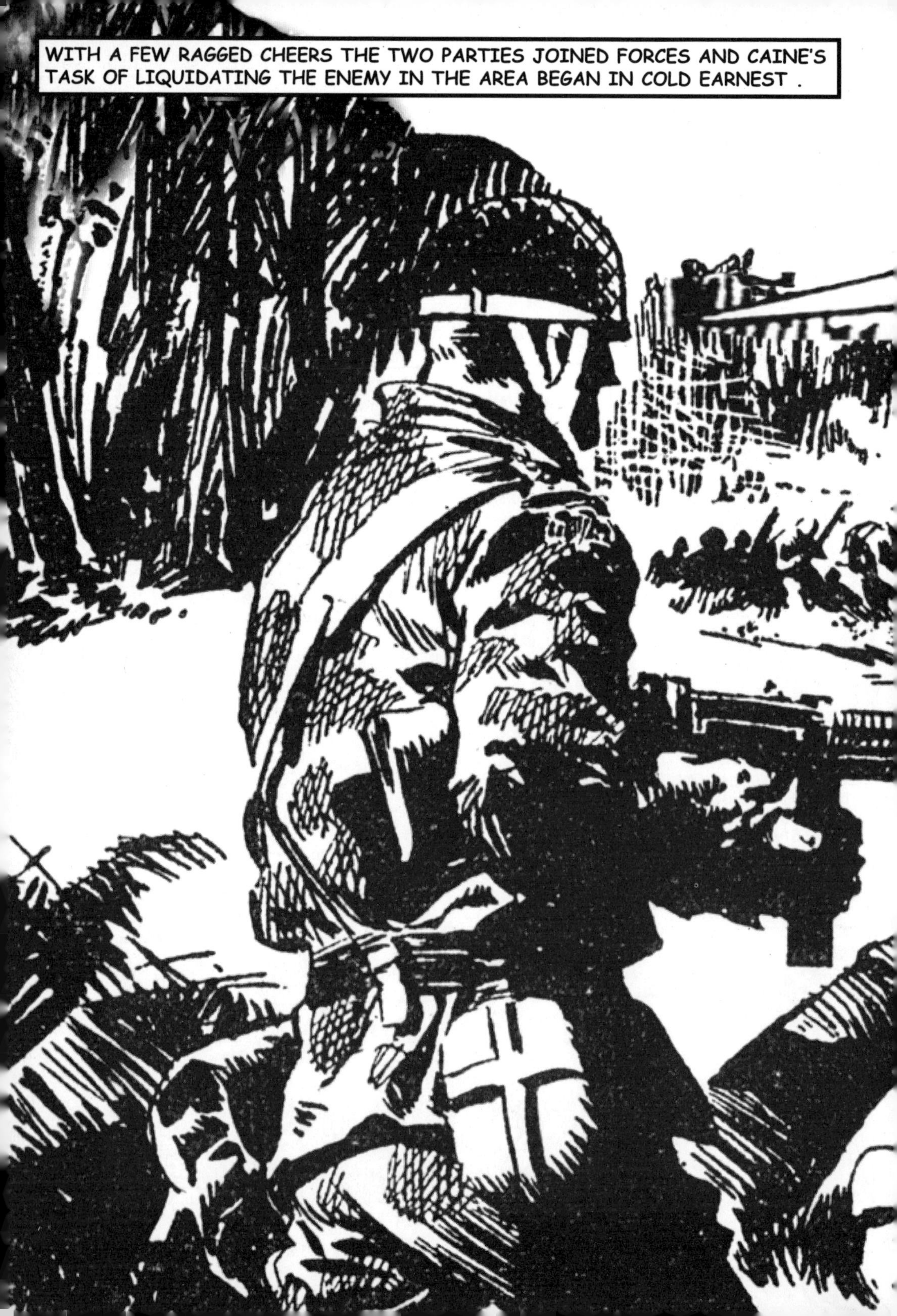
WITH A FEW RAGGED CHEERS THE TWO PARTIES JOINED FORCES AND CAINE'S TASK OF LIQUIDATING THE ENEMY IN THE AREA BEGAN IN COLD EARNEST .

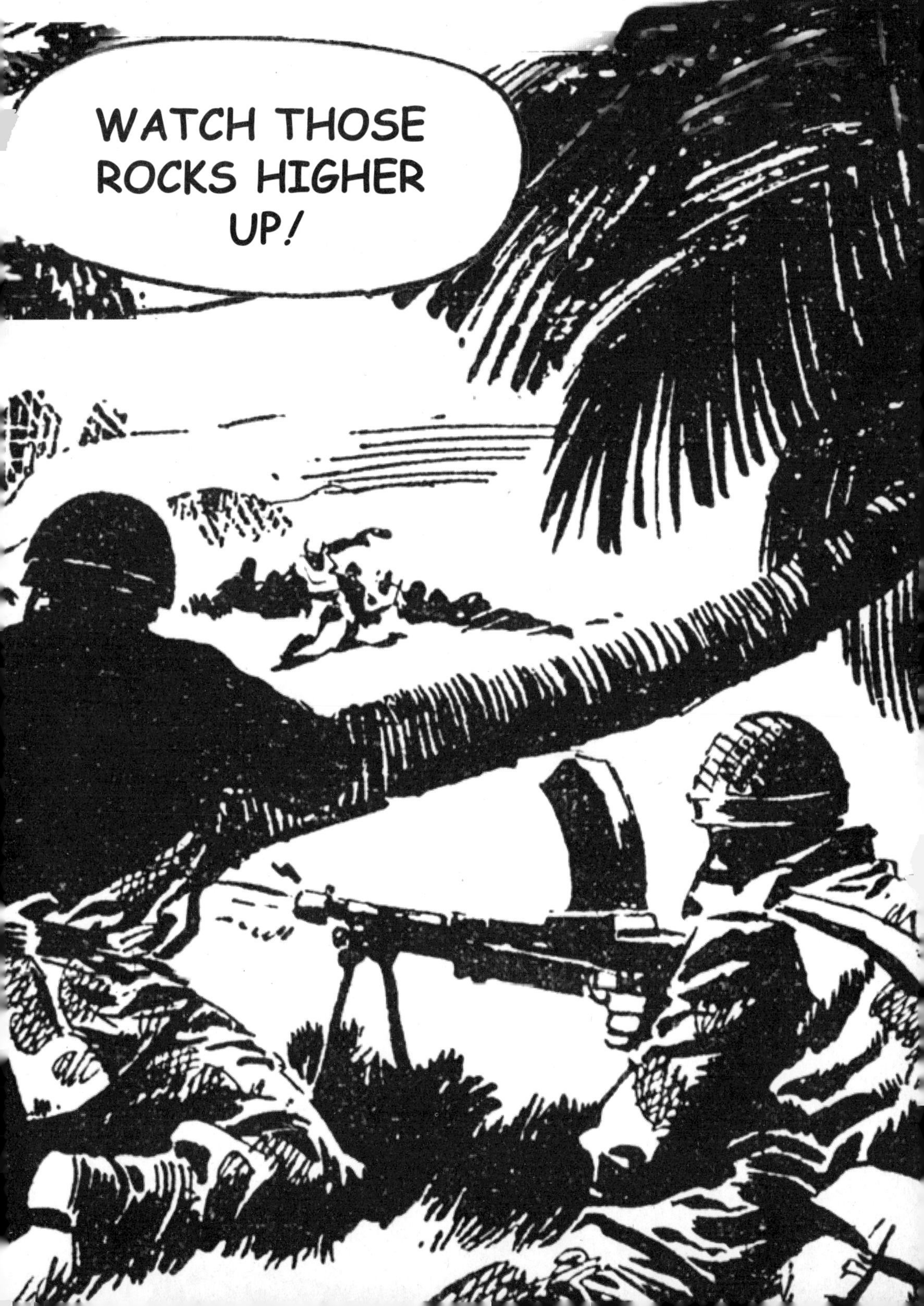
WATCH THOSE ROCKS HIGHER UP!

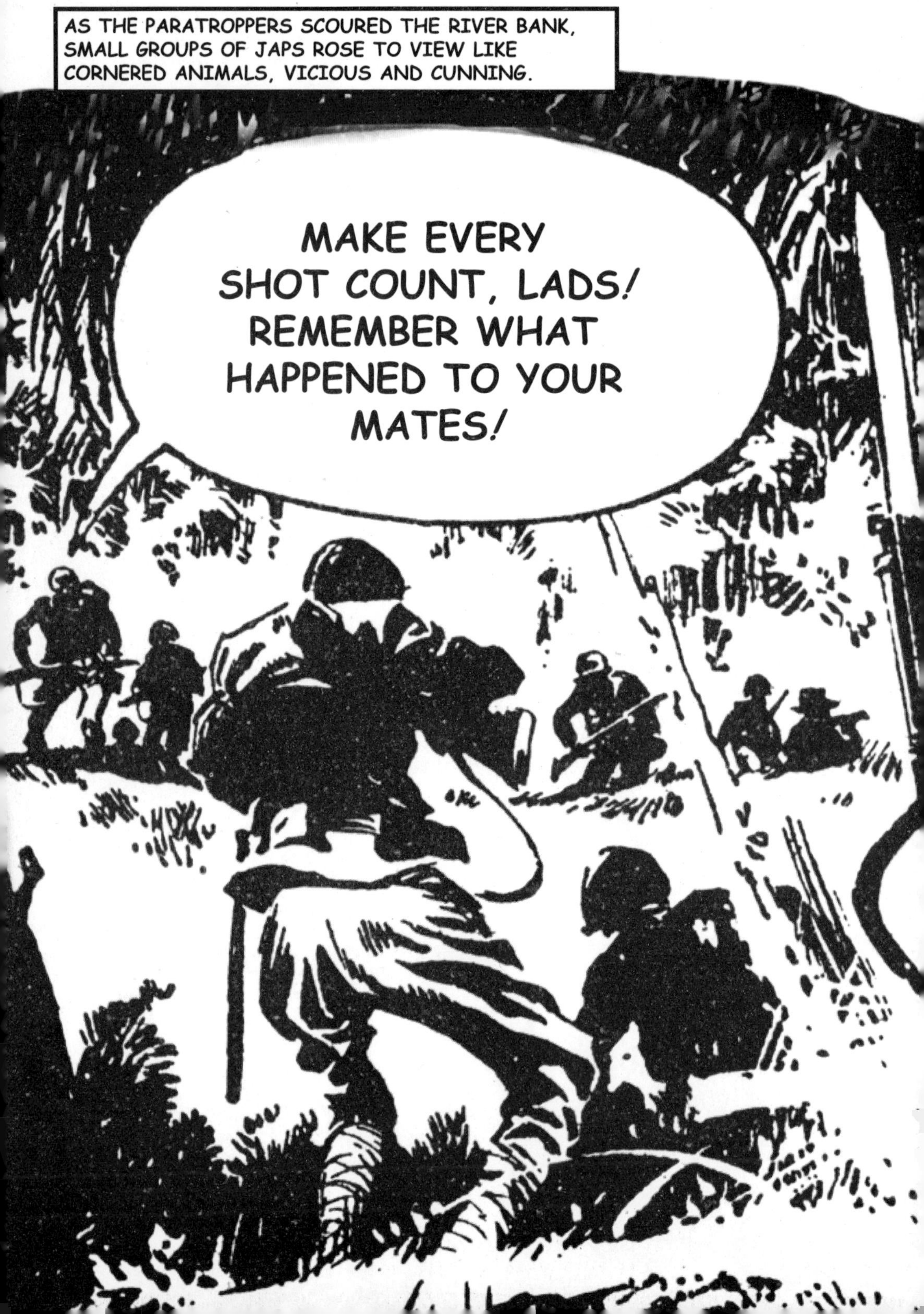
AS THE PARATROPPERS SCOURED THE RIVER BANK, SMALL GROUPS OF JAPS ROSE TO VIEW LIKE CORNERED ANIMALS, VICIOUS AND CUNNING.
MAKE EVERY SHOT COUNT, LADS! REMEMBER WHAT HAPPENED TO YOUR MATES!

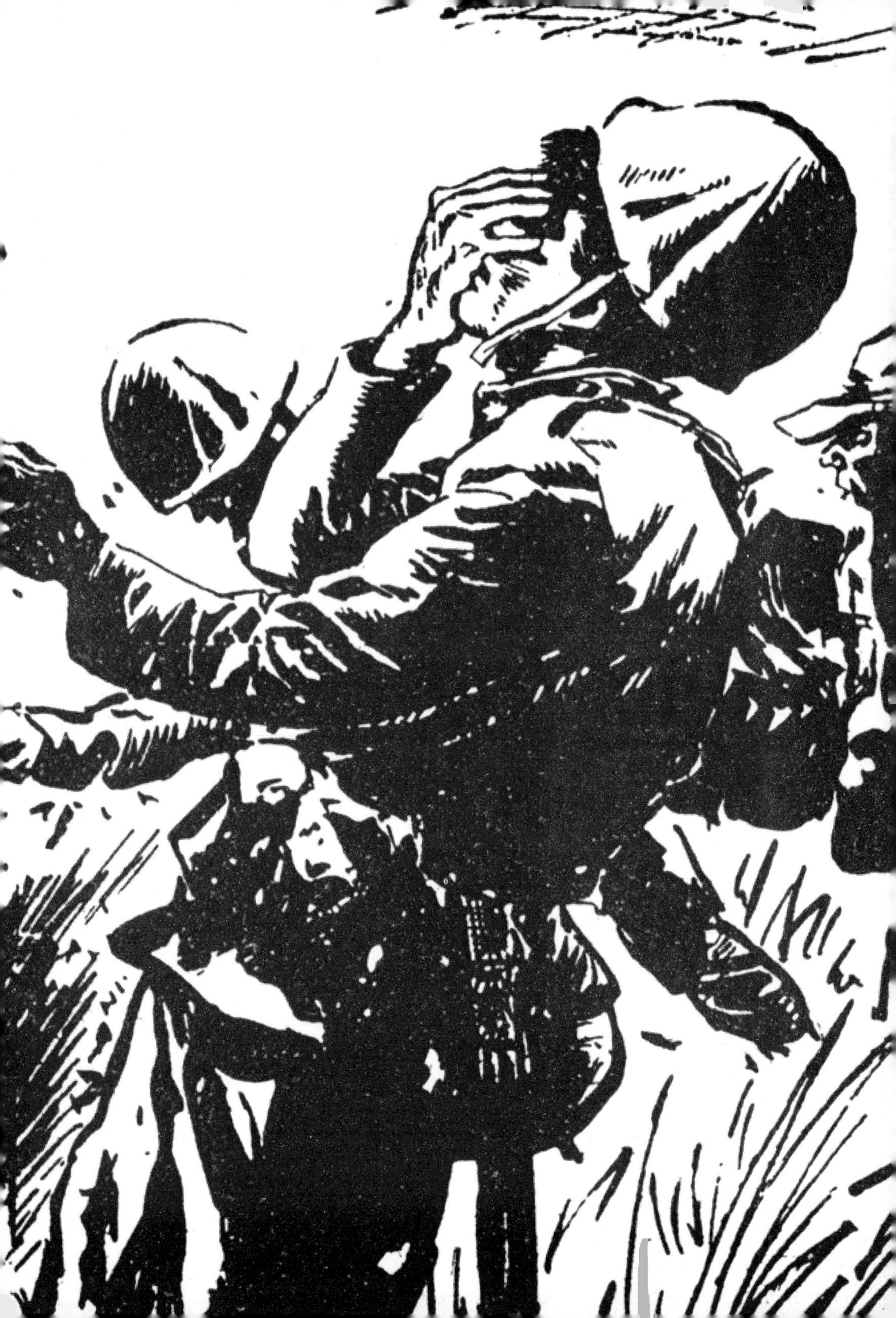

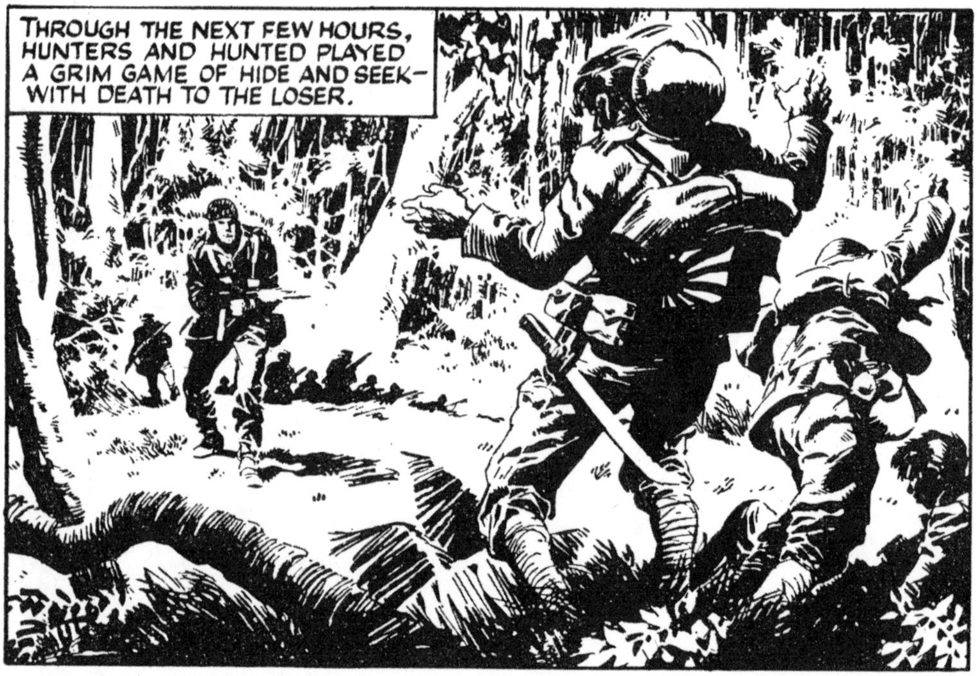
THROUGH THE NEXT FEW HOURS, HUNTERS AND HUNTED PLAYED A GRIM GAME OF HIDE AND SEEK—WITH DEATH TO THE LOSER.

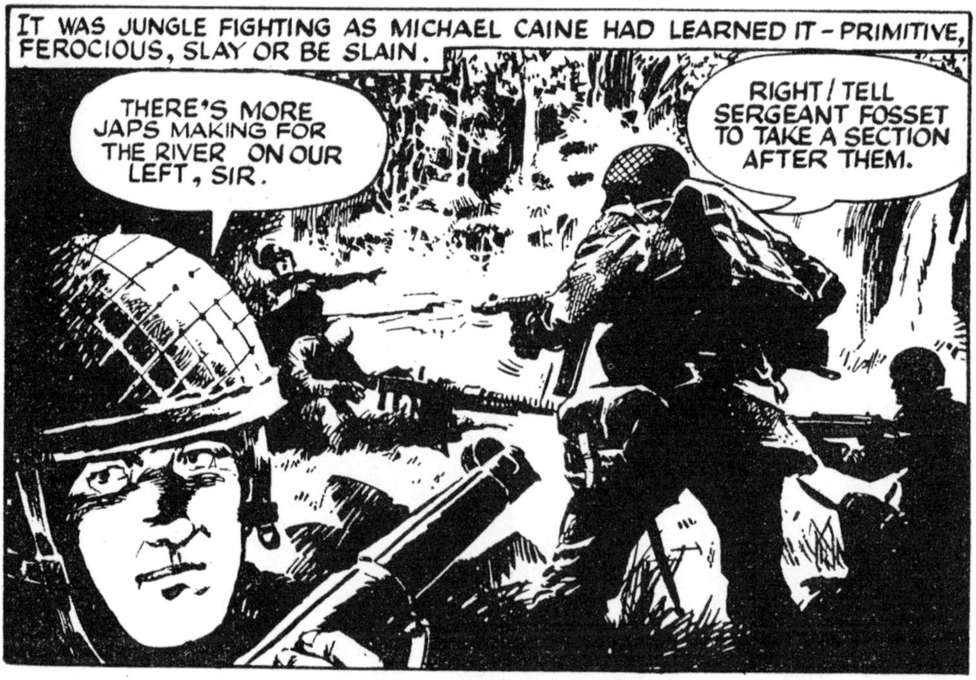
IT WAS JUNGLE FIGHTING AS MICHAEL CAINE HAD LEARNED IT - PRIMITIVE, FEROCIOUS, SLAY OR BE SLAIN.
THERE'S MORE JAPS MAKING FOR THE RIVER ON OUR LEFT, SIR.
RIGHT! TELL SERGEANT FOSSET TO TAKE A SECTION AFTER THEM.

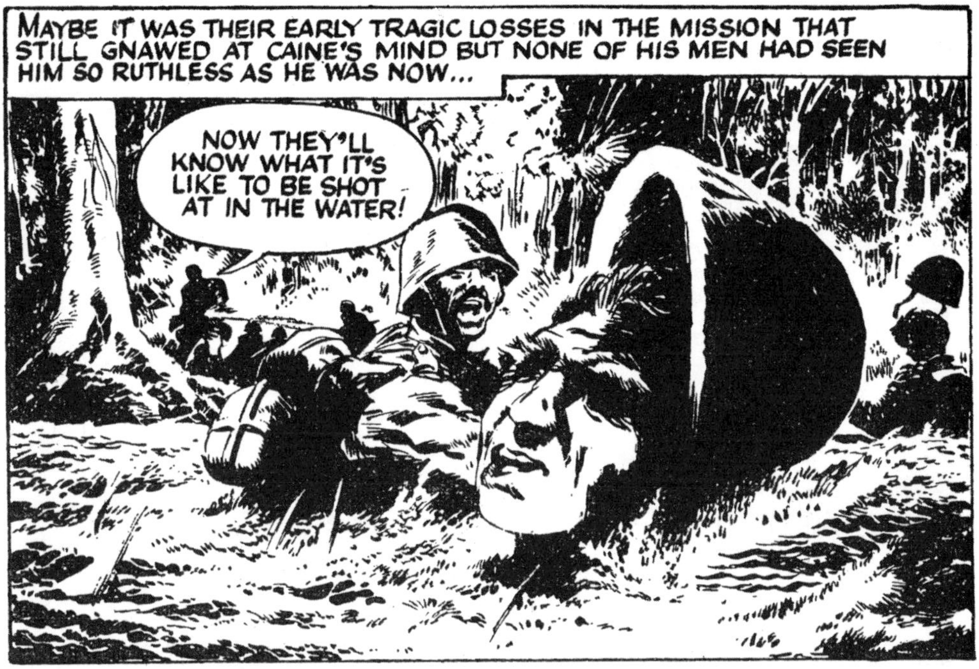
MAYBE IT WAS THEIR EARLY TRAGIC LOSSES IN THE MISSION THAT STILL GNAWED AT CAINE'S MIND BUT NONE OF HIS MEN HAD SEEN HIM SO RUTHLESS AS HE WAS NOW...
NOW THEY'LL KNOW WHAT IT'S LIKE TO BE SHOT AT IN THE WATER!

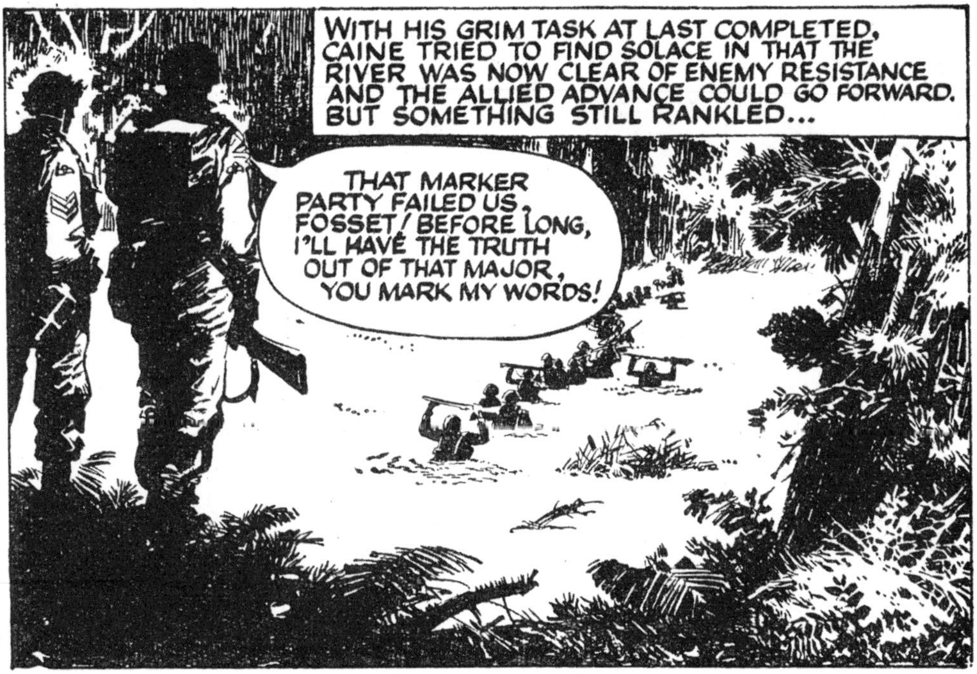
WITH HIS GRIM TASK AT LAST COMPLETED, CAINE TRIED TO FIND SOLACE IN THAT THE RIVER WAS NOW CLEAR OF ENEMY RESISTANCE AND THE ALLIED ADVANCE COULD GO FORWARD. BUT SOMETHING STILL RANKLED...
THAT MARKER PARTY FAILED US, FOSSET! BEFORE LONG, I'LL HAVE THE TRUTH OUT OF THAT MAJOR, YOU MARK MY WORDS!

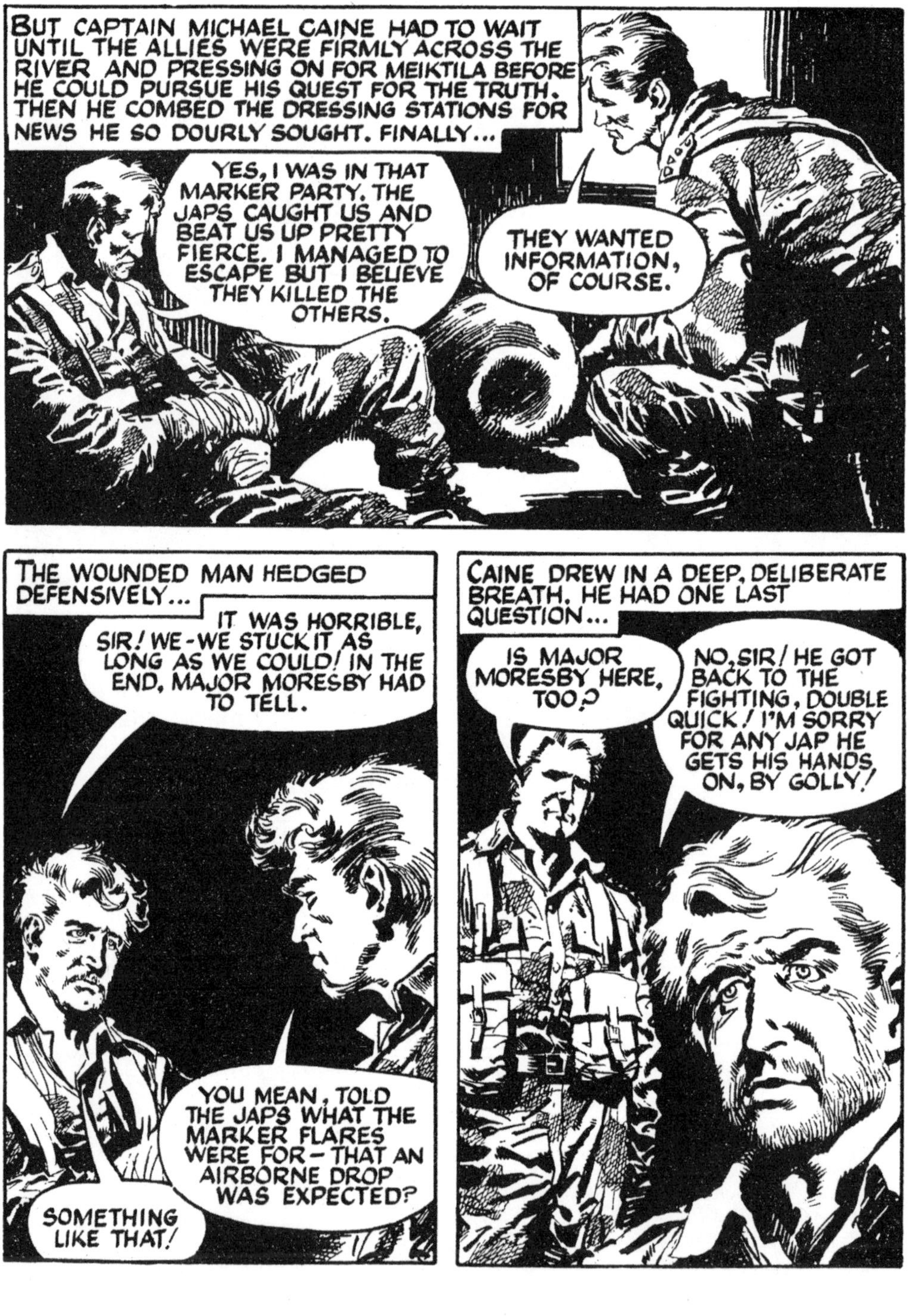
BUT CAPTAIN MICHAEL CAINE HAD TO WAIT UNTIL THE ALLIES WERE FIRMLY ACROSS THE RIVER AND PRESSING ON FOR MEIKTILA BEFORE HE COULD PURSUE HIS QUEST FOR THE TRUTH. THEN HE COMBED THE DRESSING STATIONS FOR NEWS HE SO DOURLY SOUGHT. FINALLY...
YES, I WAS IN THAT MARKER PARTY. THE JAPS CAUGHT US AND BEAT US UP PRETTY FIERCE. I MANAGED TO ESCAPE BUT I BELIEVE THEY KILLED THE OTHERS.
THEY WANTED INFORMATION, OF COURSE.
THE WOUNDED MAN HEDGED DEFENSIVELY...
IT WAS HORRIBLE, SIR! WE-WE STUCK IT AS LONG AS WE COULD! IN THE END, MAJOR MORESBY HAD TO TELL.
YOU MEAN, TOLD THE JAPS WHAT THE MARKER FLARES WERE FOR—THAT AN AIRBORNE DROP WAS EXPECTED?
SOMETHING LIKE THAT!
CAINE DREW IN A DEEP, DELIBERATE BREATH. HE HAD ONE LAST QUESTION...
IS MAJOR MORESBY HERE, TOO?
NO, SIR! HE GOT BACK TO THE FIGHTING, DOUBLE QUICK! I'M SORRY FOR ANY JAP HE GETS HIS HANDS ON, BY GOLLY!

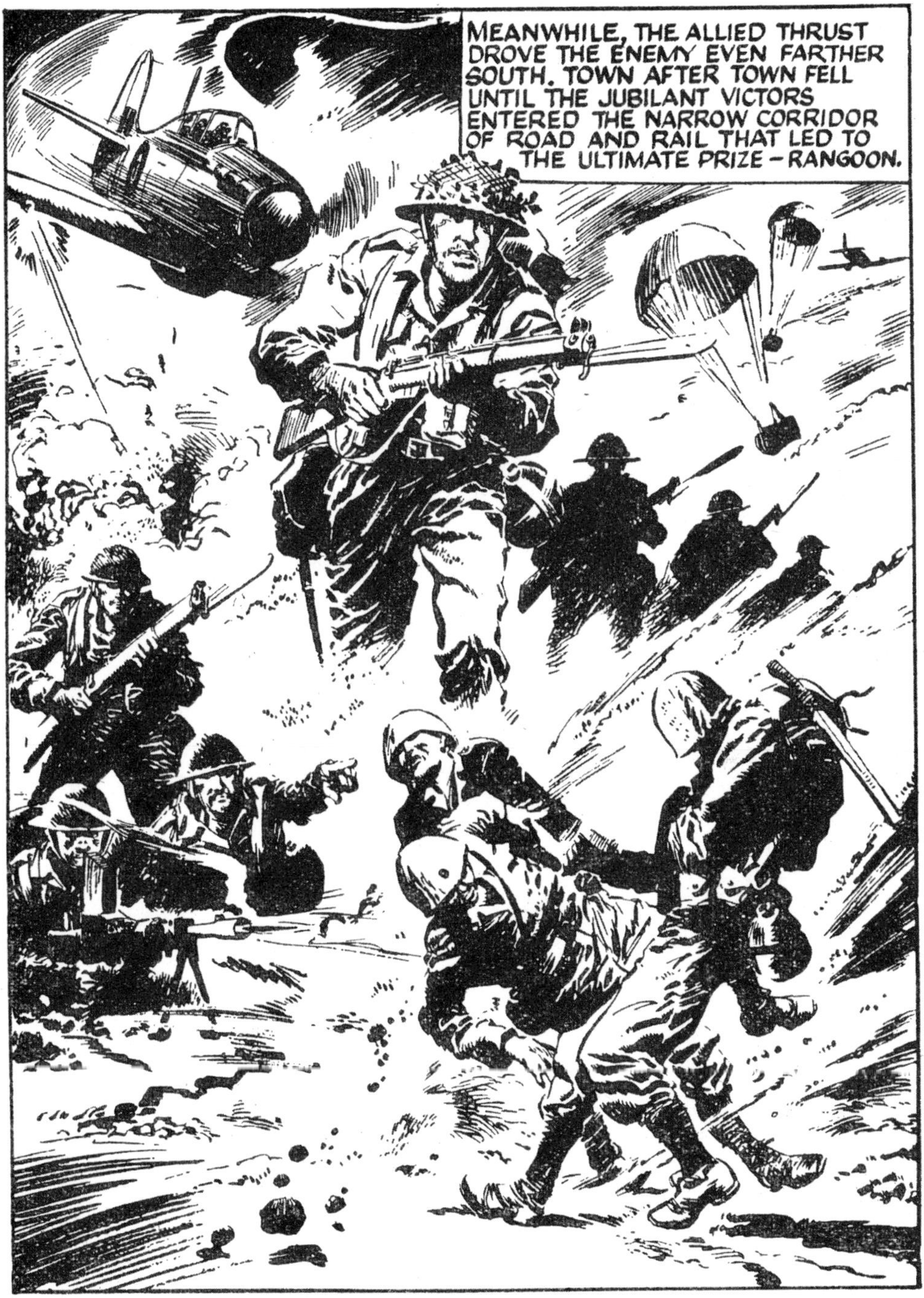
MEANWHILE, THE ALLIED THRUST DROVE THE ENEMY EVEN FARTHER SOUTH. TOWN AFTER TOWN FELL UNTIL THE JUBILANT VICTORS ENTERED THE NARROW CORRIDOR OF ROAD AND RAIL THAT LED TO THE ULTIMATE PRIZE - RANGOON.

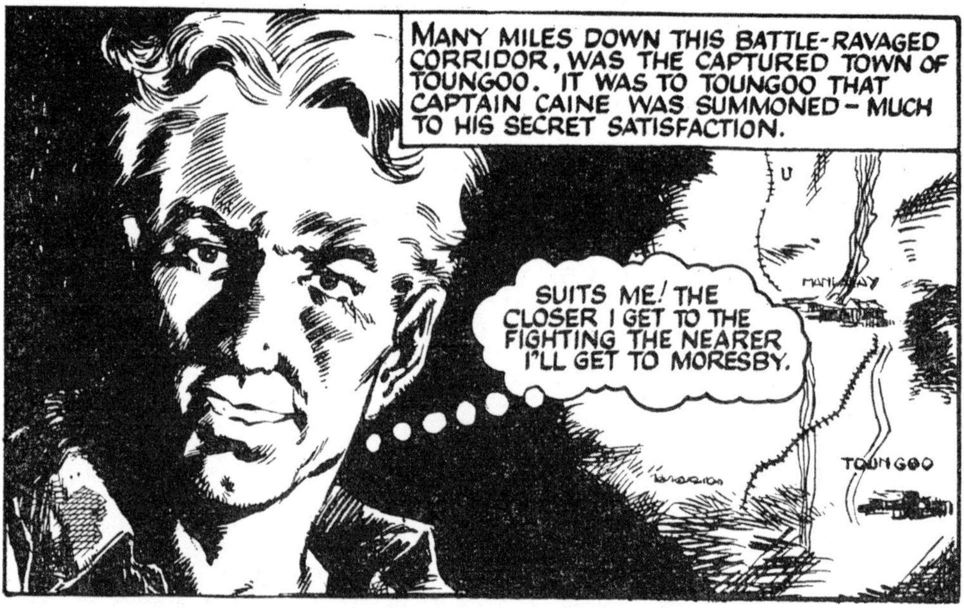
MANY MILES DOWN THIS BATTLE-RAVAGED CORRIDOR, WAS THE CAPTURED TOWN OF TOUNGOO. IT WAS TO TOUNGOO THAT CAPTAIN CAINE WAS SUMMONED - MUCH TO HIS SECRET SATISFACTION.
SUITS ME! THE CLOSER I GET TO THE FIGHTING THE NEARER I'LL GET TO MORESBY.
TOUNGOO

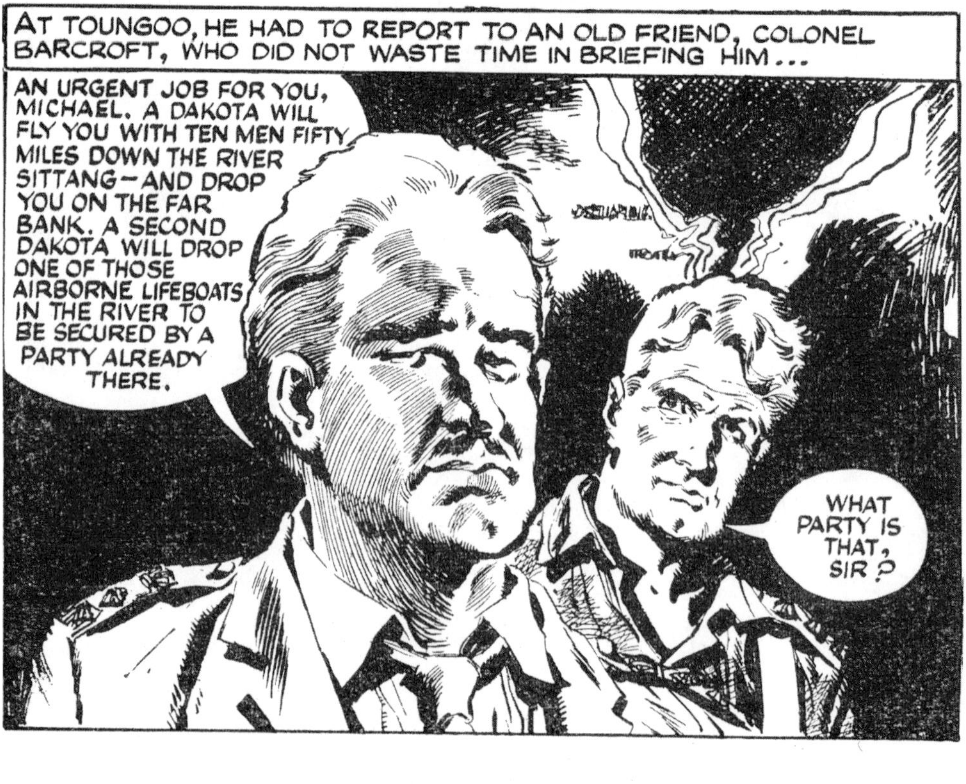
AT TOUNGOO, HE HAD TO REPORT TO AN OLD FRIEND, COLONEL BARCROFT, WHO DID NOT WASTE TIME IN BRIEFING HIM...
AN URGENT JOB FOR YOU, MICHAEL. A DAKOTA WILL FLY YOU WITH TEN MEN FIFTY MILES DOWN THE RIVER SITTANG—AND DROP YOU ON THE FAR BANK. A SECOND DAKOTA WILL DROP ONE OF THOSE AIRBORNE LIFEBOATS IN THE RIVER TO BE SECURED BY A PARTY ALREADY THERE.
WHAT PARTY IS THAT, SIR?

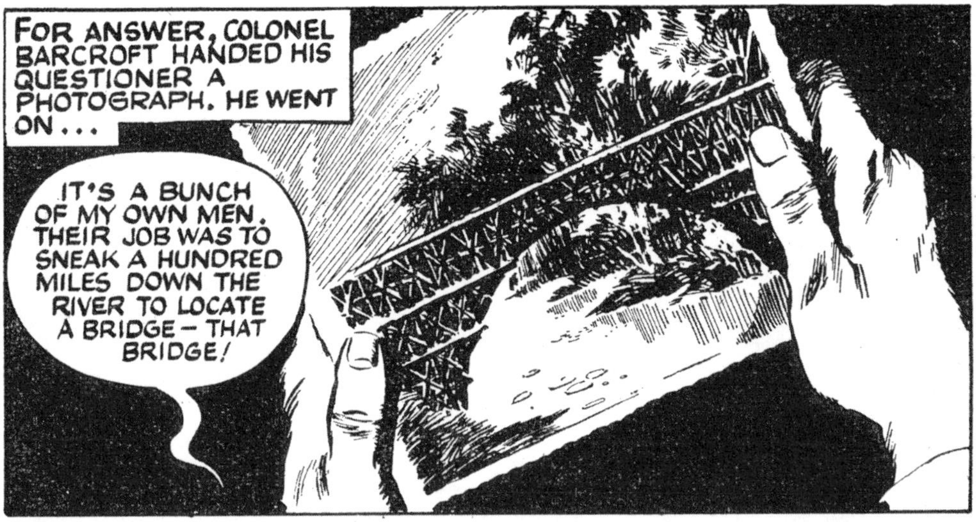
FOR ANSWER, COLONEL BARCROFT HANDED HIS QUESTIONER A PHOTOGRAPH. HE WENT ON . . .
IT'S A BUNCH OF MY OWN MEN. THEIR JOB WAS TO SNEAK A HUNDRED MILES DOWN THE RIVER TO LOCATE A BRIDGE — THAT BRIDGE!

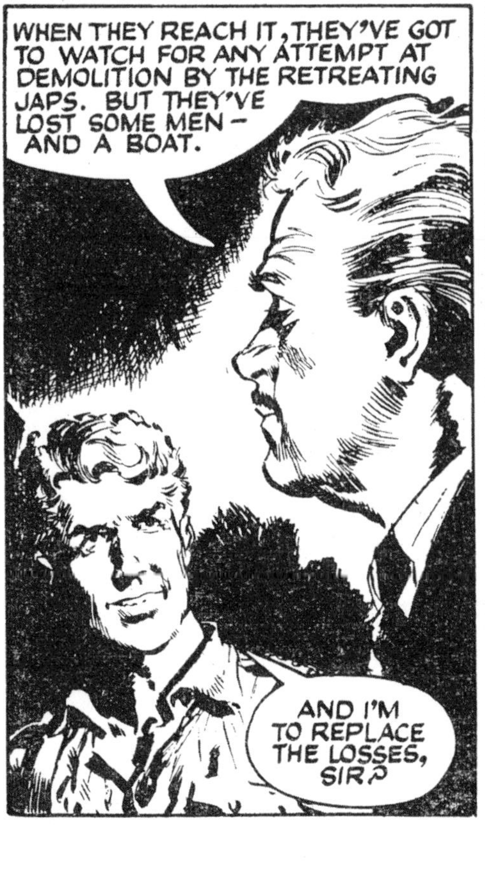
WHEN THEY REACH IT, THEY'VE GOT TO WATCH FOR ANY ATTEMPT AT DEMOLITION BY THE RETREATING JAPS. BUT THEY'VE LOST SOME MEN — AND A BOAT.
AND I'M TO REPLACE THE LOSSES, SIR?

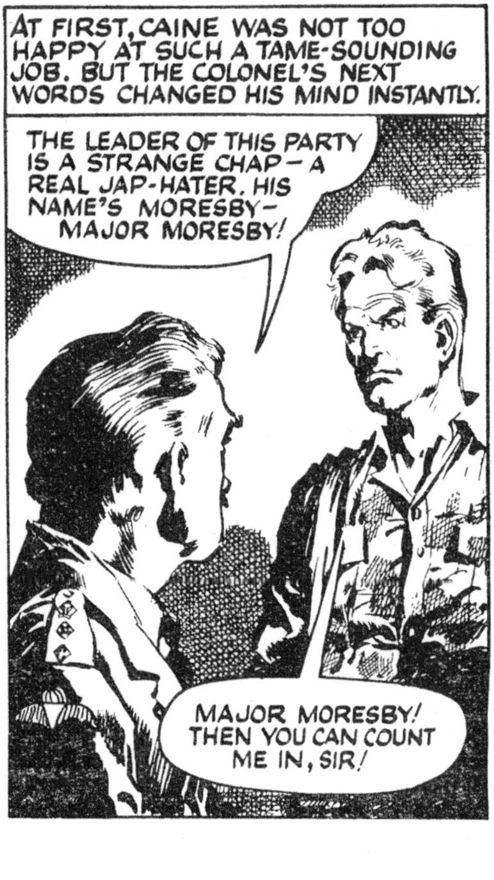
AT FIRST, CAINE WAS NOT TOO HAPPY AT SUCH A TAME-SOUNDING JOB. BUT THE COLONEL'S NEXT WORDS CHANGED HIS MIND INSTANTLY.
THE LEADER OF THIS PARTY IS A STRANGE CHAP — A REAL JAP-HATER. HIS NAME'S MORESBY — MAJOR MORESBY!
MAJOR MORESBY! THEN YOU CAN COUNT ME IN, SIR!

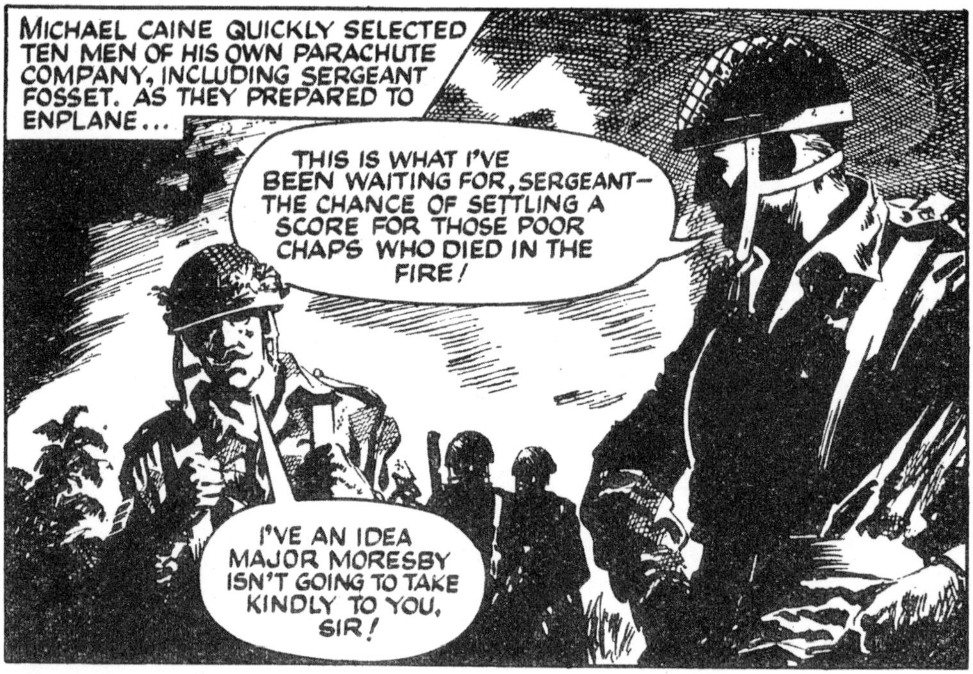
MICHAEL CAINE QUICKLY SELECTED TEN MEN OF HIS OWN PARACHUTE COMPANY, INCLUDING SERGEANT FOSSET. AS THEY PREPARED TO ENPLANE...
THIS IS WHAT I'VE BEEN WAITING FOR, SERGEANT— THE CHANCE OF SETTLING A SCORE FOR THOSE POOR CHAPS WHO DIED IN THE FIRE!
I'VE AN IDEA MAJOR MORESBY ISN'T GOING TO TAKE KINDLY TO YOU, SIR!

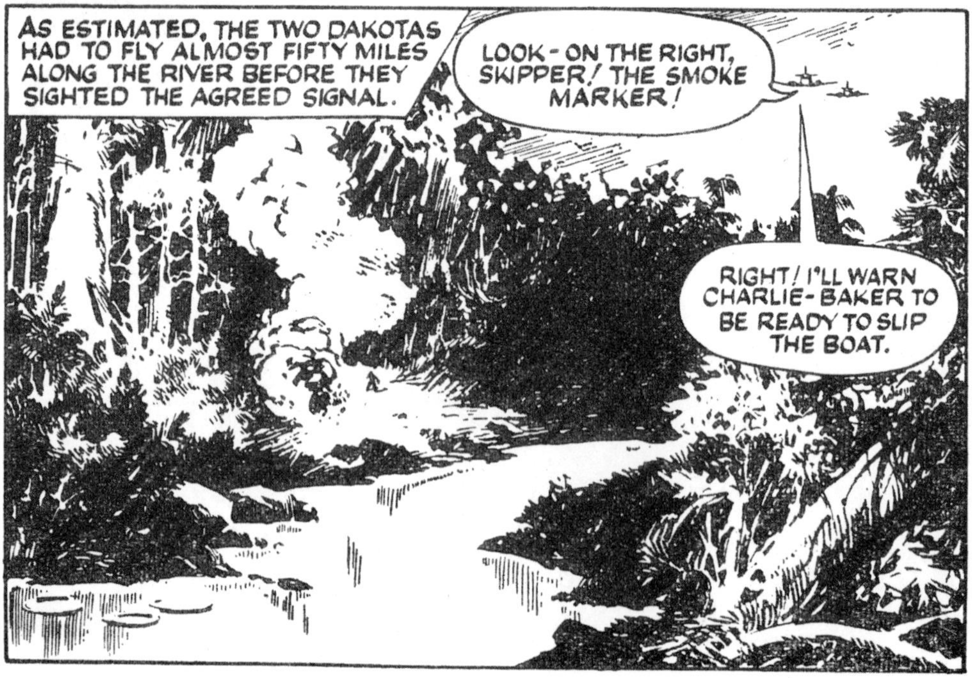
AS ESTIMATED, THE TWO DAKOTAS HAD TO FLY ALMOST FIFTY MILES ALONG THE RIVER BEFORE THEY SIGHTED THE AGREED SIGNAL.
LOOK - ON THE RIGHT, SKIPPER! THE SMOKE MARKER!
RIGHT! I'LL WARN CHARLIE-BAKER TO BE READY TO SLIP THE BOAT.

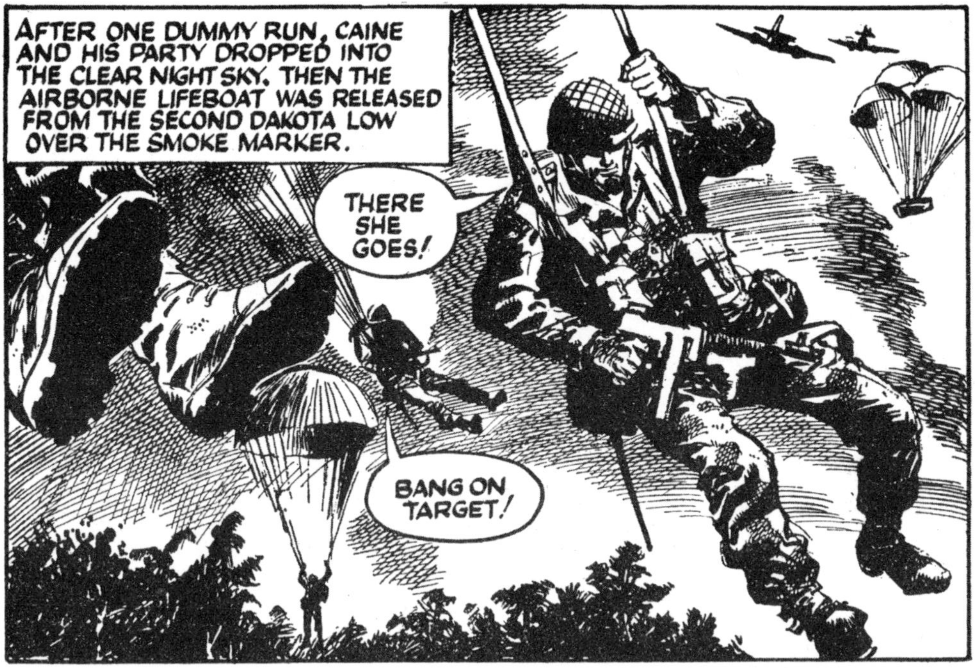
AFTER ONE DUMMY RUN, CAINE AND HIS PARTY DROPPED INTO THE CLEAR NIGHT SKY. THEN THE AIRBORNE LIFEBOAT WAS RELEASED FROM THE SECOND DAKOTA LOW OVER THE SMOKE MARKER.
THERE SHE GOES!
BANG ON TARGET!

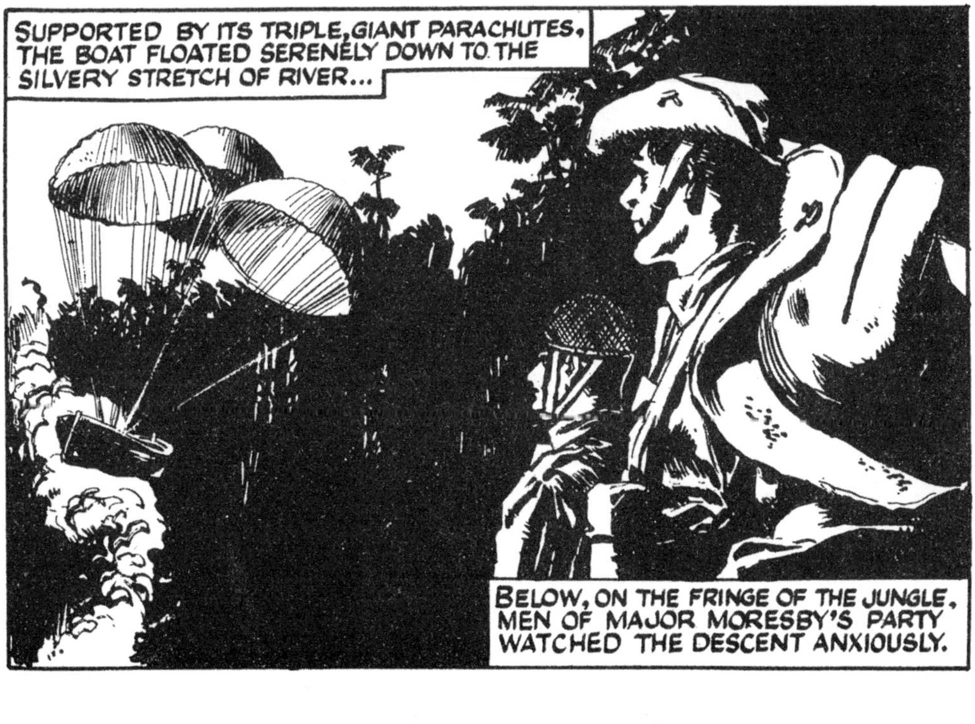
SUPPORTED BY ITS TRIPLE, GIANT PARACHUTES, THE BOAT FLOATED SERENELY DOWN TO THE SILVERY STRETCH OF RIVER...
BELOW, ON THE FRINGE OF THE JUNGLE, MEN OF MAJOR MORESBY'S PARTY WATCHED THE DESCENT ANXIOUSLY.

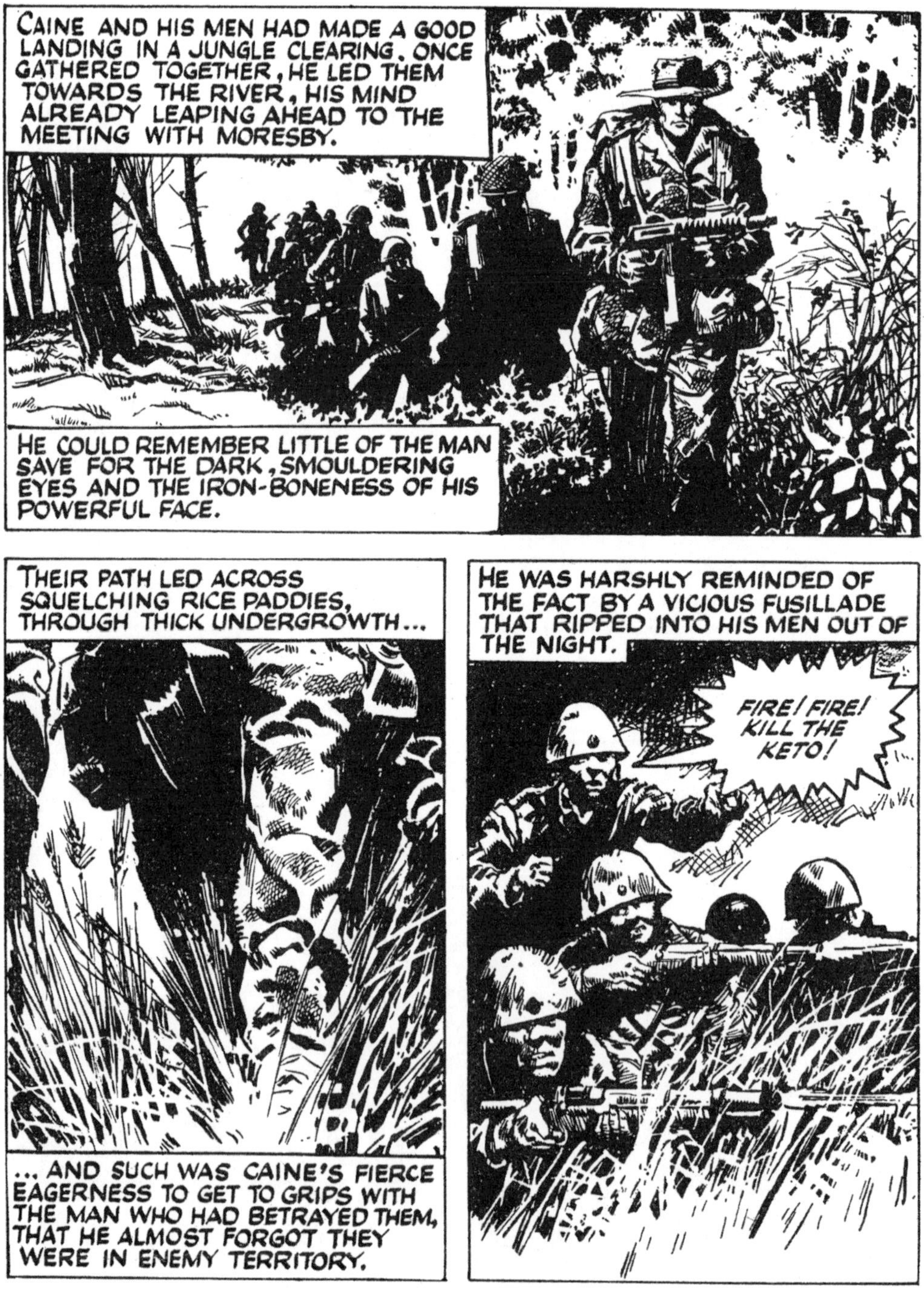
CAINE AND HIS MEN HAD MADE A GOOD LANDING IN A JUNGLE CLEARING. ONCE GATHERED TOGETHER, HE LED THEM TOWARDS THE RIVER, HIS MIND ALREADY LEAPING AHEAD TO THE MEETING WITH MORESBY.
HE COULD REMEMBER LITTLE OF THE MAN SAVE FOR THE DARK, SMOULDERING EYES AND THE IRON-BONENESS OF HIS POWERFUL FACE.
THEIR PATH LED ACROSS SQUELCHING RICE PADDIES, THROUGH THICK UNDERGROWTH...
... AND SUCH WAS CAINE'S FIERCE EAGERNESS TO GET TO GRIPS WITH THE MAN WHO HAD BETRAYED THEM, THAT HE ALMOST FORGOT THEY WERE IN ENEMY TERRITORY.
HE WAS HARSHLY REMINDED OF THE FACT BY A VICIOUS FUSILLADE THAT RIPPED INTO HIS MEN OUT OF THE NIGHT.
FIRE! FIRE! KILL THE KETO!

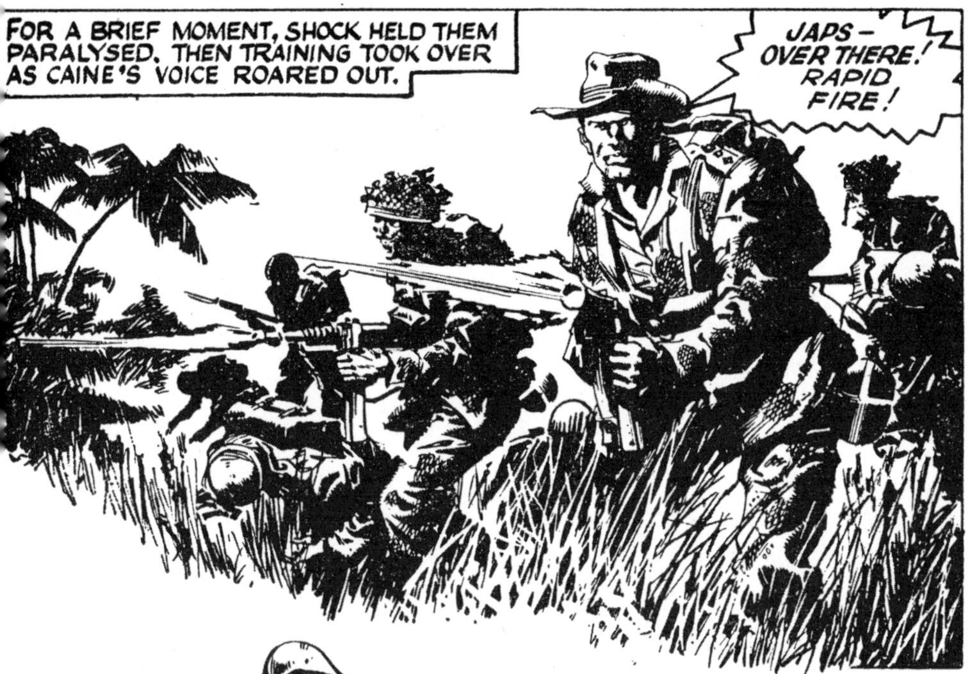
FOR A BRIEF MOMENT, SHOCK HELD THEM PARALYSED. THEN TRAINING TOOK OVER AS CAINE'S VOICE ROARED OUT.
JAPS – OVER THERE! RAPID FIRE!

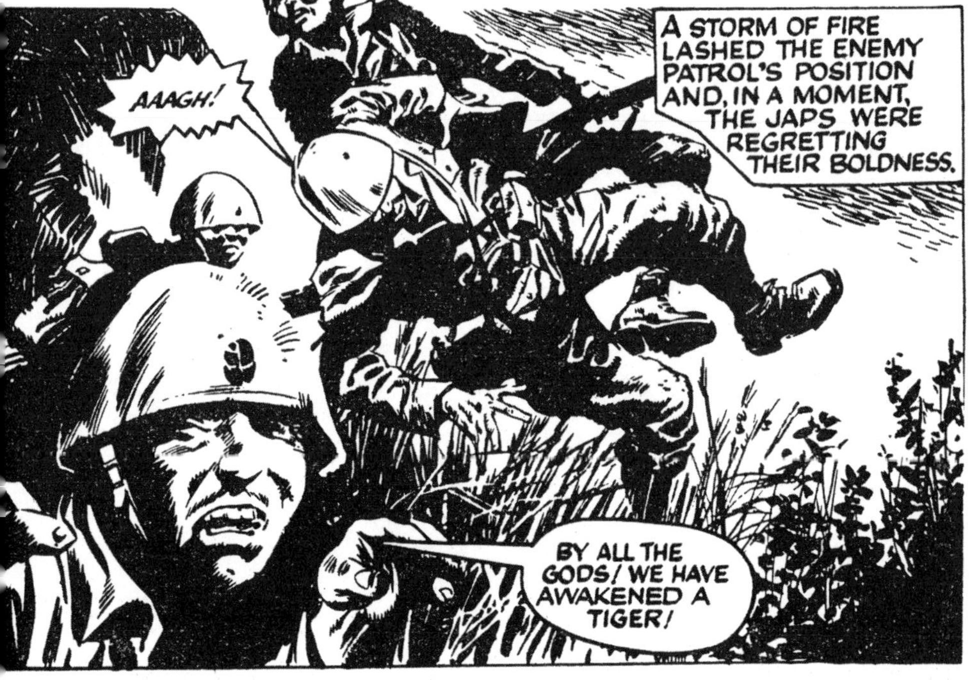
A STORM OF FIRE LASHED THE ENEMY PATROL'S POSITION AND, IN A MOMENT, THE JAPS WERE REGRETTING THEIR BOLDNESS.
AAAGH!
BY ALL THE GODS! WE HAVE AWAKENED A TIGER!

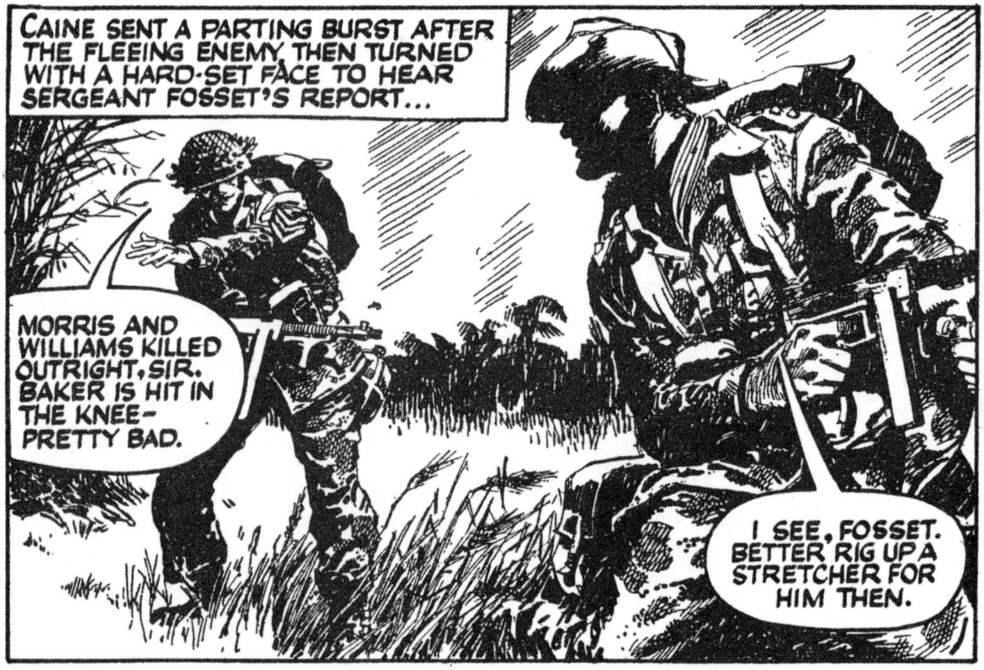
CAINE SENT A PARTING BURST AFTER THE FLEEING ENEMY, THEN TURNED WITH A HARD-SET FACE TO HEAR SERGEANT FOSSET'S REPORT...
MORRIS AND WILLIAMS KILLED OUTRIGHT, SIR. BAKER IS HIT IN THE KNEE- PRETTY BAD.
I SEE, FOSSET. BETTER RIG UP A STRETCHER FOR HIM THEN.

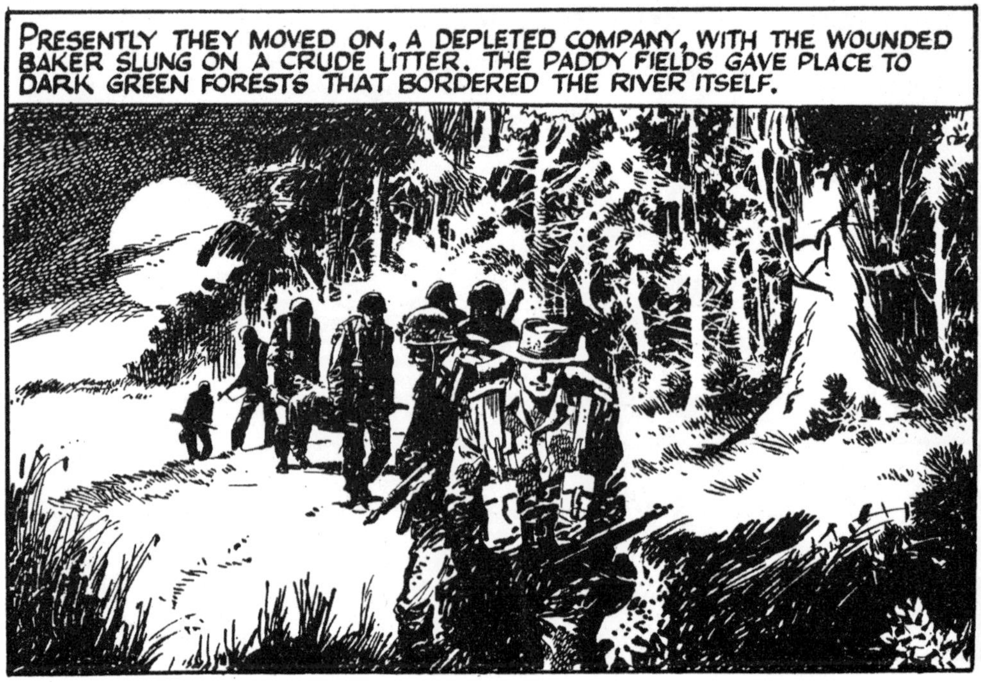
PRESENTLY THEY MOVED ON, A DEPLETED COMPANY, WITH THE WOUNDED BAKER SLUNG ON A CRUDE LITTER. THE PADDY FIELDS GAVE PLACE TO DARK GREEN FORESTS THAT BORDERED THE RIVER ITSELF.

Chapter 2. Revenge the Spur

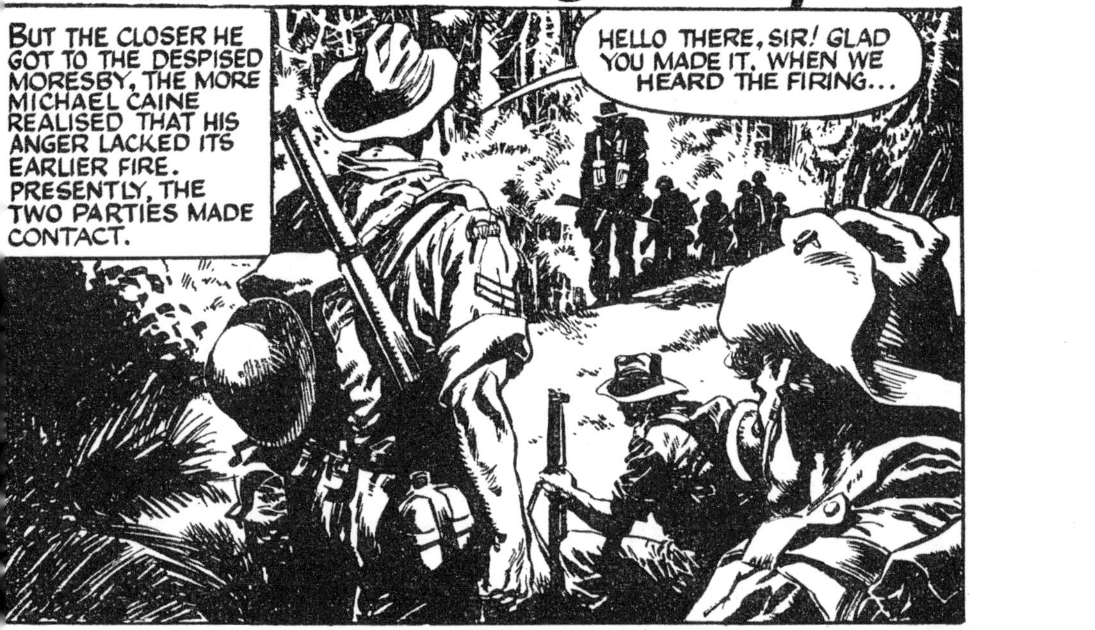
BUT THE CLOSER HE GOT TO THE DESPISED MORESBY, THE MORE MICHAEL CAINE REALISED THAT HIS ANGER LACKED ITS EARLIER FIRE. PRESENTLY, THE TWO PARTIES MADE CONTACT.
HELLO THERE, SIR! GLAD YOU MADE IT. WHEN WE HEARD THE FIRING...

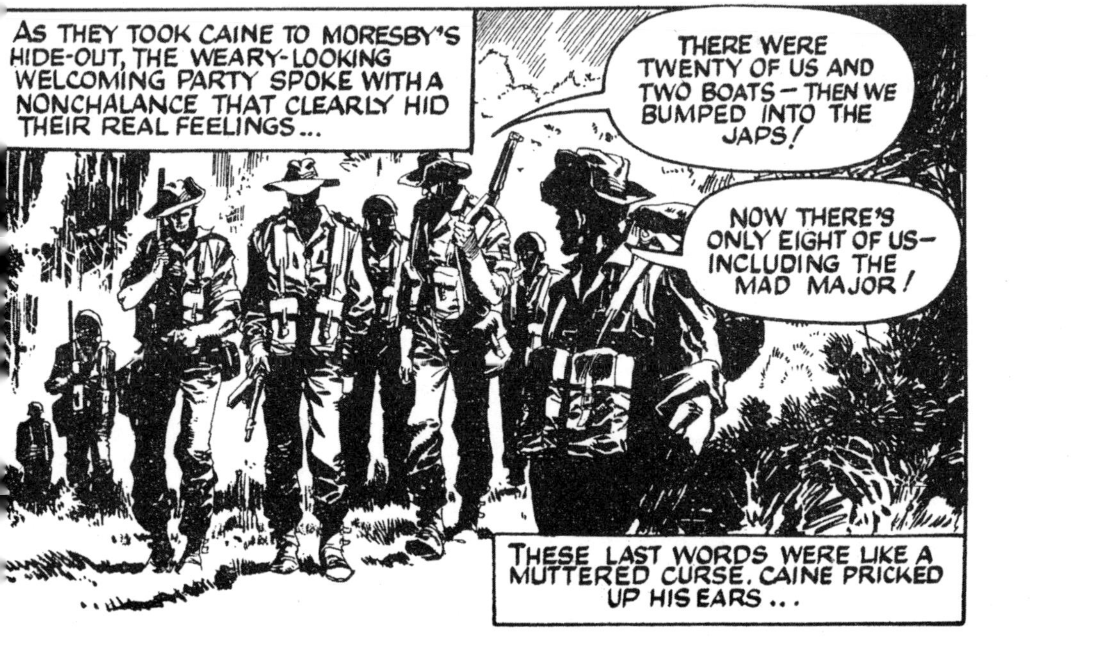
AS THEY TOOK CAINE TO MORESBY'S HIDE-OUT, THE WEARY-LOOKING WELCOMING PARTY SPOKE WITH A NONCHALANCE THAT CLEARLY HID THEIR REAL FEELINGS...
THERE WERE TWENTY OF US AND TWO BOATS — THEN WE BUMPED INTO THE JAPS!
NOW THERE'S ONLY EIGHT OF US — INCLUDING THE MAD MAJOR!
THESE LAST WORDS WERE LIKE A MUTTERED CURSE. CAINE PRICKED UP HIS EARS...

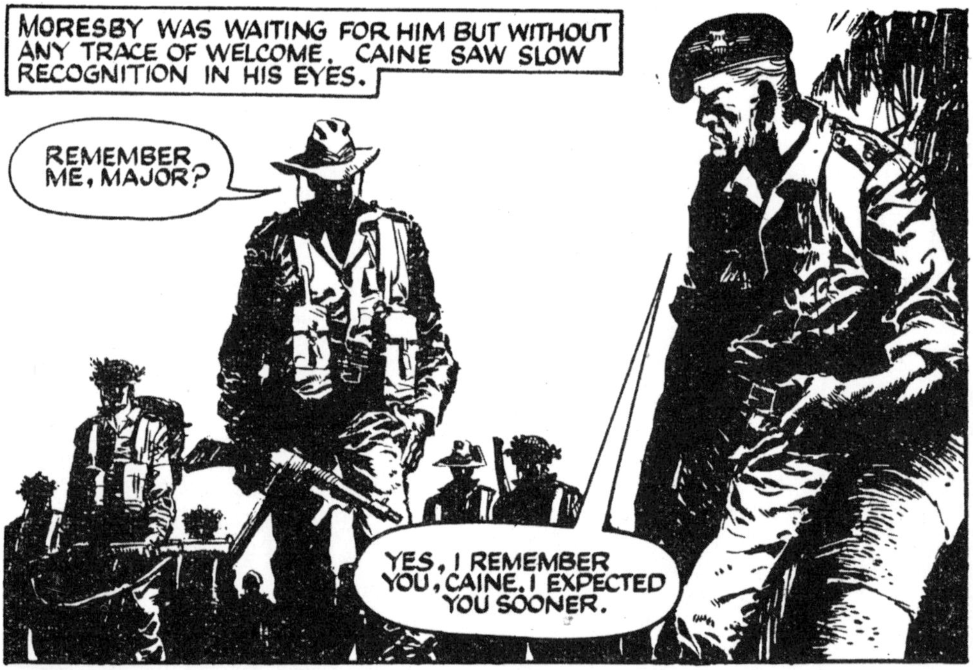
MORESBY WAS WAITING FOR HIM BUT WITHOUT ANY TRACE OF WELCOME. CAINE SAW SLOW RECOGNITION IN HIS EYES.
REMEMBER ME, MAJOR?
YES, I REMEMBER YOU, CAINE. I EXPECTED YOU SOONER.

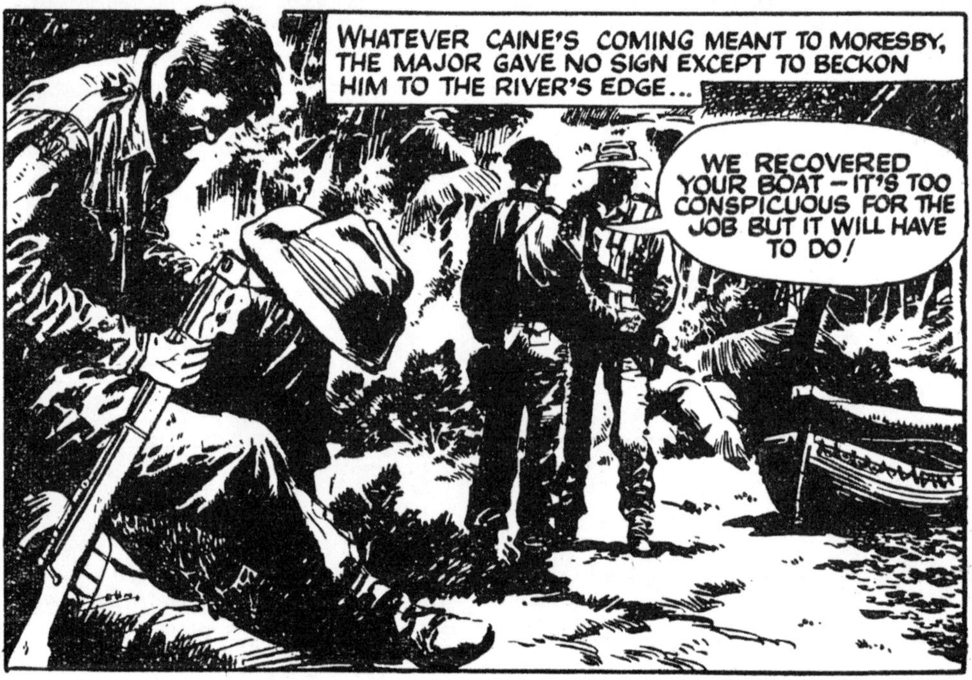
WHATEVER CAINE'S COMING MEANT TO MORESBY, THE MAJOR GAVE NO SIGN EXCEPT TO BECKON HIM TO THE RIVER'S EDGE...
WE RECOVERED YOUR BOAT – IT'S TOO CONSPICUOUS FOR THE JOB BUT IT WILL HAVE TO DO!

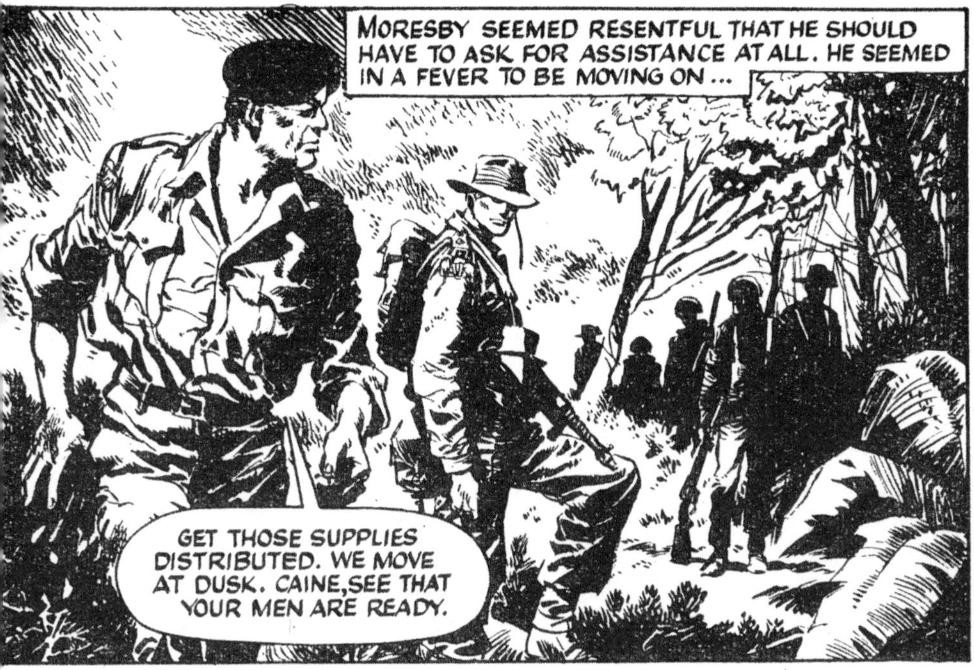
MORESBY SEEMED RESENTFUL THAT HE SHOULD HAVE TO ASK FOR ASSISTANCE AT ALL. HE SEEMED IN A FEVER TO BE MOVING ON...
GET THOSE SUPPLIES DISTRIBUTED. WE MOVE AT DUSK. CAINE, SEE THAT YOUR MEN ARE READY.

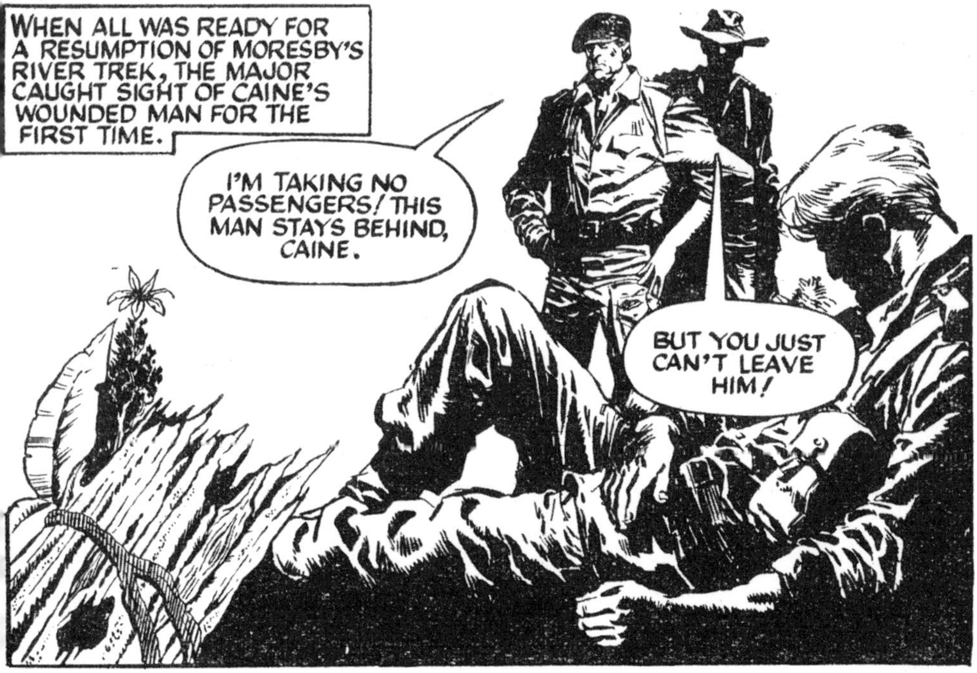
WHEN ALL WAS READY FOR A RESUMPTION OF MORESBY'S RIVER TREK, THE MAJOR CAUGHT SIGHT OF CAINE'S WOUNDED MAN FOR THE FIRST TIME.
I'M TAKING NO PASSENGERS! THIS MAN STAYS BEHIND, CAINE.
BUT YOU JUST CAN'T LEAVE HIM!

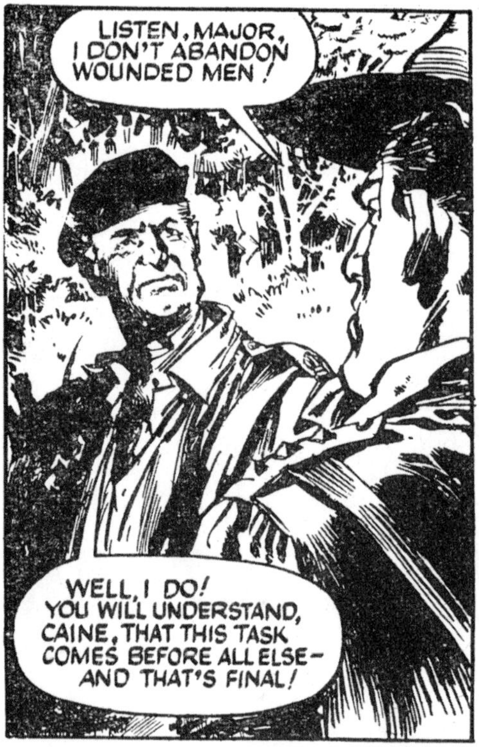
LISTEN, MAJOR, I DON'T ABANDON WOUNDED MEN!
WELL, I DO! YOU WILL UNDERSTAND, CAINE, THAT THIS TASK COMES BEFORE ALL ELSE— AND THAT'S FINAL!

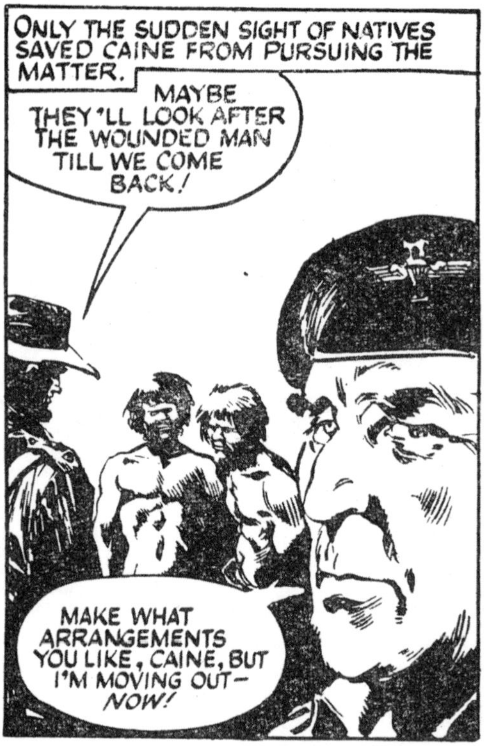
ONLY THE SUDDEN SIGHT OF NATIVES SAVED CAINE FROM PURSUING THE MATTER.
MAYBE THEY'LL LOOK AFTER THE WOUNDED MAN TILL WE COME BACK!
MAKE WHAT ARRANGEMENTS YOU LIKE, CAINE, BUT I'M MOVING OUT— NOW!

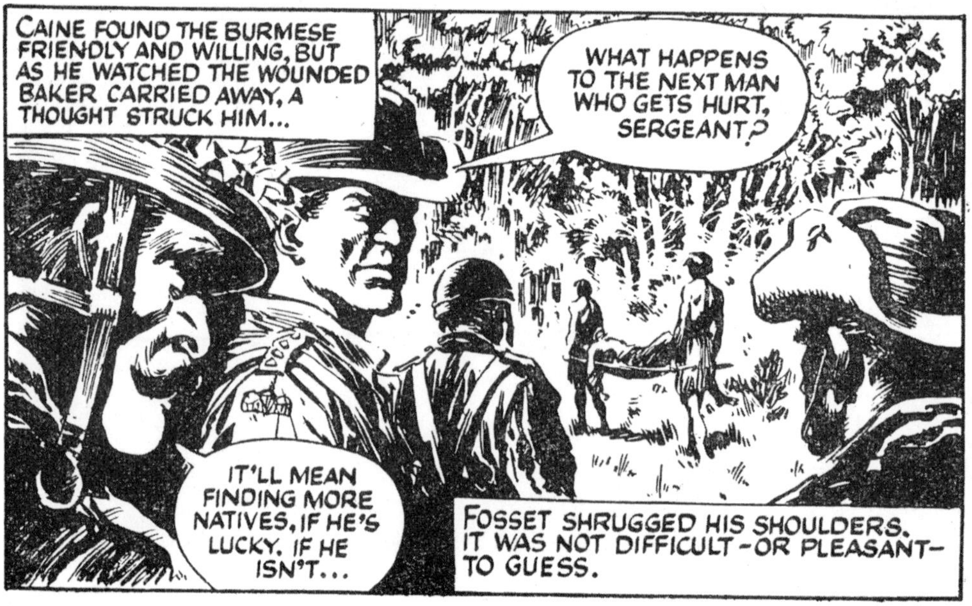
CAINE FOUND THE BURMESE FRIENDLY AND WILLING, BUT AS HE WATCHED THE WOUNDED BAKER CARRIED AWAY, A THOUGHT STRUCK HIM...
WHAT HAPPENS TO THE NEXT MAN WHO GETS HURT, SERGEANT?
IT'LL MEAN FINDING MORE NATIVES, IF HE'S LUCKY. IF HE ISN'T...
FOSSET SHRUGGED HIS SHOULDERS. IT WAS NOT DIFFICULT—OR PLEASANT— TO GUESS.

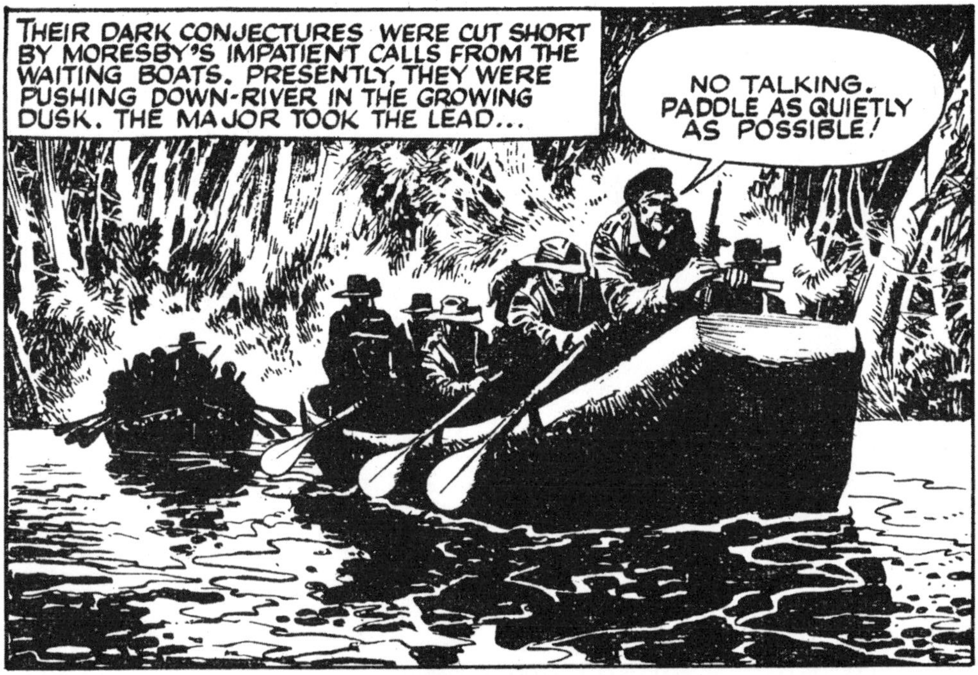
THEIR DARK CONJECTURES WERE CUT SHORT BY MORESBY'S IMPATIENT CALLS FROM THE WAITING BOATS. PRESENTLY, THEY WERE PUSHING DOWN-RIVER IN THE GROWING DUSK. THE MAJOR TOOK THE LEAD...
NO TALKING. PADDLE AS QUIETLY AS POSSIBLE!

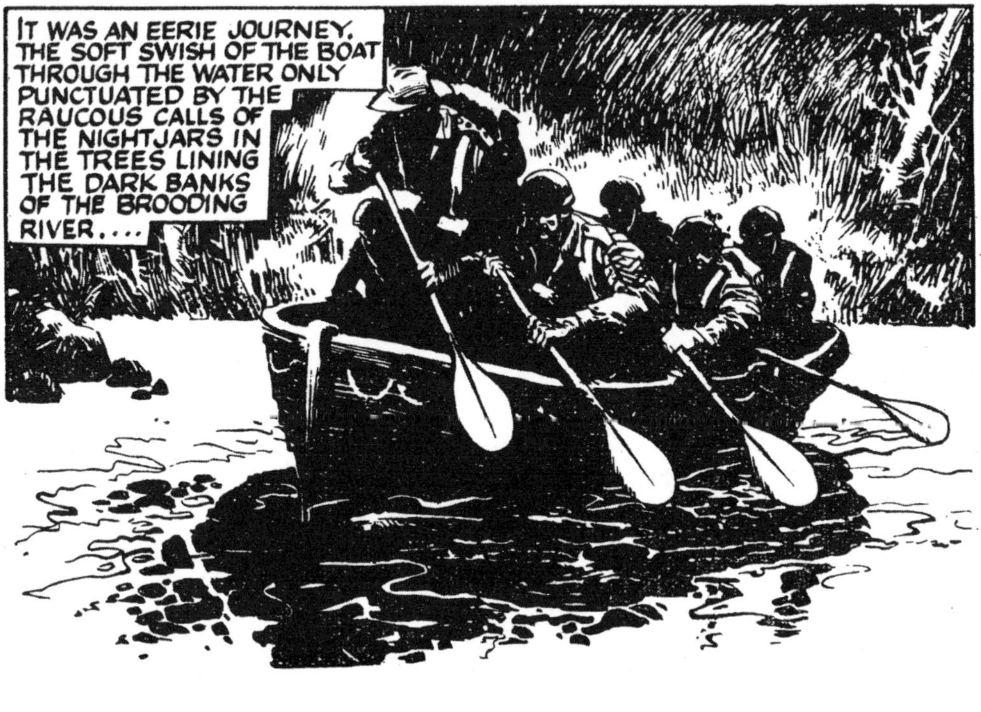
IT WAS AN EERIE JOURNEY. THE SOFT SWISH OF THE BOAT THROUGH THE WATER ONLY PUNCTUATED BY THE RAUCOUS CALLS OF THE NIGHTJARS IN THE TREES LINING THE DARK BANKS OF THE BROODING RIVER....

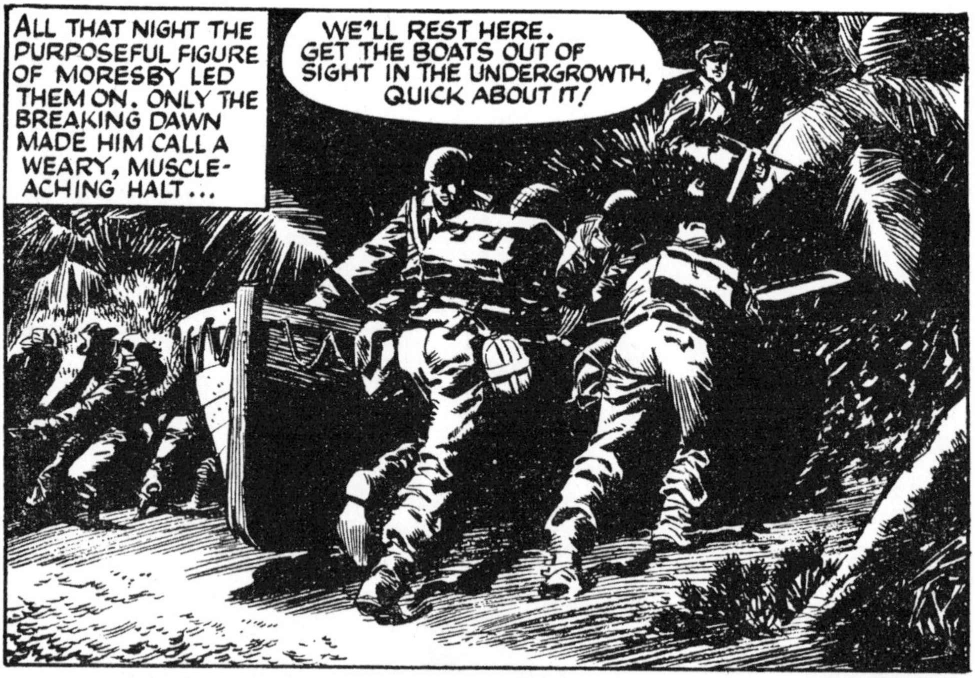
ALL THAT NIGHT THE PURPOSEFUL FIGURE OF MORESBY LED THEM ON. ONLY THE BREAKING DAWN MADE HIM CALL A WEARY, MUSCLE-ACHING HALT...
WE'LL REST HERE. GET THE BOATS OUT OF SIGHT IN THE UNDERGROWTH. QUICK ABOUT IT!

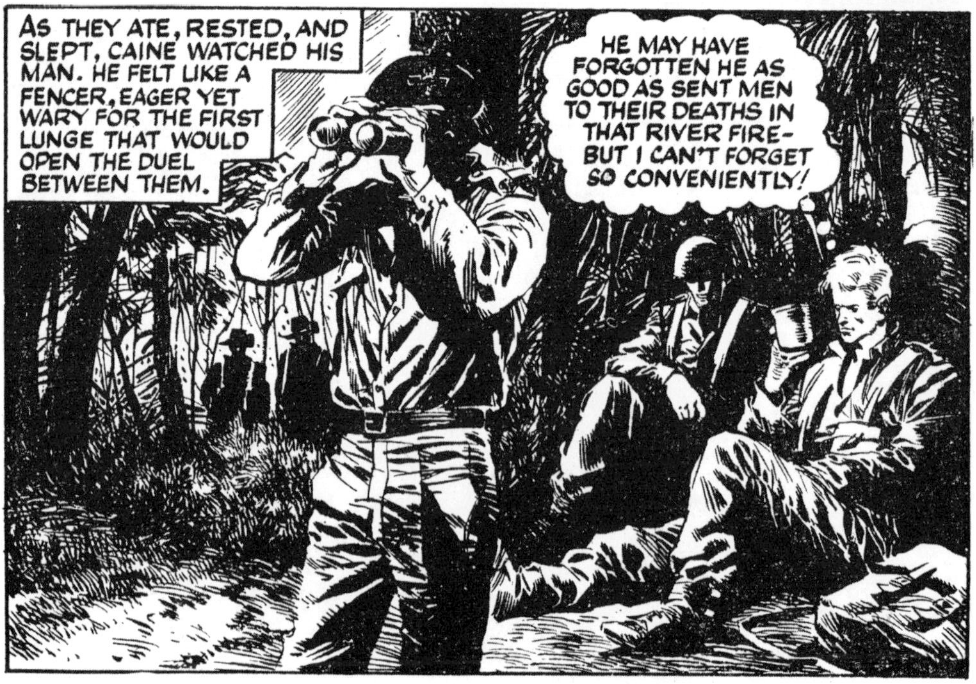
AS THEY ATE, RESTED, AND SLEPT, CAINE WATCHED HIS MAN. HE FELT LIKE A FENCER, EAGER YET WARY FOR THE FIRST LUNGE THAT WOULD OPEN THE DUEL BETWEEN THEM.
HE MAY HAVE FORGOTTEN HE AS GOOD AS SENT MEN TO THEIR DEATHS IN THAT RIVER FIRE- BUT I CAN'T FORGET SO CONVENIENTLY!

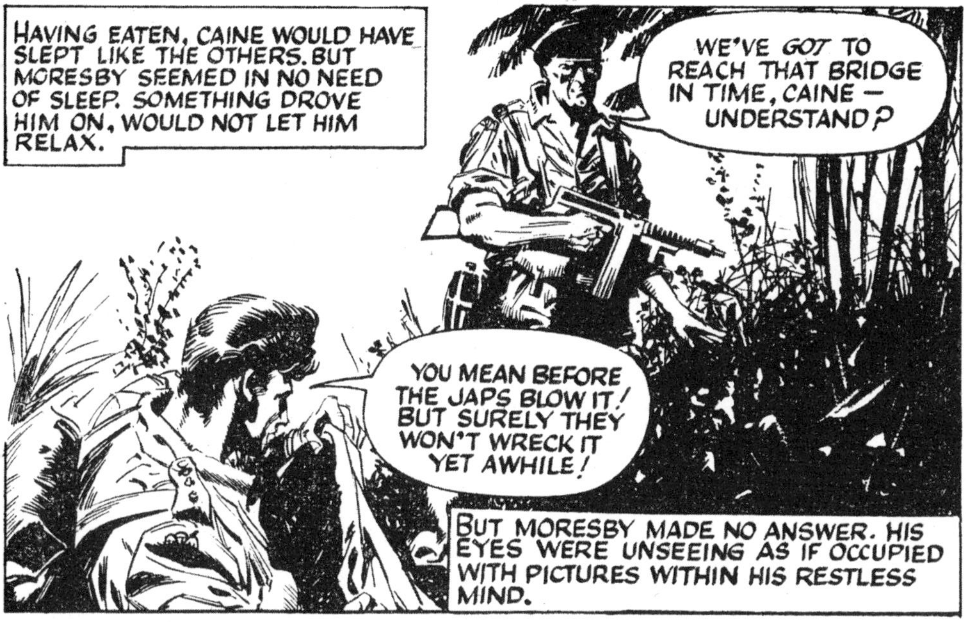
HAVING EATEN, CAINE WOULD HAVE SLEPT LIKE THE OTHERS. BUT MORESBY SEEMED IN NO NEED OF SLEEP. SOMETHING DROVE HIM ON, WOULD NOT LET HIM RELAX.
WE'VE *GOT* TO REACH THAT BRIDGE IN TIME, CAINE — UNDERSTAND?
YOU MEAN BEFORE THE JAPS BLOW IT! BUT SURELY THEY WON'T WRECK IT YET AWHILE!
BUT MORESBY MADE NO ANSWER. HIS EYES WERE UNSEEING AS IF OCCUPIED WITH PICTURES WITHIN HIS RESTLESS MIND.

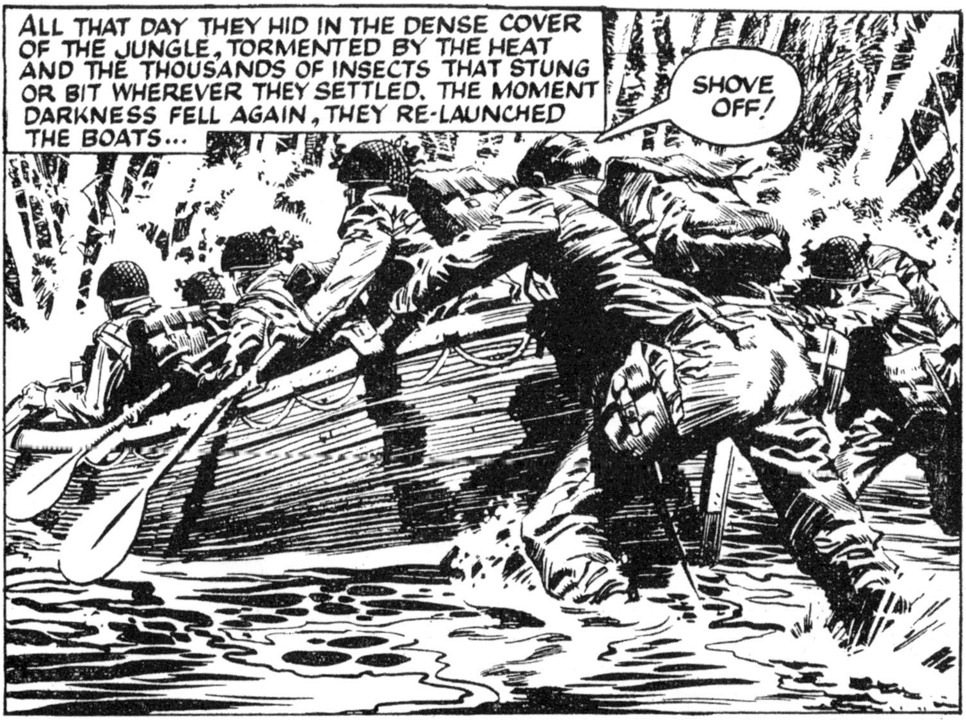
ALL THAT DAY THEY HID IN THE DENSE COVER OF THE JUNGLE, TORMENTED BY THE HEAT AND THE THOUSANDS OF INSECTS THAT STUNG OR BIT WHEREVER THEY SETTLED. THE MOMENT DARKNESS FELL AGAIN, THEY RE-LAUNCHED THE BOATS...
SHOVE OFF!

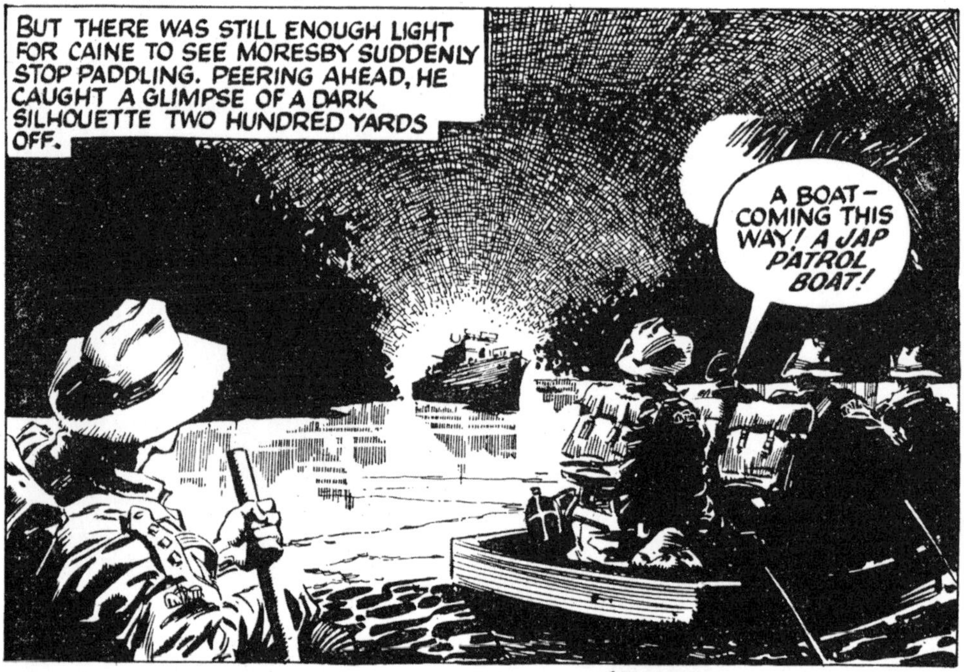
BUT THERE WAS STILL ENOUGH LIGHT FOR CAINE TO SEE MORESBY SUDDENLY STOP PADDLING. PEERING AHEAD, HE CAUGHT A GLIMPSE OF A DARK SILHOUETTE TWO HUNDRED YARDS OFF.
A BOAT— COMING THIS WAY! A JAP PATROL BOAT!

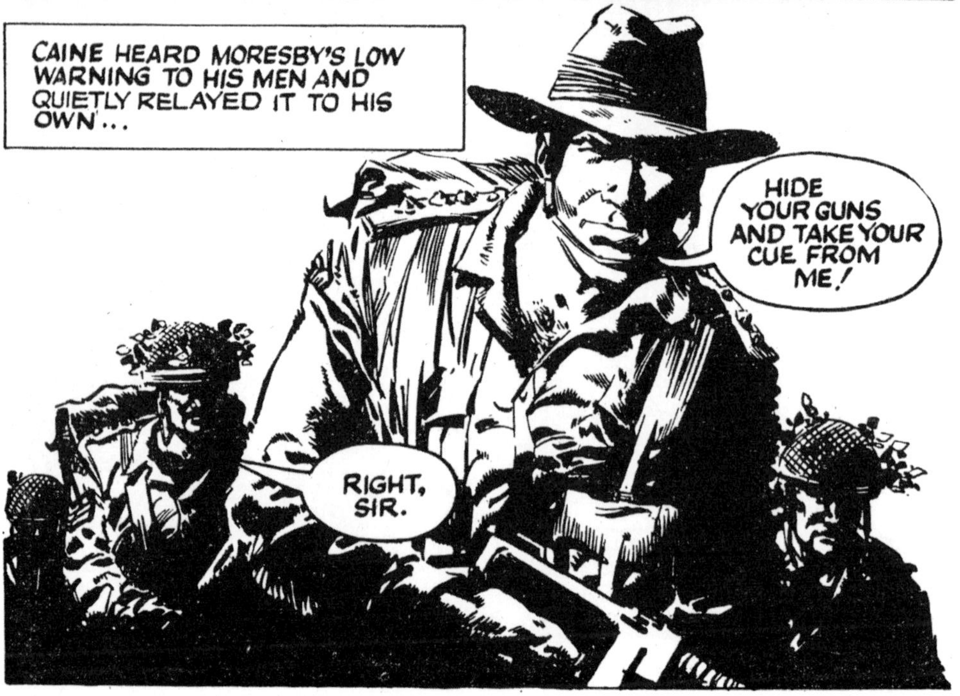
CAINE HEARD MORESBY'S LOW WARNING TO HIS MEN AND QUIETLY RELAYED IT TO HIS OWN...
HIDE YOUR GUNS AND TAKE YOUR CUE FROM ME!
RIGHT, SIR.

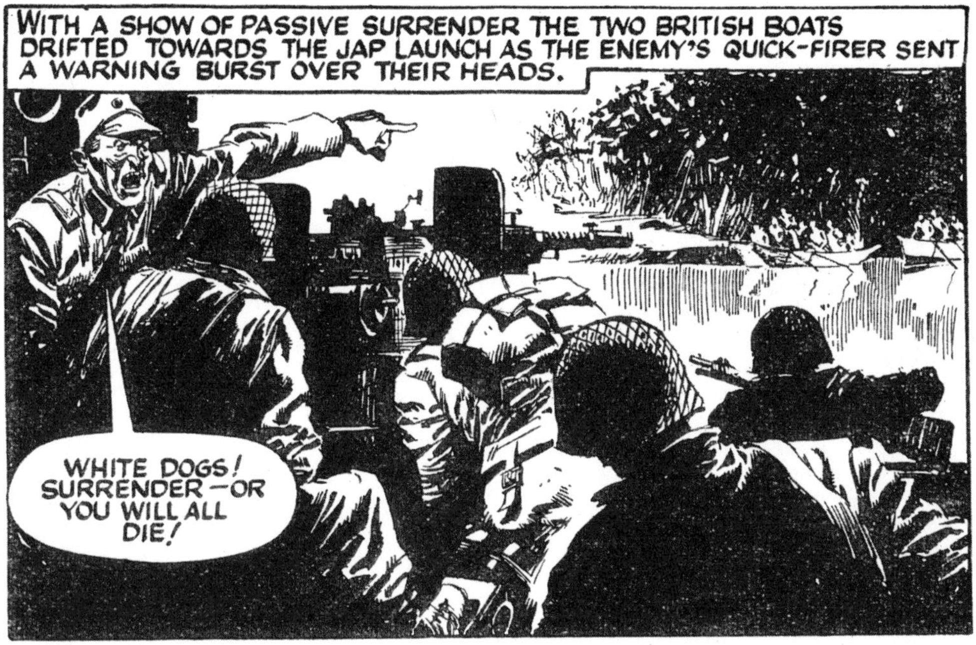
WITH A SHOW OF PASSIVE SURRENDER THE TWO BRITISH BOATS DRIFTED TOWARDS THE JAP LAUNCH AS THE ENEMY'S QUICK-FIRER SENT A WARNING BURST OVER THEIR HEADS.
WHITE DOGS! SURRENDER—OR YOU WILL ALL DIE!

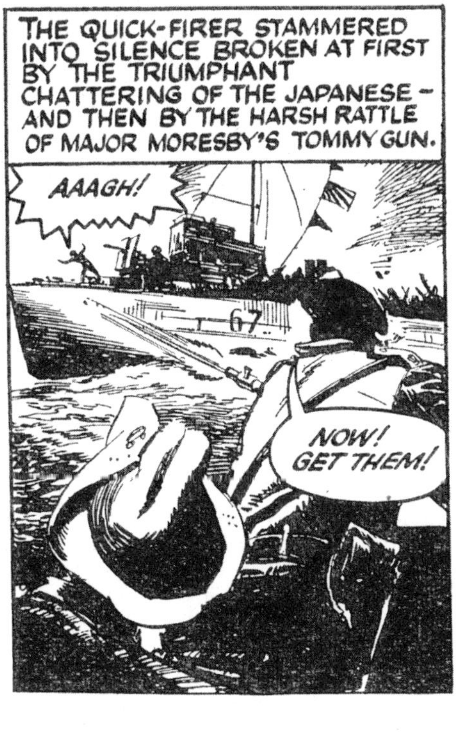
THE QUICK-FIRER STAMMERED INTO SILENCE BROKEN AT FIRST BY THE TRIUMPHANT CHATTERING OF THE JAPANESE—AND THEN BY THE HARSH RATTLE OF MAJOR MORESBY'S TOMMY GUN.
AAAGH!
67
NOW! GET THEM!

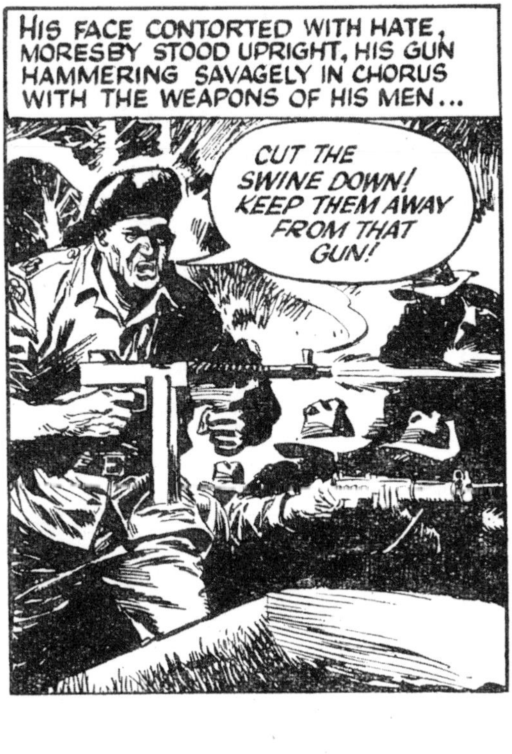
HIS FACE CONTORTED WITH HATE, MORESBY STOOD UPRIGHT, HIS GUN HAMMERING SAVAGELY IN CHORUS WITH THE WEAPONS OF HIS MEN...
CUT THE SWINE DOWN! KEEP THEM AWAY FROM THAT GUN!

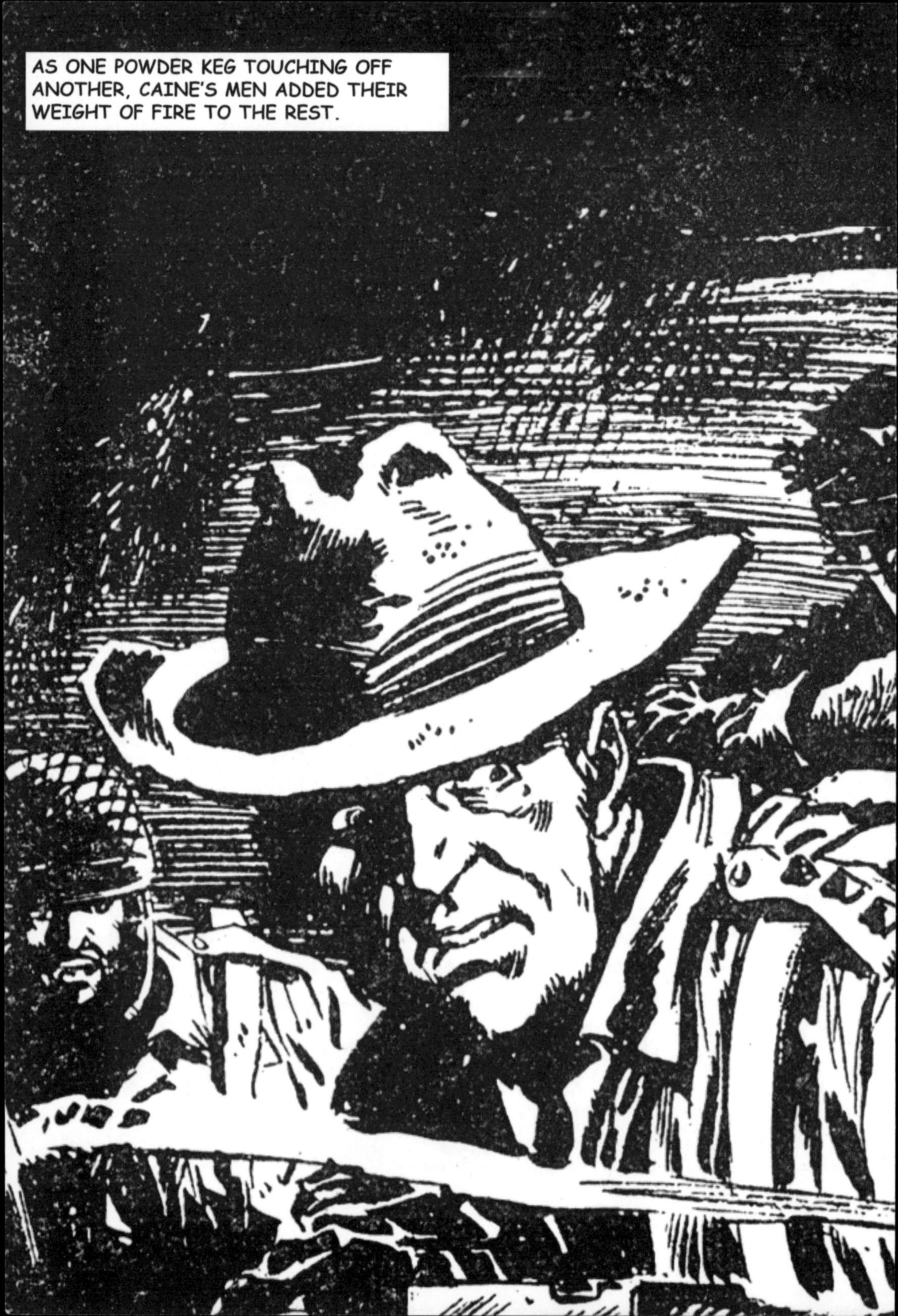
AS ONE POWDER KEG TOUCHING OFF ANOTHER, CAINE'S MEN ADDED THEIR WEIGHT OF FIRE TO THE REST.

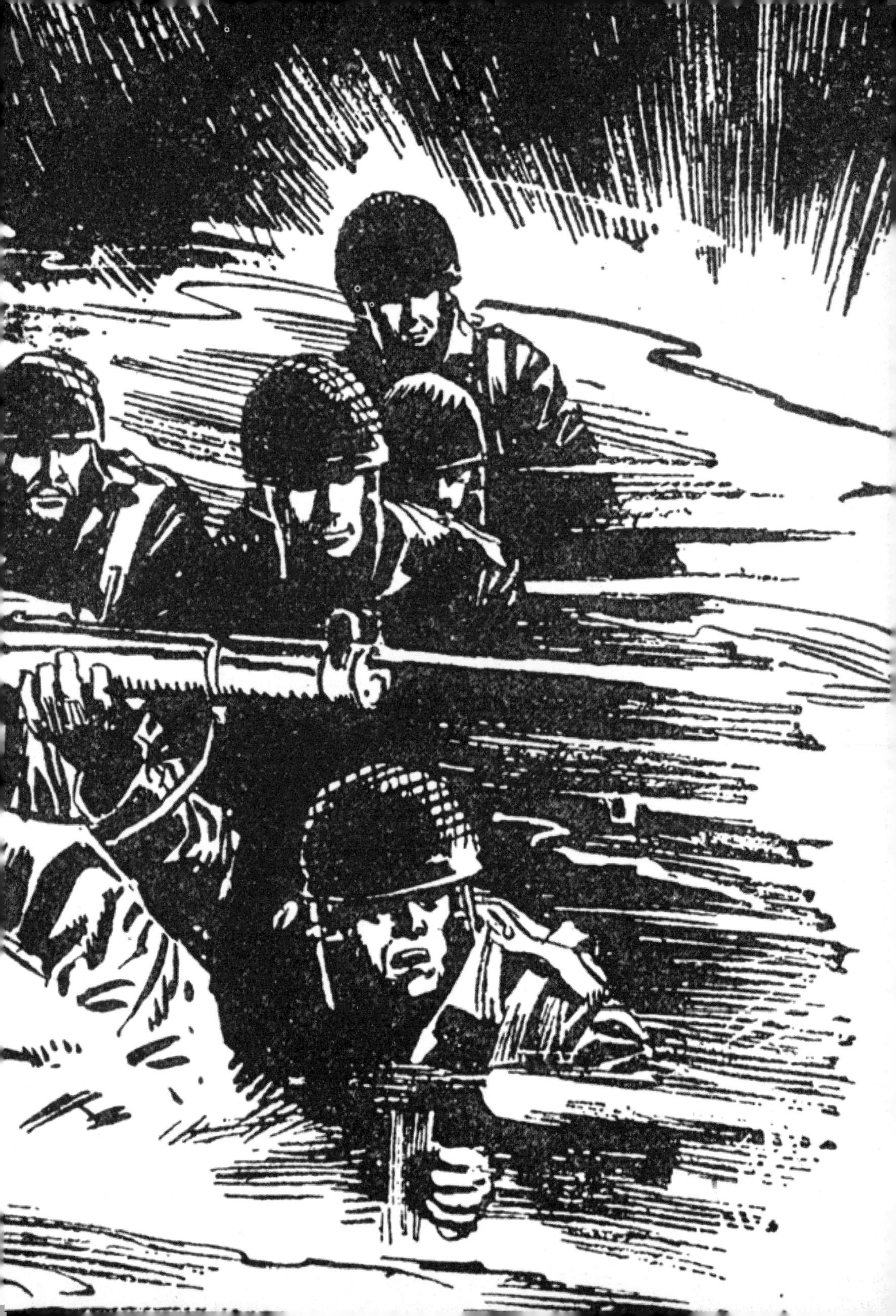

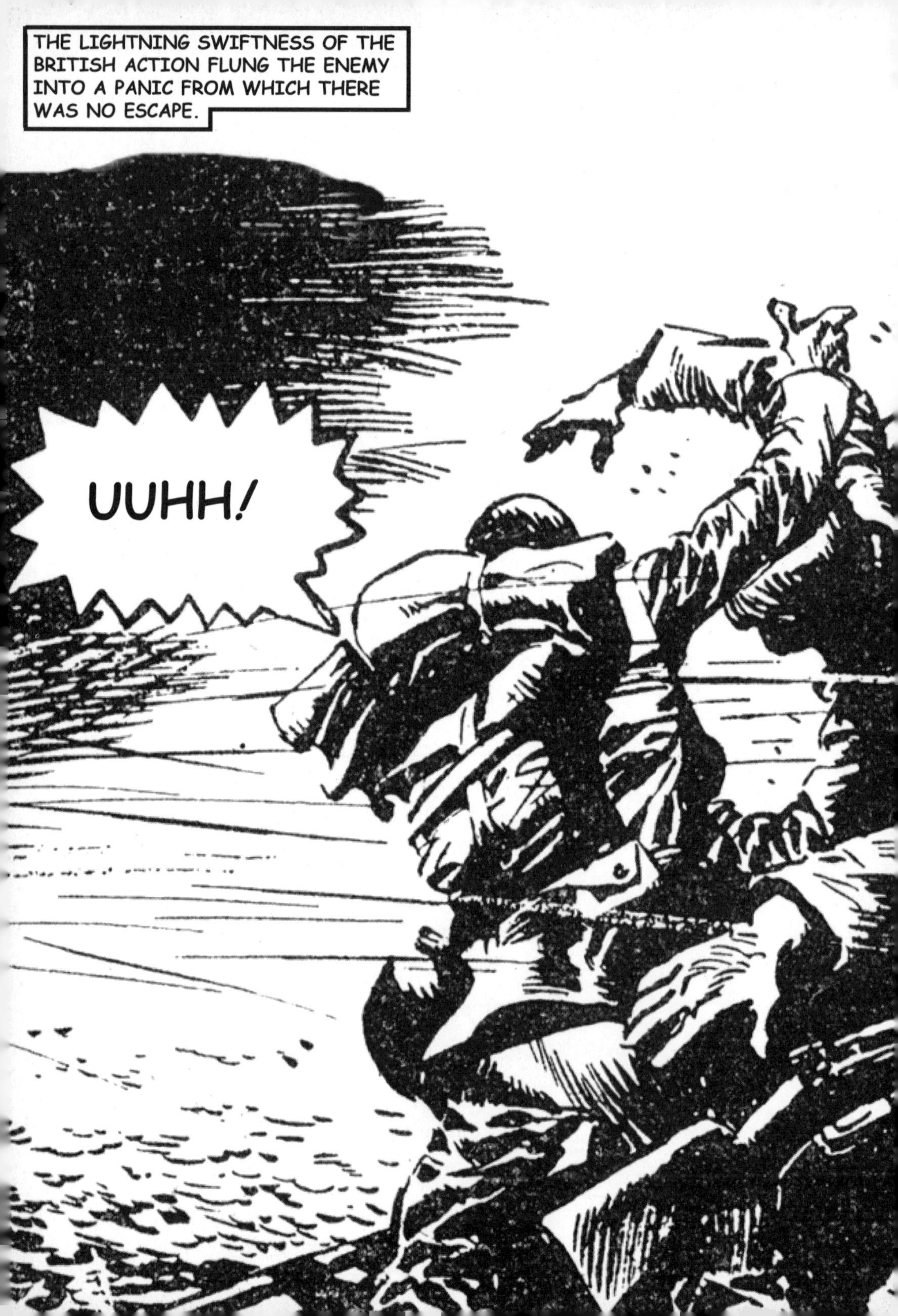
THE LIGHTNING SWIFTNESS OF THE BRITISH ACTION FLUNG THE ENEMY INTO A PANIC FROM WHICH THERE WAS NO ESCAPE.
UUHH!

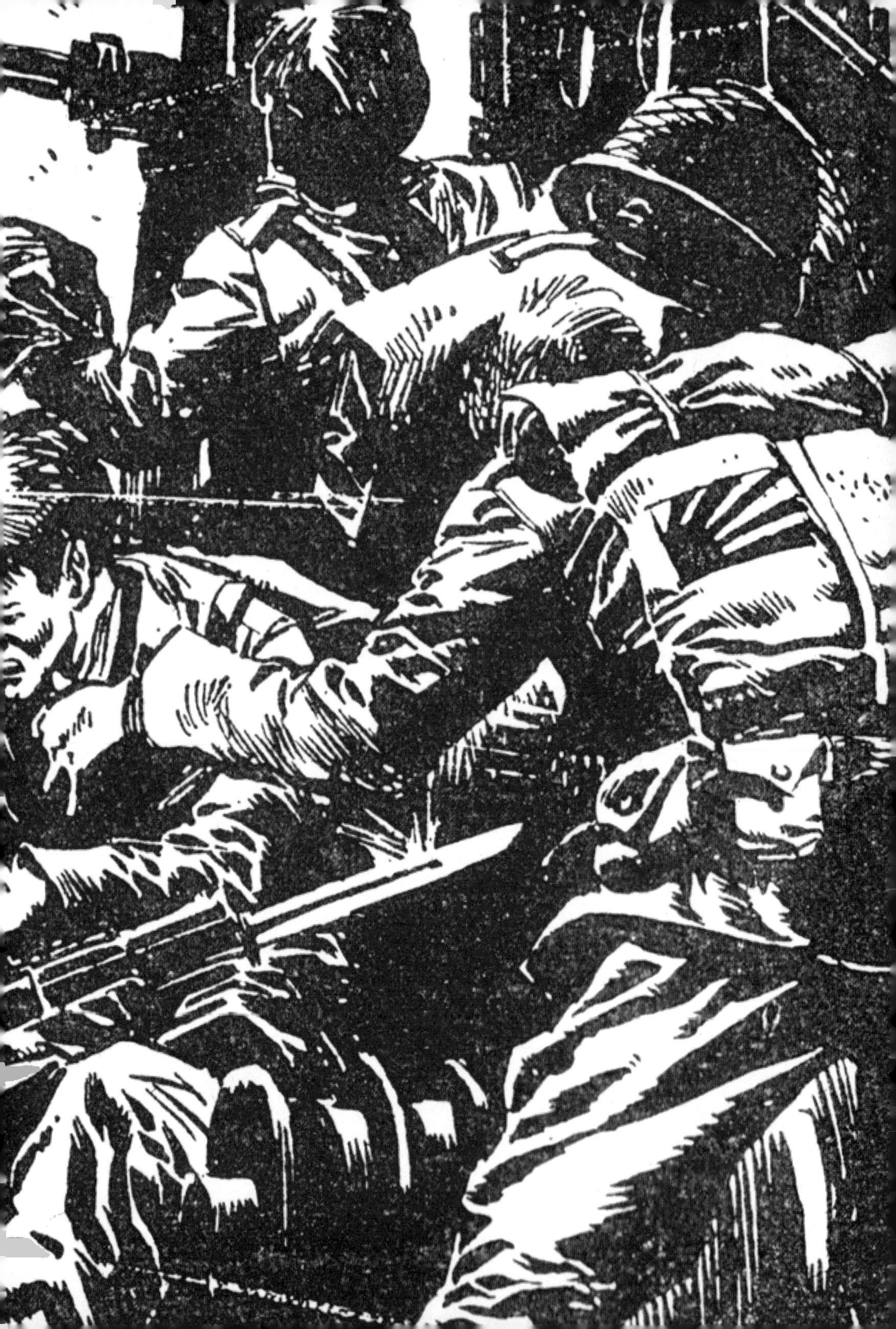

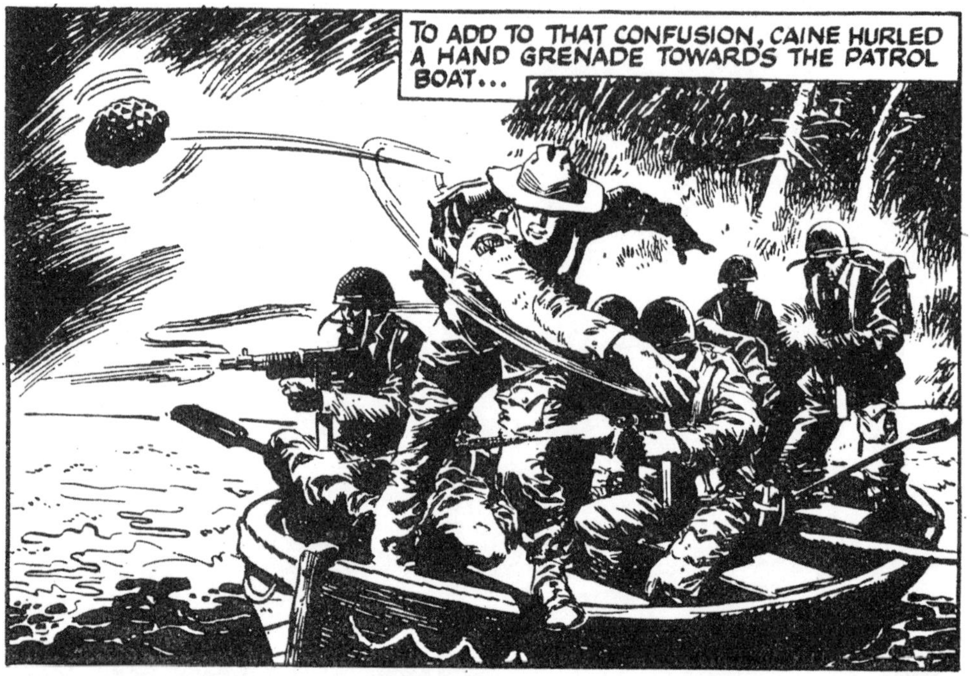
TO ADD TO THAT CONFUSION, CAINE HURLED A HAND GRENADE TOWARDS THE PATROL BOAT...

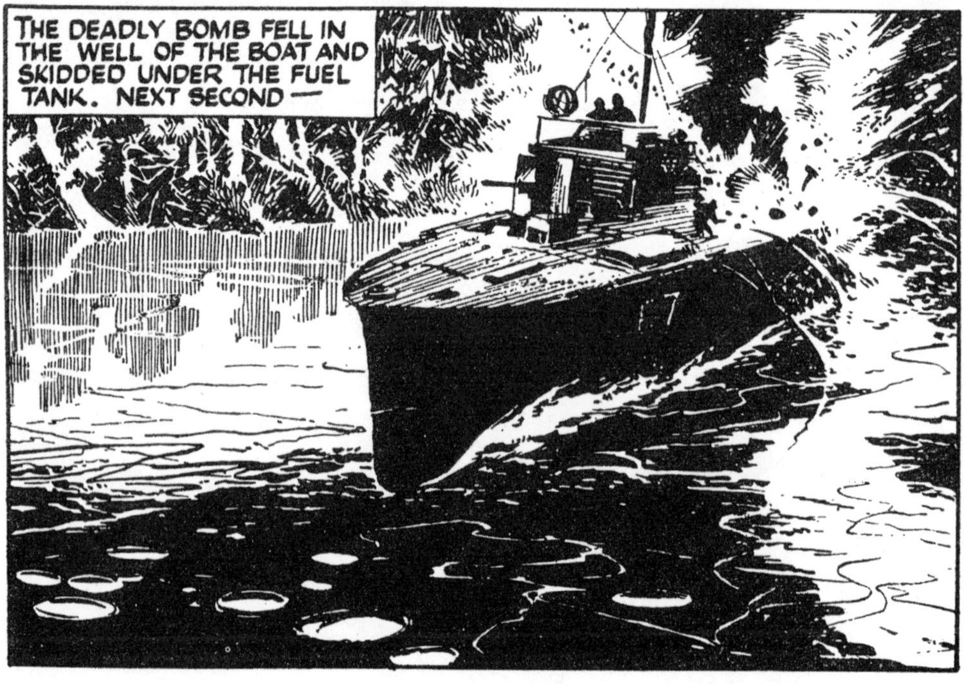
THE DEADLY BOMB FELL IN THE WELL OF THE BOAT AND SKIDDED UNDER THE FUEL TANK. NEXT SECOND —

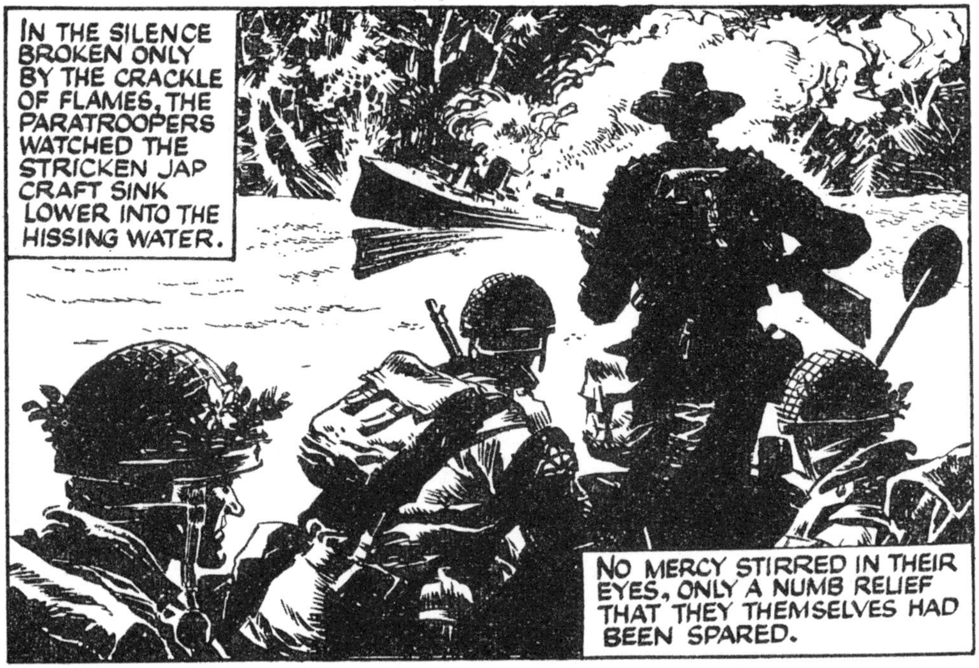
IN THE SILENCE BROKEN ONLY BY THE CRACKLE OF FLAMES, THE PARATROOPERS WATCHED THE STRICKEN JAP CRAFT SINK LOWER INTO THE HISSING WATER.
NO MERCY STIRRED IN THEIR EYES, ONLY A NUMB RELIEF THAT THEY THEMSELVES HAD BEEN SPARED.

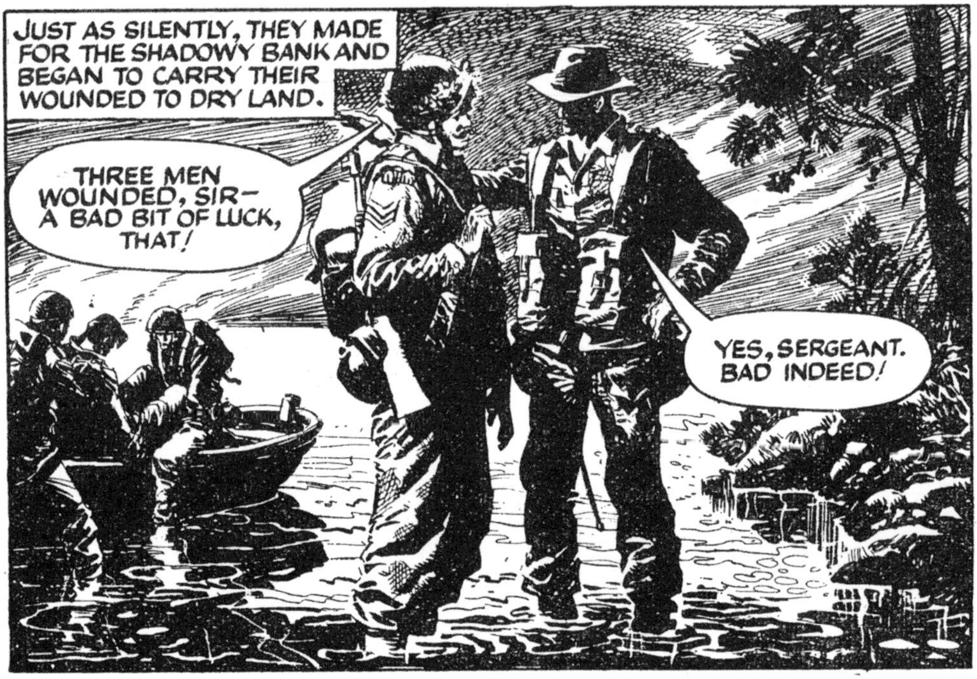
JUST AS SILENTLY, THEY MADE FOR THE SHADOWY BANK AND BEGAN TO CARRY THEIR WOUNDED TO DRY LAND.
THREE MEN WOUNDED, SIR— A BAD BIT OF LUCK, THAT!
YES, SERGEANT. BAD INDEED!

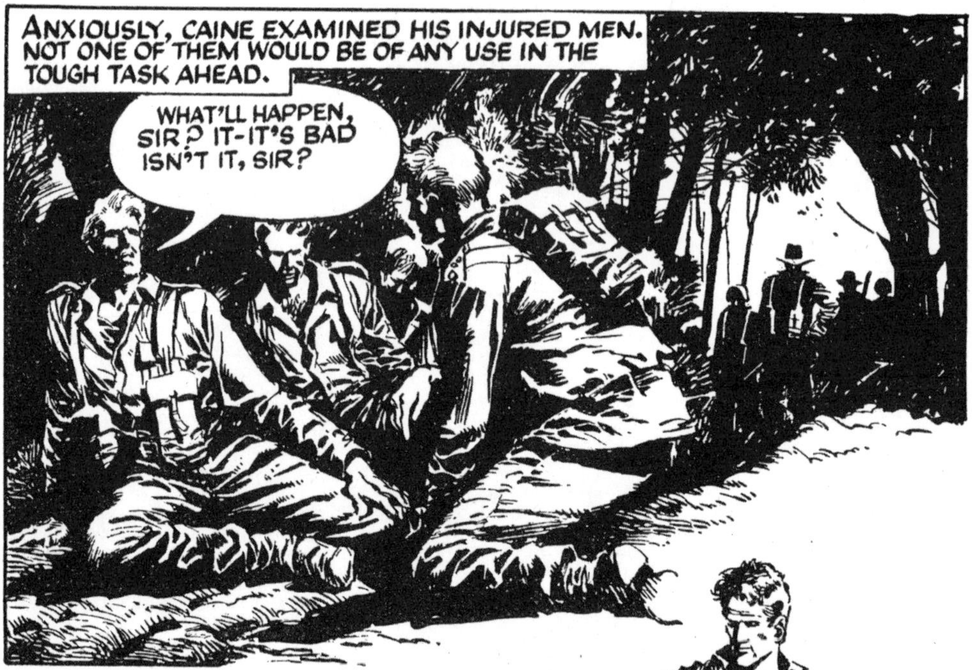
ANXIOUSLY, CAINE EXAMINED HIS INJURED MEN. NOT ONE OF THEM WOULD BE OF ANY USE IN THE TOUGH TASK AHEAD.
WHAT'LL HAPPEN, SIR? IT-IT'S BAD ISN'T IT, SIR?

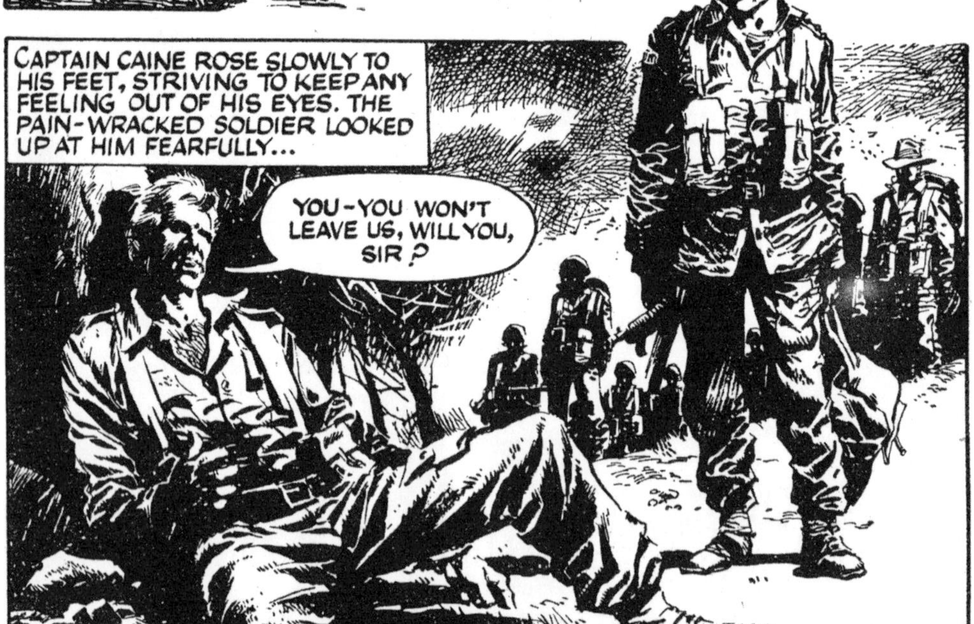
CAPTAIN CAINE ROSE SLOWLY TO HIS FEET, STRIVING TO KEEP ANY FEELING OUT OF HIS EYES. THE PAIN-WRACKED SOLDIER LOOKED UP AT HIM FEARFULLY...
YOU-YOU WON'T LEAVE US, WILL YOU, SIR?

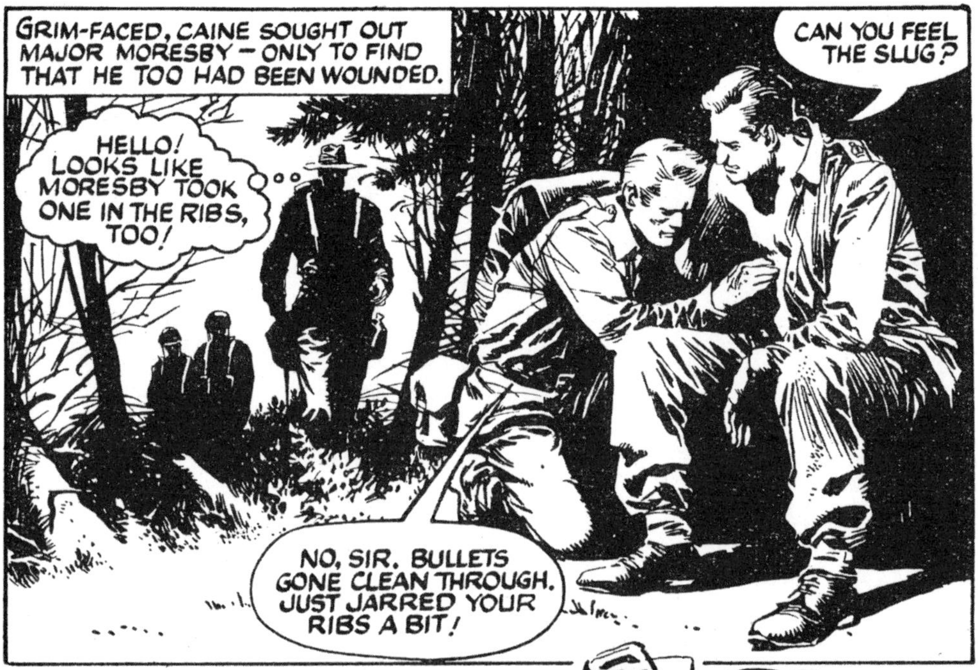
GRIM-FACED, CAINE SOUGHT OUT MAJOR MORESBY — ONLY TO FIND THAT HE TOO HAD BEEN WOUNDED.
CAN YOU FEEL THE SLUG?
HELLO! LOOKS LIKE MORESBY TOOK ONE IN THE RIBS, TOO!
NO, SIR. BULLETS GONE CLEAN THROUGH. JUST JARRED YOUR RIBS A BIT!

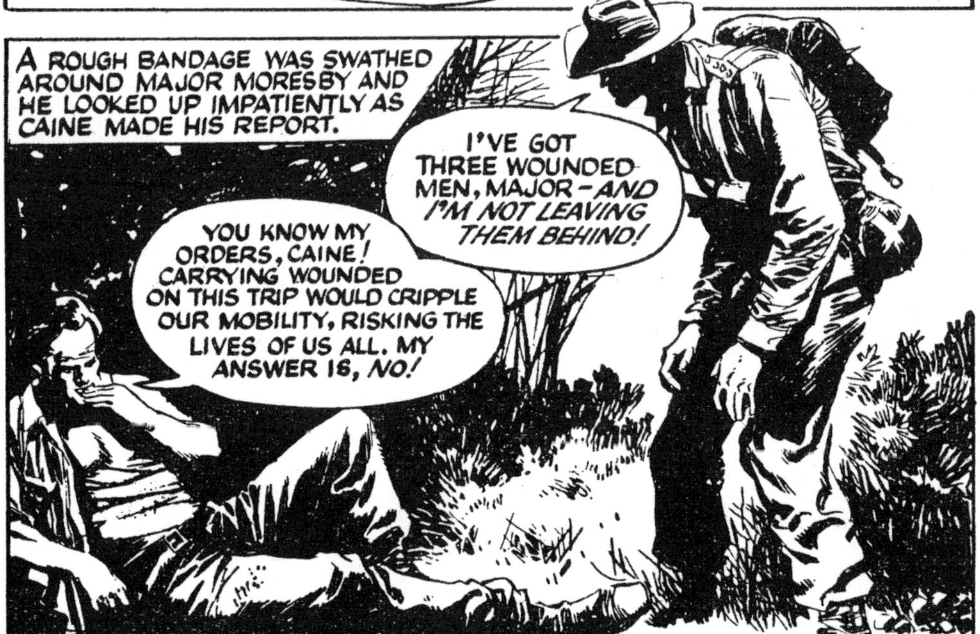
A ROUGH BANDAGE WAS SWATHED AROUND MAJOR MORESBY AND HE LOOKED UP IMPATIENTLY AS CAINE MADE HIS REPORT.
I'VE GOT THREE WOUNDED MEN, MAJOR — *AND I'M NOT LEAVING THEM BEHIND!*
YOU KNOW MY ORDERS, CAINE! CARRYING WOUNDED ON THIS TRIP WOULD CRIPPLE OUR MOBILITY, RISKING THE LIVES OF US ALL. MY ANSWER IS, *NO!*

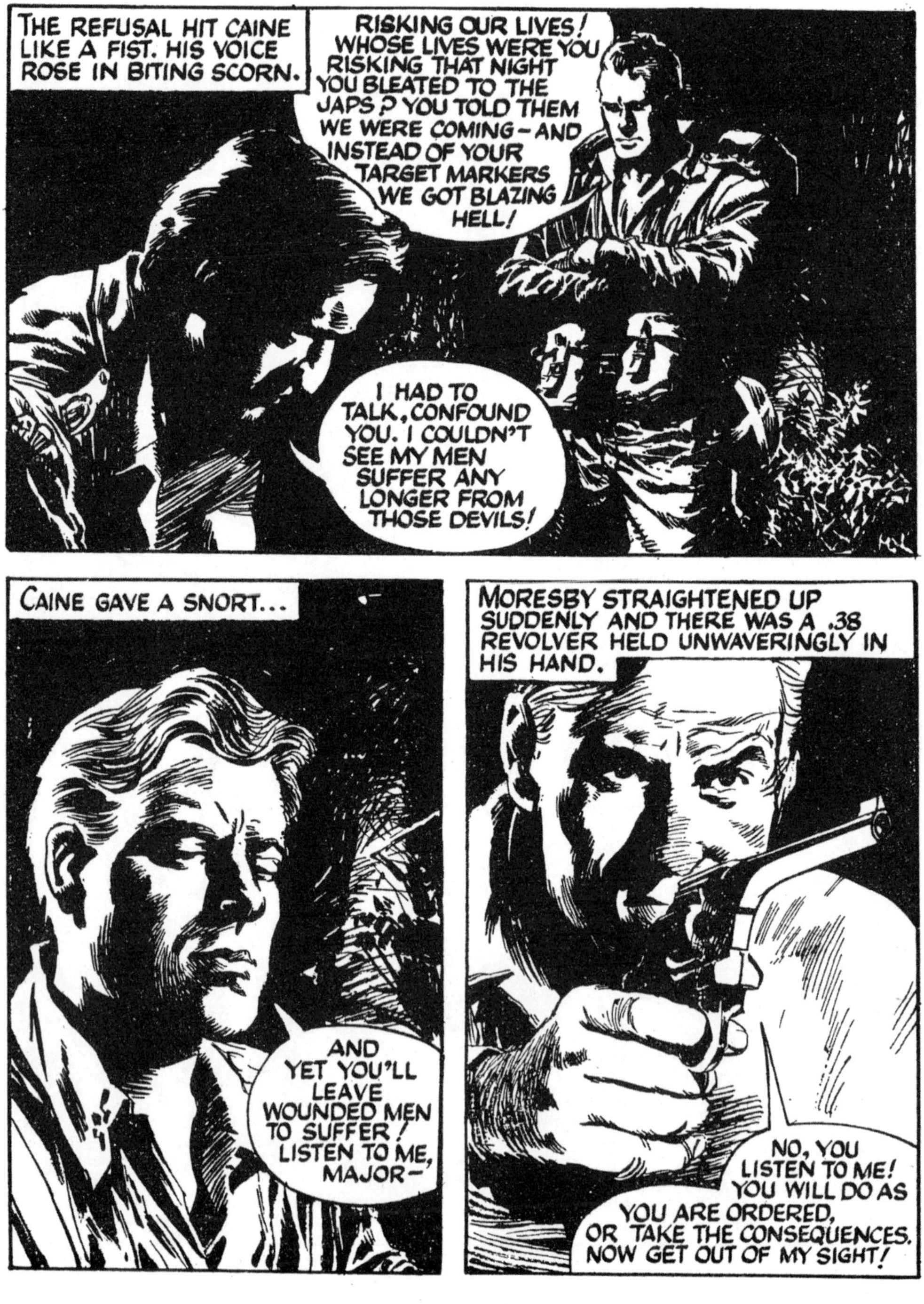
THE REFUSAL HIT CAINE LIKE A FIST. HIS VOICE ROSE IN BITING SCORN.
RISKING OUR LIVES! WHOSE LIVES WERE YOU RISKING THAT NIGHT YOU BLEATED TO THE JAPS? YOU TOLD THEM WE WERE COMING – AND INSTEAD OF YOUR TARGET MARKERS WE GOT BLAZING HELL!
I HAD TO TALK, CONFOUND YOU. I COULDN'T SEE MY MEN SUFFER ANY LONGER FROM THOSE DEVILS!
CAINE GAVE A SNORT...
AND YET YOU'LL LEAVE WOUNDED MEN TO SUFFER! LISTEN TO ME, MAJOR–
MORESBY STRAIGHTENED UP SUDDENLY AND THERE WAS A .38 REVOLVER HELD UNWAVERINGLY IN HIS HAND.
NO, YOU LISTEN TO ME! YOU WILL DO AS YOU ARE ORDERED, OR TAKE THE CONSEQUENCES. NOW GET OUT OF MY SIGHT!

Chapter 3. Victims of Vengeance

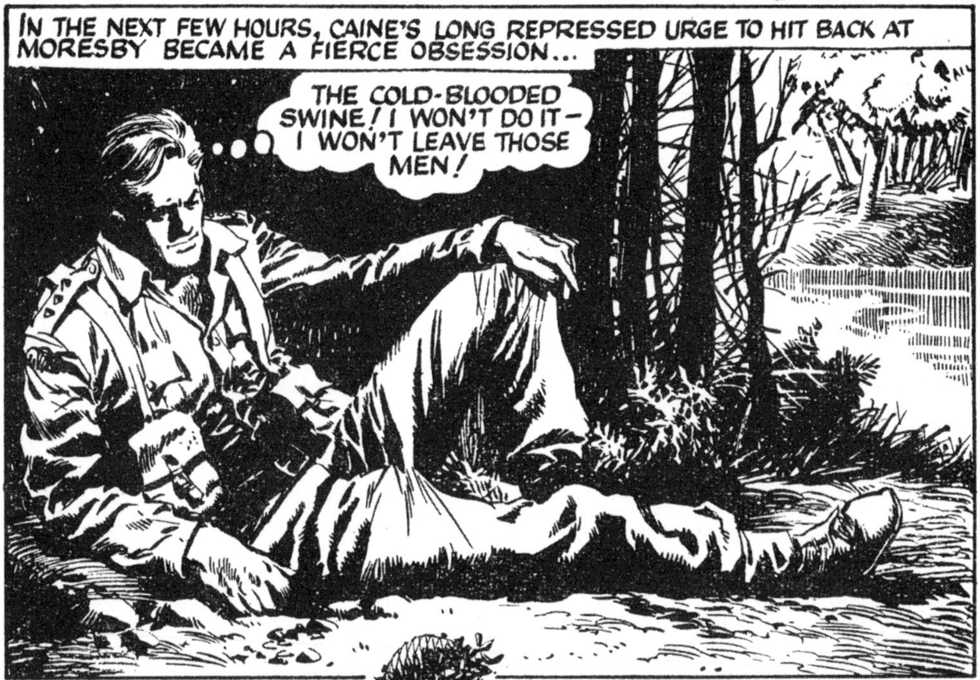
IN THE NEXT FEW HOURS, CAINE'S LONG REPRESSED URGE TO HIT BACK AT MORESBY BECAME A FIERCE OBSESSION...
THE COLD-BLOODED SWINE! I WON'T DO IT– I WON'T LEAVE THOSE MEN!

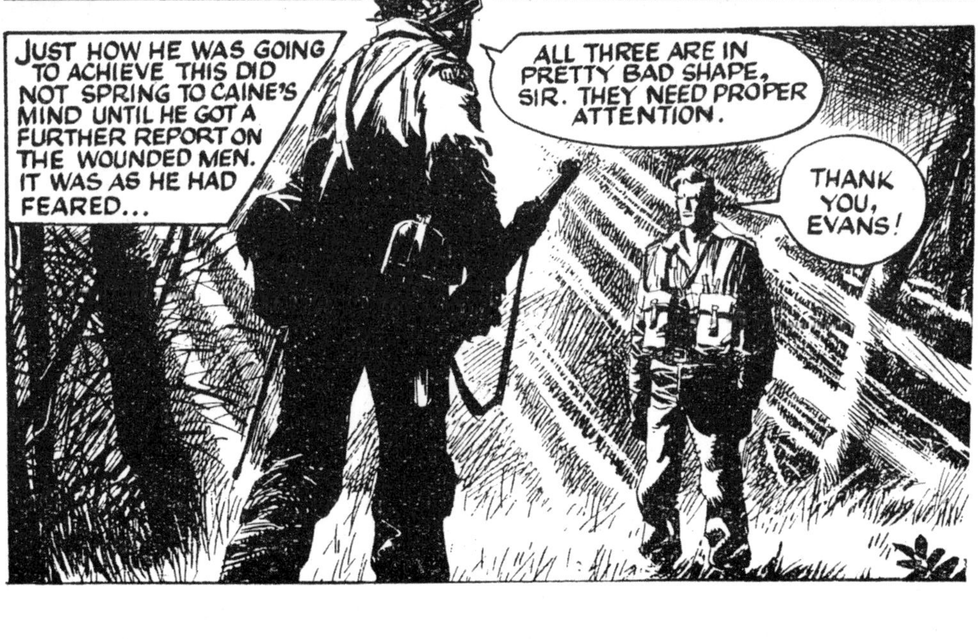
JUST HOW HE WAS GOING TO ACHIEVE THIS DID NOT SPRING TO CAINE'S MIND UNTIL HE GOT A FURTHER REPORT ON THE WOUNDED MEN. IT WAS AS HE HAD FEARED...
ALL THREE ARE IN PRETTY BAD SHAPE, SIR. THEY NEED PROPER ATTENTION.
THANK YOU, EVANS!

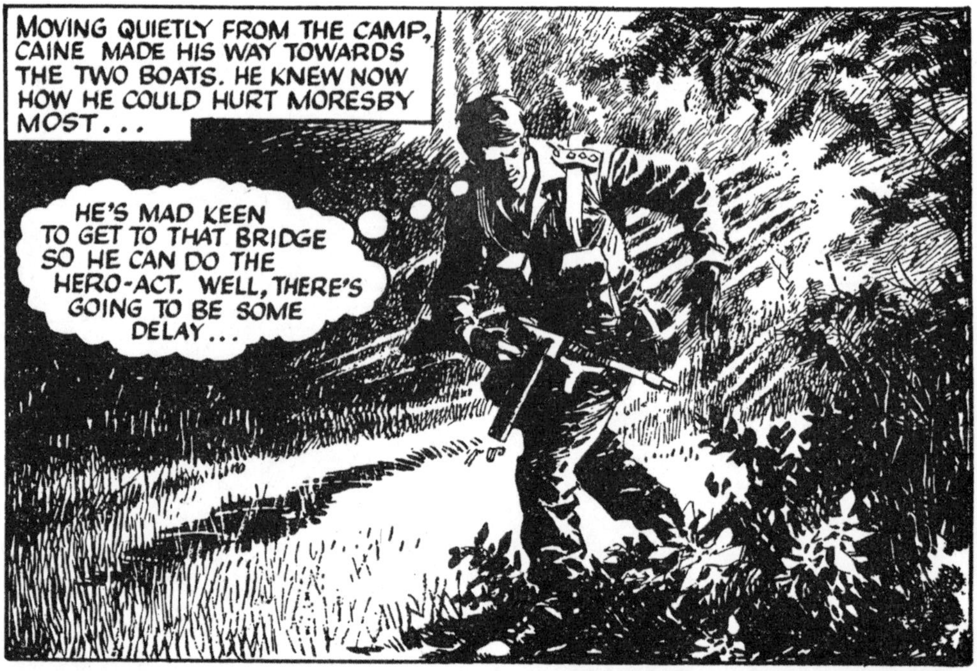
MOVING QUIETLY FROM THE CAMP, CAINE MADE HIS WAY TOWARDS THE TWO BOATS. HE KNEW NOW HOW HE COULD HURT MORESBY MOST...
HE'S MAD KEEN TO GET TO THAT BRIDGE SO HE CAN DO THE HERO-ACT. WELL, THERE'S GOING TO BE SOME DELAY...

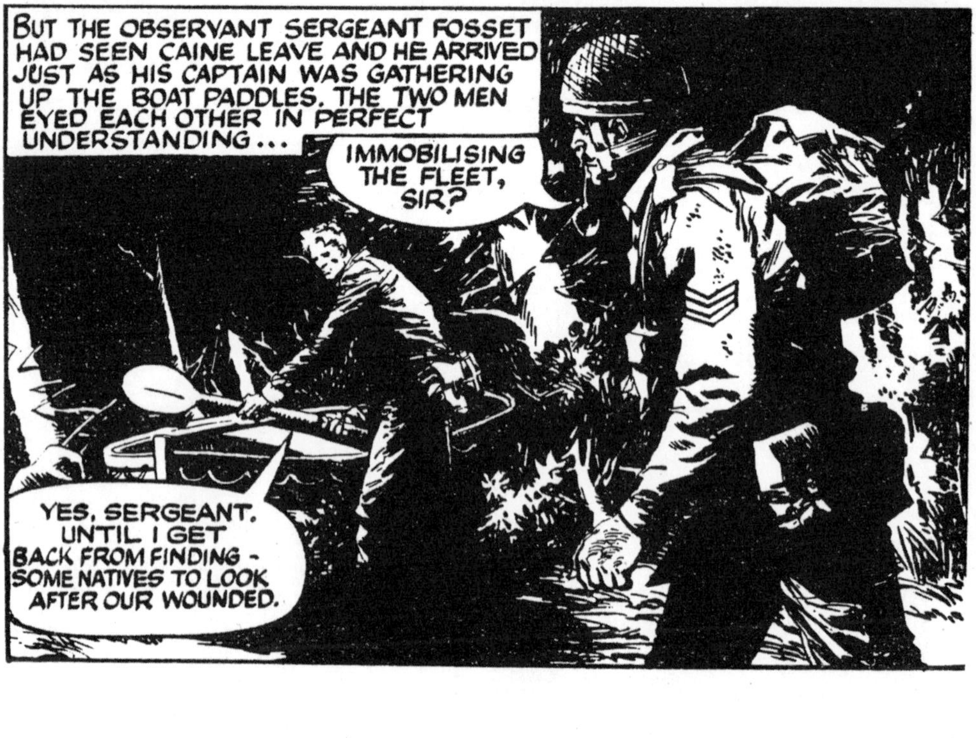
BUT THE OBSERVANT SERGEANT FOSSET HAD SEEN CAINE LEAVE AND HE ARRIVED JUST AS HIS CAPTAIN WAS GATHERING UP THE BOAT PADDLES. THE TWO MEN EYED EACH OTHER IN PERFECT UNDERSTANDING...
IMMOBILISING THE FLEET, SIR?
YES, SERGEANT. UNTIL I GET BACK FROM FINDING - SOME NATIVES TO LOOK AFTER OUR WOUNDED.

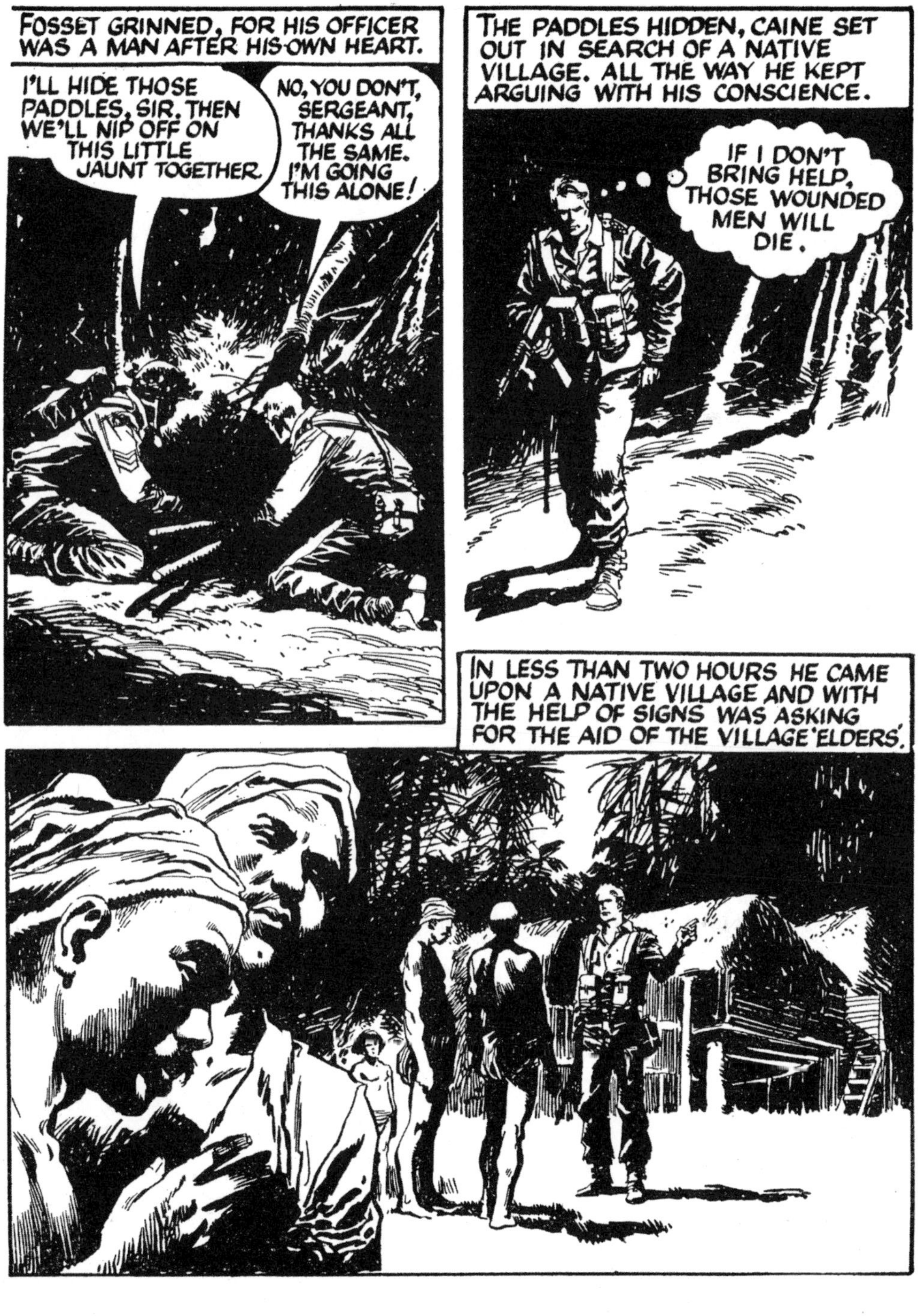
FOSSET GRINNED, FOR HIS OFFICER WAS A MAN AFTER HIS OWN HEART.
I'LL HIDE THOSE PADDLES, SIR. THEN WE'LL NIP OFF ON THIS LITTLE JAUNT TOGETHER.
NO, YOU DON'T, SERGEANT, THANKS ALL THE SAME. I'M GOING THIS ALONE!
THE PADDLES HIDDEN, CAINE SET OUT IN SEARCH OF A NATIVE VILLAGE. ALL THE WAY HE KEPT ARGUING WITH HIS CONSCIENCE.
IF I DON'T BRING HELP, THOSE WOUNDED MEN WILL DIE.
IN LESS THAN TWO HOURS HE CAME UPON A NATIVE VILLAGE AND WITH THE HELP OF SIGNS WAS ASKING FOR THE AID OF THE VILLAGE 'ELDERS'.

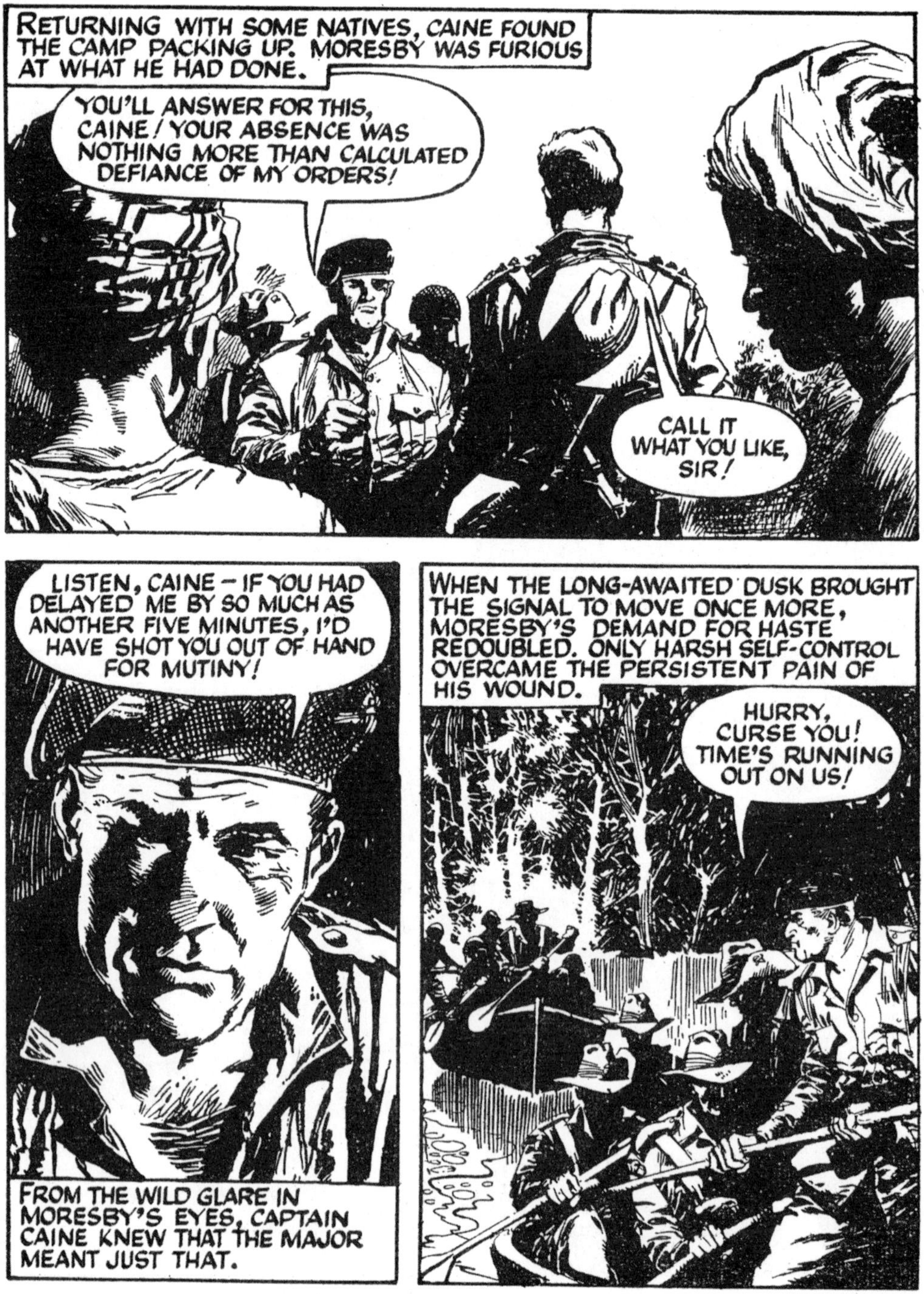
RETURNING WITH SOME NATIVES, CAINE FOUND THE CAMP PACKING UP. MORESBY WAS FURIOUS AT WHAT HE HAD DONE.
YOU'LL ANSWER FOR THIS, CAINE! YOUR ABSENCE WAS NOTHING MORE THAN CALCULATED DEFIANCE OF MY ORDERS!
CALL IT WHAT YOU LIKE, SIR!
LISTEN, CAINE – IF YOU HAD DELAYED ME BY SO MUCH AS ANOTHER FIVE MINUTES, I'D HAVE SHOT YOU OUT OF HAND FOR MUTINY!
FROM THE WILD GLARE IN MORESBY'S EYES, CAPTAIN CAINE KNEW THAT THE MAJOR MEANT JUST THAT.
WHEN THE LONG-AWAITED DUSK BROUGHT THE SIGNAL TO MOVE ONCE MORE, MORESBY'S DEMAND FOR HASTE REDOUBLED. ONLY HARSH SELF-CONTROL OVERCAME THE PERSISTENT PAIN OF HIS WOUND.
HURRY, CURSE YOU! TIME'S RUNNING OUT ON US!

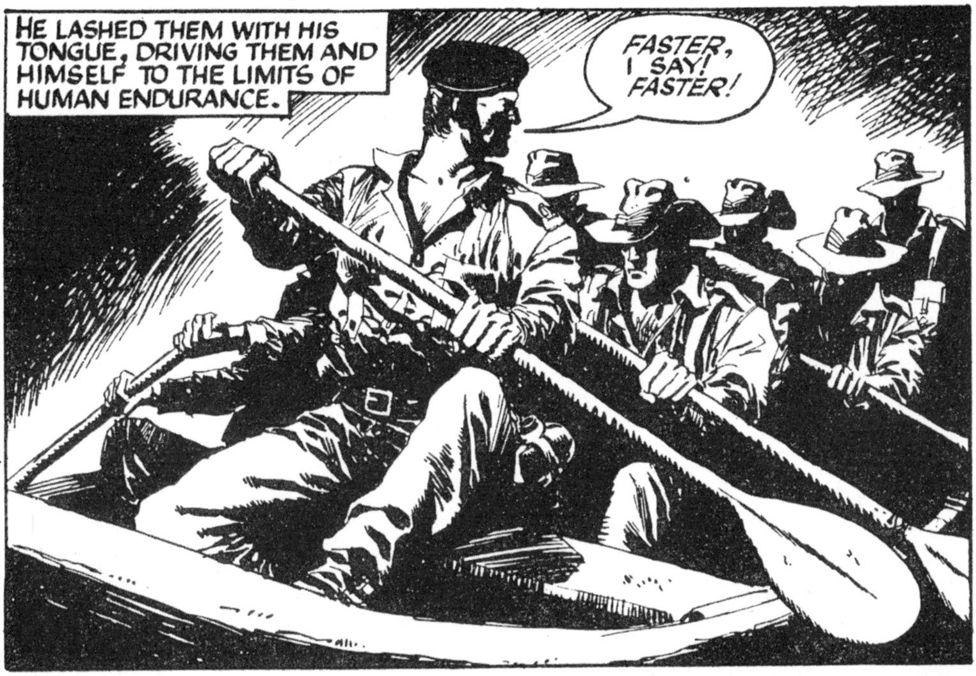
HE LASHED THEM WITH HIS TONGUE, DRIVING THEM AND HIMSELF TO THE LIMITS OF HUMAN ENDURANCE.
FASTER, I SAY! FASTER!

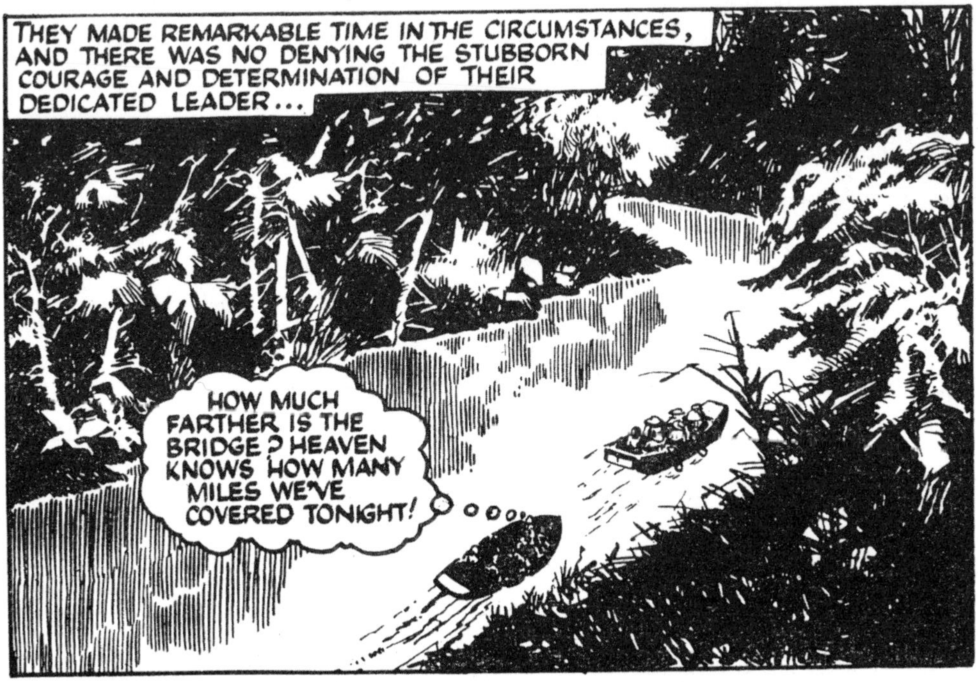
THEY MADE REMARKABLE TIME IN THE CIRCUMSTANCES, AND THERE WAS NO DENYING THE STUBBORN COURAGE AND DETERMINATION OF THEIR DEDICATED LEADER...
HOW MUCH FARTHER IS THE BRIDGE? HEAVEN KNOWS HOW MANY MILES WE'VE COVERED TONIGHT!

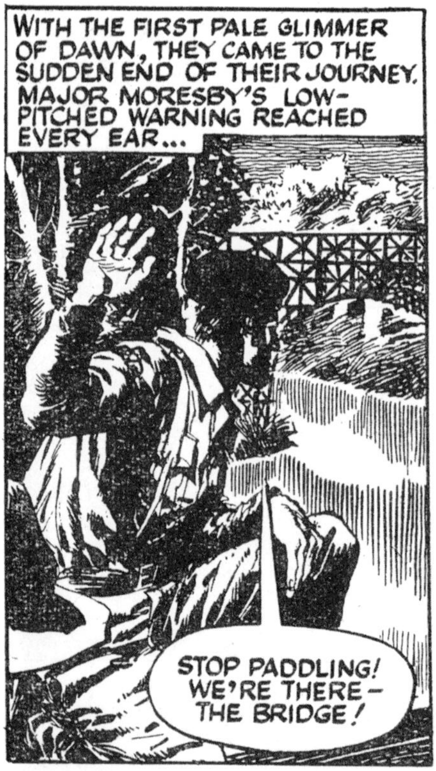
WITH THE FIRST PALE GLIMMER OF DAWN, THEY CAME TO THE SUDDEN END OF THEIR JOURNEY. MAJOR MORESBY'S LOW-PITCHED WARNING REACHED EVERY EAR...
STOP PADDLING! WE'RE THERE – THE BRIDGE!

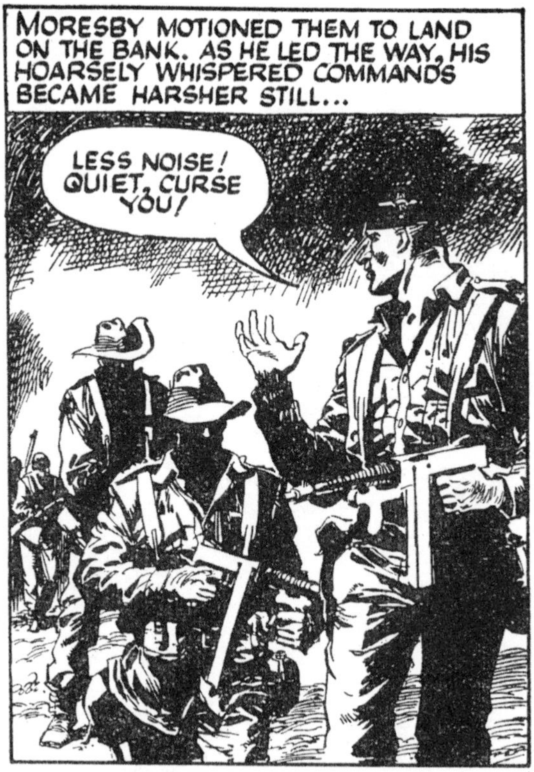
MORESBY MOTIONED THEM TO LAND ON THE BANK. AS HE LED THE WAY, HIS HOARSELY WHISPERED COMMANDS BECAME HARSHER STILL...
LESS NOISE! QUIET, CURSE YOU!

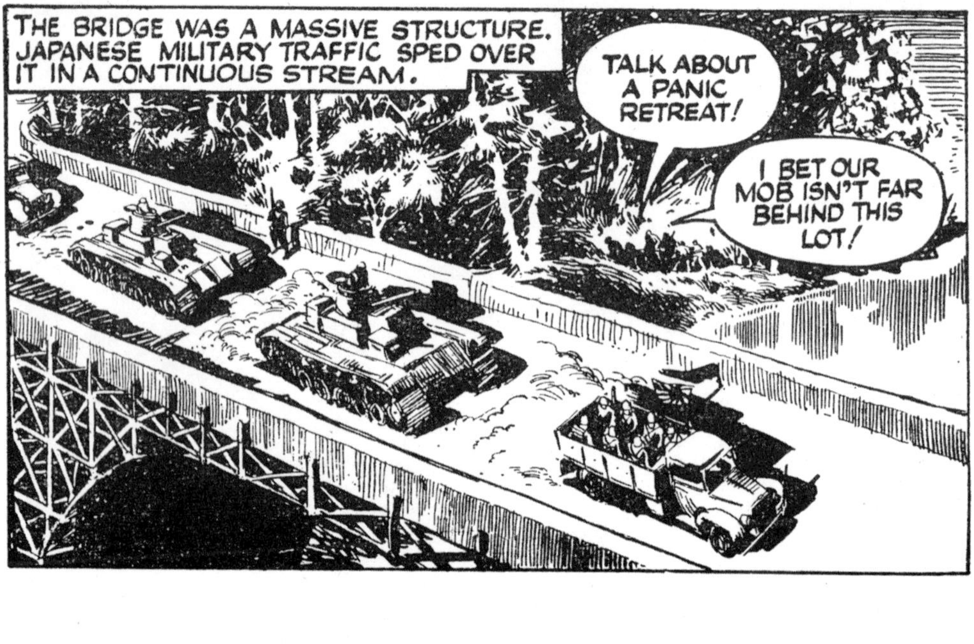
THE BRIDGE WAS A MASSIVE STRUCTURE. JAPANESE MILITARY TRAFFIC SPED OVER IT IN A CONTINUOUS STREAM.
TALK ABOUT A PANIC RETREAT!
I BET OUR MOB ISN'T FAR BEHIND THIS LOT!

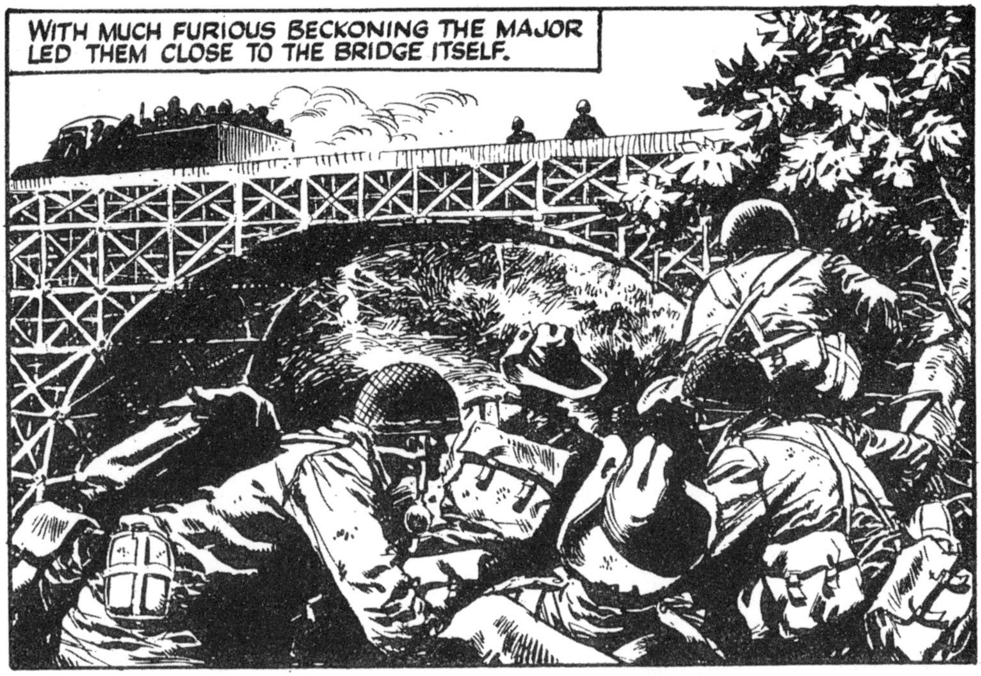
WITH MUCH FURIOUS BECKONING THE MAJOR LED THEM CLOSE TO THE BRIDGE ITSELF.

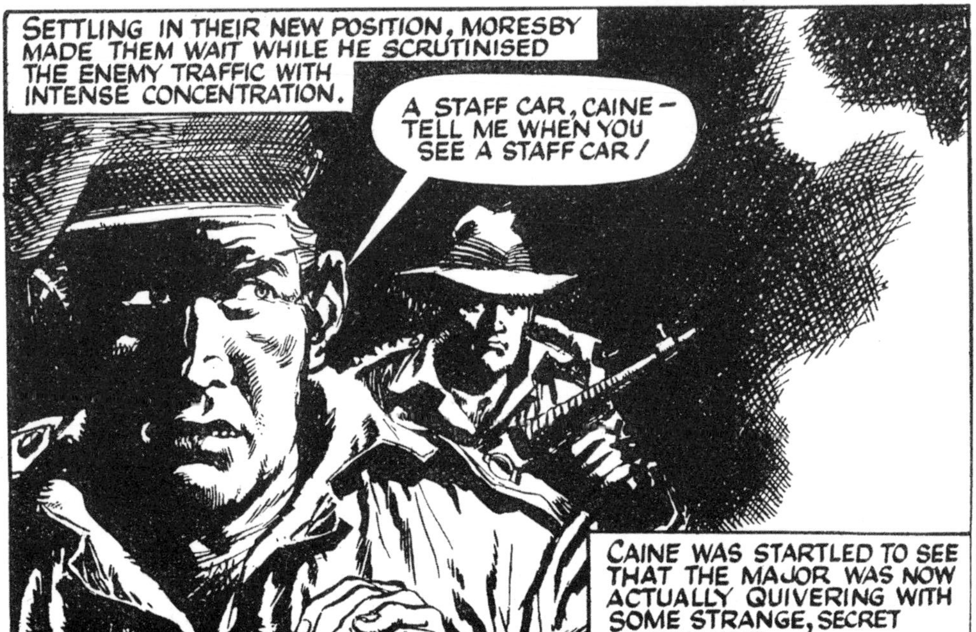
SETTLING IN THEIR NEW POSITION, MORESBY MADE THEM WAIT WHILE HE SCRUTINISED THE ENEMY TRAFFIC WITH INTENSE CONCENTRATION.
A STAFF CAR, CAINE – TELL ME WHEN YOU SEE A STAFF CAR!
CAINE WAS STARTLED TO SEE THAT THE MAJOR WAS NOW ACTUALLY QUIVERING WITH SOME STRANGE, SECRET EXCITEMENT.

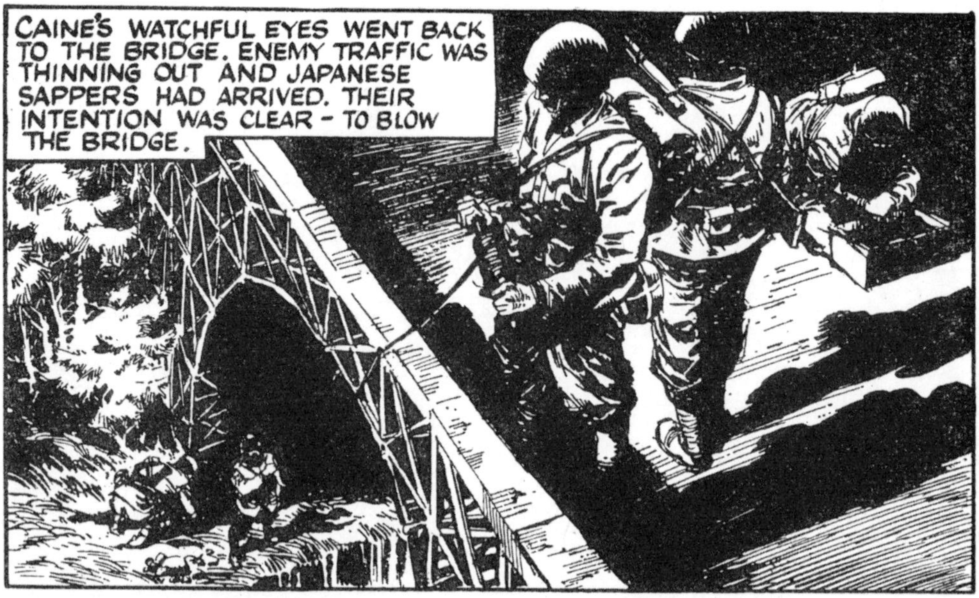
CAINE'S WATCHFUL EYES WENT BACK TO THE BRIDGE. ENEMY TRAFFIC WAS THINNING OUT AND JAPANESE SAPPERS HAD ARRIVED. THEIR INTENTION WAS CLEAR – TO BLOW THE BRIDGE.

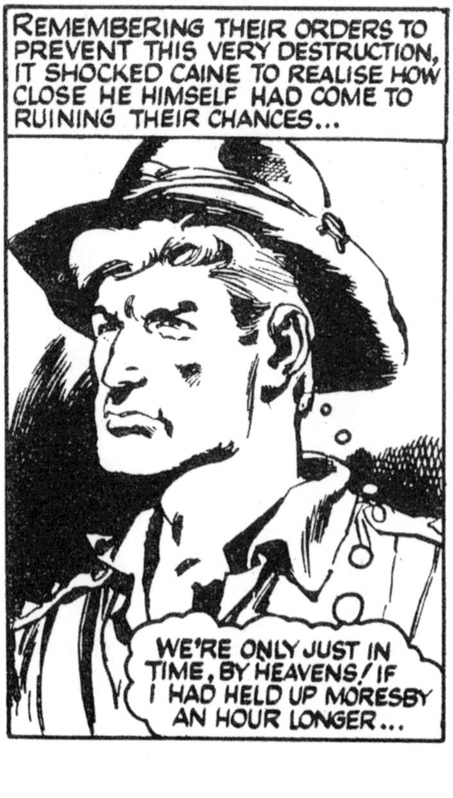
REMEMBERING THEIR ORDERS TO PREVENT THIS VERY DESTRUCTION, IT SHOCKED CAINE TO REALISE HOW CLOSE HE HIMSELF HAD COME TO RUINING THEIR CHANCES...
WE'RE ONLY JUST IN TIME, BY HEAVENS! IF I HAD HELD UP MORESBY AN HOUR LONGER...

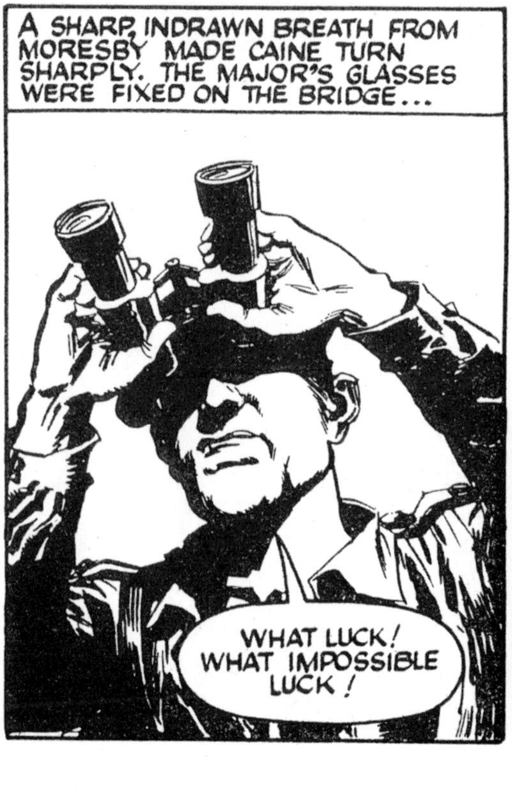
A SHARP, INDRAWN BREATH FROM MORESBY MADE CAINE TURN SHARPLY. THE MAJOR'S GLASSES WERE FIXED ON THE BRIDGE...
WHAT LUCK! WHAT IMPOSSIBLE LUCK!

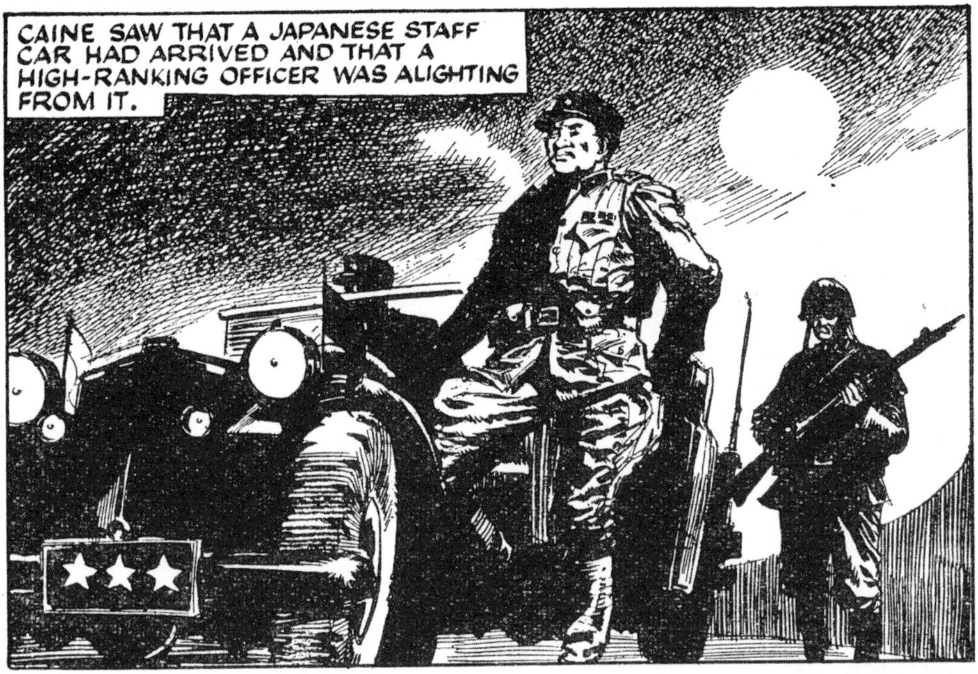
CAINE SAW THAT A JAPANESE STAFF CAR HAD ARRIVED AND THAT A HIGH-RANKING OFFICER WAS ALIGHTING FROM IT.

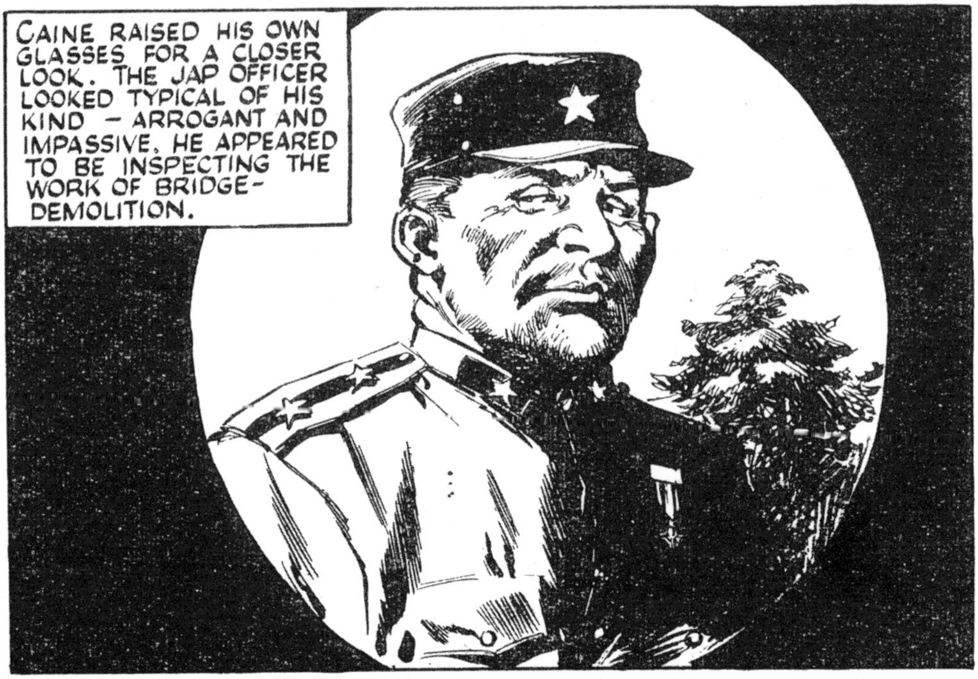
CAINE RAISED HIS OWN GLASSES FOR A CLOSER LOOK. THE JAP OFFICER LOOKED TYPICAL OF HIS KIND - ARROGANT AND IMPASSIVE. HE APPEARED TO BE INSPECTING THE WORK OF BRIDGE-DEMOLITION.

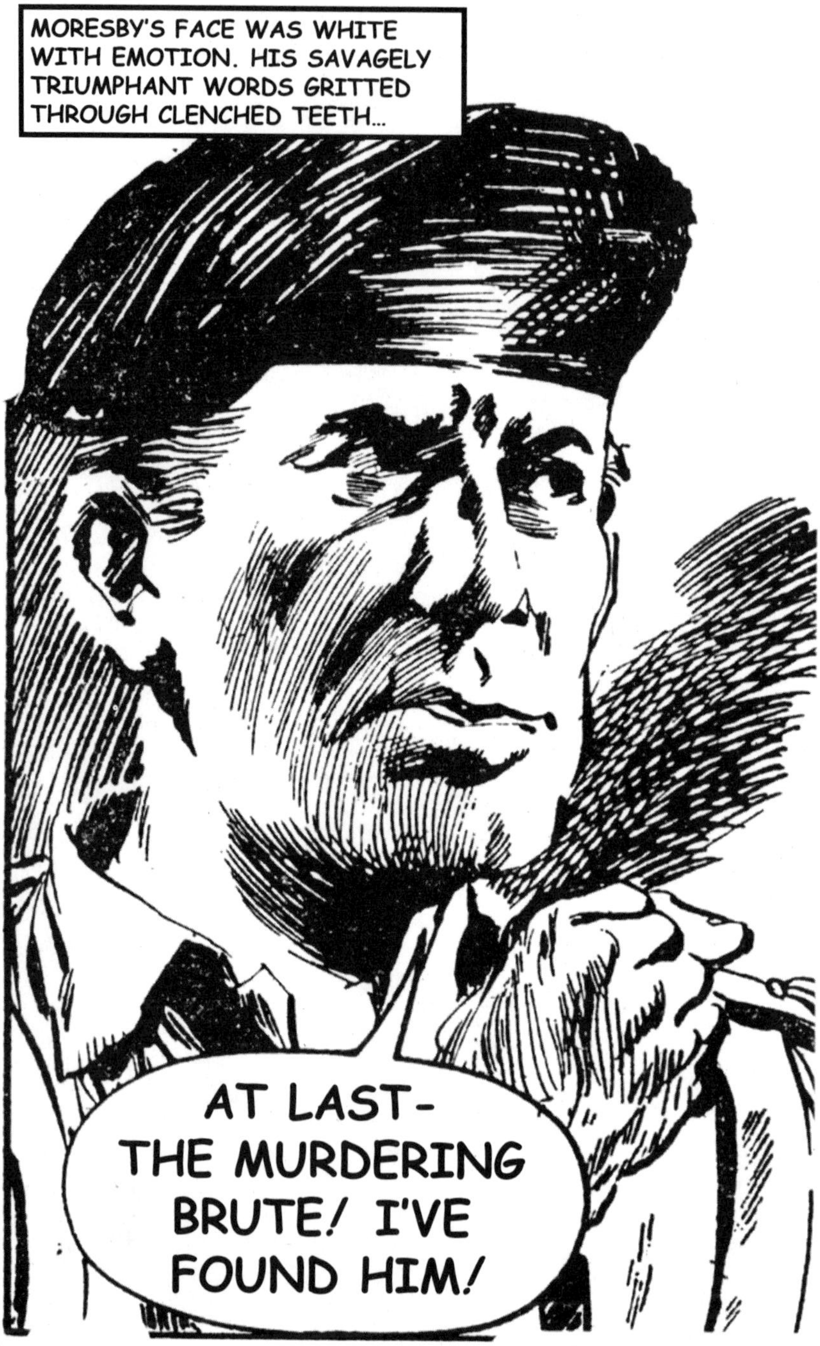
MORESBY'S FACE WAS WHITE WITH EMOTION. HIS SAVAGELY TRIUMPHANT WORDS GRITTED THROUGH CLENCHED TEETH...
AT LAST- THE MURDERING BRUTE! I'VE FOUND HIM!

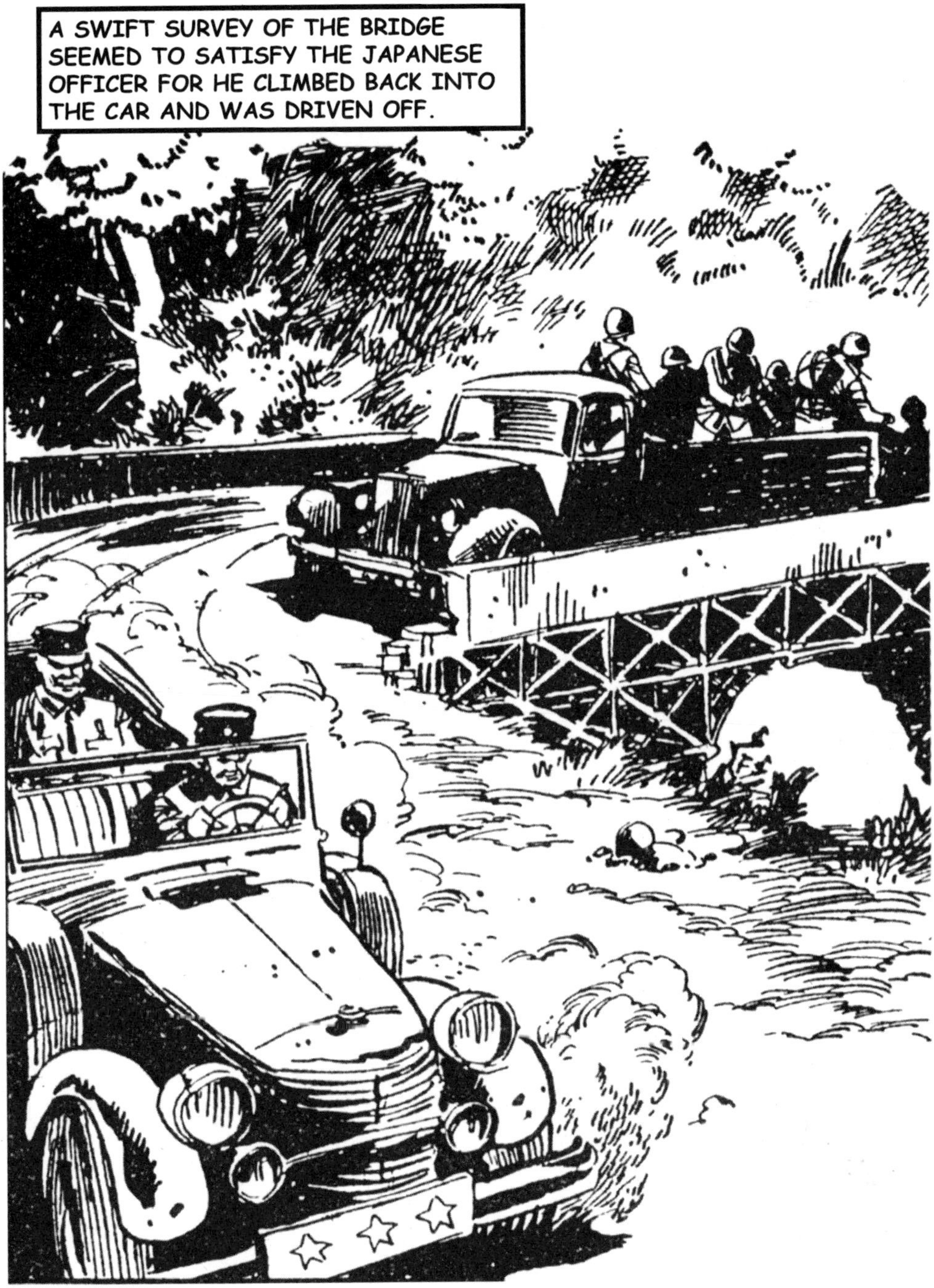
A SWIFT SURVEY OF THE BRIDGE SEEMED TO SATISFY THE JAPANESE OFFICER FOR HE CLIMBED BACK INTO THE CAR AND WAS DRIVEN OFF.

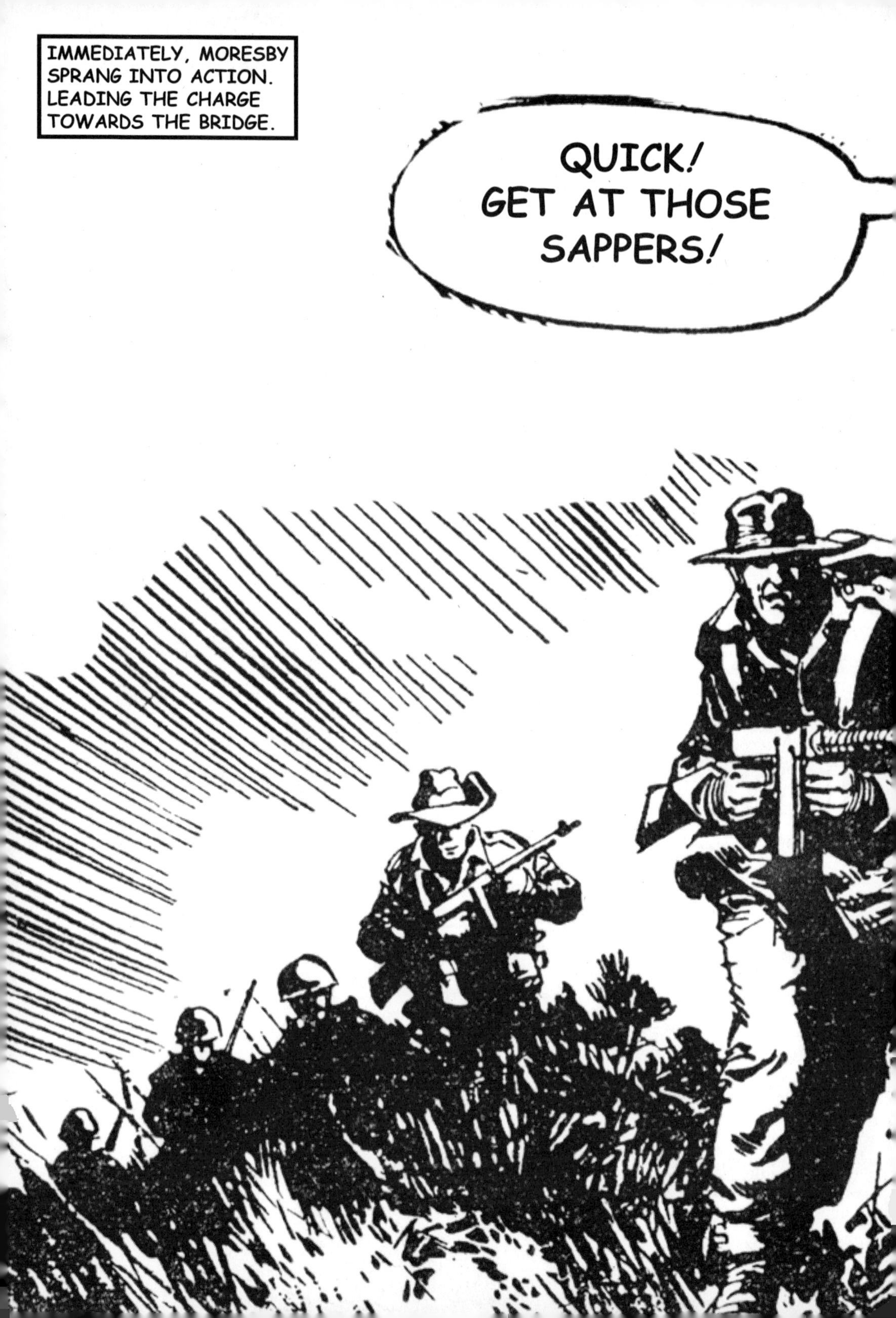
IMMEDIATELY, MORESBY SPRANG INTO ACTION. LEADING THE CHARGE TOWARDS THE BRIDGE.
QUICK! GET AT THOSE SAPPERS!

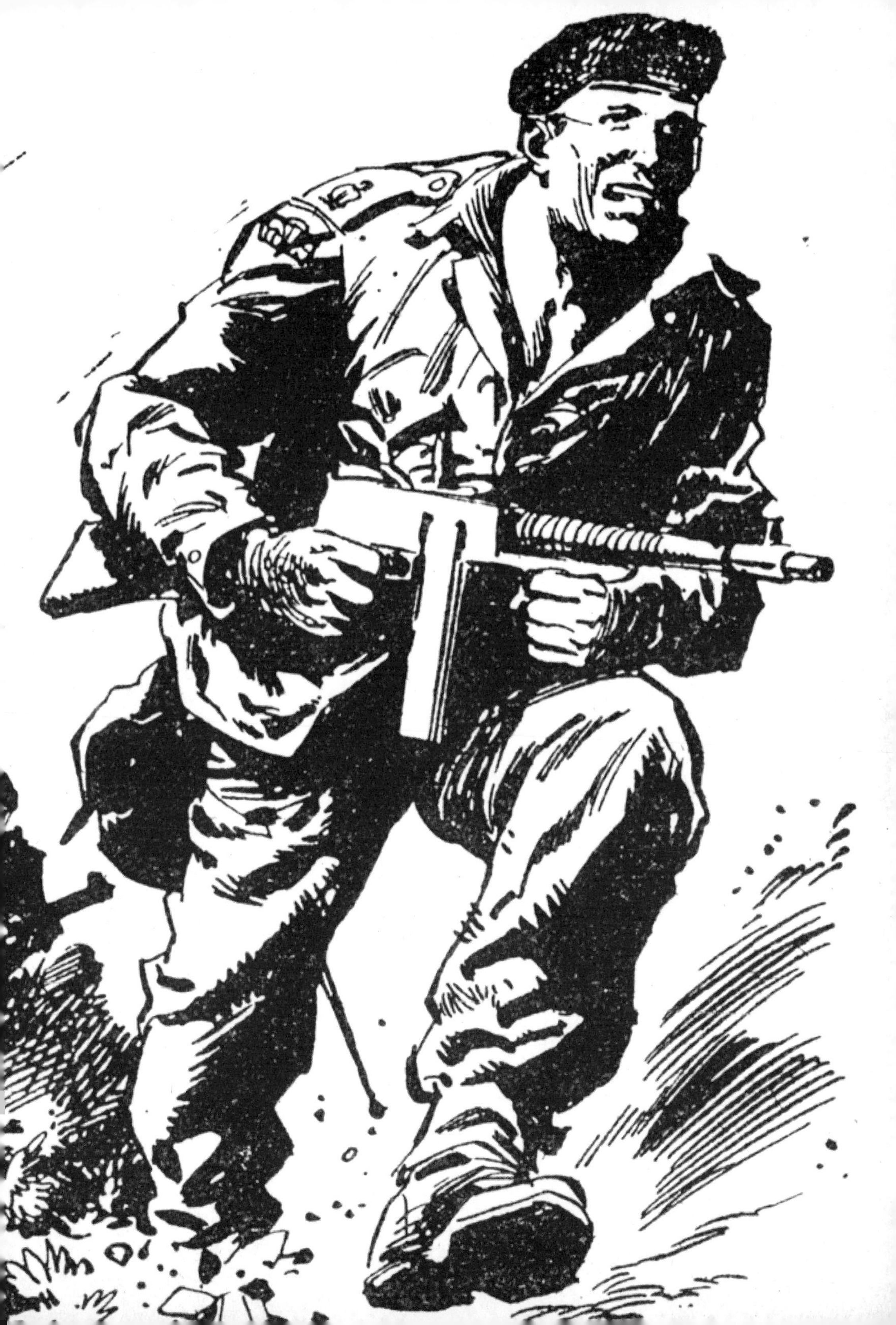

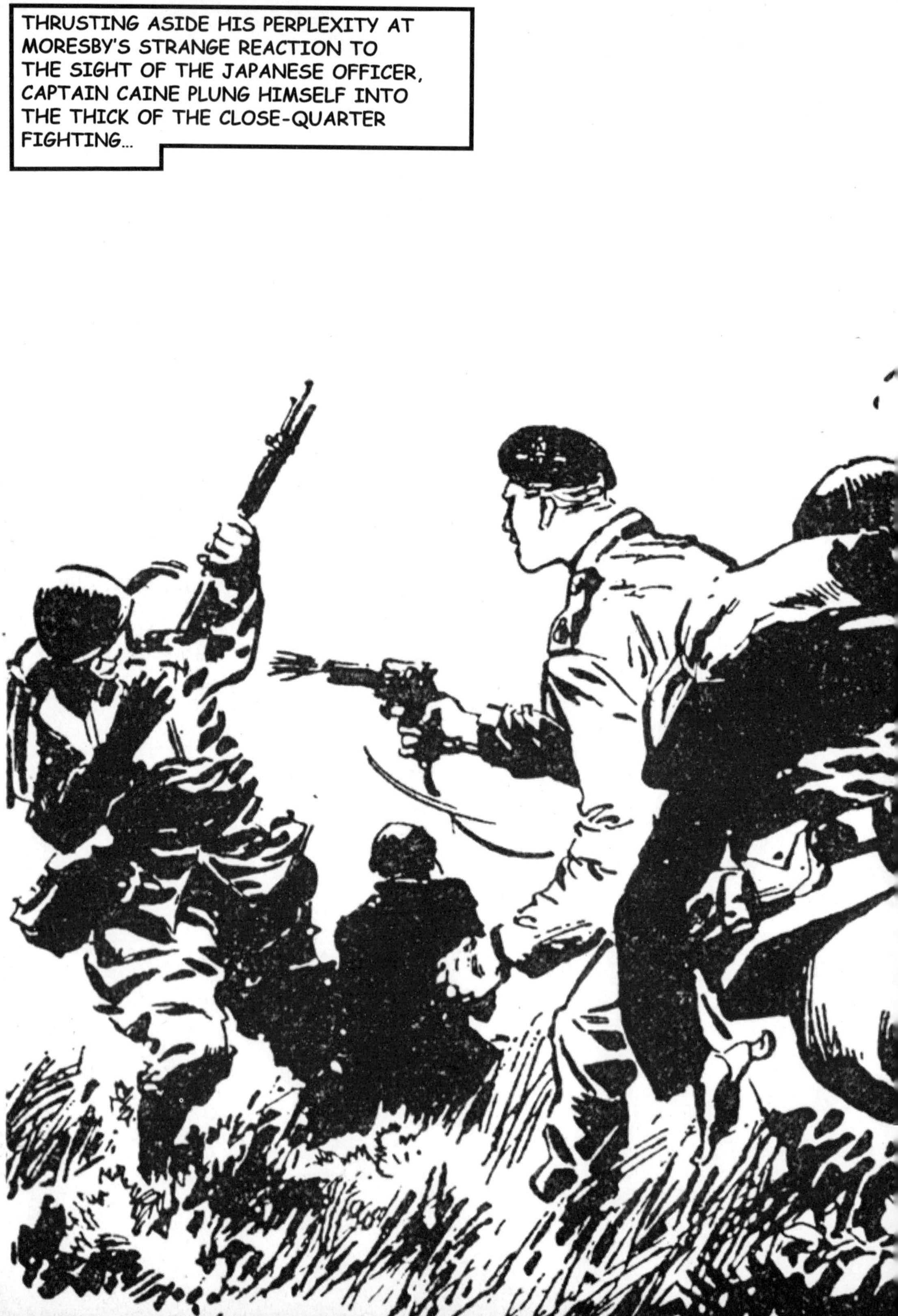
THRUSTING ASIDE HIS PERPLEXITY AT MORESBY'S STRANGE REACTION TO THE SIGHT OF THE JAPANESE OFFICER, CAPTAIN CAINE PLUNG HIMSELF INTO THE THICK OF THE CLOSE-QUARTER FIGHTING...

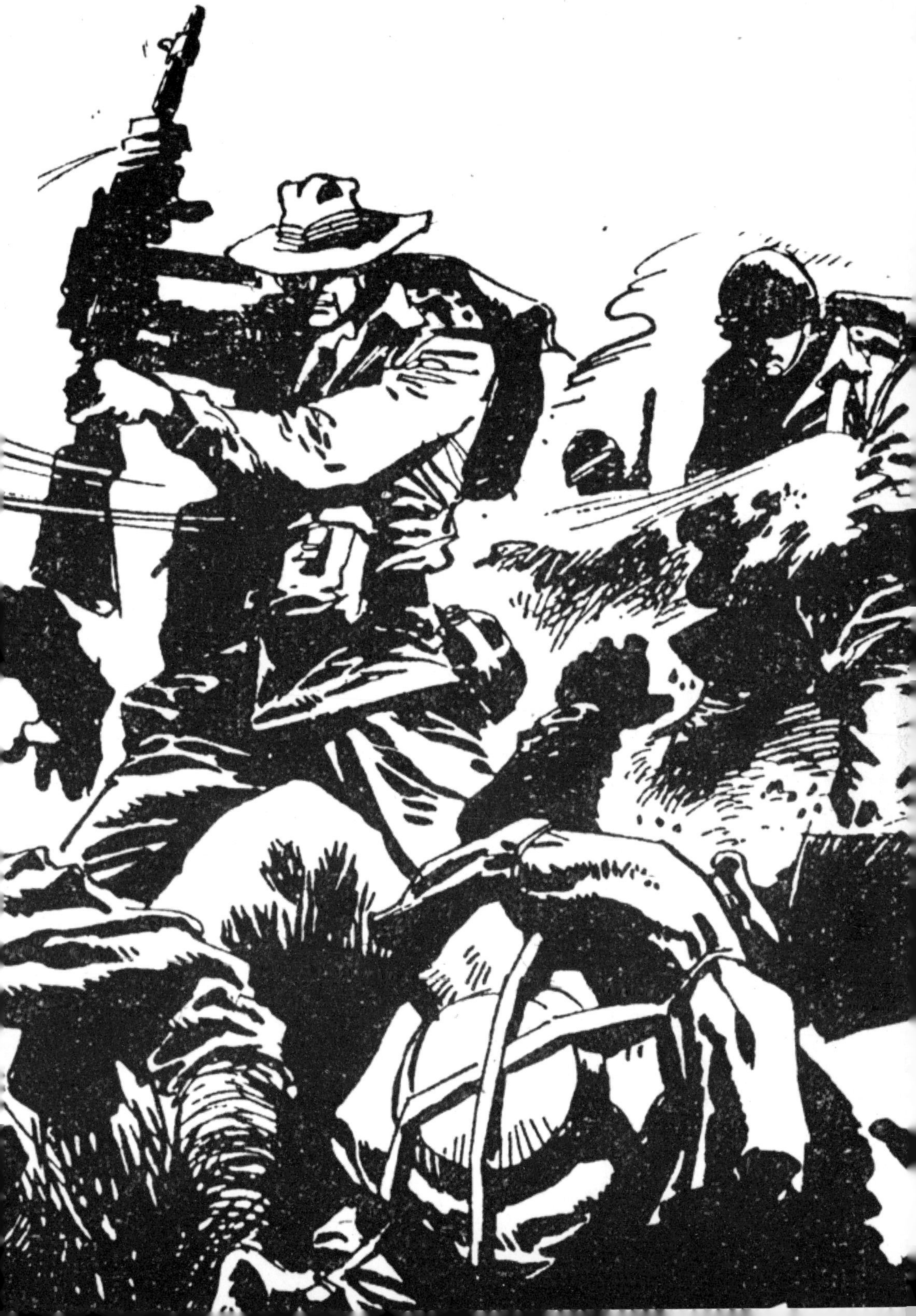

THE ASSUALT WAS SUDDEN AND OVERWHELMING. THE SMALL PARTY OF ENEMY ENGINEERS HAD LITTLE CHANCE AGAINST THE COOL FEROCITY OF THE PARATROOPERS.

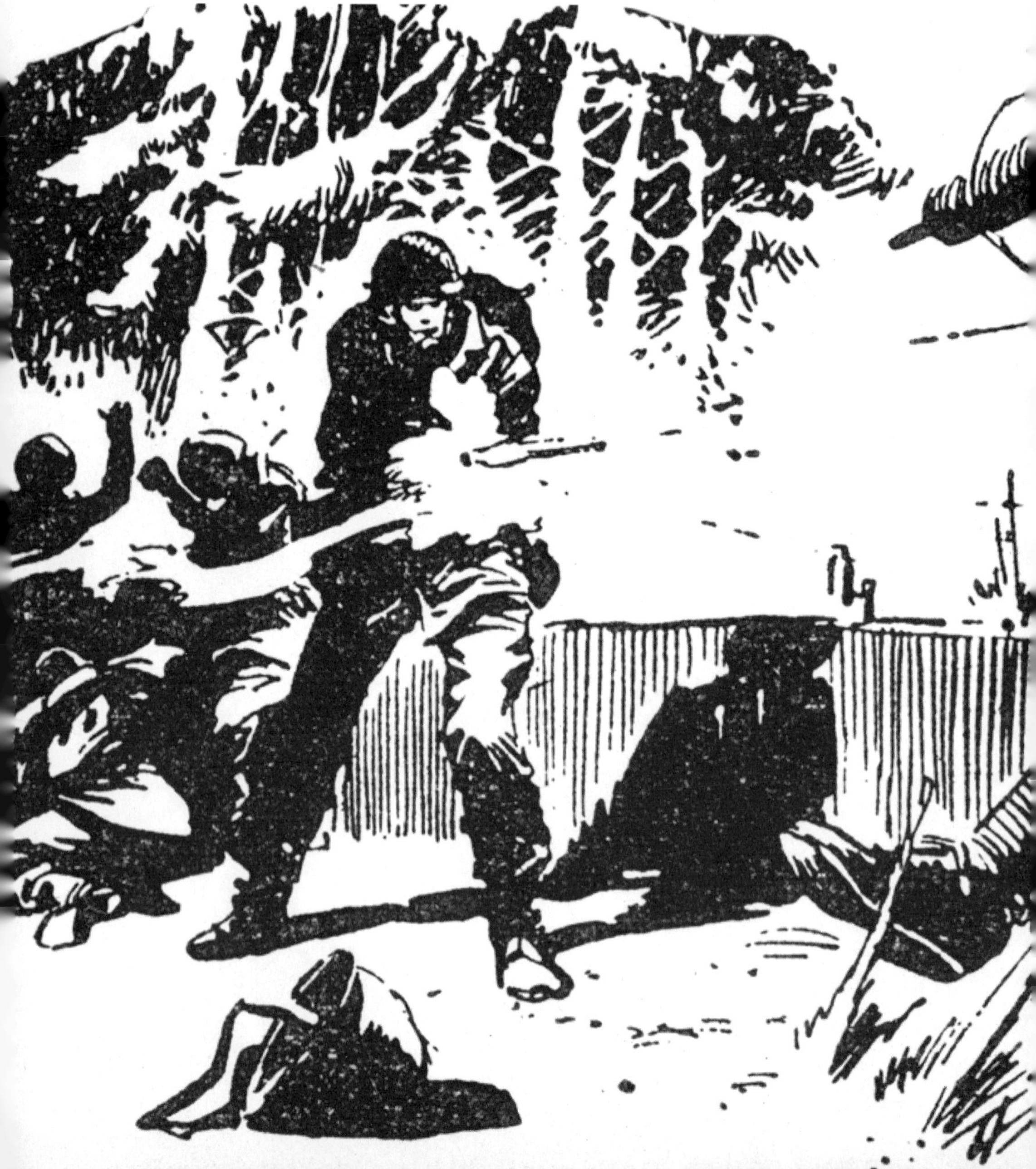

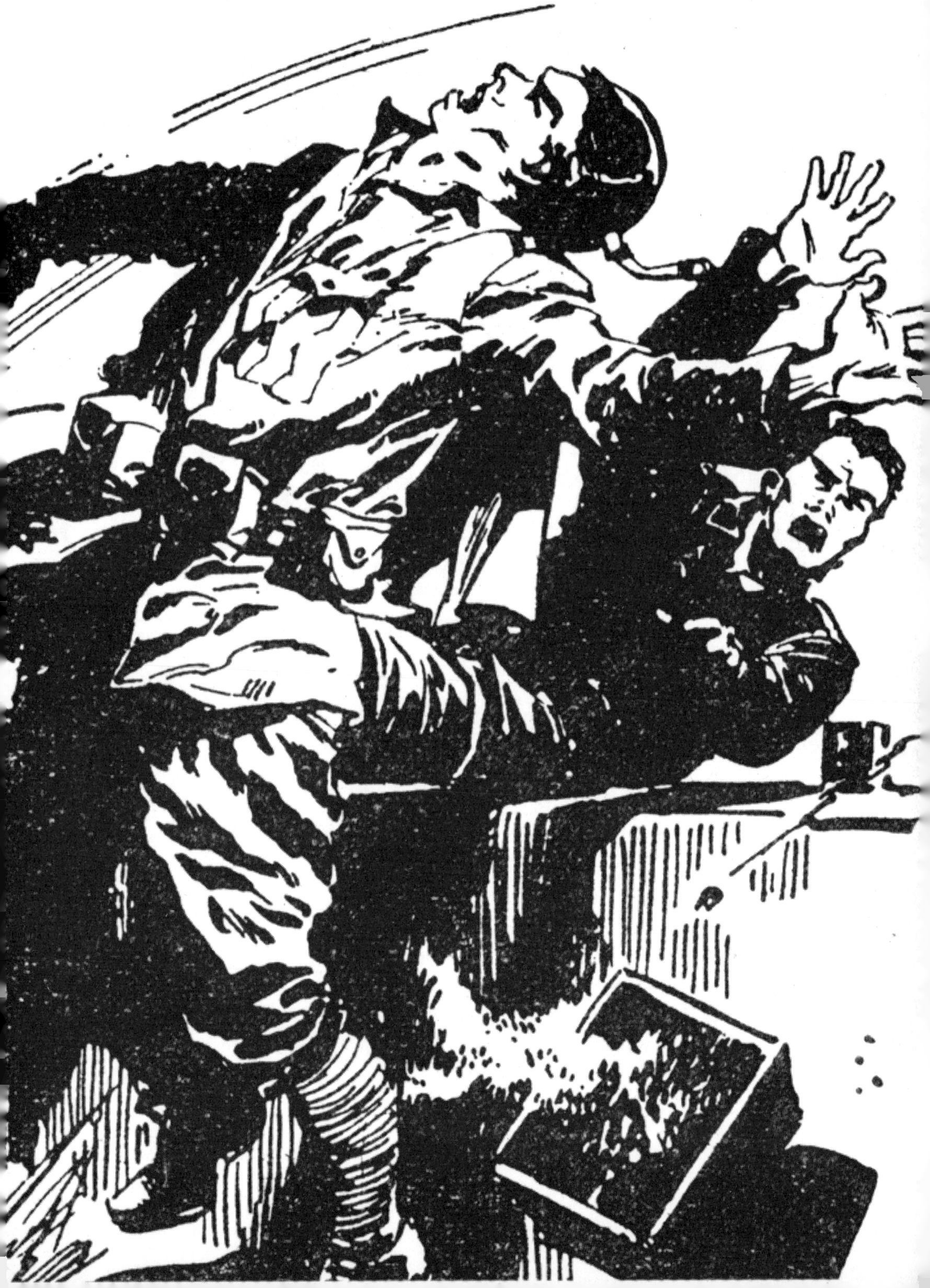

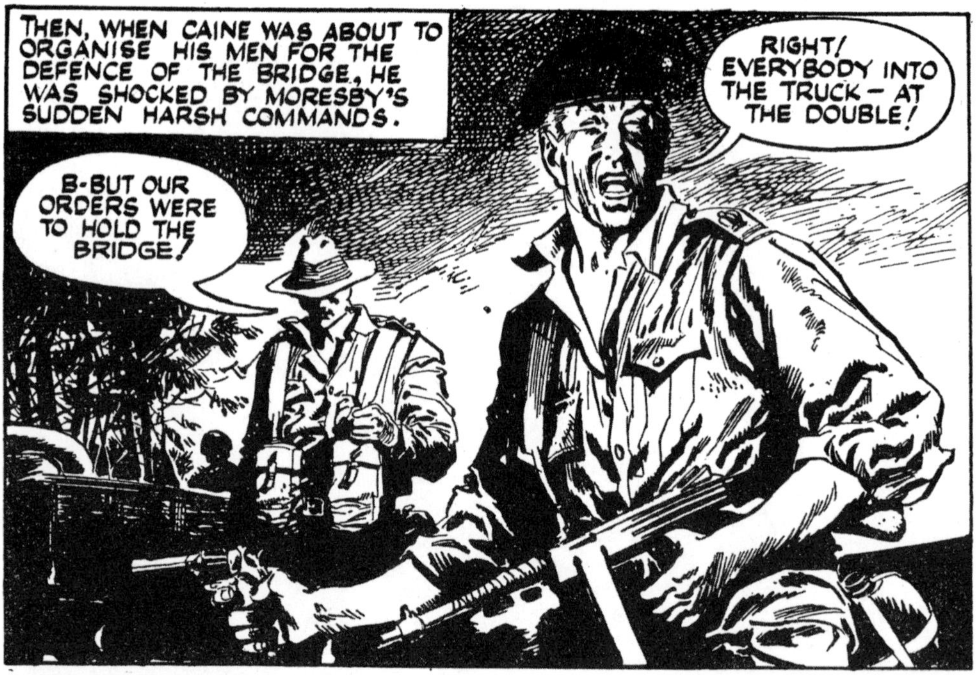
THEN, WHEN CAINE WAS ABOUT TO ORGANISE HIS MEN FOR THE DEFENCE OF THE BRIDGE, HE WAS SHOCKED BY MORESBY'S SUDDEN HARSH COMMANDS.
RIGHT! EVERYBODY INTO THE TRUCK – AT THE DOUBLE!
B-BUT OUR ORDERS WERE TO HOLD THE BRIDGE!

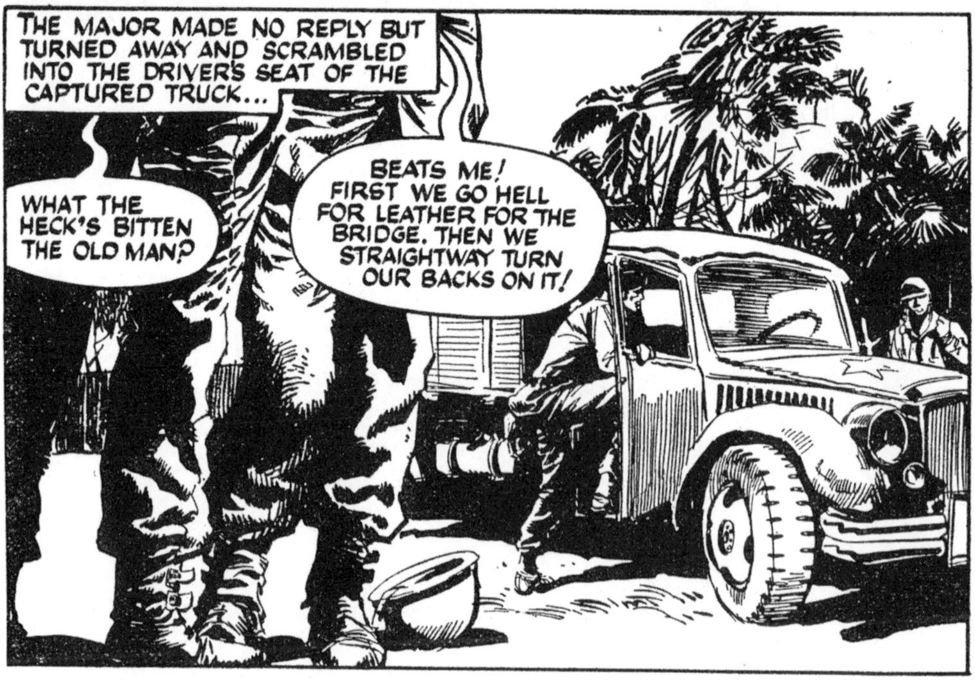
THE MAJOR MADE NO REPLY BUT TURNED AWAY AND SCRAMBLED INTO THE DRIVER'S SEAT OF THE CAPTURED TRUCK...
WHAT THE HECK'S BITTEN THE OLD MAN?
BEATS ME! FIRST WE GO HELL FOR LEATHER FOR THE BRIDGE. THEN WE STRAIGHTWAY TURN OUR BACKS ON IT!

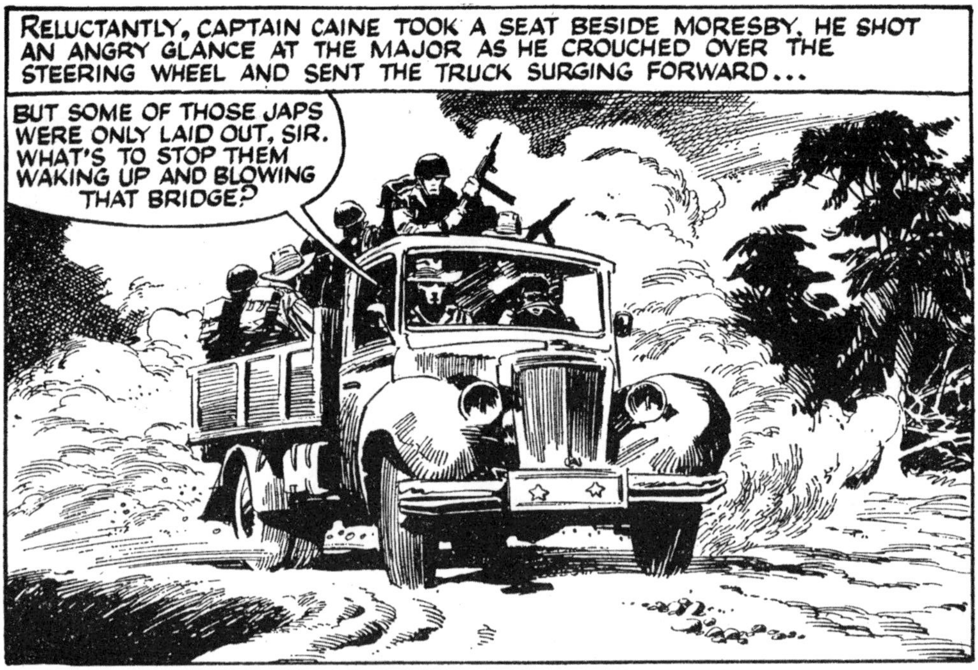
RELUCTANTLY, CAPTAIN CAINE TOOK A SEAT BESIDE MORESBY. HE SHOT AN ANGRY GLANCE AT THE MAJOR AS HE CROUCHED OVER THE STEERING WHEEL AND SENT THE TRUCK SURGING FORWARD...
BUT SOME OF THOSE JAPS WERE ONLY LAID OUT, SIR. WHAT'S TO STOP THEM WAKING UP AND BLOWING THAT BRIDGE?

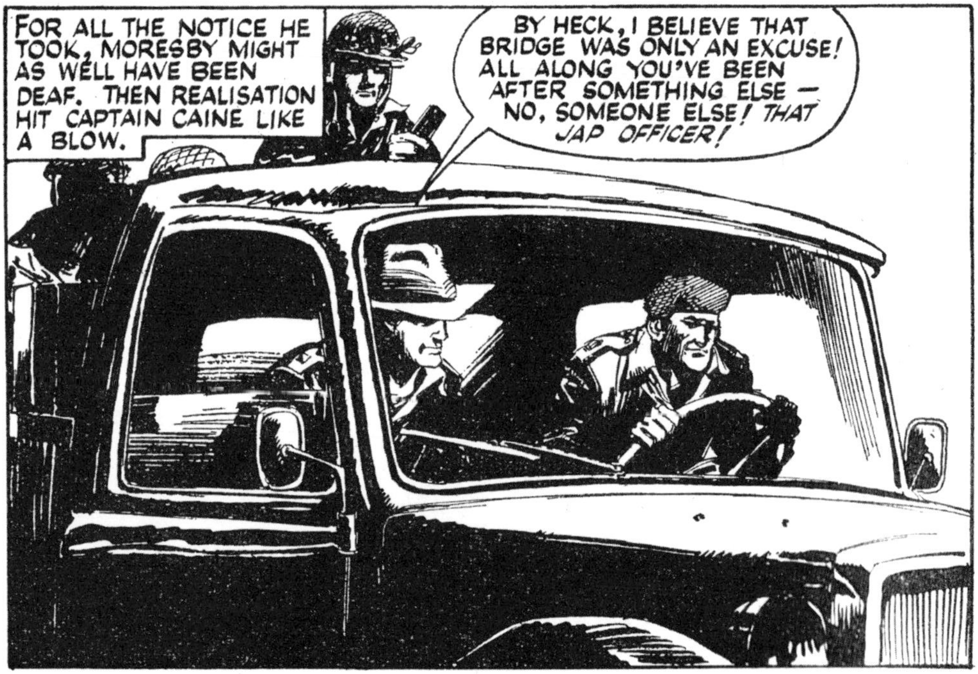
FOR ALL THE NOTICE HE TOOK, MORESBY MIGHT AS WELL HAVE BEEN DEAF. THEN REALISATION HIT CAPTAIN CAINE LIKE A BLOW.
BY HECK, I BELIEVE THAT BRIDGE WAS ONLY AN EXCUSE! ALL ALONG YOU'VE BEEN AFTER SOMETHING ELSE — NO, SOMEONE ELSE! THAT JAP OFFICER!

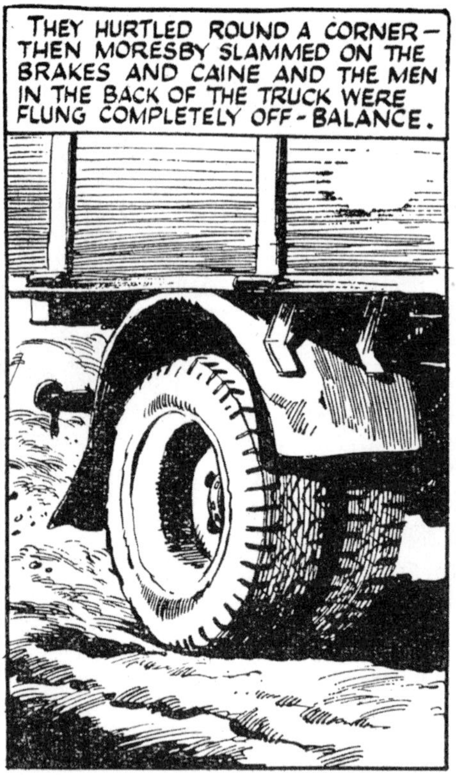
THEY HURTLED ROUND A CORNER—THEN MORESBY SLAMMED ON THE BRAKES AND CAINE AND THE MEN IN THE BACK OF THE TRUCK WERE FLUNG COMPLETELY OFF-BALANCE.

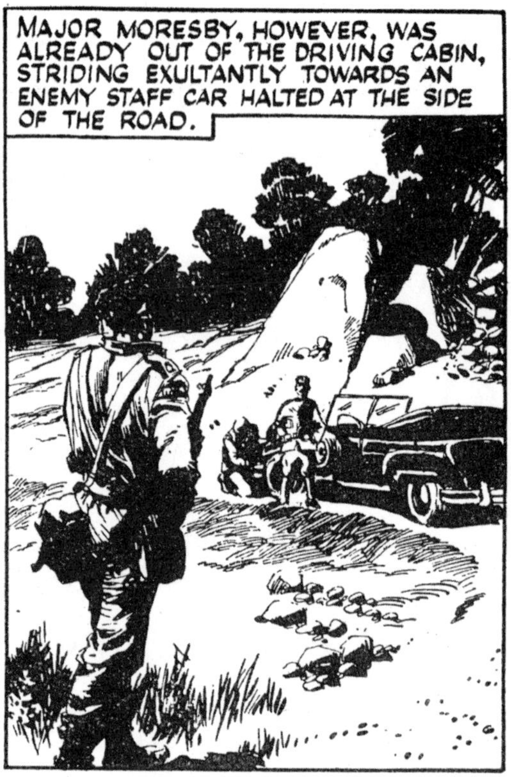
MAJOR MORESBY, HOWEVER, WAS ALREADY OUT OF THE DRIVING CABIN, STRIDING EXULTANTLY TOWARDS AN ENEMY STAFF CAR HALTED AT THE SIDE OF THE ROAD.

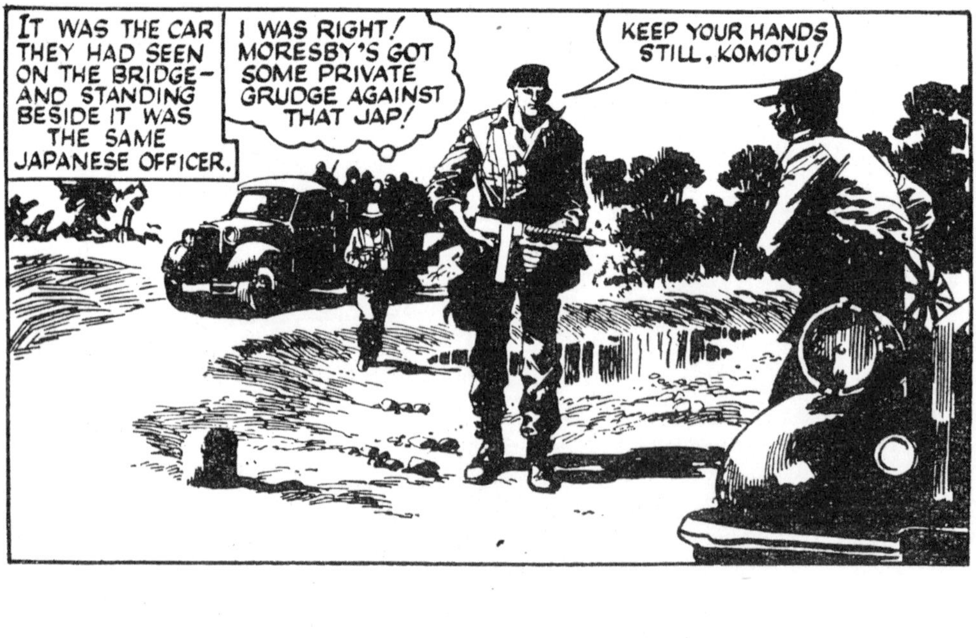
IT WAS THE CAR THEY HAD SEEN ON THE BRIDGE—AND STANDING BESIDE IT WAS THE SAME JAPANESE OFFICER.
I WAS RIGHT! MORESBY'S GOT SOME PRIVATE GRUDGE AGAINST THAT JAP!
KEEP YOUR HANDS STILL, KOMOTU!

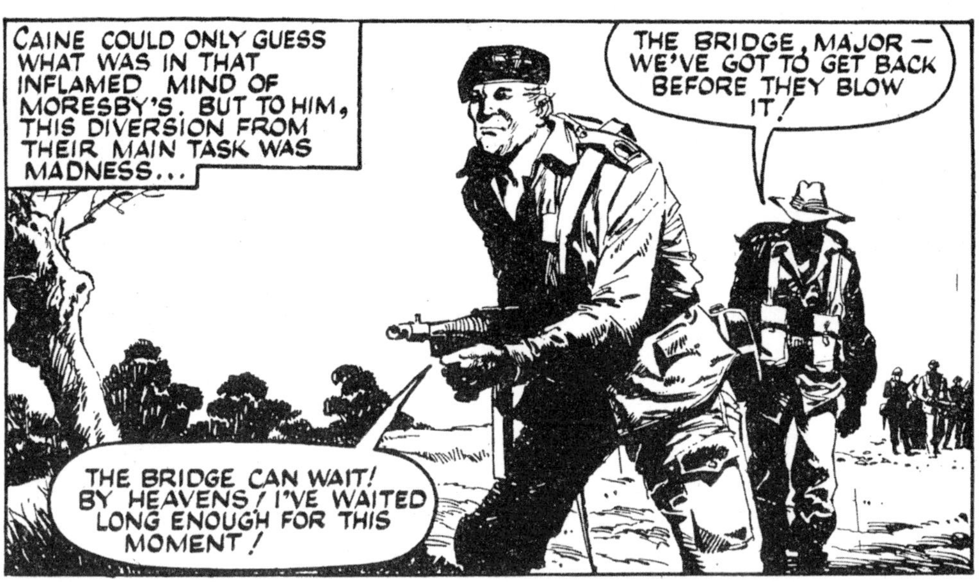
CAINE COULD ONLY GUESS WHAT WAS IN THAT INFLAMED MIND OF MORESBY'S. BUT TO HIM, THIS DIVERSION FROM THEIR MAIN TASK WAS MADNESS...
THE BRIDGE, MAJOR — WE'VE GOT TO GET BACK BEFORE THEY BLOW IT!
THE BRIDGE CAN WAIT! BY HEAVENS! I'VE WAITED LONG ENOUGH FOR THIS MOMENT!

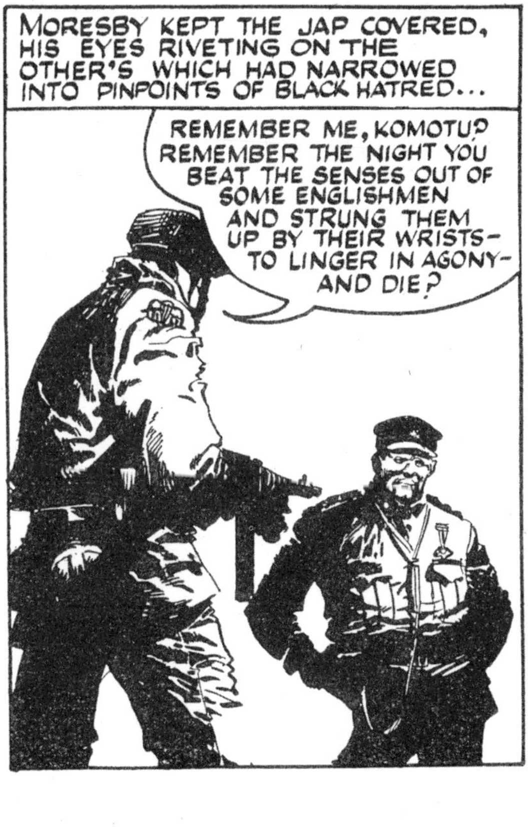
MORESBY KEPT THE JAP COVERED, HIS EYES RIVETING ON THE OTHER'S WHICH HAD NARROWED INTO PINPOINTS OF BLACK HATRED...
REMEMBER ME, KOMOTU? REMEMBER THE NIGHT YOU BEAT THE SENSES OUT OF SOME ENGLISHMEN AND STRUNG THEM UP BY THEIR WRISTS- TO LINGER IN AGONY- AND DIE?

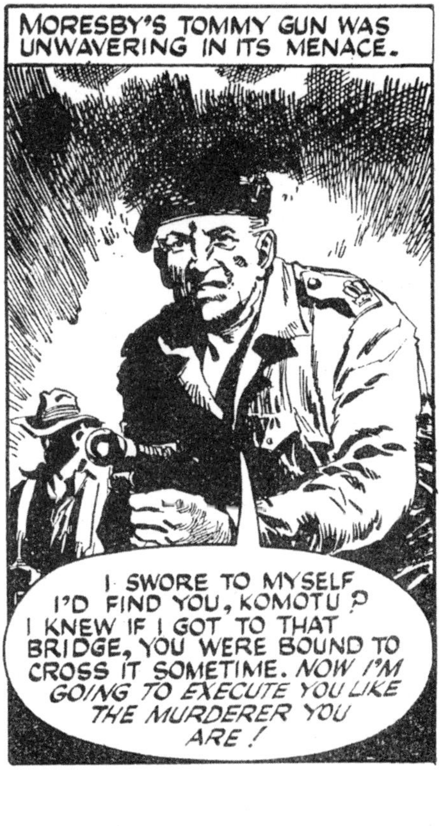
MORESBY'S TOMMY GUN WAS UNWAVERING IN ITS MENACE.
I SWORE TO MYSELF I'D FIND YOU, KOMOTU? I KNEW IF I GOT TO THAT BRIDGE, YOU WERE BOUND TO CROSS IT SOMETIME. *NOW I'M GOING TO EXECUTE YOU LIKE THE MURDERER YOU ARE!*

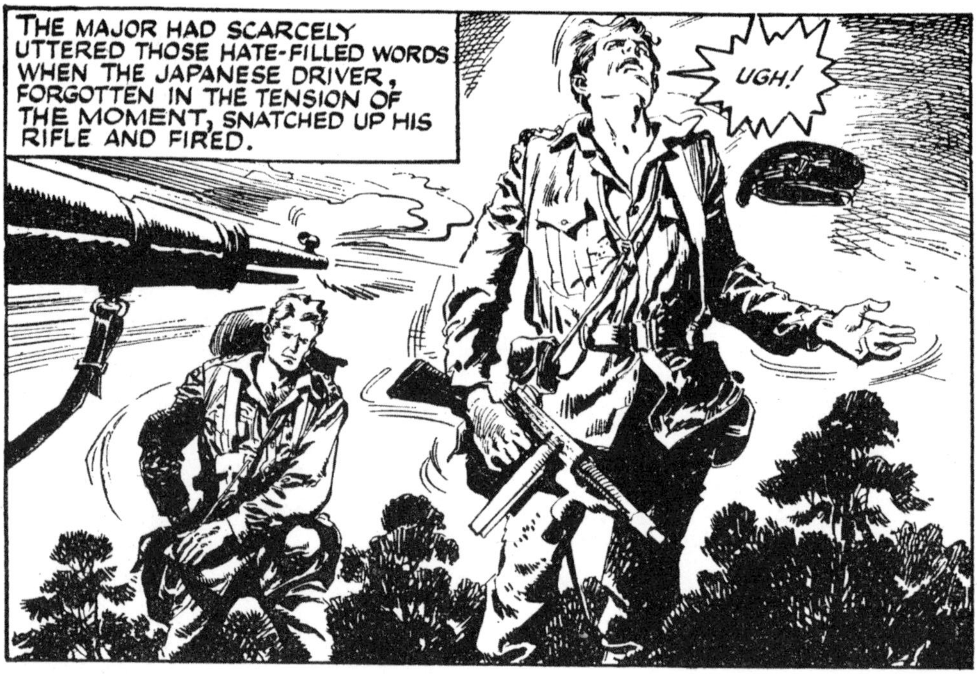
THE MAJOR HAD SCARCELY UTTERED THOSE HATE-FILLED WORDS WHEN THE JAPANESE DRIVER, FORGOTTEN IN THE TENSION OF THE MOMENT, SNATCHED UP HIS RIFLE AND FIRED.
UGH!

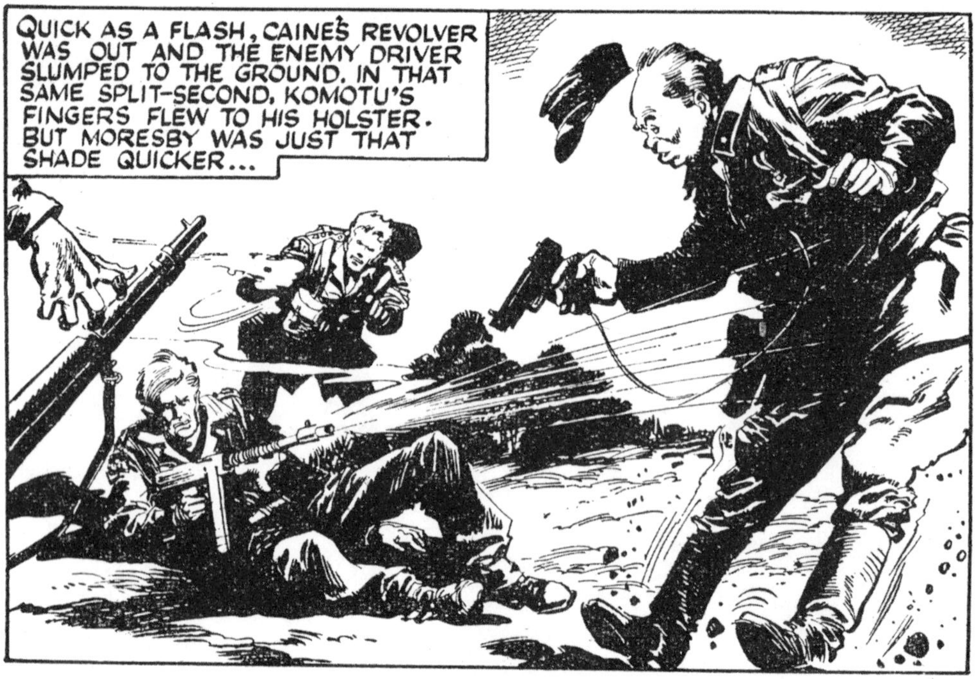
QUICK AS A FLASH, CAINE'S REVOLVER WAS OUT AND THE ENEMY DRIVER SLUMPED TO THE GROUND. IN THAT SAME SPLIT-SECOND, KOMOTU'S FINGERS FLEW TO HIS HOLSTER. BUT MORESBY WAS JUST THAT SHADE QUICKER...

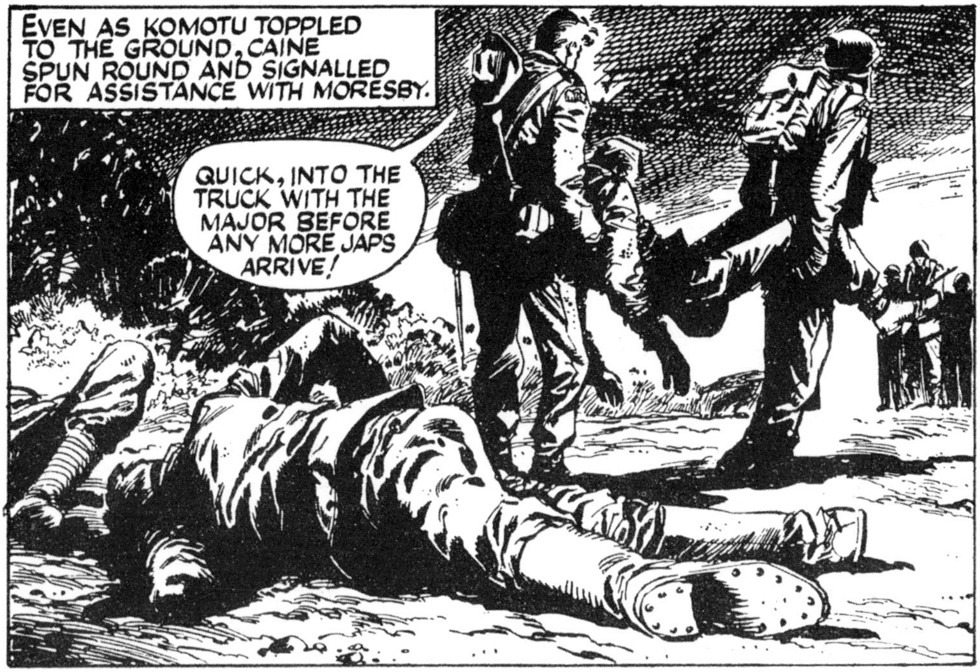
EVEN AS KOMOTU TOPPLED TO THE GROUND, CAINE SPUN ROUND AND SIGNALLED FOR ASSISTANCE WITH MORESBY.
QUICK, INTO THE TRUCK WITH THE MAJOR BEFORE ANY MORE JAPS ARRIVE!

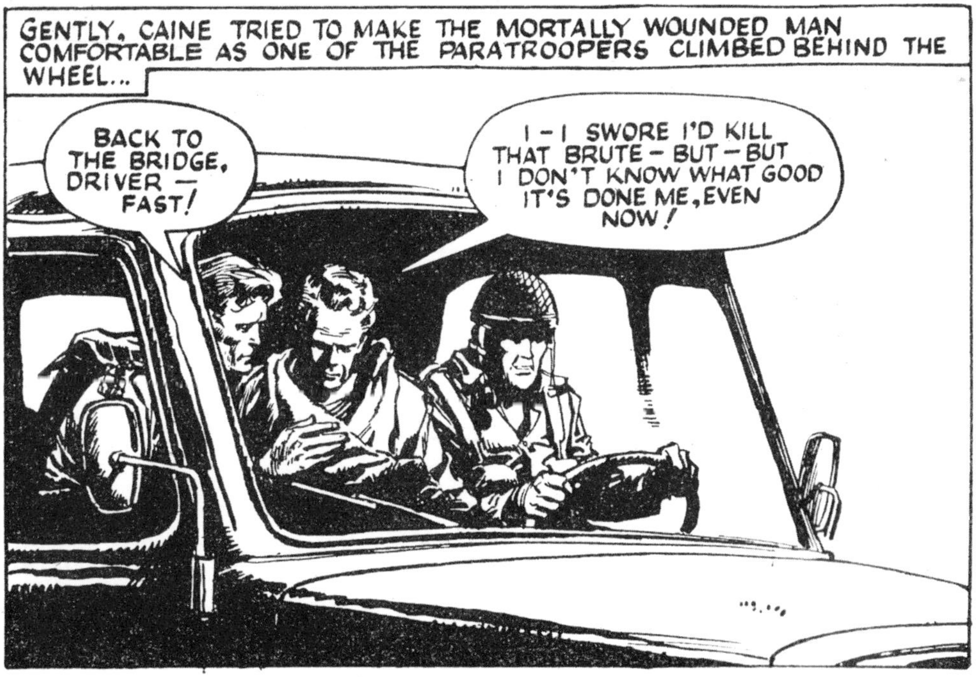
GENTLY, CAINE TRIED TO MAKE THE MORTALLY WOUNDED MAN COMFORTABLE AS ONE OF THE PARATROOPERS CLIMBED BEHIND THE WHEEL...
BACK TO THE BRIDGE, DRIVER — FAST!
I – I SWORE I'D KILL THAT BRUTE – BUT – BUT I DON'T KNOW WHAT GOOD IT'S DONE ME, EVEN NOW!

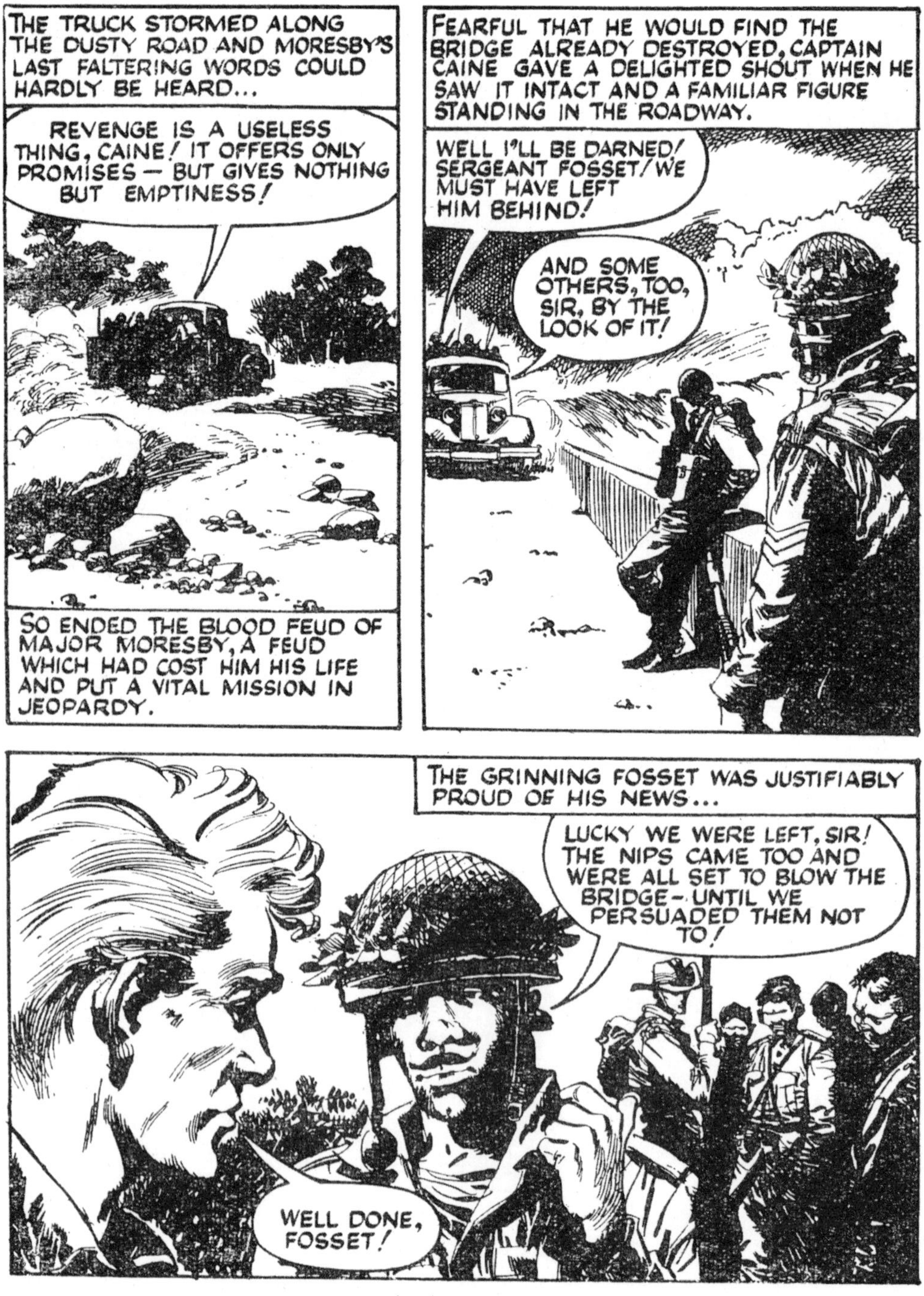
THE TRUCK STORMED ALONG THE DUSTY ROAD AND MORESBY'S LAST FALTERING WORDS COULD HARDLY BE HEARD...
REVENGE IS A USELESS THING, CAINE! IT OFFERS ONLY PROMISES — BUT GIVES NOTHING BUT EMPTINESS!
SO ENDED THE BLOOD FEUD OF MAJOR MORESBY, A FEUD WHICH HAD COST HIM HIS LIFE AND PUT A VITAL MISSION IN JEOPARDY.
FEARFUL THAT HE WOULD FIND THE BRIDGE ALREADY DESTROYED, CAPTAIN CAINE GAVE A DELIGHTED SHOUT WHEN HE SAW IT INTACT AND A FAMILIAR FIGURE STANDING IN THE ROADWAY.
WELL I'LL BE DARNED! SERGEANT FOSSET! WE MUST HAVE LEFT HIM BEHIND!
AND SOME OTHERS, TOO, SIR, BY THE LOOK OF IT!
THE GRINNING FOSSET WAS JUSTIFIABLY PROUD OF HIS NEWS...
LUCKY WE WERE LEFT, SIR! THE NIPS CAME TOO AND WERE ALL SET TO BLOW THE BRIDGE- UNTIL WE PERSUADED THEM NOT TO!
WELL DONE, FOSSET!

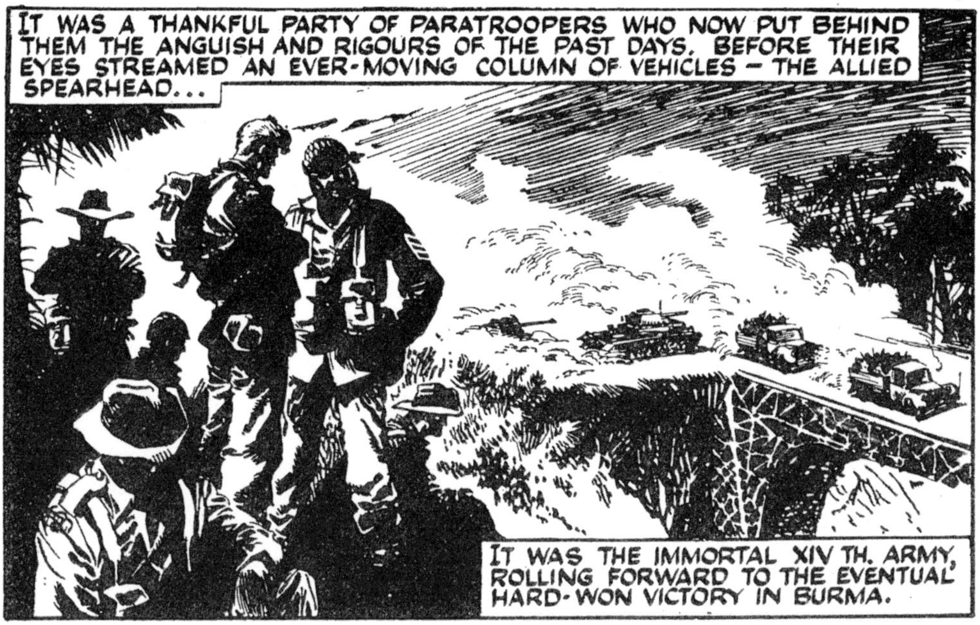
IT WAS A THANKFUL PARTY OF PARATROOPERS WHO NOW PUT BEHIND THEM THE ANGUISH AND RIGOURS OF THE PAST DAYS. BEFORE THEIR EYES STREAMED AN EVER-MOVING COLUMN OF VEHICLES – THE ALLIED SPEARHEAD...
IT WAS THE IMMORTAL XIV TH. ARMY, ROLLING FORWARD TO THE EVENTUAL HARD-WON VICTORY IN BURMA.

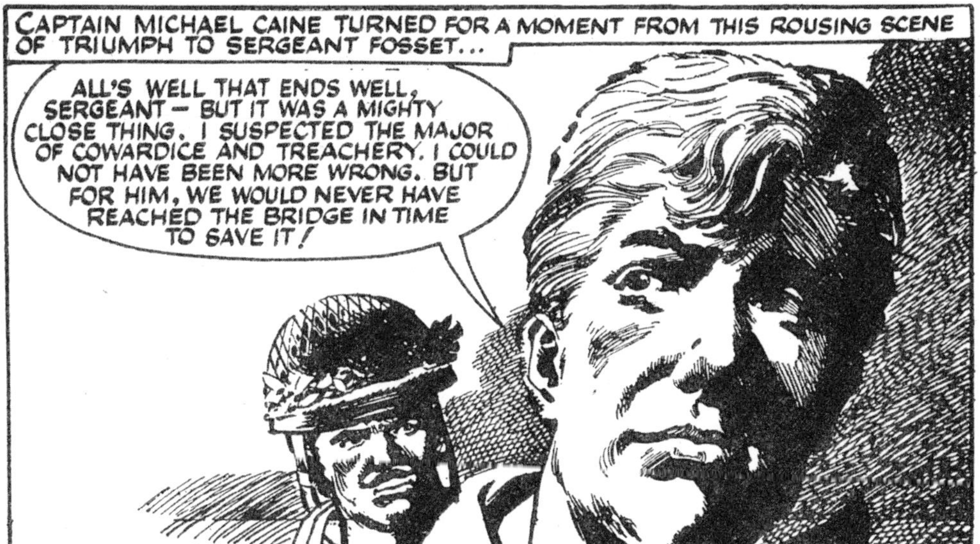
CAPTAIN MICHAEL CAINE TURNED FOR A MOMENT FROM THIS ROUSING SCENE OF TRIUMPH TO SERGEANT FOSSET...
ALL'S WELL THAT ENDS WELL, SERGEANT – BUT IT WAS A MIGHTY CLOSE THING. I SUSPECTED THE MAJOR OF COWARDICE AND TREACHERY. I COULD NOT HAVE BEEN MORE WRONG. BUT FOR HIM, WE WOULD NEVER HAVE REACHED THE BRIDGE IN TIME TO SAVE IT!

A FLEETWAY LIBRARY

BATTLE PICTURE LIBRARY

SIX OF THE BEST

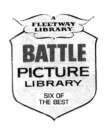

THE COVERS

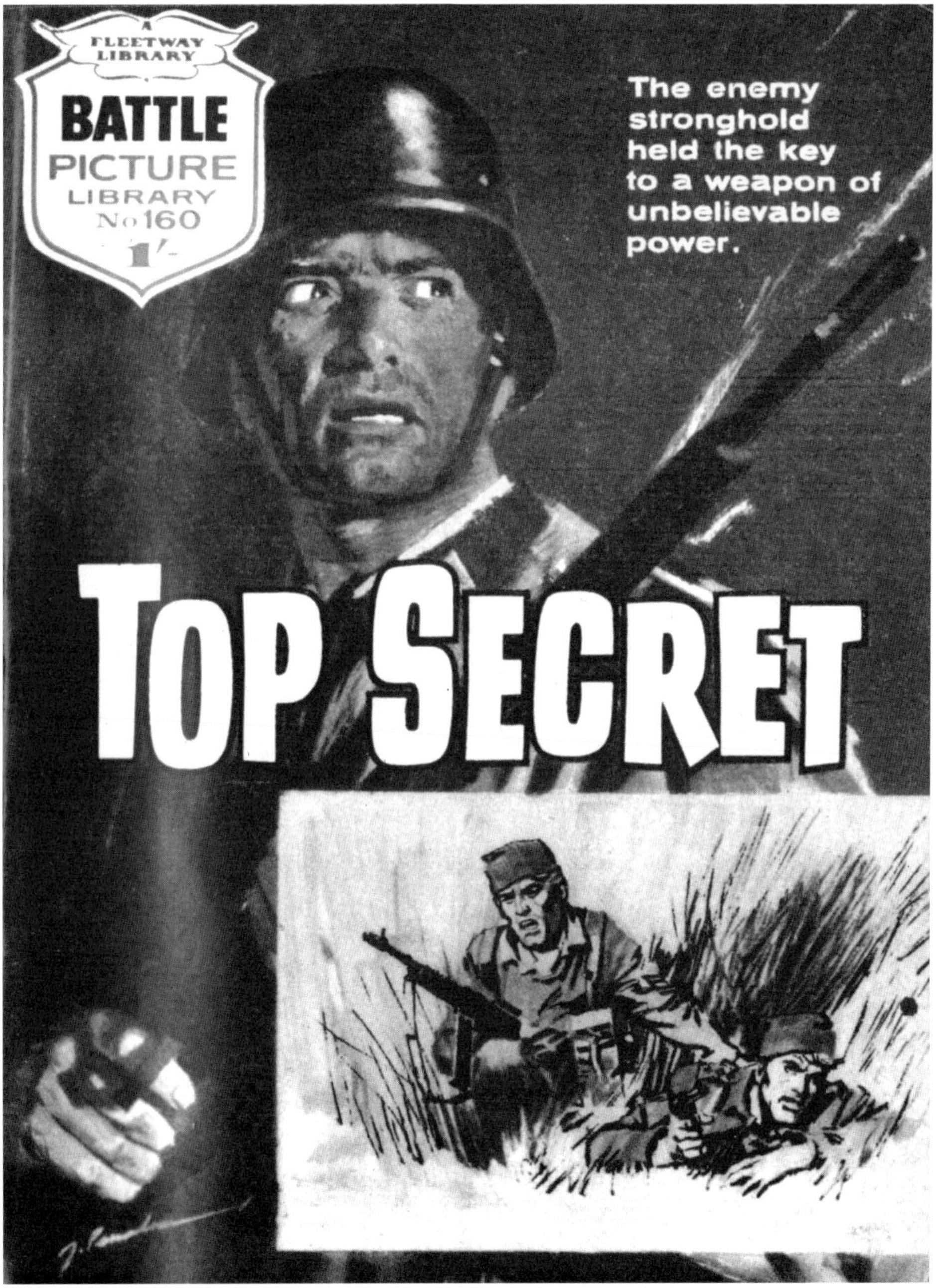
A FLEETWAY LIBRARY
BATTLE
PICTURE
LIBRARY
No 160
1/-
The enemy stronghold held the key to a weapon of unbelievable power.
TOP SECRET

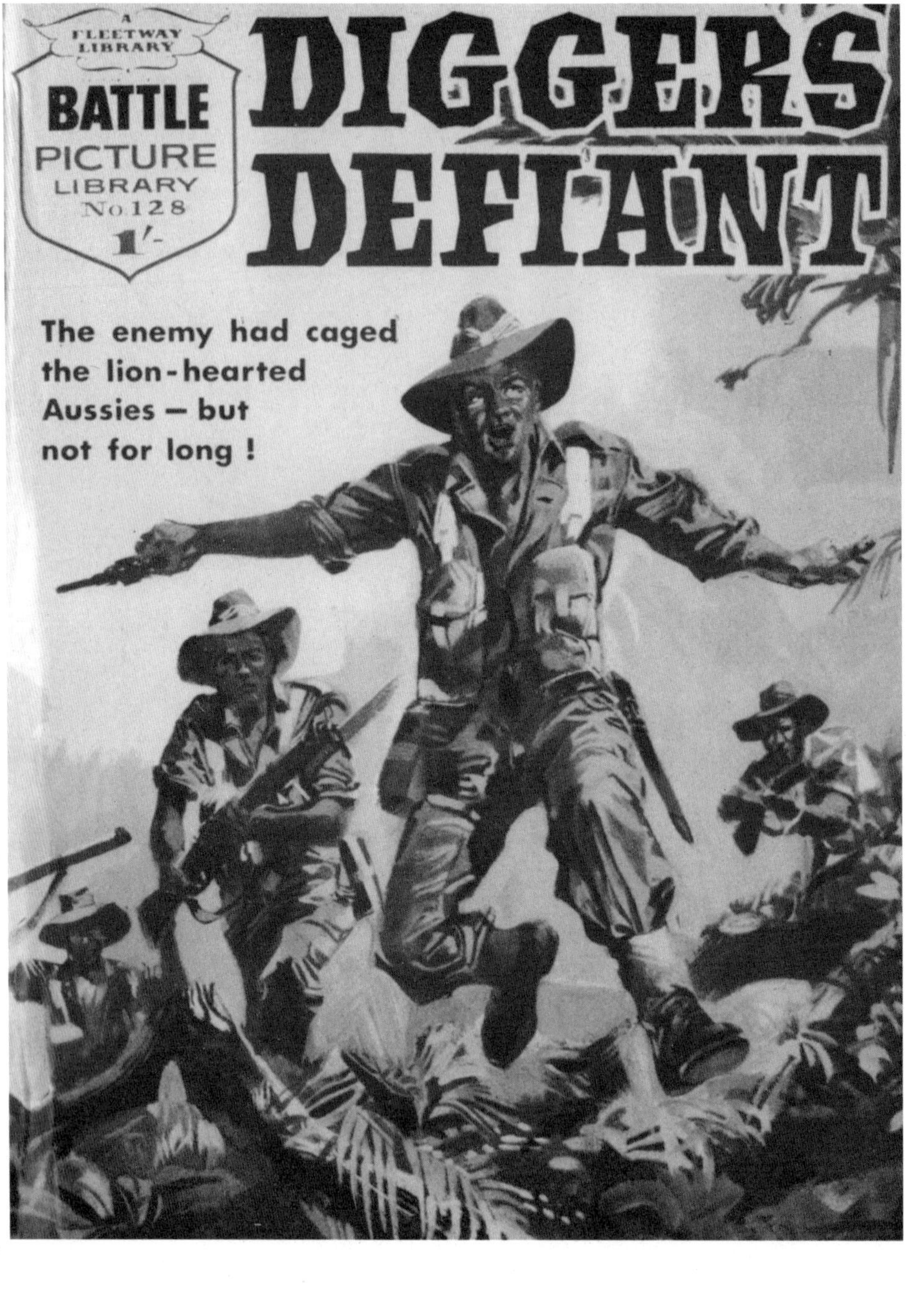
A FLEETWAY LIBRARY
BATTLE
PICTURE
LIBRARY
No.128
1/-
DIGGERS DEFIANT
The enemy had caged the lion-hearted Aussies – but not for long !

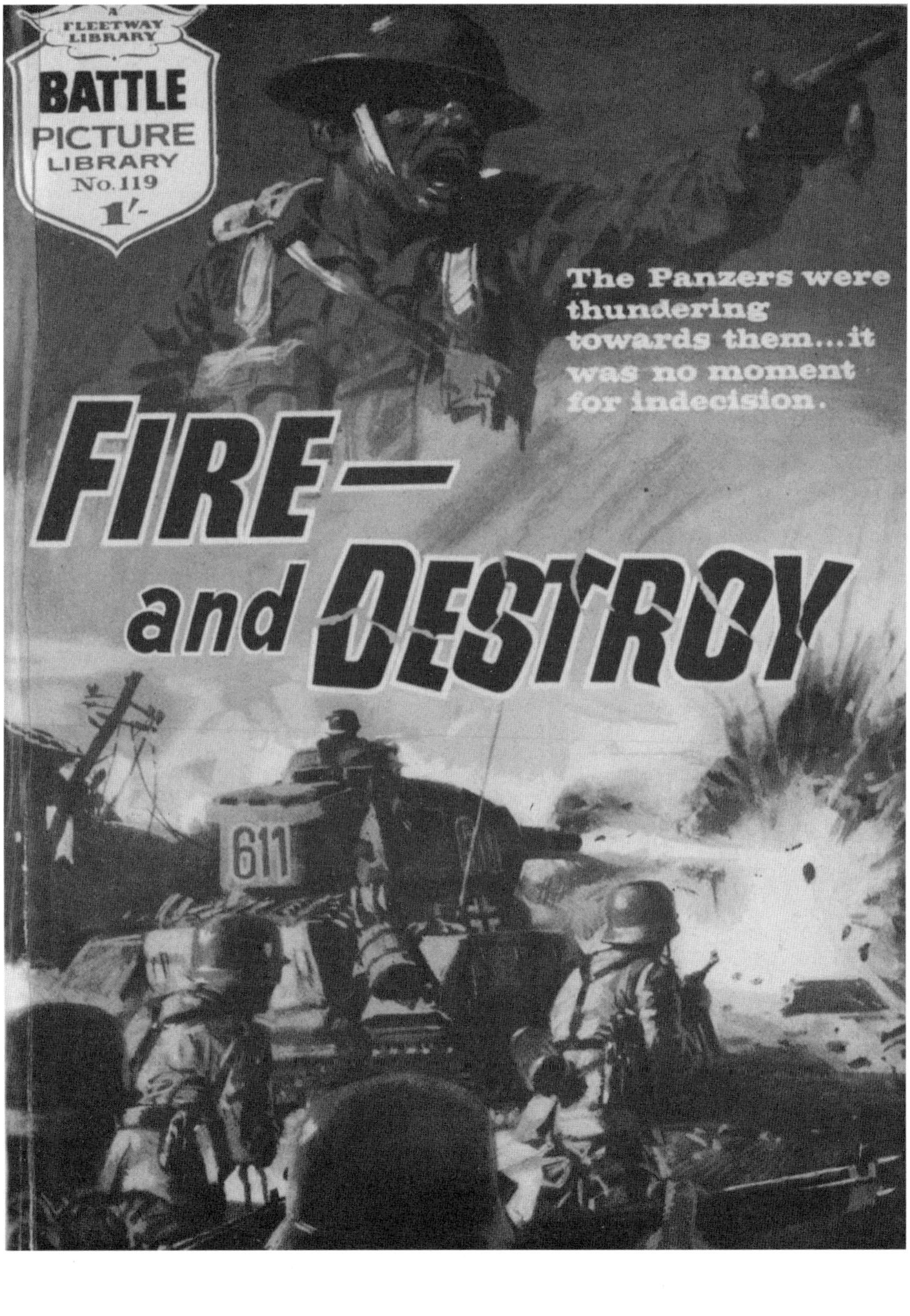
A FLEETWAY LIBRARY
BATTLE PICTURE LIBRARY
No.119
1/-
The Panzers were thundering towards them...it was no moment for indecision.
FIRE— and DESTROY
611

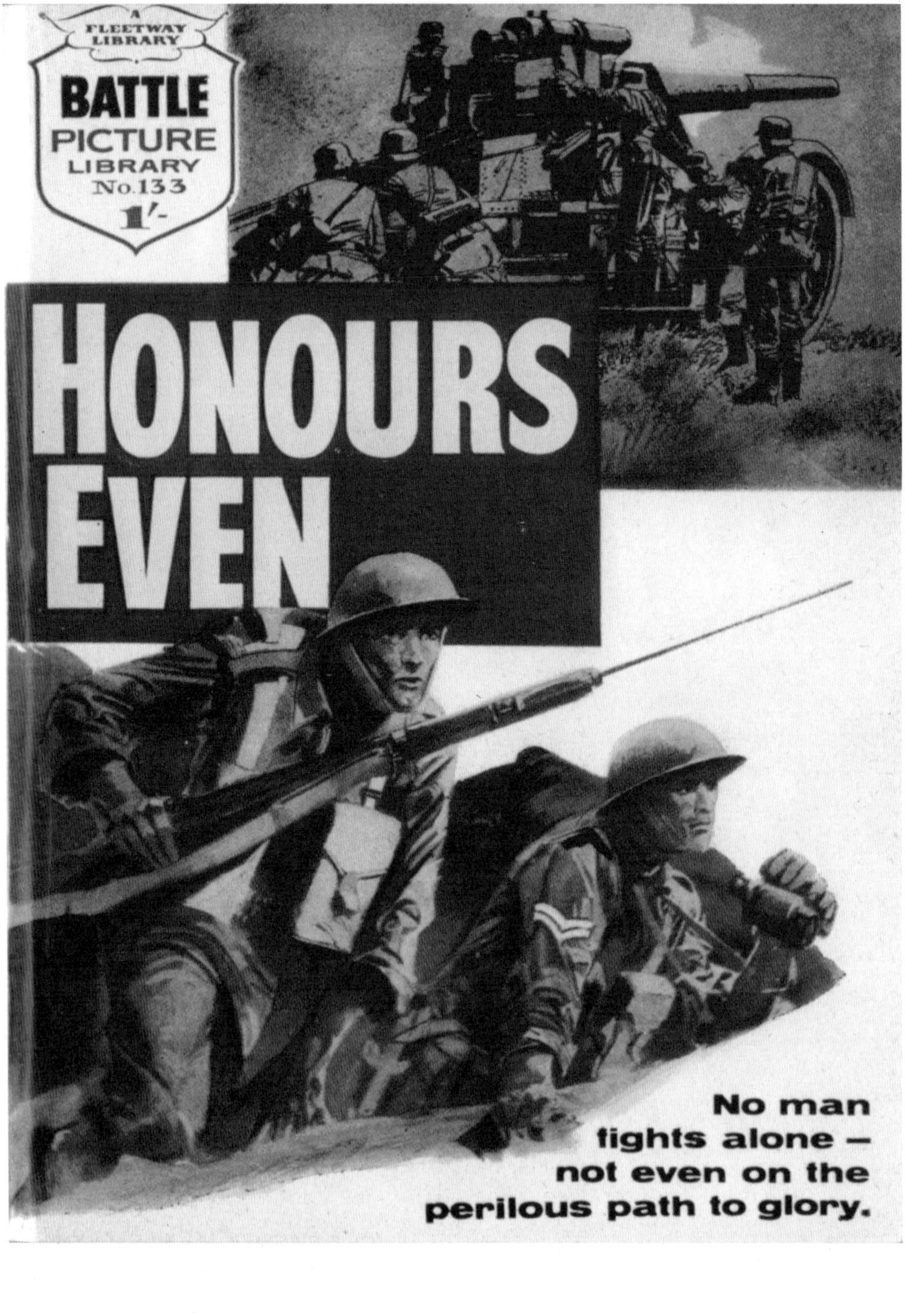
A
FLEETWAY LIBRARY
BATTLE
PICTURE
LIBRARY
No.133
1/-
HONOURS
EVEN
No man
fights alone –
not even on the
perilous path to glory.

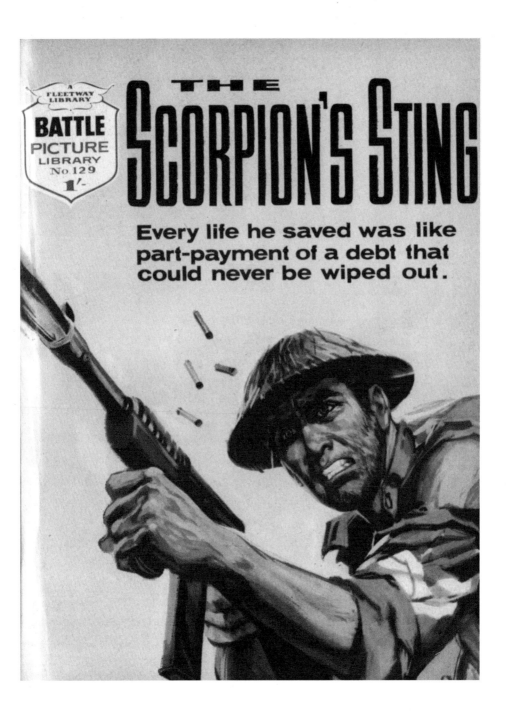

A FLEETWAY LIBRARY

BATTLE PICTURE LIBRARY No 129 1/-

THE SCORPION'S STING

Every life he saved was like part-payment of a debt that could never be wiped out.

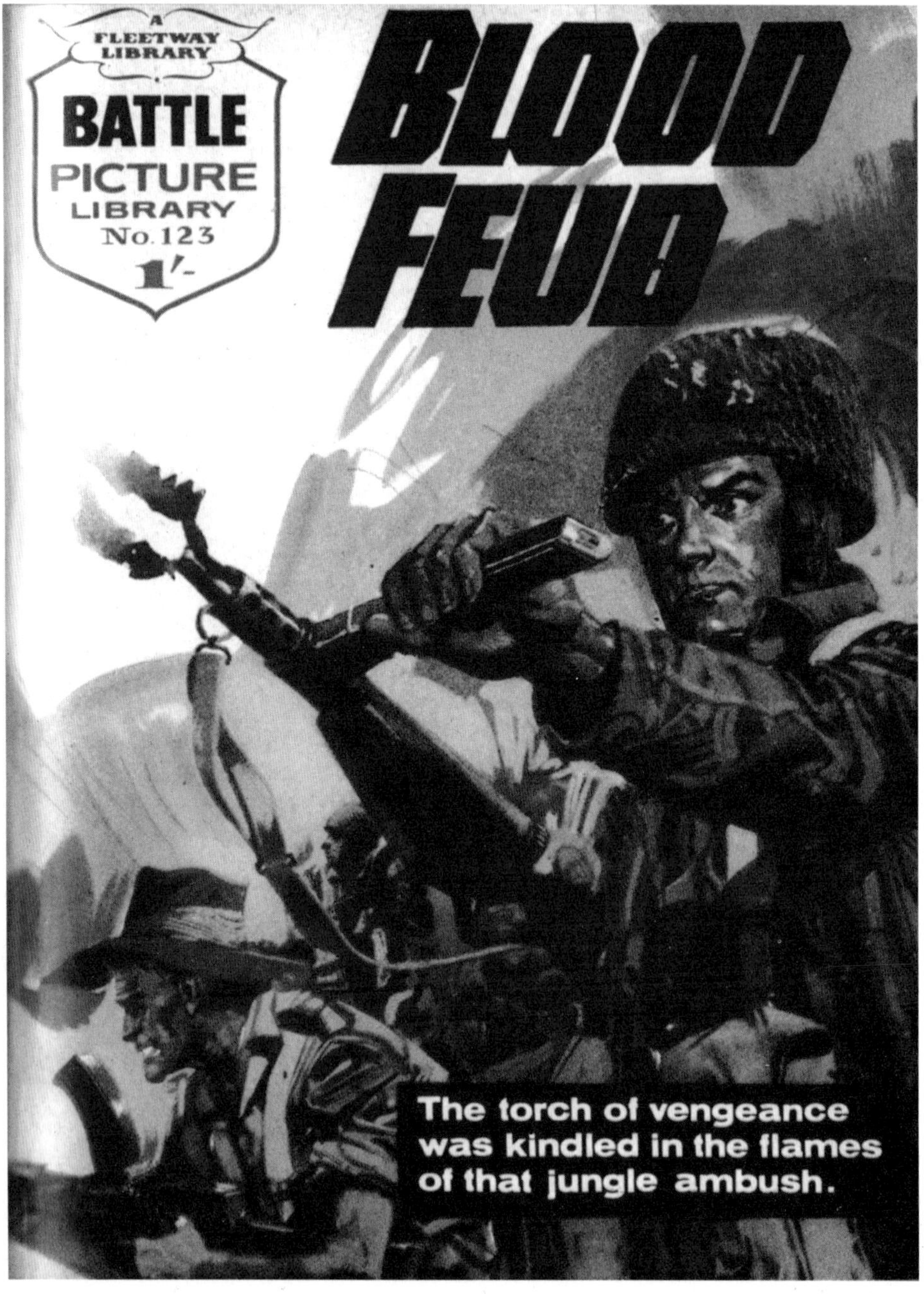
A FLEETWAY LIBRARY
BATTLE
PICTURE
LIBRARY
No. 123
1/-
BLOOD FEUD
The torch of vengeance was kindled in the flames of that jungle ambush.